New Dictionary of Scientific Biography

*Published by special arrangement with the
American Council of Learned Societies*

The American Council of Learned Societies, organized in 1919 for the purpose of advancing the study of the humanities and of the humanistic aspects of the social sciences, is a nonprofit federation comprising thirty-three national scholarly groups. The Council represents the humanities in the United States in the International Union of Academies, provides fellowships and grants-in-aid, supports research-and-planning conferences and symposia, and sponsers special projects and scholarly publications.

MEMBER ORGANIZATIONS

American Philosophical Society, 1743
American Academy of Arts and Sciences, 1780
American Antiquarian Society, 1812
American Oriental Society, 1842
American Numismatic Society, 1858
American Philological Association, 1869
Archaeological Institute of America, 1879
Society of Biblical Literature, 1880
Modern Language Association of America, 1883
American Historical Association, 1884
American Economic Association, 1885
American Folklore Society, 1888
American Society of Church History, 1888
American Dialect Society, 1889
American Psychological Association, 1892
Association of American Law Schools, 1900
American Philosophical Association, 1900
American Schools of Oriental Research, 1900
American Anthropological Association, 1902
American Political Science Association, 1903
Bibliographical Society of America, 1904
Association of American Geographers, 1904
Hispanic Society of America, 1904
American Sociological Association, 1905
American Society of International Law, 1906
Organization of American Historians, 1907
American Academy of Religion, 1909
College Forum of the National Council of Teachers of English, 1911
Society for the Advancement of Scandinavian Study, 1911
College Art Association, 1912
National Communication Association, 1914
History of Science Society, 1924
Linguistic Society of America, 1924
Medieval Academy of America, 1925
American Association for the History of Medicine, 1925
American Musicological Society, 1934
Economic History Association, 1940

Society of Architectural Historians, 1940
Association for Asian Studies, 1941
American Society for Aesthetics, 1942
American Association for the Advancement of Slavic Studies, 1948
American Studies Association, 1950
Metaphysical Society of America, 1950
North American Conference on British Studies, 1950
American Society of Comparative Law, 1951
Renaissance Society of America, 1954
Society for Ethnomusicology, 1955
Society for French Historical Studies, 1956
International Center of Medieval Art, 1956
American Society for Legal History, 1956
American Society for Theatre Research, 1956
African Studies Association, 1957
Society for the History of Technology, 1958
Society for Cinema and Media Studies, 1959
American Comparative Literature Association, 1960
Law and Society Association, 1964
Middle East Studies Association of North America, 1966
Latin American Studies Association, 1966
Association for the Advancement of Baltic Studies, 1968
American Society for Eighteenth Century Studies, 1969
Association for Jewish Studies, 1969
Sixteenth Century Society and Conference, 1970
Society for American Music, 1975
Dictionary Society of North America, 1975
German Studies Association, 1976
American Society for Environmental History, 1976
Society for Music Theory, 1977
National Council on Public History, 1979
Society of Dance History Scholars, 1979

New Dictionary of Scientific Biography

VOLUME 2
CABEO–EYSENCK

Noretta Koertge
EDITOR IN CHIEF

CHARLES SCRIBNER'S SONS
An imprint of Thomson Gale, a part of The Thomson Corporation

THOMSON

GALE

Detroit • New York • San Francisco • New Haven, Conn. • Waterville, Maine • London

New Dictionary of Scientific Biography

Noretta Koertge

For permission to use material from the product, submit your request via the Web at http://www.gale-edit.com/permissions, or you may download our Permissions Request form and submit your request by fax or mail to:

Permissions Department
Gale Group
27500 Drake Rd.
Farmington Hills, MI 48331-3535
Permissions Hotline:
248-699-8006 or 800-877-4253, ext. 8006
Fax 248-699-8074 or 800-762-4058

Cover photographs reproduced by permission.

Since this page cannot legibly accommodate all copyright notices, the acknowledgements constitute an extension of the copyright notice.

LIBRARY OF CONGRESS CATALOGING-IN-PUBLICATION DATA

New dictionary of scientific biography / Noretta Koertge, editor in chief.
   p. cm.
   Includes bibliographical references and index.
   ISBN 978-0-684-31320-7 (set : alk. paper)—ISBN 978-0-684-31321-4 (vol. 1 : alk. paper)—ISBN 978-0-684-31322-1 (vol. 2 : alk. paper)—ISBN 978-0-684-31323-8 (vol. 3 : alk. paper)—ISBN 978-0-684-31324-5 (vol. 4 : alk. paper)—ISBN 978-0-684-31325-2 (vol. 5 : alk. paper)—ISBN 978-0-684-31326-9 (vol. 6 : alk. paper)—ISBN 978-0-684-31327-6 (vol. 7 : alk. paper)—ISBN 978-0-684-31328-3 (vol. 8 : alk. paper)
   1. Scientists—Biography—Dictionaries. I. Koertge, Noretta.

Q141.N45 2008
509.2'2—dc22
[B]
                                                    2007031384

Editorial Board

C

CABEO, NICCOLÒ (*b.* Ferrara, Italy, 26 February 1586; *d.* Genoa, 30 June 1650), *natural philosophy, magnetism, mechanics, methodology.* For the original article on Cabeo see *DSB*, vol. 3.

Cabeo, a Catholic priest who had entered the Jesuit religious order as a novice in 1602, is best known for his two major publications, *Philosophia magnetica* (Magnetic philosophy, 1629) and *In quatuor libros meteorologicorum Aristotelis commentaria* (Commentary in four books on Aristotle's *Meteorology,* 1646). The first of these works addresses the phenomenon of magnetism, especially as discussed by the Englishman William Gilbert in his famous *De magnete* (On the magnet, 1600), while the second is a lengthy commentary on one of Aristotle's physical works, a form that allowed Cabeo to discuss a very broad range of topics not restricted to meteorology itself but encompassing many aspects of Aristotle's so-called sub-lunary (below the moon) region of the universe. Despite his many disagreements with Aristotle, Cabeo shared with the latter the conviction that the Earth is stationary at the center of the universe.

Career. Cabeo's academic training occurred primarily at Parma, following the usual Jesuit curriculum of the period, and included the study of logic, natural philosophy (centered on the works of Aristotle), metaphysics, and theology; he clearly also studied some mathematics. Following the completion of his studies around 1616, Cabeo taught theology, philosophy, and metaphysics at Parma until 1621; he subsequently spent several years living at the Jesuit college back in Ferrara, his birthplace, and taught some theology there in the late 1620s. At the end of his life he returned to teaching, now at the Jesuit college in Genoa. In the meanwhile, he served the ducal courts in Mantua and in Modena, made use of his mathematical expertise in work on civil engineering projects, and was an itinerant preacher. He remained throughout his life engaged in issues of mathematics and natural philosophy, debating issues of mechanics, free fall, and motion with such contemporaries and familiars as Giovanni Battista Baliani, Benedetto Castelli, and Giovanni Battista Riccioli, as well as publishing his two major treatises. His interests covered a wide range of contemporary natural philosophy, however, beyond those questions of motion associated with his older contemporary Galileo.

Magnetism and Electricity. His first book, the *Philosophia magnetica,* discussed not only Gilbert's but also Cabeo's own experimental investigations of terrestrial magnetism as well as magnetized iron and "lodestone" (the mineral magnetite). The central focus of his work, like Gilbert's before him, was therefore the study of the magnetic behaviors of compass needles. Where Gilbert, however, argued that the Earth itself is a giant magnet, whose poles reproduce the poles of an ordinary magnet and with which it interacts, Cabeo maintained instead that magnetic properties are inherent to certain sorts of matter; they did not subsist in their relationships to the great magnet, the Earth. Indeed, Cabeo denied that the Earth itself is a great magnet, even though it contains matter lending it magnetic effects. He also, again following Gilbert, discussed magnetic attraction between rubbed objects (typically, pieces of amber resin) and light objects such as bits of straw or paper; the attractive virtues of such electrified bodies appeared to be sufficiently similar to those of magnets that it seemed appropriate to investigate them together. In accounting for the production of electrical attraction by certain kinds of matter when they are rubbed, Cabeo—always, as a natural philosopher, on the lookout for causal explanations of phenomena, not simply their descriptions—suggested that the rubbing stimulates the emission of tiny particles, as an effluvium, from the rubbed body's pores, which, in its interaction with the surrounding air, tends to move light objects toward it as a result of the rarified air's subsequent behavior.

In the *Philosophia magnetica*, Cabeo considered the methodological and epistemological issues relating to his experimental investigations. He stressed that his work sought the causes behind natural effects (this being the usual goal of Aristotelian-style natural philosophy) but that he would proceed by borrowing the approach of the mathematicians because it was so clear and demonstrative. He also stressed the extent to which his discussions were based upon experimental work, his experiments having been repeated numerous times, with multiple witnesses on hand to guarantee the truth of his reports. The necessity of saying such things stemmed from the unusual nature of the phenomena Cabeo described; neither magnetic nor electrical effects were generally familiar from everyday experience, and arguments based on unusual and contrived experimental behaviors therefore needed special justification to be accepted.

Experimental Philosophy. Cabeo's use of experimental procedures in natural philosophy is also a prominent feature of his other major publication, the 1646 commentary on Aristotle's *Meteorology*. Indeed, when the work came to be reprinted (Rome, 1686), it was given a slightly revised title: Preceding the old title that described the work as comprising a commentary on Aristotle, the new edition advertised itself as *Philosophia experimentalis*, or experimental philosophy. One of Cabeo's topics concerned the behavior of falling bodies, which Galileo had made famous in his *Discorsi* of 1638. Cabeo affirmed Galileo's claim that all bodies—at least those made of the same material—tend to fall at the same rate as one another, rather than the heavier ones falling faster (the Aristotelian view). Cabeo justified his claims using reports of repeated and witnessed experimental trials. Another Galilean assertion, which Galileo had attempted to demonstrate mathematically as derivable from the simpler components principles of (roughly) horizontal inertia and vertical, uniformly accelerated fall, Cabeo characteristically attempted to test by direct trial, regarding Galileo's assertion as based too much on speculative reasoning. In his commentary Cabeo described a succession of paper panels arranged along the presumed path of a cannonball, the cannon being fired through them so as to punch a hole in each panel. The holes thus traced out the curving path of the cannonball. Cabeo said, as usual, that he had tried this many times, and with additional observers; he had also examined the curving path of a jet of water.

The full scope of Cabeo's commentary on Aristotle's *Meteorology* thus presented a full-scale example of a new style of natural philosophy, an experimental philosophy that made free use of mathematical tools. This new style was also developed by many of Cabeo's fellow Jesuits in the same period. It should not be imagined, however, that all Cabeo's work appears "modern"; besides the material already discussed, his commentary also discussed chemical and alchemical questions as well as expressing belief in the occult effects of the heavens upon the Earth, among a vast miscellany of other topics. Not only did he reject the motion of the Earth, which for him remained central in the universe, but he also denied the possibility of a vacuum in nature. Both of these debated positions were common among Jesuit natural philosophers of his time.

SUPPLEMENTARY BIBLIOGRAPHY

WORKS BY CABEO

Philosophia magnetica. Ferrara, Italy: F. Suzzi, 1629; Cologne, Germany: I. Kinckium, 1629. Note that different copies cite one or the other place of publication.

In quatuor libros meteorologicorum Aristotelis commentaria. Rome: Francisco Corbelletto, 1646.

OTHER SOURCES

Baldini, Ugo. *Legem impone subactis: Studi su filosofia e scienza dei Gesuiti in Italia 1540–1632*. Rome: Bulzoni, 1992. The appendix to chapter 11 is particularly informative as to Cabeo's presence at various Jesuit colleges.

Costantini, Claudio. *Baliani e i Gesuiti: Annotazioni in margine alla corrispondenza del Baliani con Gio. Luigi Confalonieri e Orazio Grassi*. Florence: Giunti Barbera, 1969. Contains material on Cabeo's relations with Baliani.

Dear, Peter. *Discipline and Experience: The Mathematical Way in the Scientific Revolution*. Chicago: University of Chicago Press, 1995.

Heilbron, John L. *Electricity in the 17th and 18th Centuries: A Study of Early Modern Physics*. Berkeley: University of California Press; reprint, Mineola, NY: Dover, 1999.

Ingegno, Alfonso. "Cabeo, Niccolò." In *Dizionario Biografico degli Italiani*. Vol. 15. Rome: Istituto della Enciclopedia Italiana, 1972. An excellent general treatment.

Maffioli, Cesare S. *Out of Galileo: The Science of Waters 1628–1718*. Rotterdam: Erasmus, 1994. Discusses Cabeo in relation to Castelli and Baliani on the practical hydraulics of canals and rivers.

Moscovici, Serge. *L'Expérience du mouvement: Jean-Baptiste Baliani disciple et critique de Galilée*. Paris: Hermann, 1967.

Pumfrey, Stephen. "Neo-Aristotelianism and the Magnetic Philosophy." In *New Perspectives on Renaissance Thought: Essays in the History of Science, Education, and Philosophy in*

Memory of Charles B. Schmitt, edited by John Henry and Sarah Hutton. London: Duckworth, 1990.

Sommervogel, Carlos, et al., eds. *Bibliothèque de la Compagnie de Jésus.* 12 vols. Louvain: Éditions de la Bibliothéque S.J., 1960. See vol. 2.

Thorndike, Lynn. *A History of Magic and Experimental Science.* 8 vols. New York: Columbia University Press, 1923–1958. Vols. 7 and 8 contain useful paraphrases of parts of Cabeo's works.

Peter Dear

CAIN, ARTHUR JAMES (*b.* Rugby, Warwickshire, England, 25 July 1921; *d.* Liverpool, United Kingdom, 20 August 1999), *evolutionary biology, zoology, malacology, systematics, history of taxonomy.*

Cain was a disciple of evolutionary synthesis. During the 1950s he and Philip Sheppard produced a strong case study of natural selection using the land snail, *Cepaea.* Cain became a leading advocate of selection and adaptation. He later contributed to taxonomic theory and the history of systematics.

Career in Brief. Cain was born into a working-class family. He attended Lawrence Sheriff School, Rugby, a selective boys' grammar school. In 1939 he received an academic scholarship to Magdalen College, Oxford, graduating in 1941 with a first-class honors degree in zoology.

Cain saw military service between December 1941 and November 1945, commissioned as second lieutenant in the Royal Army Ordinance Corps. In 1942 he was promoted to captain and transferred to the Royal Electrical and Mechanical Engineers. Much of his service involved radar and antiaircraft batteries in the Orkney Islands.

Cain returned to the Department of Zoology, University of Oxford. He obtained his MA (1947) and PhD (1949). From October 1946, he was departmental demonstrator. In January 1949 he was university demonstrator in animal taxonomy. Reportedly, this appointment, which lasted until 1964, was created after specific lobbying from the Systematics Association (a group committed to furthering all aspects of systematic biology). Concurrently, Cain curated the zoological collections at University Museum (1954–1964) and was lecturer in zoology, St Peter's Hall, Oxford (1958–1961).

In 1964 Cain was appointed professor of zoology, University of Manchester. This was a considerable promotion, and it removed Cain from personality conflicts growing in Oxford. Cain later delighted in the irony of his appointment: his chair's previous occupant, Herbert Graham Cannon, was a neo-Lamarckian and opponent of Darwinism. At first Cain thrived in Manchester, but politics and more personality conflicts took their toll. In this period, Cain undertook several long-term projects abroad, both relieving and aggravating the situation.

Cain soon moved to the University of Liverpool, appointed Derby Professor of Zoology in 1968. Sheppard had moved to Liverpool in 1959, and encouraged further expansion of the genetics and zoology programs. Cain retired in 1989.

As a person, Cain kept a small circle of close friends, largely professional colleagues and former students. Bryan Clarke, a student, aptly described Cain as having "an incendiary enthusiasm for evolutionary biology, a tendency toward wrathful indignation, and a deep contempt for administrators, particularly those who had once been scientists" (Clarke, 1999, p. 872). His "combative style and changeable moods" earned Cain many enemies and contributed to his delayed election into the Royal Society (1989)" (Clarke, 1999, p. 872). Lawrence Cook (2000), another student, noted, "No one ever accused him of being a good diplomat or a good administrator." At the same time, students and colleagues widely praised Cain for his encyclopedic knowledge, his demanding but inspirational mentoring, and his passion for evolutionary biology.

Department of Zoology, Oxford. Cain's graduate training concentrated on histology, the study of tissue. Returning to Oxford in 1945, he wanted to study ecology and genetics, but he later recalled being "scared stiff" by the competition between tutors in these areas (Edmund Brisco Ford and Charles Elton). Cain turned to biochemistry, studying under John Randal Baker. Cain admired Baker greatly, and his mentor had lasting influences on Cain's approach to research.

Cain's doctoral research was dictated by Baker's interest in methodological precision. How do techniques for studying cells alter them from a natural state? Baker worried over the precise limits of conclusions he could draw from laboratory data, and he was scrupulously critical when interpreting results. What artifacts might lead him astray? What were the limitations of his data? What were possible sources of error?

This critical approach proved crucial in Baker's study of the Golgi apparatus. Disputes with other histologists over the function of this organelle drew attention to the precise value of histological techniques for identifying types of lipoids. Baker assigned Cain the task of investigating the validity of such tests. In the process, Cain refined procedures for distinguishing acidic and neutral lipoids. (These later proved useful in studying cell physiology, though Cain did not pursue that avenue himself.) Baker was impressed by Cain's ability to analyze methods and determine their precise contributions to knowledge.

Cain's interests in natural history, ecology, and evolution predated the war. He was quick to seek the position of demonstrator in animal taxonomy when Oxford offered it for 1949. Recognizing he had no graduate-level qualification in systematics, Cain requested and received leave to study for six months at the American Museum of Natural History, under Ernst Mayr. Cain's participation in Mayr's program most likely was secured through David Lack.

Cain's apprenticeship with Mayr steered his biological interests, and Cain often returned to ornithological projects. While at the museum, Cain studied geographic speciation in Australian parrots and Malaysian pigeons. In 1953 he led a small expedition to the British Solomon Islands, collecting geographical varieties and searching for sibling species. As Cain later recalled, collecting was done according to an "evolutionary point of view," that is, in line with the intellectual framework advocated by Mayr. Cain's notes from his apprenticeship with Mayr formed the core of his 1954 book *Animal Species and Their Evolution.*

Natural Selection in the Land Snail, *Cepaea.* Beginning with Sheppard in the 1950s, Cain researched the evolution of the land snail, *Cepaea.* His interest in this model organism lasted forty years. The first years of research had a dramatic impact on evolutionary biology. Cain and Sheppard began their collaboration in 1949, collecting *Cepaea* from different microhabitats near Oxford. *Cepaea* is a polymorphic species. Cain and Sheppard sought correlations between morphology and environment, focusing on shell color and banding patterns, that is, on causes of conspicuousness to visual predation. Finding no correlation between these qualities and habitat type would have reinforced the commonly held view that banding pattern and coloration were adaptively neutral, that they provided no advantage to snails in their struggle for existence.

In fact, Cain and Sheppard found the reverse: a strong correlation between habitat, banding pattern, and color. This could be explained in terms of natural selection for inconspicuousness. When backgrounds were uniform, for instance, banding made snails easier for predators to see; when backgrounds were heterogeneous, banding made snails harder for predators to see. Cain and Sheppard thought they had a clear demonstration of selection. They also thought this explained why *Cepaea* was polymorphic, as selection in different parts of the range drove adaptations in different directions.

Importantly, Cain and Sheppard used their *Cepaea* work to speak authoritatively about general evolutionary theory. Their opposition held the view that traits normally were adaptively neutral. Against this view, Cain and Shep-

pard forcefully argued three points. First, natural selection was the principal cause of evolution. Second, adaptation was the best way to understand why a species evolved its traits. Third, supposedly neutral traits must be reexamined because detailed study almost certainly will produce a selection-based interpretation. For Cain, any claim that a trait had no adaptive value should be understood only as a statement of ignorance about the complexities of biological worlds.

This *Cepaea* research became a classic case study, providing supporters with a clear example of adaptation in nature. Though their conclusions were repeatedly challenged (for example, by French evolutionary biologist Maxime Lamotte), the broad significance of this research was in the conversion of *Cepaea* from an opposing to a supporting example of selection. Indeed, *Cepaea* become iconic, at least among those in English-speaking countries. This act of redemption followed other celebrated reclamations (for example, Lack on Galapagos finches, Theodosius Dobzhansky and Marion L. Queal on *Drosophila*), each drawing interest away from neutral characters and random drift as major features of evolution.

Cain and Sheppard's *Cepaea* research also bolstered "ecological genetics" and the "new" natural history as it developed in postwar Britain. These approaches combined field studies with laboratory work in genetics and physiology. It used experimental tests and correlative studies, such as fossil evidence, to complement observational results from the field.

Cain's interest in *Cepaea* lasted forty years and was not limited to studying selection. Additional research investigated the genetics of banding patterns and coloration, the relation between physiology and external morphology, microecology, variation in shell shape, seasonal changes in selection pressures, and the process of visual selection by predators, especially birds.

In the early 1960s Cain produced the first description of "area effects" in natural populations. This phenomenon concerned the distribution of variations. Cain occasionally found characters shared across adjacent populations but that could not be correlated with obvious features common to the various habitats. Cain had difficulty explaining these observations, though he was certain selection was somehow key. Perhaps, he supposed, area effects were caused by selection for environmental factors that human senses could not easily detect. Alternatively, perhaps they are caused when characters genetically linked to the ones observed are actively selected; the latter simply being dragged along. Cain collaborated with John Currey in this research but rarely moved beyond simply describing these patterns.

In 1988 Cain published his last major research paper on *Cepaea*, reporting on a twenty-year study of laboratory colonies in which population size was sharply reduced at random points in time. This simulated genetic bottlenecks and tested the prediction of some mathematical population geneticists that random sampling could lead to genetic revolutions—the "founder effect." Cain reported a failure to confirm the prediction of a founder effect. Instead, genetic diversity more or less rapidly recovered. This study was a final piece in Cain's career-long effort to downplay genetic drift in evolution.

Cain and Sheppard never explained their decision to start *Cepaea* research. Both agreed it was Cain who focused attention on *Cepaea* as a model organism. Both also admitted a predisposition toward adaptive explanations. Studying polymorphism as they did would have seemed obvious in Oxford during the 1940s. It fit nicely into the "experimental adaptationist programme" (as the historian William B. Provine refers to it) actively underway at Oxford.

Adaptationism. The origins of Cain's convictions about selection are obscure. In autobiographical notes he complained about prejudices against selection before World War II. This was especially true when closely related species were studied, with differences frequently attributed to nonadaptive characters.

Cain never doubted his selectionist position, and he happily carried the banner for his cause. In a series of letters to *Nature* during 1951, for instance, Cain eagerly argued with the zoologist George Stuart Carter over "so-called non-adaptive or neutral characters in evolution." Neutrality was a presumption and not a demonstrated conclusion, he demanded. Adaptedness should be preferred as a default hypothesis because it is more likely to be true. Only when positive evidence for random processes was presented or exhaustive tests failed to support adaptive explanations should other explanations be considered. In such disputes, Cain applied the same critical attitude Baker had used in histology: castigating writers for drawing conclusions far beyond their specific evidence and for being too quick to generalize on only a few examples. However, as the philosopher Roberta Millstein has shown, Cain demanded far more rigor for studies of neutrality and drift than he did for selection.

Cain applied his adaptationism to taxonomy by stressing the importance of constancy. Constant characters offered stable tools for taxonomic decisions, he said. Constancy could not be a passive quality in nature, as mutation and recombination constantly introduced variation. It had to be actively maintained, Cain argued, hence its presence indicated the work of natural selection. Cain was so convinced of this point that he proposed a heuristic. In the absence of contrary evidence, naturalists should

"treat constant characters as probably having a definite selective meaning" (Cain, 1959, p. 14).

In 1964 Cain published his farthest reaching proposals about adaptation. In "Perfection of Animals," he shifted from the role selection plays shaping single features to the role it plays shaping whole organisms. On one level, this paper was a broadside against the increasing dominance of reductionist molecular biology. Cain defended the alternative organism-in-environment perspective of evolutionary biology.

More subtly, Cain had broken away from thinking common descent was the most important determinant of form. Instead, he thought no character was so entrenched that it could not be reshaped during evolution. Whole body plans were subject to reshaping by natural selection. Cain explained, "the major plans of construction … are soundly functional and [are] retained merely because of that. … Their plans are adaptive for broad functional specializations; the particular features of lesser groups are, as has long been agreed, adaptive for more particular functions" (Cain, 1989, p. 4).

Cain's emphasis on selection certainly had critics. To some, he became the caricature of an adaptationist paradigm. Cain's conflict with Stephen Jay Gould, whose early study of recapitulation theory was an early broadside against Cain's "perfection" thesis, was particularly sharp. Gould and Richard C. Lewontin's attack on "spandrels" and the "Panglossian paradigm" certainly had Cain in mind. For his part, Cain regularly referred to Gould as merely a "propagandist."

A Disciple of Synthesis. Cain began his career just as the evolutionary synthesis coalesced into a distinct movement in the life sciences. His position at Oxford, and his experiences with Mayr in New York, perfectly placed him to be influenced by, and to influence, the movement on both sides of the Atlantic.

In 1954 Cain published *Animal Species and Their Evolution.* Narrowly, this book functioned as a primer on taxonomic theory, condensing Mayr's *Systematics and the Origin of Species* (1942), slightly modified. At its center was the polytypic species and the biological species concept. Cain defended the importance of geographic isolation in the formation of species, and he invoked selection-causing local adaptation as the key mechanism of evolution. Main examples came from Cain's own research. He gave no important role to neutral characters or genetic drift. Sympatric speciation was rejected for animals (at the least it was not yet demonstrated), but accepted for plants, via polyploidy. Cain elevated the subspecies (geographically definable, taxonomically distinct populations within a species) to the status of sibling species.

Animal Species departed from expectations in two important ways. Although Cain accepted the biological species concept as a criterion for species in evolutionary terms, he knew it had important practical limitations. As others did before him, Cain supplemented the biological species concept (he called it "biospecies") with additional concepts, including: "morphospecies" (defined solely by lists of characters, such as from museum collections), "paleospecies" (successive stages in a chronological sequence), and "agamospecies" (species in asexual organisms). This terminology once again reflected Cain's attention to methodological precision. Like many taxonomist colleagues before him, Cain struggled to relate taxonomic decisions and statements made by colleagues using different, often unexplained, methods. Cain worried about comparability and consistency. He wanted to know—to know precisely—what kind of species he was working with.

Cain's book sold well and broadened his audience. A decade later, he used the same book series to promote others, serving as editor of the Biological Series for Hutchinson's University Library (1967–1975). Cain oversaw publication of at least ten books, including Lawrence Cook's *Coefficients of Natural Selection* (1971), Martin Rudwick's *Living and Fossil Brachiopods* (1970), and Robert McNeill Alexander's *Functional Design in Fishes* (1967).

Theories of Classification. Cain's thinking about species concepts led him to fundamental problems, which eventually brought him to reject evolutionary systematics and binomial nomenclature. Around 1960 Cain identified with an alternative approach in the field, numerical taxonomy; however, this association was short-lived.

In *Animal Species*, Cain wrote frankly about taxonomic ranks. What's the difference, he asked, between taxonomic units such as "order" and "family"? Ultimately there were none, he said. Ranks in normal Linnean hierarchies referred to no standard unit of diversity, offering instead only convenient pigeonholes for organizational purposes.

But the discovery of evolution forced taxonomists to adopt another view about ranks. The facts of descent and phylogeny introduced notions of "relatedness" and "affinity." Organisms assigned to one group, by implication, are claimed to be more related to each other than to those assigned to different groups.

In the mid-1950s Cain started questioning the need for taxonomy to make claims about affinity and relatedness while simultaneously grouping nature into organizational units. Behind Cain's complaint, again, was his long-standing concern for precision. When taxonomists placed two morphospecies in the same taxonomic family, he worried, they did not necessarily mean to imply those morphospecies were more related to each other than to morphospecies outside that family. However, relatedness was precisely what any outsider would conclude, given a rudimentary knowledge of evolution.

Cain focused his frustration onto one taxonomic unit, the genus. (For instance, *Homo* is the genus name for a number of species, including *Homo sapiens* and *Homo erectus*.) Formal rules of nomenclature absolutely required all species names to include two pieces: a generic name (*Homo*) and trivial name (*sapiens*). To Cain, this requirement forced taxonomists to make a claim about affinity and relatedness even when they wanted only to make identifications. Consider this example: suppose one finds a fossil that seems much like the humanlike apes already known. One wants to give it a formal name, but also wishes to avoid implying a close connection with *Homo* or any other group. The rules, Cain complained, required one of two solutions: either make some generic assignment despite any reservations (for example, call it *Homo* even if it is thought that *H. sapiens* or *H. erectus* might not be its closest relations), or invent a new generic name and worry about affinities later. Neither solution seemed honest to Cain. Why be compelled to make an evolutionary claim when all he wanted was a standardized reference name for a single specimen? This logic was the foundation for Cain's later rejection of binomial nomenclature.

Cain also drew taxonomists' attention to a subtle and ultimately more worrying problem. The naming and comparing work taxonomists undertook occurred using incomplete information. For many of the similarities used in that routine, it often was difficult to identify which resulted from relatedness and which resulted from convergence (the independent evolution of similar traits in response to similar environmental challenges). This was aggravated by the frequent heavy emphasis placed on only a few characters in each group. To Cain's mind, this gave too much room for self-deception (thinking similar forms were related when in fact they had converged) and subjectivity. Cain wanted rigorous, independent tests combined with more explicit discussion in taxonomic decision making.

Cain's desire for increased rigor led him to his second substantial break in systematics. Because taxonomic decisions based on only a few characters was suspect, he argued, organisms should be compared "as a whole." He meant this in the literal sense: animals as integrated, functioning wholes. He also meant it as the study of all parts, as there was no a priori reason to privilege some characters over others. Using comparisons of all characters, he said, was the only "natural" basis for taxonomic decision making.

Cain's position was similar to advocates of "numerical taxonomy." For a few years, Cain presented himself as part of that campaign, complaining, as others did, that "phylogenists" forced evolution and systematics into an unhappy marriage. Cain soon broke with that movement, however. He complained it had became increasingly abstract and computational while less concerned with whole organisms living in natural habitats.

Cain had long-standing interests in the history of systematics, including studies of Aristotle (384–322 BCE), John Ray (1627–1705), Carolus Linnaeus (Carl von Linné, 1707–1778), and Constantine Samuel Rafinesque (1783–1840). Cain interpreted such writers in ways that added credibility to his own points of view. For this reason, and because he tended to write papers that seemed little more than long series of long quotations from original sources, Cain's historical work has not fared well with historians. Notably, Cain's technique once again followed his Oxford mentor, as when Baker wrote about the history of cell theory. Mary P. Winsor provides a superb analysis of Cain's historian interests.

Naturalist in the "Best Sense of That Word." *Cepaea* made Cain famous, but his zoological interests had much wider scope. Students called Cain one of the best naturalists of his generation. After *Cepaea,* he collected around the globe, including eastern North America (1950), British Solomon Islands (1953), and British Guiana (1959). Malacology (the study of mollusks) was his first and deepest passion. Ornithology (the study of birds) was second.

In the early 1960s Cain's research shifted to Lake Kariba (between Zambia and Zimbabwe), formed on the Zambezi River after completion of the Kariba Dam in 1960. In 1962 Cain was Oxford's representative on the Inter-Universities Committee for Research at Lake Kariba. He also served as the committee's scientific secretary in the United Kingdom. In his capacity as secretary, Cain repeatedly traveled to Africa during 1962–1965, conducting additional research in Kariba, then Johannesburg, South Africa. In 1965 he studied bird ecology in Serengeti National Park, Tanzania.

BIBLIOGRAPHY

WORKS BY CAIN

With Philip M. Sheppard. "Selection in the Polymorphic Land Snail *Cepaea nemoralis.*" *Heredity* 4 (1950): 275–294. First paper in research program on natural selection in the wild.

Animal Species and Their Evolution. London: Hutchinson's University Library, 1954.

"Function and Taxonomic Importance." In *Function and Taxonomic Importance: A Symposium,* edited by Arthur J. Cain, 5–19. London: Systematics Association, 1959.

"The Perfection of Animals." In *Viewpoints in Biology,* vol. 4, edited by John D. Carthy and C. L. Duddington. London: Butterworth, 1964. Reprinted in *Biological Journal of the Linnean Society* 36 (1989): 3–29.

OTHER SOURCES

Clarke, Bryan. "Obituary: Arthur James Cain (1921–99)." *Nature* 401 (1999): 872.

Cook, Lawrence. "A. J. Cain FRS 1921–1999." *Bulletin of the Malacological Society* 34 (2000): 2–3.

Millstein, Roberta L. "Concepts of Drift and Selection in 'The Great Snail Debate' of the 1950s and Early 1960s." In *Descended from Darwin: Insights into American Evolutionary Studies, 1900–1950,* edited by Joe Cain and Michael Ruse. Forthcoming. Thorough discussion of the *Cepaea* research and its critics.

Winsor, Mary P. "Cain on Linnaeus: The Scientist-Historian as Unanalysed Entity." *Studies in the History and Philosophy of Biology and Biomedical Sciences* 32 (2001): 239–254. Splendid study of Cain's use of history of taxonomy to express his own taxonomic theory. Also includes useful biographical information.

Joe Cain

CALDERÓN, ALBERTO PEDRO (*b.* Mendoza, Argentina, 14 September 1920; *d.* Chicago, Illinois, 16 April 1998), *mathematics, analysis, partial differential equations, singular integrals.*

Calderón was one of the most original mathematicians of the twentieth century. He had a profound influence in the development of a wide range of topics, from harmonic analysis to partial differential equations and their multiple applications. His first fundamental contribution was the theory of singular integrals, which he developed jointly with the Polish mathematician Antoni Zygmund, at the University of Chicago. The Calderón-Zygmund school projected its intellectual influence all over the mathematical world.

From Mendoza to Chicago. Calderón was born in Mendoza, Argentina. Since he was gifted in mathematics and was keenly interested in mechanics, his father sent him to a preparatory Swiss school, with the idea of having him study engineering in Zürich. But after two years he was called home, and he finished high school in Mendoza. He attended the University of Buenos Aires, from where he graduated in 1947 with a degree in civil engineering. Calderón took a research position at YPF, the Argentine state oil corporation, where he studied mathematical problems related to oil prospecting. Fortunately for mathematics, he quit YPF in 1948, just at the time when Professor Zygmund was visiting the University of Buenos Aires.

Zygmund was offering a seminar for students, and gave each participant a topic taken from his fundamental treatise *Trigonometric Series* (1935). Calderón joined the seminar, together with two other future distinguished mathematicians, Mischa Cotlar and Luis Santaló. According to Cotlar, the way Zygmund "discovered" Calderón was a memorable event. At the seminar, Calderón had to make a presentation of the Marcel Riesz theorem on the continuity of the Hilbert transform in L^P for $1 < p < ?$. His presentation, short and elegant, was liked by his fellow students, but as it went on, Zygmund grew increasingly restless and began to grimace. Finally, Zygmund interrupted Calderón to ask where he had learned that proof. A subdued Calderón answered that he had read it in *Trigonometric Series*, but Zygmund vehemently informed the audience that such proof was not in his book. After the seminar, Calderón explained to Zygmund that he had tried first to prove the theorem by himself, but thinking it was too difficult, had read a couple of lines in *Trigonometric Series* without turning the page, assuming he had figured the rest of the proof. In fact what Calderón had figured was a shorter and elegant new proof of the Marcel Riesz theorem.

The episode of the unread proof illustrates a constant in Calderón's research attitude: he always approached a problem in his own way, found his own proofs, and developed his own methods–finding new insights in the process. Zygmund realized immediately Calderón's potential, and they wrote together two joint papers while still in Buenos Aires. Not surprisingly, Zygmund invited Calderón to visit the Department of Mathematics of the University of Chicago on a Rockefeller Fellowship.

From an Outstanding Thesis to a New Theory. Calderón arrived at the University of Chicago in 1949, when its department of mathematics was considered the best in the world. The chairman of the department was Marshall Stone, and the senior faculty included A. Adrian Albert, Shiing-Shen Chern, Saunders McLane, Lawrence Graves, and André Weil. Paul Halmos, Irving Kaplansky, Irving Segal, and Edward Spanier were the junior faculty. Calderón was so awed by such star-studded firmament that he considered returning to Argentina, but Zygmund did his best to retain him—fortunately with success.

Calderón was not seeking a doctoral degree, and did not feel inclined to write a dissertation. One day Stone called him to his office and asked for his three recent papers in harmonic analysis. Stone then stapled the three papers together and said "This is your thesis!" It was a revolutionary PhD thesis indeed, since it dealt with harmonic analysis in the circle bypassing complex methods, thus opening the door to the extensions to n-dimensional Euclidean space, which were at the core of Zygmund's new program.

The Calderón-Zygmund collaboration started in Buenos Aires in 1948 and continued until Zygmund's death in 1992. It resulted in the famous theory of singular integrals in several variables. An integral is singular if it converges while its integrand tends to infinity. The classical example in one variable is the Hilbert transform of a function $f(x)$ given by $\int_{-\infty}^{\infty} \frac{f(x)}{x-y} dx$, which is known to be convergent by the theory of analytic functions in one complex variable. Calderón and Zygmund devised a real-variable method for the convergence of the Hilbert transform. The generalization to several real variables are the multidimensional singular integrals.

One of the first and most useful results of this fertile collaboration was the C-Z decomposition lemma, to deal specifically with singular integrals of integrable functions. The C-Z decomposition lemma became an indispensable tool in itself, which permeated analysis and probability theory.

Later came the memorable Calderón program, starting with the boundedness of the "first commutator," to follow with his study of the Cauchy integral on Lipschitz curves. From the successes of the Calderón program stemmed the more precise theory of Ronald R. Coifman, Yves Meyer, and Alan McIntosh, the remarkable "T-1 theorem" of Guy David and Jean-Lin Journé, and the fundamental work of Michael Lacey and Christopher Thiele on the bilinear Hilbert transform.

The methods of Calderón and Zygmund, seen at first as marginal by most analysts, became mainstream in the later 1960s. This was due to the epoch-making contributions of Calderón to the theory of partial differential equations, obtained through singular integral operators.

International Fame. Calderón achieved international fame first with the proof of the uniqueness of the Cauchy problem and then with his demonstration of the existence and uniqueness theory for hyperbolic differential equations. Both results were obtained by using singular integral operators (SIOs) and the method of the Calderón projector, which reduced elliptic boundary value problems to singular equations on the boundary. Furthermore, Calderón introduced the algebras of SIOs, which play a significant role in nonsmooth problems. Such algebras, developed by Robert Seeley, Calderón's first student, proved crucial to the proof of the Atiyah-Singer index theorem. The applications of algebras of SIOs to the theory of partial differential equations led directly to the theory of pseudodifferential operators, developed first by Joseph J. Kohn and Louis Nirenberg, and then by Lars Hormander. Calderón and Rémi Vaillancourt made important contributions to that theory.

The SIOs with kernels infinitely differentiable off the diagonal are a special case of the pseudodifferential operators. Yet Calderón was more interested in SIOs with nonsmooth kernels for potential applications to quasi-linear and nonlinear problems. In his final remarks at the 1977 international conference in his honor, held at the University of Chicago, he insisted on his viewpoint that algebras of SIOs with nonsmooth kernels (and thus not pseudo-differentials), are the ones suitable for solving concrete problems in physics and engineering, where lack of smoothness prevails.

Interest in Applied Problems. Calderón was keenly interested in the application of mathematics to physics and engineering problems. He was proud of the applied results he obtained during his brief stint at YPF in Argentina during 1947–1948, and even prouder when questions unsolved at that time were still unanswered. Calderón wrote on the applications of the Radon transform and on the phase problem 3-D Fourier transforms, crucial to 3-D crystallography. He felt good when his friend Paul Malliavin attributed his program of stochastic analysis to the influence of Calderón's paper on the uniqueness of the Cauchy problem. He was intrigued that the Calderón decomposition formula—a solution of the identity developed for complex interpolation in Banach spaces in the early 1960s—was rewritten as a decomposition of a wavelet and its inverse. In sum, he enjoyed very much seeing how his pure and applied work had influenced applied areas as diverse as signal processing, impedance tomography, geophysics, and wavelet theory.

Academic Career. The first academic position held by Calderón was as assistant professor at Ohio State University (1950–1953). After two years at the Institute for Advanced Study in Princeton, New Jersey, he joined the Massachusetts Institute of Technology (MIT) as associate professor (1955–1959). Calderón returned to the University of Chicago as professor (1959–1972; department chairman 1970–1972). He went back to MIT for three years and returned to Chicago in 1975 as university professor of mathematics until his retirement in 1985. During the late 1960s and early 1970s, he spent time in Argentina as a professor at the University of Buenos Aires and as director of the Argentine Institute of Mathematics (Instituto Argentino de Matemáticas).

Calderón had twenty-seven PhD students, among them some well-known mathematicians. In chronological order by school, they are Robert Seeley, Jerome Neuwirth, Irwin Bernstein, Israel Katz, and Robert Reitano, at MIT; Earl Berkson, Evelio Oklander, Cora Sadosky, Stephen Vagi, Umberto Neri, John Polking, Néstor Rivière, Carlos Segovia Fernández, Miguel de Guzmán, Daniel Fife, Alberto Torchinsky, Keith Powls, Carlos Kenig, Kent Merryfield, Michael Christ, and Gerald Cohen at the University of Chicago; and Josefina Dolores Álvarez Alonso, Telma Caputti, Angel Gatto, Cristián Gutiérrez, María Amelia Muschietti, and Marta Urciolo at the University of

Alberto Calderón. *Wolf Prize recipient in 1989.* **WOLF FOUNDATION. REPRODUCED BY PERMISSION.**

Buenos Aires. Now the Calderón-Zygmund school comprises mathematicians from many countries.

Honors. Calderón received the National Medal of Science (United States, 1991; Zygmund had received the same honor in 1986), the Wolf Prize (Israel, 1989, together with John Milnor), and the Böcher (1989) and Steele (1979) prizes from the American Mathematical Society, and the Consagración Nacional prize (Argentina, 1989). He was elected a Fellow of the American Academy of Arts and Sciences in 1957; a member of the National Academy of Sciences of the United States in 1968; and corresponding member of the national academies of Argentina, France, and Spain. He also received doctor honoris causa diplomas from the University of Buenos Aires (1969), the Technion Institute of Haifa (1989), Ohio State University (1995), and the Universidad Autónoma de Madrid (1997).

BIBLIOGRAPHY

Calderón's eighty-seven papers can be found online at the American Mathematical Society's MathSciNet, at http://www.ams.org/mathscinet.

WORKS BY CALDERÓN

"On a Theorem of Marcinkiewicz and Zygmund." *Transactions of the American Mathematical Society* (1950): 55–61. This paper and the two following ones are those that became Calderón's doctoral dissertation.

"On the Behavior of Harmonic Functions at the Boundary." *Transactions of the American Mathematical Society* 68 (1950): 47–54.

"On the Theorems of M. Riesz and Zygmund." *Proceedings of the American Mathematical Society* 1 (1950): 533–535.

With R. Pepinsky. "On the Phases of Fourier Coefficients of Positive Real Periodic Functions, Computing Methods and the Phase Problem in X-ray Crystal Analysis." Department of Physics, Pennsylvania State College (1952): 339–349. His first main paper on applications, solving the phase problem in 3-D crystallography. This pioneering result was not widely accessible to crystallographers since it appeared in an internal publication.

With Antoni Zygmund. "On the Existence of Certain Singular Integrals." *Acta Mathematica* 88 (1952): 85–139. Together with the two papers below, the foundation of the theory of singular integrals.

———. "Algebras of Certain Singular Integral Operators." *American Journal of Mathematics* 78 (1956): 310–320.

———. "On Singular Integrals." *American Journal of Mathematics* 78 (1956): 289–309.

"Uniqueness in the Cauchy Problem for Partial Differential Equations." *American Journal of Mathematics.* 80 (1958): 16–36. Fundamental contribution obtained through singular integral operators.

"Intermediate Spaces and Interpolation: The Complex Method." *Studia Mathematica* 24 (1964): 113–190. The definitive paper on complex interpolation.

"The Analytic Calculation of the Index of Elliptic Equations." *Proceedings of the National Academy of Sciences of the United States of America* 57 (1967): 1193–1194.

"Algebras of Singular Integral Operators." In *Proceedings of the International Congress of Mathematics (Moscow, 1966),* Moscow: Izdat "Mir," 1968, pp. 393–395. Summary of Calderón's main lecture at the 1966 ICM, one of the first large gatherings of mathematicians from East and West, and a fundamental occasion to establish significant relations among them.

With Rémi Vaillancourt. "On the Boundedness of Pseudo-differential Operators." *Journal of the Mathematical Society of Japan* 23 (1971): 374–378.

With Antoni Zygmund. "On Singular Integrals with Variable Kernels." *Applicable Analysis* 7 (1977–1978): 221–238.

"Commutators, Singular Integrals on Lipschitz Curves and Applications." In *Proceedings of the International Congress of Mathematics (Helsinki, 1978),* Helsinki, Finland: Academia Scientifica Fennica, 1980, pp. 85–89. Summary of Calderón's plenary address at the 1978 ICM on his new program.

"On an Inverse Boundary Value Problem." In *Seminar on Numerical Analysis and Its Applications to Continuum Physics.* Rio de Janeiro, Brazil: Sociedade Brasileira de Matemática, 1980, 65–73. This and the following paper deal with applications.

With Juan Enrique Santos and Jim Douglas. "Finite Element Methods for a Composite Model in Elastodynamics." *SIAM Journal of Numerical Analysis* 25 (1988): 513–532.

With Alexandra Bellow. "A Weak-Type Inequality for Convolution Products." In *Harmonic Analysis and Partial Differential Equations: Essays in Honor of Alberto P. Calderón,* edited by Michael Christ, Carlos E. Kenig, and Cora Sadosky, 41–48. Chicago: University of Chicago Press, 1999.

OTHER SOURCES

"Alberto Calderón." *Comptes Rendus de l'Académie des Sciences. Série Générale. La Vie des Science* 1 (1984): 514–515.

Christ, Michael, Carlos E. Kenig, Cora Sadosky, and Guido Weiss. "Alberto Pedro Calderón (1920–1998)." *Notices of the American Mathematical Society* 45 (1998): 1148–1153.

Lacey, Michael, and Christopher Thiele. "On Calderón's Conjecture." *Annals of Mathematics* 149 (1999): 475–496. American Mathematical Society featured review by Loukas Grafakos.

Segovia Fernández, Carlos. "Alberto Pedro Calderón, Matemático." *Revista de la Unión Matemática Argentina* 41 (1999): 129–140.

Stein, Elias M. "Calderón and Zygmund's Theory of Singular Integrals." In *Harmonic Analysis and Partial Differential Equations: Essays in Honor of Alberto P. Calderón,* edited by Michael Christ, Carlos E. Kenig, and Cora Sadosky, 1–26. Chicago: University of Chicago Press, 1999.

Uhlmann, Gunther. "Developments in Inverse Problems since Calderón's Foundational Paper." In *Harmonic Analysis and Partial Differential Equations: Essays in Honor of Alberto P. Calderón,* edited by Michael Christ, Carlos E. Kenig, and Cora Sadosky, 295–345. Chicago: University of Chicago Press, 1999.

Cora Sadosky

CALLENDAR, G.S.
SEE **Callendar, Guy Stewart**.

CALLENDAR, GUY STEWART (*b.* Montreal, Canada, 9 February 1898; *d.* Horsham, Sussex, United Kingdom, 3 October 1964), *steam and combustion engineering, climatology, glaciology, anthropogenic climate change.*

Callendar is noted for identifying, in 1938, the link between the artificial production of carbon dioxide and global warming, later called the "Callendar Effect." He was one of Britain's leading engineers, author of the standard reference book of tables and charts on the properties of steam at high temperatures and pressures, and designer of key components of the famous World War II airfield fog dispersal system, FIDO. He was keenly interested in weather and climate, taking measurements so accurate that they were used to correct the official temperature records of central England and collecting a series of worldwide weather data that showed an unprecedented warming trend in the first four decades of the twentieth century. He formulated a coherent theory of infrared absorption and emission by trace gases, established the nineteenth-century background concentration of carbon dioxide, and argued that its atmospheric concentration was rising due to human activities, which was causing the climate to warm.

Background and Education. Callendar was the third of four children and second son of Victoria Mary Stewart and the noted physicist Hugh Longbourne Callendar. When Guy was two, the family moved from Montreal to London. He received his primary education at Durston House, secondary education at St. Paul's School, and, after the war, attended City and Guilds Engineering College (part of Imperial College), where his father was chair of the physics department. His home life provided a rich creative and technical environment where he was introduced to the scientific elite of England and was able to pursue his interests in science and engineering, competitive tennis, and motor sports.

The loss of an eye in childhood rendered him unsuitable for frontline service during World War I. From 1915 to 1917, he worked in his father's laboratory at Imperial College as an assistant to the X-ray Committee of the Air Ministry, testing a variety of apparatus, including aircraft engines at the Royal Aircraft Factory (later Establishment) in Farnborough. Later he enlisted in the Royal Naval Volunteer Reserves, attaining the rank of sublieutenant. He served as a hydrophones officer and gained experience with electrical apparatus developed by his father for sound ranging and detection of submarines. Both father and son chose to work on defense projects that improved the efficiency of the military but avoided working on weapons systems. Callendar entered college in 1919, earned a certificate in mechanics and mathematics in 1922, and immediately went to work in the Physics Department at Imperial College where he assisted his father's experiments on steam at high temperatures and pressures.

After his father's death in 1930, Callendar continued his steam research at Imperial College, collaborating with the Oxford physicist Alfred Charles Glyn Egerton, under the patronage of the British Electrical and Allied Industries Research Association. Callendar participated in the International Steam Conferences in London (1929), Berlin (1930), and the United States (1934). He and Egerton led the British effort, working to reduce errors and inconsistencies in the thermodynamic properties of steam as measured by different techniques, taking measurements at ever higher temperatures and pressures, and striving to define international standard units. They published frequent updates of the famous *Callendar Steam*

Guy Stewart Callendar. COURTESY OF PROFESSOR JAMES R. FLEMING.

Tables, and their joint articles appeared in the *Philosophical Transactions* from 1933 until just after Egerton's death in 1959.

In 1930, Callendar married Phyllis Burdon Pentreath. Identical twin daughters were born the following year. The family moved from Ealing to Worthing and finally to Horsham in 1942 to a bungalow named "Redwoods" where Callendar resided the rest of his life. This final move placed him in close proximity to Langhurst, a secret research facility in West Sussex, where he worked on defense engineering projects until his retirement in 1958. His hobbies included tennis (he won a local tournament at age forty-nine), bicycling (20–40 mile trips), gardening (primarily fruit trees and conifers), and keeping an accurate and unbroken series of weather records from 1942 to 1964 at his home station, which he named "Percuil."

Wartime Research. During World War II, Callendar worked in research and development for the Petroleum Warfare Department and the Ministry of Supply. He was a key engineer and shared a patent in FIDO, an airfield fog dispersal system that provided Royal Air Force and Allied aviators with safe takeoff and landing facilities in marginal weather conditions. The FIDO system burned massive quantities of petrol to heat the fog, clear the air, and light the airfield. It used 3,000 to 5,000 gallons of fuel to land just one aircraft. Yet it was deemed worth the cost, since it allowed for flying in marginal weather conditions. FIDO was favored by pilots returning to foggy England after a mission, since they could see the airfield glowing in the distance, beckoning them home to a lighted, fog-free airport. They could also save valuable time getting their damaged planes and exhausted (and possibly wounded) crews on the ground.

During the war Callendar also examined the efficiencies of different types of electrochemical storage and generating devices. This work required that he devise tests to record and compare the efficiencies of different types of batteries and fuel cells. The challenge was immense, since the problem of providing powerful, reliable, and long-lived sources of electricity in the field was a perennial one.

In another project, Callendar collaborated with the Cambridge physicist Gordon Brims Black McIvor Sutherland, on delineating the absorption and emission characteristics of the infrared spectra of hydrocarbons and atmospheric trace gases. Captured German fuel was burned and subjected to spectroscopic analysis to determine its composition and likely place of origin, yielding strategically important knowledge. The research also resulted in fundamental new insights into the spectra of water vapor, carbon dioxide, and ozone at low concentrations and low temperatures in the atmosphere, of critical importance to studies of the Earth's heat budget.

Callendar was deeply engaged in research for the Petroleum Warfare Department that emphasized the development of flamethrowers. Thus it was impossible not to contribute to their use as offensive weapons. Nevertheless, by emphasizing FIDO and other projects involving the efficiency of fuel propellant systems and the application of thermal technology to war-related problems, Callendar attempted to isolate his work as much as possible from the killing fields. He designed internal baffles for fuel tanks, experimental devices for forest clearing, and new fuel propellant systems.

After the war, Callendar's work for the Ministry of Supply involved experimental methods for generating high-speed air currents and testing space heaters for military applications in cold climates. Throughout his years of government service, Callendar remained steadfast in his resolve to contribute to improvements in efficiency rather than weapons systems. In this he was following the pattern inculcated by his father.

Climate Research. Callendar's most significant and original scientific contribution was in climatology, specifically anthropogenic climate change. In the first half of the twentieth century, the carbon dioxide theory of climate change, established by John Tyndall (1859) and Svante Arrhenius (1896) had fallen out of favor with most scientists. This was due mainly to the lack of detailed understanding of the infrared spectra of atmospheric trace gases. The dominant opinion was that, at current atmospheric concentrations, carbon dioxide already absorbed all the available long-wave radiation; thus any increases would not change the radiative heat balance of the planet but might augment plant growth. Other physical mechanisms of climatic change, although highly speculative, were given more credence, especially changes in solar luminosity, atmospheric transparency, and the Earth's orbital elements. Callendar acknowledged the "chequered history" of the CO_2 theory: "[I]t was abandoned for many years when the prepondering influence of water vapour radiation in the lower atmosphere was first discovered, but was revived again a few years ago when more accurate measurements of the water vapour spectrum became available" (Callendar, 1949).

Beginning in 1938, Callendar revived and reformulated the carbon dioxide theory by arguing that rising global temperatures and increased fossil fuel burning were closely linked. Callendar, working on his own time and from home, compiled weather data from stations around the world that clearly indicated a global warming trend of about 0.5 C in the early decades of the twentieth century. Callendar investigated the carbon cycle, including natural and anthropogenic sources and sinks, and the role of glaciers in the Earth's heat budget. From his review of earlier measurements, Callendar established what would become the standard number of 290 parts per million (ppm) as the nineteenth-century background concentration of carbon dioxide in the atmosphere. He documented an increase of ten percent in this figure between 1900 and 1935, which closely matched the amount of fuel burned. Callendar pointed out that humans had long been able to intervene in and accelerate natural processes, and that humanity was now intervening heavily in the slow-moving carbon cycle by "throwing some 9,000 tons of carbon dioxide into the air each minute" (Callendar, 1939a). In an era before computer climate modeling, Callendar compiled all the newly available information on the detailed infrared absorption and emission spectra of atmospheric trace gases into a coherent picture of interest and relevance to meteorologists. He argued that the rising carbon dioxide content of the atmosphere and the rising temperature were due to human activities, thus establishing the carbon dioxide theory of climate change in its recognizably modern form and reviving it from its earlier, physically unrealistic and moribund status.

By the 1950s, as temperatures around the Northern Hemisphere reached early-twentieth-century peaks, global warming first found its way onto the public agenda. Concerns were expressed in both the scientific and popular press about rising sea levels, loss of habitat, and shifting agricultural zones. Amid the myriad mechanisms that could possibly account for climatic changes, G. S. Callendar was the first of many to document connections between rising surface temperatures, increasing anthropogenic CO2 emissions, infrared radiation, and global climate warming. His writings revived the theme of human agency, which had been dormant since the age of Jefferson, by pointing out that humanity had become an agent of global change by interfering with the natural carbon cycle. In the early 2000s, the theory that global climate change can be attributed to an enhanced greenhouse effect due to elevated levels of carbon dioxide in the atmosphere from anthropogenic sources, primarily from the combustion of fossil fuels, is called the "Callendar Effect" (Fleming, 2007).

Although Callendar was in declining health for the last six months of his life, he did not discuss it openly. His weather journal ended in September 1964, with a note indicating: "The sunniest September since 1911." He died suddenly on 3 October 1964 of coronary thrombosis.

Callendar was a quiet, family-oriented man, an avid sportsman, and a modest and unassuming contributor at the leading edge of research. He was a Fellow of the Royal Meteorological Society and served on its council. He was also a Fellow of the Glaciological Society. He counted many, many distinguished scientists as his friends, colleagues, and coworkers. In his early years he was deeply influenced by his famous physicist father. He received a first-rate technical education and entered into collaborations with Britain's technical elite on steam research and the infrared spectra of complex molecules.

His work on the thermodynamics of steam was foundational for steam-plant design calculations in Great Britain for over three decades. His papers on the infrared properties of trace gases drew rave reviews from leading meteorologists and climatologists and influenced the later development of the field. His work in defense-related research in two world wars and the Cold War was directed, wherever possible, toward nonviolent ends. Among many, many other accomplishments, he established the "Callendar Effect," the link between anthropogenic CO_2 and global warming.

BIBLIOGRAPHY

Callendar's unpublished papers (3 linear ft.) are in the library of the Climatic Research Unit at the University of East Anglia. The collection, including scientific correspondence, charts, research notebooks on climate and carbon dioxide, and a box of family documents and scanned photographs, has been published in digital format on DVD as The Papers of Guy Stewart Callendar, *edited by James Rodger Fleming and Jason Thomas Fleming, Boston, American Meteorological Society, 2007.*

WORKS BY CALLENDAR

"The Artificial Production of Carbon Dioxide and Its Influence on Temperature." *Quarterly Journal of the Royal Meteorological Society* 64 (1938): 223–240.

"The Composition of the Atmosphere through the Ages." *Meteorological Magazine* 74 (March 1939a): 33–39.

With Hugh L. Callendar and Sir Alfred Egerton. *The 1939 Callendar Steam Tables.* London: Published for the British Electrical and Allied Industries Research Association by Edward Arnold, 1939b. 2nd ed. 1944, 1949, and 1957.

With Gordon Brims Black McIvor Sutherland. "The Infra-red Spectra of Atmospheric Gases other than Water Vapour." *Reports on Progress in Physics* 9 (1942–1943): 18–28.

"Can Carbon Dioxide Influence Climate?" *Weather* 4 (1949): 310-314.

"On the Amount of Carbon Dioxide in the Atmosphere." *Tellus* 10 (1958): 243–248.

With Sir Alfred Egerton. "An Experimental Study of the Enthalpy of Steam." *Philosophical Transactions of the Royal Society of London*, Series A, 252 (1960): 133–164.

"Temperature Fluctuations and Trends over the Earth." *Quarterly Journal of the Royal Meteorological Society* 87 (1961): 1–11.

OTHER SOURCES

Bowen, Mark. *Thin Ice.* New York: Henry Holt, 2005.

Fleming, James Rodger. *Historical Perspectives on Climate Change.* New York: Oxford University Press, 1998.

———. *The Callendar Effect: The Life and Work of Guy Stewart Callendar (1898–1964), the Scientist Who Established the Carbon Dioxide Theory of Climate Change.* Boston, American Meteorological Society, 2007. This book contains Callendar's complete annotated bibliography, many family photographs, and an inventory of his study at the time of his death.

James Rodger Fleming

CALVIN, MELVIN (*b.* St. Paul, Minnesota, 8 April 1911; *d.* Berkeley, California, 8 January 1997), *chemistry, photosynthesis, origin of life, cancer, molecular basis of learning.*

Calvin is remembered above all for his work in photosynthesis, research that won him the Nobel Prize in Chemistry in 1961. During the latter part of the 1940s, and throughout the following decade, he led and inspired an outstanding group of researchers in unraveling a mechanism that had been a mystery for centuries. Not only was his scientific understanding outstanding, so was his leadership. Under his guidance, what was probably the first of the large integrated, modern research units in the biological sciences flourished unsurpassed for more than fifteen years.

Early Days. Born to Elias and Rose (née Hervitz) Calvin, immigrant parents from East Europe, Melvin Calvin began to show an interest in science even in his tender years. As a child, he collected rocks, watched birds, and mused about the nature and composition of the many products he saw in his parents' grocery store. It led inevitably to a lifelong dedication to chemistry.

The family moved to Detroit, where Melvin attended the Central High School before going on to take a degree in chemistry at Michigan College of Science and Technology. There followed a PhD at the University of Minnesota, where he worked with George Glockler on the electron affinity of halogens (initially iodine and later also bromine and chlorine) from space-charge effects.

Leaving Minnesota with his doctorate, Calvin used his own savings to supplement a postdoctoral fellowship from the National Research Council to work for two years with Michael Polány, as Rockefeller Fellow during the 1935–1937 period, at the University of Manchester. His research topic was the interactions between quantum mechanical theory and chemical experimentation, starting with platinum-hydrogen activation systems.

Move to Berkeley. While Calvin was still in Manchester, Joel Hildebrand of the Chemistry Department in Berkeley paid a passing visit there and met Calvin. With a glowing recommendation from Polányi, Calvin was invited to join the Berkeley faculty, where he remained for the next sixty years. Calvin's innate talent and experience were the sources of his inspiration, competence, and confidence; he was soon to benefit from being in the right place at the right time, and good luck followed in due course.

For Calvin, the period in Manchester was part of becoming a mature scientist: He gained from the experience of living outside his native country and, as a postdoctoral fellow, was recognized as one of them by his fellow scientists. He was drawn into studies on the activation of hydrogen by phthalocyanine and copper, becoming familiar with pigment chemistry and light absorption. Ten years later that experience was to prove invaluable, providing him the opportunity to embark upon what emerged as his life's great contributions to biological chemistry. But in 1937, he joined the Berkeley faculty as an assistant professor with an interest in chelate chemistry; in the war that followed just a few years later, he used his knowledge and skills as a participant in the Manhattan Project. In 1942, he married Genevieve Jemtegaard, a junior probation officer.

The Beginning of the Photosynthesis Studies. Calvin's big chance came in the autumn of 1945; to understand its significance it is necessary to go back to the history of photosynthesis and the level of understanding before Word War II. It had been known for two centuries that

Melvin Calvin. JON BRENNEIS/TIME LIFE PICTURES/GETTY IMAGES.

sunlight allows green plants to fix atmospheric carbon dioxide into all the organic compounds needed for the plants to grow and reproduce. What was not known was how it was done. There were theories—including a suggestion that the fixation of carbon dioxide first formed formaldehyde, which was then supposed to polymerize into sugars. But the basis for that idea was simply that the empirical formula for formaldehyde (CH_2O) multiplied six times gave the equally empirical formula for a hexose sugar ($C_6H_{12}O_6$); there was no experimental evidence and, indeed, plants fail to produce sugar when supplied with formaldehyde and are actually poisoned by it.

The problem, of course, was that, once inside the plant, the carbon atoms that had originated in the carbon dioxide could not be distinguished from those already there; where had the carbon dioxide carbons gone? Hope for resolution came with the discovery in the early 1930s of the first radioisotope of carbon, ^{11}C.

By virtue of its radioactivity, $^{11}CO_2$ supplied to plants would allow the incoming carbon to be located in whatever compound(s) in which it might become incorporated. The limitation was the way carbon-11 is produced (in the cyclotron, compounds containing nitrogen-14 are bombarded with protons; each impacted nitrogen atom captures a proton and then emits an (-particle to yield an atom of carbon-11) and its short half-life of only twenty minutes. Early attempts to use it, by Sam Ruben and Martin Kamen (joined later by Andrew Benson), took place in prewar Berkeley, but the experimental difficulties were immense; experiments had to be completed within two or three hours of manufacturing the nuclide.

Those studies were undertaken in the Radiation Laboratory of the University of California at Berkeley—just yards away from Calvin's office. Ernest Lawrence, director of the laboratory and inventor of the cyclotron used to produce the carbon-11, reasoned from his knowledge of nuclear physics that a longer-lived isotope (^{14}C) should exist. It was indeed discovered in 1940 but no more than minute amounts were available, and all further developments ceased when the United States entered the war in December 1941. Everybody involved had more important things to do, and by the time the war ended the original team was no longer in place.

ORL and the Bio-Organic Chemistry Group. But Lawrence had not forgotten. The Manhattan Project generated sizable quantities of carbon-14, to which Lawrence, as director of the Radiation Laboratory (the contractor for the Manhattan Project), had access. The story has it that one day in the autumn of 1945 Lawrence and Calvin were walking back to their offices after lunch in the faculty club. Lawrence suggested to Calvin that he might like to make use of the newly available carbon-14 to do two things: develop its chemistry and synthesize compounds for medical research, and use it to resolve the age-old photosynthesis puzzle: the pathway of carbon from carbon dioxide to sugars, proteins, and all the other compounds in green plants. Lawrence would supply the funding, the carbon-14, and a building, an old two-story wooden structure that had been the original home of his cyclotron and known as "ORL—the Old Radiation Lab." It was to become world-famous among plant biochemists. The Bio-Organic Chemistry Group was born.

As the prime experimental tool, Calvin's group decided to use the green microalga *Chlorella* rather than the leaves of a higher plant; as a chemist, Calvin was much happier using a suspension of a unicellular organism that could be dispensed in a pipette than trying to get uniform samples of leaves.

The basic experiment was to shine a bright light onto a suspension of the algal cells in the famous "lollipop," a thin vessel (so that light reached all the cells uniformly) into which, at the start of the experiment, was injected a solution containing $^{14}CO_2$ in the form of $NaH^{14}CO_3$. At precise times thereafter, from seconds to minutes, the

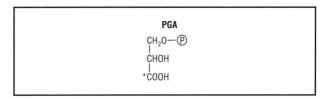

Figure 1. *3-Phophoglyceric acid. The carbon dioxide newly incoporated forms the carboxyl (COOH) group at the bottom of the structure.*

stopcock at the base of the vessel was opened to allow some of the suspension to fall into a flask of boiling ethanol, instantly killing the alga and stopping all biochemical reactions. The location of the carbon-14 in products could then be determined by appropriate analysis.

In the early days analysis depended on ion-exchange resins, a slow and tedious procedure. Nevertheless, it did allow the identification of the first compound to incorporate carbon from carbon dioxide; it turned out to be the 3-carbon sugar acid phosphate, 3-phosphoglyceric acid, thereafter known around the world as *PGA*. In short-term experiments, the carbon-14 was found almost entirely in the terminal carboxyl carbon, strongly suggesting that carbon dioxide had been added in some way to a 2-carbon receptor. The next problem was to identify it.

If the research had relied permanently on ion-exchange chromatography, the path of carbon in photosynthesis might never have been elucidated. Fortunately, in 1944, the technique of paper chromatography had been developed in Britain by Archer J. P. Martin, Raphael Consden, and Richard L. M. Synge. By 1948, word of this new and powerful technique had reached the Botany Department in Berkeley, from whence it was brought to Calvin's laboratory by a graduate student, William H. Stepka.

Resolving the Photosynthesis Puzzle. Paper chromatography revolutionized the group's analytical procedures; using a wide panoply of classical and novel analytical procedures combined with chromatography, a whole range of compounds incorporating carbon-14 from labeled bicarbonate were identified (always in minute chemical quantities), revealed, and made accessible by virtue of their ^{14}C labeling. Each large paper chromatogram was placed against a sheet of x-ray film and sealed in a lightproof envelope; in the course of days or weeks, the radioactive emissions produced a latent image on the film which, when developed, gave the exact location, size, and shape of each "spot" of a labeled compound; such "radioautograms" were the mainstay of the path-of-carbon research. It took years to identify all the radioactive spots, but in time that was done and maps were produced of how

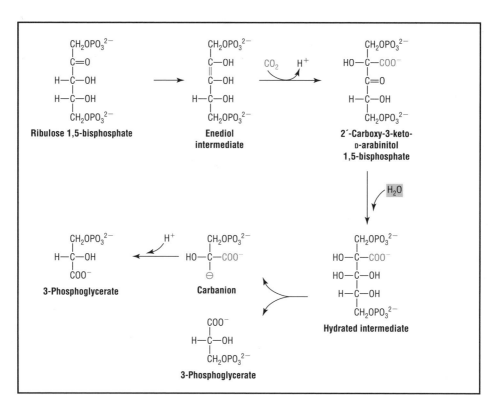

Figure 2. *The primary reaction incoporating carbon dioxide to become one of the two 3-phosphoglycerate carboxyl groups.*

compounds of interest migrated in the chromatographic system, which everybody in the lab used.

The kinetic relationships between these compounds were explored: How fast and in which order did these substances acquire carbon-14? Degradation methods were developed allowing the accumulation of radiocarbon to be measured within the individual atoms of the product molecules.

It eventually became clear that carbon dioxide was converted into hexoses by a reversal of glycolysis (breakdown of sugar into carbon dioxide and water, releasing energy), the reducing power necessary to drive the process deriving from the capture of sunlight by the energy-conversion mechanism of chloroplasts. But identifying the 2-carbon acceptor with which carbon dioxide combined was much more difficult; in short-term labeling experiments this acceptor would not itself be labeled so there was no obvious way of identifying it.

Clues ultimately came from the kinetics of the intramolecular distribution of carbon-14 within many of the compounds already shown to be products of carbon dioxide fixation. As it gradually became clear that the biochemistry of carbon fixation was a cyclic process, Calvin and his colleagues moved towards the idea of a 5-carbon acceptor, which, in accepting one molecule of carbon

dioxide, would be split into two molecules of PGA, each identical with the other except for its radioactive labeling pattern.

In two classic experiments in 1954 and 1955, Peter Massini from Switzerland and Alex Wilson, a New Zealander, showed that when the light was switched off and then on again, or the carbon dioxide concentration suddenly reduced, the kinetic behavior of compounds in the putative cycle was consistent with the operation of a cyclic pathway. By the late 1950s, the mystery of the path of carbon in photosynthesis had essentially been solved except for some details. A detailed understanding of the enzymology, particularly of the primary fixation reaction, came later from work in a variety of laboratories.

Calvin and the group's interest in photosynthesis was by no means confined to metabolic pathways; many pioneering experiments were conducted to characterize the primary photochemical events. The laboratory was one of the first two to apply the new method of electron paramagnetic resonance to photosynthetic systems, which showed there were two kinds of organic free radicals produced as a result of light absorption, one of which appeared to be either a one-electron reduced or oxidized chlorophyll species. Pursuit of such studies eventually led to the assignment of one of these signals to a pair of chlorophyll molecules which served as the primary electron donor in photosystem I, while the second was assigned to an oxidized tyrosine side chain in the protein of photosystem II.

This most exciting period of discovery yielded a famous series of twenty-three papers (the last in 1958) under the title "The Path of Carbon in Photosynthesis." ORL became the mecca for biochemists, biophysicists, and plant physiologists from around the world; graduate students (mostly, but not exclusively, from the United States) came for two or three years to carry out their thesis work, while postdoctoral visitors from around the world spent a year or two before going back home and spreading the word. In 1961, Calvin himself was awarded the Nobel Prize in Chemistry, in just and proper recognition of a remarkable achievement in inspiring his colleagues to achieve the success in which all of them shared.

As he himself recognized, he was but one of many scientists who had contributed. Foremost among them were Andrew A. Benson and James A. Bassham. Benson had for a time been part of the prewar ^{11}C effort; at the war's end he was no longer in Berkeley, and Calvin invited him back to take charge of the photosynthesis subgroup. For ten years they did it together before Benson left to become independent at another university. Thereafter, Bassham, who had joined the group as a graduate student after service in the U.S. Navy, became the de facto leader of the photosynthesis laboratory activities, with his publications world famous. He stayed for the whole of his working life.

Isotopic carbon and related activities were run by Bert M. Tolbert until he left for Colorado in 1958. Just as in the Benson/Bassham exchange, he was succeeded by Richard M. Lemmon, who had also joined as a graduate student some years earlier. Lemmon's specialty was hot atom recoil chemistry, and he, too, remained a member of the group until retirement.

After ORL. Inevitably, after the excitement of the path of carbon, the character of the Bio-Organic Chemistry Group changed. ORL itself was demolished in 1959 as part of a new chemistry development; all that remained was a plaque, although for many years Calvin kept the old door in his office. The Bio-Organic Chemistry Group was temporarily relocated several hundred yards away in the Life Sciences Building, with uncertainty about their ultimate home. Indeed, the two parts, photosynthesis and isotope work, had never been together under one roof; the latter had occupied space in the Donner Laboratory, itself a distance from ORL.

Calvin had plans for a new building. ORL was notable for its comparative lack of internal subdivisions. The researchers in the large labs were constantly talking to one another as they went about their work, while in the

center of the main laboratory stood a large white table on which the radioautograms were scrutinized, compared, and discussed. A map of the relevant compounds hung on the wall above the table. That table was the social and scientific nerve center of the group; it was where people constantly met for coffee and discussion. Not infrequently, such discussions would generate new ideas for experiments and inevitably another avenue of inquiry had been established.

It was very important that a new building had enough space to accommodate the whole group and also retained in some way the open structure. As funding became available, a three-story circular building was designed with half of the two upper floors open spaces without walls. The building, originally called the Laboratory of Chemical Biodynamics (LCB) and later Melvin Calvin Laboratory, was opened with some ceremony in November 1963. While the new building was modern, and with facilities that made the lovingly remembered ORL seem in some ways old-fashioned if not primitive, the ambience was never quite recreated.

There were a number of reasons. At the founding of the group in 1945, Calvin himself was thirty-four years old and his associates ten years younger. Some of them were still there in the 1960s and 1970s, experienced and respected scientists in their forties and fifties, each with their own research teams. Moreover, the group as a whole never again had that unity of purpose it possessed during the path-of-carbon years, and Calvin was not able to provide that same sort of leadership. Gradually, fragmentation began.

Calvin himself acquired a number of interests. He never entirely abandoned either the biochemical or the physical chemical aspects of photosynthesis, but his involvement was greatly diluted by his other activities. In the following twenty years, they encompassed the chemical origins of life, the biochemistry of learning, control of protein synthesis, cancer, moon rock analysis, novel synthetic biomembrane models for plant photosystems, and the use of certain plant oils as potential vehicle fuels. A number of these developed into discrete research activities, often accompanied by the recruitment of a scientist of some seniority and experience and with Calvin's continuing involvement and encouragement.

In addition, Calvin was at various times a consultant for Dow, Upjohn, and Diamond Shamrock as well as some start-ups, and was a member at one time of the Dow main board. During the late 1950s and early 1960s he was chairman of the National Academy of Sciences Committee on Science and Public Policy.

Furthermore, after Calvin was awarded the Nobel Prize, President Kennedy appointed him to his Science Advisory Committee. Calvin, whose life hitherto had been devoted almost totally to science and scientific discovery, suddenly found a whole new world of politics, social significance, and the rest. For him, of course, that was a new voyage of discovery, undertaken with his customary enthusiasm.

Inevitably, he found himself more and more stretched among his many concerns. Once upon a time, in the early days, he was constantly in the lab. As Andy Benson wrote:

> Melvin usually finished his lectures, office and committee work about 5:30 p.m. and stopped in at the lab with his usual question, "What's new?." Though we had just started the experiment for the day, we usually had some answer. But, the next morning when Melvin came in at 8 or before; he was an early riser; there was the first cheery question, "Well, what's new?" There was no letup. I had to keep some tidbits in reserve so that there was always something interesting to report. When important chromatograms were exposed on X-ray film we used two sheets, one to develop too early, to appease Melvin's insatiable curiosity, and one for proper documentation. (Communication to the author, 9 September 1998)

From an early date in its history, the group would meet collectively for a seminar round a long table at 8 a.m. on Friday mornings. When they first started, Calvin (who always sat at the front, on the right-hand side facing the speaker) would look round the room, point a finger at a colleague and say, "You tell us what you've been doing." No sooner was the poor unfortunate so selected halfway through his opening sentence than Calvin asked the first of many, many questions. The graduate students were petrified but dared not absent themselves. So it became the practice at the Thursday management lunch of the more senior group members to nominate the speaker for the next morning. At least that gave the victim time to collect his thoughts and arrange his material, and many a student worked nonstop through the night to do so. It was only after twenty years or so that a schedule encompassing several months was drawn up.

Calvin was perceived as being fierce in his questioning; he was not unkind or rude but certainly determined to have an answer. It was in practice an excellent training for his colleagues, some of whom adopted similar styles when later they left for academic positions elsewhere and formed their own groups.

The Friday morning seminars continued throughout Calvin's directorship of the group, but his own involvement in the details of lab activities and results declined markedly. There was much too much of it, and he was busy on too many fronts, both inside and outside the lab. Towards the end, his immediate students had something of a thin time: The fire and imagination were undimin-

ished but even for Calvin the day was only twenty-four hours long.

The Outstanding Scientist. Calvin was a superb lecturer, particularly in his earlier days when he felt able to get away with total informality. Hitching himself onto the front of the lecturer's bench or table, he would speak without notes, both he and his listeners carried away by enthusiasm for the topic. He seemed to have no concept of time and would suddenly pull himself up short, realizing he had overrun and would hastily try to bring his presentation to an orderly end.

When awarded the Nobel Prize, he was shocked to learn that protocol demanded him to give his acceptance lecture in exactly forty minutes. So, perhaps for the first time in his life, he wrote out his lecture and got his colleagues to edit and time it for him. His wife, following his text, sat next to the projectionist in order to indicate when the next slide was to be shown, thus saving Calvin the trouble of saying so and giving him a few extra precious seconds.

Those who knew Calvin and worked with him will never forget the experience. He was the most stimulating colleague one could imagine, ready to entertain any idea backed up with reason and sense. He read science voraciously; challenging him on any issue was no easy matter because he knew where the evidence had been published. But he was not averse to floating proposals that themselves were flimsily based and took being shot down with good grace—provided the ammunition was itself reliable.

Calvin retired as director in 1980 but continued to occupy an office and some laboratory space in the chemistry department. He had suffered a severe heart attack in 1949 from which he recovered completely, but after his wife died in 1987, he became rather depressed and gradually grew more frail. He died on 8 January 1997 after suffering a fall, survived by his daughters Elin and Karole, and his son Noel.

BIBLIOGRAPHY

WORKS BY CALVIN

With Gerald E. K. Branch. *The Theory of Organic Chemistry.* New York: Prentice-Hall, 1941.

With Charles Heidelberger, James C. Reid, Bert M. Tolbert, and Peter E. Yankwich. *Isotopic Carbon: Techniques in Its Measurement and Chemical Manipulation.* New York: John Wiley, 1949.

With Arthur E. Martell. *The Chemistry of Metal Chelate Compounds.* New York: Prentice-Hall, 1952.

With James A. Bassham. *The Path of Carbon in Photosynthesis.* Englewood Cliffs, NJ: Prentice-Hall, 1957.

The Path of Carbon in Photosynthesis. Nobel Lectures, Chemistry 1942–1962, Elsevier Publishing Company, Amsterdam,

1964. Also available at http://nobelprize.org/nobel_prizes/chemistry/laureates/1961/calvin-lecture.html.

Chemical Evolution: Molecular Evolution towards the Origins of Living Systems on Earth and Elsewhere. Oxford: Clarendon Press, 1969.

"Melvin Calvin: Chemistry and Chemical Biodynamics at Berkeley, 1937–1980." Archived in the History of Science and Technology Program, The Bancroft Library, University of California at Berkeley, 1984.

Following the Trail of Light: A Scientific Odyssey. Washington, DC: American Chemical Society, 1992. This book contains a bibliography listing many of Calvin's papers.

OTHER SOURCES

Moses, Vivian. "Professor Melvin Calvin" (obituary). *The Times* (London), 16 January 1997.

———. "Melvin Calvin (1911–1997)." *Nature* 385, 13 February, 1997.

———. "Melvin Calvin (1911–1997)." *Advances in Carbohydrate Chemistry and Biology* 55 (1999), 14–21.

Moses, Vivian, and Sheila Moses, eds. The Bio-Organic Chemistry Group, University of California (1945–63): Interviews for an Oral History. 1998. Recordings and transcripts archived in the Bancroft Library, University of California at Berkeley, at the Chemical Heritage Foundation, Philadelphia, and in the British Library, London.

Seaborg, Glenn T., and Andrew A. Benson. "Melvin Calvin." *Biographical Memoirs,* vol. 75. Washington, DC: National Academy of Sciences, 1998. Also available at http://www.nap.edu/books/0309062950/html/96.html.

Zallen, Doris T. "Redrawing the Boundaries of Molecular Biology: The Case of Photosynthesis." *Journal of the History of Biology* 26 (1993), 65–87. Not much on Calvin, but good for background reading.

Vivian Moses

CAMPANELLA, TOMMASO (*b.* Stilo, Calabria, Italy, 5 September 1568; *d.* Paris, France, 21 May 1639), *philosophy of nature, natural magic, astrology, medicine.* For the original article on Campanella see *DSB,* vol. 15, Supplement I.

Philosopher and theologian Campanella outlined in his extensive writings an impressive project of social reform and the reconstruction of the entire body of knowledge, seeking to reconcile the heritage of the Renaissance with the principles of the Counter-Reformation and of the new science. The primary focal points of his thought concern not only the philosophy of nature, politics, and religion, but also literature—Campanella is the author of an extraordinary collection of philosophical poetry. The principle that bestows unity and coherence upon the various parts of his complex, pluriform, and multifaceted philosophy is the constant reference to nature which, because it is the expression of rationality and divine truth, Campanella regarded as the ideal model for inspiring reforms in philosophy as well as in social and political structures.

The Early Years. Campanella was born 5 September 1568 in Stilo, Calabria, which was part of the viceroyalty of Naples and governed by the king of Spain. When he was barely fourteen years of age he entered the Dominican Order, which, given his family's very modest means, afforded him his only opportunity to pursue the studies for which he demonstrated a precocious and remarkable aptitude. In the Calabrian monasteries of the Dominicans he studied the works of Aristotle and his followers, but even in his early youth he was deeply intolerant of them. In his opinion the *Peripatetics* were too respectful of the authority of their master and were more interested in annotating Aristotle's books than in investigating first-hand the natural world; in this way, he believed, philosophic research had degenerated into sophistic and sterile disputations. On the other hand, Campanella felt an immediate attraction for the work of Bernardino Telesio. The latter's *De rerum natura iuxta propria principia* (1565, 1586; On the nature of things according to its own principles) proposed to seek truth through sensitive experience and the internal principles of nature itself, thus reestablishing the correct connections between "things" and "words." According to Campanella, the books written by human beings are partial and imperfect copies of the "book of nature," which, because it was written by God, is the sole depository of absolute truth; human books, therefore, must be continually compared and corrected in the light of the natural book.

The critique of Aristotelian philosophy on the physical, cosmological, and metaphysical levels and the defense of Telesian philosophy—strengthened with topics derived from other philosophies and authors (the pre-Socratics, Plato, Neoplatonism, Hermetism, Pliny's *Natural History*)—comprise the contents of Campanella's first work, *Philosophia sensibus demonstrata* (1591; Philosophy demonstrated by the senses). In this work of his youth and in later ones, the foundations of the Aristotelian system are demolished and replaced by new Telesian doctrines on such fundamental concepts as space, matter, movement, and the composition of celestial bodies. The work was published in Naples, a city where Campanella often met with Giambattista della Porta, one of the most famous proponents of the tradition of natural magic. But the young monk's adherence to the philosophy of Telesio rather than to scholastic and Aristotelian doctrines aroused the suspicions of theologians. Although he was imprisoned in 1592, Campanella was acquitted of the accusations against him, after which he went first to Rome and then to Florence and Bologna, where the manuscripts of his works were seized by emissaries of the Inquisition.

Settling in Padua, he met Galileo, a friend whom he would always hold in esteem. Unfortunately, Campanella was to face further and more perilous judiciary problems: In October 1594 he was incarcerated in the prison of the Holy Office in Rome. Forced to abjure "for most grave suspicion of heresy," at the end of 1597 Campanella was ordered back to Calabria, and in the summer of 1598, at nearly thirty years of age and after having been away for a decade, Campanella found himself once more in Stilo. Here he would become involved in the most dramatic events of his life, events that would influence the rest of his career. Prophetic and astrological texts, natural and heavenly signs, but especially conditions of serious social and political disorder in Calabria, persuaded Campanella that, as the century drew toward its end, a period of radical changes was approaching. He thus became the leader of a broad conspiracy that proposed to free the province from the tyranny of the king of Spain and to transform it into a republic founded on natural and rational principles. Betrayed to the Spanish authorities by two of its accomplices, the conspiracy was crushed at birth by an army sent at the order of the viceroy. Accused of the double crime of lèse-majesté and of heresy, Campanella avoided the death penalty only by feigning madness; he spent the next twenty-seven years in Neapolitan prisons.

Natural Philosophy. During his long years of imprisonment and under very harsh living conditions, Campanella devoted himself to composing his most important works. In them, nature plays a principal role even in the religious and political fields. In *Ateismo trionfato* (Atheism vanquished; Rome, 1631, and Paris, 1636) for example, Campanella set out to prove that religion is not a human invention, not a useful trick dreamed up by priests and princes in order to seize and maintain power, as the followers of Machiavelli and the "reason of State" affirmed; on the contrary, Campanella asserted, it is a *virtus naturalis* (natural power) intrinsic in mankind and in even the smallest aspect of nature. As for his political thought, early in his incarceration Campanella composed his most famous work, the *Città del Sole* (City of the Sun, 1623). The ideal city is presented as a "body of the republic" in which the individual members are part of a unified organism and contribute to the welfare of all. In order to avoid the errors and injustice of existing societies, Campanella founded his "philosophic city" on natural principles, such as an equitable division of labor based on the capabilities and the inclinations of the individuals; communal ownership of wealth; attention to procreation (eugenic norms); education available to all and made easier and more pleasant through images painted on the walls of the buildings that would gird the city in seven circles. The work was

issued in Latin translation in the corpus of the *Philosophia realis*, published in Frankfurt in 1623 by Tobias Adami, a German scholar who had come into contact with the prisoner in Naples. Political reflection is a constant feature of the thought of Campanella, who in other texts treated themes relating to the prospect of a universal monarchy and of the reunification of humanity in "a single flock under a single shepherd"; in the *Monarchia di Spagna* (Monarchy of Spain, 1640), he emphasized the providential role of the Catholic king, who, like the biblical Cyrus, has the duty to unite people in a single faith.

A prominent aspect of Campanella's philosophy of nature is natural magic, elaborated with particular effectiveness in *De sensu rerum et magia* (On the sense of things and on magic, 1620), in which Campanella expounded his vision of the natural world, considered as an organism whose individual parts are invested with life and sensitivity. Every natural being tends toward self-preservation, and to this end it is endowed, in differing degrees, with "sense," that is to say feelings and a capacity to distinguish what is useful for its own life and that should be sought and pursued, from what is perceived as destructive and that one should avoid and flee. In animal organisms the cognitive and vital functions are connected with the *spiritus*, the warm, wafting, pliant breath issuing from matter rendered extremely tenuous by the heat of the sun. It resides in the brain and, passing through very thin nerve channels, comes into contact, by means of the sensory organs, with the exhalations, motions, and light that exude from external objects; all its passions and knowledge arise from the modifications that the *spiritus* undergoes. In Book IV of the *De sensu rerum*, Campanella reinterpreted the tradition of natural magic in the light of the doctrine of the sense of things and of the *spiritus*. The magician is he who understands the sense inherent in each being and is capable of inducing certain alterations and passions into the *spiritus*. He knows how to activate the vital forces by suggesting appropriate foods, beverages, climates, sounds, and herbal and animal remedies; he understands the secrets of procreation and of illnesses; and he can explain natural divinations and the prophecies of dreams or the changes in those bitten by a rabid dog or by tarantulas, changes effected by the spread and the domination in their organism of the "spirit" of the animal that attacked them. The *spiritus* and its passions also play a central role in the *Medicina* (1653; Medicine), in which Campanella, revisiting some themes of Hippocrates and especially of Marsilio Ficino, defined medicine as "a kind of magical practice" (*quaedam magica praxis*) dedicated to avoiding or caring for illnesses through a knowledge of all human aspects—physical, psychological, emotional, and environmental.

Campanella's relations with Galileo occupied a central role in his thought. Campanella showed a steadfast interest in the astronomical and scientific discoveries of the scientist, even if he often did not agree with his positions, especially those that touched upon atomism. The most important text of this friendship is the *Apologia pro Galileo* (A defense of Galileo), written in 1616 and published in Frankfurt in 1622. In this work, which demonstrates his deep competence in theology, Campanella does not defend personal philosophic doctrines: his image of nature as a living organism is very far from that of Galileo, according to whom nature is a book written in mathematic characters; moreover, the heliocentric doctrine is scarcely compatible with Telesian physics, which maintains that the Sun is the locus of heat and the origin of movement, while Earth is the seat of cold and the prime cause of immobility and weight. Campanella's intention is to support the *libertas philosophandi* (freedom of thought) of Galileo whose fundamental right and duty is to give priority to the reading of the book of nature over that of the book of men. The discoveries of Galileo do not create a crisis in theological principles, even though Aristotelian philosophy, regarded as an erroneous reading of the book of nature, must be substituted by a different philosophy more in harmony with the new celestial phenomena.

Later Years. Campanella was released from the prison at Castel Nuovo on 23 May 1626 and then transferred to the palace of the Inquisition in Rome. The most sensational episode of his Roman sojourn is the one involving the forecasts of astrologers who predicted the imminent death of Pope Urban VIII because of unpropitious dispositions of the stars. Campanella had written a treatise on astrology, seeking to free it from Arab superstitions and to base it on natural principles. Aligning himself with the position of Thomas Aquinas, he maintained that the stars exercise an influence on the corporal *spiritus* and its passions, while the will and human reason remain free. Summoned by the pope, Campanella, hoping to avoid the perils of an eclipse, engaged in the practice of natural and stellar magic as advocated by Ficino and described by Campanella in his booklet *De siderali fato vitando* (How to avoid the fate destined by the stars). The publication of this pamphlet as the seventh book of the *Astrologicorum libri* (1629) caused a great scandal, for it risked compromising the pope himself in accusations of superstitious practices. To allay all suspicions, Urban VIII decided to act decisively against astrologers: in 1630 he ordered imprisonment for Orazio Morandi, in whose convent of Saint Praxedes the practice of astrology was enmeshed with political intrigues; Morandi died after a few months in prison, with poisoning suspected as the cause of death. In 1631 the pope promulgated the extremely harsh Papal Bull, *Inscrutabilis,* against astrology and every form of divination.

In 1634, again for political reasons, Campanella was forced to seek refuge in Paris, where he busied himself with the publication of his *Opere* (Works). Besides a second edition of *Atheismus triumphatus* (and other minor texts), 1636, and a second edition of *De sensu rerum et magia* (1636 and 1637), Campanella edited in Paris three volumes of his *Opera omnia*: the *Philosophia realis* (1637), the *Philosophia rationalis* (1638), and the monumental *Metaphysica* (1638). He also began once more to write political texts in order to demonstrate how France, difficulties and setbacks notwithstanding, was in an ascendant phase of "increasing fortune," while the Spanish-Hapsburg powers were experiencing the descending parabola of an inexorable decline. His last work was an eclogue in Latin hexameters celebrating the birth of the future Louis XIV, the Sun King, an event that occurred on Campanella's seventieth birthday. Turning again to the astrological and prophetic themes so dear to him, in these verses he foresaw the approach of a new epoch in which peace, justice, and harmony would prevail among men. He died at dawn on 21 May 1639.

SUPPLEMENTARY BIBLIOGRAPHY

Luigi Firpo, Bibliografia degli scritti di Tommaso Campanella *(Turin: V. Bona, 1940) is the only available work offering a comprehensive description of Campanella's works. Subsequent editions of his works can be found in John M. Headley,* Tommaso Campanella and the Transformation of the World *(Princeton, NJ: Princeton University Press, 1997), and the journal* Bruniana & Campelliana *(1995–).*

WORKS BY CAMPANELLA

Philosophia sensibus demonstrata. 1591. Edited by Luigi De Franco. Naples, Italy: Vivarium, 1992.

De sensu rerum et magia. Frankfurt: E. Emmelius, 1620; Paris: L. Boullenger, 1636 (Latin text).

Del senso delle cose e della magia. Edited by Antonio Bruers. Bari, Italy: Laterza, 1925 (Italian text). A new edition of the Italian text, edited by Germana Ernst, is forthcoming; publication is set for October 2007.

Apologia pro Galileo—A Defense of Galileo. 1622. Edited by Richard J. Blackwell. Notre Dame, IN; London: University of Notre Dame Press, 1994. Contains both Latin and English versions.

La Città del Sole—The City of the Sun. 1623 (*Civitas Solis,* Latin text). 2nd ed. Edited by Daniel J. Donno. Berkeley and Los Angeles, CA; London: Kessinger Publishing, 2004. In Italian and English.

Atheismus triumphatus. Rome: B. Zannetti, 1631; Paris: T. Dubray, 1636 (Latin text).

L'Ateismo trionfato. 2 vols. Edited by Germana Ernst. Pisa, Italy: Edizioni della Normale, 2004 (Italian text with the autograph manuscript by the author).

Monarchia Messiae/ La Monarchie du Messie. 1633 (*Monarchia Messiae,* Latin text). Edited by Paolo Ponzio. Translated into

French by Véronique Bourdette. Paris: Presses Universitaires de France, 2002.

Medicinalium libri VII. Lyons: I. Pillehotte, 1635.

Disputationum in quatuor partes suae philosophiae realis libri quatuor. Paris: Denis Houssaye, 1637.

Metaphysica. 1638. Anastatic reprint. Edited by Luigi Firpo, Turin, Italy: Bottega d'Erasmo, 1961.

De Monarchia Hispanica. 1640 (Italian text). *Monarchie d'Espagne et Monarchie de France.* Edited by Germana Ernst. Translated into French by Serge Waldbaum and Nathalie Fabry. Paris: Presses Universitaires de France, 1997.

De libris propriis et recta ratione studendi syntagma. 1642. Edited by Vincenzo Spampanato. Bari, Italy: Laterza, 1927. A new edition, edited by Germana Ernst, is forthcoming.

Lettere. Edited by Vincenzo Spampanato. Bari, Italy: Laterza, 1927.

Epilogo magno. Edited by Carmelo Ottaviano. Rome: Reale Accademia d'Italia, 1939.

Tutte le opere di Tommaso Campanella. Vol. 1, *Scritti letterari.* Edited by Luigi Firpo. Milan, Italy: Mondadori, 1954.

Opera latina Francofurti impressa annis 1617–1630. Edited by Luigi Firpo. Turin, Italy: Bottega d'Erasmo, 1975. Anastatic reprint of the following works, first published in Frankfurt: Vol. 1, *Prodromus philosophiae instaurandae, De sensu rerum et magia, Apologia pro Galileo.* Vol. 2, *Realis philosophiae epilogisticae partes IV, Astrologicorum libri VII.*

Opere letterarie. Edited by Lina Bolzoni. Turin, Italy: Utet, 1977.

Le poesie. Edited by Francesco Giancotti. Turin, Italy: Einaudi, 1998.

Opuscoli astrologici: Come evitare il fato astrale, Apologetico, Disputa sulle Bolle. Edited by Germana Ernst. Milan, Italy: Rizzoli, 2003. Includes the Latin text with an Italian translation.

OTHER SOURCES

Amabile, Luigi. *Fra Tommaso Campanella, la sua congiura, i suoi processi e la sua pazzia.* 3 vols. Naples, Italy: Morano, 1882. Because of their generous documentation, these volumes (and the two cited Amabile volumes below) constitute the point of departure for scholarly studies on the life and thought of Campanella.

———. *Fra Tommaso Campanella ne' castelli di Napoli, in Roma e in Parigi.* 2 vols. Naples, Italy: Morano, 1887. Anastatic reprint, Turin: Nino Aragno, 2007. A recent anastatic reprint of the five volumes by Amabile, with new documents, a foreword by Nicola Badaloni and an introduction by Tonino Tornitore.

Badaloni, Nicola. *Tommaso Campanella.* Milan, Italy: Feltrinelli, 1965.

Blanchet, Léon. *Campanella.* Paris: Félix Alcan 1920. Reprint, New York: Franklin, 1964. A comprehensive monograph that is in many ways dated but still interesting.

Canone, Eugenio, and Germana Ernst, eds. *Enciclopedia Bruniana e Campanelliana.* Pisa, Italy: Istituti editoriali e poligrafici internazionali, 2006. A collection of articles on the major philosophic concepts of Giordano Bruno (sixteen articles) and Tommaso Campanella (sixteen articles).

Ernst, Germana. *Religione, ragione e natura: Ricerche su Tommaso Campanella e il tardo Rinascimento.* Milan, Italy: Franco Angeli, 1991.

———. *Il carcere, il politico, il profeta. Saggi su Tommaso Campanella.* Pisa, Italy: Istituti Editoriali e Poligrafici Internazionali, 2002.

———. *Tommaso Campanella: Il libro e il corpo della naturaI* Rome: Laterza, 2002. A monograph that reconstructs the principal stages of Campanella's intellectual itinerary.

———. "Campanella," 2005. In *Stanford Encyclopedia of Philosophy.* Available from http://plato.stanford.edu/entries/campanella.

Firpo, Luigi. *Ricerche campanelliane.* Florence, Italy: Sansoni, 1947.

———. "Campanella, Tommaso." In *Dizionario biografico degli Italiani,* Vol. 17. Rome: Istituto dell'Enciclopedia italiana, 1974.

———. *I processi di Tommaso Campanella.* Edited by Eugenio Canone. Rome: Salerno Editrice, 1998.

Headley, John M. *Tommaso Campanella and the Transformation of the World.* Princeton, NJ: Princeton University Press, 1997. The most complete and comprehensive work on Campanella in English.

Lerner, Michel-Pierre. *Tommaso Campanella en France au XVIIe siècle.* Naples, Italy: Bibliopolis, 1995.

Mönnich, Michael W. *Tommaso Campanella: Sein Beitrag zur Medizin und Pharmazie der Renaissance.* Stuttgart, Germany: Wissenschaftliche Verlagsgesellschaft, 1990.

Walker, D. P. *Spiritual and Demonic Magic from Ficino to Campanella.* 1958. Reprinted, with an introduction by Brian P. Copenhaver. University Park: Pennsylvania State University Press, 2000.

Germana Ernst

CAMPBELL, DONALD THOMAS

(*b.* Grass Lake, Michigan, 20 November 1916; *d.* Bethlehem, Pennsylvania, 6 May 1996), *psychology, anthropology, methodology of social science, education, evolutionary theory, epistemology, science studies.*

Through his unique disposition to engage in fierce but always amicable intellectual exchange across disciplinary boundaries, inspiring teaching, and more than 240 publications, Campbell made significant contributions to a wide variety of disciplines. Campbell began his career in social and cross-cultural psychology with bench science–type contributions to such issues as leadership and subordination, conformity to groups, ethnocentrism, and xenophobia. Even more influential were his methodological innovations, in particular the *multitrait-multimethod matrix* approach to construct validity and *quasi-experimental designs* for field research. With more than 4,200 citations, Campbell and Fiske's "Convergent and Discriminant Validation by the Multitrait Multi-method Matrix" (1959) is one of the most frequently read papers in social science, and more than 300,000 copies of Campbell and Stanley's monograph on experimental and quasi-experimental designs (originally published as an article in 1963) have as of 2007 been sold (see also 1979a). This methodological work earned Campbell most of his many honors and awards. In the last fifteen years of his life, he devoted most of his attention to issues in epistemology and the philosophy and sociology of science. The *blind-variation-and-selective-retention* (BVSR) theme lies at the basis of his groundbreaking work in evolutionary epistemology (Callebaut and Pinxten, 1987; Hahlweg and Hooker, 1989) and subsequent program for a *general selection theory*, according to which all complex real systems are a result of a design or selection process (1997; cf. Wimsatt, 1986; Heyes and Hull, 2001).

Scholarly Career. Campbell's father was a farmer who moved his family first to a cattle ranch in Wyoming and then to California, where he became an agricultural extension agent. Campbell described his religious parents, Arthur and Hazel, as treating children's opinions with respect. Several of his family members belonged to Appalachian Bible-belt free churches, and although he had "by high school or early college … drifted away from whatever belief in God [he] had had as a child" (1988c, p. 21), he respected tradition, as evidenced by his presidential address to the American Psychological Association (1975a). He even "recognized in himself the zeal and persistence of an evangelical itinerant preacher" (Heyes, 2001, p. 2). After high school, he worked for a year on a turkey farm before going off to San Bernardino Valley Union Junior College, where he learned about evolutionary biology from a squirrel hunter.

In 1937 Campbell went to the University of California at Berkeley to study psychology. When he completed his undergraduate education there in 1939, he and his younger sister, Fayette, graduated first and second in their class. He was most influenced by Robert Tryon, whom he assisted as data analyst on a project examining inheritance of maze-running ability in rats; by the moderate behaviorist Edward Tolman, who treated organisms as goal-seeking; and by his "beloved Professor" Egon Brunswik, who was at the time Tolman's assistant. After Campbell served his country's war effort, he obtained his PhD from Berkeley in 1947 with a dissertation on "The Generality of Social Attitude."

Campbell's first appointment as assistant professor was at Ohio State University (1947–1950), where he taught social psychology, did research on opinion polling and leadership, and joined a regular philosophy of science table at which Kurt Wolff introduced him to the sociology

of knowledge. When the relativistic sociology of science emerged thirty years later, Campbell, unlike his contemporaries, the sociologists Robert Merton and Edward Shils, would enthusiastically engage in critical dialogue with Bloor, Collins, Knorr Cetina, Latour, and others. He even dared ask Popper, "Why are you so hard on the relativists? After all, you say, 'We don't know, we can only guess' and you agree that the facts which 'falsify' theories are but conventions agreed to among the scientists working in the field" (Callebaut, 1993, p. 5; see also 1988d).

This epistemological interest was first reflected in his inaugural colloquium "On the Psychological Study of Knowledge" at the University of Chicago, where he was an assistant professor from 1950 to 1953, working first in the Committee on Education Research and Training in Race Relations, and subsequently in James Grier Miller's Committee on Behavioral Sciences with its focus on cybernetics, general systems theory, and information theory. Campbell's work on the relationships between W. Ross Ashby's cybernetics and other natural selection analogues to learning and perception resulted in his first papers on evolutionary epistemology (1956a, b; 1959a), whereas information theory inspired his work on biases (systematic errors) on behalf of humans considered as links in communication systems (1958; cf. Wimsatt, 1980, a Campbellian exploration of biases in scientific research strategies).

Suffering under the publication pressure of the University of Chicago's tough tenure policy, Campbell moved to Northwestern University's Psychology Department in 1953, where he became tenured and spent very productive years working on social attitude measurement, ethnocentrism, and social science methodology, engaging in field work, and teaching social psychology and a seminar course on "Knowledge Processes" until his retirement as professor emeritus in 1979. During this period he was also a visiting associate professor at Yale University (1954), a fellow at the Center for Advanced Study in the Behavioral Sciences in Stanford (1965–1966), Fulbright lecturer and visiting professor in social psychology at Oxford (1968–1969), and visiting professor in psychology and social relations at Harvard University, where he delivered the William James Lectures of 1977 (circulated widely in preprint form and published later in 1987a, 1988b; see in particular 1988a).

In 1979, needing a new setting for personal reasons, Campbell moved to Syracuse University. From that time epistemology was his principal focus, resulting in a plethora of publications. In 1981 he co-organized the ERISS (Epistemologically Relevant Internalist Sociology of Science) conference, which assembled naturalistic philosophers and relativistic sociologists of science along with psychologists, anthropologists, and historians of science—a rather unusual combination at that time, which prefigured a common practice in the International Society for the History, Philosophy, and Social Studies of Biology some years later. Campbell was preoccupied with the justification of claims to knowledge and the issue of scientific validity (e.g., 1986, 1987b, 1997) and chided available evolutionary-epistemological histories of science for being "epistemologically vacuous" (1990, p. 1). He thought of ERISS as "a successful failure" in retrospect: "it failed utterly to address the agenda I had intended, mainly because the sociologists focused on a well-articulated skepticism, being unready for a speculative comparison of social systems of belief change and belief retention" (1988b, p. 25).

ERISS left no significant written record, but a conference (ERISS II) at Ghent University, Belgium, in 1984 that followed up this endeavor, with some of the same participants, did (Callebaut and Pinxten, 1987). It took several years to sort out the separate issues of realism ("theories represent aspects of the real world") and rationalism ("there are rational principles for the evaluation of theories") underlying the divide between the philosophers and the sociologists of science (Giere, 1988), which persisted into the early 2000s.

In 1982 Campbell followed his second wife, anthropologist Barbara Frankel, to Lehigh University, where he was appointed as university professor of sociology-anthropology, psychology and education. He remained active until his death, apparently from the complications of surgery, in 1996. Campbell had two sons, Martin and Thomas, with his first wife, Lola, and two grandchildren.

A Master of Many Disciplines.

A social psychologist by disciplinary identification, Campbell was a "master of many disciplines" (Thomas, 1996). His sophisticated methodological suggestions were a constructive answer to his critical questioning of certain behaviorist and logical-positivist tenets such as *perceptual foundationalism*, epitomized by the imperative to define theoretical parameters operationally. They took into account rivaling, postpositivist philosophical positions, including critical or *hypothetical realism*, which leaves a role for "Nature herself" in "editing" claims to knowledge (1973a, 1993; see also 1974b, 1988d for Campbell's assessment of Popper's philosophy), Quine's *naturalized epistemology* (1988a), Kuhn's *historicism* (1988b), and even *hermeneutics* (e.g., 1986). He thus provided "conceptual bridges between the scientific and humanistic perspectives" on the methods, metatheory, and philosophy of social science (Overman, 1988) that helped revolutionize the fundamental principles of scientific inquiry common to all the social sciences, including evolutionary economics (Nelson, 1995). He endorsed "a common denominator among a quite diverse

set of critics of logical positivism and sense data phenomenalism," namely, that there is no nonpresumptive and infallible knowledge: "All knowledge claims go beyond their evidence, are highly presumptive and corrigible" (1969b, p. 42). Even the best of physical science experimentation "probes" theory rather than "proves" it.

Campbell contributed the concept of *downward causation* to the debate on reductionism in evolutionary biology: Biological systems are hierarchically structured, and there is downward causation whenever "the distribution of lower-level events and substances" is partially determined by higher-level factors (1974a, p. 180), that is, when a higher structure operates causally upon its substructure. With his "vehicles carrying knowledge" (1979b; not to be confused with Dawkins's vehicles: Hull, 2001), he departed from the tendency of traditional epistemology (including Popper's "epistemology without a knowing subject") to treat belief and knowledge as disembodied and abstract. By calling attention to the specific physical nature of carriers of information (primordially genes in biological evolution; mosaics, paper, electronic chips, etc., in cultural evolution) and their inherent limitations, but also to the "social structural requirements of being a self-perpetuating social system," he helped pave the way for the early twenty-first century, postcognitivist emphasis on distributed, embodied, and situated cognition and activity (Hendriks-Jansen, 1996). Campbell (e.g., 1965) also was arguably the first scholar "to give cultural evolution its due weight *without* divorcing culture from biology" (Boyd and Richerson, 2005, p. 17), although he has sometimes been misunderstood as a residual dualist (but see Hull, 2001).

Through the cognitive turn in psychology of the 1970s and 1980s until the current, postcognitivist wave, Campbell remained true to a uniquely personal approach to the phenomenon of knowledge, "combining the rigor of his behaviorist education with the daring speculation of an evolutionist interested in that ephemeral organ called 'mind'" (De Mey, 1997, p. 81).

Validity, Evaluation Design, and Social Experimentation.

The behaviorism that Campbell confronted early in his career carried with it the expectation that personal traits, social attitudes, and behaviors can be observed and measured, and the conviction that the window on the world that the observable opens has epistemological primacy over scientists' theorizing. *Definitional operationalism* was the claim that single measurement operations could be regarded as defining terms in a scientific theory. In Cronbach and Meehl's (1955) *nomological network*, developed as part of the American Psychological Association's effort to develop standards for psychological testing, "laws" accordingly related observable manifestations among each other and to the network of concepts (theoretical constructs). A new construct or relation had to generate laws confirmed by observation, or reduce the number of laws required to predict observables (see Trochim, 2005).

Campbell considered definitional operationalism "positivism's worst gift to the social sciences" (cf. Hull, 1988, on the use and abuse of operational definitions in physics and biology). He objected that the term "definition" acquires its major connotations in language and logic, where the concepts of synonymity and analytic truth are appropriate. But the names for important concepts in science, he argued, are of an altogether different kind; they are

> contingent allegations of syndromes of attributes, … terms for entities given real status, and hence with innumerable attributes, known and unknown. What are loosely called "definitions" are in fact abbreviated *descriptions* used for *designation.* They contain not "essentials" nor even "defining attributes," but instead those features useful in diagnosing the presence or absence of the object or process and useful in distinguishing it from similars with which it might otherwise be confused. (1988b, p. 31)

These "diagnostic descriptions" differ depending on the user: an ordinary dictionary definition of "cat" will have little or no overlap in mentioned features with that of, say, a paleontologist, and yet refers to the same "syndrome" while privileging a different abbreviated set of features. In place of definitional operationalism, Campbell proposed *multiple operationalism* (convergent operationalism, methodological triangulation). It is "on the grounds of self-critical hard-headedness that we face up to our very unsatisfactory predicament: we have only other *invalid measures* against which to validate our tests; we have no 'criterion' to check them against" (1988b, p. 33). Allied to this reasoning is Harvard biologist Richard Levins's independent notion of our truth lying at the "intersection of independent lies" (Levins, 1966, p. 423).

The *multitrait-multimethod matrix* (MTMM) provides a concrete method for multiple operationalism (Campbell and Fiske, 1959). It is an approach to assessing the construct validity of a set of measures as part of an attempt to provide a *practical* methodology (as opposed to the nomological network idea, which was at best theoretically useful). Along with the MTMM, Campbell and Fiske introduced two types of construct validity: *convergent validity*, the degree to which concepts that should be related theoretically are interrelated in reality, and *discriminant validity,* the degree to which concepts that should not be related theoretically are, in fact, not interrelated in reality. To be able to claim that measures have construct validity one must demonstrate both convergence and dis-

crimination. Both can be assessed using the MTMM. Trochim (2005) provides an introduction.

In addition to construct validity, three other types of validity may be distinguished in Campbell's writing: *internal validity*, the attribution of cause to an intervention (see Bickman, 2000, vol. 2); *external validity*, the generalization of causal relationships (see Cook, 2000; Trochim, 2005); and *statistical conclusion* (see Elek-Fisk et al., 2000). In his view, validity was intimately related to *social activism* or planned social change (1973b), because social experimentation, say, with Head Start programs or programs to reduce highway fatalities, must be based on the concepts of validity and is never *merely* social activism (Bickman, 2000, vol. 1, p. viii). Campbell's vision of the social scientist as "methodological servant of the experimenting society" (1973b) continued to spur controversial debate (e.g., Dunn, 1998), producing arguments to which he would have subscribed in part (1982).

Selection Theory Epistemology. "Between a modern experimental physicist and some virus-type ancestor there has been a tremendous gain in knowledge," Campbell wrote in a programmatic 1960 article on evolutionary epistemology. He justified his extension of the usage of the term "knowledge" to nonhuman contexts, anathema to most philosophers and humanists at the time, as "part of an effort to put 'the problem of knowledge' into a behavioristic framework which takes full cognizance of man's status as a biological product of an evolutionary development from a highly limited background, with no 'direct' dispensations of knowledge being added at any point in the family tree" (p. 380). And he noted that this position limits one to the third-person view of "an epistemology of the other one" (cf. 1969b). While the conscious knowledge processes of humans were recognized as "more complex and subtle" than those of lower organisms, he insisted that they cannot be taken as "more fundamental or primitive," adding the ironical twist that "since the problem of knowledge has resisted any generally accepted solution when defined in terms of the conscious contents of the philosopher himself, little seems lost and possibly something gained by thus extending the range of processes considered" (1960, p. 380).

Whereas other approaches to evolutionary epistemology, such as that of Konrad Lorenz, remained silent on the actual relation of the ontogeny of knowledge to its phylogeny, or indeed on the basic character of knowledge itself in relation to the interaction of organisms with their environment (Campbell, 1975b), Campbell's EE took into account that selection operates on many levels, comprising the social and, in the human case, the cultural (as does Piaget's genetic epistemology: Parker et al., 2005). Just as EE in general was a child of the post-war penchant for interdisciplinary studies (cf. Campbell's 1969a "fish-scale model of omniscience"), Campbell's (1974b) *nested hierarchy of vicarious selection processes* was the product of systems-theoretical considerations.

In the evolutionary debates of the mid-twentieth century, an opposition between what in the early twenty-first century would be called *eliminativists* and those committed to preserving a role for "irreducible teleology" or "self-regulation" lingered on (Deacon, 2005, pp. 90–91). Authors such as Piaget and Bertalanffy rejected a view that reduced evolution to antecedent chance mutation honed by a posteriori competitive elimination, which was exactly the position Campbell embraced. When Bertalanffy pointed to "system, equifinality, emergent levels, wholes which shape parts, etc." as "truths" that "any adequate biology and psychology must take account of" (Campbell's words; 1973a, p. 1044), Campbell took on the theoretical challenge to explain these facts in terms of the natural selection model. He shared Bertalanffy's emphasis on the role of language in focusing attention on limiting perspectives of reality and hence in shaping human view of reality. But he equally believed that "the structure of the physical world limits and edits the word meanings that can be taught and that can thus become parts of a working language" (1973a, p. 1043; cf. 1988a, pp. 450–464). Moreover, Campbell took BVSR processes to be fundamental to all increases in the fit of system to environment, including all genuine increases in knowledge (see, e.g., 1974b, 1986).

Although a "confirmed Weismannian-Darwinian," Campbell was au fait with complementary and alternative developments in evolutionary theory past and present. This afforded him a much richer understanding of evolution than is currently common. In addition to the external selection that produces direct fit to the environment (1987a), his view gave prominence to *internal factors of selection* (cf. Wimsatt, 2007). When a salamander's leg is lost, it regenerates to a length that is controlled, not by the external environment, but by an evolved internal monitor. The internal selector, then, is a "vicarious representative" of the external selector. Once organisms have become internally well-adjusted systems that fit their environment moderately well, they may remain stable over long periods of time while their environment changes, as internal selection takes priority over external selection ("punctuated equilibrium").

It takes little imagination to grasp the heuristic power of viewing perceptual systems (in particular vision), human language, or cultural accomplishments as vicarious selectors. For instance, Piaget's *dialectic of assimilation and accommodation* can be interpreted in terms of internal and external selection: For a while, "the child's behavioral logic fits the world so well that he is willing to treat the world

as being appropriately described by it until he can get another, internally coherent logic that fits it better, adapting still better to the environment" (Campbell in Callebaut, 1993, p. 296). The picture becomes even more exciting if one asks how the workings of one vicarious selector impinge on another—say, vision on language, or vice versa. A related unifying theme in Campbell's writing is *pattern matching* (1966, 1997). Campbell (1974b) suggested a grand scheme of ten "more or less discrete" processes from "nonmnemonic" problem solving via vicarious locomotor devices, habit and instinct, to visually and mnemonically supported thought, observational learning and imitation, language, and cultural cumulation, including science. The many processes that "shortcut" a fuller BVSR process are, on Campbell's view, themselves "inductive achievements"—products of previous BVSR processes. In addition, they contain in their own *operation* a BVSR process at some level, "substituting for overt locomotion exploration or the life-and-death winnowing of organic evolution" (1974b, p. 421). In his characteristic, self-mocking way, he called this program "dogmatic," "utterly unjustified," and "just a leap of faith" (Callebaut, 1993, p. 297).

A BVSR process requires mechanisms for introducing variation, consistent selection processes, and mechanisms for preserving and/or propagating the selected variation. In general, the generation and preservation mechanisms are inherently at odds, hence each must be compromised (1974b, p. 421). The process is "blind" or "unjustified" (1974c) in that the occurrence of trials must be *uncorrelated* with the "solution" (which is not the same as "random"). The activities of individual scientists are surely intentional, yet "at a higher level of organization, there may be more to Campbell's thesis than one might at first think" (Giere, 1988, p. 222): An appreciation for the constraining role of cognitive resources and other nonepistemic interests suggests a picture far different from the classic view of science as a highly intentional activity. Wimsatt (1980) has suggested a rapprochement between Campbell's vicarious selectors and the heuristics dear to computationalists within cognitive science. Campbell himself (in an unpublished letter to Herbert A. Simon, October 4, 1982) agreed that he and Simon were "not all that far apart on heuristics. I suspect that my nested hierarchy of *vicarious*, presumptive, BVSR processes will map into your n-level search processes."

Among Campbell's elected offices, his presidency of the American Psychological Association in 1975 stands out. The honors and awards he received include the APA's Distinguished Contribution Award in 1969, nominations as a fellow of the American Academy of Arts and Sciences and a member of the National Academy of Sciences in 1973, and as a member of the American Philosophical Society in 1992. He received honorary degrees from the universities of Michigan (1974), Florida (1975), Chicago (1978), and Southern California (1979), Northwestern University (1983), and the University of Oslo (1985).

This brief intellectual biography has left out the preoccupations of "the householder, shopper, tourist, husband, father, friend and mortal man" that Campbell also was. He tackled these "with the same inspiring blend of deliberation and playfulness, faith and fallibilism" (Heyes, 1997, p. 299). More detailed information on Campbell's life and work as well as personal recollections are provided in Callebaut (1993), Brewer and Cook (1997), and Stanley (1998); in issues of the journals *Evolution and Cognition* (Callebaut and Riedl, 1997), *Philosophica* (Callebaut, 1997), and the *American Journal of Evaluation* (1998); and in a number of volumes that were posthumously dedicated to Campbell (Dunn, 1998; Baum and McKelvey, 1999; Bickman, 2000; Heyes and Hull, 2001). But the most valuable source of information, unparalleled in intellectual honesty, remains Campbell's exemplification of his BVSR epistemology by illustrating with his own career "the inevitable wastefulness of scientific exploration, the chancy indirectness of discovery, and the further chanciness of recognition" ("Perspective on a Scholarly Career," 1988c).

BIBLIOGRAPHY

Variations in Organization Science: In Honor of Donald T. Campbell, edited by Joel A. C. Baum and Bill McKelvey (Thousand Oaks, CA: Sage, 1999) contains an almost complete and quite reliable bibliography of Campbell's publications.

WORKS BY CAMPBELL

"Adaptive Behavior from Random Response." *Behavioral Science* 1 (1956a): 105–110.

"Perception as Substitute Trial and Error." *Psychological Review* 63 (1956b): 330–342.

"Systematic Error on the Part of Human Links in Communication Systems." *Information and Control* 1 (1958): 334–369.

"Methodological Suggestions from a Comparative Psychology of Knowledge Processes." *Inquiry* 2 (1959): 152–182.

With Donald W. Fiske. "Convergent and Discriminant Validation by the Multitrait Multimethod Matrix." *Psychological Bulletin* 56, no. 2 (1959): 81–105. Reprinted in Campbell (1988b).

"Blind Variation and Selective Retention in Creative Thought as in Other Knowledge Processes." *Psychological Review* 57 (1960): 380–400.

With Julian C. Stanley. "Experimental and Quasi-experimental Designs for Research on Teaching." In *Handbook on Research on Teaching*, edited by N. L. Gage. Chicago: Rand McNally, 1963. Reprinted as *Experimental and Quasi-experimental Designs for Research*. Chicago: Rand McNally, 1966, 2005.

"Variation and Selective Retention in Socio-cultural Evolution." In *Social Change in Developing Areas*, edited by Herbert R.

Barringer, George I. Blanksten, and Raymond W. Mack. Cambridge, MA: Schenkman, 1965.

"Pattern Matching as an Essential in Distal Knowing." In *The Psychology of Egon Brunswik*, edited by Kenneth R. Hammond, New York: Holt, Rinehart and Winston, 1966.

"Ethnocentrism of Disciplines and the Fish-scale Model of Omniscience." In *Interdisciplinary Relationships in the Social Sciences*, edited by Muzafer Sherif and Carolyn W. Sherif. Chicago: Aldine, 1969a.

"A Phenomenology of the Other One: Corrigible, Hypothetical, and Critical." In *Human Action: Conceptual and Empirical Issues*, edited by Theodore Mischel. New York: Academic Press, 1969b. Reprinted in Campbell (1988b).

"Ostensive Instances and Entitativity in Language Learning." In *Unity through Diversity: A Festschrift for Ludwig von Bertalanffy*, vol. 2, edited by William Gray and Nicholas D. Rizzo. New York: Gordon and Breach, 1973a.

"The Social Scientist as Methodological Servant of the Experimenting Society." *Policy Studies Journal* 1 (1973b): 72–75.

"'Downward Causation' in Hierarchically Organised Biological Systems." In *Studies in the Philosophy of Biology*, edited by Francisco J. Ayala and Theodosius Dobzhansky. London: Macmillan, 1974a.

"Evolutionary Epistemology." In *The Philosophy of Karl Popper*, edited by Paul A. Schilpp. LaSalle, IL: Open Court, 1974b. Reprinted in Campbell (1988b).

"Unjustified Variation and Selective Retention in Scientific Discovery." In *Studies in the Philosophy of Biology*, edited by Francisco J. Ayala and Theodosius Dobzhansky. London: Macmillan, 1974c.

"On the Conflicts between Biological and Social Evolution and between Psychology and Moral Tradition." *American Psychologist* 30 (1975a): 1103–1126.

"Reintroducing Konrad Lorenz to Psychology." In *Konrad Lorenz: The Man and His Ideas*, edited by Richard I. Evans. New York: Harcourt Brace Jovanovich, 1975b.

With Thomas D. Cook. *Quasi-Experimentation: Design and Analysis Issues for Field Settings.* Chicago: Rand McNally, 1979a.

"A Tribal Model of the Social System Vehicle Carrying Scientific Knowledge." *Knowledge: Creation, Diffusion, Utilization* 1 (1979b): 181–201. Reprinted in Campbell (1988b).

"Experiments as Arguments." *Knowledge: Creation, Diffusion, Utilization* 3 (1982): 327–337.

"Science's Social System of Validity-enhancing Collective Belief Change and the Problems of the Social Sciences." In *Metatheory in Social Science*, edited by Donald W. Fiske and Richard A. Shweder. Chicago: University of Chicago Press, 1986.

"Neurological Embodiments of Belief and the Gaps in the Fit of Phenomena to Noumena." In *Naturalistic Epistemology: A Symposium of Two Decades*, edited by Abner Shimony and Debra Nails. Dordrecht: Reidel, 1987a.

"Selection Theory and the Sociology of Scientific Validity." In *Evolutionary Epistemology: A Multiparadigm Program*, edited by Werner Callebaut and Rik Pinxten. Dordrecht: Reidel, 1987b.

"Descriptive Epistemology: Psychological, Sociological, and Evolutionary." In *Methodology and Epistemology for Social Science*, edited by E. Samuel Overman. Chicago: University of Chicago Press, 1988a.

Methodology and Epistemology for Social Science: Selected Papers, edited by E. Samuel Overman. Chicago: University of Chicago Press, 1988b.

"Perspective on a Scholarly Career." In *Methodology and Epistemology of Science*, by Donald T. Campbell; edited by E. Samuel Overman. Chicago: University of Chicago Press, 1988c. Reprinted with revisions from *Scientific Inquiry and the Social Sciences*, edited by Marilyn B. Brewer and Barry E. Collins. San Francisco: Jossey-Bass, 1981.

"Popper and Selection Theory [Review and response]." *Social Epistemology* 2 (1988d): 371–377.

"Epistemological Roles for Selection Theory." In *Evolution, Cognition, and Realism*, edited by Nicholas Rescher. Lanham, MD: University Press of America, 1990.

"Plausible Coselection of Belief by Referent: All the Objectivity That is Possible." *Perspectives on Science* 1 (1993): 88–108.

"From Evolutionary Epistemology via Selection Theory to a Sociology of Scientific Validity," edited by Cecilia Heyes and Barbara Frankel. *Evolution and Cognition* 3, no. 1 (1997): 5–38.

OTHER SOURCES

Bickman, Leonard, ed. *Validity and Social Experimentation: Donald Campbell's Legacy*. 2 vols. Thousand Oaks, CA: Sage, 2000.

Boyd, Peter J., and Peter J Richerson. *Not by Genes Alone: How Culture Transformed Human Evolution*. Chicago: University of Chicago Press, 2005.

Brewer, Marilynn B., and Thomas D. Cook. "Donald T. Campbell." *American Psychologist* 52 (1997): 267–268.

Callebaut, Werner. *Taking the Naturalistic Turn, Or How Real Philosophy of Science Is Done*. Chicago: University of Chicago Press, 1993.

Callebaut, Werner, ed. "Donald T. Campbell." *Philosophica* 60 (1997): 1–152.

Callebaut, Werner, and Rik Pinxten, eds. *Evolutionary Epistemology: A Multiparadigm Program*. Dordrecht: Reidel, 1987.

Callebaut, Werner, and Rupert Riedl, eds. Special Issue in Honor of Donald T. Campbell. *Evolution and Cognition* 3, no. 1 (1997): 1–100.

Cook, Thomas D. "Toward a Practical Theory of External Validity." In *Validity and Experimentation*, vol. 1, edited by Leonard Bickman. Thousand Oaks, CA: SAGE, 2000.

Cronbach, Lee J., and Paul E. Meehl. "Construct Validity in Psychological Tests." *Psychological Bulletin* 52 (1955): 281–302.

Deacon, Terrence W. "Beyond Piaget's Phenocopy: The Baby in the Lamarckian Bath." In *Biology and Knowledge Revisited*, edited by Sue T. Parker, Jonas Langer, and Constance Milbrath. Mahwah, NJ: Erlbaum, 2005.

De Mey, Marc. "Vision as Paradigm: From VTE to Cognitive Science." *Evolution and Cognition* 3 (1997): 81–84.

Dunn, William N., ed. *The Experimenting Society: Essays in Honor of Donald T. Campbell*. New Brunswick, NJ: Transaction Press, 1998.

Elek-Fisk, Elvira, Lanette A. Raymond, and Paul M. Wortman. "Validity Applied to Meta-Analysis and Research Synthesis." In *Validity and Social Experimentation*, vol. 1, edited by Leonard Bickman. Thousand Oaks, CA: Sage, 2000.

Giere, Ronald N. *Explaining Science: A Cognitive Approach*. Chicago: University of Chicago Press, 1988.

Hahlweg, Kai, and Clifford A. Hooker, eds. *Issues in Evolutionary Epistemology*. Albany: State University of New York Press, 1989.

Hendriks-Jansen, Horst. *Catching Ourselves in the Act: Situated Activity, Interactive Emergence, Evolution, and Human Thought*. Cambridge, MA: MIT Press, 1996.

Heyes, Cecilia M. "A Tribute to Donald T. Campbell." *Biology and Philosophy* 12 (1997): 299–301.

———. "Introduction." In *Selection Theory and Social Construction*, edited by C. Heyes and D. L. Hull. Albany: State University of New York Press, 2001.

Heyes, Cecilia, and David L. Hull, eds. *Selection Theory and Social Construction: The Evolutionary Naturalistic Epistemology of Donald T. Campbell*. Albany: State University of New York Press, 2001.

Hull, David L. *Science as a Process: An Evolutionary Account of the Social and Conceptual Development of Science*. Chicago: University of Chicago Press, 1988.

———. *Science and Selection: Essays on Biological Evolution and the Philosophy of Science*. New York: Cambridge University Press, 2001.

Levins, Richard. "The Strategy of Model Building in Population Biology." *American Scientist* 54 (1966): 421–431.

Nelson, Richard R. "Recent Evolutionary Theorizing About Economic Change." *Journal of Economic Literature* 33 (1995): 48–90.

Overman, E. Samuel. "Introduction: Social Science and Donald T. Campbell." In *Methodology and Epistemology for Social Science*, by Donald T. Campbell; edited by E. Samuel Overman. Chicago: University of Chicago Press, 1988.

Parker, Sue Taylor, Jonas Langer, and Constance Milbrath, eds. *Biology and Knowledge Revisited: From Neurogenesis to Psychogenesis*. Mahwah, NJ: Erlbaum, 2005.

Stanley, Julian C. "Biographical Memoirs: Donald Thomas Campbell." *Proceedings of the American Philosophical Society* 142 (1998): 115–120.

Thomas, Robert McG., Jr. "Donald T. Campbell, Master of Many Disciplines, Dies at 79." *New York Times*, 12 May 1996.

Trochim, William M. The Research Methods Knowledge Base, 2nd ed. Available from http://www.socialresearchmethods.net/kb/external.htm; version as of 20 October 2006.

Wimsatt, William C. "Reductionistic Research Strategies and Their Biases in the Units of Selection Controversy." In *Scientific Discovery*, Vol. 2, *Case Studies*, edited by Thomas Nickles. Dordrecht: Reidel, 1980.

————. "Heuristics and the Study of Human Behavior." In *Metatheory in Social Science*, edited by Donald W. Fiske and Richard A. Shweder. Chicago: University of Chicago Press, 1986.

————. "Echoes of Haeckel? Reentrenching Development in Evolution." In *From Embryology to Evo-Devo: A History of Developmental Evolution*, edited by Manfred D. Laubichler and Jane Maienschein. Cambridge, MA: MIT Press, 2007.

Werner Callebaut

CANTOR, GEORG FERDINAND LUDWIG PHILIP

(*b.* St. Petersburg, Russia, 3 March 1845; *d.* Halle, Germany, 6 January 1918), *mathematics, set theory, philosophy*. For the original article on Cantor see *DSB*, vol. 3.

Cantor is best known as the creator of transfinite set theory, a theory of the mathematical infinite that revolutionized mathematics at the end of the nineteenth century. But the corresponding paradoxes of set theory discovered at the end of the century, including Russell's and Burali-Forti's paradoxes, proved to be inherent in the logic and substance of Cantor's work. These raised serious questions about the consistency of set theory and prompted various approaches to secure rigorous foundations for mathematics that continued in the early 2000s to occupy mathematicians and philosophers of mathematics alike. So controversial were Cantor's ideas—both mathematically and philosophically—that Leopold Kronecker once called him a scientific charlatan, a renegade, a "corrupter of youth." Henri Poincaré considered set theory and Cantor's transfinite numbers to be "a grave mathematical malady, a perverse pathological illness that would one day be cured" (Dauben, 1979, p. 1). Taking the opposite position, Bertrand Russell regarded Cantor as one of the greatest intellects of the nineteenth century, and David Hilbert believed Cantor had created a new paradise from which mathematicians would never be driven, despite the paradoxes of set theory. Meanwhile, Cantor was plagued by recurring nervous breakdowns and ongoing academic rivalries, and his religious convictions played a significant role in his steadfast faith in the correctness of his controversial transfinite set theory; he was convinced that, no matter what the opposition might say, transfinite set theory would eventually be vindicated and accepted by mathematicians as essential to their discipline.

Family History. When Herbert Meschkowski published the first book-length study of Cantor's life and work in 1967, he included photographs of Cantor's parents, noting that his father, Georg Woldemar Cantor, was born in Denmark in 1813 or 1814, the son of a successful businessman. He was raised an Evangelical Lutheran, and he conveyed his deeply held religious views to his son. Cantor's mother, Marie Böhm, was from a family of virtuoso violinists, and she was a Roman Catholic. Meschkowski briefly addresses the significance of religion in Cantor's life in a short section of his biography (Meschkowski, 1967, "Die Religion Cantors," pp. 122–129).

One of the most contentious questions about Cantor's own religious heritage and beliefs turns on the question of whether he was Jewish. In his widely read *Men of Mathematics*, Eric Temple Bell declared that Cantor was "of pure Jewish descent on both sides" (Bell, 1937, p. 558), and went on to make some of the most unfounded and scurrilous remarks about Cantor that have ever been published. In describing the bad blood between Cantor and Kronecker, whose incompatible views on the foundations of mathematics (see below) are legendary, Bell wrote: "there is no more vicious academic hatred than that of one Jew for another when they disagree on purely scientific matters" (1937, p. 562). Cantor had been included as Jewish in a number of earlier reference works, including *The Jewish Encyclopedia* (1901); a volume edited by Siegmund Kaznelson, *Juden im Deutschen Kulturbereich* (pp. 389–390); and in the *Universal Jewish Encyclopedia*, 3 (1969, pp. 18-19).

Ivor Grattan-Guinness, after consulting many archival and hitherto unpublished manuscript documents, concluded that "Georg Cantor was not Jewish, contrary to the view which has prevailed in print and in general opinion for many years" (Grattan-Guinness, 1971, p. 351). Grattan-Guinness based his conclusion on the fact that Cantor was given Christian names, which he took to imply "that the Cantors were *not* Jewish" (p. 351), and the results of a Danish scholar, Theodor Hauch-Fausbøll, whose research at the Danish Genealogical Institute in Copenhagen had come to the same conclusion (in a document of 1937).

Walter Purkert and Hans Joachim Ilgauds were even more adamant in their biography, in which Cantor's Christian and non-Jewish racial profile is stressed. They cite the same certification reported by Grattan-Guinness from the Danish Genealogical Institute of 1937 saying that there is no record of Cantor's father in any of the records of the Jewish community there (Purkert and Ilgauds 1987, p. 15). The fact that this document was produced for the Cantor family at the height of the German persecution of Jews prior to World War II, however, casts considerable doubt on the legitimacy of this testimony. Purkert and Ilgauds leave open the question of whether ancestors of Cantor's may have converted to Christianity and say that the question is irrelevant to Cantor's mathematics, except for the fact that transfinite set theory was condemned during the Nazi period as "Jewish" mathematics.

The truth of the matter of Cantor's Jewish heritage, however, was acknowledged by Cantor himself in a letter to the French philosopher and historian of mathematics, Paul Tannery, in which he referred to his "israelitische" grandparents. And in a letter to the Jesuit priest Alex Baumgartner only recently published, Cantor wrote at even greater length about various pseudonyms he had adopted hinting at his "Portuguese Jewish origins." He noted that one in particular, Vincent Regnäs, spelled backwards, was Sänger=Cantor, which was a reference to the fact that his father was born in Copenhagen and a member of the orthodox Portuguese Jewish community there (Tapp 2005, p. 129). Although clearly of Jewish ancestry, Cantor himself was baptized and confirmed as an Evangelical Lutheran, although in later life he was not an observant follower of any particular confession.

Early Works. Cantor wrote his dissertation at the University of Berlin on number theory (*De aequationibus secudi gradus indeterminatis*, 1867), but his early research after accepting a position at the University of Halle was devoted to the theory of trigonometric series. In 1872 he published a paper establishing the uniqueness of representations of arbitrary functions by trigonometric series in cases where even an infinite number of points might be excepted from the function's domain of definition, so long as these happened to constitute what Cantor called a set of points of the first species. (An infinite set of points P was said to be of the "first species" if its set of limit points P' was finite; if not, then P', the first derived set of P, must contain an infinite number of points and also have a derived set, the second derived set of P, P''. If for some finite number ν the νth derived set P^{ν} contains only a finite number of points, then its derived set will be empty, i.e., $P^{n+1} = \emptyset$, and such infinite point sets were said to be of the first species. Infinite points sets for which none of its derived sets was finite were said to be of the second species).

Cantor's early work on trigonometric series not only launched his early interest in point sets, which led to his later abstract development of set theory, but it also required him to introduce a rigorous theory of real numbers. This too proved to be a central element of Cantor's transfinite set theory, for one of Cantor's most famous conjectures that has yet to be solved is his Continuum Hypothesis, which in one form says that the set of all real numbers (which comprise the continuum) is the next largest infinite set after the set of all integers (which comprise a denumerably infinite set; denumerably infinite sets are the least in power or cardinality of all infinite sets, like the set of all integers).

Meschkowski covered the major details of Cantor's early work in his *DSB* article, noting that the revolution in mathematics that Cantor launched can be dated to 7 December 1873, when he wrote to the mathematician Richard Dedekind to say he had found a way to prove that the set of all real numbers was non-denumerably infinite. Cantor had already proven (in a seminar with his teacher Karl Weierstrass at the University of Berlin) that the set of all algebraic numbers was denumerably infinite; if the set of all real numbers was non-denumerably infinite, this meant that there must be real numbers that were non-algebraic or transcendental. Joseph Liouville had proved the existence of such numbers in 1844; Cantor's proof was an independent verification of this discovery, without identifying any transcendental numbers in particular (the two best-known transcendental numbers are π, established by Charles Hermite in 1873, and e, proven transcendental by Ferdinand von Lindemann in 1882).

Cantor published his truly revolutionary discovery that the real numbers are non-denumerably infinite, establishing for the first time that "the infinite" was not some vast concept that simply included everything that was not finite, but that there were definite distinctions to be drawn between the relative sizes of infinite totalities, or sets. Sets such as the natural numbers, fractions, and algebraic numbers were denumerably infinite; the real numbers were non-denumerably infinite and, as Cantor conjectured, constituted a set of the next highest level of infinity after denumerably infinite sets, a conjecture he spent the rest of his life trying to prove without success (later, in the 1930s, Kurt Gödel would establish two results that explained why—although Cantor's Continuum Hypothesis was consistent with the axioms of basic set theory, it was also independent of those axioms and could not be proven, or disproven, in the context of Zermelo-Fraenkel set theory).

Meschkowski noted that Cantor's paper proving the non-denumerability of the real numbers was published in *Crelle's Journal* in 1874: "Über eine Eigenschaf des Inbegriffes aller reellen algebraischen Zahlen," a paper, Meschkowski explained, that "contained more than the title indicated." But why should Cantor have titled his paper "On a Property of the Collection of All Real Algebraic Numbers," when the clearly important, even revolutionary discovery was his proof that the real numbers were *non*-denumerably infinite? The "property" of the algebraic numbers that Cantor established in this paper was that they are only "countably infinite," but this is a minor result compared to what he had discovered about the set of all real numbers.

Why Cantor gave this paper such a consciously deceptive title was no doubt due to his mathematical rival and former teacher at the University of Berlin, Leopold

Kronecker. Kronecker was a well-known opponent of the school of analysis associated with Karl Weierstass, and he believed that the proper foundation for all of mathematics should rest on the integers alone. Kronecker rejected, for example, appeals to the Bolzano-Weierstrass theorem, upper and lower limits, and to irrational numbers in general. When Lindemann proved that *e* was transcendental, Kronecker asked what difference that made, because transcendental numbers did not exist (Weber, 1893, p. 15; Kneser, 1925, p. 221; Pierpont, 1928, p. 39; Dauben, 2005, p. 69). Worse for Cantor, Kronecker was a member of the editorial board of the journal to which he submitted his proof of the non-denumerabilty of the real numbers, and to disguise the true import of the paper was doubtless a strategic choice.

Kronecker had already tried to discourage Cantor's colleague at Halle, Eduard Heine, from publishing a paper in *Crelle's Journal* to which he objected, and Cantor could well have expected a very negative reaction from Kronecker had his paper carried a title like "Proof that the Collection of All Real Numbers is Non-Denumerably Infinite." In fact, a year later Cantor discovered something he regarded as possibly even more remarkable, that the set of points in the two-dimensional plane could be corresponded in a one-to-one fashion with those on the one-dimensional line. So counterintuitive was this result that Cantor exclaimed in a note to his colleague Richard Dedekind, "I see it, but I don't believe it!" (Dauben, 1979, p. 55). Cantor must have hoped that the infinities of points in the plane and in three-dimensional space might prove to be distinctly higher levels of infinity than the one-dimensional continuum of real numbers, but his proof of the invariance of dimension showed that the number of points in spaces of any dimension was no greater than the points on the one-dimensional line.

Kronecker objected to Cantor's proof, and for a time managed to delay its publication, something that so infuriated Cantor that he refused ever to publish in *Crelle's Journal* again. Although Meschkowski does not mention any of this in his *DSB* article, he does characterize the remarkable nature of Cantor's result: "It looked as if his mapping had rendered the concept of dimension meaningless" (p. 54). But as Dedekind soon pointed out to Cantor, although his correspondence between the points of the line and plane was one-to-one, it was *not continuous*. Cantor and others offered proofs that, indeed, a continuous mapping of points between dimensions was impossible, but a fully satisfactory proof establishing the invariance of dimension was not provided until the topologist L. E. J. Brouwer did so in 1910 (Brouwer, 1911). There was a positive side, however, to Kronecker's early opposition to Cantor's work, for it forced Cantor to evaluate the foundations of set theory as he was in the process of creating it. Such concerns prompted long historical and

Georg Cantor. SCIENCE PHOTO LIBRARY/PHOTO RESEARCHERS, INC.

philosophical passages in Cantor's major publication of the 1880s on set theory, his *Grundlagen einer allgemeinen Mannigfaltigkeitslehre* of 1883.

Cantor's *Grundlagen*. At the very beginning of this revolutionary monograph, Georg Cantor admitted how difficult it had been at first for him to accept the concept of actually infinite numbers, but he found they were absolutely necessary for the further development of mathematics:

> As risky as this might seem, I can voice not only the hope, but my strong conviction, that in time this will have to be regarded as the simplest, most appropriate and natural extension [of the concept of number]. But I realize that in this undertaking I place myself in a certain opposition to views widely held concerning the mathematical infinite and to opinions frequently defended on the nature of numbers. (Cantor, 1883, p. 165; quoted from Dauben, 1979, p. 96)

The *Grundlagen* itself provided a systematic defense of Cantor's new theory on mathematical, historical, and philosophical grounds, and made clear Cantor's metaphysical justification for the new theory, which he knew would be controversial. Although the *Grundlagen* advanced Cantor's thinking about the infinite from point sets to transfinite ordinal numbers, it did not include his later theory of transfinite cardinal numbers and the well-known alephs. Nevertheless, the *Grundlagen* was the earliest systematic treatise devoted to transfinite set theory and arithmetic. Along with Cantor's later "Beiträge zur Begrundung der transfiniten Mengenlehre" (published in two parts, in 1895 and 1897), it had a profound effect on the further development of analysis and topology, and created a virtually new discipline, set theory.

Principles of a Theory of Order Types.

Early in 1885 Cantor drafted an article for Acta Mathemaica, where a number of his early and seminal papers introducing the theory of point sets and transfinite arithmetic had just appeared in French translation, thanks to the efforts of Gösta Mittag-Leffler, the journal's editor and an early champion of Cantor's set theory. The "Principles of a Theory of Order Types" was a new effort to advance beyond well-ordered sets and their order types (the transfinite ordinal numbers) to a general theory of order types, but Mittag-Leffler declined to publish it. In explaining his grounds for rejecting the "Principles," Mittag-Leffler said he thought Cantor was at least one hundred years ahead of his time, and added: "I am convinced that the publication of your new work, before you have been able to explain new positive results, will greatly damage your reputation among mathematicians" (Mittag-Leffler in a letter to Cantor, 9 March 1885; quoted from Cantor ed. Grattan-Guinness, 1970, p. 102).

In fact, the "Principles" was filled with new terminology and philosophical reflections that were not pleasing to Mittag-Leffler. Earlier, when he had prepared the French translation of Cantor's *Grundlagen* for publication in *Acta Mathematica*, he deleted all of the historical and philosophical sections, leaving only those that dealt specifically with the theory of point sets and transfinite ordinal numbers. Readers of the French translations of Cantor's *Grundlagen* thus learned nothing about the historical and philosophical arguments that Cantor regarded as important support for his treatment of the actual infinite mathematically. Similarly, his new general theory of order types did not appear in *Acta Mathematica*, and was unknown to Meschkowski when he wrote his *DSB* article on Cantor. The rejected "Principien" was published by Ivor Grattan-Guinness in 1970.

The *Grundlagen* had only used well-ordered sets to define the transfinite ordinal numbers, but in the "Principles" Cantor presented a new and independent theory of ordered sets in general (see Cantor, 1970). While the sequence of natural numbers 1, 2, 3, … in their natural order represented a well-ordered set, Cantor had begun to consider the properties of "simply ordered" sets, like the rational numbers in their natural order, which he desig-

nated by the order-type η (between any two numbers of type η there was always another number, i.e., they were said to be "everywhere dense"), or the natural order of the real numbers, which he designated by the order-type θ (in addition to being everywhere dense, simply ordered sets of type θ were also continuous). The properties of simply ordered sets were later published by Cantor in his "Beiträge" of 1895 and 1897.

Transfinite Cardinal Numbers: The Alephs.

Although Meschkowski in his *DSB* entry for Cantor goes into considerable detail about the mathematics of transfinite set theory, he has little to say about their most famous element, the transfinite cardinal numbers, or alephs (these are only mentioned once, and as Meschkowski explains, "in all of Cantor's works we find no usable definition of the concept of the cardinal number," Meschkowski, 1971, p. 56). Indeed, transfinite cardinal numbers were not presented in the *Grundlagen*, and the evolution of Cantor's thinking about them is curious. Although the alephs are probably the best-known legacy of Cantor's creation, they were the last part of his theory to be given either rigorous definition or a special symbol. Cantor first introduced notation for sequences of derived sets P of the second species in 1879. (A set of points P was said to be of the second species if there was no finite index ν such that P^ν was empty; this meant that the intersection of all derived sets P^ν of P would be an infinite set of points, which Cantor designated P^∞, and this in turn would have a derived set $P^{\infty+1}$; this, in fact, let to an entire sequence of transfinite sets of the second species.) These point sets of the second species served to extend Cantor's idea well beyond the limitation he had earlier set himself to sets of the first species in his study of trigonometric series. However, in the early 1880s he only referred to the indexes $\infty, \infty+1, \dots$ as "infinite symbols," with no hint that they might be regarded as numbers.

By 1883, when he wrote the *Grundlagen*, the transfinite ordinal numbers had finally achieved independent status as numbers, ω being the first transfinite ordinal number following the entire sequence of finite ordinal numbers, that is, $1,2,3, \dots,\omega$. Although no explicit mention was made in the *Grundlagen* of transfinite *cardinal* numbers, Cantor clearly understood that it is the power of a set that establishes its equivalence (or lack thereof) with any other set, and upon which he would base his concept of transfinite cardinal number.

In September 1883, in a lecture to mathematicians at a meeting in Freiburg, Cantor defined the concept of transfinite cardinal number, but as yet without any particular symbol. Because he had already adopted the symbol ω to designate the least transfinite ordinal number, when Cantor finally introduced a symbol for the first transfinite cardinal number (in correspondence, as early as 1886), he represented the first transfinite cardinal as $\overset{*}{\omega}$, and the next as $\overset{*}{\Omega}$. This notation was not very flexible, and within months he began to use fraktur o's, derivatives from his omegas, to represent the sequence of cardinal numbers o_1, $o_2, o_3, \ldots$. For a time, he used an assortment of notations, including superscripted stars, bars, and his fraktur o's interchangeably for transfinite cardinal numbers. (For a detailed discussion of the evolution of Cantor's notation for the transfinite cardinal numbers, see Dauben, 1979, pp. 179–183.)

However, when the Italian mathematician Giulio Vivanti was preparing a general introduction to set theory in 1893, Cantor realized it would be timely to decide on a standard notation. He chose the Hebrew alephs (ℵ) for transfinite cardinal numbers because the Greek and Roman alphabets were already widely used in mathematics. Cantor believed his new numbers deserved something distinctive, and the Hebrew alphabet had the advantage that it was readily available among the type fonts of German printers. Moreover, this choice was particularly clever because the Hebrew aleph was also a symbol for the number one. Since the transfinite cardinal numbers were themselves infinite unities, the alephs represented a new beginning for mathematics. When Cantor introduced his transfinite cardinal numbers for the first time in the "Beiträge" in 1895, he used $\aleph_0$ to represent the first and least transfinite cardinal number, after which there followed an unending, well-defined sequence of transfinite cardinal numbers (for details, see Cantor, 1895, pp. 292–296; 1915, pp. 103–109; and Dauben, 1979, pp. 179–183, 194–218).

Cantor's Nervous Breakdowns. In his *DSB* article of 1971, Meschkowski had little to say about Cantor's famous nervous breakdowns but their role in Cantor's defense of his mathematics may have been crucial, as was his deeply held religious faith, which was also connected, at least in his mind, with his nervous breakdowns. It was in May 1884 that Cantor suffered the first of a recurring series of episodes that were to plague him for the rest of his life. The mathematician Arthur Schoenflies, when he chronicled Cantor's "mathematical crisis" over failure to resolve the Continuum Hypothesis in the 1880s, suggested that this no doubt triggered Cantor's first major breakdown (Schoenflies, 1927). Cantor's lack of progress resolving the Continuum Hypothesis or stress from Kronecker's ongoing attacks may have contributed to the breakdown, but as Ivor Grattan-Guinness concluded, based on evidence from Cantor's records at the Nervenklinik in Halle where he was treated, mathematics probably had little to do with his mental illness. Cantor suffered from acute manic depression, which was only remotely—if at all—connected to his career.

The manic phase took over with no warning and lasted somewhat more than a month (for details, see Grattan-Guinness, 1971, and Charraud, 1994). When Cantor "recovered" at the end of June 1884 and entered the depressive phase of his illness, he complained that he lacked energy and had no interest in returning to rigorous mathematical thinking. Instead, he took up the study of English history and literature, seriously advocating a popular theory of his day that Francis Bacon was the true author of Shakespeare's plays. Cantor also tried his hand without success at teaching philosophy, and about this time began to correspond with Roman Catholic theologians who had taken an interest in the philosophical implications of transfinite set theory. This correspondence was of special significance to Cantor because he was convinced that he was the messenger of the divinely inspired transfinite numbers.

Cantor and Catholic Theologians. Although Meschkowski later published a collection of Cantor's letters, a number of which reflect exchanges between Cantor and various theologians, including Cardinal Johannes Franzelin, he made only passing reference to their correspondence in his *DSB* article on Cantor. The significance of this correspondence was the subject of Christian Tapp's doctoral thesis at the Ludwig Maximilians Universität (Munich) published in 2005, which explores what Tapp calls Cantor's "dialogue" with Catholic theologians of his time.

What emerges from Cantor's letters to theologians is a much clearer picture of his understanding of the prehistory of his theory and the difficulties he knew the reception of set theory would face. In his correspondence, the philosophical foundations of set theory are discussed candidly, including the concept of infinity, the problem of the potential infinite, and Cantor's criticism of so-called proofs of the impossibility of actually infinite numbers. Cantor was especially concerned with combating objections that theologians raised in opposition to any "actual" concept of infinity apart from God's absolute infinite nature, which Cantor's transfinite numbers seemed to challenge directly. Cantor approached these matters by affirming the existence of sets as abstractions, and through a systematic critique of philosophical works, especially with respect to scholasticism and, much later, *Naturphilosophie.*

Tapp evaluates the rather eccentric interest Cantor had in Baconian studies, various claims that Bacon was a crypto-Catholic, and the relevance of the Bacon-Shakespeare question, all of which he uses to better understand Cantor's personality, if not his mathematics. He also considers a rather odd pamphlet that Cantor published privately at his own expense, *Ex Oriente Lux* (1905), in which Cantor argued that Christ was the natural son of Joseph of Arimathea (see Dauben, 1979, p. 289; Tapp, 2005, pp. 157–159). Tapp makes good use as well of information concerning often obscure individuals, some of whom no one has written about previously in relation to Georg Cantor. The new information Tapp provides leads to a very rich analysis of the "Catholic" connection in Cantor's attempts to promote and defend his transfinite set theory, especially from attacks by philosophers and theologians. In turn, Cantor's interest in "saving the Church" from mistakenly opposing transfinite mathematics for somehow being in conflict with the absolute infinite nature of God also plays a role in Cantor's thought. In addition to the various pseudonyms Cantor adopted, Tapp also considers other very original and interesting information from the correspondence, including an analysis of differences in Cantor's handwriting, to shed new light on aspects of his character and personality (for details, see Tapp, 2005).

Evaluating Cantor's Manic Depression. Much has been written about Cantor's unfortunate history of mental illness, which some such as Schoenflies have linked to his distress at not being able to prove his Continuum Hypothesis and the relentless criticism of transfinite set theory by Kronecker (Schoenfliess, 1927). The mathematician E. T. Bell explained the root of Cantor's many tribulations in completely Freudian terms, as stemming from what Bell characterized as a disastrous relationship with his father. According to Bell, it was his father's initial opposition to Cantor's wish to become a mathematician that was the source of Cantor's later mental problems (Bell, 1937, chap. 29). In 1994, Nathalie Charraud, a Lacanian psychoanalyst, after examining the records of Cantor's treatment at the neurological clinic in Halle, offered a very different interpretation of the very positive role that Cantor's father played in his son's life. She suggested that his father was a constructive force, and that the deeply religious sensibility Cantor inherited from his father prompted a connection that Cantor felt to his transfinite numbers, which he took to have been communicated to him from God directly. This, in fact, was crucial to the unwavering support Cantor always gave transfinite set theory, no matter what criticisms might be directed against it. (For details of how his religious convictions and periods of manic depression may actually have played constructive, supportive roles in the battle to establish transfinite set theory as a fundamental part of modern mathematics, see Dauben, 2005.)

Cantor and the Professionalization of Mathematics. In addition to stimulating the vigorous defense that Cantor mounted on behalf of his set theory from the outset, the opposition to Cantor's work as a mathematician had

another constructive result, namely the effort he made to establish the Deutsche Mathematiker-Vereinigung (German Mathematical Society). His motives are reflected in one of his most famous pronouncements about mathematics, that "the *essence* of *mathematics* lies precisely in its *freedom*" (Cantor, 1883, p. 182). This was largely motivated in response to Kronecker's opposition to his work; Cantor had argued in the *Grundlagen* that if a theory could be shown to be not contradictory, mathematicians should be free to pursue it; posterity would show whether its results might be fruitful or not. It was in the same spirit of freedom, hoping to promote a forum where mathematics could be discussed openly, that Cantor put considerable effort into establishing the German Mathematical Society. He was elected its first president in 1891.

Cantor's creation of transfinite set theory, despite opposition from some of the most prominent mathematicians of his day, eventually persisted, thanks in no small measure to the unwavering faith he had in the importance and correctness of the theory itself. His defense of set theory was as much historical and philosophical as it was technical, mathematically; on a very personal level, it was also religious. As Cantor himself once wrote about why he was so certain that his theory must be true:

> My theory stands as firm as a rock; every arrow directed against it will return quickly to its archer. How do I know this? Because I have studied it from all sides for many years; because I have examined all objections which have ever been made against the infinite numbers; and above all, because I have followed its roots, so to speak, to the first infallible cause of all created things. (Cantor in a letter of 21 June 1888 to Carl Friedrich Heman, professor of theology at the University of Basel; quoted from Dauben, 1979, p. 298)

Cantor suffered the last of his nervous breakdowns in the spring of 1917. He was hospitalized against his wishes, and repeatedly asked for his family to take him home. As World War I raged on, food was scarce, and a surviving photograph of Cantor shortly before his death shows a face gaunt and tired (Dauben, 1979, p. 273). On 6 January 1918, he died, apparently of heart failure. But as Edmund Landau wrote when he heard the news, Cantor and all that he represented would never die. One had to be thankful for a Georg Cantor, from whom later generations of mathematicians would learn: "Never will anyone remain more alive" (Landau, in a letter of 8 January 1918; quoted from Meschkowski, 1967, p. 270). Indeed, Cantor's creation of transfinite set theory has not only inspired mathematicians and philosophers, but the writers of poems, novels (Borges; see Hernández, 2001), and even an opera, *Cantor: Die Vermessung des Unendlichen,* by Ingomar Grünauer (Wilkening, 2006; Grattan-Guinness, 2007).

SUPPLEMENTARY BIBLIOGRAPHY

The major archival collections of Cantoriana are to be found in Germany in the archives of Halle University, and three surviving letter books now preserved in the Handschriftenabteilung of the Niedersächsische Staats- und Universitätsbibliothek, Göttingen. A substantial collection of correspondence between Cantor and the editor of Acta Mathematica, *Gösta Mittag-Leffler, is preserved in the archives of the Institut Mittag-Leffler, Djursholm, Sweden, along with letters Cantor exchanged with the English mathematician and logician Philip Jourdain. For detailed discussion of other documents relevant to Cantor's life and works, see the "List of manuscript sources" in Grattan-Guinness, 1971; and Tapp, 2005.*

WORKS BY CANTOR

Gesammelte Abhandlungen mathematischen und philosophischen Inhalts, edited by Ernst Zermelo. Berlin: Springer, 1932. Reprint, Hildesheim: Olms, 1966; Berlin: Springer, 1980. The Springer reprint includes an appendix compiled by Joseph W. Dauben, "Weitere Arbeiten von Georg Cantor," a list of works by Cantor that were not included in the *Gesammelte Abhandlungen* edited by Zermelo, as well as a list of book reviews Cantor had written, and works in which letters of Cantor have been published (pp. 487–489).

"Über eine Eigenschaft des Inbegriffes aller reellen algebraischen Zahlen." *Journal für die reine und angewandte Mathematik* 77 (1874): 258–262. Reprinted in Cantor, 1932, pp. 115–118; French translation, *Acta mathematica* 2 (1883): 205–310.

Grundlagen einer allgemeinen Mannigfaltigkeitslehre. Ein mathematisch-philosophischer Versuch in der Lehre des Unendlichen. Leipzig: Teubner, 1883. Also published (without the preface) as "Über unendliche, lineare Punktmannichfaltigkeiten" (Part 5). *Mathematische Annalen* 23 (1884): 453–488. Reprinted in Cantor, 1932, pp. 165–208. English translation by W. B. Ewald.

"Foundations of a General Theory of Manifolds: A Mathematico-philosophical Investigation into the Theory of the Infinite." In *From Kant to Hilbert: A Source Book in the Foundations of Mathematics,* vol. 2, edited by William B. Ewald. New York: Oxford University Press, 1996. This work is also analyzed in detail in Joseph W. Dauben, "Georg Cantor, Essay on the 'Foundations of General Set Theory,' 1883." In *Landmark Writings in Western Mathematics, 1640–1940,* edited by Ivor Grattan-Guinness. Amsterdam: Elsevier, 2005.

"Beiträge zur Begründung der transfiniten Mengenlehre." *Mathematische Annalen* 46 (1895): 481–512; 49 (1897): 207–246. Reprinted in Cantor, 1932, pp. 282–356. English translation by Philip E. B. Jourdain (Cantor 1915).

Contributions to the Founding of the Theory of Transfinite Numbers. Translated by Philip E. B. Jourdain. Chicago: Open Court, 1915.

"Principien einer Theorie der Ordnungstypen" (Erste Mittheilung). Edited by Ivor Grattan-Guinness: *Acta Mathematica* 124 (1970): 65–107. This paper was discovered by Ivor Grattan-Guinness among unpublished papers at the Insitut Mittag-Leffler; it was set in type but never printed, and was dated 6 November 1884.

With Richard Dedekind. *Briefwechsel Cantor-Dedekind.* Edited by Emmy Noether and Jean Cavaillès. Paris: Hermann, 1937.

OTHER SOURCES

Bandmann, Hans. *Die Unendlichkeit des Seins. Cantors transfinite Mengenlehre und ihre metaphysischen Wurzeln.* Frankfurt am Main: Lang, 1992.

Bell, Eric Temple. "Paradise Lost: Georg Cantor." In *Men of Mathematics.* New York: Simon and Schuster, 1937. Reprint, 1986, chap. 29, pp. 555–579. To be used with extreme caution; although widely read and available in numerous reprintings, it has been described as "one of the worst" books on history of mathematics, and "can be said to have done considerable disservice to the profession" (Grattan-Guinness 1971, p. 350).

Brouwer, Luitzen E. J. "Beweis der Invarianz der Dimensionenzahl." *Mathematische Annalen* 70 (1911): 161–165.

Charraud, Nathalie. *Infini et inconscient: Essai sur Georg Cantor.* Paris: Anthropos, 1994.

Dauben, Joseph Warren. *Georg Cantor: His Mathematics and Philosophy of the Infinite.* Cambridge, MA: Harvard University Press, 1979. Reprint, Princeton, NJ: Princeton University Press, 1990.

———. "Review of Walter Purkert and Hans Joachim Ilgauds: *Georg Cantor, 1845–1918* (*Vita Mathematica* 1)." Basel: Birkhäuser, 1987, in *Isis* 79, no. 4 (1988): 700–702.

———. "The Battle for Cantorian Set Theory." In *Mathematics and the Historian's Craft: The Kenneth O. May Lectures,* edited by Michael Kinyon and Glen van Brummelen. New York: Springer Verlag, Canadian Mathematical Society Books in Mathematics, 2005.

Epple, Moritz. "Georg Cantor." In *Modern Germany: An Encyclopedia of History, People, and Culture, 1871–1990,* edited by D. K. Buse and J. C. Doerr. 2 vols. New York: Garland Publishing, 1998.

Fraenkel, Abraham A. "Georg Cantor." *Jahresbericht der Deutschen Mathematiker-Vereinigung* 39 (1930): 189–266.

Grattan-Guinness, Ivor. "Towards a Biography of Georg Cantor." *Annals of Science* 27 (1971): 345–391.

———. Review of "Cantor: Die Vermessung des Unendlichen." *Annals of Science* 64 (2007).

Kaznelson, Siegmund. *Juden im deutschen Kulturbereich; ein Sammelwerk.* 2nd ed. Berlin: Jüdischer Verlag, 1959.

Hallett, Michael. *Cantorian Set Theory and Limitation of Size.* Oxford: Clarendon Press, 1984.

Hernández, Juan Antonio. *Biografía del infinito: La noción de transfinitud en George Cantor y su presencia en la prosa de Jorge Luis Borges.* Caracas: Comala.com, 2001.

Heuser-Kessler, Marie-Luisa. "Georg Cantors transfinite Zahlen und Giordano Brunos Unendlichkeitsidee." *Selbstorganisation* 2 (1991): 222–244.

Kertész, Andor. *Georg Cantor, 1845–1918: Schöpfer der Mengenlehre.* Edited by Manfred Stern. Halle: Deutsche Akademie der Naturforscher Leopoldina (*Acta historica leopoldina* 15), 1983.

Kneser, Adolf. "Leopold Kronecker." *Jahresbericht der Deutschen Mathemaiker Vereinigung* 33 (1925): 310–228.

Kohut, Adolph. *Berühmte israelitische Männer und Frauen in der Kulturgeschichte der Menschheit.* Leipzig-Reudnitz: A. H. Payne, 1900–1901.

Landman, Isaac, ed. *The Universal Jewish Encyclopedia.* New York: The Universal Jewish Encyclopedia, Inc., 1939–1943; 2nd rev. ed. New York: Ktav Publishing House, 1969.

Lauria, Philippe. *Cantor et le transfini: Mathématique et ontology.* Paris: Harmattan, 2004.

Lavine, Shaughan. *Understanding the Infinite.* Cambridge, MA: Harvard University Press, 1994.

Meschkowski, Herbert. *Probleme des Unendlichen: Werk und Leben Georg Cantors.* Braunschweig: Vieweg, 1967. A second edition of this work appeared with the variant title: *Georg Cantor: Leben, Werk und Wirkung.* Mannheim: Bibliographisches Institut, 1983.

Pierpont, J. "Mathematical Rigor, Past and Present." *Bulletin of the American Mathematical Society* 34 (1928): 23–53.

Purkert, Walter, and Hans Joachim Ilgauds. *Georg Cantor.* Leipzig: Teubner, 1985.

———. *Georg Cantor 1845–1918.* Basel: Birkhäuser, 1987.

Schoenflies, Arthur. "Die Krisis in Cantor's mathematischem Schaffen," *Acta Mathematica* 5 (1927): 1–23.

Tannery, Paul. *Mémoires scientifiques* 13: *Correspondance.* Paris: Gauthier-Villars, 1934.

Tapp, Christian. *Kardinalität und Kardinäle: Wissenschaftshistorische Aufarbeitung der Korrespondenz zwischen Georg Cantor und katholischen Theologen seiner Zeit.* Boethius: Texte und Abhandlungen zur Geschichte der Mathematik und der Naturwissenschaften, vol. 53. Stuttgart: Franz Steiner Verlag, 2005.

Weber, Heinrich. "Leopold Kronecker." *Mathematische Annalen* 43 (1893): 1–25.

Wilkening, Martin. "Ingomar Grünauers Oper 'Cantor' in Halle." *Frankfurter Allgemeine Zeitung,* 14 November 2006.

Joseph W. Dauben

CARDANO, GIROLAMO (*b.* Pavia, Italy, 24 September 1501; *d.* Rome, Italy, 1576), *medicine, mathematics, physics, philosophy.* For the original article on Cardano see *DSB,* vol. 3.

Some of the details of Cardano's life given in the first edition of the *DSB* require modification. After completing his doctorate in 1526, Cardano practiced for about a decade as a doctor in two Italian towns (Saccolongo, where he married, and Gallerate). Falling on hard times, he returned in penury to his native Milan to find himself excluded from the College of Physicians and hence from public medical practice; but he was able to obtain through the first of a line of ecclesiastical patrons, Filippo Archinto, an ill-paid post as a public teacher of a variety of arts subjects, including mathematics, in Milan. He tried to make money as an author of prognostications and

astrological works, the latter of which were published in the hope that they would attract the attention of Pope Paul III. At about the same time, Ottaviano Scoto, a Venetian publisher friend, generously printed for him two aggressively polemical works on medicine (*De malo recentiorum medicorum medendi usu; De simplicium medicinarum noxa,* both in 1536) and later brought out a work on a moral theme (*De consolatione* [1542]). Cardano then found a local sponsor to support the publication of a work of mathematics (*Practica arithmetice* [1539]), to which he took the precaution of appending a privilege to protect a list of thirty-four of his as-yet unpublished writings, thereby advertising their existence to the wider community of scholars and publishers.

This list inaugurated the second period of his life, in which he made himself an international reputation as an innovative thinker and a solid career as a practicing doctor and a teacher of medicine. A famous publisher in Nürnberg produced several of his writings, notably his mathematical *Ars magna* (1545). He made contact with the foremost scholarly publisher in Lyon, who brought out philosophical and medical works by him; these include works written explicitly to supersede the writings of Pietro Pomponazzi (the *De animorum immortalitate* of 1545 and the section of the *Contradicentia medica* on incantations that appeared first in 1548). Other unpublished works (the *De fato* and the *De arcanis aeternitatis*) are witness to his incautious interest in religious subjects that eventually brought him the unwelcome attentions of the ecclesiastical authorities. Later visits to Paris and Basel secured him further publishing outlets, making him better known abroad than in Italy. He was finally elected to the College of Physicians of Milan in 1539 and appointed to a chair of medicine at the University of Pavia shortly thereafter. His medical writings attracted the attention of the archbishop of St. Andrews, who invited him to Scotland. This allowed him to travel widely in Europe, and to return home triumphantly at the beginning of 1554. For the next six years, he enjoyed both financial security and public and professional esteem. He came to be known during this time as a mathematician, a writer on astrology, a medical authority, a natural philosopher, and a writer on moral issues.

The third phase of his life was inaugurated by the execution of his son in 1560, which caused him to lose reputation and support in Milan. Shortly after, scurrilous rumors concerning his alleged sexual misconduct started circulating in Pavia, and a challenge to his professorship was issued on the grounds of his anti-Galenic teaching. He was forced to resign his chair on 11 June 1562. Powerful ecclesiastical patrons obtained for him the chair of medicine at Bologna, which he took up in October 1562. He began to earn money again from consultations, was elected a citizen of Bologna on 26 May 1563, and set about publishing on a wide range of topics. He put into effect his project to write commentaries on the whole Hippocratic corpus. Four of these were published before 1570. He did not neglect mathematics: a large tome on proportion and on the relationship of geometry to algebra appeared in 1570.

The fourth phase of his life began with the disaster of his imprisonment by the Bologna inquisitors on 6 October 1570. As a result, he lost his professorship and the right to teach in the Papal States, and was, moreover, denied the right to publish. His protector, Cardinal Giovanni Morone, probably induced him to move to Rome, where he arrived on 7 October 1571. There he occupied himself with clearing his own name of heresy and purging his own writings, in the hope of getting the restrictions on teaching and publishing lifted, and the condemnation of his books revoked after their correction. Eventually he received a pension from the newly elected pope Gregory XIII, a qualified publishing license for his existing medical publications on 29 October 1572, the right to publish a new work for the first time since his abjuration on 14 May 1574, and the right to return to Bologna to take up his teaching again on 5 January 1576. He was received into the Roman College of Physicians in September 1574. Cardano's last known will was written on 21 August 1576, and the last date to which he refers in the writings is 1 October 1576. It is unlikely that he survived very long after this date. It is not known where he is buried.

Medical Views. Cardano was a self-proclaimed polymath, whose collected works amount to more than four million words. Whereas it is true to claim that his most enduring contribution to science lies in the field of mathematics, he saw his medical writings as worthy of as much consideration. From his practice in Saccolongo onward, he accumulated insights into pathology and therapy, which he published under the title *Contradicentia medica*, and was among the first to recognize the importance of Andreas Vesalius's anatomical work. His growing confidence as a doctor led him to challenge Galen's supremacy as a medical authority, and to supplant it with Hippocrates. Cardano set out to write commentaries on all of Hippocrates's works that he deemed authentic: four of these appeared in the course of the 1560s. He was led also to a new approach to the etiology of disease by his interest in natural philosophy.

In the *De subtilitate* of 1550, he set out a radical new general theory of nature in contradiction to that of Aristotle, but recognized that his new explanations led to an appreciation of its diversity and nonuniformity (hence the title of the work—*De rerum varietate* [1557]—written to complete the *De subtilitate*). This progression in his work from universal theory to an awareness of unexplained

Girolamo Cardano. SCIENCE SOURCE/PHOTO RESEARCHERS, INC.

residues is characteristic of much of his thought. Another strand of his inquiry into nature concerns the nature of human perception and the human mind, which he links to his investigation of the immortality of the soul (*De animorum immortalitate* [1545]). His *Dialectica* (1562), which purported to give a succinct account of all logical methods, and his work on natural magic titled *De secretis,* were both left at his death in forms that evince the incessant revisions to which he subjected his own encyclopedic enterprises.

He was also very well known during his lifetime for writings on astrology, his horoscopes, and his dream interpretation. These were not as original in method as he claimed, and their predictive power was very poor (he told the King Edward VI of England, who died at the age of sixteen in 1553, that he would have a long life). But the impulsion behind these essays was not as irrational as has often been claimed. He set out to ask how both the future and the hidden secrets of nature could be known (in medical terms, this translated itself into a close study of prognosis). His interest in human affairs through moral and historical inquiry was also connected to his investigations into the unfurling of events around him at both an individual and a universal level. Even his analysis of chance in various games was linked to his desire to measure and to quantify the likelihood of outcomes. One of his very last works, left unfinished at his death, the *De prudentia eximia,* sketched out a general theory that was tested against the course of his own life from 1570. This recourse to himself characterized also his medical and moral writings, which abound in references to his own practice and experiences. It reflects itself in his various autobiographical writings, of which the last and most famous was published posthumously by Gabriel Naudé in 1643. It was through the work of Naudé that his *Opera omnia* in ten volumes was published in 1663; but his reputation as a radical thinker had been sustained not by a strong positive interest in his novel theories of nature, but negatively by Julius Caesar Scaliger's systematic attack on his *De subtilitate* (the *Exotericae exercitationes,* which were used as a textbook in a number of German universities), and by unfounded rumors about his atheism that were propagated by antilibertine tracts of the early 1600s.

SUPPLEMENTARY BIBLIOGRAPHY

WORKS BY CARDANO

Contradicentia medica. These are versions produced from 1545 to 1663, reproduced on a DVD ROM by the Progetto Cardano, n.d.

Writings on Music. Translated by Clement A. Miller. Rome: American Institute of Musicology, 1973.

Pronostico of 1534. Edited by Germana Ernst. In *Girolamo Cardano: le opere, le fonti, la vita.* Edited by Marialuisa Baldi and Guido Canziani. Milan, Italy: Franco Angeli, 1999, pp. 457–476.

Gerolamo Cardano nel quinto centenario della nascita. Pavia, Italy: Cardano, 2001.

Liber de orthographia. Edited by Raffaele Passarella. In *Cardano e la tradizione dei saperi,* edited by Marialuisa Baldi and Guido Canziani. Milan, Italy: Franco Angeli, 2003, pp. 525–618.

De libris propriis. Edited by Ian Maclean. Milan, Italy: Franco Angeli, 2004.

De subtilitate. Books 1–7. Edited by Elio Nenci. Milan, Italy: Franco Angeli, 2004.

De immortalitate animorum. Edited by José Manuel García Valverde. Milan, Italy: Franco Angeli, 2006.

Progetto Cardano. Available from http://filolinux.dipafilo.unimi.it/cardano. A reliable bibliography of Cardano's published works can be found on this Web site, which also contains a complete list of translations of Cardano's works.

OTHER SOURCES

Albé, Patrizia. *Girolamo Cardano nel suo tempo.* Pavia, Italy: Istituto di studi superiori dell'Insubria Gerolamo Cardano 4, 2003.

Baldi, Marialuisa, and Guido Canziani, eds. *Girolamo Cardano: le opere, le fonti, la vita.* Milan, Italy: Franco Angeli, 1999.

———. *Cardano e la tradizione dei saperi.* Milan, Italy: Franco Angeli, 2003.

Fierz, Markus. *Girolamo Cardano (1501–1576), Arzt, Naturphilosoph, Mathematiker, Astronom und Traumdeuter.* Basel, Switzerland: Birkhäuser, 1977. English translation. Boston: Birkhäuser, 1983.

Grafton, Anthony. *Cardanos Kosmos: die Welten und Werke eines Renaissance-Astrologen.* Berlin: Berlin Verlag, 1999. English translation. Cambridge, MA: Harvard University Press, 2000.

Ingegno, Alfonso. *Saggi sulla filosofia di Cardano.* Florence, Italy: La nuova Italia, 1980.

Kessler, Eckhard, ed. *Girolamo Cardano: Philosoph, Naturforscher, Arzt.* Wiesbaden, Germany: Harrassowitz, 1994.

Milano, Mino. *Gerolamo Cardano: mistero e scienza nel cinquecento.* Milan, Italy: Camunia, 1990.

Schütze, Ingo. "Bibliografia degli studi su Girolamo Cardano dal 1850 al 1995." *Bruniana e Campanelliana* 4 (1998): 449–467.

———. *Die Naturphilosophie in Girolamo Cardanos De Subtilitate.* Munich, Germany: Wilhelm Fink, 2000.

Siraisi, Nancy G. *The Clock and the Mirror: Girolamo Cardano and Renaissance Medicine.* Princeton, NJ: Princeton University Press, 1997.

Ian Maclean

CAREY, SAMUEL WARREN (*b.* near Campbelltown, New South Wales, Australia, 1 November 1911; *d.* Hobart, Tasmania, 20 March 2002), *continental drift, global tectonics, Earth expansion.*

"Prof Carey," as he preferred to be known (never "Sam," except to his closest friends and colleagues), was an iconoclastic geologist who accepted and taught that the continents move relative to each other decades before this view became orthodoxy. Taking his cue from Alfred Wegener's theory of continental displacement and Arthur Holmes's version of mantle convection, he accepted the relative motion of the continents and developed and taught a theory of Earth that had some similarities with the plate tectonics view of Earth that emerged triumphant in the late 1960s. But in the late 1950s, at a time when paleomagnetic and other data were reviving interest in continental drift, he concluded that the production of new ocean floor as the continental blocks moved apart meant that Earth itself must be expanding. Through the next four decades, and well after the general acceptance of plate tectonics, he continued to elaborate and defend Earth expansion as his preferred alternative. Earth expansion attracted considerable interest in the 1960s and, even after the plate tectonics revolution, continued to have some adherents.

Early Life. Carey was born to Tasman George and Hannah Elspeth Carey at home on 1 November 1911, without doctor or midwife, in rural New South Wales in Australia after his mother had been thrown over a fence from a runaway carriage. He grew up in straitened circumstances. At the insistence of his mother, he walked to school in Campbelltown, some 3 miles distant, whatever the weather or illness, carrying his shoes in both directions in order to save wear on them. He completed his secondary school studies at Canterbury Boys High School with a focus on science; his subjects included advanced mathematics, physics, chemistry, and, at the suggestion of his physics teacher, geology. His academic achievements at Canterbury resulted in a scholarship for teacher training at the University of Sydney. This enabled him, the eldest of seven children, to enroll in 1929 as the Great Depression began. As a first-year student he intended to major in physics and mathematics, but in addition to those subjects and biology, he took geology as his fourth subject.

The teaching staff in geology, particularly Leo A. Cotton and William R. Browne, followed the lead of the influential example of the recently retired Professor Tannatt W. Edgeworth David in emphasizing both extensive fieldwork and a close knowledge of alternative theories and interpretations. Cotton, for example, wrote on polar wander and described in one of his courses Wegener's theory of continental displacement (drift) as answering many problems in the Southern Hemisphere. Carey soon concentrated on geology, in part because of his enjoyment of the physical and intellectual demands of fieldwork and his love of such activities as rock climbing, camping, and cave exploration. For his bachelor of science and master of science degrees, he undertook research on Carboniferous and Permian rocks in New South Wales, which resulted in several publications. His experience at Sydney helped shape his personal credo, exemplified later in his teaching, research, and publications: "Disbelieve if you can!" In other words, do not accept the authority of the textbook, the teacher, or the majority view; instead, challenge what is accepted, attempt to find the best explanation, and then be prepared to defend it. In his later career, this led him first to accept, elaborate, and defend a version of drift and then to reject that in favor of a theory of Earth expansion.

Fieldwork in New Guinea. Although Carey intended to apply for a scholarship to Cambridge University in England to pursue his PhD, he instead took up an offer by Oil Search Ltd. to undertake field mapping and exploration in New Guinea, north of Australia. He worked there from 1934 to 1942. His experiences as the leader of field parties of thirty New Guineans, often isolated for weeks, reinforced his independence and self-reliance. His detailed observations in New Guinea, a geologically active region of both rapid erosion and uplift including those on the

effects of the great Torricelli earthquake in 1935, underlined for him the vertical mobility of Earth's crust. He drew on these experiences in completing his doctor of science thesis in 1939 on the tectonic evolution of New Guinea and Melanesia. His examiners included Arthur Holmes and H. A. Brouwer. Carey later claimed that he had to self-censor himself regarding some of the content because it might be too radical, not only his use of the idea of moving continents, but also his now accepted "orocline concept"; that is, that many mountain belts that were initially linear in form had subsequently been bent by relative movements of the crust. He was recalled to Australia in 1942 for debriefing and then permitted to enlist for military service. He volunteered for duty in Z-Force, a special unit formed to conduct raids behind enemy lines. After first serving in New Guinea, he returned to Australia where his most memorable exploit was to demonstrate by a highly successful mock attack on allied shipping in Townsville Harbor the potential of unconventional weapons and tactics. This resulted in official approval for a successful raid on Japanese shipping in Singapore Harbor.

Working in Tasmania. In 1944 Carey became the chief government geologist for Tasmania. In that capacity he reorganized the structure of the Survey of Tasmania, wrote many reports, and directed the preparation of many geological and mineral maps. Even after departing the survey to become a professor at the University of Tasmania, as a consultant he took a keen interest in the preparation of accurate regional maps, often employing aerial photography, for the survey and for the Tasmanian Hydro-Electric Commission. Many of these maps were completed by students and staff at the university.

In 1946 he was appointed foundation professor of geology at the University of Tasmania, in which capacity he hired staff and designed a challenging curriculum that carefully integrated lectures, laboratories, and fieldwork. He regarded the introductory course as critical and taught it, beginning in 1947, for many years. He used as the text Holmes's *Principles of Physical Geology* (1944), which included a chapter on continental drift and an illustration of a possible mechanism based on convection currents in Earth's mantle. In his lectures he presented the case for continental mobility, but his teaching was based on his credo that students should make their own observations, formulate their own explanations, and then be prepared to defend them against fellow students as well as himself. For the next few years, he was occupied with the design and construction of a building for the new discipline.

A Mobilist View. Carey began publicly defending and extending a mobilist view of Earth in 1955. The view that

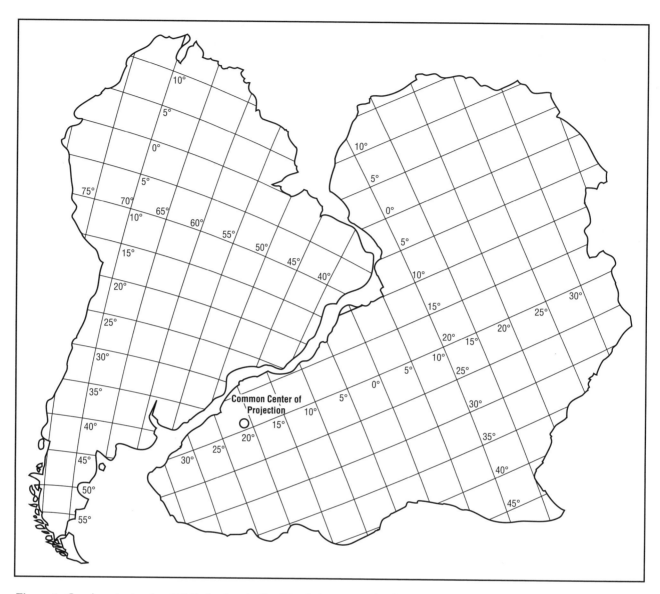

Figure 1. *Carey's projection (ca. 1936) showing the fit of South America with Africa at the 200 meter isobath, which he interpreted initially as evidence for relative motion of the two continents but later in terms of an expanding Earth.*

he put forward resembled closely the plate tectonics version of "drift," which triumphed in the late 1960s; that is, he taught and advocated the lateral motion of continents as a result of convection currents in Earth's mantle with generation of new crust and disappearance of older crust. In 1954 he submitted a paper on his orocline concept to the *Journal of the Australian Geological Society,* and it was duly sent to three referees, each a professor of geology, a Fellow of the newly formed Australian Academy of Science, and an avowed opponent of drift. Their comments were both hostile and disparaging. He vowed never to become an academician or to submit another paper to the *Journal.* The paper, "The Orocline Concept in Geotectonics," was published in 1955 in the friendlier *Proceedings of*

the Royal Society of Tasmania and was soon widely cited by mobilists. In it he argued that mountain belts may undergo subsequent deformation through large, lateral crustal movement. One of his examples, based on geological and tectonic data, was the formation of the Bay of Biscay, along the French and Spanish coast, resulting from a clockwise rotation of Spain toward the Mediterranean and the consequent curving of once-straight mountain chains. This example was later widely cited during the revival of drift in the 1960s. He also published a refutation of Harold Jeffreys's claim that the "fit" of South America to Africa used by proponents of drift as evidence for a previous connection of the two continents was relatively poor. Carey based his rebuttal on a physical fitting of scale

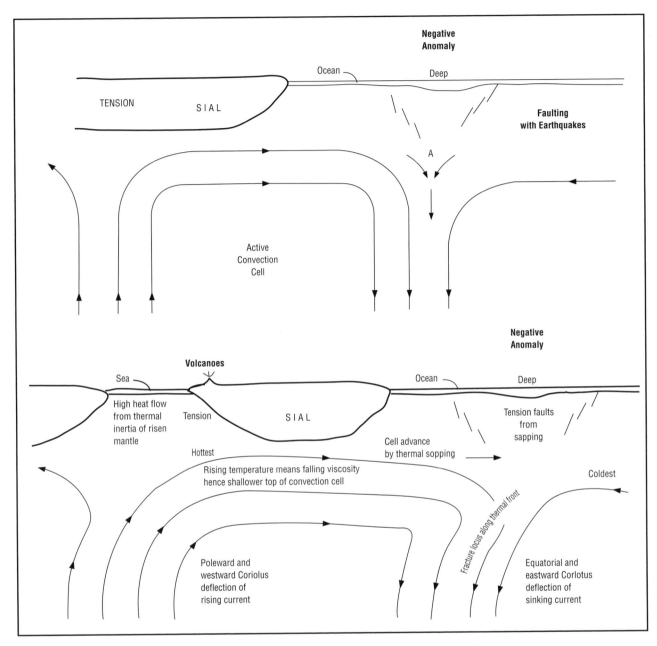

Figure 2. *Migration of continents through sapping and consumption of oceanic crust, as proposed by Carey in 1953.*

models of the two continents on a specially prepared globe and also through stereographic projection, though he noted that the fit was not absolutely perfect. There were a few small gaps, or "gores."

Carey in 1955 began convening symposia on controversial topics both to stimulate debate and to expose his students to current debates. The first in the series was on marine sedimentation. The next was the most notable.

In 1956 Carey hosted the Symposium on the Present Status of the Continental Drift Hypothesis at the University of Tasmania. The timing was fortuitous: much new

data about the topography of seafloors and the patterns of earthquake distribution were becoming available, and new paleomagnetic techniques were beginning to suggest that large-scale movements of Earth's crust had indeed taken place. This was reflected in the collection of symposium papers, published in 1958 under the title *Continental Drift, a Symposium*. Both anti- and pro-mobilists participated, but the volume reveals a softening in the stance taken by several of the former, who made explicit reference to paleomagnetic studies as an important new source of evidence. In the late 1950s and early 1960s, as debates about rival theories of Earth continued, reference was often made directly or indirectly to the symposium as a key event.

An Expanding Earth. Carey's own contribution to the symposium, composing nearly half the volume, rejected his own earlier mobilist interpretations and advocated a rapidly expanding Earth as the preferable global theory. It drew together many of his previous ideas and much of the new data. The mid-ocean ridges and associated earthquakes marked the locations where the continents had been joined together but had broken apart and where new seafloor then in-filled as the globe expanded. Likewise, the oroclines, as in the case of the rotation of Spain and the creation of the Bay of Biscay, resulted in the creation of new ocean floor, rift valleys, the Red Sea, and the Atlantic Ocean. All of this was compatible with Carey's previously held view that new seafloor was being constantly created and spread through mantle convection as explained by Holmes, but he no longer accepted that this could be counterbalanced by the disappearance of older crust into the substratum. Therefore, there must have been a net expansion of the surface of Earth. Further, the "gores" or small gaps left when the continental blocks are reassembled into a single landmass disappeared if reassembled on an Earth of somewhat smaller diameter. Carey's expanding Earth model attracted considerable attention, for it provided an elegant account for a wide range of old and new data. Moreover, the renowned physicist Paul Dirac had earlier speculated that the universal gravitational constant could diminish over time, an idea that had some currency in the late 1950s and 1960s, as in the work of Robert H. Dicke and Carl H. Brans.

Carey continued to refine his argument for an expanding Earth and to incorporate new evidence for it. *The Expanding Earth,* published in 1976, shortly before his retirement as professor, presented in a much more accessible manner the major points of his thesis along with supporting evidence. He incorporated a considerable body of relevant empirical data that had been published since the 1958 symposium and sought to answer some of the objections to expansionism, while granting the force of others. He acknowledged that a major objection to fast expansion was the absence of a known cause. To this objection he replied, "My first answer is that I do not know. Empirically I am satisfied that the earth is expanding" (Carey, 1976, p. 46).

Retirement for Carey did not mean the end of his research and writing. He continued to advocate Earth expansion as an alternative to the widely accepted theory of plate tectonics. He convened, contributed to, and edited the papers of a conference on Earth expansion (Carey, 1981). In his *Theories of the Earth and Universe*

(1988) he gave an overview of the development of geological theories, which culminated in the theory of an expanding Earth. His last major publication, *Earth, Universe, and Cosmos* (1996), contains not only a defense of an expanding Earth, but also his final thoughts on Earth science and cosmology. Besides defending and seeking to refine his expanding Earth model, Carey continued to write reflective essays on his career, his experiences, and his view on various scientific topics for his family, friends, and others. He died peacefully in Hobart at the age of ninety.

BIBLIOGRAPHY

The most complete bibliography of Carey's works is in Patrick G. Quilty and Maxwell R. Banks, "Samuel Warren Carey 1911–2002," Historical Records of Australian Science *14 (2003): 313–335. This also contains further biographical information including honorary degrees, awards and prizes, and memberships of learned societies. It is also available online from http://www.publish.csiro.au/nid/109/issue/745.htm. Official papers relating to Carey's work at the University of Tasmania are located in the university archives. Other likely repositories of papers and correspondence include the Tasmanian Hydro-Electric Commission (now Hydro Tasmania) and Oil Search Limited (with respect to his work in New Guinea in the 1930s and 1940s).*

WORKS BY CAREY

"The Orocline Concept in Geotectonics." *Proceedings of the Royal Society of Tasmania* 89 (1955): 255–288.

"Wegener's South American–African Assembly, Fit or Misfit." *Geological Magazine* 92 (1955): 196–200.

"The Tectonic Approach to Continental Drift." In *Continental Drift, a Symposium,* edited by S. Warren Carey. Hobart, Australia: University of Tasmania, 1958.

"The Expanding Earth: An Essay Review." *Earth Science Reviews* 11 (1975): 105–143.

The Expanding Earth. Amsterdam and New York: Elsevier Scientific Publishing, 1976.

Editor. *The Expanding Earth: A Symposium.* Hobart, Australia: University of Tasmania Press, 1981. Includes four contributions by Carey: "Evolution of Beliefs on the Nature and Origin of the Earth," pp. 3–7; "Tethys and her Forebears," pp. 169–187; "Earth Expansion and the Null Universe," pp. 365–372; and "The Necessity for Earth Expansion," pp. 375–393.

Theories of the Earth and Universe: A History of Dogma in the Earth Sciences. Stanford, CA: Stanford University Press, 1988.

Earth, Universe, Cosmos. Hobart, Australia: University of Tasmania Press, 1996.

OTHER SOURCES

Elliston, John. "Professor S. W. Carey's Struggle with Conservatism." In *Why Expanding Earth,* edited by Giancarlo Scalera and Karl-Heinz Jacob. Rome: Istituto Nazionale di Geofisica e Vulcanologia, 2003.

Scalera, Giancarlo. "Samuel Warren Carey: Commemorative Memoir." In *Why Expanding Earth,* edited by Giancarlo Scalera and Karl-Heinz Jacob. Rome: Istituto Nazionale di Geofisica e Vulcanologia, 2003.

H. E. Le Grand

CARNAP, PAUL RUDOLF (*b.* Ronsberg [later a part of the city of Wuppertal] Germany, 18 May 1891; *d.* Santa Monica, California, 14 September 1970), *philosophy, logic, probability theory.*

Carnap, usually known as Rudolf Carnap, was a leading exponent of the so-called Vienna Circle—probably the most fertile group of philosopher-scientists since the days of Plato's Academy—that cooperated closely in Vienna during the 1920s and early 1930s in order to establish a "scientific philosophy." The stress this group put on the importance of empirically informed ideas, the logical analysis of language in general, and the logical analysis of scientific concepts and theories in particular was instrumental in bringing about "analytical philosophy," the predominant approach as of 2007 to philosophy (not only) within the English speaking world. Carnap thus became a towering figure of twentieth-century philosophy.

Life and Education. Carnap's mother, Anna Dörpfeld, was a daughter of the educational refomer Friedrich Wilhelm Dörpfeld (on whom she published a book) and a sister of the archaeologist Wilhelm Dörpfeld, famous for his excavation work in, among others, Olympia, Troy (with Heinrich Schliemann), and Athens. Anna became the second wife of Johann Carnap, who had worked his way up to become a factory owner. Besides his sister Agnes, Carnap had ten stepsiblings his father brought into the marriage; Carnap was seven when his father died. Carnap had a modest but deeply religious family background, which might explain why, although he later became an atheist, he maintained a respectful and tolerant attitude in matters of faith throughout his life. More generally speaking, throughout his life Carnap showed a very open-minded attitude, was quite radical (leftist) in his political views, and embraced enthusiastically everything that had at least some potential to make, one way or the other, the world a better place. This explains the interest he took in Esperanto, or why he welcomed the American civil rights movement.

As the family had moved to Jena, Carnap studied mathematics, physics, and philosophy at the University of Jena (1910–1914, 1918–1919), but spent the year 1911–1912 at the University of Freiburg. In Jena he was fortunate enough not only to attend lectures by Gottlob Frege, the founder of modern mathematical logic, but also to study the philosopher Immanuel Kant (1724–1804) with Bruno Bauch, a leading figure of the neo-Kantian movement (like Jonas Cohn and Heinrich Rickert in Freiburg). Carnap also mentioned the educator Hermann Nohl (who took his doctorate with Wilhelm Dilthey) as an important influence, and Nohl's student Wilhelm Flitner became Carnap's lifelong friend. Carnap's attempt to pursue a doctoral degree in experimental physics came to a sudden halt when his advisor was killed in the early days of World War I. After having served in World War I himself, Carnap obtained his teacher certificate for secondary schools in 1920, but his first dissertation proposal—to develop an axiom system for space and time in physics—was not accepted: The physicist Max Wien referred him to the philosopher Bauch and vice versa. In 1921 he thus took his degree with Bauch on the related problem of space. While studying Bertrand Russell's books, he felt that his mission was to comply with Russell's request to study logic—for logic is to philosophy what mathematics is to physics—and to create "a school of men with scientific training and philosophical interests, unhampered by the traditions of the past, and not misled by the literary methods of those who copy the ancients in all except their merits" (Russell, quoted in Carnap, 1963, p. 13).

Carnap joined forces with Hans Reichenbach, who introduced him to Moritz Schlick, who in turn secured him a position as instructor in Vienna and thus made him a member of the Vienna Circle. From 1931 to 1935 he held the position as chair for natural philosophy at the University of Prague, which was close enough to allow him to visit Vienna frequently. In 1934 Charles W. Morris from the University of Chicago and Willard V. Quine from Harvard visited him and invited him to the United States. Carnap joined the University of Chicago in the winter of 1936 and stayed there until 1952; he replaced his old friend Reichenbach (who died prematurely) at UCLA in 1954. From 1940 to 1941, he held a visiting position at Harvard; from 1942 to 1944, he went to Santa Fe, New Mexico, on a Rockefeller research grant; from 1952 to 1954 he was a fellow of the Institute of Advanced Study at Princeton. In 1961 he retired from UCLA. He was honored in 1963 by the publication of a volume in Paul A. Schilpp's Library of Living Philosophers and received many honorary degrees.

Carnap was married twice: from 1917 to 1929 to Elisabeth Schöndube, with whom he had four children, and to Ina von Stoeger from 1935 until her death in 1964. In 1941 he became an American citizen. He died in 1970 from pneumonia that he had contracted while he was at a hospital to cure an ileus.

For purposes of this survey, Carnap's research is divided into three periods: (1) the "early Carnap" was mostly concerned with empiricism and physics; (2) the "middle Carnap" was mostly concerned with the role and the importance of a theory of language in philosophy and science; and (3) the "later Carnap" was mostly concerned with induction and probability.

The Early Period. The problem Carnap addressed in his dissertation *On Space* (*Der Raum*, 1922) was that of conflicting theories about the nature of space among mathematicians, physicists, and philosophers. His solution was to distinguish, define, and apply (accordingly) three meanings of space: (1) *Formal space* is a mathematical invention that enables the study abstract relational structures of a certain type. Under Russell's influence, he considered the theory of relations to belong to the province of logic; hence, knowledge of formal space is logical knowledge because of its relational nature. (2) *Intuitive space* stems from the faculty of "pure intuition," as neo-Kantians postulated in the wake of Kant's philosophy. Knowledge of intuitive space is based on pure intuition and is therefore independent of experience. Carnap restricted it however—like Ernst Cassirer before him—to certain topological properties, while regarding other properties (such as metrics, number of dimensions) not as intuitive, but as empirical. (3) *Physical space* is entirely dependent on experience, and any knowledge about it is hence empirical knowledge. These distinctions allowed Carnap to discuss the role of non-Euclidean geometry in Albert Einstein's general theory of relativity, without "philosophical blinders." His other early work is connected to his dissertation topic or deals with the problem of concept formation in physics.

Carnap's *Habilitation* (a second "dissertation" required by the German university system in order to qualify for a tenured position as professor), *The Logical Structure of the World* (*Der logische Aufbau der Welt*, 1928), was his first attempt at a project of "rational reconstruction." Given a certain well-established practice, the program of rational reconstruction aims at developing, from scratch, a coherent language and at providing a set of procedures that lead to the same results as the chosen practice; but this time, one proceeds reflectively and methodically and the concepts employed are more clearly defined and more exact than their informal counterparts. Rational reconstruction, therefore, does not give a "genetic" account of the chosen practice (say, psychological, historical, or sociological), but allows for a rigorous logical analysis of it. In *The Aufbau*, Carnap made the linguistic practice of employing an observational language in everyday and scientific contexts his target for a rational reconstruction. Influenced by Ernst Mach, Russell, and Gestalt psychology, and starting with nothing more than

a purely phenomenalistic language—which is quite rich in comparison to mere sense-data—of "total instantaneous experiences" (*Elementarerlebnisse*), Carnap showed how—by means of what he called *Quasi-Analyse*—individuals can rationally reconstruct their common practice of speaking about things, other minds, their properties, and their observation and experience. The main technical means of doing this were the logic of relations in general and the relation "recognition-of-similarity" (*Ähnlichkeitserinnerung*) between *Elementarerlebnisse* in particular. A little later, because of the criticism of his student Heinrich Neider and influenced by Otto Neurath and his "unity of science" program, he came to favor sentences in an objective physicalistic language ("protocol sentences")—rather than in a subjective language of *Elementarerlebnisse*—as the constitutive elements of the reconstruction. Nelson Goodman revised and refined Carnap's approach in his own *Structure of Appearance* (1951).

The Middle Period. Whereas the close interaction within the Vienna Circle (Kurt Gödel, Hans Hahn, Karl Menger, Neurath, and Schlick) as well as encounters with its satellites (Karl Popper, Alfred Tarski, and Ludwig Wittgenstein) and kindred spirits elsewhere, such as Reichenbach's group in Berlin, constantly forced Carnap to further develop his ideas, his next major publication, *The Logical Syntax of Language* (*Die logische Syntax der Sprache*, 1934), comes close to a radical transformation in his thought. Neo-Kantians had declared philosophy not to have genuine objects of its own; instead, they had demanded to study reason where reason can be found (to have emerged within the course of civilization), that is, to study theoretical reasoning within the sciences, practical reasoning within law and legislation, and so forth. Carnap took this approach one step further and deprived philosophy even of these "second-hand objects." The only legitimate project for philosophical inquiry is the logical analysis of language. Philosophy is, according to Carnap, the theory of scientific language (broadly understood so as to include the humanities insofar as they are engaged in research of which the goal is the attainment of objective truth); it is the logic of science. In modern parlance philosophy reduces to philosophy of science—any other kind of philosophy reduces to engagement with mere "pseudo-problems." The basic assumption here is that, following suggestions from David Hilbert, one has to remove any reference to scientifically dubious objects such as "thought" or "mental content" and refer instead to what provides a firm intersubjective grounding, in this case language and its rules. What formerly was taken to be a concern with "meaning" should now be reconstructed as an exclusive concern with the syntactical properties of sentences. In order to carry through this program, Carnap, drawing heavily on techniques developed by Gödel, devised a general theory of formal languages. According to this theory, formal languages serve as formal counterparts for the scientific idioms of logic and physics. Carnap used formal languages to make his results as precise as possible and focused on logic and physics because he was an adherent of logicism and physicalism. According to the former, mathematics is reducible to (formal) logic, whereas according to the latter, all sciences are ultimately reducible to physics (or, more precisely, that language X is reducible to language Y if X can be translated by purely formal means into Y).

Note, however, that Carnap did not assume that there is just one language for a science, but possibly many that best suit different purposes. This is his famous "principle of tolerance," that is, the claim that "there are no morals in logic." Everyone is free to choose the language that seems most appropriate to a particular purpose, while attempts to impose one camp's scientific idiom onto another's result in scientific "pseudo-problems." Accordingly, scientific statements such as "five is a number" should not be rendered contentually as "five is not a thing, but a number"—a pseudo-problem-propagating formulation doomed to lead to endless controversy about the ontology of numbers—but should be understood as a purely syntactical statement, namely, "according to the rules of the chosen language 'five' is not an object-word, but a number-word." In the context of the *Logical Syntax*, Carnap put forward also his account of the analytic-synthetic distinction (i.e., the difference between those sentences that are "true whatever the empirical facts may be" and those that are not), which later led to a famous controversy with Quine, who denied its meaningfulness.

Under the influence of Tarski and Morris, Carnap later admitted that syntax is not enough; that semantics and pragmatics have to be accounted for as well. Thus, when in *Meaning and Necessity* (1947) he extended his syntactical treatment to "intensional languages" —that is, languages that include modal talk, say, of possibility and necessity—he gave his treatment a semantic twist. Another aspect of modality, the analysis of possibility that comes with so-called "disposition predicates" such as "brittle," led Carnap to the important distinction between "observational" and "theoretical" language in the sciences, with the latter's concepts being declared not to be definable in terms of the observation language.

The Late Period. Carnap devoted more or less the last two decades of his life to issues in the field of probability theory and its applications (*The Logical Foundations of Probability*, 1950; *The Continuum of Inductive Methods*, 1952; *Studies in Inductive Logic and Probability*, vols. 1 and 2, 1971 and 1980, edited with Richard Jeffrey). In distinguishing "logical" or "inductive probability" (also "proba-

Rudolf Carnap. AP IMAGES.

bility1" or "credibility") from "statistical probability," that is, the relative frequency in the long run ("probability2" and thereby addressing Popper's doubt about induction, he sought to clarify the first. But also the first notion allows for two readings, one in the sciences and one in practical deliberations. Accordingly, the term $c(h,e)$—usually written "$P(h,e)$" and understood as expressing the conditional probability of h given e—can be understood as "the degree to which the hypothesis h is confirmed by the evidence e," or as "the factor by which the utility of some benefit B for a deliberating agent X must be multiplied." Using the advances of formal logic and following John Maynard Keynes, Carnap tried to devise a purely logical theory of induction by regarding $c(h,e)$ to be a measure of the extent to which h is entailed by e. For this purpose, Carnap introduced a first-order language with a finite number of monadic predicates and countably many individual constants. For such languages, Tarski's definition of entailment by "consequence" states that a sentence a entails a sentence b, if every structure A that is a model of a is also a model of b. (Note that Carnap used the related term "state-description" instead of "model.") Already in *Meaning and Necessity* Carnap had identified the meaning $M(a)$ of a sentence a with the set (in the finite case the number) of all its models; if one wants to know what the sentence "it's raining" means, look at all conceivable situations in which it rains. Now, because there is a structure preserving mapping from sentences to their meanings—under which, for example, $M(a(b)$ translates into $M(a)$ $(M(b)$—conditional probability can be interpreted as partial entailment, in which the ratio of $M(h)$ to $M(e)$ as in the right-hand side of

$$c(h \mid e) = \frac{c(h \,\&\, e)}{c(e)} = \frac{p(M(h) \cap M(e))}{p(M(e))}$$

determines the degree to which e entails h. Any probability assignment to atomic sentences results in a probability measure p as in the right-hand side of the above equation.

Thus, the problem Carnap addressed but according to the majority of his peers failed to solve satisfactorily was to impose certain "natural" constraints on the choice of c (or, equivalently, on the "measure function" m that assigns unconditional probabilities to the atomic sentences) such that from among all other candidates a unique function c would be singled out that could serve as a basis for adequately modeling our inductive practice. Initially, Carnap discussed two such functions, $c\dagger$ and c^*. One arrives at $c\dagger$ by making the plausible assumption that, because in the absence of any data, every situation is equally probable, the same a priori probabilities should be assigned to all state-descriptions. This, however, has the unfortunate consequence that learning from experience would be impossible. Carnap hence proposed to stick to c^*. One gets this function by, first, lumping together into a single "structure-description" all those state-descriptions that are isomorphic to one another, and, second, by assigning all structure-descriptions the same a priori probability (for in the absence of any data, every type of situation is equally probable). But all that Carnap could put forward in favor of c^* was that it is the only function "not entirely inadequate." In his later works, Carnap considered a continuum of inductive logics, in which a real-valued parameter λ, with $\lambda \in 0,\infty$, helps one to pick a proper function c, for λ's value is correlated to one's willingness to learn from experience. This suggests that Carnap essentially gave up the idea of basing one's inductive practice on something as objective as logic and leaned toward a subjective interpretation of probability instead; it also suggests that Carnap arrived at the insight that the problem of induction is not susceptible to a "reconstructive" solution but rather requires a "normative" one.

Throughout his career Carnap stood out as the one who actually developed in great detail ideas others were content to pursue informally. To fulfill this ambitious goal, he drew heavily on the formal machinery of both mathematics and mathematical logic. By taking meticulous care to produce results that are either verifiable or refutable, Carnap succeeded in making considerable progress in philosophy, whatever may have been the ultimate success of the particular solutions he advanced.

BIBLIOGRAPHY

Most of Carnap's literary estate is housed at the Archive for Scientific Philosophy, University of Pittsburgh, Pennsylvania, with a mirror at the Philosophisches Archiv, University of Konstanz, Germany. An edition of his collected works, to be published by Open Court, was under preparation in the mid-first decade of the 2000s.

WORKS BY CARNAP

Der Raum: Ein Beitrag zur Wissenschaftslehre. Berlin: Reuther & Reichard, 1922.

Der logische Aufbau der Welt; Scheinprobleme in der Philososphie. Berlin: Weltkreisverlag, 1928. Translated by Rolf A. George as *The Logical Structure of the World: Pseudoproblems in Philosophy.* Berkeley: University of California Press, 1961.

"Überwindung der Metaphysik durch logische Analyse der Sprache." *Erkenntnis* 2 (1932): 219–241. Translated as "The Elimination of Metaphysics through Logical Analysis of Language." In *Logical Positivism*, edited by Alfred J. Ayer. Westport, CT: Greenwood, 1978.

"Die physikalische Sprache als Universalsprache der Wissenschaft." *Erkenntnis* 2 (1932): 432–465. Translated by Max Black as *The Unity of Science.* London: Paul, Trench, Trubner, 1934.

Logische Syntax der Sprache. Vienna: Springer, 1934. Translated by Amethe Smeaton as *The Logical Syntax of Language.* London: Paul, Trench, Trubner, 1937.

Philosophy and Logical Syntax. London: Paul, Trench, Trubner, 1935.

"Testability and Meaning." *Philosophy of Science* 3 (1936): 419–471.

Meaning and Necessity: A Study in Semantics and Modal Logic. Chicago: University of Chicago Press, 1947.

"Empiricism, Semantics, and Ontology." *Revue International de Philosophie* 4 (1950): 20–40.

Logical Foundations of Probability. Chicago: University of Chicago Press, 1950.

The Continuum of Inductive Methods. Chicago: University of Chicago Press, 1952.

"Intellectual Autobiography" and "Replies and Systematic Expositions." In *The Philosophy of Rudolf Carnap*, edited by Paul Arthur Schilpp. La Salle, IL: Open Court, 1963.

Philosophical Foundations of Physics: An Introduction to the Philosophy of Science. Edited by Martin Gardner. New York: Basic Books, 1966.

"Inductive Logic and Inductive Intuition." In *The Problem of Inductive Logic*, edited by Imre Lakatos. Amsterdam: North-Holland, 1968.

With Richard Jeffrey, eds. *Studies in Inductive Logic and Probability.* Berkeley: University of California Press, 1971.

Two Essays on Entropy. Edited by Abner Shimony. Berkeley: University of California Press, 1977.

With Richard Jeffrey, eds. *Studies in Inductive Logic and Probability II.* Berkeley: University of California Press, 1980.

With W. V. Quine. *Dear Carnap, Dear Van: The Quine-Carnap Correspondence and Related Work.* Edited by Richard Creath. Berkeley: University of California Press, 1990.

Untersuchung zur allgemeinen Axiomatik. Edited by Thomas Bonk and Jesús Mosterín. Darmstadt: Wissenschaftliche Buchgesellschaft, 2000.

OTHER SOURCES

Awodey, Steven, and Carsten Klein, eds. *Carnap Brought Home: The View from Jena.* Chicago: Open Court, 2004.

Bar-Hillel, Yehousha, ed. *Logic and Language: Studies Dedicated to Professor Rudolf Carnap on the Occasion of his Seventieth Birthday.* Dordrecht, Netherlands: D. Reidel, 1962.

Cirera, Ramón. *Carnap and the Vienna Circle: Empiricism and Logical Syntax.* Translated by Dick Edelstein. Amsterdam: Rodopi, 1994.

Coffa, Alberto J. *The Semantic Tradition from Kant to Carnap: To the Vienna Station.* Edited by Linda Wessels. Cambridge, U.K.: Cambridge University Press, 1991.

Friedman, Michael. *Reconsidering Logical Positivism.* Cambridge, U.K.: Cambridge University Press, 1999.

———. *A Parting of Ways: Carnap, Cassirer, Heidegger.* Chicago: Open Court, 2000.

Giere, Richard N., and Alan W. Richardson, eds. *Origins of Logical Empiricism.* Minneapolis: University of Minnesota Press, 1996. Contains many papers on Carnap and his context.

Goldfarb, Warren, and Tom Ricketts. "Carnap and the Philosophy of Mathematics." In *Wissenschaft und Subjektivität: der Wiener Kreis und die Philosophie des 20. Jahrhunderts,* edited by David Bell and Wilhelm Vossenkuhl. Berlin: Akademie-Verlag, 1992.

Hintikka, Jaakko K., ed. *Rudolf Carnap, Logical Empiricist: Materials and Perspectives.* Dordrecht, The Netherlands: Reidel, 1975.

Proust, Joëlle. *Questions of Form: Logic and the Analytic Proposition from Kant to Carnap.* Translated by Anastasios Albert Brenner. Minneapolis: University of Minnesota Press, 1989.

Richardson, Alan W. *Carnap's Construction of the World.* Cambridge, U.K.: Cambridge University Press, 1998. Contains bibliography, pp. 230–238.

Ricketts, Tom. "Carnap's Principle of Tolerance, Empiricism, and Conventionalism." In *Reading Putnam,* edited by Peter Clark and Bob Hale. Oxford: Blackwell, 1994.

Salmon, Wesley, and Gereon Wolters, eds. *Logic, Language, and the Structure of Scientific Theories: Proceedings of the Carnap-Reichenbach Centennial.* Pittsburgh, PA: Pittsburgh University Press; Konstanz, Germany: Universitäts-Verlag, 1994.

Sarkar, Sahotra, ed. "Carnap: A Centenary Reappraisal." *Synthese* 93, nos. 1–2 (1992).

Schilpp, Paul Arthur, ed. *The Philosophy of Rudolf Carnap.* La Salle, IL: Open Court, 1963. Contains a bibliography complete up to 1962.

Spohn, Wolfgang, ed. *Erkenntnis Orientated: A Centennial Volume for Rudolf Carnap and Hans Reichenbach.* Dordrecht, The Netherlands: Kluwer, 1991.

Bernd Buldt

CAROTHERS, WALLACE HUME (*b.* Burlington, Iowa, 27 April 1896; *d.* Philadelphia, Pennsylvania, 29 April 1937), *chemistry, organic chemistry, polymer chemistry.* For the original article on Carothers see *DSB,* vol. 3.

Since the mid-1980s, a number of in-depth studies on Carothers, based on a large quantity of manuscripts, letters, and documents, have revealed some important aspects of his scientific career and work, such as his early encounter with chemistry, the origins of his polymer research, the process of his invention of nylon, and the industrial context in which Carothers worked on polymers.

Early Years. When Carothers was a high school student in Des Moines, Iowa, his early interest in chemistry began with his reading of Robert K. Duncan's popular books, *The New Knowledge: A Popular Account of the New Physics and the New Chemistry in Their Relation to the New Theory of Matter* (1905), an exposition of recent theories of matter, and *The Chemistry of Commerce: A Simple Interpretation of Some New Chemistry in Its Relation to Modern Industry* (1907), which stressed the importance of pure science for industry. While at Tarkio College in Missouri, Carothers decided on chemistry as his life's work, largely at the encouragement of his chemistry teacher, Arthur M. Pardee. The synthetic-chemical approach and industrial orientation of Roger Adams at the University of Illinois also exerted a profound influence on Carothers's style in chemistry and his career.

Before moving to the DuPont Company, Carothers had neither published nor performed any experiment in the field of polymers. In the spring of 1927, when DuPont approached Carothers to offer him a position in its newly established fundamental research program in Wilmington, Delaware, the company promised to leave the selection of research subject entirely to him. Carothers chose polymers and polymerization as his new research subject because of the need for theoretical exploration as well as the vast commercial implications of polymers. Had it not been for the DuPont job offer, it is unlikely that the young Harvard instructor would have set out on a journey into the frontier of polymer research.

Wallace Carothers. *Carothers in his laboratory at Du Pont's experimental station.* HULTON ARCHIVE/GETTY IMAGES.

Carothers had been reading recent German articles on the structure of polymers by Hermann Staudinger and his opponents. Since the early 1920s, Staudinger had proposed the theory that polymers, such as rubber, cellulose, resins, and proteins, were made up of very large molecules, what he called "macromolecules." His theory was severely criticized by many chemists, who claimed that polymers were the aggregates of relatively small molecules. The unsettled German debate over the existence of macromolecules appealed to Carothers's theoretical interest.

Wallace Carothers. *Carothers demonstrating a piece of his new synthetic rubber in laboratory.*
AP IMAGES.

Research on Macromolecules. By the time he joined DuPont in early 1928, Carothers had already developed his ideas into a coherent program for the synthesis of macromolecules by the use of established condensation reactions such as esterification. He did not intend to produce a synthetic fiber when he started working at DuPont; what he intended was simply to make molecules as large as he could in order to examine the properties of the products. If the products exhibited properties (such as elasticity and fibrousness) similar to natural polymers, then Staudinger's claim that polymers were composed of macromolecules would be supported.

Overcoming technical difficulties, his group was able to synthesize what he called "superpolymers," polymers with molecular weights of ten thousand or more. This success was soon followed by the discovery of the "cold-drawing" phenomenon peculiar to these materials. In April 1930, his co-worker Julian Hill observed that a superpolyester could be mechanically drawn out from a melt or dry-spun from a solution into fibers or threads.

This led Carothers to foresee the possibility of making artificial fibers from linear-condensation superpolymers.

Realizing its practical implication, DuPont management delayed publication of Carothers's paper on superpolymers and recommended that the result should be thoroughly protected by a well-planned patent program. This restriction appeared to abridge the academic freedom assured him at the inception of the fundamental research program. From this time on, Carothers's basic research group was obliged to shift its aim to a more practical goal, that is, to the search for polymers that could be drawn into fibers for commercial use.

During the period from 1930 to 1933, Carothers and his group systematically investigated various types of linear condensation superpolymers, including polyesters, polyanhydrides, polyacetals, polyamides, and polyester-polyamide mixtures, which were synthesized by his co-workers from hundreds of possible combinations of starting materials. After careful consideration, the company selected a superpolyamide for manufacture, first synthesized by a co-worker, Gerard Jean Berchet, in February 1935. The fiber was named "nylon" in 1938, after examining some four hundred names submitted by DuPont employees (the naming committee decided on "nylon" by arbitrarily modifying the finalist "no-run"). Nylon would become the most successful commercial product in DuPont's research and development history. A year and half before DuPont announced nylon, however, Carothers committed suicide by taking cyanide in a hotel in Philadelphia. He neither lived to hear the name nylon nor to see its enormous commercial production and subsequent impact on culture.

The nylon venture, which would become a prototype for the science-based polymer industry, also turned out to be a large-scale test of the validity of the macromolecular theory. As an industrial researcher, Carothers did not train students in polymer chemistry. Yet he introduced a number of able research chemists at DuPont to the world of polymers. From June 1928 to his death in April 1937, he had a total of twenty-five co-workers, most of them only slightly younger than the group leader, including twenty chemists with PhD degrees. The "Wilmington School" bequeathed a research tradition on polymers not only within the company, but also to American academe. Under Carothers's influence, a new generation of polymer chemists emerged in American universities. Paul J. Flory, Elmer O. Kraemer, and Carl S. Marvel were among the influential scholars who inherited Carothers's legacy.

American polymer chemistry, which first emerged from a basic research program in industry, gradually spread as an academic discipline by the late 1940s. DuPont's venture into fundamental research was rewarded by discoveries that not only had great industrial value, but

also sparked original theoretical innovations. Even beyond the perspective of a single company, industrial research turned out to play a seminal role in the birth of a new science in America.

SUPPLEMENTARY BIBLIOGRAPHY

Papers of Wallace Hume Carothers and DuPont Company documents are stored at the Hagley Museum and Library, Wilmington, Delaware. Correspondence between Carothers and Roger Adams is in the Roger Adams Papers at the University of Illinois Archives, Urbana-Champaign, Illinois.

OTHER SOURCES

Furukawa, Yasu. *Inventing Polymer Science: Staudinger, Carothers, and the Emergence of Macromolecular Chemistry.* Philadelphia: University of Pennsylvania Press and Chemical Heritage Foundation, 1998.

Hermes, Matthew E. *Enough for One Lifetime: Wallace Carothers, Inventor of Nylon.* Washington, DC: American Chemical Society and Chemical Heritage Foundation, 1996.

Hounshell, David A., and John K. Smith. *Science and Corporate Strategy: Du Pont R&D, 1902–1980.* New York: Cambridge University Press, 1988.

Morawetz, Herbert. *Polymers: The Origins and Growth of a Science.* 1985. New York: Dover, 1995.

Yasu Furukawa

CARPENTER, CLARENCE RAY (*b.* Lincoln County, North Carolina, 28 November 1905: *d.* Athens, Georgia, 1 March 1975), *primatology, field studies, Cayo Santiago Rhesus Colony.*

Carpenter's research of wild primate behavior during the 1930s was, and continued to be in the early 2000s, widely recognized within the primatological community as the first scientific primate field studies. Carpenter demonstrated that prolonged and accurate observation of primate behavior was possible and set forth methods with which to accomplish fieldwork. In turn, Carpenter encouraged the blossoming of field primatology, and indeed field studies of animal behavior more broadly, which occurred after World War II. He was also a key contributor to the formation of Cayo Santiago Rhesus Colony, an island-based field site in Puerto Rico designed for efficient observation of natural primate behavior. The colony continued to be a significant site for long-term primate research into the twenty-first century.

Carpenter and Robert M. Yerkes. After receiving his master's degree in 1929 from Duke University, Carpenter completed his PhD in 1931 working with Calvin P. Stone at Stanford University. At Stanford, Carpenter studied the sexual behavior of pigeons and its connections with physiology. This research involved gonadectomy, utilized still and motion pictures, and was funded by the National Research Council Committee for Research in the Problems of Sex (NRC-CRPS).

Carpenter's graduate work earned him a reputation for being an excellent observer, a skill that psychobiologist Robert M. Yerkes was seeking in order to extend the series of naturalistic studies of primate behavior that he had initiated in 1929. In 1931, Carpenter moved to New Haven to work with Yerkes as a fellow at Yale Laboratories of Primate Biology. Yerkes's research focused on laboratory studies of primate behavior; however, he was also a strong advocate of fieldwork due to its ability to gain knowledge of primate social behavior and to enable comparison of captive, artificial behaviors with those that occurred in nature.

For this reason, Yerkes sponsored a series of studies of wild primate behavior during the late 1920s and early 1930s. The first of these studies was conducted by Harold Bingham in 1929. This project took place in the National Parc Albert in the Belgian Congo and attempted to observe gorilla behavior in the wild. Unfortunately, insufficient field methods, lack of field experience, and the shy demeanor of gorillas resulted in few observations of gorilla behavior. During the same year, Yerkes organized Henry Nissen's field study of chimpanzees at the Pasteur Institute of Kindia in Western Africa. Nissen was more successful than Bingham at observing wild primates but also failed to gain sufficient data to make conclusions about primate social behavior.

It was within the context of these previous studies, both of which had demonstrated the need for new and improved field methods with which to make prolonged observations of primate behavior, that Carpenter joined the Yale Laboratories of Primate Biology.

Fieldwork. Carpenter continued Yerkes's series of naturalistic studies of primate behavior by spending a total of nearly eight months between 1931 and 1933 at Barro Colorado, an island in Puerto Rico. It was at this time in his career that Carpenter married his first wife, Mariana, with whom he had two sons, Richard and Lane. During his Barro Colorado fieldwork, Carpenter used his skills as an observer and existing methods of habituation to make prolonged observations of natural howler behavior, including communication, territoriality, and social interactions. These extensive observations demonstrated coordination within and between groups of howlers, including the use of vocalizations to exercise social control and to avoid intergroup aggression. Carpenter also examined howlers' locomotion and posturing, including how their feet and prehensile tail facilitated their arboreal nature.

Relationships between howlers and their environment were also studied, particularly howlers' interactions with other species. It was this kind of approach to primate research that would eventually develop into what became known as behavioral ecology.

While in Barro Colorado, Carpenter also developed new field techniques. He observed and described complex social relationships, for example, with what would become known as the dyadic method. This technique involved breaking down a social situation into its component parts. All possible relationships would be observed and described in turn, including those between males, females, and juvenile group members. Carpenter also developed a counting procedure with which to make an accurate census of the Barro Colorado howler population, thus overcoming a barrier that had marred many studies of wild animal populations.

The length and accuracy of Carpenter's observations and his ability to census primate populations ensured that his fieldwork formed a strong contrast to past primate studies. This was true for his howler study at Barro Colorado and equally so for his study of gibbons in Thailand during the Asiatic Primate Expedition in 1937. The main members of the expedition team were Harold Coolidge of the Museum of Comparative Zoology at Harvard University, Adolph H. Schultz of the Department of Anatomy at Johns Hopkins University, and Carpenter, who at that time was an assistant professor and lecturer at Bard College. Coolidge, Schultz, and Carpenter were also accompanied by Sherwood Washburn, a graduate student of Earnest Hooton at Harvard, who would go on to become a prominent anthropologist. During this expedition, Carpenter continued to emphasize the need for repetition and accuracy in field observations, an element of his fieldwork he extended by using recording technology and playback techniques to ensure precise descriptions of gibbon vocalizations and to determine the functions these calls served in primate groups.

In addition to examining gibbon vocalizations, Carpenter pursued similar questions to those he had explored during his howler research in Barro Colorado. Once again, he described both individual and group behavior and particularly focused on social coordination and control within and between groups. He also continued to study the role of territoriality in primate behavior, a topic connected to his work on vocalizations and social stability. The results of Carpenter's gibbon research were published in his 1940 monograph, which also contained an interesting introduction by Adolph H. Schultz, who proposed that gibbons were evolutionarily closer to humans than any species of monkey and thus deserved to be classified among the "higher primates." This concept was also echoed by Carpenter in the body of the monograph.

The significance of Carpenter's intellectual contributions to primate research was matched, if not exceeded, by his development of new and existing field methods. Earlier fieldwork had been criticized for producing anecdotal and unreliable observations rather than scientific research. Carpenter's work at Barro Colorado and during the Asiatic Primate Expedition developed new techniques with which to apply scientific standards of repetition and accuracy to primate fieldwork thus demonstrating field studies could indeed be scientific.

Primatologists Shirley Strum and Linda Fedigan have summarized Carpenter's multiple methodological contributions to primatology as follows: "Carpenter set a new and lasting standard for data collection. He clarified and pioneered methods of habituation for wild primates, made explicit the standards for the acceptance of naturalistic observations as facts, and developed a new approach to the analysis of complex social interactions" (p. 9). Carpenter ensured accuracy in his observations and counts by applying strict standards of repetition and note taking. He and others used this element of his fieldwork to promote the scientific value of the field during much of the early to mid-twentieth century.

Between 1930 and 1950 Carpenter frequently used his publications and speeches to discuss the ways in which fieldwork could contribute to primate research and animal behavior studies more broadly. In these public forums, Carpenter presented the laboratory and field as supplementary, each with contrasting advantages and limitations. During this period, the scientific value of the laboratory for animal behavior studies went virtually unquestioned while the potential contributions of the field had yet to be widely recognized by the scientific community.

Carpenter highlighted the specific research questions that could, and should, be pursued in the field. In his 1940 monograph concerning his gibbon research during the Asiatic Primate Expedition, Carpenter stated that: "There are problems … which can best be investigated by means of field procedures, in fact, they cannot be validly studied except by observing free ranging animals. Studies of … seasonal and diurnal variation in behavior, grouping patterns and inter-group relations and communicative behavior are some of the subjects which may first and most validly be studied in the natural habitat of the animals" (p. 29). Such specific examples were consistently embedded in Carpenter's broader view of the laboratory and field as places of equal scientific value and beholden to the same scientific standards. In 1950, he summarized this viewpoint in an article based on a conference he attended in 1948 concerning field methodology and techniques and published in *Annals of the New York Academy of Sciences*: "Let there be no mistake, in the scientific courts of appeal, we must expect all evidence, from labo-

ratory and field, to be weighed in the same critical scales and judged by the same criteria" (p. 1008).

Yerkes also used Carpenter's work to present the laboratory and field as supplementary and to highlight the limitations of captive studies and the contrasting advantages of the field. In 1935, for example, Yerkes and his wife Ada spent several pages critiquing Solly Zuckerman's study of captive primates on "Monkey Hill" at the London Zoological Gardens due to the artificiality of the behaviors observed there. They contrasted Zuckerman's study directly with Carpenter's fieldwork and used Carpenter's research to exemplify how natural primate behavior could be observed in the wild. Beyond primate studies, researchers of animal behavior, such as Theodore C. Schneirla of the Department of Animal Behavior at the American Museum of Natural History, presented Carpenter's fieldwork as proof of the value of field studies and the ability of such work to fulfill scientific standards of accuracy and repeatability.

The efforts made by Carpenter, Yerkes, and others to promote the scientific value of fieldwork during the 1930–1950 period played a significant role in the growth in fieldwork that occurred after World War II. They also contributed to a gradual recasting of the field as a place for science rather than simply a location where amateur naturalists made anecdotal and uncritical observations of animal behavior. A negative conception of fieldwork had been formed over many years, initially through exaggerated claims in travel and adventure literature concerning encounters with wild animals, such as those made by amateur naturalist Paul du Chaillu. During the twentieth century, and arguably true in the early 2000s, such negative conceptions of the field were fueled by continuing false assumptions, including an association of the field with adventure rather than science.

Cayo Santiago Rhesus Colony. Despite the value Carpenter assigned to the field, he became increasingly frustrated with what he saw as the inefficiency of fieldwork after his experiences during the Asiatic Primate Expedition. For this reason, he helped to establish an island-based primate colony on Santiago Island, Puerto Rico, between 1938 and 1940. This site would become a significant location for long-term primate research. Researchers such as Peter Marler have identified its establishment as Carpenter's central contribution to primatology.

Carpenter established the colony by transporting approximately four hundred rhesus macaques from India to Santiago Island. These primates were to serve a dual purpose by providing the opportunity to observe natural primate behavior while establishing a regenerating supply of rhesus monkeys for biomedical experiments. As such, Santiago Island represents the dramatic rise in demand for primates occurring in biomedicine during this period and the increasing restrictions placed on the exportation of primates from India. Such restrictions were imposed by the Indian government and encouraged by animal rights groups such as the Society for the Prevention of Cruelty to Animals. The island also represents one example of Carpenter's personal concern about primate supply for experimentation, a concern also reflected in his involvement during the 1950s in the Non-human Primate Committee of the Institute of Animal Resources, a branch of the Biology and Agriculture Division of the National Research Council.

After Cayo Santiago Rhesus Colony was established, Carpenter conducted research on the island, primarily focusing on the reproductive behavior of rhesus macaques. His work on the island moved away from the broadly noninterventionist approach adopted during his work in Barro Colorado and Thailand. On Santiago Island, for example, he removed the alpha male to mimic the death of an alpha in nature, thus enabling the rapid observation of an event that would potentially take years to occur without such intervention. After the removal of the alpha male, he observed how the group regained social stability.

Donna Haraway's work concerning Carpenter focused on this research, along with Carpenter's study of communication during the Asiatic Primate Expedition. Haraway interpreted Carpenter's application of such interventionist techniques as evidence of his emphasis of social control, a concern prevalent in American society during the early to mid-twentieth century. Carpenter certainly approached his study of communication, at least in part, with a focus on social control and related his conclusions to human behavior.

In contrast to Haraway's work, Montgomery uses the analytical categories of place and practice to examine Carpenter's methodological contributions to primatology and his understanding of concepts such as naturalness. Carpenter's howler and gibbon field studies, for example, emphasized avoidance of modification in order to ensure observations of natural behavior. In his 1940 monograph concerning his work during the Asiatic Primate Expedition, for example, he wrote: "The methodological problem was that of *directly observing a representative sampling of individuals and groups for long periods of time in their undisturbed natural habitat and of accurately recording and reporting the observations* … Everything possible was done to secure records of the gibbons' free, natural, undisturbed behavior and of their social responses and relationships" (p. 33, italics in original). Carpenter's application of interventionist methods on Santiago Island thus formed a clear departure from his past focus on observing behavior as it would occur without interference by the observer. Car-

penter's laboratory experience while at graduate school and his concerns about the lack of scientific status for fieldwork helps to explain this shift towards increasingly interventionist field practices. Interestingly, Carpenter continued to identify behaviors observed on Santiago Island as natural despite his increasing application of interventionist techniques. This allowed Carpenter to continue to promote fieldwork on the grounds that it provided a unique opportunity to study *natural* behavior. For a more detailed account of the ways in which Carpenter defined naturalness during his career, and the complexity behind his transition from noninterventionist to interventionist field practices, see Montgomery's dissertation and article.

Carpenter's long-term involvement in Cayo Santiago Rhesus Colony, however, was not in terms of his research but rather through his direct and indirect administrative roles. He remained in contact with researchers working on the island and during the 1970s served as a member of the Caribbean Primate Research Center (CPRC). This group was established on 1 July 1970 by the University of Puerto Rico and the National Institute of Neurological Disorders and Strokes (NINDS), which had gained control of the island colony. The CPRC included Cayo Santiago Rhesus Colony and primate groups in three other tropical locations and thus demonstrates the increasingly international nature of primate research during the last three decades of the twentieth century. It was this international aspect of primatology that Carpenter took particular efforts to embrace later in his career when his focus increasingly shifted from performing primate fieldwork to a range of administrative roles.

Other Scientific Contributions. After working on Barro Colorado, Carpenter worked at Pennsylvania State University in several capacities until 1970. He was originally employed as a psychology professor, was promoted to chair of the Psychology Department from 1952 to 1956, and was then moved to various education-based programs to focus on the use of technology in education from 1957 to 1965. In 1965, he returned to the Psychology Department, this time as a research professor for both the Psychology and Anthropology departments. These career changes reflect Carpenter's enduring interest in technology as a means of improving primate research and education alike and the multidisciplinary nature of primatology. They also exemplify Carpenter's increasing preoccupation with administration rather than primate fieldwork.

Nevertheless, Carpenter remained connected to primate field studies, returning to conduct a further census at Barro Colorado in 1959 and training Japanese primatologists in field methods in 1966 as part of the U.S.-Japan Cooperative Science Program. Carpenter also married Ruth Jones in the year of 1966, three years after the death of his first wife. Carpenter's influence on primatology while at Pennsylvania State University was further extended by his involvement as an editor for *Behaviour* and *Journal of Human Evolution* and as a proposal reviewer for the National Science Foundation's Course Development Division and Behavioral Sciences. Carpenter also provided feedback on a private basis to field researchers such as George Schaller, who went on to conduct a field study of mountain gorillas between 1959 and 1960.

Beyond field primatology, Carpenter was an influential figure in animal behavior studies conducted in a range of settings. For example, he coordinated a summer training program in Jackson Hole Wildlife Park between 1947 and 1949. These training sessions attracted professionals and students working on animal behavior studies with twenty-two individuals from eight colleges attending in 1948. Carpenter was also involved in captive studies of primates. This is seen in his 1937 article concerning captive gorillas at San Diego Zoo and in the advice he gave the Bronx Zoo about the design of their "Ape House" that opened in 1950.

During the final years of his career, Carpenter moved from Pennsylvania State University to the University of Georgia, where he assumed university duties and a position on the advisory board for the Yerkes Regional Primate Research Center, an institution focused on captive studies of primates and particularly the potential contributions of such research to biomedicine. Another enduring contribution to primate research and animal behavior studies in general was Carpenter's compilation of the Psychological Cinema Registry, a collection containing a number of significant films of animal behavior. This venture further demonstrates the interest in technology that spanned Carpenter's primatological and educational career.

The breadth of Carpenter's career led to his primate research catching the attention of colleagues in psychology, anthropology, and animal behavior studies. He collaborated with many individuals in these disciplines and appears to have been well liked by some and disdained by others. Robert Yerkes and Frank Beach, assistant curator in the Department of Experimental Biology of the American Museum of Natural History in New York, became frustrated with Carpenter's decreasing attention to field studies and by 1946 ceased to be professionally involved with his research.

For others, Carpenter's confidence and scientific achievement were inspiring. Author Nancy Robinson, for example, presented Carpenter as a scientific role model for children in her 1973 book, *Jungle Laboratory: The Story of Ray Carpenter and the Howling Monkeys.* Carpenter was also an intellectual companion to playwright and author Robert Ardrey with whom he privately shared many views

concerning territoriality and the relation of primate research to human society. Carpenter and Ardrey exchanged several letters and particularly discussed Ardrey's 1966 book, *Territorial Imperative.*

Like his social network, Carpenter's research interests were eclectic. This is perhaps best reflected in his fieldwork where he studied primate behavior with a panoramic lens, examining primate behaviors ranging from locomotion, territoriality, and vocalization to social and sexual behavior. Throughout his career, Carpenter passionately engaged with issues as diverse as pigeon sexual behavior, primate behavior, and technology's role in the classroom. Such broad interests led to diverse scientific contributions but it was within the realm of fieldwork that Carpenter's influence was most strongly felt. Both the primatological community and historians of science familiar with his work agree that Carpenter significantly shaped the development of field methods and primate research. Perhaps most importantly, Carpenter demonstrated that field studies, and particularly primate field studies, could meet scientific standards during a time in which such work was often characterized as anecdotal and inaccurate. Along with the methods Carpenter developed, this new conception of the field helped to spur the development of field primatology after World War II.

BIBLIOGRAPHY

A complete bibliography and further primary sources can be found in C. Ray Carpenter's papers at the Pennsylvania State University Library.

WORKS BY CARPENTER

"The Effect of Complete and Incomplete Gonadectomy on the Behavior and Morphological Characters of the Male Pigeon." PhD diss., Stanford University, 1931.

A Field Study of the Behavior and Social Relations of Howling Monkeys (Alouatta palliata). Comparative Psychology Monographs, vol. 10, no. 2. Baltimore, MD: Johns Hopkins University Press, 1934.

"Behavior of Red Spider Monkeys in Panama." *Journal of Mammalogy* 16, no. 3 (1935): 171–180.

"An Observational Study of Two Captive Mountain Gorillas (*Gorilla beringei*)." *Human Biology* 9, no. 2 (1937): 175–196.

"Behavior and Social Relations of Free-Ranging Primates." *Scientific Monthly* 48 (1939): 319–325.

A Field Study in Siam of the Behavior and Social Relations of the Gibbon (Hylobates lar). Comparative Psychology Monographs, vol. 16, no. 5. Baltimore, MD: Johns Hopkins University Press, 1940.

"Rhesus Monkeys (*Macaca mulatta*) for American Laboratories." *Science* 92, no. 2387 (1940): 284–286.

"Sexual Behavior of Free-Ranging Rhesus Monkeys (*Macaca mulatta*). I. Specimens, Procedures and Behavioral Characteristics of Estrus." *Journal of Comparative Psychology* 33, no. 1 (1942): 113–142.

"Sexual Behavior of Free-Ranging Rhesus Monkeys (*Macaca mulatta*). II. Periodicity of Estrus, Homosexual, Autoerotic and Non-Conformist Behavior." *Journal of Comparative Psychology* 33, no. 1 (1942): 143–162.

"Societies of Monkeys and Apes." *Biological Symposia* 9 (1942): 177–204.

"Research and Training Activities, Summer 1947." *Annual Reports of the New York Zoological Society* (1947): 53–57.

"Research and Training Activities, Summer 1948." *Annual Reports of the New York Zoological Society* (1948): 40–42.

"Animal Behavior Research and Training, Summer 1949." *Annual Reports of the New York Zoological Society* (1949): 46–67.

"General Plans and Methodology for Field Studies of the Naturalistic Behavior of Animals." *Annals of the New York Academy of Sciences* 51, no. 6 (1950): 1006–1008.

"Social Behavior of Non-human Primates." *Physiologie des Societies Animals* 34, no. 3 (1950–1952): 227–246.

Naturalistic Behavior of Nonhuman Primates. University Park: Pennsylvania State University Press, 1964.

"Approaches to Studies of the Naturalistic Communicative Behavior in Nonhuman Primates." In *Approaches to Animal Communication*, edited by Thomas A. Sebeok and Alexandra Ramsey. The Hague: Mouton, 1969.

"Breeding Colonies of Macaques and Gibbons on Santiago Island, Puerto Rico." In *Breeding Primates: Proceedings of the International Symposium on Breeding Non-human Primates for Laboratory Use.* Berne: Generva S. Karger, 1972.

OTHER SOURCES

Altmann, S. "Clarence Ray Carpenter (1905–1975)." In *Encyclopedia of Anthropology*, edited by H. James Birx. Thousand Oaks, CA: Sage Publications, 2006.

Haraway, Donna. *Primate Visions: Gender, Race, and Nature in the World of Modern Science.* New York: Routledge, 1989.

———. "Signs of Dominance: From a Physiology to a Cybernetics of Primate Society, C. R. Carpenter, 1930–1970." *Studies in History of Biology* 6 (1983): 129–219.

Marler, P. "Forward." In *The Cayo Santiago Macaques: History, Behavior and Biology*, edited by Richard G. Rawlins and Matt J. Kessler. Albany: State University of New York Press, 1986.

Mitman, Gregg. "When Nature *Is* the Zoo: Vision and Power in the Art and Science of Natural History." *Osiris* 11 (1996): 117–143.

Montgomery, Georgina M. "Place, Practice and Primatology: Clarence Ray Carpenter, Primate Communication and the Development of Field Methodology, 1931–1945." *Journal of the History of Biology* 38, no. 3 (2005): 495–533.

———. "Primates in the Real World: Place, Practice and the History of Primate Field Studies, 1924–1970." PhD diss., University of Minnesota, Minneapolis, 2005.

Rawlins, Richard. G., and Matt J. Kessler, eds. *The Cayo Santiago Macaques: History, Behavior and Biology.* Albany: State University of New York Press, 1986.

Robinson, N. *Jungle Laboratory: The Story of Ray Carpenter and the Howling Monkeys.* New York: Hastings House Publishers, 1973.

Strum, Shirley C., and Linda Marie Fedigan, eds. *Primate Encounters: Models of Science, Gender and Society.* Chicago: University of Chicago Press, 2000.

Yerkes, Robert M., and Ada Yerkes. "Social Behavior in Infrahuman Primates." In *A Handbook of Social Psychology*, edited by C. Murchison. Worcester, MA: Clark University Press, 1935.

Georgina M. Montgomery

CARPENTER, RAY

SEE **Carpenter, Clarence Ray**.

CARPENTER, WILLIAM BENJAMIN

(*b.* Exeter, England, 29 October 1813; *d.* London, England, 9 November 1885), *medicine, natural history, physiology, moral and physiological psychology.* For the original article on Carpenter see *DSB*, vol. 3.

Since the 1970s, many historians have sought to elucidate the various contexts that gave shape to the science of the Victorian period. Whereas an older historiography was contented to tell "presentist" stories focusing on "contributions" to current knowledge, this new history puts science "in its place." As George Levine (1997) puts it, this approach seeks "to understand Victorian science not only as sets of procedures for finding out what the natural world is really like but as human interventions in continuing political, social and religious struggles" (p. 15). Still, there are some historians who retain the legitimate concern of elucidating contributions to current science. Scholarship of both sorts has shed considerable light on William Benjamin Carpenter.

Scientific Contributions. The picture that emerges from traditional "presentist" scholarship is that Carpenter did make several important contributions to science. Although Thomas Laycock was first to argue that reflexes are mediated not only in the spinal cord, but also in the cerebrum ("the reflex function of the brain"), Carpenter has been credited with coining the term most often associated with this notion (*ideo-motor action*). William James incorporated the work of these British scientists, alongside related but independent insights from Germany (of Johann Herbart and Hermann Lotze), into his seminal *Principles of Psychology.* Further, the concept of ideo-motor action has recently captured the attention of cognitive psychologists. Carpenter also coined the term *unconscious cerebration,* which was meant to convey that much ideo-motor action happens outside awareness (Laycock

William Benjamin Carpenter. *Carpenter, circa 1860.*
HULTON ARCHIVE/GETTY IMAGES.

challenged Carpenter's priority on this by saying that he himself intended his original concept of the reflex function of the brain to include unconscious states). Carpenter's and Laycock's work in the area of unconscious cerebration contributed to the emergence of dynamic psychiatry and Carpenter has been cited in the recent cognitive science literature on the "new unconscious." It has also been argued that Carpenter's evolving speculations regarding the "correlation of forces" constituted an important contribution to the emergence of the doctrine of the conservation of energy. Further, some of Carpenter's contemporaries claimed that his textbooks gave to nineteenth-century British physiology a distinctive "broad and far-seeing scope" (Carpenter, 1888, p. 68) and contributed substantially to establishing physiology as a respected discipline in England. His obituary in the *Proceedings of the Royal Society of London* called his *Principles of General and Comparative Physiology* "the first attempt to recognise and lay down the lines of a science of 'Biology' in an educational form" (1886, p. iv). Finally, Leslie Spencer Hearnshaw (1964) credited Carpenter for helping to establish the discipline of physiological psychology

and calls his *Principles of Mental Physiology* "one of the classics of British psychology" (p. 20).

"Orthodox" Science. Arguably the most important recent historical work done on Carpenter (and the most promising work to be done) is of the contextualist variety. Alison Winter's work (1998, 1997), centering on issues related to authority, boundaries, and orthodoxy in science, provides a fascinating picture of Carpenter's early-career maneuvers to establish the orthodoxy of his own views, and his later-career attempts to establish the heterodoxy of others.

Winter argues that Carpenter was part of a cohort of scientists that spanned the period between early Victorian science (which was a relative "free-for-all" in which all educated Victorians could participate) and later Victorian science (a closed and professionalized version of science in which the public would be trained to respect the boundary between amateur and true scientist). In his early career, Carpenter successfully negotiated the uncertainty of the early Victorian scientific landscape—a landscape in which established scientific communities did not yet exist for most disciplines—by soliciting, creatively synthesizing, and publishing letters of recommendation from respected scientific and religious leaders who as individuals did not comprise an established scientific community and yet whose combined opinions would (and did) have the force of granting "orthodox" status to Carpenter's scientific output (that is, his first textbook, *Principles of General and Comparative Physiology*). Gaining orthodox standing was no small accomplishment. In his attempt to reduce all physiological data to single law, Carpenter was articulating an opinion that had previously been interpreted as materialistic and had doomed the careers of other scientists who were not so careful in managing the reception of their work. It was not so much "by being right about nature," Levine summarizes, that Carpenter was able to establish the orthodoxy of his beliefs, but "by careful marshalling of experts who ultimately determined what being right could mean" (1997, p. 22).

Winter also shows how, at the end of his career, Carpenter was still involved in defining orthodox science, but this time as an insider. Carpenter was at the center of debates concerning various alternative sciences (whose status was very much at this time contested) such as mesmerism, phrenology, and electrobiology. Additionally, he took interest in debunking popular occult phenomena like table-turning. It was in this context that Carpenter devised the highly influential argument that mesmerized, electrobiologized, or table-turning individuals were not actually being influenced by some yet-unknown outside force but rather were in a highly suggestible psychological state. Creatively extending Laycock's notion of the reflex function of the brain, Carpenter argued that ideas represented in the cerebrum spontaneously and reflexively create the correlative behavior if the will of the individual is not actively engaged to control the process. In Carpenter's newly coined terminology, mesmerized patients and the like were simply manifesting "ideo-motor action," a kind of cognitive automatism. This argument became standard in debunking these now "pseudoscientific" enterprises.

Carpenter's next maneuver in his battle against heterodoxy, Winter argues, was to argue that scientific education at British universities needed to be improved and expanded so that the educated middle class would no longer be susceptible to the fallacious reasoning of the pseudosciences and would respect and trust the judgments of true scientists. Thus, Carpenter, who needed to creatively open the doors of mainstream scientific approbation through the assembling of scientific authorities early in his career, was, once established, instrumental in closing the doors of the scientific laboratory to the Victorian public.

Science and Religion. Perhaps the most promising new area for contextualist investigation would be that of religion and morality. As Frank M. Turner, an eminent historian of the Victorian period, reports, a major revision in the historiography of the Victorian era has taken place vis-à-vis the "secularization thesis." This older interpretive framework looked for progressive secularization, emphasizing those elements of culture seeking to eschew religious emphases and ignoring those elements in which religion was still central. The problem with this framework, Turner reports, is that there are major segments of Victorian culture (including elements of Victorian science) that do not fit this interpretation. There is perhaps no better illustration of Turner's point than William Benjamin Carpenter. As Robert Young (1985) says, "the constant theme of [Carpenter's] writings was the reconciliation of science with a theistic view of nature" (p. 106).

Given the distorting effects of the secularization thesis, it is perhaps not surprising that no sustained treatment of the religious and moral elements of Carpenter's thought has been written for over a century. The Carpenter scholar must still turn to J. Estlin Carpenter's "Introductory Memoir" published in the anthology *Nature and Man* (1888). The purpose of this memoir was not "to estimate the precise value of his numerous contributions to knowledge, but rather to show what were the hidden purposes and guiding aims of his life" (W. Carpenter, 1888, p. 3). The "Introductory Memoir" has been a leading source of information for most of the recent historical work on William Benjamin Carpenter and also contains hints that contextualist explorations in gender and race could bear some fruit. Most significant, however, is J. Estlin's claim that "religious concerns crowned his life" (p. 45).

The evidence for the centrality of religion and morality in William Benjamin Carpenter's science is scattered in nearly everything that is written about him. Carpenter was a lifelong, committed, and relatively conservative Unitarian, a devoted church member and organist for decades (he owned an organ and would play it at home regularly), and an admirer and imitator of his father's Unitarian religion. Early in his career he was persecuted for his faith (being twice denied a position at the University of Edinburgh for his Unitarianism) and he expressed the strong belief that the Bible and science would never conflict, as both reveal God's purposes. Throughout his career he used his scientific skills to contribute to the temperance movement (he was himself a teetotaler). After retirement, he went on speaking tours and continued to write, fulfilling his desire to serve, as he put it, as a "mediator" in the emerging struggles between science and religion.

Indeed, even his most significant scientific contributions must be understood in the context of this deep religiosity. His speculations concerning the correlation of forces and his systematic and expansive style of textbook writing were shaped by his belief in the unity of a purposeful universe. While he was radical in his time for insisting that organic ("vital") and inorganic processes operate according to the same laws (a position traditionally opposed by natural theologians), he saw this approach to physiology not only as the most scientifically promising but also as only increasing awe and respect for the deity.

Carpenter's evolutionary views must also be understood in this context. Although a strong advocate of "the doctrine of progressive development" (evolution), he still was not convinced that Charles Darwin's mechanism of natural selection could explain all biodiversity. "The last mouthful chokes him," Darwin wrote to Charles Lyell in 1859, referring to Carpenter's difficulty believing that all vertebrates have a common parent. While Carpenter's hesitations were based on a mastery of the available scientific evidence, they were clearly consonant with his religious vision. Further, while Carpenter's notion of ideo-motor action emerged as part of his debunking efforts, it also fit within a broader and highly influential moral psychology. As the literature of the period attests (for example, the novel *Dracula*—see Stiles, 2006), deterministic and mechanistic doctrines such as ideo-motor action and unconscious cerebration were enormously disturbing to many Victorians, seeming to imply that human beings might be mere automata. In this context, Carpenter argued passionately and at length that human nature is different from the beasts in that we possess a self-determined will that enables us to transcend spinal and cerebral automaticity by directing attention toward moral motives. This moral psychology influenced psychologists James Sully and William James. In James's seminal and still-influential *The Principles of Psychology,* Carpenter's moral psychology is clearly reflected in several places, particularly in the chapters on habit and on will. "His book [*Mental Physiology*]," James wrote, "almost deserves to be called a work of edification" (1890, vol. 1, p. 120).

SUPPLEMENTARY BIBLIOGRAPHY

According to the National Archives of the United Kingdom (available from http://www.nationalarchives.gov.uk/), relevant archival material (mostly correspondence) appears to be scattered across the United Kingdom.

WORKS BY CARPENTER

Principles of General and Comparative Physiology Intended as an Introduction to the Study of Human Physiology: And as a Guide to the Philosophical Pursuit of Natural History. London: Churchill, 1839. Widely used textbook that appeared in many editions.

Principles of Human Physiology: With Their Chief Applications to Pathology, Hygiene, and Forensic Medicine; Especially Designed for the Use of Students. London: Churchill, 1842. Widely used textbook that appeared in many editions.

Manual of Physiology, Including Physiological Anatomy for the Use of the Medical Student. London: Churchill, 1846. Widely used textbook that appeared in many editions.

On the Mutual Relations of the Vital and Physical Forces. London: Philosophical Transactions of the Royal Society, 1850.

On the Influence of Suggestion in Modifying and Directing Muscular Movement, Independently of Volition. London, 1852.

The Physiology of Temperance and Total Abstinence; Being an Examination of the Effects of the Excessive, Moderate, and Occasional Use of Alcoholic Liquors on the Healthy Human System. London: Bohn, 1853.

"The Physiology of the Will." *Contemporary Review* 17 (1871): 192–217.

Principles of Mental Physiology: With Their Applications to the Training and Discipline of the Mind, and the Study of Its Morbid Conditions. New York: Appleton, 1874.

Science and Religion: [A Speech] Delivered before the National Conference of Unitarian and Other Christian Churches at Saratoga, U.S.A., September 19th, 1882. N.p.

The Argument from Design in the Organic World, Reconsidered in Its Relation to the Doctrines of Evolution and Natural Selection. London: Speaight, 1884.

Nature and Man: Essays Scientific and Philosophical, with an introductory memoir by J. Estlin Carpenter. London: K. Paul, Trench, 1888. See "List of Dr. Carpenter's Writings."

OTHER SOURCES

Crabtree, Adam. "'Automatism' and the Emergence of Dynamic Psychiatry." *Journal of the History of the Behavioral Sciences* 39, no. 1 (2003): 51–70.

Daston, Lorraine J. "The Theory of Will versus the Science of Mind." In *The Problematic Science: Psychology in Nineteenth Century Thought,* edited by W. R. Woodward and M. G. Ash. New York: Praeger, 1982.

Gooday, Graeme J. N. "Instrumentation and Interpretation: Managing and Representing the Working Environments of Victorian Experimental Science." In *Victorian Science in Context,* edited by B. Lightman. Chicago: University of Chicago Press, 1997.

Hall, Vance M. D. "The Contribution of the Physiologist, William Benjamin Carpenter (1813–1885), to the Development of the Principles of the Correlation of Forces and the Conservation of Energy." *Medical History* 23 (1979): 129–155.

Hassin, Ran R., James S. Uleman, and John A. Bargh, eds. *The New Unconscious.* New York: Oxford University Press, 2005.

Hearnshaw, L. S. *A Short History of British Psychology, 1840–1940.* London: Methuen, 1964.

Jacyna, L. S. "The Physiology of Mind, the Unity of Nature, and the Moral Order in Victorian Thought." *British Journal for the History of Science* 14 (1981): 109–132.

———. "Principles of General Physiology: The Comparative Dimension to British Neuroscience in the 1830s and 1840s." *Studies in History of Biology* 7 (1984): 47–92.

James, William. *The Principles of Psychology.* New York: Holt, 1890.

Levine, George. "Defining Knowledge: An Introduction." In *Victorian Science in Context,* edited by Bernard Lightman. Chicago: University of Chicago Press, 1997.

Lightman, Bernard. *Victorian Science in Context.* Chicago: University of Chicago Press, 1997.

"Obituary Notices of Fellows Deceased." *Proceedings of the Royal Society of London* 41 (1886): i–xv. An excellent brief summary of Carpenter's original scientific work.

Reed, John Robert. *Victorian Will.* Athens: Ohio University Press, 1989.

Stiles, Anne. "Cerebral Automatism, the Brain, and the Soul in Bram Stoker's Dracula." *Journal of the History of the Neurosciences* 15, no. 2 (2006): 131–152.

Stock, Armin, and Claudia Stock. "A Short History of Ideo-motor Action." *Psychological Research* 68 (2004): 176–188.

Turner, Frank M. *Contesting Cultural Authority: Essays in Victorian Intellectual Life.* Cambridge, U.K.: Cambridge University Press, 1993. See chapter 1 in particular.

———. "Practicing Science: An Introduction." In *Victorian Science in Context,* edited by Bernard Lightman. Chicago: University of Chicago Press, 1997.

Winter, Alison. "The Construction of Orthodoxies and Heterodoxies in the Early Victorian Life Sciences." In *Victorian Science in Context,* edited by Bernard Lightman. Chicago: University of Chicago Press, 1997.

———. *Mesmerized: Powers of Mind in Victorian Britain.* Chicago: University of Chicago Press, 1998.

Young, Robert M. *Darwin's Metaphor: Nature's Place in Victorian Culture.* New York: Cambridge University Press, 1985.

Russell D. Kosits

CARROLL, LEWIS
SEE **Dodgson, Charles Lutwidge**.

CARSON, HAMPTON LAWRENCE

(*b.* Philadelphia, Pennsylvania, 5 November 1914; *d.* Honolulu, Hawaii, 19 December 2004), *cytogenetics, evolutionary theory.*

Carson was one of the pioneers in applying cytogenetic analysis of chromosome structure, particularly inversion patterns, to tracing evolutionary migrations, population divergences, and speciation. He was a member of the National Academy of Sciences, the American Academy of Arts and Sciences, the Society for the Study of Evolution (president, 1971), American Society of Naturalists (president, 1973), the Genetics Society of America (president, 1981), and the American Association for the Advancement of Science. He was a Fulbright research scholar at the University of Melbourne (1961) and served as a visiting professor of biology at the University of São Paulo, Brazil (1961, 1977). He was also a member of the Wheelock Expedition to Labrador (1934). To Carson, one of his greatest honors was receiving the Joseph Leidy Medal from the Academy of Natural Sciences in Philadelphia (1985).

Background and Education. Carson came from an old Philadelphia family with a strong professional background (his great-grandfather, Dr. Joseph Carson, was a botanist and professor of materia medica at the University of Pennsylvania and his father a prominent lawyer). He credited his initial interest in natural history to examining insects and other organisms under his great-grandfather's small antique microscope. Carson graduated with a major in zoology (1936) and subsequently pursued his PhD (1936–1943) at the University of Pennsylvania. His interest shifted from birds to insects as models for investigating mechanisms of evolutionary change. Carson spent the rest of his career working on the cytogenetics and geographic distribution of several insect species, mostly the fruit fly *Drosophila*. He remained an avid field biologist all his life, going on one of his last field trips in 2004, at the age of ninety.

His full-time teaching positions included twenty-seven years at Washington University in St. Louis, where he served as assistant, associate, and full professor (1943–1970), and as professor of cell and molecular biology at the University of Hawaii, where he remained for the rest of his career (he became emeritus in 1985). Carson was active in publishing (his last papers were on mate-choice in *Drosophila* in 2002, 2003) and presenting seminars (his final one was a Sesquicentennial Lecture in the Biology Department at Washington University in April 2004). He died from metastasized bladder cancer in December 2004.

Carson entered the University of Pennsylvania as a freshman in 1932, intending to become a lawyer. Harbor-ing an interest in natural history, he soon took up bird-watching seriously. He studied under Clarence E. McClung, a cytologist of note who had been among the first to suggest that the accessory chromosome (later known as the "X" chromosome) was associated with sex determination. Under McClung, a meticulous investigator with little taste for large-scale theorizing, Carson first studied development of the apical cell in spermatogenesis in insects. The apical cell is close to the sperematogonia, the cells that actually give rise to sperm, and McClung, who believed in the inheritance of acquired characteristics, thought that influences from the environment could be transferred to the spermatagonia via the apical cell. After two years, Carson had not found much, and the aloof McClung retired in 1934.

Carson then studied under Charles W. Metz, a student from Thomas Hunt Morgan's laboratory at Columbia (PhD, 1916), who was McClung's successor as head of the laboratory. Metz specialized in the genetics of diptera, including *Drosophila* and *Sciara*. Unlike McClung, Metz took more direct interest in his students, and in particular fostered Carson's growing interest in genetics and its relationship to evolution. That interest was given considerable boost from two books: Cyril D. Darlington's *Recent Advances in Cytology* (1932) and Theodosius Dobzhansky's *Genetics and the Origin of Species* (1937). Darlington's book spoke directly to Carson's interest in the relationship between cytology and evolution. Unlike many cytologists of his day, Darlington was willing to theorize and speculate about cell structures and functions in a free and uninhibited way. In particular, he emphasized the importance of understanding the cytological structure of chromosomes as bearing on the nature of variation and selection. Darlington pointed out that variations in chromosome structure (inversions, deletions, transpositions, and duplications) could be as important as point mutations as a source of variation on which selection could act. He thus stressed the importance of cytological investigation of those structural rearrangements and their effects on phenotypic variation. However, senior biologists viewed Darlington's book with suspicion and outright hostility. Carson reported that he had to keep his copy of *Recent Advances* inside his desk drawer because most of the faculty thought it was "dangerous" material for graduate students to read.

In contrast, Dobzhansky's book, based on his Jessup Lectures at Columbia, was far more acceptable to the genetics establishment. Dobzhansky suggested a variety of ways in which genetics, including chromosomal rearrangements, could provide the foundation for understanding the mechanism of variation and thus of evolution. In particular, Dobzhansky was just beginning his use of chromosome morphology to distinguish between genetically heterogeneous populations of *Drosophila* in the wild. For Carson, the synthesis of genetics and evolution through cytology was greatly reinforced when, in 1939, Dobzhansky visited the Penn labs to give a seminar. As Carson recalled, Dobzhansky

> walked into my lab and I had an inversion configuration from *Sciara* under the microscope, which I thought was a transposition. In other words, a section of bands was not in the right place. It was moved down the chromosome, but the rest of the chromosome was in the expected order, and he said, "Oh, Carson, that is two inversions, but they're overlapping one another." He made a diagram to show how that worked. (quoted in Anderson, Kaneshiro, and Giddings, 1989, p. 6)

Through Dobzhansky, Carson was also introduced to the Russian school of population genetics, particularly the work of Nikolai I. Dubinin, which among other things made clear the importance of combining field and laboratory work.

At Metz's suggestion, Carson undertook for his thesis a study of the geographic distribution of inversions in polytene chromosomes (chromosomes that have replicated many times without the daughter strands separating, thus producing a much-enlarged, and more visible structure under the microscope) of *Sciara*. Among the various consequences of inversions, crossing-over, or exchange of genetic information between two homologous chromosomes is greatly reduced or prevented in the inverted region. What this meant from an evolutionary perspective was that blocks of advantageous genes, especially ones that functioned together adaptively (epistatically), would be preserved as a group. Thus inversions could be seen as an important evolutionary mechanism for preserving adaptive groups of genes. Carson proceeded to survey a number of populations of *Sciara* in the eastern United States, noting that different populations could be characterized by the frequency of particular inversions. Although Carson did not yet have an explicitly evolutionary focus for his research, the idea of using a detailed cytological record of inversions as a means of exploring evolutionary relationships was already beginning to emerge in his thinking.

As Carson was finishing his dissertation in November 1942, Viktor Hamburger, chair of the Zoology Department at Washington University in St. Louis, offered him a position as assistant professor. In January 1943, Carson drove to St. Louis to take up his new position. His wife Meredith and young son Eddie, were to follow shortly by train. Carson's first teaching assignment was two advanced lecture/laboratory courses, one in parasitology and the other in protozoology. His only preparation was having taken a course in each subject while at Penn, and his only

resources were the course and lab outlines and slides left by his predecessor.

From *Sciara* to *Drosophila*. Carson found the intellectual atmosphere in the Zoology Department at Washington University congenial and stimulating. Hamburger encouraged faculty members and graduate students to organize informal gatherings and journal clubs, to which he would often invite his former European colleagues when they visited St. Louis. Carson recalls meeting the embryologists Johannes Holtfreter and Salome Gluecksohn-Waelsch, and the geneticist Curt Stern, as well as local faculty such as the biochemists Carl and Gerti Cori (future Nobel laureates for their work on the initial stages of carbohydrate metabolism) and the neurophysiologist George Bishop (a specialist in the physiology of the central nervous system), all of whom took interest in his work.

Of more immediate and practical importance was his association with two colleagues, the plant geneticist Edgar Anderson, Engelmann Professor in the Henry Shaw School of Botany (counterpart to the Zoology Department and housed in the same building), and another recent arrival in the Zoology Department, Harrison D. "Harry" Stalker, a student of Curt Stern's at Rochester. Anderson was a superb field naturalist as well as a well-trained geneticist (he was a student of Edward M. East at Harvard's Bussey Institution). He was also, like Carson, interested in the relationship between genetics and evolution, and was to propose, in 1949, the influential theory of introgressive hybridization as a mechanism of evolution in plants. Carson attended Genetics and Natural History, a course developed by Anderson in which students went on field trips and were told simply to observe "the sunflower" in the field and find something interesting to study about its genetics. Carson found numerous polytene chromosomes inside the sunflower heads, which he playfully claimed at first to belong to sunflower seeds. He later told Anderson and the class that they were actually from the salivary glands of the larvae of a very small fly that lived in the sunflower seed. The mixture of genetics and field work appealed to Carson's naturalist background.

Carson's association with Stalker proved to be more serious and long-lasting. Stalker was interested in the morphometrics of *Drosophila* and had written to Alfred H. Sturtevant at the California Institute of Technology, who had worked out the first chromosome map in *Drosophila melanogaster* in 1911. Stalker had asked Sturtevant what species of *Drosophila* needed to be worked on, and Sturtevant had suggested *D. robusta*, because it had numerous inversions that affected size, growth rates, and other morphometric characteristics. Stalker had no familiarity with cytology, and because Carson had worked on inversions in *Sciara*, Stalker suggested they collaborate: he would do the morphometrics and Carson could work out the inversions. Sturtevant generously sent them a manuscript of a paper in which he had outlined some of the inversions he had observed in *robusta,* telling the young investigators they could do with the findings anything they wanted, as he was not going to publish it. Carson's collaboration with Stalker produced a series of papers over the decade 1945–1955, using inversions—the type, frequency, and changes over time—to determine the structure and evolution of natural populations. For example, they noted correlations between specific inversion figures, inherited phenotypic characters (determined by controlled laboratory breeding experiments), and geographic distribution (north-south or altitudinal gradients). This work followed directly in the vein of Dobzhansky's study of *Drosophila pseudoobscura* populations across the southwest. Such studies suggested that certain gene arrangements were more adaptive under one set of environmental conditions (seasonal, or climatic) than others. Such changes opened the door to investigation in the laboratory of exactly how certain gene complexes could be selected for or against by environmental factors. On the genetic side these findings also supported laboratory work, showing that the final phenotypic form of most traits are the result of interaction between environmental factors and multigene complexes.

Carson and Stalker worked together in complementary ways. Stalker had a down-to-earth view of science that emphasized data collection, and shied away from large-scale theorizing. He was a careful and thorough quantitative biologist who firmly believed that if enough data were available theoretical conclusions would follow logically. He was skeptical of generalizations, and as Carson reported, he "always had a dozen reasons why an idea or research plan or theoretical notion was no good" (Anderson, Kaneshiro, and Giddings, 1989, p. 10). Carson was interested in theoretical issues, in using organisms and their chromosomes to answer larger questions about the evolutionary process, particularly the mechanism of speciation. Gradually, Carson began to work on other projects, though he and Stalker remained close friends throughout their careers.

The Hawaiian *Drosophila* Project. In 1962 Carson had a conversation with Wilson Stone from the University of Texas about a project Stone and Elmo Hardy from the University of Hawaii were organizing to study the distribution and genetic makeup of the various species of *Drosophila* in the Hawaiian archipelago. In 1963 Stone invited Carson (and Stalker) to take part in a grant he was preparing with Marshall Wheeler for National Science Foundation (NSF) funding. Carson and Stalker agreed, and the Hawaiian project was to become the focus of their work, particularly Carson's, for the rest of his career (Stalker eventually bowed out, especially after Carson

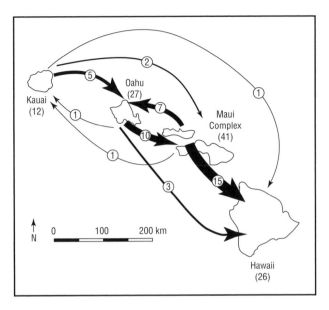

Figure 1. *Large-scale postulated migrations of Drosophila in the Hawaiian archipelago, as judged by Carson from examining inversion patterns of polytene chromosomes, moved from northwest to southeast, as founder individuals colonized new islands as they formed. The width of the arrows and the circled numbers indicate the number of hypothesized founders, while the numbers in parentheses indicate the number of species endemic to each island.*

moved to Hawaii). Initially Stone's and Hardy's aim was to develop methods of collecting and rearing the various species in the laboratory, because none of the methods used with North American species seemed to work with the Hawaiian groups (they were more fragile and easily damaged by collecting with nets; the larvae did not eat the usual banana-fruit food and would not pupate in the culture vials). A good part of the group's initial work was directed to solving these problems.

Once a multitude of technical problems were resolved, it became clear that the Hawaiian *Drosophila* offered an incredibly rich field and laboratory system with which to study evolution. Carson began to find all sorts of new inversion patterns. Comparing them to each other and with the mainland North American species, he and Stalker made several important and novel observations. Of the 250 species found within the archipelago all but about twelve were endemic, meaning they had evolved in the Hawaiian archipelago and were found nowhere else. The Hawaiian group comprised about one-fourth of all the *Drosophila* species in the world known at that time. Because the oldest of the Hawaiian islands (Kauai, the northwest end of the archipelago) is only 5.6 million years old, and the youngest (Hawaii, at the southeastern end) is only about 700,000 years old, evolutionary radiation has been extensive and rapid. Hybridization studies, carried out largely by the Texas colleagues of the project, showed that no fertile hybrids were produced from crosses between any of the Hawaiian species.

Carson was able to use his examination of inversions in a large number of species to propose a pattern of migration between the islands that proceeded from the oldest (Kauai) to the youngest (Hawaii) island. The basic method was simple: Carson compared inversions in different species to each other and to a standard chromosome arrangement from *Drosophila grimshawi,* chosen as the likely progenitor of the others. For practical purposes Carson concentrated on a large subset of species called the "Picture-Wing" Group, a name derived from the characteristic markings on their wings, noting differences in inversion patterns of their chromosomes. The more similar the pattern, he reasoned, the more recently two species diverged. As might be expected, the patterns differed most widely between species on the two most distant islands, Kauai and Hawaii, with intermediates in the intervening islands. However, backward migrations also seemed to have occurred, as suggested by the arrows labeled 1 and 7 in Figure 1. These studies, in the 1960s, led Carson to consider the relationship between migration events by "founder" organisms and the formation of new species.

Founder-Flush and Speciation. The Hawaiian *Drosophila* system allowed Carson to address several important theoretical questions about the process of speciation that had been of interest to him and had been widely debated among evolutionary biologists ever since Darwin. By the mid-twentieth century most investigators more or less agreed on several points: divergent speciation required the migration of some "founder" individuals out of the parent species' range to a new locale. The founder group most likely to lead to the formation of a new and successful divergent line would be one that harbored considerable genetic diversity, allowing it to adapt more readily to new conditions. It was also held that the founder population would have to remain geographically isolated from the parent population for a long enough period that genetic variations could accumulate to a sufficient degree that the two populations could no longer interbreed (what is called allopatric speciation). Finally, it was clear to many evolutionists that the basic mechanism of microevolution—selection acting on slight individual genetic differences—was not likely by itself to lead to speciations. Some other processes and conditions were necessary, but what those conditions were and how speciation actually took place were not well worked out. Carson's "founder-flush" model was one attempt to provide a new model.

Based in part on some of the work of Ernst Mayr, and his own studies of the Hawaiian *Drosophila,* Carson's

model suggested that migration of a few, or even one (such as a gravid female) organism could be enough to initiate a founder event. His own studies on inversions showed that there was considerable genetic variation (individuals heterozygous for one or more inversions) in natural populations (there was debate as to whether there was more variation at the center or periphery of a population's range). Along with Mayr, Carson thought genetic divergence of the founder population would be enhanced not only by heterozygosity but also by the random sampling error introduced by migration of just a few organisms from the original population. In the new environment, freed from the constraints imposed by rigorous competition and selection in the large, dense, parent population), the variability in the founder population might confer a greater chance of survival. Borrowing Mayr's concept of a "genetic revolution" in a founder population, Carson saw inversions, in particular, as serving two very different roles that would both foster and preserve new variability. On the one hand, because the genome functions as an integrated whole, new combinations of inversions could lead to new phenotypes that might prove adaptive to the new environment. On the other hand, inversions preserved successful combinations of genes and thus helped to stabilize the founder population's genetic makeup.

Under these conditions a founder population could undergo rapid expansion, producing what Carson called a "flush" period. During the flush period Carson saw the process that actually transformed the old species into a new one by means of Sewall Wright's shifting-balance concept, in which the population shifted from its old to a new genetic constitution and to a new adaptive landscape. The flush period led eventually to high density and "overpopulation," followed by a "crash" period, in which the population would shrink considerably in size. In each crash period random sampling error could again produce a significant change in the population's genetic composition that could (but not necessarily would) lead to further divergence. The Hawaiian *Drosophilas,* in their multiple migrations among the islands provided the perfect example of how a founder-flush model for speciation could occur. Carson first put forth his "founder-flush" model at the 1955 Cold Spring Harbor Symposium on Quantitative Biology.

Following Dobzhansky, Carson tested his founder-flush model with laboratory experiments, using population chambers where environmental conditions could be controlled, and into which he could introduce flies in all sorts of combinations (a single gravid female, or flies with known inversions) and observe changes in genotypes/phenotypes over a specified number of generations. For example, in one experiment he placed into an inbred population of flies with recessive mutant markers one male fly whose mother was from the population but whose father was from a wild-type laboratory strain. Keeping food, space, and all other conditions constant, he noted that a population flush ensued so that within nine generations the population size had tripled. He reasoned that introducing the wild-type genes had produced, through hybridization, a new gene pool with higher Darwinian fitness in at least some of the genotypes produced by mixing the wild-type with the inbred mutant strain. Thus a population flush could be induced by introducing novel genetic elements, as well as by other more conventional causes such as decreased predation or increased food supply.

Carson's work was highly influential, stimulating a whole generation of evolutionary biologists to investigate the process of speciation from a population genetic perspective. As the historian William Provine has remarked, Carson's

> theorizing has always been very closely tied to experimental evidence. He began thinking about founder effects and genetic revolutions at a time when direct evidence from natural populations was almost entirely absent. My … conclusion … is that the evidence from natural populations and from laboratory experiments concerning founder effects and genetic revolutions grew and changed dramatically between 1955 and 1975, in large part from Carson's own researches and those stimulated by him. (Provine, 1989, p. 69)

Among those who owe a considerable debt to Carson are Alan Templeton (his undergraduate student at Washington University), Brian Charlesworth, Nicholas H. Barton, and William L. Brown, even when those individuals sometimes disagreed strongly with his ideas.

Assessment. Carson's work systematically brought together the ideas of a number of evolutionary thinkers, both from the past and from among his contemporaries. Four of particular importance were represented by portraits on the wall of his office at the University of Hawaii: Charles Metz, John T. Gulick (who grew up in Hawaii and after reading Darwin recognized the importance of the Hawaiian biota for evolutionary theory), Theodosius Dobzhansky, and Sewall Wright. (A fifth portrait was of Viktor Hamburger, who gave Carson's career such a promising start.) Others from whom he drew inspiration included Cyril D. Darlington (for uniting cytogenetics and evolutionary theory) and Ernst Mayr (for his synthetic views on species and speciation). Carson thought of himself as a synthesizer, bringing together not only genetics, cytology, and evolutionary theory, but also the combined field and laboratory approaches so necessary to understanding evolution of real populations in nature. As he wrote in 1980, his work in cytogenetics and evolution

"shows how advancing understanding tends to unify knowledge by the removal of the artificial walls that man erects as he fumbles along…. At this juncture we would do well to sharpen our perception to identify barriers [to our thinking] as yet only dimly seen" (Carson, 1980, p. 92).

BIBLIOGRAPHY

A complete bibliography of Carson's publications from 1934 to 1989 can be found in Genetics, Speciation, and the Founder Principle, *edited by Luther Val Giddings, Kenneth Y. Kaneshiro, and Wyatt W. Anderson, pp. 28–41. New York: Oxford University Press, 1989.*

WORKS BY CARSON

With Harrison D. Stalker. "Gene Arrangements in Natural Populations of *Drosophila robusta* Sturtevant." *Evolution* 1 (1947): 113–133.

"The Genetic Characteristics of Marginal Populations of Drosophila." *Cold Spring Harbor Symposium on Quantitative Biology* 20 (1955): 276–286.

"The Species as a Field for Gene Recombination." In *The Species Problem,* edited by Ernst Mayr, 23–38. Science Publication no. 50. Washington, DC: American Association for the Advancement of Science, 1957.

"Response to Selection under Different Conditions of Recombination in Drosophila." *Cold Spring Harbor Symposium on Quantitative Biology* 23 (1958a): 291–306.

"Increase in Fitness in Experimental Populations Resulting from Heterosis." In *Proceedings of the National Academy of Sciences of the United States of America* 44 (1958b): 1136–1141.

"Genetic Conditions Which Promote or Retard the Formation of Species." *Cold Spring Harbor Symposium on Quantitative Biology* 24 (1959): 87–105.

"The Population Flush and Its Genetic Consequences." In *Population Biology and Evolution: Proceedings of the International Symposium, June 7–9, 1967, Syracuse, New York,* edited by Richard C. Lewontin, 123–137. Syracuse, NY: Syracuse University Press, 1968.

"Chromosome Tracers of the Origin of Species." *Science* 168 (1970): 1414–1418.

"The Genetics of Speciation at the Diploid Level." *American Naturalist* 109 (January–February 1975): 83–92.

"Cytogenetics and the Neo-Darwinian Synthesis." In *The Evolutionary Synthesis: Perspectives on the Unification of Biology,* edited by Ernst Mayr and William Provine, 86–95. Cambridge, MA: Harvard University Press, 1980.

With Alan R. Templeton. "Genetic Revolutions in Relation to Speciation Phenomena: The Founding of New Populations." *Annual Reviews of Ecology and Systematics* 18 (1984): 97–131.

"Inversions in Hawaiian *Drosophila*." In *Drosophila Inversion Polymorphism,* edited by Costas B. Krimbas and Jeffrey R. Powell, 407–453. Boca Raton, FL: CRC, 1992.

"A New Era in Science at Washington University, St. Louis: Viktor Hamburger's Zoology Department in the 1940s." *International Journal of Developmental Neuroscience* 19 (2001): 125–131.

"Mate Choice Theory and the Mode of Selection in Sexual Populations." In *Proceedings of the National Academy of Sciences of the United States of America* 100 (2003): 6584–6587.

OTHER SOURCES

Anderson, Wyatt, Kenneth Y. Kaneshiro, and Luther Val Giddings. "Hampton Lawrence Carson: Interviews toward an Intellectual History; List of Publications from 1934 to 1989." In *Genetics, Speciation, and the Founder Principle,* edited by Luther Val Giddings, Kenneth Y. Kaneshiro, and Wyatt W. Anderson, 3–41. New York: Oxford University Press, 1989. The interviews provide useful insight into the various influences that stimulated Carson from his student days onward.

Dobzhansky, Theodosius. "Adaptive Changes Induced by Natural Selection in Wild Populations of *Drosophila.*" *Evolution* 1 (1947): 1–16.

Provine, William B. "Founder Effects and Genetic Revolutions in Microevolution and Speciation: An Historical Perspective." In *Genetics, Speciation, and the Founder Principle,* edited by Luther Val Giddings, Kenneth Y. Kaneshiro, and Wyatt W. Anderson, 43–76. New York: Oxford University Press, 1989. Has a section on Carson's work but the article as a whole traces the much wider discussion of founder effects.

Garland E. Allen

CASIMIR, HENDRIK BRUGT GERHARD

(*b.* The Hague, Netherlands, 15 July 1909; *d.* Heeze, Netherlands, 4 May 2000), *physicist, quantum physics, statistical physics.*

Casimir's major achievements in physics lie in the field of quantum physics (theory of nuclear and electron spins, intermolecular forces, "Casimir effect") and statistical physics (superconductivity, Onsager relations). He also introduced what became known as the "Casimir operator" in the theory of groups, and played an important role in the international world of industrial research.

Early Life. The son of Rommert Casimir and Teunsina Dina Borgman, Hendrik (Henk) Casimir grew up and went to school in The Hague. Casimir's early environment was that of an intellectual milieu: His father was an important educational reformer and pedagogue who combined his work as the head of a progressive secondary school in The Hague with an extraordinary professorship in pedagogy at the University of Leiden. Already at a young age Casimir showed extraordinary abilities, both in the sciences and in languages. He combined these talents with an extraordinary memory, which allowed him to recite favorite texts throughout his life. Starting in 1926, he studied physics at the University of Leiden in the

Netherlands. After finishing the first phase of his studies in record time, ending with the *candidaatsexamen* in 1928, he began his specialization, theoretical physics, under Paul Ehrenfest. As was the case with so many of his fellow students, Casimir became deeply influenced by Ehrenfest's personality and his unique style of doing physics.

At the initiative of Ehrenfest, Casimir spent much time with Niels Bohr in Copenhagen, Denmark, in the period from 1929 to 1931. In his autobiography, *Haphazard Reality* (1983), Casimir tells how Ehrenfest introduced him to Bohr: "I bring you this boy. He has already some ability, but he still needs thrashing" (p. 91). The Copenhagen years were formative ones for young Casimir. He witnessed firsthand how the new and still rudimentary quantum mechanics was developed into a mature theory. Working with Bohr, he made the acquaintance of all the major physicists of the time. From the stories and anecdotes related in the autobiography, a picture emerges of a close-knit group of young people having a wonderful time, not just doing physics but engaging in all sorts of social activities in Copenhagen as well.

In November 1931, Casimir obtained his doctorate with a dissertation on the rotation of rigid bodies in quantum mechanics. It contains, among other things, the introduction of what became known as the Casimir operator in the theory of representations of groups. After completing his doctoral work, Casimir first remained in Leiden as Ehrenfest's assistant, but in the fall of 1932, he left for Zürich, Switzerland, to become Wolfgang Pauli's assistant at the Swiss Federal Institute of Technology. He enjoyed his new position and was planning to stay in Zürich for at least two years, but in the spring of 1933, Ehrenfest implored him to return to Leiden in the fall, saying "Please, Caasje, put your broad shoulders under the wagon of Leiden physics" (*Haphazard Reality*, p. 147). The reason for this request became obvious when Ehrenfest committed suicide on 25 September of that year, an act that he had been planning for quite some time. Casimir took on Ehrenfest's duties until the fall of 1934, when Hendrik Anthony Kramers was appointed as Ehrenfest's successor.

The Leiden Laboratory. In the meantime, Casimir had developed an interest in experimental physics. He assisted his wife, an experimental physicist, with her work in the Kamerlingh Onnes Laboratory of the University of Leiden. Casimir's experimental activities eventually led to his appointment, in 1936, as *conservator* (managing director) of the laboratory. He worked in the section that was led by Wander J. de Haas, who codirected the laboratory with Willem Keesom. Notable in this period is his work with Cornelis Jacobus Gorter on superconductivity, reported in

Hendrik Casimir. *From left to right: Walter Wilhelm Georg Bothe, Francis Henri Jean Siegfried Perrin, Hendrik Brugt Gerhard Casimir, and Luis Walter Alvarez.* EMILIO SEGRE VISUAL ARCHIVES/AMERICAN INSTITUTE OF PHYSICS/PHOTO RESEARCHERS, INC.

their paper, "On Supraconductivity I" (1934), in which they introduced a two-fluid model for this phenomenon, and his paper (with Frits K. du Pré) on a thermodynamic theory of paramagnetic relaxation, "Note on the Thermodynamic Interpretation of Paramagnetic Relaxation Phenomena" (1938). In this work a magnetic crystal is treated as a combination of two systems with two different temperatures: the lattice with its phonons and electrons, on the one hand, and the spins, on the other. These two systems have different relaxation times, with the spin lattice relaxation time determining the time in which the two temperatures become equal. Finally, a paper with de Haas and Gerard J. van den Berg, "The Electrical Resistance of Gold Below 1°K" (1938), described a newly discovered effect: a temperature dependent residual electrical resistance in metals that seemed to diverge as the temperature approached absolute zero. Only many years later was this phenomenon explained by Jun Kondo as the result of an interaction between the conducting electrons and magnetic impurities; it became known as the Kondo effect.

Not related to experimental work in the Kamerlingh Onnes Laboratory was Casimir's book, *On the Interaction between Atomic Nuclei and Electrons* (1936), in which he summarized earlier work on electron and nuclear spins and their interactions. It was his contribution to an essay contest by Teyler's Foundation in Haarlem, the Netherlands, and it earned him a gold medal.

Philips Company. Not long after the German invasion and occupation of the Netherlands in May 1940, the University of Leiden was closed down by the occupiers. Work in the Kamerlingh Onnes Laboratory continued, however, though under increasingly difficult circumstances. Casimir's decision in 1942 to accept the offer of a position at the Physics Laboratory of the Philips Company in Eindhoven, in the south of the Netherlands, was undoubtedly influenced by these difficulties. A deteriorating relationship with his director, de Haas, may have played a role as well.

In the Philips Laboratory, which from its creation in 1914 provided a stimulating atmosphere in which fundamental as well as applied research flourished, Casimir clearly found his place. After only four years he became one of its three directors and ten years after that, in 1956, he became a member of the top executive committee of the Philips Company. In that capacity he was in charge of all Philips laboratories worldwide. By appointing him a member of the executive committee, the leaders of Philips showed their dedication to fundamental as well as applied research. Especially at the central laboratory in Eindhoven, much fundamental research was being done, and so it became an attractive place for new PhDs to start their professional careers. Casimir supervised, stimulated, and where necessary gave direction to the research, always considering both the company's interests and the scientific merit of the work.

Casimir's move from the academic world to the world of industry was not received favorably by all of his colleagues. A prominent example is Pauli, who began addressing him facetiously as "Herr Direktor." There was concern that the industrial environment would put an end to Casimir's research in theoretical physics, a concern that would prove to be largely unfounded. In fact, some of his most important work in theoretical physics dates from the Philips days; most famous is the discovery, in 1948, of the Casimir effect: the attractive force between two perfectly conducting uncharged plates in vacuum.

Intermolecular Forces and the Casimir Effect. In the Philips laboratory, experiments had been done on the stability of colloids, with results that seemed to contradict theoretical predictions, in particular those concerning the long-range behavior of the attractive intermolecular forces acting between the colloidal particles. One of the experimenters, the physical chemist Jan Theodoor Gerard Overbeek, suggested to Casimir that the problem might be solved by modifying the London-van der Waals electromagnetic theory of molecular forces between electrically neutral particles by taking into account the finite propagation speed of electromagnetic interactions. For this, Casimir quickly realized, one needed a quantum-electrodynamical theory for the interaction energy between polarizable particles. Together with his collaborator, Dirk Polder, he succeeded in creating such a theory, using the still-rudimentary formalism of quantum electrodynamics. Their final result was deceptively simple. They found an attractive force that for large distances R decreases as R^7 instead of the usual R^6 of the London-Van der Waals forces. It did not take long before Casimir had the insight that these forces could also be calculated by looking at the vacuum energy fluctuations of the electromagnetic field. Although the zero-point energy of the vacuum is infinite, the presence of, for instance, two metal plates will create a finite disturbance that will manifest itself as a force on the plates. A short calculation led Casimir to a very simple expression for the attractive force per unit area between two perfectly conducting parallel plates in a vacuum, now known as the Casimir effect:

$$F(R) = \frac{\overline{h}c\pi^2}{240} \frac{1}{R^4}.$$

There is a simple way to grasp the mechanism behind this effect, namely by considering the space between the plates as a resonance cavity. Only the radiation modes that "fit" between the two plates will be present in this cavity; the other ones will be damped out. Thus, there are fewer modes between the plates than outside of them, so that the radiation pressure on the outside will exceed that on the inside, leading to an effective attraction. An amusing analogous phenomenon will appear when two ships are reasonably close together under the right weather conditions, which are little wind and strong waves: the ships will then drift towards each other. The Casimir effect, which is extremely difficult to test (the effect becomes measurable only for distances of the order of one hundred atom diameters), became a widely discussed phenomenon, especially since its experimental verification in the 1990s.

Onsager Relations. Another important contribution by Casimir from the Philips period is his generalization of Lars Onsager's theory of irreversible phenomena, in particular the so-called Onsager reciprocal relations. In irreversible thermodynamics, one distinguishes between "forces" (for instance, gradients) and the "fluxes" caused by those forces. In a very general way one may write $I_i = \sum_k L_{ik}X_k$, with I_i the fluxes and X_k the forces. Onsager had found the general relations $L_{ik} = L_{ki}$, a result based on time reversal invariance of the underlying microscopic processes. Casimir succeeded in generalizing this to situations where effects that are not time-reversal invariant play a role. In the presence of a magnetic field, for instance, one has $L_{ik}(B) = L_{ki}(-B)$.

Other Activities. As part of his work at the Philips Company, Casimir traveled a great deal, visiting the various Philips laboratories and also attending scientific meetings. He developed a large network and became widely respected, not only for his work in physics, but also as a mediator between industry and the world of science in academia (as opposed to industrial science). In 1966, he became the first president of the European Industrial Research Management Association (EIRMA), which was cofounded by him. After his retirement from Philips in 1972, Casimir began spending more time on organizational and other nonscientific matters. He served as president of the Royal Netherlands Academy of Arts and Sciences from 1973 to 1978 and was one of the founding members of the European Physical Society, as well as its president from 1972 to 1975. He was also frequently asked to be the chairman or keynote speaker at conferences and other gatherings. His after-dinner speeches were famous for their wit and erudition. His sense of humor was also evident in one of his most widely read nonscientific papers: a pseudo-linguistic essay on Broken English as the international language of science. (It was reprinted in Casimir's autobiography.)

Casimir was a man of power and influence, but he was also a kind and even somewhat shy person, with a genuine interest in other people. His interests ranged far and wide, as is witnessed by his many articles on cultural topics and by his co-editorship of *De Gids*, one of the oldest Dutch literary journals. In the Netherlands, he became the grand old man of physics, one of the last of the generation that helped to shape modern physics in the heroic years of the 1920s and 1930s. He was a member of several scientific organizations and academies and received many honors, including eight honorary doctorates and two of the highest Dutch Royal decorations.

BIBLIOGRAPHY

Casimir's papers are in Rijksarchief in Noord-Holland, Haarlem, the Netherlands. Bibliographies of Casimir's work are on pp. 193–217 of Sarlemijn and in the Hargreaves article, both cited below.

WORKS BY CASIMIR

Rotation of a Rigid Body in Quantum Mechanics. Groningen, Netherlands: Wolters, 1931.

With Cornelis J. Gorter. "On Supraconductivity I." *Physica* 1 (1934): 306–320.

On the Interaction between Atomic Nuclei and Electrons. Haarlem, Netherlands: Bohn, 1936.

With Wander J. de Haas and Gerard J. van den Berg. "The Electrical Resistance of Gold Below 1°K." *Physica* 5 (1938): 225–229.

With Frits K. du Pré. "Note on the Thermodynamic Interpretation of Paramagnetic Relaxation Phenomena." *Physica* 5 (1938): 507–511.

"On Onsager's Principle of Microscopic Reversibility." *Reviews of Modern Physics* 17 (1945): 343–350.

With Dirk Polder. "The Influence of Retardation on the London-van der Waals Forces." *Physical Review* 73 (1948): 360–372.

"On the Attraction between Two Perfectly Conducting Plates." *Proceedings of the Koninklijke Akademie van Wetenschappen* B51 (1948): 793–795.

Haphazard Reality: Half a Century of Science. New York: Harper and Row, 1983. This autobiography appeared first in English and then in a slightly rewritten Dutch version, *Het toeval van de werkelijkheid: Een halve eeuw natuurkunde* (Amsterdam, Netherlands: Meulenhoff Informatief, 1983).

Waarneming en visie, over wetenschap en maatschappij. Amsterdam, Netherlands: Meulenhoff Informatief, 1987.

Mens en Kosmos: Essays. Amsterdam, Netherlands: Meulenhoff, 1993.

OTHER SOURCES

Hargreaves, C. M. "Casimir, Hendrik Brugt Gerhard." *Biographical Memoirs of Fellows of the Royal Society* 50 (2004): 39–45.

Lamoreaux, Steve K. "Hendrik Brugt Gerhard Casimir." *Proceedings of the American Philosophical Society* 146 (2002): 285–290.

Polder, Dirk. "Hendrik Brugt Gerhard Casimir: 15 juli 1909–4 mei 2000. Levensbericht door D. Polder." In *Koninklijke Nederlandse Akademie van Wetenschappen: Levensberichten en herdenkingen 2001.* Amsterdam: Koninklijke Nederlandse Akademie van Wetenschappen, 2001.

Rechenberg, Helmut. "Hendrik Brugt Gerhard Casimir (1909–2000): The Physicist in Research, Industry and Society." *European Journal of Physics* 22 (2001): 441–446.

Sarlemijn, A., ed. *Tussen academie en industrie: Casimirs visie op wetenschap en researchmanagement.* Amsterdam: Meulenhoff Informatief, 1984.

A. J. Kox

CASPERSSON, TORBJÖRN OSKAR

(*b.* Motala, Sweden, 15 October 1910; *d.* 7 December 1997), *cytochemistry, genetics, cytology.*

One of the greatest challenges the biological sciences confront is the development of instruments and techniques that can provide information about the physical processes occurring in biological systems at very small dimensions. Success in developing new instruments and techniques for biological inquiry requires both skill in developing instruments and a deep understanding of biological problems so as to measure signals that reflect biological processes and avoid many potential artifacts. Caspersson pioneered in the development of techniques for identifying and measuring chemical components within biological systems from their optical characteristics—absorption of radiation, especially ultraviolet light—and made important discoveries that became the foundation for major advances, especially in cell biology and genetics. Caspersson's career in cytology and genetics was characterized by a drive to measure biophysical materials precisely and the project of building instruments to make those measurements.

Research on Nucleic Acids for MD. Caspersson was born on 15 October 1910 in the town of Motala in southeastern Sweden. He studied medicine and biophysics at the Karolinska Institutet in Stockholm, from which he received his MD in 1936. Beginning with a lectureship, he remained at the Karolinska Institutet for his entire career, and from the mid-1940s, he directed a major laboratory in cell biology and genetics.

Caspersson carried out his initial research as a docent in the laboratory of Einar Hammarsten, who was professor of chemistry and one of the few investigators in the 1930s who focused his research on nucleic acids. Hammarsten had developed new procedures for the preparation of nucleic acids and with his collaborators applied physical and chemical techniques in the attempt to determine their constitution. Caspersson determined that the results of Hammarsten's preparations could be trapped by various filters and ascertained "the astonishing fact that the complexes of nucleic acids must be larger than the protein molecules" (Caspersson, 1934). Hammarsten and Caspersson then collaborated with organic chemist Rudolf Signer in Bern who measured the weight by flow birefringence. In conflict with then accepted views, they concluded that DNA was a large molecule with a molecular weight between 500,000 and 1,000,000 (Signer, Caspersson, and Hammarsten, 1938).

Among Caspersson's other early projects were developing procedures for assaying the potency of liver extracts by measuring blood formation in chicken embryos and an examination of changes in blood in florescent cells of embryonic liver. Soon, though, his primary focus was on the structure of chromosomes, which he prepared for study by digesting attached proteins with proteolytic enzymes. He then examined the remaining nucleic acids under ultraviolet light, where they appeared to be disks connected by a thread.

For his research leading to his medical degree, Caspersson turned to the question of measuring the quantities of proteins and nucleic acids in various specimens and the changes in these quantities over time as cells went through different stages of the cell cycle. Since different biological materials, especially proteins and nucleic acids, absorb maximally light of different wavelengths, he recognized that by measuring the absorption of light of various wavelengths in a given specimen he could determine the quantities of the materials present in that specimen.

The critical challenge was to be able to make precise measurement from very small objects. He argued theoretically that this should be possible on objects as small as three times the wavelength of the light whose absorption was measured (this meant that accurate measurements could be obtained to a resolution of 0.5μ with ultraviolet light). To do this he integrated a spectroscope with a microscope fitted with a quartz lens to produce a monochromatic ultraviolet microscope. He then confronted a number of problems, such as the loss of light due to scattering in the specimen, which could generate erroneous measurements. Accordingly, much of his effort went into overcoming these sources of error. He approached the problem of scatter by generating an additional apparatus to measure the quantity of scatter directly. To compensate

Torbjörn Oskar Caspersson. FONDAZIONE BALZAN "PREMIO," MILANO.

for the lack of homogeneity in specimens, he developed procedures for photographing specimens and performing measurements on the photographs.

Since nucleic acids absorb light very strongly at 2,600 angstroms (the mid-ultraviolet range), Caspersson was able to use the device to locate them in different parts of individual cells and measure their quantities. In these studies for his medical degree, he showed that regions on chromosomes that differentially absorbed the Feulgen stain (known as *euchromatin bands*) also exhibited high absorption at 2,600 angstroms (Caspersson, 1936). Caspersson determined that these regions also had a high protein content (revealed by absorption at 2,800 Å) that was dissolved when enzymes such as trypsin, known to digest proteins, were applied.

This supported the claim that chromosomes were long polypeptide chains on which molecules of nucleic acid were attached. Caspersson suggested that deoxyribonucleic acid (DNA) figured in gene replication as smaller groups polymerized into larger aggregates, providing a structure on which extended protein molecules could be reproduced (Caspersson and Schultz, 1938). Although focusing on nucleic acids, Caspersson did not at the time view DNA as the genetic material. Rather, he endorsed the widely accepted view that genes must be made of proteins "because of their inexhaustible possibility of variation" (1936, p. 138).

When Caspersson began his research in the 1930s what came to be known as DNA and ribonucleic acid (RNA) were often identified as originating in animals and plants (especially yeast) respectively, although RNA was also known to occur in some animal cells. As a result, they were often referred to as animal and plant nucleic acids respectively. One result of Caspersson's research was the demonstration that RNA as well as DNA was a regular constituent of animal cells. Although spectroscopic measurements alone could not discriminate DNA from RNA, Caspersson used the Feulgen reaction, which was specific for DNA, to differentiate the two nucleic acids. He localized RNA to locations that did not show the Feulgen reaction but revealed spectroscopically the presence of nucleic acids.

Collaboration with Jack Schultz. Hammarsten received extensive support from the Rockefeller Foundation for his research and, as was customary for up-and-coming researchers with great promise, he had promoted Caspersson for a Rockefeller Fellowship to do further research in a laboratory in the United States. But in fall 1937, before those plans could be finalized, Jack Schultz came to the Karolinska on a Rockefeller Fellowship to spend two years working with Caspersson. Schultz had completed his PhD in Thomas Hunt Morgan's genetics laboratory at the California Institute to Technology, where he had been working with Sturtevant and Bridges. Interested in relating genetics and development, Schultz had formulated the hypothesis that a concentration of DNA along the chromosomes would block the expression of nearby genes (assumed to consist of proteins). He sought out Caspersson's help on the idea that spectroscopic techniques would permit the localization of DNA and hence the genes whose expression was blocked, on chromosomes in mutant fruit flies that he brought with him to Stockholm.

Regions of chromosomes stain differentially in the Feulgen reactions, with some regions (euchromatin) manifesting orderly bands of light and dark regions and others (heterochromatin) exhibiting a much more disorganized pattern. The heterochromatic bands stain most deeply in the interphase chromosome and Caspersson demonstrated that it had the greatest concentration of nucleic acid. These heterochromatin regions were also the locus of the abnormalities in gene reproduction due to chromosomal rearrangements in the different strands of *Drosophila* Shultz had been studying. Caspersson and Schultz now

linked these regions with nucleic acid metabolism (Caspersson and Schultz, 1938).

Moreover, in female *Drosophila* eggs with an additional Y chromosome (XXY) Caspersson and Shultz established that the amount of nucleotides in the cytoplasm was greater than the amount found in normal (XX) females, suggesting that although the additional Y chromosome did not appear to be expressed in the phenotype, it did affect nucleic acid metabolism. Moreover, from the fact that the Y chromosome had extensive heterochromatin regions, they attributed to the heterochromatin region a role in nucleic acid synthesis, and proposed such synthesis played a role in gene replication.

In subsequent work, Caspersson and Schultz continued this line of research, ascertaining from absorption spectra that concentrations of RNA are high in the cytoplasm of rapidly growing tissues (*Drosophila* larva) but low in mature tissues, which instead have a high protein concentration. This pointed to a central role of RNA in cytoplasmic protein synthesis, a conclusion that Jean Brachet reached at the same time based on other techniques.

The conclusion, however, was not universally accepted. Shortly after Caspersson's and Brachet's research, Albert Claude, in pioneering research using the ultracentrifuge to segregate fractions from cells, isolated small particles he called microsomes, which he found to be high in RNA content. He, however, rejected suggestions that they figured in protein synthesis.

In their subsequent work, Caspersson and Schultz turned their attention to the nucleolus and the cytoplasm around the nuclear membrane, where they also found high concentrations of RNA. They carried out these measurements in diverse species—sea urchin eggs, periblem cells of spinach root tip, and salivary gland cells of *Drosophila melanogaster*. In all species, in the nucleolus they found local maxima in the wavelengths indicating nucleic acids and a secondary local maximum in the wavelengths indicative of proteins. In the sea urchin, the cytoplasm around the nuclear membrane showed a similar pattern, but with a higher local maximum in the protein region. In peripheral protoplasm there was only a temporary plateau in an otherwise steady drop from a high level of absorption in the shorter wavelengths, indicating low concentrations of RNA.

Caspersson and Schultz attempted to interpret their findings so as to provide a model of gene action. Although their data did not support transport of RNA from the nucleus to the cytoplasm, they viewed the existence of a gradient between the nuclear regions of the cytoplasm and the peripheral regions as supporting the claim that synthesis occurred in the cytoplasmic regions adjoining the nucleus. They also viewed the evidence as supporting the claim that "the activity of nucleoli is closely associated with an intense synthesis of the cytoplasmic ribonucleic acids" and given the additional association of RNA with protein synthesis, they concluded that "the nucleo-cytoplasmic relationships may provide some insight into the mode of action of the genes" (p. 514).

Making use of a linkage others had established between the heterochromatin region of the X and Y chromosomes and the nucleolus, Schultz, Caspersson, and Aquilonius used chromosomal rearrangements and duplicated regions to try to understand differences in absorption spectra identified in male and female *Drosophila.* They claimed to find a correlation between structural properties of nucleoli and nucleic acid content, indicating that both forms of nucleic acid have a role in structure formation: "the genotypic control of the structural characteristics of the nucleolus may be mediated by changes in its nucleic acid content" (p. 522). While drawing attention to the presence of nucleic acids and proposing a role for them in protein synthesis, the specific function Caspersson proposed for RNA remained auxiliary to that of the proteins, which he continued to view as the genes. He proposed that proteins migrated from the chromosomes to the membrane of the cell nucleus, where they induced the synthesis of RNA, which in turn supported the production of proteins in the cytosol (Caspersson and Thorell, 1941).

Continuing Spectrographic Studies during World War II. The beginning of World War II interrupted the further collaboration of Caspersson and Schultz (who returned to the United States) and prevented Caspersson from pursuing his delayed Rockefeller Fellowship (it had by then been arranged that he would spend such a fellowship with W. H. Lewis at Johns Hopkins University). Instead, with support from the Rockefeller Foundation, he continued his ultraviolet spectrographic studies of cells through the war.

One continuing focus of his research was measuring quantities of protein in the nucleus. From the evidence he gathered, he further articulated a complex scheme of protein synthesis. He contended that the swelling and disappearance of chromosomes during the telophase of mitosis was due to the generation of protein from the gene-carrying parts of the chromosomes. He viewed the synthesis of proteins as also providing the mass of the nucleolus. From the nucleolus, proteins were transported to the periphery of the nucleus, where they figured in the generation of ribonucleic acids which in turn supported the synthesis of cytoplasmic proteins. He concluded: "Polynucleotides are a base for the protein synthesis in the cell. A central function for the cell nucleus is to be the centre for the protein production. The heterochromatin is an [organ] regulating the production of the proteins of the cytoplasm. This regulation works via the nucleolus" (letter to Miller, program

officer of the Rockefeller Foundation, 1 September 1940). He later termed heterochromatin-nucleolus-nuclear membrane as the cellular "system of protein synthesis" and protein synthesis as the prime function of the nucleus as a whole.

In addition to determining the nucleic acid and protein content of the nucleus, Caspersson set out to determine how it varied through the cell cycle. Using grasshopper testis, he traced changes in the absorption spectrum during the cell cycle, showing that nucleic acid concentrations increased during prophase and then remained constant while the ratio of nucleic acid to protein increased, indicating a loss of protein as meiosis proceeded. Although he did not construe nucleic acids as the genetic material, he viewed increases in nucleic acids as indicating when gene replication occurred.

During the war, Caspersson recruited a number of junior researchers, including Holger Hydén, Bo Norberg, Arne Engström, and Bo Thorell into his laboratory, and with them he began to apply these measurement techniques to other cell types (especially tumor cells and nerve cells) and to develop and deploy related measurement techniques such as photoelectric methods, x-ray ultramicrospectrography, and cathode-ray fluorescence. Caspersson construed tumor cells as performing protein synthesis without the operation of normal inhibitory mechanisms and thus as providing a particular type of specimen in which to investigate protein synthesis.

Creating an Institute and Developing Instruments. In 1944, Caspersson was appointed to a professorship for cell research specially created by an act of the Swedish parliament. Funding from the Nobel Institute provided funding for a new Medical Nobel Institute building to house the laboratories of Caspersson and Hugo Thorell, an enzyme chemist who was another protégé of Hammarsten. Grants from the Wallenberg Foundation and the Rockefeller Foundation provided for an extension of the building devoted to an Institute for Cell Research under Caspersson's direction. Once he had adequate facilities, the size of Caspersson's research group grew considerably, with upwards of fifteen scientists and twenty technicians carrying out research at a given time. In addition, Caspersson began to attract a substantial cadre of international researchers, who generally came to work for a period of nine to twelve months in his laboratory. The new laboratory also permitted introduction of new instruments, including an electron microscope, acquired for the objective of demonstrating virus particles in infected mammalian cell preparations that corroborate the results of ultraviolet measurements in such cells. Although Caspersson never performed electron microscope investigations himself, Venezuelan Humberto Fernández-Morán used the microscope extensively in his early studies of nerve structure.

Although the development of new instruments and techniques for using them had been a feature of Caspersson's career from the beginning, it began to be a major preoccupation when he acquired the new laboratory facility and expanded his research group. Caspersson included an instrument workshop facility as a major component in the design of the building and became focused on building equipment that generated extremely precise measurements, was automated, and capable of supporting large-scale research.

In his annual reports to the Rockefeller Foundation, which continued to provide him substantial support until 1961, he routinely began with a discussion of the development of new instruments or improvements in existing ones and relegated the results of experimental studies to the latter part of the report. In his December 1953 report to the Rockefeller Foundation, he emphasized the division between the development of instrumentation and basic research:

> work in the institute … has been carefully divided so that half the resources were devoted to developmental work on the side of the instruments and the other half to work on biological problems with the intracellular regulation of protein synthesis as key note. This arrangement has always very strictly been carried through, in spite of the fact that it has often been evident that the biological work on short sight would have benefited from a larger share of the efforts, what would undoubtedly also have made the work more easy to manage financially. The reason for this politics was that the biophysical techniques in question are the primary condition for the work, and furthermore they represent in my personal view one of the ways, which has to be gone sooner or later if we will ever get close to the basic problems of gene reproduction and gene function and thus a quite general approach from the beginning should prove most fruitful at the end. (p. 1)

Among the instruments on which Caspersson and his collaborators worked were a high vacuum x-ray microspectrograph, a universal microspectrophotometer, and instruments for photoelectric scanning. Although Caspersson emphasized both the accuracy and usefulness of the new instruments, they did not receive significant uptake in the research community. Nurnberger (1955) commented critically:

> Caspersson's photographic micrabsorption technique described in 1936 remains, to this day, the simplest and only readily available ultraviolet method for estimating mean or average concentrations of nucleic acid (and proteins) in large cell areas or, likewise of obtaining approximate absorption coefficient for extremely small areas of the order of $1\mu^2$. Though Caspersson has recently developed a highly flexible photoelectric scanning apparatus to replace the photographic system, it is doubtful whether equipment of such complexity will find popularity in any except the best equipped laboratories where show facilities are adequate to the technical problems implied.

The tenor of Nurnberger's evaluation seems to have been shared more generally, and indeed the responsible program officers at the Rockefeller Foundation expressed growing frustration over the years at his continually unfulfilled promises to focus more on basic scientific problems.

Caspersson defended his investment in development of precise and automatic quantitative measurement as providing the main avenue for understanding cellular processes such as protein synthesis. But while he was developing these cytochemical techniques, other approaches were being pursued elsewhere. The approach of cell fractionation through centrifugation, for example, made it possible to isolate ever more specific fractions from cells, with which it was possible both to perform chemical analysis as well as carry out specific chemical reactions in isolation from each other. When supplemented with radioactive tracers, these fractions provided a means to study the process of protein synthesis in a much more direct manner than Caspersson envisaged.

Collaboration with Zech on Chromosome Banding. Although for a prolonged period Caspersson's contributions were primarily on the instrumental side, beginning in the late 1960s, he collaborated with Lore Zech in studies that treated metaphase plant chromosomes with different alkylating and intercalating substances. In the course of these studies they found distinctive light and dark banding patterns under ultraviolet light in chromosomes from *Vicia faba* (a variety of bean) and *Trillium erectum* (a perennial wildflower) stained with quinacrine mustard, a process that came to be known as Q-banding (Caspersson et al., 1968). They showed that the banding pattern could be recorded photoelectrically with fluorescence microscopes either directly or from photographs (which avoided problems with fading of the stain under ultraviolet illumination). In the wake of Caspersson and Zech's research, a number of other staining techniques were developed that revealed similar banding patterns on chromosomes.

At the time of this research, human geneticists lacked adequate ways to distinguish human chromosomes from each other either in normal or pathological conditions. In subsequent studies Caspersson and Zech found that despite the fact that human chromosomes were much smaller than the plant chromosomes on which they had been working, they could adapt their techniques to study them (Caspersson, Lomakka, and Zech, 1971).

In very small regions of chromosomes they found very brightly fluorescing regions that also exhibited individual variation that they found to be heritable. The largest such region was found on the distal part of the long arm of the Y chromosome, which Caspersson and Zech noted would provide a means for prenatal sex determination and a tool for screening for XYY males. But more importantly, the whole length of each human chromosome exhibited a faint fluorescence pattern that was distinctive of the particular chromosome and highly consistent across normal individuals. Caspersson and Zech presented curves resulting from passing a slit along the length of each chromosome and recording from the area within the slit, with each chromosome producing a distinctive curve. These consistent patterns provided a basis for detecting chromosomal abnormalities. For this purpose Caspersson developed a simpler, more readily used instrument for recording fluorescence patterns. This contribution had its primary uptake in medical genetics as it enabled investigators to determine which chromosomes were altered in various clinical populations, thereby giving rise to the field of human cytogenetics.

Professional and Personal Life. It is noteworthy that Caspersson adopted the name Institute for Cell Research for his laboratory beginning in 1947. This was a period in which researchers from a variety of different biological disciplines began to train their investigations on the functions of various organelles that were identified within cells. Terms such as *cell research* and *cell biology* began to be used to designate the domain of inquiry as distinct from classical cytology that had focused primarily on cell structure. In 1947, Caspersson played a central role in hosting the sixth International Congress for Experimental Cytology in Stockholm. At this meeting the congress renamed itself the International Society for Cell Biology. In 1950, he and John Runnström, head of the Wenner-Gren Institute for Experimental Biology and Cell Research at the University of Stockholm, established *Experimental Cell Research*, the first of several new journals devoted to cell research and cell biology to be founded during the ensuing decade.

In 1936, Caspersson married Siv Gunnarson (1911–1999), a child psychiatrist who was for many years chief medical officer at the Child Guidance Center, Stockholm, and a pioneer in developing interdisciplinary treatment teams for disturbed children. The couple had two children: Gunnel and Lena. Caspersson received many honorary degrees, including ones from Brandeis University, the University of Giessen, the University of Ghent,

the University of Helsinki, and the University of Rotterdam. He died on 7 December 1997.

BIBLIOGRAPHY

Archival materials from Caspersson's collaboration with Schultz are housed in the Library of the American Philosophical Society in Philadelphia. Archival materials relating to his support from the Rockefeller Foundation are housed in the Rockefeller Archive Center.

WORKS BY CASPERSSON

"Druckfiltrierung von Thymonucleinsäure." *Biochemische Zeitschrift* 270 (1934): 161–163.

"Über den chemischen Aufbau der Strukturen des Zellkernes." *Skandinavisches Archiv für Physiologie* 73, supplement no. 8 (1936): 1–151.

With R. Signer and E. Hammarsten. "Molecular Shape and Size of Thymonucleic Acid." *Nature* 141 (1938): 122.

With J. Schultz. "Nucleic Acid Metabolism of the Chromosomes in Relation to Gene Reproduction." *Nature* 142 (1938): 294–295.

With J. Schultz. "Pentose Nucleotides in the Cytoplasm of Growing Tissues." *Nature* 143 (1939): 602–603.

With J. Schultz. "Ribonucleic Acids in Both Nucleus and Cytoplasm, and the Function of the Nucleolus." *Proceedings of the National Academy of Sciences of the United States of America* 26 (1940): 507–515.

With J. Schultz and L. Aquilonius. "The Genetic Control of Nucleolar Composition." *Proceedings of the National Academy of Sciences of the United States of America* 26, no. 8 (1940): 515–523.

With B. Thorell. "Der endozelluläre Eiweiss- und Nukleinsäurestoffwechsel in Embryonalem Gewebe." *Chromosoma* 2 (1941): 132–154.

With L. Santesson. "Studies on Protein Metabolism in the Cells of Epithelial Tumours." *Acta Radiologica* 46, supplement (1942): 1–105.

"A Universal Ultramicrospectrograph for the Optical Range." *Experimental Cell Research* 1 (1950): 595–598.

Cell Growth and Cell Function. New York: Norton, 1950.

With S. Farber, G. E. Foley, J. Kudynowski, E. J. Modest, E. Simonsson, et al. "Chemical Differentiation along Metaphase Chromosomes." *Experimental Cell Research* 49 (1968): 219–222.

With L. Zech, C. Johansson, and E. J. Modest. "Identification of human chromosomes by DNA-binding fluorescent agents." *Chromosoma* 30 (1970): 215–227.

With G. Lomakka and L. Zech. "The 24 Fluorescence Patterns of the Human Metaphase Chromosomes—Distinguishing Characters and Variability. *Hereditas* 67 (1971): 89–102.

OTHER SOURCES

Klein, G. G., and E. Klein. "Torbjörn Caspersson: Some Personal Perspectives." *Cytometry* 5 (1984): 318.

Nurnberger, J. I. "Ultraviolet Microscopy and Microspectroscopy." In *Analytical Cytology: Methods for*

Studying Cellular Form and Function, edited by R. C. Mellors. New York: McGraw Hill, 1955.

William Bechtel

CATTELL, JAMES MCKEEN

CATTELL, JAMES MCKEEN (*b.* Easton, Pennsylvania, 25 May 1860, *d.* Lancaster, Pennsylvania, 20 January 1944), *psychology, scientific journal editing.* For the original article on Cattell see *DSB,* vol. 3.

Cattell's scientific work and programmatic statements—with their focus on quantification, potential applicability, and a concern for human behavior—helped shape the course of twentieth-century "scientific" psychology. His editorial and institutional activities, especially his fifty-year editorship of *Science,* provided an organizational infrastructure that supported the American scientific community through the same period.

Education and Early Scientific Successes. At Lafayette College (AB, 1880), Cattell studied Baconian ideas with philologist Francis Andrew March and, on his own, Comtean positivism. His later approach to science combined a Comtean emphasis on quantification with a Baconian appreciation for the hypothesis-free collection of empirical "facts" and the usefulness of science. His scientific work thus featured methods that produced quantitative data about (potentially applicable) psychological phenomena, even if he often could not explain them. At Lafayette (which his father, William C. Cattell, served as president, and of which his maternal grandfather, James McKeen, was the major benefactor) Cattell also developed a self-righteous expectation of deference from others, an attitude that often alienated his peers and colleagues.

Hoping to emulate March's scholarly career, Cattell studied at the universities of Göttingen and Leipzig before assuming a fellowship at Johns Hopkins University in 1882. There he showed great experimental skill by timing individuals' reading of letters and words and claiming that people naturally read whole words, rather than syllables. (This study later reinforced the "whole-word" approach to reading education.) In 1883, he lost his fellowship and returned to Leipzig. In 1886, he became the first American to earn a German PhD in experimental psychology with Wilhelm Wundt, who is often credited with establishing the new science. Cattell's dissertation research measured reaction times under varying conditions more precisely than any previous study. As he worked, he soon found that Wundt's preferred methods—which involved *innere wahrnehmung* (internal perception, or simply perceiving subjective events, a procedure often confused with the more rigorous *selbstbeobachtung* and mistranslated as

James McKeen Cattell. ARCHIVES OF THE HISTORY OF AMERICAN PSYCHOLOGY. REPRODUCED BY PERMISSION.

introspection)—gave inconsistent results. He thus abandoned these procedures to emphasize the behavior of his subjects—a term he apparently introduced in reports on psychological experiments—and set a precedent that many later psychologists followed.

In 1886, Cattell became a Fellow-Commoner at St. Johns College, Cambridge. Following visits to Francis Galton's Anthropometric Laboratory in London, Cattell assimilated into his approach to science Galton's interest in differences among individuals. Galton developed this interest into a program of positive eugenics, an idea that Cattell found congenial; Cattell and his wife—Josephine Owen, an Englishwoman who had studied music in Leipzig—had seven children.

Experimental Accomplishments and Disappointments. In 1889, Cattell assumed a professorship at the University of Pennsylvania, where he performed two elaborate series of experiments. With biologist Charles S. Dolley, he continued his reaction-time studies in an attempt to measure the velocity of the nervous impulse. With philosopher George S. Fullerton, he extended traditional psychophysical techniques whose proponents claimed they measured the relation between (physical) stimulus and (mental) sensation, and used his results to argue against any mentalistic interpretation of his (or others') experiments.

Cattell moved to Columbia University in 1891, where he developed an influential program of "mental tests." He and his collaborators used standard laboratory procedures—measuring (among other traits) reaction times, short-term memory, and the sensitivity of the senses—to gather quantitative data on psychological differences. But the studies lacked a functional view of how these traits helped people live their lives, and because the tests produced no useful results, psychologists soon abandoned them. Cattell then left the laboratory, but in 1901 his earlier experimental achievement led to his election as the first psychologist in the National Academy of Sciences. Three years later, while addressing "The Conceptions and Methods of Psychology," he urged his colleagues to apply their science to practical problems, and those who later developed an explicitly applied psychology often emphasized Cattell's inspiration.

Editorial Achievements. From 1894, when he founded *The Psychological Review* with Princeton colleague James Mark Baldwin, Cattell owned, edited, and eventually published many major scientific journals. In late 1894, he took control of the failing weekly *Science*, and in 1900 it became—even though privately owned—the official journal of the American Association for the Advancement of Science (AAAS). This arrangement greatly increased AAAS membership, *Science*'s circulation, and Cattell's advertising income. Before 1920, he used *Science* to initiate debates over major policy issues, including the work of federal scientific bureaus, plans for the Carnegie Institution of Washington's $10 million endowment, and the governance of higher education. After 1915, *Science* emphasized discussions about support for scientific research and both the National Research Council and the AAAS's own Committee of One Hundred on Scientific Research. These concerns attracted additional readers, and this growing readership (and its weekly publication schedule) in turn led many American scientists to publish their best work in *Science*.

Cattell took over another failing journal, *The Popular Science Monthly*, in 1900, and used his *Science*-based network to attract contributors. (In 1915, he sold the journal's name, but continued it as *The Scientific Monthly*.) In 1903, Cattell began collecting data for what emerged in 1906 as the first edition of *American Men of Science*, a directory of the country's scientific workers. He also used these data in his studies of scientific eminence, which he repeated, with modifications, for the six later *American Men of Science* editions he oversaw. In 1904, he sold his share of *The Psychological Review* and, in 1907, took over *The American Naturalist*. He initially hoped that the *Nat-*

uralist would encourage positive eugenics, but he soon came to rely on the editorial guidance of Columbia colleague Thomas H. Morgan, and the journal instead promoted Mendelian genetics. In 1915, he founded *School and Society* to serve educators as *Science* served scientists. He edited these publications through the 1930s—and *Science* through the early 1940s—and they defined his position in the American scientific community.

Institutional Failures. Even as American scientists respected Cattell's scientific and editorial achievements, they resented his self-righteous approach. This attitude at times emerged as a defense of academic freedom, and in 1913, he collected a series of *Science* articles in a volume, *University Control.* But his verbal and written statements often included public attacks on others, which cost him friends. When Columbia president Nicholas Murray Butler tried to force Cattell to retire in 1913, friends admitted Cattell's personal shortcomings but rushed to his defense. Nevertheless, he gradually alienated most of them, including his long-time supporters at Columbia, anthropologist Franz Boas and philosopher John Dewey. In 1917, when the university finally fired Cattell, ostensibly for opposing U.S. conscription policy during World War I, he found few supporters. He sued Columbia for libel and, in 1922, won a monetary settlement. He used some of it to found the Psychological Corporation, which tried to implement his interest in applied psychology. Cattell, however, emphasized the firm's organization and never could explain how psychologists actually applied their science. The corporation floundered until 1926, when psychologists with significant experience with "real world" problems assumed its control.

Through the 1920s and 1930s, Cattell continued to edit his journals and chair the AAAS Executive Committee, and he acted as psychology's grand old man. His last years, however, proved disappointing. *Science* grew duller and attracted both growing criticism and fewer readers, younger scientists lost interest in his continued studies of scientific eminence, and he continued to alienate others. Under his leadership the AAAS hired and fired four permanent secretaries through the 1930s, and a public personal attack (as president of the 1929 International Congress of Psychology) on Duke University researcher William McDougall scandalized American psychologists. In 1941, the AAAS Executive Committee finally forced Cattell from its chair. Although he edited *Science* until his death, his continued relationships with AAAS officials were cool at best.

SUPPLEMENTARY BIBLIOGRAPHY

The Library of Congress holds an exceptionally valuable collection of Cattell papers. (It tripled in size in the early 1970s, after Nathan Reingold submitted his original DSB *article on Cattell. The original article also could not benefit from the post-1970 spurt of research on psychology's past and—led largely by Reingold—on the twentieth-century American scientific community.) Cattell's papers are also held in Central Files, Columbia University, New York. Although Columbia University's Manuscripts Library and the Columbiana Collection both also hold collections of Cattell material, the records of all Columbia faculty and administrative officers available in the university's Central Files are much more valuable.*

WORKS BY CATTELL

James McKeen Cattell: Man of Science, edited by A. T. Poffenberger. 2 vols. Lancaster, PA: The Science Press, 1947. Collects many of Cattell's most important scientific and programmatic papers and includes an incomplete bibliography.

"APA's First Publication: Proceedings of the American Psychological Association, 1892–1893." *American Psychologist* 28 (1973): 277–292. A facsimile reprint of a major report that Cattell edited for publication in 1894.

An Education in Psychology: James McKeen Cattell's Journal and Letters from Germany and England, 1880–1888, edited by Michael M. Sokal. Cambridge, MA: MIT Press, 1981.

OTHER SOURCES

Pillsbury, Walter B. "Biographical Memoir of James McKeen Cattell, 1860–1944." *National Academy of Science Biographical Memoirs* 25 (1949): 1–16. Includes an incomplete bibliography.

The Psychological Researchers of James McKeen Cattell: A Review by Some of His Students. New York: The Science Press, 1914.

Sokal, Michael M. "The Unpublished Autobiography of James McKeen Cattell." *American Psychologist* 26 (1971): 626–635.

———. "*Science* and James McKeen Cattell, 1894–1945." *Science* 209 (1980): 43–52.

———. "The Origins of the Psychological Corporation." *Journal of the History of the Behavioral Sciences* 17 (1981): 54–67.

———. "James McKeen Cattell and the Failure of Anthropometric Mental Testing, 1890–1901." In *The Problematic Science: Psychology in Nineteenth-Century Thought*, edited by William R. Woodward and Mitchell G. Ash. New York: Praeger, 1982.

———. "James McKeen Cattell and American Psychology in the 1920s." In *Explorations in the History of Psychology in the United States*, edited by Josef Brožek. Lewisburg, PA: Bucknell University Press, 1984.

———. "Life-Span Developmental Psychology and the History of Science." In *Beyond History of Science: Essays in Honor of Robert E. Schofield*, edited by Elizabeth W. Garber. Bethlehem, PA: Lehigh University Press, 1990. Provides an interpretive overview of Cattell's life and career.

———. "James McKeen Cattell, the New York Academy of Sciences, and the American Psychological Association, 1891–1902." In *Aspects of the History of Psychology in America: 1892–1992*, edited by Helmut E. Adler and Robert W. Rieber (*Annals of the New York Academy of Sciences*, vol. 727, 1994), pp. 13–35.

———. "Stargazing: James McKeen Cattell, *American Men of Science*, and the Reward Structure of the American Scientific Community, 1906–44." In *Psychology, Science, and Human Affairs: Essays in Honor of William Bevan*, edited by Frank Kessel. Boulder, CO: Westview, 1995.

———. "Baldwin, Cattell, and the *Psychological Review*: A Collaboration and Its Discontents." *History of the Human Sciences* 10 (1997): 57–89.

———. "Promoting Science in a New Century: The Middle Years of the AAAS." In *The Establishment of Science in America: 150 Years of the American Association for the Advancement of Science*, by Sally Gregory Kohlstedt, Michael M. Sokal, and Bruce V. Lewenstein. New Brunswick, NJ: Rutgers University Press, 1999.

———, and Patrice A. Rafail, eds. *A Guide to Manuscript Collections in the History of Psychology and Related Areas*. Millwood, NY: Kraus, 1982. Describes collections in which much of Cattell's correspondence with his psychological contemporaries may be found.

Michael M. Sokal

CAUCHY, AUGUSTIN-LOUIS (*b.* Paris, France, 21 August 1789; *d.* Sceaux [near Paris], 23 May 1857), *mathematics, mathematical physics, celestial mechanics.* For the original article on Cauchy see *DSB,* vol. 3.

Since the publication of Hans Freudenthal's lengthy *DSB* article in 1971, several books and a host of articles have appeared exploring Cauchy's extensive contributions to mathematical science. Four books are devoted exclusively to Cauchy, by Judith Grabiner (1981), Amy Dahan-Dalmédico (1992), Bruno Belhoste (1991), and Frank Smithies (1997). Grabiner provides a detailed account of Cauchy's contributions to the foundations of calculus. In addition to presenting an extended analysis of Cauchy's science, Dahan-Dalmédico situates Cauchy within the French scientific milieu of the late eighteenth century and first part of the nineteenth century. Belhoste presents a comprehensive biography of Cauchy, giving a balanced account of his life, mathematical science, and philosophy that supersedes Claude Alphonse Valson's uncritical biography of 1868. Smithies concentrates on Cauchy's seminal role in the creation of complex function theory.

The last volume of Cauchy's *Oeuvres complètes* appeared in 1976, containing several *mémoires détachés* as well as a range of miscellaneous material. The volume ends with a detailed bibliography relating to Cauchy. In 1981 there appeared a substantial fragment of several previously unpublished lectures that Cauchy delivered in the early 1820s at the École Polytechnique in Paris on the subject of ordinary differential equations. In 1989 a conference was held at the École Polytechnique itself to commemorate the bicentennial of Cauchy's birth. The proceedings of the conference were published as the first issue of *Revue d'Histoire des Sciences* in 1992 and included a bibliography of historical literature that had appeared since 1976.

Contributions to Analysis. Historical research on eighteenth-century calculus has resulted in an increased appreciation of Cauchy's groundbreaking contributions to the foundations of analysis. Craig Fraser (1989), Marco Panza (1996), and Giovanni Ferraro (2004) have documented the conceptual gulf that separated the formal-analytic approach of Leonhard Euler and Joseph-Louis Lagrange from the arithmetic and conceptual style of Cauchy. Not only did Cauchy put calculus on a rigorous technical foundation that became standard, his work also contributed to a radical new philosophical conception of analysis and its place in exact science.

Grabiner (1981) examines the origin of Cauchy's calculus techniques in the work of earlier mathematicians, especially Lagrange, and provides English translations of some of his key results concerning functions and integrals. Smithies (1986) examines Cauchy's understanding of rigor in relation to the eighteenth-century belief in the "generality of algebra." Both Ivor Grattan-Guinness (1970) and Umberto Bottazzini (1986) include extended accounts of Cauchy's foundation within broader surveys of the history of analysis. Bottazzini's (1992) introduction to a reprint of the first part of Cauchy's 1821 treatise on algebraic analysis discusses technical, historical, and conceptual issues involved in an understanding of Cauchy's achievement. Thierry Guitard (1986) considers the relationship of the work of André-Marie Ampère and Cauchy, while Christian Gilain (1989) presents a detailed study of Cauchy's teachings on analysis from 1816 to 1830 at the École Polytechnique.

The novel conception of analysis at the base of Cauchy's work brought with it a new understanding of mathematical existence. Solutions to differential equations were no longer assumed to be given but rather constructed through specified processes of analysis. Gilain (1981) provides a historical account of existence questions for ordinary differential equations; his essay appears as the introduction to the 1981 edition of Cauchy's lectures. A useful overview of existence theorems is given by Morris Kline (1972, chapters 28 and 29), who also situates Cauchy within the broader development of nineteenth-century analysis. Kline (p. 671) asserts that during this period partial differential equations "became and remain the heart of mathematics" and describes a fundamental existence theorem from the subject first obtained by Cauchy. A detailed account of Cauchy's work on partial differential equations is given by Dahan-Dalmédico (1992, chapter 7).

Two special topics concerning Cauchy's calculus should be mentioned. The first is the relationship of his ideas to those of his contemporary Bernhard Bolzano, a subject that is explored by Grattan-Guinness (1970), Hans Freudenthal (1971) and Hourya Sinaceur (1973). The other concerns the place of infinitesimals in Cauchy's calculus and the possible relevance of such modern theories as nonstandard analysis to an historical appraisal of his achievement. Studies here have been written by Imre Lakatos (1978), Gordon Fisher (1978), Detlef Laugwitz (1978, 1989) and Detlef D. Spalt (2002). Laugwitz's thesis is that certain of Cauchy's results that were criticized by later mathematicians are in fact valid if one is willing to accept certain assumptions about Cauchy's understanding and use of infinitesimals. These assumptions reflect a theory of analysis and infinitesimals that was worked out by Laugwitz and Curt Schmieden during the 1950s.

Cauchy was a formative figure in the creation of complex analysis, one of the most impressive branches of mathematics to emerge in the nineteenth century. The subject was a prominent one in Freudenthal's original article and has since attracted considerable historical attention. Detailed accounts are given by Bottazzini (1986, chapter 4), Belhoste (1991, chapter 7), Grattan-Guinness (1990, chapter 10.2) and Smithies (1997). Cauchy's investigations grew out of a new conception of integration. In the eighteenth century, integration was understood as the algorithmic inverse of differentiation: The primitive or integral of a given function was the function that when differentiated produced the given function. What later became known as the definite integral was understood as the difference between the values of the primitive at two values of the independent variable. By contrast, Cauchy envisaged the integral as the limit of a sum and recognized that it was necessary to show that such a limit exists. In the investigation that was stimulated by the new definition, he was led to consider definite integrals in which the limits of integration are complex numbers. This point of view was combined with the formal theory he had developed for complex functions and singular integrals. A stream of important researches beginning in 1814 culminated in 1825 with the appearance of his masterpiece, "Sur les intégrales prises entre des limites imaginaires." This work laid the foundation for the calculus of residues and was the basis of subsequent researches by Cauchy up to the late 1840s.

Physical Science and Continuous Media. A prominent area of historical work since the 1970s has been the study of the mathematization of physical science in France in the early nineteenth century. Dahan-Dalmédico (1992) identifies several different styles of mathematization that were at work and gives an account of Cauchy's contributions to hydrodynamics and elasticity. An important

Augustin-Louis Cauchy. © BETTMANN/CORBIS.

theme of Belhoste's (1991) biography is that even results that have traditionally been viewed as part of pure analysis were connected to techniques and problems arising in physical science. Cauchy's various contributions to analysis and applied mathematics are described in some detail by Grattan-Guinness (1990).

Cauchy's interest in continuous media originated in a study beginning around 1815 of the propagation of waves at the surface of a liquid of specified depth. Continuum mechanics as a coherent branch of mathematical science was set forth in a major paper composed in 1822 as well as in several lengthy papers written later in the decade. In the original *DSB* article Freudenthal wrote, "Never had Cauchy given the world a work as mature from the outset as this," and asserted that a developed theory of elasticity was his most important contribution to science, elevating him to the ranks of the greatest scientists. The circumstances of the competitive scientific research environment of the period as well as an account of Cauchy's theory are provided by Belhoste (1991). Dahan-Dalmédico (1992, part 4) examines the interconnected researches of Siméon-Denis Poisson, Claude Navier, and Cauchy. The role of Cauchy's theory in the history of tensor calculus is described by Dieter Herbert (1991, chapter 2).

During the late 1820s Cauchy turned to the elaboration of a molecular model of a continuous media, follow-

ing the prevailing notions of Laplacian physics. This research was closely connected to an interest in Auguste Fresnel's wave theory of light, a topic that occupied Cauchy's attention increasingly during the 1830s. An account of this transition in Cauchy's scientific thought as well as an exposition of his optical theory is given by Dahan-Dalmédico (1992, chapter 13). Cauchy's conception of a molecular or punctiform optical ether is analyzed by Jed Buchwald (1980), who also situates Cauchy's optical researches in the context of Fresnel's theory.

Algebra, Theory of Errors. In the field of algebra, Luboš Nový's (1973) history of this subject contains a detailed discussion of Cauchy's results on permutation groups; this account is a shortened version of the author's studies in Russian from 1966. Dahan-Dalmédico (1980–1981) considers this subject as well as the relationship of Cauchy and Évariste Galois. The latter relationship is also the focus of an article by René Taton (1971). Thomas Hawkins (1975) documents some of Cauchy's results in linear algebra concerning the eigenvalues of linear transformations, a subject that the author calls "spectral theory."

Cauchy's contributions to the theory of errors were comparatively minor but still noteworthy. Two studies related to what is known as the Cauchy distribution have been published by Stephen Stigler (1974) and Ivo Schneider (1987). Cauchy's disagreement with his contemporary I. J. Bienaymé about the value of Pierre-Simon Laplace's theory is documented by Christoper C. Heyde and Eugene Seneta (1977).

Reception and Reputation. Since 1971 a sizable literature has developed on the reception of Cauchy's mathematical science in various countries of Europe. Jesper Lützen (1990) considers the French scene at the middle of the century, Bottazzini (1989) examines Cauchy and Italian analysis, H. Niels Jahnke (1987) and Reich (2003) explore the reception of Cauchy's ideas in Germany, and Adrian Rice (2001) looks at the introduction of his calculus into Britain. Schubring (2005) provides a contextual study of Cauchy's work on the foundations of analysis, confirming his status as a critical figure in the development of nineteenth-century mathematical thought.

René Taton wrote a short introduction to the reprint in 1970 of Valson's biography of Cauchy. Taton opened with the comment that, after Carl Friedrich Gauss, whose preeminence was beyond discussion, Cauchy was one of the leading mathematicians of the first half of the nineteenth century. In the period since 1970 it is significant to note that Cauchy has attracted considerably more historical attention than has Gauss, a fact that speaks to the historical importance of the French savant. The evidence that has accumulated suggests that Taton's ranking might be challenged, and that while Gauss's achievements were certainly monumental, it was Cauchy who was the preeminent mathematician of his time.

SUPPLEMENTARY BIBLIOGRAPHY

WORKS BY CAUCHY

Oeuvres complètes. Series 2, vol. 15. Paris: Gauthier-Villars, 1974.

Équations différentielles ordinaires: Cours inédit. Fragment. Paris: Études Vivantes; New York: Johnson Reprint Corporation, 1981. With an introduction by Christian Gilain.

Cours d'analyse de l'École Royale Polytechnique. Première partie: Analyse algébrique. Vol. 7 (1990) of *Instrumenta Rationis.* Reprint of the 1821 edition with an introduction by Umberto Bottazzini. Bologna, Italy: Editrice, 1992.

OTHER SOURCES

Belhoste, Bruno. *Augustin-Louis Cauchy: A Biography.* Translated by Frank Ragland. New York: Springer, 1991.

Bottazzini, Umberto. *The Higher Calculus: A History of Real and Complex Analysis from Euler to Weierstrass.* Translated by Warren Van Egmond. New York: Springer, 1986.

——————— "I matematici italiani e la 'moderna analisi' di Cauchy." *Archimede* 41 (1) (1989):15–29.

———. Introduction (in English) to *Cours d'analyse de l'École Royale Polytechnique. Première partie: Analyse algébrique,* by Augustin-Louis Cauchy, xi–clvii. Bologna, Italy: Editrice, 1992.

Buchwald, Jed. "Optics and the Theory of the Punctiform Ether." *Archive for History of Exact Sciences* 21 (1980): 245–278.

Dahan-Dalmédico, Amy. "Les travaux de Cauchy sur les substitutions: Étude de son approche du concept de groupe." *Archive for History of Exact Sciences* 23 (1980–1981): 279–319.

———. *Mathématisations: Augustin-Louis Cauchy et l'École Française.* Paris: A. Blanchard, 1992.

Ferraro, Giovanni. "Differentials and Differential Coefficients in the Eulerian Foundations of the Calculus." *Historia Mathematica* 31 (2004): 34–61.

Fisher, Gordon. "Cauchy and the Infinitely Small." *Historia Mathematica* 5 (1978): 313–331.

Fraser, Craig. "The Calculus as Algebraic Analysis: Some Observations on Mathematical Analysis in the 18th Century." *Archive for History of Exact Sciences* 39 (1989): 317–335.

Freudenthal, Hans. "Did Cauchy Plagiarize Bolzano?" *Archive for History of Exact Sciences* 7 (1971): 375–392.

Gilain, Christian. Introduction to *Équations différentielles ordinaires: Cours inédit. Fragment,* by Augustin-Louis Cauchy, xi–lvi. Paris: Études Vivantes; New York: Johnson Reprint Corporation, 1981.

———. "Cauchy et le cours d'analyse de l'École Polytechnique." *Bulletin de la Société des Amis de la Bibliothèque de l'École Polytechnique* 5 (1989): 1–145.

Grabiner, Judith V. *The Origins of Cauchy's Rigorous Calculus.* Cambridge, MA: MIT Press, 1981.

Grattan-Guinness, Ivor. "Bolzano, Cauchy, and the 'New Analysis' of the Early Nineteenth Century." *Archive for History of Exact Sciences* 6 (1970): 372–400.

———. *The Development of the Foundations of Mathematical Analysis from Cauchy to Riemann.* Cambridge, MA: MIT Press, 1970.

———. *Convolutions in French Mathematics, 1800–1840.* 3 vols. Basel, Switzerland: Birkhäuser, 1990.

Guitard, Thierry. "La querelle des infiniment petits à l'École Polytechnique au XIXᵉ siècle." *Historia Scientiarum* 30 (1986): 1–161.

Hawkins, Thomas. "Cauchy and the Spectral Theory of Matrices." *Historia Mathematica* 2 (1975): 1–29.

Herbert, Dieter. *Die Entstehung des Tensorkalküls von den Anfängen in der Elastizitätstheorie bis zur Verwendung in der Baustatik.* Stuttgart, Germany: Franz Steiner Verlag, 1991.

Heyde, Chris C., and Eugene Seneta. *I. J. Bienaymé: Statistical Theory Anticipated.* New York: Springer, 1977.

Jahnke, H. Niels. "Motive und Probleme der Arithmetisierung der Mathematik in der ersten Hälfte des 19. Jahrhunderts— Cauchys Analysis in der Sicht des Mathematikers Martin Ohm." *Archive for History of Exact Sciences* 37 (1987): 101–182.

Kline, Morris. *Mathematical Thought from Ancient to Modern Times.* New York: Oxford University Press, 1972.

Lakatos, Imre. "Cauchy and the Continuum: The Significance of Nonstandard Analysis for the History and Philosophy of Mathematics." *Mathematical Intelligencer* 1 (1978): 151–161.

Laugwitz, Detlef. "Infinitely Small Quantities in Cauchy's Textbooks." *Historia Mathematica* 14 (1978): 258–274.

———. "Definite Values of Infinite Sums: Aspects of the Foundations of Infinitesimal Analysis around 1820." *Archive for History of Exact Sciences* 39 (1989):195–245.

Lützen, Jesper. *Joseph Liouville, 1809–1882: Master of Pure and Applied Mathematics.* New York: Springer, 1990.

Nový, Luboš. *Origins of Modern Algebra.* Leyden, Netherlands: Noordhoff International Publishing, 1973.

Panza, Marco. "Concept of Function, between Quantity and Form, in the 18th Century." In *History of Mathematics and Education: Ideas and Experiences,* edited by Hans Niels Jahnke et al., 241–274. Göttingen, Germany: Vandenhoeck & Ruprecht, 1996.

Reich, Karin. "Cauchy und Gauß. Cauchys Rezeption im Umfeld von Gauß." *Archive for History of Exact Sciences* 57 (2003): 433–463.

Rice, Adrian. "A Gradual Innovation: The Introduction of Cauchian Calculus into Mid-Nineteenth-Century Britain." *Proceedings of the Canadian Society for the History and Philosophy of Mathematics* 13 (2001): 48–63.

Schneider, Ivo. "Laplace and Hereafter: The Status of Probability Calculus in the Nineteenth Century." In *The Probabilistic Revolution.* Vol. 1, *Ideas in History,* edited by Lorenz Krüger et al., 191–214. Cambridge, MA: MIT Press, 1987.

Schubring, Gert. *Conflicts between Generalization, Rigor, and Intuition Number Concepts Underlying the Development of Analysis in 17–19th Century France and Germany.* New York: Springer, 2005.

Sinaceur, Hourya. "Cauchy et Bolzano." *Revue d'Histoire des Sciences* 26 (1973): 97–112.

Smithies, Frank. "Cauchy's Conception of Rigor in Analysis." *Archive for History of Exact Sciences* 36 (1986): 41–61.

———. *Cauchy and the Creation of Complex Function Theory.* New York: Cambridge University Press, 1997.

Spalt, Detlef D. "Cauchys Kontinuum: Eine historiografische Annäherung via Cauchys Summensatz." *Archive for History of Exact Sciences* 56 (2002): 285–338.

Stigler, Stephen. "Studies in the History of Probability and Statistics XXXIII. Cauchy and the Witch of Agnesi: An Historical Note on the Cauchy Distribution." *Biometrika* 61 (1974): 375–380.

Taton, René. Introduction to *La vie et les travaux du Baron Cauchy,* by Claude Alphonse Valson. Paris: A. Blanchard, 1970.

———. "Sur les relations scientifiques d'Augustin Cauchy et d'Évariste Galois. *Revue d'Histoire des Sciences* 24 (1971): 123–148.

Craig Fraser

Margaret Cavendish. © BETTMANN/CORBIS.

CAVENDISH, MARGARET, DUCHESS OF NEWCASTLE (*b.* Colchester, England, 1623 [?]; *d.* Welbeck Abbey, Nottinghamshire, 15 December 1673), *atomism, materialism, vitalism, women in science.*

Cavendish was the first woman to write about science in English. She developed a unique natural philosophy, as well as publishing poetry, romances, plays, and essays. Her importance as a thinker has been recognized by the inclusion of the second edition of her most important treatise, the 1668 *Observations upon Natural Philosophy,* in the Cambridge *Texts in the History of Philosophy* series. Cavendish's natural philosophy is the first example of the reception and reconstitution of the ideas of New Science by a woman. Her significance lies in her priority and in her originality: She felt her sex ultimately enabled rather than hindered her ability to be a natural philosopher and to be the peer of masculine interpreters of nature.

Family Connections. Gender shaped both the articulation and content of her philosophy. Cavendish was poorly educated, although she was a member of a prominent gentry family, the Lucases of Colchester in Essex who had risen to preeminence during the Tudor period. Her widowed mother, Elizabeth Lucas, preferred her daughters to be schooled in virtue rather than learning and the tutors she employed "were rather for formality then benefit" (Margaret Cavendish, *A True Relation of my Birth, Breeding and Life* [1656], in Bowerbank and Mendelson, *Paper Bodies,* 43). Cavendish embraced an epistemology that privileged introspection and imagination over logic and experimentation. She was skeptical that perception based only on the senses could do anything but delude the observer. Her most developed natural philosophy was a kind of vitalistic materialism that she composed as a response to and repudiation of mechanistic materialism. Cavendish was not a brilliant natural philosopher. Her style was abstruse and some of her theories are strange, even in the context of her own time. But her idiosyncrasies reveal how gender and culture functioned in the seventeenth century, a period when women were increasingly excluded from all intellectual activities.

Cavendish was first exposed to new scientific ideas by her brother, John Lucas; her husband, William Cavendish, the Duke of Newcastle; and her brother-in-law, Sir Charles Cavendish. William was a patron of the arts and letters. Sir Charles was an amateur mathematician. After Margaret Cavendish joined the royal court in exile in 1644, she met and married Newcastle. He entertained Pierre Gassendi, Marin Mersenne, and René Descartes, and had a long association with Thomas Hobbes. Cavendish's direct contact with these thinkers was limited, but her husband and brother-in-law discussed their ideas with her and encouraged her to write her own philosophic musings.

Early Atomism and Materialism. Her first work, the 1653 *Poems and Fancies,* contains a verse rendition of atomism. Most scholars have characterized her atomism as an extreme form of mechanistic materialism; four differently shaped atoms—square, round, long, and sharp—constitute earth, water, air and fire. But even Cavendish's earliest philosophy contained vitalistic elements. The universe she described was seething with active principles and their conflicts. Atoms were reified as the functional equivalent of fairies: their motion causes thought and feeling. Like fairies, atoms were sentient and vital. In a companion work, the 1653 *Philosophic Fancies,* Cavendish explored how vital matter can produce an abundance of possible beings living on alternative worlds. Her early works self-consciously merged philosophy and fancy in materialistic speculations.

By 1655, Cavendish began to devote herself systematically to natural philosophy. The 1655 *Philosophical and Physical Opinions* began with a rejection of mechanical atomism. Her revised natural philosophy was materialistic and vitalistic. Matter came in three forms: rational matter, sensitive matter (which together composed something Cavendish calls innated matter), and inanimate matter, which was inert. All three were integrated in physical objects and vary only in their level of perception and self-movement. This doctrine of matter would continue to be the basis for all of Cavendish's subsequent scientific thought. She immediately faced the religious and moral difficulties associated with a philosophy of living matter in a companion work to *Opinions,* the 1656 *Natures Pictures.* The multiplicity of genres, including romances, comic tales, fantasies, and poetry in this work allowed Cavendish to give free rein to speculations about nature and God, and the role of gender in natural philosophy. In *Natures Pictures,* Cavendish justified her right to write natural philosophy and argued for a special kind of female knowledge.

Cavendish and New Science. After Cavendish's return to England with the Restoration, she developed her ideas in the 1664 *Philosophical Letters* by critiquing the work of Hobbes, Descartes, Van Helmont, and Henry More. She argued that particulate matter, as described by the mechanical philosophers, could never achieve order and harmony. Instead, Cavendish envisioned a material wholeness where parts, composed of the three forms of matter inextricably commingled, self-moving and self-conscious, were differentiated only by their own motions. She rejected the Hobbesian principles of force and determinism and instead argued that harmony rather than war is the natural state of the universe. Whereas Hobbes dis-

tinguished man from beasts by crediting man alone with speech and ratiocination, Cavendish contended that all beings, including beasts, possess reason and intelligence, at least of their own kind. There is a continuity of animate matter from stones to humans, which included those creatures usually regarded as irrational—animals, children, and, by implication, women.

Cavendish also denied the claims of the new experimental philosophers. She reacted with horror when the members of the Royal Society followed the Baconian vision of penetrating nature. The 1666 *Observations upon Experimental Philosophy* was a critique of Robert Hooke's *Micrographia*. Cavendish believed it was impossible to reveal the interiority of nature; the attempt was presumptuous as well as useless. But Cavendish was not content to merely criticize the experimenters. She also felt the need to parody their behavior and to assert her own right to be a female natural philosopher. Published in the same volume with *Observations* was a parody of the Royal Society called *The Blazing World*. In this fantastical romance, a young lady becomes Empress of the Blazing World, whose inhabitants are beast-men. She organized them into scientific societies. These hermaphroditical creatures are both metamorphosed experimenters and the objects they study. In *The Blazing World*, Cavendish imagined a world where a female natural philosopher could not only exist, but rule.

The year after Cavendish published *Observations* and *The Blazing* World, she asked to be invited to visit the Royal Society. She became the first and only woman to visit the Society in the seventeenth century, and the members feared her notoriety and eccentricity would reflect on them. Indeed, her visit functioned as a tangible vindication of her own philosophy and status and a subversion of male pretensions in natural philosophy. Whereas most scholars accept the notion that Cavendish was overwhelmed by the experience, a more nuanced reading of the incident shows that Cavendish was ridiculing the Royal Society by treating their displays as a kind of circus side-show. Her last work, the 1668 *Grounds of Natural Philosophy* demeaned the Royal Society and once again stated her material philosophy. She was eulogized by the playwright Thomas Shadwell: "Philosophers must wander in the dark, All did depend on Her, but She on none, For her Philosophy was all her own" (Thomas Shadwell, in *A Collection of Letters and Poems Written by Several Persons of Honour and Learning, Upon Divers Important Subjects, to the late Duke and Duchess of Newcastle (London, 1678)*, 166).

BIBLIOGRAPHY

WORKS BY CAVENDISH

Philosophical Fancies. London, 1653.

Poems and Fancies. London, 1653.

Philosophical and Physical Opinions. London, 1655.

Natures Pictures. London, 1656.

Philosophical Letters. London, 1664.

Grounds of Natural Philosophy. London, 1668.

Observations upon Experimental Philosophy. To which is added, The Description of a New Blazing World. London, 1666; rev. London, 1668.

The Blazing World and Other Writings. Edited by Kate Lilley. London: Penguin, 1994.

Paper Bodies: A Margaret Cavendish Reader. Edited by Sylvia Bowerbank and Sara Mendelson. Ontario: Broadview Press, 2000.

Observations upon Experimental Philosophy. Edited by Eileen O'Neill. Cambridge, U.K.: Cambridge University Press, 2001.

OTHER SOURCES

Battigelli, Anna. *Margaret Cavendish and the Exiles of the Mind.* Lexington: University Press of Kentucky, 1998. Argues Cavendish's scientific thought arose from the experience of exile.

Campbell, Mary Baine. *Wonder & Science: Imagining Worlds in Early Modern Europe.* Ithaca, NY: Cornell University Press, 1999. Intriguing discussion of Cavendish and Thomas Hooke.

Clucas, Stephen, ed. *A Princely Brave Woman: Essays on Margaret Cavendish, Duchess of Newcastle.* Hampshire, U.K.: Ashgate Press, 2003. Collection of articles, several devoted to natural philosophy.

———. "The Atomism of the Cavendish Circle: A Reappraisal." *The Seventeenth Century* 9 (1994): 247–273. Argues that Cavendish's atomism developed from native English traditions.

Harris, Frances. "Living in the Neighborhood of Science. Mary Evelyn Margaret Cavendish and the Greshamites." In *Women, Science and Medicine: 1500–1700,* edited by Lynette Hunter and Sarah Hutton: Stroud, U.K.: Sutton Publishing, 1997.

Hutton, Sarah. "Anne Conway, Margaret Cavendish and Seventeenth Century Scientific Thought." In *Women, Science and Medicine: 1500–1700,* edited by Lynette Hunter and Sara Hutton, 218–234. Stroud, U.K.: Sutton Publishing, 1997.

———. "In Dialogue with Thomas Hobbes: Margaret Cavendish's Natural Philosophy." *Women's Writing* 4 (1997): 421–432.

James, Susan. "The Innovations of Margaret Cavendish." *British Journal for the History of Philosophy* 7 (1999): 219–244. Excellent introduction to Cavendish's natural philosophy.

Keller, Eve. "Producing Petty Gods: Margaret Cavendish's Critique of Experimental Science." *English Literary History* 64 (1997): 447–472.

Mendelson, Sara Heller. *The Mental World of Stuart Women.* Amherst: University of Massachusetts Press, 1987. Good short summary of Cavendish's thought.

Mintz, S.I. "The Duchess of Newcastle's Visit to the Royal Society." *Journal of English and Germanic Philology* 51 (1952): 168–176. Classic but now out-of-date discussion of Cavendish's visit to the Royal Society.

Rees, Emma. *Margaret Cavendish: Gender, Genre, Exile.* Manchester: Manchester University Press, 2003.

Rogers, John. "Margaret Cavendish and the Gendering of the Vitalist Utopia." In *The Matter of Revolution: Science, Poetry, and Politics in the Age of Milton.* Ithaca, NY: Cornell University Press, 1996. Connects Cavendish's natural philosophy and liberal political theory.

Sarasohn, Lisa. "A Science Turned Upside Down: Feminism and the Natural Philosophy of Margaret Cavendish." *Huntington Library Quarterly* 47 (1984): 299–307. Discusses the relationship of Cavendish's materialism and feminism.

Spiller, Elizabeth. "Reading through Galileo's Telescope: Margaret Cavendish and the Experience of Reading." *Renaissance Quarterly* 53 (2000): 192–221. Post-structuralist analysis of Cavendish's use of experimental imagery.

Whitaker, Katie. *Mad Madge: The Extraordinary Life of Margaret Cavendish, Duchess of Newcastle, the First Woman to Live by Her Pen.* New York: Basic Books, 2002. Detailed biography of Cavendish's life.

Lisa T. Sarasohn

CELSUS, CORNELIUS (AULUS)

CELSUS, CORNELIUS (AULUS) (*b.* southern France toward the end of the 1st century BCE; *d.* Rome, 1st century CE), *collection of knowledge.* For the original article on Celsus see *DSB,* vol. 3.

Celsus is often considered the most important Latin medical writer of antiquity for several reasons. His *Prefatio* is particularly important for medical historians, because in it he traces the history of medicine from its origins to his time. Of equal importance is the information he furnished about surgical techniques and medical authors of the Hellenistic-Roman period, which otherwise would not be known.

Celsus created a medical language in Latin. He synthesized and documented an entire series of works, achievements, and medical techniques of the Greco-Roman era which is our sole source of knowledge of them. He demonstrated great independence of thought and judgment. Finally, he described and represented the Roman ideal of the physician-friend (*medicus amicus*).

Life. Little is known about the details of his life except for his name (*nomen: Cornelius*) and his surname (*cognomen: Celsus*). Nothing else can be regarded as certain: not his given name (*praenomen*), his place of birth, the dates of composition of his work, or his profession. The ancient sources never gave his *praenomen,* only Cornelius Celsus. In later manuscripts it was usually given as the initial *A.,* that is sometimes interpreted as Aulus, sometimes, less plausibly, as Aurelius.

Neither the ancient documents nor Celsus himself mentioned a clear and definite birthplace. The hypothesis has been advanced that it was located somewhere in the region of Hispania Tarraconensis and Narbonnese Gaul (northeast Spain and southwest France), a conjecture based on discoveries in that region of a series of inscriptions recording various *Cornelii Celsi* and on the description of Gallic therapeutic techniques in *De medicina*. As for the date of composition of his work, the only certainty, which is also supported by linguistic evidence, is that Celsus lived and wrote between the last years of the first century BCE and the middle years of the next. Possibly he was most active between 21 and 39 CE.

Historians often debate the question of Celsus's profession; that is, whether he was a physician, but without reaching any definitive conclusion. The issue is somewhat secondary and in any case should be approached differently. On the one hand, no one doubts the technical knowledge of Celsus; on the other hand, there is a tendency to agree that this knowledge is not necessarily the result of a regular course of study leading to a medical degree. In any case neither course nor degree was required of professionals in the ancient world, nor does it presuppose the actual practice of medicine for money. Essentially, what is certain and of interest is Celsus's possession and mastery of precise medical knowledge; all the rest is irrelevant. There emerges from the *De medicina* a personality of notable substance whose primary characteristics seem to be a deep respect for life and for humanity, an ideological independence, and breadth in his historico-cultural interests.

Work. Although it is vague and therefore has been interpreted in various ways, the most comprehensive description of Celsus's work may be found in the *Institutio oratoria* of Quintilian (late first century CE):

> How much has Varro passed down to us, almost the whole of human knowledge! What rhetorical instrument did Cicero lack? What more can we say if even Cornelius Celsus, a man of modest ability, not only has written of all these arts, but he has left to us the precepts of military art, agriculture, and medicine presented in so coherent a manner that we must believe that he had a thorough knowledge of them. (XII.11.24)

From this passage of Quintilian one learns that Celsus wrote on agriculture, military art, medicine, and also "all these arts." Scholars disagree on the meaning of the expression "all these arts" (Latin: *his omnibus … artibus*), especially the sense of the word *artibus*. In essence, they offer three interpretations: (1) the "arts" are those three of which Quintilian speaks in the preceding paragraph, 9, of the same book, that is, philosophy, law, and rhetoric; (2)

Celsus. NATIONAL LIBRARY OF MEDICINE/PHOTO RESEARCHERS, INC.

the term *arts* is the equivalent of *instruments* or of the "precepts of oratory" and is to be understood as "all of rhetoric"; (3) *artes* are the techniques and instruments of the orator, that is, philosophy, law, and historical *exempla*.

At the very least, this passage from Quintilian provides undeniable evidence that Celsus wrote on medicine, military art, and agriculture, and probably, also on rhetoric, philosophy, law, and history. In the early twenty-first century eight books of medicine survive in their entirety, as well as many fragments that have come down indirectly through other works and writers and whose content could be categorized as dealing with agriculture, military art, rhetoric, and philosophy.

De medicina: **Content.** The eight books that comprise the *De medicina* are divided according to the three principal branches of treatment in Celsus's time: diet, pharmacology, and surgery. Books One through Four treat diet, Five and Six pharmacology, and the final two surgery. A substantial preamble introduces the work. Although they were well developed at the time, the more theoretical fields such as anatomy, physiology, and pathology, and individual specializations (which had become so subdivided that they occasioned the satire of contemporary poets such as Martial) are not accorded their own space or a book devoted specifically to them. But when it was necessary and the occasion arose, Celsus would then treat anatomy, the functioning of the different organs, and the dynamics of the various functions as well as specialized topics such as ophthalmology (e.g., the treatment of cataracts) and gynecology (e.g., embryotomy and embryology).

De medicina: **Sources.** A general consideration of the sources of *De medicina* is important because it provides important parameters for evaluating the scientific level of the *De medicina* and of its audience, and it throws light on the personality of its author. For the medical topics Celsus cites a total of eighty-five sources specifically by name and a number of anonymous references: Gauls, Greeks, a pupil of Chrysippus (*Chrysippi discipulus*), country folk (*agrestes, rustici*), and a certain person (*quidam*). The greatest names of early medicine occupy a preeminent place among the Celsian sources: Hippocrates, Diocles, Erasistratus, Herophilus, Heracleides of Tarentum, and Asclepiades of Bithynia.

Several pieces of evidence support the thesis of a direct, first-hand reading of previous or contemporary sources:

1. the implicit or explicit affirmation of a direct reading of the work indicated by verbs in the first person such as *invenio* "I find," *video* "I see," *deprehendi* "I understood," or through the mention of specific titles of works;

2. comparisons among the different authors upon whom he draws, with reference to the variations in the treatments of their subjects;

3. awareness of the terminological diversity in the sources, with the explicit statement that he noticed these differences through direct reading;

4. interpretation of individual passages within a broader context, that indicates extensive reading beyond the immediate object of study, a method clearly used with regard to Hippocrates and Erasistratus;

5. translation of passages from the Hippocratic corpus in conformity with Celsus's literary and stylistic exigencies.

His attitude toward his sources is sometimes complimentary, sometimes critical. It is never passive.

De medicina: **Audience.** Anyone who examines the *De medicina* will conclude that it was intended for an audience of wealthy and cultured persons. The professional status of Celsus's reader is far less certain: Was this a layperson, a medical student, or a physician?

Proof of the elevated cultural level of Celsus's reading public is provided by the historical and philosophical content, especially that of the preamble, and also by the linguistic and literary refinements of the language. Indirect evidence of a cultured audience can be inferred by noting that the intended reader of the books dealing with diet (in particular Book One) is called *imbecillus,* that is, a person of fragile health and one represented by city-dwellers and by almost all persons of letters.

The patient Celsus had in mind is wealthy. The first four books in particular recommend costly treatments (oil baths for cases of tetanus, travel as therapy for hemoptysis). The writer identifies civic duties, writing, reading, and mental work in general as dangerous activities—or at least activities that the patient being treated should avoid. The convalescence that Celsus recommends requires a long time, as well as expensive activities and nourishment (for example, the *gestatio* "passive movement by a means of transport," a varied food diet, etc.). The emphasis on the aesthetic consequences of therapy, especially surgery, is also significant in establishing the social and cultural level of his audience.

Particularly in Books Five and Six Celsus would appear to address lay readers and/or patients when he states that he intends to explain what should be done in a first operation, when he suggests remedies that do not involve either physicians or medications, when he approves even remedies alien to accepted medical practice, and when he lingers over details that would be superfluous if he were speaking to a professional physician, as when he stipulates that, unless otherwise specified, water is always understood to be the medium.

Other parts of the work, however, appear to be written for a physician or a medical student. Among these are not only the complex and delicate surgical operations impossible for a layperson such as the removal of limbs or parts of them and plastic surgery, but also the recommendations for medical deontology such as one reads in chapters three, five, and six of the third book and, especially, the description of an ideal physician.

The model of the physician that emerges from Celsus's *De medicina* is one who can easily identify with the cultured reader and presume to treat wealthy patients. For Celsus the ideal physician as described in various passages of Book Three should be cultured, not greedy for gain, expert, dedicated to few patients, a convincing speaker, and a friend to patients. In conclusion, the audience Celsus addresses is composed of the *medicus amicus,* the physician-friend who attends and treats the Roman aristocracy of the period.

De medicina: **Reception.** Although one can point to express mentions of Celsus's work in Columella, Pliny the

Elder and, albeit at second or third hand, Galen (second century CE), the *De medicina* enjoyed scant success among medical authors in Roman antiquity. It seems to have acquired recognition, prestige, and its canonization in official medical and professional circles only in late antiquity and the High Middle Ages: complete passages, sometimes quoted explicitly, sometimes not, found their way into academic texts intended for medical professionals, such as chapter 2.8 of the *Gynaecia Muscionis* (Moschion's gynaecia; a translation of Soranus's from the sixth century CE) or the numerous passages that a sixth-century translator introduced into the Latin version of the *Synopsis of Oribasius*. The utilization of Celsus in medical circles in the High Middle Ages finds further confirmation in some brief extracts that appear in a twelfth-century codex of the *Definitiones medicae* (Medical definitions) in the library of the Lincoln Cathedral, cod. Lat. 220. Other medieval authors to use the *De medicina* are Simon of Genoa (end of the thirteenth century) and Pietro D'Abano (thirteenth–fourteenth centuries).

From the Renaissance to the present day the reception of Celsus has been remarkable. After the *Editio princeps* of 1478, editions and reprints multiplied, more or less richly glossed and commented: There were nineteen in the fifteenth and sixteenth centuries alone. Praise for both its content and its language has been unanimous and numerous; Johann F. Clossius even set the work in elegiac couplets. In the Renaissance Celsus's language and the terminology that he coined became both a model to imitate and a source to be drawn upon by the humanist physicians of that period and of the centuries to follow, from Antonio M. Brasavola to Bartolomeo Eustachi to Andreas Vesalius to Gabriele Falloppia to Girolamo Cardano.

SUPPLEMENTARY BIBLIOGRAPHY

Conde Parrado, Pedro. Hipócrates latino. *El De medicina de Cornelio Celso en el Renacimiento*. Valladolid, Spain: Universidad de Valladolid, 2003.

Langslow, David. *Medical Latin in the Roman Empire*. Oxford: Oxford University Press, 2000.

Marx, Friedrich. *A. Cornelii Celsi quae supersunt*. Leipzig, Germany: Teubner, 1915.

Mazzini, Innocenzo. *A. Cornelio Celso. La chirurgia (libri VII e VIII del De Medicina)*. Pisa, Italy: Istituti Editoriali e Poligrafici Internazionali, 1999.

Mudry, Philippe. *La Préface du "De medicina" de Celse. Texte, traduction et commentairey*. Geneva: Droz, 1982.

Sabbah, Guy and Philippe Mudry, eds. *La médecine de Celse. Aspects historiques, scientifiques et littéraires*. Saint-Étienne, France: Publications de l'Université de Saint-Étienne, 1994.

Schulze, Christian. *Celsus*. Hildesheim, Germany: Olms, 2001.

Serbat, Guy. *Celse: De la médecine*. Vol.1. Paris: Les belles Lettres, 1995.

Spencer, William G. *Aulus Cornelius Celsus, De Medicina*. London: Heinemann, 1960.

Innocenzo Mazzini

CHAMBERS, ROBERT (*b.* Peebles, Scotland, 10 July 1802; *d.* St. Andrews, Scotland, 17 March 1871), *biology, geology, popular science*. For the original article on Chambers see *DSB,* vol. 3.

Chambers helped popularize science by writing for general interest publications—particularly *Chambers's Edinburgh Journal*—to report on scientific discoveries, giving the public access to ideas that were available only to scientists who regularly attended professional meetings or read published transactions of such forums. He had no formal training in the sciences and little interest in advancing the professional status of scientists, but his skillful reporting enabled readers to learn how the ideas that flowed from scientific innovation affected the world around them, and his series of articles in the *Journal* presenting his rudimentary ideas on evolution served as a prelude to his most important work, *Vestiges of the Natural History of Creation*.

Although the son of a cotton manufacturer, Robert Chambers grew up poor because of a series of reversals in his family's heirloom business. Robert's family moved to Edinburgh; initially Robert remained behind to continue his education, but soon he rejoined his family. The move to Edinburgh eventually proved fortuitous: It was a time of scientific and intellectual ferment, called the "Scottish Enlightenment," growing out of the Medical School of Edinburgh University. Advances in medicine created interest in a wide range of fields, including chemistry, physiology, and botany. The Royal Society of Edinburgh, founded in 1783, further stimulated the growth and professionalization of Scottish science, and Robert benefited from this environment.

In addition to his family's difficulties, both he and William were hexadactyls; they were born with six fingers on each hand and six toes on each foot. This condition was properly remedied in William's case but Robert's condition was more difficult to treat; surgery left him lame and he was unable to participate in childhood games. He became more introspective, and his avid reading enabled him to be well versed in a broad range of subjects, with his condition a constant reminder of how biological processes could go awry. He sought explanations for his affliction, as he considered his inherited condition.

With his brother William, Chambers published pamphlets filled with poetry and Scottish folklore. They sold these penny papers to a public eager to buy inexpensive

Robert Chambers. GEORGE BERNARD/PHOTO RESEARCHERS, INC.

reading material. The income derived from such sales gave Robert time to write. After carefully examining popular periodicals, he wrote numerous articles on literature and topical subjects as well as Scottish folklore. *The Kaleidoscope* and *Edinburgh Literary Amusement* (which sold for three pence in 1821), are early examples of such publications.

Finally, having acquired the comfort and security of a satisfactory income, Robert was able to marry and begin a family of his own. He devoted more time to reading works of science, and his natural curiosity and interest in cosmology drew him to the nebular hypothesis of Pierre-Simon, Marquis de Laplace (1749–1827), which explained the origin and evolution of the universe.

Development of Scientific Interest. William Chambers's business was flourishing, and because there was a market for popular literature, in 1832 he started *Chambers's Edinburgh Journal,* a well-produced weekly journal printed on quality paper that workingmen could afford. The *Journal* soon included articles on science, such as the "Influence of

Steam Navigation" and the "Character of Fish." During the next few years (1833–1835), the number of scientific reports in the *Journal* increased, with articles on the migration of birds, the naturalist Charles Waterton's description of the sloth, and the safety lamp of Sir Humphry Davy (1778–1829). Robert Chambers's contributions illustrated his voracious reading of scientific literature and interest in incorporating the information he acquired into his articles in the *Journal*. In his scientific reports he explored similarities between plant and animal nutrition, but his major efforts were in geology and paleontology. This was a prelude to Chambers's series "Ages of Animal Life" (1836–1837), the most significant articles he contributed to the *Journal,* containing the essence of his views on evolution, which he later developed more completely in *Vestiges of the Natural History of Creation* (1844).

Chambers's lack of practical scientific training and sophistication, which made him vulnerable to errors, also made his work more appealing to the popular audience because of his enthusiasm and fresh approach, unencumbered by the formal restraints and demands that vigorous scientific investigation requires. Although aware of some of the theory's weaknesses, Chambers was strongly influenced by Laplace's "nebular hypothesis," which suggested that the universe had been formed much earlier than stated in scripture, and that it had undergone considerable change. Chambers also read geological works, including those by the Scot James Hutton (1726–1797), that convinced him that Earth's crust had also changed over time.

Chambers's initial articles in geology did not create much of a stir. They set the stage for his later work on the transformation of species. In "Werner and Hutton" he discussed Abraham Gottlob Werner's (1750–1817) "catastrophism" and Hutton's "uniformitarianism," making these complex and contrasting theories more understandable for readers. Chambers explained how Charles Lyell (1797–1875) incorporated Werner's ideas about the power of heat into Hutton's geology, which emphasized the action of water. A subsequent series, "Theory of the Earth," further weighed the relative merits of Wernerian and Huttonian geology, indicating how the results of geological inquiry provided the "light" that illuminated the study of the history of "animated nature." He described stratified rock formations, including the grawache series of rocks containing trilobites, which he referred to as the first living forms inhabiting Earth, and old red sandstone containing "vertebrated animals." He found it remarkable that this stratum contained shellfish and other "inferior" animals. Other strata contained amphibians of the "lizard and turtle tribes," or were "mixed with fish, crocodiles, and reptiles" ("Popular Information on Science, Theory of the Earth—Third Article," in the *Journal,* 27 May 1837, p. 139).

Chambers's mistakes in taxonomy were balanced by the sense of wonder he skillfully conveyed to readers. He indicated that new species replaced the extinct forms and discussed the extinction of species and competition in "Popular Information on Science, First Forms of Animal and Vegetable Life" (in the *Journal*, 8 July 1837, pp. 186–187 and "Popular Information on Science, Second Ages of Animal Life" 22 July 1837, pp. 202–203). The articles contained the same type of scientific errors and flawed reasoning later found in *Vestiges* but brought provocative ideas to the public as well as Chambers's remarkable but untutored insight into the relations between different species and how organic change may have taken place. He continued to furnish evidence of evolutionary change, describing the Pterodactyls as "perhaps the greatest wonder of the Reptile Age" with "the wings of a bat, the neck of a bird, and a head furnished with long jaws full of teeth, so that in this last part of its organisation it bore some resemblance to the crocodile ("Second Ages of Animal Life," p. 202). The "Ages of Animal Life" series contained vivid descriptions of fossil forms and speculation on how one form was transformed into different organisms. The similarity of language and ideas in passages in this series and passages in *Vestiges* is striking. In the concluding article in the series, (Fourth Ages of Animal Life," 23 December 1837, pp. 379–380), Chambers focused on the current forms of mammals, indicating that "the earth, then, being now fitted for the animals associated with man … was … the object … of all the changes that had taken place" (p. 380). Because these essays generated little controversy, Chambers felt emboldened to go into retreat in St. Andrews, and while in seclusion there, he wrote *Vestiges*.

Vestiges is even more explicit in explaining how species were transformed. Chambers expressed his objective more clearly in this work than in his *Journal* articles. He intended the book to be a complete explication of evolution, one that could be understood by laypeople, not just professional scientists. As a precaution, he insisted he should not be identified as the author because he feared that eventually an issue of this magnitude would create unnecessary problems and endanger his family's business interests. Only William, his wife, his publisher, and a literary go-between knew the secret of his authorship during his lifetime. It was not until he died that he was revealed as author. In retrospect, it should not have been surprising that he was the author of *Vestiges*, because the faithful readers of his earlier articles in the *Journal* had read similar passages almost a decade before in weekly installments.

Although Thomas Henry Huxley believed in a rudimentary form of evolution by the time he was asked to review *Vestiges* (in 1854, for *British and Foreign Medico-chirurgical Review*, 13, p. 333), he felt that the "progression" theory in *Vestiges* was deeply flawed. He felt the work did not serve the cause of evolution and actually did it harm because of its errors in biology and geology, and he deplored its faulty logic as well as the idea that amateurs could engage in scientific investigation. In contrast, Alfred Russel Wallace had a more favorable view of *Vestiges* than Huxley and even Charles Darwin had, and remained a steadfast supporter of the work throughout his career.

Although Darwin's reaction to *Vestiges* was not favorable when it was first published in 1844, he developed an understanding of the value of Chambers's contribution to evolutionary thought, although he fully recognized its shortcomings. He realized the importance of allowing fresh ideas about organic change being properly aired. However, he was primarily concerned with his own theory, viewing all developments in evolutionary biology from this perspective. He did not give full consideration to Chambers and his book early on, mainly because of his feelings that the concepts in *Vestiges* were very different from his own. However, because Chambers's work was directed toward a popular audience, his ideas reached a wide audience years before the evolutionary theories of Darwin and Wallace were published. Thus, Chambers prepared the public for the more rigorous scientific ideas of those who followed, making it easier for the ideas of professional evolutionists to be accepted.

SUPPLEMENTARY BIBLIOGRAPHY

Chambers's articles in Chambers's Edinburgh Journal *represent his important early writing.*

WORKS BY CHAMBERS

"Popular Information on Science, First Forms of Animal and Vegetable Life." *Chambers's Edinburgh Journal* 6 (8 July 1837): 186–187.

"Popular Information on Science, Second Ages of Animal Life." *Chambers's Edinburgh Journal* 6 (22 July 1837): 202–203.

"Popular Information on Science, Third Ages of Animal Life." *Chambers's Edinburgh Journal* 6 (1837): 298–299.

"Popular Information on Science, Fourth Ages of Animal Life." *Chambers's Edinburgh Journal* 6 (23 December 1837): 379–380.

OTHER SOURCES

Schwartz, Joel. "Darwin, Wallace, and Huxley, and *Vestiges of the Natural History of Creation*." *Journal of the History of Biology* 23, no. 1 (Spring 1990): 127–153. Analyzes the different reactions of prominent Victorian naturalists to Chambers's work.

———. "Robert Chambers and Thomas Henry Huxley, Science Correspondents: The Popularization and Dissemination of Nineteenth Century Natural Science." *Journal of the History of Biology* 32, no. 2 (Fall 1999): 343–383. Discusses Chambers's early life in the context of the Scottish Enlightenment and illustrates the similarities between passages in his *Journal* articles and those in *Vestiges*.

Secord, James. *Victorian Sensation: The Extraordinary Publication, Reception, and Secret Authorship of "Vestiges of the Natural History of Creation."* Chicago: University of Chicago Press, 2000. Discusses *Vestiges* from the perspective of cultural history.

Joel S. Schwartz

CHANDRASEKHAR, SUBRAH-MANYAN (*b*. Lahore, Punjab, British India [later Pakistan], 10 October 1910; *d*. Chicago, Illinois, 21 August 1995), *physics, astrophysics, applied mathematics.*

A Nobel Laureate honored for his extraordinarily wide-ranging contributions to physics, astrophysics, and applied mathematics, Chandrasekhar is well known for his discovery of the limiting mass (Chandrasekhar limit) of a star that could become a white dwarf.

Career. Chandrasekhar, known simply as "Chandra" in the scientific world, was one of ten children of Chandrasekhara Subrahmanyan Ayyar and Sitalakshmi Balakrishnan. Ayyar was an officer in the British government services. Sitalakshmi, a woman of great talent and self-taught intellectual attainments, played a pivotal role in her son's career. Chandrasekhar's uncle Sir Chandrasekhara Venkata Raman was the recipient of a Nobel Prize for the celebrated discovery concerning the molecular scattering of light known as the "Raman Effect."

Chandrasekhar's early education took place under the tutelage of his parents and private tutors. When he was twelve, his family moved to Madras, where he began his regular schooling at the Hindu High School in Triplicane, which he attended from 1922 to 1925. Chandrasekhar then received his university education at Presidency College in Madras and earned a bachelor's degree with honors in 1930. He was awarded a three-year Government of India scholarship for graduate studies at Cambridge in England.

Chandrasekhar left India for England in July 1930 to undertake research under the supervision of the pioneering theoretical astrophysicist Ralph Howard Fowler. He spent the third year of his graduate scholarship in Copenhagen, Denmark, at Niels Bohr's Institute of Theoretical Physics before completing his work on his Cambridge PhD in the summer of 1933. In October he was elected a fellow of Trinity College, Cambridge, a position he held from 1933 to 1937. He visited the United States for the first time from January to March 1936 at the invitation of Harlow Shapley, the director of the Harvard College Observatory at Harvard University. In the late summer of 1936, Chandrasekhar returned to India for a short visit to

marry Lalitha Doraiswamy, whom he had met while both were undergraduate students at the Presidency College. They wed on 11 September 1936.

In January 1937, Chandrasekhar joined the faculty of the University of Chicago at the Yerkes Observatory, Williams Bay, Wisconsin. Chandrasekhar and Lalitha lived in Williams Bay for the next twenty-seven years. In 1964, they moved to Chicago, living in the Hyde Park neighborhood near the university. Elected a Fellow of the Royal Society of London and named the Morton D. Hull Distinguished Service Professor in 1946, Chandrasekhar remained at the University of Chicago until his death. Chandrasekhar and Lalitha became U.S. citizens in 1953.

Chandrasekhar is known for a distinctive pattern of research that encompassed diverse areas, each of which occupied a period of five to ten years. Each period of study resulted in a series of long papers and ended with a monograph. Speaking of his monographs and his motivation for research, Chandrasekhar, in the autographical account published with his Nobel lecture, said:

> After the early preparatory years, my scientific work has followed a certain pattern motivated, principally, by a quest after perspectives. In practice, this quest has consisted in my choosing (after some trials and tribulations) a certain area which appears amenable to cultivation and compatible with my taste, abilities, and temperament. And when after some years of study, I feel that I have accumulated a sufficient body of knowledge and achieved a view of my own, I have the urge to present my point of view, ab initio, in a coherent account with order, form, and structure.

Thus Chandrasekhar's researches, principally motivated by *a quest after perspectives,* a quest after attaining a complete understanding of an area and internalizing it, covered a wide range of investigations that are summarized here chronologically.

Stellar Structure, White Dwarfs (1929–1939). Chandrasekhar's scientific career began while he was still an undergraduate at Presidency College, when he published his first paper, "The Compton Scattering and the New Statistics," in 1929. The new statistics refers to the Fermi-Dirac quantum statistics that he was made aware of in a dramatic encounter with Arnold Sommerfeld during the latter's visit to Presidency College in the fall of 1928. The new quantum mechanics, which had stunned Europe, had not yet made its way to India. Sommerfeld was invited to speak to the science students and Chandrasekhar, who was among them, made arrangements to see him the following day in his hotel room.

Chandrasekhar had mastered the atomic theory as laid out in Sommerfeld's classic book on old quantum

Subrahmanyan Chandrasekhar. *Chandrasekhar in his office, 1939.* **AP IMAGES.**

theory, *Atomic Structure and Spectral Lines.* He approached Sommerfeld with the brash confidence of a young undergraduate to impress upon the master his knowledge as well as his intense desire to pursue a research career in physics. But Sommerfeld shocked him by telling that the old quantum theory in his book was no longer of any use. It was replaced by the revolutionary new quantum mechanics due to the work of Erwin Schrödinger, Werner Heisenberg, Paul M. Dirac, and others. While Chandra had also studied on his own the classical Maxwell-Boltzmann statistics, Sommerfeld told him that too had undergone a fundamental change in the light of the new quantum mechanics. Seeing a crestfallen young student facing him, Sommerfeld offered Chandra the galley proofs of his as yet unpublished paper that contained an account of the new Fermi-Dirac quantum statistics and its application to the electron theory of metals.

Chandrasekhar would later characterize this encounter as the "single most important event" in his sci-

entific career. He immediately embarked on a serious study of the new developments in atomic theory. Sommerfeld's paper was sufficient for him to learn about Fermi-Dirac statistics and write, within a few months, his first paper. He sent it for publication in the *Proceedings of the Royal Society of London* to be communicated through Ralph H. Fowler in Cambridge, England. Fowler had published a pioneering paper on the theory of white dwarfs (dense collapsed configurations of stars, with planetary dimensions but as massive as the Sun, in their terminal stages) that contained still another application of the new statistics to the stellar matter in the form of degenerate electrons in white dwarfs and solved a long-standing problem about their equilibrium structure. So for Chandra, at the time, Fowler was someone who knew Fermi-Dirac statistics and consequently someone who could understand his paper and support its publication. The paper was indeed published in the *Proceedings.* However, this chance circumstance was to have a profound influence on Chandra's future scientific career. The following year, when he was unexpectedly offered the Government of India scholarship to continue his research in England after his graduation, he did not have to think hard before choosing Cambridge University and Fowler as his thesis advisor.

In studying Fowler's paper, Chandrasekhar discovered that Fowler's pressure-density relation in the white dwarf configuration, when combined with conditions for it to be in equilibrium under its own gravity, led to some far-reaching conclusions: (i) the radius of a white dwarf was inversely proportional to the cube root of the mass—implying thereby that every finite-mass star has a finite radius; (ii) the density is proportional to the square of the mass; (iii) the central density would be six-times the mean density ρ_m.

Chandrasekhar prepared a paper to present to Fowler on his arrival in Cambridge. But on his long voyage to England, he began to ponder the implications of the last of the three conclusions that seemed to raise a number of key questions, which proved crucial to the subsequent theory of white dwarfs. If the central densities were so high, would not the electron energies, increasing as one moved away from the center of the Fermi sphere, reach magnitudes comparable to their rest masses? If they did, the special-relativistic variation of mass with velocity would be important and would have to be taken into account. What would be the consequences?

He made a quick calculation and found that relativistic effects were indeed important. In the extreme relativistic limit, the pressure-density relation changed from the nonrelativistic case in such a way that it was no longer true that a star of any mass could have a finite radius. The total mass of the equilibrium configuration (at the limiting zero radius) was uniquely determined in terms of fundamental atomic constants and mean molecular weight μ of the stellar matter. Using the known values of the atomic constants, the mass turned out to be $5.76/\mu^2$ solar masses. In 1930, the canonical value for μ was 2.5, giving a mass of 0.91 solar masses (which later became 1.44 solar masses when μ was revised to 2). This was the origin of the critical mass or Chandrasekhar limit.

Chandrasekhar brought two short papers with him to Cambridge. One dealt with the extension of Fowler's non-relativistic degenerate configurations, the other with relativistic effects leading to the startling conclusion regarding the critical mass: *If the mass was greater than the critical mass, the star would not become a white dwarf. It would continue to collapse under the extreme pressure of gravitational forces to reach a point of infinite mass density, clearly unphysical.* After a few more years of hard work, he established the critical mass condition on a rigorous basis and reported his findings at the January 1935 meeting of the Royal Astronomical Society of London. His findings raised challenging, fundamental questions: What happens to the more massive stars when they continue to collapse? Are there terminal stages of stars other than the white dwarfs?

Astronomers' appreciation of the importance of this discovery was withheld because of the objections of Arthur Stanley Eddington, an older, well-established, and renowned scientist. Soon after Chandrasekhar's presentation at the meeting, Eddington ridiculed the whole idea of relativistic degeneracy. He characterized Chandrasekhar's theory as amounting to *reductio ad absurdum* behavior of the star, tantamount to *stellar buffoonery*. For Eddington, white dwarf stage was the ultimate terminal stage for *all stars irrespective of their masses*. He found it disturbing that if the mass of a star was greater than a certain limit, the collapse will continue and the star will not rest in peace. It was contrary to his view of nature.

While eminent physicists with no exception agreed that Chandrasekhar's derivations based on fundamental concepts of quantum mechanics and special relativity were flawless, Eddington's authority prevailed among astronomers until observations confirmed the theory. It was a traumatic incident in young Chandrasekhar's life. While he was convinced about the validity of his results and the challenge they presented to those interested in stellar evolution, he thought it better not to go on confronting and arguing with Eddington. He wrote the monograph *An Introduction to the Study of Stellar Structure* in 1939, giving a full account of the theory of white dwarfs, and passed on to a new area of research.

Stellar Dynamics: Stochastic and Statistical Approaches (1938–1943). Stellar dynamics deals with the distribution of matter and motion in stellar systems such as the Milky Way, the galaxy which is the home of Earth's solar system with the Sun as one of at least 200 billion other stars and their planets, and thousands of clusters and nebulae. The focus of stellar dynamics is the interpretation of the characteristic features of stellar systems in terms of the forces that govern motions of the individual stars.

In his monograph *Principles of Stellar Dynamics*, Chandrasekhar laid the foundations of the dynamical theory as a branch of classical dynamics—a discipline in the same general category as celestial mechanics. As in celestial mechanics, the forces that govern the motion of stars in a stellar system are principally gravitational. The motion of an individual star is then affected, first, by forces that are due to a smoothed-out distribution of matter in the system and, second, from the effect of chance encounters with neighboring stars. The continuous motion under the gravitational potential due to the smoothed-out distribution undergoes abrupt change due the chance encounters.

An important question from the point of view of what can be observed is how the cumulative effect of chance encounters affects the orbit of a star measured by what is called "time of relaxation" of the stellar system. Conventional wisdom assumed it could be theoretically calculated by considering the cumulative effect of a large number of two-body encounters. A closer analysis convinced Chandrasekhar that such an idealization did not provide a good approximation to the physical situation in the stellar system. The gravitational field fluctuated in space and time. New methods of treating the problem based on statistics were required. He laid the foundations of such new methods in one of his most celebrated and widely quoted papers, "Stochastic and Statistical Problems in Astronomy," published in 1943. The probability methods reviewed in this paper have found application beyond astronomy in a wide variety of problems and fields as different as colloidal chemistry and stellar dynamics. A series of papers and the monograph *Principles of Stellar Dynamics* marked the end of this period and the beginning of a new subject.

Radiative Transfer (1943–1950). Chandrasekhar used to say that 1943 through 1948 were some of the happiest and most satisfactory years of his scientific life. His researches culminating in the monograph *Radiative Transfer* produced a series of papers in rapid succession. The subject evolved on its own, on its own initiative and momentum, and attained elegance and a beauty which, according to his own admission, was not to be found in any of his other work.

The subject of radiative transfer deals in a general way with the transport of energy in stellar atmospheres that absorb, emit, and scatter radiation as it emerges from the star. The characteristics of the emerging radiation, such as the variations in intensity over the stellar disc and the energy distribution over different wavelengths (spectral distribution) are the features that can be observed and measured. The latter are of extreme importance for an astrophysicist in his attempt to understand the constitution and structure of stellar atmospheres. The theoretical analysis of the transfer phenomena demanded new mathematical developments in the theory of integro–differential and functional equations. It demanded new approximation techniques to solve them to find the observed characteristics. Chandrasekhar's pioneering effort during these years and his monograph provided the necessary foundation. His work also included a study of the formation of absorption lines due to scattering of light in moving atmospheres, a subject of great interest in astrophysics dealing with a variety of objects such as novae,

Wolf-Rayet stars, planetary nebulae, solar corona, and solar prominences.

In a related subject, the explanation of the polarization of light by Earth's atmosphere was a problem that had remained unsolved since the classic work of Lord Rayleigh in 1871. In explaining the blue color of the sky based on Maxwell's equations, Rayleigh had made the approximation of a single scattering of the radiation and predicted nonvanishing polarization in all directions, except directly towards or away from the Sun. It was known, however, that there existed two, sometimes three, neutral points of zero polarization on the Sun's meridian circle, called the Babinet, Brewster, and Arago points. Chandrasekhar, in a series of papers in 1946, formulated the scattering problem with polarization and found solutions for the sunlit sky exhibiting precisely the character of the observations, in particular the above-described neutral points.

Negative Hydrogen Ion (1944–1958). The negative hydrogen ion (quantum mechanically, the bound state of a neutral hydrogen atom and an electron) was a subject of great astrophysical importance. Hans A. Bethe in 1929 and independently Egil A. Hylleraas in 1930 had demonstrated theoretically that such a stable configuration could exist, which in turn pointed to its possible existence in the Sun's atmosphere, where there was an abundance of neutral hydrogen atoms as well as a supply of electrons due to the ionization of other elements. Theory anticipated that under such circumstances, there should be bound negative ions of hydrogen, and they should have an effect on the absorption spectrum of the Sun. Rupert Wildt in 1938 had indeed produced strong evidence for the presence of negative ions of hydrogen in sufficient quantities to be the principal source of continuous absorption in the solar atmosphere and in the atmospheres of certain types of stars.

After the pioneering work of Bethe and Hylleraas, several others tried to determine the electron affinity to the hydrogen atom (binding energy) with greater precision by trying out wave functions with more parameters than the original calculations of Bethe and Hylleraas. These efforts, however, had led to ambiguous results. Chandrasekhar realized that the form of the wave function used by the later authors, based upon an analogy with the wave function that was immensely successful in explaining the helium atom, was not appropriate for the physical situation in the case of the negative hydrogen ion. With a more general parameterization, he was able to obtain a more precise and stable value for the binding energy and subsequently the value for the continuous absorption coefficient of the negative hydrogen ion and the consequent cross-sections for radiative processes leading to its ionization. These results played an extremely important role in scientists' understanding of the continuous spectrum of the sun and the stars.

Turbulence and Magneto-Hydrodynamics (1950–1960).

After completing the monograph *Radiative Transfer* Chandrasekhar embarked on a new area, the study of turbulence, a phenomenon widespread in nature in the flow of liquids and gases. It is a familiar fact that a steady linear flow of water in a tube persists for velocities below a certain limit and, when the velocity exceeds this limit, the steady flow ceases spontaneously. Complex, irregular, and fluctuating motion sets in. Similar phenomena in solar and stellar atmospheres are to be expected and have been found observationally.

The theory of turbulence has been and continues to be one of the most intractable subjects. Chandrasekhar's work began with a closer analysis of Werner Heisenberg's elementary theory of turbulence, which provided an easily visualizable picture of what takes place in a turbulent medium. Heisenberg had provided an equation for determining the "spectrum" of turbulence encoded in a function of wave numbers of the eddies in the turbulence. Chandrasekhar obtained an explicit solution to the equation in the case of statistically stationary turbulence and offered further simplifications of the equation making it amenable to solutions in a more general case.

The theory of turbulence and hydrodynamics needed a reconsideration of the fundamental problems concerning the adequacy of their formulation in the context of astrophysical problems or adequacy of their formulation when dealing with the physics of the stellar interiors. In the early 1950s, Chandrasekhar undertook such reconsideration and developed appropriate mathematical formulations, their relation to underlying physics and approximation schemes best suited to the problems. Of particular importance was the generalization of hydrodynamics to include magnetic fields whose all-pervasive character in astrophysical settings (especially on the galactic scale) was becoming of great importance. Along with Enrico Fermi, he wrote two seminal papers, one on the estimation of the magnetic field in the spiral arms of the our galaxy, and the other on the gravitational stability of cosmic masses of infinite conductivity in the presence of a magnetic field.

The methods and approximation schemes developed in the astrophysical context became equally useful in the applications to laboratory experiments concerning the stability of viscous flow in the presence of a magnetic field and the hydrodynamic stability of helium II between rotating cylinders. As usual, a series of papers on the subject ended with the monograph *Hydrodynamic and Hydromagnetic Stability*.

Ellipsoidal Figures of Equilibrium (1960–1968).

As a consequence of his work with Fermi, it became clear to Chandrasekhar that stars with magnetic fields were unlikely to be spherical. In order to study the stability of such stars, methods used in radial oscillations of spherical stars were inadequate. The methods used in their work based on the so-called virial theorem needed to be generalized to be useful in the context of nonspherical rotating fluid masses. Chandrasekhar developed the needed theory and, along with Norman Lebovitz, applied the theory to the problem of oscillations of a class of historically well-known objects, the Jacobi ellipsoid and the Maclaurin spheroid and a wider class of ellipsoidal figures discovered by Richard Dedekind and Georg Friedrich Bernhard Riemann. The collaboration resulted in a series of classic papers, culminating in Chandrasekhar's *Ellipsoidal Figures of Equilibrium,* acclaimed as one of the most elegant expositions on the subject.

Relativistic Astrophysics (1965–1975).

During and after the near completion of his work on hydrodynamic and hydromagnetic stability, Chandrasekhar began to think of turning to general relativity, a subject he was introduced to in his first year as a graduate student in Cambridge. Charmed though he was by Eddington's exposition of relativity, full of fun and humor, he had shied away from a serious study of relativity for more than thirty years. This was partly because, at the time, relativity did not seem to be relevant for problems of stellar structure, internal constitution of stars, and other problems in astronomy.

The situation had changed by the 1960s. Rapid discoveries were taking place in astronomy. Quasars, pulsars, radio galaxies, cosmic x-ray sources, and cosmic microwave background radiation created a new arena of research for practical-minded relativists. On the theoretical side, a new discipline, relativistic astrophysics, was shaping up, dominated by youthful personalities that included Kip Thorne, Roger Penrose, James Hartle, James Bardeen, Stephen Hawking, Brandon Carter, and others. "Chandrasekhar (or Chandra, as he encouraged us to call him) was our young-at-heart co-worker," says Kip Thorne, "as new to relativity as we. We had the flexibility of youth, the freedom from preconceived notions that is a modest compensation for lack of experience. Chandra had the wisdom of decades of research in fundamental, Newtonian physics and astrophysics—a wisdom that gave him guidance on what problems were worth studying and how to approach them" (in Chandrasekhar, *Selected Papers*, vol. 5, p. xii).

Once he decided to turn to general relativity, it was not long before he brought general relativity to its "natural home"—astronomy. It was a well-established fact that massive stars, during the course of their evolution, and when they have exhausted their nuclear source of energy, collapse into equilibrium configurations of finite dimensions (white dwarfs, neutron stars). The question arose concerning their stability. If one assumes that they are spherical, nonrotating gaseous masses, their stability against radial oscillations is governed by γ, where γ is the average ratio of specific heats. As long as $\gamma > 4/3$, Newtonian theory predicted that no matter what the mass of the star, it could be in a dynamically stable configuration with a radius that decreased with increasing mass, reaching zero only when the mass becomes infinite.

An appeal to quantum Fermi-Dirac statistics and degeneracy pressure, including special relativistic effects, did not alter this conclusion, except that the vanishing radius is reached at a finite limiting mass, the Chandrasekhar limit (1.44 solar masses in the case of white dwarfs and 2–3 solar masses in the case of neutron stars). The singular nature of the solution, namely, a star with finite mass shrinking to a point of zero radius, was clearly unphysical; it also contradicted observations, because white dwarfs and neutron stars existed in nature with finite radii. Such an unphysical solution, a consequence of relativistic degeneracy, had led Eddington in the thirties to characterize Chandrasekhar's theory of white dwarfs as the *reductio ad absurdum* behavior of the stars.

In the mid-1960s, Chandrasekhar made a major discovery. He showed that this difficulty was no longer an issue within the framework of general relativity. In addition to γ, the stability depended upon the radius of the star as well. For any finite γ, dynamical instability always intervened and prevented the star collapsing to a singularity. If a massive star was to collapse into a stable configuration of a finite mass and a finite radius, it had to explode and eject a substantial fraction of material to interstellar space. Such a mass ejection could be a cataclysmic event, such as supernova explosion. If the remnant mass was in the narrow permissible range, it would then settle into a stable state of a white dwarf or a neutron star. A priori, it was highly unlikely that a massive star of several solar masses would always eject, in a violent explosion, just the right amount. It was more likely that the collapse would continue, leading to the formation of a black hole. Thus, if general relativity had a say in the matter, the existence of black holes had to be accepted as a reality.

After this major discovery, Chandrasekhar devoted himself to a systematic development of post-Newtonian approximation schemes stemming from general relativity. It marked the beginning of a correct description of radiation reaction and the discovery of a radiation-reaction-driven instability, conservation laws in general relativity, and how they are incorporated in successive post-Newtonian approximations.

Mathematical Theory of Black Holes, and Newton's *Principia* (1975–1995). After carrying out post-Newtonian approximation nearly as far as it could go, Chandrasekhar decided to undertake a systematic exploration of uniformly rotating stars within the framework of general relativity. In a series of papers with John Friedman, he developed a general formalism that paralleled Newtonian theory and revealed departures from it. In the process of studying the stability of such rotating stars under perturbations, their work led to the study of the physical situation outside a black hole (technically, the study of deformations of vacuum solutions external to a black hole).

Chandrasekhar's study of black holes, which began with an analysis of the equations governing the perturbations of the Schwarzschild black holes, was to develop into a complete body of work of his own published in the form of a treatise, *The Mathematical Theory of Black Holes*. He was prompted to undertake this study because there was a great deal of mystery shrouding the subject with different sets of equations attributed to different authors (Zerilli equation, Bardeen–Press equation, Regge-Wheeler equation). Chandrasekhar's coherent and self-contained account clarified the mystery and established the relations between the different sets of equations.

In the 1980s, during and after the completion of his book, Chandrasekhar had two young collaborators in Basilis Xanthopoulos and Valeria Ferrari. Together they discovered an underlying unity in the mathematical description of black holes and colliding gravitational waves. Earlier K. Khan and Roger Penrose had discovered the formation of a spacelike singularity in the collision of two plane gravitational waves. The nature of this singularity was very much like the one in the interior of the black hole. Subsequent extensions to more complicated waves and coupled gravitational and electromagnetic waves had led to problems that needed new ideas in the form of a rigorous mathematical theory of colliding waves patterned after the mathematical theory of black holes. With Ferrari and Xanthopoulos, Chandrasekhar formulated such a theory.

After the tragic, violent death of Basilis Xanthopoulos on 27 November 1990, Chandrasekhar continued to work with Ferrari on nonradial oscillations of stars in the framework of general relativity, until the end of his life. Concurrently, during the last decade of his life, he was devoted to the study of Sir Isaac Newton's *Principia* (1687) and in 1995, just before he died of a heart attack, his monumental treatise *Newton's* Principia *for the Common Reader* was published.

BIBLIOGRAPHY

WORKS BY CHANDRASEKHAR

"The Compton Scattering and the New Statistics." *Proceeding of the Royal Society,* A, 125 (1929): 231–237.

An Introduction to the Study of Stellar Structure. Chicago: University of Chicago Press, 1939. Reprinted New York: Dover Publications, 1967. Translated into Japanese and Russian.

"Stochastic Problems in Physics and Astronomy." *Reviews of Modern Physics* 15 (1943): 1–89. Reprinted in *Selected Papers on Noise and Stochastic Processes,* edited by Nelson Wax. New York: Dover Publications, 1954, 3–91.

Principles of Stellar Dynamics. Chicago: University of Chicago Press, 1943. Reprinted New York: Dover Publications, 1960.

Radiative Transfer. Oxford: Clarendon Press, 1950. Reprinted New York: Dover Publications, 1960. Translated into Russian.

Hydrodynamic and Hydromagnetic Stability. Oxford: Clarendon Press, 1961. Reprinted New York: Dover Publications, 1981. Translated into Russian.

Ellipsoidal Figures of Equilibrium. New Haven, CT: Yale University Press, 1968. Reprinted New York: Dover Publications, 1987. Translated into Russian.

The Mathematical Theory of Black Holes. Oxford: Clarendon Press, 1983. Translated into Russian.

"Autobiography." In *Les Prix Nobel: The Nobel Prizes 1983,* edited by Wilhelm Odelberg. Stockholm: Nobel Foundation, 1984. Also available from http://nobelprize.org.

Eddington: The Most Distinguished Astrophysicist of His Time. Cambridge: Cambridge University Press, 1983.

Truth and Beauty: Aesthetics and Motivations in Science. Chicago: University of Chicago Press, 1987.

Newton's Principia *for the Common Reader.* Oxford: Clarendon Press, 1995.

Selected Papers. 7 Volumes. Chicago: University of Chicago Press, 1989–1997. Chandrasekhar's original papers.

A Quest for Perspectives: Selected Works of S. Chandrasekhar, with Commentary, edited by Kameshwar C. Wali. London: Imperial College Press, 2001. A subset chosen from the *Selected Papers* volumes.

OTHER SOURCES

Fowler, Ralph H. "On Dense Matter." *Monthly Notices of the Royal Astronomical Society* 87 (1926): 114.

Wali, Kameshwar C. *Chandra: A Biography of S. Chandrasekhar.* Chicago: University of Chicago Press, 1992.

The following three books contain articles by various experts providing a grand tour of the colossal scientific edifice Chandrasekhar left behind and subsequent developments in their fields of expertise.

Srinivasan, G., ed. *From White Dwarfs to Black Holes: The Legacy of S. Chandrasekhar.* Chicago: University of Chicago Press, 1999.

Wald, Robert M. *Black Holes and Relativistic Stars.* Chicago: University of Chicago Press, 1998.

Wali, Kameshwar C., ed. *S. Chandrasekhar: The Man behind the Legend.* London: Imperial College Press, 1997.

Kameshwar C. Wali

CHARGAFF, ERWIN (*b.* Czernowitz, Austria-Hungary, 11 August 1905; *d.* New York, New York, 20 June 2002), *molecular biology.*

Chargaff is best known for his discovery of DNA "base ratios," also known as "Chargaff's rules," in the late 1940s, while working at Columbia University in New York City. The discovery of base-ratios was later interpreted stereochemically by James Watson and Francis Crick in 1953 to also mean "base-pairings," eventually becoming the most important feature of DNA structure, namely, the feature that explains DNA's capacity for precise duplication. The base-ratios require that each base on one of DNA's double helix's two strands "pairs" with a complementary base only, as specified by Chargaff's rules (see below, the chemical details of the various rules) from the other strand. Though DNA emerged since the mid-1960s as the best-known symbol of the new field of molecular biology, Chargaff preferred, even insisted, on calling himself a cell chemist, so as to emphasize the primacy of his chemical training and practices in his work on biological material. Indeed, Chargaff's discoveries were both enabled and constrained by his training as a chemist who specialized in microanalytic studies of a wide variety of cellular components, including factors in blood coagulation, lipids and lipoproteins, the metabolism of amino acids and inositol, and the biosynthesis of enzyme phosphotransferases.

Early Years. Chargaff was born to Hermann Chargaff (1870–1934), owner of a small bank, and Rosa Silberstein Chargaff (1878–1943), in the multicultural town of Czernowitz, capital of the easternmost province of the Austro-Hungarian Empire, Bukovina. Famous as the Vienna of Eastern Europe, Czernowitz was the birth place of many cultural luminaries, most notably the foremost post–World War II poet in the German language, Paul Celan. To this day, former residents retain a distinct pride in their multicultural background and maintain their own Website. Czernowitz's cultural diversity stemmed from a balance among several ethnic groups: the German-speaking Austrian bureaucracy at the top of the social hierarchy; Ruthenian peasants and landed gentry who spoke Romanian or Ukrainian; and Jews in various stages of emancipation, ranging from culturally assimilated, well-to-do German speakers, such as Chargaff's parents, to poor shtetl dwellers who spoke Yiddish and bits of the local dialects of Romanian, Ukrainian, Polish, or Russian, and made up a quarter of the urban population, but a majority of its middle class. With the outbreak of World War I, Czernowitz was to change hands many times, having been occupied by the Russian Army in 1914, incorporated into Romania in 1919, ceded to the Soviet Union in 1939, occupied by Nazi Germany in 1941, and by the

Soviet Union in 1945. Since 1991, it has been part of Ukraine, and called Chernivtsi. Chargaff relocated with his family to Vienna in 1914, and attended there a well-known humanistic gymnasium, the Maximilian, where his literary talents and ambitions could flourish. However, the great inflation of 1923, which ravaged the Central European middle classes, made it no longer possible for Chargaff to become a writer and he studied instead a profession that guaranteed a living: chemistry, famous for its employment opportunities in the chemical industry.

After his graduation with a PhD in analytical chemistry from the University of Vienna in 1928, Chargaff did two years of postdoctoral research at Yale University with R. Anderson, an editor of the *Journal of Biological Chemistry,* from whom he learned research methods in bacterial chemistry. Despite a productive experience and job offers in the United States, Chargaff chose to return to Europe, being apparently overwhelmed by "culture shock." (He mentioned in his autobiography the endless commotion of New York City, especially during Prohibition and the Great Depression, as well as Yale's "caste provincialism.") Because he described his subsequent quest for a position in Berlin as doing "what desperate Viennese always threatened to do," it is obvious that Chargaff, having arrived in the United States as a nonimmigrant, had been unprepared for his initial encounter with American culture.

Return to Europe. For the next two and a half years (1930–1933) Chargaff enjoyed "the best years of his life" as a privatdozent, or occupant of the first ladder in a professorial career at the University of Berlin's Department of Public Health, where its head, Martin Hahn, appreciated Chargaff's past experience at Vienna and Yale in bacterial and analytic chemistry. The admissions committee was particularly impressed with Chargaff's cultivated manner and proficiency in central European literature. Rubbing shoulders in weekly colloquia with scientific luminaries such as the Nobel laureate chemists Fritz Haber and Otto Warburg, as well as other scientists, most notably Albert Einstein, Max von Laue, James Franck, Max Planck, Walther Nernst, and fellow Viennese Lise Meitner and Erwin Schrödinger, Chargaff also enjoyed the innovative and lively cultural life that became a hallmark of the Weimar Republic. He was convinced that he had found a suitable place for both his scientific and cultural aspirations, concluding reluctantly, like many before him, that Berlin surpassed even his native Vienna.

However, by the time Chargaff was ready to submit his *Habilitationschrift* in 1933 (a formal condition for becoming a university professor), the scene had changed profoundly due to the Nazis' rise to power. Despite his apolitical disposition and Austrian passport, Chargaff, who came from a family of Austrian Empire Jews who had

assimilated into German culture as part of their upward mobility a generation earlier (his father Germanized the Spanish-Jewish last name of Chargaff's paternal grandfather Don Isaak Chargaf by adding an "f"), realized that he had to leave Berlin immediately. He accepted an invitation to work at the Pasteur Institute in Paris, whose director, Albert Calmette, correctly realized that Chargaff's expertise in bacterial chemistry could help exonerate him from accusations of responsibility for fatalities resulting from contaminated BCG (Bacille Calmette-Guerin) vaccines (Calmette was coinventor of that vaccine).

After two years at the Pasteur Institute, which Chargaff later described as "decadent," he once again had to move when the increasing flow of refugees from Nazi Germany sparked displays of xenophobia (it was more of an antiforeigner than an anti-Semitic bias, though the two are often linked; France elected Leon Blum, a French Jew, as prime minister in 1936, a year after Chargaff had left; the derogatory term addressed at refugees that Chargaff recalled was "metheques" which means "foreign half-caste)" in France. Besides, research in France was not as well paid as in Germany, and careers for foreigners were next to impossible. After unsuccessfully scouting for job opportunities in the United Kingdom, with help from the Rockefeller Foundation's European office in Paris, Chargaff returned to the United States, where he was eventually able to find a research position at Columbia University's Department of Medicine at the College of Physicians and Surgeons, working on the chemistry of blood coagulation for a project run by surgeons. However, the chairman of the Department of Biochemistry, Hans Clarke, who knew German biochemistry from his own experience there before World War I, and who had already hired several refugees, most notably the department's star, Rudolf Schoenheimer, in 1933, understood Chargaff's potential and integrated him into the large Department of Biochemistry.

Move to Columbia. Chargaff was to remain at Columbia for the rest of his career, concluding as chairman of the Department of Biochemistry (1970–1974) and retiring as a recipient of the National Medal of Science (1975). However, his relationship to his department remained strained, in part because he inevitably compared it with his experiences in Vienna, Berlin, and Paris, as well as at Yale. During those early years, as a gifted and hardworking young man, Chargaff was spotted and appreciated by senior scientists, in the central European manner, according to which heads of research institutes invited promising young researchers to work with them, thus securing their future in a career that was supposed be based on excellence in research only.

By contrast, U.S. research departments were more decentralized, and opportunities for promotion often depended on a variety of extraneous factors, such as one's negotiating position or networking position in the discipline at large, as well as in one's department. Ironically, Chargaff turned out to be very capable of securing research grants, of interacting professionally with a wide range of scientists in other institutions and countries, lecturing well, and possessing all the ingredients for a successful career in the United States. But he could not avoid being trapped in the cultural values of another place and another time, of the Vienna of his serene childhood, prior to the demise of the Austro-Hungarian Empire, recalling the resulting social and political upheaval and the painful loss of his family's former upper-middle-class status during the inflation of the early 1920s.

A major reason that Chargaff remained trapped by the values of his past was his experience in the 1920s as a follower of Vienna's leading cultural critic, Karl Krauss. Young Chargaff naively absorbed Krauss's apocalyptic vision, which dramatized the corruption of Vienna's leaders, often contrasting it with earlier, more benign times. Krauss's lamentations of the loss of Vienna's former cultural glory resonated only too well with Chargaff's own experience, and Chargaff, who referred to Krauss as "my only teacher," hoped to emulate him as a writer and cultural critic at large. However, the social upheaval of post–World War I Vienna, when fascists and communists violently battled in the streets, and especially the Great Inflation of 1923, demanded that Chargaff choose a profession that would guarantee a living. He chose chemistry, a science that offered sure employment, especially in the large chemical industry, but he came to resent what he considered a betrayal of his initial, or more genuine, literary vocation, and thus he came to regard science as a "second best," a mere profession.

The relevance of this seemingly peculiar fact for understanding Chargaff's career in science pertains not only to his later emergence, since the 1960s, as a cultural critic of "Big Science," a critique inspired by Krauss's apocalyptic model. Rather, Chargaff's perception of the loss of his true vocation led to his refusal to become fully absorbed by science. This moral distinction between vocation and profession, elaborated by Max Weber, led Chargaff to compensate for the abandoning of his "first love" or literary vocation by spending a great deal of his time on literary and cultural matters. This guilt-laden attitude also meant that, while Chargaff discharged his formal responsibilities in research and teaching in a dutiful manner, he refused to spend time on "career building" such as networking or cultivating mentors and peers. Though always busy with the responsibilities of a leading scientist, Chargaff seemed to be waiting for an opportunity to become a full-time writer, which he accomplished in the 1960s, and

Erwin Chargaff. *Portrait of Erwin Chargaff smoking a pipe, circa 1991.* **HULTON ARCHIVE/GETTY IMAGES.**

especially after his retirement in 1975. This conduct of letting cultural values override scientific priorities manifested itself in the two most important episodes of Chargaff's life, namely the discovery of DNA base ratios and his critique of molecular biology as Big Science.

Chargaff thus became one of very few scientists who immediately understood the implications of Oswald Avery's seminal paper, published in 1944, on DNA's ability to effect a genetic change in bacteria by itself, due to Chargaff's extensive prior experience with diverse facets of cell chemistry, but also due to his research for the war effort, which required the study of tropical pathogens' nucleic acids, starting in 1942. Placed at a great university in a great city, Chargaff had access to many graduate and postdoctoral students, to the effect that he was not only able to reorient his entire research program to focus on DNA, but could benefit from the work of many talented young scientists, many of whom became leaders in biochemistry and molecular biology (including, for example, those invited to speak at Chargaff's retirement symposium: Aaron Benditch, George Brawerman, Seymour Cohen, David Elson, Boris Magasanik, David Shemin, and David Sprinson). The availability of research grants from both governmental agencies and private foundations and, after World War II, new equipment capable of measuring minute quantities were also key factors in enabling Chargaff to discover many structural features underlying DNA's genetic function.

Research on DNA Bases. In a series of innovative experiments in the mid- and late 1940s, focused on measuring DNA's base composition in a variety of species and organs, Chargaff established that the ratio of purines to pyrimidines (two- versus one-ring nitrogenous bases) was 1; that the ratios of adenine to thymine and guanine to cytosine, respectively, was also 1 (the former base in each pair is a purine and the latter a pyrimidine); that DNA base ratios are similar across organs in the same organism; and that DNA composition or percentage of each base is species-specific. He further established such specificity for a wide range of species, ranging from bacteria to humans. These results refuted previous beliefs, according to which DNA structure was a repetition of the same four bases, and hence monotonous or unable to account for biological diversity. Prior to Chargaff's work, scientists believed that the molecular basis of biological specificity resided in proteins, which were composed of twenty types of amino acids and thus possessed a structure more conducive to account for biological diversity, for example, the endless varieties of antibodies produced in immunological reactions.

At the time, Avery's and Chargaff's discoveries on DNA function and structure, respectively, were greeted with little interest because their transdisciplinary nature, combining biochemistry with genetics and microbiology, eluded the expertise of most scientists, who remained compartmentalized within disciplinary boundaries. Besides, most scientists still believed in the protein primacy of the genetic material, widely acknowledged to be a combination of protein and nucleic acids. Besides Chargaff's laboratory, which focused on a microanalytic approach to DNA base composition, the only other laboratory to include DNA structure as a major research project was the Biophysics Unit of the Medical Research Council at King's College, London, which had also begun in 1946, though work there on DNA intensified in 1950 with the arrival of Rosalind Franklin. Chargaff agreed to supply DNA samples to biophysicist Maurice Wilkins from King's College, London, who wished to duplicate Franklin's work. (The lab director, John T. Randall, transferred the study of DNA by x-ray diffraction to Franklin because Wilkins, who focused on optical studies, did not have such expertise.)

Like many other scientists who collaborated across disciplines at the time, Chargaff and Wilkins limited their exchange to correspondence and sample exchange, but did not seek to explore the ramifications of each other's projects. Thus Wilkins was slow to conclude that Chargaff's

"base ratios" were the key to DNA structure, while sharing his view with Watson late in January 1953. But the question persists as to why Chargaff himself did not attempt to better establish how the biophysical structurists in London were using his discovery of base ratios, especially because he himself mentioned that their meaning must be essential to DNA function.

Chargaff's base ratios were given a stereochemical interpretation as "base pairings" as part of the double-helix structure proposed by Watson and Crick in April 1953. Subsequently, after the mode of DNA replication was confirmed in the late 1950s and 1960s, DNA structure became an icon of the new biology, with base pairings its most salient feature, because it is the feature that explains DNA's ability to duplicate correctly, by matching the correct base across its two strands, according to Chargaff's rules.

It is not obvious why the scientific community chose to highly value the base-pairing interpretation of Chargaff's base ratios, while at the same time opting to devalue Chargaff's results—results which made that interpretation possible in the first place. Many scientists thus strangely believe that Chargaff missed the greater discovery of the double helix, even though it is only too obvious that he had no intention to enter either crystallography or stereochemistry.

In any event, it is difficult to envisage the emergence and persistence of such a large disparity between base ratios and base pairings without myriad social processes such as discipline formation and social change in science after World War II. However, Chargaff's own cultural constraints, such as his outlook of science as a "mere" profession and his perception of himself as a potential writer, sparing his better moments for literature—not for inquiring what others are doing or for forging alliances and opportunistic collaborations—go a long way to explain the differential reception of scientific discoveries related to DNA structure and function.

Chargaff took both Crick and Watson to task for providing inadequate and misleading citations to his work in their papers on DNA structure in 1953, to the effect that in the early twenty-first century readers do not understand its enormous importance for any DNA model. (Linus Pauling and Robert Corey's model, also in 1953, and other preceding models of DNA failed, in part, because they ignored Chargaff's rules.). Chargaff also attempted to comprehend the new style of doing science that developed after World War II, He commented that "molecular biology is the practise of biochemistry without a license," (Chargaff, 1963, p. 176) with the obvious implication that the licensing system went bankrupt after the war, when the rapid rise in the number of scientists encouraged rapid mobility across disciplines, institutions, or techniques (Abir-Am, 1980).

Chargaff's critique of the rising field of molecular biology, an interdisciplinary field that came to focus on nucleic acids (DNA and several types of RNA) and their relationships with proteins, was first published in 1963 as a dialogue between an old biochemist and a young molecular biologist. It captured a generational transition between those trained prior to World War II, who retained loyalty to their formative disciplines (especially chemists such as Chargaff), and those trained after the war, often physical or medical scientists attracted to molecular biology by the availability of a wide range of new technical opportunities, such as artificial isotopes, ultracentrifuges, electrophoreses, several forms of chromatography, electron microscopes, and x-ray diffraction equipment. However, this change was also numeric, because the rapid growth of science in the 1950s—due to increased funding opportunities after the war, and again after the *Sputnik* launch in 1957—propelled large numbers of individuals into new fields, to the effect that scientists such as Chargaff, then fifty years of age, rapidly became a minority.

Chargaff's witty reference to "DNA tycoons" or those who "made a killing in RNA," captures the rising practice of scientific empire building, in which science had lost its earlier character as a search for truth and contemplation of nature via carefully designed experiments, having become immersed in slick and quick pursuits of power, money, and managerial control. Not only was science being destroyed by the invasion of numerous unlicensed practitioners, but the new allure of models in biology, artificial constructs that "legislate for nature," was viewed by Chargaff as having destroyed the very concept of the molecule—a concept at the heart of science, in his view. As the revolution of molecular biology destroyed Chargaff's last refuge in science, both in terms of a science that became a mass occupation and in terms of molecules that no longer reflected nature but derived their reality from artificial models, he was propelled to fight back while recovering his long lost vocation as a cultural critic.

Chargaff eventually expanded his critique of molecular biology as Big Science to its recombinant-DNA phase. He published articles such as "Triviality in Science: A Brief Meditation on Fashions" (1976) and "In Praise of Smallness: How Can We Return to Small Science?" (1980), promoting the notion that "small is beautiful" with the rare voice of an "outsider on the inside." Whether denouncing big, slick, industrial, artificial, genetically centered outlooks that prevailed in the United States since the 1960s, or lamenting the passing of the small, noble, empirical, and biochemically centered outlook of pre–World War II science, Chargaff's experience of cultural displacement and loss of vocation, in the interwar period, led him full circle to find and lose again his refuge in twentieth-century DNA science.

In the last two decades of his life Chargaff began writing books in German, and became a frequent radio and TV interviewee in central Europe. A documentary was made of his life in 1996 by an Austrian filmmaker. A literary archive was established for his writings in Marbach, Germany. Chargaff died in 2002 at age ninety-six at his home in Central Park West in New York City, where he had lived for almost seven decades, always dreaming of his lost life in interwar Europe.

BIBLIOGRAPHY

Chargaff's scientific archive is at the American Philosophical Library in Philadelphia.

WORKS BY CHARGAFF

"On the Nucleoproteins and Nucleic Acids of Microorganisms." *Cold Spring Harbor Symposium on Quantitative Biology* 12 (1947): 28–34.

"Chemical Specificity of Nucleic Acids and Mechanism of Their Enzymatic Degradation." *Experentia* 6 (1950): 201–209.

Essays on Nucleic Acids. Amsterdam: Elsevier, 1963. See especially chapter 11, which includes the composite dialogue between an old chemist and a young molecular biologist.

"A Quick Climb up Mount Olympus." *Science* 159 (1968): 1448–1449. Review of James D. Watson's *The Double Helix,* 1968.

"The Paradox of Biochemistry." *Columbia Forum* (Summer 1969): 15–18.

"Preface to a Grammar of Biology." *Science* 172 (1971): 637–642.

"Bitter Fruits from the Tree of Knowledge: Remarks on the Current Revulsion from Science." *Perspectives in Biology and Medicine* 16 (Summer 1973): 486–502.

"Voices in the Labyrinth: Dialogues around the Study of Nature." *Perspectives in Biology and Medicine* 18 (Winter 1973): 251–285.

"A Fever of Reason: The Early Way." *Annual Review of Biochemistry* 44 (1975): 1–18.

"Profitable Wonders: A Few Thoughts on Nucleic Acid Research." *Sciences* (August–September 1975): 21–26.

"Triviality in Science: A Brief Meditation on Fashions." *Perspectives in Biology and Medicine* 19 (Spring 1976): 325–333.

"Experimenta Lucifera." *Nature* 266 (1977): 780–781.

Heraclitean Fire: Sketches of a Life before Nature. New York: Rockefeller University Press, 1978.

"Strands of the Double Helix." *New Scientist* (17 August 1978): 484.

"In Praise of Smallness: How Can We Return to Small Science?" *Perspectives in Biology and Medicine* 23 (Spring 1980): 370–385.

"Swindle: Scientific and Otherwise." *Science and Society BioEssays* 2, no. 3 (1985): 132–135.

"A Dialogue and a Monologue on the Manufacture of Souls." *Perspectives in Biology and Medicine* 31 (Autumn 1987): 81–93.

"In Retrospect: A Commentary by Erwin Chargaff." *Biochemica et Biophysica Acta* 1000 (1989): 15–16.

Ein Zweites Leben. Stuttgart, Germany: Klett-Cotta, 1990.

OTHER SOURCES

Abir-Am, Pnina G. "From Biochemistry to Molecular Biology: DNA and the Acculturated Journey of the Critic of Science Erwin Chargaff." *History and Philosophy of Life Sciences* 2 (1980): 3–60.

———. "Noblesse Oblige: Lives of Molecular Biologists." *Isis* 82 (1991): 326–343.

———. "The Molecular Transformation of Twentieth-Century Biology." In *Science in the Twentieth Century,* edited by John Krige and Dominique Pestre, 495–524. London: Harwood, 1997.

Appelfeld, Aharon. "Buried Homeland." *New Yorker* (23 November 1998): 48–57.

Cohen, Seymour S. "Presentation of Academy Medal to Erwin Chargaff." *Bulletin of the New York Academy of Medicine* 56, no. 7 (1980): 601–606.

Crick, Francis. *What MAD Pursuit: A Personal View of Scientific Discovery.* New York: Basic Books, 1988.

Deichmann, Ute. *Biologists under Hitler.* Cambridge, MA: Harvard University Press, 1996.

Dubos, Rene J. *The Professor, the Institute, and DNA.* New York: Rockefeller University Press, 1976.

Eisenberg, Henryk. "Never a Dull Moment: Peripatetics through the Gardens of Science and Life." *Comprehensive Biochemistry* 37 (1990) 265–348.

Felstiner, John. *Paul Celan: Poet, Survivor, Jew.* New Haven, CT, and London: Yale University Press, 1995.

Forsdyke, Donald R., and James R. Mortimer. "Chargaff's Legacy." *GENE* 261 (2000): 127–137.

Judson, Horace Freeland. *The Eighth Day of Creation: Makers of the Revolution in Biology.* Expanded ed. Plainview, NY: CSHL Press, 1996. See especially the appendix on Chargaff.

Maddox, Brenda. *Rosalind Franklin, the Dark Lady of DNA.* London: Harper Collins, 2002.

Magasanik, Boris. "A Midcentury Watershed: The Transition from Microbial Biochemistry to Molecular Biology." *Journal of Bacteriology* 181, no. 2 (1999): 357–358.

McCarty, MacLyn. *The Transforming Principle: Discovering That Genes Are Made of DNA.* New York: W.W. Norton, 1985.

Rezzori, Gregor von. "Memoirs of an Antisemite." *New Yorker* (26 April 1969): 42–83.

Sayre, Anne. *Rosalind Franklin and DNA.* New York: W.W. Norton, 1985.

Srinivasan, Parithychery R., Joseph S. Fruton, and John T. Edsall, eds. *The Origins of Modern Biochemistry: A Retrospect on Proteins.* Special Issue of *Annals of the New York Academy of Sciences* 325 (1979): 1–373.

Watson, James D. *A Passion for DNA: Genes, Genomes, and Society.* Oxford: Oxford University Press, 2000.

Wilkins, Maurice. *The Third Man of the Double Helix.* Oxford: Oxford University Press, 2003.

Pnina G. Abir-Am

CHARNEY, JULE GREGORY (*b.* San Francisco, California, 1 January 1917; *d.* Boston, Massachusetts, 16 June 1981), *dynamic meteorology, numerical weather prediction.*

Charney was a leader of the Meteorology Project at the Institute for Advanced Study, Princeton, New Jersey, one of several centers focused on the development of numerical weather prediction in the mid-twentieth century. Numerical weather prediction, whereby future atmospheric conditions are forecast using computer-solvable models, was one of the most important scientific accomplishments in twentieth-century meteorology. Charney later played a critical role in international meteorological cooperation, spearheading the Global Atmospheric Research Program in the 1960s and 1970s. In other meteorological work, he made fundamental contributions through examinations of drought and the development of persistent high pressure areas known as blocks. Charney's theoretical work extended to oceanography; his work on ocean currents was particularly important.

Early Years. Charney was born in San Francisco to Stella and Ely Charney—Yiddish-speaking, Russian Jewish émigrés who worked as laborers in the garment industry. As secular Jews, religion played no role in their family life. Intellectual pursuits, however, were highly prized, and the Charney home was full of lively discussions and music that would become integral parts of Charney's life.

When Charney was five years old, his family settled in the Los Angeles area where he attended public schools. He excelled in mathematics, showing a tremendous ability to reduce complex problems to a number of smaller, simpler ones for which he would propose solutions—an ability critical for his later success in solving atmospheric dynamics problems. By the time Charney entered the University of California, Los Angeles (UCLA) in 1934, he had taught himself two to three years of university mathematics. Unfortunately, the teaching-intensive mathematics department had no mechanism for offering accelerated course work. Charney did exceedingly well in his studies with little effort, less faculty encouragement, and no direction. After completing his BS in mathematics in 1938, he remained for graduate studies and completed his MS in mathematics in 1940 with a thesis on curved spaces.

Meteorology Beckons. During this time, Charney made his first contact with meteorology when he attended a seminar given by the Norwegian Jörgen Holmboe, a former member of the Bergen School of Meteorology—the twentieth century's premier meteorological research school. Charney was impressed. He knew nothing about meteorology, but it appeared to be a science worth pursuing. He also realized that atmospheric motions were subject to the laws of physics and represented by partial differential equations—a delightful pairing of the applied mathematics and physics theory beloved by Charney.

The first in a series of events that would profoundly affect Jule Charney's professional life occurred in 1940. Norwegian Jacob Bjerknes, a Bergen School meteorologist of international reputation who had become exiled in the United States after Germany invaded Norway, established a meteorology program under the auspices of the UCLA Physics Department and brought Holmboe and Morris Neiburger in as faculty members. Their immediate purpose was to provide accelerated meteorology training to young military officers for the war effort. The United States needed several thousand weather forecasters and had only four hundred before the war started.

By 1941 the military draft offered Charney a choice: enlist in a military service or find a defense-related job. Holmboe presented Charney with the option of joining the new meteorology program as a teaching assistant (exempting him from military service) and taking graduate meteorology courses at the same time. Unsure about making a commitment, Charney consulted California Institute of Technology physicist Theodor von Kármán and asked if he should shift to meteorology or take a position in the aeronautics industry. Von Kármán recommended meteorology—he felt aeronautics had veered too far into engineering. The combination of the draft, Holmboe's invitation, and von Kármán's recommendation nudged Charney into meteorology, a switch he made that July.

Graduate School. Charney's initial heavy teaching load allowed little time for research, yet the curriculum must have grounded him in the fundamentals of atmospheric dynamics. Once the demand for new meteorologists cooled in 1944, Charney returned to a more regular graduate student schedule.

He also identified his research topic: the problems of genesis and development of extratropical cyclones, that is, low-pressure circulations in the middle latitudes, an extremely important area of meteorological research. Charney was convinced that he could develop a basic model that would produce cyclones if he could carry out some very complicated mathematics. In his model, the westerlies (air moving from west to east in the zone between 30° and 60° north latitude) would be in near geostrophic balance (the horizontal pressure gradient balancing the Coriolis force) and show an increase in speed with height until they reached a maximum at the tropopause (approximately 10 kilometers above Earth's surface). Charney's chosen topic was extremely difficult, but it was perfect for his abilities and psychological need for a challenge. He was convinced that rewards in absence of hard work were meaningless—the greater the challenge, the happier he was.

Charney attacked his dissertation research, concentrating on the dynamics of the lower 10 kilometers of the atmosphere. To simplify the problem, he assumed an approximate balance between the pressure gradient and Coriolis forces (quasi-geostrophic approximation).

This assumption reduced the problem to one that could be solved by a second-order differential equation. However, no tabulated solution existed for this equation, so Charney had to solve it on a mechanical calculator using finite difference methods. In 1946, Charney finally found the solution and completed his dissertation.

He also married his first wife, Elinor Kesting Frye. Their twenty-year marriage produced two children—Nora and Peter—and Elinor's son Nick from her first marriage took Charney's name. Charney would marry again in 1967. His nine-year marriage to painter and color theorist Lois Swirnoff ended in divorce.

As evidence of the outstanding quality of his work, the *Journal of Meteorology* published his dissertation as a single article ("The Dynamics of Long Waves in a Baroclinic Westerly Current") entirely filling one of its 1947 issues. Meteorologists immediately recognized its importance; the model and results made meteorological sense even if many of them could not follow the mathematics he had used in the solution.

En Route to Norway. His PhD complete, Charney wanted to further his studies with the leading meteorological theorists of the time, the Norwegians. Awarded a prestigious National Research Fellowship, he left Los Angeles to study with Halvor Solberg at the University of Oslo. While en route, Charney stopped at the University of Chicago to visit with Swedish American meteorologist Carl-Gustaf Rossby—one of the most eminent meteorologists in the United States—who was the discoverer of large-scale waves in the atmosphere.

Rossby's dynamic view of meteorology meshed nicely with Charney's, making it a much better fit than UCLA's more geometrical approach. While chatting with Rossby, Charney found out that Solberg would not be in Norway when he arrived because he was due shortly in Chicago. Therefore, Rossby encouraged Charney to postpone his fellowship and stay with Chicago's Meteorology

Department for a few months. Charney accepted, and later considered the time with Rossby to be *the* defining experience of his professional life. Not only did Rossby provide tremendous intellectual stimulation, but he was available at almost any time for discussions ranging over a wide variety of issues. For the first time in his life, Charney felt he had discovered true intellectual rapport with another person. Their close working relationship continued until Rossby's death in 1957.

After a year at Chicago, Charney continued on to the University of Oslo. Working with meteorologists Arnt Eliassen and Ragnar Fjørtoft, he began seeing a way to reduce the number of equations required to describe the atmosphere. Charney's primary focus was to eliminate all equations that were not meteorologically important and to find a numerical solution for those remaining.

This was not a new idea. Vilhelm Bjerknes and his Bergen School had been working on a rational physics- and mathematics-based meteorology since before World War I. Lewis Fry Richardson had also picked up the challenge, publishing the result of his flawed attempt to solve the hydrodynamic equations defining atmospheric motion by iterative methods in his 1922 book, *Weather Prediction by Numerical Process.* Now Charney wanted to put forecasting on a firmer mathematical basis.

By assuming a geostrophic and hydrostatic atmosphere, Charney simplified the problem down to a single equation involving only air pressure, from which sound and gravity wave solutions were excluded. His work would be particularly important several years later because a special case of the quasi-geostrophic approximation model—the equivalent barotropic model—was used in the first numerical forecast in 1950. Charney's 1948 article "On the Scale of Atmospheric Motions" set the stage for advancements in numerical weather prediction.

Numerical Weather Prediction. With Charney's year in Norway almost up, he received an invitation from Hungarian-born mathematician John von Neumann to join the Meteorology Group at the Institute for Advanced Study in Princeton. Von Neumann had met Charney in August 1946 during a meeting to which Rossby had been invited. Rossby had insisted that Charney come along. At the meeting, von Neumann tried to convince meteorologists that the atmospheric "problem" was ideal for solving on his new electronic digital computer. Charney had been intrigued by von Neumann's proposal, and it had driven part of his work in Norway. Hearing of Charney's research, von Neumann invited him to join the Princeton team.

Charney took over the rudderless Meteorology Project in spring 1948, immediately offering the project a better sense of direction. He insisted that the team start with a very well-defined, simple model that could be

assembled with workable algorithms that would operate in small steps. Once the simplified model worked, they would add more factors one at a time until the model became more realistic and complex. Charney had already prepared his quasi-geostrophic prediction equations, but they needed to be adapted to the computer. The result was a 500 millibar (approximately 5,500 meters above sea level) barotropic model, that is, a single-parameter, single-level model based solely on the horizontal motion of the initial circulation field.

While the model was ready, von Neumann's computer was not, so project members gave their model a trial run on Aberdeen (Maryland) Proving Ground's ENIAC computer in April 1950. The results of this first "expedition" produced forecast maps that looked meteorological, but needed refinements. Over the next four years, project members continued to improve their atmospheric models, which were finally run operationally in May 1955 at the Joint Numerical Weather Prediction Unit, a combined U.S. Weather Bureau–Navy–Air Force organization that was an outgrowth of the Meteorology Project.

The creation of numerical weather prediction was a tremendous achievement whose success was due to Charney's attention to the details of hydrodynamic factors in the atmosphere and von Neumann's computational techniques. Charney's quasi-geostrophic model had been critical to getting the project started and he had been absolutely determined to see the model progress from research project to daily operations. He also wanted to ensure that the theoretical models were not only internally consistent mathematically, but represented observational evidence.

Charney was forced to make assumptions during the development of his model. He first removed all vertical motion in the atmosphere from consideration and then reduced movement to one dimension. He added in friction and topography while trying to make the model more "realistic," but found those factors had little effect for twenty-four-hour forecasts and removed them. The numerical weather prediction models run by the Meteorology Project proved it was possible to predict cyclogenesis (the birth and development of a low-pressure circulation system), which is the precursor to the formation of weather-producing fronts. The models also proved that a geostrophic system could successfully create an elementary simulation of the atmosphere's general circulation pattern. Charney also showed that model complexity was constrained by computing power. As computing power increased, the models included more variables and became more sophisticated.

The results of Charney's research were widely felt throughout the meteorology community. Although he had had to make simplifying assumptions, Charney had not done so in the absence of supporting theory. His assumptions enabled dynamic meteorologists to understand the atmosphere's very complex physical processes and analyze the motion of large-scale systems. Therefore, Charney's assumptions not only reduced the number of years required to produce operational computer-created forecasts, but their basis in systematic quantitative arguments was equally important for meteorological theory.

The MIT Years. The work of the Meteorology Project completed, Charney moved on to the Massachusetts Institute of Technology (MIT) faculty in 1956. While at MIT, he continued his research on problems in dynamic meteorology including the vertical propagation of planetary waves (very long waves of energy that encircle the globe), the stability of jet streams, the generation of hurricanes, geostrophic turbulence, and climate dynamics in desert areas.

In addition to his theoretical research, Charney was also active in organizational work. He was a leading member of the Committee on Atmospheric Sciences at the National Academy of Sciences and was involved in the decision to form the National Center for Atmospheric Research in Boulder, Colorado, which became one of the premier sites for meteorological research in the United States in the early 1960s.

In 1968, Charney accepted the chair of the committee directing the Global Atmospheric Research Program (GARP)—a huge international undertaking that proposed to observe "the entire atmosphere of the Earth and the sea surface … in detail for the first time." Charney had been mulling over the possibility of such a project since the early 1960s. He had realized that meteorology was a global science, but it was decidedly lacking in the global observations that would allow atmospheric scientists to cooperate across national boundaries. Even a short-term observational experiment would give meteorologists a tremendous data set with which to work.

Although several smaller experiments took place during the early 1970s, notably the GARP Atlantic Tropical Experiment (or GATE), the main yearlong event—the Global Weather Experiment—started in December 1978. This five-hundred-million-dollar project involved four polar orbiting and five geosynchronous satellites, more than three hundred ocean buoys, and more than three hundred constant-level balloons that would drift on air currents approximately 14 kilometers above Earth's surface while measuring temperature and upper level winds. The experiment was a huge success. These data—so critical for meteorological research—were almost immediately used to improve operational weather forecasting.

With his GARP responsibilities behind him in 1978, Charney turned to what would be his last major research

project, which examined the creation of blocks (masses of high-pressure air that prohibit the normal flow of atmospheric systems). Although blocking highs had been readily identifiable features for many years, no accepted theory for their life cycle existed until Charney began to examine them in the context of a seminar he was teaching at UCLA. Charney and one of the students, John DeVore, developed and published a dynamical theory of blocking in 1979. As had been the case throughout Charney's life, this scientific study encouraged further investigations, particularly among the ranks of fluid dynamicists.

The supervisor of many graduate students during his MIT years, Charney left behind many academic progeny. They continued the various strands of his research agenda after his death at age sixty-four from lung cancer.

BIBLIOGRAPHY

WORKS BY CHARNEY

"The Dynamics of Long Waves in a Baroclinic Westerly Current." *Journal of Meteorology* 4 (1947): 135–162.

"On the Scale of Atmospheric Motions." *Geofysiske Publikasjoner* 17, no. 2 (1948): 1–17.

"On a Physical Basis for Numerical Predictions of Large-Scale Motions in the Atmosphere." *Journal of Meteorology* 6 (1949): 371–385.

With Ragnar Fjørtoft and John von Neumann. "Numerical Integration of the Barotropic Vorticity Equation." *Tellus* 2 (1950): 248–257.

With Robert G. Fleagle, Vincent E. Lally, Herbert Riehl, et al. "The Feasibility of a Global Observation and Analysis Experiment." *Bulletin of the American Meteorological Society* 47 (1966): 200–220.

With John G. DeVore. "Multiple Flow Equilibria in the Atmosphere and Blocking." *Journal of the Atmospheric Sciences* 36 (1979): 1205–1216.

OTHER SOURCES

Harper, Kristine C. "Research from the Boundary Layer: Civilian Leadership, Military Funding and the Development of Numerical Weather Prediction (1946–1955)." *Social Studies of Science* 33 (October 2003): 667–696.

Lindzen, Richard S., Edward N. Lorenz, and George W. Platzman, eds. *The Atmosphere—A Challenge: The Science of Jule Gregory Charney.* Boston: American Meteorological Society, 1990. This volume contains Charney's curriculum vitae, an oral history interview conducted approximately one year before his death, articles about his work and life, and reprints of several of Charney's most significant articles.

Nebeker, Frederik. *Calculating the Weather: Meteorology in the 20th Century.* San Diego, CA: Academic Press, 1995. See especially chapters 10 and 11.

Phillips, Norman A. "Jule Charney's Influence on Meteorology." *Bulletin of the American Meteorological Society* 63 (1982): 492–497.

———. "Jule Gregory Charney, January 1, 1917–June 16, 1981." *Biographical Memoirs*, vol. 66. Washington, DC: National Academy of Sciences, 1995.

Richardson, Lewis Fry. *Weather Prediction by Numerical Process.* Cambridge, U.K.: Cambridge University Press, 1922. Reprinted by Dover Publications, New York, 1965, and by Cambridge University Press, 2006.

Kristine C. Harper

CHATT, JOSEPH (*b.* Hordern, County Durham, England, 6 November 1914; *d.* Hove, Sussex, England, 19 May 1994), *inorganic and organometallic chemistry of transition elements, nitrogen fixation.*

Joseph was one of the originators of the field of transition-metal organometallic chemistry and was an innovator in the areas of synthesis, understanding electronic effects, and the study of the mechanisms of the reactions of transition-metal compounds. In nitrogen fixation, his group prepared more novel dinitrogen complexes than any other, into the early 2000s, and he led the way in building inorganic models for the mechanism of biological nitrogen fixation.

Education and Early Career. Joseph Chatt, eldest son of Joseph and M. Elsie Chatt, began his education in a very inauspicious manner, in the village school of Welton, not far from Carlisle in the northwest of England. He stayed there until he was fourteen. This school was very conventional, teaching no science as such, and as his father was a farmer, he received little encouragement to study science at home. However, his uncle was the chief chemist in a steelworks near Newcastle upon Tyne, and Joseph learned some basic chemistry and physics on his holiday visits there. His home did not have an electricity supply, but when his uncle sent him a book on electricity and magnetism, Chatt fitted up his bedroom with an electric light powered by a dichromate cell and switched the light on and off from the door by raising and lowering an electrode using a piece of string. Not only did his uncle inspire an interest in science, but the area where he lived, Caldbeck Fells, is comprised of many old and metalliferous rocks. Chatt searched out rock types, an interest that stayed with him. After moving on to secondary school, he came into contact with a chemistry teacher who encouraged him in many ways, not least in inorganic analysis to determine what metals his rock samples contained, but also in other branches of chemical science, and Chatt used this disinterested help to explore chemistry for himself, in a way that would not be permitted on grounds of safety to young chemists in the early 2000s. Chatt claimed to be the last person to have observed the direct reaction of sodium metal and concentrated sulphuric acid, because it is unlikely that anyone since would have dared to try such a potentially dangerous experiment.

Not only was Chatt an unusually highly motivated pupil, but the masters at his secondary school, the Nelson School at Wigton, were very perspicacious. They realized that this pupil was exceptional, even taking into account that he had arrived at the school three years older than the usual intake. He matriculated in about two years rather than the normal five. Although the family's circumstances were straitened, he won scholarships sufficient to allow him to study at Cambridge University, something that his farming family would never have envisaged. He obtained a place at Emmanuel College Cambridge through the efforts of his mathematics master, who though the university already had its formal quota of new students, personally made a tour of the individual colleges until he found one that was prepared to accept his exceptional pupil.

Chatt would have started his studies at Cambridge in October 1934, but he was unable to do so until he had passed the then-obligatory examination in Latin, which he had not studied before. With yet more help from his secondary school, he passed this exam and entered the Cambridge in January 1935. He obtained his PhD in the summer of 1940, when World War II had been in progress for about a year.

During World War II, Chatt was unable to follow his academic interests. His 1940 appointment to an academic post at St. Andrews University, Scotland, seems to have lapsed completely. He never took it up, and instead performed various functions related to the war effort. The government authorities dictated these, and none of them seems to have been very appropriate. His weak ankle, which troubled him for the whole of his adult life, clearly prevented him from active service in the armed forces. However, Chatt was obliged to do as he was directed in the national interest, and he finally finished as chief chemist in a factory concerned mainly with the production of alumina. Once the war was over, he resigned and went to the Imperial College of Science and technology in London as an ICI (Imperial Chemical Industries) Fellow.

Coordination Chemistry around 1940. When Chatt began his research work, chemistry research was almost entirely concerned with organic chemistry. Inorganic chemistry, which had interested him because of the multitude of elements he had detected in his rock samples, was regarded as a finished subject. Textbooks on inorganic chemistry were generally compendia of preparations, colors, and physical properties. Organometallic chemistry was a subject of limited interest and was restricted to elements such as silicon and magnesium, which are main-group elements. There was skepticism as to whether transition-metal organometallic compounds would be stable enough to exist under ambient conditions. Very few academics were interested in the subject, but one of the few was Frederick G. Mann, whose lectures Chatt admired. Mann was interested in the nature of various types of chemical bond and believed that information on their quality might be derived from a parameter called the parachor, related to the dipole moment of a molecule, itself a measure of charge separation. The measurement of the parachor required the preparation of solutions in organic liquids. However, inorganic compounds are usually not soluble in such liquids, and certainly not in those common in the 1930s. Mann realized that forming complexes of inorganic compounds with agents such as tertiary phosphines, many of which are rather vile smelling and reactive materials, would produce adducts that were soluble in organic liquids. Chatt did his PhD research work on phosphine complexes of palladium, among other related species, and this led to his lifelong interest in basic transition-metal chemistry, transition-metal organometallic chemistry, and the nature of the coordinate bond.

This last subject requires a little explanation. The interest that Mann had in the parachor has long been superseded. However, a coordinate bond between a metal ion acceptor and a donor such as ammonia has been recognized for several decades to be the result of the sharing between the donor and acceptor of a pair of electrons (a lone pair). The extent to which this donation of negatively charged electrons leaves a positive charge on the donor and produces a negative charge on the acceptor has been the subject of research for perhaps sixty years, starting with the the effective founder of the field, Alfred Werner. The amount of charge transfer varies considerably with both the kind of donor and the kind of acceptor. Chatt was one of the first to concern himself experimentally with this problem, using the kinds of compound he had first studied with Mann, and to solve it he employed the most recent advances in preparative inorganic chemistry and in various branches of spectroscopy. His work paralleled that of Dwyer and especially Nyholm, who became a close friend when the latter moved to University College, London. Wilkinson also worked, in part, in related areas, and so did Pearson and Basolo.

Inorganic Chemistry at ICI. Chatt's brief stay at Imperial College had been very frustrating. The aftermath of the war, with its shortages both of money and of materials, prevented him from doing any significant work. However, his enthusiasm was noted by the then chairman of ICI, Wallace Akers, who was a keen supporter of academic research, and who was also convinced that the company would benefit from having a general group of first-class academic researchers working in new areas in the company's own laboratories. He persuaded the company to establish such a laboratory, in some temporary buildings on the grounds of a country house called The Frythe, near Welwyn, Hertfordshire, some twenty miles north of London. ICI recruited Chatt directly form his fellowship at Imperial College, and gave him the objective of setting up an academic-style inorganic chemistry laboratory. The name, The Frythe, became synonymous with innovative inorganic chemistry research of the highest order. Although Chatt initially headed a department of one, namely, himself, he built up a famed research group, two of the most eminent members of which, among several others, were Luigi M. Venanzi and Bernard L. Shaw. At The Frythe, Chatt was able to work and publish uninterruptedly on his own projects. He was able to apply his meticulous methodology and integrity to completely novel projects. That ICI did not take commercial advantage of what he produced, though others in other countries did, was a great pity for the company.

During World War II, Chatt had become interested in the peculiar addition compounds that seemed to form between elements such as platinum, on the one hand, and olefins and acetylenes, on the other, organic compounds that contain multiple carbon-carbon bonds but no lone pairs of electrons of the kind recognized in ammonia. The study of these addition compounds gave rise to a series of papers titled "The Nature of the Coordinate Link," published between 1950 and 1984. Just how an olefin could bind to a transition metal ion when it had no lone pairs, and what the structure of such a complex might be, was very much of a mystery. The ideas generated in these papers remain into the early 2000s a fundamental part of the inorganic chemists' theoretical armory. It was inferred by Chatt, as described in "Olefin Coordination Compounds," Parts I (1949) and III (1953), that the electrons forming the carbon-carbon multiple bond could act as lone pairs, and that the negative charge transferred from the olefin to the metal in this process could be partly neutralized by the transfer of other electrons on the metal ion back to the olefin (back-bonding). Such a coordinate bond thus has two parts, formed by transfer of electrons in opposite directions. Not only that, but donors such as the tertiary phosphines, to which Mann had introduced him, were shown to be able to bond to metal ions in a comparable way. There has been some disagreement as to who first publicized this idea of simultaneous transfer of electrons in both directions when forming a coordinate bond, particularly when olefins and acetylenes are involved, and people such as Linus Pauling and Michael J. S. Dewar were important contributors. There is, however, no doubt that Chatt was instrumental in developing it and showing its wide applicability.

The consequences of this work were very wide-reaching. Chatt was one of the first to use infrared spectroscopy to characterize inorganic chemical compounds and to use the frequencies of given infrared absorptions to infer the nature of the bonds producing such absorptions. This later became common, but at that time there were few, if any, commercial infrared instruments available. The ICI workshops constructed one specifically for the use of Chatt's group, which also did extensive work on the dipole moments of complexes in order to infer charge distributions. This latter technique, the measurement of dipole moments, is no longer widely employed.

Many new complexes, often phosphine complexes, were produced at The Frythe. Together with Sten Ahrland, who came from the Scandinavian school of chemistry that had developed very advanced techniques for measuring stability constants, he employed the Scandinavian methods to compare the intensities of the interactions between various donors (such as ammonia, phosphines, and the related arsines) and various metal-ion acceptors (both transition-metal and non-transition-metal ions) when forming metal complexes. From this work came the generalization that acceptors in these complexes fall into two groups, those designated Class A, which seem to comprise those that do not partake of significant backbonding, magnesium being a typical example, and those designated Class B, which do. Typical examples of the latter are the platinum group metals. These ideas were later extended and generalized by Ralph G. Pearson to produce the concepts of hard and soft Lewis acids and Lewis bases, which still form a useful part of the inorganic chemist's theoretical armory.

This was not the end of The Frythe's influence. Together with Pearson and novices Bernard L. Shaw and Harry B. Gray, both now internationally recognized, Chatt was a participant in one of the first major studies of the mechanism of substitution of groups in inorganic complexes. Such studies were common in organic chemistry, stimulated by the work of researchers such as Ingold, and the results were well understood in electronic terms, comparable studies on inorganic compounds could not be made until the development of novel complexes such as those studied at The Frythe. In the early 2000s, such work is common, but then it was groundbreaking.

There was at least one further development that can be traced back to The Frythe. Chatt reasoned that developing a metal-carbon bond in complexes of donors such as his favorite phosphines with metal ions, for example those of platinum and palladium, could strengthen the supposedly very weak metal-carbon bond. This did indeed turn out to be the case, and the result was a series of elegant and original papers titled "Alkyls and Aryls of the Transition Metals" (1959–1966). This work finally exploded the idea that transition-metal bonds to carbon in, say, alkyl compounds, are inherently very weak, and

led to a veritable explosion in preparative chemistry, both inorganic and organic, that changed ideas about transition-metal compounds and had a profound influence on industrial chemistry and catalysis. Almost as a by-product, the first hydride complex (a complex containing a bond between a transition-metal ion and a hydrogen atom) containing no moieties with metal-carbon bonds was characterized at The Frythe. Metal carbonyl hydrides had been recognized for more than fifty years. Many other classes of hydride complex were later known.

This work not only was a fundamental part of the renaissance of inorganic chemistry in the 1950s and 1960s, but it changed completely the prevailing ideas about inorganic compounds and their structures, about transition-metal catalysis, and even about significant aspects of organic synthesis. Nevertheless, in 1962, perhaps because of a less favorable economic climate and with a more focused management, ICI decided to reorganize its research activities, and the decision was made to close The Frythe laboratory and draft Chatt back to northern England to involve him in industrial organic chemicals. This he declined to accept, and when the laboratory was closed, he looked for other employment.

Nitrogen Fixation Research. By this time Chatt already had an international reputation and, in 1961, had been elected to the Royal Society. It was rumored that he would move to the United States, but the then-secretary of the Agricultural Research Council, Sir E. Gordon Cox, persuaded the council to set up a research laboratory for him, to absorb the little biological nitrogen fixation work the council was already funding, and to launch a full-scale effort in both biology and chemistry to uncover the mechanism of biological nitrogen fixation. The conversion of atmospheric nitrogen (or dinitrogen, N_2), a very unreactive compound that comprises about 80 percent of atmospheric air, to ammonia (NH_3) is achieved industrially using catalysts and elevated temperatures and pressures, but microorganisms can achieve such a conversion in the soil under ambient conditions. Exactly how they do so was then (and remained into the early 2000s) an unsolved problem.

The laboratory, internationally known as the Unit of Nitrogen Fixation, became the leading one of its kind in the world. Initially situated at Queen Mary College in London, that site was ultimately determined to be unsuitable, and in 1964, the unit moved to the University of Sussex in Brighton, East Sussex, with the encouragement of the head of the School of Chemistry and Molecular Science, Colin Eaborn. There the unit was set up in two separate but closely connected sections, the chemistry led by Chatt and the biology led by John R. Postgate, with Chatt as overall director. Eventually, at its zenith in the 1980s, the unit comprised some sixty persons and was notable for its breadth of expertise, ranging from inorganic chemistry at one extreme through biochemistry and microbiology to molecular biology at the other. After a considerable amount of encouragement from Chatt and Postgate, all the various researchers in the unit developed the ability to discuss meaningfully most aspects of the nitrogen fixation problem, whatever their basic discipline, and this unique property attracted a constant stream of researchers from all over the world. The Agricultural Research Council ran the unit on a very loose rein, something that was exceptional by the 1990s, and remained so as of 2006. Nevertheless, this approach was rewarded with a stream of fundamental discoveries that have had an enormous impact on our understanding of both the chemistry and biology of nitrogen fixation. Despite the successes achieved, the successor to the council eventually decided that the direct economic payback for all this academic work was too little, and the unit was allowed to fade away after 1996, when many of its staff were transferred to the John Innes Centre at Norwich. However, what Chatt achieved in chemistry and Postgate in biology is still widely appreciated and used.

Perhaps the most important biological discovery was the ability to transfer a plasmid containing the genes necessary to fix nitrogen from *Klebsiella pneumoniae* to *Escherichia coli.* Although this work was within Postgate's section, Chatt was skilled enough subsequently to present to the council a case for expanding the unit's genetics effort by about 50 percent. He was successful, and this discovery was the basis for advances in the understanding of the function, genetics, and regulation of biological nitrogen fixation and similar properties of other processes in a large variety of organisms.

The chemistry work, led by Chatt, was at least as influential. It had been believed for some years prior to the 1960s that the enzyme responsible for the biological conversion of dinitrogen to ammonia was a metalloenzyme, possibly containing iron and (or) molybdenum. However, no one had detected any sign of the direct interaction of dinitrogen with a metal compound that might be regarded as a model for the metalloenzyme function. In 1965, Albert D. Allen and Caesar V. Senoff announced the first dinitrogen complex, based upon ruthenium, and containing the moiety Ru—N≡N. Cobalt and iridium dinitrogen complexes appeared soon after. The conversion of the bound dinitrogen to ammonia turned out to be much more difficult and was not achieved until later.

The unit's chemistry work started in 1965 and took off when the unit moved into its own building in 1969. In that year, in a paper titled "A Series of Nitrogen Complexes of Rhenium(I)," Chatt and his collaborators described the first two extensive series of dinitrogen complexes, based upon rhenium and osmium, both also containing the customary phosphine donors. They also described related nitride complexes, which contain a single nitrogen atom combined with a metal ion.

These dinitrogen complexes proved rather recalcitrant as far as making the dinitrogen react. However, the Chatt group adduced evidence to show that the complexed dinitrogen was probably polarized so that the external nitrogen atom carried a negative charge, a consequence of the two-way flow of electrons between a donor and an acceptor of the kind discussed above. This was surely a way to render the dinitrogen more reactive, and in 1972, the group reported the first reaction of a well-defined dinitrogen complex, of tungsten, a congener of the biological metal molybdenum, to produce a well-defined complex product containing a new nitrogen-carbon bond. The mechanism of this reaction was described subsequently in detail by the Chatt group in "The Mechanism of Alkylation of Dinitrogen Coordinated to Molybdenum(0) and Tungsten(0)." This study remained the major kinetic investigation of a reaction of this kind into the twenty-first century. It led to the establishment of a cyclic system for making amines directly from dinitrogen. In 1972, the controlled protonation of coordinated dinitrogen was achieved, and the protonation all the way to ammonia was reported in 1975. These and many related studies were the basis for what was later described as the Chatt cycle to explain the protonation of dinitrogen, both in these complexes of molybdenum and also in nitrogenase enzymes. As of 2007, it remained an open question whether extension to the nitrogenase enzymes is justified or not.

Later Life and Honors. Chatt retired from the Unit of Nitrogen Fixation in 1978 and gradually withdrew from professional activities. His work was regularly quoted in the literature, and much of it remained current. He was active outside his immediate area of employment all his professional life. For example, he was secretary of the Chemical Society (later the Royal Society of Chemistry) and for over twenty years a member of IUPAC, during which time (1959–1963) he occupied effectively the chair of the Commission on the Nomenclature of Inorganic Chemistry. He was honored by election to several academies, including the New York Academy of Sciences (1978), the American Academy of Arts and Sciences (1985), and the Indian Chemical Society (1984). He received several medals and lectureships, including the American Chemical Society Award for Distinguished Service in the Advancement of Inorganic Chemistry in 1971 and the Wolf Prize for Chemistry in 1981. Her Majesty the Queen appointed him to the rank of Commander of the British Empire (CBE) in 1978.

The Royal Society of Chemistry endowed a lectureship in his name. By its terms, every second year a distinguished chemist, without regard to nationality, is invited to deliver the lecture at several venues within the United Kingdom.

BIBLIOGRAPHY

Documents relating to Chatt's professional career are deposited at the John Innes Centre, Colney Lane, Norwich, NR4 7UH. A complete bibliography is obtainable from the library of the Royal Society, London; see Eaborn, C., and G. J. Leigh, cited below.

WORKS BY CHATT

"Olefin Coordination Compounds. Part I, Discussion of Proposed Structures: The System Ethylene-Trimethylborine." *Journal of the Chemical Society* (1949): 3340–3348.

"The Nature of the Co-ordinate Link. Part I, Halogen-Bridged, Binuclear Platinous Complexes." *Journal of the Chemical Society* (1950): 2301–2310.

"The General Chemistry of Olefin Complexes with Metallic Salts." In *Cationic Polymerization and Related Complexes,* edited by P. H. Plesch. Cambridge, U.K.: Heffer, 1953.

With L. A. Duncanson. "Olefin Coordination Compounds. Part III, Infra-red Spectra and Structure of Acetylene Complexes: Attempted Preparation of Acetylene Complexes." *Journal of the Chemical Society* (1953): 2939–2947.

With L. A. Ducanson and B. L. Shaw. "A Volatile Chlorohydride of Platinum." *Proceedings of the Chemical Society* (1957): 343.

With S. Ahrland, N. R. Davies, and A. A. Williams. "The Relative Affinities of Coordinating Atoms for Silver Ions. Part I, Oxygen, Sulphur, and Selenium." *Journal of the Chemical Society* (1958) 264–276.

With S. Ahrland, N. R. Davies, and A. A. Williams. "The Relative Affinities of Coordinating Atoms for Silver Ions. Part II, Nitrogen, Phosphorus, and Arsenic." *Journal of the Chemical Society* (1958): 276–288.

With B. L. Shaw. "Alkyls and Aryls of the Transition Metals. Part I, Complex Methylplatinum(II) Derivatives." *Journal of the Chemical Society* (1959): 705–716.

With F. Basolo, H. B. Gray, R. G. Pearson et al. "Kinetics of the Reaction of Alkyl and Aryl Compounds of the Nickel Group with Pyridine." *Journal of the Chemical Society* (1961): 2207–2215.

With J. M. Davidson. "The Tautomerism of Arene and Ditertiary Phosphine Complexes of Ruthenium(0), and the Preparation of New Types of Hydridocomplexes of Ruthenium (II)." *Journal of the Chemical Society* (1965): 843–855.

With J. R. Dilworth and G. J. Leigh. "A Series of Nitrogen Complexes of Rhenium(I)." *Chemical Communications* (1969): 687–688.

With G. A. Heath and G. J. Leigh. "The Formation of a Nitrogen to Carbon Bond in a Reaction of a Dinitrogen Complex." *Journal of the Chemical Society, Chemical Communications* (1972): 444–445.

With A. J. Pearman and R. L. Richards. "The Reduction of Mono-coordinated Molecular Nitrogen to Ammonia in a Protic Environment." *Nature* 253 (1975): 39–40.

With R. A. Head, G. J. Leigh, and C. J. Pickett. "The Mechanism of Alkylation of Dinitrogen Coordinated to Molybdenum(0) and Tungsten(0)." *Journal of the Chemical Society, Chemical Communications* (1977): 299–300.

With P. B. Hitchcock, A. Pidcock, C. P. Warren et al. "The Nature of the Coordinate Link. Part XI, Synthesis and phosphorus-31 nuclear magnetic resonance spectroscopy of platinum and palladium complexes containing side-bonded (E)-diphenyldiphosphene. *X*-Ray crystal and molecular structures of [Pd{(E)-PhP=PPh}(Ph$_2$PCH$_2$CH$_2$PPh$_2$)] and [Pd{[(E)-PhP=PPh][W(CO)$_5$]$_2$}(Ph$_2$PCH$_2$CH$_2$PPh$_2$)]." *Journal of the Chemical Societ, Dalton Transactions* (1984) 2237–2244. This was the last paper in the series, "The Nature of the Coordinate Link."

OTHER SOURCES

Brock, William H. *The Fontana History of Chemistry.* London: Fontana Press, 1992. See especially pp. 591–618.

Dixon, R. A., and J. R. Postgate. "Transfer of Nitrogen Fixation Genes by Conjugation in *Klebsiella Pneumoniae.*" *Nature* (London) 234 (1971): 47–48.

Eaborn, C., and G. J. Leigh. "Joseph Chatt, C.B.E., 6 November 1914–19 May 1994." *Bibliographic Memoirs of Fellows of the Royal Society* 42 (1996): 96–110.

Hussain, W., G. J. Leigh, and C. J. Pickett. "Stepwise Conversion of Dinitrogen Coordinated to Molybdenum into an Amine and an Imido-complex: Relevance to the Reactions of Nitrogenase." *Journal of the Chemical Society, Chemical Communications* (1982): 747–748.

Leigh, G. J. "A Celebration of Inorganic Lives. Interview of Joseph Chatt." *Coordination Chemistry Reviews* 108 (1991): 1–25

———. "Professor Joseph Chatt CBE FRS." *Coordination Chemistry Reviews* 154 (1996): 1–3

———. In *Nitrogen Fixation at the Millennium,* edited by G. J. Leigh: Elsevier, Amsterdam, Netherlands; Boston, 2002, Chapter 11, Dinitrogen Chemistry.

———. J. N. Murrell, W. Bremser, and W. G. Proctor. "On the State of Dinitrogen Bound to Rhenium." *Chemical Communications* (1970): 1661.

———. and N. Winterton, eds. *Modern Coordination Chemistry: The Legacy of Joseph Chatt.* Cambridge, U.K.: Royal Society of Chemistry, 2002.

G. Jeffrey Leigh

CHERENKOV, PAVEL ALEKSEYE-VICH

(*b.* Novaya Chigla, Voronezh province, Russia, 28 July 1904; *d.* Moscow, USSR, 6 January 1990), *experimental physics, optics, nuclear and elementary particle physics, accelerators, cosmic rays.*

The Soviet physicist Cherenkov (sometimes also spelled *Čerenkov* or *Tscherenkow*) is known primarily for the 1934 discovery of the Cherenkov effect, a distinctive type of electromagnetic radiation emitted when charged particles travel faster than light would travel through a particular medium. The effect serves as the basis for Cherenkov counters, commonly used detectors of high-energy particles in elementary particle accelerators. For his role in the discovery, Cherenkov shared the 1958 Nobel Prize in Physics. His scientific career can also be seen as a striking illustration of Communist "affirmative action" policies in the Soviet Union—reverse privileges in education that strongly encouraged the promotion of representatives of the lower classes into the ranks of the scientific profession. These educational opportunities, not ordinarily available to the son of a peasant, enabled Cherenkov to embark on what would become an illustrious career in science.

From Peasant Laborer to Scientist. Cherenkov's parents, Aleksey and Mariya, were peasants in the village of Novaya Chigla in southern Russia. His mother died and his father remarried when Pavel was two years old. With eight siblings from his father's two marriages, Cherenkov grew up in poverty and had to start work as a manual laborer at the early age of thirteen, having completed just two years of elementary schooling. After the Bolshevik Revolution and the civil war that followed, a new Soviet secondary school opened in the village in 1920, which allowed Cherenkov to resume his education while continuing to earn a living through occasional work at a grocery store. The door to further schooling beyond the incomplete secondary level was opened for him by the revolutionary Bolshevik government's radical reform of the entire educational system.

In their attempts to democratize access to higher education, the Bolsheviks were not satisfied with simply removing formal barriers of gender, ethnicity, and religion. They also tried to compensate for economic disadvantages by preferential treatment of students from worker and peasant backgrounds. The latter measures included free tuition, stipends for low-income students, class quotas, preparatory courses (*rabfaks*, or workers' faculties, for those who had not finished secondary school), and last but not least, softening of the formal criteria required for advancement from one educational level to another. It became possible, in principle, to enroll in a university without a formal high school diploma, start a graduate program without fully completing undergraduate education, and be hired as a professor without a PhD degree or equivalent. Many Soviet scientists of the Cherenkov generation skipped one or another of these formal steps while embarking on their academic careers. Cherenkov took advantage of promotional opportunities available for lower-class students and in 1924, apparently

without completing secondary education, enrolled in the Pedagogical Department of Voronezh State University.

Graduation in 1928 enabled Cherenkov to become a teacher of physics and mathematics at an evening school for workers in Kozlov (now Michurinsk), a small town in Tambov province. But 1928 was also the year when a new, more radical cultural revolution broke out in the Soviet Union, and attempts intensified to draw more women, minorities, and lower-class students not only into colleges but also into the ranks of scientific researchers and to rapidly train a new and massive generation of scientists for the ongoing crash industrialization effort. "Affirmative action" measures were applied to the greatly expanded *aspirantura*, or graduate studies programs, at universities and institutes for research. Soviet educational policies at the time did not recognize academic degrees such as the PhD. The job of a graduate student, or *aspirant*, was not to write a thesis but instead to learn the trade of scientific research while working as a junior apprentice alongside established scientists. In 1930 Cherenkov was admitted as aspirant to one such program at the Physico-Mathematical Institute of the USSR Academy of Sciences in Leningrad.

Earlier that year Cherenkov married Marya Putintseva, daughter of a professor of Russian literature from Voronezh. Other events, typical of the revolutionary era, also affected his life. His father-in-law was dismissed as a "bourgeois professor" and sent to work in a labor camp, while Cherenkov's own father was deprived of property and exiled as a kulak. *Kulak* literally means "a wealthy peasant," but the label did not have to correspond to the true state of affairs—it received a very liberal and broad application and could also be applied to poorer peasants during the chaotic and violent collectivization of Soviet agriculture around 1930. In theory, associations with persecuted relatives could have undermined some of the advantages Cherenkov received due to his low class origin, but there is no evidence that he was affected in this way, at least not significantly.

Cherenkov Radiation. Living the life of a young up-and-coming physicist in the revolutionary Soviet society meant also to be particularly receptive to the on-going radical revolution in fundamental laws of physics. The news of the 1919 triumphant confirmation of Einstein's relativity theory was among the first to arrive in the country at the end of the Civil War and created a wave of public astonishment and obsession, made perhaps even stronger than in the rest of Europe by metaphorical associations with the concurrent political revolution. The year 1923 brought yet another radical crack in the established foundation of physics: the Compton Effect—electrons kicked out of their atoms by incoming x-rays—confirmed an even more daring prediction by Einstein that electromagnetic radiation behaves like an assembly of particle-like light quanta. In 1925 quantum mechanics revealed the new strange laws of microscopic particles at the atomic levels that contradicted not only the classical Newtonian mechanics but also seemingly the laws of reason and causality. Quantum mechanics' relativistic generalization in the 1928 Dirac equation explained the Compton Effect and the electron spin, but also led to prediction of the yet unknown anti-electron and antimatter in general, which were seen as wild speculations even by the majority of otherwise radically inclined theorists. Shockingly, in 1932 anti-electron turned out in cosmic rays, and the discovery of the neutron—another previously unknown elementary particle—that same year shifted physicist's interests to the emerging field of nuclear physics.

Although the news about the most recent breakthroughs often came to them with a certain delay, the young Soviet physicists jumped at every opportunity to contribute to the great developments in physics, often ahead of their more senior peers. In 1922 Alexander Friedmann revealed for the first time that Einstein's relativity, when applied to cosmology, means that the Universe is not stable, but expands in what came to be called the Big Bang explosion. Upon receiving the first news about quantum mechanics, theorists Yakov Frenkel, Vladimir Fock, Igor Tamm, and Lev Landau immediately joined the new revolutionary theory and made important contributions to it. In 1928 Georgiy (George) Gamow pioneered the application of quantum mechanics to atomic nucleus with his theory of alpha-decay.

Despite its elite affiliation, the Physico-Mathematical Institute of the USSR Academy of Sciences, where Cherenkov began his aspirant studies, had been a very small and almost nominal institution. The main events in Soviet physics occurred elsewhere, in much larger and better funded universities and research institutes associated with industry. In 1932, however, the situation was about to change with the appointment of Sergei Ivanovich Vavilov (1891–1951) as the director of the institute's Department of Physics.

A physics professor from Moscow State University and a newly elected member of the USSR Academy of Sciences, Vavilov was an expert in experimental research on luminescence—a kind of quantum interaction between light and matter typically observed as a property of some substances to glow long after being exposed to light or some other excitation (the phenomenon is used in luminescent screens). In the course of his research, Vavilov became a firm believer in Einstein's light quanta and made their study his lifelong commitment in experiment. As director, he harbored broader ambitions and wanted to develop in his institute the most exciting and cutting-edge

fields, in particular the study of the atomic nucleus. His appointment at the Physico-Mathematical Institute was connected with the plans by the academy to greatly expand and separate the institute into two independent ones, for physics and mathematics respectively.

The institute's only specialist in nuclear physics, Gamow (1904–1968), decided to stay in the West and did not return after attending the 1933 Solvay conference in Brussels. In a bold administrative move, and also in the spirit of revolutionary times, Vavilov entrusted several aspirants to start nuclear research on their own, while appointing himself the pro forma head of the nuclear laboratory to ensure administrative protection. Cherenkov received a more precise assignment, a fusion between Vavilov's own research program in luminescence and the new interest in nuclear physics. He was asked to study what happens to luminescent solutions of uranium salts excited not by ordinary light, as in the common method, but by much more energetic gamma rays from a radioactive source.

Cherenkov Radiation. Earlier in the 1920s, when economic conditions were extremely poor, Vavilov with coworkers developed a clever observational method for registering extremely faint luminescence—almost at the threshold of single light quantum—by using an experimenter's naked eye adapted to greater sensitivity by several hours spent in complete darkness. Cherenkov mastered this technique and applied it in his study of luminescence induced by gamma rays in uranium salt solutions. An extremely diligent and meticulous observer, he noticed that gamma rays also produced a faint background blue glow in ordinarily nonluminiscent pure solvents, such as sulfuric acid or water. Vavilov's expertise helped him to recognize the effect as a new phenomenon, different from luminescence. The institute's unpublished annual report for 1933 first mentioned the discovery of a new radiation in pure liquids by aspirant Cherenkov working under Vavilov's supervision. The publication came in 1934 as two back-to-back papers in *Doklady* (Reports) of the USSR Academy of Sciences: one by Cherenkov on the experimental discovery of the "blue light," and another by Vavilov with theoretical discussion of the observed results. Vavilov attributed the radiation to *Bremsstrahlung*, or "stopping radiation," emitted by rapidly decelerating Compton electrons that had been dislodged from their atoms by incident gamma rays.

Also in 1934 the Soviet government enacted a major buildup of the academy's research infrastructure, including the reorganization of its Physico-Mathematical Institute into separate institutes for physics and mathematics and their relocation, along with a number of other institutes, from Leningrad to Moscow. Vavilov's numerous

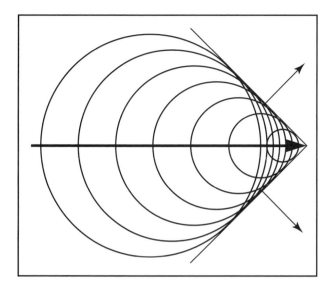

Cherenkov radiation.

Ilya Mikhailovich Frank (1908–1991) explain the true cause of the phenomenon in 1937.

Cherenkov (or Vavilov-Cherenkov) radiation is produced when Compton electrons, kicked by high-energy gamma quanta, move through a substance relatively uniformly (rather than decelerating rapidly, as Vavilov had thought) and faster than light would travel in the substance. It is the optical analog of shock waves in acoustics, the sound produced in the air by an ultrasonic projectile or jet, which also propagates at a certain angle relative to the direction of the projectile's movement (see Figure 1).

As was realized post-factum, the phenomenon is rather general and must have been seen by many physicists, starting with Pierre and Marie Curie, who had worked with gamma radiation prior to Cherenkov but either did not attribute special importance to the glow or, like Lucien Mallet (1885–1981) in 1926, considered it luminescence. Also, as early as 1904 Arnold Sommerfeld (1868–1951) had calculated waves emitted by an electron traveling faster than the speed of light, according to the turn-of-the-century electron theory, and arrived at the formulas almost identical to those derived by Tamm and Frank. Sommerfeld's calculation seemed meaningless and was forgotten almost immediately because of Einstein's relativity theory of 1905, which prohibits any physical object from moving faster than light. The limitation, however, refers to *light in a vacuum*, whereas, as explained by Tamm and Frank, objects can travel faster than the *phase speed of light in a medium* (always less than the speed of propagation in a vacuum) without entering into any conflict with Einstein's postulate. So although Cherenkov radiation seemed to contradict relativity theory, it was in fact fully compatible with it.

Cherenkov radiation can be produced by any electrically charged particles, not just electrons, if they propagate through a medium with sufficient velocity. It is often seen, for example, in photos of nuclear reactors as bright blue light emanating from water. The effect proved especially useful for registering high-energy elementary particles encountered in cosmic rays or produced in particle accelerators. Detectors using this principle, Cherenkov counters, were designed and became widely used soon after World War II, and they helped physicists find new elementary particles, such as the antiproton discovered in 1955. Cherenkov also pointed out that the radiation could be used to measure the velocities of particles, an idea later realized in the so-called RICH detectors. The 1958 Nobel Prize in Physics "for the discovery and the interpretation of the Cherenkov effect" was shared between the experimentalist Cherenkov and the theoreticians Tamm and Frank. Vavilov had died in 1951 and thus could not be nominated for the Nobel Prize. In the Soviet Union the discovery of the new radiation was recognized by a Stalin Prize awarded

administrative chores, including the task of organizing the Physical Institute of the Academy of Sciences (FIAN)—eventually the nation's main research center in fundamental physics—no longer allowed him to engage actively in hands-on research. Cherenkov, who also moved to Moscow, continued his studies of the new effect despite the strong skepticism he encountered. In the preceding decades, physicists had witnessed several embarrassing cases of widely publicized "discoveries" of spurious rays. Some influential Soviet colleagues and foreign visitors also mocked FIAN's search for an almost non-visible radiation in complete darkness as "spiritism" and "ghost-hunting." With Vavilov's backing, Cherenkov defiantly persevered. His English-language article reporting the chief results of the investigation was rejected by *Nature* in 1937 but published later that year by the *Physical Review*.

Soviet educational policies started returning to more traditional forms around that time, with diminishing attention to class criteria and a renewed emphasis on regularity and quality of training. In particular, from 1934 on, graduate students were once again required to defend a thesis for the *kandidat nauk*, the Russian equivalent of the PhD degree. After receiving his degree in 1935 Cherenkov remained at FIAN as a research associate and in 1940 defended his second thesis for a higher academic degree, the *doktor nauk*. In the course of these studies he discovered further characteristics of the new radiation, including its specific anisotropy—the radiation propagated at a very particular angle relative to the direction of the incident gamma ray. This feature helped the FIAN theoreticians Igor Yevgenyevich Tamm (1895–1971) and

Pavel Cherenkov. AP IMAGES.

to Vavilov, Cherenkov, Tamm, and Frank in 1946. Generally Russian-language sources attribute partial credit for the experimental discovery to Vavilov and often prefer the term *Vavilov-Cherenkov radiation.*

Later Years. Cherenkov worked at FIAN for the rest of his life. He participated in FIAN's Elbrus expedition in 1934 that established the first Soviet high-altitude cosmic ray station in the Caucasus Mountains and studied the new phenomenon of cosmic ray showers in the atmosphere. In the 1940s he constructed Wilson chamber detectors for the Pamir Mountains cosmic rays expedition and station. During World War II, as the German armies approached Moscow, FIAN was evacuated to Kazan on the Volga River, where Cherenkov worked on acoustical systems for air defense. During the patriotic upsurge of the war, many scientists joined the Communist Party, which also became less exclusive. Cherenkov became a Communist in 1944 and remained a loyal party member for the rest of his life.

From 1946 to 1958 Cherenkov assisted Vladimir Iosifovich Veksler (1907–1966) in designing new types of particle accelerators, the synchrotron (1947) and the first Soviet betatron (1948). A larger 250 MeV synchrotron

started operating in FIAN in 1951, for which the main contributors, including Veksler and Cherenkov, received that year's Stalin Prize. Most of the research done by Cherenkov during those years was classified—not necessarily for good reasons but simply because of its relation to nuclear physics at a time when the development of atomic weapons constituted one of the country's top security priorities. Starting in 1959 Cherenkov directed his own laboratory at FIAN, which studied how photons interacted with mesons and nucleons (a series of investigations recognized by the USSR State Prize in 1977). He also helped organize and design a new acceleration laboratory with a 1.2 Gev synchrotron in Troitsk, near Moscow, in the 1970s. Between 1951 and 1977 he taught as professor at the Moscow Institute of Physical Engineers (MIFI), which educated specialists for the field of nuclear energy.

After World War II, as the use of Cherenkov's 1934 discovery and his fame grew in the West, his reputation and standing in his own country remained very modest, overshadowed by more illustrious colleagues. Perhaps, owing to his peasant background, he was still perceived as an outsider by elitist representatives of the Soviet intelligentsia. His lifestyle was also rather unprivileged: At the time of his 1958 Nobel Prize the Cherenkov family with two children still lived in a so-called communal apartment (a flat with rooms occupied by several different families and with shared facilities), which was a typical arrangement for common urban dwellers in the overcrowded Soviet cities from the 1920s to the 1960s. They moved into a separate flat—the ultimate sign of a middle class standing in the Soviet society—only in 1962.

His election to the USSR Academy of Sciences—the most prestigious body in Soviet science—also came rather late. Cherenkov became a corresponding member of the academy in 1964 and a full member in 1970. In 1985 he was elected to the U.S. National Academy of Sciences as a foreign member. Until the end of his life he tried to avoid using the phrases "Cherenkov effect" and "Cherenkov detectors," which had become standard terminology in physics. He was also very reluctant to allow the use of his name and fame for public relations purposes and for the promotion of scientific projects. He did, however, represent the Soviet Union internationally—in the Soviet Peace Committee, in the Soviet OSCE (Organization for Security and Co-operation in Europe) Committee, and in the Pugwash Conferences on Science and World Affairs—in a manner compatible with his membership in the Communist Party. Cherenkov remained occupied with scientific research at FIAN almost until his death at age eighty-five. His two children, a son and a daughter, also became scientists.

BIBLIOGRAPHY

WORKS BY CHERENKOV

"Vidimoe svechenie chistykh zhidkostei pod deistviem gamma-radiatsii" [Visible glow of pure liquids under gamma irradiation]. *Doklady AN SSSR*, t. 2 (1934): 451–457.

"Visible Radiation Produced by Electrons Moving in a Medium with Velocities Exceeding That of Light." *Physical Review* 52 (1937): 378–379.

"Spatial Distribution of Visible Radiation Produced by Fast Electrons." *Comptes Rendus de l'Académie des Sciences de l'URSS* 21 (1938): 319–321.

With Igor E. Tamm and Ilya. M. Frank. "Svechenie chistykh zhidkostei pod deistviem bystrykh elektronov" [The glowing of pure liquids under the influence of fast electrons]. *Izvestiia AN SSSR, Seriia Fizicheskaia* 1–2 (1938): 29–31.

"Radiation of Particles Moving at a Velocity Exceeding that of Light, and Some of the Possibilities for Their Use in Experimental Physics." Nobel Lecture, 11 December 1958. Available from http://nobelprize.org.

OTHER WORKS

Afanasiev, Georgy N. *Vavilov-Cherenkov and Synchrotron Radiation: Foundations and Applications.* Dordrecht and Boston: Kluwer, 2004.

Bolotovsky, Boris M. *Svechenie Vavilova-Cherenkova.* Moscow: Nauka, 1964.

Cherenkov, Pavel Alekseevich (1904–1990): Materialy k bibliografii uchenykh. Moscow: Nauka, 1997. Contains a full bibliography plus a biographical essay and a list of secondary literature.

Frank, Ilya M. "A Conceptual History of the Vavilov-Cherenkov Radiation." *Soviet Physics Uspekhi* 27 (1984): 385–395.

Gorbunov, Andrei N., and E. P. Cherenkova, eds. *Pavel Alekseevich Cherenkov: Chelovek i otkrytie.* Moscow: Nauka, 1999. Recollections about Cherenkov.

"Izluchenie Vavilova-Cherenkova: 50 let otkrytiia" [Recollections and materials published on the occasion of the discovery's 50th anniversary]. *Priroda* 10 (1984): 74–86.

Jelley, John V. *Čerenkov Radiation and Its Applications.* New York: Pergamon Press, 1958.

Nobel Lectures, Including Presentation Speeches and Laureates' Biographies: Physics: 1942–1962. Amsterdam: Elsevier, 1964.

Tamm, Igor E., and Ilya M. Frank. "Coherent Visible Radiation of Fast Electrons Passing through Matter." *Comptes Rendus de l'Académie des Sciences de l'URSS* 14 (1937): 109–114.

Vavilov, Sergi I. "O vozmozhnykh prichinakh sinego gamma-svecheniia zhidkostei" [On the possible causes of blue gamma-glow of liquids]. *Doklady AN SSSR*, t. 2 (1934): 457–461.

Alexei Kojevnikov

CHERN, SHIING-SHEN (*b.* Jia Xin, Chekiang Province, China, 26 October 1911; *d.* Tianjin, China, 3 December 2004), *mathematics, differential geometry.*

Chern was a highly influential figure in pure mathematics. From the 1940s onward he redefined the subject of differential geometry by drawing on, and contributing to, the rapid development of topology during the period. Despite spending most of his working life in the United States, he was also a source of inspiration for all Chinese mathematicians, and contributed in many ways to the development of the subject in China.

Early Life. Shiing-Shen Chern was born in the final year of the Qing dynasty, and educated at a time when China was only beginning to set up Western-style universities. His father was a lawyer who worked for the government. Chern first showed his mathematical ability when he was a student at the Fu Luen Middle School in Tsientsin, where he did all the exercises in classical English textbooks on algebra and trigonometry. He then went to Nankai University at the age of fifteen. There, mathematics was a one-man department run by Li-Fu Chiang, who had been a student of Julian Coolidge, and this ensured that Chern studied a great deal of geometry, particularly the works of Coolidge, George Salmon, Guido Castelnuovo, and Otto Staude. He became a postgraduate in 1930 at Tsinghua University in Beijing, where he met his wife Shih-Ning, the daughter of a professor. At Tsinghua Chern came under the influence of Dan Sun, one of the few mathematicians in China publishing research in mathematics. Sun's subject was projective differential geometry, which caught Chern's interest, and he studied in detail the works of the German mathematician Wilhelm Blaschke. After Blaschke visited Tsinghua in 1932 and lectured on differential-geometric invariants, Chern won a fellowship to study with him in Hamburg, Germany, for two years, and he received his DSc there in 1936 for work on the theory of webs, a subject central to Blaschke's work at the time. These were turbulent times in Germany: in Hamburg Chern met the mathematician Wei-Liang Chow, who had left Göttingen because of the flight of the best mathematicians from that university, and during the same period Blaschke was forced to resign from the German Mathematical Society for opposing the imposition of Nazi racial policies.

While in Hamburg, Chern studied the works of Elie Cartan and in 1936 spent a year in Paris with him. Cartan, who turned sixty-seven that year, was the dominant figure in geometry at the time, and had introduced new techniques that few people understood. The language in which to properly express Cartan's work was not then available, and it was ten years before the notation and terminology of fiber bundles allowed Chern to explain these concepts in a satisfactory way. The regular "Séminaire

Julia" that year was devoted to expounding Cartan's work and Chern there met André Weil and other young French mathematicians who were the founders of the Bourbaki group that came to dominate French mathematics after World War II.

Move to the United States. In the summer of 1937 he took up the position of professor at Tsinghua, crossing the Atlantic, the United States, and the Pacific to do so, only to find that the Sino-Japanese war had begun. His university had moved, with the universities of Peking and Nankai, to Kunming. There, despite all the deprivations of war and virtually cut off as he was from the outside world, he found the time to work deeply through Cartan's work and came to his own vision of where geometry should be going. He was also able to teach many students who were to go on to make substantial contributions in mathematics and other fields—among them Chen Ning Yang, whose work in theoretical physics won him a Nobel Prize in 1957. Eventually, Chern was able to make his way to the Institute for Advanced Study in Princeton, New Jersey, on a series of military flights through India, Africa, Brazil, and Central America.

In Princeton, Hermann Weyl and Oswald Veblen already had a high opinion of Chern because of his papers. Chern soon got in touch with Claude Chevalley and Solomon Lefschetz and also with Weil in nearby Lehigh University. In Weil's words, "We seemed to share a common attitude towards such subjects, or towards mathematics in general; we were both striving to strike at the root of each question while freeing our minds from preconceived notions about what others might have regarded as the right or the wrong way of dealing with it" (Weil, 1992, p. 74). Chern and Weil worked and talked together to reveal the topological character of some of the new ideas in algebraic geometry. These included the Todd-Eger classes, whose definition was at the time derived in the old-fashioned spirit of Italian geometry, but which nevertheless caught Chern's imagination. These discussions provided the foundation of his most famous work on what became known as Chern classes (though he would always insist that the letter c by which they were denoted stood for "characteristic classes"). The ideas he developed at that time emerged in a concrete form in his new intrinsic proof (1944) of the general Gauss-Bonnet theorem—by his own account, one of his favorite theorems.

When World War II ended in 1945, Chern began another lengthy, complicated return to China, reaching Shanghai in March 1946. There, he was asked to set up an institute of mathematics as part of the Academia Sinica. He did this very successfully—several outstanding mathematicians were nurtured there—but the institute was located in Nanjing, and the turmoil of the civil war was

making southern China ever more dangerous. As a result, Weil, by then in Chicago, and Veblen and Weyl in Princeton became concerned about his fate, and both Chicago and Princeton's Institute for Advanced Study offered Chern visiting positions, culminating in a full professorship at Chicago. So in 1949 he returned to the United States, this time with his family, to spend most of his working life there.

Chern's topological interests in Nanjing and Chicago deepened as he absorbed the rapid postwar development in algebraic topology, and his talk at the 1950 International Congress of Mathematicians (1952) shows how dramatic the interaction of differential geometry and topology had become by then. It is a thoroughly modern statement, totally different in outlook from the work of fifteen years earlier.

Work in California and China. In 1960, Chern moved again, to become a professor at the University of California at Berkeley—attracted by an expanding department and a milder climate. There he immediately started a differential geometry seminar that continues in the early twenty-first century, and he attracted visitors both young and old. His own PhD students included Shing-Tung Yau, who won a Fields Medal in 1982.

In 1978, the year he turned sixty-seven, Chern, Isadore Singer, and Calvin Moore prepared a response to the National Science Foundation's request for proposals for a mathematical institute that would reflect the "need for continued stimulation of mathematical research" in an environment that considered American mathematics to be in a "golden age." Their ideas were approved in 1981 and Chern became the first director of the Mathematical Sciences Research Institute, a post he held from 1982 until 1985. It was a huge success, and Chern supported it thereafter in many ways, not least from the proceeds of his 2004 Shaw Prize. A new building, Chern Hall, was dedicated in his memory on 3 March 2006.

Throughout his years in the United States Chern's interest in Chinese mathematicians continued. He aimed to put Chinese mathematics on the same level as its Western counterpart, "though not necessarily bending its efforts in the same direction" (Citation, Honorary Doctorate, Hong Kong University of Science and Technology, 7 November 2003, available from http://genesis.ust.hk/jan_2004/en/camera/congregate/citations_txt05.html). During the 1980s, he initiated three developments in China: an International Conference on Differential Geometry and Differential Equations, the Summer Education Centre for Postgraduates in Mathematics, and the Chern Programme, aimed at helping Chinese postgraduates in mathematics to go for further study in the United States. In 1984 China's Ministry of Education invited him

Shiing-Shen Chern. *Shiing-Shen Chern at conference with Chinese President Jiang Zemin.* AP IMAGES.

to return to his alma mater, Nankai University, and create the Nankai Research Institute of Mathematics. The university built a residence for him, "The Serene Garden," and he and his wife lived there every time they returned to China. While director he invited many overseas mathematicians to visit; he also donated more than 10,000 books to the institute, and his $50,000 Wolf Prize to Nankai University.

In 1999 Chern returned to China for good, where he continued to do mathematics, grappling until just before his death with an old problem about the existence or otherwise of a complex structure on the six-dimensional sphere. The finest testament to his achievement in his final years was to be seated next to President Jiang Zemin in the Great Hall of the People in Beijing at the opening of the 2002 International Congress of Mathematicians. During the course of his lifetime, mathematics in China had changed immeasurably.

Chern received many awards for his work including the U.S. National Medal of Science in 1975, the Wolf Prize in Mathematics in 1983, and the Shaw Prize in 2004. He died on 3 December 2004 at age ninety-three; his wife of sixty-one years had died four years earlier. He was survived by a son, Paul, and a daughter May Chu.

Proof of the Gauss-Bonnet Theorem. Chern's mathematical work encompasses a period of rapid change in geometry, and he was exceptionally able to capitalize on his extensive knowledge of the mathematics of both the first and the second half of the twentieth century. His subject of differential geometry had its origins in the study of surfaces inside the three-dimensional Euclidean space with which everyone is familiar. It involves the notions of the length of curves on the surface, the area of domains within it, the study of geodesics on the surface, and various concepts of curvature. By the late nineteenth century other types of geometry were being studied this way, such as projective geometry and web geometry, the subject on which Chern cut his mathematical teeth. An *n-web* in the plane consists of *n* families of nonintersecting curves that fill out a portion of the plane. For example, a curvilinear coordinate system such as planar Cartesian coordinates or polar coordinates defines a 2-web. By a change of coordinates any planar 2-web can be taken to the standard Cartesian system, but this is not so for webs of degree three and higher and invariants which have the nature of curvature obstruct this.

Most proofs related to the subject that appeared during this period involve intricate calculations, and Chern indeed was a master at such proofs. However, in the 1920s new inputs in differential geometry arrived from its importance in Einstein's theory of general relativity. One of these was the shift in emphasis from two-dimensional geometry to the four-dimensional geometry of space-time. Coupled with the nineteenth-century formulation of mechanics, which involved high-dimensional configuration spaces where kinetic energy defined a similar structure to a surface in Euclidean space, the ruling perspective in differential geometry was to work in n dimensions. A second change brought on by relativity was the requirement that the equations of physics should be written in a coordinate-independent way. This required the introduction of mathematical objects that had a life of their own, but which could still be manipulated by indexed quantities so long as one knew the rules for changing from one coordinate system to another. The most fundamental change, however, was the movement from extrinsic geometry to intrinsic geometry: four-dimensional space-time was not sitting like a surface in a higher-dimensional Euclidean space; its geometry could be observed and described only by the beings that lived within it. The intrinsic viewpoint also paved the way for the global viewpoint—the spaces one needed to study, not least space-time itself, could have quite complicated topology and one wanted to understand the interaction between the differential geometry and the topology: to see what constraints topology imposes on curvature, or vice-versa.

This was the context of Chern's proof of the general Gauss-Bonnet theorem (1944), which was a pivotal event in the history of differential geometry, not just for the theorem itself but also for what it led to. The classical theorem of the same name concerns a closed surface in Euclidean three-space. It states that the integral of the Gaussian curvature is 2π times the Euler number. The Euler number for a surface divided into F faces, E edges and V vertices is V-E+F. For a sphere this is 2, and the Gauss-Bonnet theorem gives this because the Gaussian curvature of a sphere is 1, and its area is 4π.

This link between curvature and topology has several features: one is Gauss's *theorema egregium*, which says that a certain expression of curvature of the surface, the Gauss curvature, is intrinsic—it can be determined by making measurements entirely within the surface. That being so, clearly whatever its integral evaluates to depends only on the intrinsic geometry. In contrast, there is a very natural and useful extrinsic interpretation of this integral as the degree of the Gauss map: the unit normal to the surface at each point defines a map to the sphere, and its topological degree (the number of points with the same normal direction) is the invariant. The problem was to extend this result to (even-dimensional) manifolds in higher dimension. In 1926 Heinz Hopf had generalized the Gauss map approach to hypersurfaces in Euclidean n-space, but the task was to prove the theorem for any even-dimensional

Riemannian manifold. The concept of *manifold,* commonplace in mathematics today and signifying a higher-dimensional analogue of a surface, was by no means clear when Chern was working on this theorem. Indeed, the definition was formulated correctly by Hassler Whitney only in 1936, and Cartan even in 1946 considered that "the general notion of manifold is quite difficult to define with precision" (Cartan, 1949, p. 56).

The novel content of the proof came from studying the intrinsic tangent sphere bundle, and using the exterior differential calculus that Chern had learned at the hands of Cartan. The language of fiber bundles was necessary to describe in an intrinsic way the totality of tangent vectors to a manifold—it was what Cartan lacked and was only developed amongst topologists in the period 1935–1940. Chern's theorem, proved with the use of this concept, provided a link between topology and differential geometry at a time when the very basics of the topology of manifolds were being laid down.

Discovery of the Chern Classes. The successful attack on the Gauss-Bonnet theorem led him to study the other invariants of bundles, to see whether curvature could detect them. He started with Stiefel-Whitney classes but their more algebraic properties "seemed to be a mystery" (Weil, 1992, p. 74), and what are now called Pontryagin classes, where curvature could make an impact, were not known then, so Chern moved into Hermitian geometry and discovered the famous Chern classes whose importance in algebraic geometry, topology, and index theory cannot be underestimated. As he pursued his work on characteristic classes and curvature, Chern always recognized that there was more than just the topological characteristic class to be obtained, and this emerged later in a strong form in his work on Chern-Simons invariants with James Simons (1971). Nowadays the Chern-Simons functional is an everyday tool for theoretical physicists.

The Chern classes, coupled with the Hodge theory that in the postwar period was given a more rigorous foundation by Kunihiko Kodaira and Weyl, provided a completely new insight into the interaction of algebraic geometry and topology. But Chern was always happy to work in algebraic geometry. His studies in Hamburg involved webs obtained from algebraic curves—a plane curve of degree d meets a general line in d points. There is a duality between points and lines in the plane: the one-parameter family of lines passing through a point describes a line in another plane. So the curve describes d families of lines, which is a web. Chern in fact later returned to this theme in far more generality in collaboration with the algebraic geometer Phillip Griffiths (1978). Nevertheless, it was the new differential and topological viewpoint on the traditional geometry in the complex domain that motivated most of his contributions. One of these was his work in several complex variables on value distribution theory. In joint work with Raoul Bott (1965) he introduced the use of connections and curvature on vector bundles into this area. In fact, their formulation of the notion of a connection in that paper is so simple and manageable that it has become the standard approach in the literature. In this context a vector bundle is a smooth family of abstract vector spaces parameterized by the points of a manifold (like the tangent spaces of a surface) and a connection is an invariant way of taking the derivative of a family of vectors.

Another link between the algebraic geometric and differential geometric world that Chern contributed to is in the area of minimal surfaces, the simplest examples of which are the surfaces formed by the soap films spanning a wire loop. Chern was the first to attempt a rigorous proof of what is classically known as the existence of isothermal coordinates on a surface. On any surface, such as a surface sitting in Euclidean space, one can find two real coordinates which are described by a single complex number. This immediately links the differential geometry of surfaces with complex analysis, and the most direct case is that of a minimal surface. The physicist Yang learned about this taking a course from Chern in China in 1940: "When Chern told me to use complex variables … it was like a bolt of lightning which I never later forgot" (Yang, 1992, p. 64). In later work, Chern discussed minimal surfaces in higher dimensional Euclidean spaces and in spheres and showed how in quite intricate ways the algebraic and differential geometry intertwine.

Other Mathematical Work. Chern's work on characteristic classes earned him a large audience of mathematicians in a variety of disciplines, but he did not neglect the other aspects of differential geometry, especially where unconventional notions of curvature were involved. Some of this arose from early attempts to extend general relativity—for example, Weyl geometry and path geometry. The latter considers a space which has a distinguished family of curves on it that behave qualitatively like geodesics—given a point and a direction there is a unique curve of the family passing through the point and tangent to the direction. Veblen and his school in Princeton had worked on this and it was through this work that they probably first heard of Chern. Curvature invariants in complex geometry also came up in his work with Jürgen Moser (1974) on the geometry of real hypersurfaces in a complex vector space, picking up on a problem once considered by Cartan. When, in the mid-1970s, soliton equations such as the KdV equation, together with its so-called Bäcklund transformations, began to be studied, he was well prepared to apply both his expertise in exterior differential

systems and his knowledge of classical differential geometry to provide important results.

Sometimes his choice of topics was unorthodox, but reflected both his curiosity and respect for the mathematicians of the past. Bernhard Riemann in his famous inaugural lecture of 1854, *On the Hypotheses which Lie at the Basis of Geometry,* discussed various competing notions of infinitesimal length but concluded that it would "take considerable time and throw little new light on the theory of space, especially as the results cannot be geometrically expressed; I restrict myself therefore to those manifoldnesses in which the line element is expressed as the square root of a quadric differential expression" (Riemann, 1873, p. 17). His "restricted" theory is what is known as Riemannian geometry in the early twenty-first century. The alternatives have come to be called Finsler metrics; Chern took Riemann at face value and set out with collaborators to investigate the geometry of these (2000).

In a life as long and full as Chern's, there are many more highly significant contributions. He also returned to some favorite themes over the decades. One was Blaschke's use of integral geometry and generalizations of the attractive Crofton's formula, which measures the length of a curve by the average number of intersections with a line. Despite his geometrical outlook, Chern's proofs were usually achieved by the use of his favorite mathematical objects—differential forms. He had learned this skill with Cartan and was an acknowledged master at it.

One of the enduring features in Chern's life was his accessibility and offers of encouragement to young mathematicians: As Bott remarked, "Chern treats people equally; the high and mighty can expect no courtesy from him that he would not also naturally extend to the lowliest among us" (Bott, 1992, p. 106). His relaxed style and willingness to help young researchers earned him loyalty from generations of mathematicians. One such appreciative student bought his weekly California State Lottery tickets with the single thought "If I win, I will endow a professorship to honor Professor Chern." In 1995 he won $22 million and the Chern Visiting Professors became a regular feature on the Berkeley campus.

BIBLIOGRAPHY

WORKS BY CHERN

"A Simple Intrinsic Proof of the Gauss-Bonnet Formula for Closed Riemannian Manifolds." *Annals of Mathematics* 45 (1944): 747–752.

"On the Curvatura Integra in a Riemannian Manifold." *Annals of Mathematics* 46 (1945): 674–684.

"Differential Geometry of Fiber Bundles." In *Proceedings of the International Congress of Mathematicians, Cambridge, Mass., 1950.* Vol. 2. Providence, RI: American Mathematical Society, 1952.

"An Elementary Proof of the Existence of Isothermal Parameters on a Surface." *Proceedings of the American Mathematical Society* 6 (1955): 771–782.

With Richard Lashof. "On the Total Curvature of Immersed Manifolds." *American Journal of Mathematics* 79 (1957): 306–318.

With Raoul Bott. "Hermitian Vector Bundles and the Equidistribution of the Zeroes of Their Holomorphic Sections." *Acta Mathematica* 114 (1965): 71–112.

Complex Manifolds without Potential Theory. Princeton, NJ, Toronto, and London: Van Nostrand, 1967. 2nd edition, New York and Heidelberg: Springer-Verlag, 1979, and revised printing of the 2nd edition, New York: Springer-Verlag, 1995.

With James Simons. "Some Cohomology Classes in Principal Fiber Bundles and Their Application to Riemannian Geometry." *Proceedings of the National Academy of Sciences of the United States of America* 68 (1971): 791–794.

With Jürgen K. Moser. "Real Hypersurfaces in Complex Manifolds." *Acta Mathematica* 133 (1974): 219–271. Erratum: 150 (1983): 297.

With Phillip A. Griffiths. "An Inequality for the Rank of a Web and Webs of Maximum Rank." *Annali della scuola normale superiore di Pisa classe di scienze* 5 (1978): 539–557.

With Jon G. Wolfson. "Harmonic Maps of the Two-Sphere into a Complex Grassmann Manifold II." *Annals of Mathematics* 125 (1987): 301–335.

With David Bao and Zhongmin Shen. *An Introduction to Riemann-Finsler Geometry.* New York: Springer, 2000.

OTHER SOURCES

Bott, Raoul. "For the Chern Volume." In *Chern, a Great Geometer of the Twentieth Century,* edited by Shing-Tung Yau. Hong Kong: International Press, 1992.

Cartan, Elie. *Leçons sur la Géométrie des Espaces de Riemann.* 2nd ed. Paris: Gauthier-Villars, 1946.

Hitchin, Nigel J. "Shiing-Shen Chern 1911–2004." *Bulletin of the London Mathematical Society* 38 (2006): 507–519. Contains a complete list of Chern's works.

Jackson, Allyn. "Interview with Shiing Shen Chern." *Notices of the American Mathematical Society* 45 (1998): 860–865.

Riemann, Bernhard. "On the Hypotheses which Lie at the Bases of Geometry." Translated by William K. Clifford. *Nature* 8 (1873): 14–17, 36, 37.

Weil, André. "S. S. Chern as Geometer and Friend." In *Chern, a Great Geometer of the Twentieth Century,* edited by Shing-Tung Yau. Hong Kong: International Press, 1992.

Yang, Chen Ning. "S. S. Chern and I." In *Chern, a Great Geometer of the Twentieth Century,* edited by Shing-Tung Yau. Hong Kong: International Press, 1992.

Nigel J. Hitchin

CHEVALLEY, CLAUDE (*b.* Johannesburg, Transvaal, South Africa, 11 February 1909; *d.* Paris, France, 28 June 1984), *algebra, class field theory, group theory.*

The most resolute modernizer among the founders of Bourbaki, and the most given to austere axiomatic abstraction, Chevalley was influential in setting the broad agenda of Bourbaki's project and for major advances in number theory and the theory of Lie groups. He was the chief representative of mathematical logic in France in the 1930s not for any work of his own but for promoting the ideas of his friend Jacques Herbrand, who died in a mountain-climbing accident in 1931 at age twenty-three. Chevalley had philosophical, cultural, and political interests, in which "his mathematician friends had the impression that he proceeded as in mathematics, by the axiomatic method: having posed some axioms he deduced consequences from them by inflexible logic and unconcerned with obstacles along the route which would have led anyone else to go back and change the axioms" (Dieudonné, 1999, p. 113).

Early Life and Education. Chevalley was born into socially rising French Protestant circles little more than a hundred years after Protestants gained full citizenship. His paternal grandfather was a Swiss-born clockmaker naturalized as French. His uncles on that side were a legal councilor to the king of Egypt and a head doctor at l'Hôpital des Enfants-Malades in Paris (France's first children's hospital). His father, Daniel Abel Chevalley, passed the *agrégation* at the École Normale Supérieure de Saint-Cloud to become professor of English at the Lycées Voltaire and Louis-le-Grand in Paris. He became a diplomat in South Africa, Norway, and the Caucasus and Crimea, and returned to academic research after retirement. Chevalley's maternal grandfather was a village pastor in the Ardèche who became a professor of the Faculty of Protestant Theology of Strasbourg and eventually a founder and the dean of the Faculty of Protestant Theology of Paris. His mother, born Anne Marguerite Sabatier, was also an Anglicist and coauthor with her husband of the first edition of the *Concise Oxford French Dictionary*. His parents married in 1899 and besides their son had a daughter Lise, who lived to have children but died in 1933. Daniel also died in 1933, while Marguerite lived to 1969. They were active in the Association France-Grande-Bretagne—a group founded during World War I and prominent enough that when the Germans took Paris in 1940 there was barely time to destroy the records before the Gestapo came for them.

Chevalley traveled with his parents until he began school at Chançay and then in Paris at the Lycée Louis-le-Grand, where he gained his love of mathematics and began to study the standard analysis textbook, Édouard Goursat's 1902 *Cours d'analyse*. In 1926 he entered the École Normale Supérieur (ENS) in Paris at the early age of seventeen. He formed an important friendship with Herbrand, who had also been admitted at seventeen, one year before him. The two were drawn to number theory, and to German mathematics, in 1927 when they met André Weil. They took courses from the same excellent but dated mathematicians as Weil. Jacques-Salomon Hadamard's seminar gave them glimpses of recent mathematics, and they taught themselves more from original sources than they learned in courses. Chevalley studied especially with Émile Picard, graduated in 1929, and published a note on number theory in the *Comptes Rendus de l'Academie des Sciences* that year. In 1929–1930 Herbrand did his military service and produced the work that Chevalley later said formed the basis of the new methods in class field theory. Herbrand spent 1930–1931 in Germany studying logic, and died on holiday in the Swiss Alps on the way back. Chevalley spent 1931–1932 studying number theory especially with Emil Artin at Hamburg and Helmut Hasse at Marburg and came back to earn his doctorate from the University of Paris in 1933 with a thesis on the work he did in Germany.

Class Field Theory. Class field theory had been at the top of the agenda in number theory since Teiji Takagi around 1920 proved a series of decades-old conjectures of Leopold Kronecker and David Hilbert. The proofs were extremely complicated, and the results were at once productive of concrete arithmetic theorems and promising of further theoretical advances. The subject was prestigious and daunting. Chevalley's work on it showed a typical difference from Weil, who used modern number theory to expand themes from classical analysis while Chevalley worked to remove analysis in favor of algebra and point-set topology. Weil's impulse was more classically geometrical and Chevalley's more algebraic.

Carl Friedrich Gauss already used what are now called the Gaussian numbers $Q[i]$ in arithmetic. These are expressions $p+qi$ where p and q are any ordinary rational numbers and i is the imaginary square root of -1. In particular the Gaussian integers $Z[i]$ are those $a+bi$ where a and b are any ordinary integers. An ordinary prime number may not be prime in the Gaussian integers, as for example the ordinary prime 5 factors as $5 = (2+i)\times(2-i)$.

Yet the Gaussian integers do have unique prime factorization analogous to the ordinary integers. This is the prime factorization of 5 as a Gaussian integer. Using other algebraic irrationals in place of i gives other algebraic number fields K in place of the Gaussian numbers $Q[i]$. And each algebraic number field K contains a ring A of algebraic integers analogous to the Gaussian integers $Z[i]$

although generally not so easy to describe. If rings of algebraic integers always had unique prime factorization, then there would be wonderful consequences, such as a one-page proof of Fermat's last theorem. They do not. Class field theory began as an astonishing way to measure and work with failures of prime factorization.

Each algebraic number field K extends to a certain larger field $L(K)$ called the Hilbert class field, so that the Galois group of $L(K)$ over K measures the failure of unique prime factorization in the ring A. Furthermore, roughly speaking, all the algebraic integers in A have unique prime factorization in $L(K)$. If A itself has unique prime factorization then $K=L(K)$ and the Galois group is the trivial {1}. A nontrivial Galois group for $L(K)$ shows failure of prime factorization in A, and a larger Galois group shows greater failure. Explicit descriptions of Hilbert class fields were known—some using classical complex analysis. Other arithmetic properties of the ring A are expressed by the Galois groups of other extensions of K, which are also called class fields of various kinds.

The German number theorists would study any given algebraic number field K and its ring of algebraic integers A in connection with other related fields called local fields, so-called because these fields often concentrate attention on a single prime factor. One of Chevalley's typical contributions was to stress the sense in which every one of them concentrates on a single prime—if, for example, the rational number field Q is taken to include one "infinite prime" along with the finite primes 2, 3, 5, 7, and so on. A less vivid term for infinite primes is Archimedean places. For each ordinary prime number p the p-adic numbers Q_p focus on the single factor p. From this point of view the real numbers R focus on absolute value, which at first glance is nothing like a prime factor, but there are extensive axiomatic analogies. Chevalley stressed how much simpler the theory becomes when "infinite primes" are put on a par with the finite.

The theory of prime factorization in any one local field is extremely simple because there is only one prime. The algebraic number fields K are global, as each one of these fields involves all the usual finite primes at once plus some infinite. Number theorists would calculate various class fields for K by quite complicated use of related local fields. Chevalley multiplied the number of basic definitions manyfold and yet simplified, unified, and extended the theory overall by introducing class fields directly for the local fields themselves. He earned his doctorate from the University of Paris in 1933 with a thesis on class field theory over finite fields and local fields.

The dissertation won Chevalley research support in Paris through 1937. For several reasons he worked on eliminating classical complex analysis from class field theory: the local fields related to prime numbers p favored algebraic methods. Chevalley extended ideas from Wolfgang Krull and Herbrand to unify class field theory by generalizing algebraic number fields K to infinite degree extensions of Q (that is, extensions involving infinitely many independent algebraic irrationals) and these also favored algebraic tools. And Chevalley was personally drawn to modern, pure, uniform algebraic methods replacing classical complex analysis.

Chevalley advanced each of these goals by his creation of *idèles* linking local and global. Roughly speaking, an *idèle* of a global field K is a list of ways that a nonzero element of K might look in each of the local fields related to K. This list may or may not actually be generated by an element of K, just as an ideal of a ring may or may not be generated by a single ring element. So *idèles* are more flexible and more easily accessible than elements, and arithmetic conclusions about K follow from knowing which *idèles* correspond to elements. Weil added a related notion of *adèle*, and the two notions are today central to algebraic number theory.

Local fields and the Galois groups of infinite degree field extensions both have pro-finite topologies. For example, in the 5-adic integers Z_5 a number counts as closer to 0 when it is divisible by a higher power of p (that is, when it equals 0 modulo a higher power). This was a triumph for the axiomatic definition of a topological space. All of these spaces satisfy the axioms. Topological notions of continuity, compactness, and so forth, are very useful in studying them. Yet they are far from ordinary spatial intuitions. For one thing, they are everywhere disconnected. The only connected parts of such a space are the single points, and yet these disconnected points "cluster around" one another. Chevalley applied the axioms completely unconcerned with classical geometric intuitions. *Idèles* also have an algebraically defined topology, although a version by Weil suited to Fourier analysis has replaced Chevalley's version.

Bourbaki. Hadamard's seminar ended in 1933. Gaston Julia allowed Weil, Chevalley, and other ENS graduates to run a new seminar in his name on recent mathematics ignored by the dominant mathematicians of Paris at the time. These meetings gave rise to a plan to replace the venerable Goursat (1902) by a new up-to-date textbook on analysis. And so Henri Cartan, Claude Chevalley, Jean Delsarte, Jean Dieudonné, René de Possel, and André Weil met on Monday 10 December 1934 at the Café Capoulade. The textbook project quickly expanded to a project for a book series on the basics of all pure mathematics, which would reestablish French dominance in mathematics. The group adopted the collective pseudonym of Nicolas Bourbaki, and the series became the phenomenally influential *Elements of Mathematics*. Chevalley's

mother hosted two early Bourbaki congresses at the family property at Chançay.

Dieudonné says that Chevalley was early a leader because "at the start only Weil and he had the vast mathematical culture required to conceive a plan for the whole, while each of the others only gradually acquired the necessary panoramic view" (1999, p. 107). Probably through Herbrand's influence, Chevalley was an ardent advocate of Hilbert-school axiomatic rigor indifferent to any nonmathematical reality. This was common ground in Bourbaki, and Bourbaki had a large role in making it widespread today—despite complaints in some quarters that Bourbaki's *Elements* promoted sterile abstraction. Chevalley outdid even Weil in this style, so that Weil reviewed Chevalley as "algebra with a vengeance; algebraic austerity could go no further … a valuable and useful book … [yet] severely dehumanized" (1951).

Chevalley did not see himself that way. He joined the personalist group "l'Ordre Nouveau," not to be confused with a later extreme right group by the same name. They promoted personal liberty and growth and rejected all of anarchism, despotism, Marxism, and "le capitalism e sauvage," or unrestrained capitalism.

Career. The single result most widely associated with Chevalley is the Chevalley-Warning theorem, far from his deepest theorem, and suggested by a less specific conjecture of Artin. The name credits Chevalley for seeing its importance as early as 1936. Any finite field has some prime number p as characteristic and then the number of elements is some power p^n of p. Chevalley's part of the theorem says: for any polynomial $P(X_1, \ldots, X_j)$ with degree less than the number of variables, the number of roots in any finite field F is divisible by the characteristic of F. In particular, every homogeneous polynomial has a solution $<0, \ldots, 0>$ so if the degree is less than the number of variables then it has nonzero solutions. This is important to projective geometry over finite fields.

Chevalley did his first teaching in 1936 at Strasbourg, replacing Weil, who had gone to the Institute for Advanced Study in Princeton, New Jersey, and then at Rennes in a teaching-research position (*maître de conférences*) 1937–1938, replacing Dieudonné who had gone to Nancy. In 1938 he was invited to the Institute for Advanced Study and he was there when World War II broke out in Europe. The French ambassador felt he might best serve France by remaining in the United States, where he was the only French scholar at the time.

Princeton University made him a professor, and he remained there until 1948, when he moved to Columbia University, where he stayed until 1955. American students found him terse and demanding, so that few undertook research with him. In 1933 Chevalley had married his first-cousin Jacqueline. There were no children, and the marriage dissolved in 1948. That same year he married his second wife, Sylvie, a professor and theater historian in New York. Their daughter Catherine was born in 1951 and became a philosopher and historian of science. When the family returned to France, Sylvie would become librarian and archivist for the Comédie Française.

In the 1940s Chevalley took up algebraic geometry and Lie groups and most especially the union of these themes in the Lie algebras of algebraic groups. He followed Weil in seeking algebraic geometry not only over the complex numbers but over an arbitrary field. In other words he wanted to eliminate classical complex analysis here too, in favor of purely algebraic methods. He would return to this in his 1950s Paris seminar, described below.

His greatest mathematical influence was in Lie groups and centered on his use of global topological methods regarding a Lie group as a manifold. Lie groups had always been defined as (real or complex) manifolds that are simultaneously groups, but workers from Sophus Lie (1842–1899) on had routine methods for looking at the group operation in an infinitesimal neighborhood of the unit element, while they looked at the space as a whole on a more ad hoc basis as needed. In precise terms, they had better tools for Lie algebras than for Lie groups directly.

The real line R is a Lie group with real-number addition as group law, and the unit circle S^1 is a Lie group with angle addition as group law. A small neighborhood of the unit is the same in the two cases: In R it is 0 plus or minus some small real number. In S^1 it is 0° plus or minus some small number of degrees. So R and S^1 have the same Lie algebra. The difference is global: traveling away from 0 in R leads to ever new real numbers; while traveling away from 0° in S^1 eventually circles back to 0°. Lie thought of his groups globally. Henri Poincaré (1854–1912) created his tools for topology largely to handle the global topology of Lie groups. Chevalley's Princeton colleague Hermann Weyl made group representations central to his work, reflecting the global properties of groups. But no one before Chevalley succeeded at making global topology so explicitly fundamental to Lie group theory.

On the one hand this organized the theory so well that Chevalley (1946) became "the basic reference on Lie groups for at least two decades" (Dieudonné and Tits, 1987, p. 3). On the other hand it combined with Chevalley's interest in finite fields and algebraic geometry. As the global theory was less analytic, it could generalize. An algebraic group is rather like a Lie group, possibly over some field other than the real or complex numbers. Each algebraic group has a kind of Lie algebra, but over most fields not all of these Lie algebras come from groups. Chevalley found a remarkable procedure whereby every simple Lie algebra (that is, one that is not abelian and con-

tains no nontrivial ideals) over the complex numbers corresponds to a simple algebraic group over any field (that is, a group with no nontrivial quotients). A huge feat in itself, this fed into one of the largest projects in twentieth-century mathematics. Applied to any finite field it gives finite simple groups now called Chevalley groups; it was a useful organizing device, and gave some previously unknown finite simple groups. It became a tool in the vast and now completed project of describing all the finite simple groups. Further Chevalley hoped his algebraic group methods applied to algebraic number fields and related fields would be useful in arithmetic. Alexander Grothendieck's algebraic geometry soon made them so.

A Guggenheim grant took Chevalley back to Paris for the year 1948–1949. He happily rejoined the Bourbaki circle and shared research with them. He was also happy to leave the anticommunist atmosphere of America during the 1948 Soviet blockade of Berlin, the 1949 Soviet atomic bomb test, and the imminent rise of McCarthyism. A Fulbright grant took him to Japan for 1953–1954, including three months at Nagoya. Chevalley had worked with Japanese mathematicians in Hamburg and later in Princeton and always maintained close ties to Japan.

Return to France. A 1954 campaign to place Chevalley at the Sorbonne "unleashed passions in the mathematical community scarcely comprehensible today" (Dieudonné, 1999, p. 110). Some believed new opportunities should go to those who had stayed and fought or been captured in the army or the resistance. Others opposed Bourbaki's influence. Chevalley was appointed in 1955 to the nearby Université de Paris VII, where he retired in 1978.

He began a seminar in 1956 at the École Normale Supérieur, initially with Cartan, and made it an early home for Grothendieck's project to rewrite the foundations of algebraic geometry. Chevalley among others anticipated aspects of Grothendieck's scheme theory, and the seminar proceedings include the first published use of the word *scheme* (*schéma*) in its current sense in algebraic geometry. He claimed "Grothendieck had advanced algebraic geometry by fifty years" (Seshadri, 1999, p. 120).

Chevalley continued to deepen his work on groups. He determined all of the semisimple groups over any algebraically closed field, that is, all of the groups that cannot be reduced in a certain way to simple groups. When the field has characteristic 0, or in other words contains a copy of the rational numbers Q, both the result and the proof were very like those known fifty years before over the complex numbers using methods of Lie algebras. But when the field has a finite prime characteristic p, so that it contains a copy of the finite field of p elements, the older proof did not work at all. Lie algebras in finite characteristic were not fully classified themselves, they were known to be much more complicated than in characteristic 0, and Chevalley found they tell much less about the Lie groups. Surprisingly, then, when Chevalley completed the proof for finite characteristic the result was independent of which finite characteristic, and rather parallel to characteristic 0. Since Lie algebra methods were unusable, he produced purely group theoretic and algebra-geometric methods and the deepest work of his career. In the 1960s he turned to more detailed work on finite groups and produced and inspired new developments on them.

He retained his philosophical and political ideas though he had lost the friends who shared them; the last of his philosophical friends, Albert Lautman, died in the Resistance. Having become skilled at the game of Go in Japan, Chevalley promoted it among his friends and students, some of whom organized the first Go club in France in 1969. He supported the student movement of 1968 and charitable progressive projects of a kind associated with French Protestantism though he did not keep the religious faith. Chevalley had small respect for academic honors. He accepted the Cole Prize of the American Mathematical Society in 1941, and honorary membership in the London Mathematical Society in 1967. Dieudonné wrote, "No one who has known Chevalley can fail to see how his [philosophical-political] principles agreed with his entire character. When his articles exalt 'revulsion at accommodations, at self-satisfaction or satisfaction with humanity in general, and at every kind of hypocrisy' he describes himself" (1999, p. 112).

BIBLIOGRAPHY

WORKS BY CHEVALLEY

"Sur la théorie des idéaux dans les corps algébriques infini." *Academie des Sciences, Comptes Rendus Hebdomadaires* 189 (1929): 616–618.

With Arnaud Dandieu. "Logique hilbertienne et psychologie." *Revue philosophique de la France et de l'Étranger* 113 (1932): 99–111. Depicts Hilbert's proof theory as an apt reaction to Bertrand Russell's realist logicism on one hand and Luitzen Egbertus Jan Brouwer's intuitionism on the other.

"Démonstration d'une hypothèse de M. Artin." *Abhandlungen aus dem Mathematischen Seminar der Universität Hamburg* 11 (1936): 73–75.

"La théorie du corps de classes." *Annals of Mathematics,* ser. 2, 41 (1940): 394–418.

Theory of Lie Groups. Vol. 1. Princeton, NJ: Princeton University Press, 1946.

Introduction to the Theory of Algebraic Functions of One Variable. New York: American Mathematical Society, 1951.

Théorie des groupes de Lie. Vol. 2, *Groupes algébriques.* Paris: Hermann, 1951.

Théorie des groupes de Lie. Vol. 3, *Théorèmes généraux sur les algèbres de Lie.* Paris: Hermann, 1955.

Fondaments de la géométrie algébrique. Paris: Secrétariat Mathématique, 1958.

OTHER SOURCES

Dieudonné, Jean. "Claude Chevalley." *Transformation Groups* 4, nos. 2–3 (1999): 105–118. This includes an extensive bibliography compiled by Catherine Chevalley.

Dieudonné, Jean, and Jacques Tits. "Claude Chevalley (1909–1984)." *Bulletin of the American Mathematical Society* 17 (1987): 1–7. A masterful mathematical survey.

Goursat, Édouard. *Cours d'analyse mathématique.* 2 vols. Paris: Gauthier-Villars, 1902–1905.

Guedj, Denis. "Nicholas Bourbaki, Collective Mathematician: An Interview with Claude Chevalley." *Mathematical Intelligencer* 7, no. 2 (1985): 18–22.

Hasse, Helmut. "History of Class Field Theory." In *Algebraic Number Theory: Proceedings of an Instructional Conference Organized by the London Mathematical Society (a NATO Advanced Study Institute) with the Support of the International Mathematical Union,* edited by John Cassels and Albrecht Fröhlich, 266–279. London: Academic Press, 1967.

Seshadri, Conjeevaram. "Claude Chevalley: Some Reminiscences." *Transformation Groups* 4, nos. 2–3 (1999): 119–125.

Weil, André. Review of *Introduction to the Theory of Algebraic Functions of One Variable,* by C. Chevalley. *Bulletin of the American Mathematical Society* 57 (1951): 384–398.

Colin McLarty

CHIONIADES, GEORGE (OR GREGORY) (*b.* Constantinople, c. 1240–1250; *d.* Trebizond, c. 1320), *astronomy.*

Byzantine scholar, physician (iatrosophist), and astronomer, George Chioniades was born probably at Constantinople between 1240 and 1250 and died at Trebizond around 1320. His life is not well known. According to his correspondence, it is known that he traveled between Constantinople, Trebizond, and Tabriz during 1295 to 1310. Monk and priest, he was named bishop of Tabriz, probably around 1304 or 1305, to defend Christians living in the Mongol Empire. The change of name from George to Gregory may have occurred at that time. It may have been on the occasion of this nomination that he wrote a profession of Christian faith, preserved in *Vaticanus gr.* 2226. In this document, he refuted accusations of having adopted foreign beliefs from having stayed so long among the Persians, the Chaldeans, and Arabs. He also defended himself against having accepted astrological fatalism contrary to the Christian religion. Around 1310 or 1314, he spoke of himself as an old man. On his death some of his classical books passed into the hands of

Constantine Loukites, Protonotarius of Trebizond, with whom Chioniades maintained friendly relations.

His name is associated with the introduction of the Persian astronomical tables to Constantinople. According to the preface of the *Persian Syntaxis* of George Chrysococces (written around 1347), Chioniades, desiring to learn astronomy in order to better practice medicine (or iatromathematics), went to Trebizond where he obtained financial support from Alexis II Comnenus (1297–1330) to travel to Persia, then under Mongol domination. Going to the court, he learned the language of the country and obtained authorization to learn astronomy in return for his services. He then returned to Trebizond with astronomical books he translated into Greek. His books passed into the hands of the priest Manual of Trebizond, with whom George Chrysococces was learning astronomy.

It is difficult to know exactly what the astronomical work of Chioniades was, and his exact role in the introduction of Persian astronomy to Constantinople, for few texts under his name have come down to the present. A manuscript in New York (Smith West. Add. 10, Columbia University) contains autograph notes of George Chioniades: some commentaries on John of Damascus, and elementary astronomical and astrological diagrams containing Arabic terms mentioning the Persians. The *Persian Syntaxis* of George Chrysococces was based, according to its author, on a "Persian Syntaxis, better than the others," which Chioniades had Hellenized, without adding commentaries to it (Usener, 1914 p. 357). The principal source has been identified by Raymond Mercier. It consists of the *Zīj ī-Ilkhānī* of Naṣīr ad-Dīn aṭ-Ṭūsī. (c. 1270). Chioniades therefore must have put into Greek the tables of the *Zīj ī-Ilkhānī*, without explanation, but this version has not come down to us.

Besides, an important corpus of Byzantine astronomical texts, adapted from Arabic and Persian, was preserved in manuscripts of the thirteenth and fourteenth centuries, and David Pingree has seen in these adaptations of the work of George Chioniades. These manuscripts are principally the *Vaticanus gr.* 211 (end thirteenth century), the *Vaticanus gr.* 191 (c. 1302), *Laurentianus* 28/17 (copied after 1346 by Theodore Meliteniotes), the *Vaticanus gr.* 185 (c. 1345), the *Vaticanus gr.* 1058 (c. 1345–1360), and some others of later date.

The oldest, the *Vaticanus gr.* 211, contains a Byzantine version of the *Zīj al-'Alā'ī* of the Arabic astronomer al-Fahhād (c. 1176), executed according to the teaching of Shams Bukhārī (c. 1295–1296), a Byzantine version of the *Zīj as-Sanjārī* of the Arabic astronomer al-Khazīnī (c. 1115), tables of these two treatises, and several other texts and diagrams, notably the pre-Copernican figures deriving from the *Tadhkhira* of Naṣīr ad-Dīn aṭ-Ṭūsī. This manuscript, contemporary with Chioniades, preserves

several titles in Arabic. The *Vaticanus gr.* 191 contains notes and calculations dated 1302, as well as unidentified tables starting in 1093.

The *Laurentianus* 28/17 contains the teaching of Shams Bukhārī on the *Zīj al-'Alā'ī*, as well as the *Zīj as-Sanjārī*, but without any table. The copy was partly made from the *Vaticanus gr.* 211, partly from an original of the thirteenth century, now lost. The *Vaticanus gr.* 185 also has the tables of 1093, and the *Vaticanus gr.* 1058 repeats the texts of the *Vaticanus gr.* 211. Finally, a treatise on the astrolabe of Siamps the Persian (Shams Bukhārī), dedicated to the emperor Andronicus II, appears in a number of manuscripts of the fourteenth and fifteenth centuries (for example, *Marcianus gr.* 309 and *Vaticanus gr.* 210).

What was Chioniades's part in these adaptations? The question is difficult to decide. His name was mentioned only in the account by Chrysococces and his handwriting, known from the autograph noted above, nowhere appears in the manuscripts of the thirteenth century that contained adaptations of the Persian treatises. Chioniades may be the author of the translations preserved in *Vaticanus gr.* 211 and in *Laurentianus* 28/17, but the astronomical notes of *Vaticanus gr.* 191 are certainly due to another Byzantine scholar.

The various hands that one encounters in the manuscripts, the variations in the adaptations of the Persian names allow one to think that more than one person had worked on this material. Chioniades certainly had collaborators, secretaries, and students. His successors included the priest Manuel of Trebizond, the teacher of Chrysococces, who is perhaps the author of the Ephemerides compiled at Trebizond for the year 1336, preserved in the manuscript *Monacensis gr.* 525; George Chrysococces, principal source of information about Chioniades; Theodore Meliteniotes, copyist of the *Laurentianus* 28/17, and author of an *Astronomical Tribiblos,* of which Book Three is devoted to the Persian tables.

Whoever was the author of these Byzantine adaptations of Persian astronomical treatises, they were written in a rather unelegant style, with technical words simply transcribed in Greek. Difficult to understand for a Byzantine reader, they would meet only a limited diffusion and were replaced from 1347 by the *Persian Syntaxis* of George Chrysococces.

Chioniades was also a physician (his *Profession of Faith* designates him as iatrosophist). A list of antidotes translated from Persian is preserved under his name in *Ambrosianus* Q 94 sup. (fourteenth century).

BIBLIOGRAPHY

Mercier, Raymond. "The Greek 'Persian Syntaxis' and the *Zīj ī-Ilkhānī*." *Archives Internationales d'Histoire des Sciences* 34, no. 112:3 (1984): 35–60.

———. *An Almanac for Trebizond for the Year 1336, Corpus des Astronomes Byzantins* VII. Louvain-la-Neuve, Belgium: Academia-Bruylant, 1994.

Neugebauer, Otto. "Studies in Byzantine Astronomical Terminology." *Transactions of the American Philosophical Society,* n.s., 50, pt. 2. (1960): 3–45.

Paschos, Emmanuel A., and Panagiotis Sotiroudis. *The Schemata of the Stars. Byzantine Astronomy from 1300 A.D.* Singapore: World Scientific, 1998.

Pingree, David. "Gregory Chioniades and Palaeologan Astronomy." *Dumbarton Oaks Papers* 18 (1964): 135–160.

———. *The Astronomical Works of Gregory Chioniades,* Vol. I: *The Zīj al-'Alā'ī,* part 1: *Text, Translation, Commentary;* part 2: Tables, *Corpus des Astronomes Byzantins* II, 2 vols. Amsterdam: Gieben, 1985–1986.

Tihon, Anne. "Les tables astronomiques persanes à Constantinople dans la première moitié du XIVe siècle." *Byzantion* 57 (1987): 471–487.

Usener, Hermann. "Ad historiam astronomiae symbola." In *Kleine Schriften* III, Leipzig- Berlin: Teubner, 1914.

Westerink, L. G. "La profession de foi de Grégoire Chioniadès." *Revue des Études Byzantines* 38 (1980): 233–245.

Anne Tihon

CHRYSIPPUS (*b.* Soli, Asia Minor, c. 280 BCE; *d.* Athens, c. 205 BCE), *theory of matter, logic, cosmology, psychology, Stoicism.*

The third leader of the Stoic school of philosophy in Athens, Chrysippus consolidated and expanded the influence of the Stoic school, making it one of the most influential philosophies of the Greco-Roman world. He made particularly important contributions to cosmology, the theory of matter, logic, and psychology; his doctrines became standard in Stoicism and so a major influence on later Greek natural philosophy.

Cosmology. Building on the theories of Plato (in the *Timaeus*) and Aristotle, as well as the work of his predecessors in the school, Chrysippus held that the cosmos is a unique and closed physical system surrounded by an indefinite void but with no emptiness within its boundaries. The cosmos is a physical plenum containing four basic elements (earth, air, fire, and water), but ultimately composed of two principles: an active, causal principle identified with god and reason; and a passive principle, prime matter without quality. The cosmos is spherical, with the heavenly bodies rotating around the unmoving, central Earth. It is structured by the rational, divine principle and so is both a thoroughgoing teleological system (with the interests of humans and gods paramount) and a wholly deterministic system: there are no uncaused events

or states and all are in principle explicable. The cosmos is an ordering of all the matter in the cosmos; it has a beginning and an end, whereas the matter and principles persist forever. The creation and dissolution of the cosmic order is cyclical, beginning with a watery phase in which the seed of future changes is contained and ending with a fiery conflagration, after which an identical cosmogenesis begins again.

The Four Elements. Earth, air, fire, and water had been identified as the basis of all other forms of matter by Empedocles, a tradition accepted in varying forms by Plato and Aristotle. Like Plato and Aristotle, Chrysippus did not regard the four forms of matter as truly elemental: Each is a product of the two corporeal principles (god and prime matter) that are perfectly blended with each other. Each form of matter is characterized by one defining quality rather than two as Aristotle had held (fire is hot, water is moist, air is cold, earth is dry). One of Chrysippus's innovations was the theory that the cosmos coheres with itself as a natural unity owing to the omnipresence of pneuma, a breathlike substance composed of fire and air perfectly blended. Early Stoics had given a predominant causal role to a creative form of fire. The varying degrees of tension in pneuma explain the differing levels of organization of material objects (things such as rocks, plants, animals, and rational animals). The orderliness and causal interdependence of everything in the cosmos was a vital feature of Stoic cosmology.

The cohesion imparted by pneuma is also reflected in the stoic theory of natural motion. Aristotle had held that earth and water have a natural downward motion, while fire and air naturally move upward. Chrysippus and his predecessors claimed that all the elements are centripetal, with the lighter elements simply being drawn less vigorously to the center than is earth.

Logic. Chrysippus was the greatest logician in the ancient world, after Aristotle. He did not follow Aristotle's lead in the development of a syllogistic logic based on terms (subjects or predicates) as the basic unit. Rather, the statement, or proposition, is fundamental to Chrysippus's logic. This facilitated his development of a forerunner of sentential logic. All valid inferences are reducible ultimately to one of the five indemonstrable argument forms.

1. If A then B. A. Therefore B.
2. If A then B. Not B. Therefore not A.
3. Not both A and B. A. Therefore not B.
4. Either A or B. A. Therefore not B
5. Either A or B. Not A. Therefore B.

Chrysippus is also responsible for even more impressive work in the field now called semantics, in rhetoric, and in the theory of argument forms.

Psychology. From the beginning Stoic psychology was corporealist. The soul is made of pneuma that pervades the entire body, and the mind is a highly concentrated and refined form of this pneuma centered in the heart (in this respect following Aristotle rather than Plato). The perceptual and motor functions are carried out through what has become known as the circulatory system, which forms a network throughout the body. Functionally, the mind (called the commanding part, or *hēgemonikon*) is fully unified. There is no division between a part responsible for reasoning and a separate locus of desire and perception. The Stoic theory was resistant to growing evidence from medical dissections (especially the discovery of the optic nerve) that the brain had a better claim to be the seat of thought and awareness. Chrysippus was more impressed by the importance of the network of arteries centered on the heart, which offered an explanation for the way the mind communicated with the entire body. Because the central nervous system was not yet understood, this consideration was hard to reject on scientific grounds. The Platonizing doctor Galen of Pergamum relied on dubious philosophical considerations in his support for the brain as the seat of thought, being most concerned to confirm the theory of Plato's *Timaeus* against Chrysippus, whose view continued to be the principal alternative to Plato's for many centuries. Galen also argued vigorously for the tripartition of the soul and the sharp separation of desire and cognition. Chrysippus's conviction that the mind was in the heart was wrong, though the reasoning behind the view was not unreasonable. But his claim that the mind is material and that cognitive, perceptual, emotional, and other functions are highly unified is more in keeping with modern scientific psychology than the medical tradition represented by Galen.

Chrysippus's philosophical brilliance transformed Stoicism and made it into the most influential school for centuries, until the revival of Platonism and Aristotelianism displaced it—in time for those schools to become dominant in their influence on medieval and early-modern science. He was also a prolific author (though none of his 700 books has been preserved intact) and a skilled organizer of intellectual activity in his school, using his position as head to give it an agenda that long outlasted his own career.

BIBLIOGRAPHY

Algra, Keimpe. *The Cambridge History of Hellenistic Philosophy.* Cambridge, U.K.: Cambridge University Press, 1999. Chrysippus features centrally in any general account of ancient Stoicism.

Bréhier, Émile. *Chrysippe et l'ancien stoïcisme.* Paris: Presses Universitaires de France, 1951.

Goulet, Richard. "Chrysippe de Soles." In *Dictionnaire des philosophes antiques,* vol. 2, edited by Richard Goulet, 329–361. Paris: CNRS Éditions, 1994. The best summary overview is found here.

Inwood, Brad, ed. *The Cambridge Companion to the Stoics.* Cambridge, U.K.: Cambridge University Press, 2003.

Tieleman, Teun. *Chrysippus' On Affections: Reconstruction and Interpretations.* Leiden, Netherlands: Brill, 2003.

von Arnim, Hans, ed. *Stoicorum Veterum Fragmenta,* vols. 2–3. Leipzig, Germany: Teubner, 1903. The basic textual evidence is collected in this work.

Brad Inwood

CHUNG YAO CHAO
SEE **Zhao, Zhongyao**.

CLARK, JOHN DESMOND (*b.* London, United Kingdom, 10 April 1916; *d.* Oakland, California, 14 February 2002), *paleoanthropology, archaeology.*

Clark conducted groundbreaking research into the prehistoric archaeology of Africa and through his discoveries he convinced archaeologists of the importance of Africa for understanding world prehistory. During his long career he made significant contributions to the knowledge of human origins through his excavations, his efforts to develop archaeological institutions in Africa, and the students he trained.

Education. Desmond Clark first became interested in archaeology as a child growing up in Buckinghamshire. His father, a chemist with an interest in history, often took Desmond to see the ruins of hill-forts, monasteries, and castles. These interests were later encouraged by Clark's mathematics teacher at Monkton Combe School in Bath. In 1934, Clark entered Christ's College, Cambridge University, where he studied history and then archaeology and anthropology with Miles Burkitt and Grahame Clark. Under their tutelage Clark learned the basics of Paleolithic archaeology, the importance of artifact typology, and the role of the environment in shaping material culture and human behavior. While at Cambridge, Clark also spent two seasons excavating an Iron Age hill camp at Maiden Castle under the guidance of archaeologist Mortimer Wheeler, keeper of archaeology at the Museum of

John D. Clark. AP IMAGES.

London, who taught Clark rigorous excavation methods and the importance of keeping careful records. During his last year at Cambridge Clark became engaged to Betty Cable Baume, who was studying modern languages at Newnham College, and they married in 1938.

Clark received a BA in anthropology and archaeology with First Class Honors in 1937 but quickly found that there were few university or museum positions available in Britain. However, late that year he received an offer from the governor of Northern Rhodesia to become curator of the David Livingstone Memorial Museum and secretary of the Rhodes-Livingstone Institute for Social Anthropology in Livingstone, near Victoria Falls in Northern Rhodesia (later Zambia). Clark accepted and arrived in Livingstone in January 1938. At the time the museum consisted of early maps of Africa, cultural artifacts, and documents belonging to David Livingstone. Clark quickly began to put the museum's collection of archaeological and ethnological material in order and prepared a handbook for the collection.

The Africa Years. When Clark arrived in Livingstone there were only a few archaeologists who were investigating African prehistory. Astley John Hilary Goodwin, Clarence van Riet Lowe, and Neville Jones had begun to work out the sequence of archaeological artifacts and periods of southern Africa, while further north in Kenya Louis and Mary Leakey were searching for evidence of the earli-

est humans in Africa. Rhodesian Man had been discovered at a mining site called Broken Hill in 1921, attracting worldwide attention, and Paleolithic artifacts had been found in the Old Terrace Gravels of the Zambezi River. Clark conducted excavations of these Zambezi River deposits in collaboration with geologist Basil Cooke in 1938, and together they began to unravel the sequence of stone industries and fossils at the site. Clark also learned of excavations conducted at Mumbwa in the Kafue Valley by Italian scientists in 1930 and decided to reinvestigate the site in 1939. These careful excavations disclosed a remarkable archaeological sequence stretching from the Middle Stone Age to the Iron Age that Clark used to illustrate the impact of paleoenvironments on early human behavior. The results of these researches, published in 1942, were not only significant for their detail but also for the careful drawings of artifacts that Clark's wife Betty prepared.

World War II interrupted Clark's career, and in 1941, he joined the Field Ambulance Unit of the Northern Rhodesia Regiment. He was sent to Ethiopia and Somalia and saw action against the Italians, but conditions were such that Clark had frequent opportunities to search for prehistoric artifacts, and by the end of the war he had accumulated an extensive knowledge of the archaeology of the region, which led to the publication of *The Prehistoric Cultures of the Horn of Africa* in 1954. While in Nairobi, where the headquarters of the British East Africa Command was located, he visited Louis and Mary Leakey to discuss African prehistory and to conduct a small excavation. Clark was discharged from the army in 1946 and returned to Livingstone to resume his duties there. His wife Betty had run the museum during his years away and continued to serve as its secretary after his return. The decision had recently been made to separate the Rhodes-Livingstone Institute, which was moved to the capital Lusaka, from the museum, which was renamed the Rhodes-Livingstone Museum and opened with a new building in 1951.

During his travels across Africa before and during the war, Clark became aware of the growing threat to archaeological sites by settlement, farming, treasure hunting, and other activities. In order to insure the preservation of archaeological sites, Clark established the Northern Rhodesia National Monuments Commission and served as its first secretary. With the end of the war, it was also easier for scientists across Africa to travel, attend meetings, and organize new institutions. Clark regularly attended meetings of the South African Archaeological Society, but it was the organizing of the first Pan-African Congress on Prehistory by Louis Leakey that brought the greatest number of researchers together and did the most to encourage archaeology in Africa. The meeting was held in Nairobi in 1947 and was attended by archaeologists, geologists, and paleontologists from all over Africa as well as Europe. Clark presented his research at the congress and served as its assistant secretary. The congress not only elevated the stature of archaeological research in Africa in the eyes of European and American researchers, but it also brought together researchers from Africa in fruitful ways that accelerated the progress of prehistoric research on the continent. Clark's own stature was elevated through his participation in the First Pan-African Congress, and at the Second Pan-African Congress, held in Algiers in 1952, Clark was appointed president of the prehistory section.

Beginning in 1948, Clark had also initiated new excavations along the Zambezi River Valley around Victoria Falls, where he collected numerous stone artifacts and worked out a stratified sequence of successive stone tools types or industries. In 1950, Clark took a leave of absence from his duties at the Rhodes-Livingstone Museum and returned to England. Working with Miles Burkitt at Cambridge University, Clark drew upon the material he had collected in the Horn of Africa and his excavations of the Zambezi gravels to complete his PhD degree in 1951. After completing his dissertation, Clark returned to Livingstone and resumed his studies.

While exploring along the Kalambo River near Lake Tanganyika in 1953, Clark discovered a rich archaeological site at a location called Kalambo Falls. He conducted a cursory investigation in 1953 and then again in 1955, but his first serious season of digging was undertaken in 1956 when he was able to get financial support from the Wenner-Gren Foundation. Work continued intermittently at the site until 1966, and the wealth of material found at the site, combined with Clark's extensive and careful records of his discoveries, made his work there a valuable contribution to African archaeology and made Clark a recognized expert in African prehistory. His excavations uncovered a long succession of deposits beginning with Acheulean hand-axes, followed by materials from the Middle Stone Age, and finally by Iron Age artifacts. However, no hominid or animal remains were ever found at the site.

A great deal was learned about the climate and environmental conditions existing at the various periods being uncovered because Clark had assembled colleagues from a variety of different disciplines to participate in the excavations. The newly invented method of carbon-14 dating was also used to obtain absolute dates for the different layers, which greatly improved the understanding of the chronology of African prehistory, although the dates obtained were later found to be somewhat incorrect. Studying the material found, interpreting what it indicated about cultural and technological developments in prehistoric Africa, and preparing his results for publication was a long and arduous task. The first volume of *Kalambo Falls Prehistoric Site* was published in 1969, with

a second volume appearing in 1974. Clark continued working on the third and last volume through the later years of his life, and it was finally published in 2001.

Clark's career took another significant advance forward in 1955 when he arranged for the Third Pan-African Congress on Prehistory to be held in Livingstone. Again the meeting was well attended by scientists from Africa and abroad, with Clark even leading participants on field trips to archaeological sites in the vicinity. It was during the Livingstone meeting that Clark first met Sherwood Washburn, who was conducting research on baboons at Victoria Falls and the Wankie (later Hwange) Game Reserve. The success of the meeting, combined with Clark's extensive fieldwork in various parts of Africa as well as his accomplishments at the Rhodes-Livingstone museum, gave Clark an international reputation. In 1952, he had been elected a Fellow of the Society of Antiquaries and in 1955, he became president of the South African Archaeological Society. He was appointed to the Order of the British Empire in 1956 and was later named a Commander of the Order of the British Empire in 1960. He was also made a Fellow of the British Academy in 1961.

Clark published a series of articles in the years immediately after the Pan-African Congress in Livingstone, including a catalogue for the David Livingstone exhibition and several encyclopedia articles on African prehistory. He also expanded the collections of the Rhodes-Livingstone Museum and added two young British archaeologists, Ray Inskeep and Brian Fagan, to the museum staff. Then in 1959, the Portuguese diamond mining company Companhia de Diamantes de Angola invited Clark to excavate sites in northern Angola where mining operations had discovered large quantities of artifacts. Although the colonial government in Northern Rhodesia was not happy about Clark working in a region not under British colonial administration, his discoveries in Angola added important new data to his knowledge of African prehistory.

The Berkeley Years. Clark's career took a dramatic turn in 1960 when the Department of Anthropology at the University of California at Berkeley invited him to join their program to teach Old World Archaeology, and especially the archaeology of Africa. Sherwood Washburn, who had met Clark at the Pan-African Congress in Livingstone, had recently joined the department and had just started a program in paleoanthropology. Recognizing that he was at the mid-point of his career and that such an opportunity might not present itself again, Clark accepted the offer and joined the department in the fall of 1961. He joined such talented researchers as Washburn, Theodore McCown, and F. Clark Howell, and with the addition of Glynn Isaac to the department in 1966, Berkeley became a center for the study of African prehistory and paleoanthropology.

Clark now had access to funds that allowed him to conduct a much wider variety of research projects. In July 1961, just before going to Berkeley, Clark traveled to Burg Wartenstein in Austria to participate in a symposium sponsored by the Wenner-Gren Foundation on the subject of African Ecology and Human Evolution. He joined nineteen other participants from a variety of disciplines to discuss the implications of new ecological, evolutionary, and primatological discoveries for the study of human origins and human prehistory. The symposium was so successful that Clark, Walter W. Bishop, and F. C. Howell organized another international colloquium in 1965 at the Wenner-Gren conference center at Burg Wartenstein. The papers presented at the colloquium and the volume that was subsequently published, *Background to Evolution in Africa* (1967), helped to shape the newly emerging discipline of paleoanthropology.

Through an invitation to conduct work in Syria by the Antiquities and Museums Directorate of Syria, Clark spent two seasons in 1964 and 1965 excavating a Lower Paleolithic site in the Orontes Valley. From 1965 to 1968, Clark supervised the investigation of lake bed deposits in the Karonga region of Malawi in northern Africa. These excavations brought together archaeologists, paleontologists, and geologists who worked together to reconstruct the cultural, environmental, and geologic conditions in the area during the Pleistocene. From 1970 to 1973, Clark excavated Neolithic sites in the central Sahara and the Sudanese Nile Valley, where he investigated the origins of agriculture and the development of sedentary ways of living, and the ways that changes in climate contributed to such changes in human behavior. He also continued to write during this period. After many years of collecting information about the relationship between early human material culture and ancient environmental conditions, Clark published an *Atlas of African Prehistory* in 1967. The atlas consisted of a series of maps that show the distribution of archaeological sites in different geological periods in relation to topography, vegetation, climate, and other factors.

At Berkeley, Clark and his colleagues were attracting students and prestige to their program in African prehistory and paleoanthropology because of the quality of the training and research offered there. They were able to hire Glynn Isaac as a faculty member in 1966, which further strengthened the department's expertise in African paleoanthropology. The program was influential not only for its renowned teaching and research faculty, but also for its efforts to train African nationals who might return to Africa and encourage an indigenous tradition of research there. Throughout his career, Clark remained dedicated to the support of African researchers and the formation of research institutions in Africa.

Clark departed for Ethiopia in 1974 with a large team of international colleagues from a variety of disciplines to undertake an extensive excavation project. The team, coordinated by Clark, investigated Middle and Late Stone Age sites, but on the Gadeb Plain in central Ethiopia the team discovered Oldowan and Acheulean artifacts in deposits dated at 1.5 million years old. In addition to heading the research, Clark helped to find money for the construction of research facilities to be located in Ethiopia. Then in 1980, Clark conducted a cursory exploration of the deposits along the Middle Awash River. He found an abundance of Oldowan and Acheulean artifacts and plans were made to begin serious excavations the following year, but rebel fighting and difficulties with the Ethiopian authorities made that impossible.

While work in Ethiopia was suspended, Clark participated in excavations in India and Korea. He was also invited by the Institute of Vertebrate Paleontology and Paleoanthropology and the Chinese Academy of Sciences to join collaborative Chinese-American excavations of early Pleistocene hominid occupation sites in the Nihewan basin in the Chinese province of Hebei for four successive seasons between 1989 and 1992.

Clark formally retired from teaching at Berkeley in 1986, but he remained active in collaborating with researchers on new excavations. Circumstances in Ethiopia improved so that a team of researchers led by Clark and Tim White, also a Berkeley professor of paleoanthropology, was able to return in 1990 to work in the Middle Awash region. In 1994, the team found the fossil bones of a new hominid species that was estimated by radiometric dating methods to have lived 4.5 million years ago. The new hominid was so different from any species then known that a new genus was created and the creature was named *Ardipithecus ramidus*. This remarkable discovery was followed in 1996 by the excavation of some new hominid remains, and in 1997, Yohannes Haile-Selassie, who was then a Berkeley graduate student, found a skullcap of this hominid. This new hominid species was later named *Australopithecus garhi* and was determined to be 2.5 million years old. While Clark remained a part of the Middle Awash research team throughout the 1990s, his role in the actual excavations diminished over the years as a result of his failing eyesight and his age.

During the latter portion of his career, Clark received numerous awards. He received his DSc degree from Cambridge University in 1975 and honorary doctorates from both the University of Witwatersrand and the University of Cape Town in 1985. The Royal Anthropological Institute awarded Clark the Huxley Medal in 1974, and he was awarded the Grahame Clark Medal for Prehistory by the British Academy in 1997. It brought great satisfaction to Clark, who had been a long-time friend and colleague of

Louis and Mary Leakey, when he received the L. S. B. Leakey Foundation Prize in 1996. Clark was also a member of many scientific societies. He became a fellow of the American Academy of Arts and Sciences in 1965, four years after his arrival at Berkeley. He served as a member of the L. S. B. Leakey Foundation's Scientific Executive Committee from 1980. In 1986, Clark became a foreign associate of the National Academy of Sciences, and in 1993, he became a full member after obtaining American citizenship.

Clark achieved great prominence during his career and is considered to have made significant contributions to the knowledge of the archaeology of prehistoric Africa and to the development of the discipline of paleoanthropology during the last half of the twentieth century. Clark arrived in Africa at a time when African archaeology was in its infancy, and because he was one of only a handful of professionally trained archaeologists working on the continent, he was in a unique position to make important advances. By taking advantage of unexpected opportunities to travel and excavate in different parts of Africa, he achieved a remarkably comprehensive knowledge of the prehistoric cultures of the entire continent, from the early Paleolithic to the advent of agriculture. One of Clark's primary contributions to archaeological methodology was his conviction that one needed to determine the environmental conditions prevailing at a particular time and place in prehistory in order to properly interpret the cultures of the past and the ways they actually used the artifacts that archaeologist found. He wanted to reconstruct the behavior of early peoples and how they used their tools. In this work, he reflects the influence of his old professor Grahame Clark.

Clark also promoted and facilitated the pursuit of archaeological research in Africa by expanding the role of existing institutions such as the Rhodes-Livingstone Museum or by helping to establish new institutions such as the Pan-African Congresses as mechanisms to foster research and to bring researchers together. As a leader of major expeditions, he offered colleagues and students opportunities to conduct groundbreaking research and during his tenure at Berkeley, he trained several generations of students who have gone on to make significant contributions of their own. While colleagues and historians held Clark and his achievements in high regard, there were aspects of his work that were criticized. Some scholars have noted that Clark was slow to accept the great age assigned to archaeological sites after the development of the radiocarbon (carbon-14) dating method, and he viewed the extremely early dates given for early hominid sites by the potassium/argon dating method with caution. However, through his many books, articles, and presentations at meetings, which he continued working on right until his death, Desmond Clark made archaeologists rec-

ognize the importance of Africa in world prehistory and the centrality of Africa for the study of human origins.

BIBLIOGRAPHY

WORKS BY CLARK

Stone Age Sites in Northern Rhodesia and Possibilities of Future Research. Livingstone, Northern Rhodesia: Rhodes-Livingstone Institute, 1939.

The Stone Age Cultures of Northern Rhodesia. Cape Town: South African Archaeological Society, 1950.

The Prehistoric Cultures of the Horn of Africa. Cambridge: Cambridge University Press, 1954.

The Prehistory of Southern Africa. Harmondsworth, U.K.: Penguin, 1959.

Prehistoric Cultures of Northeast Angola and Their Significance in Tropical Africa. Lisbon: Companhia de Diamantes de Angola (Diamang), 1963.

The Distribution of Prehistoric Culture in Angola. Lisbon: Companhia de Diamantes de Angola (Diamang), 1966.

Atlas of African Prehistory. Chicago: University of Chicago Press, 1967.

With Walter W. Bishop, eds. *Background to Evolution in Africa.* Chicago: University of Chicago Press, 1967.

Kalambo Falls Prehistoric Site, vol. 1, *The Geology, Palaeoecology and Detailed Stratigraphy of the Excavations.* Cambridge: Cambridge University Press, 1969.

The Prehistory of Africa. London: Thames & Hudson, 1970.

Kalambo Falls Prehistoric Site, vol. 2, *The Later Prehistoric Cultures.* Cambridge: Cambridge University Press, 1974.

The Cambridge History of Africa: From the Earliest Times to c. 500 B.C. London: Cambridge University Press, 1982.

Kalambo Falls Prehistoric Site, vol. 3, *The Earlier Cultures: Middle and Earlier Stone Age.* Cambridge: Cambridge University Press, 2001.

OTHER SOURCES

Cooke, H. P., J. W. Harris, and K. Harris. "J. Desmond Clark: His Career and Contribution to Prehistory." *Journal of Human Evolution* 16 (1987): 549–581.

Daniel, Glyn, and Christopher Chippindale, eds. *The Pastmasters: Eleven Modern Pioneers of Archaeology: V. Gordon Childe, Stuart Piggott, Charles Phillips, Christopher Hawkes, Seton Lloyd, Robert J. Braidwood, Gordon R. Willey, C. J. Becker, Sigfried J. De Laet, J. Desmond Clark, D. J. Mulvaney.* New York: Thames and Hudson, 1989.

Phillipson, David W. "John Desmond Clark 1916–2002." *Proceedings of the British Academy* 120 (2003): 65–79.

Wendorf, Fred. "J. Desmond Clark." In *Encyclopedia of Archaeology: The Great Archaeologists*, edited by Tim Murray. Santa Barbara, CA: ABC-CLIO, 1999.

———. "J. Desmond Clark." *Biographical Memoirs*, vol. 83. Washington, DC: National Academies Press, 2003.

Matthew Goodrum

CLARK, DESMOND

SEE **Clark, John Desmond**.

CLARK, KENNETH BANCROFT (*b.* Panama Canal Zone, 24 July 1914; *d.* Hastings-on-Hudson, New York, 1 May 2005), *psychology, child development, social action.*

CLARK, MAMIE PHIPPS (*b.* Hot Springs, Arkansas, 18 October 1917; *d.* Hastings-on-Hudson, New York, 11 August 1983), *psychology, child development, social action.*

Kenneth Bancroft Clark and Mamie Phipps Clark, two African American psychologists, were leaders in the struggle for civil rights in the United States whose joint work was a central piece of the U.S. Supreme Court decision in 1954 (*Brown v. Board of Education of Topeka*) to declare school segregation unconstitutional. They studied the effects of segregation on child development.

Early Years. Kenneth Clark was born in 1914 in the Canal Zone of Panama where his father, Arthur, a Jamaican by birth, was a supervisor for the United Fruit Company. His mother, Miriam Hanson Clark, also Jamaican, brought Kenneth and his sister Beulah to New York City when he was four-and-a-half and she was two. Clark grew up in a sequence of apartments in the northern edge of Harlem in the early 1920s, then a predominantly white community.

By the mid-1920s, Clark recalls, "junior high school was the beginning of [his] segregated educational experience." (All uncited quotations are from oral histories; see note at head of bibliography.) Only when he was considering high schools did he experience the pain of racism in the city's school system: his guidance counselor urged him to attend one of Harlem's vocational schools, rather than to pursue an academic track. Clark rejected this advice and entered George Washington High School in Washington Heights, where he was one of ten African Americans in his graduating class.

Upon graduation in 1931, Clark chose to go to Howard University, the elite African American university in Washington, DC. An African American intellectual community that believed in the possibilities of a non-racist America thrived at Howard during the late 1920s and 1930s, and a gifted group of Howard teachers and students helped lay the groundwork for the flowering of the civil rights movement of the 1950s and early 1960s. Scholars including E. Franklin Frazier, Alain LeRoy Locke, Ralph Bunche, Charles Hamilton Houston, Sterling Allen Brown, and the psychologist Francis Cecil Sumner (whom Clark considered his "intellectual father"),

inspired and taught a new generation of black leaders, academics, and activists. Convinced that racism could and would be overcome and that an integrated society was both necessary and possible, they held a basically optimistic view of the possibilities of America—that political and legal integration was achievable and that equal opportunity, coupled to an expanding economy, could lessen—even abolish—the virulence of America's racism.

Mamie Phipps had come from a quite different background. Born in 1917 in the resort spa of Hot Springs, Arkansas, she grew up in a middle-class household, part of a small elite of African Americans in a relatively liberal southern town. Despite her family's social prominence, Mamie Phipps attended a segregated school and was "always aware of which way you could go, which way you couldn't go, and what you could do and what you couldn't do." Mamie Phipps entered Howard in 1934 at sixteen, planning to become a mathematics major and teacher, but, in her sophomore year, the intellectual environment at Howard convinced her that the social sciences were more intellectually challenging. By that time she had met Kenneth Clark, then a graduate student and teaching assistant in the psychology master's program. Clark reinforced her growing interest in the social sciences and, as they started to date, convinced her that psychology had scientific rigor and could satisfy her desire to work with children.

By the end of Mamie Phipps's junior year, in the summer of 1937, Kenneth Clark had been accepted at Columbia University in the psychology department, the first African American student permitted to enroll in its graduate program. For much of the academic year, Kenneth Clark and Mamie Phipps corresponded virtually every day. The separation became too painful for them and, during the spring break in 1938, they eloped, to be married by a justice of the peace in Virginia.

After graduation in the spring of 1938 Mamie Phipps Clark began her master's degree at Howard and became interested in a series of studies by Ruth and Gene Horowitz on "self-identification" in nursery school children, and considered how she might merge her own interest in children with her broadening perspectives on racism and segregation. She could use the data on children for a thesis on "The Development of Consciousness of Self in Negro Pre-school Children."

In a matter of months in 1939, the Clarks prepared four papers and got them accepted in the prestigious academic journals of that period. The first, written by Mamie Clark, appeared in the *Archives of Psychology*. The latter three were jointly authored with Kenneth Clark and appeared in the *Journal of Social Psychology* and the *Journal of Experimental Education*. They developed a joint proposal, submitted to the Julius Rosenwald Fund, to develop "newer methods of a coloring test and a doll's test" to continue their research on identity and race. The foundation awarded a fellowship to them just after Mamie Clark graduated in 1940, which meant that Mamie and Kenneth Clark could now work together in New York.

In the same year, 1940, Kenneth Clark was completing his doctoral degree, and Mamie Clark entered Columbia's psychology department as its second African American student. Mamie had opted to work with Henry Garrett precisely because, as Mamie Clark put it, he was "not by any means a liberal on racial matters" (quoted in O'Connell and Russo, 1983, Vol. 1, p. 268). Kenneth tried to dissuade her, but she told him "I want to work with the man who had these racial attitudes." In addition, having entered college intending to be a mathematics major, she was quantitatively oriented, and Garrett was the statistician on the faculty, so there was a convergence of interests, racial issues aside. She carried out her dissertation, "The Development of Primary Mental Abilities with Age," under Garrett's direction, using schoolchildren from the public school system in New York. Shortly after receiving his degree, Kenneth Clark taught at the Hampton Institute for a semester before becoming, in 1941, the first African American instructor appointed to the City College of New York. Two years later Mamie Clark received her PhD.

Work at the Northside Center. By 1945 Mamie Clark decided to strike out on her own and abandon her plans to work in the white-oriented social service system because of the racism she encountered there. She considered organizing a child guidance clinic that would address an obvious need in the growing Harlem community. That turned out to be the Northside Center for Child Development. Members of the Rosenwald and Stern families, and other leading white, principally Jewish, philanthropists served on its board, along with public figures in African American social service and legal worlds, including Judge Robert Carter and James Dumpson. Although ostensibly a mental health center, its history over the next several decades reflected the continuing controversies not only about racial justice but also community psychiatry, deinstitutionalization, and community action. For the organization's first forty years, Kenneth Clark used it as a base for his varied activities in education, psychology, and the antipoverty and urban renewal programs. The Northside Center was at the center of virtually every important political and social debate of the post–World War II era: de facto school segregation, juvenile delinquency, community action and the antipoverty programs of the Johnson era, educational reform and community control, urban renewal and housing reform, mental health and community psychiatry, Jewish-black relations, violence, and drug addiction and AIDS.

Mamie Clark, the executive director of Northside from its founding in 1946 to her retirement in 1979, inspired and shaped the center's structure and clinical program. Kenneth Clark, Northside's cofounder and research director from 1946 through 1966 and a board member until his death in 2005, advanced a broader social agenda through his wide variety of activities in New York's contentious political arena. Northside was, in this sense, a laboratory in which both of the Clarks' ideas and values were put into practice and tested. As Dumpson, a longtime board member and president and close friend of the Clarks, pointed out, Northside was a microcosm of the world the Clarks desired: a world of social equality, humanity, integration, and caring for all children and their families, without regard to race and circumstance. It was a place where black children, in particular, could learn to value their own worth and abilities and believe that they could shape their own future. Kenneth Clark said at the time, "We don't want psychiatry to be a panacea or substitute for social justice; what we conceived of when we started Northside was helping children to develop the kind of strength and belief in themselves, and the kind of personality stability which are necessary for them to contribute to making a better society" (Samuels, 1954). "A more just society" for Harlem's children was Northside's core agenda.

To outside observers it may have appeared that Kenneth and Mamie Clark operated in separate spheres—she inside and he outside Northside. Yet, as the Clarks and anyone who knew them well observed, they were essentially partners who depended on each other's insights, strengths, and values. They provided a source of empowerment for the children served, and their parents, and for the community of which Northside was part. But the full range and depth of their work has not always been apparent. Kenneth Clark said that Northside operated on many levels. It could only meet a tiny fraction of Harlem's needs, but it could serve as the catalyst for other organizations and activities with a broader impact on the quality of life of the children of Harlem.

School Integration North and South. Reforming education and providing reading and other academic support was a critical part of Northside's program. Monday, 17 May 1954—the day the U.S. Supreme Court announced that it had made a unanimous decision in *Brown v. Board of Education,* that "separate education facilities are inherently unequal," and hence, unconstitutional—marked the culmination of fifteen years' effort by the Clarks starting with the development of their famous doll tests. In 1951 the National Association for the Advancement of Colored People (NAACP) Legal Defense and Educational Fund (LDEF) had turned to social scientists in an unorthodox and innovative attempt to marshal expert testimony for a

Kenneth Clark. © ROBERT MAASS/CORBIS.

systematic fight against school segregation. Thurgood Marshall, the general counsel for the NAACP-LDEF, who had led the team of lawyers in arguing the *Brown* case, and his colleagues were unable to find senior academics willing to publicly testify, and Robert Carter, later a federal judge in New York and board member of Northside, asked Otto Klineberg at Columbia for advice. Klineberg led him to Kenneth Clark, then still in his thirties. Clark recalled the beginning of that story:

> Around February or March of 1951 I got a call from Bob Carter of the NAACP … and they wanted help from the psychologists to prove that segregated education could never be equal and that segregation, in itself, was harmful, without regard to whether facilities were equal or not. [Columbia's] Otto [Klineberg] had told him I had this manuscript which I had prepared for the [Mid-Century] White House Conference [on Children, 1950] and whatever help psychologists could give would be found in this manuscript. … So Bob Carter and I met for the first time. He told me the problem they faced; … that segregation, in

itself, damaged the personality of the Negro child. They had come upon this question themselves. They had formulated their legal approach and the only thing they didn't know was whether they could get any support for it from psychologists. … So they went back to Otto and he said your man is Kenneth Clark.… [But] he took the manuscript and read it and called me about a week later, all excited, I'll never forget his words. He said, 'This couldn't have been better if it had been done for us.'"

Clark, then an assistant professor at City College, marshaled other social and behavioral scientists to prepare and support an appendix to the NAACP brief, "summarizing the evidence on the effects of segregation and the consequence of desegregation." Both he and Mamie Clark testified in NAACP cases in Virginia (Kenneth Clark also testified in South Carolina and Delaware) about the results of the doll test and the negative impact of public school segregation. Mamie Clark said she was asked to testify in the Prince Edward County, Virginia, desegregation case in order to rebut directly the testimony offered in that court in support of inherent racial differences presented by Henry Garrett, her Columbia advisor and former president of the American Psychological Association.

As a result of his testimony during the school desegregation lawsuits in Virginia and elsewhere, Kenneth Clark became involved in New York public school desegregation politics during the mid-1950s. One attorney representing a southern state asked him why he was focusing so much on southern segregation when the schools in his own city were just as segregated. In response, in a speech to the New York Urban League in February 1954, at Harlem's Hotel Theresa, Kenneth Clark challenged New York's political leadership to acknowledge its own role in perpetuating a segregated system. He called upon the city's board of education to cooperate in a "study of the extent and effects of segregation in the public schools of New York City's Harlem" (Urban League Dinner speech, 1954)

In April 1954, shortly after his speech at the Hotel Theresa and a month before the Court's decision in *Brown,* Clark organized a conference at Northside Center called "Children Apart." More than two hundred representatives of sixty schools, social welfare agencies, religious organizations, unions, parents' organizations, and Harlem community groups attended. So did B'nai B'rith and the NAACP. The meeting attracted wide media coverage because of its implicit and explicit condemnation of the resistance of the city's governmental and educational leadership to acknowledging, much less confronting, the "increasing segregation" of the city's school system and the continued denial of an equal education to its African American and Puerto Rican children. In the conference's principal address, Kenneth Clark noted the subtle and not-so-subtle impact of educational policies, social theory, and housing patterns on the education of African American children. Segregation was a fact of life no less real in New York than in Mississippi. The following month came the *Brown* decision.

The ebullient optimism of the first post-*Brown* years quickly began to dissipate as civil rights leaders and educators ran up against entrenched opposition to change throughout the country. Kenneth Clark continued to believe that segregation would ultimately be defeated, but he began to voice concern about lack of commitment from local and national white leadership in the north and south. He singled out for special criticism "professional educators and their national organizations," "church organizations," "Southern labor unions," and "Northern white liberals." Educators "have been conspicuous by their silence, ambiguity, or equivocation on this issue" (Clark, 1956).

The next year, 1957, the long-simmering controversy over de facto school segregation in New York City burst onto the pages of local newspapers when Bernice and Stanley Skipworth and four other Harlem parents refused to send their children to JHS 136 at 135th Street and Edgecomb Avenue and JHS 139 at 140 West 140th Street because the schools were segregated, underfunded, and therefore of inferior quality. The nation's attention was riveted on Little Rock, Arkansas, where state and local authorities had refused to allow nine children to attend Central High School until President Dwight D. Eisenhower was forced to call out the National Guard to protect them. New York's own school authorities refused to allow black children in segregated elementary schools to move to predominantly white schools in other areas of the city. A comparison with Little Rock was never far from Kenneth and Mamie Clark's personal consciousness, for they had taken it upon themselves to provide a home and schooling in Hastings-on-Hudson to one of the "Little Rock Nine," Minnie Jean Brown, who had been expelled in the middle of the school year for throwing some chili onto a white student at Little Rock High School.

For Kenneth Clark, the Skipworth case was "a major development in the struggle of Negroes in northern communities to obtain equal and non-segregated education" (1959, pp. 11–12). Until this time, the New York City board of education, like most northern liberals, rarely acknowledged the impact on children of de facto segregation in northern urban communities. In court, the board of education no longer contested the fact that segregation existed, but did deny the claims of African American parents that de facto segregation was as destructive and harmful as was southern de jure segregation. Kenneth Clark was convinced that Judge Justine Wise Polier's decision acknowledging the inferiority of segregated schools in

New York could provide an opening to attack invidious northern de facto segregation, just as the U.S. Supreme Court's decision of 1954 had provided the basis for challenging de jure segregation in the South.

Harlem's youth were even more segregated in school by the early 1960s than they had been in the mid-1950s. The flight of white children to the city's private and parochial school systems and to the suburbs had heightened the frustration of black parents committed to integration. Because of Kenneth Clark's own long involvement in the desegregation effort of the 1950s and 1960s, he understood perhaps better than anyone the centrality of education in the broader struggle for equality and political power.

In the years between 1964 and the fall of 1968, the dissipation of school activists' confidence in integration as the best means of addressing the obvious inequalities in the public schools led to calls for community control. "Most of those in the minority communities who are now fighting for community control have been consistent fighters for integration," Kenneth Clark pointed out. "Their support for decentralization is not, therefore, to be seen in terms of a desire for separatism or a rejection of integration, but … it is a strategy of despair determined by the broken promises of the white community" (draft of "Introduction" by Dr. Kenneth B. Clark to "Community Control and the Urban School," 24 March 1970, Kenneth B. Clark MSS). While he himself refused to abandon the long-range goal of integration, he supported "the demand for community control" as "primarily a desperate attempt [by African American parents] to protect their children in the schools they are required to attend."

Critique of Arthur Jensen. By the late 1960s, in the wake of the social turmoil and disaffection that accompanied the late civil rights movement, a few psychologists and educators had begun to argue that the lack of measurable economic progress by African Americans during the 1960s could be explained by genetic factors. One of the prime pieces of evidence cited in this academic war by authors such as education professor Arthur Jensen at the University of California at Berkeley and Nobel Prize–winning engineer William Shockley of Stanford University, was that average test scores of African American youth were lower than whites. This focus on IQ testing was part of a much wider, scholarly attack against some of the more progressive aspects of the 1960s War on Poverty and Great Society programs. Head Start, the Office of Economic Opportunity, funding for minority college scholarships, affirmative action programs of various sorts, had been rooted in the assumption that differences between African American and white achievement in the country were attributable, in large part, to social, environmental, and historical oppression. By the late 1960s, however, certain academics maintained that African Americans, far from being at a disadvantage, had received too many special privileges. This white backlash seized on evidence offered and theories attributed to perceived differences in IQ between groups as "objective" proof of the fallacy of the environmental argument. Social programs could not, they argued, compensate for what they regarded as essentially innate and genetic inferiority.

The appearance of Jensen's article "How Much Can We Boost IQ and Scholastic Achievement?" in the 1969 *Harvard Educational Review* seemed to give the cloak of legitimacy to his views on the inherent inferiority of African Americans. It was given further credence by a "scientific" statistical reanalysis of data gathered by other psychologists and educators. Kenneth Clark was greatly concerned about the potential impact on educators, administrators, policy makers, and the broader public, many of whom lacked the training or familiarity with such statistical claims to evaluate Jensen's work. Clark, then president of the Metropolitan Applied Research Center, decided to "convene a small meeting of authorities to discuss the scientific and policy implications of the resurgence of this point of view," especially focusing on the view that compensatory programs like Head Start were failing and that investment in education for minority youth was wasted money. "Jensen's position has been consistent with the reduction of compensatory programs in education, a slowdown in school desegregation and an increase in white attitudes of superiority. In addition," Clark wrote, "teachers who apply Jensen's recommendations will abandon their efforts to impart the necessary symbolic skills and will stress only rote learning for minority groups pupils" (Kenneth B. Clark and Lawrence Plotkin to Professor Doxie Wilkerson, 26 September 1969; Kenneth B. Clark MSS).

Clark pointed out that Jensen's theories were consistent with past theories based on assumptions of racial inferiority, his "statistical apparatus notwithstanding." "Because the concept of race itself is so elusive for certain distinct physical characteristics." Clark maintained that "genetic differences identifiable by race have so far proved impossible to determine." Even if one could determine racial differences, African Americans themselves could not be identified as "a biological or 'racial' entity," but as "a socially defined group with common characteristics generated by social and institutional exclusiveness [which] has existed for too brief a time to develop any meaningful genetic character by inbreeding" (1974, pp. 109–110).

Kenneth Clark and the War on Poverty. By the mid-1960s, the optimism that the white community could recognize the evils of segregation and remove traditional barriers to African Americans' full participation in American life had eroded. No longer could the Harlem community depend upon the ambivalent and halting actions of even the most enlightened of northern white liberals. Harlem had to turn inward, to its own resources and institutions, and develop new ways to combat the ingrained racism and resistance to change that had left Harlem's children in segregated schools, poor housing, and economic crisis. The problems of Harlem were understood to have their roots in segregation, the conditions of housing, the lack of job opportunities, the transformation of the city's economic base from manufacturing to services, the deterioration of the school system, and drugs, among many other things.

The origins of "the war against poverty" and community action programs can be traced back to the 1960 election of John F. Kennedy as president and the subsequent appointment of Robert Kennedy as attorney general in 1961. The coming of the "New Frontier" marked heightened federal attention to domestic issues. Just as concern about the unemployed had generated the social programs of the New Deal a generation before, so the growing attention to the problem of youth and juvenile delinquency during the 1950s—a common concern in postwar periods—helped stimulate the programs of the early 1960s to restructure northern cities. Social scientists had long been asking questions about the relationship between youth, social class, and crime.

The President's Committee on Juvenile Delinquency, established by Attorney General Kennedy in 1961, issued policy guidelines for funding proposals for "demonstration projects for the prevention and control of juvenile delinquency" that emphasized that "the sources of delinquent behavior lie in the individual *and* in his social situation." In urban slums, "the sections of our cities frequently populated by Negroes and other low-income minority groups," it said, "even the healthiest personalities can be overwhelmed by delinquency patterns which are environmentally supported." Federal and local efforts should be aimed, therefore, at "actions aimed primarily at changes in social arrangements affecting target areas youth rather than changes in the personality of the individual delinquent" (U.S. Department of Health, Education, and Welfare Administration, 1963). In this approach were the seeds of the broader War on Poverty of the later Lyndon Johnson presidency. In sharp contrast to the earlier delinquency programs that sought to address the problems of youths already in trouble with the law or society, this new federal initiative sought to support programs "whose potential target is *all* youth in these most vulnerable areas of our cities" through "the *prevention* of those conditions which are seen as causal to delinquency." In the policy and academic arenas, social ramifications of poverty had

Mamie Phipps Clark. © CONDE NAST ARCHIVE/CORBIS.

replaced individual pathology as the paradigm for explaining delinquency.

A host of Harlem organizations joined Kenneth Clark in producing a statement, "A Program for Harlem's Youth." Over the course of 1962, Kenneth Clark and others began to develop a "comprehensive youth services program in the Central Harlem community." Clark wrote the planning grant, and the President's Committee on Juvenile Delinquency funded it at the end of 1962. The $230,000 established Harlem Youth Opportunities, Inc., known as HARYOU, to become one of the principal federally funded programs in the coming War on Poverty. HARYOU held out the possibility of hope that Harlem might be on the verge of a renaissance and a renewed control of its own destiny.

Rather than start from the answers, HARYOU began with questions. The first tack was a comprehensive survey to determine what facilities were available for youth, how they were being utilized, and to determine what new programs were needed. At the meeting of the Citizens' Advisory Council of the President's Committee on Juvenile Delinquency, Clark announced that "HARYOU is not an agency, not an action program, not a demonstration. It is only planning—thinking, looking, researching to understand the problems of youth in Harlem and to develop a solid, comprehensive program providing opportunities for the maximum adjustment of Harlem youth."

HARYOU, under Clark's direction, continued to develop a planning document, citing the enormous discrepancies in social services, educational opportunities, employment opportunities, housing, recreational facilities, and other services directly affecting Harlem's youth and the social consequences of increased mortality and educational deficiencies. Mamie Clark was chair of a HARYOU committee that assessed the "nature and quality of existing services for youth in the Harlem community," identifying existing services for adoption, daycare, employment and vocational guidance, family services and financial assistance, hospitals, mental health programs, recreation, group work programs, settlements, neighborhood centers, and vacation services.

Kenneth Clark wrote much of HARYOU's final report, *Youth in the Ghetto,* issued in 1964, and his book *Dark Ghetto,* published the year after, grew out of it. Given Clark's theories on social power it is no accident that the HARYOU report was subtitled *A Study of the Consequences of Powerlessness,* for it was born out of his growing frustration with traditional dependence for dealing with problems of poverty in the black "ghettos" of America on the benevolence of the private philanthropy and governmental bureaucracies. His hope for an integrated assault on social pathology was undermined by years of disappointment, and he was now convinced that Harlem would have to turn inward, to its own resources and political base to affect meaningful change. Only through drawing on its own strengths as an African American community with the potential for real political power could the rapidly accelerating problems associated with poverty, social dislocation, drugs, crime, inadequate housing, and disastrous schools be seriously addressed. But he also retained skepticism about this approach. Without a massive infusion of funds and an end to Harlem's isolation, in the long run no meaningful systemic change could occur. But he saw no way to go except to attempt to meet immediate needs with available resources—to try, as he often said, not to sacrifice another generation of children.

Ironically, HARYOU, and specifically Kenneth Clark, now became the target of a massive and well-coordinated campaign from within the community (or so it appeared) that sought to undermine them as an independent force. Adam Clayton Powell, then the chairman of the House Education and Welfare Committee, was mobilizing federal and local official support to dislodge Clark and take over HARYOU by merging it with his own antipoverty organization, Associated Community Teams (ACT). He sought to portray the Clarks as profiteers who had benefited from public monies that might otherwise go to more worthy antipoverty programs (such as his own).

Privately, Kenneth Clark revealed that Powell offered him an opportunity to share the spoils of federal largess and was offended when Clark turned him down. On 7 July 1964, the newly merged HARYOU-ACT board failed to elect Clark as one of its officers and, three weeks later on 29 July, Clark resigned from the organization he had founded. The impact of Kenneth Clark's resignation brought to the fore HARYOU's political importance; it was perhaps the largest source of federal antipoverty money in the nation, and Powell had felt he had a right to direct its use. Clark saw HARYOU as "the last chance

available for thousands of young people in Harlem," and Powell's political maneuvering endangered that chance. For liberals, white and black, the message was particularly troubling, because Clark represented both the scholarly and professional communities. "Dr. Kenneth Clark was recently crushed by practical politicians when he tried to steer the local anti-poverty program on an independent professional course," said Woody Klein in the *Nation* magazine (1964). Klein, a reporter from the *New York World-Telegram* who had broken the story of the HARYOU-ACT split in the *Nation* piece, described "the mild-mannered, 50-year-old City College of New York psychology professor [who had] … stepped out of his role as scholar when he publicly accused Powell of trying to make HARYOU a 'political pork barrel'"(p. 27).

Temporarily stymied on the political stage, Clark turned to writing what became his most noted book, *Dark Ghetto: Dilemmas of Social Power,* published in 1965, and then laid plans to reenter the fight over Harlem from another direction. With funding from the Ford Foundation and the Carnegie Corporation, among others, he organized the integrated Metropolitan Applied Research Center (MARC). It was to provide a new base for leadership in the school decentralization struggle, work with national civil rights leaders, undertake major research into racial segregation, accept a request from the school board of Washington, D.C., to propose reform of that system, help organize black elected officials nationally, found the Joint Center for Political Studies in Washington, D.C., and so on.

The confluence of internal battles in HARYOU and the outside attack on Mobilization for Youth (a federally funded antipoverty agency on the Lower East Side of New York City) combined to undermine the faith of the Harlem community in federal antipoverty programs that had once seemed so promising. When, in August 1964, President Johnson, with much fanfare and media attention, launched his War on Poverty, many in Harlem reacted with cynicism and anger at first. From Kenneth Clark's perspective, such cynicism was legitimate. In a study sponsored by the Stern Family Fund, he analyzed the conditions under which antipoverty programs failed or succeeded, including the tactics of participation by the poor on governing boards and in confrontation with white power. In *A Relevant War against Poverty,* Clark and Jeannette Hopkins—on leave from Harper & Row to work with him as vice president for publications, on a Carnegie–Harper & Row cosponsored urban affairs publications program at MARC—concluded that federally funded antipoverty programs foundered on the inability and unwillingness of the powerful in the society to "share even a modicum of real power with those who have been powerless." The "poor and the powerless are perceived and treated as if they are objects to be manipulated, taunted, played with, and punished by those with power." The poor "are required to be grateful for the verbalizations and crumbs of power and are rejected as incorrigibly inferior, childlike, or barbaric if they rebel against and otherwise disturb the convenience of their more powerful benefactor." Despite the rhetoric of meaningful empowerment, "Antipoverty programs … were doomed to failure because they reflected a total lack of commitment to eliminate poverty, to share power with the powerless." At root, the antipoverty programs were based on racist assumptions and paternalistic traditions that saw the objects of charity as "inferior human beings" and "did not want to, and would not, operate in terms of the rationale and goals of the potential equality of all human beings. They did not seek to accept and strengthen the humanity of the deprived through compassion, empathy, and a serious sharing of power" (Clark, 1974a, p. 159).

Theoretical Analysis of Inequality. Kenneth Clark was formulating his analysis of the nature of power relationships in the larger city and nation as a whole, leading to his book *Pathos of Power* (1974). In the mid-1960s, Clark was defining "social power" as "the force or energy required to bring about, to sustain, or to prevent social, political, or economic change" (1974a, p. 75.). To him, it was a neutral force like electricity that could be used positively or negatively. Beginning with the assumption that established politicians and white groups had little interest in upsetting the status quo, he sought to understand the place of Harlem in this power equation. Harlem was first and foremost a ghetto, Clark observed, and as such, was a creation and manifestation of the white system's intent on maintaining existing power relations by isolating and confining troublesome blacks. Harlem and other segregated communities were evidence and proof of the powerlessness of their African American residents, whether or not at times they were able to appear to transcend the boundaries, as in the Harlem Renaissance of the arts in the 1920s. "The confinement of powerless individuals to restrictive ghettos in the North can be seen as an example of power by control" (1974a, p. 78).

He studied the approaches necessary to confront the oppression of African Americans in the American South and in the North. In the South, the civil rights movement had been able to mobilize hundreds of thousands of black middle-class and working-class people in an alliance with northern and southern liberal whites and an eager generation of young people, white and black, to tear down the citadels of segregation. In the North, without the clearer, more vulnerable, more dramatic targets of de jure segregation, such unity had been elusive, if not impossible, to achieve. What new strategies could work in the North? The antipoverty programs were a revealing and discouraging test.

Later, in his 1971 presidential address to the American Psychological Association (APA), he reviewed the theoretical basis for Northside's expansionist definition of therapy, developed during the 1960s. He looked at the schism that had developed between professionals there with psychiatrists tending to maintain a strong commitment to Freudian and other traditional forms of psychoanalysis and those who were seeking theoretical legitimacy for community empowerment as part of the therapeutic process. He argued that "Freudian theory does not appear to offer a theoretical basis for a psychology concerned [with] social change or a psychotechnology other than one-to-one psychoanalytic therapy," indeed, it inhibited "the quest for a more enlightened social policy," because "morally and rationally determined social change could not proceed from the premise that man is a totally or primarily nonrational organism whose most powerful drives are instinctive and animalistic" (1974a, p. 161).

Clark turned to other interpersonal theorists, specifically to Alfred Adler, who, he felt, showed a "concern with man's social interaction." Adler placed a greater "emphasis on the human struggle for self-esteem," concerns "much more compatible with my main research and action" (1974a, p. 75). In contrast to Sigmund Freud—who, in Clark's view, saw humans as essentially powerless to alter and shape their social environment—Adler demanded greater personal and social control over one's fate. The ability to "bring about, to sustain, or to prevent social, political or economic change" had to be at the heart of any successful psychological theory. "The core Adlerian idea which persists in its influence on my thinking concerns the nature of psychological power in understanding human beings and human society." Clark held that "Bertrand Russell's assertion that 'the fundamental concept in social science is Power, in the same sense in which Energy is a fundamental concept in physics' reinforced the influence of Adlerian theory in my thinking" (1974a, p. 75).

The APA paper stirred up a hornet's nest of protest in the profession and in the press, ostensibly because of its prescription of medical, specifically drug, intervention in preventing extreme behavior among top political leadership. Commentators all but ignored his theoretical arguments on power and powerlessness in psychotherapy.

Kenneth Clark cautioned the broader mental health community of the dangers professionals faced if they did not reform their own attitudes, beliefs, and assumptions: "We can no longer afford our past rationalizations, our past defenses, for that matter, even our past prejudices." Psychiatrists, social workers, psychologists, and other mental health workers had "to break down the distinctions between mental health as a personal problem … and mental health as a problem of social stability…. [W]e can no longer afford the luxury of looking at mental health problems in terms of the adjustment of a particular individual [but rather] we must now see the problem of our cities, the problem of equality in nature, the moral substance of our society, and the problem of individual adjustment as one or—at worst—interrelated." Clark continued, "the goal of mental health, therefore, can no longer be one in which we help individuals to adjust to their environment no matter what the quality of their environment" (transcript of remarks at "The Child, the Family, and the City," Conference organized by the Metropolitan Applied Research Center, Delmonico Hotel, New York, NY, Kenneth B. Clark MSS). Empowerment of the client, through personal growth or political action, had to be central to any serious therapeutic process: "The individual has to be helped to attain the strength to mobilize his own energies and resources to bring about the changes in the environment which are consistent with human dignity."

In 1983 Mamie Clark died of cancer; she was sixty-five years old. In 2005 Kenneth Clark died at the age of ninety.

Ironically, Kenneth and Mamie Clark probably had a deeper and broader impact on American society than on the field of psychology. Kenneth, one of the premier public intellectuals of the twentieth century, and Mamie were unswerving advocates of racial integration as being critical to the social and psychological health of both white and black Americans. The Clarks' research, testimony, and activism were critically important in the U.S. Supreme Court's landmark 1954 *Brown* decision, and more broadly, helped to stimulate social scientists to use their research to influence social policy. Due in part to the Clarks' example, psychologists paid increasing attention to the roles of race and gender in the post–World War II period.

BIBLIOGRAPHY

This essay is based primarily on the Kenneth Clark Manuscripts at the Library of Congress, and the Mamie Phipps Clark and the Northside Center for Child Development Manuscripts at the New York Public Library, RG 220 (the Records of the President's Committee on Juvenile Delinquency) at the National Archives, as well as the oral histories of Kenneth and Mamie Clark at the Columbia University Oral History Collection.

WORKS BY KENNETH CLARK

"Desegregation: An Appraisal of Evidence." *Journal of Social Issues* 9, no. 4 (1953): 2–76.

"The Negro in New York City—The Role of Education." Speech for Urban League Dinner, Hotel Theresa, 15 February 1954, Kenneth B. Clark MSS.

"The Present Crisis in Race Relations." Paper delivered at the Annual Dinner of the Unitarian Service Committee, Inc., 19 May 1956, Boston, MA. Northside Center for Child Development MSS, New York Public Library.

"Present Problems in Public School Desegregation in New York City." In *Harlem Works for Better Schools*, Pamphlet, New York [c. 1959], Kenneth B. Clark MSS.

The Negro Protest: James Baldwin, Malcolm X, Martin Luther King Talk with Kenneth B. Clark. Boston: Beacon Press, 1963. Published as *King, Malcolm, Baldwin: Three Interviews.* Middletown, CT: Wesleyan University Press, 1985.

Prejudice and Your Child. 2nd ed. Boston: Beacon Press, 1963.

Dark Ghetto: Dilemmas of Social Power. New York: Harper & Row, 1965.

With Talcott Parsons, eds. *The Negro American.* Boston: Houghton, Mifflin, 1966.

An Intensive Program for the Attainment of Educational Achievement in Deprived Area Schools of New York City. New York: Metropolitan Applied Research Center, 1968.

With Julian Bond and Richard G. Hatcher, eds. *The Black Man in American Politics: Three Views.* Washington, DC: Metropolitan Research Center for the Institute for Black Elected Officials, 1969.

As general editor, with Jeannette Hopkins. *A Relevant War against Poverty: A Study of Community Action Programs and Observable Social Change.* New York: Harper & Row, 1969.

With Harold Howe, et al. *Racism and American Education: A Dialogue and Agenda for Action.* New York: Harper & Row, 1970.

A Report to the Parents and Other Citizens of Washington, D.C., on the Status of the Academic Achievement Design at This Stage of the 1970–71 School Year. New York: Metropolitan Applied Research Center, 1971.

The Educationally Deprived: The Potential for Change. New York: Metropolitan Applied Research Center, 1972.

A Possible Reality: A Design for the Attainment of High Academic Achievement for Inner-City Students. New York: Emerson Hall, 1972.

Pathos of Power. New York: Harper & Row, 1974a.

Response to Chancellor's Report on Programs and Problems Affecting Integration of the New York City Public Schools, February 1974: Report. New York: Metropolitan Applied Research Center, 1974b.

With John Hope Franklin. *The Nineteen-Eighties—Prologue and Prospect.* Washington, DC: Joint Center for Political Studies, 1981.

Toward Humanity and Justice: The Writings of Kenneth B. Clark, Scholar of the 1954 Brown v. Board of Education *Decision.* Edited by Woody Klein. Westport, CT: Praeger, 2004.

OTHER SOURCES

Benjamin, Ludy T., Jr. *A History of Psychology in Letters.* 2nd ed. Malden, MA: Blackwell, 2006.

Benjamin, Ludy T., and Ellen M. Crouse. "The American Psychological Association's Response to *Brown v. Board of Education:* The Case of Kenneth B. Clark." *American Psychologist* 57, no. 1 (2002): 38–51.

Black, Sheila R., et. al. "Contributions of African Americans to the Field of Psychology." *Journal of Black Studies* 35, no. 1 (2004): 40–64.

Bowser, Benjamin P., and Louis Kushnik. *Against the Odds: Scholars Who Challenged Racism in the Twentieth Century.* Amherst: University of Massachusetts Press, 2002.

Evans, G. "'Incorrigible Integrationist': Kenneth Clark Reflects on a Lifetime of Question-Asking." *Chronicle of Higher Education* 32 (21 May 1986): 3.

Freeman, Damon. "Not So Simple Justice: Kenneth Clark and the *Brown* Decision." Paper presented at the annual meeting of the Association for the Study of African American Life and History. Pittsburgh, PA, 2004.

Jackson, John P., Jr. *Social Scientists for Social Justice: Making the Case against Segregation.* New York: New York University Press, 2001.

Jones, James M., and Thomas F. Pettigrew. "Kenneth Clark (1914–2005)." *American Psychologist* 60, no. 6 (2005): 649–51.

Keppel, Ben. *The Work of Democracy: Ralph Bunche, Kenneth B. Clark, Lorraine Hansberry, and the Cultural Politics of Race.* Cambridge, MA: Harvard University Press, 1995.

———. "Kenneth B. Clark in the Patterns of American Culture." *American Psychologist* 57, no. 1 (2002): 29–37.

Klein, Woody. "Defeat in Harlem." *Nation* 199, no. 2 (1964): 27–29.

Lal, Shafali. "Giving Children Security: Mamie Phipps Clark and the Racialization of Child Psychology." *American Psychologist* 57, no. 1 (2002): 20–28.

O'Connell, Agnes N., and Nancy Felipe Russo, eds. *Models of Achievement: Reflections of Eminent Women in Psychology.* 3 vols. New York: Columbia University Press, 1983–2001.

Phillips, Layli. "Recontextualizing Kenneth B. Clark: An Afrocentric Perspective on the Paradoxical Legacy of a Model Psychologist-Activist." In *Evolving Perspectives on the History of Psychology,* edited by Wade E. Pickren and Donald A. Dewsbury. Washington, DC: American Psychological Association, 2002.

Pickren, Wade E., and Henry Tomes. "The Legacy of Kenneth B. Clark to the APA: The Board of Social and Ethical Responsibility for Psychology." *American Psychologist* 57, no. 1 (2002): 51–59.

Samuels, Gertrude. "Where Troubled Children Are Reborn." *New York Times Magazine,* 13 June 1954.

U.S. Department of Health, Education, and Welfare Administration, Office of Juvenile Delinquency and Youth Development. "Policy Guides to the Presentation of Proposals for Funding under Public Law 87-274" (3 September 1963).

Gerald Markowitz

CLARK, WILFRID EDWARD LE GROS

(*b.* Hemel Hempstead, Hertfordshire, United Kingdom, 5 June 1895; *d.* Barton Bradstock, Dorset, United Kingdom, 28 June 1971), *comparative anatomy, primatology, paleoprimatology, paleoanthropology, neuroanatomy.*

Clark's knowledge of anatomy covered a wide area from fossil skeletal remains of nonhuman and hominid primates to the comparative structural and functional anatomy of organ systems throughout the primate order. A particular interest was the brain: His experimental anatomy that contributed to insights into the connections of the thalamus, the hypothalamus, and the sensory input to the brain was fundamental to the development of neuroanatomy. In fact, Clark had a profound influence on the teaching of anatomy as he moved from a topographical learning by heart to an emphasis on the connection between structure and function. In the field of paleoanthropology, Clark was a key figure in uncovering the Piltdown forgery and in establishing the australopithecines as hominids.

In general, Clark's work is of interest to the historian as it spans one of the major transitions in paleoanthropology, when it was updated with the methodological and conceptual changes that had taken place in biology in the course of the evolutionary synthesis, to form "a new physical anthropology" (after Sherwood L. Washburn). Clark's work is also a pleasure to study due to his clarity and economy of language. This advantage has been attributed to a speech impediment that as a young man threatened his plan of an academic career. His effort in overcoming the handicap was of such a nature that it turned his oratory and writing skills into an example for others. His lucidity in style may be enjoyed in the *History of Primates: An Introduction to the Study of Fossil Man* (1949), which was addressed to a more general public.

Education and Early Anatomical Work. Clark spent his first nine years in Newnham, Gloucestershire, but after the death of his mother, his father accepted the rectory of Washfield, near Triverton, in Devon. He attended a preparatory school at Malvern Wells and entered Blundell's School in Triverton in 1910. He was the youngest of three sons of the Reverend Travers Clark, who intended Wilfrid to follow in the footsteps of his grandfathers, both of whom had been at St. Thomas's Hospital. Indeed, Clark entered St. Thomas's Hospital Medical School (1912) on an entrance scholarship. He enjoyed a close relationship and shared many interests with his brothers. It was after one of their frequent walking and nature observation tours in Dartmoor (his father had retired at Teignmouth) on 4 August 1914 that they heard of the declaration of war. After qualifying at Medical School in 1917, Clark entered the Royal Army Medical Corps. Serving in France until the end of World War I, he returned to St. Thomas's Hospital to study for his surgical qualifications in 1919.

A turning point came in 1920 when he left for northwestern Borneo as principal medical officer to Sarawak for three years, where his elder brother was minister of state. In fact, his services as physician and surgeon were valued so highly that he was tattooed on the shoulders with the insignia of the Sea Dyaks of Borneo. There, Clark also followed the advice of the influential anatomist Grafton Elliot Smith and took the opportunity to study the tree-shrews (*Tupaia*) and tarsiers (*Tarsius*) of the region, on which his early work was centered (e.g., Clark, 1924a, 1924b). He returned to England and, in 1923, accepted the post as reader of anatomy at St. Bartholomew's Hospital, where he was named professor in 1927.

His continued work on the tree-shrew and tarsier led him to accept Elliot Smith's view that the modern tree-shrew resembled most the earliest primates that first differentiated from the mammalian/insectivore stem. They had to be considered primates, not insectivores. This theory, based on dissections, was published in *Early Forerunners of Man: A Morphological Study of the Evolutionary Origin of the Primates* (1934), dedicated to Elliot Smith, who had been a great inspiration to him. The book reviewed the different anatomical body systems for the information they provided on the phylogeny of the primates. After having again moved to St. Thomas's as professor of anatomy in 1930, Clark finally left for Oxford University's chair of anatomy in 1934. The following year, his work on primate evolution secured him the election to a Fellowship of the Royal Society.

Australopithecus. From the mid-1920s onwards, australopithecine remains were discovered in South Africa and subsequently East Africa. Although the australopithecine discoverers came to regard the new creatures as missing links between apes and humans, the anthropological communities in general judged them to be fossil apes with no particular relation to humans. This judgment was motivated mainly by three factors: brain expansion was considered to have been the hominid specialization that led away from the pongid line; Asia, rather than Africa, was favored as the cradle of humankind; and the persistence of non-Darwinian mechanisms of evolution. The small-brained but bipedal australopithecines from Africa thus did not fit the expected pattern, and their morphological similarities to hominids were explained by parallel evolution rather than close kinship.

Prior to the update of paleoanthropology through the evolutionary synthesis, it was commonplace to accept mechanisms other than natural selection and adaptation, such as the inheritance of acquired characters and orthogenesis, for hominid evolution. The typological approach dominant at that time also meant that rather than recognizing intraspecific variation in the often fragmentary fossil record, there was a tendency to describe every new fossil hominid as a separate species, if not genus.

One obstacle to the acceptance of australopithecines as hominids was that, up to that point, the oldest hominid fossils had been discovered in Asia. Another was the so-called Piltdown Man. During the years of 1911 and 1912, several cranial fragments and the right half of a mandible containing molar teeth were reportedly unearthed by Charles Dawson and others in a gravel pit at Piltdown in Sussex, England. While the mandible was ape-like, the braincase was modern looking. In contrast, *Pithecanthropus erectus* (later *Homo erectus*) from Java, consisting of a femur, calvarium, and some teeth, discovered by the Dutch physician Eugène Dubois at Trinil in 1891–1892, though suggesting bipedal locomotion, had a small cranial capacity.

Piltdown was thus welcome support for the widespread assumption that the expansion of the brain had preceded the acquisition of a fully upright posture in the course of human evolution. The fact that already at the Pliocene-Pleistocene boundary there had been a human type of an essentially modern skull size put into question the ancestral status of *Pithecanthropus* and other early hominid remains, which seemed to date from about the same period, but were less modern in brain anatomy. Once the australopithecines came to be viewed as hominids and even as ancestral to modern humans, they catalyzed the turn of focus from Asia to Africa as the cradle of humankind and made the Piltdown assemblage look odder than ever. The eventual unmasking of the Piltdown forgery removed the final conceptual stronghold of the brain-first theory.

Following the general trend, in the *Early Forerunners of Man* Clark discussed the australopithecines as fossil remains of African anthropoid apes. He cautioned that parallel evolution had been a central mechanism in the evolutionary radiation of the primates, thus the separation of the hominid from the anthropoid line might have taken place earlier than an estimate based on comparative anatomy alone would suggest. Here, Clark positioned himself against evolution by selection among random variations and followed the American paleontologist Henry Fairfield Osborn in his assumption of evolutionary trends programmed into the germ plasm that would lead the evolution of related forms into similar directions. Even at the risk of vitalism, Clark thought such orthogenesis preferable over pure contingency as a shaper of primate evolution. Parallel evolution could explain the human-like traits of *Australopithecus* without inferring that australopithecines were hominids.

During World War II, Robert Broom, who with Raymond Dart was the main discoverer of australopithecine remains, started a voluminous correspondence with Clark despite the slow mail service. Clark, whose main research was at that time connected to the war effort notwithstanding his pacifist principles (muscle and nerve regeneration, ergonomics), received information on all the latest discoveries and casts of the man-ape (or ape-man, as Clark would reckon later) material, to the effect that he became Broom's mouthpiece at British scientific meetings. With each new fragment of australopithecines discovered, insights into their morphology grew, so that eventually their affinities to humans in dentition, way of locomotion, and precision in hand movement could no longer be doubted or explained by parallel evolution.

Therefore, at the first Pan-African Congress on Prehistory in Nairobi in 1947, Clark presented the insights gained from his studies of the australopithecine material during a short South Africa visit: "The general conclusion was reached that the *Australopithecinae* must at least be regarded as having a fairly close relationship to the ancestral stock which gave rise to the *Hominidae*" (1947a, p. 101). Even more significantly, Clark carried out a detailed analysis of australopithecine teeth compared with pongid and hominid dentition, which was later drawn on by Donald Johanson and Timothy White in their reorganization of the African fossil record from Ethiopia and Laetoli (Clark, 1950). Australopithecines were to be regarded as hominids, and Clark was aware of the fact that the taxonomist and evolutionary synthesist Ernst Mayr (1950) had even gone as far as including them in the genus *Homo*. As a happy ending to the australopithecine story, Broom's book *Finding the Missing Link* appeared in 1950, and Clark's *The Fossil Evidence for Human Evolution: An Introduction to the Study of Paleoanthropology* in 1955. Both advocated the important role of the australopithecines in hominid evolution.

The New Physical Anthropology. Clark's book represented a review of the current status of fossil evidence, and it was required reading for a generation of students in physical anthropology. *The Fossil Evidence for Human Evolution* is a remarkable work in more than one way. It proves the author's deep and wide knowledge of the fossil record, history of discoveries, related literature, and associated controversies, as well as the various methods applied to their analysis. It may also be valued, as has indeed been expressed by many reviewers, for its dispassionate and cautious stance. Clark provided the different views held by anthropologists with regard to questions of taxonomy and phylogeny, and while he emphasized the reasons for his own judgments, these were always presented as working hypotheses rather than definitive claims.

Clark's book was indicative of changes that had taken place in paleoanthropology with respect to other areas than the australopithecine question. Besides attributing

less importance to evolutionary parallelism, it strongly relied on the paleontologist George Gaylord Simpson, who rewrote human paleontology on the basis of a biological concept of species and the new systematics. Simpson and others interpreted the hominid fossil record within the framework of variation within populations and possible reproductive isolation between groups (polymorphic species as reproductive, ecological, and genetical units). The existence of taxonomic entities established on these criteria could then be explained by the mechanisms of natural selection, adaptation, and genetic drift. Clark stressed the need for an appreciation of modern evolutionary and genetic concepts and the significance of functional anatomical studies. His book clearly represented a much-needed introduction to human evolution that recognized fully the advances made in modern biology. He also followed the trend of reducing the number of taxa and including more variation within each taxon.

The Fossil Evidence for Human Evolution might also be symptomatic of post–World War II paleoanthropology in that Clark took a clear stance against views according to which the modern human "races" had long independent histories and had evolved separately since the beginning of the Pleistocene. Correspondingly, he rejected the attempt to recognize in some fossils of supposedly Pleistocene age the precedents of existing races:

> No fossil skeleton that is indisputably older than the end of the Pleistocene has yet been discovered which can be certainly identified as of Negroid or Mongolian stock, and the skulls of Australoid type found at Wadjak, Talgai, Cohuna, and Aitape have all been assigned a Pleistocene date on evidence which is regarded by some authorities as geologically inadequate. (1964, p. 55)

If paleoanthropology was still a source of moral lessons, these differed markedly from their prewar counterparts, as might be glimpsed from *History of the Primates*, which ends with a warning to the general reader:

> If Man has gained his intellectual dominance over his fellow creatures by concentrating his evolutionary energies on the development of his brain, it remains to be seen whether he can now maintain his position by contriving a method of living in orderly relations with members of his own species. If he fails to do so, he may yet follow the example of many other groups of animals which have achieved a temporary ascendancy by an exaggerated development of some particular structural mechanism. He may become extinct. (1950a, p. 112)

In *The Fossil Evidence for Human Evolution*, Clark devoted a chapter to the dangers and fallacies of the quantitative assessment of taxonomic relationships (such as relying on too few measurements, using characters that are irrelevant for the establishment of taxonomic relationships, treating characters in isolation rather than in combination, or simply wrong statistics). His reliance on overall morphological patterns for the allocation of fossils to taxa brought him into opposition with South-African-born Solly Zuckerman's statistical approach to taxonomy. Unlike Zuckerman, who had spent a decade in Clark's Department of Anatomy at Oxford University (1934–1945), Clark was convinced that the interrelationship of anatomical features and their interpretation in functional terms was the most robust method to arrive at taxonomic relationships.

The work of Zuckerman, who launched one of the last attacks against the australopithecines' hominid status, was nonetheless also illustrative of a new paleoanthropology. After his move from Oxford to Birmingham University, Zuckerman was involved in a research program for the application of biometry to paleoanthropology. With regard to the australopithecines, Zuckerman's analysis of teeth indicated a close relationship to chimpanzees, which turned the australopithecine controversy into a battle between the descriptive and the statistical method. Zuckerman was in favor of biometry, genetics, and natural selection, while Broom had no regard for any of the three. Clark agreed with Broom that the biometry applied to *Australopithecus* teeth was meaningless (see also Clark, 1950). Ironically, the controversy ended when biometricians came to Broom's support by finding fault with Zuckerman's figures; apparently he had forgotten to divide his numbers by the square root of two (Ashton and Zuckerman, 1950, 1951).

Besides his role in establishing the australopithecines as hominids, Clark also worked and published extensively on the fossil primate remains from East Africa that were made famous by Louis S. B. Leakey (e.g., Clark and Leakey, 1950; Clark and Thomas, 1952). Furthermore, he took part in the dismantling of the Piltdown forgery mentioned earlier. Despite their anthropoid morphology, the Piltdown teeth's wear was more characteristic of human beings. However, Clark's analysis brought to light that the molar teeth in the mandible and the canine had undergone postmortem artificial abrasion so as to give the impression of natural attrition during a hominid way of life. Clark concluded that teeth and jaw were in fact those of an orangutan. In combination with Kenneth Page Oakley's evidence through chemical analysis of fluorine and nitrogen content that showed that the jaw and cranium were not of the same age and not as old as claimed, and with the insight that the bones had been artificially colored, the Piltdown chimera was finally removed from the fossil record (Clark, Weiner, and Oakley, 1953; Weiner, Clark, Oakley, et al., 1955).

In 1959, the new anatomy department Clark had begun to create at Oxford was finally opened, and Clark published *The Antecedents of Man: An Introduction to the Evolution of the Primates*. It was based on the Munro lectures he had delivered at the University of Edinburgh in 1953 on the subject of the paleontology of the primates and the problem of human ancestry. It was intended to replace *The Early Forerunners of Man*, which had been out of print for a long time, among other things because stocks had been destroyed in the bombing raids of World War II. The new encompassing work covered primate comparative anatomy, comparative embryology, paleontology, and cranial and dental anatomy in a way that students and nonexperts also may appreciate. Here, Clark argued against a teleology that might arise because the student of human evolution always knows how the story will end. Mechanisms proposed earlier to explain seeming evolutionary trends in the direction of living hominids, such as orthogenesis, were rejected.

However, whereas Clark denied the idea of inherent directional tendencies, which invoked a mysterious agency infused into the germ plasm of the evolving organism, impelling it along a predetermined course of evolution, he did see orthoselection as a possibility. It denoted the adaptation of a population to a narrow and restricted environment to a degree of specialization where further development could only mean a continuation of the trend. However, although the principle of the irreversibility of evolution was held as true for most cases, one had to allow for the possibility of retrogression.

While comparative anatomy and paleontology were presented as the main approaches through which to reconstruct primate phylogeny, blood reactions and protein structure analysis were accepted as important complementary tools (Nuttall, 1904; Goodman, 1963; the latter in later editions of *Antecedents of Man*, e.g., 3rd ed., 1971). In fact, the protein structure analysis functioned as collateral evidence that often confirmed long-standing insights from comparative anatomy. Once again, to determine taxonomic relationships, the comparative anatomist had to consider the organism as an entire functional unit:

> This *principle of taxonomic relevance* is rather liable to be overlooked, particularly in the uncritical attempts which are sometimes made to quantify degrees of relationship by statistical comparisons of isolated measurements. Each natural group of animals is defined by a certain pattern of morphological characters which its members possess in common and which have been found by detailed studies to be sufficiently distinctive and consistent to distinguish its members from those of other related groups. The possession of this common morphological pattern can be taken to indicate a

community of origin (in the evolutionary sense) of all the members of the group. (1971, p. 12)

A word of caution was also spoken with regard to the distinction between adaptive and nonadaptive traits, of which the latter had been considered as taxonomically more relevant, since in Clark's integrative view it was often impossible to tell whether a trait might not be part of an intricate adaptational complex. In general, the book is illustrative of the post-synthesis era, with an emphasis on populations (rather than individual specimens) and the tendency to (again) interpret *Australopithecus, Homo erectus, Homo sapiens* as forming an evolutionary sequence (or at least as closely approaching such a sequence). These ideas can be generalized to primate evolution as a whole, where Clark recognized an overall evolutionary trend made up of tree-shrew, lemur, tarsier, monkey, ape, human, without suggesting that evolution had proceeded through these exact stages.

Obviously, the more linear interpretation of the hominid fossil record went along with taxonomic lumping. In fact, with regard to australopithecine taxonomy, Clark took the conservative view, rejecting subfamily status (*Australopithecinae*) and the subdivision into several genera (*Australopithecus, Plesianthropus, Paranthropus*). Rather, he adhered to the opinion that the australopithecine fossil remains represented species and varieties of one genus.

Final Years and Honors. Clark retired in 1962 but remained associated until his death in an honorary capacity with the Department of Anatomy at Oxford University, which he had transformed during the nearly thirty years as its head into one of the best schools in the country. Sadly, the year after his retirement his wife died, the former Freda Constance Giddey, with whom he had two daughters. Clark was remarried the following year, to Violet Browne. Once retired from the position of Dr. Lee's professor of anatomy, he continued to make good use of his writing skills when telling the story of the australopithecine discoveries and controversies in chapters two through four of *Man-Apes or Ape-Men? The Story of Discoveries in Africa* (1967), in which he had played an important role. The remainder of the book summarized the interpretations of the teeth, skull, pelvis, and limb bones and provided an attempt at reconstructing the australopithecine ecology and evolutionary origins.

This was the time of the man-the-hunter paradigm. This hunting hypothesis shared wide popularity among anthropologists as an explanation for the evolution of adaptive behaviors. The human hallmarks of bipedalism, tool use, social cooperation and coordination, strategic reasoning (increased intelligence), and the differentiation of sex roles came to be explained on the basis of the male hunting way of life. The logic was that when human

infants grew ever more dependent on their mothers due to postnatal neurological development, the male hunters had to become more efficient to care for the offspring as well as the encumbered females. Clark drew a picture of the australopithecines as tool-making hunters who must have had some form of social organization and communication system to be successful on the hunt in the open country. Life in the savannah was hostile and proto-"men" who were able to kill dangerous and sizable beasts might have turned against each other from time to time. However, Clark did not go as far as the American playwright, screenwriter, novelist, and popular writer of anthropology, Robert Ardrey, who claimed that men were inherently killer-apes, having inherited an instinct for murderous aggression that had been the driving force of all evolutionary progress (Ardrey, 1961, 1966).

Having tasted the sweetness of historical writing, Clark added to the account of the scientific career of the australopithecines that of his own. He wrote the story of his successes and contributions to science as "the doyen of British anatomy," interspersed by fragmentary autobiographic memories, under the Whitmanian motto of a *Chant of Pleasant Exploration* (1968). Despite two world wars, it is a chant and not a hymn, and it is pleasant rather than sad: "One is left with the impression of a contemplative man who has explored the world both physically and intellectually, and who is not dissatisfied with what he found" (Day, 1969, p. 168). Clark died suddenly in Burton Bradstock, Dorset, on 28 June 1971, while visiting a friend from his student days.

Clark was a great authority in the world of anatomy and held honorary degrees from the universities of Durham, Edinburgh, Malaya, Manchester, Melbourne, Oslo, and Witwatersrand. He became a Fellow of the Royal College of Surgeons in 1919, was Arris and Gale Lecturer in 1932, and Hunterian Professor in 1934 and 1945. He was also editor of the *Journal of Anatomy*. He was president of the International Anatomical Congress in 1950, of the Anatomical Society of Great Britain in 1952, and the Anthropological Section of the British Association for the Advancement of Science in 1939 and 1961. He held honorary memberships in foreign academies and societies, among them the American Philosophical Society and the National Academy of Science in Washington. He was knighted in 1955, and the recipient of the Viking Fund Medal in 1956 and of the Royal Medal of the Royal Society in 1961.

BIBLIOGRAPHY

WORKS BY CLARK

"Notes on the Living Tarsier (*Tarsius spectrum*)." In *Proceedings of the General Meetings for Scientific Business of the Zoological Society of London,* vol.1. London : Longmans, Green, 1924a.

"On the Brain of the Tree-Shrew (*Tupaia minor*)." In *Proceedings of the General Meetings for Scientific Business of the Zoological Society of London,* vol. 2. London : Longmans, Green, 1924b.

"Studies on the Optic Thalamus of the Insectivora: The Anterior Nuclei." *Brain* 52 (1929): 334–358.

"The Thalamus of *Tarsius*." *Journal of Anatomy* 64 (1930): 371–414.

"The Brain of Insectivora." In *Proceedings of the General Meetings for Scientific Business of the Zoological Society of London,* vol.2. London : Longmans, Green, 1932.

"An Experimental Study of Thalamic Connections in the Rat." *Philosophical Transactions of the Royal Society,* series B Biological Sciences, 222 (1933): 1–28.

Early Forerunners of Man: A Morphological Study of the Evolutionary Origin of the Primates. London: Ballière, Tindall, 1934.

"Evolutionary Parallelism and Human Phylogeny." *Man* 36 (1936): 4–8.

With John Beattie, George Riddoch, and Norman M. Dott. *The Hypothalamus: Morphological, Functional, Clinical, and Surgical Aspects.* Edinburgh: Oliver and Boyd, 1938.

The Tissues of the Body: An Introduction to the Study of Anatomy. Oxford: Clarendon Press, 1939.

"Pan-African Congress on Prehistory: Human Palaeontological Section." *Man* 47 (1947a): 101.

"The Importance of the Fossil Australopithecinae in the Study of Human Evolution." *Science Progress* 35 (1947b): 377–395.

"Observations on the Anatomy of the Fossil Australopithecinae." *Journal of Anatomy* 81 (1947c): 300–333.

History of the Primates: An Introduction to the Study of Fossil Man. London: Printed by order of the Trustees of the British Museum, 1949. (2nd ed., London: Trustees of the British Museum, 1950a; 10th ed., London: British Museum, 1970).

"Hominid Characters of the Australopithecine Dentition." *Journal of the Royal Anthropological Institute of Great Britain and Ireland* 80 (1950): 37–54.

With Louis S. B. Leakey. "Diagnoses of East African Miocene Hominoidea." *Quarterly Journal of the Geological Society of London* 105 (1950): 260–262.

With D. P. Thomas. *The Miocene Lemuroids of East Africa.* Fossil Mammals of Africa no. 5. London: British Museum (Natural History),1952.

Clark, Wilfrid Edward Le Gros, Joseph S. Weiner, and Kenneth Page Oakley. "The Solution of the Piltdown Problem." *Bulletin of the British Museum (Natural History), Geology Series* 2 (1953): 141–146.

With Weiner, Joseph S.; Kenneth Page Oakley, et al. "Further Contributions to the Solution of the Piltdown Problem." *Bulletin of the British Museum (Natural History), Geology Series* 2 (1955): 225–287.

The Fossil Evidence for Human Evolution: An Introduction to the Study of Paleoanthropology. Chicago: University of Chicago Press, 1955. (2nd ed., University of Chicago Press, 1964).

The Antecedents of Man: An Introduction to the Evolution of the Primates. Edinburgh: Edinburgh University Press, 1959 (3rd ed., Edinburgh: University Press, 1971).

Man-Apes or Ape-Men? The Story of Discoveries in Africa. London: Holt, Rinehart & Winston, 1967.

Chant of Pleasant Exploration. Edinburgh: E. & S. Livingstone, 1968.

OTHER SOURCES

Ardrey, Robert. *African Genesis: A Personal Investigation into the Animal Origins and Nature of Man.* New York: Atheneum, 1961.

———. *The Territorial Imperative: A Personal Inquiry into the Animal Origins of Property and Nations.* New York: Atheneum, 1966.

Ashton, E. H., and Solly Zuckerman. "Some Quantitative Dental Characteristics of Fossil Anthropoids." *Philosophical Transactions of the Royal Society,* series B Biological Sciences, 234 (1950): 485–520.

———. "Statistical Methods in Anthropology." *Nature* 168 (1951): 1117–1118.

Broom, Robert. *Finding the Missing Link: An Account of Recent Discoveries Throwing New Light on the Origin of Man.* London: Watts, 1950.

Day, M. H. Review of *Chant of Pleasant Exploration. Man,* n.s., 4, no. 1 (1969): 168.

Goodman, Morris. "Man's Place in the Phylogeny of the Primates as Reflected in Serum Proteins." In *Classification and Human Evolution,* edited by Sherwood Larned Washburn. London: Methuen, 1963.

Mayr, Ernst. "Taxonomic Categories in Fossil Hominids." In *Origin and Evolution of Man.* Cold Spring Harbor Symposia on Quantitative Biology 15. Cold Spring Harbor, NY: The Biological Laboratory, 1950.

Nuttall, George H. F. *Blood Immunity and Blood Relationship: A Demonstration of Certain Blood-Relationships amongst Animals by Means of the Precipitin Test for Blood.* Cambridge, U.K.: Cambridge University Press, 1904.

Washburn, Sherwood Larned. "The New Physical Anthropology." *Transactions of the New York Academy of Sciences,* series 2, 13 (1951): 298–304.

Weddell, G. "In Memoriam: Wilfrid Edward Le Gros Clark." *Journal of Anatomy* 111 (1972): 181–184.

Zuckerman, Solly. "Wilfrid Edward Le Gros Clark, 1895–1971." *Biographical Memoirs of Fellows of the Royal Society* 19 (1973): 217–233. See this memoir for a more comprehensive bibliography.

Marianne Sommer

CLAUDE, ALBERT (*b.* Longlier, Luxembourg, Belgium, 23 August 1899, *d.* Brussels, Belgium, 22 May 1983), *cytology, cancer research.*

Claude had a lifelong interest in cancer research. Starting with investigations into the causes of cancer, he revolutionized the cytology of his time. By adapting and developing the most advanced biophysical and biochemical methods, such as differential high speed centrifugation, electron microscopy, and enzyme mapping, Claude characterized a class of small cytoplasmic particles, the microsomes, demonstrating that cells are endowed with a pervasive network of membranes, the endoplasmic reticulum. Eventually, microsomes were found to consist of chunks of this reticulum with even smaller particles attached to them, which came to be called ribosomes. Claude was the first to visualize the Rous sarcoma virus by means of electron microscopy. Later in his life, he turned his interest to the characterization of the cellular Golgi apparatus. In 1974, together with Christian de Duve and George E. Palade, he was awarded the Nobel Prize in Physiology or Medicine for his achievements in exploring the ultrastructure of the cell.

Origin and Early Years. Albert Claude was born in 1899 (according to his autobiography, but 1898 according to the civil register) in Longlier, a little village of the Belgian Ardennes, in the province of Luxembourg. He was the youngest of four children; he had two brothers and one sister. His father, Valentin Claude, was a baker by training. His mother, Glaudicine Watriquant, developed breast cancer when Albert was three years old. He closely experienced the inexorable progress of her illness; she died when he was seven. Other than this tragic event, his childhood was marked by the peaceful surroundings of the woods and pastures of the Ardennes. He spent his first school years at the primary school in Longlier. The school accommodated some forty children of mixed age in one room under a single teacher. In his autobiography—quipping at his own achievements—Claude praised this "pluralistic system" as "excellent." A few years after his mother's death, Claude and his family moved to Athus, a steel-mill region in a corner of Belgium between France and the Grand Duchy of Luxembourg. There, Albert went to a German-language school for a couple of years before being called back to Longlier to help with the care of an uncle paralyzed by a cerebral hemorrhage. With that, his formal education came to an end. He never attended a secondary school. When World War I broke out, he became an apprentice and subsequently earned his living as an industrial designer. As a patriotically minded young Belgian, Claude worked in the *résistance* and also for the British Intelligence Service. When the war was over, he was decorated for his courage.

Claude's dream had always been to study medicine. However, he lacked the high school diploma that would have documented the required skills, particularly in Greek and Latin. So he decided to prepare to enter the School of Mining in Liège. But when the noted biochemist Marcel Florkin became head of the Direction of Higher Education in Belgium's Ministry of Public Instruction for a short period, a law was passed that allowed veterans to

Albert Claude. *Albert Claude speaking at a press conference.* AP IMAGES.

enter the university without the high school diploma and further examinations. Claude immediately seized the opportunity and registered, in 1922, with the Faculty of Medicine at the University of Liège. In his spare time, he frequented the laboratory of his zoology professor Désiré Damas, and later, in the course of his clinical studies, the physiological laboratory of Henri Fredericq. It was there also that he came in contact with Florkin. In the course of these formative years, he occupied himself intensely with observing cells through the microscope, gazing at "the mysterious ground substance where the secret mechanisms of cell life might be found," as he expressed it in his Nobel Lecture, "The Coming Age of the Cell." He also tried to isolate the eosinophilic granules of leukocytes, but failed. In 1928 Claude received his doctoral degree.

For his doctorate, he had worked on the transplantation of mouse cancers into rats. This work on heterologous transplants earned him a travel fellowship from the Belgian government. Claude decided to spend a postdoctoral year in Berlin. In Ferdinand Blumenthal's Institute for Cancer Research at the University of Berlin, he took up the issue of a possible transfer of mouse mammary cancer by bacteria. After having shown that the effect must be due to a contamination of the bacterial culture by cancer

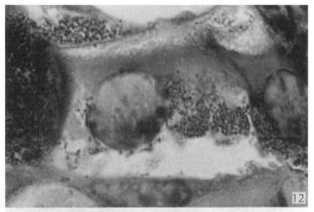

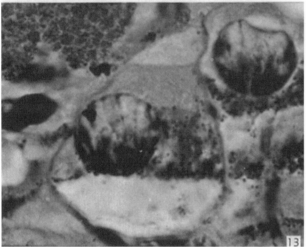

Figure 1. Amphiuma liver. Intracellular segregation of the morphological constituents of hepatic cells after 60 minutes of centrifugation at 18,000 g. STUDIES ON CELLS: MORPHOLOGY, CHEMICAL CONSTITUTION, AND DISTRIBUTION OF BIOCHEMICAL FUNCTIONS. HARVEY LECTURES 1947-1948 (EDITED 1949).

cells, Claude left the institute and went on to study the technique of tissue culture with Albert Fischer, a Danish guest scientist at the Kaiser Wilhelm Institute for Biology in Berlin-Dahlem.

At the Rockefeller Institute in New York. Back in Belgium in 1929, Claude received a fellowship from the Belgian American Educational Foundation (Commission for Relief in Belgium, CRB) for a research stay in the United States. He applied to the Rockefeller Institute, and Simon Flexner accepted his proposal to work on the isolation and identification of the Rous sarcoma virus. In September 1929 he sailed from Antwerp to New York. He came to work with James Murphy, a former coworker of Peyton Rous and, at the time of Claude's arrival in New York, head of the Pathology Laboratory at Rockefeller. Rous had speculated that his filterable agent transmitting chicken

tumors might be some sort of ultrabacterium or virus. But around 1915 he left the field after fruitless efforts to find similar agents affecting mammals. Murphy and Claude now proceeded from the assumption that the tumor-causing agent might be an endogenous cellular component, perhaps an enzyme of sorts, which had "gone wild" for some unknown reason. For several years, Claude attempted to isolate, enrich, and characterize Rous's chicken tumor I agent by traditional biochemical means of aluminum hydroxide adsorption and gelatin precipitation, to no great avail. Around 1935 it came to his attention that two British groups had sedimented the filterable agent causing avian sarcomas by means of high-speed centrifugation. Encouraged by Murphy, he switched to the new technology of differential sedimentation and, within a comparably short time, managed to enrich the tumor agent by a factor of almost 3,000. The substance he had sedimented contained, in addition to phospholipids and proteins, a nucleic acid of the ribose type.

Differential Centrifugation. At the same time, however, a new research horizon was opened by a control experiment. Claude realized that, from samples of healthy chicken embryo tissue, a sediment could be obtained that was indistinguishable in its chemical composition from the infectious sample. In his Nobel Prize report of 1974, Claude's former coworker Keith Porter referred to this event as a classic situation characteristic of the process of research: The control becomes the real experiment. Two interpretations were possible at this point. The infectious fraction might consist predominantly of an inert material that was also present in normal cells. Despite enrichment, further chemical analysis appeared hopeless in this case. Alternatively, normal cells might contain noninfectious cellular precursors of the chicken tumor agent, and in this case, the analysis of these precursors was of paramount importance. Considering these options, Claude decided to abandon the Rous sarcoma agent and to turn his attention to the differential fractionation of healthy tissue by high-speed centrifugation.

For a long time, cytomorphology had been the domain of increasingly sophisticated microscopic observation. As cellular components, nuclei and mitochondria had been visualized *in situ*. Subsequently, the latter had been isolated from cells by Robert Bensley and Normand Hoerr in Chicago. The tissue of choice of a nascent *in vitro* cytology—with early attempts going back to Otto Warburg—became the liver. In a first analysis, Claude identified his particulate cytoplasmic fraction as precursors or fragments of mitochondria. Soon, however, he had to give up this assumption. Under appropriate buffer and centrifugation conditions, a fraction of large granules could be separated from a fraction of small granules. Claude renamed his small cytoplasmic particles *microsomes*. The problem was

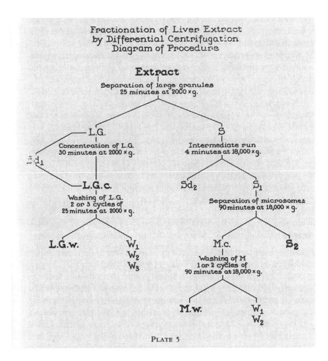

Fractionation of Liver Extract
by Differential Centrifugation
Diagram of Procedure

PLATE 5

Figure 2. Diagram od fractionation of mammalian liver cells by means of differential centrifugation at various speeds.
STUDIES ON CELLS: MORPHOLOGY, CHEMICAL CONSTITUTION, AND DISTRIBUTION OF BIOCHEMICAL FUNCTIONS. HARVEY LECTURES 1947-1948 (EDITED 1949).

this: They could be sedimented at high speed from a tissue homogenate, but after resuspension, they could no longer be visualized by the light microscope. Faced with this situation, Claude resorted to a remarkable and convincing trick. He subjected intact cells—liver cells of *Amphiuma*—to high-speed sedimentation and subsequently fixed and stained them differentially. When cut parallel to the sedimentation direction, the content of such cells appeared in layers: at the bottom, glycogen; in the middle, the nucleus and mitochondria as well as secretory granules; above them, the microsomes; and finally, the cell sap (Figure 1). The microsomal layer appeared in the color of the cytoplasmic ground substance.

When introducing differential centrifugation as a means of separating the cell into its different components (Figure 2), Claude followed what he termed a "balance sheet–quantitative analysis method." It consisted of meticulous measurements of activity and composition of the original homogenate and of all the different fractions obtained. Tumor activity could of course no longer be used as a measure after Claude switched to the analysis of healthy tissue toward the end of the 1930s. Throughout the 1940s, Claude, together with his Rockefeller colleagues Rollin Hotchkiss, George Hogeboom, Walter Schneider and George Palade, worked hard to establish what they

called "biochemical mapping." It consisted of adapting particular quantifiable enzyme tests to measure the activities of the different fractions. Soon it turned out that major enzymes of the respiratory chain segregated with Claude's large granule fraction that consisted of mitochondria and a class of less-well-defined secretory granules. One of the big problems of differential fractionation at the time was that these two cellular components—mitochondria and secretory granules—were barely distinguishable from each other in solution. Help came, toward the end of the 1940s, from the use of a centrifugation solution of a different composition. Instead of the usual electrolyte buffers containing various amounts of salts, Hogeboom, Schneider, and Palade found sugar solutions to be a medium in which, first, sedimented mitochondria retained the filamentous structure known from *in situ* staining of cells, and, second, appeared to be poor in secretory vesicles. Now, the respiratory enzymes could be mapped onto these purified mitochondria with more confidence.

Consequently, in terms of their function, the mitochondria came to be addressed by Claude as the "real power plants of the cell." The problem, however, was that enzyme mapping did not provide any clear-cut hints as to the function of the other class of isolated cytoplasmic particles, the microsomes. They steadfastly resisted this type of biochemical characterization. Claude was well aware of the work on microsomes of his Belgian colleague Jean Brachet and his coworkers Hubert Chantrenne and Raymond Jeener, who suspected the ribonucleic acid-rich particles to be involved in protein synthesis. But Claude could not convince himself of this option and stuck to the idea that microsomes might be involved in some phase of the anaerobic pathway in cellular energy generation. Consequently, he did not engage in the *in vitro* analysis of protein biosynthesis that was initiated by other groups with the advent of radioactive labels such as carbon (^{14}C) and hydrogen (^{3}H) after the end of World War II.

Electron Microscopy. In 1942 Claude started to add another advanced instrument to the arsenal of his analytical procedures: He secured access to the electron microscope of the Interchemical Corporation in New York, the only instrument of that type (a Model B, from the Radio Corporation of America [RCA]) then in the city. Together with Interchemical's electron microscopist, Ernest Fullam, Claude tried to adapt the technique for the observation of biological specimens. After three years of meticulously tuning their preparation procedures—staining, fixation, dehydration, proper support—Claude and Fullam were able to present the first pictures of isolated mitochondria. In parallel and in cooperation with Rockefeller scientist Keith Porter, Claude brought whole cells under the electron microscope. For future research on cellular ultrastructure, the correlation of *in vitro* and *in situ*

Figure 3. *Electron micrograph of a chick embryo fibroblast-like cell, grown in tissue culture.* STUDIES ON CELLS: MORPHOLOGY, CHEMICAL CONSTITUTION, AND DISTRIBUTION OF BIOCHEMICAL FUNCTIONS. HARVEY LECTURES 1947-1948 (EDITED 1949).

representations turned out to be essential. Tissue culture specialist Porter succeeded in growing fibroblast-like embryonic chicken cells on a glass coated with a thin plastic film. The film, together with the cells, could then be transferred to an electron microscope grid, and after staining and fixation, inserted in the instrument. At their periphery, the cells were flattened enough to be penetrated by the electron beam. Besides filamentous mitochondria, a fine-spun, lace-like network of cytoplasmic threads became visible in the body of these cells. It came to be known as *endoplasmic reticulum* (Figure 3).

At this point, the Rous sarcoma agent reemerged as a subject of Claude's research. The possibility of making visible the contents of cells at a resolution of about 200 Å led Claude to pick up the thread where he had left it late in the 1930s. In 1946–1947, together with Porter and Edward Pickels, he succeeded in preparing sarcoma cells

for electron microscopy. It turned out that they were crammed with small, electron-dense particles (Figure 4). Nothing of that sort could be seen in healthy control cells. Thus, for the first time, the chicken tumor agent had been rendered visible and its viral nature strongly corroborated.

During the academic year 1947–1948, Claude was invited to deliver one of the prestigious Harvey Lectures under the auspices of the Harvey Society in New York. He opened the lecture with a homage to the nineteenth-century Italian astronomer and lens-maker Giovanni Battista Amici. "In the history of cytology," he concluded, "it is repeatedly found that further advance had to await, as in the case just mentioned, the accident of technical progress" (Claude, 1950, p. 121). With this reference to Amici, Claude articulated his own research philosophy. For him, methods and results had to be equally emphasized. And indeed, he was a master in taking advantage of the "accident of technical progress" and using it to shape a new experimental cytology. To begin with, the *in vitro* fractionation approach to the cell met with fierce objection from many a traditional cytologist and morphologist who did not believe that valuable knowledge would be likely to result from the creation of what they called, as Brachet remembers, a "cellular mayonnaise." But Claude was convinced of the analytical power of penetrating the ultrastructure of the cell and assigning particular functions to particular cellular compartments.

Back in Belgium: The Institut Jules Bordet. In 1946, while spending a research year in the United States, Brachet visited Claude in New York and asked him, in the name of the rector of the Free University of Brussels, whether he would be willing to come back to Belgium and join the Faculty of Medicine at the University of Brussels. Claude hesitated. It was four years before he finally agreed to leave the Rockefeller Institute, where he had spent the two most important decades of his research career. In 1950 he was entrusted with the scientific direction of the Institut Jules Bordet, the cancer research center in Brussels. He soon regretted having left New York, where he had assumed U.S. citizenship in 1941, and where he had been living with his only daughter Philippa after his divorce from his wife Julia Gilder whom he had married in 1935. To Brachet, he once confessed briefly, but clearly: "It was a mistake." Despite the frictions in his new academic environment, Claude worked hard to modernize and develop cancer research at the University of Brussels between 1950 and 1970. For himself, he created a modern laboratory for experimental cytology and oncology in order to pursue the analysis of cellular ultrastructure. There, he engaged in research on the Golgi apparatus, whose existence had been corroborated by the electron microscope, but whose function remained enigmatic. He was able to show that the Golgi membranes are

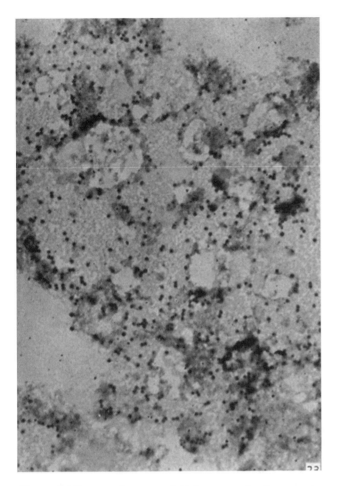

Figure 4. *Electron microscopy of chicken tumor I cells, grown in tissue culture* STUDIES ON CELLS: MORPHOLOGY, CHEMICAL CONSTITUTION, AND DISTRIBUTION OF BIOCHEMICAL FUNCTIONS. HARVEY LECTURES 1947-1948 (EDITED 1949).

continuous with the endoplasmic reticulum, that they are perpetually turned over and regenerated, and that in the liver cell, they are essentially involved in lipoprotein packaging and transport. Besides working on the Golgi, he continued to refine the techniques of electron microscopic specimen preparation, together with his collaborator and eventual successor at the Institut Jules Bordet, Jànos Frühling.

Louvain-la-Neuve and the Nobel Prize. After retiring in 1971, at the age of seventy-two, from the University of Brussels and from the directorship of the Institut Jules Bordet, Claude continued his laboratory work at the Catholic University of Louvain-la-Neuve, where he was invited to become professor and was given a laboratory for cell biology and oncology in 1972. There, he continued to work quietly on the ultrastructure of the Golgi complex. In 1974, together with Christian de Duve from the University of Louvain and the Rockefeller University and

George Palade, from Rockefeller as well, Claude received the Nobel Prize in Physiology or Medicine for his discoveries concerning "the structural and functional organization of the cell." Before that, he had received the Baron Holvoet Prize of the Fonds National de la Recherche Scientifique of Belgium (1965), the Louisa Gross Horwitz Prize of Columbia University in New York (1970), and the Paul Ehrlich and Ludwig Darmstaedter Prize (1971), as well as honorary doctorates from the Universities of Modena, Brno, Liège, Louvain, Gent, and the Rockefeller University. All these honors did not distract him from continuing the experimental work that he steadfastly pursued until he died, at his home in Brussels, in 1983.

Those who knew Albert Claude personally report that he was an individualist with slightly eccentric manners. Among his friends were painters, including Diego Rivera and Paul Delvaux, and musicians such as Edgard Varèse. He was, according to his colleague Brachet, a man full of contrasts. He could ask questions that scared his interlocutors. Despite his eccentricity, however, he engaged in fruitful scientific collaborations. Claude therefore can rightfully be called the pioneer of modern, interdisciplinary experimental cytology.

BIBLIOGRAPHY

A complete bibliography is included in the article by Jean Brachet, cited below.

WORKS BY CLAUDE

"Greffes cancéreuses hétérologues." *Comptes Rendus de la Société de Biologie* 99 (1928): 650–654, 1061–1063.

"Properties of the Causative Agent of a Chicken Tumor." *Journal of Experimental Medicine* 61 (1935): 41–57.

"Concentration and Purification of Chicken Tumor I Agent." *Science* 87 (1938): 467–468.

"A Fraction from Normal Chick Embryo Similar to the Tumor Producing Fraction of Chicken Tumor I." *Proceedings of the Society for Experimental Biology and Medicine* 39 (1938): 398–403.

"Particulate Components of Normal and Tumor Cells." *Science* 91 (1940): 77–78.

"Particulate Components of Cytoplasm." *Cold Spring Harbor Symposia on Quantitative Biology* 9 (1941): 263–271.

"The Constitution of Protoplasm." *Science* 97 (1943): 451–456.

With Ernest F. Fullam. "An Electron Microscope Study of Isolated Mitochondria." *Journal of Experimental Medicine* 81 (1945): 51–61.

With Keith R. Porter and Ernest F. Fullam. "A Study of Tissue Culture Cells by Electron Microscopy." *Journal of Experimental Medicine* 81 (1945): 233–246.

"Fractionation of Mammalian Liver Cells by Differential Centrifugation." *Journal of Experimental Medicine* 84 (1946): 51–89.

With Keith R. Porter and Edward G. Pickels. "Electron Microscope Study of Chicken Tumor Cells." *Cancer Research* 7 (1947): 421–430.

"Studies on Cells: Morphology, Chemical Constitution, and Distribution of Biochemical Function." *The Harvey Lectures* 43 (1950): 121–164.

"Interrelation of Cytoplasmic Membranes in Mammalian Liver Cells: Endoplasmic Reticulum and Golgi Complex." *Journal of Cell Biology* 39 (1968): 24a.

"Growth and Differentiation of Cytoplasmic Membranes in the Course of Lipoprotein Granule Synthesis in the Hepatic Cell: 1. Elaboration of Elements of the Golgi Complex." *Journal of Cell Biology* 47 (1970): 745–766.

"Autobiography." In *Les Prix Nobel en 1974*, edited by Wilhelm Odelberg. Stockholm: Nobel Foundation, 1975.

"The Coming Age of the Cell." *Science* 189 (1975): 433–435.

OTHER SOURCES

Brachet, Jean. "Notice sur Albert Claude." *Académie Royale de Belgique, Annuaire 1988*: 93–135.

de Duve, Christian. "Tissue Fractionation: Past and Present." *Journal of Cell Biology* 50 (1971): 20D–55D.

———, and George E. Palade. "Albert Claude, 1899–1983." *Nature* 304 (1983): 588.

Florkin, Marcel. "Pour saluer Albert Claude." *Archives Internationales de Physiologie et de Biochimie* 80 (1972): 633–647.

Lejeune, Louis, Yves Mathieu, Henri Weyrich, et al. *Le Professeur Albert Claude: Longlier, son village.* Neufchateau: Weyrich Edition and Communication, 1999.

Löwy, Ilana. "Variances in Meaning in Discovery Accounts." *Historical Studies in the Physical and Biological Sciences* 21 (1990): 87–121.

Moberg, Carol L. "James B. Murphy, the Rous Sarcoma Agent, and Origins of Modern Cell Biology." In *Creating a Tradition of Biomedical Research*, edited by Darwin H. Stapleton. New York: Rockefeller University Press, 2004.

Palade, George E. "Albert Claude and the Beginnings of Biological Electron Microscopy." *Journal of Cell Biology* 50 (1971): 5D–19D.

Porter, Keith R. "The 1974 Nobel Prize for Physiology or Medicine." *Science* 186 (1974): 516–518.

Rheinberger, Hans-Jörg. "From Microsomes to Ribosomes: 'Strategies' of 'Representation.'" *Journal of the History of Biology* 28 (1995): 49–89.

———. "Cytoplasmic Particles in Brussels (Jean Brachet, Hubert Chantrenne, Raymond Jeener) and at Rockefeller (Albert Claude), 1935–1955." *History and Philosophy of the Life Sciences* 19 (1997): 47–67.

Hans-Jörg Rheinberger

CLAVIO, CRISTOFORO

SEE **Clavius, Christopher**.

CLAVIUS, CHRISTOPH (*b*. Bamberg, Germany, 25 March 1538; *d*. Rome, Italy, 6 February 1612), *astronomy, cosmology, mathematics, education*. For the original article on Clavius see *DSB*, vol. 3.

Clavius offered the last serious defense of the ancient Ptolemaic cosmology and published one of the earliest critiques of Copernican theory. Along with his students, he authenticated Galileo's early telescopic discoveries and prominently recognized their epochal significance in his widely used textbook of elementary astronomy. Clavius attained international esteem for his exposition of Euclid's *Elements* and spent much of his career establishing an important place for mathematical studies in Jesuit schools. He was also a member of the papal commission that planned and executed the Gregorian calendar reform of 1582 and through subsequent publications became the principal expositor and defender of the Gregorian calendar.

Biographical Background. Other than his birth date in Bamberg, Clavius's origins are unknown, including his original family name, which might have been Clau, Schlüssel, or some variant. Any details of his early life in Bamberg are also absent, and he never returned there, although he took an interest for the rest of his life in the city and its fortunes amidst the Counter-Reformation. Horst Enzensberger's "Società, cultura e religione a Bamberga" (1995) provides a sketch of the intellectual and political context that must have shaped Clavius's early life. He entered the Society of Jesus on 12 April 1555 and was then sent to study at the University of Coimbra, which he entered in 1556. His first recorded astronomical observation took place at Coimbra: the total solar eclipse of 21 August 1560. By May 1561 he had returned to Rome to begin advanced studies in theology and other subjects at the Jesuit Collegio Romano and was ordained in 1564. Clavius began teaching mathematics at the Collegio Romano, as he would for nearly all his career, as early as 1563. With rare good fortune for a person in that era, he witnessed on 9 April 1567 a second total solar eclipse in Rome. His account of the eclipse, published in his *Sphere* commentary, attracted attention in its day because of his controversial conclusion that it was an annular eclipse. At the turn of the twenty-first century, F. Richard Stephenson, J. Eric Jones, and Leslie Morrison used his report to investigate long-term variations in the rotation rate of the Earth (1997). During a brief stint in Messina working with Francesco Maurolico, in 1574, he acquired many unpublished mathematical treatises, including Maurolico's treatise on the nova of 1572 and a manuscript on light, which Clavius would eventually publish. Aside from another sojourn at the Jesuit College in Naples in 1596, Clavius spent the rest of his long career in Rome, where he died on 6 February 1612. A more complete biography can be found in James Lattis's *Between Copernicus and Galileo* (1994).

Mathematics. Clavius published his edition of Euclid's *Elements* in 1574. More a commentary enhancing access to the work than a philological edition of the Greek text, it achieved great popularity and influence. Revising and republishing it at least five times, Clavius went beyond the strict bounds of Euclid's material to introduce new materials, including his own proof of Euclid's fifth postulate and his solution to the problem of squaring the circle. Vincent Jullien (1997) and Sabine Rommevaux (2005) show the broad significance of Clavius's *Euclid* for many seventeenth-century mathematicians, not only Jesuits, and Paolo Palmieri (2001) finds connections between Clavius's theory of proportions and Galileo's own struggles with the concept.

Clavius's other original mathematical contributions include a digression on combinatorics in his *Sphere* commentary in 1581, which Eberhard Knobloch (1979) judges a seminal text, and his publication of the *Spherics* of Theodosius (in 1586). He also published a variety of practical textbooks on arithmetic, geometry, gnomonics, and the construction of instruments. Music, one of the four mathematical sciences of the traditional Quadrivium (along with arithmetic, geometry, and astronomy), was another area of interest for Clavius. His surviving works include eleven motets and two songs, none of which have yet received significant study.

Astronomy. Clavius authored one of the most influential astronomy textbooks in history, his *Commentary on the Sphere of Sacrobosco,* which remained a standard for astronomy instruction for three-quarters of a century. It was published at least sixteen times between 1570 and 1618 by printers spread across Europe. He revised the text seven times, often expanding it greatly in scope and detail and taking note of new discoveries and controversies.

In lengthy digressions in his *Sphere*, Clavius defended the Ptolemaic cosmology (a blending of Aristotelian physics and mathematical models of Ptolemy's *Almagest* into a physical cosmos) against a variety of critics. The critics included both skeptics who doubted that knowledge about celestial causes is even possible, as well as those who advocated alternatives to the Ptolemaic cosmos. Clavius's "realist" views, which hold that it is possible to deduce celestial causes from observations of the motions of celestial bodies, resonated strongly (if only at the epistemological level) with those of Johannes Kepler, as Nicolas Jardine discusses in "The Forging of Modern Realism" (1979). Prominent among the alternative cosmologies criticized by Clavius stands Copernicus's heliocentric cosmos. Clavius's criticisms of the Copernican cosmos

Christoph Clavius. *18th Century engraving.*

included its inconsistencies with common sense, Aristotelian physics, and the testimony of Scripture, as well as a flawed methodology that would, he said, prevent it from providing reliable astronomical knowledge.

Despite his antipathy toward the Copernican cosmos, Clavius's *Sphere* expressed admiration for Copernicus's mathematical skill, and he ultimately incorporated several ideas from Copernicus's work into his own version of the Ptolemaic cosmology, most notably Copernicus's model for representing what later would be called the precession of the equinoxes, which motion Copernicus attributed to the Earth, but which Clavius located in the outer spheres of the Ptolemaic cosmos. Clavius also confronts and rejects the cosmological theory of homocentric spheres at considerable length and with even greater vigor than he devotes to Copernican theory, and goes on to reject other cosmic concepts as well. His treatment of these rivals to Ptolemaic cosmology shows that the cosmological debates of the late sixteenth and early seventeenth centuries were far more complex than a simple confrontation between Ptolemy and Copernicus.

Clavius also used his *Sphere* as a vehicle for commentary on the remarkable novas of 1572, 1600, and 1604. In the 1585 (and every subsequent) edition, he published his conclusion that the nova of 1572 must have been located in the firmament of the fixed stars—thus demonstrating, contrary to Aristotle, that celestial matter was capable of qualitative change. He based his conclusion firmly on observations reported by correspondents widely placed across Europe showing that all had observed the nova to be in the same location with respect to nearby stars, putting, in effect, an upper limit on the parallax of the nova. Clavius's measurement of the location of the nova was thus in agreement with but independent of Tycho Brahe's more famous conclusion. Galileo's celebrated discoveries of 1609 and 1610 were also reported in the *Sphere*. In April 1611, Cardinal Bellarmine requested of Clavius an opinion concerning Galileo's sensational telescope discoveries, which the astronomers of the Collegio Romano then confirmed with their own telescopes. In his final version of the *Sphere*, published in 1611, Clavius noted Galileo's findings, including the phases of Venus and moons of Jupiter, and famously recognized their significance by calling upon astronomers to accommodate them in astronomical theory. A fuller account of Clavius's astronomical career and significance is found in Lattis's *Between Copernicus and Galileo*.

Although Clavius's *Sphere* was the book by which his astronomical teaching reached the world at large, it is not, as Ugo Baldini (2000) points out, an adequate measure of the level of his astronomical research. Clavius never finished his more advanced treatise in theoretical astronomy, but the surviving parts (fragments of his solar and lunar theories) are interesting and perhaps unique examples of how advanced astronomical theory was taught in the late sixteenth century. The surviving solar theory has been published by Baldini in *Legem impone subactis* (1992), and further discussed, along with the lunar theory, in his *Saggi sulla Cultura della Compagnia di Gesù* (2000). Baldini, in his *Saggi*, judges it doubtful that, even if it had been finished, his theoretical work would have resulted in anything other than an ad hoc adjustment to the established Ptolemaic theories. Clavius found even the geocentric system of Tycho to be incomprehensible as a representation of reality and remained committed to the Ptolemaic cosmos. Clavius's level of expertise was also very high in the area of instrument design as indicated by his several books on the construction and use of astrolabes, sundials, and meridian instruments. Baldini and Juan Casanovas (1996) identify the sole surviving example of one of Clavius's instruments, namely a celestial globe constructed in 1575, in which he adopted from Copernicus the location of the vernal equinox and updated star positions.

Galileo drew heavily on Jesuit sources during his early academic career, as is documented by William Wallace in *Galileo and His Sources* (1984), and had personally conferred with Clavius. His cordial relationship with Galileo endured through the end of Clavius's life and generally extended to the other Jesuit astronomers of the Collegio Romano who collectively celebrated Galileo's telescope discoveries with a ceremony at the Collegio Romano on 18 May 1611. Although Clavius had endorsed and confirmed the observations themselves, he originally expressed reservations about the full meaning of Galileo's discoveries. Yet the doubts of the senior astronomer seem not to have dampened the enthusiasm of the younger ones, which included Christoph Grienberger, Odo van Maelcote, Paul Guldin, Paolo Lembo, and Gregory of St. Vincent. Relations between Galileo and the Collegio Romano astronomers soured only after Clavius's death in the wake of Cardinal Bellarmine's restrictions on the teaching of Copernicanism and the controversies that grew out of Galileo's feuds with Jesuits Orazio Grassi and Christoph Scheiner.

Gregorian Calendar. Sometime between 1572 and 1575, Pope Gregory XIII convened a commission to make recommendations on the reform of the Julian calendar, and the young Clavius was tapped to serve as the commission's technical expert. As such, he reviewed and explained the various issues and proposed reform schemes and specified the technical terms of the reform that the commission eventually decided on. This, however, was only the beginning of the work, because Clavius went on to write and publish the fundamental works promulgating and explaining the new Gregorian calendar and the transition process from the old calendar to the new. A collection of articles explaining various aspects of the calendar reform appears in *Gregorian Reform of the Calendar* (Coyne, et al, 1983). Many critics, among them Joseph Scaliger and Michael Maestlin, found fault with the calendar reform, and the task fell to Clavius to respond to them in print. An overview of Clavius's role in the reform and his responses to the critics can be found in Carmelo Oñate Guillen's "Christopher Clavius y el Calendario Gregoriano" (2000). A proper history of the Gregorian calendar reform has as of 2007 yet to be published.

Institution Building. Jesuit scholars achieved great respect for their contributions to mathematical sciences, and Clavius was the architect of the mathematical curriculum in the Jesuit educational establishment. His influence on the *Ratio studiorum*, the plan of studies for Jesuit schools, published in final form in 1599, established mathematics as a vital component in an era when mathematical subjects were rarely or inconsistently taught in many institutions of higher learning. His concerns went beyond curriculum parameters and extended to measures intended to enhance the prestige of mathematical work and the respect accorded its specialists. Dennis Smolarski surveys Clavius's pedagogical efforts and his influence on the development of the *Ratio studiorum*. In addition to establishing a curriculum that specified the study of Euclid, arithmetic, astronomy, cosmography, optics, timekeeping, and instrument construction, Clavius's lifetime of writing provided teachers, Jesuit and otherwise, with textbooks to cover almost the entire mathematical curriculum. By the end of his career, Clavius's efforts had led to a required rotation of mathematics courses in the hundreds of Jesuit schools and to a growing number of skilled teachers and practitioners of the mathematical sciences. Alistair Crombie, in "Mathematics and Platonism" (1977), largely credits Clavius's policies and efforts for Jesuit achievements in science during the seventeenth century. Clavius's impact also went well beyond Europe, carried by mathematically trained Jesuit missionaries such as Matteo Ricci and Johann Adam Schall. Notwithstanding his significance for helping scholars understand the development of early modern science, Clavius's greatest legacy and impact might be found in his efforts as a teacher and builder of educational institutions.

SUPPLEMENTARY BIBLIOGRAPHY

WORKS BY CLAVIUS

Opera mathematica, 5 vols. Mainz: Eltz, 1612. Clavius's collected works.

Bibliothèque de la Compagnie de Jésus, compiled by Carlos Sommervogel. Paris: Alphonse Picard, 1891. Reprint, Paris, 1960. Contains a complete listing of Clavius's publications.

Christoph Clavius: Corrispondenza, ed. Ugo Baldini and Pier Daniele Napolitani. Pisa: University of Pisa Press, 1992.

Theorica solis. In *Legem impone subactis,* Ugo Baldini. Rome: Bulzoni, 1992. Contains the surviving portion of his solar theory.

OTHER SOURCES

Baldini, Ugo. "La nova del 1604 e i matematici e filosofi del Collegio Romano: Note su un testo inedito." *Annali dell'Istituto e Museo di Storia della Scienza di Firenze* 6, fasc. 2 (1981): 63–98.

———. "Christoph Clavius and the Scientific Scene in Rome." In *Gregorian Reform of the Calendar,* edited by George V. Coyne, Michael A. Hoskin, and Olaf Pederson. Vatican City: Specola Vaticana, 1983.

———. *Legem impone subactis: Studi su filosofia e scienza dei Gesuiti in Italia, 1540–1632.* Rome: Bulzoni, 1992.

———, ed. *Christoph Clavius e l'attività scientifica dei Gesuiti nell'età di Galileo.* Rome: Bulzoni, 1995.

———, and Juan Casanovas. "La sfere celeste di Cristoforo Clavio." In *Osservatorio Astronomico di Capodimonte, Almanacco 1996.* Napoli: Arte Tipografica, 1996.

———. *Saggi sulla Cultura della Compagnia di Gesù.* Padova: CLEUP, 2000.

Casanovas, Juan. "L'astronomia nel Collegio Romano nella prima metà del seicento." *Giornale di Astronomia* 10 (1984): 149–155.

———. "Il P. C. Clavio professore di matematica del P. M. Ricci nel Collegio Romano." In *Atti del Convegno Internazionale di Studi Ricciani,* edited by Maria Cigliano. Macerata: Centro Studi Ricciani, 1984.

Coyne, George V., Michael A. Hoskin, and Olaf Pedersen. *Gregorian Reform of the Calendar: Proceedings of the Vatican Conference to Commemorate its 400th Anniversary, 1582–1982.* Vatican City: Specola Vaticana, 1983.

Crombie, Alistair C. "Mathematics and Platonism in the Sixteenth-Century Italian Universities and in Jesuit Educational Policy." In *Prismata,* edited by Yasukatsu Maeyama and Walter G. Saltzer. Wiesbaden: Franz Steiner Verlag, 1977.

Döring, Klaus, and Georg Wöhrle, eds. *Vorträge des ersten Symposions des Bamberger Arbeitskreises "Antike Naturwissenschaft und ihre Rezeption" (AKAN).* Wiesbaden: Otto Harrassowitz, 1990.

Enzensberger, Horst. "Società, cultura e religione a Bamberga e in Franconia ai tempi di Christoph Clavius." In *Christoph Clavius e l'attività scientifica dei Gesuiti nell'età di Galileo,* edited by Ugo Baldini. Rome: Bulzoni, 1995.

Flindell, E. Fred. "Christophorus Clavius." In *The New Grove Dictionary of Music and Musicians,* edited by Stanley Sadie. London: Macmillan, 1980.

Garibaldi, Antonio C. "Il Problema della quadratice nella matematica dei Gesuiti da Clavius alla metà del secolo XVII." In *Christoph Clavius e l'attività scientifica dei Gesuiti nell'età di Galileo,* edited by Ugo Baldini. Rome: Bulzoni, 1995.

Jardine, Nicolas. "The Forging of Modern Realism: Clavius and Kepler against the Skeptics." *Studies in History and Philosophy of Science* 10 (1979): 141–173.

Jullien, Vincent. "Quelques aspects du caractère incontournable des *Éléments* d'Euclide au XVIIe siècle." *Science et Techniques en Perspective,* IIe série, 1 (1997): 221–265.

Knobloch, Eberhard. "Musurgia universalis: Unknown Combinatorial Studies in the Age of Baroque Absolutism." *History of Science* 17 (1979): 258–275.

———. "Sur la vie et l'oeuvre de Christophore Clavius (1538–1612)." *Revue d'Histoire des Sciences* 41 (1988): 331–356.

———. "Christoph Clavius: Ein Astronom zwischen Antike und Kopernicus." In *Vorträge des ersten Symposions des Bamberger Arbeitskreises "Antike Naturwissenschaft und ihre Rezeption" (AKAN),* edited by Klaus Döring and Georg Wöhrle. Wiesbaden: Otto Harrassowitz, 1990.

———. "Sur le rôle de Clavius dans l'histoire des mathematiques." In *Christoph Clavius e l'attività scientifica dei Gesuiti nell'età di Galileo,* edited by Ugo Baldini. Rome: Bulzoni, 1995.

Lattis, James M. "Homocentrics, Eccentrics, and Clavius's Refutation of Fracastoro." *Physis* 28 (1991): 699–725.

———. *Between Copernicus and Galileo: Christoph Clavius and the Collapse of Ptolemaic Cosmology.* Chicago: University of Chicago Press, 1994.

Lucchetta, Giulio A. "Componenti platoniche e aristoteliche nella filosofia della matematica di Clavius." In *Christoph Clavius e l'attività scientifica dei Gesuiti nell'età di Galileo*, edited by Ugo Baldini. Rome: Bulzoni, 1995.

Maeyama, Yasukatsu, and Walter G. Saltzer, eds. *Prismata: Naturwissenschaftsgeschichtliche Studien*. Wiesbaden: Franz Steiner Verlag, 1977.

Oñate Guillen, Carmelo. "Christopher Clavius y el Calendario Gregoriano." *Letras de Deusto* 30 (2000): 55–70.

Palmieri, Paolo. "The Obscurity of the Equimultiples: Clavius' and Galileo's Foundational Studies of Euclid's Theory of Proportions." *Archive for History of Exact Sciences* 55 (2001): 555–597.

Remmert, Volker R. "'Sonne Steh Still uber Gibeon.' Galileo Galilei, Christoph Clavius, katholische Bibelexegese und die Mahnung der Bilder." *Zeitschrift für Historische Forschung* 28 (2001): 539–580.

Rommevaux, Sabine. *Clavius. Une clé pour Euclide au XVIe siècle*. Paris: Vrin, 2005.

Smolarski, Dennis C. "The Jesuit *Ratio studiorum,* Christopher Clavius, and the Study of Mathematical Sciences in Universities." *Science in Context* 15 (2002): 447–457.

Stephenson, F. Richard, J. Eric Jones, and Leslie V. Morrison. "The Solar Eclipse Observed by Clavius in A.D. 1567." *Astronomy and Astrophysics* 322 (1997): 347–351.

Wallace, William A. *Galileo and His Sources: The Heritage of the Collegio Romano in Galileo's Science*. Princeton, NJ: Princeton University Press, 1984.

James M. Lattis

CLEMENTS, FREDERIC EDWARD

(*b.* Lincoln, Nebraska, 16 September 1874; *d.* Santa Barbara, California, 26 July 1945), *botany.* For original article on Clements see *DSB,* vol. 3.

Clements is best known for his theory of community development or plant succession. He claimed that a plant community underwent a predictable series of developmental stages that was comparable to the development of an organism. The final stage or climax community was determined by the climatic conditions of a geographic area. For Clements, the plant community was, in fact, a "complex organism" with a physiology that could be studied with the same precision as an organism in the laboratory. These organismal ideas were both influential and controversial during Clements's lifetime. They focused considerable attention on plant succession as a major research area for American ecologists during the early decades of the twentieth century, when the discipline was becoming established. Although widely rejected by later ecologists, Clements's organicism and physiological perspective persisted in attenuated form even after World War II.

Plant Communities. Historians are in general agreement that Clements drew his idea of the plant community as a complex organism from Herbert Spencer and other late nineteenth-century social thinkers who employed similar organic analogies. This idea was central to Clements's attempt to create a science of ecology based on the model of laboratory physiology with its rigorous experimental and quantitative methods. Historian Sharon Kingsland asserts that the organismal idea also allowed Clements to situate human activities within ecology. Knowing the natural patterns of development in plant communities provided a way to understand and correct the pathological disturbances caused by human activities. Damaged lands could be rescued from overgrazing and other unwise agricultural practices, but only if agriculture was based on sound ecological principles. Throughout his career Clements emphasized the practical role that ecology could play in setting public policy regarding land use and resource management. As Kingsland points out, Clements's view of the social dimension of ecology was in tune with the Progressive Era ideas of efficiency and scientific management and also with later New Deal policies. This belief in the public role of ecology met a critical challenge during the Dust Bowl years of the 1930s.

The importance of the prairie and the Dust Bowl for Clements's career has been the focus of considerable interest by historians. Both Donald Worster and Ronald Tobey emphasize the formative influence of growing up on the prairie for Clements's thinking about succession. Both of these historians portray Clementsian ecology as a broad, philosophical perspective on nature exemplifying what Thomas Kuhn referred to as a scientific "paradigm." According to Worster and Toby, Clements's paradigm was established in opposition to a less deterministic theory of succession proposed by Henry Chandler Cowles at the University of Chicago and the later "individualistic" concept of the plant community championed by Henry Allan Gleason of the New York Botanical Garden. Both historians present the Dust Bowl as a critical challenge to the explanatory power of Clements's theory of succession. By emphasizing his determinism Worster and Tobey claim that Clements's had an almost metaphysical commitment to the lawlike development of vegetation that could not adequately account for the calamitous effects of the Dust Bowl.

This historical interpretation has been challenged by Christopher Eliot, who argues that Clements was much more attuned to the complexity of nature than his critics allege and that textbook descriptions of the Clements-Gleason controversy present a caricature of differences between the two ecologists' philosophical commitments and explanatory strategies. Nonetheless, the traumatic episode of the Dust Bowl undoubtedly weakened the hold that Clements's ideas had on plant ecologists, and encouraged criticism by Gleason and others. According to Tobey, Clementsian ecology experienced a life cycle of its own. Once established during the first decade of the twentieth century, it rapidly expanded through a social network of grassland ecologists located primarily in the Midwest. The Clementsian paradigm guided the research of this loose network of researchers from the end of World War I until the end of the 1930s. According to Tobey, this network of researchers decayed because of the combined effects of the Dust Bowl, the rise of competing approaches in ecology, and Clements's retirement and death.

Fate of Clements's Research Group. Taking a less sociological approach than Tobey, and focusing more closely on the small group of scientists who worked directly with Clements, this author has examined the fate of the Clementsian research school and why it failed to perpetuate itself after Clements's death. First at the University of Nebraska (1897–1907) and then at the University of Minnesota (1907–1917), Clements was a dynamic teacher who trained a devoted group of students. Several of these junior scientists continued to work with him for many years. When Clements became a research associate with the Carnegie Institution of Washington in 1917 he gained the financial support needed to establish and maintain his alpine laboratory near Pikes Peak, Colorado. Although the research group that Clements assembled was quite productive, subordinates found it difficult to develop independent lines of research. Clements may have been a benevolent dictator, much admired by his former students and coworkers, but he was a dictator nonetheless. Scientists at the alpine laboratory always worked on projects that were designed by Clements. To be successful, a subordinate had to struggle to break free from this dominance. For example, John Weaver, who was Clements's most successful student, refused an offer to become a full-time researcher at the alpine laboratory. Although he continued to collaborate and publish with Clements, Weaver maintained some autonomy by keeping his faculty position at the University of Nebraska. When Clements hired the taxonomist Harvey Monroe Hall to assist him in developing a new program in experimental taxonomy, Hall also resisted working directly with Clements at the alpine laboratory. Instead, Hall continued to work near Berkeley, where he had been a professor at the University of California. For Clements, experimental taxonomy was to be a part of ecology focusing on experimentally converting one plant species into another. Hall never accepted Clements's ideas on inheritance of acquired characteristics, and unlike Clements he developed strong ties with plant geneticists. For Hall, experimental taxonomy was an interdisciplinary field combining not only ecology and taxonomy, but also genetics and cytology. Patricia Craig has carefully documented the concomitant rise of Hall's

influence and the erosion of Clements's status within the Carnegie Institution during the 1930s. Ultimately, Hall gained complete control of the Carnegie Institution's program in experimental taxonomy and moved it to a new laboratory at Stanford University. Ironically, Hall's group eventually refuted Clements's neo-Lamarckian claims about experimentally transmuting species. At the expense of Clements, Hall's coworkers successfully brought experimental taxonomy into the mainstream of evolutionary biology after World War II.

The case of experimental taxonomy is enlightening for several reasons. It illustrates the challenges that Clements faced in gaining and retaining financial support for his research. Initially the Carnegie Institution considered Clements's approach to experimental taxonomy to be innovative and important, but enthusiasm for the theoretical foundation of this work diminished throughout the 1930s. As Donald Burnette has documented, Clements was also ultimately unsuccessful in attracting other potential patrons to support this type of research near his winter residence at Santa Barbara. Despite strong local interest in building a botanical garden, Clements was unable to convince wealthy patrons to support his research plans for building an experimental garden to study the effects of transplantation. Although Clements was peripherally involved in its establishment, the Santa Barbara Botanic Garden was designed to serve aesthetic and horticultural interests, rather than research in experimental taxonomy.

Experimental taxonomy is also a good example of the general fruitfulness of Clements's novel ideas, but it illustrates how difficult it was for his followers to take these ideas in new directions. The idea of an experimental taxonomy ultimately gained widespread acceptance, but it was developed largely by outsiders who broke with Clements on important theoretical issues. This general pattern was also evident in the later response to Clements's organismal idea of the community. British ecologist Sir Arthur Tansley, who was a friend and early supporter of Clements, was critical of Clements's claim that the community was a complex organism. Although he sometimes found organismal analogies useful, Tansley believed that Clements's claim was too rigid and dogmatic. He also vigorously opposed the philosophical holism that became associated with Clementsian ecology during the 1930s. According to Tansley, Clements's organicism and holism had become articles of faith that impeded the process of science. For example, to dogmatically claim that emergent properties of the organismal community can never be explained in terms of the parts effectively closed off potentially fruitful lines of inquiry. In response, Tansley proposed the term *ecosystem* as a philosophically more acceptable alternative to the complex organism. The term quickly caught on, particularly in the United States.

Ironically, some ecosystem ecologists—notably Eugene Odum—returned to holism and organicism. Thus, although Clements's idea of complex organism did not survive intact after World War II, in attenuated form his thinking continued to have influence during the later part of the twentieth century.

SUPPLEMENTARY BIBLIOGRAPHY

Burnette, Donald R. "Failed Boundary Objects: The Case of Frederic E. Clements and the Santa Barbara Botanic Garden." Unpublished manuscript submitted to the *Journal of the History of Biology*.

Craig, Patricia. *Centennial History of the Carnegie Institution of Washington*. Vol. 4, *The Department of Plant Biology*. New York: Cambridge University Press, 2005.

Eliot, Christopher. "Method and Metaphysics in Clements's and Gleason's Ecological Explanations." *Studies in History and Philosophy of the Biological and Biomedical Sciences* 38 (2007): 85–109.

Hagen, Joel B. "Experimentalists and Naturalists in Twentieth-Century Botany: Experimental Taxonomy, 1920–1950." *Journal of the History of Biology* 17 (1984): 249–270.

———. *An Entangled Bank: The Origins of Ecosystem Ecology*. New Brunswick, NJ: Rutgers University Press, 1992.

———. "Clementsian Ecologists: The Internal Dynamics of a Research School." *Osiris* 8 (1993): 178–195.

Kingsland, Sharon E. *The Evolution of American Ecology, 1890–2000*. Baltimore, MD: Johns Hopkins University Press, 2005.

Tobey, Ronald C. *Saving the Prairies: The Life Cycle of the Founding School of American Plant Ecology, 1895–1955*. Berkeley: University of California Press, 1981.

Worster, Donald. *Nature's Economy: A History of Ecological Ideas*. 2nd ed. Cambridge, U.K.: Cambridge University Press, 1994.

Joel Hagen

CO-CHING CHU
SEE **Zhu Kezhen**.

COCKAYNE, LEONARD (*b.* Norton Lees, near Sheffield, England, 7 April 1855; *d.* Wellington, New Zealand, 8 July 1934), *ecology, phytogeography, horticulture.*

Cockayne, who from the late 1890s was well known within the rapidly emerging European school of ecologists, achieved world recognition in 1919 for *The Vegetation of New Zealand*, published at Leipzig in Germany as

volume 14 of *Die Vegetation der Erde*, a project conceived and edited, from 1896 to 1928, by Adolf Engler, professor of botany and director of the botanical garden at Berlin, and Oscar Drude, professor of botany at the Dresden Polytechnic and director of the Dresden botanical gardens. This masterwork was the culmination of several decades of Cockayne's intensive and largely independent study of the New Zealand flora and his early recognition of the uniqueness of New Zealand as a locus for understanding change induced by human activity in native floras generally. From this work he developed a theory of hybridization as the driving force in evolution.

Early Life, Education, and Migration. Brought up as a very-much-younger son in a middle-class mid-Victorian northern English mercantile family, Cockayne later attributed his lifelong, and largely autodidactic, interests and achievements in botany to an early childhood spent in solitary "self-given nature-studies in the remnant of ancient British woodland" that occupied the bottom of a gully near Thorpe House, his family home at Norton Lees. After a fragmented and mediocre schooling on classical lines, which he disliked intensely, Cockayne was admitted in 1873 to medical studies at the Manchester Royal Infirmary and the Manchester Royal School of Medicine and Surgery. When his health broke down in 1875, he turned to botany. He later recalled that he attended a course of lectures in the subject, "which at that time was almost entirely systematic [classification]," and passed a degree examination at the University of London. From this, he said, he acquired "a fair amount of botanical jargon and so could use a flora to some extent" (Thomson, 1983, 30–33).

At this point in his life Cockayne decided to migrate to Australia. His reasons for doing so are unclear. It has been suggested that he was prompted by poor health and a sense of academic failure. In addition, an overseas career may have seemed promising to one with his natural abilities and intellectual independence, in terms of opportunities not open to him in Britain. Whatever the case, Cockayne spent four years teaching school in Australia before migrating to New Zealand in 1881. He arrived there with no formal qualifications but with a considerable knowledge of, and a deep interest in, botany.

After teaching the subject in schools for two or three years, an independent income from his deceased father's estate allowed him to concentrate on something quite new for New Zealand, experimental plant research. Cockayne, with his habits of independent thought, quickly recognized that a relatively recently colonized country like New Zealand presented an opportunity to study in some detail the evolution of a new flora, induced by European settlement, and the evolving relationships between that flora and those who induced it. Cockayne considered that such studies would be "of the greatest scientific and economic interest not only with regard to New Zealand botany, pure and applied, but also because they may shed much needed light upon the evolution of floras and vegetation in general." Cockayne's early realization that many of the plants introduced into New Zealand and into much of the New World from the Old were "some of them the most aggressive weeds in Europe," served to heighten his interest (Cockayne, 1927, 145–146).

Severe economic depression and a highly conservative political and scientific and academic establishment, however, encumbered New Zealand science at that time. The meager university teaching of the day was based on English scholastic rather than European experimental models. Cockayne had already found the former to be highly uncongenial to his mode of independent inquiry. He became increasingly impatient with his botanical colleagues, whom he considered to be shackled to the outdated "name, classify, describe" Linnaean paradigm of systematic botany that he had left behind in England. He taught himself to read German so that he could tap into the mainstream of European botanical thought and used a portion of his patrimony in 1892 to purchase a property on which he established his Tarata Experimental Garden, near Christchurch in the South Island of New Zealand. There he assembled a variety of both indigenous and exotic plants, of botanical rather than aesthetic value, gathered from the temperate regions of the globe. But he decided, "New Zealand species were to play a larger part in the plant population than had hitherto been the case" (Thomson, 1983, 38). In itself, this was a novel approach among New Zealand gardeners, most of whom were of British extraction, and who had been largely intent upon replicating the flora of their homelands in their adopted country. At Tarata he began to focus on plants and their relation to their surroundings, gathering his data from actual observations in the field. This was something of a paradigm shift in New Zealand botanical thinking at that time. He also extended his knowledge of plant propagation, which he shared unstintingly through his associations with local and international horticultural societies. To the end of his life he saw himself, at heart, as a gardener.

European Connections. From his experimental work and from wider field observations, Cockayne gained insights into the distinctive nature of the New Zealand flora and the changes induced in it by European colonization. These could not be explained by the current, predominantly English, evolutionary paradigms, which advocated that innately "superior" European species would inevitably outcompete and in due course displace "inferior" indigenes, whether they be floral, faunal or human.

Cockayne looked instead to the emerging science of ecology to gauge the effects on the indigenous biota of invasions by European colonists and their alien plants, animals, and agricultural practices. The European invasion of New Zealand, a relatively small, isolated archipelago in the South Pacific, had been documented more or less continuously, although somewhat haphazardly, from the contact period following James Cook's rediscovery of the country in the late eighteenth century. Working from this record, and his own systematic observations and experimentation, Cockayne used an ecological paradigm to interrogate earlier narrowly based Darwinian-Hookerian-Wallacean evolutionary theories about the assumed superiority of European flora, and to develop an alternative explanation of human- and animal-induced transformations in the New Zealand flora after colonization.

Cockayne was particularly influenced by Eugenius Warming, the Danish botanist whose *Plantesamfund,* published in 1895 and translated into German the following year as *Lehrbuch der ökologischen Pflanzengeographie,* Cockayne considered to be a founding document in the emerging science of ecology. The German botanist Karl Ritter von Goebel, director of the botanical gardens at Munich, who visited New Zealand in 1898, recognized the wider ecological significance of Cockayne's work and strongly encouraged him to persevere in the face of a considerable degree of local indifference.

Meanwhile, Cockayne had been obliged to sell Tarata in 1903 when his health again failed and his finances became stretched. When he had recovered his health he embarked on a program which took him into the field for an average of one hundred days a year, a pace that he maintained until 1925 when he reached seventy years of age. Over the next thirty years his ideas would eventually dominate both the research and the debate on the mechanisms underlying induced changes in the indigenous flora of New Zealand and contribute significantly to an understanding of global floral transformations. This was largely due to the increasingly extensive nature of his botanical fieldwork and a growing appreciation, particularly in Germany, of its wider ecological implications.

His finances were another matter. Realizing that he could not maintain the scale of his researches from his personal purse he approached the New Zealand government, seeking appointment as its official botanist. In this von Goebel and the botanist and plant geographer Friedrich Diels, a protégé of Adolf Engler, who had met Cockayne during a visit to New Zealand in 1902, supported him. Cockayne's radical views and rather abrasive ways of expressing them appear to have worked against him. Although his son Alfred was appointed assistant government biologist in 1904, Cockayne never received a similar position. But in 1907 "arrangements, very satisfactory from a scientific point of view [were] entered into between the Government and Dr. L. Cockayne, which would enable him to continue and extend the work he had so long conducted at his own expense." That arrangement provided the support needed to produce a groundbreaking ecological study that would bring Cockayne world recognition.

Contribution to *Die Vegetation der Erde*. Following the publication of two major ecological studies, one in 1900 on South Island grasslands and another in 1902 on the Chatham Islands, an isolated group lying off New Zealand's eastern coast, Cockayne received an invitation in 1904 from Professor Engler to contribute a New Zealand volume to the major and successful global botanical study then under way in Germany, *Die Vegetation der Erde*. Armed with Engler's synopsis of the proposed work, Cockayne set about acquiring, over the next nine years, a firsthand botanical knowledge of New Zealand's many unexplored and imperfectly known regions. Along the way he used data he had gathered on hybridization, particularly from New Zealand's ancient Gondwanan forests, for his landmark *Observations Concerning Evolution, Derived from Ecological Studies in New Zealand*, published in 1912. He was elected a Fellow of the Royal Society in the same year, on the proposal of Sir Joseph Hooker, and received the Hector Medal from his New Zealand colleagues in 1913 in recognition of his achievement. This and later fundamental research into the role of hybridization in the evolutionary process led in due course to the award of the Darwin Medal by the Royal Society.

He completed his field research for *The Vegetation of New Zealand* in June 1913 and sent his manuscript to Germany in March 1914. Publication was unfortunately forestalled by the war that engulfed Europe over the next four years. It is a measure of the strength of personal and scientific bonds that although the best of German and New Zealand manhood were pitted against each other in that pointless slaughter, Cockayne's great work was eventually in print in Germany in January 1921. It set out, for the first time in ecological terms, the nature of the New Zealand flora, the changes that had occurred to it from ancient times to the present, and Cockayne's understanding of the mechanisms, both natural and human-induced, underlying those changes. It was not only a radical departure from anything that had hitherto been published on the New Zealand flora, but because it drew on a unique scientific record from the time of the earliest European contact with a suite of primeval ecosystems, it also provided a comprehensive analysis of ecological processes and threw fresh light on global environmental changes stemming from human impacts.

Following highly favorable reviews in a succession of scientific journals, the first edition sold out within a year. Engler and his Leipzig publisher Wilhelm Englemann promptly invited Cockayne to prepare a second edition. He used data he had gathered since 1913 to produce an extensively rewritten and revised edition that was published in 1928 and remained into the twenty-first century a standard academic work on the ecology of the New Zealand flora. Cockayne also wrote, at the behest of the New Zealand Department of Education, a popular version of his masterwork as *New Zealand Plants and Their Story*. First published in 1910, it underwent four editions and was still in print in 1967. In it Cockayne the conservationist advocated careful stewardship of New Zealand's indigenous flora, "one of the most interesting in the world," against what he saw as poorly considered introductions of exotic floral and faunal species.

Cockayne had never, since his medical school days, enjoyed robust health. Shortly after publication of the 1928 edition of his masterwork, his eyesight began to fail. With his colleagues G. Simpson and J. Scott Thomson, he produced one final major paper in 1932, "Some New Zealand indigenous-induced weeds and indigenous-induced modified and mixed plant-communities." This comprehensive and unsurpassed study demonstrated that human interventions could cause some species normally found in cooperative rather than competitive indigenous plant communities to become aggressively weedy.

The University of Munich awarded Cockayne an honorary PhD in 1903 for his pioneering work in phytoecology. He was elected Fellow of the Linnaean Society of London in 1910 and Fellow of the Royal Society of London in 1912. The New Zealand Institute, in his adopted country, awarded him its Hector Memorial Medal in 1913 and the Hutton Memorial Medal in 1914. He was eventually elected Fellow of the Institute in 1919, following publication of the first edition of his *magnum opus*. After the publication of a second and extensively revised edition in 1928, he received the Mueller Memorial Medal from the Australasian Society for the Advancement of Science and in 1929 was made a Companion of the [British] Order of St. Michael and St. George (CMG). In 1928, the Royal Society awarded him its Darwin medal for his work on plant hybridization as an explanatory mechanism in the dynamics of ecosystems. In 1931, his lifelong work in horticulture was recognized with the award of the Veitch Memorial Medal by the Royal Horticultural Society. It was only towards the end of his life, in 1931, that his extensive achievements in ecology and phytogeography were finally acknowledged by the University of New Zealand with the award of an honorary DSc, almost three decades after the value of his initial contributions to global ecological science were first recognized in Germany.

Following his death in July 1934, Cockayne was buried in the grounds of the Otari Native Plant Museum, near Wellington, which provides a fitting memorial to his vast knowledge of the ecology of New Zealand's indigenous flora.

BIBLIOGRAPHY

WORKS BY COCKAYNE

The Vegetation of New Zealand. Die Vegetation der Erde 14. Leipzig: Wilhelm Englemann, 1921. 2nd ed. 1928. The two editions are worth consulting as they illustrate the progression of the author's ideas in the light of his advancing research.

New Zealand Plants and Their Story. Wellington: Government Printer, 1910. 2nd ed. 1919. 3rd ed. 1927. Posthumous 4th ed. 1967. Regarded as a popular classic, the first three editions again illustrate progressions in the author's ecological thinking.

Cockayne, Leonard, Simpson, G. and Scott Thomson, J, "Some New Zealand indigenous-induced weeds and indigenous-induced modified and mixed plant-communities." *Journal of the Linnean Society – Botany* 49 (June, 1932): 13–45. Regarded as a landmark in ecological literature.

OTHER SOURCES

Allan, H. H. "Leonard Cockayne (1855–1934)." *Proceedings of the Linnaean Society of London* 147 (1935): 167–171.

Hill, A. W. "Leonard Cockayne 1855–1934." *Obituary Notices of Fellows of the Royal Society* 1 (1935): 457–467. Contains a short bibliography.

Moore, L. B. "The Cockayne Memorial Lecture, 1965: Leonard Cockayne, Botanist." *Transactions of the Royal Society of New Zealand,* General series, 2 (1965): 1–18.

Thomson, A. D. "A Bibliography of the Work of Leonard Cockayne." *New Zealand Journal of Botany* 20:3 (1982): 205–219. Comprehensive but not exhaustive.

———. *The Life and Correspondence of Leonard Cockayne.* Christchurch: Caxton Press, 1983. Written by a botanist. Fragmentary, but useful background material. Illustrated, with facsimiles of some original correspondence.

———. "Cockayne, Leonard 1855–1934." In *Dictionary of New Zealand Biography,* updated 16 December 2003. Available from http://www.dnzb.govt.nz/.

Neil Clayton

COIGNET, MICHIEL (MICHAËL)

(also Connette, Cognet, Quignet) (*b.* Antwerp, Brabant [later Belgium], 1549; *d.* Antwerp, 24 December 1623), *mathematics, winegauging, navigation, instrument making.*

Although Coignet was an able mathematician, his prime contribution to science lies in the development and explanation of scientific instruments, such as astrolabes, nocturlabes, sectors, reduction compasses, and various navigational instruments.

Coignet's father, Gillis, a well-to-do mathematical instrument maker, died in 1562 or 1563 when Michiel was merely 13 years of age. Michiel must have received a good mathematical training at a young age; in 1568, he started a school in which he taught French and mathematics. He was married to Maria vanden Eynde, with whom he had ten children. In 1606, after the death of his first wife, he married Magdalena Marinus, with whom he had another four children.

His first publication (1573) was an adaptation of Valentin Mennher's *Livre d'arithmétique* (first published 1561). To this Coignet appended his own *Cent questions ingenieuses*, in which he deals with algebra and spherical trigonometry. In 1580, he published *Nieuwe onderwijsinghe op de principaelste puncten der zeevaert* (New instruction on the most important issues of navigation) as an appendix to Merten Everaert's translation of Pedro de Medina's *Arte de navegar.* Both books would be republished three times in Amsterdam (1589, 1593, 1598). In 1581, the French translation *Instrvction novvelle* was published. Thomas Blundiville plagiarized *Instrvction novvelle* and published it as part of his *Exercises* (1594), which was republished eight times. This seems to indicate that Coignet's book had its greatest influence in England.

In the book Coignet describes the use of the most commonly known instruments, the cross-staff and the mariner's astrolabe. Coignet's is the first book in which the description of a cross-staff with more than one transversal, which allowed for smaller angles to be measured, is found. His improved instruments also allowed pilots to read positional data off the instrument instead of calculating.

Early-sixteenth-century ships from the Low Countries did not travel beyond Scandinavia or the Canary Islands, so navigators could get by with only a compass, instruments to determine latitude, and knowledge of the coastline. But Dutch and Flemish merchants would have much wider opportunities if their ships could navigate the oceans to the Americas and Indies. The major challenge was determining longitude. Coignet's book treated Reiner Gemma Frisius's solution to find longitude. Theoretically this amounts to knowing the time difference between a fixed point (e.g., the harbor of departure) and the local time, which allows the longitudinal difference to be calculated. Unfortunately, Coignet's method was based on the use of sand-filled hourglasses, which are notoriously inexact, especially when used on a rolling ship. He described a nautical hemisphere, which is a meteoroscope adapted for use at sea. In principle the problem of longitude could be solved using the hemisphere. The nautical hemisphere is made of a round horizontal plate with a compass inset. Three arcs, two of which can move, are erected on the plate. One arc represents the meridian; the second, which can revolve around the east-west axis, represents the equinoctial; and the third, which revolves around the pole, represents the altitude. The second arc is mounted with a small arc that indicates time between 6:00 a.m. and 6:00 p.m. These movable arcs allow the user to mechanically solve the PZX or position triangle. The instrument was developed further in works by William Barlow (1597) and Edward Wright (1599). As of 2007, the only known surviving hemisphere was made by Charles Whitwell and was kept in Florence in the Museo di storia della Scienza.

In 1595, Coignet became mathematician to the Hapsburg Archduke Albert and Isabella, who were governors of the Spanish Netherlands. His advice was sought during the sieges of Hulst and Ostend. In this period he had some private pupils, among them Federico Saminiati and Marino Ghetaldi.

From 1601 onward Coignet edited the new editions of *Epitome Theatri Orbis Terrarum* by Abraham Ortelius. He wrote a new introduction and added another thirteen maps. Coignet also wrote an introduction for de Jode's *Speculum Orbis Terrarum* (1593). This introduction is the first known description of projection methods used by mapmakers, although Coignet essentially limits himself to stereographic projections.

It is in this period, between 1600 and 1610, that he seems to have written his first manuscripts on the sector. The sector is a development from the reduction compass and the proportional compass, which were used to mechanically perform calculations. The scales on the legs of all three instruments are such that the principles of similar triangles can be used. A sector consists of two pivoting arms on which scales are engraved. With these scales computations can be carried out by which equations of the type $\frac{f(x_1)}{f(x_2)} = \frac{a}{b}$, in which three parameters are known, can be solved.

The invention of the sector is usually ascribed to Galileo. However, at least one man can, on the basis of published material, claim priority: Thomas Hood. In the very same year that Galileo made his invention public, Hood published *The Making and Use of the Geometrical Instrument, Called a Sector* (1598), in which he described a sector for use in surveying. The hitherto earliest known sectors are English sectors: James Kynvyn's of 1595 and Robert Beckit's and Charles Whitwell's, both from 1597. Hood never claimed priority and even wrote that the instrument was already in use.

Coignet also has a claim to priority. However, one of the many problems here is that Coignet's manuscripts

about the sector were probably written after 1600. These manuscripts show the development of his sector. They can be divided into three categories: (1) the manuscripts in which he describes his *reigle platte;* (2) the ones with a modified version of Mordente's reduction compass; (3) those in which he describes a genuine sector. The reigle is a rather small rule on which scales are engraved. The use of the rule is analogous to that of the sector, but the operations are carried out with pen and paper. Originally there were only four scales on the rule; later it was "enrichy de huict diuisions" (enriched with 8 divisions) (*La géometrie,* 1626, introduction).

In a later stage, Coignet adapted the reduction compass invented by Fabrizio Mordente. In the partially printed manuscript of 1608, *Della forma et parti del compasso di Fabritio Mordente*, Coignet describes a rule that can be used in conjunction with the compass, in which case, the operations performed with such a rule are actually the same as for a sector. It is likely that this modification dates back to the 1580s. This he developed into a proper sector, which has sighting vanes at the end of the legs. It allows the sector to be used not only for calculations, but also for observations relating to surveying. The first sector of this type was made for Archduke Albert, indicating that it was constructed no later than 1596. Later, possibly after 1610, he developed his instrument into a sector that bears a close resemblance to Galileo's. Coignet had now transferred the twelve scales of the reigle platte to a set of two sectors, each carrying three scales on either side.

Coignet's sector had thus reached its final stage. The importance of his sector lies less in its final appearance (which is very similar to Galileo's) than in the fact that its development can be easily traced from additions and incorporation of ideas taken from other instruments to its final form. Although less visible, these aspects are also present in other instruments that Coignet describes. Additions, adaptations, and incorporation of different functions led to an instrument that was seen as an improvement. Some of these changes proved to be impractical and were soon forgotten, while others became common. This becomes obvious in Coignet's instruments and instrument descriptions. Thus Coignet's work is a prime example of how the mind of an early modern instrument maker worked.

BIBLIOGRAPHY

WORKS BY COIGNET

Cent questions ingénieuses et récréatives pour délecter & aguiser l'entendement, de feu Valentin. Mennher Allemand. Souldées & amplifiées par les raisons géométriques requises à icelles par Michiel Coignet. Antwerp: J. van Waesberghe, 1573.

Nieuwe onderwijsinghe op de principaelste puncten der zeevaert. Antwerp: Henry Hendrix, 1580. (Reprints: C. Claesz, 1589, 1593, and 1598).

Instrvction novvelle des poincts plus excellents & nécessaires, touchant l'art de nauiger. Antwerp: Henry Hendrix, 1581.

"De Regulae Pantometrae Fabrica & usu Libri Septem," (unpublished manuscript). c. 1600–1610. Bodleian Library Oxford, MS, Canon Misc 243.

Ortelius, Abraham, *Epitome theatri orbis terrarum Abrahami Ortelij*, edited by Michiel Coignet. Antwerp: J. Keerbergen, 1601. (Numerous reprints and translations).

Della forma et parti del compasso di Fabritio Mordente Salernitano. Con gli usi di esso, raccolti da Michele Coignet Mathematico del Serenissimo Archiduca Alberto. Per quali si risolvono molte propositioni, cavate dalla primi sei libri d'Euclide (unpublished manuscript). 1608. Bibliotheca Estense Modena, MS Gamma G.4.34 (Campori, 548).

Usus Duodecim Diuisionum Geometricarum (unpublished manuscript). 1610–1612. Koninklijke Bibliotheek Albert I Brussel, MS II769.

El uso de las doze diuisiones geometricas (unpublished manuscript). 1618. Stadsbibliotheek Antwerpen, B264708.

Tabula Geographica Indicans Iter Novum inter Mediolanum et Antverpiam, Abraham Verhoeven, 1621.

La géomérie réduite en une facile et briefve pratique, par deux excellens instrumens, dont l'un est le pantomètre ou compas de proportion de Michel Connette, et l'autre est l'usage du compas à huict pointes inventé par Fabrice Mordente composé en italien par M.C.… Traduits enfrançois par P.G.S. mathématicien, edited by P. G. S. Paris: Charles Hulpeau, 1626.

M. Michel Connette, sur les propositions géométriques extraictes des six premiers liures des "Élémens d'Euclide, Paris: C. Hulpeau, 1626.

OTHER SOURCES

Barlow, William. *The Navigator's Supply.* Amsterdam: Theatrum Orbis Terarum, 1597 (New York: Da Capo Press, 1972).

Bosmans, Henri. "Le Traité des Sinus de Michel Coignet." *Annales de la Société Scientifique de Bruxelles* 25 (1901): 91–170.

———. "Michel Coignet, ami et correspondant de Galilée." *Revue des questions scientifiques*, 3rd series, 16 (1909a): 644–647.

Davids Carolus Augustinus. *Zeewezen en wetenschap: De wetenschap en de ontwikkeling van de navigatietechniek in Nederland tussen 1585 en 1815*, Amsterdam: Bataafsche Leeuw, 1986.

de Jode, Gerard. *Speculum Orbis Terrarum.* Antwerp: A. Coninx, 1593.

Meskens, Ad. "Michiel Coignet's Nautical *Instruction.*" *The Mariner's Mirror* 78 (1992): 257–276.

———. "Winegauging in Late 16th- and Early 17th-Century Antwerp." *Historia mathematica* 21 (1994): 121–147. In the 1570s through 1590s Coignet was a wine-gauger.

———. *Familia universalis: Coignet.* Antwerp: Koninklijk Museum voor Schone Kunsten, 1998. Deals with Michiel Coignet and other members of his family; extensive bibliography and inventory of instruments by Michiel Coignet.

Prims, F. "Michiel Coignet." *Antwerpiensia* 19 (1948): 103–114.

Rose, P. L. "The Origins of the Proportional Compass from Mordente to Galileo." *Physis* 10 (1968): 53–69.

Ad Meskens

COLLONGUES, ROBERT

COLLONGUES, ROBERT (*b.* Toulouse, France, 1 January 1924; *d.* Villejuif, France, 10 May 1998), *solid-state chemistry, materials science, high temperature devices, metal oxides crystal-growth.*

Collongues, the heir to a long research tradition dating back to Henry Le Chatelier in the early twentieth century, contributed to the emergence of solid-state chemistry in France. Around 1950, Collongues's early works on crystal-structure defects in iron oxides led him to reappraise the concept of non-stoichiometry and to focus on order-disorder phenomena. Then he promoted the crystal-growth of metal oxides by developing high temperature devices during the 1960s. He became a world leader in refractory materials and single crystal-growth in the 1960s, moved into solid-state ionics during the 1970s, and shifted to optical materials after 1980. His most notable contribution was the founding of a major French research school that promoted solid-state chemistry at the national and international levels.

Childhood and Education. Robert was the only son of Marie-Louise Trouvé (1898–1979) and Gaston Collongues (1895–1986). During World War I, Gaston was enrolled as a soldier and wounded in 1916. He received a medal (Légion d'honneur) in 1961. Marie-Louise worked as an employee of the administration (*préfecture*) of the department of Haute-Garonne in Toulouse. Robert was a brilliant student interested both in sciences and literature. At the secondary school Pierre de Fermat in Toulouse, he received two baccalauréats (GCE A-levels) in 1941: letters and mathematics. After a three-year preparation for the competitive exams of engineering schools, he joined the École supérieure des industries chimiques de Nancy (Chemical engineering school of Nancy), France. There he enjoyed laboratory classes and got acquainted with metallurgy thanks to an engineer internship in a steelworks. In June 1947, he received his chemical engineer degree, on 5 September he married Nelly Sarazin (1921–2001), a student in Nancy, who became a mathematics teacher. They would have three children: Alain (1949), Catherine (1952), and François (1957). In October 1947, Collongues became a PhD student in the laboratory of Professor Georges Chaudron in Paris.

Chaudron and the LCTC. After World War II, Chaudron was a major figure in the French chemical community, both as a university professor and an industrial advisor. Chaudron had been trained in metallurgy and inorganic chemistry in Le Chatelier's laboratory from 1913 to 1921. In 1939, he became head of the Laboratoire central des traitements chimiques (LCTC, Central laboratory for chemical treatments), which had been founded two years before by Georges Urbain in Vitry-sur-Seine, a southern suburb of Paris. Between 1950 and 1962, Chaudron was the director of the most famous French chemical engineering school, the École nationale supérieure de chimie de Paris (ENSCP; National superior school of chemistry at Paris), which allowed him to recruit students. From 1951 on, he also worked as a techno-scientific advisor for the Commissariat à l'énergie atomique (CEA, atomic energy commission) at Saclay. In 1954 he was elected to the French Académie des sciences in the chemistry section and became president of the Académie for the year 1971–1972.

In 1947, when Collongues joined Chaudron's laboratory, the LCTC was dedicated to the synthesis and study of metals, metallic alloys, and inorganic solid compounds, especially metal oxides. One major feature of this research center was the hybridization of solid-state physics and physical chemistry methods used to study crystal structures—especially x-ray diffraction—with metallurgical methods used to characterize inorganic compounds, particularly thermal analysis and magnetism measurements. Chaudron helped to popularize among chemists the notion of "solid solution" commonly used by metallurgists. He thus promoted an interdisciplinary style of research without claiming that he was founding a new discipline.

A second feature of Chaudron's laboratory was its connections with industrial companies. In a period when French scientific research was mostly supported by a state agency created in the 1930s, the Centre national de la recherche scientifique (CNRS; National center for scientific research), which encouraged fundamental research, Chaudron was eager to solve technical issues encountered in steel industries, aeronautics, mechanics, and refractory materials companies. In return he received money from these companies, although the LCTC was also the recipient of generous state funding from the CNRS.

Finally, as one of the leaders of the French metallurgy community, Chaudron had international relations with European metallurgists and solid-state physicists. He met many times with Nevill Mott from the University of Bristol in England. He was in touch with the solid-state reactions community, especially the Swedish school of thought headed by Johan Hedvall. Through inorganic chemistry, he was also connected with European chemists

and organized a famous international CNRS conference in Paris during 1948 on chemical "reactions in solid state." Thus, Chaudron's laboratory was one of the rare places in France that intimately combined academic and applied researches and was open to foreign influences.

Early Career. Collongues was assigned a rather fundamental subject for his PhD, dealing with defects in iron monoxide. This research lasted for seven years, the usual lapse of time for a PhD project in France at that time. In 1954, he defended his thesis, titled *Contribution à l'étude des propriétés et des modes de décomposition de la phase protoxyde de fer* (Contribution to the study of properties and the decomposing ways of the iron monoxide phase).

Iron monoxide was known to be a non-stoichiometric compound: Instead of following the FeO stoichiometry, its general formula was $Fe_{1-x}O$, with $0<x<0.1$. Below 570°C, the protoxide is decomposed and gives metallic iron and magnetite:

$$4\ FeO \rightarrow Fe3O4\ (I)$$

Collongues's aims were threefold: (1) understanding the mechanisms of (I) by analysis of the kinetics of the reaction; (2) drawing a parallel between the iron monoxide and the steel phase diagrams in order to extend the definition of "solid solution" from intermetallic to ionic compounds; and (3) understanding the physical properties of the solid solution in terms of structure defects. Up to the 1960s, the metal oxides were usually prepared as solid polycrystalline powders, that is, ceramics made up of many grains randomly packed together. Each grain was a single crystal with a typical size of one micrometer or less. Using metallography (metallurgical optical reflection microscopy), Collongues observed the micrometric domains and growing surfaces, and with x-ray diffraction (the Debye-Scherrer powder method) he determined the atomic structure of polycrystals. Collongues was not the first one to study iron monoxide in LCTC. In 1939, Jacques Bénard had defended his PhD thesis, *Étude de la décomposition du protoxyde de fer et de ses solutions solides* (Study of the decomposition of iron monoxide and its solid solutions). Bénard had used the same techniques to show that (I) occurred without structural changes and without matter transport (i.e., without diffusion). Collongues, however, went further: He tried to link the physical properties (density and electrical conductivity) to the chemical composition and experimental conditions (temperature, quantity of impurities). For this purpose, he used the notion of "defects"—investigated by the American physicist Frederick Seitz, building on earlier work by the Russian investigator Yakov Frenkel and the Germans Wilhelm Jost, Carl Wagner, and Walter Schottky—and ventured a comparison between the defect crystal structure and a solid solution, which led him to describe the crystal as a dynamic (diffusion and reactions), non-ideal (non-stoichiometric), and disordered (order-disorder phenomena) structure.

Collongues's PhD research was not really innovative in terms of methods and concepts. The techniques he used to draw phase diagrams and study crystal structures were taken from early twentieth century metallurgy and crystallography. In addition, his approach—based on notions such as defects and structure-dependent properties—followed the path opened by solid-state physics during the 1930s. Yet Collongues opened up a research avenue because he extended the techniques and methods traditionally used to study alloys or model crystals to the investigation of ionic compounds such as non-stoichiometric metal oxides. Thus, he and others—such as Ferdinand A. Kröger at Royal Philips Electronics at Eindhoven in the Netherlands, or John Goodenough from the Lincoln Laboratory (MIT)—paved the way towards the science of new materials.

High-Temperature Research. Early in 1953, Chaudron's laboratory was renamed Centre d'étude de chimie métallurgique (CECM; Center for the study of metallurgical chemistry), a name emphasizing the close connection between chemistry and metallurgy, without, however, mentioning solid-state physics. In fact, two research programs were developed at the same time. On the metallurgy side, the aim was to obtain metals in their purest state; for instance, aluminium was purified by using the "zone melting" method developed by William Pfann at the Bell Laboratories in New Jersey for germanium in 1952. On the chemistry side, the investigative effort concerned solid-state metal oxides. The laboratory was divided into four different groups.

When Collongues completed his PhD in 1954 at the age of thirty and obtained a permanent position at the CNRS, Chaudron created a fifth research group: the High Temperature Section. Devoted to the study of metal oxides, it was placed under Collongues's supervision. His first two PhD students were women, and later on his group included several female researchers, which was quite unusual in the 1950s. Jeanine Théry continued previous research on iron oxides and ferrites at still higher temperatures than before while Monique Perez y Jorba tackled a new material, zirconia (ZrO_2). With a melting point of around 2,680°C, this zirconium oxide is extremely resistant to high temperature, but undergoes a dramatic structural transition around 1,050°C that at the time made it useless for technological purposes. Nevertheless, the CEA, considering zirconia materials as potentially heat resistant, contracted Collongues to study them. Zirconium oxide was finally stabilized by the addition of rare

or alkaline earth elements. Up to the 1990s, zirconium and its alloys were massively used to produce tubes in nuclear power plants. Thus, until 1973, Collongues's research group responded to the demand on high performance materials from atomic and military programs.

In the 1960s, Collongues himself considered designing refractory materials for spacecraft. But in order to meet industrial demands for heat-resistant materials, he had to produce higher temperatures in controlled conditions. With the help of new PhD students, he designed a number of sophisticated furnaces: an "image furnace" in 1960; a high-frequency plasma furnace in 1961 (following the pioneer work of the American Thomas B. Reed in 1960); and a direct induction furnace during 1962–1964. These new devices were built and operated thanks to the recruitment of skillful collaborators by the CECM and to the financial support of industrial firms interested in the development of such furnaces. During the 1960s, the group thus built up an expertise in temperatures ranging from 2,000 to 20,000°C. Its reputation was reinforced by the creation of an international journal, the *Revue internationale des hautes températures et des réfractaires* (High temperatures and refractory materials international review) edited by Collongues from 1963 to 1976 and dedicated to high temperatures production and refractory crystal compounds. However, the audience of the journal, written in French, was limited to the French-speaking European solid-state chemistry communities.

Crystal-Growth. From 1962 to 1973, Collongues developed a new expertise in single crystal-growth. Here again the innovative strategy was based on the transposition of traditional chemical metallurgy techniques to metal oxides. The group performed the synthesis of single crystals of metal oxides measuring a few centimeters, the first one being calcium oxide, synthesized in 1964 by using the flame fusion method (also called Verneuil's method) related to a plasma furnace. While the physical measurements usually performed on powder crystals could only give average numbers in space, which hid the possible anisotropic properties, with centimeter-size single crystals the crystal was large enough to allow measurements on one single-oriented domain. Moreover, single crystals provided further information on atomic structures. Collongues's group was thus able to make more precise structure determinations and to measure new anisotropic properties. Moreover, Collongues performed this kind of determinations in a systematic way on a wide variety of metal oxides (zirconium, aluminium, germanium, titanium, and lanthanides).

In 1966, Collongues's research group included twenty people (out of 111 people for the entire CECM). Although all members and Collongues himself still had to pay allegiance to the supreme reigning master, Chaudron, Collongues gained personal recognition. He became a professor at the Université de Paris (without a chair in 1964, and with a chair in 1967), was awarded several national science prizes in the 1960s, and in 1966 was appointed a member of the CNRS National Committee in the inorganic chemistry section. The same year he organized an international conference, "Les mécanismes de fusion et de solidification" (Mechanisms of fusion and solidification).

Solid State Ionics. In 1972, Collongues left the niche where he had "grown up" professionally to create his own laboratory, the Laboratoire de chimie appliquée de l'état solide (Laboratory of chemistry applied to the solid state), established within the ENSCP in Paris, where Bénard had succeeded Chaudron as a director. This institution, located in the Quartier Latin not far from the Sorbonne and other research centers, provided better opportunities for creating links and recruiting students. This strategic move was synchronized with a shift of research interests from refractory to electrical materials, prompted by one single and very promising material: beta-alumina. This ordinary ternary oxide was an inexpensive material largely available in the form $(Al_2O_3)_{11}(Na_2O)_x$, the structure of which had been determined by x-ray diffraction in the 1930s. During the 1960s, it was of interest only to a few crystallographers and ceramists because its good refractory properties qualified it for high temperature furnaces.

In 1962, two members of Collongues's group, Jeanine Théry and Daniel Briançon, identified and described a new form of β-alumina, named β''-alumina. The discovery was hardly noticed until suddenly, in 1967, three scientists from the Ford Motor Company at Dearborn, Michigan, reinvented β-alumina. Their first articles revealed that β-alumina's structural peculiarities led to a high ionic conductivity and that, consequently, β-alumina could be used to make sodium-sulfur batteries for electrical vehicles. These unconventional batteries have two liquid electrodes (sodium and sulfur) and a solid electrolyte. In order to liquefy sodium and sulfur and reach high conductivity, the cell has to work at high temperatures (350-400°C). β-alumina and other compounds of its family first appeared to be ideal for solid-state electrolytes because they were both high ionic conductive and refractory materials. Despite a number of technological problems (reactivity of liquid sodium at 400°C, electrodes' leakage), solid-state batteries have some distinct advantages over traditional electrolyte: a longer life-time; an easier way of miniaturizing, for example in a thin-film form; a usefulness both in low-power and high-energy forms; a combination of two functions: separating the electrodes and conducting the ions.

When the energy storage issue became crucial in the early 1970s during the oil crisis, β-alumina became a star material, intensely investigated by hundreds of chemists and physicists from both industry and academic laboratories in the United States and in Europe who created a new sub-discipline named solid-state ionics dedicated to "superionic" conducting materials. β-alumina provided a model-material for developing methods of investigation and understanding the physical laws of high ionic conductivity. In the United States, Robert Huggins (Stanford University), Michael Whittingham (Exxon Research), and Bruce Dunn (General Electrics) were leading figures in the field. Because Collongues's group already had an expertise in β-alumina, big French companies such as Compagnie générale d'electricité (later renamed Alcatel), Renault, and Electricité de France contracted the group to study its ionic conductivity. New spectroscopic and crystallographic techniques had to be used to detect atomic movements. Therefore, Collongues started a fruitful partnership with solid-state physics and spectroscopy laboratories, the members of his group providing their know-how in the synthesis and the structural characterizations of β-alumina single crystals and the physicists performing more technical characterizations and dealing with physical theories. In the series of eight international conferences on fast ion transportation held from 1972 to 1992, Collongues and his group always had significant results to present.

However, in the mid-1980s, the intense exploratory activity on β-alumina came to an end for several reasons: No commercial application was under way, as some technical problems remained unsolved; new high ionic conductors became more promising than β-alumina; and above all the concern of the companies and states for energy storage declined after the two oil crises. For a few years, Collongues's group went hunting other families of ionic solid conductors, such as the NASICON (Na superionic conductor) family, but it was a swan's song.

Optical Materials. The group moved on to new research topics. An opportunity had opened up in 1979 when a team in the laboratory observed that a laser effect could be obtained with a family of compounds produced by inserting rare earths inside a β-alumina single crystal matrix: the LNA (Nd-doped lanthanum-hexaluminate) with a chemical formula $LnMgAl_{11}O_{19}$ (Ln = La_{1-x}, Nd_x [La = Lanthanum; Nd = Neodymium]). The discovery of its potential laser effect resulted from the use of Electron Paramagnetic Resonance (EPR), a technique introduced in the laboratory in 1972 by a newcomer, Jacques Livage, on his return from a postdoctoral stay at the Clarendon Laboratory in Oxford where he worked with John Owen on paragmagnetic electronic resonance. For optical materials Collongues left the scientific leadership to others, especially Daniel Vivien, because he did not feel comfortable enough with the instrumentation (EPR) and related theories. Nevertheless, he supervised the transition from ionic conductors to optical materials as a laboratory manager in charge of research strategies. He did not hesitate to raise funds from the French Ministère de la défense (Ministry of defense) as well as from medical companies; he bought new equipment and favored the shift toward quantum chemistry. In the last years of his directorship, from 1988 to 1993, Collongues worked out a smooth transition in which he allowed more and more autonomy to Vivien, who scientifically was at the heart of the laser project and who became his successor at the head of the laboratory.

The French Research Style. Collongues's career exemplifies the French way of doing materials research. In the 1960s, there was a strong governmental incentive in the United States to create interdisciplinary laboratories investigating all kinds of materials from metals to ceramics to semiconductors and intimately combining science and engineering, but in France the shift from metallurgy to new materials was carried out by a few individuals working in CNRS laboratories under disciplinary labels such as chemistry. A new discipline named solid-state chemistry that embraced all inorganic solid compounds emerged out of the mainstream of inorganic chemistry at the intersection of metallurgy, ceramics, glass materials, and high temperature production. Interdisciplinarity and collaboration between physics and chemistry were the key words. However, most of Collongues's investigations did not require quantum mechanics (except for optical materials). In keeping with a long tradition of applied chemistry initiated by Le Chatelier, Collongues developed physical techniques to study materials structures, and he often used industrial opportunities to start new research programs. Over his long career, he investigated a wide range of materials: single crystal-growth in the 1960s, solid-state ionics during the 1970s, and optical materials after 1980. Each research cycle reused a part of the expertise acquired during the previous one, while new techniques were introduced in the group by the newcomers.

Thus, Collongues exemplified the strengths and weaknesses of the French research system. While the CNRS secured job positions and research funds, his group could also rely on industrial contracts but was not encouraged to patent. Researchers were not prone to mobility and tended to stay in the laboratory where they started their career. Thus through teaching and supervising from one generation to the other, they gradually formed a local research school. According to his former students, Collongues was an outstanding teacher, always including new research results in his courses and engaging in discussions with his students. In the laboratory, he was extremely demanding and very strict about clean and well-controlled syntheses, but open-minded enough to accept proposals from his collaborators even if he did not fully understand them. Among his seventy former PhD students, half went into industrial careers. A few of them stayed in the group, while others were encouraged to create new independent laboratories of solid-state chemistry: Jean-Claude Gilles became professor at the École supérieure de physique et de chimie industrielle de Paris (Paris superior school of industrial physics and chemistry) in 1972, Alexandre Revcolevschi at the University of Orsay near Paris in 1977, and Jean-Pierre Boilot at the École Polytechnique (Polytechnical School, Palaiseau) in the early 1980s. Jacques Livage created a laboratory at the University of Paris 6 and became one of the world leaders of a new branch of materials chemistry that he himself labeled "chimie douce" (soft chemistry) in 1978. By using ambient temperature and low energy bio-inspired chemical reactions, soft chemistry allows the synthesis of a wide range of new materials.

Despite his huge influence on a generation, Collongues never enjoyed international recognition. He did not travel much and was not eager to speak English. His name can hardly be associated with a discovery or a new theory, but he was one of the major cogwheels of the solid-state chemistry machinery in France. Collongues's research school competed—both scientifically and institutionally—with other French groups in the field of materials chemistry, such as the research school headed by Paul Hagenmuller in Bordeaux, the group founded by Félix Trombe at Meudon-Bellevue, and the group around Jean Flahaut at the University of Pharmacy in Paris. However, the rivalry did not prevent cooperation among the groups, and so a French community of solid-state chemistry emerged with a common language and specific methods. These were characterized by close connections between chemistry and physics, between fundamental and applied research, the synthesis and characterization of new solid compounds, and focus on the linear model linking atomic structure to physical properties and properties to applications.

For Collongues's retirement in 1993, the members of the LCAES—most of them being his former students—organized a weekend in the countryside and played several cheerful spectacles to express their admiration and affection to the old master. Soon after, in 1994, Collongues discovered that he had a lung cancer. For four years, he fought with strong energy against the disease, analyzing the results of medical tests just as he used to do with chemical ones, giving the impression while speaking with doctors that he was their colleague rather than a patient. He died at the hospital of Villejuif near Paris on 10 May 1998.

BIBLIOGRAPHY

Unpublished documents of Collongues can be found in the archives of the Académie des sciences in Paris. Particularly Notice des titres et travaux scientifiques (1979), written by Collongues himself, gives his complete bibliography up to 1979.

WORKS BY COLLONGUES

"Les composés non stœchiométriques." In *Quelques problèmes de chimie minérale,* edited by Instituts Solvay. Bruxelles: R. Steeps, 1956.

"Argent." In *Nouveau traité de chimie minérale,* edited by Paul Pascal. Vol. 3. Paris: Masson, 1957.

"Alliages de cuivre et d'argent." In *Nouveau traité de chimie minérale,* edited by Paul Pascal. Vol. 20, 2nd fascicule. Paris: Masson, 1958.

La non-stœchiométrie. Paris: Masson, 1971.

With A.-M Anthony. "Modern Methods of Growing Single Crystals of High-Melting-Point Oxides." In *Preparative Methods in Solid State Chemistry,* edited by Paul Hagenmuller. New York: Academic Press, 1972.

Le solide cristallin. Paris: Presses universitaires de France, 1973.

With Alexandre Revcolevsch. "Le Four à image." In *Les hautes températures et leurs utilisations en physique et chimie,* edited by Georges Chaudron and Félix Trombe. Paris: Masson, 1973.

With F. Galtier and J. Reboux. "Le Four à plasma." In *Les hautes températures et leurs utilisations en physique et chimie,* edited by Georges Chaudron and Félix Trombe. Paris: Masson, 1973.

With Jean-Pierre Boilot. "β aluminas." In *Solid electrolytes,* edited by Paul Hagenmuller and W. Van Gool. New York: Academic Press, 1978.

With A.-M. Lejus. "Lanthanide oxides. Structural anisotropy. Physical and Mechanical Properties." *Current Topics in Materials Science* 3 (1979).

With A. Kahn and D. Michel. "Superionic conducting oxides." *Annual review of Materials Science* 9 (1979): 123-150.

With J-F. Delpech, C. Détraz, et al. *La matière aujourd'hui.* Interrogés par [interviewed by] Emile Noël. Paris: Seuil, 1981. Translated by W. J. Duffin as *Emile Noël Discusses Aspects of Matter in Science Today.* Cottingham, North Humberside, U.K.: W. J. Duffin, 1985.

OTHER SOURCES

Bensaude-Vincent, Bernadette, and Arne Hessenbruch. "Materials Science: A Field about to Explode?" *Nature Materials* 3, no. 6 (June 2004): 345–346.

Cahn, Robert W. *The Coming of Materials Science.* Amsterdam, London, New York: Pergamon, 2001. An Anglo-Saxon overview of the development of materials science—including solid-state chemistry and metallurgy—from about 1900 to 2000.

Cornet, Michel. "Histoire du Centre d'études de chimie métallurgique." *Cahiers pour l'histoire du CNRS* 5 (1989): 59–109. Available from http://www.cecm.cnrs.fr/Bibliocecm/historique_cecm.html. A recollection of the history of the CECM by one of its members.

"History of Materials Research." 2004. Available from http://hrst.mit.edu/hrs/materials/public.

Hoddeson Lillian, Ernst Braun, Jürgen Teichman, et al., eds. *Out of the Crystal Maze: Chapters from the History of Solid State Physics.* Oxford, New York: Oxford University Press, 1992. A U.S.-centered overview of the emergence of solid-state physics.

Picard, Jean-François. *La république des savants: La recherche française et le CNRS.* Paris: Flammarion, 1990. About the French scientific community in the post–World War II period.

Teissier, Pierre. "Le laboratoire de Robert Collongues (1950–2000): Une école de recherche aux débuts de la chimie du solide." *L'Actualité Chimique* no. 294 (February 2006): 50–59.

Bernadette Bensaude-Vincent
Pierre Teissier

COLONIENSIS, A.
SEE **Albertus Magnus, Saint**.

CONDON, EDWARD UHLER (*b.* Alamogordo, New Mexico, 2 March 1902; *d.* Boulder, Colorado, 26 March 1974), *physics, theoretical physics, quantum physics, spectroscopy, atomic and molecular structure, solid state physics, industrial physics, government administration.*

Condon's long and varied career combined major discoveries in theoretical physics with professional forays into academe, industry, and the federal government and political engagement on issues related to science, particularly the dangers of the nuclear age. His most noteworthy scientific achievements included the quantum tunneling explanation of alpha particle radioactivity. More generally, Condon experienced and participated in most of the major developments in the history of twentieth-century American physics: the quantum revolution and its reception in the United States; the building of patronage networks for training and research support; industrial research; war and the transformation of relations between science and government; the rise of the Cold War and military patronage of science; and the politics of the nuclear age.

Origins and Early Career. Condon was born in Alamogordo, New Mexico, not far from the site of the Trinity test, the world's first nuclear detonation, four decades later. The son of William Edward Condon, a railroad builder, and Carolyn Uhler Condon, the future physicist experienced a peripatetic early childhood as his family moved from one construction job to the next. The moves continued even after Condon's parents divorced, until Condon and his mother settled in Oakland, California. There Condon attended high school and nourished early interests in science and journalism. He then attended college at the University of California, Berkeley, but soon dropped out to embark on a career as a newspaper reporter. His two years as a journalist ended in disgust, however: Not only did he have to write what he later termed "lurid and sensationalist" pieces about the Communist Labor Party for the right-wing *Oakland Enquirer,* but he was also forced to testify as a witness against the party in a criminal syndicalism trial. Disillusioned, he turned to physics out of strong interest and, he later recalled, "as a means of escape from the corruption of the world" (Morse, 1976, p. 126).

Condon returned to the University of California, Berkeley, in the fall of 1921, and while in college he married Emilie Honzik in 1922. He earned his bachelor's degree in three years and completed his doctorate at Berkeley in 1926 under Raymond T. Birge, who was then studying the band spectra of diatomic molecules. Condon's dissertation provided a general theoretical explanation of the regularities in band spectral intensities observed by Birge and other researchers, by extending James O. Franck's explanation of the dissociation of a diatomic molecule due to absorption of a photon. Condon described a more complex absorption process involving simultaneous changes in the molecule's electron state and vibrational state. After receiving his PhD, Condon spent a postdoctoral year in Germany on a Rockefeller-funded fellowship from the National Research Council (NRC), de rigeur for young, ambitious American theoretical physicists. The Condons, with infant daughter Marie in tow, spent the fall of 1926 in Göttingen, where Condon worked with Max Born and mastered the newly invented theory of quantum mechanics. They then moved on to Munich for the spring of 1927, where Condon enjoyed the tutelage of Arnold Sommerfeld and revised his doctoral research with a more fully worked out quantum mechanical explanation of the band spectra of diatomic molecules. Later known as the Franck-Condon principle, the interpretation rested on the basic assumption that electron excitation due to photon absorption occurs almost instantaneously, without a change in the relative position of the much heavier nuclei. The excited molecule finds itself in a non-equilibrium position with regard to the vibrations of its constituent atoms; the absorption thus leads to changes in both the electronic and vibrational states of the molecule. Subsequently, the molecule frequently loses vibrational energy more quickly due to interactions with other molecules, before losing electron excitation energy by emission of a photon and thereby returning to the electron ground state. This

understanding provided a quantum theoretical explanation of the long-observed Stokes rule in photoluminescence, that is, the downward shift in light frequency between absorption and emission. Condon's work allowed exact calculations of band intensities, correctly predicted a new type of band spectrum, and established the main foundation for physical explanations of the complex interaction between absorption, emission, and atomic vibrations in molecular spectra.

Condon returned from Germany as part of the group of young, talented American physicists who would soon transform the United States, then still somewhat of a scientific backwater, into a leader in physics. Despite his early success, however, Condon underwent a crisis of confidence. Overwhelmed by the rate of progress in theoretical physics and the seeming impossibility of keeping up with the literature, he feared himself inadequate for a research career. Falling back upon his journalistic roots, Condon initially took work at the publications bureau for Bell Telephone Laboratories. This industrial experience provided him a first lesson in communicating the significance of physics to management, as he spent the fall of 1927 trying to convince Bell's higher-ups of the importance of Clinton J. Davisson's and Lester H. Germer's in-house experiments on the diffraction of electrons beams by single crystals of nickel. Ten years later, Davisson shared the Nobel Prize in Physics with George P. Thomson for this experimental confirmation of the wave nature of electrons.

Condon's own hiatus from research did not last long. Quantum mechanics was new to the United States, and Condon found himself in great demand as a speaker at various university seminars and colloquia. He soon received half a dozen offers for academic positions, and he joined the physics faculty of Princeton University in 1928. There Condon enjoyed an extremely productive first year that included an elaboration of his earlier work on the Franck-Condon principle as well as the coauthoring, with Philip M. Morse, of *Quantum Mechanics* (1929), the first English-language textbook on the subject. His most important discovery by far, however, was the barrier leakage (often referred to as quantum tunneling) explanation of radioactivity that he and Ronald W. Gurney worked out in 1928. Classical physics could not explain how an alpha particle acquired sufficient energy to overcome the binding forces of the nucleus and be emitted from an atom. By contrast, Gurney and Condon demonstrated that according to the new probabilistic quantum mechanics, an alpha particle had a finite chance of escaping from the nucleus without having to surmount an energy barrier by "leaking" under it through an area of prohibited energies. The two physicists likened the process to that of a ball leaving a valley by "slipping through the mountain" rather than having to climb over the surrounding ranges in order to escape. Soviet physicist George Gamow independently developed the same interpretation of alpha radioactivity, which also explained the fundamentally probabilistic nature of radioactive decay and the wide range of lifetimes observed experimentally for various radioactive nuclei. The Gamow-Condon-Gurney theory of alpha decay soon became famous as the first successful application of quantum mechanics to nuclear phenomena.

Condon was briefly wooed to the University of Minnesota by a full professorship; he spent the 1929–1930 academic year there before returning to what he felt was the livelier intellectual atmosphere of the Physics Department at Princeton. Over the next seven years, he continued to pursue work in nuclear physics, quantum mechanics, and atomic and molecular spectra. In "Theory of Scattering Protons by Protons" (1936), written with Gregory Breit and Richard D. Present, Condon made another important theoretical contribution, this time toward understanding what physicists later called the strong nuclear interaction. By analyzing experimental data on proton-proton scattering from Merle Tuve, Lawrence Hafstad, and Norman Heydenburg at the Carnegie Institution of Washington, Breit, Condon, and Present demonstrated the charge-independence of nuclear forces, namely that proton-proton and proton-neutron nuclear interactions are nearly equal, with differences resulting only from the weaker Coulomb and spin effects. Meanwhile, Condon's interest in atomic spectra led him to produce another classic textbook, *The Theory of Atomic Spectra* (1935), coauthored with George H. Shortley. The Princeton years also witnessed rapid growth in the Condon household with the birth of sons Paul Edward and Joseph Henry. Princeton doctoral students, including Morse and Frederick Seitz, later recalled the warm sociability and hospitality of the Condon home, a large, rambling household with a regular flow of guests located in a less fashionable area of town, in marked contrast to the cold civility that normally dominated life at Princeton.

From Industrial to War Research. Despite his professional achievements, Condon received no rank promotions or salary increases as a faculty member throughout the 1930s, and additionally, as someone used to the relaxed, casual customs of the West, he disliked the atmosphere of snobbery and elitism that he perceived at Princeton. In addition, Karl T. Compton's departure for the Massachusetts Institute of Technology (MIT) in 1930 had left Princeton's Physics Department with a void in leadership, and Condon found the scholarly environment increasingly unsatisfactory. Condon had not forgotten his days at Bell, and he remained interested in industrial physics. When Westinghouse Electric and Manufacturing Company offered him new challenges, a change of scenery, and a much higher salary, he leapt at the oppor-

tunity and moved to Pittsburgh to become Westinghouse's associate director of research in the fall of 1937.

Westinghouse hired Condon as part of an effort to catch up with the likes of General Electric, AT&T, and DuPont by building a strong industrial research program. Under Condon's guidance, Westinghouse established a reputation in nuclear physics, mass spectrometry, and microwave electronics. Using the company's five-million-volt electrostatic generator, physicists in Condon's group measured various light elements' threshold energies for neutron emission when bombarded by protons. After the discovery of nuclear fission by Otto Hahn, Fritz Strassmann, and Lise Meitner in 1938, physicists at Westinghouse discovered the phenomenon of photofission (fission of uranium by gamma ray absorption, rather than neutron bombardment), and they established the neutron energy threshold for the fissioning of U-238. In mass spectrometry, Condon was a pioneer in encouraging the general use of mass spectrometry in industrial science, and he also pushed Westinghouse to develop spectrometers as a commercial product. Condon established a thriving program in microwave research as well, which soon yielded wartime applications.

In addition to implementing an active research agenda, Condon also launched the Westinghouse Research Fellowships, a program modeled on the NRC postdoctoral fellowships and designed to nurture young talent and encourage physicists to consider careers at Westinghouse. World War II brought the fellowship program to a temporary close in 1942, but during its four years of operation under Condon's tenure, it succeeded in training and recruitment. Condon hired some two dozen fellows, and nearly two-thirds of them ultimately accepted full-time employment at Westinghouse.

Condon proved less successful at the business end of industrial science. Westinghouse's roots in a strong engineering tradition meant that its managers had little knowledge of physics and its commercial potential, and Westinghouse generally did a poor job of exploiting its physics research program for commercial purposes. Management's ignorance gave Condon free rein in running his research group, but the company's leadership was often unresponsive to his ideas about commercial applications. Despite his urging, Westinghouse failed to enter the growing market for radioactive isotopes in the 1930s. Condon's efforts to have Westinghouse manufacture and sell portable spectrometers also came to naught. For the most part, during Condon's years at the company, physics research provided Westinghouse with a public image of innovation and cutting-edge science but less in the way of practical applications. The one major exception was the microwave research program, where the pull of World War II and wartime military needs mattered more than managerial strategy. Radar became a major source of revenue, with radar equipment bringing in more than $200 million in sales by the end of 1945.

War mobilization also brought Condon, along with most of the rest of the American physics community, into a new relationship with the state. In 1940, the National Defense Research Committee (NDRC) set up the Radiation Laboratory at MIT in order to pursue research and development of radar. By this time, Westinghouse's program in microwave electronics had already begun to yield major improvements in the performance of the Sperry Gyroscope Company's klystron, and this work led to collaborative efforts with the radar project at MIT. Condon spent much of 1940–1941 shuttling back and forth between Pittsburgh and Cambridge, Massachusetts, as head of Westinghouse's microwave research. Meanwhile, the company cut back on its other scientific programs in order to concentrate on the war effort. Westinghouse shut down its nuclear physics program in 1941 and suspended its research fellowships in 1942.

World War II ushered in the age of prominent advisory positions and high-level government and military contacts that came to define much of physicists' political existence during the Cold War years. Radar quickly drew Condon into this new and evolving era. As war preparedness spread throughout the United States in the summer and fall of 1941, Condon briefly served with Richard C. Tolman and Charles C. Lauritsen on the NDRC's rocket program, from which emerged the California Institute of Technology's Jet Propulsion Laboratory. He was also a member of S-1, the committee set up in 1941 to explore the feasibility of the atomic bomb. Then, in 1943, Condon joined the Manhattan Project as associate director of Los Alamos, the secret New Mexico laboratory led by J. Robert Oppenheimer with the mission of building the atomic bomb. Condon's stint at Los Alamos ended after a disastrous six weeks, but his affiliation with the Manhattan Project continued. At the University of California, Berkeley, Ernest O. Lawrence's Radiation Laboratory was using Westinghouse mass spectrographs in its efforts to purify U-235 through electromagnetic separation. The Westinghouse connection took Condon to Berkeley, where he headed the Theoretical Physics Division at the Radiation Laboratory from August 1943 to February 1945.

The brevity of Condon's tenure at Los Alamos resulted from repeated clashes with General Leslie R. Groves over security restrictions and living conditions on the mesa. Condon found military control and coordination at Los Alamos inadequate in almost every respect, and he challenged Groves on matters ranging from water supply, to schools for the children of laboratory personnel, to secrecy requirements and the policy of compartmentalization. His brief and bitter experience at Los Alamos led

him to develop a healthy disdain for the military's ability to run scientific operations. In later years he liked to regale friends and colleagues with tales that demonstrated the shortcomings of the military mentality, and in public he became a sharp critic of military constraints on scientific research. Groves, for his part, never forgave Condon. In June 1945, just before Condon was about to leave for Moscow as part of an American scientific delegation invited to celebrate the 220th anniversary of the Russian Academy of Sciences, Groves pressured Westinghouse to keep Condon at home, and he had the scientist's passport revoked at the last minute. Condon nearly lost his job because the company feared losing military contracts if it kept him on the payroll, and the incident helped precipitate his move to the National Bureau of Standards (NBS) after the war.

Nuclear Age Politics. After World War II ended with the atomic devastation of Hiroshima and Nagasaki, Americans uneasily contemplated the grim prospect of future conflicts fought with nuclear weapons. Manhattan Project scientists became particularly active participants in the early postwar debate over atomic energy, augmenting their new partnership with the state with attempts at public education and direct political mobilization in what quickly became known as the atomic scientists' movement. Condon eagerly lent his voice and energy to the movement, and he became an outspoken and prominent advocate of civilian and international control of atomic energy. A self-identified liberal with strong civil libertarian leanings, Condon devoted his postwar political exertions to speaking out on issues related to science, namely atomic energy, security and secrecy, and international cooperation in science. As part of the scientists' movement, he worked with physicist Leo Szilard to organize against the May-Johnson bill, a hastily constructed piece of legislation proposed immediately after the war to place atomic energy under strict military control with heavy secrecy requirements. The new connections the atomic scientists forged with Congress soon landed Condon an official position as technical adviser to the Senate Special Committee on Atomic Energy in November 1945. Through Szilard, Condon also met Henry A. Wallace, the secretary of commerce and former vice president of the United States, and Wallace tapped Condon to become the next director of the NBS.

At the end of 1945, the May-Johnson bill was scrapped in favor of the McMahon bill, which placed atomic energy under the purview of the civilian Atomic Energy Commission (AEC). In the spring of 1946, as he and other scientists fought for the McMahon bill, Condon spoke out vigorously about the need to oppose secrecy and promote international cooperation in science. An attitude of openness, Condon argued, not only allowed progress in scientific knowledge but also promoted trust between nations, a sorely needed commodity in a time of growing tension between the United States and the Soviet Union. The military mentality of secrecy, by contrast, led to "suspicion and mistrust," as well as to a misplaced belief that other nations could attain nuclear weapons only through espionage and not their own scientific capacities. Condon urged Americans to "chase this isolationist, chauvinist poison from our minds," reject the military mind-set, and seek international control of atomic energy and international cooperation in science as part of the larger pursuit of world peace (Wang, 1999, p. 22).

Scientists' political mobilization helped ensure passage of the McMahon bill, and President Truman signed the measure, the Atomic Energy Act, into law in August 1946. The exigencies of the Cold War, however, ultimately defeated scientists' hopes that American nuclear policy would focus on peaceful applications, and by the late 1940s, it was clear that the development of nuclear weapons constituted the AEC's top priority. More generally, with funding for basic research in the physical sciences dominated by the AEC and the Office of Naval Research (ONR), the linkages between science and the military strengthened during the cold war years. Under Condon's leadership, the NBS took part in the consolidation of the science-military relationship. Although an opponent of what he saw as a dangerous postwar trend toward militarism in U.S. foreign policy, Condon nevertheless avidly sought military contracts to supplement regular congressional appropriations and expand the bureau's work.

Cold War Federal Science. The National Bureau of Standards was founded in 1901 to establish and maintain physical standards, analyze and test industrial materials, and conduct research related to measurement. As with other government agencies founded in the late-nineteenth and early-twentieth centuries in the United States, the bureau's scientific research functions were largely limited to solving a narrow range of practical problems connected directly to its mission. Nonetheless, by the time Condon became director, the NBS possessed a well-respected record of research in atomic and molecular spectroscopy, metallurgy, organic chemistry, and electrical and high-temperature measurement. Its wartime achievements included the variable-time radio proximity fuse, guided missile development, and work on natural and synthetic rubber, optical glass, and high-frequency radio propagation.

Although only in his early forties, Condon was an elder statesman in American science by the time he took charge at the NBS. He became a member of the National Academy of Sciences in 1944, served as vice president of the American Physical Society in 1945, and became president of the society in 1946. Condon arrived at the

Edward Condon. UNIVERSITY OF COLORADO, PHOTOGRAPHY DEPARTMENT. REPRODUCED BY PERMISSION.

National Bureau of Standards in late 1945 with ambitions of dramatically expanding its research functions and transforming it into a world-class scientific institution. As he attempted to implement this program, however, the bureau faced intense competition from rival visions for postwar science. Some scientists who were traditional conservatives, such as Frank B. Jewett, president of the National Academy of Sciences and former president of Bell Laboratories, distrusted governmental control of science and hoped for a return to the prewar dominance of the private sector—namely, philanthropic foundations and industry—as the primary sponsor of basic research. Most scientists, however, were impressed by their wartime experiences and bullish on the prospects of continued science-state cooperation, and they placed their faith in some kind of statism. Legislative proposals for a National Science Foundation first appeared during the war, and scientists of varying political stripes backed different versions of a government-funded foundation that would support basic research. During the debate over the McMahon bill, the atomic scientists hoped that an AEC under civilian control would provide generous funding for research in nuclear physics and related fields. The military, eager to capitalize on the relationship with science built during the war, also entered the field, and the ONR, established in 1946, quickly became a major supporter of the physical sciences.

In this competitive political environment, Condon's aspirations for the NBS to become a leader in postwar science policy never had much of a chance. Stymied by the narrowly defined mission of its organic act and congressional unwillingness to grant the NBS greater administrative discretion, the bureau lacked the necessary institutional and political support to achieve Condon's aims. Meanwhile, with the legislation for the National Science Foundation tied up in political conflict and with cold war priorities on the upswing, military and defense-related patronage from the ONR and the AEC came to dominate research in the physical sciences. By 1950, when the National Science Foundation was finally established and the organic act of the NBS amended, the vacuum in science funding had long since been filled by defense spending and a military-based political economy for Cold War science.

Although Condon outspokenly criticized what he saw as a dangerously confrontational foreign policy on the part of the United States, he was not so averse to military patronage of science as to forego opportunities for his agency. Under the Manhattan Project, he had sharply attacked military regimentation and the subordination of science to military decision making, but as director of the Bureau of Standards, he exhibited few qualms about seeking defense dollars. Like many physicists, his initial suspicions of military funding eased as he found that ONR and other military patrons seemed to provide generous funding with few strings attached. As Paul Forman, Stuart W. Leslie, and other historians have pointed out, however, this symbiosis of science and state did not leave science independent of military considerations—instead, it subtly redirected the research priorities of the physical sciences toward the needs of the national security state. Under Condon's leadership, the bureau pursued research in materials science, solid state physics, guided missile development, radio wave propagation, and other areas of intense interest to the military. By the time Condon left the NBS in 1951, the die was cast. In 1953, 80 percent of the bureau's budget came from either the Department of Defense or the Atomic Energy Commission.

Cold War Political Persecution. Although Condon managed the Bureau of Standards in a manner consistent with Cold War political orthodoxy, his outspokenness on atomic energy, internationalism, and international cooperation in science led to years of confrontation with the House Committee on Un-American Activities (HUAC), the self-appointed congressional guardian against internal political subversion. Better known for making sensational accusations than carefully investigating actual security threats, HUAC became a powerful symbol of the anti-Communist fervor that swept through U.S. politics and culture in the era of the post–World War II red scare. At the outset of the postwar period, the committee possessed little power or influence. In 1947, HUAC chairman J.

Parnell Thomas latched upon atomic espionage as one of several issues the committee could exploit in order to raise its profile. As part of that effort, in the spring and summer of 1947, Thomas began to attack publicly Condon's political associations and memberships in the American-Soviet Science Society (an organization dedicated to the exchange of published scientific literature) and other supposed communist front organizations. Then, on 1 March 1948, a HUAC subcommittee issued a report that labeled Condon "one of the weakest links in our atomic security" and challenged W. Averell Harriman, Henry A. Wallace's successor as secretary of commerce, to either justify Condon's continued federal employment or fire him (Wang, 1999, p. 132).

HUAC could cite no specific instances of inappropriate actions or violations of the law on Condon's part, and its allegations consisted primarily of insinuations about Condon's political beliefs and associations, particularly his support for international cooperation in science and the open exchange of scientific ideas, which J. Parnell Thomas equated with advocating espionage. Because Condon was a high-level presidential appointee, however, the case constituted serious political business, and it made newspaper headlines across the country. Thus began the most prominent Cold War political attack on an American scientist before the Oppenheimer case of 1954. The Department of Commerce immediately defended Condon by announcing that its loyalty board had cleared the NBS director in late February. (Under the loyalty program created by the Truman administration in March 1947, all federal employees had to undergo loyalty clearance.) Over the next several months, the scientific community rallied behind Condon with statements of support and letters to the White House, and he also received backing from the American Civil Liberties Union, Henry A. Wallace, and U.S. representatives Helen Gahagan Douglas and Chet Holifield from California. The Atomic Energy Commission signaled its endorsement in mid-July, when it upgraded Condon's security clearance from pending to regular status. Then, in September, the president himself demonstrated his outright support. As he prepared to hit the campaign trail, Harry S. Truman shook hands with Condon on stage at the annual meeting of the American Association for the Advancement of Science before delivering a nationally broadcast address in which he slammed attacks on scientists as "unfounded rumors, gossip and vilification" that were "un-American, the most un-American thing we have to contend with today" (Wang, 2001, p. 40).

The atomic scientists feared that HUAC's attack might be the beginning of a renewed assault on civilian control of atomic energy. The AEC, however, enjoyed the protection of the Joint Committee on Atomic Energy, and Thomas could not intrude too far onto the turf of another, more powerful congressional committee. For

HUAC, targeting Condon served more mundane objectives as the committee sought higher appropriations and tried to make political hay during an election year. The furor temporarily died down after two HUAC members lost their reelection bids and Thomas resigned from Congress in disgrace after being indicted for payroll padding.

Yet in the ideologically charged atmosphere of the early Cold War years, when even mildly liberal political views could become pretexts for persecution, Condon remained vulnerable. In April 1951, Richard B. Vail, an obscure, second-term representative from Illinois and a member of HUAC, renewed the committee's earlier charges. At the same time, under a revision in the executive order governing the federal loyalty program, Condon faced a reexamination of his loyalty clearance. Unwilling to undergo another round of wrenching political scrutiny, Condon resigned from the National Bureau of Standards in August to become the director of research and development at Corning Glass Works. There he wanted to delve into solid state physics, and he eventually produced four papers on the physics of the glassy state. Unfortunately for Condon, however, physics no longer offered the retreat from ugly political realities that it had three decades earlier, when he abandoned journalism for college. Vail continued to attack Condon, and in the 1952 election season HUAC subpoenaed him for a hearing. Condon answered all questions and emerged politically unscathed, but he still could not escape from anti-communist political pressures despite his move to the private sector. In 1954, he successfully applied for a security clearance in connection with classified research at Corning, but when the news became public, the secretary of the navy abruptly withdrew his security clearance, apparently at the behest of then vice president Richard M. Nixon, a former member of HUAC.

Condon initially resolved to fight for his security clearance, but frustrated by the seemingly endless battle and the heavy personal toll it extracted, he abandoned the struggle. Instead, he decided to return to university life, but there, too, a powerful academic blacklist affected his prospects. Scared off by Cold War political pressures, both New York University and the University of Pennsylvania turned Condon down for permanent positions. Washington University in St. Louis, however, doggedly refused to cave in to anti-communist orthodoxy. Under the leadership of the physicist and university chancellor Arthur H. Compton, it became somewhat of a refuge for scholars deemed too politically dangerous by other institutions, and after Compton stepped down from his administrative post in 1953, his successor continued the university's vigorous defense of academic freedom. Condon joined Washington University in 1954, and he became chairman of the Physics Department in 1956.

Later Years. Condon did not stay put for long. In 1963, he moved on to a faculty position at the University of Colorado in Boulder, where he also held a position as fellow at the Joint Institute for Laboratory Astrophysics. Although he published few scientific papers during these later years, Condon continued to contribute to the profession as the editor of *Reviews of Modern Physics* from 1957 to 1968, and he also served as president of the American Association of Physics Teachers in 1964. Condon remained politically active as well. During the tumultuous years of the Vietnam War, he served as president of the Society for Social Responsibility in Science in 1968 and 1969 and as national co-chairman of SANE, the Committee for a Sane Nuclear Policy, in 1970. The only flashpoint of controversy came when he agreed to head the Air Force's investigation of unidentified flying objects (UFOs) in the late 1960s. He had no trouble obtaining a security clearance, but the community of UFO believers never forgave his official report, which found no evidence of extraterrestrial visits to Earth. Condon had not lost his sense of humor, and he memorialized his experiences with the project for the *Bulletin of the Atomic Scientists* in an essay puckishly titled, "UFOs I Have Loved and Lost" (1969).

Condon retired in 1970 and thereby brought his long and distinguished career to a close. He had lived through and helped to shape a transformative era in physics, one that witnessed the profound intellectual advances of the quantum revolution as well as the institutional metamorphosis of physics from a largely academic undertaking at the beginning of the century, to the rise of industrial physics in the interwar years, to the large-scale, state-funded enterprise that became post–World War II physics. During the process of institutional transformation, physicists' social and political roles also changed, as the dilemmas of world war and the nuclear age offered physicists public visibility, high-powered advisory positions, and pressing opportunities for grassroots political activism. Condon's life, then, provides a window on the broader history of physics in the United States during the twentieth century.

BIBLIOGRAPHY

Condon's personal papers, a large collection of seventy-five linear feet of material, are held at the American Philosophical Society in Philadelphia. Correspondence relevant to his life and career can be found in a wide range of archival collections besides his own papers. Two of the most important are the Records of the Westinghouse Electric Corporation at the Historical Society of Western Pennsylvania in Pittsburgh, Pennsylvania, and Records of the National Institute of Standards and Technology (formerly the National Bureau of Standards), RG 167, at the National Archives in College Park, Maryland. In addition, Charles Weiner conducted an extensive series of oral history interviews with Condon in the late 1960s and early 1970s. The transcripts are held by the Niels Bohr Library at the American Institute of

Physics, College Park, Maryland. A full bibliography can be found in Philip M. Morse, "Edward Uhler Condon, 1902–1974," Biographical Memoirs *(National Academy of Sciences) 48 (1976). 125–151.*

WORKS BY CONDON

"Nuclear Motions Associated with Electron Transitions in Diatomic Molecules." *Physical Review* 32 (1928): 858–872.

With Ronald W. Gurney. "Wave Mechanics and Radioactive Disintegration." *Nature* 122 (22 September 1928): 439.

With Ronald W. Gurney. "Quantum Mechanics and Radioactive Disintegration." *Physical Review* 33 (1929): 127–140.

With Philip M. Morse. *Quantum Mechanics.* New York: McGraw-Hill, 1929.

With George H. Shortley. *The Theory of Atomic Spectra.* New York: Cambridge University Press, 1935.

With G. Breit and R. D. Present. "Theory of Scattering of Protons by Protons." *Physical Review* 50 (1936): 825–845.

OTHER WORKS

Britten, Wesley E., and Halis Odabasi, eds. *Topics in Modern Physics: A Tribute to Edward U. Condon.* Boulder: Colorado Associated University Press, 1971. Recollections of Condon are in the Preface and Foreword.

Lassman, Thomas C. "Industrial Research Transformed: Edward Condon at the Westinghouse Electric and Manufacturing Company, 1935–1942." *Technology and Culture* 44 (2003): 306–339.

———. "Government Science in Postwar America: Henry A. Wallace, Edward U. Condon, and the Transformation of the National Bureau of Standards, 1945–1951." *Isis* 96 (2005): 25–51.

Morse, Philip M. "Edward Uhler Condon, 1902–1974." *Biographical Memoirs* (National Academy of Sciences) 48 (1976): 125–151. A memorial essay.

Wang, Jessica. *American Science in an Age of Anxiety: Scientists, Anticommunism, and the Cold War.* Chapel Hill: University of North Carolina Press, 1999. Wang has concentrated on Condon's politics, especially his long, drawn-out confrontation with HUAC.

———. "Edward Condon and the Cold War Politics of Loyalty," *Physics Today* 54 (2001): 35–42.

Jessica Wang

CONWAY, ANNE (née Finch) (*b.* Kensington, United Kingdom, 14 December 1631, *d.* Ragley Hall, Warwickshire, United Kingdom, 23 February 1679), *philosophy.*

Conway (née Finch) was the daughter of Sir Heneage Finch and his second wife, Elizabeth Bennett. Born shortly after her father's death, she was the youngest of her father's six surviving children, among whom two of her half brothers had distinguished careers: Heneage Finch

became Lord Chancellor and was created first Earl of Nottingham; Sir John Finch was to serve as British ambassador to the Ottoman Empire. In 1650, she married Edward Conway, who inherited the title of third Viscount Conway in 1655, and was created Earl Conway after her death. The Conways had extensive landed interests in Warwickshire and County Antrim and recovered their political fortunes at the Restoration. Her husband apparently shared her interest in the new philosophy of Descartes. They had one child, Heneage, who died in infancy. Toward the end of her life Anne Conway composed a short treatise, *Principia philosophiae antiquissimae et recentissimae*, which was published anonymously in Latin translation in 1690, and was translated back into English in 1692.

In order to pursue her interests in science and philosophy, Anne Conway had to overcome two major obstacles: As a woman, she was barred from attending university, and severe ill health inhibited her participation in the intellectual debates of her time. However, a combination of fortunate individual circumstances enabled her to overcome these disadvantages. She received tuition in philosophy from England's most prominent enthusiast for Cartesian natural philosophy, Henry More, who became a personal friend. For much of her life she found a sympathetic mentor in her half brother, Sir John Finch, a Paduan-trained anatomist and a Fellow of the Royal Society with strong links to the Accademia del Cimento in Florence. She was conversant with the experimental science of the Royal Society in London, and the debates surrounding it. For example, she knew the writings of Robert Boyle (1627–1691) and was acquainted with one of the society's most acerbic detractors, Henry Stubbe (1632–1676), who was physician to the Conways. It was the visit of the Irish healer Valentine Greatrakes (1628–1682), whom she consulted in 1666, which sparked a controversy about experimental method between Stubbe and members of the Royal Society. Her ill health also brought her into contact with some of the leading medical thinkers of her time: William Harvey, Thomas Willis, and Francis Glisson. She also consulted Francis Mercury van Helmont (1614–1698), son of Jan Baptiste van Helmont, who subsequently became a friend and mentor. She shared van Helmont's interest in kabbalism, and it was through him that she came into contact with Quakerism, to which she converted shortly before her death in 1679.

With its critique of Hobbes, Descartes, Henry More, and Spinoza, Conway's *Principia philosophiae* is situated at the center of philosophical and scientific debates of the seventeenth century. The metaphysical system it propounds anticipates Leibniz (who is known to have read it), while the natural philosophy it contains suggests the influence of Helmontianism. The treatise sets out a tripartite order of being in which all created things derive from

God. Creation is not *ex nihilo* (creation from nothing) but a continuous emanation of God's perfection, effected through the agency of an intermediate species, Middle Nature, which shares properties of both God and creation. As the efficient cause by which God creates things, and the final cause, by which nature is organized for the best, Middle Nature bears resemblance to Henry More's "Spirit of Nature."

According to Anne Conway, the basic "stuff" of creation is an infinity of monads, each of which contains an infinite number of infinitely divisible particles. The monads may be combined in such a way that some groupings take on more corporeal attributes and some retain more spiritlike attributes. All created things are combinations of these spiritlike and bodylike particles, characterized by extension, solidity, and motion. Soul and body are not radically distinct from one another but exist as part of a continuum of substance, all of which is endowed with life and perception. So, whether they are physical objects such as dust and stones, or complex beings such as animals and humans, all things are living organisms. Because all of created nature and its constituents are composed of one substance and are characterized by mutability and perfectibility, it is theoretically possible for one creature to transmute into another. Nevertheless, Anne Conway maintains the integrity of the species of created things. But she does argue that particular creatures may transmute gradually, by successive changes in successive lives: A horse might, by striving to perfect itself within the limits of its species, through successive incarnations, gradually become a man.

Anne Conway's philosophy of nature exhibits some distinctly Helmontian aspects: For example, she shares the Helmontian view that created substance was originally a form of spirit, and accepts that solids originate as fluids, that individual creatures develop from "universal seeds and principles" (*semina et principia*), and that all creatures are composites of active (male) and passive (female) principles. She also utilizes the Helmontian theory of imagination to explain the communication of thoughts and perceptions by the transmission of images. Although she does not employ van Helmont's doctrine of the *archeus*, there are echoes of van Helmont's "*archeus influens*" in her conception of the dominant or "ruling" spirit, which determines the character of the individual creature.

The anonymous publication of Conway's *Principles* means that it is impossible to assess its impact. Only in the late twentieth century has there been any serious interest in the treatise. (Leibniz's copy of the *Principia* is in the collection of his books in Hanover. He was given it by their mutual friend Francis Mercury van Helmont, and knew her authorship because he inscribed it with her name.)

BIBLIOGRAPHY

A complete bibliography is contained in the Hutton biography, cited below. There is no ms of her Principles, *but some letters are extant: Cambridge, Christ's College, MS 21 (Letters of Anne Conway and Henry More); London, British Library MS Additional 23,216 (Letters from Henry More and others); London, British Library MS Additional 23,215 (Letters to Anne Conway from John Finch and Thomas Baines); and London, British Library MS Additional 23,215 (Letters to Anne Conway from Quakers).*

WORKS BY CONWAY

Principiae Philosophiae Antiquissimae & recentissimae de Deo, Christo & Creatura id est de Spiritu & materia in genere. Amsterdam, 1690.

The Principles of the Most Ancient and Modern Philosophy: Concerning God, Christ, and the Creature; That is, concerning Spirit and Matter in General. English translation by "J. C." London, 1692. Modern English translation by Allison P. Coudert and Taylor Corse. Cambridge, U.K.: Cambridge University Press, 1996.

The Conway Letters: The Correspondence of Anne, Viscountess Conway, Henry More and Their Friends, 1642–1684, edited by Marjorie Nicolson, revised by Sarah Hutton. Oxford: Clarendon Press, 1992.

OTHER SOURCES

Hutton, Sarah. *Anne Conway, a Woman Philosopher.* Cambridge, U.K.: Cambridge University Press, 2004.

———. "Of Physic and Philosophy: Anne Conway, Francis Mercury van Helmont and Seventeenth-Century Medicine." In *Religio Medici Medicine and Religion in Seventeenth-Century England,* edited by Andrew Cunningham and O. Grell, pp. 218–246. Aldershot, U.K.: Scholar Press, 1996.

Sarah Hutton

COON, CARLETON STEVENS (*b.* Wakefield, Massachusetts, 23 June 1904; *d.* West Gloucester, Massachusetts, 3 June 1981), *physical anthropology, archaeology, ethnography.*

Coon was a prominent American anthropologist who traveled throughout the world to investigate little-known peoples and their cultures at a period when physical and cultural anthropology were undergoing significant change. He wrote extensively on physical anthropology and conducted many archaeological excavations, but he is best known for his scientific research into the evolution of human races and the biological causes for human racial diversity. His views on race, however, made his opinions and research controversial.

Early Years and Education. Carleton Coon was born in Wakefield, Massachusetts, the son of John Lewis Coon and Bessie Carleton. He was descended from a Cornishman who arrived in the United States in the 1830s, and two of Coon's ancestors fought in the Civil War. His father was a cotton broker, and sometimes during his business trips abroad he would take the young Carleton with him. Some of these early trips were to Egypt, which may have sparked Coon's later interest in Egyptology. Coon attended the prestigious Phillips Academy in Andover, Massachusetts, where he learned to read classical Greek and began to teach himself Egyptian hieroglyphics. He entered Harvard University where he began studying Egyptology with George Reisner, but during his sophomore year he took a course in anthropology taught by Earnest A. Hooton and this led Coon to pursue a degree in anthropology. He graduated magna cum laude from Harvard in 1925 and immediately began his graduate studies there.

Coon traveled to Morocco in 1924 and there he encountered the Rif Berbers who became the subject of his dissertation research. He returned to Morocco the following year to begin his studies of these people, thus beginning a long career of adventurous fieldwork expeditions to exotic places. In 1926 Coon married Mary Goodale, who accompanied her new husband on his fieldwork in North Africa. Coon completed his PhD in 1928 and his dissertation, titled *Tribes of the Rif*, was published in 1931. He became a lecturer in anthropology at Harvard in 1928 but he also continued his anthropological research abroad. He collected information about the warlike Ghegs of northern Albania from 1929 to 1930 and traveled in Ethiopia and Yemen in 1933 and 1934. Coon enjoyed living a life of adventure and danger, and his research and other writings reflect this. In 1932 he published *Flesh of the Wild Ox*, a novel describing his time among the Rif Berbers, which was treated by some anthropologists as an accurate account of Riffian life. Following the success of his first novel Coon wrote a second novel titled *The Riffian* (1933), but few anthropologists took note of this work, and Coon was more explicit that it was partially fictional.

Years at Harvard. Coon was appointed an instructor at Harvard in 1935 and became a professor of anthropology there in 1938. Prompted by his editor, Coon wrote a popular book on anthropological fieldwork titled *Measuring Ethiopia and Flight into Arabia* (1935), in which he described the logistics of his expedition to Ethiopia and Yemen and the problems he encountered in taking anthropometric measurements there. In 1939 he published a reworked version of William Z. Ripley's *The Races of Europe* (originally published in 1899), where he identified seventeen different racial groups in Europe and exam-

ined the craniometric data on European populations. His career was abruptly interrupted, however, by the outbreak of World War II, and in 1941 Coon took a leave of absence from Harvard in order to join the newly formed Office of Coordinator of Information, later renamed the Office of Strategic Services (OSS). He was engaged in espionage and the smuggling of arms to French resistance groups in North Africa. There has even been speculation that Coon was involved in the assassination in 1942 of Vichy Admiral Jean-François Darlan in Aliers (Giles, 1997; 1999). Coon returned to the United States in 1943 and received a commission as a major in the U.S. Army, and when he was discharged in 1945 he received the Legion of Merit. He was also made a *membre d'honneur* of the Association de la Libération Française du 8 Novembre 1942 by the French government.

Interests in Archaeology. Coon returned to Harvard after the war, but in 1948 he accepted a position as professor of anthropology at the University of Pennsylvania and also became curator of ethnology at the University of Pennsylvania Museum. Whereas much of his research thus far had been in physical anthropology, Coon expanded into archaeology as well. He had conducted an excavation in caves near Tangiers in Morocco in 1939 where he unearthed a Neanderthal maxillary bone, and he returned to the site in 1947 with a team of Harvard archaeologists led by Hugh Hencken. Over the next ten years Coon conducted excavations at Paleolithic and Neolithic sites in Iraq (1948), Iran (1949 and 1951), Afghanistan (1954), and Syria (1955) with researchers from the University of Pennsylvania Museum. Coon was one of the first anthropologists to use the newly developed radiocarbon (carbon-14) dating method to date the artifacts found at Belt Cave in Iran. These incursions into archaeology led Coon to publish *The Seven Caves* in 1957, a popular account of his excavations of prehistoric humans sites. Coon's interest in and extensive knowledge of human prehistory led to the installation in 1949 of a Hall of Man exhibit at the University of Pennsylvania Museum, where he depicted the evolution of humans and the development of human culture in prehistory. In 1959 he traveled to Tierra del Fuego with a team of physiologists to study how the local peoples had adapted to be able to endure such a cold environment while wearing very little clothing. During one of his last archaeological expeditions, where he excavated a cave at Yengema in Sierra Leone in 1965, almost a thousand Paleolithic and Neolithic implements were found.

Human Evolution. The question of human racial diversity was a prominent scientific subject for Coon, and during the 1950s he published widely on the question of race and its biological foundations. Like many anthropologists of this generation, Coon sought a Darwinian explanation

Carleton Coon. AP IMAGES.

Coon's ideas about the origin of human races were influenced by the polycentric hypothesis of the German physical anthropologist Franz Weidenreich, who had supervised excavations of *Homo erectus* fossils from the site of Zhoukoudian in China in the 1930s. According to Weidenreich, geographical isolation had led different populations of *Homo erectus* in Asia to develop distinct racial features, and because these populations were sedentary these racial groups had persisted for very long periods of time. Weidenreich argued, like Coon, that these racially and geographically distinct populations of *Homo erectus* had then evolved into *Homo sapiens* while retaining their racial characteristics. However, whereas Weidenreich argued that the geographical isolation of these different races was not complete and that some exchange of genes did occur between groups, thus insuring that humans remained one single species, Coon seemed to allow for much less genetic exchange between populations, thus making the human races more separate. For this reason Coon's conception of human evolution is sometimes called the "candelabra model," because several distinct races branch off from an original ancestral species and continue forward in time with little biological contact with one another.

Weidenreich and Coon's conception of human evolution fit very well with the prevailing notions of evolution in populations promoted by supporters of the modern evolutionary synthesis such as Ernst Mayr, professor of biology at Harvard, and George Gaylord Simpson, professor of paleontology and the American Museum of Natural History. However, Coon's ideas did not sit well with the prevailing political and social attitudes of the day, which had begun to downplay the significance of the concept of race in the aftermath of World War II and the civil rights movement. Even more controversial was Coon's suggestion that the different racial groups present in *Homo erectus* evolved into modern *Homo sapiens* at different times, thus explaining why some racial groups were culturally less advanced than others. Coon argued from the evolution of increased brain size that the Caucasoids had evolved into modern humans first, followed by the Mongoloids, Congoids, Capoids, and lastly the Australoids. This unfortunately implied that the darker-skinned races were not as evolutionarily advanced as the lighter-skinned peoples of the world. This has led many readers of Coon's work to suppose that Coon harbored racist sentiments and that he even condoned racism, but the matter is hardly as simple as that and Coon's thoughts on race and racism are much more complex and nuanced than his critics allow. The book did spark considerable controversy both within the anthropological community and among the broader public. Coon later backed away from some of the ideas expressed in this book, yet he did succeed in

for racial variation in humans. Coon's collaboration with the anthropologist Stanley Garn and biologist Joseph Birdsell on *Races: A Study of the Problems of Race Formation in Man* (1950) was an early example of Coon's attempt to explain human racial differences on the basis of adaptations to environmental conditions. This work had a considerable influence on the development of the "new physical anthropology" that was just emerging at this time through the efforts of people such as Sherwood Washburn, who were trying to apply the principles of the modern evolutionary synthesis to the problems of physical anthropology. Coon addressed the broad issue of human evolution in *The Story of Man* (1954), where he traced the causes of human biological and cultural changes from the Pleistocene to the present.

His most comprehensive work on the subject, however, was *The Origin of Races* (1962). In this work Coon assembled material from cultural and physical anthropology, linguistics, and human paleontology to argue that the five major races of humans (Caucasoids, Mongoloids, Congoids, Capoids, and Australoids) had existed for at least half a million years. On the basis of fossil evidence Coon suggested that these racial divisions existed before the evolution of modern *Homo sapiens* and were observable already in *Homo erectus*.

showing that race could be studied using evolutionary biology and the hominid fossil record.

Coon returned to the problem of human races in 1965 with *The Living Races of Man*, written in collaboration with the anthropologist Edward Hunt, which examined physiological adaptation in human populations. This work generated considerably less controversy than *The Origin of Races* and once again argued that evolutionary biology could be productively applied to explaining the origin of human racial diversity. Coon's final work on the topic of human races, *Racial Adaptations: A Study of the Origins, Nature, and Significance of Racial Variations in Humans* (1982), was published the year after his death and marks the culmination of his work on the subject. The work repeats many of the ideas presented in his earlier books, but Coon did introduce new data derived from recent biochemical research. Although much of his research focused on the problem of the evolution and physical characteristics of the human races, Coon continued to write popular books on cultural anthropology. *Caravan: The Story of the Middle East* (1951) introduced readers to the Islamic peoples of the Middle East, and *The Hunting Peoples* (1971) discussed the existing hunting and gathering cultures of the world.

Later Years. Coon's marriage with Mary ended in divorce in 1944, and in 1945 he married Lisa Dougherty Geddes, a cartographer; she drew many of the maps that appear in Coon's later books. He received many honors during his long career, including the Viking Fund Medal and Award in Physical Anthropology in 1951 and the Athenaeum Literary Award in 1962. He was a fellow of the American Academy of Arts and Sciences and was elected to the National Academy of Sciences in 1955. He was a member of the American Anthropological Association and the American Association of Physical Anthropologists, where he served as president from 1962 to 1963 but resigned over the controversy raised by issues surrounding his book *The Origin of Races*. Coon was a member of Sigma Xi and was belatedly made a member of Phi Beta Kappa in 1950 on the occasion of his twenty-fifth class reunion.

Coon retired from his position at the University of Pennsylvania in 1963 and moved to West Gloucester, Massachusetts, although he continued to travel and to publish extensively. He became a research associate in ethnology at the Peabody Museum at Harvard in 1968. In 1980 Coon published *A North African Story*, a memoir recounting his activities as an OSS agent during World War II. The manuscript was written in 1943 but could not be published at the time due to the sensitive material it contained. Here Coon describes his wartime adventures and demonstrates how his experience as an anthropologist in Morocco proved to be invaluable preparation for his

successful operation in German-occupied North Africa. The year after the publication of *A North African Story*, Coon's autobiography appeared. In *Adventures and Discoveries* (1981) Coon describes his early life in Massachusetts, his writings and museum exhibits, his numerous appearances between 1952 and 1957 on the popular CBS television program *What in the World*, where he discussed archaeology and anthropology, and his thoughts about his scientific career.

BIBLIOGRAPHY

The C. S. Coon Papers are in the National Anthropological Archives, National Museum of Natural History, Smithsonian Institution, Washington, D.C. The C. S. Coon Correspondence in Expedition Records–Near East is held in the University Museum Archives, University of Pennsylvania, Philadelphia. C. S. Coon Correspondence is in the library of the American Philosophical Society, Philadelphia.

WORKS BY COON

Tribes of the Rif. Cambridge, MA: Harvard African Studies, 1931.

Flesh of the Wild Ox: A Riffian Chronicle of High Valleys and Long Rifles. New York: William Morrow, 1932.

The Riffian. Boston: Little, Brown, 1933.

Measuring Ethiopia and Flight into Arabia. Boston: Little, Brown, 1935.

The Races of Europe. New York: Macmillan, 1939.

The Mountains of Giants: A Racial and Cultural Study of the North Albanian Mountain Ghegs. Cambridge, MA: Peabody Museum, 1950.

With Stanley M. Garn and Joseph B. Birdsell. *Races: A Study of the Problems of Race Formation in Man.* Springfield, IL: Charles C. Thomas, 1950.

Caravan: The Story of the Middle East. New York: Holt, 1951.

The Story of Man. New York: Knopf, 1954; rev. ed., 1962.

The Seven Caves. New York: Knopf, 1957.

The Origin of Races. New York: Knopf, 1962.

As editor, with Edward E. Hunt. *Anthropology A to Z.* New York: Grosset & Dunlap, 1963.

With Edward E. Hunt. *The Living Races of Man.* New York: Knopf, 1965.

The Hunting Peoples. Boston: Little, Brown, 1971.

A North Africa Story: The Anthropologist as OSS Agent, 1941–1943. Ipswich, MA: Gambit, 1980.

Adventures and Discoveries: The Autobiography of Carleton S. Coon. Englewood Cliffs, NJ: Prentice-Hall, 1981.

Racial Adaptations: A Study of the Origins, Nature, and Significance of Racial Variations in Humans. Chicago: Nelson-Hall, 1982.

OTHER SOURCES

"Coon, Carleton Stevens." In *The National Cyclopaedia of American Biography.* Vol. 1 (1953–1959), pp. 108–109. New York: J. T. White, 1960.

Giles, Eugene. "Coon, Carleton S(tevens) (1904–1981)." In *History of Physical Anthropology: An Encyclopedia*, edited by Frank Spencer. New York: Garland, 1997.

———. "Coon, Carleton Stevens." In *American National Biography*, edited by John A. Garraty and Mark C. Carnes. Vol. 5, pp. 429–431. New York: Oxford University Press, 1999.

Howells, William W. "Carleton Stevens Coon." In *Biographical Memoirs* (National Academy of Sciences). Vol. 58, pp. 109–130. Washington, DC: National Academies Press, 1989.

Hunt, Edward E. "Carleton Stevens Coon: 1904–1981." *American Journal of Physical Anthropology* 58 (1982): 239–241.

Jackson, John P. "'In Ways Unacademical': The Reception of Carleton S. Coon's *The Origin of Races*." *Journal of the History of Biology* 34 (2001): 247–285.

Schmidt, Nancy J. "Carleton Coon: A Pioneer in Anthropological Literary Genres." *Anthropology and Humanism Quarterly* 10 (1985): 40–45.

Matthew R. Goodrum

COPERNICUS, NICHOLAS (*b.* Toruń, Poland, 19 February 1473; *d.* Frauenburg [Frombork], Poland, 24 May 1543), *astronomy, cosmology.* For the original article on Copernicus see *DSB,* vol. 3.

Scientists value accuracy, precision, consistency, coherence, and other like characteristics. There was not a great deal that Nicholas Copernicus contributed or, arguably, could have contributed to the greater factual accuracy and precision of astronomy. But inconsistencies and the incoherence of geocentric astronomy motivated him and eventually led him to propose the motions of Earth and of all the planets around the sun. His detailed effort to construct a planetary, heliostatic system with Earth in motion around the Sun may be seen properly as having inaugurated a revolution in cosmology. The resulting astronomical system, however, remained conservative, largely dependent on Ptolemy and other geocentric mathematical astronomers for the construction of models that were designed to preserve the ancient axiom regarding the perfectly uniform, circular motions of the heavenly bodies. This postscript focuses on revisions to Copernicus's biography and to accounts of his education, books that he owned or used, path to the heliocentric theory, and his revision and adaptation of Aristotelian natural philosophy to heliocentrism.

Accounts of His Education. The details of Copernicus's biography have undergone some revision although accounts of his life sometimes have been held hostage to the provincial or nationalistic sentiments of some contem-

poraries and later scholars. Still, such biases motivated biographers to search for documents that have contributed to a fuller picture of his life and work. There is little doubt now that Copernicus's principal vernacular language was German, the commercial language of many of the towns along the Vistula River. The records of his administrative duties in Varmia in northeastern Poland suggest, however, that he knew more Polish than earlier experts were willing to concede. On some occasions, he may even have served as an interpreter between German and Polish-speaking representatives to meetings involving diplomatic negotiations between officials of Varmia, the Polish crown, and the Teutonic Knights.

Such possibilities to the contrary notwithstanding, Copernicus wrote some letters and reports in German, and all of his works on astronomy in Latin with occasional remarks in Greek. He devoted much time and effort to mastering technical details of astronomy and learning Greek so that he could consult ancient authorities where Latin translations were either unavailable or unreliable. Educated in a scholastic-humanist environment, he perceived problems that he thought he could solve by discovering errors, removing inconsistencies, and constructing an alternative but equally competent mathematical system.

Scholars assume that Copernicus received an education in the liberal arts at Kraków, but they tend to be vague or incomplete about what such an education entailed. Like most medieval universities, Kraków required students to attend the equivalent of eight classes on logic including lectures and exercises. Aside from learning the technicalities of valid reasoning, students also received instruction in how to construct arguments and recognize fallacies. The university curriculum additionally placed great emphasis on natural philosophy by means of lectures on Aristotle's treatises on physics and cosmology. Kraków was exceptional in offering extensive instruction on mathematical subjects with special emphasis on astronomy and astrology. There is no doubt that Copernicus learned the fundamentals of astronomy and geometry at Kraków, for while a student at the university (1491–1495) he purchased books containing the Alfonsine Tables and a copy of a Latin translation of Euclid's *Elements*. Scholars also introduced humanism at Kraków in the fifteenth century, and influenced Copernicus to develop his interest in the examination of ancient astronomy and mathematics. Although Kraków was propitious for the learning of fundamentals, Copernicus recognized that he would be able to advance his interests and career further only by completing his studies in Italy.

His uncle, the Bishop of Varmia, helped to arrange an ecclesiastical position for Copernicus that would provide the income needed to study law at Bologna. When he went there in 1496, Copernicus met Domenico Maria Novara, an astronomer who had links to the great fifteenth-century humanist-astronomer Regiomontanus. According to one source, Copernicus resided with Novara and assisted him in his astronomical observations. While in Bologna, Copernicus also began to study Greek, a language that he learned primarily, however, by translating a collection of letters that a friend arranged to have published in 1509.

His Sources. By 1500 Copernicus evidently had completed his formal instruction in the law, and he visited Rome during the Jubilee Year. He gave a lecture on mathematics, but unfortunately nothing is known about the details. He returned briefly to Varmia in 1501 to obtain permission to study medicine for two years. Copernicus went to the University of Padua where he evidently concentrated on that part of the curriculum concerned with practical medicine, especially diagnosis and the preparation of drugs. He left Padua without a degree, for which he would have required a third year. It was probably during those last two years that he acquired many of the books that he later used in Varmia. With his permitted time about to elapse, he went to the University of Ferrara in 1503, where two professors at the university prepared him for an examination in canon law. Copernicus passed the examination on the first try, returned to Varmia with his doctorate in canon law, and almost immediately joined the retinue of his uncle at the episcopal residence in Lidzbark Warmiński. He remained there until 1510.

During those seven years Copernicus found the time to work his way through several of the books that he had purchased in Italy, and also consulted books in the collection of the episcopal library. The most important by far was Regiomontanus's *Epitome* of Ptolemy's *Almagest.* Relying on Cardinal Bessarion's defense of Plato, Giorgio Valla's encyclopedia, Pliny's *Natural History*, and other works, Copernicus undertook the study that led him, probably around 1508 or 1509, to the heliocentric cosmology and his first sketch of the system, the *Commentariolus,* completed by 1514 at the latest.

Understanding His Cosmology. Copernicus's path to a heliocentric cosmology is a matter of speculation. Some scholars believe that a mathematical analysis of models and technical details led him to his theory. Others believe that more qualitative and relatively less technical considerations led him to the conclusion that the celestial spheres of ancient Aristotelian cosmology and ancient astronomy could be ordered uniformly only by imagining Earth with its Moon in motion around the Sun. Transforming that solution into a technically competent system

required several decades to accomplish, and the final results were not altogether satisfactory.

Whichever scenario one prefers, everyone agrees that Copernicus depended heavily on his predecessors, astronomical tables, Regiomontanus, Giorgio Valla, and, after 1515, Ptolemy's own book in a printed Latin translation with its observations to accomplish his reformation or restoration of ancient astronomy. The principal goal or task of that tradition was to construct models that preserved the perfectly uniform, circular motions of the celestial spheres while agreeing with the observations within the then limits of accuracy. The goal, it turns out, was unachievable. That fact to the contrary notwithstanding, Copernicus's effort persuaded Michael Mästlin, Johannes Kepler, and Galileo Galilei, among others, that his cosmological solution was correct. This conviction spurred them to complete what Copernicus had begun.

The details, of course, fascinate experts. For purposes of clarification and accuracy, it is necessary to distinguish between Copernicus's vision and astronomers' modern understanding. Copernicus accepted the ancient idea that planets are attached to or embedded in spheres. They do not float through space. The spheres support, contain, and move the planets. He was silent on the separate questions about the nature of the spheres and whether or not they are solid or hard. Spheres or orbs were considered to be three-dimensional bodies (whatever their nature), and so were solid in the same abstract sense in which any three-dimensional body is said to be a solid, but Copernicus did not elaborate. By assuming celestial spheres as the carriers of the planets, Copernicus committed himself to some features of Aristotle's conception of the heavens. He knew that he had to justify his departures from Aristotle, which he did by constructing a number of arguments that relied on standard techniques of medieval logic and on other ancient authors, especially Pliny, Cicero, and a Greek dictionary known as the *Suidae lexicon.*

Some later authors were persuaded by such arguments, but for about a century most could not overcome the arguments based on common sense, and so they judged his theory to be absurd. The principal objections were physical. How is it possible for Earth to move so rapidly and its motion be insensible and imperceptible?

His Motivation. What motivated Copernicus to discover and then propose an idea that he could expect nearly everyone to reject? There are generally two approaches to this question, as briefly mentioned above. Some distinguish between Copernicus's cosmological theory and his technical, mathematical system. According to the first, numerous inconsistencies in the ancient-medieval astronomical-cosmological tradition troubled Copernicus. For example, why are the planets arranged around Earth

Nicholas Copernicus. SCIENCE SOURCE / PHOTO
RESEARCHERS, INC.

according to two different principles? Mercury and Venus
move with the Sun, and so both have a zodiacal period of
one year. This fact also supported three alternative order-
ings of Mercury and Venus—between Earth and the Sun
(Ptolemy), around the Sun (Martianus Capella), and
beyond the Sun (Plato). Mars, Jupiter, and Saturn were
placed beyond the Sun in that order, according to their
sidereal periods. On this reading, Copernicus assumed that
the planets should be ordered according to one principle.
The Capellan arrangement probably inspired him to consider ordering all of the planets around the Sun, placing
Earth with its Moon in orbit to fill the large gap between
Venus and Mars. His calculation of the sidereal periods of
Mercury and Venus would have confirmed their ordering,
thus working out a unique arrangement of all of the planets ordered according to a single principle, sidereal periods.

Those who favor the second approach point to the fact
that Copernicus was working with mathematical models
and studying Regiomontanus's *Epitome.* Among Copernicus's books (now mostly at Uppsala University Library) is a
codex that contains notes, tables, and the results of calculations in Copernicus's own hand. One set of numbers in particular provides clues about how Copernicus transformed
Ptolemy's geocentric models into the heliocentric ones
found in *Commentariolus.* He may have been inspired by

two propositions in the *Epitome* to recognize a geo-heliocentric and a strictly heliocentric conversion of Ptolemy's
models. On this reading, he would have rejected the geo-
heliocentric alternative because it entails the intersection of
the spheres of Mars and the Sun, an unacceptable alternative, and so would have settled on the heliocentric conversion. There seems to be little question in the early
twenty-first century that Copernicus did rely on those two
propositions in the *Epitome* to convert the models, but he
may not have recognized that possibility until after he had
already formulated the heliocentric theory. Unfortunately,
his copy of the *Epitome* has disappeared.

His first effort with double-epicycle models for the
planets and the Moon later gave way to the mature presentation in *De revolutionibus.* Earth orbited by the Moon
on a double-epicycle circles the mean sun (eccentric to the
true or apparent Sun). Each of the superior planets moves
on a small epicycle around the center of Earth's orbit,
eccentric models describe the motions of the inferior planets. In addition, following Ptolemy, he also provided separate accounts for the motions of the planets in latitude.
Many subsequent astronomers admired the mathematics
and used the models without adopting Copernicus's physical assumptions about the motions of Earth.

Copernicus and his genuine followers were convinced
of the truth of his system for primarily four reasons. First,
his arrangement of the planets yields a natural explanation
for the observation of the bounded elongations of Mercury and Venus. Second, the motion of Earth explains the
observation of the retrograde motions of all of the planets
as an optical illusion. The third reason is the ordering of
the planets around the sun according to sidereal periods;
Copernicus was most proud of this result. The fourth, following on the third, is the ability to estimate the relative
linear distances of the planets from the Sun, and in this
respect the calculations based on Copernicus's numbers
are very close to the modern ratios.

The theory had disadvantages, of course. There were
principally four. The first is the absence of a coherent
physical theory to account for the motions of Earth. The
second is the failure to observe stellar parallax, a consequence that should follow from Earth's annual orbit but
which is unobservable with the naked eye. The third
includes a number of mathematical weaknesses, such as
problems with the measurement of the Sun's eccentricity,
the need to use epicycles, and the construction of models
that contain a hidden equant. Finally, the heliocentric theory contradicted some passages of the Bible literally interpreted. For one or all of these reasons, most astronomers
and philosophers rejected the theory for several decades.

His Ideas in Natural Philosophy. Scholars also disagree
about Copernicus's ideas in natural philosophy. What he

says is very sketchy, making it necessary to reconstruct his intentions. Some believe that he merely revised Aristotelian principles, adapting them to heliocentrism. Others have demonstrated his reliance on other ancient authorities, and argue that his views derive from Neoplatonic and Stoic sources. Copernicus's arguments in *De revolutionibus*, Preface and Book I, seem intended to persuade Aristotelians to reexamine their assumptions about the simple motions of simple natural elemental bodies, and to recognize that several problems remained unsolved. For that reason some scholars, while acknowledging that Copernicus relied on Neoplatonic and Stoic sources, believe that he used them in conjunction with his reading of Aristotle, and perhaps scholastic commentaries reported and developed at Kraków, to fashion a sketchy account that was sufficiently and superficially Aristotelian enough to allay the anticipated rejection. The strategy failed in part because of a "Letter" added anonymously by Andreas Osiander right after the title page. Osiander advocated a strictly mathematical interpretation of the hypotheses and rejection of any physical interpretation.

For several decades many readers believed that Copernicus himself wrote the "Letter." Whatever Osiander's intention may have been, many astronomers found the approach congenial with their own views about astronomy and their equally firm conviction about a geocentric cosmos. It is impossible to say whether the strategy rescued Copernicus's book and the theory from immediate and wholesale condemnation. His few supporters were spared official censure for several decades. Ironically, by the time church and theological authorities censured the work, evidence in support of the theory was growing. The publication of Kepler's tables (1627) virtually assured that practicing astronomers would find it more difficult than before to separate the observational consequences from the models and hypotheses on which they were based, especially in Kepler's corrected version of the heliocentric theory.

Whether Copernicus ever saw what Osiander had done is unknown. In 1543 when the book appeared he was near death, perhaps in a coma, when Rheticus brought a copy to him. Recent investigations by Polish scholars have also shed light on Copernicus's death and burial. Excavation of the cathedral where he was buried has unearthed what the investigating scientists believe to be Copernicus's remains. By means of forensic reconstruction they have generated an image of Copernicus's head and face at the time of his death. By the mid-seventeenth century Copernicus became an icon for the lone scientist standing against what the world regards as common sense and for the courageous exercise of imagination in pursuit of the truth. In his own mind and words, he saw himself as having tried to restore and achieve the goals of ancient astronomy. Indeed, as an astronomer he was a conserva-

tive, but that cannot undo the fact, also contrary to his intention perhaps, that he introduced a revolution in cosmology that in turn contributed to the rise of modern science, a consequence that some refer to as the scientific revolution.

SUPPLEMENTARY BIBLIOGRAPHY

There are two modern editions of Copernicus's works, one of which is also issuing parallel volumes with translations in several modern languages.

WORKS BY COPERNICUS

Locationes mansorum desertorum. Edited by Marian Biskup. Olsztyn, Poland: Pojeziere, 1970. Copernicus's record of abandoned farmsteads in Varmia.

Three Copernican Treatises. Translated by Edward Rosen. 3rd ed., revised. New York: Octagon Books, 1971. Contains translations of *Commentariolus*, *Letter against Werner*, and Rheticus's *First Report* (*Narratio prima*), and a biography of Copernicus with annotated bibliography.

Opera omnia. 4 vol. Vols. 1–2, and 4: Warsaw: Polish Scientific Publishers, 1973–1992. Volume 1 is a photographic copy of Copernicus's manuscript. Volume 2 is the critical edition. Jerzy Dobrzycki completed the edition of *Commentariolus* for volume 3, but it has yet to appear in print. Volume 4 contains facsimiles of manuscripts of Copernicus's minor works.

Nicolaus Copernicus Gesamtausgabe. 9 vols. Vols. 1–2, edited by Heribert M. Nobis and Bernhard Sticker. Hildesheim, Germany: H.A. Gerstenberg, 1974–1984. Vol. 3, edited by Heribert M. Nobis; vol. 5, edited by Heribert M. Nobis and Menso Folkerts; vol. 6, edited by Menso Folkerts; vols. 8–9, Berlin: Akademie Verlag, 1994–2004. The critical edition of *Commentariolus* will appear in volume 4. No information is available on volume 7. A brief historical summary of the project is available from http://www.geschichte.uni-muenchen.de/wug/gnw/coped.shtml (in German).

On the Revolutions of the Heavenly Spheres. Translated by Alistair Matheson Duncan. New York: Barnes and Noble, 1976. Preferred by some experts over Rosen's translation.

Complete Works. 4 vols. The first volume, as in the modern Latin editions, is a photographic copy of Copernicus's manuscript. Vol. 2, *On the Revolutions*, edited by Jerzy Dobrzycki, translated by Edward Rosen with commentary. Warsaw: Polish Scientific Publishers; London: Macmillan, 1978. Also published Baltimore, MD, and London: Johns Hopkins University, 1978, reissued 1992. Vol. 3, *Minor Works*, edited by Paweł Czartoryski, translated with commentary by Edward Rosen and Erna Hilfstein. Warsaw: Polish Scientific Publishers; London: Macmillan, 1985. Reissued, Baltimore, MD, and London: Johns Hopkins University, 1992. Volume 3 contains Rosen's revised translation of *Commentariolus*, and supersedes the translation in *Three Copernican Treatises*. The *Commentariolus* was also translated by Noel Swerdlow (1973) but embedded in a commentary for which it is primarily important. Vol. 4, *The Manuscripts of Nicholas Copernicus' Minor Works Facsimiles*, edited by Paweł Czartoryski. Warsaw: Polish Scientific Publishers, 1992.

OTHER SOURCES

Birkenmajer, Aleksander. *Études d'histoire des sciences en Pologne, Studia Copernicana*, Vol. 4. Wrocław, Poland: Polish Academy of Sciences, 1972. Articles and French translations of papers first written in Polish.

———. "Commentary." In Nicolaus Copernicus, *Opera omnia*, Vol. 2. Warsaw: Polish Scientific Publishers, 1975. The authoritative Polish commentary written in Latin on Book I of *De revolutionibus*.

Birkenmajer, Ludwik Antoni. *Mikołaj Kopernik.* Kraków, Poland: Skad Gowny w Ksiegarni Spoki Wydawniczej Polskie, Skład Główny w Księgarni Spółki Wydawniczej Poslkir, 1900. Materials toward a biography of Copernicus that Birkenmajer never wrote and that contains indispensable details and references. A partial and rough English translation was supervised by Jerzy Dobrzycki and Owen Gingerich (1976).

———. *Stromata Copernicana.* Kraków, Poland: Nakładem Polskiej adademji umiejętnosci, Nakładem Polskiej akademji umiejętności, 1924. Another indispensable and somewhat more synthetic collection of chapters related to Copernicus's education and works.

Biskup, Marian, ed. *Regesta Copernicana.* Translated by Stanisław Puppel. Studia Copernicana, Vol. 8. Wroclaw, Poland: Zakład Naradovy, 1973. Chronology of documents related to Copernicus's family and career. The English version adds a few documents to the Polish version.

———. "Biography and Social Background of Copernicus." In *Nicholas Copernicus, Quincentenary Celebrations, Final Report*, edited by Zofia Wardęska. Studia Copernicana, Vol. 17. Wrocław, Poland: Polish Academy of Sciences, 1977, pp. 137–152. Important reflections by a leading Polish historian.

Clutton-Brock, Martin. "Copernicus's Path to His Cosmology: An Attempted Reconstruction." *Journal for the History of Astronomy* 36 (2005): 197–216. Important review that amplifies Swerdlow's analysis (1973).

Curtze, Maximilian. *Reliquiae Copernicanae.* Leipzig, Germany: B.G. Teubner, 1875. Important documents by one of the earliest Copernican scholars who examined the collection of Copernicana at Uppsala University Library.

———, ed. *Mitteilungen des Coppernicus-Vereins für Wissenschaft und Kunst zu Thorn.* Several volumes issued between 1878 and 1882 that contain editions and studies on Copernicus. Snabrück, Germany, 1878–1882.

Czartoryski, Paweł. "The Library of Copernicus." *Studia Copernicana* (1978): 354–396. Indispensable foundational study of the books that Copernicus owned or used. Corrects many of Ludwik Birkenmajer's attributions.

Di Bono, Mario. "Copernicus, Amico, Fracastoro and Tusi's Device: Observations on the Use and Transmission of a Model." *Journal for the History of Astronomy* 26 (1995): 133–154. Challenges the standard orthodoxy about Copernicus's reliance on Arabic predecessors.

Dobrzycki, Jerzy. "Commentary." In Nicolaus Copernicus, *Opera omnia*, Vol. 2. Warsaw: Polish Scientific Publishers, 1975. The authoritative Polish commentary written in Latin on Books II–VI of *De revolutionibus*.

Dobrzycki, Jerzy, and Owen Gingerich, eds. *Nicholas Copernicus: Studies on the Works of Copernicus and Biographical Materials.* Ann Arbor, Michigan: Bell and Howell Learning and Information (formerly University Microfilms International), 1976. Translation of several important chapters of Ludwik Birkenmajer's *Mikołaj Kopernik*.

Evans, James. *The History and Practice of Ancient Astronomy.* New York: Oxford University Press, 1998. Outstanding introduction to the field.

Fiszman, Samuel, ed. *The Polish Renaissance in Its European Context.* Bloomington: Indiana University, 1988. Important collection of papers, some of which are on Copernicus and his background.

Gąssowski, Jerzy, ed. *Poszukiwanie Grobu Mikołaja Kopernika, Castri Dominae Nostrae Litterae Annales.* Vol. 2. Pułtusk, Poland: Baltic Research Center in Frombork, 2005. Results of most recent research on Copernicus's burial place and on the forensic analysis of his presumed remains. For images of the reconstruction of Copernicus's head and face, see http://archeologia.ah.edu.pl/Frombork_eng.html.

Gierowski, Józef, ed. *The Kraków Circle of Nicholas Copernicus.* Translated by Janina Ozga. Copernicana Cracoviensia, Vol. 3. Kraków, Poland: Jagiellonian University Press, 1973. Articles on Copernicus's teachers and fellow students.

Gingerich, Owen. *The Eye of Heaven: Ptolemy, Copernicus, Kepler.* New York: American Institute of Physics, 1993. Studies on Copernicus and his reception.

———. "The Copernican Quinquecentennial and Its Predecessors." In *Commemorative Practices in Science: Historical Perspectives on the Politics of Collective Memory*, edited by Pnina Abir-Am and Clark Elliott. *Osiris*, second series, 14 (1999): 37–60. A witty guide to the history of Copernican celebrations and scholarship through 1973.

———. *An Annotated Census of Copernicus' De Revolutionibus (Nuremberg, 1543 and Basel 1566).* Leiden, Netherlands: Brill, 2002. Indispensable for studying the reception of the Copernican theory.

———. "Supplement to the Copernican *Census*." *Journal for the History of Astronomy* 37 (2006): 232. Announces that Brill will issue a corrected reprint that will update some entries and add a total of twenty-two copies.

Goddu, André. "The Logic of Copernicus's Arguments and His Education in Logic at Cracow." *Early Science and Medicine* 1 (1996): 26–68.

———. "Copernicus's Annotations—Revisions of Czartoryski's 'Copernicana.'" *Scriptorium* 58 (2004): 202–226, with eleven plates. Corrects Czartoryski (1978), provides a detailed description of Copernicus's hand, proposes one addition to the authentic Copernicana, and verifies another.

———. "Hypotheses, Spheres, and Equants in Copernicus's *De revolutionibus*." In *Les éléments paradigmatiques thématiques et stylistiques dans la pensée scientifique*, edited by Bennacer el Bouazzati. Casablanca: Najah El Jadida, 2004, pp. 71–95. Attempts to resolve disputes among the experts.

———. "Reflections on the Origin of Copernicus's Cosmology." *Journal for the History of Astronomy* 37 (2006): 37–53. Orders the stages in Copernicus's discovery.

Goldstein, Bernard. "Copernicus and the Origin of His Heliocentric System." *Journal for the History of Astronomy* 33 (2002): 219–235. Important challenge to Swerdlow's reconstruction (1973).

Hilfstein, Erna, ed. *Starowolski's Biographies of Copernicus.* Studia Copernicana, Vol. 21. Wrocław, Poland: Polish Academy of Sciences, 1980. Edition and study of early biographies.

Hipler, Franz, ed. *Spicilegium Copernicanum.* Festschrift des historischen Vereins für Ermland zum vierhundertsten Geburtstage des ermländischen Domherrn Nikolaus Kopernipus. Braniewo, Poland: Eduard Peter, 1873.

———. "Analecta Warmiensia." *Zeitschrift für die Geschichte und Altertumskunde Ermlands* 5 (1874): 316–488. Indispensable edition and study of catalogs of Polish libraries from the fifteenth through the early seventeenth centuries.

Knoll, Paul. "The Arts Faculty at the University of Cracow at the End of the Fifteenth Century." In *The Copernican Achievement,* edited by Robert S. Westman. Berkeley and Los Angeles: University of California Press, 1975, pp. 137–156.

———. "The World of the Young Copernicus: Society, Science, and the University." In *Science and Society,* edited by Nicholas Steneck. Ann Arbor: University of Michigan, 1975, pp. 19–51.

Knox, Dilwyn. "Ficino, Copernicus and Bruno on the Motion of the Earth." In *Bruniana and Campanelliana,* Richerche filosofiche e materiali storico-testuali 5 (1999): 333–366. Considers the sources for Copernicus's doctrine of natural elemental motion.

———. "Ficino and Copernicus." In *Marsilio Ficino: His Theology, His Philosophy, His Legacy,* edited by Michael Allen and Valery Rees. Leiden, Netherlands: Brill, 2002, pp. 399–418. Important article by the most authoritative scholar on Copernicus's ancient and Renaissance sources.

Kokowski, Michał. *Copernicus's Originality: Towards Integration of Contemporary Copernican Studies.* Warsaw and Kraków: Polish Academy of Sciences, 2004. Important attempt by a young Polish scholar to revise current historiography.

Kuhn, Thomas. *The Copernican Revolution.* Cambridge, MA: Harvard University Press, 1957. Accessible account that sparked a reevaluation of Copernicus's achievement.

Markowski, Mieczysław. *Filozofia przyrody w drugiej połowie XV wieku* [Natural philosophy in the second half of the fifteenth century]. *Dzieje filosofii średniowiecznej w Polsce* [History of Medieval philosophy in Poland], Vol. 10. Wrocław, Poland: Polish Academy of Sciences, 1983. The most important survey of the teaching on natural philosophy at the University of Kraków in the fifteenth century.

Moraux, Paul. "Copernic et Aristote." In *Platon et Aristote à la Renaissance.* XVIe Colloque International de Tours. Paris: J. Vrin, 1976, pp. 225–238. Most thorough article to date on Copernicus's acquaintance with the works of Aristotle.

Papritz, Johannes, and Hans Schmauch, eds. *Kopernikus-Forschungen.* Deutschland und der Osten, Vol. 22. Leipzig, Germany: S. Hirzel, 1943. Important materials related to Copernicus's biography.

Prowe, Leopold. *Nicolaus Coppernicus.* 2 vols. Berlin: Weidmann, 1883–1884. Reprinted, Osnabrück, Germany: Zeller, 1967. Dated but still valuable biography with documents.

Rose, Paul. *The Italian Renaissance of Mathematics.* Geneva: Droz, 1975. Important for the humanistic background to Copernicus's achievement, especially chapters 2–5.

Rosen, Edward. *Copernicus and the Scientific Revolution.* Malabar, Florida: Robert E. Krieger, 1984. Defends Copernicus's role in the scientific revolution, and provides documents translated into English.

———. *Copernicus and His Successors.* London and Rio Grande, OH: Hambledon Press, 1995. Important collection of previously published articles.

Rosińska, Grażyna. "Nicolas Copernic et l'école astronomique de Cracovie au XVe siècle." *Mediaevalia philosophica Polonorum* 19 (1974): 149–157. One of many important articles by a leading Polish scholar.

Schmeidler, Felix. *Kommentar zu "De revolutionibus."* Volume 3/1 of *Nicolaus Copernicus Gesamtausgabe,* edited by Heribert M. Nobis. Berlin: Akademie Verlag, 1998. The standard German commentary.

Studia Copernicana. 37 volumes to date. Warsaw: Polish Academy of Sciences, 1970–1999. Contains several volumes on Copernicus as well as a subsidiary series titled *Colloquia Copernicana.* There is also a Brill's series of *Studia Copernicana,* 2 volumes to date. Leiden, Netherlands, and Boston: Brill, 2002.

Swerdlow, Noel. "The Derivation and First Draft of Copernicus's Planetary Theory: A Translation of the Commentariolus with Commentary." *Proceedings of the American Philosophical Society* 117 (1973): 423–512. The commentary is authoritative.

———. "An Essay on Thomas Kuhn's First Scientific Revolution, the Copernican Revolution." *Proceedings of the American Philosophical Society* 148 (2004): 64–120. A contextual and positive evaluation of Kuhn (1957) that is illuminating and insightful about Copernicus's achievement.

Swerdlow, Noel, and Otto Neugebauer. *Mathematical Astronomy in Copernicus's De Revolutionibus.* 2 parts. New York: Springer Verlag, 1984. The most authoritative and thorough examination of Copernicus's mathematics with a very important introduction.

Westman, Robert. ed. *The Copernican Achievement.* Berkeley and Los Angeles: University of California Press, 1975. Several important papers, including one by Westman on Wittenberg interpreters of Copernicus's theory.

———. "The Melanchthon Circle, Rheticus, and the Wittenberg Interpretation of the Copernican Theory." *Isis* 66 (1975): 165–193. One of Westman's groundbreaking studies on the reception of the Copernican theory.

———. "The Astronomer's Role in the Sixteenth Century: A Preliminary Study." *History of Science* 18 (1980): 105–147. Emphasizes one claim made by Copernicus that can be regarded as properly revolutionary.

———. "Copernicus and the Prognosticators: The Bologna Period, 1496–1500." *Universitas* 5 (1993): 1–5. Brief but suggestive summary of additional motives behind Copernicus's reformation of astronomy.

Wyrozumski, Jerzy, ed. *Das 500 jährige Jubiläum der krakauer Studienzeit von Nicolaus Copernicus.* Kraków, Poland: Internationales Kulturzentrum, 1993. Important studies on Copernicus's education.

Zinner, Ernst. *Entstehung und Ausbreitung der copernicanischen Lehre,* edited by Heribert Nobis and Felix Schmeidler. 2nd ed. Munich, Germany: C.H. Beck, 1988. Revised, corrected, and annotated version of Zinner's important studies.

André Goddu

CORNUBIENSIS, RICHARD RUFUS

SEE **Rufus, Richard of Cornwall**.

COWDRY, EDMUND VINCENT (*b.* Fort Macleod, Alberta, Canada, 18 July 1888; *d.* 25 June 1975), *cytology, gerontology, cancer research.*

Cowdry is remembered in the historical record predominantly for his involvement in founding the discipline of gerontology in the United States in the 1930s. He was also involved in the worldwide spread and popularization of the idea of the scientific study of aging as a distinct scientific and medical field. However, his long career and prolific writings played a role in many fields of twentieth-century life sciences, including cytology, eugenics, bacteriology, and cancer research. Scientific posterity tends to reward discoverers of objects and processes but leaves little room for those scientists who play an important organizational, administrative, or editorial role in the production of scientific knowledge. Cowdry was one such synthesizing figure, repeatedly bringing many diverse researchers and their work together into new configurations. His facilitation of major meetings, resulting in many edited volumes in numerous editions, served as points of consolidation and mobilization in several areas of twentieth-century life science.

Microscopic Morphology. Cowdry was born in 1888 in the small Canadian town of Fort Macleod, Alberta. He attended the University of Toronto, graduated with a bachelor of arts degree in 1909, and then moved to Chicago to pursue graduate work in anatomy. Cowdry's dissertation, "The Relations of Mitochondria and Other Cytoplasmic Constituents in Spinal Ganglion Cells of the Pigeon," completed and published in 1912, established his expertise in microscopic morphology and his lifelong interest in mitochondria. After receiving his PhD in 1913, Cowdry was appointed as an associate in anatomy at Johns Hopkins University. In 1917 he became a professor of anatomy at the Peking Union Medical College established in Beijing, China, by the Rockefeller Foundation. In 1921 Cowdry became an associate member at the Rockefeller Institute for Medical Research in New York.

Before the era of formalized postdoctoral training, this kind of appointment was an important career step for young biologists, and it was formative for Cowdry. Simon Flexner, the director of the Rockefeller Institute at that time, was interested in recruiting anatomists not with an interest in traditional morphological description, but with skills applicable to researching the cellular basis of pathologies.

The application of cytology to questions of physiology and pathology opened a chapter of Cowdry's career that was dedicated to the study of disease mechanisms at the level of the cell. Under the auspices of the Rockefeller Foundation, he made several research trips to Africa. Microscopic morphology here served the purpose of identifying the organism and mechanism of infection of heartwater, a common disease affecting goats, sheep, and cows (which later also became known as cowdriosis). In South Africa, he observed inclusion bodies in the nuclei of kidney cells of affected animals. When these nuclear inclusions were isolated and injected into ticks, animals bitten by the ticks subsequently developed the disease, a classic demonstration of Robert Koch's postulates for identification of the cause of disease. It was also the first demonstration of a rickettsial infection outside of the human body. Cellular morphologies associated with infection are still identified with Cowdry's name, Cowdry type A and type B inclusion bodies. He also traveled to Tunisia to study the etiology of malaria, and to Kenya to study yellow fever.

During the 1920s, Cowdry pursued research into cellular morphology, for example, publishing a detailed description of the secretory cells of the kidney tubules, and continuing his interest in cellular organelles such as the mitochondria, which he felt had been neglected in relation to the cell nucleus. He explored the use of vital stains, rather than fixatives that killed the cell, as a means to observe the mitochondria, whose role in the life of the cell was at that time unclear. Importantly, he also began what would become a lifelong habit of editing volumes that gathered the more specialized work of eminent scientists together into a text that could serve as a textbook or handbook for a wider audience. More than simply a propensity for the role of editor, Cowdry saw this work as a strike against overspecialization in the life sciences, which he thought was resulting in the loss of knowledge that fell between the narrow areas of individual specialization. Furthermore, he thought that students were being increasingly faced with the need to choose and specialize without even gaining an appreciation of the larger picture. Cowdry's introductions to many of these volumes reflect these sentiments.

Cytology Textbooks. Cowdry's edited volumes, beginning with *General Cytology: A Textbook of Cellular*

Structure and Function for Students of Biology and Medicine in 1924, drew on well-known scientists with particular expertise in one aspect of the subject at hand. Taken individually, these contributions would be quite narrow, but together they constituted an overview of the contemporary state of knowledge and research in a field that could be used by students and scientists as a textbook or handbook. *General Cytology,* for example, is an interesting contrast to the third edition of a classic textbook of the cell, *The Cell in Development and Heredity* (1925), by Edmund B. Wilson, first published in 1896. The single-authored authoritative overview was becoming harder and harder to do as the number of scientists and the production of literature in the life sciences increased, and in Cowdry's volume, Wilson is just one contributor among thirteen authors. While Wilson's book still looked back to European scientists and literature, particularly in theoretical debates about the cell's role in development and heredity, Cowdry's looked resolutely and inclusively at present-day work in progress, attempting to survey the leading edge of current knowledge in the field in the United States; the authors (including Cowdry himself, who contributed a chapter as well as editing the volume) represented the elite of American biology at that time.

Access to and participation in this elite was afforded by Cowdry's place at the Rockefeller Institute for Medical Research; his lack of training at a European university and his travels to Africa and China set him apart from just one earlier generation of American biologists, most of whom went through an obligatory graduate or postgraduate stint in a European laboratory. Contributors such as Thomas Morgan (1866–1945) and Frank Rattray Lillie (1870–1947) were in their own right central to developments in early twentieth-century life sciences, but here their individual perspectives were subsumed to the greater project of providing multiple entries on the study of the cell. Importantly, new biochemical and genetic approaches were introduced that presented the cell as a research object open to a wide variety of experimental questions, from the nature of membranes to the more classic questions of mechanisms of division and differentiation. *General Cytology,* resulting from a meeting of the contributing authors at the Marine Biological Laboratory at Woods Hole, Massachusetts, in 1922, was thus a snapshot of American biology—and cytology in particular—at this time: rapidly expanding and fragmenting beyond the purview of any one scientist.

General Cytology was supplemented in 1928 by *Special Cytology: The Form and Functions of the Cell in Health and Disease,* again subtitled *A Textbook for Students of Biology and Medicine.* Cowdry's own interest in working with the cell as a living subject rather than the dead stained one of classical anatomy and histology is evident in his selection of authors; for example, he solicited two chapters by

practitioners of the relatively new technique of tissue culture, in which small pieces of tissue from complex animals were cultured outside of the body such that the living populations of cells could be grown and observed in vitro for prolonged periods. Alexis Carrel (1873–1944), then a senior figure at the Rockefeller Institute, was one of these contributors. Carrel put a great deal of emphasis on the dependency of the cell on the local particular conditions of the culture medium—mimicking the specific conditions in the body that any given cell occupied as part of a specialized tissue and organ with its own particular relationship to circulating body fluids. Indeed, Carrel claimed that frequent replacement of the culture medium around a cell culture could lead to the immortality of cells in culture. This focus on the interdependency of cellular form and function in specific local bodily conditions, and the study of the cell and its medium as an experimental system for the exploration of biological mechanisms of aging deeply influenced Cowdry's own scientific thinking and writing in later years.

In 1928 Cowdry joined the Washington University School of Medicine in St. Louis, Missouri, as head of the cytology program and cochair of the Anatomy Department. He continued to receive Rockefeller Foundation funding for his cytology laboratory, and served on the Rockefeller Foundation Yellow Fever Commission. He would be based in St. Louis for the rest of his career, and became an American citizen in 1930. After his arrival in St. Louis, Cowdry began his involvement in American science at the national level, with his appointment in 1930 as chairman of the Division of Medical Sciences of the National Research Council. He also continued to display great editorial zeal, in 1930 coordinating the volume *Human Biology and Racial Welfare,* which promised to break down the barriers between specialized sciences "which have a definite bearing on human welfare and are referred to collectively as 'human biology.'" This volume was an effort to collect scientific studies of human biology that could serve as a basis for enhancing human progress, and was directed at a lay audience. The contributions ranged from Cowdry's own mild claim that human biology and therefore human well-being should not just be studied in the abstract, but should focus concretely on "the vital unit" of the cell—because that is where disease mechanisms (and therapies) such as the relationship between diabetes and insulin were to be found—to the most starkly eugenic writings of figures such as Edwin Grant Conklin and Charles Davenport. As with the earlier *Cytology* volumes, Cowdry clearly had the connections and standing to call on the elite figures of the American life sciences for contributions. Cowdry's social and scientific network, just at this historical point of the ascendancy of eugenics in American science, is reflected in this collection. However, this volume departed from the earlier ones in the broadness of its scope, crossing not just the subspecialties of biology and medicine, but including contributions from social scientists as well.

Arteriosclerosis and Aging Research. In his role as chairman of the Division of Medical Sciences of the National Research Council, Cowdry was approached for advice in 1931 by Ludwig Kast, first president of the Josiah Macy, Jr., Foundation, just as the foundation was formulating its first project to address processes of aging and degenerative changes. After wide consultation, Cowdry and the Macy Foundation decided to tackle this broader subject by first examining arteriosclerosis, the hardening and thickening of arterial walls often associated with aging. Research on the topic was haphazard, and Cowdry was attracted to the idea of coordinating various specialists to work as a team on formulating not just the state of the field, but also the research questions in need of exploration. *Arteriosclerosis: A Survey of the Problem,* edited by Cowdry, was published in 1933, and contained the contributions of twenty-three experts offering in-depth, discipline-specific assessments of research into the disease. The stamp of Cowdry's earlier participation in Rockefeller Institute–coordinated efforts to understand infectious disease in Africa is clear; in the introduction to *Arteriosclerosis,* he wrote that the volume "brings to bear upon a chronic disease that kind of team work which has proved such an effective instrument in the investigation of acute infections" (p. ix). The volume had a unifying effect on research in the field in the practical sense of putting all the diverse approaches in one handbook, but also in the less tangible sense of making arteriosclerosis into a distinct disease to be researched like any other—analogous to infectious diseases whose causes had been isolated and for which therapies and vaccines had successfully been developed—and not an amorphous and inevitable process of change in the aging body.

In 1935, at Cowdry's own urging, the Macy Foundation asked him to take the same approach to the larger topic of aging itself. Interest in the scientific study of aging was spurred in part by the perception of old age as a pressing social problem in the wake of the Great Depression and the institution of the Social Security Act of 1935. Cowdry invited a wide range of specialists to a meeting at Woods Hole in 1937. With the additional support of the Union of American Biological Societies (of which he was then president) and the National Research Council, Cowdry aimed to turn attention to the fact that while the problems of growth, "the upswing of the curve of vital processes" were being energetically tackled, the problems of aging and the downswing of the curve toward death were by contrast "shamefully neglected" ("Woods Hole Conference on the Problems of Aging," *Scientific Monthly* 45 [1937]: 189–191). The pattern set by Cowdry's earlier projects was repeated here: individuals well known for

their specific contribution to narrow areas within the proposed topic were invited to come together, exchange views and manuscripts, and then contribute to an edited volume. As with *Human Biology and Racial Welfare,* the conference attendees and chapter authors were not limited to the biological sciences. Cowdry tapped John Dewey, a Macy Foundation board member and extremely well-known philosopher and educator, to write the introduction to the volume *Problems of Aging,* published in 1939. In an introduction that could easily have been penned in the early twenty-first century, Dewey commented that biological processes condition social life, and social contexts shape biological life, and the specificities of this biological and social interaction were the heart of the "problem" of aging.

This perspective was reflected in the book's makeup, which considered aging in plants, animals, insects, and humans, and included clinical, psychological, and anthropological research alongside the physiology and biology of the aging body. Moreover, the specificity of some of the chapters, concerning, for example, the skin, the eye, or lymphatic tissue, reflected the tenor of Cowdry's own contribution, "Ageing of Tissue Fluids," which emphasized the importance of local tissue-fluid interactions in any given process of senescence. Referring back to his editorial work on *Arteriosclerosis,* Cowdry wrote that this book showed "unmistakably that the burden of years is not evenly felt by blood vessels of all sorts" (Cowdry, 1939, p. 665). Both the susceptibility to aging and the speed of senescent processes were heterogeneous within the same body. In short, any adequate survey or broad understanding of a general subject such as aging had to start with the local particularities and work up to synthesis, just as he had argued years before that any understanding of human welfare had to begin with specific details of cellular life and disease.

Individual authors disagreed about the specific nature of the "problem" of aging, in particular whether old age resulted from distinct degenerative diseases and was therefore purely pathological, or if it was a more systemic and normal process of aging. Nonetheless, this volume marks a founding event for the discipline of gerontology; it gathered scholarship discussing aging in a coherent fashion as a distinct scientific problem, and was legitimated by the backing of philanthropic and government organizations and the stamp of famous individual contributors. The formation of a scientific field did not stop at a meeting and a book; Cowdry also served as the second chairman of the Club for Research on Ageing, initially made up of the original participants, with regular reunions funded by the Macy Foundation. In 1945 several members of this club formed the Gerontological Society, whose aim was to publish a journal to distribute research findings to a wider audience. Cowdry also became the president of the

Edmund Vincent Cowdry. *Edmund Vincent Cowdry talking to a Swiss guard.* AP IMAGES.

International Association of Gerontology, and the principal organizer of the Second International Gerontological Congress in 1951. In 1958 he chaired a meeting on aging in Los Angeles and edited a book with contributions from participants on the subject of the medical care of elderly people, *The Care of the Geriatric Patient,* which was translated into Spanish and appeared in revised editions for many decades. Later in his life he worked to popularize the kind of work that resulted from the field of gerontology, writing a popular book titled *Aging Better* (1972). He also campaigned locally and vociferously with the university administration about inadequate pensions forcing his retired colleagues to live in penury.

Cancer Research. Cowdry's short autobiographical notes contain the offhand comment that his wife Alice once asked him why he did not work on something important, such as cancer; as a result, he wrote, he had labored with a split personality between cancer research and aging. This is perhaps an understatement, because he also continued to contribute to the formation of the basic practice of cytology as well. In 1934 he wrote *A Textbook of Histology: Functional Significance of Cells and Intercellular Substances* with characteristic emphasis not just on cells and their morphology, but their dynamic existence in relation to

their structural and fluid milieu. The production of detailed handbooks continued in 1943 with *Microscopic Technique in Biology and Medicine;* both of these texts continued to be reissued in multiple editions, and contributed to the training of countless students of biology and medicine, and were translated into Chinese and Russian. Cowdry's activities in cancer research were both local, involving his own laboratory, and international, continuing his flair for large-scale meeting administration. In 1939 Cowdry became director of research for the Barnard Free Skin and Cancer Hospital in St. Louis, and in 1950 director of the Wernse Cancer Research Laboratory at the medical school. He organized the Fourth International Cancer Congress in St. Louis in 1947, and then served seven years as the U.S. representative on the International Cancer Research Commission established at the 1947 meeting. In 1951 and 1952 he was an advisor on cancer to the government of India, funded by a Truman administration initiative for international assistance to less-developed nations. In 1955 he wrote the monograph *Cancer Cells,* which combined his cytological experience with his personal and administrative work in cancer research.

The papers of Edmund Vincent Cowdry are held at the Bernard Becker Medical Library of Washington University in St. Louis, and reflect the remarkably energetic and productive life of a scientist who excelled at organizing groups of scientists to consolidate and invigorate the research fields of cytology, aging, and cancer. His career reflects the influence of philanthropic organizations on the life sciences in the first half of the twentieth century and the growth of government funding for biomedical research after World War II. Another key to understanding Cowdry's career lies in several popular pieces he wrote in the 1930s about the analogy to be drawn between the cells of the body and the citizens of a nation, including an unpublished manuscript called "Citizen Cells: How Cells Manage Their Social Problems." Thoroughly convinced that like cells, individuals could be more than the sum of their parts if organized properly, he worked ceaselessly to bring scientists, medical practitioners, and social scientists together across disciplinary divides and international borders to generate new collaborative work. In an age of increasing specialization, he contributed his own particular observations and experiments to the science of cells, but he also remained a committed generalist, working ceaselessly to keep broad overviews of science and its techniques in plain view for practitioners and students.

BIBLIOGRAPHY

WORKS BY COWDRY

Editor. *General Cytology: A Textbook of Cellular Structure and Function for Students of Biology and Medicine.* Chicago: University of Chicago Press, 1924.

Editor. *Special Cytology: The Form and Functions of the Cell in Health and Disease: A Textbook for Students of Biology and Medicine.* New York: Hoeber, 1928.

Editor. *Human Biology and Racial Welfare.* New York: Hoeber, 1930.

Editor. *Arteriosclerosis: A Survey of the Problem.* New York: Macmillan, 1933.

A Textbook of Histology: Functional Significance of Cells and Intercellular Substances. Philadelphia: Lea and Febiger, 1934.

Editor. *Problems of Aging; Biological and Medical Aspects.* Baltimore, MD: Williams and Wilkins, 1939.

Microscopic Technique in Biology and Medicine. Baltimore: Williams and Wilkins, 1943.

Cancer Cells. Philadelphia: Saunders, 1955.

Editor. *The Care of the Geriatric Patient.* St. Louis, MO: Mosby, 1958.

Etiology and Prevention of Cancer in Man. New York: Appleton-Century-Crofts, 1968.

Aging Better. Springfield, IL: Charles Thomas, 1972.

OTHER SOURCES

Achenbaum, W. Andrew. *Crossing Frontiers: Gerontology Emerges as a Science.* Cambridge, U.K.: Cambridge University Press, 1995.

Freeman, Joseph T. "Edmund Vincent Cowdry, Creative Gerontologist: Memoir and Autobiographical Notes." *Gerontologist* 24 (1984): 641–645.

Katz, Stephen. *Disciplining Old Age: The Formation of Gerontological Knowledge.* Charlottesville: University Press of Virginia, 1996.

Maienschein, Jane. "Cytology in 1924." In *The Expansion of American Biology,* edited by Keith Benson, Jane Maienschein, and Ronald Rainger, 23–51. New Brunswick, NJ: Rutgers University Press, 1991.

Hannah Landecker

COWLES, HENRY CHANDLER (*b.* Kensington, Connecticut, 27 February 1869; *d.* Chicago, Illinois, 12 September 1939), *plant ecology, botany, conservation.*

Cowles was one of the pioneers of the science of ecology in the United States. At the turn of the twentieth century he produced two seminal studies on plant succession and the dynamics of community change that served as both an introduction to the science and an inspirational model for a generation of newcomers to the field. He held the first chair in plant ecology at the University of Chicago, one of the first such positions anywhere, and he influenced numerous American plant and animal ecologists through his early writings, his courses, and his field excursions. He was also instrumental in the founding of

the Ecological Society of America in 1915, just two years after its British counterpart, and he was active in a number of regional conservation campaigns involving the protection of wildflowers, the establishment of forest preserves, and the preservation of the Lake Michigan sand dunes.

Early Life and Career. Cowles was born in Kensington, Connecticut, a small village near the manufacturing town of New Britain. His father, Henry Martyn Cowles, a farmer whose family had been established in the area since the seventeenth century, served as a deacon of the Congregationalist Church, superintended Sunday school instruction, and held a variety of local offices. Cowles's mother, Eliza Whittlesley, was from Ohio, although she had relatives in central Connecticut who also traced their roots back two centuries. Henry worked on the family farm and nurtured a growing interest in natural history, particularly botany. He attended New Britain High School, where he received a solid training in the classics, and he continued his classical education at Oberlin College in Ohio. Encouraged by science instructor Albert A. Wright, Cowles supplemented his studies with courses in botany, becoming proficient at plant taxonomy, and he developed a strong interest in geology. Wright had already helped secure a place for another promising Oberlin science student, Charles Chamberlain, in the graduate program of the newly reconstituted University of Chicago. Cowles followed Chamberlain to Chicago after his graduation in 1893, and the two obtained their doctorates there and remained on the Botany Department faculty for their entire careers.

Cowles, however, went to Chicago fully expecting to study geology under the formidable duo of Thomas C. Chamberlin and Rollin Salisbury, who had just come to Chicago from the University of Wisconsin. Chamberlin had been president of the University of Wisconsin when Chicago's president, William Rainey Harper, persuaded him to come to head the new Department of Geology. He brought his colleague Salisbury with him, and the two continued their productive collaboration in Chicago, where Salisbury eventually agreed to head a newly created Geography Department.

Geographical and geological exploration, initially under federally sponsored expeditions and then in association with state geological surveys and the U.S. Geological Survey, had attracted much attention from young scientists in the last decades of the nineteenth century. John Wesley Powell's study of the Grand Canyon provided the initial inspiration for much work on fluvial erosion patterns, culminating, just about the time that Cowles was completing his undergraduate education, in Harvard geographer William Morris Davis's theory of cycles of erosion, that is, stages in the life cycle of a landscape (youthful, mature, old) from a condition of varied relief and high stream gradients to one of uniform level plains and low stream gradients. Chamberlin and Salisbury emphasized postglacial erosion cycles in the American Midwest, stressing the general idea, initiated by Powell and elaborated by Davis, that the process of stream erosion led to the wearing away of a surrounding landscape to its base level, a theoretical inland extension of sea level.

After a year studying this approach to geology at Chicago, Cowles left to spend the 1894–1895 academic year teaching the sciences at Gates College in Neligh, Nebraska, a short-lived, church-affiliated school. He may have left Chicago for financial reasons, but the available records are not clear on this point. He returned in the fall of 1895, with fellowship support, and resumed his studies in geology. He also began attending the lectures of John Merle Coulter, slated to head the university's new Botany Department. Cowles soon fell under Coulter's influence. Harper had recruited Coulter, like Chamberlin, from the ranks of college presidents. He was still president of Lake Forest College when he began lecturing at Chicago, and he had been the president of Indiana University before that. Coulter earned his scientific reputation as botanist on the Hayden expedition to the western territories in the 1870s and as a leader in the developing field of plant morphology, as well as a promoter of what was called the "new botany," that is, an approach that emphasized laboratory research, microscopical investigations, and physiological studies, as opposed to the older emphasis on description and classification.

One of the new fields that Coulter promoted was ecology. Impressed by Danish botanist Eugenius Warming's recently published textbook in this field, *Plantesamfund*, Coulter had sections of the book translated a day in advance so that he could lecture on them. Cowles, impatient to learn more, taught himself Danish in order to read ahead in Warming's book. From that point on, he was committed to the science of ecology. With his background in geology, Cowles sought a research topic that could link vegetation studies with studies of land forms. Fortunately for him, the perfect research site was close at hand in the extensive region of sand dunes along the Lake Michigan shore to the south and east of Chicago. Twenty years earlier Coulter had been one of the first botanists to catalog the plant species of the region, but Cowles's interests extended to the plant societies, as Warming had called them. He completed his doctoral dissertation under Coulter in 1898, publishing it in serial form in Coulter's *Botanical Gazette* the following year under the title "Ecological Relations of the Vegetation on the Sand Dunes of Lake Michigan." Coulter hired him immediately to teach plant ecology, perhaps the first such appointment anywhere, and he remained in that position until his retirement.

Cowles followed his work on sand dune vegetation with "The Physiographic Ecology of Chicago and Vicinity," an equally ambitious study of the plant societies of the Chicago region that included a bit more theoretical discussion concerning the nature of ecology and his approach to the field. These two works established his reputation as a leader in plant ecology, but they did not initiate a prolific program of research and writing. Cowles continued active research for several years, but he produced no more major publications. Aside from a few suggestive articles, most of them based on brief talks at scientific meetings, and a 1911 textbook, which emphasized individual plant adaptations rather than community processes, Cowles's original contributions to ecology ended in 1901. He kept up with the field during the next two decades, but he focused his attention on teaching, which included extensive fieldwork. His classes made frequent excursions in and around the Chicago area, taking advantage of the readily accessible regional system of railways and streetcar lines. In addition, he taught field classes during most summers, which took his students from northern Michigan to the Gulf coast and from Maine to New Mexico, Colorado, and Alaska.

By all accounts Cowles was a dynamic teacher who was at his best in the field, giving impromptu lectures as he led his charges through forests, dunes, ravines, bogs, and streams. His genial personality and relaxed style, an asset for undergraduate teaching, did not lend itself as well to the supervision of graduate students, and he tended to rely more on intuitive impressions, rather than rigorous quantitative methods, in his own fieldwork. His best-known students were perhaps William S. Cooper, who went on to direct a productive program in plant ecology at the University of Minnesota, and Arthur Vestal, who established plant ecology at the University of Illinois, but Cowles also influenced Paul Sears, Burton Livingston, and Stanley Cain, among botanists, and Victor Shelford and Charles C. Adams, among zoologists, and he exerted an indirect influence on numerous American biologists, geographers, and ecologists to the middle of the twentieth century—perhaps hundreds, according to Charles Adams and George Fuller in a tribute to their former teacher.

In 1900, Cowles married Elizabeth L. Waller of Louisville, Kentucky, a former Chicago botany student. Their only child, Harriet Elizabeth, was born in 1912. Wife and daughter often accompanied Cowles on field excursions, including the extended summer field courses.

In the summer of 1911, Henry and Elizabeth traveled to England for the International Phytogeographical Excursion in the British Isles organized by plant ecologist Arthur Tansley. They were accompanied by fellow Americans Frederic and Edith Clements and a host of European botanists. Two years later Cowles returned the favor by organizing the International Phytogeographical Excursion in the United States. He planned the itinerary, with some help from Clements and others, and then escorted his European colleagues on a whirlwind tour of the country, from the New Jersey salt marshes to the Great Plains, Colorado, California, and the Pacific Northwest, with a high point being a visit to his beloved sand dunes on the shore of Lake Michigan. Besides Tansley, the party included Adolf Engler, Carl Schröter, and Edward Rübel, among others, and the excursion convinced the Europeans of the significant contributions of Americans to this rapidly developing branch of science. Two years later, Cowles, with Victor Shelford and others, helped organize the Ecological Society of America, inspired in part by Tansley's establishment of its British equivalent in 1913.

Physiographic Plant Ecology. Cowles thought of ecology as the study of the organic processes that accompany the dynamic physiographic changes which Chamberlin and Salisbury described. Hence he chose to call his specialty "physiographic plant ecology." His article on the Lake Michigan sand dune vegetation began as follows: "The province of ecology is to consider the mutual relations between plants and their environment. Such a study is to structural botany what dynamical geology is to structural geology." He further noted that just as the physiographer focuses on changing topographic forms, the ecologist employs the methods of physiography and focuses on the changing flora. With this connection in mind, he decided that a most fitting subject for ecological research would be the plant communities on the shifting sands of the dunes along the southern and eastern Lake Michigan shoreline.

Succession, the process by which the composition of vegetation changes in a regular and predictable fashion—as, for example, when a plowed field is abandoned and allowed to return to prairie or forest, or when a patch of forest recovers after a wind storm, or when a pond slowly fills in—had been observed for centuries, but few researchers had studied the process in detail. On sand dunes, Cowles reasoned, substrate and vegetation interact in a most intense and direct manner, and the ecologist can follow the sequence of changes that may occur at one location over a long span of time by tracing those same changes horizontally as one proceeds inland from the shore. At the Indiana end of Lake Michigan the region of sand dunes extended some thirty miles along the shore, and older, established dunes could be found in places as distant as five miles inland. There was a striking sequence of changing vegetation, from the youngest dunes, supporting only scattered cottonwoods and dune grasses, to older dunes populated by prairie grasses, shrubs, and pines, to still older dunes, farther inland, supporting a mixed oak forest on a rich layer of humus.

Cowles carefully documented the characteristics of each successive plant society, noting local differences in soil, water, wind, and other factors. Cowles utilized Warming's classification scheme for plant societies—xerophytic, mesophytic, hydrophytic—based upon the level of moisture available in the soil, although he later found it inadequate to account for all differences in vegetation. Warming also had alluded to a final stage in succession, an endpoint. Cowles designated this final, and relatively stable, stage as the *climax,* thus introducing the term that would dominate much of American plant ecology for half a century.

Studies of succession and the climax are associated more with Cowles's contemporary Frederic E. Clements, who was a much more prolific writer and developed a strong following, first at the universities of Nebraska and Minnesota, and then at a number of research centers in the West associated with the Carnegie Institution. Clements's work followed more closely a tradition within plant geography, initiated by Alexander von Humboldt and elaborated upon by numerous European phytogeographers in the nineteenth century, that identified whole assemblages of plants, usually called *formations*, with the climatic regimes in which they are found. For Clements, then, the climax was ultimately an expression of the general climate in a region; there was one climax formation associated with each region and climate, and once achieved it remained stable indefinitely. Because Cowles identified ecology closely with physiography, and since he chose to focus more at the local than the regional level, he tended to view plant societies as continually changing, along with the land forms with which they are associated.

The climax, for Cowles, was more an ideal, like the base level in physiography, than a fixed and inevitable endpoint. Just as no landscape is ever permanent, no plant society remains the same in one place for very long. Chamberlin's work, rooted, like that of Powell and Davis, in the progressive evolutionary perspective of the late nineteenth century, viewed geological processes as proceeding in an orderly and regular fashion, as though following an inevitable pattern of development. Clements, equally influenced by the progressive evolutionary views of Herbert Spencer and others, tended to see the climax as an organic entity, a kind of superorganism, a mature stage in a process that begins with disturbance and instability and ends with internal stability and resistance to disturbance.

Although Cowles sympathized with aspects of this view, and he sometimes referred to the climax as the stable and inevitable result of a successional sequence, he did not view the climax as a superorganism, and he saw the entire process as dynamic and continually changing, a view, one might say, more in keeping with the progressive politics and social theories of his Chicago colleagues in and around the university, where he was associated with individuals and civic organizations that included urban planners, settlement house workers, and social reformers attempting to monitor and grasp the problems of a rapidly industrializing and urbanizing society.

Cowles never fully developed his ideas about plant succession; there is no mature statement of his views. In a talk titled "The Causes of Vegetative Cycles," delivered in 1910 as the outgoing president of the Association of American Geographers, Cowles stressed the complexity of vegetation change and the continual interaction of physiographic, climatic, and biotic processes. Within large regional climatic regimes, Cowles argued, there are always smaller processes taking place that involve local responses to topography, water relations, and the contingencies of plant and animal distribution patterns. When invited to write the volume on ecology in a two-volume botany textbook coauthored with Chicago colleagues Coulter and Charles R. Barnes, Cowles sidestepped the topic of plant societies and succession entirely and focused instead on the adaptations of individual plants, and individual plant structures, to their immediate environmental conditions. This was a viewpoint inspired by the work of German botanist Gottlieb Haberlandt, whose ideas Cowles incorporated into a course on Ecological Anatomy which he had been offering at the university regularly for over a decade.

Scientific Organization, Public Service, and Conservation. Cowles was instrumental in the organization of numerous scientific societies. As a natural public speaker and genial host he was also a frequent choice to hold office. He served as president of the Ecological Society of America in 1918 and the Botanical Society of America in 1922. He helped organize the Association of American Geographers, serving as its president in 1910. He also offered his services generously to local and regional organizations. He was very active in the Illinois State Academy of Science, the Geographic Society of Chicago, and the Chicago Academy of Sciences, serving as president of the latter from 1922 to 1934.

As an ecologist and ardent field naturalist living in a region undergoing rapid urban and industrial development, he turned his attention as well to issues of conservation and preservation. He helped found the Wild Flower Preservation Society and the Prairie Club, a kind of midwestern counterpart to the Sierra Club, and he contributed to the establishment of the Illinois state park system and the Cook County Forest Preserves, which still provide a welcome green ring around the city of Chicago. He was very active in the movement to preserve the Indiana sand dunes, testifying eloquently at the 1916 hearings held by Stephen Mather, a colleague in local conservationist organizations who had become head of the U.S. National Park Service.

Cowles also rendered his services frequently as an expert witness in legal disputes. He testified in litigation involving river pollution in Illinois, and from 1912 to 1921, as a result of a suggestion to federal attorneys by a former student, he became involved in lawsuits conducted by the U.S. Department of Justice. Many of these cases had to do with land fraud in Arkansas and Louisiana. The most complex case, settled in the U.S. Supreme Court in the early 1920s, involved a dispute between Texas and Oklahoma brought on by the discovery of oil in the bed of the Red River, which forms the border between the states. In that case Cowles was pitted indirectly against Frederic Clements, through the testimony of a Texas botanist.

In later years Cowles relegated much of the ecology teaching to his former student George Damon Fuller while he took on more administrative responsibilities. He filled in as department chair for Coulter during the latter's absence in 1923–1924, and, following Coulter's retirement, he assumed the chairmanship of the Botany Department from 1925 to 1928, although his official position was listed as secretary.

Cowles's health began to fail in the late 1920s, due to the onset of Parkinson's disease. By the 1930s, he could no longer perform his duties at the university, and he officially retired in 1934. He died in his home in Chicago on 12 September 1939. When, in the height of the Great Depression, the editors of *Ecology*, the journal of the Ecological Society of America, solicited monetary contributions to support a special double issue in Cowles's honor for July 1935, over three hundred people responded, most of them adding words of praise for Cowles. The resulting issue contained several notable articles, including one by Clements on "Experimental Ecology in the Public Service" and another by Tansley on "The Use and Abuse of Vegetational Concepts and Terms," which introduced the term *ecosystem* to the language of ecology.

BIBLIOGRAPHY

The Henry Chandler Cowles Papers can be found at the Department of Special Collections, University of Chicago.

WORKS BY COWLES

"Ecological Relations of the Vegetation on the Sand Dunes of Lake Michigan." *Botanical Gazette* 27 (1899): 95–117, 167–202, 281–308, 361–391. Cowles's PhD dissertation.

"The Physiographic Ecology of Chicago and Vicinity: A Study of the Origin, Development, and Classification of Plant Societies." *Botanical Gazette* 31 (1901): 73–108, 145–182. Published also, with an accompanying map and minor changes to the text, as *The Plant Societies of Chicago and*

Vicinity. The Geographic Society of Chicago Bulletin, no. 2. Chicago: The Geographic Society of Chicago, 1901.

"The Causes of Vegetative Cycles." *Botanical Gazette* 51 (1911): 161–183. Reprinted in *Annals of the Association of American Geographers* 1 (1912): 3–20.

A Textbook of Botany for Colleges and Universities, vol. 2, *Ecology.* New York: American Book Co., 1911. The two-volume textbook lists John M. Coulter, Charles R. Barnes, and Henry C. Cowles as authors, but Cowles was the sole author of volume 2, which focuses almost exclusively on the anatomical and physiological adaptations of individual plant structures.

OTHER SOURCES

Adams, Charles C., and George D. Fuller. "Henry Chandler Cowles: Physiographic Plant Ecologist." *Annals of the Association of American Geographers* 30 (1940): 39–43.

"American Environmental Photographs, 1891–1936." Images from the University of Chicago Library. Library of Congress. Available from http://memory.loc.gov/ammem/award97/icuhtml/aephome.html. An online collection of over 4,000 photographs taken by Cowles and his colleagues on field trips and excursions; includes images of Cowles, Clements, Tansley, and other ecologists.

Cassidy, Victor M. *Henry Chandler Cowles: Pioneer Ecologist.* Chicago: Kedzic Sigel Press, 2007. A biography of Cowles and a selection of his major publications.

Cittadino, Eugene. "'A Marvelous Cosmopolitan Preserve': The Dunes, Chicago, and the Dynamic Ecology of Henry Cowles." *Perspectives on Science* 1 (1993): 320–359.

———. "Borderline Science: Expert Testimony and the Red River Boundary Dispute." *Isis* 95 (2004): 183–219. Discusses Cowles's role as expert witness in a U.S. Supreme Court case.

Cooper, William S. "Henry Chandler Cowles." *Ecology* 16 (1935): 281–283. Introduction to the special issue of *Ecology* dedicated to Cowles.

Engel, J. Ronald. *Sacred Sands: The Struggle for Community in the Indiana Dunes.* Middletown, CT: Wesleyan University Press, 1983. Chapter 4, "The Birthplace of Ecology," focuses on Cowles and his influence.

Eugene Cittadino

COX, ALLAN VERNE (*b.* Santa Ana, California, 17 December 1926; *d.* Woodside, California, 27 January 1987), *geophysics, geomagnetic reversal timescale, geomagnetism, paleomagnetism, plate tectonics.*

Cox's most important scientific work concerned the development of the reversal timescale, work that he did with Richard Doell and G. Brent Dalrymple, and work that he accomplished during the half-dozen years after obtaining his PhD in 1959. Cox and Doell, both paleomagnetists, teamed up with Dalrymple, a geochronologist, and developed increasingly accurate reversal timescales.

The timescale they and their competitors in Australia, Ian McDougall, Don Tarling, Hans Wensink, and F. H. Chamalaun, produced from 1963 through 1966 played a pivotal role in the confirmation of seafloor spreading.

Early Years. Cox was born on 17 December 1926 in Santa Ana, California, approximately 30 miles southeast of Los Angeles. His father was a housepainter. Although he had no formal education in electronics, he liked repairing radios for friends, and Cox remembered that their garage was always filled with electronic equipment. He had one sibling, a sister, Lois. His mother attended high school while raising her children, and graduated from high school the same year as Allan. After Cox had finished fifth grade at a local grammar school, his parents sent him to a Lutheran parochial school in a nearby town. He left after only three years, later attributing his drifting away from religion to his unrewarding stay at the school. Returning to public school, he attended local high school in Santa Ana, where he was inspired by his chemistry teacher, who had to compress a chemistry class into six weeks because of obligations to the U.S. Navy. Cox found the hard work refreshing, and decided that he wanted to be a chemist. He built a chemistry laboratory in his basement. Cox also read widely during his high school years, both fiction and nonfiction, and most every book in the local library on Sigmund Freud.

Encouraged to attend college by his teachers who recognized his abilities, Cox enrolled at the University of California at Berkeley in summer 1944 immediately after graduating from high school, planning to major in chemistry. However, he left after only one quarter and enlisted in the U.S. Merchant Marines for three years. With time to spare, he continued to read widely in different fields, including philosophy, anthropology, and science. He returned to Berkeley in 1948, thought about majoring in philosophy, but decided to continue majoring in chemistry. Although he enjoyed his chemistry courses, he did not get to know his professors and found the department impersonal. He also was demoralized by the rise of McCarthyism, felt alienated, and his grades suffered.

In winter 1950, during his junior year, Cox was introduced to the geologist Clyde Wahrhaftig, who was studying rock glaciers in the Alaska Range for the U.S. Geological Survey (USGS). Wahrhaftig asked Cox to be one of his assistants for the upcoming summer. Cox accepted. Unlike his experience in Berkeley's chemistry department, Cox found his coworkers in Alaska open and friendly. Cox also enjoyed the fieldwork, and found the geological problems intellectually stimulating. He began reading geology for pleasure.

Cox continued to major in chemistry, but found it even harder to concentrate on his studies. The 1950–1951 academic year proved to be his undoing, and undergoing a personal crisis, he left school in spring 1951 before completing his courses and spent a month by himself hiking through the Sierra Nevada. As a result, he lost his student deferment, and was drafted by the U.S. Army. Before reporting for active duty in October 1951, he spent another summer with Wahrhaftig and his colleagues studying rock glaciers in Alaska. He decided that he would study Earth science once he left the army. Wahrhaftig continued to send Cox reading in geology during Cox's army years. Cox spent another summer (1954) working with Wahrhaftig in Alaska, and they eventually coauthored a major paper (1959) on rock glaciers in the Alaska Range.

After his discharge from the army, Cox returned to Berkeley in fall 1954, and obtained a BA degree in geophysics in June 1955. He decided on geophysics instead of geology, partly because he already had taken almost enough courses in mathematics and physics to complete majors in both subjects. He found his professors in the Earth sciences much more personal than his previous professors. He particularly liked Perry Byerly's class in geophysics. After doing very well on his midterm exam, Cox was asked by Byerly if he had thought about a career in geophysics. Cox later remarked that his decision to become a geophysicist grew out of his talks with Byerly and the personal attention he received.

Cox obtained a Stanford Oil Company of California scholarship in geophysics, and became a graduate student at Berkeley in geophysics in September 1955. Although he found Byerly's subject of seismology interesting, he wanted to find something less mainstream or "Big Science." John Verhoogen offered him just such an opportunity. Verhoogen's former student, Richard Doell, had set up a paleomagnetics laboratory at Berkeley, and Verhoogen identified Cox as Doell's successor. Doell was completing his PhD work when Cox was a senior. Doell showed him how to use the magnetometer, find appropriate rocks in the field, and prepare them for measurement on the magnetometer. Cox agreed to work in paleomagnetism. With Doell and Cox, Verhoogen was doubly blessed with two wonderful students. Doell completed his PhD in spring 1955, left Berkeley for a one-year position in geophysics at the University of Toronto, and Cox took over the magnetics laboratory.

Work on Paleomagnetism. When Cox began working in paleomagnetism, practitioners were working on two central problems. The first was continental drift and polar wander. A group of scientists at Cambridge University—S. Keith Runcorn, Edward Irving, K. M. Creer, and Jan Hospers—had begun using paleomagnetism to test continental drift and polar wander. Creer developed what came to be called an apparent polar wander (APW) path for Great Britain based on his own findings and those of Irving and Hospers. He argued for polar wander and continental drift, invoking the latter to explain discrepancies between his APW path and his reworking of John Graham's 1949 finding from North America. Graham, a U.S. paleomagnetist, had begun working in the subject in the late 1940s at the Carnegie Institution in Washington.

Irving found paleomagnetic support that India had drifted from the Southern to the Northern Hemisphere as Alfred Wegener and others had proposed. Runcorn collected samples in North America and found discrepancies between the pole positions of North America and Great Britain that could be explained in terms of continental drift, but he attributed them to systematic errors and opted for polar wander without drift. Irving moved to the Australian National University in 1954, set up a paleomagnetic laboratory, began to develop a polar wander path for Australia, and argued for continental drift and polar wander, given discrepancies in APW paths or paleopoles for North America, Great Britain, India, and Australia (1956).

Runcorn, who moved to Newcastle, changed his mind (1956) and adopted polar wander and continental drift. P. M. Du Bois, one of Runcorn's students, collected samples from North America and argued (1955) in favor of continental drift. Graham also continued working in paleomagnetism, sampling rocks from the Grand Canyon during the summer of 1954. Creer soon joined Runcorn at Newcastle, and, in 1956, began paleomagnetic work in South America. A. E. M. Nairn, recruited by Runcorn, started working in Africa in 1956. Another group of paleomagnetists from Great Britain, begun and overseen by Patrick M. S. Blackett, and run on a daily basis by John A. Clegg, began supporting continental drift in 1954. They confirmed Irving's Indian results (1956), added more results from Spain and France, and argued in favor of continental drift. Back in the United States, Graham (1965) and Doell (1956) independently obtained samples from the Grand Canyon. Both tentatively endorsed polar wander but rejected continental drift.

The other problem was that of reversals. About one-half of the rocks that had been paleomagnetically studied had normal polarity and the other half had reversed polarity. Reversals were interpreted in either of two ways; either as reversals of the geomagnetic field or as self-reversals. Graham (1953) favored self-reversals as a general explanation for reversed rocks. Having found what he thought were reversed rocks, he asked Louis Néel, future Nobel laureate for his theoretical work on ferromagnetism and antiferromagnetism, if there were ways for rocks to undergo a self-reversal. Néel (1951) suggested four possible mechanisms, and in 1951, Seiya Uyeda found a self-reversing rock from a volcano in Japan that confirmed the existence of one of Néel's mechanisms. However, Hospers and Antonio de la Roche from France defended field reversals during the early 1950s, and most paleomagnetists agreed with them. Hospers and Roche had begun to develop reversal timescales. Runcorn, Irving, and Creer also found reversed rocks, and preferred field reversals.

Verhoogen, learning of Irving's determination of an Eocene paleopole for India, encouraged Cox to obtain an Eocene-aged paleopole for North America to compare it with the Indian paleopole. Parke D. Snavely Jr., who had mapped and named the Siletz River volcanics of northwestern Oregon in 1949, suggested that Cox sample them, in part, because they could be dated paleontologically. Cox began collecting samples in 1955, and submitted his results in a note to *Nature* in January 1957. He studied eight flows spread through about 4,000 feet. He found normal and reversed rocks. He applied appropriate field tests and magnetically cleaned his samples. His data were clearly reliable. He calculated a paleopole at latitude 37° north and longitude 50° west. But there was a problem, at least for those who supported mobilism: the pole position for the Siletz River volcanics was very close to Irving's similarly aged Indian paleopole. Cox opted for rapid polar wander, rejected continental drift, and noted that if polar wander is very rapid, it would be very difficult to obtain robust paleomagnetic evidence for continental drift. Indeed, Cox decided to no longer actively work on continental drift.

Work on Reversals. Cox decided to turn to the problem of reversals. He found the problem intrinsically interesting, and had found reversals among his Siletz River volcanics. At the time Verhoogen was inclined toward self-reversals. At first Cox agreed, but began to question the idea of self-reversals after reading Hospers's papers. With the help of Harold Malde of the USGS, he collected samples from the Snake River Plain of Idaho. He found normal and reversed rocks, and tested various self-reversal hypotheses, including those developed by Néel. None applied, and he also discovered that the stratigraphic position of the normal-reversed horizon he found agreed with the position found by others working on different continents. This led him to favor field reversals in his 1959 PhD thesis, "The Remanent Magnetization of Some Cenozoic Volcanic Rocks."

Doell, who had moved from Toronto to the Massachusetts Institute of Technology, returned to Berkeley in 1958 to teach a summer class. He and Cox discussed recent work in paleomagnetism, found that they were in general agreement, and decided they would work together on a long-range project at the USGS in Menlo Park, California. They began their project in April 1959, and were greatly helped by James Balsley, then chief of the Geophysics Branch of the USGS. Cox already had decided to work at the USGS. Balsley, who had worked in paleomagnetism and favored self-reversals, knew both Cox and Doell, and wanted to get the USGS involved in rock magnetism.

Balsley was also instrumental in getting Cox and Doell to write a lengthy review of paleomagnetism. Balsley was asked by the Geological Society of America to write such a review, but he declined and recommended Cox and Doell. They finished the review in 1960. Unlike almost every major paleomagnetist except for Graham, they were unwilling to favor continental drift. Although some of its paleomagnetic support, in particular Irving and Green's 1957 APW path for Australia, was highly suggestive of continental drift during the Permo-Carboniferous, they argued that more work was needed before acceptance of continental drift was warranted. Cox also continued to maintain that proximity of the contemporaneous paleopole positions of the Siletz River volcanics and India weakened the support for continental drift. Irving (1959) had proposed a clockwise rotation of the Oregon region that would place the paleopole of the Siletz River volcanics in line with other North American paleopoles and away from the Indian paleopole. Cox rejected Irving's alternative explanation. Although Cox and Doell (1961) were slightly more inclined toward mobilism in a second review, they still were unwilling to accept continental drift. Indeed, Cox (1965) continued to resist continental drift during the next few years as evidenced by his review of Irving's 1964 textbook on paleomagnetism, in which he suggested that Irving had exaggerated the paleomagnetic support for continental drift.

Cox and Doell decided to determine the time intervals between successive reversals of the geomagnetic field during the past several million years, which would accomplish by tracking the recent history of reversals through the study of temporally overlapping lava flows. This meant that they would need someone trained in radiometric dating of young rocks. They tried without success to get Jack Evernden and Garniss Curtis at Berkeley; both were working on other projects. Learning about Dalrymple from Wahrhaftig, they successfully recruited him at the end of 1962. Dalrymple, who received his PhD in 1963 under Evernden, began working on the project in early 1963. However, even after the National Science Foundation granted the USGS $120,000 to support Cox, Doell, and Dalrymple's project, they were refused permission to build their own mass spectrometer until early 1964. Indeed, they threatened to resign unless they received permission. Once they managed to get their spectrometer fully operational in August 1964, they were able to begin dating their samples much more quickly than when dependent on the use of other instruments.

When they began their project, they, like everyone else including their competitors at the Australian National University (ANU), mistakenly assumed that field reversals were periodic instead of episodic. Both groups began to realize that reversals might be episodic by 1964, but Cox, Doell, and Dalrymple were the first to incorporate the idea into a reversal timescale. In their third timescale, which was published in June 1964, they distinguished between long-term reversals, which they called epochs, and short-term reversals, which they called events. Epochs lasted from 0.9 to 1.4 million years; events were about one-tenth as long. Deciding to name reversal-epochs after deceased geophysicists who had increased the understanding of Earth's magnetism, they called the current normal epoch the Brunhes, the first reversed epoch the Matuyama, and the third epoch the Gauss. The Brunhes, they claimed, began 0.9 million years ago; the Matuyama lasted for 1.4 million. Naming events in terms of the location of the rocks used in their discovery, they identified two events: the normal Olduvai within the Matuyama, and the reversed Mammoth in the Gauss.

Continuing to refine their timescale, Cox collected samples in the Galapagos Islands and on Nunivak Island off the coast of Alaska in the Bering Sea, and Doell and Dalrymple returned to the Jemez Mountains in New Mexico to obtain more samples. The samples from the Jemez Mountains included three reversed ones with ages ranging from 0.71 and 0.73 million years, an intermediately magnetized one aged 0.88 million years, and a normally magnetized one aged 0.89 million years. Doell and Dalrymple (1966) concluded that they had found another event, which they named the Jaramillo. They had two options. They could keep the boundary between the Brunhes and Matuyama at 1.0 million years and place the new event within the Brunhes as a reversed event, or they could redefine the boundary between the Brunhes and Matuyama at 0.7 million years, and place the event within the reversed Matuyama as a normal event, which ended 0.89 million years ago. They chose the latter because they thought it would be stratigraphically more useful. McDougall, H. L. Allsopp, and Chamalaun (1966) of the ANU group independently discovered the same event, but their paper did not appear until after Doell and Dalrymple's paper. The ANU group found three normally magnetized samples aged 1.01 million years, which established when the Jaramillo event began.

Dalrymple told Fred Vine about the discovery of the Jaramillo event at the Geological Society of America's November 1965 meeting. Vine, who had obtained changing seafloor spreading rates using their previous timescale that did not include the Jaramillo, immediately realized that the new timescale would give him constant spreading rates. Thus, their timescale played an important role in confirming seafloor spreading, and thereby continental drift. Ironically, Cox had decided not to use paleomagnetism to test continental drift when he turned to the problem of reversals, but ended up providing unexpected paleomagnetic support for it after all.

Although Cox's most significant scientific achievement was the work he did with Doell and Dalrymple, he continued to contribute to the understanding of secular variation, nondipole features of Earth's magnetic field, and the origin of reversals, and he discovered a geomagnetic excursion. He also worked in tectonics, even returning to the Oregon Coast range. With the triumph of plate tectonics, Cox accepted Irving's rotational analysis of the mountain range, and he and his students developed more and more refined reconstructions of the region. Cox wrote more than a hundred papers, and two textbooks. The first, *Plate Tectonics and Geomagnetic Reversals* (1973), contained many of the important early papers surrounding the development and early application of plate tectonics and development of the reversal timescale. The second, *Plate Tectonics: How It Works* (1986), coauthored with Robert Brian Hart, remains one of the best introductions to the working of plate tectonics.

Cox spent much of his career at Stanford University. Securing a position as research associate at Stanford in 1961, he became professor of geophysics in 1967, and dean of its School of Earth Sciences in 1979, a position that he continued to hold at his death in 1987. Cox was a popular teacher with both graduates and undergraduates. In recognition of his working with undergraduates, Stanford University established the Allan Cox Medal for Faculty Excellence Fostering Undergraduate Research. The Geological Society of America also established the Allan V. Cox Student Research Award, which is given annually in recognition of outstanding student research involving application of geophysical principles and techniques.

Cox was elected to the National Academy of Sciences in 1969 and to the American Philosophical Society in 1984. He was awarded the John Adam Fleming Medal of the American Geophysical Union (1969), the Arthur L. Day Medal of the Geological Society of America (1975), the Arthur L. Day Prize of the National Academy of Sciences (1984), and the Vetlesen Prize from Columbia University, which he shared with Doell and Runcorn (1971). He also served as president of the American Geophysical Union (1978–1980).

Cox continued to display a wide range of interests in the arts. He loved ballet, theater, music, and visual arts. He even became the artist Walter De Maria's geological consultant for some of his outside installations, such as The Lightning Field in New Mexico. He loved the outdoors, and spent part of most summers backpacking in the Sierra Nevada.

Cox took his own life the night of 27 January 1987. An expert cyclist, he rode his bicycle off a descending mountain road before it started to curve, crashing head-on into a large tree. The parents of a boy with whom Cox had allegedly had repeated sexual contact since the child was fourteen had recently told him that they had reported him to the police. The child's father had studied for his PhD under Cox. This crisis seems to have precipitated Cox's suicide: he had mentioned suicide to others, and several books on how to make wills were found at his home the day after his death.

BIBLIOGRAPHY

Cox's papers are housed at the Stanford University Archives.

WORKS BY COX

"Remanent Magnetization of Lower to Middle Eocene Basalt Flows from Oregon." *Nature* 179 (1957): 685–686.

With Clyde Adolph Wahrhaftig. "Rock Glaciers in the Alaska Range." *Geological Society of America Bulletin* 70 (1959): 383–436.

With Richard R. Doell. "Review of Paleomagnetism." *Geological Society of America Bulletin* 71 (1960): 645–768.

———. "Paleomagnetism." *Advances in Geophysics* 8 (1961): 221–313.

With Richard R. Doell and G. Brent Dalrymple. "Reversals of the Earth's Magnetic Field." *Science* 144 (1964): 1537–1543.

Review of *Paleomagnetism and Its Application to Geological and Geophysical Problems* by E. Irving. *Science* 147 (1965): 494.

With Richard R. Doell and G. Brent Dalrymple. "Time Scale for Geomagnetic Reversals." In *The History of the Earth's Crust,* edited by Robert A. Phinney. Princeton, NJ: Princeton University Press, 1968.

Plate Tectonics and Geomagnetic Reversals. San Francisco: W.H. Freeman, 1973.

With Robert Brian Hart. *Plate Tectonics: How It Works.* Palo Alto, CA: Blackwell Scientific Publications, 1986.

OTHER SOURCES

Banerjee, Subir K. "The Scientific Work (1957–1987) of Allan Cox." *Journal of Geophysical Research* 93(B10) (1988): 11563–11568.

Coe, Rob, and Brent Dalrymple. "Allan Cox 1926–1987." *Eos* 68, no. 19 (1987): 513–514.

Doell, Richard R., and G. Brent Dalrymple. "Geomagnetic Polarity Epochs: A New Polarity Event and the Age of the Brunhes-Matuyama Boundary." *Science* 152 (1966): 1060–1061.

Glen, William. *The Road to Jaramillo: Critical Years in the Revolution of Earth Science.* Stanford, CA: Stanford University Press, 1982.

Irving, E. "Palaeomagnetic Pole Positions." *Geophysical Journal of the Royal Astronomical Society* 2 (1959): 51–79.

Krauskopf, Konrad B. "Allan V. Cox." *Biographical Memoirs, National Academy of Sciences* 71 (1977): 17–31.

McDougall, Ian, H. L. Allsopp, and F. H. Chamalaun. "Isotopic Dating of the Newer Volcanics of Victoria, Australia, and Geomagnetic Polarity Epochs." *Journal of Geophysical Research* 74 (1966): 6107–6118.

Netzer, Baie. "Officials Say Cox's Death Was Suicide." *Stanford Daily,* 30 January 1987.

Henry Frankel

CRAFTS, JAMES MASON (*b.* Boston, Massachusetts, 8 March 1839, *d.* Ridgefield, Connecticut, 20 June 1917), *organic chemistry, thermometry.*

Crafts was one of the most prominent American chemists of the late nineteenth century, teaching at Cornell University and the Massachusetts Institute of Technology (MIT). He is most famous for discovering, with the French chemist Charles Friedel, a series of chemical reactions of aromatic compounds with organic halides in the presence of aluminum trichloride that proved extremely useful in the preparation of new organic compounds.

Early Years. Crafts was born in Boston to Royal Altemont Crafts, a prosperous textile merchant, and Marian Mason, daughter of Jeremiah Mason, a prominent lawyer and senator from New Hampshire. During his childhood he was acquainted with members of the academic community in Boston, and he received a bachelor of science degree from Harvard in 1858. After an additional year of study at Harvard, he studied in Europe for short periods at both the Freiberg school of mines and in Heidelberg with Robert Bunsen, before spending four years in Paris with Charles-Adolphe Wurtz at the École de médicine. During this period, Crafts met Charles Friedel (1832–1899), a prominent student of Wurtz and after 1856 curator of the mineral collection at the School of Mines. Crafts would share an extremely fruitful collaboration with Friedel that resulted in seventy-five coauthored papers published between 1863 and 1889.

Upon returning to the United States in 1865, Crafts became an inspector of mines in Mexico, and in 1867 he was chosen as professor of chemistry at the recently formed Cornell University. In 1868, he married Clémence Haggerty, with whom he would have four daughters. His experience in creating a new course in analytical chemistry led him to write a full textbook on qualitative analysis, integrating practical and theoretical chemistry and dedicated to Wurtz, which appeared in 1869. In 1870, Crafts accepted the chair of general and analytical chemistry at MIT, where, following the model of Bunsen's laboratory in Heidelberg, he modernized the teaching laboratories by installing ventilation systems and steam tables. He taught organic chemistry at an advanced level using the research literature; the choice of text was left to the students, and the majority chose August Kekulé's large and comprehensive German textbook. In his 1872 annual report, Crafts wrote that in his course he emphasized the details of theory in organic chemistry because that would serve better to ground students in general chemical theory.

Research and Academic Success. Because of health problems, in 1874 Crafts became a nonresident professor at MIT and returned to Paris to pursue research once again with Wurtz and Friedel. He intended his stay in Paris to be only one or two years, but the success of the collaboration with Friedel compelled him to stay. In 1880, he resigned his position with MIT, and he remained in Paris until 1891.

This period was the most productive of his scientific life. In 1877 with Friedel, Crafts reported in a series of three papers the discovery a new class of chemical reactions of aromatic compounds with aluminum trichloride and organic halides. As Crafts would later remember, the general reaction was discovered by the accidental observation of the reaction of amyl chloride with metallic aluminum. Among the products were hydrochloric acid, aluminum trichloride, and a mixture of various hydrocarbons. Friedel and Crafts noticed that the hydrogen and chlorine atoms in the hydrochloric acid formed must come from different hydrocarbons, and the hydrocarbon residues were combining with each other to yield the mixture of hydrocarbons in the presence of the aluminum trichloride.

$$C_5H_{11}Cl + C_6H_6 \xrightarrow{AlCl_3} C_6H_5(C_5H_{11}) + HCl$$

$$C_6H_5COCl + C_6H_6 \xrightarrow{AlCl_3} C_6H_5COC_6H_5 + HCl$$

This reaction led them to suspect that aluminum trichloride would work as a general reagent to couple organic chlorides with other organic compounds. In their first attempt, they combined amyl chloride with benzene and succeeded in substituting a hydrogen atom on benzene with an amyl group to give amyl benzene as the principal product:

$$C_6H_6 + C_5H_{11}Cl + AlCl_3 \rightarrow HCl + C_6H_5C_5H_{11}$$

Friedel and Crafts quickly expanded on the general implications of this reaction and found that any organic chloride would add to the aromatic ring in the presence of aluminum trichloride, and that other halogens and nonaluminum metal chlorides would work equally well. In the second paper, they reported that acid chlorides would also react with aromatic compounds to give aromatic ketones:

$$C_6H_5COCl + C_6H_6 + AlCl_3 \rightarrow HCl + C_6H_5COC_6H_5$$

Crafts later reported that these reactions were very easy to execute and that the reactions described in the first three papers of 1877 took only five or six weeks to complete, despite what he regarded as insufficient laboratory conditions. Between 1877 and 1889, Friedel and Crafts published over sixty papers describing the scope and power of this new synthetic technique.

While in Paris, Crafts also began an independent project on measurement of the relationship between the vapor pressure of iodine and temperature. He was soon led into research on establishing fixed reference points for high temperature thermometry. Crafts returned to the United States and MIT in 1892, where he resumed teaching organic chemistry. In 1895, he became head of the Chemistry Department. Two years later he was elected president of MIT.

As a teacher, Crafts was highly regarded by his students, who eagerly sought him out for advice on both laboratory and personal matters. In his 1899 MIT graduation address, Crafts emphasized the importance of a close relationship between teacher and student. Good students, Crafts said, "find [themselves] trying to pass beyond the boundaries marked out by routine and textbooks, and, in companionship with your teachers, trying to discover something new. This is the chief end of education; not so much to make you learned as to make you original and able to stand on your own feet" (Ashdown, 1928, p. 916).

In 1900, after a successful term as president, he resigned to return to full-time research in thermometry. Designing his own apparatus, Crafts determined the relationship between temperature and the vapor pressure of various substances water, naphthalene, and benzophenone, and found that naphthalene was nearly equivalent to water for establishing fixed points of reference for a temperature scale. His work on thermometry served to correct earlier attempts at constructing a fixed temperature scale. After 1911, he abandoned laboratory work because of ill health and wrote his final comprehensive articles on thermometry near the time of his death in 1917.

BIBLIOGRAPHY

WORKS BY CRAFTS

A Short Course in Qualitative Analysis with the New Notation. New York: Wiley, 1869.

With Charles Friedel. "Sur une nouvelle méthode générale de synthèse d'hydrocarbures, d'acétones, etc." *Comptes rendus hebdomadaires des séances de l'Académie des sciences* 84 (1877):

1392–1394; 1450–1453; 85: 74–77. The first papers announcing what would become known as the "Friedel-Crafts" reaction.

"Points fixes de thermométrie entre 100° extraterrestrial 400°: Tensions de la vapeur de la naphthaline, de l'eau, et de la benzophénone." *Journal de chimie physique* 11 (1913): 429–477. Crafts's major work on thermometry.

OTHER SOURCES

Ashdown, Avery A. "James Mason Crafts." *Journal of Chemical Education* 5 (1928): 911–921. Contains excerpts from Crafts's 1872 report to MIT and from three addresses as president.

Cross, Charles R. "James Mason Crafts, 1839–1917." *Biographical Memoirs of the National Academy of Sciences* 9 (1919): 159–177. Contains a complete bibliography.

Richards, Theodore W. "James Mason Crafts (1839–1917)." *Daedalus: Proceedings of the American Academy of Arts and Sciences* 53 (1917–1918): 801–804.

Peter J. Ramberg

CRAIG, WALLACE (*b.* Toronto, Canada, 20 July 1876; *d.* Woods Hole, Massachusetts, 25 April 1954), *ethology, animal psychology.*

Craig's comparative studies of the behavior of pigeons provided special insights into the nature of instincts and their role in the social life of birds. His ideas had an important influence in the 1930s, via Konrad Lorenz's instinct theory, on the conceptual foundations of the young science of ethology.

Early Development. Craig was born to a Scottish father and an English mother. He attended high school in Chicago and from there went on to study at the University of Illinois, where he majored in zoology and wrote a bachelor's thesis titled "On the Early Stages of the Development of the Urogenital System of the Pig." Such morphological research had no lasting appeal for him, however. More to his liking were the kinds of research promoted by his zoology professor, the pioneer ecologist Stephen Alfred Forbes, who stressed the importance of studying living nature instead of laboratory specimens.

After receiving his BS degree in 1898, Craig was appointed resident naturalist at the biological field station that Forbes had established at Havana, Illinois. His job was to make systematic collections of plankton and fish at various locations on the Illinois River and adjacent waters. He found, however, that the techniques at his disposal failed to reveal much about the lives of the fish. Deciding that animal psychology was the subject that interested him most and that the best place to pursue it would be at

the University of Chicago under Charles Otis Whitman, he enrolled as a graduate student at Chicago in 1901, after receiving his MS degree at Illinois earlier the same year for a thesis titled "On the Fishes of the Illinois River System at Havana, Ill."

Whitman, Craig's chosen mentor, was a biologist of great distinction and a pioneer in the study of animal behavior. At the time Craig came to study with him, Whitman was engaged in reconstructing the history of the pigeon family through an analysis of the heredity, variation, and development of the structural and behavioral characteristics of different pigeon species and their hybrids. Craig took Whitman as the model for his own scientific practices and thinking. He conducted his doctoral research on pigeons in Whitman's personal aviary.

Craig chose as his dissertation topic the vocal expressions of pigeons, as exemplified in the blond ring dove (*Turtur risorius*). He provided a detailed description of the sounds and body movements of the bird in all stages of its life and over the course of its annual and breeding cycles. Craig envisioned this work as preliminary to a larger comparative study of the sounds and gestures of different pigeon species. He expected this research would illuminate problems of animal psychology and sociology as well questions of heredity, development, and evolution.

Pigeon Instinct and Behavior. Craig's mentor, Whitman, was best known to later students of animal behavior for his recognition that instinctive behavior patterns could be used just like structures and organs to reconstruct the evolutionary history of a group of related organisms. Craig's own most significant work dealt less with reconstructing phylogenies than with analyzing pigeon social behavior and the nature of instinctive behavior generally. In 1908, the year that he finished his dissertation, Craig published in the *American Journal of Sociology*, "The Voices of Pigeons Regarded as a Means of Social Control." His goal was to explain how social influences, acting upon the instinctive machinery and limited learning abilities of individual pigeons, permit the organization of pigeon society to be remarkably flexible and adaptable. It was not sufficient, he maintained, to regard the individual animal as a being endowed with a set of social instincts. One had also to understand the way that the instincts of many individuals are brought into harmony in the animal society as a whole. With an emphasis on the role that bird song played in directing the behavior of other birds, but with mention of how colors, bodily structures, specific behavior patterns, and various expressions of emotion also served in this capacity, he explained how avian social behavior is structured.

Craig argued that the mating cycle of ringdoves is a mutual process in which the actions of each bird have to be finely tuned to those of the other. In pigeons, he allowed, there is always a ceremony prior to pairing. Through this, both the female and the male are made ready for the mating process, a complicated cycle of behavior patterns that involves copulation, egg-laying by the female, sitting on the eggs by both parents, and then feeding of the young. For all this to happen, Craig said, the birds have to go through the whole sequence of activities in the proper order and at the same time.

In the course of his paper on avian sociology, Craig also called attention to some of the features of the phenomenon that the Austrian naturalist Konrad Lorenz would later make famous under the name "imprinting." Young doves, Craig reported, do not recognize instinctively their own kind. Under normal circumstances, they learn the form, colors, gestures, and call notes distinctive of their species through contact at an early age with their parents. However, when eggs of wild species are hatched by the domestic ringdove, the young raised by the ringdoves thereafter associate with ringdoves and seek to mate with them instead of with members of their own species. Whitman had exploited this phenomenon as a means of hybridizing different species. Craig cited it as an example of how social influences interact with instincts in creating a harmonious bird society.

In the fall of 1908, Craig went to the University of Maine to teach philosophy and psychology. In his first years there he continued to publish the results of his graduate research. In 1911, one of his papers described the social behavior of the passenger pigeon, a bird that was virtually extinct. In another paper the same year, he discussed the influence of the male bird in stimulating oviposition in the female. He found this influence to be more psychological than physiological. In ringdoves, he had reported in 1909, the female's egg-laying does not depend upon actual copulation with the male. The male's mere presence—or, alternatively, stroking of the female by the experimenter—can induce the female to lay eggs.

The most important publication of Craig's career was his 1918 paper, "Appetites and Aversions as Constituents of Instincts." There he made a critical distinction between the appetitive behavior that initiates an instinctive behavior cycle and the "consummatory action" by which the cycle is concluded. He defined an "appetite" as "a state of agitation which continues so long as a certain stimulus, which may be called the appeted stimulus, is absent" (p. 91). As he explained, once the animal receives the stimulus for which it has been searching, the stimulus elicits a consummatory action or reaction, causing the appetitive behavior to cease and leaving the animal in a state of relative rest.

At the time that Craig wrote, instincts were commonly viewed as chains of innate reflexes. He readily acknowledged that innate reflex actions are a part of instinctive behavior patterns, but he insisted there was more to the story. By his account, appetites, not reflex actions, were what set instinctive behavior cycles going in the first place. Furthermore, the reactions at the beginning or in the middle of the cycle were often not innate but instead had to be learned at least in part through experience. The only part of the cycle that was always innate was the consummatory action, the end of the sequence.

Fighting Behavior. Among Craig's other publications was a 1921 paper, "Why Do Animals Fight?" He wrote this paper to refute various writers who cited biological facts and arguments to justify human warfare. He was not the only author to object to such claims. A number of biologists before him had argued that Darwinian evolutionary theory did not sanction militarism. But Craig's approach was different. Instead of couching his argument in terms of evolutionary theory (which he regarded as too speculative), he turned to empirical evidence concerning animal fighting. He acknowledged that animals fight their own kind. The question at issue, he said, was why they do so. His approach to the subject, consistent with all that he had learned from Whitman, was to consider fighting as a form of behavior that needed to be analyzed in the context of the entire life history of a particular species and then addressed further through comparison with closely related species. Not surprisingly, Craig's choice for his discussion was the pigeon family, the long-term focus of his scientific attention.

The primary conclusion Craig drew from his pigeon studies was that pigeons have no special appetite for fighting. A pigeon does not seek the fighting situation, he reported, nor does it seek to prolong the situation while engaged in it. Fighting is a negative reaction or aversion— a way of getting rid of a bothersome stimulus. The bird has appetence for such other things as water, food, mates, and nest, and it shows distress when it is unable to secure them, but it never shows an appetence for enemies or for battle.

Disappointments. Craig's discussion of instincts attracted the favorable notice of two influential psychologists: William McDougall (in his *An Outline of Psychology* [1923 and subsequent editions]) and Edward C. Tolman (in his *Purposive Behavior in Animals and Men* [1932]). Likewise, Craig's analysis of the social function of bird calls was featured by the linguist Grace Andrus de Laguna in her book, *Speech: Its Function and Development* (1927). Craig's own career, however, did not benefit from this attention. Soon after arriving at Maine he had found that financing a pigeon-centered research program required more monetary resources than he could muster. The university was unable to provide him money for his research, and he had no other resources upon which to draw. By 1920, he was actively trying to find a new post. Seeking the freedom and support to complete a monograph, "Social Behavior and Emotional Expression in the Blond Ring Dove and Other Pigeons," he tried unsuccessfully to get a one-year research position at Charles B. Davenport's Station of Experimental Evolution at Cold Spring Harbor, New York.

Craig left Maine in 1922, not because he had found a new position but because he was losing his hearing and felt that his effectiveness as a classroom teacher had suffered because of it. He taught animal psychology as a visiting lecturer at Harvard in the spring of 1923. He hoped to find a research position in zoology. What he found instead was work as a librarian at Harvard University. He spent four years in the Department of Biophysics of the Cancer Commission of Harvard Medical School and two more years at Harvard College Library. Thereafter he seems to have had no steady employment. He and his wife lived for two years in Scotland before moving in June 1937 to Albany, New York, where Craig's longtime friend, Charles C. Adams, then director of the New York State Museum, promised to help him publish a monograph on the song of the wood pewee. The monograph appeared in 1943.

Influence. Although Craig was without scientific employment in the 1930s, his ideas on instinct were put to significant use in that decade by the young Austrian naturalist Konrad Lorenz. Craig and Lorenz, put in contact with each other by the American ornithologist Margaret Morse Nice, were corresponding by early 1935. Lorenz depended heavily on his ongoing exchanges with Craig in constructing his important, programmatic paper of 1937, "The Establishment of the Instinct Concept." Craig's analysis of appetitive behavior helped Lorenz realize that the active organism is not simply responding to external stimuli in a chain-reflex fashion but is instead seeking the stimuli that release its instinctive behavior patterns. Lorenz's use of Craig's ideas proved to be selective, however. For example, he failed to pick up on Craig's denial that animals have an appetite for fighting. In later writings, most specifically in his popular book, *On Aggression,* first published in German in 1963, the Austrian ethologist represented aggression as an instinct that builds up in the organism and needs to be discharged.

Delivering a lecture in 1951 at Harvard on animal behavior, the British ethologist William H. Thorpe expressed appreciation of the important early contributions to the field made by the American biologists Charles O. Whitman, William Morton Wheeler, and Wallace Craig. Although the audience was a large one, only one or two people in the room seemed to know who Craig was.

Thorpe, who supposed that Craig was dead, was astonished to find that Craig was not only alive but actually in attendance at the lecture.

Craig had come to Cambridge, Massachusetts, from Albany in 1944. There, with the support of a grant from the American Philosophical Society, he lived an impoverished existence while working on a manuscript titled "The Space System of the Perceiving Self." He never completed the work, however, and as of 2007 it was not known whether any copies of it still exist. He and his wife moved to Woods Hole, Massachusetts, in 1953. He died there the following year from pancreatic cancer.

Craig's career illustrates some of the problems of attempting to pursue a career as a student of animal behavior in the first third of the twentieth century. His work was of high quality, but he lacked the confidence and resources needed to be a discipline builder at a time when the disciplinary status of animal behavior studies remained uncertain. Nonetheless, his theory of instinct played an important role in Lorenz's classic formulation of the 1930s regarding how instincts work. Craig's work stands as an early milestone in the study of instincts and of the interplay between instincts and social influences in animal life.

BIBLIOGRAPHY

The Library of the University of Illinois, Urbana-Champaign has a copy of Craig's unpublished BS thesis, "On the Early Stages of the Development of the Urogenital System of the Pig" (1898). The Forbes Biological Station of the Illinois Natural History Survey at Havana, Illinois, has a copy of Craig's unpublished MS thesis, "On the Fishes of the Illinois River System at Havana, Ill." (1901). For Craig's scattered manuscript correspondence, see the archives listed in Burkhardt, Patterns of Behavior, *p. 490. A nearly complete list of Craig's published writings is to be found in Kalikow and Mills, below.*

WORKS BY CRAIG

"The Voices of Pigeons Regarded as a Means of Social Control." *American Journal of Sociology* 14 (1908): 86–100.

"The Expressions of Emotion in the Pigeons. I. The Blond Ring Dove (*Turtur risorius*)." *Journal of Comparative Neurology and Psychology* 19 (1909): 29–80.

"The Expressions of Emotion in the Pigeons. II. The Mourning Dove (*Zenaidura macroura* Linn.)." *Auk* 28 (1911): 398–407.

"The Expressions of Emotion in the Pigeons. III. The Passenger Pigeon (*Ectopistes migratorius* Linn.)." *Auk* 28 (1911): 408–427.

"Oviposition Induced by the Male in Pigeons." *Journal of Morphology* 22 (1911): 299–305.

"Appetites and Aversions as Constituents of Instincts." *Biological Bulletin of the Marine Biological Laboratory* 34 (1918): 91–107.

"Why Do Animals Fight?" *International Journal of Ethics* 31 (1921): 264–278.

"A Note on Darwin's Work on the Expression of the Emotions in Man and Animals." *Journal of Abnormal Psychology and Social Psychology* 16 (1921–1922): 356–366.

"The Song of the Wood Pewee *Myiochanes virens* Linnaeus: A Study of Bird Music." *New York State Museum Bulletin* no. 334 (1943): 1–186.

OTHER SOURCES

Burkhardt, Richard W., Jr. *Patterns of Behavior: Konrad Lorenz, Niko Tinbergen, and the Founding of Ethology.* Chicago: University of Chicago Press, 2005. Devotes a chapter to the work of Whitman and Craig and its relation to subsequent developments in ethology.

De Laguna, Grace Andrus. *Speech: Its Function and Development.* New Haven, CT: Yale University Press, 1927.

Kalikow, Theodora J., and John A. Mills. "Wallace Craig (1876–1954), Ethologist and Animal Psychologist." *Journal of Comparative Psychology* 103 (1989): 282–288.

McDougall, William. *An Outline of Psychology.* New York: Charles Scribner's Sons, 1923.

Tolman, Edward C. *Purposive Behavior in Animals and Men.* New York: Century Company, 1932.

Richard W. Burkhardt, Jr.

CRAM, DONALD J. (*b.* Chester, Vermont, 22 April 1919; *d.* Palm Desert, California, 17 June 2001), *physical organic chemistry.*

As a young adult, Cram became enamored of research in chemistry. In the aftermath of World War II, he thrived in the new style of American science: he led a large group of graduate students and postdoctoral associates at the University of California at Los Angeles (UCLA); applied successfully for grants from funding agencies such as the National Science Foundation; and mastered the new instrumentation, such as nuclear magnetic resonance and mass spectrometry. He saw chemistry as an artistic endeavor, heeding the structural lessons offered by natural products in order to improve upon nature. His devising of inclusion complexes for both ground states (equilibrium) and transition states (catalysis) won him the Nobel Prize in Chemistry for 1987 jointly with Charles J. Pedersen and Jean-Marie Lehn. He had successfully joined the powerful new host-guest chemistry which his colaureates had pioneered a few years earlier.

Early Life. Cram was the youngest of four children. At the age of just four, he lost his father to pneumonia, yet he nevertheless enjoyed a bucolic and idyllic childhood, immersed in books. Cram's mother, with Victorian upper-class English values, taught him to read at four and a half. Cram was a precocious child, curious, self-assured, and

troublesome, whose self-education was very American, that of a latter-day Benjamin Franklin. This rawboned New Englander was already fully grown by the age of sixteen: he was six feet tall, weighed 195 pounds, and excelled in competitive sports such as tennis, football, and ice hockey. He also had had eighteen different employers by the age of sixteen, at which time his family dispersed.

Cram became a drifter, first in Florida, then in Massachusetts and New York. He completed his secondary schooling while supporting himself as a manual worker. Having won a four-year scholarship, he returned to Florida for study at Rollins College in Winter Park. Still unfocused, Cram read widely, studying chemistry and philosophy, but he also invested time and energy in extracurricular activities, such as learning to fly an airplane, singing in a choir and a barbershop quartet, acting in plays, and producing-announcing a radio program. During the summers from 1938 through 1941, Cram earned money, first as a salesman in some of the worst neighborhoods of New York City, then as a laboratory analyst for the National Biscuit Company.

Cram's first college chemistry professor, Guy Waddington, told him he had the stuff of a good industrial investigator, not an academic one. Thus prodded, Cram, with his contrarian spirit, ultimately became a professor of chemistry. He entered the University of Nebraska and obtained his master's degree in 1942 under the supervision of Norman O. Cromwell.

After Pearl Harbor, Cram (C) went to work for Merck and Co., eventually in its penicillin project. Max Tishler, (T), who became a father figure, recruited him. Their first meeting proceeded in this manner : "T: So you are interested in doing research? What can you do? / C: In my master's work at Nebraska, I worked on rearrangements of … / T: What is the base-catalyzed condensation of benzaldehyde and acetophenone? / C: Benzalacetophenone—I made a ton … / T: Why are you here without your Ph.D.? / C : My draft board told me to leave school and get a job to aid the war effort. I fully intend to return to … / T: As far as I am concerned, you are hired."

Immediately after the war ended, Tishler arranged for Cram (C) to enter Louis F. Fieser's laboratory at Harvard University; eighteen months later, Cram had obtained his PhD. After a short, three-month stint as a postdoctoral fellow in John D. (Jack) Roberts's laboratory at the Massachusetts Institute of Technology, he went in 1947 to UCLA, again as a postdoctoral fellow, with Saul Winstein, who became a mentor to Cram. Cram remained at UCLA, rising through the ranks to become a full professor in 1956.

Researcher and Educator. Winstein, Roberts, Paul D. Bartlett, and a few others brought American physical organic chemistry to a level of excellence that eventually surpassed that of the pioneering British school of Christopher K. Ingold and Edward Hughes. The mainstay of this American accent was the synthesis of novel molecules tailor-made for testing working hypotheses or new principles. The sheer number of molecules that Cram's group synthesized over the duration of his career is very impressive, more than ten thousand by his own count.

Winstein became not only a colleague of Cram's, but a trusted friend and a competitor. Their joint evening seminar became legendary. It lasted for hours and the presenter would be submitted to a harsh and relentless stream of questions and comments. The aggressivity was not personal; its only aim was to ascertain the reliability of the results and their importance. Those seminars brought to the fore Cram's qualities as a pedagogue, a critical and quick thinker who had an encyclopedic knowledge of organic chemistry. They also expressed a playfulness that was as basic to his personality as was his extreme competitiveness.

Cram took very seriously his responsibilities as an educator. He would disseminate in classrooms the new knowledge he was acquiring in the laboratory. Something of an iconoclast, Cram would challenge established wisdom whenever he felt it was mistaken. When both he and George S. Hammond were postdoctoral fellows at UCLA, they resolved to reform and update the teaching of organic chemistry. Instead of cataloging reactions in the traditional manner in terms of reactants, reaction conditions, and products, they emphasized mechanisms, based on recently established knowledge. Rationality would supersede empiricism.

Their joint textbook, titled simply *Organic Chemistry*, like the manual by Fieser it was intended to replace, appeared in 1959. Its very organization set it apart from its predecessors. It started with the structure of organic compounds, their nomenclature, and their grouping into major classes. Proceeding logically, its ensuing chapters presented a modern treatment of chemical bonding, stereochemical definitions, and graphical representations, followed by correlations between structure and equilibrium properties or chemical reactivity. These early chapters served to introduce reaction mechanisms. Moreover, the "Cram and Hammond" (as it became known among chemists) did not shy away from topics earlier deemed difficult or too specialized, such as molecular rearrangements, heterocyclic chemistry, polymers, and spectroscopy.

This text won a large measure of peer respect for its authors and it did well in sales. But its lasting value was not commensurate. It failed to make as durable, as deep an impact as, say, Linus C. Pauling's *General Chemistry* (1944), to which it can validly be compared. The underlying reason was, in retrospect, that the predominant

audience for organic chemistry was found in service courses rather than in classes intended for chemistry majors. Starting in the 1960s, American undergraduate students took organic chemistry during their sophomore year. For a great number, it was an inescapable prerequisite for application to medical school.

To many among these premedical students, Cram and Hammond was too confusing, packed as it was with, to them, bewildering information. They needed lighter fare. Accordingly, their instructors favored a competing manual, *Organic Chemistry* (1959), by Robert Thornton Morrison and Robert Neilson Boyd, surely less hearty and less sapid, but an easier read and much easier to ingest by rote memorization—its authors had seen to it by building in systematic repetition. "Morrison and Boyd" became the standard. Nonetheless, with his usual energy, that of the apostle intent on spreading the faith, Cram would go on to write a few other textbooks in subsequent years.

Cram's Rule. If innovative in teaching and textbooks, following Pauling's lead, Cram ambitioned to become a research leader in physical organic chemistry. Winstein, his mentor and colleague, privileged the topic of reaction mechanisms and the tool of kinetics. Cram had thus to find another niche for himself. He chose to devise new molecular structures, with a stereochemical outlook. Pauling's influence was again blatant.

Cram's entry into academic research was marked by his serendipitous discovery of the phenonium ion rearrangement. Upon loss of a leaving group from a reactant dissolved in a highly polar solvent, assistance could be provided by an adjacent benzene ring within the reactant molecule, which would provide some of its mobile (electrons to compensate in part for the electronic deficiency at the carbon losing the departing group. This aromatic ring would thus bridge the two adjacent carbons, the one it was originally bonded to and that which had borne the departing group, forming a so-called phenonium ion:

Cram had analyzed for this purpose the products from solvent-induced ionization of the isomeric L-*threo* and *erythro*-3-phenyl-2-butyl tosylate. He proposed a phenonium ion intermediate of the type described above. Winstein came to his support with kinetic data for this reaction, demonstrating rate acceleration from participation of the neighboring benzene ring.

A controversy ensued. Herbert C. Brown questioned the intermediacy of a nonclassical, bridged phenonium ion in these processes. Both rate enhancement and product stereospecificity had to be explained. While Cram proposed a bridged structure that prevented nucleophilic attack from one side, Brown countered that the same result could come from a "windshield wiper" effect caused by rapid 1,2-phenyl shifts. The difference between the two models is mostly a matter of language. Even Brown's classical cations are stabilized through hyperconjugation.

The ion-pair phenomena encountered in carbocation stereochemistry led Cram to pose the general question of the stereochemical capabilities of carbanions. This led him to discover phenomena that, with his taste for lexical invention he termed isoinversion, conducted tour mechanism, and ion-pair reorganization. It also allowed him take advantage of stabilization of a carbanionic center by an adjacent sulfur atom.

Chemists use the term *asymmetric induction* to describe the transfer of molecular asymmetry, with its attendant physical property of rotatory power, from a pre-existing chiral molecule or chiral center to a newly forming chiral molecule or center. In 1951 Vladimir Prelog of the Eidgenössische Technische Hochschule in Zürich proposed a rule for predicting the stereochemical outcome of addition of nucleophiles, Nu: (that is, an atom or a group of atoms Nu bearing an electronic lone pair) to (-keto esters. Prelog's rule predicted the stereoselectivity in this addition from an intuitively satisfactory arrangement of the alkyl substituents and the trans-coplanar carbonyl C=O groups.

In 1952 Cram and his coworker, Fathy Ahmed Abd Elhafez, published a paper, "Studies in Sterochemistry," that presented their rule of "steric control of asymmetric induction in the synthesis of acyclic systems." They based it on much earlier work, dating to the beginning of the twentieth century by a Frenchman, Marc Tiffeneau, and a Scot, Alexander McKenzie. Whereas Prelog had investigated a similar problem, he had concerned himself with systems in which the chiral centers, inducing and induced, bore a 1,4 relationship to one another. Cram's Rule had premises and made predictions similar to Prelog's.

Cram and Elhafez examined nucleophilic addition to the carbon atom of a carbonyl group adjacent to (1,2 relationship) a chiral center that consisted of a carbon atom bearing three different substituents, ranked small, medium, and large according to their relative bulk. Cram's rule was "that diastereoisomer will predominate which would be formed by the approach of the entering group [Nu:] from the *least hindered side* of the double bond when the rotational conformation of the C-C bond is such that the double bond is flanked by the two least bulky groups attached to the adjacent asymmetric center." (See Figure 1.)

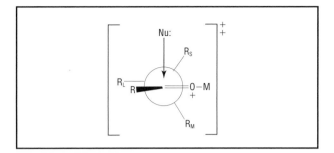

Figure 1. *Cram acyclic model.*

Cram's rule predicted the major stereoisomers produced in more than two dozen reactions. It was a convenient and a rather empirical mnemonic. In Cram's own words (written in December 1977), "the explanation offered is reasonable, arbitrary, unprovable, and provocative."

This last adjective, nicely consonant with Cram's personality, was indeed well chosen. Among the numerous organic and theoretical chemists who rose to the challenge posed by this conjecture, predicting the stereochemical outcome of C=O addition reactions, were John Cornforth, Hugh Felkin, Nguyen Trong Anh, Odile Eisenstein, Piotr Cieplak, and Shuji Tomoda.

Cram's rule expressed its author's familiarity with molecular models, the inferences he made from a close examination of their features, and his erudition about the major reactions of organic chemistry showing asymmetric induction. Which brings up a key issue: the role of molecular models in Cram's thinking about organic molecules and their reactivities—in this case the stereochemical bias responsible for an observed stereoselectivity.

CPK Models as Inspiration. Some of Cram's former coworkers, when queried about his singularity as a scientist, gave pride of place to his reliance on CPK molecular models. Cram himself emphasized how important they had been to his thinking during the planning stages in his research. Those models were made initially of hard wood (1 inch per angstrom) and plastic (0.5 inch per angstrom). Individual atoms were shaped as spheres or portions thereof, with a radius proportional to van der Waals radius. Wooden atoms were connected by steel rods and clamps, plastic atoms with snap fasteners. CPK models embodied the detailed structural knowledge that Pauling had accumulated, by the end of the 1930s, from his numerous determinations of molecular structures using x-ray crystallography and electron diffraction.

CPK models had originated in 1960 within the U.S. National Institutes of Health's biophysics and biophysical chemistry study section. Its members had given their principal consultant, Walter L. Koltun, the responsibility of convening an ad hoc committee to design and develop new models for biological molecules and macromolecules based on the earlier ones devised by Robert B. Corey and Pauling. Hence, the newer variety became known as CPK models. By comparison with the earlier CP models, they were not only lighter, but more accurate in their bond angles because of their increased rigidity and better connectors, which Koltun had devised.

These space-filling (or compact) CPK models contrasted with the skeletal, ball-and-stick models. The former aim at realism with respect to the overall molecular shape, the latter are a three-dimensional rendition of the molecular formula. These representations complement one another. In the 1960s, every organic chemist used skeletal models. The version devised by André S. Dreiding from the University of Zürich was ubiquitous and to be seen in many offices. Conversely, only the best-funded research groups could afford a set of the considerably more expensive CPK models.

Cram's recourse to the latter is instructive in two ways. His imagination was highly visual. He handwrote more than four hundred manuscripts for scientific publications and also handsomely illustrated them. The figures Cram devised for his articles and communications would usually be quite eloquent, telling the story independently of the text.

On the other hand, CPK models originated in molecular biology. Cram's forte was to borrow an idea from the album of nature and run with it until he scored. For example, he would scrutinize the structural details of an enzymatic binding site and then design biomimetic synthetic analogues to explore all the consequences of a given arrangement.

As he wrote in his Nobel lecture (and note his nautical metaphor),

> from the beginning, we used Corey-Pauling-Koltun (CPK) molecular models, which served as a compass on an otherwise uncharted sea full of synthesizable target complexes. We have spent hundreds of hours building CPK models of potential complexes, and grading them for desirability as research targets. Hosts were then prepared by my co-workers to see if they possessed the anticipated guest-binding properties. Crystal structures of the hosts and their complexes were then determined to compare what was anticipated by model examination with what was experimentally observed. (Cram, 1992, p. 420)

One may add here, in a more speculative but nevertheless equally relevant vein, that Cram's playfulness was very much in evidence when he put together a mole-

Donald J. Cram. *Donald J. Cram smiling after winning Nobel Prize for chemistry.* BEN MARTIN/TIME LIFE PICTURES/GETTY IMAGES

cule from the CPK building blocks. This highly time-consuming activity resembles that of a child with tinkertoys such as Lego, or an Erector set (Meccano). In doing this activity, Cram behaved as a genuine molecular architect, relying, as is the wont of architects, on three-dimensional mock-ups built to scale. To Cram, the CPK models not only bridged biochemistry and organic chemistry, the natural and the artificial, they also bridged his mental imagining of molecules and their actualization, first in laboratory flasks, second as crystal structures obtained from x-ray diffractometry.

It is no accident that Cram opted for a career in chemistry. This science had a Promethean, transgressive appeal for him. To be able to circumvent natural rules and obstacles, to impose one's will upon matter, to sculpt it into one's own imaginings, was the type of undertaking he relished. Forcing molecules into his preconceptions gave him the utmost satisfaction.

Cyclophanes and Inclusion Complexants. Thus, Cram's next big research topics was cyclophanes—significantly, he coined that name. These are molecules in which two or more aromatic rings are bridged in such a manner as to bring them into close contact and interaction. For instance, [2.2]paracyclophane is a molecule in which two benzene rings are held face-to-face by opposite bridges consisting each of two methylene CH_2 units. Such close contact brings together the clouds of π electrons associated with each benzene ring; then, π-π complexes can be shown to occur. If, to give an example, a molecule of tetracyanoethylene withdraws π electrons from one of the benzene rings, the electronic deficiency is partly compensated by donation of π electrons from the second benzene ring:

After Charles J. Pedersen had published his serendipitous production of crown ethers, reporting on their cation-complexing abilities (1967), after Jean-Marie Lehn had synthesized his cryptands and publicized their uncanny aptitude at selectively encapsulating metallic ions (1969), Cram decided around 1970 to enter this new field. To Cram, this supramolecular chemistry, as Lehn had named it, was immensely engaging. It was challenging, broke new ground, and required big resources, both human and material. It upstaged nature and promised to rival enzymatic processes in their speed and efficiency. In brief, Cram saw the opportunity for a culmination to his career. He entered the new area with characteristic determination and vitality, and by 1980, he had already published around fifty papers on it. An early accomplishment was chiral catalysis of the Michael addition, achieving 99 percent stereospecificity.

Cram's style of supramolecular research started with biomolecules: "The biotic world is such a wonderful world; it shows what can be done," he said. He would put together, for instance, a molecule with the same kinds of functional groups and in the same arrangements as in the enzyme α-chymotrypsin, with a view to seeing if it would catalyze trans-acylation. As always, he relied on CPK models when designing these new molecular types.

For this host-guest chemistry, Cram defined topologically a host (guest) as having convergent (divergent) binding sites. Another principle of his, arguably his main contribution to this field, was preorganization, that is, hosts already showing holes of various sizes, held open within a rigid framework, typically one containing rigid and planar benzene rings. This ensured that binding of guests was less energy-demanding. But creating them was

not an easy task. As Cram remarked, "holes don't like to exist," a twentieth-century variant of the ancient adage, "nature abhors a vacuum." He had not only to contend with sometimes lengthy and sophisticated syntheses, and with van der Waals forces both attractive and repulsive; he also had to convince his sometimes skeptical coworkers of the feasibility of some revolutionary-looking molecular construct. In Cram's words, "they were pessimistic about our finding ways of preparing carcerands. However, when a literature search revealed that (some) derivatives were already known and easily made, they warmly endorsed the carcerand concept" (Cram, 2001).

Cram's contribution was a numerous manifold of increasingly complex host systems capable of binding molecules, not only ions, that emulated enzymatic sites. The carcerand concept was a generalization of his initial devising of "spherands," that is, guests with cation-binding oxygen atoms preset in an octahedral array (see Figure 2). Some of Cram's hosts were capable of enantiomeric recognition and were thus applicable to resolution of racemic mixtures.

Hemicarcerands have a small gap in the wall of the carcerand. Molecules can travel through this gap only if the temperature is high enough. Once inside, however, the molecules cannot escape if the temperature has been lowered. The ultimate test of hemicarcerands came when Cram allowed a molecule of α-pyrone to enter the carcerand cage. Inside, the α-pyrone was photochemically

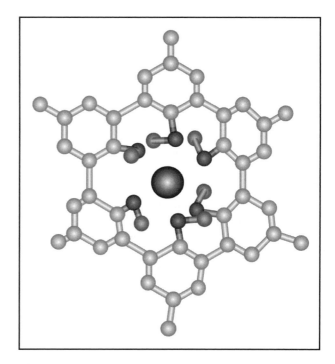

Figure 2.

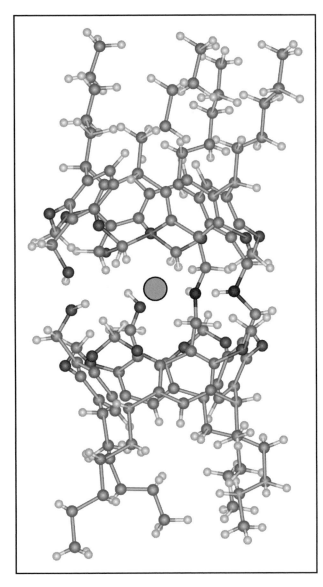

Figure 3.

converted into cyclobutadiene and carbon dioxide, which escaped (see Figure 3). Cyclobutadiene is normally so highly reactive that it can neither be isolated nor studied. Cram's carceplex, however, kept it from reacting for quite long periods and allowed the molecule to be observed spectroscopically for the first time. This was possibly, Cram's finest result.

In 1979 Orville L. Chapman, a fellow professor of Cram in the UCLA Department of Chemistry, revealed privately that he was lobbying the Nobel Committee on behalf of a Cram-Lehn ticket. The lobbying would bear fruit in 1987.

A hard worker, Cram enjoyed life to the full. As a transplant to Southern California, he loved to take advan-

tage of the sunny, seasonless climate. He played a mean game of tennis, having trained with the top tennis coach at UCLA. His zest for challenges of any kind caused him to embrace other sports in which he would set ambitious goals for himself and then proceed to meet them. He went downhill skiing in the Sierras, swam numerous laps in the UCLA pool, and sailed as well. Perhaps his favorite sport was surfing on the nearby beaches. It was a passion that he related to his other passion—chemistry. In both those avocations he yearned to be or feel "on the crest of a wave."

BIBLIOGRAPHY

WORKS BY CRAM

With Fathy Ahmed Abd Elhafez. "Studies in Stereochemistry. 10. The Rule of 'Steric Control of Asymmetric Induction' in the Synthesis of Acyclic Systems." *Journal of the American Chemical Society* 74 (1952): 5825–5835.

With George S. Hammond. *Organic Chemistry*. New York: McGraw-Hill, 1959.

Fundamentals of Carbanion Chemistry. New York: Academic Press, 1965.

Letter to *Citation Classics,* no. 11 (13 March 1978): 248. Available from http://www.garfield.library.upenn.edu/classics1978/A1978EM93500002.pdf.

Interview by Leon Gortler. 14 January 1981. Transcript, Chemical Hertitage Foundation, Philadelphia, PA.

"Preorganization—From Solvents to Spherands." *Angewandte Chemie International Edition in English* 25 (1986): 1039–1134.

From Design to Discovery. Profiles, Pathways and Dreams: Autobiographies of Eminent Chemists series, edited by Jeffrey I. Seeman, Washington, DC: American Chemical Society, 1990.

"The Design of Molecular Hosts, Guests, and Their Complexes." In *Nobel Lectures, Chemistry 1981–1990*, edited by Bo G. Malmström. Singapore: World Scientific Publishing, 1992. Contains his 1988 Nobel lecture.

With Martin E. Tanner and Robert Thomas. "The Taming of Cyclobutadiene." *Angewandte Chemie International Edition in English* 30 (1991): 1024–1027.

With Siavash K. Kurdistani and Roger C. Helgeson. "Stepwise Shell Closures Provide Hosts that Expose or Protect Guest from Outer-phase Reactants." *Journal of the American Chemical Society* 117 (1995): 1659–1660.

With T. A. Robbins. "Comparisons of Activation Energies for Guest Escapes from the Inner Phases of Hemicarcerands with Varying Numbers of Bowl-Linking Groups." *Journal of the Chemical Society, Chemical Communications* (1995): 1515–1516.

With Roger C. Helgeson, Kyungsoo Paek, Carolyn B. Knobler, et al. "Guest-Assisted and Guest-Inhibited Shell Closures Provide Differently Shaped Carceplexes and Hemicarceplexes." *Journal of the American Chemical Society* 118 (1996): 5590–5604.

With Juyoung Yoon. "The First Water-Soluble Hemicarceplexes." *Journal of the Chemical Society. Chemical Communications* (1997): 497–498.

With Roger C. Helgeson and Carolyn B. Knobler. "Correlations of Structure with Binding Ability Involving Nine Hemicarcerand Hosts and Twenty-four Guests." *Journal of the American Chemical Society* 119 (1997): 3229–3244.

"Donald Cram Speaks on His Research Philosophy." (2001). Available from http://www.chem.ucla.edu/research/org/CRAM/Cram_RschPhil.html.

OTHER SOURCES

Franklin, James. "Diagrammatic Reasoning and Modelling in the Imagination: The Secret Weapons of the Scientific Revolution." In *1543 and All That*, edited by Guy Freeland and Anthony Corones. Dordrecht, Netherlands, and Boston: Kluwer, 2000. While Cram is not mentioned, this is an excellent paper on the seminal role of models for scientists.

Hawthorne, M. Frederick. "Obituary: Donald J. Cram (1919–2001)." *Nature* 412 (2001): 696.

Pierre Laszlo

CREMER, ERIKA (*b*. Munich, Germany, 20 May 1900; *d*. Innsbruck, Austria, 21 September 1996), *chemical kinetics, atomic energy, chromatography, gas liquid chromatography, reaction kinetics, catalysis, adsorption, thin-layer technology.*

Cremer is a pioneer in gas chromatography. At the beginning of her scientific work there were studies on chain-mechanisms of chemical reactions, accounting to some extent for explanations of fast reactions such as in detonating gases containing hydrogen. To reaction kinetics and catalysis she added the field of adsorption, which became the basis for chromatographic methods. In applications such as column, liquid, thin-layer, and high-pressure chromatography and others, this is a widely used analytical method in various aspects of chemistry and life science.

Cremer was the daughter of Max Cremer, a professor of physiology. Her mother, Elisabeth (née Rothmund), descended from a dynasty of scientists. Erika had two brothers: Hubert was a mathematician at Technical High School Aachen; Lothar was a professor in acoustics at Technical High School Berlin.

Cremer attended the Lyzeum Boretius in Berlin beginning in October 1911, took her final examination at Elisabeth-Oberschule in Berlin in mathematics, physics, and chemistry with excellent marks ("Sehr Gut") on 21 February 1921, and then studied chemistry and physics at Kaiser Wilhelm University in Berlin. The introductory course Inorganic Experimental Chemistry (Anorganische Experimentalchemi) was given by Walther Hermann Nernst. Cremer was impressed by the opposing opinions of Nernst and Albert Einstein as she heard them expressed in the Physics Colloquium of Max von Laue.

In her thesis—"Über die Reaktion zwischen Chlor, Wasserstoff und Sauerstoff im Licht" (About the reaction between chlorine, hydrogen, and oxygen in light), supervised by Nernst's successor, Max Bodenstein—Cremer proposed a reaction scheme and drew as a possible conclusion the idea that the explosion process was due to chain branching. Nikolaj N. Semjonov, a professor of physical chemistry in Leningrad since 1931, learned of Cremer's thesis and invited her for a research visit at his institute for several weeks in 1932. Cremer later said that the idea of accounting for explosions in terms of chain branching had been her priority. When Semjonov, together with Cyril Norman Hinshelwood, received the Nobel Prize (1965, Chemistry) for research in chemical kinetics, Cremer was convinced that the Nobel Prize should have been awarded to her for her thesis work, just as Marie Curie had been awarded the Nobel Prize (1911, Chemistry) for her doctoral thesis study of radioactivity in 1903. She felt that Bodenstein had not given enough attention to the results of her thesis.

Cremer had personal contacts with many leading figures among Berlin's natural scientists. Strangely enough she seems to have had strong reservations against the Austrian Lise Meitner. She assumed that Meitner—after leaving Germany following the Anschluss of Austria and emigrating to Sweden—had more or less willingly diminished the credit due to Otto Hahn and Fritz Strassmann by handing a letter written by Hahn about his discovery of uranium fission to Niels Bohr, and by publishing a note together with her nephew Otto Robert Frisch in London soon thereafter.

Cremer had to overcome difficult times in her academic career after her promotion to PhD on 11 October 1927, and had to cancel several projects because of poor working conditions. However, because of her private and financial background and her obvious abilities she was able to collaborate in excellent groups during this time, partly as an unsalaried postdoctorate. At first she worked with Karl Friedrich Bonhoeffer; at other times she was in Freiburg with Georg Karl von Hevesy, who made available valuable samples of rare earth oxides for her investigations of catalytic reactions. Together with Hevesy as first author she published a paper "Über die Sulfate des Zirkoniums und Hafniums" (About the sulfates of zirconium and hafnium) in 1930. In October of that year Cremer returned to Berlin and started several projects in the new Kaiser-Wilhelm-Institut für Physikalische Chemie und Elektrochemie together with Michael Polanyi. However, she was still working without a funded position. The ascendancy of the Nazis to power ended her cooperation with Polanyi, who emigrated to England. Nothing in Cremer's public life reveals reservations on her part regarding National Socialism.

On 10 February 1939 Cremer was awarded a Dr. phil. habil. in Berlin for her investigation "Bestimmung der Selbstdiffusion in festem Wasserstoff aus dem Reaktionsverlauf der Ortho-Para-Umwandlung" (Determination of self-diffusion in solid hydrogen by the reaction scheme of ortho-para-conversion). She was now a member of the Uranverein (Uranium Society), a research group dealing with problems of using atomic energy. Carl Angelo Knorr, who since August 1940 had been building up physical chemistry at the University of Innsbruck and who knew Cremer from Munich, called her now to strengthen his group in Innsbruck. At this time Cremer had several offers for different positions. She continued her research for the habilitation in Innsbruck in an atmosphere she enjoyed because of scenic mountains and because of the rigorous catholic-conservative atmosphere. On 9 December 1940 she received a *Lehrbefugnis* (*doctor habilitatus*) for physical chemistry and was designated *Dozentin mit Diäten* (member of staff) on 8 April 1942. At the end of World War II the unmarried Cremer was the only representative of physical chemistry in Innsbruck. Nevertheless, her academic career proceeded sluggishly: On 6 February 1948 she received the title *außerordentlicher Universitätsprofessor* (extraordinary professor); on 21 March 1951 she was appointed to *außerordentlicher Universitätsprofessor für Physikalische Chemie;* and only on 11 February 1959 was she appointed *ordentlicher Universitätsprofessor* (professor with a chair) of physical chemistry.

In Innsbruck, Cremer took part in Knorr's research on catalytic hydration of acetylene. During this work she came upon the idea of applying methods described for liquids in liquid column chromatography to gases as gas chromatography. Theoretical considerations led to the conclusion that even very small differences in absorption energies should lead to the possibility of separating different gaseous samples, if the mixture to be separated is led by an inert carrier near to the surface of the adsorbing medium. Because this occurred during the war it was not possible to publish her invention of gas chromatography, although she got as far as reading the galley proofs of a note for the journal *Die Naturwissenschaften* and returning them to the journal in February 1945. After the liberation of Austria she told her PhD student Fritz Prior to verify her idea experimentally, and he built under her supervision the first gas chromatograph (Deutsches Museum). Cremer did not initially assign appropriate importance to what was in fact a genuinely brilliant idea. This episode illustrates how difficult it sometimes is for a scientist to recognize the real importance of one's own inventions. In

1952 the British chemists Archer John Porter Martin and Richard Laurence Millington Synge together were awarded the Nobel Prize in Chemistry for their invention of partition chromatography, a process formulated as "the partition of a substance between two liquids…as a new analytic tool."

Cremer continued investigating experimental and theoretical aspects of gas chromatography and did research in reaction kinetics, catalysis, adsorption, and thin-layer technology. In spite of her modest academic position at a provincial university she was able to actively participate in the international scientific community because of her excellent research as a physical chemist. Her numerous student courses enhanced her productivity as a researcher. She was frequently able to compensate for the lack of expensive instruments and substances that could not be provided by the small and resource-limited Austria.

After returning from a one-year leave as visiting professor at the Massachusetts Institute of Technology in Cambridge, Massachusetts (1953–1954), Cremer worked to build up a radiochemistry group at her institute. Cremer's school trained several well-known physical chemists who were successful both in industry and in academic science.

In 1964 Cremer was elected corresponding member of the mathematic-scientific class of the Austrian Academy of Sciences, and a full member in 1973. The academy in 1970 decorated her with the Erwin Schrödinger Award. In 1958 she received the Wilhelm Exner Medal of the Austrian Gewerbeverein, in 1965 she became doctor honoris causa of the Technical University Berlin. Additional recognitions included in 1974 the American M. S. Tswett Chromatography Medal, in 1978 the Tswett Medal of the USSR. She retired on 30 September 1970.

BIBLIOGRAPHY

WORKS BY CREMER

With Fritz Prior. "Anwendung der chromatographischen Methode zur Trennung von Gasen und zur Bestimmung von Adsorptionsenergien." *Zeitschrift fur Elektrochemie* (1951): 55, 66–69.

"How We Started to Work in Gas Adsorption Chromatography." *Chromatographia* 9 (1976): 364–366.

OTHER SOURCES

Bobleter, Ortwin. "Erika Cremer 1900–1996: A 96-Year Life of Research." *Chromatographia* (1996): 581–582.

Lambert, David, and Tony Osmond. *Great Discoveries and Inventions.* London: Orbis, 1985.

Miller, Jane A. "Women in Chemistry and Physics." In *Women of Science: Righting the Record,* edited by G. Kass-Simon and Patricia Farnes. Bloomington: Indiana University Press, 1990.

Neckel, Adolf. "Erika Cremer." In *Almanach der Österreichischen Akademie der Wissenschaften 1996/97.* Vol. 147, pp. 505–515. Vienna, 1998.

Oberkofler, Gerhard. *Erika Cremer (1900–1996): Ein Leben für die Chemie.* Innsbruck, Austria: Studien Verlag, 1998.

Pohl, W. Gerhard. "50 Jahre Gaschromatographie: Erika Cremer und Fritz Prior revolutionierten die Analytische Chemie." *Chemkon* 5 (1998): 7–8.

Schwarzl, Sonja M. "Zum Beispiel: Erika Cremer." *Nachrichten aus der Chemie* 49 (September 2001): 1106–1108.

Hans Mikosch
Gerhard Oberkofler

CRICK, FRANCIS HARRY COMPTON
(*b.* Weston Favell, Northampton, United Kingdom, 8 June 1916; *d.* La Jolla, California, 28 July 2004), *molecular biology, the genetic code, the neuroscience of consciousness.*

Crick was one of the central figures, one might say *the* central figure, in the molecular revolution that swept through biology in the latter half of the twentieth century. Having with James Watson discovered the structure of deoxyribonucleic acid (DNA), Crick went on to play a central role in the elucidation of the genetic code and the mechanism of protein synthesis. These achievements won him a share in the Nobel Prize in Physiology or Medicine in 1962. Much sought after as a lecturer, he became the "molecular evangelist," seeking to convert biochemists and biologists to the new science. He traveled extensively, broadcast on radio, and frequently wrote for *Scientific American.* His later years were spent in California, where he plunged into the complex world of neuroscience. Crick was vivacious, party-loving, gregarious, hospitable, and a gentleman. But he could react in a forthright manner to pomposity, pretentiousness, and stupidity. Those who knew him well did not find him arrogant or immodest.

Crick was the firstborn of Harry Crick, boot and shoe manufacturer, and Annie Elizabeth Wilkins, the elder daughter of F. W. Wilkins, a gentlemen's outfitter. Educated to the age of fourteen at Northampton Grammar School for Boys, he then entered Mill Hill School as a scholar and boarder. By the age of sixteen he had passed the Higher Certificate exams, gaining a distinction in physics, but stayed on a further two years. Failing to win a scholarship at either Cambridge or Oxford, he was accepted into the physics course at University College London. There he graduated with a second-class degree and began research on the viscosity of water. When World War II broke out in 1939, his physics department was evacuated to Wales, but he stayed behind.

Naval Research. Crick was among the six thousand scientists selected to support the armed forces as civilian scientists, and in 1940, he began work at the Admiralty Research Laboratory on the outskirts of London. In the winter of 1942, he was one of a five-man team of physicists and mathematicians sent to Havant, close to Portsmouth. There this team set to work to revitalize the Royal Navy's mine design program. Put in charge of the design of mine-firing mechanisms, Crick displayed imagination and skillful planning in challenging the enemy's use of mines as offensive weapons. Crick's performance in this work won him the respect of his seniors. Although at war's end Crick returned to London as a civil servant in the Admiralty, he felt dissatisfied with military research and decided to make a change.

Casting around for suggestions, he reflected on the principal subject matter of his scientific chats with colleagues. Instead of being physics it was biology: How do chromosomes perform their amazing "dance" in cell division? What is it that distinguishes a crystalline virus capable of reproduction from other organic crystals incapable of reproduction? What can neurophysiology reveal about the mystery of consciousness? Behind these concerns lay his ambition to show that "detailed scientific knowledge" that has already made many religious beliefs untenable, can banish the mystery of life and of consciousness too. While these mysteries "remain unexplained," he judged, "they can serve as an easy refuge for religious superstition." Removing these "unfortunate vestiges of earlier beliefs" would enable us to "find our true place in the universe." "Obviously," he confessed, "a disbelief in religious dogma was a very deep part of my nature" (Crick, 1988, p. 11).

A New Career: Crystallography. Crick's ambition was to learn the art of x-ray crystallography in order to study the structure of proteins, for in them surely lay the secret of life itself. The Medical Research Council (MRC) agreed to support him, however, only if he would first immerse himself in biology. That meant studying the whole cell, not just extracted material. After he spent two years at the Strangeways Laboratory fulfilling this requirement, his wish to study the structure of proteins was granted, and in 1949, he moved to the MRC Unit for the Study of the Molecular Structure of Biological Systems in Cambridge University's Cavendish Laboratory. There his first achievement was to administer a frontal attack on the methods of interpretation of x-ray data being used by his bosses, Sir Lawrence Bragg and Max Perutz, in their brave attempt to find the structure of hemoglobin. Teaching himself, Crick had mastered the application of Fourier theory to the data of x-ray diffraction patterns. Now he possessed an unrivaled insight into the strengths and limitations of these

Francis Harry Compton Crick. *Francis Harry Compton Crick with DNA structure model.* A. BARRINGTON BROWN/PHOTO RESEARCHERS, INC.

techniques and a remarkable ability to visualize molecular structures and their symmetry relations in space. This was manifested in his success simultaneously with William Cochran in deriving the main features of the x-ray diffraction pattern that a helical molecule should yield. Next he introduced the idea of supercoiling of helices to account for anomalous diffraction data from the α-keratin of wool that had proved so difficult to accommodate in helical models.

Armed with this knowledge, Crick realized that conventional approaches to the structural interpretation of diffraction patterns have limited value when dealing with DNA fibers, for these consist of long chain molecules packed in a regular order only in the fiber direction. Therefore they lack the three-dimensional lattice of a single crystal. That said, there are strict limitations on the different conformations that long chain molecules can take because they are oriented and packed tightly together in the fiber direction. So it is possible to guess a plausible structure, predict its diffraction pattern and check this against the diffraction data without carrying out the traditional, lengthy calculations, and without knowing the phases of the reflections. Linus Pauling's success with his alpha helix in 1951 was the classic example of this "stochastic method," as Pauling called it.

The Structure of DNA. In the fall of 1951, Crick was diverted somewhat from his protein research by the arrival of a young American, James D. Watson. Now Crick had found a collaborator, who like him recognized DNA as the chief if not the sole hereditary material, and after two attempts at building a model by the stochastic method, they arrived at the essentially correct structure in the spring of 1953. Their first attempt in 1951 had proved a fiasco and had caused the ire of Professor Bragg. Not until Pauling was about to publish his own structure for DNA had Bragg in February 1953 permitted Watson and Crick to make a second attempt. Now they opted for a two-chain cylindrical molecule, the helical chains on the outside of the cylinder held together by hydrogen bonds between the bases on the inside. This pairing of bases was specific, always adenine paired with thymine and guanine with cytosine, thus accounting for the strange 1:1 ratios between these pairs of bases described by the biochemist Erwin Chargaff.

The Watson-Crick structure was a proposal, based upon—and therefore supported by—the data of Rosalind Franklin, Raymond Gosling, and Maurice Wilkins published alongside it. Definitive proof of the structure, however, took almost another quarter of a century, owing to the difficulty of synthesizing small stretches of DNA in the form of single crystals.

Watson and Crick's first communication was exceedingly brief and went over the heads of most biologists, unfamiliar as they were with x-ray crystallography. The second paper, written largely by Crick, brought their proposal down to earth because it explained the relevance of their unusual two-stranded model to biologists. There they explained

> the precise sequence of the bases [on one chain] is the code which carries the genetical information. If the actual order of the bases on one of the pair of chains were given, one could write down the exact order of the bases on the other one, because of the specific pairing. Thus one chain is, as it were, the complement of the other, and it is this feature which suggests how the deoxyribonucleic acid molecule might duplicate itself. . . . The hypothesis we are suggesting is that the template is the pattern of bases formed by one chain … and that the gene contains a complementary pair of such templates. (Watson and Crick, 1953b, p. 966, 967)

But could DNA carry the enormous variety of genetic determinants involved? Providing the pairing rules were followed, any conceivable sequence was possible on one chain, the other carrying the complementary sequence. Here was speculation on a grand scale.

Despite all the excitement about DNA—the steady stream of visitors coming to see the model, among them Pauling from California and Gerald Pomerat from the Rockefeller Foundation—the impact of Watson and Crick's proposal within the Cavendish laboratory was mixed. Members of the university's Subdepartment of Crystallography—quite distinct from the Medical Research Council Unit—were unimpressed. But Bragg became very excited. He had been looking forward to Crick's departure from the lab once his doctoral thesis was completed. Now he began to appreciate Crick's potential. But Crick was scheduled to spend the next academic year at the Protein Institute in Brooklyn, New York, to help the team there studying the structure of the protein ribonuclease. Then he had the option to work with Linus Pauling at the California Institute of Technology.

Fortunately Crick was able to complete his doctoral dissertation and defend it before leaving for Brooklyn. It was formally awarded to him in absentia in 1954. Meanwhile his future was uncertain. Not until the spring of that year did he receive a new seven-year contract from the Medical Research Council and decide to return to Cambridge.

Crick stayed with the MRC Unit in Cambridge when in 1957 it was moved out of the Cavendish into the hut

close by then, in 1962, to the new Laboratory of Molecular Biology two miles from the center of Cambridge. Meanwhile his friends' nomination of him for a fellowship at King's College Cambridge in 1956 failed, as did his application for the chair of genetics at Cambridge University as Ronald Fisher's successor in 1957. The fellowship he accepted at the projected Churchill College in 1960 turned sour when the decision was taken to build a college chapel. Crick resigned over the issue in 1961, but was persuaded to accept an honorary fellowship subsequently. He was a member of Gonville and Caius College, subsequently was given dining rights, and made an honorary fellow in 1976.

The Genetic Code and Protein Synthesis. Given that the gene's specificity or "information" is encoded in a base sequence of DNA, how is that translated into the immediate gene product: a polypeptide chain composed of a specific sequence of amino acids? Stimulated by the physicist George Gamow, Crick joined in the effort to use cryptography to solve the problem, but all the schemes considered suffered from limitations on the variety of possible amino acid sequences. Nature's proteins showed no such limitations.

Cogitating on the coding problem, Crick began to ponder the relation between the nucleic acids and the proteins, and to make this the subject of his lecture, "On Protein Synthesis," delivered to the Society for Experimental Biology in 1957. Here he laid out the framework that was to constitute the core principles of what became the classical period of molecular biology. First came the *Sequence Hypothesis* stating that "the specificity of a piece of nucleic acid is expressed solely by the sequence of its bases, and that this sequence is a (simple) code for the amino acid sequence of a particular protein" (1958, p. 152). Second came the *Central Dogma:* "the transfer of information from nucleic acid to nucleic acid, or from nucleic acid to protein may be possible, but transfer from protein to protein, or from protein to nucleic acid is impossible. Information means here the *precise* determination of sequence …" (p. 153).

Given these restrictions on information transfer, how can a match be achieved between a triplet of bases and the amino acid for which the triplet is the cipher? Crick had already discussed this problem earlier and had suggested the existence of "adaptor molecules," small molecules with hydrogen-bonding sites attached to the appropriate amino acid by special enzymes. His prediction was fulfilled by the discovery of transfer RNA (tRNA).

This framework served its purpose admirably at the time. The extraordinarily complex picture that has since emerged has understandably introduced qualifications. But the discovery in 1970 of a type of RNA that can transfer sequence information back to DNA (reverse transcriptase) did not flout Crick's definition of the Central Dogma. The great surprise came eight years later. This was the discovery that whole chunks of the RNA transcribed from the gene are often excised before translation of the message into protein begins. Crick commented on these discoveries, accepting that the early ideas were too simple. In this sense he admitted that some of his critics were proved right.

When Sydney Brenner joined the MRC Unit in 1957, their remarkable collaboration began. Also attracted to the unit as visitors that year were the world experts on the genetics of bacterial viruses (bacteriophages or "phages") Seymour Benzer and George Streisinger. They attempted to discover the code by establishing the base sequence in a gene and the corresponding amino acid sequence in its protein product. But Crick and Brenner continued their own study of the genetics of phage mutations.

In February 1961, Crick began a series of experiments based on an idea he had about the manner in which a mutation can be "suppressed" by a further mutation. The results led him to support Brenner's suggestion that such "suppressions" are due not to *substitution* of a different base in a sequence of bases on the DNA molecule, but to *addition* or *deletion* of a base. After conducting extensive experiments for some five months, Crick attended a meeting in the Alps. There he mentioned this idea, and the hypothesis "that the code is read in short groups, starting from one end of the gene. The exact starting point is supposed to determine which group is read" (Crick, 1961a, p. 188).

Back in Cambridge Crick carried out further experiments to clinch the case for the "short groups" being composed of three bases or a multiple thereof. In their classic paper summarizing this work, the Cambridge group claimed that the genetic code "is of the following general type": three bases (or a multiple of three) codes for one amino acid. It is not an overlapping code, "probably 'degenerate'; that is, in general, one particular amino-acid can be coded by one of several triplets of bases," and "the sequence of the bases is read from a fixed starting point.... There are no special 'commas' to show how to select the right triplets" (Crick et al., 1961, 1227).

Meanwhile he had listened in Moscow to Marshall Nirenberg describe the stunning result of his work with Johann Matthaei on the synthesis of the polypeptide polyphenylalanine (polyPhe), using as template the synthetic RNA polyuridylic acid. PolyU, they concluded, codes for polyPhe. The Cambridge group had revealed the general nature of the code, and Nirenberg and Matthaei had identified the specific cipher for one of the twenty amino acids.

This discovery of the code was the last time Crick worked at the bench. After exploring embryological development with Peter Lawrence, he turned to the mysteries of the chromosome, excited by the discussions ongoing over the enormous amount of nongenetic DNA therein. Here was a chance to provide a model the structure of which might suggest why there is so much repetitive DNA in chromatin and how gene expression is regulated. Unfortunately his structure was proved to be entirely wrong, but it served as the stimulus to attract Roger Kornberg and Aaron Klug to the subject. Kornberg turned the field upside-down by situating the histone on the inside of the chromosome in the form of beads (nucleosomes) and around these beads the DNA is wound. Crick went on to collaborate with Klug on a model that could achieve the ten-thousand-fold compacting suffered by human chromosomes during nuclear division.

From 1959 he had helped Jacob Bronowski and Jonas Salk formulate the plans for the projected Salk Institute in La Jolla, California, and was a nonresident fellow to the institute from 1962 until 1974. The academic year 1976–1977 he spent on sabbatical there. In 1977, he accepted the position of Kieckhefer Distinguished Professor at the Salk, holding it for the rest of his life. Although he avoided whenever possible undertaking administrative work and sitting on committees, he was a powerful influence in deciding policy both in Cambridge and in La Jolla. He refused honorary degrees, the CBE, and a knighthood, but in 1991, he accepted the very exclusive Order of Merit from Queen Elizabeth II. However, he has frequently been referred to erroneously as Sir Francis and even as Lord Crick.

The Brain and Consciousness. For many years Crick had been following developments in neurophysiology from a distance. It was the move to California that helped him to extricate himself from old agendas and turn to new ones. His long-term goal was to tackle "the problem of consciousness," concentrating on visual perception in primates. He had "rather little expectation of producing any radically new theoretical ideas at such an advanced age," but he thought he "might interact fruitfully with younger scientists." At this time in his life, he felt he "had a right to do things" for his own amusement, so long as he "could make an occasional useful contribution" (*What Mad Pursuit*, p. 152).

He approached the subject without prejudice, ready to consider mathematical-computational and physiological approaches. Having Tomaso Poggio, David Marr, and Graeme Mitchison visit and work with him at the Salk Institute, he immersed himself in the computational approach. But he became skeptical of some of the mathematical modeling of visual processing. His strongest criticisms were directed at those cognitive psychologists who showed no concern for the lack of biological realism in their schemes. Repeatedly he stressed how inappropriate was the analogy drawn between the standard digital computer and the brain. And when he joined the group in the Psychology Department of the University of California at San Diego studying parallel distributed processing—as distinct from the serial processing of standard computers—he repeatedly stressed the need to consider whether their schemes were applicable to the manner in which the brain is wired.

An example of a computational approach that led to an interesting hypothesis was Crick and Mitchison's paper on the function of dreaming. They found that computer simulations of neural nets when subjected to heavy use become overloaded and unable to continue functioning normally. Cutting off any input, and permitting the nets to cycle over and over, mysteriously restored normal function. Might this not happen in the brain also? Is that what happens when people dream, sensory input being cut off, and rapid eye movements (REM sleep) occurring? Accordingly they suggested that the function of REM sleep is to "unlearn" unwanted "modes of excitation." They called it "reverse learning."

Crick laid most emphasis upon physiological and anatomical approaches to the brain, for these involved opening the "black box." He had been delighted at the way David Hubel and Torsten Wiesel used the technique of single-cell recording to reveal the "functional anatomy" in the visual centers of the brain. Looking ahead, he urged that greater effort be put into developing new techniques for unraveling the brain's immensely intricate anatomy.

For the last fourteen years of his life, Crick collaborated with Christoff Koch, professor of cognitive and behavioral biology at Caltech, on the subject of consciousness. Putting aside the difficult problem of explaining how neural events can yield the subjective states of consciousness known as qualia, they looked for the neural correlates of consciousness (NCC). What particular neural activity is present during conscious activity, but absent from activity that is not conscious? Their ambition was to achieve a "framework" that would do for consciousness what the DNA double helix did for molecular biology.

This framework, they claimed, was the first "coherent scheme for the NCC." Underlying it was the idea of competing coalitions of neurons, some at the back of the brain, others at the front. The mechanisms of attention "bias the competition among these nascent coalitions." Crick had the conviction that most of what people assume is conscious activity is in fact zombie-like activity. People have the sense of consciously coming to decisions, but they are really the product of unconscious computation. What they are conscious of is only the end result of that computation. As for the function of consciousness, Crick and Koch suggested it serves "to produce the best current interpretation" of the sensory data. Like an "executive summary" it overcomes the problem of data overload thus making possible a swift response.

Crick as Author. From the earliest of his scientific papers, Crick showed good organization and clarity of expression. Not surprisingly, he was the one asked to write the first draft of so many of the jointly authored papers. In writing for general audiences, he knew how to explain the science at their level without being condescending. He started several book projects, but traveling so frequently to meetings and being on the international lecture circuit he was rarely sufficiently settled to carry them through. His first book *Of Molecules and Men* contained his John Danz lectures. They were devoted to critiquing vitalism by marshaling the successes of molecular biology. The lectures ended with a denunciation of religious education, denial of the existence of an immortal soul, and a prevision of "a time when vitalism will not seriously be considered by educated men" (p. 99).

Very different in tone was *Life Itself: Its Origin and Nature.* This was distilled from his many discussions with Leslie Orgel, his colleague at the Salk Institute, and enlarges on an idea they had in 1973 and called "directed panspermia." They suggested that life did not originate on this Earth, but was brought to it in the form of microorganisms carried in an unmanned spaceship from a "higher civilization" elsewhere. This would account for the fact that the genetic code on this Earth is universal, barring a few trivial variants. It assumes that the primitive environment of the Earth was too hostile for the emergence of life here. As an exercise in imagination it was intended to provoke the reader. Crick doubted whether it was likely to be true.

Asked by the Sloan Foundation to write about his life, Crick decided to use his experiences "to teach some general lessons about how research is done, and what mistakes to avoid." Hence, the book begins with a quotation from Oscar Wilde: "Experience is the name everyone gives to their mistakes." The book's title he took from his first public talk on the structure of the proteins: *What Mad Pursuit.* Crick described the experience early in his career at Cambridge of witnessing Bragg's failure to discover the alpha helix that made such a deep impression on him. The most striking error he identified was that of assuming that the nucleoprotein particles in the cytoplasm, later called ribosomes, contain the genetic message. Here, fortunately, aided by their colleague Francois Jacob from the Pasteur Institute, Crick and Brenner were among the first to realize there must be a separate RNA messenger (mRNA).

His last book, *The Astonishing Hypothesis,* was the product of his long-felt need to reconstitute the moral and legal framework of society on a scientific basis. Hence the need to understand human nature, but to achieve this, he claimed, requires a scientific understanding of the nature of consciousness. Only then can people hope to understand humanity's place in nature. Continuing with outmoded concepts will only lead, he foresaw, to a world so overpopulated as to spell disaster. After explaining with consummate skill many of the complex features of the brain, he ended with "Dr. Crick's Sunday Morning Service." Here he expressed his hope that scientific research will make it possible to argue that "the idea that man has a disembodied soul is as unnecessary as the old idea that there was a Life Force" (p. 261).

Crick died in 2004 after a courageous fight against colon cancer. Following a private family memorial, a public memorial was held at the Salk Institute to honor his remarkable contributions to twentieth-century science. Crick's marriage to Ruth Doreen Dobbs in 1940 was dissolved seven years later. In 1949, he married Odile Speed. He was survived by his wife, his son Michael from his first marriage, and Gabrielle and Jacqueline from his second, plus six grandchildren.

BIBLIOGRAPHY

For a complete list of Crick's published papers see: http://www.pitt.edu/rhpsdept/people/primary_faculty.html#Olby. For manuscript sources see: The Wellcome Library for the History and Understanding of Medicine. Online catalogue of Western Manuscripts and Modern Papers. Reference PP/CRI/A to M. A copy of these papers is at the Mandeville Special Collections Library 0175-S, University of California at San Diego, MSS 600. The Crick Family Papers are only available at UCSD, MSS 660.

WORKS BY CRICK

With W. Cochran. "Evidence for the Pauling-Corey _-Helix in Synthetic Polypeptides." *Nature* 169 (1952): 234–235.

"Is α-Keratin a Coiled Coil?" *Nature* 170 (1952): 882–883.

With W. Cochran and V. Vand. "The Structure of Synthetic Polypeptides: I. The Transform of Atoms on a Helix." *Acta Crystallographica* 5 (1952): 581–586.

With James D. Watson. "The Molecular Structure of Nucleic Acids: A Structure for Deoxyribonucleic Acid." *Nature* 171 (1953a): 737–738.

With James D. Watson. "Genetical Implications of the Structure of Deoxyribonucleic Acid." *Nature* 171 (1953b): 964–967.

With James D. Watson. "The Complementary Structure of Deoxyribonucleic Acid." *Proceedings of the Royal Society,* Series B, 223 (1954): 80–96.

"The Structure of the Synthetic α-Polypeptides." *Science Progress* 42 (1954): 205–219.

"The Structure of the Hereditary Material." *Scientific American* 191 (1954): 54–61.

With B. S. Magdoff and V. Luzzati. "The Three-Dimensional Patterson Function of Ribonuclease II." *Acta Crystallographica* 9 (1956): 156–162.

With James D. Watson. "The Structure of Small Viruses." *Nature* 177 (1956): 473–476.

"On Degenerate Templates and the Adaptor Hypothesis: A Note for the RNA Tie Club." Unpublished paper distributed to members of the RNA Tie Club, 1956. Crick Papers, Wellcome Library. Online catalogue of Western Manuscripts and Modern Papers. Reference PP/CRI/H/1/38.

With J. C. Griffith and L. E. Orgel. "Codes without Commas." *Proceedings of the National Academy of Sciences of the United States of America* 43 (1957): 416–421.

"On Protein Synthesis." In "The Biological Replication of Macromolecules." *Symposia of the Society of Experimental Biology* 12 (1958): 138–163.

With Leslie Barnett, S. Brenner, and R. J. Watts-Tobin. "General Nature of the Genetic Code for Proteins." *Nature* 192 (1961): 1227–1232.

"The Genetic Code." *Scientific American* 207 (1962): 66–74.

"Discussion." *Deoxyribonucleic Acid. Structure, Synthesis and Function, Proceedings of the 11th Annual Reunion of the Société de Chimie Physique,* June 1961, p. 188.

Of Molecules and Men. Seattle: University of Washington Press, 1966.

"Central Dogma of Molecular Biology." *Nature* 227 (1970): 561–563.

"General Model for the Chromosomes of Higher Organisms." *Nature* 234 (1971): 25–27.

With P. A. Lawrence. "Compartments and Polyclones in Insect Development." *Science* 189 (1975): 340–347.

"Split Genes and RNA Splicing." *Science* 204 (1979): 264–271.

"Thinking about the Brain." *Scientific American* 241, no. 3 (1970): 219–232.

Life Itself: Its Origin and Nature. New York: Simon and Schuster, 1981.

With G. Mitchison. "The Function of Dream Sleep." *Nature* 304 (1983): 111–114.

What Mad Pursuit: A Personal View of Scientific Discovery. New York: Basic Books, 1988.

With C. Koch. "The Problem of Consciousness." *Scientific American* 267 (1992): 152–159.

The Astonishing Hypothesis: The Scientific Search for the Soul. New York: Simon and Schuster, 1994.

With C. Koch. "A Framework for Consciousness." *Nature Neuroscience* 6 (2003): 119–126.

OTHER SOURCES

Ashe Lincoln, F. *Secret Naval Investigator.* London: William Kimber, 1961.

Blackmore, Susan. *Conversations on Consciousness.* Oxford: Oxford University Press, 2006.

Brenner, Sydney. *My Life in Science.* London: BioMed Central, 2001.

Chadarevian, Soraya de. *Designs for Life: Molecular Biology after World War II.* Cambridge, U.K.: Cambridge University Press, 2002.

Cowie, Captain J. S. *Mines, Minelayers, and Minelaying.* London: Oxford University Press, 1949.

Judson, Horace F. *The Eighth Day of Creation: Makers of the Revolution in Biology.* Expanded edition. Cold Spring Harbor, NY: Cold Spring Harbor Laboratory, 1996.

Olby, Robert. "Francis Crick, DNA, and the Central Dogma." *Daedalus* 99 (1970): 938–987. Reprinted with a postscript and comments from Dr. Crick and his aunt, Mrs. Arnold Dickens. In *The Twentieth-Century Sciences: Studies in the Biographies of Ideas,* edited by Gerald Holton. New York: Norton, 1972.

Ridley, Matthew. *Francis Crick: Discoverer of the Genetic Code.* London: Harper Collins, 2006.

Watson, James D. *The Double Helix: A Personal Account of the Discovery of the Structure of DNA.* Norton Critical Edition. New York: Norton, 1980.

Robert C. Olby

CRONQUIST, ARTHUR (*b*. San Jose, California, 19 March, 1919; *d*. Provo, Utah, 22 March, 1992), *botany, plant taxonomy, monography, phytogeography, systems of classification of flowering plants.*

Cronquist provided the framework for ushering in a generation of plant systematists using phylogenetic analysis, molecular data, and bioinformatics. Best known for his system of classification of angiosperms (flowering plants), Cronquist should equally be credited for his body of work in floristics, the taxonomic study of the flora of a given geographic region. Two factors enabled Cronquist to become one of the foremost botanists in the twentieth century. The first was his ability to assimilate botanical information: Cronquist readily translated field observations and assessments of variation present in herbarium specimens into concisely written species descriptions and clear, usable, taxonomic keys. The second factor was Cronquist's forty consecutive years at the New York Botanical Garden in the Bronx, New York, where he had access to a comprehensive herbarium and one of the best botanical libraries in the world. Cronquist would eventually incorporate his vast knowledge of angiosperm families gained from years of floristic studies into significant work focused on general systems of angiosperm classification.

Early Years. Arthur Cronquist was born in San Jose, California, and grew up near Portland, Oregon, and Pocatello, Idaho. Cronquist's parents divorced when he was a young child, and he and his older sister were raised by his mother, Fern, who held a position with the Union Pacific Railroad in Pocatello. His involvement with the Boy Scouts of America played an important role in focusing his interest on the outdoors and prompting him to learn the natural history of the Pacific Northwest. Cronquist enrolled in the Southern Branch of the University of Idaho (later Idaho State University) in Pocatello and was influenced there by Professor Ray J. Davis, who was working on the *Flora of Idaho.* After completing a bachelor's degree in 1938, Cronquist entered Utah Agricultural College (later Utah State University) at Logan and completed his master's degree in 1940 under the direction of Dr. Bassett Maguire. The subject of Cronquist's master's thesis was the *Aster foliaceous* complex, and it marked the beginning of his lifelong interest in the Asteraceae (sunflower family). Because a childhood accident left Cronquist with incomplete use of his right arm, he was ineligible to serve in the armed forces in World War II and instead enrolled in a doctoral program at the University of Minnesota in Minneapolis. For his dissertation, directed by Dr. C. O. Rosendahl, Cronquist revised the genus *Erigeron* and strengthened his expertise in Asteraceae.

New York Botanical Garden. Focusing on a large family of flowering plants was instrumental in Cronquist securing a junior staff position at the New York Botanical Garden in 1943. Dr. Henry Gleason was completing *The New Britton and Brown Illustrated Flora* (3 vols., 1952) and drafted Cronquist to work on a treatment of Asteraceae for this work before Cronquist completed his dissertation in 1944. Cronquist then spent two years at the garden before teaching botany at the University of Georgia (1946–1948) at Athens and at State College of Washington in Pullman (later Washington State University) (1948–1951). It is no surprise that Cronquist elected not to remain a university botanist, because his true interests were centered on floristic work. Floristic treatments provide the tool required by the ecologist, forester, and members of the general public who need to know plant names and readily retrieve information regarding plants and include keys and descriptions used to identify plants in a given geographic region. A position at a botanical garden provided the flexibility of schedule needed to complete extensive field seasons as well as access to extensive herbarium and library holdings needed for floristic studies. After serving as a botanist with the Belgian government for a year, Cronquist rejoined the scientific staff at the New York Botanical Garden in 1952 and he remained there until 1992.

Cronquist's return to the garden in 1952 rekindled his productive collaboration with Henry Gleason. Gleason's *New Britton and Brown Illustrated Flora,* which contained Cronquist's treatment of Asteraceae, appeared that year. Later, Gleason and Cronquist completed the *Manual of Vascular Plants of Northeastern United States and Adjacent Canada* (1963), known to a generation of plant taxonomy students as "the Green Bible." In 1964 Gleason and Cronquist published *The Natural Geography of Plants.*

Gleason was the most influential individual in Cronquist's career and immediately recognized his colleague's gifts for synthesizing botanical information and reaching an audience outside his own discipline.

The link between systematic botanists and the general public is via published floras. Floras consist of keys to identify plants and descriptions of all species found in a particular region, and they also commonly include other pertinent information valuable to the general public such as ethnobotanical uses of plants, whether the plant is native or introduced, and notes on the ecological occurrence of species. Monographic and revisionary studies of taxonomic groups constituted the bulk of scientific work completed in systematic botany during the 1940s and 1950s. (Monographs provide a detailed analysis and synthesis of the existing taxonomic data for a family, tribe or genus of plants, plus additional results of the monographer's original research of the taxonomic group.) These studies provided the framework for biosystematic studies in the 1960s, but the results of the monograph or revision are not readily available to the consumer of plant names. Cronquist completed revisionary studies but primarily as part of his preparations for floristic projects. Cronquist, who had summer jobs as a youth with the U.S. Forest Service in Idaho working on a range management project and was also an assistant to the Park Naturalist at Sequoia National Park in California, recognized that, too often, plant systematists produced works primarily for others in their own discipline. His return to the New York Botanical Garden propelled Cronquist into the position of being the foremost floristic botanist of his time, and besides his collaborations with Gleason, he contributed heavily to the *Vascular Plants of the Pacific Northwest* (1957–1969) and *Intermountain Flora* (1971–1992). Cronquist also excelled in instructing the next generation of floristic workers. His first doctoral student, Theodore Barkley, was a co-editor of *Flora of the Great Plains* (1986) and lead editor of the three Asteraceae volumes for the *Flora of North America* (2006).

Work on Classification. Cronquist expanded his interests to include general systems of classification and began publishing on the subject in 1957. His *The Evolution and Classification of Flowering Plants* (1968; 2nd ed.,1988) represents his views and approaches for understanding the relationships among flowering plants. In 1981 Cronquist's *An Integrated System of Classification of Flowering Plants,* a detailed classification of plant families, was presented to the botanical community. His system was incorporated into both the *Flora of North America* and *Flora of Australia* (1982–). The views presented in *An Integrated System* were very much shaped by Cronquist's warm working relationships with Armen Takhtajan of Russia, Robert F. Thorne of the United States, and Rolf Dahlgren of Sweden.

Many plant systematists refer to the relationships outlined in *An Integrated System* as the Cronquist-Takhtajan system, since the men so strongly collaborated with one another. Cronquist's ability to synthesize information and write with ease placed him in the position to publish a thorough summary of the state of plant classification. However, a case could be made that Dahlgren could have also contributed a significant future volume on the subject had it not been for his untimely death in an auto accident. Cronquist's *An Integrated System* provided the model classification that the present generation of plant systematists test, using phylogenetic analysis of molecular data.

Cronquist also used his considerable skills as a writer to reach a generation of general botany students. *Introductory Botany,* published in 1961 (2nd ed., 1971), was tailored for use in a two-semester course, and *Basic Botany,* published in 1973 (2nd ed., 1982), was widely adopted for use in one-semester courses. In both texts Cronquist framed the details of plant structure, function, and diversity within the context of organic evolution.

During his career, Cronquist was consulted on a number of legal cases, including a legal battle to prevent land development near Jackson Hole, Wyoming, and at least one creationism case. He also provided testimonies and statements regarding the taxonomy of *Cannabis* for several criminal cases involving the prosecution of individuals for possession of marijuana. Cronquist corresponded with Ernest Small, a Canadian colleague and expert of hemp use, on *Cannabis* taxonomy and its legal dimensions in American society.

Awards and Honors. Cronquist was active in numerous professional societies until his death. Many a presenter at professional meetings would shudder when Cronquist was in attendance. He often would ask questions in his distinctive, booming voice during presentations instead of waiting for the presenter to finish. After the presentation, Cronquist often chatted with his "target" and displayed his considerable warmth and charm as well as his full two meter (six-foot, eight-inch) stature. Throughout his career Cronquist was a guiding force for the American Society of Plant Taxonomists (ASPT), attending his last ASPT meeting in San Antonio, Texas, in 1991. Cronquist was the president of ASPT in 1962 and was second recipient of the Asa Gray Award, ASPT's highest honor, in 1985. Cronquist was also president of the Botanical Society of America (1973) and the Torrey Botanical Club (1976). Other professional awards and honors bestowed upon Cronquist include the Leidy Medal of the Academy of Natural Sciences, in Philadelphia (1970), honorary vice president of the XII International Botanical Congress, held in Leningrad (1975), and the Medal for Botany of the Linnean Society of London (1986). Probably the greatest reward Cronquist ever received was a lifetime of pursuing his boyhood passions of plants and natural history. Arthur Cronquist died peacefully of heart failure while examining specimens of *Mentzelia* in the Brigham Young University herbarium.

BIBLIOGRAPHY

The Arthur Cronquist Collection housed in the Records of the Herbarium of the New York Botanical Garden in The Bronx, New York, consists of correspondence, manuscripts and typescripts, research papers, institutional and legal records, photographs, and artwork spanning Cronquist's activities at the New York Botanical Garden from 1942 to 1992. The full scope of Cronquist-related materials at the Botanical Garden can be found at http://library.nybg.org/finding_guide/cronweb3.php. Theodore Barkley, "Arthur Cronquist (1919–1992)," Taxon *42 (1993): 480–488, includes a complete list of Arthur Cronquist's publications.*

WORKS BY CRONQUIST

With C. Leo Hitchcock, Marion Ownbey, and J. W. Thompson. *Vascular Plants of the Pacific Northwest.* Seattle, WA: University of Washington Press, 1957–1969.

With Henry A. Gleason. *Manual of Vascular Plants of Northeastern United States and Adjacent Canada.* Princeton, NJ: Van Nostrand, 1963.

With Henry A. Gleason. *The Natural Geography of Plants.* New York: Columbia University, 1964.

Introductory Botany. 2nd ed. New York: Harper and Row, 1971.

With Arthur H. Holmgren, Noel H. Holmgren, and James L. Reveal. *Intermountain Flora: Vascular Plants of the Intermountain West, U.S.A.* New York: Hafner Publishing, 1971–1992.

An Integrated System of Classification of Flowering Plants. New York: Columbia University Press, 1981.

Basic Botany. 2nd ed. New York: Harper and Row, 1982.

The Evolution and Classification of Flowering Plants. 2nd ed. Bronx, NY: New York Botanical Garden, 1988.

OTHER SOURCES

Barkley, Theodore. "Arthur Cronquist (1919–1992)." *Taxon* 42 (1993): 480–488.

"In Memoriam: Arthur Cronquist: an Appreciation." *Bulletin of the Torrey Botanical Club* 119 (1992): 458–463.

Takhtajan, Armen L. "In memory of Arthur Cronquist (1919-1992)." *Brittonia* 48 (1996): 376–378.

Melanie DeVore

CROSSE, ANDREW (*b.* Broomfield, Somersetshire, United Kingdom, 17 June 1784; *d.* Broomfield, 6 July 1855), *electricity, chemistry, geology, natural law.*

Crosse was among the earliest electrochemists to use electricity in mineral solutions to form naturally occurring crystals under experimental conditions. His observations of tiny insects within a laboratory environment supposed to be hostile to life precipitated an international controversy about the role of miracles and natural law in the formation of life. Despite the unwanted notoriety, Crosse was regarded as an eminent gentleman-philosopher whose avocation in experimental science promoted scientific learning in provincial regions of Great Britain in the first half of the nineteenth century.

Education and Early Electrical Experiments. Andrew Crosse lived with his parents, a younger brother, and half sister at a small estate, Fyne Court, in the parish of Broomfield, Somersetshire, England. His father, Richard Crosse, was a politically liberal high sheriff for Somersetshire whose scientific friends included Benjamin Franklin and Joseph Priestley. Like his father, Andrew's mother, Susannah Mary Porter, supported her son's scientific interests by employing a clerical tutor and, after her husband's death, supplying Andrew with electrical apparatus for use in experiments.

For secondary school studies, Andrew Crosse attended Reverend Samuel Seyer's Royal Fort School in Bristol, where young Crosse befriended other sons of the landed gentry. In 1802, he enrolled at Brasenose College, Oxford, as a gentleman commoner—a status that conferred certain special privileges such as dining with the college's fellows. After taking his degree and upon reaching his majority, he returned home in 1805 to manage his family's estate and nurse his terminally ill mother. He continued to live at Fyne Court with his brother and half sister until he married Mary Anne Hamilton in 1809. Over the next decade Mary Anne gave birth to seven children, with only four surviving into adulthood.

After leaving Oxford, Crosse abandoned plans to pursue a career in law to devote his time to electrical experiments at his estate. He outfitted a laboratory in the music hall of Fyne Court where he routinely conducted his experiments. He befriended literary and scientific men, most notably the chemist Humphry Davy and the amateur experimental electrician George John Singer, who supplied Crosse with a battery table of fifty large Leyden jars along with other equipment. In the organ gallery of the music hall Crosse assembled an instrument designed to measure atmospheric electricity, consisting of a cylindrical electrical machine and brass ball suspended over a large capacitor. He connected the ensemble to one-third mile of copper wires strung along the trees of his estate and observed that fog produced a much larger potential than other atmospheric conditions. His production of noisy and bright discharges in these experiments caused neighbors to dub him "the thunder and lightning man" (C. Crosse, p. 114). He reported his observations in lectures he delivered at the Taunton Mechanics Institute, Bristol, of which he was chairman. Singer described the experiments in *Elements of Electricity and Electro-Chemistry* (1814), a widely circulated textbook.

During this time, Crosse also conducted electrocrystallization experiments in which he sustained voltaic currents in mineral solutions that caused crystals to form on the current-carrying platinum wires. He began these studies as early as 1807, when he visited the nearby Holwell Cave and became fascinated by its rich stalactites and stalagmites. After several years, he produced more than two hundred varieties of crystals that included aragonite, malachite, and quartz. In 1836, he reported on his formation of crystals, improvements on the voltaic battery, and observations on atmospheric electricity to the Geological and Chemical Sections of the British Association for the Advancement of Science (BAAS) at Bristol. His audiences favorably received the evidence that his experiments seemed to provide in support of theories explaining naturally occurring geological formations by electrical action. Crosse emerged as "one of the great show-beasts of the meeting," having achieved national repute as a scientific philosopher of eminence (C. Crosse, p. 150).

The *Acari Controversy*. Crosse's new public recognition turned into notoriety when his next set of experiments caused an international sensation. While making further electrocrystallization experiments at Fyne Court in 1836, he unexpectedly observed the appearance, development, and propagation of tiny mites within conditions that he believed were destructive to life. He gave no opinion about the cause, but his observations prompted others to speculate about such agents as miracles and spontaneous generation. In the experiments, Crosse dripped a dilute solution of silicate of potash (potassium silicate) and hydrochloric acid on a porous stone of red iron oxide, electrified with current passing from a voltaic battery through platinum wires. Over the course of several weeks, he observed tiny white specks on the stone that gradually developed into mature insects. Advised by the British comparative anatomist and paleontologist Richard Owen, he concluded they were cheese mites and assigned them to the genus *Acarus*. An unauthorized account about the "Extraordinary Experiment" appeared in the local *Somerset County Gazette* and, reprinted by newspapers across Europe, made Crosse's discovery famous.

But readers generally denounced the news of an electrician allegedly professing natural—rather than divine—agency in the creation of life. Scientific experts were drawn into the fray, with one widely circulated report claiming that the famous chemist Michael Faraday had

successfully replicated the experiment, but Faraday publicly denied any interest in the question. An experiment by John Edward Gray and John George Children, zoologists at the British Museum, however, failed to generate the *Acarus*; their null results thus lent support to the deistic side of the debates. Others showed more sympathy toward the possibility of spontaneous generation. Crosse's friend, the Sandwich surgeon William Henry Weekes, reported having successfully reproduced the *Acari* (as Weekes termed the insects) in his trials. References to Crosse's experiments in further popular texts, including Robert Chambers's anonymous and widely controversial *Vestiges of the Natural History of Creation* (1844), John Newbery's children's book, *The Newtonian Philosophy*, Henry Noad's *Lectures on Electricity* (1844), and Alfred Smee's *Elements of Electro-biology* (1849), helped to make the galvanic insects famous among Victorian readers.

Later Researches. Retreating from the debates, Crosse returned to private research and his life as a liberal, local magistrate and country squire of means. At Fyne Court, he and his wife managed a dispensary where they offered electrotherapy to Broomfield villagers suffering from rheumatism and paralysis. Despite his retreat from scientific society, he maintained his intellectual friendships, hosting several distinguished guests, including Faraday, at his private laboratory. He also attended the less publicized meetings of the Electrical Society in London, of which he was a member, and the Somerset Archaeological and Natural History Society, of which he was a vice president. Mary Anne Crosse died in 1846, and on 22 July 1850, Andrew married Cornelia Augusta Hewitt Burns, a member of his London intellectual circle who shared in his scientific interests. Their marriage produced one son, born in 1852.

As with his earliest experiments, Andrew Crosse's last set of electrical experiments lent support to the latest theoretical developments in geology. In experiments he conducted in the 1850s, he employed a sustaining Daniell's battery to electrify a gold coin resting on a slab of marble in a weak sulfuric acid solution. He observed carbonic gas bubbles emerging from the decomposing marble and flecks of gold oxide separating from the coin, and he argued that the mechanical action of the bubbles was sufficient to dislodge the flecks. The interpretation resonated with a turn toward mechanical explanations of geological phenomena. However, when he presented his argument at the 1854 BAAS meeting in Liverpool, members reacted with skepticism. After the meeting, he returned to his experimental trials to resolve the criticisms, but a terminal paralytic seizure interrupted his work. Cornelia, who had assisted him, completed the unfinished experiments. Through a paper read to the Chemical Section of the

BAAS at Glasgow in 1855, she presented results that vindicated her husband's argument.

Andrew Crosse acquired national eminence for his electrical studies and international notoriety for stirring debates over divine versus natural causes. His private avocation at his country estate epitomized a form of country-house scientific research in Britain that gradually diminished alongside the rise of professional scientific institutions and the building of specialized laboratories toward the end of the nineteenth century. Accompanying his public fame is the popular image of Crosse as the embodiment of Mary Shelley's Dr. Frankenstein character; however no evidence exists confirming that Crosse may have inspired the gothic novel. His experiments, no doubt, contributed to the culture of electricity in which Frankenstein also participated. Posthumously, his manor house—largely destroyed by a fire in 1894—was given to the National Trust in 1967. Primarily through the efforts of the Somerset Trust for Nature Conservation, the remaining structure, including the undamaged music hall, was restored in 1977 for tenancy by the trust and for other public uses.

BIBLIOGRAPHY

WORKS BY CROSSE

"Experiments in Voltaic Electricity." *Philosophical Magazine* 46 (1815): 421–446.

"Mr. Crosse's Experiments." *Bristol Advocate* 1, no. 21 (4 February 1837): 165.

"Description of Some Experiments Made with the Voltaic Battery." *The Transactions and the Proceedings of the London Electrical Society, from 1837 to 1840*, 1841, 10–16.

OTHER SOURCES

Anonymous [Shelley, Mary Wollstonecraft]. *Frankenstein, or The Modern Prometheus*. 3 vols. London: Lackington, Hughes, Harding, Mayor and Jones, 1818.

Bragg, William. "Extraordinary Experiment." *Somerset County Gazette* 1, no. 1 (31 December 1836): 3.

Crosse, Cornelia A. H. *Memorials, Scientific and Literary, of Andrew Crosse, the Electrician*. London: Longman, 1857.

Hunt, Robert. "Crosse, Andrew (1784–1855)," revised by J. A. Secord. In *Oxford Dictionary of National Biography*, edited by H. C. G. Matthew and Brian Harrison. Oxford: Oxford University Press, 2004. Also available (by subscription only) at http://www.oxforddnb.com/view/article/6799.

Mead, Audrey. *Andrew Crosse: Scientific Squire of Broomfield*. Broomfield: Somerset Trust for Nature Conservation, n.d.

———. *The Story of Fyne Court and Broomfield*. Reprint. Broomfield: Somerset Wildlife Trust, 1997.

Morus, Iwan. *Frankenstein's Children: Electricity, Exhibition, and Experiment in Early-Nineteenth-Century London*. Princeton, NJ: Princeton University Press, 1998.

Noad, Henry M. *Lectures on Electricity: Comprising Galvanism, Magnetism, Electro-Magnetism, Magneto- and Thermo-Electricity*. Rev. ed. London: G. Knight, 1849.

Opitz, Donald L. "Crosse, Andrew." In *The Dictionary of Nineteenth-Century British Scientists*, edited by Bernard Lightman. Bristol: Thoemmes Continuum, 2004.

Secord, James A. "Extraordinary Experiment: Electricity and the Creation of Life in Victorian England." In *The Uses of Experiment: Studies in the Natural Sciences*, edited by David Gooding, Trevor Pinch, and Simon Schaffer. Cambridge, U.K.: Cambridge University Press, 1989.

Singer, George John. *Elements of Electricity and Electro-Chemistry*. London: Longman, Hurst, Rees, Orme, and Brown, and R. Triphook, 1814.

Smee, Alfred. *Elements of Electro-Biology, or, The Voltaic Mechanism of Man; of Electro-Pathology, Especially of the Nervous System; and of Electro-Therapeutics*. London: Longman, Brown, Green, and Longmans, 1849.

Telescope, Tom, *Pseud.* [John Newbery]. *The Newtonian Philosophy, and Natural Philosophy, and Natural Philosophy in General, Explained and Illustrated in Familiar Objects*. Rev. ed. London: Thomas Tegg and Son, 1838.

Weekes, William H. "Details of an Experiment in Which Certain Insects, Known as the *Acarus crossi*, Appeared." *Proceedings of the London Electrical Society* 1 (1842): 240–256.

Donald L. Opitz

CROWFOOT, DOROTHY
SEE **Hodgkin, Dorothy Mary**.

CULLEN, WILLIAM (*b.* Hamilton, Scotland, 15 April 1710; *d.* Kirknewton, near Edinburgh, 5 February 1790), *chemistry, physiology, natural history, psychology.* For the original article on Cullen see *DSB*, vol. 3.

Cullen was one of the leading chemists of eighteenth-century Europe. Although he taught many talented students, the nineteenth and early twentieth centuries remembered him primarily for the supporting role that he played in the isolation of fixed air (carbon dioxide) by his protégé Joseph Black. Such an approach was part of a larger historiography that framed most eighteenth-century chemists, Cullen and Black included, as opening acts for the new chemical nomenclature that was proposed in France at the end of the century. Although histories written in this tradition have shed much light on select topics such as heat and gas, they usually bracket most of the theories and practices that do not resemble those used by modern chemists. Recent work on Cullen and his times, however, has revealed that chemistry was an exciting enterprise that was practiced both in the laboratory and in a wide variety of local settings such as mineral wells, farmer's fields, infirmaries, and factories. When viewed from this perspective, Cullen turns out to be an extremely original and influential thinker.

Early Career. Cullen was first educated at home and then at Hamilton Grammar School. He briefly attended the University of Glasgow in 1729, but in the same year moved on to a short-lived apprenticeship with John Paisley, a highly regarded Glaswegian surgeon-apothecary. By the end of the year he had traveled to London where he was appointed surgeon on a ship that eventually sailed to Jamaica. He returned to Scotland three years later and set up a practice outside Hamilton. During the mid-1730s he attended several courses in the University of Edinburgh Medical School, but he remained a surgeon until he acquired an MD from the University of Glasgow in 1740. The next year he married Anna Johnstone, and he continued to practice as a physician until he was appointed professor of medicine at Glasgow in 1750.

From that point forward he championed the cause of chemistry, and in 1755 he was appointed to Edinburgh's chair in the subject. He quickly became one of the most popular lecturers. In 1766 he moved to the chair in the theory of medicine and in 1773 he settled into the chair of the practice of medicine and remained there for the rest of his career. Although he held different posts in the medical school, it was chemistry that underpinned his empirically minded approach to health and disease. His reputation and publications on these topics led to his being appointed to the Royal College of Physicians in Edinburgh (1756) and the Royal Society of London (1777). He was a longstanding member of Edinburgh's Philosophical Society and remained active as a fellow when it became the Royal Society of Edinburgh (1783). By the time of his death in 1790 he was one of the foremost chemists in Britain and, arguably, Europe.

Like many of his mid-eighteenth-century contemporaries, Cullen classified all observable matter into five principles: salts (acids and alkalines), inflammables, waters, earths, and metals (he added an "aer" principle in the 1760s). The compounds formed by these principles were held together by forces of attraction called affinities. Although he sometimes mentioned particles or corpuscles, Cullen refrained from linking microscopic manifestations of matter to Newtonian forces. In this sense he was part of a large wave of mid-century British chemists who rejected iatromechanism, that is, the belief that illness could be reduced to laws of motion or mechanical physics. Such theories had been promoted earlier in the century, but had failed to be therapeutically useful. Instead he used heat, water, and "menstrua" (acids and alkalis) as solvents to break down material conglomerates to various combinations of the five principles. Drawing from gravimetric practices forged in metallurgy, he used weight and ratios to determine the material composition of minerals, drugs, and bodily substances. As early as the 1750s he had developed different types of diagrammatic schemes that allowed him to represent visually the compounds formed by the combination or separation of different chemical species. It was these practices that Joseph Black, one of Cullen's protégés, would go on to refine when he performed experiments that confirmed the existence of fixed air (carbon dioxide).

Cullen was a keen promoter of in situ and in vitro experimentation, and his main concern was to define and categorize all of the matter comprehended under each principle into a reasonable classification of genera and species. He often called such arrangements "doctrines," and they were collectively known as a "system." Such an approach was inherently nominalistic and allowed him to continually reclassify genera and species based upon new experiments. Although he experimented on many topics, he remained interested in formulating his own "doctrine of salts" throughout his career. Because saline experimentation was the leading decompositional method used during the eighteenth century, he worked diligently to understand the composition of a wide variety of acids and alkalis. His research on this topic utilized the affinity tables first developed by Étienne-François Geoffroy in France during the 1710s. Drawing from a superior knowledge of books, monographs, and journals published across Europe, he fused his observations on affinity with the ideas offered by leading continental chemists such as Geoffroy, Hermann Boerhaave, and Georg Ernst Stahl. In addition to giving his own classification of salts, he also expanded Geoffroy's tables by adding fifteen new columns. By the late 1750s he was distributing printed copies of the table in his chemistry lectures. It was enthusiastically received by his students, including Black, Donald Monro, George Fordyce, and Benjamin Rush.

The Usefulness of Chemistry. Throughout his career Cullen worked diligently to show that chemistry was relevant to the larger improvement of Scotland's national economy. He gave lectures on georgics during the 1760s, and these inspired several leading agriculturalists, Lord Kames and John Anderson, for example, to use chemistry to study soil fertility. His research into Scottish potash production was also appreciated by industrialists involved in the linen, ceramic, and sulfuric acid industries. Yet even though these and other efforts put extra money in his pocket and strengthened his ties with government officials, his main experimental interests were guided by a practical concern for how chemical principles could be used to ameliorate disease. He held that substances contained "active principles" that had both positive and negative effects upon the human body. In particular he was influenced by a school of thought called neo-humoralism, which held that these principles could be used to regulate the hard and soft tissues of the body, thereby creating a balance of health. His overriding concern for identifying and systematizing the therapeutic effects of these principles led him to oversee original physiological experiments that guided the addition and removal of pharmaceutical cures contained not only in his own publications but also in the various editions of the widely read Edinburgh *Pharmacopoeia* (which he edited from 1773 to 1775). Indeed, his efforts to link in vitro experiments conducted in Edinburgh's Medical School with observations made in the city's Royal Infirmary made him one of Britain's leaders in clinical medicine.

Because drugs were made from mineral, plant, and animal substances, Edinburgh's primary site for systematic instruction in natural history was the Medical School. Cullen was an early convert to the utility of Carl Linnaeus's binomial nomenclature and used it not only to create medical systems but also to order his botanical and mineralogical specimens. For minerals, however, Cullen replaced Linnaeus's external characters (mainly color and shape) with those based on the principles of chemistry. His thoughts on this matter were influenced by the chemical mineralogies developed in continental Europe, especially in the work of Johann Pott and Axel Cronstedt. Throughout his career he actively followed international publications on this subject, especially works published by chemists connected to mining academies situated on or near the Baltic Sea. His expertise on mineralogy was respectfully acknowledged by Scotland's landed aristocracy, for whom he sometimes assayed ores and soils. This mineralogical legacy was institutionalized when the Reverend Dr. John Walker, one of Cullen's many protégés, was appointed as the Medical School's professor of natural history in 1779—one of the first chairs of the subject to be established in Europe. Both Walker and Black followed in their mentor's footsteps and taught their students how to use chemical characters to classify minerals and geological strata. Under Cullen's guidance they also became mineralogical advisors to some of Scotland's most powerful patrons, including Lord Bute, Lord Kames, and Lord Hopetoun.

Cullen's therapeutic approach was based upon a vitalistic physiology that treated the nervous system as the cause of chemical and mechanical processes. Although he recognized that the mind could influence the body and vice versa, he held that thought and matter were categorically different substances. Cullen's nervous system included not only the brain, spinal cord, and nerves but also different types of muscle fibers (especially those of the heart and stomach). As all of these "nervous fibers" regulated the hardness or softness of body tissue, they played a key role in maintaining health. In fact, Cullen coined the term *neurosis* to label most forms of sickness that could not be attributed to a fever or a localized disease. For such disorders he promoted both chemical and "hygenic" cures. To induce chemical cures he prescribed drugs with active principles that were known to stimulate or relax nervous fibers. He was particularly fond of the stimulatory (tonic) power of fixed air, and he regularly advised his patients to drink mineral water from spas that contained it. Hygenic cures regulated peace of mind via environmental factors. To relax nervous fibers he advised leisurely strolls in the country and spending time at spa resorts. He also prescribed novels to excite the nerves of those suffering from depression or a debilitating sickness—the most famous recipient of this cure being the philosopher Dugald Stewart.

Pedagogy and Publications. Cullen was extremely devoted to being a good lecturer. In many ways the world was his classroom. He was one of Britain's first medical professors to lecture in the vernacular (as opposed to using Latin), and he not only gave lectures in university halls but also took his students on excursions around the Firth of Forth and the Pentland Hills (where they collected pharmaceutical simples). No matter where he might be, he was always ready to conduct an experiment—the louder and brighter, the better. From the start his students were impressed with the pedagogical efficacy of his chemically based medical systems and the enthusiasm that he had for the subject. They diligently took notes that were transcribed and bound as manuscripts that were then treated just like medical textbooks, many of which are now housed at the University of Edinburgh and the Wellcome Library in London. Once students had taken his introductory classes Cullen then supervised final dissertations on subjects that were relevant to his own industrial and medical interests. Thus, during the 1750s and 1760s Cullen's chemical and physiological ideas were spread via manuscript notebooks, dissertations, and the high praise sung by his former students in Edinburgh, London, and Philadelphia.

Cullen's ideas also spread throughout Europe and its colonies via his correspondence and publications. By the end of his career he was receiving hundreds of letters per year requesting advice on everything from mining to depression. Many of his responses were more essays than letters, and they often were circulated among aristocratic households and European academic societies. Cullen's first publication was an article on the fall in temperature caused by evaporation, which appeared in the *Essays and Observations, Physical and Literary* (1756). It was soon combined with Black's essay on magnesia alba and converted into a pamphlet that went through at least two editions. Because Cullen made much of his money from fees paid by students who attended his lectures, he was initially reluctant to put his ideas into print. However, his lectures were so popular that a pirated version of his *materia medica* course appeared. This episode, and the legal wrangling that went along with it, baptized him into the world of medico-scientific print and no doubt motivated him to publish his other lectures before he lost money on more pirated editions. He went on to write *Synopsis nosologiae methodicae* (1769), *Institutes of Medicine* (1772), and his four-volume magnum opus *First Lines of the Practice of Physic* (1777–1784). His books went through multiple revisions and printings, and they were translated into several European languages (including Latin, German, French, and Dutch). His work was also included in medical anthologies well into the nineteenth century. Cullen's chemical ideas were also spread via chemistry books and articles written or translated by devoted students such as William Hunter, William Withering, Thomas Trotter, Charles Blagden, and John Brown.

SUPPLEMENTARY BIBLIOGRAPHY

The largest collection of Cullen's personal notes and letters, along with bound copies of student notes taken in his lectures, are housed in the libraries of the University of Edinburgh, the Royal Medical Society of Edinburgh, the Royal College of Surgeons of Edinburgh, the University of Glasgow, and the Wellcome Trust, London.

WORKS BY CULLEN

"Of the Cold Produced by Evaporating Fluids, and Some Other Means of Producing Cold." In *Essays and Observations, Physical and Literary, Read before a Society in Edinburgh and Published by Them.* Vol. 2, pp. 145–156. Edinburgh, 1756.

Synopsis nosologiae methodicae. Edinburgh, 1769.

Lectures on the materia medica. London: Printed for T. Loundes, 1772.

Institutes of Medicine. Edinburgh: Printed for Charles Elliot and T. Cadell, 1772.

First Lines of the Practice of Physici. Edinburgh: Printed for W. Creech, 1777–1784.

"A Cullen Manuscript of 1753." Edited by Leonard Dobbin. *Annals of Science* 1 (1936): 138–156. Cullen's classification of salts.

OTHER SOURCES

Bowman, Inci Altug. *William Cullen (1710–90) and the Primacy of the Nervous System.* PhD diss., Indiana University, Bloomington, 1975.

Bynum, William F., and Roy Porter, eds. *Brunonianism in Britain and Europe.* London: Wellcome Institute for the History of Medicine, 1988.

———, and Vivian Nutton, eds. *Theories of Fever from Antiquity to the Enlightenment.* London: Wellcome Institute for the History of Medicine, 1981.

Christie, John R. R. "Historiography of Chemistry in the Eighteenth Century: Hermann Boerhaave and William Cullen." *Ambix* 41 (1994): 4–19.

Clow, Archibald, and Nan L. Clow. *The Chemical Revolution: A Contribution to Social Technology.* London: Batchworth Press, 1952.

Cowen, David L. *Pharmacopoeias and Related Literature in Britain and America, 1618–1847.* Aldershot, U.K.: Ashgate, 2001.

Craig, William Stuart. *History of the Royal College of Physicians of Edinburgh.* Oxford: Blackwell, 1976.

Doig, Andrew, et al., eds. *William Cullen and the Eighteenth Century Medical World.* Edinburgh: Edinburgh University Press, 1993.

Donovan, Arthur L. *Philosophical Chemistry in the Scottish Enlightenment: The Doctrines and Discoveries of William Cullen and Joseph Black.* Edinburgh: Edinburgh University Press, 1975.

———. "Pneumatic Chemistry and Newtonian Natural Philosophy in the Eighteenth Century: William Cullen and Joseph Black." *Isis* 67 (1976): 217–228.

———. "William Cullen and the Research Tradition of Eighteenth-Century Scottish Chemistry." In *The Origins and Nature of the Scottish Enlightenment,* edited by R. H. Campbell and Andrew S. Skinner, 98–114. Edinburgh: J. Donald, 1982.

Eddy, Matthew D. 'The Doctrine of Salts and Rev John Walker's Analysis of a Scottish Spa, 1749–1761." *Ambix* 48 (2001): 137–160.

———. "Scottish Chemistry, Classification, and the Early Mineralogical Career of the 'Ingenious' Rev. Dr. John Walker (1746–1779)." *British Journal for the History of Science* 35 (2002): 411–438.

———. "Set in Stone: The Medical Language of Mineralogy in Scotland." In *Science and Beliefs: From Natural Philosophy to Natural Science,* edited by David Knight and Matthew D. Eddy, 77–94. Aldershot, U.K., and Burlington, VT: Ashgate, 2005.

Golinski, Jan V. "Utility and Audience in Eighteenth-Century Chemistry: Case Studies of William Cullen and Joseph Priestley." *British Journal for the History of Science* 21 (1988): 1–31.

Lawrence, Christopher. "Ornate Physicians and Learned Artisans: Edinburgh Medical Men 1726–1776." In *William Hunter and the Eighteenth-Century Medical World,* edited by W. F. Bynum and Roy Porter, 153–176. Cambridge, U.K.: Cambridge University Press, 1985.

Monro, Donald. "An Account of a Pure Native Crystalised Natron, or Fossil Alkaline Salt…." *Philosophical Transactions* 61 (1771): 567–573. Contains a chart listing Cullen's saline affinities.

Morrell, Jack B. "The University of Edinburgh in the Late Eighteenth Century: Its Scientific Eminence and Academic Structure." *Isis* 62 (1971): 158–171.

Risse, Guenter B. *Hospital Life in Enlightenment Scotland: Care and Teaching at the Royal Infirmary of Edinburgh.* Cambridge, U.K.: Cambridge University Press, 1986.

———. *New Medical Challenges during the Scottish Enlightenment.* Amsterdam: Rodopi, 2005.

Stott, Rosalie. "Health and Virtue; or, How to Keep Out of Harm's Way: Lectures on Pathology and Therapeutics by William Cullen, c. 1770." *Medical History* 31 (1987): 123–142.

Taylor, Georgette. "Unification Achieved: William Cullen's Theory of Heat and Phlogiston as an Example of His Philosophical Chemistry." *British Journal for the History of Science* 39 (2006): 477–501.

Thomson, John, W. Thomson, and David Craigie. *An Account of the Life, Lectures, and Writings of William Cullen, M.D.* 2 vols. Edinburgh, 1869. The best source on Cullen's life.

Withers, Charles W. J. "William Cullen's Agricultural Lectures and Writings and the Development of Agricultural Science in Eighteenth-Century Scotland." *Agricultural History Review* 37 (1989): 144–156.

———, and Paul Wood, eds. *Science and Medicine in the Scottish Enlightenment.* East Linton, U.K.: Tuckwell Press, 2002.

Wright, John. "Materialism and the Life Soul in Eighteenth-Century Scottish Physiology." In *The Scottish Enlightenment: Essays in Reinterpretation*, edited by Paul Wood, 177–197. Rochester, NY: University of Rochester Press, 2000.

Matthew D. Eddy

CUVIER, GEORGES

(baptized Jean-Léopold-Nicolas-Frédéric, but known as Georges) (*b.* Montbéliard, Württemberg [now in France], 23 August 1769; *d.* Paris, France, 13 May 1832), *zoology, paleontology, geology.* For the original article on Cuvier see *DSB*, vol. 3.

It is difficult to overestimate the huge impact of Cuvier on zoology, paleontology, and geology, and indeed on all the sciences encompassed by the Muséum d'Histoire Naturelle and the Institut National (later the Académie Royale des Sciences) in Paris, during his lifetime and in subsequent decades. Because Paris was then the center of the scientific world, and French its international language, his impact was felt even more widely. This was epitomized, for the scientific and social elites, by the cosmopolitan gatherings at his famous weekly salon; and, for the wider educated public, by the sales of his more accessible publications and particularly the editions of his "Preliminary Discourse" in its original French and in many translations. In an effective amalgam of Enlightenment rigor and Romantic imagination, Cuvier boosted the prestige of the sciences of nature throughout the European cultural sphere.

There has been a large body of important scholarly research on Cuvier since Franck Bourdier's *DSB* entry was published in 1971. Although the factual outlines of his account are generally accurate, his evaluation of Cuvier's scientific research has become seriously inadequate. In particular, Cuvier's work in Earth sciences deserves much fuller treatment. This postscript supplements the earlier entry and should be read in conjunction with it.

During his lifetime Cuvier was regarded as a towering figure in the natural sciences, not only in France but throughout the scientific world. The generally negative evaluation of his work later in the nineteenth century, and through much of the twentieth, was due mainly to the perception that he had been on the losing side in two major theoretical debates, in that he adamantly opposed all "transformist" (in modern terms, evolutionary) claims about organisms, and also championed "catastrophist" claims about Earth's past history. Furthermore, he was misrepresented as a biblical literalist: in French political and cultural struggles over the relation between church and state, he was misused posthumously as an icon of religious conservatism, while his older colleague and adversary Jean-Baptiste de Lamarck was equally misused as an icon of enlightened secularism. It was only in the late twentieth century that historians of the sciences, returning to the original sources, began to recover the grounds for Cuvier's outstanding reputation during his lifetime, and to appreciate his huge and enduring importance in the development of the modern natural sciences.

Cuvier was a beneficiary of the meritocratic policies of the Directorate and later regimes in France, which in contrast to the patronage networks of the Old Regime aimed to make "careers open to talent." He moved to Paris and joined the Muséum d'Histoire Naturelle not long after it was founded (or rather, "democratized" from the old royal museum and botanic garden). He worked initially as an assistant to the professor of anatomy and then as his successor; he had the chair renamed "comparative" anatomy, thereby enlarging its scope to cover the whole animal kingdom. For the rest of his life the museum provided him with a secure position (and a home), and also with outstandingly rich and varied collections of specimens relevant to his research. However, his spectacularly successful career within the museum, and far beyond it, was not only the product of exceptional scientific talents; it also required intensive political work, in which he was equally talented, among the Parisian elites. In parallel with his scientific career he built a prominent public career as an administrator, particularly in the field of higher education, serving each of the successive regimes in France with equal diligence. His willingness to do so has sometimes been criticized as revealing an unprincipled opportunist; it can better be attributed to the traditional Lutheran principle, which he would have absorbed in his youth, that every citizen had a duty to serve the state, even if the regime was uncongenial, for the greater good of maintaining a peaceable society. Having witnessed mob violence in

Normandy during the Revolution, Cuvier had good reason to value social stability.

Cuvier used his prominent position in French society to promote his own concept of what constituted sound and reliable scientific research. In his reports on work submitted to the institute for its approval, in his lengthy obituaries (*éloges*) of its deceased members, and in his compilation of his major *Rapport historique* (1810) on the recent progress of all the natural sciences, he commended research that was based on a detailed investigation of the relevant evidence and, conversely, criticized theorizing that lacked any such solid empirical foundations. He was certainly not averse to theorizing as such, and in his own research he worked hard to establish theoretical inferences from his detailed observations. But he was implacably hostile to the kind of speculative theorizing represented (in his opinion) by Lamarck, publicly deriding it when the opportunity arose.

Concept of Embranchment. Cuvier's main scientific research was in two distinct areas, linked only loosely with each other. Within zoology he worked on the traditional problems of animal classification. Here his most enduring achievement was to establish the reality of several sharply distinct kinds of anatomy underlying the bewildering diversity of animal forms. His four *embranchements* of the animal kingdom, first outlined in 1812 and set out more fully in his *Règne animal* (Animal kingdom; 1817), subsequently became the model for the more numerous and diverse phyla of modern zoology. Because all the vertebrates, from fish to mammals, constituted only one of his four *embranchements*, the "invertebrates" (as Lamarck had named all the others) were in effect elevated in relative significance, and the human species was no longer so unambiguously the pinnacle of the living world. At a more detailed level, Cuvier undertook substantial research on the comparative anatomy of all the vertebrate classes, from fish to mammals; but he also contributed importantly to the *embranchement* of the mollusks, which was poorly understood at the start of his career. His research on all these extremely diverse animals allowed full scope for his outstanding manual skills in dissection and biological drawing.

Cuvier's concept of *embranchement* was based on his belief that equivalent (or, in modern terms, homologous) parts could in principle be identified within any one of these great divisions of the animal kingdom (for example, a reptile's foreleg, a bird's wing, and the human arm), but that no such equivalents could possibly be identified between them, except as functional analogues (for example, the eyes of fish and of cephalopod mollusks). This was the kind of issue at stake between Cuvier and Étienne Geoffroy Saint-Hilaire, in their famously bitter and public dispute in 1830. Geoffroy Saint-Hilaire, Cuvier's colleague at the museum and his collaborator in their youth, claimed that true homologies could be detected between *embranchements,* there being an underlying common ground plan. The primary issues between the two naturalists were not those of transformism or evolution, but of comparative anatomy or morphology.

In some of Cuvier's early work he used the traditional language of the *échelle des êtres* (scale of beings), describing specific animals as being intermediate between others in the supposedly linear but atemporal "animal series" (with the human species as its highest point). But in practice he soon replaced this with an emphasis on the distinctness of animal taxa at all levels from the species and genus to the *embranchement*. Cuvier's apparent change of outlook in this respect may be related to the concurrent adoption of "scale" language by advocates of transformism such as Lamarck; but it was derived primarily from Cuvier's strong sense of the functional—and therefore anatomical—integration of the body in every kind of animal, as formalized in his concepts of the "correlation of parts" and the "subordination of characters."

Cuvier's insistence on the reality of organic species as the basic natural units of the animal kingdom was not the product of creationist thinking, or related in any way to issues of biblical interpretation. Instead it grew out of his conviction that each species is uniquely suited, by its functional anatomy, to a particular way of life, distinct even from those of closely similar species. It was therefore inconceivable to him that any one species could be transformed imperceptibly into another, no matter how much time was allowed, because no intermediate forms could or would be viable. This inference seemed to him to be confirmed by the absence of any such intermediates among living organisms (or rather, among the specimens in his museum collections). A celebrated case in point was the sacred ibis of the ancient Egyptians. Cuvier claimed that mummified specimens collected during Napoleon's military expedition in 1798–1799 were indistinguishable from the same birds still living in Egypt. He was well aware that the intervening span of perhaps three millennia was extremely brief compared with the likely total span of Earth's history; but he argued that even a brief interval should show some slight change, if in fact the same "transformist" (or evolutionary) process was responsible for the far greater changes needed to account for the total diversity of animal form. Lamarck's concept of the organic world as a theater of continual flux, lacking distinct natural units or stable categories of any kind, therefore seemed to Cuvier to subvert the foundations of classification, and hence of all the natural-history sciences. This contrast in fundamental concepts of nature is more than adequate to account for Cuvier's hostility to the kinds of transformist theorizing that were being advocated during his lifetime.

Georges Cuvier. *Lessons of anatomy of the baron Georges Cuvier in the Jardin des Plantes of Paris (Museum of Natural History), circa 1800.* **BOYER/ROGER VIOLLET/GETTY IMAGES.**

(Whether he would have reacted in the same way to Charles Darwin's theory, first formulated privately a decade after Cuvier's death, is a counterfactual question of some interest and importance.)

Work on Fossils. The second area of research in which Cuvier's impact was incalculable was in the sciences of Earth. Unlike his work in comparative anatomy, this was unplanned and unanticipated. It was prompted by two serendipitous events around the time of his arrival in Paris. The newly founded Institut National was sent some engravings from Madrid, depicting fossil bones from South America that had recently been assembled into a skeleton. Cuvier, the youngest member of the institute's natural-scientific "First Class," was asked to report on them. He concluded sensationally that the unknown mammal, which he named *Megatherium,* was a giant edentate quite distinct from any known living species. At the same time, specimens recently brought to the museum from a collection in the defeated Netherlands enabled him to confirm Johann Friedrich Blumenbach's inference that the Indian and African elephants were separate species, and, more importantly, that the Siberian fossil "mammoth"

was distinct from either. Cuvier's work on both these sets of fossil bones turned his attention to the already hotly debated question of extinction. He argued that the huge megatherium and mammoth were unlikely to be still alive (as "living fossils") yet unreported, even from remote regions, either by explorers or by indigenous peoples. Rigorous comparative anatomy of living and fossil animals might therefore help to test the reality of extinction. Because there were no reliable reports of human remains being found alongside the fossils, Cuvier suspected that extinction must be a natural event or process (not all cases being due, like the famous dodo, to human activities).

By the turn of the century Cuvier had compiled a growing inventory of fossil mammals that were, he claimed, distinct in their anatomy from any living species. Adopting Jean-André Deluc's language, he described them all as inhabitants of a prehuman "former world," separated from the "present world" of human societies by some great "revolution" that had caused a mass extinction. In 1800 he announced his intention to study all known fossil bones, in order to clarify this previously obscure aspect of natural history. He issued an international appeal to "savants and amateurs" to send him further specimens (or at least accurate drawings of them) from their own collections, in return for which he would offer authoritative identifications. Despite the wartime conditions there was a huge response. Cuvier made rigorous comparisons between all these fossil bones and the skeletons of extant species in the great collections at the museum. In a long series of papers (1804–1810) in the new *Annales du Muséum,* he claimed that the fossils were distinct, and argued that they all belonged to extinct species or even genera. In 1812 he republished these papers in his great four-volume *Recherches sur les ossemens fossiles* (Researches on fossil bones).

When lecturing in 1805 to the educated Parisian public, and later when writing the attractively readable "Discours préliminaire" prefixed to his *Ossemens fossiles,* Cuvier proposed an ambitious research program to reconstruct Earth's history by emulating analogically the methods of human historiography. He called himself "a new species of antiquarian," who was using fossil bones instead of human artifacts as historical evidence. He therefore argued that naturalists such as himself could and should aspire to "burst the limits of time," by making the prehuman history of Earth reliably knowable to humans confined to the present, just as astronomers such as Pierre-Simon de Laplace (to whom he dedicated his *Ossemens fossiles*) had already "burst the limits of space" by making the movements of the solar system accurately knowable to humans confined to one small planet (the reference in both cases was to extensions to human knowledge, not to the magnitudes of either time or space). These two key analogies, with historiography and with astronomy, caught the imagination of scientific savants and the educated public; Cuvier's "Discourse" was published in several European languages, as a short and readable book detached from the technically demanding papers in the rest of *Ossemens fossiles.*

Cuvier argued that "quadrupeds," although rare as fossils, were the best material with which to test the reality of extinction, because their living species were much more fully known than those of, say, the marine molluscs, which are abundant as fossils. In particular, large terrestrial quadrupeds (such as mammoths) were the least likely to survive as "living fossils" without being seen and reported. His reasoning was explicitly probabilistic: the greater the number of large fossil quadrupeds that were identified, the more probable it became that they were all truly extinct. But Cuvier's case depended on eliminating any possibility that he was reassembling fossil bones that in reality had belonged to different animals. So here he drew on his anatomical concept of the functional integration of the animal body, and deployed it in an instrumental role to ensure the reliability of his reconstructions, and hence that of his distinctions between living and fossil species. (In consequence, the clearest statement of his anatomical principles is in his geological "Discourse," rather than in any of his zoological works.) This then reinforced his claims about the reality of a mass extinction.

Views on the History of Earth. Because any such mass extinction was a putative event in Earth's history, it was reasonable to try to relate it to recorded human history. Cuvier argued that it dated from a point too early for human activities to have been responsible for killing off the extinct animals, but recent enough for human societies to have preserved a faint memory of the natural event that had done so. Adopting the role of an antiquarian, Cuvier reviewed the multicultural evidence for a "deluge" or watery catastrophe near the start of human civilizations. He claimed that such textual records could be found in several independent traditions, from as far away as China. The ancient Jewish story of Noah's Flood (for which he relied on rigorous German biblical scholarship) was just one of the many that he analyzed. Like the rest, he treated it as a faint and perhaps garbled record, but of a genuine event; he gave it no special status and inferred that it had preserved contemporary Egyptian traditions (which were not directly accessible, because the hieroglyphic script was as yet undeciphered). So Cuvier concluded that a massive global catastrophe of some kind had affected the continents near the dawn of human history, wiping out a whole fauna of previously well-adapted animals. Human history was thus hitched on to the tail end of Earth's history, with the putative deluge as the crucial connecting link recorded both in human and in natural records.

Cuvier was mainly concerned to establish the historicity of the deluge event. For its physical cause he tentatively adopted either of two earlier suggestions: Deluc's conjecture that a sudden crustal collapse had submerged the former continents, leaving the former ocean floors high and dry to replace them; or Déodat de Dolomieu's notion of a huge tsunami, far larger than any witnessed in human history, sweeping briefly across the continents. Following the same two naturalists, Cuvier dated this boundary event at no more than about ten millennia in the past (compatible with the modern dating of the end of the last Pleistocene glaciation, which is now held responsible for many of the features then attributed to a deluge). Cuvier assumed the role of an ancient historian once again, when he debunked claims that the written records of some civilizations extended unbroken over a far longer period than this.

Cuvier was in no doubt that the putative deluge, although ancient in terms of human history, was very recent in terms of the history of Earth. Like all serious naturalists, since at least the time of Georges-Louis Leclerc de Buffon, he took it for granted that Earth's total timescale was vast beyond human imagination (though there was no reliable way to quantify it). His reasoning was certainly not cramped by the traditional brief cosmic timescale that the "chronologers" of earlier centuries had derived from ancient texts such as Genesis. On the other hand he was convinced that the timescale was finite: He was critical of those (such as Lamarck) who invoked a vast timescale, or even hinted that the world might be eternal, just in order to solve their explanatory problems. Cuvier argued for a catastrophe not because he allowed too little time, but because he believed there was abundant positive evidence for such an event.

In his earliest research Cuvier tacitly treated all his fossil bones as the relics of a single undifferentiated "former world." However, he was soon made aware that they came from different kinds of deposit, which were not all of the same age: those found in river gravels were obviously more recent than those found in the rock formations through which the river valleys had been cut. Among the latter were bones from the gypsum formation outcropping around Paris; Cuvier showed that they belonged to mammals of totally unknown genera (for example, his "palaeotherium"), much less like any living species than those (for example, mammoths) from the river gravels. Colleagues such as Alexandre Brongniart, who were familiar with "geognostic" (later called "stratigraphical") field research elsewhere in Europe, then made Cuvier aware that rock formations containing the bones of strange reptiles (but no trace of any mammals) were still lower in the pile and therefore still older. Cuvier therefore inferred that fossil bones recorded a genuine history of quadrupeds: first reptiles, which had then been joined by mammals of progressively more familiar kinds and finally by human beings. Once again, the historicity of the sequence was more important to him than its cause; he was content to leave the latter unresolved, though he was convinced that the new forms of life could not have been introduced by Lamarck's kind of transformism.

Early in the new century Cuvier collaborated with Brongniart on a study of the Parisian rock formations (it was almost the only outdoor fieldwork that Cuvier, by choice an indoor museum naturalist, ever did after he settled in Paris). Their methods were similar to those that William Smith in England had recently developed (and later termed *stratigraphical*), but the two Frenchmen went much further. Fossils were for them far more than merely "characteristic" of specific formations: they were relics of Earth's history and indicators of former environments. In the Paris region they found that formations with fossil mollusks of clearly marine origin alternated with others containing shells similar to those now inhabiting fresh water (and also Cuvier's bones of land mammals). They therefore inferred that this pile of formations represented a temporal sequence of shallow seas alternating with freshwater lakes or lagoons; and also—because the boundaries

between the two kinds of formation were often sharp—that they represented a series of sudden environmental changes. So there had been a sequence of local "revolutions" similar in kind to the much later and apparently worldwide one at the dawn of human history. This implied that such repeated "catastrophes" must be part of the ordinary course of nature, just as much as the repeated extinctions that they might have caused. Once again, Cuvier's inference that the events had been sudden was not forced on him by any imagined brevity of time in Earth's history: he and Brongniart concluded that catastrophes had only occasionally punctuated long periods of generally tranquil conditions, because there was clear evidence that the rock formations themselves had accumulated very slowly and in calm conditions.

This joint study by Cuvier and Brongniart (published in outline in 1808 and fully in 1811) was so important for Cuvier's broader research goals that he reprinted it in 1812 in his *Ossemens fossiles,* immediately following his introductory "Discourse" and preceding any of his analyses of fossil quadrupeds. He commended it explicitly as a model of how the history of Earth and life could be reconstructed, reliably and in detail. It also gave a broader context for his own lively reconstructions—for which he even used the metaphor of "resurrection"—of the strange mammals whose bones were found in the Parisian gypsum formation. By this time he was well aware that all the Parisian formations collectively constituted just the uppermost portion (subsequently named "Tertiary") of a far thicker pile outcropping beyond the Paris region. But he argued that the Paris rocks deserved to be treated as an exemplar, precisely because they were the most recent: being the nearest to the present they were potentially the easiest to decipher, and could act as a key to the even stranger worlds of still earlier periods of Earth's history.

After the first publication of his *Ossemens fossiles* in 1812, Cuvier withdrew from this kind of geological research, leaving Brongniart to pursue it further. He himself extended his inventory of extinct quadrupeds, consolidating it with the help of masses of new specimens (or pictures of them) sent to him from around the world. After the wars ended in 1815, his earlier conjecture that an age of reptiles had preceded the age of mammals in the history of life was vindicated by English discoveries of several strange new fossil reptiles. William Daniel Conybeare analyzed the marine ichthyosaur and plesiosaur on explicitly Cuvierian lines, and William Buckland described his megalosaur and Gideon Algernon Mantell his iguanodon (both defined by Richard Owen, much later, as "dinosaurs") as terrestrial forms from the same remote era (in modern terms, the Jurassic period). These were all reported in time for Cuvier to incorporate them in the much enlarged second edition (1821–1824) of his *Ossemens fossiles,* reissued in 1825 as the third and last in his lifetime. This massive work became the indispensable starting point for all further research of this kind in subsequent decades.

Human Paleontology. In his last years Cuvier became involved in an important controversy in geology (coincidentally around the same time as his zoological controversy with Geoffroy Saint-Hilaire). It concerned the place of the human species in the history of Earth; more specifically, the authenticity of claims that human fossil bones had been found in the same deposits as the bones of the most recent extinct mammals such as mammoths. Earlier reports of this kind had been rejected by Cuvier (and many other naturalists), with good reason, on the grounds that the human bones were not unambiguously in the same deposits or of the same age as the animal bones. However, new reports from southern France (from 1828), by Jules de Christol and Paul Tournal, were more difficult to dismiss, because they were based on much more careful methods of excavation. Yet Cuvier did resolutely dismiss them, asserting that there was still no reliable evidence that humans had coexisted with the extinct mammals. The issue at stake was the dating of human origins in relation to the catastrophe or deluge that—so Cuvier claimed—had caused the mass extinction of the most recent set of fossil mammals.

Cuvier's position in this argument was complex and ambiguous. In his 1805 lectures in Paris, he had surprised his audience by agreeing with his predecessors Deluc and Dolomieu in dating Earth's last "revolution" no more than a few millennia in the past, making it compatible with the traditional dating of Noah's Flood derived from biblical "chronology." In view of Napoleon's recent rapprochement with the papacy, this helped to deflect counterrevolutionary political criticism away from the then novel and insecure science of geology. Yet Cuvier's multicultural argument for the reality of a deluge event does not suggest that in dating it to the dawn of human history he was primarily concerned to vindicate the historicity of Genesis. If the story of Noah's Flood was indeed one of many faint but genuine traces of a real event, human societies must already have been in existence beforehand, for it to be recorded at all. So the discovery of human fossils mixed with the bones of the putative animal victims of the deluge could have been seen as confirming, not undermining, the biblical narrative.

This suggests that Cuvier's adamant denial of the contemporaneity of humans and the extinct mammalian fauna was powered by sources other than a desire to defend the truth and authority of Genesis. The obvious alternative is that his stance on this issue served to reinforce the reality of extinction as a natural process: that the mass extinction at the last "revolution" was due not to the arrival of the human species but to an environmental catastrophe that these well-adapted animal species were unable to survive. The natural status of extinction was then confirmed by the evidence of still earlier events of the same kind and of a fossil record that charted a long and complex history of life itself. Cuvier was well aware that one major causal factor in that history remained an enigma: his concept of extinction as a natural process explained the disappearance of animals known only as fossils, but he had no comparable explanation of their origins. Like many of his contemporaries he was carefully noncommittal about the latter, noting only, for example, that certain forms "began to exist" at certain times in Earth's history. However, there is no evidence that he had in mind any kind of unmediated divine intervention; far more probably he guessed that a natural process of some unknown kind was involved, but certainly not Lamarck's notion of imperceptibly slow transformist change, nor Geoffroy Saint-Hilaire's conjecture about the sudden appearance of "hopeful monsters" as a result of embryonic macromutation.

The misconception that Cuvier's work was primarily powered by religious concerns arose—particularly in the anglophone world—after Robert Jameson in Edinburgh published an English edition (1813) of Cuvier's "Discourse" (with a rather poor translation), claiming that the vindication of the Flood narrative in Genesis was a major purpose of the Frenchman's research (Jameson's later editions were progressively enlarged with further editorial accretions). This served to recruit Cuvier on to the conservative and counterrevolutionary side in British politics, but it entailed a gross distortion of Cuvier's own cultural and scientific goals. His personal religious position is difficult to discern: his pious daughter was recorded, after her tragically early death, as having prayed for her father's conversion, which hardly suggests that he was the ardently religious figure of conventional historical myth. More probably his commitment to the Lutheran tradition of his youth was relatively formal, but on a cultural level he remained loyal to that small fraction within the mainly Reformed (Calvinist) Protestant minority in French society. Late in his life, as one of the few Protestants prominent in public life in France, he was highly effective in supporting this minority on the political and cultural level, serving as its official link with the French government and helping to secure its civil rights.

SUPPLEMENTARY BIBLIOGRAPHY

WORKS BY CUVIER

Rapport historique sur les progrès des sciences naturelles depuis 1789, et sur leur état actuel. Paris: impr. impériale, 1810.

With Alexandre Brongniart. "Essai sur la géographie minéralogique des environs de Paris." In *Mémoires de la classe des sciences mathématiques et physiques de l'Institut Impérial de France, année 1810* (1811): 1–278.

Recherches sur les ossemens fossiles de quadrupèdes, où l'on rétablit les caractères de plusieurs espèces d'animaux que les révolutions du globe paroissent avoir détruites. 4 vols. Paris: Deterville, 1812.

With Pierre-André Latreille. *Le règne animal distribué d'après son organisation, pour servir de base à l'histoire naturelle des animaux et d'introduction à l'anatomie comparée.* Paris: Deterville, 1817.

Discours sur les révolutions de la surface du globe, et sur les changemens qu'elles ont produits dans le règne animal. Paris, 1826. The first separate edition in French.

Dehérain, Henri. *Catalogue des manuscrits du fonds Cuvier conservés à la Bibliothèque de l'Institut de France.* [1] Paris: Honoré Champion, 1908, and [2] Hendaye: Observatoire d'Abbadie, 1922. A chronological listing, with summaries, of [1] scientific, and [2] administrative letters to Cuvier.

The Letters of Georges Cuvier: A Summary Calendar of Manuscript and Printed Materials Preserved in Europe, the United States of America, and Australasia. Edited by Dorinda Outram. Chalfont St. Giles, U.K.: British Society for the History of Science, 1980. A valuable though incomplete listing of letters from Cuvier.

Outram, Dorinda. "Storia naturale e politica nella corrispondenza tra Georges Cuvier e Giovanni Fabbroni." *Richerche storiche* 13 (1982): 185–235. Transcriptions of one of Cuvier's many important exchanges of correspondence.

Georges Cuvier: Annotated Bibliography of His Published Works. Compiled by Jean Chandler Smith. Washington, DC: Smithsonian Institution Press, 1993. A comprehensive listing, including contemporary translations.

Rudwick, Martin J. S. *Georges Cuvier, Fossil Bones, and Geological Catastrophes: New Translations and Interpretations of the Primary Texts.* Chicago: University of Chicago Press, 1997. English translations of Cuvier's "Discours préliminaire" and many earlier writings.

OTHER SOURCES

Appel, Toby A. *The Cuvier-Geoffroy Debate: French Biology in the Decades before Darwin.* New York: Oxford University Press, 1987. Also includes much on their earlier interactions and initial collaboration.

Buffetaut, Eric, J. M. Mazin, and E. Salmon, eds. *Actes du symposium paléontologique G. Cuvier.* Montbéliard, France: Ville de Montbéliard, 1982. A valuable collection of articles.

Bultingaire, Léon. "Iconographie de Georges Cuvier." *Archives du Muséum National d'Histoire Naturelle,* 6th ser., 9 (1932): 1–12. Fine reproductions of many portraits.

Burkhardt, Richard W., Jr. *The Spirit of System: Lamarck and Evolutionary Biology.* Cambridge, MA: Harvard University Press, 1977. Includes much on Cuvier.

Coleman, William. *Georges Cuvier Zoologist: A Study in the History of Evolution Theory.* Cambridge, MA: Harvard University Press, 1964. Still the finest analysis of Cuvier's zoological work.

Corsi, Pietro. *The Age of Lamarck: Evolutionary Theories in France, 1790–1830.* Berkeley: University of California Press, 1988. Includes much on Cuvier.

Laurent, Goulven. *Paléontologie et évolution en France de 1800 à 1860: Une histoire des idées de Cuvier et Lamarck à Darwin.* Paris: Éditions du Comité des Travaux Historiques et Scientifiques, 1987.

Negrin, Howard Elias. *Georges Cuvier: Administrator and Educator.* New York: New York University, 1978 [University Microfilms, dissertation no. 78-3124].

Outram, Dorinda. "The Language of Natural Power: The 'Éloges' of Georges Cuvier and the Public Language of Nineteenth-Century Science." *History of Science* 16 (1978): 153–178.

———. *Georges Cuvier: Vocation, Science, and Authority in Post-Revolutionary France.* Manchester, U.K.: Manchester University Press, 1984. An important analysis of Cuvier's construction of his career.

———. "Uncertain Legislator: Georges Cuvier's Laws of Nature in Their Intellectual Context." *Journal of the History of Biology* 19 (1986): 323–368.

Rudwick, Martin J. S. "Researches on Fossil Bones: Georges Cuvier and the Collecting of International Allies" (1997) and "Georges Cuvier's Paper Museum of Fossil Bones" (2000). Reprinted in his *The New Science of Geology: Studies in the Earth Sciences in the Age of Revolution.* Aldershot, U.K.: Ashgate/Variorum, 2004.

———. *Bursting the Limits of Time: The Reconstruction of Geohistory in the Age of Revolution.* Chicago: University of Chicago Press, 2005. Includes much on Cuvier's earlier work.

———. *Worlds before Adam: The Reconstruction of Geohistory in the Age of Reform.* Chicago: University of Chicago Press, 2008. Includes much on Cuvier's later work.

Taquet, Philippe. "Georges Cuvier, ses liens scientifiques européens." In [Anon., ed.] *Montbéliard sans frontières.* Montbéliard, France: Société d'Émulation de Montbéliard, 1994, 287–309.

———. *Georges Cuvier: Naissance d'un génie.* Paris: Odile Jacob, 2006. The first volume (to 1795) of a projected major biography.

Theunissen, Bert. "The Relevance of Cuvier's *lois zoologiques* for His Palaeontological Work." *Annals of Science* 43 (1986): 543–556.

Martin J. S. Rudwick

D

D'ALEMBERT (DALEMBERT), JEAN LE ROND

(*b.* Paris, France, 16 November 1717; *d.* Paris, France, 29 October 1783), *mathematics, mechanics, astronomy, physics, philosophy.* For the original article on d'Alembert see *DSB,* vol. 1.

Since the first edition of *DSB,* d'Alembert has been the object of several studies, giving a better knowledge of his scientific works, especially in mathematics. Publication of the first two volumes of his œuvres complètes, concerning celestial mechanics, has put into evidence some of his unpublished early texts about lunar theory and it has given rise to critical studies. His correspondence with Euler, published in Euler's *Opera Omnia,* has been also an important source of information.

As a scientist, d'Alembert made decisive contributions in mathematics and in various fields of mechanics. His leading scientific publications consist of six treatises (published from 1743 to 1756, two of them being reedited later); twenty-two memoirs in the collections of the Berlin Academy, the Paris Academy of Sciences, and the Turin Academy (from 1748 to 1774); and the fifty-eight memoirs gathered in the eight volumes of his *Opuscules mathématiques* (from 1761 to 1780). Other scientific writings appeared in the form of letters to Joseph-Louis Lagrange in the *Memoirs* of the Turin Academy and in those of the Berlin Academy (between 1766 and 1782). And d'Alembert also took the opportunity in some of the numerous entries he contributed to the *Encyclopédie* to clarify or develop scientific concepts. In addition, he left several unpublished works: early memoirs of mathematics and celestial mechanics, *plis cachetés* deposited at the Paris Academy, and a ninth volume of his *Opuscules.*

Having entered the Paris Academy of Sciences in 1741, d'Alembert only reached the highest rank of *pensionnaire* on 10 November 1765, but he enjoyed some of its prerogatives from 1756, when he became *pensionnaire surnuméraire.* He held the positions of *sous-directeur* and *directeur* in 1768 and 1769 respectively. As an academician, he was in charge of reporting on a large number of works submitted to the Academy, and he sat on many prize juries. In particular, one may believe that he had a decisive voice concerning the choice of works about lunar motion, libration, and comets for the astronomy prizes awarded to Leonhard Euler, Lagrange, and Nikolai Fuss between 1764 and 1780.

D'Alembert exchanged scientific correspondences with Euler (mainly between 1746 and 1751), Gabriel Cramer (between 1748 and 1751), and Lagrange (from 1759). He helped the latter to enter the Berlin Academy as a director, he protected Pierre Simon Laplace's early career, and he was a friend of Marie-Jean-Antoine-Nicolas de Caritat, Marquis de Condorcet.

Mathematics. For imaginary (that is, complex) numbers, d'Alembert demonstrated the stability of the symbol $p + q\sqrt{-1}$ (*p* and *q* real) with respect to elementary algebraic or analytical operations, in an unpublished memoir of 1745 and in his *Réflexions sur la cause générale des vents* (1747). Before the end of 1746, he demonstrated that any polynomial with degree $n \geq 1$ and real coefficients has at least one root either real or of the form $p + q\sqrt{-1}$ ($q \neq 0$), and that nonreal roots can be associated in pairs (namely $p + q\sqrt{-1}$ and $p + q\sqrt{-1}$). Later (1772), he extended the former property to polynomials with complex coefficients. These results induce that any polynomial of the *n*th degree with complex coefficients has *n* complex roots separate or not, and also that any polynomial with real coefficients can be put in the form of a product of binomials of the first degree and trinomials of the second degree with real coefficients. Though d'Alembert's analytical demonstration presents a few gaps, it stands as the first attempt to establish the fundamental theorem of algebra on rigorous bases, other demonstrations being given later by Carl Friedrich Gauss.

The study concerning polynomials with real coefficients was involved in the first of three memoirs devoted to integral calculus (published in 1748, 1750, 1752), in connection with the reduction of integrals of rational fractions to the quadrature of circle or hyperbola. In the same memoirs, d'Alembert began to deal with integrals that can reduce to the rectification of ellipse or hyperbola, in the continuation of Colin Maclaurin's works, but using merely algebraic methods. Furthermore he considered another class of integrals, which included $\int \frac{dx}{x\sqrt{P}}$, where *P* is a polynomial of the third degree, an early approach to elliptic integrals whose theory was later started by Adrien-Marie Legendre. Works on the same topic can also be found in the *Opuscules mathématiques* and in other late memoirs.

The 1750 and 1752 memoirs additionally dealt with differential equations, a topic that appeared also in several of d'Alembert's texts on mechanics and astronomy. In particular, he gave an original method, using multipliers, for solving systems of linear differential equations of the first order with constant coefficients, and he introduced the reduction of linear differential equations of any order to systems of equations of the first order.

D'Alembert was the first to solve partial differential equations, in his *Réflexions sur la cause générale des vents*. He considered a system of two differential expressions supposed to be exact differential forms in two independent variables, which should be equivalent to two independent linear partial differential equations of the second order with constant coefficients. He used the condition for exact differential forms and introduced multipliers leading to convenient changes of independent variables and unknown functions. His solution involved two arbitrary functions, to be determined by taking into account the boundary conditions of the physical problem. He applied this method to vibrating strings in two memoirs published in 1749, and to fluids in a 1749 manuscript at the origin of his *Essai d'une nouvelle théorie de la résistance des fluides* (1752). That gave rise to a discussion with Euler about the nature of curves expressing boundary conditions. Another method, based on variable separation, appeared in a third memoir of d'Alembert about vibrating strings (1752), and a more general study of partial differ-

Jean d'Alembert. *Jean d'Alembert, circa 1745.* HULTON ARCHIVE/GETTY IMAGES.

ential equations, including equations of the first order—also studied by Euler—was undertaken in the twenty-sixth memoir of the *Opuscules mathématiques* (1768). These works were continued by Lagrange and Laplace.

Motion of a Solid Body around Its Mass Center and Astronomical Applications. In his first treatise, the *Traité de dynamique* published in 1743, d'Alembert introduced the principle that came to be called "d'Alembert's principle," which he next applied in several fields. One of them is the motion of a solid body around its center of mass.

D'Alembert started studying this problem in his fourth treatise, *Recherches sur la précession des équinoxes, et sur la nutation de l'axe de la Terre, dans le système newtonien* (1749). His purpose was to show that Newtonian attraction could explain a small motion of the Earth's axis connected to the lunar node motion, which had just been discovered by James Bradley. First he separated the motion of the Earth attracted by the Sun and the Moon into two independent motions: the motion of the Earth mass center (relevant from the three-body problem) and the rotation of the Earth around its mass center, considered as a fixed point. Then applying his principle to the Earth, supposed to be a solid body of revolution about its polar axis (called axis of figure), he established two differential equations of the second order giving the motion of the figure axis in space and a third one expressing angular displacement around the figure axis. He also proved the existence of an instantaneous axis of rotation moving both in space and in the Earth, but close to the figure axis.

Using approximations in solving his differential equations, d'Alembert was the first to obtain analytical expressions for the two angles positioning the Earth's polar axis with respect to the ecliptic plane. They accounted for the observed motions of the axis: precession known from antiquity and Bradley's nutation.

Several common features exist between d'Alembert's nutation theory and Edgar W. Woolard's (1953), in the differential equations taken into account and in the solving methods. By comparing analytical amplitudes of precession and nutation to observed ones, d'Alembert gave values of two physical constants: the ratio of lunar and terrestrial masses, and a constant equivalent to modern dynamical flattening. Using the latter, he discussed the compatibility between the theory of the Earth's figure, the observed motion of its polar axis, and the values of its geodetic flattening recently obtained by Pierre-Louis Moreau de Maupertuis and Pierre Bouguer.

In the third book of his *Recherches sur différens points importans du système du monde* (1754), and in several later memoirs, d'Alembert attempted to apply his theory of precession-nutation to the lunar libration. But, though in a memoir published in 1759 he extended his differential equations to an ellipsoid with three unequal axes, he failed to account for the empirical laws found by Jean-Dominique Cassini. Finally, the complete theoretical explanation of Cassini's laws was given by Lagrange in the 1780s, using differential equations similar to d'Alembert's in the 1759 memoir, but a different method for solving them.

In the second memoir of the *Opuscules mathématiques* (1761), d'Alembert gave the way to obtain six differential equations of the second order representing the complete motion of any solid body in space. The position of the solid was defined by six functions of time: the coordinates of a particular point (for example, the mass center) in a system of rectangular axes fixed in space, and three angles (analogous to Euler's angles) positioning the directions of body-fixed axes with respect to the space-fixed system. In the twenty-second memoir (1768), he simplified his equations by using what is called principal axes of inertia as body-fixed axes.

The problem of the motion of a solid around its mass center gave rise to a long polemic between d'Alembert and Euler. In 1751, Euler published his work about precession-nutation without referring to d'Alembert's 1749 treatise, but he agreed to write in the next volume of the same

Memoirs of the Berlin Academy that his French colleague had been the first to solve that particular problem. Nevertheless, he never recognized d'Alembert's priority in solving the general problem of the motion of a solid around its mass center, as the latter required. In fact, Euler's general solution, also published in the 1760s, is very different from d'Alembert's and, as Wenceslaus Johann Gustav Karsten wrote in the preface of Euler's *Theoria Motus Corporum Solidorum seu Rigidorum*, both scientists contributed equally to solve the problem.

Three-Body Problem. The three-body problem was the subject of an intense competition between Euler, Alexis-Claude Clairaut, and d'Alembert in the late 1740s and early 1750s. After preliminary attempts withdrawn from publication, d'Alembert published two memoirs about this topic in 1749, the second one (read at the Paris Academy of Sciences in February–March 1748) beginning the application of the first one (read in June 1747) to lunar theory. He achieved this lunar theory in August 1748, but like Clairaut's and Euler's at the same time, his theoretical calculations yielded only the half value of the observed mean motion of the lunar apsides. He did not take part in the controversy raised by Clairaut about the Newtonian formulation of universal gravitation, but he tried to account for the discrepancy between theory and observation by a force acting complementarily in the vicinity of the Earth. The unpublished manuscript of that 1748 lunar theory was deposited at the Paris Academy in May 1749, after Clairaut had stated his successful calculation of the apsidal mean motion.

Nevertheless, d'Alembert's work was the first attempt at constructing a literal theory of the Moon (that is a theory involving explicitly four angles, functions of time, and constant mean orbital elements of the Moon and the Earth, kept under a literal form) and it presented a theoretical interest in the calculation of periodic inequalities. He resumed it from the end of 1749 on and then achieved an expression of the apsidal mean motion compatible with the observed value. His new theory was finished in January 1751, but he did not submit it to the St. Petersburg Academy of Sciences for the 1751 prize, because of the presence of Euler on the jury. The prize was awarded to Clairaut, and d'Alembert published his theory later in the first book of the *Recherches sur différens points importans du système du monde* (1754).

In d'Alembert's lunar theory, the geocentric motion of the Moon disturbed by the Sun is expressed by four differential equations: the first two expressing the motion of the body in projection on the ecliptic plane, the last two expressing the motion of the nodal line and the variations of the inclination of the instantaneous orbital plane on the ecliptic plane. Independent variable z is analogous to ecliptic longitude. The first equation is formulated as $\frac{d^2 t}{dz^2} + N^2 t + M = 0$ where unknown function t is simply connected to radius vector of the projection; N is a constant, $1 - N$ being proportional to the apsidal mean motion; and M depends on the position of the body through the disturbing forces. The whole system has to be solved by an iterative process; at each step, M is considered as a known function of z, and constant N is determined so that the differential equation in t could not have any solution increasing indefinitely with z. This determination of the apsidal mean motion at the differential equation level is one of the leading characteristics of d'Alembert's method compared to Clairaut's. In the 1748 theory, only the first step of the iterative process was performed, whereas further steps are necessary to obtain a good value of N.

D'Alembert derived two sets of lunar tables from his theory: the first one was published in 1754 with the theory; the second one was published separately in 1756. A third set of tables, based on an empirical process, was published in the *Opuscules mathématiques* (1761).

The method introduced in the first memoir of 1749 was applied to planetary motions in the second and fifth books of *Recherches sur différens points importans du système du monde* (1754, 1756), and to comets in the *Opuscules mathématiques*. These latter also contain interesting developments about lunar theory, some of them connected to the problem of the secular acceleration of the Moon.

SUPPLEMENTARY BIBLIOGRAPHY

A bibliography of d'Alembert has been published by Anne-Marie Chouillet in Analyse et dynamique: Études sur l'œuvre de d'Alembert, *edited by Alain Michel and Michel Paty (see below). A critical complete edition of d'Alembert's works is in progress in France (first volume published in 2002); information is available from http://dalembert.univ-lyon1.fr.*

WORKS BY D'ALEMBERT

Traité de dynamique. Paris: David l'aîné, 1743.

Traité de l'équilibre et du mouvement des fluides. Paris: David l'aîné, 1744.

Réflexions sur la cause générale des vents. Paris: David l'aîné, 1747.

"Memoirs addressed to the Berlin Academy." In *Histoire de l'Académie royale des Sciences et Belles lettres.* Berlin: Ambroise Haude, 1747–1771. For memoirs discussed in this article, see the volumes for the years 1746, 1747, 1748, 1750, 1763, 1765, and 1769.

"Memoirs addressed to the Paris Academy of Sciences (France)." *Histoire de l'Académie Royale des Sciences.* Paris: Jean Boudot, 1702–1797. For memoirs discussed in this article, see the volumes for the years 1745, 1754, 1757, 1764, 1765, 1767, 1768, and 1771.

Recherches sur la précession des équinoxes, et sur la nutation de l'axe de la Terre, dans le système newtonien. Paris: David l'aîné, 1749.

Essai d'une nouvelle théorie de la résistance des fluides. Paris: David l'aîné, 1752.

Recherches sur différens points importans du système du monde. 3 vols. Paris: David l'aîné, 1754–1756.

Opuscules mathématiques; ou, Mémoires sur différens sujets de géométrie, de méchanique, d'optique, d'astronomie, &c. 8 vols. Paris: David, 1761–1780.

Œuvres complètes. Series 1, vol. 6. *Premiers textes de mécanique céleste (1747–1749).* Edited by Michelle Chapront-Touzé. Paris: CNRS Éditions, 2002. Contains his 1748 lunar theory and other early unpublished texts about the three-body problem.

———. Series 1, vol. 7. *Précession et nutation (1749–1752).* Edited by Michelle Chapront-Touzé and Jean Souchay. Paris: CNRS Éditions, 2006.

OTHER SOURCES

Auroux, Sylvain, and Anne-Marie Chouillet, eds. "D'Alembert (1717–1783)." *Dix-huitième Siècle* 16 (1984): 7–203. Special issue, with contributions from seventeen authors.

Chapront-Touzé, Michelle. "D'Alembert, Jean Le Rond." In *Biographical Encyclopedia of Astronomers*, edited by Thomas A. Hockey. New York and London: Springer, 2007. Contains complementary information about d'Alembert's works in astronomy and celestial mechanics.

De Gandt, François, Alain Firode, and Jeanne Peiffer, eds. "La formation de d'Alembert (1730–1738)." *Recherches sur Diderot et sur l'Encyclopédie* 38 (2005): 7–224. A special issue, with contributions from eleven authors.

Demidov, Serghei S. "Création et développement de la théorie des équations différentielles aux dérivées partielles dans les travaux de J. d'Alembert." *Revue d'histoire des sciences* 35 (1982): 3–42.

Emery, Monique, and Pierre Monzani, eds. *Jean d'Alembert, savant et philosophe: Portrait à plusieurs voix; actes du colloque.* Paris: Editions des Archives Contemporaines, 1989.

Firode, Alain. *La dynamique de d'Alembert.* Montreal: Bellarmin; Paris: Vrin, 2001.

Fraser, Craig G. *Calculus and Analytical Mechanics in the Age of Enlightenment.* Aldershot, U.K.: Variorum, 1997.

Gilain, Christian. "Sur l'histoire du théorème fondamental de l'algèbre." *Archive for History of Exact Sciences* 42 (1991): 91–136.

———. "D'Alembert et l'intégration des expressions différentielles à une variable." In *Analyse et dynamique: Études sur œuvre de d'Alembert*, edited by Alain Michel and Michel Paty. Laval, Quebec: Les Presses de l'Université Laval, 2002.

———. "Équations différentielles et systèmes différentiels: De d'Alembert à Cauchy." *Oberwolfach Reports* 1 (2004): 2741–2743.

Grimberg, Gérard. "D'Alembert et les équations aux dérivées partielles en hydrodynamique." PhD diss., Université Denis Diderot, Paris, 1998.

———. "D'Alembert et les équations différentielles aux dérivées partielles en hydrodynamique." In *Analyse et dynamique:*

Études sur l'œuvre de d'Alembert, edited by Alain Michel and Michel Paty. Laval, Quebec: Les Presses de l'Université Laval, 2002.

Hankins, Thomas L. *Jean d'Alembert: Science and the Enlightenment.* Oxford: Clarendon Press, 1970.

Maheu, Gilles. "La vie et l' œuvre de Jean d'Alembert: Étude bio-bibliographique." PhD diss., École des Hautes Études en Sciences Sociales, Paris 1967.

Michel, Alain, and Michel Paty, eds. *Analyse et dynamique: Études sur l'œuvre de d'Alembert.* Laval, Quebec: Les Presses de l'Université Laval, 2002. With contributions from eleven authors.

Paty, Michel. *D'Alembert; ou, La raison physico-mathématique au siècle des Lumières.* Paris: Les Belles Lettres, 1998.

Viard, Jérôme. "Le principe de d'Alembert et la conservation du 'moment cinétique' d'un système de corps isolés dans le *Traité de dynamique*." *Physis* 39 (2002): 1–40.

Wilson, Curtis. "D'Alembert versus Euler on the Precession of the Equinoxes and the Mechanics of Rigid Bodies." *Archive for History of Exact Sciences* 37 (1987): 233–273.

Michelle Chapront-Touzé

DAL MONTE, GUIDOBALDO

SEE **Monte, Guidobaldo, Marchese del.**

DAMIANUS OF LARISSA (*fl.* probably fifth to sixth centuries CE), *optics.*

Damianus is the name of the author of a short monograph in optics, the *Optical Hypotheses*. Nothing is known of the author, and the work is never mentioned in the ancient technical corpus. The latest cited authority is Ptolemy. The text is therefore later than the second century CE, but several features of the exposition suggest that Damianus was affiliated with some Neoplatonic school of late antiquity, most likely the one that flourished at Alexandria in the fifth and sixth centuries CE with Ammonius and his pupils.

Contents of the Treatise. The *Optical Hypotheses* were very likely aimed at providing a concise introduction to some basic notions in optics. It may be that they are a redaction of an introductory lecture to some major technical work. In fact, the manuscript tradition assigns them a role among the prefatory material to the Euclidean *Optics*. A historically sound assessment of the value of Damianus's text must take such a crucial feature into account. The treatise is divided into fourteen parts of vari-

able length. The contents of each part are summarized at the very beginning in a list of one-sentence chapters. The most complete title found in the manuscripts is in fact *Chapters of the Optical Hypotheses of Damianus of Heliodorus of Larissa.* A tentative identification of this Heliodorus with Ammonius's brother must remain a conjecture unless new evidence is found.

The main thesis of the treatise is the identity of sight and solar light. Chapter 13 is devoted to an extensive treatment of this topic with numerous examples. In this way, a common set of assumptions provides foundations both to optics and to an investigation of the properties of solar rays. The contents of the treatise can be summarized as follows. Sight is something emitted from the eye (chapter 1), and what is emitted is in fact light (2). Sight moves in a straight line (3), and the visual rays comprise a right-angled cone (4–5). The cone is made of a discrete set of rays (6) and anything seen is viewed under an acute or right angle (7); what is seen from a larger angle seems larger (8). We see primarily by means of the light along the axis of the cone, because of the forward character of the visual power (10). The vertex of the visual cone is inside the pupil (11). We see either directly or by broken rays, the latter either reflected or deflected (that is, refracted) (12). Visual and solar rays behave identically and propagate instantaneously (13). Reflections and deflections of both visual and solar rays occur at equal angles (14). Such statements are proved either inductively through a number of examples or by providing theoretical, and mainly teleological, explanations. The latter ascribe some kind of necessity to phenomena that had been since long established by means of technical devices or experiments. This happens, for instance, in chapter 3. In it, a teleological argument (whose source is very likely Hero) grounded on the principle of economy corroborates Ptolemy's experimental proof that sight moves in a straight line.

Geometrical explanations, when present in the *Optical Hypotheses,* are particularly simple and not supported by any mathematical proofs. A case in point is the reason why the cone of vision is right-angled. This is because Nature prefers a well-defined form, namely the right angle, to an indeterminate one, as any acute or obtuse angle is (the source is Proclus). Statements employing a refined technical lexicon are present, but they might well have served to give the *Optical Hypotheses* an aura of exactness: the assertion that reflection at equal angles occurs with respect to any homeomeric line, or the quotation of Archimedes' definition of straight line serve as examples. A remarkable "mistake" is Damianus's claim that deflection also occurs at equal angles. The claim is argued on the sole basis of an asserted similarity between reflection and deflection. To save Damianus from such a seemingly obvious blunder, it has been proposed that the equal angles were the ones that the refracted ray forms with the normal to the surface and the incident ray when produced. Another explanation could be that A" double refraction may produce in suitable conditions equality of angles of incidence and refraction. Of some interest is the term *diaklasis* (deflection) employed by Damianus. The same word is typical of the very late commentator Olympiodorus, a pupil of Ammonius.

Damianus's Sources. The *Optical Hypotheses* offer some interesting pieces of documentary information. Damianus ascribed (chapter 14) to Hero a proof of the equal-angle rule for reflection. The proof is identical with the one attested in the treatise that has come down to us, in Latin translation only and attributed to Ptolemy, under the title *De speculis*. Damianus asserted (chapter 3) that Ptolemy showed by some device that sight moves in a straight line and forms a right-angled cone (possibly a misconception for right cone). Most likely, this happened in the first book of Ptolemy's *Optics,* which is now lost. Plenty of examples in the *Optical Hypotheses* already, in fact, appear in what remains of Ptolemy's treatise. Damianus also quoted (chapters 5, 8, and 12 respectively) almost exactly proposition 1 and definition 4 of the Euclidean *Optics,* and definition 6 of the *Catoptrics.* Two examples in the *Optical Hypotheses* coincide with examples in the introduction preceding one redaction of Euclid's *Optics.* Finally, a reference, in the context of a citation of the isoperimetric theorem, to the circle as "the most spacious" plane figure tallies with terminology typical of Neoplatonic commentators. The identity of the basic assumptions in optics and in a theory of the propagation of solar rays is already in Geminus. Other, similar examples can be adduced: Damianus's text is just a bit more than a patchwork of quotations from standard works. However, it need not follow that the author directly drew from all the sources here mentioned. Most of the examples were commonplace in the optical literature, and it is likely he worked on epitomes and compilations.

BIBLIOGRAPHY

WORK BY DAMIANUS

Damianos Schrift über Optik, mit Auszügen aus Geminos, griechisch und deutsch herausgegeben von Richard Schöne. Berlin: Reichsdruckerei, 1897. The critical edition of Damianus's text. The editor wrongly relied on manuscripts carrying a Byzantine recension and neglected what very likely will turn out to be the best manuscript. A new edition is much needed.

OTHER SOURCES

Eastwood, Bruce S. "Metaphysical Derivations of a Law of Refraction: Damianos and Grosseteste." *Archive for History of Exact Sciences* 6 (1969/1970): 224–236, in particular 225–232. A full discussion of the bewildering rule of equal angles in refraction is here offered, and the first proposal expounded in the text above is made.

Hultsch, Friedrich. *Berliner philologische Wochenschrift* 46 (12 November 1898): 1413–1417. This review of Richard Schöne's editions includes several corrections. It supplements Schöne's prolegomena on important points and contains the interpretation of Damianus's equal-angle rule as a double refraction. Hultsch wrote also the notice in Pauly-Wissowa, G., et al., eds., *Paulys Real-Encyclopädie der Classischen Altertumswissenschaft.* 2nd ed., 1st Series. 24 vols. in 43 tomes. Stuttgart, Germany: J.B. Metzler, 1894–1963, Vol. IV, Tome 2: 2054–2055, where he proposed that Damianus was Heliodorus's son and pupil and that the former abridged a work of the latter. Hultsch's view that Heliodorus's work was in thirteen chapters relies on a wrong assessment of the contents of some manuscripts.

Knorr, Wilbur R. "Archimedes and the Pseudo-Euclidean *Catoptrics:* Early Stages in the Ancient Geometric Theory of Mirrors." *Archives Internationales d'Histoire des Sciences* 35 (1985): 28–105, in particular 89–96. A general assessment of Damianus's treatise, with particular emphasis on its dating, may be found in this text. Knorr proposes the identification of Heliodorus with Ammonius's brother, and refutes with a detailed discussion Heiberg's contention that the author of the introduction to a redaction of the Euclidean *Optics,* usually but on no grounds believed to be Theon, had drawn from Damianus's work.

Tannery, Paul. "Rapport sur une mission en Italie." *Archives des missions scientifiques et littéraires,* 3ᵉ série, 13 (1888): 405–455. Reprinted in Id., *Mémoires Scientifiques,* tome II (1912), n. 44: 269–331. Detailed information on those of the manuscripts that were copied by the famous calligrapher Angelus Vergecius may be found in this work.

Todd, Robert B. "Damianus." In *Dictionnaire des Philosophes Antiques,* edited by Richard Goulet. Paris: CNRS Editions, 1994.

———. "Héliodore De Larissa." In *Dictionnaire des Philosophes Antiques,* edited by Richard Goulet. Paris: CNRS Editions, 2000. An account of Damianus's work and a discussion of its connection with late Platonism in this text.

———. "Damianus (Heliodorus Larissaeus)." In *Catalogus Translationum et Commentariorum: Mediaeval and Renaissance Latin Translations and Commentaries* 8, edited by Virginia Brown. Washington, DC: Catholic University of America Press, 2003. This is a valuable exposition of the *Fortleben* of Damianus's work, with an overview of the manuscript tradition.

Fabio Acerbi

DANSEREAU, PIERRE MACKAY (*b.* Outremont, Quebec, Canada, 5 October 1911), *biogeography, ecology, environmental studies.*

Dansereau pioneered the study of plant ecology in Canada, drawing on both European and North American perspectives. Beginning in the 1930s with studies of phytosociology (the study and classification of plant communities), he progressively broadened his perspective to encompass biogeography, ecological land-use planning, and the urban environment. As both a specialist in plant ecology and a scientist concerned with broader questions of human society and the natural environment, he has urged attention to synthetic perspectives that combine knowledge of nature and of humanity, to be achieved through interdisciplinary environmental studies.

Early Life and Research. Dansereau was born in Outremont, a suburb of Montreal. The Dansereau family was prominent in Quebec society: his grandfather was cofounder and editor of *La Presse,* Montreal's largest newspaper, and his father, Lucien Dansereau, was a successful public works engineer. His mother, Marie Archambault, although also French Canadian, was born near Albany, New York. The oldest of five, with a sister and three brothers, his childhood was secure and happy.

Dansereau obtained his early education at the Collège Sainte-Marie, a Jesuit college in Montreal. Its focus on classics gave him little exposure to science. Following the wishes of his parents he began to study law, but after a year his interests turned to farming, and so he enrolled at the Institut Agricole d'Oka, an agricultural college affiliated with the Université de Montréal. There he also studied with Frère Marie-Victorin, founder of the Montreal Botanical Garden and author of *La flore laurentienne* (1935), who awakened his interest in biology and geography. He would later describe himself as not merely a student, but a disciple of Marie-Victorin. Field trips, particularly to the Gaspé Peninsula in southeast Quebec, sharpened his interest in botany. Upon graduation in 1936, Dansereau began studies at the Université de Genève in Switzerland, where he studied with the ecologist Josiah Braun-Blanquet, receiving a DSc in plant taxonomy in 1939. From Braun-Blanquet he gained a grounding in the Zürich-Montpellier school of phytosociology, including its distinctive approach to identifying and classifying plant communities, and understanding their dynamics, on the basis of species composition. On his return to Quebec he would contribute to introducing North American ecologists to this perspective.

In 1935 Dansereau married Françoise Masson; they have enjoyed a long and happy marriage, Françoise accompanying Pierre on scientific travels while pursuing her own political and social concerns. They have had no children. In the early 1930s Dansereau exhibited his interest in political and social issues as coleader of Jeune-Canada, a group of university students urging that Quebec assert more firmly its autonomy and French iden-

tity. The organization was active for several years but by the late 1930s had dispersed.

Between 1940 and 1950 Dansereau taught at the Université de Montréal while serving as botanist, and subsequently assistant director, at the Montreal Botanical Garden. In addition, between 1943 and 1949 he was director of the provincial biogeography service. During this decade, a significant focus of his research was the application of phytosociological methods to vegetation in Quebec, particularly maple forests. But he soon broadened his research beyond his European training. With a few other geographically oriented ecologists, he experimented with describing and classifying vegetation in terms of structure, presenting graphically the distinctive forms, or physiognomy, of the principal vegetation types. This approach would, he suggested, be more biologically meaningful than descriptions based on plant taxa.

This work epitomized Dansereau's growing interest in applying a geographical perspective to plant communities by understanding, through comparison, how their characteristic forms were related to the geology and climate of regions. In linking ecology with biogeography, he drew from the French geographer Emmanuel de Martonne and his classic text, *Traité de Géographie Physique* (1905). Dansereau also expressed this geographical orientation by pursuing research in a variety of environments. In 1945 he traveled to Brazil to teach and conduct research. He would maintain a lifelong affinity for that country. In 1950 he studied Arctic plant communities on Baffin Island in the Arctic Ocean. In the course of his career he would conduct research across North and South America, as well as in Australia, New Zealand, the Philippines, and the Canary Islands; he has also lectured on every continent except Antarctica.

Although the 1940s were productive for Dansereau in terms of research, his position at the Université de Montréal was not secure. He had introduced ecology to what was at the time a fairly conservative institution, and the status of the discipline remained, at best, provisional. Frustrated, Dansereau moved in 1950 to the University of Michigan. His five years there as professor of botany proved among the most satisfying and stimulating of his career. (He also during this time taught for short periods at Stanford University and the University of Vermont). In his research he pursued a variety of avenues, including work on forest dynamics and vegetation change. He explored other areas as well: the taxonomy and phenomenology of vegetation and aspects of the relation between ecology and evolution, including the ecology of natural selection.

In a series of publications, particularly his synthesis of the ecological and biogeographical sciences titled *Biogeography: An Ecological Perspective* (1957), Dansereau displayed his interest in the common ground of disciplines concerned with the environment and the potential for collaboration. This theme, already evident in his work on representation and classification of vegetation structure, would become increasingly evident in his writings, particularly as environmental concerns began to reshape the intellectual and public context of ecology. Nevertheless, while seeking synthesis over specialization, he continued to insist on the need to ground one's work in a specific discipline.

In 1955 Dansereau returned to the Université de Montréal, serving until 1961 as director of its Botanical Institute and dean of the Faculty of Sciences. Again, however, he found the intellectual environment less open than he had hoped, and not just in scientific terms. Meanwhile, his American sojourn had not diminished his commitment to Quebec political and social concerns, and in 1956 Dansereau became president of Le Rassemblement, a movement for democratization and social justice. (The vice president was Pierre Trudeau, who would go on to serve as prime minister of Canada between 1968 and 1984). In response, Maurice Duplessis, the authoritarian premier of Quebec, insisted that the university strip Dansereau of his deanship. Dansereau kept his deanship, but the university accommodated Duplessis by urging Dansereau to stick to his science.

Ecology and Urban Society. In 1961 Dansereau returned to the United States to teach at Columbia University and serve as assistant director of the New York Botanical Garden. Life in the metropolis opened up new perspectives and opportunities. Captivated by the complexities of the urban ecosystem, he explored the application of ecological concepts to cities, insisting that, as an ecologist, he found cities as interesting as "natural" communities.

Dansereau also pursued his interest in interdisciplinary environmental studies, seeking to define a common ground shared by ecological and social perspectives. In his view, solutions to environmental challenges demanded not just science, but attention to culture and psychology; for Dansereau, this implied a need for dialogue between scientists and individuals in government, business, and civil society. In 1968 he organized a wide-ranging symposium on the urban environment, published in 1970 as *Challenge for Survival*. He also urged formation of an interdisciplinary environmental science, in which specialists in the Earth and biological sciences would collaborate with experts in agriculture, economics, and other fields. Anticipating the advent of university environmental studies programs and departments, this approach, he argued, would entail reorganization of academic structures and curricula.

During the 1960s an increasingly humanistic perspective became evident in Dansereau's work. He engaged in wide-ranging reflections on such topics as the relations between the scientific and other cultures and the social responsibilities of scientists. This was not entirely novel for Dansereau: he had exhibited since the 1930s a concern for social and ethical issues. In the 1960s he extended this concern, combining ecological ideas with those of a variety of writers and public intellectuals of the time, including Jean Gottman, Kenneth Boulding, and particularly Lewis Mumford, whose humanistic sensibility toward society and technology he admired.

Dansereau was, of course, not alone among North American ecologists in responding to the novel political prominence of their discipline by exploring its wider implications. But the depth and seriousness with which he drew from humanistic as well as scientific perspectives was more unusual. This, he felt, was consistent with his critical perspective on scientific conventions, especially the notion that objectivity demanded depersonalization of scientific expression. In Dansereau's view, that notion denied the essential social identity of scientists while separating their work from other forms of learning. As he often affirmed, authentic knowledge could be derived as much from artistic as from scientific sources—indeed, Dansereau felt, the search for such knowledge demanded attention to all of one's faculties and senses, a perspective he would characterize as acting as a "barefoot scientist."

For Dansereau, the French philosopher Pierre Teilhard de Chardin served as a model of this reconciliation of scientific and other forms of knowledge and perception. He had first encountered Teilhard's ideas in the 1930s, through Marie-Victorin. He subsequently maintained an active interest, writing several essays and conference presentations on Teilhard's ideas and serving in the late 1960s as president of the American Teilhard de Chardin Association. While he did not follow Teilhard in all the details of his arguments regarding the convergence of evolution and religion, he admired his effort to reconcile the scientific and the spiritual.

Ecology in Montreal. In 1968 Dansereau returned to the Université de Montréal as professor of ecology and director of the Centre de recherches écologiques de Montreal. Four years later, he moved across town to the Université du Quebec à Montréal as program director of the Centre de recherché en sciences de l'environnement.

In Montreal he initiated a variety of efforts to apply his ideas regarding the reconciliation of ecology and human society. In the early 1970s he led a large study of the terrain set aside for the proposed Mirabel Airport, north of Montreal. A vast area of land had been expropriated, far more than that required for the airport itself, and

Dansereau saw an opportunity to reconstitute its use on an ecological basis. Accordingly, he assembled an interdisciplinary group of specialists who examined the region's natural and social environment and integrated the results with the area's economic potential and the cultural factors shaping its use. The study, known as the EZAIM project (Écologie de la zone de l'aéroport international de Montréal), was, Dansereau believed, a successful experiment in integrating ecological considerations into land-use decisions.

In 1971 Dansereau proposed a new model of the ecosystem: the *boule-de-flèches* (ball of arrows). An elaboration of conventional trophic models, it incorporated in six trophic levels both natural and human factors; in particular, the two top levels—investment and control—incorporated the influence of psychological functions such as will and agency. In effect, the model sought to encompass the ecological significance of deliberate action and thus, Dansereau argued, could be applied as readily to an ecosystem dominated by humans, such as a city, as to more "natural" ecosystems. This was not a predictive or quantitative model; rather, it served to exhibit how, in ecological contexts, humans were unique—their resource use determined not just by need, but by social and cultural factors—but that this uniqueness could nevertheless be incorporated within an understanding of ecosystems. It was in this sense consistent with the interest then emerging among some ecologists in finding ways to incorporate human use of the environment within ecology, as exemplified, for example, by UNESCO's Man and the Biosphere Program.

Dansereau also became involved in other activities relating to science and the human environment. In 1968 he was named to the Science Council of Canada; he was also appointed vice president of a federal commission on housing and urban development. This work provided additional avenues through which he expressed his view that human-dominated ecosystems could be attractive and productive habitats. This perspective was itself founded on a lifelong optimism, an outlook that was the product of a happy childhood but also, he has stressed, grounded on science and on the history of humans learning to live with and adapt to nature. This optimism, however, had to be founded on accepting responsibility for alleviating social and economic injustices and for reducing one's own consumption through an embrace of "joyous austerity."

In 1976 Dansereau was named professor emeritus at the Université du Quebec à Montréal; at age ninety-five in 2006, he continued to write and participate in public affairs. He has received many honors: a member of the Royal Society of Canada since 1949, he was named a Companion of the Order of Canada in 1969, and a grand

officer of the Order of Québec in 1992. In November 2001 Dansereau was inducted into the Canadian Science and Engineering Hall of Fame. He has also received fifteen honorary degrees.

BIBLIOGRAPHY

A large collection of unpublished materials relating to the life and work of Dansereau are held at the archives of the Université du Québec à Montréal. A bibliography of Dansereau's works is available at the Web site of the Union for Sustainable Development, http://www.udd.org/Anglais/lefonds.html.

WORKS BY DANSEREAU

"Description and Recording of Vegetation upon a Structural Basis." *Ecology* 32 (1951): 172–229.

Biogeography: An Ecological Perspective. New York: Ronald Press, 1957.

"Ecological Impact and Human Ecology." In *Future Environments of North America,* edited by F. Fraser Darling and John P. Milton. Garden City, NY: Natural History Press, 1966.

Challenge for Survival: Land, Air, and Water for Man in Megalopolis. New York: Columbia University Press, 1970.

Inscape and Landscape. Toronto: Canadian Broadcasting Corporation, 1973.

La lancée, 1911–1936. Sainte-Foy, Quebec: Éditions Multimondes, 2005. First volume of a planned three-volume autobiography.

OTHER SOURCES

L'archives de Radio-Canada. *Dansereau, l'écologiste aux pieds nus.* Available from http://archives.radio-canada.ca/IDD-0-16-639/sciences_technologies/pierre_dansereau. Extensive audiovisual archive of Dansereau's life and work (in French).

Dumesnil, Thérèse. *Pierre Dansereau, l'écologiste aux pieds nus.* Montreal: Éditions Nouvelle Optique, 1981.

National Film Board of Canada. *An Ecology of Hope.* 2001. A documentary film about Dansereau's life and work.

Vaillancourt, Jean-Guy. "Pierre Dansereau, écologue, écosociologue, et écologiste." *Sociologie et sociétés* 31 (1999): 191–193.

Stephen Bocking

DART, RAYMOND ARTHUR (*b.* Brisbane, Queensland, Australia, 4 February 1893; *d.* Johannesburg, South Africa, 22 November 1988), *paleoanthropology, anatomy.*

Dart fundamentally changed research into human origins through his discovery of *Australopithecus africanus,* a new species of hominid that Dart considered the evolutionary link between the anthropoid apes and modern humans. His years of research and his sustained effort to convince others of the importance of the australopithecines in the history of human evolution helped to focus the attention of paleoanthropologists toward Africa as the continent where the earliest human ancestors would be found. His work on the origins of tool use, although now discredited, offers historians important insights into twentieth century debates over the role of tools in human evolution.

Education and Training. Dart was born in a suburb of Brisbane called Toowong, the son of Samuel Dart and Eliza Anne Brimblecombe. Dart's maternal and paternal grandfathers had both emigrated from Devonshire, in England, to Australia in the mid-nineteenth century, one to search for gold and the other to grow sugarcane. After attending the prestigious Ipswich Grammar School, he left to study medicine at the University of Queensland in 1911. Dart had been raised in a strict religiously fundamentalist family, but at university he encountered evolution theory and acquired a love for zoology. He completed his Honors degree in 1913 and his MS in 1915.

In 1914, he entered the University of Sydney, where he was a tutor of biology in St. Andrew's College as well as a demonstrator of anatomy and later secretary of the Sydney University Medical Society. That same year the British Association for the Advancement of Science held its annual meeting in Sydney. At the meeting Dart met the prominent neuroanatomist and physical anthropologist Grafton Elliot Smith, himself a graduate of the University of Sydney, and William Johnson Sollas. From 1915 to 1917, Dart assisted James Thomas Wilson, head of the Anatomy Department, in his anatomical studies of the human brain. Dart's achievements were such that he was made vice principal of St. Andrew's College during his last year at the university.

Dart continued with his studies despite the outbreak of World War I, and he completed his medical degree in 1917. Soon thereafter he enlisted in the Australian Army Medical Corp and shipped out to England in 1918. He spent the last year of the war stationed in France, but after demobilization in 1919, Dart left for University College, London, to join Grafton Elliot Smith in the Department of Anatomy, where he served as senior demonstrator. Soon after he joined the department, however, Elliot Smith encouraged Dart to accept an opportunity from the Rockefeller Foundation to teach and pursue research in the United States. Dart arrived at Washington University in St. Louis, Missouri, late in 1920. Robert J. Terry, the head of the Anatomy Department at the time, was assembling a large collection of human skeletons of different races at the university, and this demonstrated to Dart the value of anatomical collections, which would prove important

later in his career. Dart spent a brief period demonstrating anatomy in Cincinnati, Ohio, and there he met a medical student named Dora Tyree. They married at Wood's Hole, Massachusetts, in September 1921, just before Dart was to leave for England.

After his return to University College, Dart became interested in physical anthropology and began exploring the collection of brains housed at the Royal College of Surgeons. Elliot Smith had become deeply involved in anatomical studies of the Piltdown Man fossils, which drew Dart into the growing debate about their meaning. But then in 1922, Elliot Smith suggested that Dart apply for the Chair of Anatomy at the newly established University of the Witwatersrand, in Johannesburg, South Africa. Dart was not keen to leave England, but he and Dora left for South Africa in December 1922. The medical school's facilities were still under construction when Dart arrived, and he spent his early years at the university simply assembling the materials needed for a functioning department. In addition to his duties as professor of anatomy, Dart was dean of the Faculty of Medicine at the university from 1925 to 1943, and from 1934 to 1948 he served on the South African Medical and Dental Council.

Discovery of *Australopithecus*. Dart's life and career took a dramatic turn in 1924 when in November of that year he received a crate full of fossils blasted from the Northern Lime Company's quarries in Buxton, near the town of Taungs (the spelling was later changed to Taung). Among the various fossils in the crate were two pieces of breccia; in one Dart recognized an endocranial cast (the fossilized cast of the brain), and in the other he could see the interior of the front of a cranium, the bones of the face still encased in stone. Earlier in the year one of Dart's medical students, Josephine Salmons, had brought him a fossilized baboon skull that had been found at the Taung quarry. The existence of fossil primates at the site had captured Dart's attention, and he arranged for any other interesting fossils to be sent to him. The endocranial cast and partial cranium were particularly interesting because Dart quickly recognized that they belonged to some sort of primate.

Over the next four weeks, Dart carefully removed the stone to reveal the front portion of the skull of a hitherto unknown primate. The creature had humanlike teeth, and from the position of the foramen magnum, the opening where the spinal cord enters the skull, it was clear the creature walked upright. There were also humanlike features present in the endocranial cast. But there were also apelike features to the skull, most noticeably the small braincase. Interpretation of the fossil was made difficult by the fact that the remains were from a juvenile, perhaps only five or six years old, but Dart was convinced that he possessed an extinct species of anthropoid ape that evolutionarily represented an intermediate stage between apes and humans.

In January 1925, Dart sent a short article announcing his discovery to the journal *Nature*. The article, which was published in February, described the anatomical features of the fossil, the geological evidence for its antiquity, and Dart's conclusion that the creature would best be described as a "man-like ape" and might very well be ancestral to modern humans. Dart named this new species *Australopithecus africanus*, or southern ape from Africa. The discovery attracted considerable interest and generated much debate. Despite the fact that Charles Darwin had suggested in the *Descent of Man* (1871) that humans had evolved from an apelike ancestor in Africa, many anthropologists of the early twentieth century thought that humans had evolved in Asia. *Pithecanthropus erectus* had been discovered by Eugène Dubois on the island of Java in the 1890s, and Henry Fairfield Osborn's conviction that fossil human ancestors would be found in China was confirmed when successive excavations led by Davidson Black, Franz Weidenreich, and Pei Wenzhong recovered numerous specimens of *Sinanthropus pekinensis* (Peking Man) from the site of Zhoukoudian in China in the 1920s and 1930s. As a result, few anthropologists were looking to Africa for evidence of human evolution.

The response to *Australopithecus africanus* was also influenced by differing conceptions of human evolution itself. Some anthropologists thought that in the process of human evolution bipedalism (walking upright) had evolved first and that led to an increase in the size of the brain as the hands were used to make tools. The small-brained but upright-walking *Pithecanthropus erectus* fossil supported this view. However, there was a significant contingent of anthropologists, led in England by Arthur Keith, who believed that intelligence and a large brain had evolved first and that had led to bipedalism. They dismissed *Pithecanthropus* as a human ancestor and pointed instead to the Piltdown Man (*Eoanthropus dawsoni*) fossils unearthed between 1908 and 1911 to support their view. From this perspective, the small brained *Australopithecus africanus* did not correspond to their conception of a human ancestor.

A week after *Nature* published Dart's account of *Australopithecus africanus,* the journal published responses by several influential British physical anthropologists to Dart's discovery. Dart's old mentor at University College, Grafton Elliot Smith, Arthur Keith, anatomist at the Royal College of Surgeons, and Arthur Smith Woodward, Keeper of Geology and the British Museum (Natural History) each thought the discovery was significant but were skeptical about Dart's suggestion that *Australopithecus* was a human ancestor. Dart did find one valuable supporter, however. Robert Broom, a Scottish-born physician who

had emigrated to South Africa early in life and become an expert in paleontology, learned of Dart's discovery and immediately traveled to Johannesburg to see the fossil for himself. After inspecting the fossil and discussing it with Dart, Broom became convinced that *Australopithecus* was not merely an extinct species of ape but was in fact an intermediate form between the anthropoid apes and humans. Broom wrote two influential articles in 1925, one in *Nature* and the other in *Natural History*, that provided observations and arguments that strengthened Dart's assertion that *Australopithecus africanus* was a human ancestor. But this still failed to convert other anthropologists to Dart's view.

Dart received an important opportunity to make his case more directly when he was invited to prepare an exhibit for the South African pavilion at the British Empire Exhibition held at Wembley, in London, during the summer of 1925. Dart had plaster casts of the skull prepared along with a chart that represented *Australopithecus africanus* as ancestral to *Pithecanthropus* and in an evolutionary tree that showed other early human types such as Neanderthal. The casts and the chart appeared under a banner boldly proclaiming "Africa: The Cradle of Humanity," which prompted a very negative reaction from Arthur Keith and others who were unwilling to accept such a strong claim for Dart's fossil. Late that summer Aleš Hrdlička, a leading physical anthropologist at the Smithsonian Institution, traveled to South Africa to examine the specimen for himself and to visit the site where it had been found. He acknowledged *Australopithecus*'s significance for understanding primate evolution, but he was unwilling to accept Dart and Broom's stronger claims.

As the initial excitement over the discovery faded, Dart continued to study the skull, working to free the lower jaw from the rest of the face so as to be able to more closely examine the teeth, which would help to determine if *Australopithecus* was more apelike or on the path to becoming human. Meanwhile, his duties at the university were consuming much of his time, so work on *Australopithecus* proceeded slowly. Moreover, Robert Broom had realized that in order to truly convince other scientists of their interpretation of *Australopithecus* it would be necessary to find a more complete skeleton and fossils of adult specimens. Dart finally succeeded in freeing the lower jaw from the skull in 1929, and he prepared casts of the jaw to be sent to experts around the world. The British Association for the Advancement of Science also met in Johannesburg that year, and though Dart hoped that some of his critics would examine the fossil and change their minds, most continued to consider *Australopithecus* an extinct species of ape and not a human ancestor.

Then toward the end of 1929, the Italian Scientific Expedition, led by Attilio Gatti, invited Dart to accompany their research team on an eight-month research expedition through central and southern Africa. The expedition explored the ruins of Great Zimbabwe and the archaeological site of Solwezi. These experiences increased Dart's interest in anthropology and archaeology more broadly. He closely followed the excavation of the archaeological site of Mapungubwe, located in the Northern Transvaal, which began in 1932. Dart also briefly explored evidence of a cultural connection between ancient India and China and the peoples that had built Great Zimbabwe and Mapungubwe. A further opportunity to study the indigenous cultures of southern Africa arose in 1937, when Dart was asked to join a team that planned to assemble a group of Bushmen from the Kalahari Desert that would be displayed at an exhibition celebrating the British Empire to be held in Johannesburg. Little scientific information had previously been collected about the physical and cultural attributes of the Bushmen, and Dart spent a month studying their physical traits. Their culture and technology also impressed Dart as living examples of Middle Stone Age cultures, much like that probably possessed by the so-called Boskop Man, whose fossilized remains had been discovered in the Transvaal in 1914.

Dart had devoted only limited time to working on *Australopithecus* during the 1930s. A promising opportunity arose to present the specimen to colleagues in Europe when Dart's wife Dora, who had suspended her medical studies when they had married, decided to go to England in 1930 to continue her medical training, which she had resumed in Johannesburg. She took the *Australopithecus* fossil with her and showed it to several scientists. Dart joined her briefly in 1931 and used the occasion to visit Grafton Elliot Smith, Arthur Keith, and Arthur Smith Woodward, but they were far more interested in the recently discovered Peking Man fossils from China. Even his presentation delivered at the Zoological Society of London in February, where he displayed the skull, generated little excitement. Although Dart returned to Johannesburg somewhat discouraged, important events soon changed the status of *Australopithecus africanus*.

Robert Broom had hoped to find further specimens of *Australopithecus* ever since his first encounter with Dart's discovery. Broom's ability to pursue that search improved in 1934 when he was appointed curator of vertebrate paleontology and physical anthropology at the Transvaal Museum in Pretoria. He achieved spectacular success in 1936 when he found a partial skull of a creature very like *Australopithecus* in a quarry at a site called Sterkfontein. Despite its similarities to Dart's fossil, Broom considered it a separate species and named it *Plesianthropus transvaalensis*. Then in 1938, Broom obtained a partial skull and other bones at Kromdraai, just across the valley

from Sterkfontein, which differed enough from his previous discovery that he created another new species, *Paranthropus robustus*. The outbreak of World War II diverted both Dart and Broom from devoting much further time to searching for fossils, but they now had fossils from three different specimens of australopithecine upon which to build a better case for their being human ancestors.

Dart spent the years just prior to and during the war teaching and conducting research in comparative neurology. His marriage to Dora ended in 1933, but he married Marjorie Frew, the head librarian at the university's medical library, in 1936. Broom, however, was busy preparing a monograph with Gerrit Willem Hendrik Schepers on the various australopithecine fossils that had been collected thus far. Attitudes about *Australopithecus* began to change after the war, in part due to the publication of Broom and Schepers' *The South African Fossil Ape-Men: The Australopithecinae* (1946), which presented detailed descriptions of the fossils and an argument in support of their intermediate status between apes and humans. Equally significant was the visit to South Africa by Wilfrid Le Gros Clark in 1947 to examine the *Australopithecus* fossils firsthand. Le Gros Clark, professor of anatomy at Oxford University, possessed an extensive knowledge of primate comparative anatomy. His investigation of Dart and Broom's fossils led him to conclude that Dart and Broom were correct, and the australopithecines did possess features that indicated they were an evolutionary link between early anthropoids and modern humans. Le Gros Clark's prominence in Britain influenced many to take *Australopithecus* seriously as a human ancestor.

Makapansgat and the Osteodontokeratic. Dart's relative inactivity in studying his fossil during the 1930s and 1940s came to an end in 1947 when James Kitching of the Bernard Price Institute for Palaeontological Research, which had been established at the University of Witwatersrand in 1945 to encourage research into paleontology, unearthed a portion of an *Australopithecus* cranium along with an enormous quantity of animal bones at a limestone quarry located in Makapansgat, in the center of Transvaal province. The discovery reignited Dart's interest in human paleontology and sparked a new period of intensive research into the culture and evolutionary status of the australopithecines. The presence of charred material at the site led Dart to name the newly discovered fossil *Australopithecus prometheus*. Again Dart examined the fossil for evidence of its relationship to apes and humans, but the quantity and nature of the animal bones found at the site also drew Dart's attention.

Kitching had found baboon skulls at Makapansgat that had been fractured in such a way that Dart suspected they had been struck by some kind of club. Moreover a

240

survey of the animal bones present at the site showed an unusual number of ungulate leg bones. The abundance of bones from big game animals indicated that perhaps *Australopithecus* had been a hunter. Then Dart examined the fractures on the baboon skulls and concluded they resulted from the skulls being smashed by a leg bone used as a club. Thus it appeared that *Australopithecus* had hunted big game animals and used some of their bones as weapons, both of which were behaviors that were distinctly human and not apelike. In 1948, Dart, Kitching, and Alun Hughes (who was Dart's assistant in the Anatomy Department) began a systematic search through the debris piles at the Makapansgat limeworks searching for additional *Australopithecus* fossils and further evidence of *Australopithecus* tool use. Work at Makapansgat continued through the 1960s and proved remarkably productive.

Additional *Australopithecus* fossils were periodically discovered, but increasingly Dart's attention was devoted to collecting and interpreting the animal bones found at Makapansgat. Gradually Dart became convinced, from the kinds of bones he was finding and evidence that some of these bones had been modified, that he had discovered tools that had been used by the australopithecines of Makapansgat. No stone tools had been discovered at Makapansgat, or at any other australopithecine site, and Dart began to suspect that the evidence at Makapansgat showed that before the existence of stone tools bone had been used to make tools. He identified examples of leg bones, horns, and jaw bones that seemed to have been used as clubs, picks, knives, and saws. Dart argued that due to the difficulty of manufacturing tools from stone and the fact that bone tools worked very well for many of the same kinds of tasks that stone tools were later used for, it made sense that *Australopithecus* would have used bone tools. At the Third Pan-African Congress on Prehistory, held in 1955 in Livingstone, Northern Rhodesia, Dart displayed a collection of these bone implements and presented a paper which outlined his arguments that *Australopithecus* had possessed an osteodontokeratic (bone-tooth-horn) culture.

There was immediate criticism of Dart's osteodontokeratic tools and of the idea that the australopithecines had been tool users or tool makers. Sherwood Washburn argued, as did others, that the modifications to the bones Dart noted were not from their being used as tools but resulted from the bones being gnawed by carnivores before becoming fossilized. More seriously, Kenneth Oakley argued against the notion that *Australopithecus* was capable of making tools and was skeptical that they even used tools. Dart responded by rejecting the carnivore gnawing hypothesis and vigorously defended his evidence for an *Australopithecus* osteodontokeratic culture. Dart devoted tremendous energy and time to collecting and examining bone tools from Makapansgat between 1953

Raymond Arthur Dart. *Raymond Arthur Dart and the original Tuang specimen of Australopithecus africanus.* **JOHN READER/PHOTO RESEARCHERS, INC.**

and 1965, resulting in a steady stream of articles supporting the osteodontokeratic tools of *Australopithecus* and his argument that *Australopithecus* had been a tool user.

There is considerable historical evidence to suggest that Dart's interest in and ardent defense of the osteodontokeratic was related to his early failure to convince colleagues that *Australopithecus* was a human ancestor on the basis of the anatomy of the fossils. Once he had evidence that the australopithecines were tool users, he realized he had powerful support for his interpretation of the *Australopithecus* fossils because tool use represented a level of intelligence and culture that only humans and "protohumans" would possess. Despite Dart's immense efforts, however, few researchers ever accepted the validity of the osteodontokeratic, and it was later shown, partially on the basis of studies conducted by Charles Kimberlin (Bob) Brain in the 1970s, that Dart's bone tools were actually produced by natural weathering and carnivore gnawing.

Dart retired from teaching in 1958 but remained active in research through the 1960s. He wrote an autobiographical account of his studies in *Adventures with the*

Missing Link, which was published in 1959. He was made a Fellow of the Royal Society of South Africa in 1930 and served as an officer in many of the early Pan-African Congresses on Prehistory. Dart had a lasting institutional impact by gathering around himself a talented group of researchers who made the University of Witwatersrand a center for the study of paleoanthropology. Dart's broader influence on paleoanthropology was to help shift the search for the earliest evolutionary ancestors of modern humans from Asia to Africa, a process that Robert Broom and Louis Leakey also contributed to. Thus, Dart's research opened the way for significant paleontological and archaeological discoveries in Africa.

BIBLIOGRAPHY

The Raymond A. Dart Papers are split between the Department of Anatomy and Human Biology, University of the Witswatersrand Medical School, Johannesburg, South Africa, and the University Archives, University of the Witswatersrand, Johannesburg, South Africa.

WORKS BY DART

"*Australopithecus africanus*: The Man-Ape of South Africa." *Nature* 115 (1925): 195–199.

"The Makapansgat Proto-human *Australo-pithecus prometheus*." *American Journal of Physical Anthropology* 6, n.s., (1948): 259–283.

"The Predatory Implemental Technique of Australopithecus." *American Journal of Physical Anthropology* 7, n.s., (1949): 1–38.

"Cultural Status of the South African Man-Apes." In *Annual Report of the Smithsonian Institution*. Washington, DC: U.S. Government Printing Office, 1955.

The Osteodontokeratic Culture of Australopithecus prometheus. Transvaal Museum Memoir, no. 10. Pretoria: Transvaal Museum, 1957.

Africa's Place in the Emergence of Civilisation. Johannesburg: South African Broadcasting Corporation, 1959.

With Dennis Craig. *Adventures with the Missing Link*. New York: Viking Press, 1959.

OTHER SOURCES

Broom, Robert. "Some Notes on the Taungs Skull." *Nature* 115 (1925): 569–571.

———. "On the Newly Discovered South African Man-Ape." *Natural History* 25 (1925): 409–418.

———, and Gerrit Willem Hendrik Schepers. *The South African Fossil Ape-Man: The Australopithecinae*. Pretoria: Transvaal Museum, 1946.

Fischer, Ilse. *Professor Raymond Arthur Dart: A Bibliography of His Works*. Johannesburg: University of the Witwatersrand, Department of Bibliography, Librarianship, and Typography, 1969. Includes brief biography.

Tobias, Phillip V. *Dart, Taung and the "Missing Link": An Essay on the Life and Work of Emeritus Professor Raymond Dart*. Johannesburg: Witwatersrand University Press, 1984.

———. "Ape-like Australopithecus after Seventy Years: Was It a Hominid?" *Journal of the Royal Anthropological Insititute* 4 (1998): 283–308.

Wheelhouse, Frances. *Raymond Arthur Dart: A Pictorial Profile*. Sydney: Transpareon Press, 1983.

———, and Kathaleen S. Smithford. *Dart: Scientist and Man of Grit*. Sydney: Transpareon Press, 2001.

Matthew R. Goodrum

DARWIN, CHARLES ROBERT (*b*. The Mount, Shrewsbury, England, 12 February 1809; *d*. Down House, Downe, Kent, England, 19 April 1882), *natural history, geology, evolution*. For the original article on Darwin see *DSB*, vol. 3 (note error in date of birth given there).

When Gavin de Beer wrote the article on Darwin in the original *DSB* there were only a handful of historical studies available, including his own biography. Over the next few decades there was an explosion of interest in the process by which Darwin developed his theory of evolution by natural selection, fueled by the publication of his notebooks, edited by de Beer himself. There have also been many studies of the impact of Darwin's ideas, inspired in part by a recognition that earlier perceptions had been shaped by the success of the selection theory in the mid-twentieth century. Michael Ruse coined the term "Darwin industry" to denote the group of historians who devoted themselves to the study of his work. Many of Darwin's papers have since been published, including a combined volume of the notebooks originally edited by de Beer. There are editions of his diaries, of the marginalia he scribbled in the books he read, and an ongoing project to publish his whole correspondence. Both the *Origin of Species* and the notebooks have been provided with a concordance. The flow of technical literature has slackened off, but the flood of biographical studies has continued unabated, those by Janet Browne and by Adrian Desmond and James Moore having attracted particular attention.

There have been important developments in the understanding of many aspects of Darwin's work and its implications. Historians such as Jonathan Hodge have alerted scholars to the strong thread that runs through Darwin's work based on a traditional view of heredity and reproduction. There have been major debates on the role of ideology in his thinking and new developments in the understanding of his changing religious views. De Beer's effort to trace a straightforward link between Darwin's original theory and modern Darwinism have come under suspicion as researchers have become more aware of the existence of alternative ideas about how evolution might work.

Darwin's Early Career. Darwin's period of medical study at Edinburgh has traditionally been dismissed as of little significance. But he also worked on natural history there, and this has led Hodge and Phillip R. Sloan to challenge the impression given in his autobiography that these were wasted years. Darwin claimed to have been unimpressed by the Lamarckian anatomist Robert Grant, although it is now known that the two worked closely together, and that Darwin was impressed by Grant's claim that the "zoophytes" (Hydrozoa and corals) serve as a bridge between the plant and animal kingdoms. Darwin's early reading focused his attention on issues that would shape his later thinking, especially his ideas about generation or sexual reproduction. He became committed to the view that reproduction is a creative activity of the vital forces in the body, a position quite unlike the modern focus on the rigid transmission of genetic units. Here his thinking reflects the fascination with the creativity of sex that ran through his grandfather Erasmus Darwin's theories.

Sandra Herbert has made a major study of Darwin's geological work and has shown how he turned the methodology of Charles Lyell into a theoretical program for understanding all Earth movements. There have been important studies of Darwin's biogeographical work on the *Beagle* voyage. Working on Darwin's original notes, Frank Sulloway has undermined the myth of a "eureka" experience on the Galápagos Islands by showing that the finches there could not have played such a crucial role. Darwin's own specimens were not even labeled to show which island they were collected on, and he had to rely on collections made by others on the ship to reconstruct the distribution. Only after his return to England, when the ornithologist John Gould informed him that the finches really did constitute a group of distinct but closely related species, did Darwin realize their full significance.

Herbert and Martin Rudwick have made detailed studies of Darwin's active role in the London geological community following his return, including his abortive theory on the parallel roads of Glen Roy. But behind the scenes he had begun to think hard about the question of transmutation. Sulloway argues that the insights that led Darwin to the idea of branching evolution were probably arrived at after the *Beagle* had returned to England in October 1836, although a few historians speculate that he may have accepted transmutation during the later part of the voyage. Ernst Mayr called this the first Darwinian revolution: The Galápagos results convinced him that new species are formed by the natural transformation of old ones, although as yet he had no idea what the process of change might be. Over the next few years he searched for

a plausible mechanism, and his development of the theory of natural selection constitutes a second revolution.

The Discovery of Natural Selection. Howard Gruber has explored Darwin's notebooks from this period to argue that the discovery of the selection theory can be seen as a major example of creative thinking. Darwin sometimes projected an image of himself as a patient observer, and his opponents have always accused him of being incapable of deep thought. But he also said that the *Origin* was "one long argument," and Mayr among others has stressed that he was anything but a simple fact-gatherer. Ruse and Silvan Schweber focus on Darwin's desire to appear a good scientist as defined by contemporary discussions of the scientific method by Sir John Frederick William Herschel and William Whewell. They argue that he developed natural selection by a creative process of synthesis and testing. David J. Depew and Bruce H. Weber see the selection theory as the product of a new statistical mode of explanation and also stress his innovative work in the area of methodology. Darwin wanted to create a theory based on natural law in the Newtonian tradition, but by the very nature of the problems he addressed he was forced to transform this program by introducing statistical and historical elements into his explanations. Robert J. Richards sees the historical element as derived from German idealist philosophy, but others, including Hodge, relate it to Lyell's uniformitarian methodology.

Darwin started from his knowledge of biogeography, and with a conviction that evolution must be a branching process in which one species is divided by geographical barriers and the separate populations then become transformed in different directions. He wondered if species might be "born" with a built-in lifespan, after which they become extinct. He soon realized, however, that some more active mechanism of change was needed and by July 1837 he was convinced that transmutation must come about by the accumulation of individual variations over many generations. He explored the direction already taken by Jean-Baptiste de Lamarck and Erasmus Darwin: Might a change in the environment produce modifications either by affecting the reproductive process or by changing the organisms' habits? He soon decided that Lamarckism was inadequate. For a variety of reasons, he decided that although the environment might well be the stimulus, the majority of the changes it produced were not purposeful.

Studies by Hodge, David Kohn, and Phillip Sloan have revealed the extent to which Darwin was influenced by his views on "generation" or reproduction. The key to transmutation was the creative power of sexual reproduction. The theory of heredity he later called "pangenesis" (published in 1868) was formulated at this early stage.

Older studies lament Darwin's "failure" to anticipate genetics, on the assumption that if he had developed the concept of the gene he would have avoided the problems that beset the selection theory in the late nineteenth century. Modern scholars accept that the foundations of his thought lie in a premodern concept of heredity.

James Secord and Peter J. Vorzimmer show how the C notebook shows Darwin studying work of animal breeders, where changes could actually be observed within a species. He later suggested that he observed the breeders applying a process of artificial selection and then saw how this model could be transferred to natural evolution. L. T. (Lloyd Thomas) Evans and Ruse have explored the analogy between artificial and natural selection because—as Darwin himself later realized—it offers such a neat model for how natural selection operates. But although the process of selection seems clearly illustrated in such cases, Darwin's notebooks show that there was no direct borrowing of the selection model from the breeders. Throughout the C and D notebooks he remained convinced that adaptive variations must somehow be elicited automatically in a changed environment (Lamarckism), and did not see the breeders work as a useful analogy. Accounts of the discovery of the selection mechanism by Camille Limoges, Herbert, and Richard A. Richards have argued that he could not have been inspired by the model of artificial selection. Darwin became so used to citing the work of animal breeders as a model in his later accounts of the theory that he actually came to believe that this was how he was led to the idea of selection.

At this point he read Thomas Robert Malthus on population and realized the significance of the struggle for existence. Here the discussion enters the debate over the extent to which his thinking reflected the ideology of free-enterprise capitalism. Robert M. Young has been the most powerful advocate of the view that the selection theory does reflect the prevailing ideology of the time, a position backed up in the biography by Desmond and Moore. Schweber argues for an influence derived from the individualism of Adam Smith's economics, while noting that scientific factors had already begun to make Darwin think in terms of individual variation within a population—the innovation that Mayr calls "population thinking"—the transition from seeing a species as based on an ideal type to seeing it as a population of distinct individuals. Depew and Weber see the rise of Darwinism as the creation of a statistical mode of explanation as opposed to the old Newtonian view of causation based on law. The claim for a direct input from Darwin's social environment must be balanced against the evidence for a growing awareness that for science to tackle certain kinds of questions, a new type of explanation based on statistically modeled changes was needed.

De Beer's account minimized the influence of Malthus, treating the population principle as only a catalyst helping Darwin to put together insights already gained from his observations of nature. The connection is certainly not as direct as is sometimes implied: Peter J. Bowler showed that Darwin's concept of the struggle for existence does not appear in Malthus's work, and in this sense he had to think creatively with the insight provided by the population principle. Malthus did not anticipate the logic of what became known as social Darwinism, and thus could not provide the whole model for the selection theory. Edward Manier and Schweber point to the breadth of Darwin's reading, which reveals other ways in which the ideology of the time could have filtered into his thinking. He read Smith and also David Brewster's review of Auguste Comte's positivist philosophy, which argued for the need to base all theories on mathematical foundations—exactly what was provided by the arithmetical logic of the population principle. Looking for a way of measuring variation, he turned to the work of the Belgian anthropologist Lambert Quételet, who pioneered the application of statistics to the human population. Darwin's theory was not a slavish copy of Malthus's political philosophy, but it may nevertheless have been steeped in the ideology of the time. As Desmond and Moore stress, this was a time of social conflict in Britain, so Darwin could see on the streets the struggle that the political economists were trying to understand.

Studies by Gruber and Herbert show the M and N notebooks revealing Darwin's adoption of a materialist perspective, at least on how his theory would apply to humankind. These notes anticipate many of the topics later articulated in the *Descent of Man*. Darwin saw no room for the traditional notion of a soul existing on a purely spiritual plane: The mind was a product of the material activity of the brain, just as the phrenologists held. He suspected that much of human unconscious behavior may be instinctive, programmed into human brains by the effect of evolution on humanity's ancestors. The ways in which individuals express their emotions reveal their animal ancestry, as in the case of snarling to express anger. He was convinced that evolution would throw light on moral values by showing how certain forms of social behavior have been programmed into humans by natural selection. Morality was merely a rationalization of these social instincts. Such ideas would undermine the whole traditional view of human nature.

Yet Darwin still felt that the laws of nature were instituted by a wise and perhaps even benevolent God. Far from recognizing the full horror of a worldview based on struggle, he stressed that the end result of evolution was to keep species well adapted to their environments in an ever-changing world. As Walter Cannon and Young argue, he transformed rather than destroyed the old natural

Charles Darwin. *Darwin, circa 1875.* **AP IMAGES.**

theology of William Paley (1743–1805). Even struggle and death had a positive value in the divine plan. Robert Richards argues that Darwin was also committed to the idea of progress. He suggests that historians influenced by modern Darwinism have failed to appreciate that Darwin still saw evolution as a steady pressure to mount the scale of organization. Selection was a force that would tend to raise the standard of organization whenever the circumstances were appropriate. But he was also aware that the advance could take place in a number of directions, not just along a single line leading toward humanity.

Development of the Theory. Over the next twenty years Darwin worked on his theory, soon moving to live in the countryside at Downe. He was not a complete recluse, however, and the vast extent of the correspondence network he built up (later published) provided him with sources of information on subjects relevant to his theorizing. As Manier argues, he was trying to build up a community of scientists who would speak the new language of evolution.

Darwin's work on barnacles provided him with many insights, including the importance of embryological characters for determining relationships. His thinking incorporated an element of what would later be called the recapitulation theory, although the extent to which he can be associated with the full-blown version of this theory is controversial. Richards has argued that Darwin adopted the "law of parallelism," whose influence had been charted by Stephen Jay Gould. This form of recapitulation theory implies a linear model of evolution, with the lower animals being treated as immature versions of the more perfect human form. Many historians are suspicious of Richards's effort to tie Darwin in with the developmental way of thinking so prevalent in Germany.

An important change took place in Darwin's thinking in the 1850s. It has often been assumed that as soon as he formulated the selection theory, he must have recognized that it implied a much harsher vision of nature as a scene of unrelenting struggle and suffering. But Dov Ospovat argued that the early form of the theory still revealed its roots in Paley's vision of natural theology. Only in the 1850s did he realize that a compromise could not be maintained. The principle of population implies that the struggle for existence continues even in a stable environment, so there can never be any escape from the relentless threat of death. As Frank Burch Brown, Kohn, and Neal Gillespie show, Darwin's worldview thus became gradually more pessimistic. Moore notes how this move was encouraged by the death of his beloved daughter Anne in 1851.

Ospovat also notes that this growing recognition of the power of struggle allowed Darwin to explain the trends toward divergence and specialization being discovered by Richard Owen in the fossil record. Both Owen and William B. Carpenter recognized this trend by comparing the fossil sequences with the process of embryological specialization observed by Karl Ernst von Baer. In effect, Darwin applied the principle of the "division of labor" to explain why it was advantageous for species to diversify. Browne and Kohn note that biogeography also transformed Darwin's thinking on this issue. His "principle of divergence" arose from a recognition that successful genera expand and diversify, wiping out the species that had previously occupied the territory. Here again Darwin came face to face with the relentless pressure of natural selection. Sulloway notes that by focusing on the pressure to specialize, Darwin was led to marginalize his early emphasis on the role of geographical isolation in speciation, as in the Galápagos. Nevertheless, by 1856 he had created a much more sophisticated theory and had amassed a vast amount of supportive evidence and had begun to write a "big book" on the topic, now published and edited by Robert Stauffer. This was the project interrupted by the arrival of Alfred Russel Wallace's paper in 1858. There has been much debate over the degree of similarity between the two men's theories of natural selection, summarized by Malcolm Kottler. Some scholars argue

that there were significant differences between them, but no one disputes that Darwin recognized important parallels and began writing the *Origin of Species.*

The Reception of Darwin's Theory. Surveying the recent work on the reception of the *Origin of Species* moves into broader realms of the interactions between Darwin and the scientific, cultural, and social developments of the time. A survey of the Darwinian revolution by Ruse provides a useful overview, as do the biographies of Darwin by Browne and Desmond and Moore. Recent studies of the early Darwinians such as Thomas Henry Huxley should also be consulted.

For the scientific debate, David Hull edited and commented on a collection of reviews of the *Origin.* Scholars such as Vorzimmer, Jean Gayon, and William Provine have traced the debates over natural selection from Darwin's time into the era of modern genetics. The emergence of the so-called modern synthesis of Darwinism and genetics was the topic of an important collection of essays edited by Mayr and Provine. Here is a complex series of debates centered on challenges to the traditional assumption that Darwin's "failure" to recognize the significance of Gregor Mendel's laws of heredity left him vulnerable to attacks such as the one launched by Fleeming Jenkin in 1867. In the early 2000s, recognition of the role played by a pregenetical model of heredity and variation in Darwin's thinking about selection makes it difficult to imagine how he could have appreciated the potential value of Mendelism. Nor is it clear that his theory of pangenesis necessarily undermined the credibility of the selection mechanism, although Jenkin's attack did force him to question his longstanding assumption that favorable variations were very rare. The process by which the theory of natural selection was synthesized with genetics was long and complex because it involved the destruction of a developmental viewpoint in which the transmission of characters was thought to be inextricably connected with the mechanism by which those characters are generated in the embryo.

Many modern historians would accept that it was the prevalence of this developmental model in late nineteenth-century biology, not a specific problem associated with "blending inheritance" that accounts for the widespread reluctance to take the theory of natural selection seriously during Darwin's own lifetime. Peter Bowler has outlined several alternative theories of evolution developed in the late nineteenth-century "eclipse of Darwinism." In particular he develops Gould's account of the ways in which the recapitulation theory was used to imply that evolution must be directed along predefined channels, just like the development of the embryo. Bowler has also suggested that an appreciation of the extent to which

Darwin's own explanation of the process was rejected must force us to reconsider the reasons why the basic idea of evolution became popular at the time. Darwinism was translated into a theory of necessary progress, and the more radical implications of the selection theory remained dormant until the twentieth century. Along similar lines, Ruse has written a provocative book arguing that Darwinism succeeded only because the theory of evolution piggybacked on the rising tide of enthusiasm for the idea of progress.

In terms of the wider public response, Alvar Ellegard provided a detailed study of the reaction to Darwin in the British periodical press. Gillian Beer has pioneered the study of Darwin's influence in the literary sphere. Moore has challenged the established view that evolutionism became sucked into a "war" between science and religion, noting the extent to which liberal Christians welcomed the theory because they saw it as a model for social progress in the modern world. The challenges posed by this vision to the more traditional Christian view of the origin of humanity were highlighted in Darwin's own study of human origins, the *Descent of Man*. Richards has written a detailed account of the development of evolutionary explanations of the human mind, which compares Darwin's ideas on the topic with those of other thinkers such as Herbert Spencer. He stresses the extent to which Darwin and Spencer saw themselves as providing morality with a new foundation, certainly not as destroying all traditional values. Darwin did, however, come to accept the prevailing view that the nonwhite races retain more traces of humanity's ape ancestry, although initially he had adopted more liberal views on this issue.

Curiously, however, there have been comparatively few attempts to integrate Darwin's ideas on human origins with the history of paleoanthropology, although a survey by Bowler stresses the innovative nature of his belief that the development of an upright posture was the key breakthrough in the separation of the first hominids from the apes. Virtually all other commentators before the mid-twentieth century took it for granted that it was the expansion of the human brain that drove the separation—Darwin was the first to suggest that the initial step might have been triggered by an adaptive change necessitated by the hominids' move onto the open plains.

There have been endless debates about the role played by Darwin's theory in the promotion of "social Darwinism." Historians such as Young, who stress the ideological input into Darwin's own thinking, have naturally pointed to the use of Darwinian rhetoric to justify policies in which struggle is the driving force of progress. There have been many accounts of social Darwinism making the same point, from the classic study by Richard Hofstadter to more recent work by Mike Hawkins. But historians such as Robert Bannister and Bowler have urged caution, noting that some appeals to the metaphor of the struggle for existence did not depend on the application of the selection theory, even when Darwin's name was invoked. Spencer's enthusiasm for individual competition was linked to a Lamarckian mechanism of self-improvement, for all that he coined the term "survival of the fittest."

There have been comparatively few accounts of the detailed biological investigations Darwin carried out in the later part of his life, apart from those contained in the biographies. Helena Cronin and Kottler have written on the theory of sexual selection, especially Darwin's long-standing debate with Wallace on the topic (significantly in the context of the "eclipse" of Darwinism; few other biologists took that theory seriously until the mid-twentieth century). On a more personal level, Ralph Colp has written on Darwin's illness. Moore has discredited the story, popular among modern creationists, that he underwent a deathbed conversion back to Christianity. Moore has also provided an analysis of the symbolism associated with the events surrounding his funeral. When he died in 1882 the scientific community was anxious to exploit his status as the most famous biologist of the century to obtain for him the honor of being buried in Westminster Abbey.

SUPPLEMENTARY BIBLIOGRAPHY

There have been many modern editions of The Origin of Species, *usually based on either the first or the sixth editions, and translations into most major languages.*

WORKS BY DARWIN

Charles Darwin's Natural Selection: Being the Second Part of His Big Species Book Written from 1856 to 1858. Edited by Robert C. Stauffer. London: Cambridge University Press, 1975.

The Collected Papers of Charles Darwin. Edited by Paul H. Barrett. 2 vols. Chicago: University of Chicago Press, 1977.

A Concordance to Darwin's Origin of Species, First Edition. Edited by Paul H. Barrett, Donald J. Weinshank, and Timothy T. Gottleber. Ithaca, NY: Cornell University Press, 1981.

The Correspondence of Charles Darwin. Edited by Frederick Burkhardt and Sydney Smith. Cambridge: Cambridge University Press, 1985–. Thirteen volumes published thus far, series still in progress.

A Calendar of the Correspondence of Charles Darwin, 1821–1882. Edited by Frederick Burkhardt, Sydney Smith, David Kohn, et al. New York and London: Garland, 1985.

Charles Darwin's Notebooks, 1836–1844: Geology, Transmutation of Species, Metaphysical Enquiries. Edited by Paul H. Barrett, Peter Jack Gautrey, Sandra Herbert, et al. London: British Museum (Natural History); Ithaca, NY: Cornell University Press, 1987.

Charles Darwin's Beagle Diary. Edited by Richard D. Keynes. Cambridge, U.K.: Cambridge University Press, 1988.

Charles Darwin's Marginalia. Vol. 1. Edited by Mario di Gregorio and Nick Gill. New York: Garland, 1990–.

A Concordance to Charles Darwin's Notebooks, 1836–1844. Edited by Donald J. Weinshank et al. Ithaca, NY: Cornell University Press, 1990. Available from www.darwin-online.org.uk.

OTHER SOURCES

Bannister, Robert C. *Social Darwinism: Science and Myth in Anglo-American Social Thought.* Philadelphia: Temple University Press, 1979.

Beer, Gillian. *Darwin's Plots: Evolutionary Narrative in Darwin, George Eliot, and Nineteenth-Century Fiction.* London: Routledge and Kegan Paul, 1983.

Bowler, Peter J. "Malthus, Darwin, and the Concept of Struggle." *Journal of the History of Ideas* 37 (1976): 631–650.

———. *The Eclipse of Darwinism: Anti-Darwinian Evolution Theories in the Decades around 1900.* Baltimore: Johns Hopkins University Press, 1983.

———. *Evolution: The History of an Idea.* Berkeley: University of California Press, 1984. Rev. ed., 2003.

———. *Theories of Human Evolution: A Century of Debate, 1844–1944.* Baltimore: Johns Hopkins University Press, 1986.

———. *The Non-Darwinian Revolution: Reinterpreting a Historical Myth.* Baltimore: Johns Hopkins University Press, 1988.

———. *Charles Darwin: The Man and His Influence.* Oxford: Basil Blackwell, 1990.

Brown, Frank Burch. "The Evolution of Darwin's Theism." *Journal of the History of Biology* 19 (1986): 1–45.

Browne, Janet. "Darwin's Botanical Arithmetic and the 'Principle of Divergence,' 1854–1858." *Journal of the History of Biology* 13 (1980): 53–89.

———. *Charles Darwin: A Biography.* 2 vols. London: Cape, 1995–2002.

Cannon, Walter F. "The Bases of Darwin's Achievement: A Reevaluation." *Victorian Studies* 5 (1961): 109–134.

Colp, Ralph. *To Be an Invalid: The Illness of Charles Darwin.* Chicago: University of Chicago Press, 1977.

Cronin, Helena. *The Ant and the Peacock: Altruism and Sexual Selection from Darwin to Today.* Cambridge, U.K.: Cambridge University Press, 1991.

Crook, Paul. *Darwinism, War, and History: The Debate over the Biology of War from the "Origin of Species" to the First World War.* Cambridge, U.K.: Cambridge University Press, 1994.

Depew, David J., and Bruce H. Weber. *Darwinism Evolving: Systems Dynamics and the Genealogy of Natural Selection.* Cambridge, MA: MIT Press, 1995.

Desmond, Adrian, and James R. Moore. *Darwin.* London: Michael Joseph; New York: Viking Penguin, 1991.

Ellegard, Alvar. *Darwin and the General Reader: The Reception of Darwin's Theory of Evolution in the British Periodical Press, 1859–1872.* Göteburg, Sweden: Acta Universitatis Gothenburgensis, 1958. Reprint, Chicago: University of Chicago Press, 1990.

Evans, L[loyd] T[homas]. "Darwin's Use of the Analogy between Artificial and Natural Selection." *Journal of the History of Biology* 17 (1984): 113–140.

Gayon, Jean. *Darwinism's Struggle for Survival: Heredity and the Hypothesis of Natural Selection.* Cambridge, U.K.: Cambridge University Press, 1998.

Gillespie, Neal C. *Charles Darwin and the Problem of Creation.* Chicago: University of Chicago Press, 1979.

Gould, Stephen Jay. *Ontogeny and Phylogeny.* Cambridge, MA: Harvard University Press, 1977.

Gruber, Howard E. *Darwin on Man: A Psychological Study of Scientific Creativity, by Howard E. Gruber, Together with Darwin's Early and Unpublished Notebooks, Transcribed and Annotated by Paul H. Barrett.* New York: E. P. Dutton, 1974.

Hawkins, Mike. *Social Darwinism in European and American Thought, 1860–1945: Nature as Model and Nature as Threat.* Cambridge, U.K.: Cambridge University Press, 1997.

Herbert, Sandra. "The Place of Man in the Development of Darwin's Theory of Transmutation." Pts. 1 and 2. *Journal of the History of Biology* 7 (1974): 217–258; 10 (1977): 155–227.

———. *Charles Darwin, Geologist.* Ithaca, NY: Cornell University Press, 2005.

Hodge, Michael J. S. "The Structure and Strategy of Darwin's 'Long Argument.'" *British Journal for the History of Science* 10 (1977): 237–246.

———. "Darwin and the Laws of the Animate Part of the Terrestrial System (1835–1837): On the Lyellian Origins of His Zoonomical Explanatory Program." *Studies in the History of Biology* 6 (1983): 1–106.

———. "Darwin as a Lifelong Generation Theorist." In *The Darwinian Heritage,* edited by David Kohn. Princeton, NJ: Princeton University Press, 1985.

———, and David Kohn. "The Immediate Origins of Natural Selection." In *The Darwinian Heritage,* edited by David Kohn. Princeton, NJ: Princeton University Press, 1985.

———. "Generation and the Origin of Species (1837–1937): A Historiographical Suggestion." *British Journal for the History of Science* 22 (1989): 267–282.

Hofstadter, Richard. *Social Darwinism in American Thought.* Rev. ed. New York: George Braziller, 1959.

Hull, David L. *Darwin and His Critics: The Reception of Darwin's Theory of Evolution by the Scientific Community.* Cambridge, MA: Harvard University Press, 1973.

Kohn, David. "Theories to Work By: Rejected Theories, Reproduction, and Darwin's Path to Natural Selection." *Studies in the History of Biology* 4 (1980): 67–170.

———. "Darwin's Principle of Divergence as Internal Dialogue." In *The Darwinian Heritage,* edited by David Kohn. Princeton, NJ: Princeton University Press, 1985.

———. "Darwin's Ambiguity: The Secularization of Biological Meaning." *British Journal of the History of Science* 22 (1989): 215–240.

———, ed. *The Darwinian Heritage.* Princeton, NJ: Princeton University Press, 1985.

Kottler, Malcolm Jay. "Darwin, Wallace, and the Origin of Sexual Dimorphism." *Proceedings of the American Philosophical Society* 124 (1980): 203–226.

———. "Charles Darwin and Alfred Russel Wallace: Two Decades of Debate over Natural Selection." In *The Darwinian Heritage*, edited by David Kohn. Princeton, NJ: Princeton University Press, 1985.

Limoges, Camille. *La sélection naturelle: Étude sur le première constitution d'un concept (1837–1859)*. Paris: Presses Universitaires de France, 1970.

Manier, Edward. *The Young Darwin and His Cultural Circle: A Study of Influences which Helped Shape the Language and Logic of the First Drafts of the Theory of Natural Selection*. Dordrecht: Reidel, 1978.

———. "History, Philosophy, and Sociology of Biology: A Family Romance." *Studies in the History and Philosophy of Science* 11 (1980): 1–24.

Mayr, Ernst. "Darwin and Natural Selection: How Darwin May Have Discovered His Highly Unconventional Theory." *American Scientist* 65 (1977): 321–327.

———. *The Growth of Biological Thought: Diversity, Evolution, and Inheritance*. Cambridge, MA: Belknap Press, 1982.

———. *One Long Argument: Charles Darwin and the Genesis of Modern Evolutionary Thought*. Cambridge, MA: Harvard University Press, 1991.

———, and William B. Provine, eds. *The Evolutionary Synthesis: Perspectives on the Unification of Biology*. Cambridge, MA: Harvard University Press, 1980.

Moore, James R. *The Post-Darwinian Controversies: A Study of the Protestant Struggle to Come to Terms with Darwin in Great Britain and America, 1870–1900*. New York: Cambridge University Press, 1979.

———. "Charles Darwin Lies in Westminster Abbey." *Biological Journal of the Linnean Society* 17 (1982): 97–113.

———. *The Darwin Legend*. Grand Rapids, MI: Baker, 1994.

Ospovat, Dov. "The Influence of Karl Ernst von Baer's Embryology, 1828–1859: A Reappraisal in Light of Richard Owen and William B. Carpenter's 'Paleontological Application of von Baer's Law.'" *Journal of the History of Biology* 9 (1976): 1–28.

———. *The Development of Darwin's Theory: Natural History, Natural Theology, and Natural Selection, 1838–1859*. Cambridge, U.K., and New York: Cambridge University Press, 1981.

Provine, William B. *The Origins of Theoretical Population Genetics*. Chicago: University of Chicago Press, 1971.

Richards, Richard A. "Darwin and the Inefficiency of Artificial Selection." *Studies in the History and Philosophy of Science* 28 (1997): 75–97.

Richards, Robert J. *Darwin and the Emergence of Evolutionary Theories of Mind and Behavior*. Chicago: University of Chicago Press, 1987.

———. *The Meaning of Evolution: The Morphological Construction and Ideological Reconstruction of Darwin's Theory*. Chicago: University of Chicago Press, 1992.

Rudwick, Martin J. S. "Darwin and Glen Roy: A 'Great Failure' in Scientific Method?" *Studies in the History and Philosophy of Science* 5 (1974): 97–185.

———. "Charles Darwin in London: The Integration of Public and Private Science." *Isis* 73 (1982): 186–206.

Ruse, Michael. "The Darwin Industry: A Critical Evaluation." *History of Science* 12 (1974): 43–58.

———. "Charles Darwin and Artificial Selection." *Journal of the History of Ideas* 36 (1975): 339–350.

———. "Darwin's Debt to Philosophy: An Examination of the Influence of the Philosophical Ideas of John F. W. Herschel and William Whewell on the Development of Charles Darwin's Theory of Evolution." *Studies in the History and Philosophy of Science* 6 (1975): 159–181.

———. *The Darwinian Revolution: Science Red in Tooth and Claw*. Chicago: University of Chicago Press, 1979.

———. *Monad to Man: The Concept of Progress in Evolutionary Biology*. Cambridge, MA: Harvard University Press, 1996.

Schweber, Silvan S. "The Young Darwin." *Journal of the History of Biology* 12 (1979): 175–192.

———. "Darwin and the Political Economists: Divergence of Character." *Journal of the History of Biology* 13 (1980): 195–289.

———. "John Herschel and Charles Darwin: A Study in Parallel Lives." *Journal of the History of Biology* 22 (1989): 1–71.

Secord, James A. "Nature's Fancy: Charles Darwin and the Breeding of Pigeons." *Isis* 72 (1981): 163–186.

Sloan, Phillip R. "Darwin's Invertebrate Program, 1826–1836." In *The Darwinian Heritage*, edited by David Kohn. Princeton, NJ: Princeton University Press, 1985.

———. "Darwin, Vital Matter, and the Transformism of Species." *Journal of the History of Biology* 19 (1986): 369–445.

Sulloway, Frank J. "Geographic Isolation in Darwin's Thinking: The Vicissitudes of a Crucial Idea." *Studies in the History of Biology* 3 (1979): 23–65.

———. "Darwin and His Finches: The Evolution of a Legend." *Journal of the History of Biology* 15 (1982): 1–54.

———. "Darwin's Conversion: The *Beagle* Voyage and Its Aftermath." *Journal of the History of Biology* 15 (1982): 325–396.

Vorzimmer, Peter J. *Charles Darwin: The Years of Controversy; The Origin of Species and Its Critics, 1859–1882*. Philadelphia: Temple University Press, 1970.

Young, Robert M. *Darwin's Metaphor: Nature's Place in Victorian Culture*. Cambridge, U.K.: Cambridge University Press, 1985.

Peter J. Bowler

DAVY, HUMPHRY

(*b.* Penzance, Cornwall, England, 17 December 1778; *d.* Geneva, Switzerland, 29 May 1829), *chemistry*. For the original article on Davy see *DSB*, vol. 3.

Since David Knight's entry on Davy was published, Knight's biography has appeared, as has the first part of the long-awaited biography by the late June Fullmer, while Sophie Forgan has edited a collection of essays on him. Considerable work has been undertaken on Davy's connection with English Romanticism and his presidency of the Royal Society, but comparatively little has been written on his chemical researches. However, due to the discovery of previously unknown archives, Davy has proved an invaluable site for endeavoring to understand the complexities of applying science for practical purposes during a period of rapid industrialization. An underlying theme of all these studies has been to provide a unity to Davy's life and career that might, at first glance, appear disjointed. Davy's character has emerged as much less attractive than the romantic image of him once suggested, but this is in line with recent studies of other Romantic figures depicting them to be rather self-obsessed.

English Romanticism. As is well-known, Davy met Samuel Taylor Coleridge and Robert Southey while was working on gases at Thomas Beddoes's Pneumatic Institution in Bristol in the late 1790s. Through these friendships, Davy came to edit and see through the press that seminal text of English Romanticism, the second edition of *Lyrical Ballads* (1800), by William Wordsworth. Knight has long emphasized the importance of Davy's relationship with the Romantics, both for them and for him, though Fullmer played down its significance. Scholars of English literature have, likewise, dealt variously with this aspect of Davy's life. In particular, Richard Holmes has emphasized the importance of Davy's friendship with Coleridge who, after all, attended Davy's chemistry lectures at the Royal Institution "to increase my stock of metaphors." Holmes also drew attention to the importance of Davy's role in arranging for Coleridge to lecture at the Royal Institution. Hitherto usually depicted as failures, Holmes argued that his talks initiated Coleridge's career as a lecturer, which helped support him financially.

The other aspect of Davy's Romanticism that has been studied is the way in which Mary Shelley used him as the model for the character and views of Professor Waldman in her novel, *Frankenstein; or, the New Prometheus* (1818). In the story, Victor Frankenstein studies with Waldman at the University of Ingolstadt and his lecture, which so inspired Frankenstein to search for the secret of life, follows closely in its rhetoric Davy's "Discourse Introductory to a Course of Lectures on Chemistry" of 1802. As Davy's career developed, his visible interest in and connections with the Romantic movement became more attenuated, but as Knight pointed out in his original entry, these early themes reemerged in Davy's last writings. As a postscript to Davy's involvement with the Romantics, it should be noted that Wordsworth borrowed Davy's sword from his brother (and neighbor in Ambleside), John Davy, when Wordsworth was installed as poet laureate in 1845.

The Safety Lamp. Davy's invention of a form of the miners' safety lamp is perhaps the most widely known thing about him. This is partially because the lamp worked, saved lives, and increased production in the very practical world of coal mining. But public knowledge of the lamp has also been due to the way in which Davy was able to establish the claim that it was the successful application of science that allowed him to invent the lamp. Recent study of Davy's work on the lamp, however, has raised serious questions about how much science was needed for the invention of the lamp. The only piece of scientific knowledge involved was that an explosion would not pass through narrow tubes, and this was discovered independently by Davy, the mining engineer George Stephenson in Killingworth Colliery near Newcastle, and by Smithson Tennant at Cambridge University. Davy and Stephenson developed miners' lamps at precisely the same time, in the closing months of 1815. There were some design differences between them. Davy ultimately used wire gauze to enclose the flame, while Stephenson's lamp retained holes punched in tin sheets. Nevertheless, both designs worked, and a bitter priority dispute arose. Davy was able to win it by linking the lamp to the agenda of the president of the Royal Society, Joseph Banks, who sought to promote the practical value of science in England for industry, for war, and for the exploitation of the empire. Davy had little difficulty in enlisting the support of the metropolitan elite of science and, by aligning himself with their Baconian ideology, neither of which Stephenson was in a position to do. Therefore, he was able to defeat Stephenson's claims.

Davy's victory allowed him to use the lamp an example of the value of science in practical matters. Because of the importance, until the 1980s, of coal mining to Britain, the lamp came to enjoy an iconic status as the premier example of the supposed dependence of technology on science. Indeed, an image of the lamp was used at the symbol of the 20th International Congress of the History of Science held in Liège, Belgium, in 1997. But Davy also reaped immediate rewards for his success. He was created a baronet in 1818, and the following year France's Académie des Sciences elected him one of its eight foreign associates. (He had received only one vote when nominated after his visit to Paris in 1814.) The greatest prize was that by becoming so closely associated with the Banksian agenda, Davy had put himself in a position to succeed Banks as president of the Royal Society.

Royal Society President. It is hard to tell who would have been a suitable successor to Banks after his forty-two-year reign as a fairly autocratic president; it would have been a difficult task for even the most skilled of administrators, which Davy certainly was not. With his self-confidence generated by the Romanic conception of the individual's self-assertion, Davy was perhaps the only person who felt

Humphry Davy. © MICHAEL NICHOLSON/CORBIS.

himself capable of succeeding Banks. When Banks died on 19 June 1820 Davy was in Italy, and his friend William Hyde Wollaston was elected president. Davy rushed back to London and Wollaston, realizing the magnitude of the task he faced, stood aside for Davy to be elected at the end of November.

As David Miller has shown, Davy inherited a faction-ridden society that had a significant contingent of nonscientific members who had been friends of Banks. Besides being seen as someone who would continue the Banksian program, Davy was supported by the scientific faction, which believed that Davy would seek to make the society more scientific. This was almost certainly Davy's intention, but various actions—such as being perceived as cutting the number of fellows elected annually—brought him into conflict with other factions and ultimately with those many fellows connected with the Admiralty. Davy's major initiative to resolve this problem was his founding, with the secretary of the Admiralty, John Wilson Croker, the Athenaeum Club in 1824. In doing this Davy hoped to establish an institution equally prestigious to the Royal Society that those nonscientific men who had previously aspired to fellowship in the society would be happy to join. While the Athenaeum was (and remains) a success, its founding did not reduce Davy's problems in running the Royal Society.

Davy's political problems in the Royal Society are illustrated in their most acute form by his attitude toward the election of Michael Faraday as a fellow. Faraday had joined the Royal Institution as laboratory assistant in 1813; had accompanied Davy on his continental tour from 1813 to 1815; and had assisted him with some of his researches, including work on the lamp. In 1821, when Faraday was superintendent of the Royal Institution, he made his first major discovery of electromagnetic rotations. This caused some problems between him and Davy, because the latter did not think that Faraday had properly acknowledged Wollaston's role in the discovery. Worse was to follow in 1823 when, following an experiment suggested by Davy, Faraday unexpectedly liquefied chlorine, the first time that a gas had been liquefied. Davy sought to take some of the credit for this, but Faraday refused to oblige. When Faraday was nominated in the spring of 1823 by his friend Richard Phillips to be a fellow of the Royal Society, Davy opposed his election. There were good political reasons for Davy to oppose Faraday's election, but they may well have been given an edge by personal considerations. As Davy was trying to bring an end to Banksian nepotism, he needed to be seen publicly to oppose Faraday's election, because otherwise it would be assumed that Davy was using his power to elect his protégé. To prevent this perception Davy took the quite extraordinary step of having a public row with Faraday in the courtyard of Somerset House, the home of the Royal Society, telling Faraday to take his nomination certificate down. Faraday once again stood up to Davy's bullying and pointed out that because he had not put it up he could not take it down. Faraday was elected in early 1824 and admitted by Davy. There is a narrow line between patronage and exploitation and, following this row, Davy crossed that line by using, as discussed below, Faraday's undoubted ability without considering his best interests. It is little wonder, then, that Faraday later commented that afterward he was "by no means in the same relation as to scientific communication with Sir Humphry Davy" (Jones, 1870, vol. 1, p. 353).

Practical Failures. The major failure of the Royal Society during Davy's presidency was its inability to provide effective scientific advice to the government. In the case of the protection of the copper sheeting of Royal Navy vessels and in the project to improve optical glass, Davy and the Royal Society failed to provide the Admiralty with appropriate advice and in the former case managed to disable the fleet, while the latter failure led to the abolition of the Board of Longitude.

In early 1823 the navy asked the Royal Society for advice about how to prevent the corrosion of the copper bottoms of its ships. With postwar retrenchment this had become a major issue for the navy, because if it could extend the time between replacements of the copper, considerable savings would be made. Although a Royal Society committee was formed, Davy bypassed it entirely and found, in his last piece of scientific research, that if zinc or cast iron were attached to the copper, its electrochemical polarity would be reversed and thus could not be corroded by seawater. Davy instructed Faraday to do the follow-up work. The "protectors," as they were called, were tested, under Faraday's supervision, on three ships in Portsmouth dockyard. The results appeared so satisfactory that the Admiralty issued the order that all ships should be equipped with protectors. Unfortunately, what no one had noticed was that because the poisonous salts from the copper were no longer entering the water, there was nothing to kill the barnacles and the like in the vicinity of a ship. This meant that barnacles could now attach themselves to the bottom of a vessel, thus impeding severely its steerage, much to the anger of the captains who wrote to the Admiralty to complain about Davy's protectors. Davy, following the success of the miners' lamp and of his rhetorical strategy to secure priority in its invention, became a victim of his own rhetoric about the value of science for practical purposes. Assuming that something that worked in the controlled conditions of the laboratory would work in practice, as had happened with the lamp, Davy believed that electrochemical protection would also work in the uncontrolled outside environment; hence, neither Davy nor the Admiralty saw the need for serious testing, and so the perfunctory nature of the testing led to the subsequent disaster.

Between the time of the apparent success of electrochemical protection and its practical failure, Davy, as chairman of the Board of Longitude, established a joint committee between the board and the Royal Society to find a means of replicating Joseph von Fraunhofer's process of producing high-quality optical glass. Faraday, again at Davy's behest, spent the latter part of the 1820s trying to make glass with little success. Once again Davy's name became associated with failure in the eyes of the Admiralty, and in 1828 Parliament abolished the Board of Longitude, which since its founding in 1714 had been the sole conduit in England for the state's support of science.

The pressure on Davy was immense, and in 1826 he began suffering from a serious illness that led him, on 6 November 1827, to resign the presidency. Faraday, who had been an uncomfortably close witness to Davy's failures in the 1820s, learned from his experiences. Whenever he provided scientific advice to the state and its agencies, it was always in the most cautious manner, contrasting sharply with Davy's style. When offered the presidency of the Royal Society in 1858, he had no hesitation in immediately declining, adding that if he accepted he "would not answer for the integrity of my intellect for a single year"

(Tyndall, 1868, p. 267). That he had his firsthand knowledge of Davy's experiences in mind cannot be doubted.

SUPPLEMENTARY BIBLIOGRAPHY

Significant deposits of previously unknown papers relating to Davy's work have been found in the National Archives (formerly the Public Record Office) in Kew, Surrey; the Northumberland Record Office in Newcastle upon Tyne; the Tyne and Wear Archive Service in Newcastle upon Tyne; and the County Durham Lambton Estate Office.

Field, J. V., and Frank A. J. L. James. "Frankenstein and the Spark of Being." *History Today* (September 1994): 47–53.

Forgan, Sophie, ed. *Science and the Sons of Genius: Studies on Humphry Davy.* London: Science Reviews, 1980.

Fullmer, June Z. *Young Humphry Davy: The Making of an Experimental Chemist.* Philadelphia: American Philosophical Society, 2000.

Holmes, Richard. "The Coleridge Experiment." *Proceedings of the Royal Institution* 69 (1997): 307–323.

James, Frank A. J. L. "Davy in the Dockyard: Humphry Davy, the Royal Society, and the Electro-chemical Protection of the Copper Sheeting of His Majesty's Ships in the Mid 1820s." *Physis* 29 (1992): 205–225.

———. "How Big Is a Hole?: The Problems of the Practical Application of Science in the Invention of the Miners' Safety Lamp by Humphry Davy and George Stephenson in Late Regency England." *Transactions of the Newcomen Society* 75 (2005): 175–227.

Jones, Henry Bence. *The Life and Letters of Faraday.* 1st ed. 2 vols. London: Longmans, Green and Co, 1870.

Knight, David. *Humphry Davy: Science and Power.* 2nd ed. Cambridge, U.K.: Cambridge University Press, 1998.

Miller, David Philip. "Between Hostile Camps: Sir Humphry Davy's Presidency of the Royal Society of London, 1820–1827." *British Journal for the History of Science* 16 (1983): 1–47.

Tyndall, John. "On Faraday as a Discoverer." *Proceedings of the Royal Institution* 5 (1868): 199–272.

Frank A. J. L. James

DAY, ARTHUR LOUIS (*b.* Brookfield, Massachusetts, 30 October 1869; *d.* Bethesda, Maryland, 2 March 1960), *geophysics, geochemistry, petrology, seismology, volcanology, glass and ceramic research.*

Day was one of the leading figures of physically and chemically based Earth sciences in the first half of the twentieth century. As the longstanding director of the Geophysical Laboratory of the Carnegie Institution of Washington, he set the standards of modern experimental petrology. Also owing largely to Day is the setup of the optical glass industries in America and the organization of America's first comprehensive seismological survey.

From Yale to Berlin. Arthur was the son of Daniel Putnam Day from Brookfield, Massachusetts, and his wife Fannie Maria Hobbs Day. Encouraged by a young high school teacher, he entered the Sheffield Scientific School of Yale University, graduating with a BA in 1892. Although his true interest at this time was mechanical engineering, not a scientific career, he remained at Yale because of an appointment as Sloane Fellow in physics, and in June 1894 he earned his PhD. Shortly before, in 1893—following the retired Edward S. Dana—Day became an instructor in physics at Sheffield Scientific School. After four years, despite an offer to become an assistant professor in physics, Day resigned his instructorship. From 1897 on, he never taught again at a university.

Vacation trips during this time had more lasting effects on Day's career. In the summer of 1893, he visited the World's Fair in Chicago where he was deeply impressed by the immense collection of electrical apparatus. In the summer of next year he set off for Europe. He spent two months at Braunschweig (Brunswick, Germany), and in 1895 he toured through Norway and Sweden. Looking for an appropriate opportunity to do research work in physics, Day returned to Braunschweig in the summer of 1897 where he was recommended—by an American who had just finished his studies in physics—not to go to a German university but, rather, to the Physikalisch-Technische Reichsanstalt in Berlin (the German Bureau of Standards), one of the best-equipped physics laboratories of the time.

The result was that Day was soon made the first foreign member of the Reichsanstalt's regular staff. And his connections to German physics became still closer. On 20 August 1900 he married Helene (Helen) Kohlrausch, the daughter of the then-president of the Reichsanstalt, Friedrich Kohlrausch. They had three daughters (Margaret, Dorothy, and Helen), and one son, Dr. Ralph Kohlrausch Day (b. 1904), who followed his father in becoming a physicist engaged in glass industries. Day's second marriage, on 27 March 1933, was to his secretary Ruth Sarah Easling of Corning, New York, with whom he had no children.

High-Temperature Physics—Petrology. Because of his experience in high-temperature research at the Reichsanstalt—and persuaded by the geologist Carl Barus, a former student of Friedrich Kohlrausch—Day was called as a physical geologist to the newly established physical laboratory of the U.S. Geological Survey in 1900. Its formal leader was George Ferdinand Becker, with whom Day carried out initial experiments on the effects of

crystallization pressure (crystallization force). From 1904 to 1906 he received early funds from the newly established Carnegie Institution of Washington. And on 1 January 1907, he was appointed the first director of the institution's new Geophysical Laboratory, a position that he held until his retirement in 1936.

At the new laboratory Day first continued the lines of scientific investigations he had set up at the Geological Survey laboratory. This focused in particular on his experiments concerning the extension of the standard thermometer scale, which he started at the Physikalisch-Technische Reichsanstalt, mainly in collaboration with the German physicist Ludwig Holborn, an expert in the field of precise measurements of high and low temperatures. After more than ten years of work, Day succeeded in the extension of the standard gas thermometer scale from 1,200 to 1,600 degrees Celsius in a series of experiments that he completed in 1911. His practical temperature scale defined in terms of closely spaced melting points of pure substances became essential in studying the thermal behavior of common minerals that melt at very high temperatures.

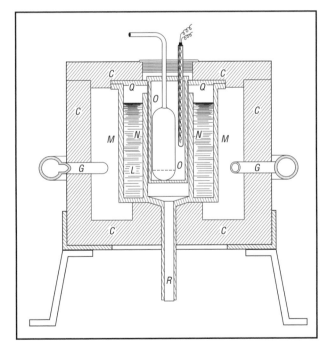

Figure 1. *Boiling apparatus of the type Day used in all his experiments on the extension of the standard thermometer scale and the melting points of minerals. Here is an apparatus for boiling zinc from his early work with Ludwig Holborn. M and N: Boiling kettle proper of two concentric iron cylinders, of which the inner one (N) contained the bulb of the gas thermometer and the (electric) thermo-element, protected by a porcelain tube. Z: Ring-shaped space, filled with zinc. Q and C: Iron cover and jacket of fire-clay. R: Tube where the zinc vapor passed off. G: Blowpipes furnishing the heat.*

A second major concern—together with Eugene T. Allen and Joseph P. Iddings—was to determine the thermal stability of the major feldspars of the plagioclas series (albite-anorthite), using the cooling-curve method. And by a third series of experiments Day studied the physico-chemical behavior of phases in systems of important oxides and sulfides in Earth's crust; the first one was the so-called portland cement system, that is, the calcium oxide-silica system, including alumina. These experiments provided a source of information not only to geology but also to the steel, cement, and glass industries.

Volcanology—Glass Works. In 1911, Day turned his attention to volcanology. Between 1912 and 1916 he visited the volcanic areas of Hawaii, Italy, and Lassen Peak in California. His initial question was of the water content of volcanic gases, a controversial topic in contemporary volcanological discussion. Together with Ernest S. Shepherd he collected gas samples directly from the liquid lava of Hawaii's Kilauea in 1912. They successfully proved that water vapor was the most abundant component of volcanic gases, that is, that these gases were not, as widely assumed, anhydrous. The crucial point was that water is often chemically fixed to other substances within the hot gases so that it became detectable first in the course of cooling.

Day resumed his volcanological studies in 1920, shifting his attention also to hot springs. He studied volcanic activity of the geysers region in California and, in collaboration with Allen, the hot springs of Yellowstone National Park. Annual visits to Yellowstone Park over the years furnished material for Day's last, comprehensive study, the monumental volume on *Hot Springs of the Yellowstone National Park* (1935). Day's very last paper of 1939 was also dedicated to the hot-spring problem. He continued this work for some years. After an unfortunate physical breakdown in 1946, however, Day was forced to give up his research.

A central concern of Day's work throughout his life—probably the most important one for himself—was the application of his scientific results to industrial goals, that is, of his experiences on the melting behavior of silicates to glass manufacturing. An early paper, written with Shepherd in 1906, was on quartz glass. And beginning in 1905 he served as a research consultant of Corning Glass Works (Corning, New York). This work became immediately important for Day and the Geophysical Laboratory when the United States entered World War I in April 1917. High quality optical glass was in urgent demand for equipment such as gun sights, periscopes, and field glasses. In 1917, the Geophysical Laboratory joined forces with Bausch and Lomb Optical Company at Rochester, New York, and by the end of the year, they produced up

to 40,000 pounds of government-accepted glass per month. According to Day, about 97 percent of all optical glass used by the American forces in World War I was made under the direction of the Geophysical Laboratory. Finally, for fifteen months, Day took a leave of absence from the Geophysical Laboratory to become vice president of Corning's manufacturing department in the spring of 1919.

Organizing Science. Upon returning to the Geophysical Laboratory in 1920, Day took the institution in a new direction. From 1921—when the Carnegie Institution founded its Seismological Laboratory in Pasadena, California—to 1936, Day served as the chairman of Carnegie's Advisory Committee in Seismology. He organized what was then the largest cooperative effort in the history of American science. Among the cooperating institutions were the Seismological Society of America, the California Institute of Technology, the U.S. Coast and Geodetic Survey, Stanford University, and the Mount Wilson Observatory. Several comprehensive reports on seismological problems in the western United States were the result of the enterprise. Finally in 1925 Day paved the way for the Geophysical Laboratory to enter radioactive research. Charles Snowden Piggot developed a coring gun that was able to obtain sediment samples from the ocean bottom to test for radioactivity.

Arthur Day's ability to initiate new lines of research and to organize cooperation in science made him a central figure in early twentieth-century American science. In 1911 he was elected to the National Academy of Sciences, serving as its home secretary from 1913 to 1918 and vice president from 1933 to 1941. He also presided over the Philosophical Society of Washington (1911), the Washington Academy of Sciences (1924), and the Geological Society of America (1938). Among his memberships in foreign scientific societies were the London Geological Society and the Academies of Science of Sweden, Norway, and the USSR. Day received honorary degrees from Groningen University (1914), Columbia University (1915), Princeton University (1918), and the University of Pennsylvania (1938), and his numerous awards included the Wollaston Medal of the Geological Society of London, the Penrose Medal of the Geological Society of America, and the Bakhuis Roozeboom Medal of the Royal Academy of Amsterdam. In 1948 Day established a fund for an Arthur L. Day Medal to be awarded annually by the Geological Society of America.

BIBLIOGRAPHY

Day's papers are mostly at the Archives of the Carnegie Institution. Some are also at the Ceramic Society. An autobiography of Day is held by the Center for History of Physics of the American Institute of Physics.

WORKS BY DAY

With Ludwig Holborn. "Ueber das Luftthermometer bei hohen Temperaturen." *Wiedemann's Annalen der Physik und Chemie*, n.s., 68 (1899): 817–852. English translation, "On the Gas Thermometer at High Temperatures." *American Journal of Science* 4, no. 8 (1899): 165–193.

With Eugene T. Allen and Joseph P. Iddings. *The Isomorphism and Thermal Properties of the Feldspars.* Part 1, *Thermal Study*; Part 2, *Optical Study.* With an introduction by George F. Becker. Carnegie Institution of Washington, Publication no. 31. Washington, DC: Carnegie Institution, 1905.

With George F. Becker. "The Linear Force of Growing Crystals." *Proceedings of the Washington Academy of Sciences* 7 (1905): 283–288.

With Ernest S. Shepherd. "The Phase-Rule and Conceptions of Igneous Magma." *Economic Geology* 1 (1905): 286–289.

———. "The Lime-Silicia Series of Minerals." With optical study by F. E. Wright. *American Journal of Science* 4, no. 22 (1906): 265–302.

———. "Quartz Glass." *Science* 23 (1906): 670–672.

"Some Mineral Relations from the Laboratory Viewpoint." *Bulletin of the Geological Society of America* 21 (1910): 141–178.

"Die Untersuchung von Silikaten." *Zeitschrift für Elektrochemie* 17 (1911): 609–617.

With Robert B. Sosman and Eugene T. Allen. *High Temperature Gas Thermometry. With an Investigation of the Metals.* Carnegie Institution of Washington, Publication no. 157. Washington, DC: Carnegie Institution, 1911.

With Ernest S. Shepherd. "Water and the Magmatic Gases." *Journal of the Washington Academy of Sciences* 3 (1913): 457–463.

"Optical Glass and Its Future as an American Industry." *Journal of the Franklin Institute* 190 (1920): 453–472.

With Eugene T. Allen. *Hot Springs of the Yellowstone National Park. Microscopic Examinations by Herbert Eugene Merwin.* Carnegie Institution of Washington, Publication no. 466. Washington, DC: Carnegie Institution, 1935.

["Day-volume"]. *American Journal of Science.* Fifth series, Vol. 35a (= 235a), 1938. A special issue of the journal dedicated to Day, its longstanding associate editor, in 1938; also referred to as Publications of the Geophysical Laboratory of the Carnegie Institution, no. 100. The volume contains twenty-three papers on geophysics, geochemistry, and volcanology.

"The Hot-Spring Problem." *Bulletin of the Geological Society of America* 50 (1939): 317–336.

OTHER SOURCES

Abelson, Philip H. "Arthur Louis Day." In *Biographical Memoirs of the National Academy of Sciences of the United States of America* 47 (1975): 27–47. With a mostly complete bibliography.

"Arthur L. Day." In *J. C. Poggendorff. Biographisch-Literarisches Handwörterbuch der exakten Naturwissenschaften,* edited by

Hans Wußing. vol. 8, pt. 1. Berlin: Wiley-VCH, 1999. Contains some bibliographical additions.

Sosman, Robert B. "Memorial to Arthur Louis Day." *Proceedings of the Geological Society of America* 75 (1964): 147–155. With a mostly complete bibliography.

Sullivan, Eugene C. "American Contemporaries: Arthur Louis Day." *Industrial and Engineering Chemistry*, News Edition, 14 (1936): 341.

Yoder, Hatten S., Jr. "Arthur Louis Day." In *Dictionary of American Biography*, Supplement 6, edited by John A. Garraty, 152–154. New York: Charles Scribner's Sons, 1980.

———. "Development and Promotion of the Initial Scientific Program for the Geophysical Laboratory." In *The Earth, the Heavens and the Carnegie Institution of Washington. History of Geophysics*, vol. 5, edited by Gregory A. Good, 21–28. Washington, DC, 1994.

Bernhard Fritscher

DE FINETTI, BRUNO (*b.* Innsbruck, Austria, 13 June 1906; *d.* Rome, Italy, 20 July 1985), *probability theory, statistics, mathematics.*

De Finetti was a probability theorist who contributed to statistics, mathematics, financial and actuarial science, and economics. He pioneered the subjectivistic interpretation of probability, according to which probabilities describe a person's propensity to bet, not objective frequencies independent of humans. He also proved a famous representation theorem concerning exchangeable probability assignments, which ground common patterns of inductive inference.

Although he was born in Austria, de Finetti's parents were Italian. He pursued his university education in Italy and graduated in mathematics from Milan University in 1927. During his academic career he held chairs at Trieste University and the University of Rome. In a long series of publications he promoted the account of subjective probability prominent in decision theory. His views resemble those of Frank Ramsey and Leonard Savage, but he formulated them independently and they have distinctive features. Some probability theorists hold that subjective probabilities are compatible with objective probabilities, but de Finetti denied the existence of objective probabilities and advanced subjective probabilities as a replacement for them. His *Theory of Probability* ([1970] 1974–1975) is a comprehensive presentation of his position on probability.

Subjective Probability. De Finetti held that probability exists because of ignorance of events and does not have a foundation in the objective features of events. The illusion of objective probabilities may be explained by properties of subjective probabilities.

According to de Finetti, a person's probability assignment is defined in terms of betting ratios. These are ratios of stakes that bettors risk. Suppose that one person offers to bet that an event occurs and another person accepts the bet. The person betting that the event occurs stakes x, and the person betting that the event does not occur stakes y. The betting ratio for the bet is $x/(x + y)$. The probability a person assigns to an event is a betting ratio for the event that the person is willing to use no matter whether he is betting that the event occurs or betting that it does not occur. For example, suppose that a filly Fleetfoot is in a race at Belmont Park today. The probability for a person that Fleetfoot wins depends on the person's betting ratio for that event. Suppose that the person is willing to pay a maximum of $0.80 for a bet that pays $1.00 if Fleetfoot wins and $0 if she does not win. Then the person adopts a betting ratio of $0.80/($0.80 + $0.20), that is, 0.80, for bets that Fleetfoot wins. Hence the probability of Fleetfoot's winning is 0.08 for that person.

A set of betting ratios for events is coherent if and only if it does not permit a Dutch book, that is, a system of bets that guarantees a loss. De Finetti showed that coherence among betting ratios requires that they conform to the standard laws of the probability calculus. A coherent set of betting ratios yields a subjective probability function on a set of events. Subjective probabilities obey the laws of probability and so may replace objective probabilities in probability theory.

De Finetti defined conditional probabilities in terms of conditional bets. A bet that Fleetfoot will win if the favorite withdraws is a conditional bet. It is called off if the condition is not met. For coherence, a betting ratio for a conditional bet must equal a ratio of betting ratios for nonconditional bets. The ratio must conform with the usual account of conditional probability, according to which, for events A and B and a probability assignment P, the following equality holds: $P(A \text{ given } B) = P(A \& B)/P(B)$.

The version of the subjective theory of probability that de Finetti formulated included finite additivity of probabilities but not countable additivity of probabilities. Many probability theorists view countable additivity as an essential component of probability theory. De Finetti excluded it because coherence among betting ratios does not require it. The requirement of coherence yields exactly the laws of probability, he held. As Jan von Plato (1994) observes, de Finetti argued that because coherence requires only finite additivity, countable additivity is optional.

Some probability theorists argue that many people do not have a precise assignment of betting ratios for events and so do not have a probability function on events. To accommodate this observation, de Finetti allowed replac-

ing a single value for an event's betting ratio with upper and lower bounds for the betting ratio.

De Finetti's definition of subjective probability met the operational standards of his era. An alternative interpretation of his definition takes it as a method of inferring probabilities from betting ratios instead of as a method of specifying the meaning of subjective probability. A subjective probability may be a rational degree of belief rather than a betting ratio in a coherent system of betting ratios. Rational degrees of belief conform to the laws of probability. Assuming that degrees of belief govern betting behavior, an agent has a reason to hold degrees of belief conforming to those laws. Failure to conform creates the possibility of a Dutch book. This argument for conformity assumes that prevention of Dutch books is an optimal strategy. However, prevention of Dutch books may have costs that make it sub-optimal. For example, preventing Dutch books also prevents systems of bets that guarantee gains. Whether prevention of Dutch books is optimal depends on circumstances, as Alan Hájek (2005) observes. Fortunately, besides the Dutch book argument there are nonpragmatic and purely epistemic arguments for holding degrees of belief that conform to the probability laws, at least in the case of ideal agents. These arguments show that conformity is a cognitive goal for reasonable people.

As von Plato explains, de Finetti took two approaches to quantitative probability. The first, already described, defined it in terms of betting ratios. The second, intended as a complementary approach, defined it using qualitative, or comparative, probability. For the second method, de Finetti formulated axioms that govern comparisons of probability and showed that if a person satisfies those axioms, there is a unique probability function that represents the person's comparisons of probability.

Exchangeability. De Finetti contributed to probability theory major results concerning exchangeability and used them to explain inductive inference. A probability assignment for sequences of trials is exchangeable if and only if it assigns the same probability to all sequences of the same length and number of successes. Exchangeability implies that for all positive integers n, all permutations of the results of a sequence of length n have the same probability. Hence a sequence with exactly two successes followed by a failure has the same probability as a sequence with exactly two successes separated by a failure. If a probability assignment is exchangeable, it displays a type of symmetry. Also, the success rate in a sequence of trials is a sufficient statistic, that is, it captures all information about the sequence relevant to inferences about success rates in future sequences. For example, given an exchangeable probability assignment for sequences of trials, the probability of a result on the next trial depends only on the number of previous trials and the number of successes in those trials. If probabilities of sequences of a biased coin's tosses are exchangeable, then after observing a sequence of tosses, one needs only the number of heads and tails in the sequence to assess the probability that the next toss of the coin will yield heads.

Theorists also attribute exchangeability directly to sequences of trials. For example, a set of sequences of coin tosses has the property of exchangeability if the same probability attaches to obtaining a certain number of heads in all sequences of the same length. In general, a sequence of random variables (which de Finetti preferred to call random quantities) has the property of exchangeability if the probability assignment governing it is exchangeable.

According to Sandy L. Zabell (2005, pp. 9, 56), William Ernest Johnson introduced exchangeability. However, de Finetti made exchangeability prominent by proving a major representation theorem involving it. Zabell's notation (p. 3) is being used here to present the theorem.

An indicator random-variable uses numbers to indicate whether an event occurs, for example, whether a coin toss yields heads. The number 1 may stand for heads and the number 0 may stand for tails. Let $X_1, X_2, X_3 \ldots$ be an infinite sequence of indicator random-variables having the value 0 or 1. The sequence is exchangeable if all finite subsequences of the same length with the same number of ones have the same probability.

De Finetti showed that if the infinite sequence $X_1, X_2, \ldots X_n, \ldots$ is exchangeable, then the relative frequency of successes in n trials, that is the number of successes divided by n, will with probability 1 have a limit as n goes to infinity. Also, a mixture of binomial probabilities having that random limit Z as success parameter represents the probability distribution of the sequence. In other words, given any exchangeable probability assignment for finite sequences, there is a unique probability distribution over a mixture of binomial probabilities that gives the probability of r successes in n trials. This theorem is called a representation theorem because the probability distribution represents the consequences of an exchangeable probability assignment. As von Plato remarks, de Finetti held that the representation theorem shows how to replace unknown objective probabilities of independent events with subjective probabilities.

As a corollary of his representation theorem, de Finetti showed that in almost every case, after observing a sufficiently long initial segment of the sequence $X_1, X_2, \ldots X_n, \ldots$, the posterior distribution of the limit Z will be highly peaked about the observed relative frequency, and future trials will be expected to occur with a relative frequency very close to the observed relative frequency. As

Zabell explains, de Finetti used this mathematical result as a justification of inductive reasoning. Suppose that a person has coherent attitudes toward events so that her attitudes yield a probability function for the events. Also, suppose that with respect to the probability function, future events form an exchangeable sequence. Then if an event occurs with a certain relative frequency in a long sequence of trials, the person will assign a high probability to that event's occurring with approximately the same relative frequency in remaining future trials. In that sense, the person will expect the future to resemble the past.

Given an exchangeable probability assignment, the probability of success on a trial given a sequence of previous trials depends solely on the number of successes observed and does not depend on their order in the sequence. Exchangeability thus rules out sensible forms of inductive inference that attend to the order of successes. An exchangeable probability assignment is warranted only when order has no significance, as with a sequence of coin tosses. To treat other cases, de Finetti introduced a generalization of exchangeability he called partial exchangeability. Persi Diaconis and David Freedman (1980) evaluate partial exchangeability. Other generalizations of exchangeability taking account of the effects of order are topics of current research in statistics. As Zabell notes, to each type of exchangeability corresponds a judgment concerning a type of symmetry, the sufficiency of a statistic, a representation theorem, and a corresponding method of inductive inference.

De Finetti had multiple talents, and his contributions outside probability theory are numerous. Some of his early work was in genetics. It introduced de Finetti diagrams, which are still used for graphing genotype frequencies. Also, de Finetti formulated a mean-variance theory of portfolio selection. To evaluate an investment, it combines an assessment of the investment's expected return with an assessment of its risk. Mean-variance portfolio selection seeks the best overall balance of expected return and risk. De Finetti's theory is among the earliest theories of this type.

De Finetti received many honors, including honorary membership in the Royal Statistical Society. In 2006 the University of Rome organized an international symposium called the Bruno de Finetti Centenary Conference. Speakers demonstrated the continuing influence of de Finetti's ideas in a variety of fields.

BIBLIOGRAPHY

For listings of de Finetti's works, consult the Bruno de Finetti Web site (http://www.brunodefinetti.it/index_en.htm), the bibliography in von Plato (1994), and the Bruno de Finetti Collection at the University of Pittsburgh.

WORKS BY DE FINETTI

"Probabilism: A Critical Essay on the Theory of Probability and on the Value of Science" [1931]. Translated by Maria Concetta di Maio, Maria Carla Galavotti, and Richard Jeffrey. *Erkenntnis* 31 (1989): 169–223.

"Foresight: Its Logical Laws, Its Subjective Sources" [1937]. Translated by Henry Kyburg. In *Studies in Subjective Probability*, edited by Henry Kyburg and Howard Smokler, 93–158. New York: Wiley, 1964.

"On the Condition of Partial Exchangeability" [1938]. Translated by Paul Benacerraf and Richard Jeffrey. In *Studies in Inductive Logic and Probability*, vol. 2, edited by Richard Jeffrey, 193–205. Berkeley: University of California Press, 1980.

Theory of Probability [1970]. 2 vols. Translated by Antonio Machí and Adrian Smith. New York: Wiley, 1974–1975.

Probability, Induction, and Statistics: The Art of Guessing. New York: Wiley, 1972.

OTHER SOURCES

Diaconis, Persi, and David Freedman. "De Finetti's Generalization of Exchangeability." In *Studies in Inductive Logic and Probability*, vol. 2, edited by Richard Jeffrey, 233–249. Berkeley: University of California Press, 1980.

Galavotti, Maria Carla. "The Notion of Subjective Probability in the Work of Ramsey and de Finetti." *Theoria* 57 (1991): 239–259.

———, and Richard Jeffrey, eds. "Bruno de Finetti's Philosophy of Probability." Double issue. *Erkenntnis* 31, nos. 2, 3 (1989). The essays in this collection treat de Finetti's interpretation of probability and his mathematical results concerning exchangeability.

Hájek, Alan. "Scotching Dutch Books?" *Philosophical Perspectives* 19 (2005): 139–151.

Jeffrey, Richard. "Reading *Probabilismo*." *Erkenntnis* 31 (1989): 225–237. A discussion of de Finetti ([1931] 1989).

———. "Conditioning, Kinematics, and Exchangeability." In his *Probability and the Art of Judgment,* 117–153. Cambridge, U.K.: Cambridge University Press, 1992.

Milne, Peter. "Bruno de Finetti and the Logic of Conditional Events." *British Journal for the Philosophy of Science* 48, no. 2 (1997): 195–232.

von Plato, Jan. *Creating Modern Probability: Its Mathematics, Physics and Philosophy in Historical Perspective.* Cambridge, U.K.: Cambridge University Press, 1994. Chapter 8 treats de Finetti's theory of subjective probability and his representation theorem involving exchangeability.

Zabell, Sandy L. *Symmetry and Its Discontents: Essays on the History of Inductive Philosophy.* Cambridge, U.K.: Cambridge University Press, 2005. Chapters 1 and 2 treat exchangeability, de Finetti's representation theorem involving it, and the theorem's implications for inductive reasoning.

Paul Weirich

DE GIORGI, ENNIO (*b.* Lecce, Italy, 8 February 1928; d. Pisa, Italy, 25 October 1996), *calculus of variations, partial differential equations, foundations of mathematics.*

De Giorgi was the greatest Italian mathematician of the second half of the twentieth century. His activity ranged from the calculus of variations to the theory of partial differential equations, with a strong interest in foundations of mathematics.

De Giorgi was born in Lecce, in southern Italy in 1928. After his high school studies in Lecce, he moved to Rome in 1946 to begin his university studies in engineering. The following year he switched to mathematics, and graduated in 1950 under the direction of Mauro Picone. After a fellowship at the Istituto per le Applicazioni del Calcolo, he became an assistant of Picone at the University of Rome in 1951.

The Theory of Perimeters and the 19th Hilbert Problem. In the 1953–1955 period, De Giorgi obtained his first important mathematical results on the theory of perimeters, a notion of (n-1)-dimensional measure for oriented boundaries of n-dimensional sets introduced by Renato Caccioppoli, who had a great influence on his mathematical formation. These results led to the proof of the isoperimetric inequality for arbitrary measurable sets, published in 1958.

De Giorgi in 1955 obtained a counterexample to the uniqueness for regular solutions of the Cauchy problem for a linear partial differential equation with smooth coefficients, a question that had been open for about half a century. De Giorgi's paper had a remarkable impact on the mathematical community and inspired other counterexamples to uniqueness, constructed by Jean Leray in 1966.

The most important result obtained by De Giorgi is the proof of the Hölder continuity of the solutions of elliptic equations with bounded measurable (possibly discontinuous) coefficients. This result, obtained in 1955 and published in complete form in 1957, was the last—and perhaps the hardest—step in the solution of the 19th problem posed by Hilbert in 1900: whether the solutions of regular minimum problems of the calculus of variations for multiple integrals are smooth, and even analytic if the data are analytic. Indeed, every minimizer satisfies a quasilinear elliptic equation, called euler equation, and De Giorgi's theorem provides the tools that allow to study these solutions by using well known results on elliptic equations.

This theorem had an enormous impact in the theory of nonlinear elliptic equations. The same result for parabolic equations was proved independently by John F. Nash in the same period by totally different methods. It is remarkable that a few years later, in 1968, De Giorgi himself showed by a counterexample that the same result does not hold for uniformly elliptic systems with discontinuous coefficients.

Results on Minimal Hypersurfaces. In 1958, De Giorgi became professor of mathematical analysis at the University of Messina. After one year Alessandro Faedo invited him to the Scuola Normale of Pisa, where De Giorgi had the Chair of Algebraic and Infinitesimal Mathematical Analysis for almost forty years. In 1960, he was awarded the Caccioppoli Prize, established in the same year by the Italian Mathematical Union.

During the 1960s, De Giorgi's scientific activity was mainly devoted to the theory of minimal hypersurfaces. His main success was the proof of the analyticity almost everywhere of minimal boundaries in any number of spatial dimensions. This is a striking example of the use of the theory of perimeters in the calculus of variations. He considered this result as a victory in one of his most audacious scientific challenges. His technique was immediately adapted by William K. Allard and Frederick J. Almgren to obtain partial regularity results for more general geometrical objects and has become widely known and used in contexts quite far from the initial one: nonlinear equations and systems of elliptic and parabolic type, harmonic maps, geometric evolution problems, and so forth.

In 1965, De Giorgi obtained an extension of Bernstein's theorem to dimension three: The only solutions of the minimal surface equation defined on the whole three dimensional space are necessarily affine. This result was soon extended to dimensions up to seven by James Simons, who also constructed what is called a locally minimizing cone in dimension eight. De Giorgi then proved, in 1969, with Enrico Bombieri and Enrico Giusti, that Simons's cone is also globally minimizing. Furthermore, using this cone, they constructed a solution of the minimal surface equation that is not affine and is defined in the whole Euclidean space of dimension eight. This striking result shows that Bernstein's theorem cannot be extended to dimensions larger than seven. In the same year De Giorgi proved, with Enrico Bombieri and Mario Miranda, the analyticity of the solutions of the minimal surface equation in any space dimension.

In 1971, together with Lamberto Cattabriga, De Giorgi proved that any partial differential equation with constant coefficients and real analytic right-hand side has a real analytic solution in dimension two, while in dimensions larger than two there are examples, as simple as the heat equation, for which there is no analytic solution.

Gamma-Convergence. In the 1973–1985 period, De Giorgi developed the theory of Gamma-convergence,

designed to give a unified answer to the following question, which arises in many problems of applied mathematics: Given a sequence F_k of functionals, defined on a suitable function space, does there exist a functional F such that the solutions of the minimum problems for F_k converge to the solutions of the corresponding minimum problems for F?

In 1973, the Accademia dei Lincei awarded him the Prize of the President of the Italian Republic. That year, with Sergio Spagnolo, De Giorgi showed the variational character of the notion of G-convergence of elliptic operators, introduced by Spagnolo in 1967–1968, and its connection with the convergence of the energy functionals associated with the elliptic operators. In an important paper published in 1975, De Giorgi passed from the "operational" notion of G-convergence to a purely "variational" one. Instead of a sequence of differential equations, he considered a sequence of minimum problems for functionals of the calculus of variations. Without writing the corresponding Euler operators, he established what is to be considered as the variational limit of this sequence of problems and also obtained a compactness result. This is the starting point of Γ-convergence.

The formal definition of this notion, together with its main properties, appeared a few months later in a paper with Tullio Franzoni. In the next ten years, De Giorgi was engaged in the development of the applications of this theory to many asymptotic problems of the calculus of variations, like homogenization problems, dimension reduction, phase transitions, and so on. De Giorgi, usually very temperate when speaking of his results, was very proud of this creation and considered it a conceptual tool of great importance.

Gradient Flows and Free Discontinuity Problems. At the beginning of the 1980s, in a series of papers with Antonio Marino and Mario Tosques, De Giorgi proposed a new method for the study of gradient flows, which can be applied to many problems with nonconvex nondifferentiable constraints. In 1983, De Giorgi gave a plenary lecture on Γ-convergence at the ICM in Warsaw. On that occasion he publicly expressed one of his deepest beliefs, declaring that the human thirst for knowledge was, in his opinion, the "sign of a secret desire to see some ray of the glory of God." In the same year, during a ceremony at the Sorbonne, De Giorgi received the degree *honoris causa* in mathematics of the University of Paris.

De Giogi proposed, in a 1987 paper with Luigi Ambrosio, a very general theory for the study of a new class of variational problems characterized by the minimization of volume and surface energies. In a later paper he called this class "free discontinuity problems," referring to the fact that the set where the surface energies are concentrated is unknown and can often be represented as the set of discontinuity points of a suitable auxiliary function. Surprisingly, in the same period David Mumford and Jayant Shah proposed, in the framework of a variational approach to image analysis, a minimum problem for which this theory is perfectly suited. The existence of solutions to this problem was proved by De Giorgi in 1989, in collaboration with Michele Carriero and Antonio Leaci. In 1990, De Giorgi was awarded the prestigious Wolf Prize in Tel Aviv.

From the mid-1970s, De Giorgi also worked on foundations of mathematics, adopting a nonreductionist point of view. For this work the University of Lecce awarded him the degree *honoris causa* in philosophy in 1992.

Personal Attributes. De Giorgi had a striking mathematical intuition, combined with the prodigious ability to obtain from it a complete proof, with all minor details. He had a very large number of students. His activity had a tremendous influence on the developments of the calculus of variations and of the theory of partial differential equations. Although he was surrounded by the deep admiration of his colleagues, friends, and students, he remained a very modest person. His office was always open to people who wanted to discuss with him some mathematical problem. On these occasions he often seemed inattentive, but he was always able to grasp the heart of the matter and to suggest new approaches—which worked.

De Giorgi was very active in the protection of human rights. He was a deeply religious man. His attitude toward a continuous search, his natural curiosity, and his open-mindedness to all ideas made it easy for him to have a constructive dialogue with others. From 1988, De Giorgi began to experience health problems. In September 1996, he was taken to a hospital in Pisa and, after undergoing surgery, he died on 25 October.

BIBLIOGRAPHY

WORKS BY DE GIORGI

Selected Papers. Published with the support of Unione Matematica Italiana and Scuola Normale Superiore. Edited by L. Ambrosio, G. Dal Maso, M. Forti, M. Miranda, and S. Spagnolo. Berlin: Springer, 2006.

"Su una teoria generale della misura *(r-1)*-dimensionale in uno spazio ad *r* dimensioni." *Annali di Matematica Pura ed Applicata (4)* 36 (1954): 191–212.

"Un esempio di non unicità della soluzione di un problema di Cauchy, relativo ad un'equazione differenziale lineare di tipo parabolico." *Rendiconti di Matematica e delle sue Applicazioni (5)* 14 (1955): 382–387.

"Sulla differenziabilità e l'analiticità delle estremali degli integrali multipli regolari." *Memorie dell'Accademia delle Scienze di Torino. Parte Prima, Classe di Scienze Fisiche, Matematiche e Naturali (3)* 3 (1957): 25–43.

"Sulla proprietà isoperimetrica dell'ipersfera, nella classe degli insiemi aventi frontiera orientata di misura finita." *Atti dell'Accademia Nazionale dei Lincei, Memorie della Classe di Scienze Fisiche, Matematiche e Naturali, Sezione I (8)* 5 (1958): 33–44.

"Un esempio di estremali discontinue per un problema variazionale di tipo ellittico." *Bollettino dell'Unione Matematica Italiana (4)* 1 (1968): 135–137.

With E. Bombieri and M. Miranda. "Una maggiorazione apriori per le ipersuperficie minimali non parametriche." *Archive for Rational Mechanics and Analysis* 32 (1969): 255–267.

With E. Bombieri and E. Giusti. "Minimal Cones and the Bernstein Problem." *Inventiones Mathematicae* 7 (1969): 243–268.

With L. Cattabriga. "Una dimostrazione diretta dell'esistenza di soluzioni analitiche nel piano reale di equazioni a derivate parziali a coefficienti costanti." *Bollettino dell'Unione Matematica Italiana (4)* (1971): 1015–1027.

With S. Spagnolo. "Sulla convergenza degli integrali dell'energia per operatori ellittici del secondo ordine." *Bollettino dell'Unione Matematica Italiana (4)* 8 (1973): 391–411.

"G-operators and Γ-convergence." *Proceedings of the International Congress of Mathematicians*, no. 2 (Warsaw, 1983), 1175–1191. Warsaw and Amsterdam: Pwn and North-Holland, 1984.

With M. Carriero and A. Leaci. "Existence Theorem for a Minimum Problem with Free Discontinuity Set." *Archive for Rational Mechanics and Analysis* 108 (1989): 95–218.

OTHER SOURCES

Ambrosio, L., G. Dal Maso, M. Forti; et al. "Ennio De Giorgi." *Bollettino dell'Unione Matematica Italiana (8)* 2-B (1999): 1–31. Includes a complete list of De Giogi's works.

Gianni Dal Maso

DE LAUGING, A.
SEE **Albertus Magnus, Saint**.

DEACON, GEORGE EDWARD RAVEN
(*b.* Leicester, United Kingdom, 21 March 1906; *d.* Guildford, United Kingdom, 16 November 1984), *oceanography.*

Deacon was one of the leading British oceanographers in the mid-twentieth century. He was the first to show the extent of the circumpolar Antarctic Convergence, and his work helped to define the characteristics of the Southern Ocean. He became an influential figure in developing theories of global ocean circulation. He also directed pioneering studies of waves during World War II, and later directed Britain's National Institute of Oceanography for over two decades. In 1971, he was knighted and received the Royal Geographical Society's Founder's Medal.

The *Discovery* Committee. Deacon had no training as an oceanographer, though that certainly was not uncommon for oceanographers of that era. The son of devout nonconformists George Raven Deacon and Emma Deacon (née Drinkwater), he grew up with a strong appreciation for education and religion. As a youth, he excelled in mathematics, physics, and chemistry at Leicester Boys' School. He entered King's College, London, in 1924 as a student in the chemistry honors course. He planned to become a teacher, so he pursued a Diploma in Education and taught grammar school two days a week. He published his first paper in 1927 in the *Journal of the Chemical Society*, based on research he conducted in his spare time. When he finished, he found a job lecturing in chemistry and mathematics at Rochdale Technical School. Meanwhile, responding to a newspaper advertisement, he applied for a post to take part in the ocean investigations of RRS *Discovery*, the ship made famous by Captain Robert Falcon Scott's National Antarctic Expedition from 1901 to 1904.

The British government appointed the *Discovery* Committee in 1924 to address the economic importance of the Falkland Islands dependencies. This remote region's most important natural resources were the whales in the surrounding seas. The committee's purpose was to coordinate scientific studies of the whales, their biology, and their environment, with the aim of putting the industry on a sustainable basis. Its work was to be financed from taxes on whale products. By the time Deacon was hired as a chemist, the committee already had set up a laboratory near one of the major whaling stations at Grytviken in South Georgia, and *Discovery* had made a preliminary survey of the surrounding whaling area.

Deacon jumped at the chance to go to sea, both for the scientific work he could do and for the possibility of adventure. He started in late 1927, first aboard *William Scoresby*, the supporting vessel for *Discovery*. It was a smaller, faster ship that was intended for chasing down whales to mark them for migration studies. Deacon's job was to sample the water, to determine its temperature, salinity, oxygen content, and concentrations of chemicals at various depths. Because of its small size, *William Scoresby* was not very well-suited for Deacon's chemical analyses. Thus much of his work was done on land, in South Georgia. Soon, however, *Discovery* was replaced by a new ship constructed specifically for scientific research in the open ocean, *Discovery II*. After joining the ship in 1930, Deacon found it equipped with a chemical laboratory, allowing him to conduct most of his analysis aboard ship and to develop his ideas about ocean circulation. He worked intensively with the *Discovery II*, either on board taking samples or on land studying them, through the 1930s. He was the ship's principal scientist from 1935 to 1937.

The Hydrology of the Southern Ocean. In the course of the *Discovery* investigations, Deacon's work strayed far from the narrow studies of whales. In 1931, between voyages, he came to England and submitted a manuscript about the hydrology of the southern Atlantic Ocean, ultimately published in 1933. He later added his studies of other parts of the seas surrounding Antarctica. With Deacon on board, *Discovery II* circumnavigated the entire continent of Antarctica in 1932–1933, and Deacon could describe the circulation of water over a huge area. The result was his major work, *The Hydrology of the Southern Ocean,* finally published in 1937 in Discovery Reports. This work earned him a doctorate from the University of London, election as a Fellow of the Royal Society in 1944, and it became the standard text on the Antarctic water masses.

The Hydrology of the Southern Ocean synthesized a great number of descriptive observations with some recent theoretical work, especially from Albert Defant's 1929 book, *Dynamische Ozeanographie.* Deacon used the data from all around the continent to construct a larger picture of ocean circulation and the interaction of water masses. These masses differed in temperature, salinity, and density. The principal interaction was the Antarctic Convergence, where cold southern waters met relatively warm northern ones. Deacon demonstrated definitively that the Antarctic Convergence did indeed surround the whole continent. He concluded that the cold water formed from the continent spread northward at shallow depths until it reached the convergence, where it dropped deeper and continued northward beneath the warm water mass above it, with another warm mass below it. Deacon referred to this cold water as the Antarctic intermediate current. From the north, the warm deep water crept southward past the convergence underneath the intermediate current, but on top of even colder water, dubbed the Antarctic bottom water.

Although the Southern Ocean might have been difficult to identify to a lay person glancing at a conventional map of the world, Deacon's work implied that it could be studied as a specific entity, with the Antarctic Convergence as its boundary. His work became the basis for the discussions of Antarctic waters in the influential 1942 textbook, *The Oceans*, by Harald Sverdrup, Martin Johnson, and Richard Fleming. Thus Deacon's work on the Southern Ocean's circulation and its interactions with the seas north of the Antarctic Convergence became a crucial component of oceanographers' views of global circulation from the 1940s onward.

The War Years. In 1939, Deacon asked the British government what he could do for the war effort. The Admiralty put him to work on HMS *Osprey*, a center of research on Asdic (sonar) and undersea warfare. Deacon helped to design and test equipment for detecting ships with underwater sound, including some work on the sloop HMS *Kingfisher*. During this period, in 1940, he married Margaret Elsa Jeffries, who had also worked for the *Discovery* Committee. Soon the intense German air raids forced Deacon's laboratory to move to Ayrshire, the Anti-Submarine Experimental Establishment. It was there that the Deacons had their only child, Margaret.

In 1944, Deacon took charge of a new unit within the Admiralty Research Laboratory dedicated to studying ocean waves and swell. Deacon headed up Group W (for Waves) to help predict conditions for planning amphibious assaults. In the course of its research, Group W developed an instrument to analyze the spectrum generated from incoming waves, making it possible to distinguish between waves originating from different sources. For example, they now knew when waves generated by storms from Florida reached the coast of Cornwall, as opposed to waves from storms off Cape Horn. Deacon did much to promote this work and mentored the young scientists involved by encouraging them to publish their results, including an influential paper by Norman F. Barber and Fritz J. Ursell that he communicated to the Royal Society.

Group W undertook several other projects during the war. One of them was the Beach Reconnaissance Intelligence Committee, for which the group tried to make accurate devices to measure beach slopes and judge their effects on wave refraction. Deacon and his colleagues were using new techniques to account for a large array of influences over local conditions. By the war's end, the work at Group W had set the tone for postwar research on physical oceanography. As in the United States, British oceanographers explored the explicitly physical parameters of their research, such as the transmission of sound waves, the propagation of surface waves, the influence of storms, and of a variety of new applications of spectral analysis. Deacon, however, still had no secure employment. Though he initially reverted to his post under the *Discovery* Committee, in 1947 he took what he thought was a more stable position as a scientist working for the Admiralty.

National Institute of Oceanography. Keenly aware of the importance of physical oceanography in naval operations, the Royal Navy wanted a new center of research. During

the war, scientists and officers alike envisioned a major institute, focusing primarily on the physics of the seas, equipped with a vessel big enough to conduct first-rate research. Deacon agreed that physical oceanography needed long-term support, though he argued that it would be useful to have a marine biologist on staff as well. After a sluggish start, in 1949 Britain's National Oceanographic Council was formed, with a National Institute of Oceanography dedicated to studying all aspects of oceanography. Deacon became its first director.

Deacon ultimately spent over two decades at the institute. The *Discovery* Committee disbanded as the institute came into being, and its ships now came under Deacon's control. Eventually, in 1962, yet a third *Discovery* became part of the research arsenal of British oceanographers. The institute became involved in many international projects after World War II. Just as the *Discovery* Committee had existed to serve British interests in the Southern Hemisphere, the far-flung holdings of the British Empire gave the institute a mandate to conduct research worldwide in the service of Britain.

International Oceanography. As head of the institute, Deacon spearheaded British involvement in many international oceanographic projects. The first large-scale effort was the International Geophysical Year (IGY) of 1957–1958. Deacon saw the IGY as a way to investigate subjects needing worldwide observational networks. Oceanographers acquired data on mean sea level, long waves propagated through the oceans, and the problems of large-scale general circulation. He was somewhat annoyed that the IGY planners had not set aside a seat for oceanography on the international committee that formulated the program. Nonetheless, he became chairman of a less prominent group, the Working Panel on Oceanography, which coordinated oceanographic studies.

When leading oceanographers from other countries, notably the American Roger Revelle, wanted to take advantage of the international cooperation of the IGY and develop a more permanent arrangement, Deacon initially resisted. He felt that the body that eventually became the Scientific Committee for Oceanic Research (SCOR) was too broad in scope. He wondered if SCOR would usurp the role of the existing International Association of Physical Oceanography, an organization that Deacon held dear. He firmly believed that physical oceanography was at a crucial stage of development, and he did not wish to see it decline in importance. But Revelle and others proved persuasive, and Deacon ultimately conceded that a coordinating body like SCOR was needed in order to put international recommendations about marine science on firm scientific grounds. When the Intergovernmental

Oceanographic Commission was founded in 1960, SCOR became its principal advisory body.

Deacon tempered his enthusiasm for international cooperation with a healthy skepticism about the value of collecting heaps of data. Some proposals for international work, particularly those made by Soviets, seemed unimaginative and redundant. The past century and a half of ocean exploration already had yielded a huge storehouse of observations, like those of the *Discovery* cruises. He also was keenly aware of the financial difficulties at his own institute, and he resented that the superpowers did not seem to appreciate the struggles that smaller countries such as Britain faced. For Deacon, maintaining the status of British oceanography meant tackling important problems, not just collecting data.

Deacon's institute took on major financial responsibilities for international projects, trying to keep up with better-funded institutions in the United States and Soviet Union. One of these was the International Indian Ocean Expedition in the early 1960s. The institute sent *Discovery* to the region to make observations and spent an extraordinary amount of money overhauling a vessel to do experimental fishing, the *Manihine*. This was primarily designed to satisfy patrons who supported the expedition because of its practical aims. These years were so difficult financially for the institute that Deacon lost his appetite for large-scale investigations. He was much more comfortable working with organizations like the North Atlantic Treaty Organization's (NATO's) Science Committee. In NATO, he could concentrate on physical oceanography without having to promise economic benefits and without negotiating scientific plans with Russian scientists.

Later Years. Despite Deacon's successes in the 1960s, they were trying years. For one, there was the constant financial problem at the institute. Also, the entire British scientific establishment was reorganized by the Science and Technology Act of 1965. Despite Deacon's efforts to keep it alive, the National Oceanographic Council disappeared, and the institute became part of the Natural Environment Research Council. It dealt a severe blow to his scientific autonomy and that of the institute. Even worse was a personal loss, as Deacon's wife died of cancer in 1966. In 1971, he retired as director.

In the ensuing years, Deacon returned to the subject that had brought him to oceanography in the first place: the Southern Ocean. He went to sea aboard an American ship, *Glacier*, in 1975, and again aboard *Discovery* in 1979. When Britain and Argentina went to war over the Falkland Islands in the 1980s, Deacon drew on his long experience to advise the government on oceanic conditions. His final work was a book titled *The Antarctic Cir-*

cumpolar Ocean, published toward the end of 1984. Some days later, he had a heart attack and died shortly after.

BIBLIOGRAPHY

Papers of George Edward Raven Deacon. Deacon Library, National Oceanography Centre, Southampton, England. This archival collection includes a large number of letters to and from Deacon to colleagues all over the world.

WORKS BY DEACON

The Hydrology of the Southern Ocean. Discovery Reports 15. Cambridge, U.K.: Cambridge University Press, 1937.

The Antarctic Circumpolar Ocean. Cambridge, U.K.: Cambridge University Press, 1984.

OTHER SOURCES

Barber, Norman F. and Fritz Ursell. "The Generation and Propagation of Ocean Waves and Swell, I: Wave Periods and Velocities," *Philosophical Transactions of the Royal Society of London, Series A, Mathematical and Physical Sciences* 240, no. 824 (1948): 527–560.

Charnock, H. "George Edward Raven Deacon." *Biographical Memoirs of Fellows of the Royal Society* 31 (1985): 112–142.

Deacon, Margaret. "Sir George Deacon: British Oceanographer." *Oceanus* 28 (1985): 90–94.

Hamblin, Jacob Darwin. *Oceanographers and the Cold War: Disciples of Marine Science.* Seattle: University of Washington Press, 2005.

Mills, Eric L. "Creating a Global Ocean Conveyor: George Deacon and *The Hydrology of the Southern Ocean.*" In *Extremes: Oceanography's Adventures at the Poles,* edited by Helen M. Rozwadowski. Canton, MA: Science History Publications, in press.

Jacob Darwin Hamblin

DEFANT, ALBERT JOSEPH MARIA

(*b.* Trient, Austria [later Trento, Italy], 12 July 1884; *d.* Innsbruck, Austria, 24 December 1974), *meteorology, oceanography.*

Defant played a key role in changing oceanography from a descriptive to a physics-based science and in bringing atmospheric and oceanic research closer together. His work covered a wide range, from raindrop sizes and precipitation to radiation, to the turbulent structure and the large-scale circulation of the atmosphere, and further on to water-level changes in lakes and in the ocean, to processes in sea straits, to internal waves, and to the large-scale circulation of water masses in the ocean. Understanding the causes and finding adequate mathematical descriptions motivated his work. He was also a most talented teacher and science organizer.

Albert Defant. *Defant in 1957.* COURTESY OF CHRISTINE DEFANT.

The Meteorologist. Defant was born on 12 July 1884 in Trient, which belonged to the Austrian Empire at that time (after 1919 Trento in Italy). The name Defant is of Ladin origin, from the Romance language, which is spoken in certain regions of Trient and South Tyrol. His parents were Josef and Maria Defant. His father was a teacher who later became an inspector overseeing the schools in North and South Tyrol. Albert Defant went to school in Trient and Innsbruck, Austria, and began studying mathematics, physics, and geophysics at the University of Innsbruck in 1902. Wilhelm Trabert was the professor who had the greatest influence in guiding his interests. Defant proved to be thorough and patient in processing and analyzing field data, but he also acquired an excellent knowledge of the mathematical treatment of data and physical processes. He received his Doctor of Philosophy with distinction in 1906, with a thesis on the spectral properties of raindrop sizes, and added a schoolteacher's degree in mathematics and physics in 1907.

He then moved to Vienna to work at the Austrian Central Institution for Meteorology and Geodynamics, first as an assistant, then from 1909 as head of the weather department and from 1911 to 1918 as adjunkt (senior

researcher). He found a stimulating environment because this was the time when Austrian meteorology was at its height, with many excellent atmospheric scientists working in Vienna. In 1909, he obtained his *Habilitation* (the permission to teach at Vienna University). During the early years in Vienna atmospheric physics was in the center of his interests, with an emphasis on processes in the region such as mountain wind systems, including foehn, wave phenomena, thunderstorms, radiation properties in the mountain range, and snow density in the Alps. About twenty publications in professional journals resulted from this research. His work also made him a member of the weather prediction community, and he tackled the practical aspects of weather prediction successfully as is documented by his first book on weather and weather prediction in 1918 (second edition 1926).

During the later years in Vienna his interests shifted gradually to two other themes: changes in the general atmospheric circulation and related physical processes, and water-level changes in lakes and enclosed or semi-enclosed seas. The second topic was at the beginning of his admirable work in oceanography, which dominated his research during the later part of his life. During this early phase he developed a new method which permitted him to determine the detailed structure of resonant oscillations (seiches) in lakes, investigated causes of water-level changes, and particularly studied tidal effects in the Adriatic and the Mediterranean Sea, the North Sea, the Red Sea, and the Persian Gulf.

The time in Vienna also brought changes to his private life. In 1909, he married Maria (called Mimi) Krepper. They had three children, Edgar, Erika, and Friedrich.

In 1919, Defant accepted the chair for cosmic physics (emphasizing meteorology and geophysics) at the University of Innsbruck. In the following years the most important themes of his atmospheric research emerged: the structure of high-reaching cyclones and anticyclones, free and forced waves in the atmosphere, and in particular the meridional heat transport, which balances the heat gain at low latitudes and the heat loss at high latitudes. With the sensible meridional heat flux being much too small to achieve this meridional transport, he showed quantitatively that large organized turbulent structures could achieve the transfer of heat to high latitudes. These findings (Defant, 1921) prepared the ground for studies on climate change of later generations of atmospheric scientists.

He published an important book on statics and dynamics of the atmosphere in 1928. But even during this most productive phase in atmospheric research, he continued carrying out oceanic tide studies, and his reputation in that field resulted in an invitation to join two cruises of the German surveying ship *Panther* in 1925 and 1926 in the North Sea. The acquaintance with the practical work at sea gained during these cruises was to constitute an important basis for his future work.

The Oceanographer. In 1926, he finally moved into oceanography when he accepted the chair of oceanography at the University of Berlin in Germany and became the director of the Institute and Museum for Marine Research (Institut und Museum für Meereskunde), then the center of ocean science in Germany. He was the successor of Alfred Merz, the promoter and organizer of the famous South Atlantic Expedition (1925–1927) on the Research Vessel *Meteor*. Unfortunately, Alfred Merz had died during the expedition in Buenos Aires, Argentina, in 1925. When accepting the position in Berlin, Defant had agreed to guide the analysis of the data from the expedition and to take care of the Scientific Results series. He joined the last three legs of the cruise to gain firsthand experience with the data gathering. During that cruise he also became familiar with the joint activities of a multidisciplinary community onboard, consisting of physical oceanographers, chemists, biologists, and geologists.

His work in Berlin was concentrating on the physics of the ocean and in particular on the *Meteor* Scientific Results series, both as a data evaluator and author and as an editor. His ability to analyze observational data with a broad knowledge in physics and mathematics led to an improved understanding in many branches of oceanography. The first large-scale systematic survey in the Atlantic during the *Meteor* expedition (1925–1927) had provided a data set with unprecedented quality and spatial coverage. Defant, together with his colleague Georg Wüst, set a standard of excellence in the presentation of oceanographic data. It was not by chance that Defant concentrated on the upper ocean with the interface to the atmosphere where he could bring in his combined knowhow in atmospheric and oceanic processes. His analysis of the water masses and the flow field in the Atlantic formed the basis of knowledge about the upper-ocean circulation. It came to be known as an important component of the global overturning circulation of water masses, which form and sink in the northern Atlantic and are transported at great depths to all oceans and, after modification, become part of an upper-ocean flow to the north Atlantic. There global transports have a major impact on climate change. In particular, he was the first one to use the density field for determining the geostrophic flow in the North Atlantic Ocean down to 2000 meters, including evidence of the extent and structure of the return flow east of the Gulf Stream.

The *Meteor* data set and the results obtained by Defant and Wüst from these data were considered of such fundamental nature that the National Science Foundation in Washington, DC, arranged for the translation of three volumes of the *Meteor* results series by William J. Emery. They were published in 1979, 1981, and 1985. Defant also used data from *Meteor* anchor stations to identify vertical displacements of equal-density surfaces and showed that they were mainly caused by internal tidal waves and by inertial waves. Furthermore, Defant contributed to the understanding of the role of water masses of Arctic and Antarctic origin and particularly helped to realize the significance of the southward deep-water overflow across the Greenland-Scotland Ridge, which was subsequently considered an essential component of the global overturning circulation. His work on tides continued during that time, and he also became an expert in the understanding of the flow in ocean straits. He wrote two important books on dynamical oceanography in 1928 and on the physics of the ocean in 1931.

He also had a major impact on ocean and atmosphere science by being the leader in building up oceanography in Germany in the early part of the twentieth century, furthering links with the meteorological community and connecting researchers in Germany with the atmospheric and oceanic research communities in other countries. He was an impressive personality. His guidance as a director was described as being cordial, but at the same time pushing successfully for the best scientific quality possible.

World War II changed working conditions and cut his close connections in particular to his Scandinavian colleagues, but he continued his work in Berlin until 1943 when the institute was first hit by bombing. He managed to save the major part of the institute's oceanographic library by transferring it to the small town of Wunsiedel in the center of Germany. He did some teaching in Vienna and then stayed in Wunsiedel, continuing the work on a fundamental book on physical oceanography on which he had started in 1935, based on his teaching at the University of Berlin. At the end of the war the institute in Berlin was completely destroyed, terminating ocean research in that city. The library in Wunsiedel later became the basis of oceanographic libraries at the marine science institute in Kiel, Germany, and at the German Hydrographic Office in Hamburg.

The Third Phase. Defant returned to Innsbruck in 1945, where he had been offered the chair for meteorology and geophysics. Nevertheless, ocean-related research continued to dominate his work. In 1949, his wife died. Shortly thereafter, he followed an invitation to the Scripps Institution of Oceanography in La Jolla, California in 1949–1950. He served as *Rektor* (president) of Innsbruck University in 1950–1951. In 1952, he married his second wife Maria Theresia Schletterer. After official retirement in 1955, he continued to be an active researcher and teacher by accepting visiting professorships at the University of Hamburg, Germany, until 1956 and at the Free University of Berlin from 1956 to 1958. He wrote a state-of-the-art chapter on tides for the *Encyclopedia of Physics* in 1957.

The publication of his book on physical oceanography had been impossible during the postwar years. With the help of Carl-Gustaf Rossby in Sweden and support from the Office of Naval Research in the United States, he was able to prepare an English version, partly during a stay at the International Institute of Meteorology in Stockholm, Sweden, in 1957–1958. He also had the help of his son Friedrich Defant, an atmospheric scientist who later headed the meteorology department at the oceanographic institute in Kiel, Germany. The two volumes of *Physical Oceanography* were finally published in 1960 and 1961 and became a standard text in oceanography for a long time. Defant himself considered these volumes his lifework. His scientific activities and publishing continued until the mid-1960s. Albert Defant died on 24 December 1974 in Innsbruck.

International Relations and Honors. Defant's work was strongly influenced by the ocean/atmosphere researchers in Scandinavia, in particular by Vagn Walfrid Ekman, Björn Helland-Hansen, Johan Wilhelm Sandström, and Jonas Ekman Fjeldstad. Defant was on the same route, which was leading from geographical description to a mathematics-physics approach in ocean research. His excellent scientific and personal relationship with Scandinavian scientists is documented by numerous honors: the Vega Medal of the Royal Swedish Geographic Society, Stockholm (1932); the Galathea Medal of the Royal Danish Geographic Society, Copenhagen (1936); memberships in the Finnish Academy of Sciences, Helsinki (1942), the Royal Academy of Sciences, Göteborg, Sweden (1939), the Royal Swedish Academy of Sciences, Stockholm (1945), and the Norwegian Academy of Sciences and Letters, Oslo (1964).

Defant was also held in high esteem in many other countries, documented by the Agassiz Medal of the National Academy of Sciences, Washington, DC (1933) and the Golden Honorary Medal of the Oceanography Society of Japan, Tokyo (1975, posthumous), as well as honorary memberships in the Russian Geographic Society, Leningrad (1938), the Royal Netherlands Geographic Society, Amsterdam (1939), and the New York Academy of Sciences (1949).

With his scientific achievements and his leadership in organizing top-class research, the scientific honors in Germany and Austria were manifold: Memberships in the German Academy of Sciences Leopoldina, Halle (1919), the Prussian Academy of Sciences, Berlin (1935), the Göttingen Academy of Sciences (1935), the Austrian Acad-

emy of Sciences, Vienna (1939), the Academy of Sciences and Literature in Mainz (1949), and the Bavarian Academy of Sciences, Munich (1951); honorary memberships in the Society for Science and Medicine, Innsbruck (1926), the Pomeranian Geographic Society, Greifswald (1939), and the German Scientific Commission for Marine Research (1956).

He received numerous scientific medals and awards: the Ludwig Haitinger Award of the Royal Academy of Sciences, Vienna (1912), the Ackermann Award of the University of Leipzig (1928), the Arrhenius Award of the University of Leipzig (1943), the Honorary Ring of the Austrian Society of the United Nations League, Vienna (1947), the Golden Wiechert Medal of the German Geophysical Society (1956), the Joachim Jungius Medal of the University of Hamburg (1963), the Golden Anniversary Medal of the University of Innsbruck (1974), and the Austrian Decoration for Science and Art, Vienna (1974). He was granted a honorary doctorate by the Free University of Berlin (1958), and was made *Ritter der Friedensklasse des Ordens "Pour le mérite"* in 1962, a distinguished award dating back to a proposal by Alexander von Humboldt in 1842, which has been given only to a select number of scientists and artists. A Festschrift was dedicated to him on the occasion of his seventieth birthday in the *Archiv für Meteorologie, Geophysik und Bioklimatologie* in 1954.

BIBLIOGRAPHY

Defant's works included 222 papers and 12 books or contributions to books, and he was editor of three publication series. Some of his most important contributions are given below.

WORKS BY DEFANT

Wetter und Wettervorhersage [Weather and Weather Prediction]. Vienna: Fr. Deutike, 1918. 2nd ed. 1926.

Die Zirkulation der Atmosphäre in den gemässigten Breiten der Erde [The Circulation of the Atmosphere in Moderate Latitudes]. Geografiska Ann. 3, 209–266, 1921.

Lufthülle und Klima [Atmosphere and Climate]. Enzyklopädie der Erdkunde, edited by Erich Obst. Vienna: Fr. Deutike, 1923.

Gezeitenprobleme des Meeres in Landnähe [Problems of Ocean Tides near the Land]. Probleme der Kosmischen Physik, vol. 6. Hamburg: H. Grand, 1925.

"Statik und Dynamik der Atmosphäre" [Statics and Dynamics of the Atmosphere]. In *Handbuch der Experimentalphysik*, 25, 1, Geophysik, edited by Wilhelm Wien and Friedrich Harms. Leipzig. Akademische Verlagsgesellschaft, 1928.

"Physik des Meeres" [Physics of the Sea]. In *Handbuch der Experimentalphysik*, Geophysik, vol. 2, edited by Wien and Harms, Leipzig, 1931.

"Die Troposphäre." In *Schichtung und Zirkulation des Atlantischen Ozeans*. Wissenschaftliche Ergebnisse der deutschen atlantischen Expedition auf dem Forschungsschiff

"Meteor" 1925–1927, vol. 6, part 1. Berlin: Walter de Gruyter, 1936. Translated by William J. Emery. *The Troposphere: Stratification and Circulation of the Atlantic Ocean.* Scientific Results of the German Atlantic Expedition of the Research Vessel "Meteor" 1925–1927, vol. 6, part 1. New Delhi: Amerind and Springfield, VA: Available from the U.S. Dept. of Commerce, National Technical Information Service, 1981.

"Flutwellen und Gezeiten des Wassers" [Tidal Waves and Tides of the Water]. In *Encyclopedia of Physics*, vol. 48, *Geophysics II*, edited by Julius Bartels and Siegfried Flügge. Berlin: Springer-Verlag, 1957a.

With F. Defant. *Atmospherische Dynamik* [Atmospheric Dynamics]. Frankfurt am Main: Akademische Verlagsgesellschaft, 1957b.

Ebb and Flow. Ann Arbor Sciences Library. Ann Arbor: University of Michigan Press, 1958. 2nd ed. 1960.

Physical Oceanography, vol. 2. New York: Pergamon Press, 1960. Vol. 1. 1961.

OTHER SOURCES

Böhnecke, G. "In Memoriam Albert Defant 1884–1974" [In Memory of Albert Defant 1884–1974]. "*Meteor*" *Forschungsergebnisse. Reihe A: Allgemeines, Physik und Chemie des Meeres* no. 18 (1976): 1–8. Includes a bibliography.

Pichler, H. "Albert Defant zum Gedenken." [In Memory of Albert Defant]. *Innsbrucker Universitätsnachrichten,* vol. 8, 1978: 126-129.

Gerold Siedler

DEL MONTE, GUIDOBALDO

SEE **Monte, Guidobaldo, Marchese del**.

DELBRÜCK, MAX LUDWIG HENNING (*b.* Berlin, Germany, 4 September 1906; *d.* Pasadena, California, 10 March 1981), *viral and bacterial genetics, molecular biology.*

Delbrück shared the Nobel Prize for Physiology or Medicine in 1969 for his pioneering work in viral and bacterial genetics. He was one of the founders of molecular biology as well as a guiding and exacting spirit in its early development, particularly through the so-called Phage Group.

Early Life. Delbrück was a product of Germany's academic and intellectual aristocracy. The great German chemist Justus Liebig was among his maternal forebears, and his father was Hans Delbrück, who had served briefly in the Prussian parliament and the Reichstag and was a professor of history at the University of Berlin. The youngest of seven children, Delbrück grew up in the Grunewald suburb of Berlin amid family and friends who included Adolf von Harnack, a cofounder and president of the Kaiser Wilhelm Gesellschaft (Kaiser Wilhelm Society), and Karl Bonhoeffer, his brother-in-law and a professor of psychiatry at the University of Berlin. Delbrück later reflected that in this bustling, politically engaged milieu, he turned to science—his first love was astronomy—as a way of establishing his own identity.

Starting in 1924 Delbrück studied astronomy, physics, and mathematics at several universities; then, in 1926, he enrolled at Göttingen University in Germany, where he remained to pursue doctoral work in theoretical physics. He was caught up in the enthusiasm for the new quantum mechanics and came to know several of the young scientists—including J. Robert Oppenheimer, Pascual Jordan, and Victor Weisskopf— who had come to the university to pursue the new theory. ("I learned at an early age that science is a haven for the timid, the freaks, the misfits," Delbrück later mused, explaining, "If you were a student in Göttingen in the 1920s and went to the seminar 'Structure of Matter' … you could well imagine that you were in a madhouse.… Every one of the persons there was obviously some kind of severe case" ("*Homo Scientificus*"). He failed in an attempt to write a doctoral thesis on novae because he found the mathematics too difficult. He managed to obtain his doctorate in 1930 with a study that extended to lithium the quantum mechanical theory of the homopolar bond that had recently been developed for hydrogen.

Growing Interest in Biology. In 1929 Delbrück had joined the physics faculty at Bristol University in England, and after gaining his PhD the following year, he received a Rockefeller Foundation postdoctoral fellowship that enabled him to spend the spring and summer of 1931 studying with Niels Bohr in Copenhagen, Denmark, and then the fall and winter with Wolfgang Pauli, in Zürich, Switzerland. While in Copenhagen he was inspired to start learning biology as a result of hearing Bohr propose that living systems might operate under the principle of complementarity, exhibiting features comparable to the duality of light as a wave and a particle. An organism might, for example, be investigated as a collection of molecules or as a behavioral whole, but not as both simultaneously. In mid-1932, after he spent another six months in Bristol, Delbrück's growing interest in biology was strengthened upon listening to Bohr lecture in Copenhagen on "Licht und Leben" (Light and life), suggesting, in line with his ideas about complementarity, that biological understanding would require concepts that could not be reduced to those of atomic physics. What fascinated

Delbrück was precisely that biology might ultimately yield such concepts, some new principle inherent in the human observer's attempt to comprehend vital nature. He would tell Bohr in 1962 that the question of complementarity in biology had given him his primary motivation for his work.

Delbrück returned to Berlin in 1932 to become an assistant to Lise Meitner at the Institute for Chemistry within the Kaiser Wilhelm Gesellschaft. Part of his research involved the scattering of gamma rays by a Coulomb field. Although inapplicable to the case that stimulated the effort, the results were theoretically sound and were later dubbed "Delbrück scattering" by Hans Bethe, who confirmed them. He also further explored biology by organizing a private discussion group of physicists, biologists, and biochemists. In pursuit of complementarity in biology, he resolved to investigate a simple biological system—something akin to the hydrogen atom in physics—and press its analysis until paradoxes appeared, just as they had emerged in the exploration of atomic physics. The system he was lured to was the gene.

Delbrück collaborated with two members of the discussion group, the Russian geneticist Nicolai Timofeeff-Ressovsky and the physicist Karl Günter Zimmer, to study the effect of ionizing radiation on genes. In 1935 the three men published "Uber die Natur der Genmutation und der Genstruktur" (The nature of genetic mutations and the structure of the gene), a paper that combined experimental data and—Delbrück's interpretive contribution—the quantum theoretical idea of atoms residing in "energy wells" to account for both genetic stability and the occurrence of mutations in response to energetic ionizing radiation. Although ultimately proved wrong in several important respects, the paper indicated that genes were not abstract entities but relatively stable macromolecules susceptible to analysis by physical and chemical methods. Published in an obscure journal, the paper, Delbrück later said, got "a funeral first class." However, the physicist Erwin Schrödinger, the Nobel laureate in physics for his contributions to quantum mechanics, called prominent attention to it in his influential book *What is Life?*, which was published in 1944 (a German translation *Was ist Leben?* was published in 1946). Schrödinger contended that he had been inspired to write the book by Delbrück's paper. The book, a tour de force of how physical reasoning might be applied to biological problems, stimulated a number of young physicists to emulate Delbrück by becoming molecular geneticists.

War Years in America. The merits of his research did not earn Delbrück a regular academic post in Nazi Berlin. Unlike his family, he was doggedly apolitical, alienated from state and society by World War I—in which he had

lost his oldest brother—and by the ugly political passions that had bubbled, not always beneath the surface, in Weimar Germany. Even so, in the 1930s he made no secret of the fact that he found the Nazis contemptible, as did members of his family, some of whom opposed them actively. Despite his impeccable German (and nominally Christian) credentials, he was deemed politically unreliable and was unable to obtain a university post. Coveting one greatly, Delbrück went to considerable lengths to prove that he was not Jewish, and he submitted to courses at Nazi indoctrination camps—all to no avail. However, the paper on genetic mutations led to an opportunity to escape the difficulty—a Rockefeller Foundation Fellowship to spend the 1937–1938 academic year in the United States, mainly at the California Institute of Technology (Caltech) in Pasadena, to study genetics with Thomas Hunt Morgan, who in 1933 had been awarded a Nobel Prize for his pioneering work on the genetics of *Drosophila* (fruit flies).

Delbrück found fruit-fly genetics not to his liking because it was too ridden with elaborate jargon. But he was exhilarated when, by chance, he met the Caltech biochemist Emery Ellis, who was working with bacteriophage, a virus that preys on bacteria. If the phage were permitted to infect bacteria contained on a flat plate, they would multiply in the infected cells, killing them, and the dead cells would reveal themselves as clear areas called "plaques" on a lawn of bacterial growth. In 1935 the biochemist Wendell Stanley succeeded in crystallizing a tobacco virus, which indicated, as Delbrück put it, that a virus is a "living molecule." In Delbrück's view, bacteriophage presented a simple system—the hydrogen atom for biology—he had been looking for. With Ellis's plaque methods, bacteriophage's actions of infection and reproduction through time could be quantitatively scrutinized and analyzed.

Delbrück promptly embarked on a program of phage research, remaining in the United States for another year via an extension of his Rockefeller fellowship to 1939 and then—amid the outbreak of war in Europe—indefinitely, with an appointment in January 1940 to the faculty of Vanderbilt University in Nashville, Tennessee. Collaborating with Ellis while still at Caltech, he refined the treatment of the one-step growth curve (the spread of infection from a single particle) and devised the so-called single-burst experiment, which permitted a comparison of phage multiplication in individual cells. He also devised mathematical formulas for calculating the rate of adsorption of free phage by bacteria under different experimental conditions and, using Siméon Denis Poisson's statistics of random sampling, for assessing the proportion of virus particles able to produce plaques. These methods proved to be crucial for the subsequent development of phage research.

In the summer of 1941 Delbrück went to the Cold Spring Harbor Laboratory, on Long Island in New York, to work on bacteriophage with Salvador Luria, whom he had met in 1940. A refugee from Italy, Luria had been eager to collaborate with Delbrück since reading the paper on genetic mutations. In 1942 Luria and Delbrück began to think about whether bacterial resistance to phage originated from the bacteria's contact with the phage or from spontaneous mutation. Luria had the idea of resolving the issue by comparing the numbers of resistant bacteria in independent cultures, each seeded with only a few sensitive cells. Resistance induced by contact with the phage would yield numbers of resistant cells within the limits expected by random sampling. In contrast, resistance arising from mutation would generate numbers of resistant cells with much larger variation. In sum, a fluctuation greater than that of sampling error in the numbers of resistant bacteria would mean that these variants had arisen before they were exposed to the phage and were therefore mutants.

Delbrück enthusiastically endorsed Luria's idea with a fully developed mathematical theory of the proposed experiment that enabled calculation of the rate of mutation from the data. Luria's experiment showed unambiguously that bacterial resistance is the product of spontaneous mutation, not of some Lamarckian adaptation. Delbrück and Luria's paper "Mutations of bacteria from virus sensitivity to virus resistance," published in 1943, was a landmark in the history of bacterial and phage genetics. It offered the first solid evidence that bacterial inheritance is governed by genes, an unpopular view at the time among leading microbiologists, and it laid out powerful methods and modes of analysis by which bacterial genetics could be studied efficiently.

The Phage Group. Also in 1943, Delbrück and Luria took into their partnership Alfred Hershey—Luria and Hershey would be Delbrück's co-recipients of the Nobel Prize—a chemist on the faculty of the Washington University School of Medicine in St. Louis, Missouri. Hershey's arrival initiated what came to be known as the Phage Group, an informal network of viral and bacterial geneticists. In 1944 Delbrück negotiated a "phage treaty," a kind of standardization agreement intended to make the results of phage research comparable across different laboratories. According to the agreement, members of the Phage Group would deal mainly with a set of seven phage (T1 through T7) and use the bacterium *E. coli* as the object of infection.

Delbrück modeled the Phage Group after the network of physicists centered on Niels Bohr that had created quantum physics, later reflecting how it was formed to imitate "the Copenhagen spirit" in physics. He helped

Max Delbrück. HULTON ARCHIVE/GETTY IMAGES.

recruit a number of scientists, especially physicists, into postwar molecular biology, both indirectly, by the showcasing Schrödinger gave him in *What is Life?*, and directly, by organizing in 1945 what became an annual summer phage course at Cold Spring Harbor that continued for twenty-five years. Intended for biologists, biochemists, and physicists, it inculcated the Phage Group's quantitative and statistical approach to biology, and it drew a steadily increasing number of students, ranging from young postdoctoral fellows to senior physicists, for a total of some four hundred by the end. In 1947 he initiated a series of phage meetings that continued until his incapacity in 1981 and that eventually drew hundreds of scientists. Also in 1947 he returned to the California Institute of Technology as professor of biology, and he made Caltech into a center of the new quantitative molecular biology.

DNA. After the war Delbrück continued to hope that the study of the genetics of microorganisms would expose some deep paradox that would compel the forging of a new principle. Although the evidence had kept accumulating that genetics was chemistry, Delbrück tended not to think biochemically. He and Luria were well aware of the evidence developed by Oswald Avery's group at the Rockefeller Institute for Medical Research that the genetic material might be DNA. However, they did not credit what Avery and others had learned about the transforming principle in pneumococcus with broad applicability to phage research or even other types of bacteria. They did not see how DNA could carry hereditary information. And, in any case, they did not attach great importance to whether genes were proteins or nucleic acid.

Once James Watson and Francis Crick together pieced out the structure of DNA in 1953, it was clear that the key to the transmission and expression of genetic information inhered not in some new physical laws but in a supple, compact, and beautiful molecule whose functions were explicable in terms of conventional chemistry. This denoument disappointed Delbrück because it did not reveal any profound new principle of nature. He thought the structure of DNA was marvelous, to be sure. But, as he wrote in 1986 in *Mind from Matter*: "Upon the discovery of the DNA double helix, the mystery of gene replication was revealed as a ludicrously simple trick. In peole who had expected a deep solution to the deep problem of how in the living world like begets like, it raised a feeling similar to the embarrassment one feels when shown a simple solution to a chess problem with which one has struggled in vain for a long time."

Later Career. In 1950 Delbrück began moving away from phage research, believing that it was well established and could take care of itself. He began turning his attention to problems of sensory perception and its transduction into physiological activity. Looking for a model organism with which to investigate the subject, he first tried the bacterium *Rhodospirillum,* which swims towards a light source. After a few experiments, however, he decided to switch to *Phycomyces,* a simple fungus that sprouts large aerial stalks called sporangiophores that exhibit a number of behavioral responses to different stimuli, notably growing toward light, against gravity, into the wind, and away from nearby objects. In 1953 Delbrück began his first experiments with the fungus and in 1956 published a paper, "System analysis for the light growth reactions of *Phycomyces,*" that proposed a kinetic model of adaptation to light. The model proved to be influential for analyzing other sensory systems and the paper became a classic. Delbrück gradually established a *Phycomyces* group, recruiting members mainly from physics. Sufficient work had accumulated by 1969 to warrant a review of the field. He had hoped that the work with *Phycomyces* might reveal paradoxes that would lead to a new principle of nature, but he

was no more satisfied in this endeavor than he had been with genetics.

Delbrück felt acutely the terrible losses suffered by friends and relatives who had stayed in Germany. He considered those who had remained and resisted the regime—like his brother-in-law Karl Bonhoeffer, who had survived, and Karl's brother Dietrich, who was murdered by the Nazis—prisoners of conscience, and he donated his Nobel Prize money to Amnesty International "as a debt to all prisoners of conscience." From 1961 to 1963 he took leave of absence from Caltech to help establish the Institute for Genetics at the University of Cologne in Germany. He organized four research groups there, including one led by himself, to study the photochemical effects of ultraviolet light on DNA. He also established phage courses on the Cold Spring Harbor model. He maintained connections with the Genetics Institute as honorary professor, returning every year or so to give a series of lectures or a seminar. Later he served as an adviser in natural science on the founding committee of the new University of Konstanz in Germany, founded in 1966.

Otherwise, Delbrück hewed to a largely apolitical life, keeping the house clear of radio, television, and magazines. He held to the belief, as he declared in an autobiographical fragment, that "the pursuit of scientific truth, of poetic truth or of mystic truth, is ultimately far more important and influential in shaping man's fate than the power game of those with political aspirations who try to change the world directly." Among the truths he tried to puzzle out in his later years was how mind emerged from matter, which was the subject of a series of lectures that he gave at Caltech in 1972 and of an essay that he presented to the Nobel Conference in 1977. In the end, he could find no explanation for the remarkable fact that the brain, if selected for its survival value, could nevertheless range over disparate abstract subjects such as cosmology, genetics, and number theory.

Delbrück's insulation from the world was made all the more possible by his American circumstances. He was favored by the increasingly abundant resources of American science, and also by his marriage. His biographers, Ernst Peter Fischer and Carol Lipson, report that his wife "sheltered him, allowing him to concentrate on science," adding, "Manny ran the house, looked after the car, did the income tax, and later on guided the children" (1998). Yet if politics and public affairs meant little or nothing to Delbrück, neither did material goods or fame. He lived modestly. He was uncomfortable with kudos. When he won the Nobel Prize, he acknowledged the congratulations that poured in from friends by mailing out a handwritten excerpt from a Japanese poem that he had read at the end of the press conference occasioned by the award:

The temple bell echoes the impermanence of all things …

Before long the mighty are cast down

And are as dust before the wind.

While an advocate of cooperation, Delbrück himself sometimes behaved more in the irascible manner of Wolfgang Pauli, who was quantum physics's uncompromising intellectual conscience, than in the way of the tactful Bohr. Delbrück's criticism could be devastating. He might comment on a seminar by stalking out after five minutes or, worse, by telling the speaker afterwards that this was "the worst seminar I ever heard." (He kept a bottle of brandy in his desk for the restoration of the distressed.) Some thought of him as hypercritical and arrogant. Still, he was widely respected for his nagging questioning, his tendency to poke holes in seemingly settled results or new claims. Scientists on both sides of the Atlantic, encountering fresh ideas or data, would commonly wonder, "What will Max think?"

Delbrück was also on the whole an unusually engaging, humorous, and generous colleague, devoting "great effort and intelligence," Hershey once noted, "to encouraging, appreciating, and steering the work of others, probably often at the expense of his own." He was playful and unpretentious, never the distinguished professor, always "Max." He and his wife, the former Mary Adeline Bruce, the daughter of a prosperous mining engineer, familiarly known as "Manny," whom he married in 1941, were warmly hospitable in their Pasadena home to students, colleagues, and other visitors. Max and Manny often led weekend camping trips to the desert accompanied by an entourage of undergraduates, graduates students, postdoctoral fellows, staff, dogs, and children, including their own four. A camper might awaken in the middle of the night to see Delbrück standing naked, his binoculars balanced on the car, observing the sky.

When Delbrück learned that he had multiple myeloma—the disease that eventually killed him—he gathered his students together for a seminar on the subject and, as the disease progressed, told his son Jonathan that he was embarked on his "last great adventure." A few months before his death, he suffered a stroke that impaired his vision on one side. He was fascinated by the limitation and made himself available to students for "some tests they cannot do with the monkeys."

BIBLIOGRAPHY

Unpublished letters and other papers of Delbrück and an oral interview with him are in the Max Delbrück Papers at the archives of the California Institute of Technology in Pasadena. Requests for use of these materials can be made at http://archives.caltech.edu.

WORKS BY DELBRÜCK

"Uber die Natur der Genmutation und der Genstruktur" [The nature of genetic mutations and the structure of the gene]. *Nachrichten von der Gesellschaft der Wissenschaften zu Gottingen* 6 (1935): 189–245.

With Salvador Luria. "Mutations of bacteria from vrius sensitivity to virus resistance." *Genetics* 28, no. 6 (1943): 491–511.

With Werner Reichardt. "System analysis for the light growth reactions of *Phycomyces*." In *Cellular Mechanisms in Differentiation and Growth*, edited by Dorothea Rudnick, 3–44. Princeton, NJ: Princeton University Press, 1956.

"*Homo Scientificus* According to Beckett." Lecture at California Institute of Technology. Chemistry and Society Lecture Series, 24 February 1971. Available from http://barnesworld.blogs.com/delbruck1971.pdf.

Mind from Matter? Oxford, U.K.: Blackwell Scientific Publishing, 1986.

OTHER SOURCES

Cairns, John, Gunther S. Stent, and James D. Watson, eds. *Phage and the Origins of Molecular Biology.* Cold Spring Harbor, NY: Cold Spring Harbor Laboratory of Quantitative Biology, 1966.

Fischer, Ernst Peter, and Carol Lipson. *Thinking about Science: Max Delbrück and the Origins of Molecular Biology.* New York: Norton, 1988. The most comprehensive treatment of Delbrück, the man and the scientist. Fischer was one of his last graduate students.

Hayes, William. "Max Ludwig Henning Delbrück, September 4, 1906–March 10, 1981." *National Academy of Sciences Biographical Memoirs* 62 (1993): 67–117. A valuable short treatment of Delbrück.

Judson, Horace Freeland. *The Eighth Day of Creation: Makers of the Revolution in Biology.* New York: Simon and Schuster, 1979.

Luria, Salvador E. *A Slot Machine, a Broken Test Tube.* New York: Harper and Row, 1984.

Mullins, Nicholas C. "The Development of a Scientific Specialty: The Phage Group and the Origins of Molecular Biology." *Minerva* 10 (1972): 51–82.

Olby, Robert. *The Path to the Double Helix.* London: Macmillan, 1974.

Schrödinger, Erwin. *What is Life? The Physical Aspect of the Living Cell.* New York: Macmillan, 1944.

Strasser, Bruno J. *La fabrique d'une nouvelle science: La biologie moléculaire à l'âge atomique, 1945–1964* [The making of a new science: Molecular biology in the atomic age, 1945–1964]. Florence, Italy: Olschki, 2006.

Daniel J. Kevles

DELLA FRANCESCA, PIERO

SEE **Piero della Francesca**.

DESCARTES, RENE DU PERRON (*b.* La Haye, Touraine, France, 31 March 1596; *d.* Stockholm, Sweden, 11 February 1650), *natural philosophy, scientific method, mathematics, optics, mechanics, physiology.* For the original article on Descartes see *DSB,* vol. 4.

Since the 1970s there has been enormous interest in Descartes's scientific thought. There have been numerous new studies of his physics and its foundations, and its relation to scholastic thought about the physical world. Recent studies have emphasized the systematic nature of Descartes's scientific thought, and the way in which the various pieces of his thought fuse to make a unified whole. Also, as historians come to understand the period better, they have come to see what is distinctively Cartesian in this point of view, and how Descartes's scientific thought differs radically from that of other contemporaries, such as Galileo.

Natural Philosophy. In both *Le monde, ou Traité de la lumière* (1630–1633) and the later and more formal *Principia philosophiae* (1644), Descartes put forward a genuine natural philosophy, as opposed to the kind of mixed mathematical investigations found in his *Dioptrics* or his mechanical writings. (See the treatment of those domains in "Descartes: Mathematics and Physics" in *DSB* vol. 4.) Central to this natural philosophy is a conception of a world created and sustained by God and governed by laws of nature. Indeed, Descartes was arguably the first to make the idea of a law of nature central to his conception of physics. This view, in turn, grounded a program for explaining the present state of the world by showing how it could be derived from an initial state, evolving in accordance with those laws of nature. In these respects, among others, Descartes's program offers an interesting contrast to the very influential view of nature found in contemporaries such as Galileo.

There was a standard distinction between pure mathematics and mixed mathematics that dates far before the seventeenth century. Pure mathematics included geometry and arithmetic and was the pure study of mathematical objects such as geometrical objects and numbers. Mixed mathematics, however, included such domains as astronomy, optics, music, mechanics, and, by the seventeenth century, motion. Mixed mathematics was mathematical insofar as it treated its subjects with the tools of mathematics, but it differed from pure mathematics insofar as it applied to the physical world. It also differed from

physics or natural philosophy, terms generally synonymous in the period. For an Aristotelian physicist, natural philosophy was limited to the natural world, the world of things with *natures,* such as the Aristotelian elements (fire, air, water, and earth), living things, and appropriate mixtures. This differs from the mixed mathematical science of mechanics, which treats machines, which are artificial and have no nature properly speaking. For Descartes and some of his contemporaries, though, the distinction between the natural and the artificial had been broken down, thus making this distinction between mixed mathematics and natural philosophy irrelevant. (See the treatment of this issue in "Descartes" in *DSB* vol. 4.) However, natural philosophy was also distinguished from the mixed mathematical sciences by virtue of the fact that in natural philosophy, one dealt with the true causes and explanations of things, and not just their mathematical descriptions at least in principle.

Descartes worked on both sides of the divide. His *Dioptrics* (1637) and essay on mechanics (*Explication des engins par l'aide desquels on peut avec une petite force lever un fardeau fort pesant* of 1637) can be read as essays in mixed mathematics, though even in these texts Descartes shows his interest in understanding the true cause of the phenomena. But in *Le monde* (1630–1633) and more especially in the *Principia philosophiae* (1644) his goal was a complete natural philosophy, beginning with first principles and deriving a complete account of the world from them.

At the bottom level are the first principles, what he called his *first philosophy* or his *metaphysics*. These included the existence and nature of the soul or mind (the first thing we come upon when we philosophize in order), followed by God, and finally the existence and nature of matter or body. These are treated in part I and the beginning of part II of the *Principia philosophiae*, though they are treated at greater length in the *Meditations* (1641). (These were discussed less systematically in *Le monde*, though they did enter into the details of the arguments.) Whereas the soul would enter into his account of the human being, it is God and the nature of body that were most at issue in his account of the physical world.

Descartes argued that the nature of body was to be extended. For him that meant that in the strictest sense bodies had geometrical properties and nothing else: Bodies were the objects of geometry made real, and nothing else. And so, apparent properties of bodies such as hot or cold, wet or dry (to take the Aristotelian primary qualities), or color, are just sensations in the mind, grounded in the size, shape and motion of the smaller parts that make up bodies. It also follows from this conception that bodies have no inherent tendency to move in any particular direction. The natural tendency fire has to rise or earth to fall must be explained, again, in terms of the size, shape and motion of the parts that make up the bodies in question, as they interact with the other bodies in their environment. Another consequence of this conception of body is that there is no empty space. Any volume constitutes an extension, and because one cannot have an extension without a substance in which it inheres, Descartes argued that any volume will be an extended substance and therefore a body. For that reason Descartes did not recognize space as something over and above body: To talk about space is just to talk about bodies in an abstract way. To say that a body D can occupy the same space that is now occupied by a body C is to say that it could happen that D hold the same relation to some other bodies A and B that C now bears to those bodies. And because all space is occupied, even though the universe as a whole is infinite, Descartes argued that all motion is ultimately circular, as bodies move out of the way of other bodies in order to make way for the other bodies to enter the spaces where they had formerly been.

Laws of Motion. Motion can be defined in terms of the relation of bodies to one another. However, to understand the laws of motion, Descartes turned to the general cause of motion, God. Whereas the laws of nature (laws of motion) are first introduced in chapter 7 of *Le monde*, the most systematic presentation was later in the *Principia philosophiae*. The discussion there began with a characterization of God as the "universal and primary cause [of motion], which is the general cause of all motions which are in the world" (*Principia* part II § 36). God's activity in sustaining the world from moment to moment gives rise to an important general rule: "from the sole fact that God moved the parts of matter when he first created them, and now conserves matter as a whole in the same way and with the same order with which he first created it, it is most consistent with reason that we think that he always conserves the same amount of motion in it" (*Principia* part II § 36). This amount is what he called quantity of motion, the sum of the size times the speed of the particles that make up the universe. (Note here that this is *not* what later came to be called momentum. Directionality, what Descartes called *determination* is not governed by this law, only speed, a scalar quantity.)

Descartes did not identify this general conservation law as a law. It is a very general constraint that governs the universe as a whole, and did not say anything about the behavior of particular bodies. For that reason, in the following sections Descartes introduced three specific constraints, each of which was explicitly identified as a *law of nature* (*lex naturae*). The first law is that "each and every thing, insofar as it can [*quantum in se est*] perseveres in the same state, nor is it ever moved unless by an external cause." More specifically, Descartes inferred from this that

"what is once moved, always proceeds to move" (*Principia* part II § 37). This is a law of the persistence of motion in an individual body, understood as a special case of the persistence of any property bodies have. The second reads: "every motion in itself is straight and therefore that which moves circularly always tends to recede from the center of the circle which it describes" (*Principia* part II § 39). This is a law of the persistence of directionality in an individual body. These two laws are often regarded as Descartes's law of inertia, connecting them to Newton's first law of motion. But this is misleading. For Descartes and his contemporaries, inertia was the property bodies have by virtue of which they tend to come to rest. For Descartes these laws dealt with the property bodies have by virtue of which they remain in rectilinear motion. The third law governs the collision of bodies:

> When a moving body comes upon another, if it has less force for proceeding in a straight line than the other has to resist it, then it is deflected in another direction, and retaining its motion, changes only its determination. But if it has more, then it moves the other body with it, and gives the other as much of its motion as it itself loses. (*Principles*, part II, § 40)

Unlike the conservation principle and the first two laws, all of which deal with the persistence of certain features of bodies, this law can be thought of as reconciling the behavior of two bodies whose motion and direction would tend to be conserved, but because of the impenetrability of bodies, cannot. Descartes followed this with seven rules of impact, showing how the third law can be applied to the case of direct collision under certain assumptions, such as that the bodies are perfectly hard and isolated from all other bodies. In the examples Descartes made it clear how collisions are meant to be governed by his general conservation principle, and how he thought the forces involved are to be calculated. Descartes's collision rule turned out to be very problematic. It is not at all clear what exactly he meant by force in the law, and how bodies that contain only extension can have either a force for proceeding or a force of resistance. The rules of impact drew serious criticisms from a number of later people, most notably Christiaan Huygens and Gottfried W. von Leibniz, who showed that they are inconsistent with a relativistic conception of motion and with certain plausible wider constraints that one might want to impose on a scientific theory.

Even though the laws were somewhat suspicious, particularly the collision law and the rules of impact that are connected with it, the overall view of natural philosophy and the physical world were important and influential. What Descartes offered was a conception of a world governed by laws of nature, grounded in God. Even though

Descartes himself did not present them in mathematical form, because they could in principle be given in terms of size, shape, and motion, it was a conception of a law-governed universe that was well-suited to a mathematical physics. Another important feature of the view was that the basic laws are understood in terms of the conservation of certain features of bodies. This conception of physics would characterize the conception of physics found later in Leibniz's system.

Structure of the World. With these laws in place, Descartes then proceeded to account for the current state of the world in outline. He began with an hypothesis about the initial state of the world, an assumption of random sized initial bodies in chapter 6 of *Le monde* and of uniform sided initial bodies in *Principia* part III § 46. He then showed how from this initial state and the laws of nature, these initial bodies would divide themselves into bodies of three different sizes, which he called elements. Because the world is a plenum, and all motion circular, the universe will become divided into an infinity of vortices of fluid matter, each with a sun (or star) at the center which will be the source of light, understood as centrifugal pressure in the vortex. In *Le monde* (chapter 9) the larger masses of matter from the initial creation form planets and comets, the former staying within a single vortex and rotating around its sun, the latter migrating from one vortex to another, moving at the interstices between vortices. In part III of the *Principia philosophiae*, Descartes argued that these larger masses are formed from suns (stars) which become encrusted with sunspots, and are either captured by vortices (and become planets) or wander from one vortex to another (and become comets).

In part four of the *Principia* Descartes dealt with the structure of the Earth in some detail. Descartes argued that the Earth has three regions. Because it originated as a star, encrusted by sunspots, it still retains at its center the same celestial matter found in other stars. Above that is the dense and opaque material that derives from the sunspots that encrusted the original star. The top layer is a mixture of different elements, resulting from the interaction between the second layer and the particles in the vortex surrounding the Earth. All the bodies in human experience are made up of the parts of this third layer. Such terrestrial bodies are not heavy in themselves, but only because they are driven toward the center of the Earth by the heavenly matter that surrounds the Earth and forms a vortex around it. Descartes went on to deal with a wide variety of terrestrial phenomena, including the formation of mountains and valleys, the nature of the air, oceans and their tides, the properties of various chemicals and metals and why they are found where they are in the Earth, the properties of fire and how it is generated, and the properties of glass. The account of the bodies found on Earth ends with a lengthy account of the magnet, giving an ingenious mechanistic model that attempts to unify a wide variety of empirical data about the behavior of magnets by way of a few simple hypotheses.

The main body of the *Principia* ends with terrestrial physics. However, Descartes had intended to end with an account of living things, derived in the same way that he attempted to derive the properties of the Earth, arguing genetically from some initial assumptions and the laws of nature, in a broadly evolutionary fashion. Descartes was working on these issues in his last years, though never fully integrated his account of the life sciences into his natural philosophy. (See the treatment of Descartes's work in the life sciences in "Descartes: Physiology" in *DSB* vol. 4.)

Contrast with Galileo. Though often paired with Galileo as one of the founding fathers of the New Science of the seventeenth century, Descartes actually saw himself as doing something radically different. In a letter to Marin Mersenne from 11 October 1638, Descartes conveyed his comments on Galileo's program, with particular reference to the *Discorsi* (1637). He wrote:

> I find in general that he philosophizes much better than is common, insofar as he avoids as much as he can the errors of the schools, and tries to examine physical matters using mathematical reasons. In that I am entirely in agreement with him…. But it seems to me that he is greatly lacking insofar as he continually makes digressions and never stops to explain a matter in its entirety. This shows that he hasent examined them in arder, and without having considered the first causes of nature, he has only looked for the reasons for certain particular effects, and thus that he has built without a foundation.

This nicely captures the spirit of the natural philosophical approach that Descartes took in contrast to the mixed mathematical approach that he saw in Galileo. For Descartes, what was important was bringing the explanation of phenomena back to their ultimate causes, building a science grounded in first principles. When possible, he was happy to derive mathematically rigorous representations of nature, like Galileo, as he did, for example, with the sine law of refraction. (See the treatment of refraction in "Descartes: Mathematics and Physics" in the original *DSB*). But for Descartes, the mathematical expressions were empty unless accompanied by an account of the true causes.

SUPPLEMENTARY BIBLIOGRAPHY

WORKS BY DESCARTES

Regulae ad directionem ingenii. Edited by Giovanni Crapulli. Gravenhage, Netherlands: Martinus Nijhoff, 1966. This is a scholarly edition of the text.

Theory of Vision. *Diagram of Rene Descartes' Theory of Vision.* **COURTESY OF MARYE ANNE FOX.**

Régles utiles et claires pour la direction de l'esprit en la recherche de la vérité. Edited and translated by Jean-Luc Marion and Pierre Costabel. The Hague: Martinus Nijhoff, 1977. This is a translation of the *Regulae* with an extensive commentary on the scientific themes.

Ecrits physiologiques et médicaux. Edited by Vincent Aucante. Paris: Presses Universitaires de France, 2000.

Tutte le lettere 1619–1650. Edited by Giulia Belgioioso et al. Milan: Bompiani, 2005. This is a new edition of all Descartes's correspondence, in original language with Italian translation and excellent notes on the scientific and mathematical letters.

OTHER SOURCES

Aiton, Eric J. *The Vortex Theory of Planetary Motions*. London: Macdonald, 1972.

Ariew, Roger. *Descartes and the Last Scholastics*. Ithaca, NY: Cornell University Press, 1999.

Armogathe, Jean Robert, and Giulia Belgioioso. *Descartes, Principia Philosophiae: 1644–1994: Atti del convegno per il 350° anniversario della pubblicazione dell'opera*. Naples, Italy: Vivarium, 1996. This is a major collection of writings on Descartes's scientific work from a conference given on the anniversary of the publication of the *Principia*.

———, and Vincent Carraud. *Bibliographie Cartésienne : 1960–1996*. Lecce, Italy: Conte Editore, 2003.

Aucante, Vincent. *La philosophie médicale de Descartes*. Paris: Presses Universitaires de France, 2006.

Belgioioso, Giulia, ed., et al. *Descartes, Il Metodo e I Saggi : Atti del convegno per il 350° anniversario della pubblicazione del Discours de la méthode e degli Essais*. Rome: Istituto della enciclopedia italiana, 1990. This is a major collection of writings on Descartes's scientific work from a conference given on the anniversary of the publication of the *Discourse* and *Essays*.

Clarke, Desmond M. *Descartes: A Biography*. Cambridge, U.K.: Cambridge University Press, 2006.

Des Chene, Dennis. *Physiologia: Natural Philosophy in Late Aristotelian and Cartesian Thought*. Ithaca, NY: Cornell University Press, 1996.

———. *Spirits and Clocks: Machine and Organism in Descartes*. Ithaca, NY: Cornell University Press, 2001.

Duchesneau, François. *Les modèles du vivant de Descartes à Leibniz*. Paris: J. Vrin, 1998.

Garber, Daniel. *Descartes' Metaphysical Physics, Science and Its Conceptual Foundations*. Chicago: University of Chicago Press, 1992.

Gaukroger, Stephen. *Descartes: Philosophy, Mathematics and Physics*. Sussex and Totowa, N.J.: Harvester Press and Barnes and Noble Books, 1980. This is an important collection that contains a number of essays that have become classics, including essays by John Schuster, Michael Mahoney, Martial Gueroult, and Alan Gabbey.

———. *Descartes: An Intellectual Biography*. Oxford: Oxford University Press, 1995.

———, John Schuster, and John Sutton. *Descartes' Natural Philosophy, Routledge Studies in Seventeenth-Century Philosophy*. London: Routledge, 2000. This is a large collection of late twentieth century studies focused on Descartes's science.

———. *Descartes' System of Natural Philosophy*. Cambridge, U.K.: Cambridge University Press, 2002.

Daniel Garber

DEWAR, MICHAEL J. S. (*b.* Ahmednagar, India, 24 September 1918, *d.* Gainesville, Florida, 10 October 1997), *chemistry, computational chemistry, theoretical and experimental study of organic reaction mechanisms.*

Dewar was one of the first, if not the first, organic chemist to master and apply molecular orbital theory. He pioneered many of the fundamental concepts that are now taken for granted, and over a period of four decades he developed and perfected the semi-empirical methods that are still in use. He developed a reputation for coming up with marvelously original and unorthodox ideas and for impeccable integrity.

Early Years and Career Summary. Dewar was born to Scottish parents in Ahmednagar, India, on 24 September 1918. His father was employed in the British government of India, the Indian Civil Service. Michael attended boarding school in England, having won a prestigious scholarship to Winchester College. In 1936, he entered Balliol College at Oxford, where he at first studied the classics. Before long, however, he developed a passion for organic chemistry. He earned a first-class honors undergraduate degree and his doctoral degree, and then stayed at Oxford as a postdoctoral fellow with Sir Robert Robinson in the Dyson Perrins Laboratory. Robinson left an indelible impression on the young chemist and remained his role model for the rest of Dewar's life. It was at Oxford that Michael met Mary Williamson, a historian who later became well recognized as a scholar of English Tudor history. They married in 1944 and had two children, Robert and Steuart.

During the war, Dewar conducted defense research, serving as a temporary colonel. In 1945, Dewar became research director of the physical chemistry laboratory at Courtaulds in Maidenhead, near London. There he wrote *The Electronic Theory of Organic Chemistry*. Published in 1949, the work provided the first treatment of organic chemistry in terms of molecular orbital theory in a fashion accessible to the bench chemist.

In 1951, Dewar accepted a chair at Queen Mary College at the University of London, and he played an essential role in its development into a credible research program. He shocked British university circles when he moved to the University of Chicago in 1959. Soon thereafter, in 1963, he accepted the first Robert A. Welch chair at the University of Texas at Austin. He and his former student Rowland Pettit attracted many international and sabbatical visitors, transforming the university's formerly undistinguished chemistry department into a pilgrimage site for those interested in theoretical chemistry or organic mechanisms. In 1980, along with his wife, he became a U.S. citizen. Dewar was elected to the National Academy of Sciences in 1983. He left Austin in 1989, moving to a half-time appointment at the University of Florida at Gainesville. He retired in 1994 and died in 1997.

Post-War Accomplishments. Dewar had a well-deserved reputation for finding original solutions to intractable problems. In 1945, when he was still a postdoctoral fellow at Oxford, he deduced the correct structure for stipitatic acid, a small organic molecule that had remained an enigma to the best organic chemists of the day. Dewar correctly deduced that it contained a new kind of seven-membered ring, for which he coined the term *tropolone*. He then suggested that another puzzling compound, the alkaloid colchicine, had a similar structure. This, too, turned out to be correct. The discovery of the nonbenzenoid but aromatic tropolone structure gave birth to the field of nonbenzenoid aromaticity, which witnessed feverish activity all over the world for several decades. It made a permanent contribution to the way in which chemists look at cyclic pi-electron systems. Dewar soon became a standard fixture on the international chemistry circuit, featured frequently as plenary lecturer at virtually every important international conference.

Also in 1945, Dewar introduced the concept of a π complex in connection with his studies of the benzidine rearrangement. This notion automatically accounted for the ease of 1,2-shifts in carbocations and their absence in radicals and carbanions and explained the structure of "nonclassical" carbenium ions, which were just beginning to become well-known. Moreover, it offered a correct description of the electronic structure of complexes of transition metals with olefins, which then became known as the Dewar-Chatt-Duncanson model. At Courtaulds, Dewar developed a taste for the utility of models in practical chemistry. He measured the first absolute rate constants in a vinyl polymerization and in an autoxidation, and executed numerous other kinetic and mechanistic studies. In his free time, Dewar developed the concepts described in his first book, *The Electronic Theory of Organic Chemistry* (1949). This work started a revolution in the way in which organic chemists viewed their subject. By 1951, Dewar had developed a semiquantitative version of his theory for the practicing organic chemist who typically knew little or nothing about molecular orbitals. Unfortunately, his decision to publish it as a series of mathematical theorems in six back-to-back articles in the *Journal of the American Chemical Society* resulted in a wide appreciation of his erudition but little comprehension by the average organic chemist of the time. As a result, this approach, called "perturbational molecular orbital theory," never became the everyday tool for practicing organic chemistry that it was designed to be. Even though the theory is clearly superior to the purely qualitative resonance structure theory, the latter remains more popular. Dewar was therefore regarded as a chemical genius whose

Michael Dewar. *Michael Dewar in the laboratory.* © BETTMANN/CORBIS.

contributions, like Einstein's, were considered to be understandable to only a focused group of active theorists.

Queen Mary College Tenure. At Queen Mary College, Dewar continued his highly original work on the theory of organic chemistry. He tended to start controversies by adopting unorthodox and sometimes extreme views, for instance when he denied the existence of hyperconjugation. His work served to correct the simplistic descriptions accepted by many at the time and ultimately led to formulation of the more sophisticated pictures that are accepted in the early twenty-first century. In some cases, his strikingly novel views were ultimately recognized as literally correct, for instance his insistence that the classical inductive effect is insignificant and is best replaced by direct field effects, an insight that was based on his new experimental results.

Dewar's experimental program was also extensive. His research group performed the first quantitative evaluation of reactivity in aromatic substitution, designed to test the semiquantitative perturbation molecular orbital theory he developed. Dewar solved the electronic structure of phosphononitrile chlorides, developed and characterized borazaro-aromatic compounds, examined the structure and properties of liquid crystals, and pioneered the now highly popular studies of self-assembled monolayers of thiols on a metal surface. He built an electron paramagnetic resonance spectrometer for use in his research, at a time when it was just beginning to be recognized as useful in chemistry.

Chicago Interim. Dewar soon found the administrative duties associated with the chairing of a modern research-focused department burdensome. He solved the problem by giving up his chair at Queen Mary College and moving to the University of Chicago as a professor. Michael and Mary were already familiar with the United States from their 1957 half-year visit to Yale, which included an automobile trip around the country. During this visit they had met many American scientists, establishing many lasting friendships and collaborations. They were delighted with the country and with the spirit of its scientists, and were exuberant in their praise. Although he was elected a fellow of the Royal Society in 1960, Michael was adamant about remaining in the United States. Nevertheless, the Dewars spent each summer in England.

At Chicago, Dewar added new projects. He showed that charge transfer only makes a minor contribution to the stability of charge-transfer complexes, contrary to the general belief at the time. Most importantly, he created the field for which he is most likely best known: the development of increasingly sophisticated semi-empirical molecular orbital methods for organic chemistry. For this, he needed much more computer time than he could easily obtain at the University of Chicago, and this prompted his move to the University of Texas at Austin, with which his name is most strongly associated.

University of Texas: Career Peak. In Austin, his interests widened further. His experimental work now ranged from carbenium ions, semiconductors, and liquid crystals to nuclear quadrupole resonance and photoelectron spectroscopy; gradually, however, the attractions of sophisticated and highly useful applications of molecular orbital theory proved irresistible. A steady stream of world-renowned chemists found their way to Austin to engage Dewar's insight to solve their own scientific problems. Ultimately, Dewar moved away from experiments to focus entirely on the improvement of semi-empirical molecular orbital methods. Although structure and many molecular properties were treated, his primary interest always was chemical reactivity, and he devoted most of his efforts to

characterizing the structure and energetics of transition states of organic reactions.

Dewar has contributed much to current understanding of pericyclic reactions, hydrogen bonding, and sigma conjugation. Because the semi-empirical methods were computationally less demanding than the alternative ab initio methods, he was able to explore more realistic reaction models and to perform full geometrical optimizations of equilibrium and transition state geometries for large molecules well before others could do so. Toward the end of his active career, Dewar explored increasingly more complex phenomena, such as superconductivity, the structure of organometallics, and biological reactivity in enzymes and carbohydrates.

In the early twenty-first century, continued advances in computer technology and computer codes permitted ab initio calculations for large molecules at a level of sophistication that is far beyond anything that was available when Dewar developed his semi-empirical methods. Although this development rendered many applications of his semi-empirical approach obsolete, his models remained in use for very large molecules and for rapid preliminary scans. The power of modern computers permitted the development of a whole new family of semi-empirical methods based on density functional theory. One can easily imagine that if he had lived into the early 2000s, Dewar would have relished participating in the development of this current generation of parameterized methods, which have penetrated into all areas of chemistry, including nanoscience and molecular biology.

Teaching Methods. Dewar was also the quintessential teacher, cajoling and mentoring his students to maximize their growth as chemists. He insisted that they always stretch their goals to allow for understanding at the highest possible level. Few things pleased him more than the sudden look of understanding on the face of a previously unconvinced student. Although he was an exceedingly gentle man, he did not shy away from delivering necessary messages that his students and colleagues might not have wanted to hear, always in a spirit of inducing improvement. As a result, many of his students occupy important positions in the field.

Dewar was a formidable and witty debater who reveled in controversy and enjoyed nothing more than a good verbal match. He enjoyed expressing himself candidly, sometimes shocking others with his surprising ideas on all possible subjects. For example, he was known to declare with conviction that everyone ought to study Latin at an early age. He would give three reasons: (i) Latin is complex enough to teach children how to reason through intricate problems; (ii) because they tend to hate Latin, children learn at an early age how to cope with adversity;

and (iii) in almost all cases Latin will be totally useless for them later, so it does not matter if they develop great aversion to it and fail to learn it. Another example is his rationale for breaking the speed limit while driving. He argued that accidents only occur when cars are moving on the road, never in the garage, and that it was best to minimize the time spent on the former activity and maximize the time spent on the latter. There were many others, presented with a disarming twinkle in his eye and a tongue in cheek.

Other Interests. Dewar's wide interests in chemistry were matched by an even wider range of outside interests, from astronomy and geology to Asian cooking. In his youth, Dewar was an avid outdoorsman, but he had to give up rock climbing after a back injury. In his later years, his physical exercise consisted primarily of carrying large pitchers of Manhattans and martinis at the legendary parties the Dewars loved to give.

Dewar's outspokenness pervaded all of his life and assured him a steady supply of adversaries. In his later years at Austin, he found it increasingly difficult to deal with the University of Texas's overwhelming red tape. He finally decided to join the Quantum Theory Project at the University of Florida in Gainesville. Unfortunately, the disruption associated with this move preempted the completion of what might have been some of his finest work. The tragedy of Mary's premature death by lung cancer—after her lifelong opposition to smoking—left him devastated. Some of the difficulty of this period is reflected in his memoirs, published by the American Chemical Society, "A Semi-Empirical Life," which provides an uncharacteristically embittered and convoluted picture of a truly great man, who had been a warm and happy person.

Titles and Awards. Dewar's professional recognition started early with his scholarships to Winchester and Balliol. He became a Gibbs Scholar in his second year at Oxford, the youngest ever. He received his first major award from the Chemical Society in 1954, in recognition of the influence of *The Electronic Theory of Organic Chemistry* and of the stunning 1952 series of articles in the *Journal of the American Chemical Society* that outlined the perturbational molecular orbital theory of organic chemistry. He was elected a Fellow of the American Academy of Arts and Sciences in 1966, and a member of the National Academy of Sciences soon after accepting U.S. citizenship. He was also elected to the Royal Society of Chemistry at age forty-two and was named an honorary Fellow of Balliol College (Oxford) and of Queen Mary and Westfield College (University of London).

Despite his distaste for flying, Dewar accepted thirty-two named lectureships and visiting professorships around the world and served as a stimulating consultant to industry both in the United States and abroad. His list of professional society awards serves as a nearly complete list of those available to organic chemists at the time:

Tilden Medal of the Chemical Society (1954)

Harrison Howe Award of the American Chemical Society (1961)

Robert Robinson Medal, Chemical Society (1974)

G. W. Wheland Medal of the University of Chicago (first recipient, 1976)

Evans Award, Ohio State University (1977)

Southwest Regional Award of the American Chemical Society (1978)

Davy Medal, Royal Society of London (1982)

James Flack Norris Award of the American Chemical Society (1984)

William H. Nichols Award of the American Chemical Society (1986)

Auburn–G. M. Kosolapoff Award of the American Chemical Society (1988)

Tetrahedron Prize for Creativity in Organic Chemistry (1989)

World Association of Theoretical Organic Chemists MedalChemical Pioneer Award, American Institute of Chemists (1990)

American Chemical Society Award for Computers in Chemistry (1994)

As a recipient of the Davy Medal, he is one of only six Americans to have been so selected. Dewar was especially proud of the achievements of his more than fifty doctoral students and sixty postdoctoral fellows, whose names are given in the more than six hundred referenced scientific papers and eight books that Dewar published.

BIBLIOGRAPHY

WORKS BY DEWAR

The Electronic Theory of Organic Chemistry. Oxford: Clarendon, 1949.

"A Review of the π-Complex Theory." *Bulletin of the Chemical Society* 18 (1951): C71–C79.

"A Molecular Orbital Theory of Organic Chemistry. I. General Principles." *Journal of the American Chemical Society* 74 (1952): 3341–3345.

With H. N. Schmeising. "A Re-Evaluation of Conjugation and Hyperconjugation: The Effects of Changes in Hybridization of Carbon Bonds." *Tetrahedron* 5 (1959): 166.

With Patrick J. Grisdale. "Substituent Effects. IV. A Quantitative Theory." *Journal of the American Chemical Society* 84 (1962): 3548–3553.

With Alice L. H. Chung. "Ground States of Conjugated Molecules. I. Semi-Empirical SCF MO Treatment and Its Application to Aromatic Hydrocarbons." *Journal of Chemical Physics* 42 (1965): 756–766.

With N. C. Baird. "Ground States of Sigma-Bonded Molecules. IV. The MINDO Method and Its Application to Hydrocarbons." *Journal of Chemical Physics* 50 (1969): 1262.

With Edwin Haselbach. "Ground States of Sigma-Bonded Molecules. IX. The MINDO/2 Method." *Journal of the American Chemical Society* 92 (1970): 590.

With W. Thiel. "Ground States of Molecules. 38. The MNDO Method. Approximations and Parameters." *Journal of the American Chemical Society* 99 (1977): 4899–4907.

With E. G. Zoebisch, E. F. Healy, and J. J. P. Stewart. "AM-1: A New General Purpose Quantum Mechanical Molecular Model." *Journal of the American Chemical Society* 107 (1985): 3902–3909.

"The Semi-Empirical Approach to Chemistry." *International Journal of Quantum Chemistry* 44 (1992): 427–447.

OTHER SOURCES

Michl, Josef, and Marye Anne Fox. "Michael J. S. Dewar." *National Academy of Sciences Biographical Memoirs*. Vol. 77 (1999): 64–77. Washington, DC: National Academy Press.

Josef Michl
Marye Anne Fox

DICKE, ROBERT HENRY (*b.* St. Louis, Missouri, 6 May 1916; *d.* Princeton, New Jersey, 4 March 1997), *cosmology, gravity physics, quantum optics.*

Dicke contributed to central developments in modern physics, including quantum optics, the precision tests of gravity physics, and the observational establishment of the big bang cosmology. Space is filled with a smooth sea of radiation that had relaxed to thermal equilibrium when our expanding universe was far denser and hotter than it is now. As part of war research in the 1940s, Dicke invented main parts of the technology for detection of this radiation. In 1964 he proposed the search that led to its identification. The precision measurements of this fossil are an essential basis for the richly developed evidence that the universe is evolving and that the evolution is well described by the physics of general relativity theory. Commencing in the 1950s Dicke pioneered the renaissance of interest in research in the physics of gravity. At that time scholars had an elegant theory, general relativity, but few tests and little research aimed at improving the situation. He led the program of experiments that now give a well-checked understanding of gravity in terms of space-time structure. His work on quantum optics in the 1940s and 1950s included the demonstration that collisions of radiating atoms with an inert "buffering" gas can suppress the

Doppler effect—the tendency of motions of radiating bodies to shift the radiation to the blue or red—thus producing more sharply defined frequency standards. Dicke's analysis of the quantum mechanics of radiation by a system of particles includes the prediction of rapidly emitting "superradiant" states. He held fifty patents, on subjects from clothes dryers to lasers. The company he cofounded, Princeton Applied Research, packaged his advances in phase-sensitive detection in the now-ubiquitous "lock-in amplifier."

Great scientists can leave problems as well as solutions. Dicke passed on an example from the generation before him: Discover whether or how physics in the laboratory depends on the rest of the universe. At the end of the nineteenth century Ernst Mach argued for such a relation, that inertial motion is determined by the motion of all the matter in the universe. This was one of Albert Einstein's guides to general relativity theory, and it led him to propose the basis for modern cosmology: The observable universe is close to homogeneous. (Imagine a thought experiment: In an island universe a particle could escape and move arbitrarily far into asymptotically flat space-time, where in general relativity theory the particle would be predicted to have all normal physical properties, including inertia, but no other matter nearby to give significance to inertial motion. Einstein disliked this possibility. And it is now known that the universe indeed has no observable edge).

General relativity theory predicts that the rotation of the Earth "drags" a locally nonrotating telescope relative to the distant stars, as Mach might have expected, but the theory predicts that measurements that are confined to a small laboratory are quite unaffected by external conditions. Dicke suspected that there is more than this, that the unity of physics suggests the behavior of the universe affects physics in the laboratory. He termed this concept Mach's principle. (The name has been applied to many ideas; here it is taken to signify what Dicke had in mind.) Dicke's searches for manifestations of Mach's principle, in situations ranging from the laboratory to the expanding universe, yielded nothing convincing. But a century after Mach, superstring theory was again leading people to seek this aspect of unity that so fascinated Dicke.

The Radiation Laboratory and the Dicke Radiometer. In 1941, after completion of graduate work in physics at the University of Rochester, Dicke followed one of his professors, Lee Alvin DuBridge, to war research at the Radiation Laboratory at the Massachusetts Institute of Technology. DuBridge was director; Dicke worked on microwave radar (then meaning wavelengths in the range 30 cm to 3 mm), which offered better resolution than earlier generations of radar at longer wavelengths. The results had an important effect on the course of World War II and on advances in technology after the war. Dicke's contributions, notable for his imaginative and effective way of doing physics, are summarized in the book *Principles of Microwave Circuits,* a standard reference for microwave engineering after the war.

Among Dicke's inventions at the Radiation Laboratory is a radiometer capable of detecting microwave radiation produced by a warm body. He took the radiometer to Florida to demonstrate that humid air radiates strongly near 1-centimeter wavelength. The significance for war research was that the strong emission means humid air is a strong absorber, which at the time limited the push to shorter wavelength radar. In 1946 he with colleagues at the Radiation Laboratory published applications of his radiometer to astronomy, showing among other things that the amount of "radiation from cosmic matter" at wavelengths 1 to 1.5 centimeters is less than that equivalent to blackbody radiation at temperature 20 K (Dicke et al., 1946). This is notable for its relation to the theory published two years later by George Gamow, then at the George Washington University, on the physical conditions under which thermonuclear reactions in the early stages of expansion of an initially hot universe would produce an observationally interesting abundance of elements heavier than hydrogen. Gamow's theory required that the early universe was filled with thermal radiation. The radiation would have cooled as the universe expanded, but would still be present. Gamow's student, Ralph Asher Alpher, with Robert Herman, at the Applied Physics Laboratory at Johns Hopkins University, improved the calculation and translated Gamow's condition into the present temperature, about 5 K. That is not much below the upper limit from Dicke's radiometer, and it is close to what is now measured. Dicke made the connection between the theory and the measurement two decades later.

Quantum Optics. After the war Dicke returned to Princeton University, where he had spent two years as an undergraduate. He was appointed Cyrus Fogg Brackett Professor of Physics in 1957 and Albert Einstein Professor of Science in 1975. In his first decade back at Princeton Dicke put aside his interest in astronomy, working instead on quantum optics and techniques of precision measurements of atomic structure. His style is illustrated by his demonstration of what came to be called Dicke buffering (1953).

The Doppler shift of the frequency of a photon emitted by a moving particle can be associated with the change of kinetic energy of the particle due to the recoil from the momentum transferred to the photon. Dicke showed that if inert "buffering" particles confine the motions of the radiating particles to distances smaller than the photon wavelength, the Doppler effect is suppressed and the

Robert Dicke. © UPI/BETTMANN/CORBIS.

momentum recoil is taken up by the system of buffering particles. Dicke and his student Robert Romer (PhD 1955) demonstrated the effect for ammonia molecules confined to a narrow container, and he and another student, James Pleister Wittke (PhD 1955), used the line-narrowing effect in a precision measurement of the frequency of the 21-centimeter radiation produced by atomic hydrogen. The same physics applies to the line-narrowing effect Rudolf Mössbauer discovered in 1958 in the emission and absorption of gamma ray photons by atomic nuclei. Lipkin, in *Quantum Mechanics: New Approaches to Selected Topics,* points out that the physics was already demonstrated in the 1930s, by Bragg scattering of neutrons by a crystal, where the recoil momentum again is taken up by the crystal rather than individual ions. The surprise greeting Dicke's and Mössbauer's results illustrates the difficulty of seeing subtle physics common to very different situations.

Gravity Physics. Dicke turned to the study of gravity while on sabbatical leave at Harvard from 1954 to 1955. He was struck by the scarcity of experimental work in this subject, and he set about improving the situation in an elegant series of experiments, beginning with a repetition of a fundamental measurement made a half century earlier by Roland von Eötvös in Hungary.

Eötvös and colleagues improved the test of the idea that objects with different compositions fall with the same gravitational acceleration. They showed that a broad variety of materials fall with the same acceleration to an accuracy of about three parts in 10^9. Dicke could do better with modern technology: the measurement with younger colleagues at Princeton improved the bound by two orders of magnitude. The advance was impressive, and it is an impressive measure of Eötvös's skill that the improvement was not greater. The experiment added support to Einstein's idea that an observer may "transform away" gravity by falling freely, which of course requires that all matter falls at the same rate. Dicke emphasized that the experiment limits the idea that Einstein's theory might be adjusted to allow the physical properties of matter to depend on the nearby mass distribution, as might be suggested by Mach's principle, for that could make the energy of a test particle vary with position, and the gradient of this energy would be a long range "fifth force" (adding to gravity and the strong, weak, and electromagnetic interactions). This fifth force could not significantly depend on composition, for that would violate the Eötvös-Dicke experiment.

Other examples show the range of Dicke's ideas. His student James Brault (PhD 1962) made the first accurate measurement of the gravitational redshift of light from the Sun. It avoided the Doppler shifts produced by turbulence in the solar atmosphere by the choice of a spectral line that originates high in the solar atmosphere where turbulence is suppressed. The measurement was important because the gravitational redshift is one of the classical tests of general relativity, and at the time it was not well checked.

Another student, Lloyd Kreuzer (PhD 1966), tested the close equivalence of active and passive gravitational masses, which measure how strongly an object gravitationally attracts neighboring matter and how strongly the object is gravitationally attracted to neighboring matter. The measurement avoided gravitational influences outside the experiment by floating a test object in a tank of fluid with different composition but the same density, at neutral buoyancy. That means the passive gravitational mass densities are the same. If the active mass densities were significantly different, then moving the object through the fluid would have produced an observable change in the gravitational field.

Dicke led the idea of placing corner reflectors—that bounce light directly back—on the Moon, for use in precision measurements of its orbit. In 1969 the *Apollo 2* astronauts placed the first array of reflectors. By 2005 Dicke's concept had grown into an array of reflectors on the Moon and on artificial satellites, at distances measured by laser pulse timing to better than one-centimeter accuracy, for applications from gravity physics to continental drift and the Global Positioning System.

Dicke liked concepts as well as experiments. He was taken by the enormous value of the ratio of the electro-

magnetic and gravitational forces of attraction of the proton and electron in a hydrogen atom,

$$\frac{e^2}{Gm_e m_p} = 2 \times 10^{39}$$

and by P. A. M. Dirac's proposal (in 1937) that this might be because the strength of the gravitational interaction (in the denominator) is decreasing as the universe expands. Maybe gravity is weak now because the universe has been expanding for a long time. Dicke took this as a possible example of Mach's principle, with the chance of a test: evolution of the strength of gravity might be detectable in the structures of stars and planets. For example, in the 1960s geologists were finding increasingly persuasive evidence for continental drift. Might continents be drifting because gravity is weakening, allowing the Earth to expand and rearrange its surface?

With a student at Princeton, Carl Brans (PhD 1961), Dicke developed a theory for the evolution of the strength of the gravitational interaction. It assumes a long-range scalar field in addition to the metric tensor of general relativity. They found that their approach was closely related to earlier work by Pascual Jordan at Hamburg University; it is best called the Jordan-Brans-Dicke (JBD) theory. Dicke was largely motivated by his concept of Mach's principle; Jordan emphasized Dirac's proposal. Jordan and Dicke corresponded, and met, but worked separately on tests of JBD. The theory predicts slightly smaller values than general relativity for the gravitational deflection of light by the Sun and the relativistic contribution to the precession of the perihelion of the orbit of Mercury.

When Brans and Dicke published their version of JBD in 1961, measurements of the solar deflection of starlight were quite inadequate for a test. That changed with advances in radio interferometric measurements of the angular positions of distant radio sources passing close to the Sun in the sky, which by 1975 showed that the deflection is within one percent of the general relativity prediction and inconsistent with JBD for parameters Dicke considered reasonable. In 1961 the measured rate of precession of Mercury's orbit—after correction for the effects of the planets—was consistent with general relativity and larger than JBD by 3.3 times the probable error. Brans and Dicke suggested that that could be due to an error in the mass of Venus, but the *Mariner 2* flyby a year later fixed the mass well enough to eliminate that possibility. Not being one to abandon an idea without all due checks, Dicke undertook his last great experiment: measure the shape of the Sun well enough to test for the effect an oblate interior mass distribution could have on the motion of Mercury. The work with several generations of colleagues commenced in 1963 and ended two decades later in the complexities of solar structure. JBD as conceived was ruled out. But interesting ideas are durable: in the years 2000 to 2004 there are some 150 references to the Brans-Dicke paper in the literature of physical science on subjects ranging from superstring cosmology to laboratory tests of gravity physics.

Cosmology. Dicke liked the idea of an expanding universe. He noted that Mach's principle suggests that expansion could drive evolution of local physics, which would be a wonderful thing to discover. The idea has continued to drive research, though by 2005 there was no convincingly established evidence of evolution of the parameters of physics.

Dicke (1961) pointed out that an acceptable home for beings such as humans would have to have an age on the order of 10 billion years, roughly what is observed. It takes about that long for nuclear burning in several generations of stars to produce the heavy elements out of which we are made. Since we depend on the heat from a star, and the rate of formation of stars is now less than the stellar death rate, humans could not have lived in the universe when it grew much older. Dicke informally termed this a simple consistency condition. By the year 2005 some in the physical science community agreed, while others argued that Dicke's consideration is part of an anthropic principle that accounts for the selection of our universe from an ensemble.

Dicke also liked to ask what the universe was doing before it was expanding. That led him to consider that if the universe were oscillating, then during the collapse phase starlight would be blueshifted, and a small fraction of the blueshifted starlight would serve to photodissociate the heavy elements formed in the production of the starlight by nuclear burning in stars, returning a fresh supply of hydrogen after the bounce. If the rest of the starlight survived the bounce it would be a thermal sea of radiation. That is, an oscillating universe could be irreversible in the sense that it produces entropy near the bounce, mainly in the form of a sea of blackbody radiation. If so the universe cannot have been bouncing forever, so Dicke's question just changes to what the universe was doing before it was bouncing, but he was willing to accept the change as a modest advance. In 1964 Dicke persuaded two young members of his group, Peter Roll and David Wilkinson, to build a Dicke radiometer to look for the radiation, and he suggested that Jim Peebles think about the theoretical consequences of the detection or nondetection of the radiation. That had a lasting effect on all three, though most particularly Wilkinson and Peebles, who devoted much of their careers to measurements of the radiation and analyses of the significance of its properties. By 2005 these programs had grown into a rich physical science.

The story of the discovery and validation of the interpretation of the radiation has been told elsewhere and may be briefly summarized here. In 1965 news of the Roll-Wilkinson experiment in progress reached Arno Allan Penzias and Robert Woodrow Wilson at the Bell Laboratories in Holmdel, New Jersey, not far from Princeton. They saw that Dicke's idea might solve a problem they encountered in a search for diffuse microwave radiation from the halo of our Milky Way galaxy. They used an instrument that was built for satellite communications experiments. It had capabilities similar to the Princeton experiment, and it indicated more noise than expected from sources within the instrument. Their improvements to the receiver did not remove the excess noise. They knew that the noise was not likely to be from the galaxy because the noise was isotropic, while the solar system is near the edge of its galaxy of stars. Penzias and Wilson did the right thing—they built well and took great care in exploring possible instrumental explanations of an unexpected result—and were awarded the Nobel Prize in 1978 for the detection of this radiation.

This fossil radiation is distinguished by its thermal—blackbody—spectrum. Radiation emitted in the universe as it is now cannot relax to this state because space is optically thin, which scientists know because objects at cosmologically large distances are observed at microwave wavelengths. The fossil radiation, which would have relaxed to a thermal spectrum in the dense, optically thick, early universe, is perturbed at recent times by out-of-equilibrium matter, but the effect is slight because the heat capacity of the radiation is much larger than that of the matter. The Penzias and Wilson measurement at 7-centimeter wavelength fixed the temperature of the radiation, if thermal, within the uncertainty of their measurement. The Roll and Wilkinson experiment showed that the intensity at 3.2 centimeters is consistent with a thermal spectrum. Wilkinson led many of the experiments that by 1970 showed consistency with the long wavelength Rayleigh-Jeans part of the spectrum and the 1990 satellite measurement that demonstrated close agreement with the full blackbody form. Herb Gush led an experiment at the University of British Columbia that, also in 1990, independently demonstrated this beautiful result: space is filled with thermal radiation left from the early stages of expansion of the universe.

Why did the discovery of this fossil radiation take so long? One may also ask, why were people surprised by the physics of Bragg scattering when applied to Dicke's microwave photons or Mössbauer's gamma ray photons? It is because scientists tend to narrow the field of view to see more deeply. The discovery of the fossil radiation certainly was aided by Dicke's knowledge of microwave physics—he had invented key elements—and of cosmology—he had given considerable thought to its possible relation to the rest of physics. It also helped that Dicke liked fresh ideas, even if speculative, provided they appealed to his sense of physics and they suggested experimental tests. In science one cannot spend all one's time exploring the roads less traveled: In the chaos how could scientists marshal the tight webs of evidence that show the true roads? But they can follow Dicke by pausing on occasion to consider what they are doing.

BIBLIOGRAPHY

No complete compilation of Dicke's papers exists. The *Theoretical Significance of Experimental Relativity (1964) includes the papers on gravity physics that Dicke considered most important. A partially comprehensive bibliography of his publications is available from the Smithsonian/NASA Astrophysics Data System Database, available online from http://adsabs.harvard.edu/abstract_service.html.*

WORKS BY DICKE

With Carol G. Montgomery and Edward M. Purcell, eds. *Principles of Microwave Circuits.* New York: McGraw-Hill, 1948. A standard reference for microwave engineering after World War II.

With R. Beringer, R. L. Kyhl, and A. B. Vane. "Atmospheric Absorption Measurements with a Microwave Radiometer." *Physical Review,* series 2, 70 (1946): 340-348. The demonstration that "there is very little (<20 K) radiation from cosmic matter" at microwave wavelengths.

"The Effect of Collisions upon the Doppler Width of Spectral Lines." *Physical Review,* series 2, 89 (1953): 472-473. Dicke buffering.

"Coherence in Spontaneous Radiation Processes." *Physical Review,* series 2, 93 (1954): 99-100. Dicke superradiance.

With R. H. Homer. "New Technique for High-Resolution Microwave Spectroscopy." *Physical Review,* series 2, 99 (1955): 532-536. The first experimental demonstration of Dicke buffering.

With James P. Wittke. "Redetermination of the Hyperfine Splitting in the Ground State of Atomic Hydrogen." *Physical Review,* series 2, 103 (1956): 620-631. The first application of Dicke buffering in a precision measurement.

With W. F. Hoffmann and R. Krotkov. "Precision Optical Tracking of Artificial Satellites." *I.R.E. Transactions on Military Electronics* 4 (1960) 28-37. Explores the possibility of testing gravity physics by tracking earth satellites.

"Dirac's Cosmology and Mach's Principle." *Nature* 192 (4 November 1961): 440-441.

With P. G. Roll and R. Krotkov. "The Equivalence of Inertial and Passive Gravitational Mass." *Annals of Physics* 26 (1964): 442-517. Dicke's version of the classic Eotvos experiment.

The Theoretical Significance of Experimental Relativity. New York: Gordon and Breach, 1964. In this work and the next, Dicke summarizes his assessments of gravity physics and cosmology.

Gravitation and the Universe. Memoirs of the American Philosophical Society, vol. 78. Philadelphia: American Philosophical Society, 1970.

With J. G. Williams, P. L. Bender, C. O. Alley, et al. "New Test of the Equivalence Principle from Lunar Laser Ranging." *Physical Review Letters* 36 (1976): 551-554. An example of the continuing tests of gravity physics.

OTHER SOURCES

Happer, W., and P. J. E. Peebles. "Robert Henry Dicke: 6 May 1916-4 March 1997." Biographical Memoirs. *Proceedings of the American Philosophical Society* 150, no. 1 (March 2006): 181-186.

———, P. J. E. Peebles, and D. T. Wilkinson. "Robert Henry Dicke: May 6, 1916—March 4, 1997." In *Biographical Memoirs,* vol. 77. Washington, DC: National Academy of Sciences, 1999. Also available from www.nap.edu/html/biomems/.

Kragh, Helge. *Cosmology and Controversy.* Princeton, NJ: Princeton University Press, 1996. A broad view of the history.

Lipkin, Harry J. *Quantum Mechanics: New Approaches to Selected Topics.* New York, American Elsevier Pub. Co., 1973.

Wilkinson, D. T., and P. J. E. Peebles. "Discovery of the Cosmic Microwave Background." *Physica Scripta* T85 (2000): 136-141. The history of the discovery of the thermal cosmic background radiation, from the Princeton viewpoint.

P. J. E. Peebles

DIDYMUS (*fl.* second half of the first century CE), *musical theory.*

A musical theorist and grammarian, Didymus was author of a treatise called *On the Difference between the Aristoxenians and the Pythagoreans* (of which only few fragments survive, quoted by Porphyry of Tyre), and perhaps of a work *On Pythagorean Philosophy* mentioned by Clement of Alexandria. He is famous above all for his intervallic divisions of the Greek musical scale recorded by Ptolemy in his *Harmonics,* where he is called "the musician." His biographical data are uncertain, but he seems to inclined to the Pythagorean musical tradition.

Despite his possible connections with some Alexandrian scholars (he is said to have been son of a certain Heraclides, perhaps the Heraclides Ponticus the Younger who studied in Alexandria), Didymus is almost certainly to be distinguished from the famous Didymus nicknamed *Chalkenteros* (Brazen-guts) for his indefatigable industry with regards to books, who lived in the first century BCE. It seems more probable that he was the one said by the Byzantine encyclopedia *Suda* (s.v. Didymus) to have lived in the time of Nero and to have been a grammarian and good musician, with a talent for singing.

Both Ptolemy and his commentator Porphyry quote his activity as musical theorist, the former with regard to some improvements tentatively introduced by him in the monochord (the Pythagorean device for measuring intervals between notes expressing them as mathematical ratios) and concerning the numbers that make up the division of the octave; the latter in a section that discusses the different schools of harmonic theory and their methodologies, and as the source—together with Archytas—for a passage that comments on Pythagoreans' mistakes in computing musical concords (*symphoniai*). Furthermore, see the reference to a certain Didymus who described the rhythm (*rhythmos*) as "a configuration (*schematismos*) of a particular sound" in Bacchius's *Introduction to the Art of Music* (p. 313, 9 f. Jan), which may reasonably allude to the same person.

Despite his criticism, Ptolemy's recording of Didymus's scalar divisions beside those of more famous musical theorists—such as Archytas, Aristoxenus of Tarentum, and Eratosthenes—shows that his work in harmonics (the science of the elements out of which melody is built) was regarded as something of considerable importance in antiquity. According to Ptolemy, Didymus failed to mathematically identify the intervals that make up the octave because he relied on the misleading help of the monochord, whose difficulties in making more accurate measurements were not solved by his correction (*diorthosis*) "in that he concentrated solely on making the bridge easier to manipulate, being unable to find any cure for the other more numerous and more serious defects" (Didymus, trans. Barker, 1989, p. 342). His procedure was the positioning of the bridge so that the opposite sides of the string could produce usable sounds. But this system, though helpful for demonstrating basic Pythagorean ratios (as the double, corresponding to the octave, the hemiolic, corresponding to the fifth, and the triple ratios, corresponding to the octave and a fifth) did not allow him to construct exactly the mathematical proportions of smaller intervals in the tetrachord (the basic scalar system of ancient Greek music, which spans a fourth). According to Ptolemy's judgment, his divisions of the diatonic, chromatic, and enharmonic tetrachords (the three main genera of tetrachordal divisions) were calculated without considering beforehand the way in which they were used in practice (*chresis*), the only thing that makes it possible for them to be brought into conformity with the impressions of perception (*aisthesis*).

In Porphyry's *Commentary on the Harmonics of Ptolemy*, Didymus is mentioned in the section that compares the various schools of harmonic theory by reference to the status assigned by each to perception (*aisthesis*) and reason (*logos*), together with Ptolemais of Cyrene. In his treatise, titled *On the Difference between the Aristoxenians and the Pythagoreans* (which was probably Porphyry's source for the quotations of Ptolemais's fragments), Didymus distinguished at least three main approaches to the

theoretical musical inquiry. At one extreme are those who concentrated on perception alone, ignoring reason completely; on the other extreme those who esteemed reason as the highest judge, the Pythagoreans, attending to perception only to the extent that it suffices to give them a starting point for further theoretical investigations. Between these two extremes there is Aristoxenus, who gave an equal importance to both principles.

The empiricists were called by Didymus instrumentalists (*organikoi*) and vocal trainers (*phonaskikoi*), names that suggest that they were practical musicians who only occasionally devoted themselves to theory, depicted as people who offered no demonstration and no coherent theory on this topic. Their description is similar to some others offered by more ancient sources, such as Plato *Republic* book seven (530c–531c), where these theorists were characterized as "those worthy persons who bully the strings and interrogate them with torture" (Didymus, trans. Barker, 1989, p. 56), and the Hibeh Papyrus on music (1.13), in which they claim the theoretical branch to be their own special business although they spent their entire life on strings. As a matter of fact, these pieces of evidence suggest a quite old and lasting empirical tradition in the theoretical inquiry on music, which is still echoed in Didymus's treatise. The Pythagoreans, instead, though deriving the catalyst of their investigation from perceptibles, constructed their theorems through reason on its own, dismissing perception when it bears witness against their conclusions.

Between these two approaches, as in Ptolemais's fragments, is Aristoxenus, who treated both principles, perception and reason, as having equal power. According to him, these criteria have to be as accurate as possible, because "music … is perceptual (*aistheton*) and rational (*logikon*) at the same time" (Didymus, second extract, trans. Barker, 1989, p. 244). It has to be noticed that the description of the Aristoxenian procedure in Didymus's fragments finds several echoes in what survives of genuine Aristoxenian works.

Furthermore, among those theorists whose approach to harmonics was based more on reason than perception, Didymus quoted Archestratos, who is mentioned also by Philodemus (first century BCE) as a devotee of musical theory who regarded the nature of sounds, notes, and intervals as philosophical aspects of music.

BIBLIOGRAPHY

WORKS BY DIDYMUS

Porphyrios kommentar zur Harmonielehre des Ptolemaios. Edited by Ingemar Düring. Göteborg, Sweden: Elanders, 1932. Reprint, New York: Garland, 1980. This is the most recent critical edition of Porphyry's Greek text that includes Didymus's fragments.

Greek Musical Writings. Vol. 2: *Harmonic and Acoustic Theory.* Edited by Andrew Barker. Cambridge, U.K.: Cambridge University Press, 1989. It includes the English translation of Didymus's fragments.

OTHER SOURCES

Barker, Andrew. "Greek Musicologists in the Roman Empire." In *The Sciences in Greco-Roman Society,* edited by Timothy D. Barnes, 53–74. Edmonton, Canada: Academic Printing and Publishing, 1994.

———. "Didymus [3]." In *The Oxford Classical Dictionary,* edited by Simon Hornblower and Antony Spawforth. Oxford: Oxford University Press, 1996.

Cohn, Leopold. "Didymus [11]." *Real-Enzyklopädie der klassischen Altertumswissenschaft* 5, no. 1 (1903): 473–474.

Düring, Ingemar. *Die Harmonielehre des Klaudios Ptolemaios.* Göteborg, Sweden: Elanders, 1930. Reprint, New York: Garland, 1980.

———. *Ptolemaios uns Porphyrios über die Musik.* Göteborg, Sweden: Elanders, 1934. Reprint, New York: Garland, 1980.

Jan, Karl von. *Musici Scriptores Graeci. Aristoteles, Euclides, Nicomachus, Bacchius, Gaudentius, Alypius et melodiarum veterum quidquid exstat.* Leipzig, Germany: Teubner, 1895. Reprint, Hildesheim, Germany: G. Olms, 1962.

Zaminer, Frieder. "Didymus [1] von Alexandreia B. Musiktheorie." In *Der Neue Pauly: Enzyklopadie der Antike* 3, edited by von Hubert Cancik and Helmet Schneider. Stuttgart, Germany: Metzler, 1997.

Eleonora Rocconi

DIETZ, ROBERT SINCLAIR (*b.* Westfield, New Jersey, 14 September 1914; *d.* Tempe, Arizona, 19 May 1995), *marine geology and geomorphology, plate tectonics, planetary science.*

Widely known for pioneering contributions to the geology of the seafloor and to geological aspects of the theory of plate tectonics, Dietz also made important scientific contributions to the recognition of impact structures, particularly of ancient, eroded impact scars on Earth, which he named *astroblemes* (star wounds). He also contributed to and used new methods of seafloor exploration, including scuba and bathyscaph. Dietz published prolifically in scientific and popular scientific journals and was both a synthesizer of key research and a generator of controversial speculation.

Early Life. Robert Sinclair Dietz was the second youngest of seven children (the eldest a girl, then six boys); his father Louis was a civil engineer and his mother Bertha a devout Christian Scientist. Dietz reminisced that by high school he had rejected all religion, developed a serious interest in science, and become an ardent amateur naturalist and rock hound; his interest in astronomy, and especially the Moon, commenced at this time. Dietz's mother died when he was in high school, and his father died a few years later.

In 1933, Dietz hitchhiked west from New Jersey to the University of Illinois, attracted by the Chicago World's Fair and cheap tuition. Dietz intended to major in geology and to pursue his interests in astronomy at Illinois, although its astronomy department was weak at the time. He took the two available astronomy classes and studied every lunar photograph he could obtain. Dietz decided that lunar craters must be formed by meteorite impact and submitted a PhD proposal to study craters on the Earth and Moon. His professors, however, turned it down, steering Dietz instead toward marine geology.

On the Illinois geology faculty was a first-generation marine geologist, Francis Parker Shepard, who conducted research in the summer at the Scripps Institution of Oceanography in La Jolla, California. Dietz befriended fellow student K. O. (Kenneth Orris) Emery, and together they were Shepard's first two graduate students, both going on to prominent careers. For his MS degree (1938), Dietz studied phosphorite deposits off the coast of southern California, and for his PhD (1941) degree he examined deep-sea clays. Dietz spent a good portion of his graduate student years at Scripps and some time at the Smithsonian Institution in Washington, DC, as well.

Career. Once graduated from Illinois with his PhD, Dietz returned to Scripps and applied for work with the navy-sponsored Division of War Research in San Diego. However, he had enrolled in the ROTC at Illinois and was already a first lieutenant in the U.S. Army Reserve, so the navy would not hire him. Instead, in August 1941, he was called to active duty as a ground officer in the U.S. Army Air Corps. After Pearl Harbor, he applied for and went through flight training, serving thereafter as an instructor in Hondo, Texas, for about eighteen months and then transferring to a photographic mapping squadron. Most of his photo-mapping work was in South America, where he was fascinated with aerial views of Earth.

During the 1940s, Dietz worked on papers interpreting lunar craters and certain ancient circular structures on Earth as impact features. While based in Texas, Dietz flew repeated proficiency and recreational flights to Meteor Crater, a 183-meter (six-hundred-foot) deep depression in Arizona, which helped convince him that meteor craters existed on Earth. Contradicting the prevailing "cryptovolcanic" hypothesis for the origin of certain ancient circular structures on Earth, Dietz called them "cryptoexplosion" structures and used shatter cones as critical evidence for impact.

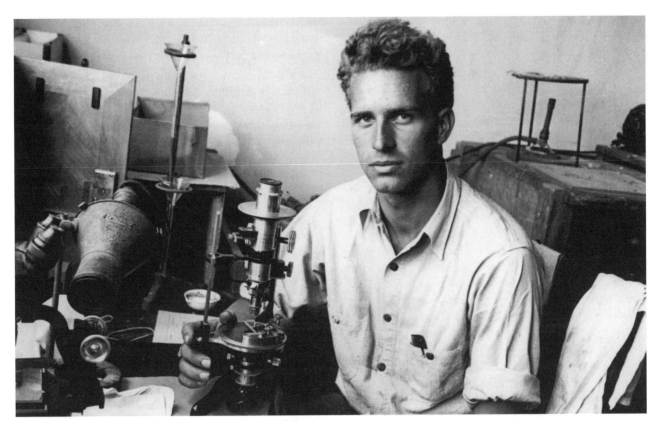

Robert S. Dietz. *Dietz at the Scripps Institution of Oceanography in 1938.* ARCHIVES AT SCRIPPS INSTITUTION OF OCEANOGRAPHY, UC SAN DIEGO.

From the late 1930s through the 1950s, most of Dietz's publications and reports focused on aspects of marine geology and technology. In 1946, Dietz joined the U.S. Navy Electronics Laboratory (NEL) in San Diego as a civilian scientist, becoming head of the Sea-Floor Studies Section; Henry W. Menard, hired in 1949 by this group, chronicled some of its history in his memoir, *The Ocean of Truth* (1986). Dietz worked with a wide range of marine geologists during this postwar exploratory oceanographic era, including a cast of leading oceanographers at NEL and Scripps.

Dietz's first assignment at NEL was to lead the oceanographic research effort of Admiral Richard E. Byrd's fourth and last Antarctic expedition, Operation Highjump, in 1946 and 1947. Dietz also co-led the Mid-Pacific (MidPac) expedition, sponsored by the navy and the Scripps Institution in 1950. Always looking for better ways to study the ocean floor, in 1952 he authorized the first U.S. purchase of "aqua-lungs," invented by Jacques-Yves Cousteau and Emile Gagnan in France. NEL researchers and colleagues from Scripps then made the first offshore geological map of the seafloor using scuba gear. In 1953, Dietz was a Fulbright Fellow at the University of Tokyo, which inspired him to name the chain of

mountains he mapped in the northern mid-Pacific after Japanese emperors—the Emperor Seamounts.

From 1954 to 1958, Dietz was assigned to the U.S. Office of Naval Research (ONR) in London as scientific liaison conducting overt scientific intelligence in western Europe, covering all earth sciences. During the London years Dietz began collaborating with Swiss engineer Jacques Piccard in developing the bathyscaphe *Trieste* for ultra-deep-sea diving. The collaboration culminated in 1960, when the *Trieste* dived seven miles, an experience described in their popular and widely translated book, *Seven Miles Down* (1961). During his London assignment, Dietz's writing consisted primarily of technical reports on scientific meetings and on the status of science in various countries.

While in London, Dietz kept up with science in the United States and had a keen interest in developments regarding interpretation of continents and ocean basins and of the nature and topography of the seafloor. By 1958, at a meeting in France on the topography and geology of the deep sea, Dietz was entertaining the possibility of continental drift, was aware of accumulating evidence (some of which he had helped collect) that the seafloor was relatively young, and was cognizant of detailed descriptions of seafloor topography. Thus it should not be surprising that he and Harry Hammond Hess independently arrived at the idea of *seafloor spreading* (Dietz's term) in the early 1960s.

Dietz returned in 1959 to the Navy Electronics Laboratory in San Diego, moved in 1963 to the U.S. Coast and Geodetic Survey in Washington, DC, and through a series of bureaucratic reorganizations ended his government service at the National Oceanic and Atmospheric Administration (NOAA) in Miami. Dietz formed a team of marine scientists at NOAA similar to the seafloor studies group at NEL. He also held several visiting professorship positions in the 1970s as he became disenchanted with his government position; Dietz felt that the "o" in NOAA was receiving less attention than the "a" and that his agency's efforts in geology and geophysics were minimal. In 1977, he retired from government service and moved permanently to Arizona State University at Tempe, where he was professor of geology and then emeritus professor, remaining active until his death. Especially during his later years, he became deeply involved in the creation-evolution debate.

Scientific Contributions. Dietz made major contributions in three general areas of Earth and planetary sciences: marine geology and geomorphology; continental drift and plate tectonics; and planetary geology, particularly the study of impact structures. He traveled widely in the United States and around the world, was a keen observer, and had a gift for finding adventure. He was an independent and broad thinker who relished the discussion of ideas and who commonly recognized the significance of new concepts before their originators.

One of the first professional marine geologists, Dietz made significant contributions in mapping and interpreting the sea floor, particularly of the North Pacific and the Arctic basins, as well as the Hawaiian swell. He recognized the importance of diving technology, and with colleagues at Scripps and NEL, he helped map submarine fans (fan-shaped deposits at the mouths of submarine canyons) off California and contributed to early recognition of the significance of submarine canyons and turbidity currents. Dietz published important analyses of the geomorphic evolution of continental margins, and he later considered the geologic architecture of these margins.

As early as 1953, Dietz was thinking about how the Hawaiian chain of islands and seamounts might be moving on a "conveyor belt." By 1958, he was entertaining ideas about continental drift, and in 1961, he published his pioneering concept of seafloor spreading, independently proposed by Hess. Dietz went on to analyze the long-term evolution of continents, especially of their boundaries with the ocean. With student and illustrator John C. Holden, he published several influential and widely cited papers on geological aspects of plate tectonics, the most famous being their geological reconstruction of the ancient supercontinent of Pangea.

From his days as a student, Dietz thought of Earth in a planetary sense and commonly compared Earth with its Moon, speculating on why they looked so different when they should have had a shared history. An early proponent of the idea that the Moon's craters were impact-generated rather than volcanic, Dietz expected such craters to have been formed also on Earth. However, he noted, Earth is geologically active and has an ocean and atmosphere, so these craters would have been eroded, deformed, and recycled. Certain ancient circular structures on Earth had characteristics that Dietz, along with a few other renegades, assigned to impact rather than volcanism. In this field, he is best known for having interpreted the Sudbury structure in Canada as a deformed and eroded impact structure.

Earth scientists and historians of science have noted that the second half of the twentieth century featured two major conceptual shifts in Earth sciences. The better known is the plate tectonics revolution, in which Dietz played a significant role. The second is the birth of planetary geology—the shift in viewing the Earth from an Earth-bound perspective to seeing it as a planet in a planetary system, and Dietz was involved here as well. Moreover, he was an important proponent of the scientific view that catastrophes are a natural part of Earth's history. Dietz spent a good part of his time in later years refuting creationist views, co-authoring *Creation-Evolution Satiricon* (1987) with John Holden and even offering a monetary reward for solid evidence of Noah's Ark.

Among many honors for his diverse contributions, he received the American Geophysical Union's Bucher Medal (1971) and the Geological Society of America's Penrose Medal (1988). Moreover, an Antarctic mountain, a Pacific seamount, and a Phoceaid asteroid have been named in his honor.

BIBLIOGRAPHY

For unpublished documents pertaining to Dietz, see Robert Sinclair Dietz Papers, 1905–1995, Archival Collection MC 28, Scripps Institution of Oceanography Archives, University of California, San Diego. An online catalog of the collection is available at http://scrippsarchives.ucsd.edu/sio/archives/guides/index.html.

WORKS BY DIETZ

"The Meteoritic Impact Origin of the Moon's Surface Features." *Journal of Geology* 54 (1946): 359–375.

"Geomorphic Evolution of Continental Terrace (Continental Shelf and Slope)." *Bulletin of the American Association of Petroleum Geologists* 36 (1952): 1802–1819.

"Shatter Cones in Cryptoexplosion Structures (Meteorite Impact?)." *Journal of Geology* 67 (1959): 496–505.

"Astroblemes." *Scientific American* 205 (1961): 50–58.

"Continent and Ocean Basin Evolution by Spreading of the Sea Floor." *Nature* 190 (1961): 854–857.

"Vredefort Ring Structure: Meteorite Impact Scar?" *Journal of Geology* 69 (1961): 499–516.

With Jacques Piccard. *Seven Miles Down: The Story of the Bathyscaph Trieste.* New York: Putnam, 1961.

"Collapsing Continental Rises: An Actualistic Concept of Geosynclines and Mountain Building." *Journal of Geology* 71 (1963): 314–333.

"Wave-base, Marine Profile of Equilibrium, and Wave-built Terraces: A Critical Appraisal." *Geological Society of America Bulletin* 74 (1963) 971–990.

"Sudbury Structure as an Astrobleme." *Journal of Geology* 72 (1964): 412–434.

"Reconstruction of Pangea—Breakup and Dispersion of Continents, Permian to Present." *Journal of Geophysical Research* 75 (1970): 4939–4956.

With John C. Holden. *Creation-Evolution Satiricon: Creationism Bashed.* Winthrop, WA: Bookmaker, 1987.

"Earth, Sea, and Sky: Life and Times of a Journeyman Geologist." *Annual Review of Earth and Planetary Sciences* 22 (1994): 1–32.

OTHER SOURCES

Bourgeois, Joanne, and Steven Koppes. "Robert S. Dietz and the Recognition of Impact Structures on Earth." *Earth Sciences History* 17 (1998): 139–156.

Menard, Henry W. *The Ocean of Truth: A Personal History of Global Tectonics.* Princeton, NJ: Princeton University Press, 1986.

Sorkhabi, Rasoul B. "Robert S. Dietz—An Appreciation." *Journal of the Geological Society of India* 44 (1994): 121–126.

Joanne Bourgeois

DIEUDONNÉ, JEAN (*b.* Lille, France, 1 July 1906; *d.* Paris, France, 29 November 1992), *analysis, algebra, history of mathematics, Bourbaki.*

Dieudonné was distinguished as much for vast mathematical knowledge as for his own innovations. He influenced twentieth-century mathematics through his role in the Bourbaki group, his nine-volume *Treatise on Analysis*, his four-volume collaboration with Alexander Grothendieck, and his historical writing. He wrote tens of thousands of pages. More than any other mathematician in Bourbaki, Dieudonné stressed the simplifying role of axiomatics, which David Hilbert also stressed, as opposed to the generalizing role. Fundamental, classical theorems often use far less than the classical assumptions. Dieudonné would drop the irrelevant assumptions and

prove the theorems from just the relevant axioms. Of course the results are also more general, but Dieudonné aimed more to organize and unify than to generalize.

Youth. Dieudonné deeply admired and respected his father, Ernest, who had supported a family from the age of twelve and rose from a modest employee to become general director of a textile manufacturing group. Ernest valued education, strove to make up for what he had missed, and married Léontine Lebrun who taught grade school until Jean was born. A few years later came a sister, Anne Marie. Jean's mother taught him to read before he went to school. He favored dictionaries, encyclopedias, and universal histories. He began school in Lille, but in 1914 when the city declared itself indefensible and surrendered to the Germans he went to Paris to the Lycée Condorcet.

He spent 1919–1920 as a fellow of Bembridge School on the Isle of Wight to learn English. The school was founded in 1910 on the principles of John Ruskin, who would address social ills by "making a carpenter … happier as a carpenter" and making the elite a better elite (Hicks, 1974, p. 57). Dieudonné encountered algebra there and found his calling as a mathematician.

With the war over, he returned to Lille and the Lycée Faidherbe. In 1924 he was accepted at both the École Polytechnique and the École Normale Supérieure (ENS) and chose the latter. There he took courses from great mathematicians at the Sorbonne and the Collège de France, notably including C. Emile Picard and Jacques Hadamard. These were older men; France had lost the intermediate generation in World War I. Hadamard's seminar raised topics from recent mathematics, but most instruction was in nineteenth-century analysis. Dieudonné graduated and took first place in the mathematics agrégation examination for teaching at a lycée. Accepted to the doctoral program at the ENS, Dieudonné did his military service from 1927 to 1928 and began research.

Princeton University made him a Proctor Visiting Fellow for 1928–1929. He studied with Hermann Weyl, and with Godfrey H. Hardy who visited for that same year. A Rockefeller Foundation grant for 1930–1931 let him study with Ludwig Bieberbach in Berlin and George Pólya in Zurich.

In 1931 Dieudonné completed his thesis at the ENS supervised by Paul Montel. He calculated bounds on the locations of zeros of a complex meromorphic function $f(z)$ or its derivative $f'(z)$ given specified bounds for values of $f(z)$ on specified domains. This was the subject of virtually all his publications prior to Bourbaki.

With his record at the ENS, Dieudonné was extremely employable even in hard times. His role in

Bourbaki made him a sought-after professor, although he had no interest in and small gift for teaching. He would eventually hold professorships at five universities in the United States and France, plus visiting professorships at eleven universities in Europe, Asia, and North and South America. He began as an instructor at Bordeaux in 1932 and went to Rennes from 1933 to 1937, first as an instructor and then in a teaching-research position (maître de conférences).

Bourbaki. In the fall of 1934, Odette Clavel dropped her program at a Sunday afternoon concert. Dieudonné picked it up, handed it to her, and married her on 22 July 1935. Fifty-six years later he described the marriage as fifty-six years of happiness. They had a son and a daughter: Jean-Pierre and Françoise. Dieudonné admitted to taking too much time away from them for work.

On Monday, 10 December 1934, Dieudonné joined a handful of ENS graduates called by André Weil to the now-vanished Café Capoulade to plan a thoroughly collaborative, definitive new analysis textbook. It would not have separate chapters by separate experts, but the whole group would write every part of it using the latest tools and the latest standards of rigor out of Hilbert's school in Germany. It would reestablish French preeminence in mathematics. The others at the café were Henri Cartan, Claude Chevalley, Jean Delsarte, and René de Possel.

The mutation of their project foreshadowed their eventual impact on mathematics. They aimed to replace the text they had all studied and taught, Edouard Goursat's 1902–1905 *Cours d'Analyse Mathématique.* Goursat reached classical problems, notably envelopes of families of curves or families of surfaces, the Dirichlet problem, the heat equation, and Fredholm's equation, by sketchy methods of real and complex algebra, real and complex integration, and formal power series. The young mathematicians quickly saw that rigor would mean vast prerequisites. The projected analysis text turned into an entirely self-contained multivolume work on the methods most widely used across mathematics.

They formed a society under the fictitious name of Nicolas Bourbaki and began the *Elements of Mathematics* with volumes on set theory, algebra, topology, functions of one real variable, topological vector spaces, and integration. Dieudonné always insisted that the *Elements* are not encyclopedic because they select only the most useful generalities and reach no serious theorems, but they became the encyclopedia of a new conception of mathematics organized around methods rather than theorems. Despite many critics then and now, the new organization of mathematics became the worldwide norm for graduate training as it proved to be more accessible to students and finally more productive of new great theorems.

The methodical axiomatic style spread so quickly to other authors that a story has grown that the *Elements* themselves never worked as textbooks. But there were circles in the 1950s where, as Pierre Cartier recalled, "every time that Bourbaki published a new book, I would just buy it or borrow it from the library, and learn it. For me, for people in my generation, it was a textbook. But the misunderstanding was that it should be a textbook for everybody" (Senechal, 1998, p. 25).

Dieudonné personified Bourbaki. He was a powerful personal force within the group: He worked as a kind of sergeant at arms and did much of the writing. Sections of the *Elements* went through repeated drafts by different members and were critiqued by all, but Dieudonné wrote every final draft as long as he was an active member. The only works under the name of Bourbaki not approved by the group were the conceptual papers by André Weil (Bourbaki, 1949) and by Dieudonné (Bourbaki, 1950), and Weil and Dieudonné's historical notes to the *Elements* (Bourbaki, 1960). Pierre Cartier says: "When Dieudonné was the 'scribe of Bourbaki' every printed word came from his pen. With his fantastic memory he knew every single word. You could say 'Dieudonné what is the result about so and so?' and he would go to the shelf and take down the book and open it to the right page. After Dieudonné retired no one was able to do this" (Senechal, 2005, p. 28).

Dieudonné often praised the way collaboration reshaped his research: "if I had not been submitted to this obligation to draft questions I did not know a thing about, and to manage to pull through, I should never have done a quarter or even a tenth of the mathematics I have done" (1970, p. 144). He published a little more on zeros of functions, but Bourbaki took him into abstract algebra and point-set topology and a modicum of the new logic.

With Henri Cartan, Dieudonné wrote a series of notes on *teratopology* or counterexamples to plausible guesses in point-set topology. He began work that he would later extend with Laurent Schwartz on topologies for infinite dimensional vector spaces with applications to functional analysis.

Dieudonné's innovations were often extremely useful without being deep or hard. He gave the idea of *paracompact* topological spaces, where every open cover has some open locally finite refinement—that is, a cover by open subsets of sets in the original cover and such that any point lies in just finitely many of these subsets; he proved every separable metrizable space is paracompact. He defined *partitions of unity* for covers. That is, on suitable spaces (which, depending on details, are basically the paracompact spaces) given any locally finite cover of the space by open subsets U_i, each set U_i of the cover can be assigned a smooth function f_i which is 0 outside U_i and bounded between 0 and 1 inside it, and at every point the sum of the values of the functions is 1. A partition of unity on a cover gives a systematic way to take local constructions on each set of the cover and add them together to get smooth constructions on the whole space.

Bourbaki is especially identified with the idea of a mathematical *structure*. Dieudonné was clear: "I do not say it was an original idea of Bourbaki—there is no question of Bourbaki's containing anything original" (1970, p. 138). But Dieudonné and Weil led the group in codifying ways that a few kinds of structure recur throughout mathematics; for example, the addition of real numbers, and of vectors, and multiplication of matrices are all associative binary operations. Or, for another example, divisibility of integers and inclusion of subsets are both transitive relations. Bourbaki from the first volume of the *Elements* in 1939 sought a general theory of all the ways a set can be structured: by operations on the set, or relations among its members, or a topology on the set. But the theory they produced was not general enough to apply to all the mathematical objects they needed, and it was too complicated to use when it did apply. After working with Grothendieck, Dieudonné concluded that Bourbaki's theory of structures "has since been superseded by that of category and functor, which includes it under a more general and convenient form" (1970, p. 138).

Early Years at Nancy. The University of Nancy made Dieudonné an instructor in 1937 and then promoted him to maître de conférences. He held that post until 1946, although he was mobilized for the war in September 1939 and many university jobs were relocated to Clermont-Ferrand when the Germans made France north of the Somme a *zone interdite*, forbidden to the French, under Belgian administration. He returned to Nancy by 1943 while it was still *zone interdite* (Eguether, 2003, p. 25). After the war, Dieudonné spent 1946–1948 as a professor at the University of São Paulo, Brazil, and returned to Nancy as a professor from 1948 to 1952. Fellow founder of Bourbaki Jean Delsarte was then dean of the Science Faculty and was assembling a brilliant collection of Bourbaki members or future members at Nancy.

Delsarte and Dieudonné brought Laurent Schwartz to Nancy. Schwartz was working on his distributions, which made rigorous the generalized functions used by physicists, such as the Dirac delta function. His basic tool was to set up a relation between, roughly speaking, the space of all real-valued smooth functions f on the real line and the space of all generalized functions φ on the same line. Exploring the foundations of his idea, he co-authored a paper on topological vector spaces with Dieudonné; the two of them recommended certain open questions from that paper to their student Grothendieck. Grothendieck in response created the idea of a nuclear

space, and Dieudonné later described his student's answers as "the greatest advance in functional analysis after the work of Banach" (1981, p. 220).

Work on Groups. The *classical groups* are certain groups of matrices with clear geometric sense—at least, they have a clear geometric sense when the matrices have real or complex numbers as entries. For example, the *real general linear group* $GL_n(R)$ consists of all invertible n by n matrices of real numbers and is geometrically the group of all linear maps from the n-dimensional real vector space to itself. Mathematicians since the mid-nineteenth century had studied these, and also analogous groups with entries in fields other than the real or complex numbers. From the late 1940s into the 1950s Dieudonné used the relatively new axiomatic theory of vector spaces, in its geometrical interpretation, to simplify the proofs and clarify the subject and solve some fundamental problems in it.

This led to Dieudonné's deepest and most imaginative personal work in mathematics, his work on *formal groups*. The spaces of classical algebraic geometry are defined by polynomial equations, as for example $x^2+y^2-1=0$ defines the unit circle. Roughly speaking, a coordinate function on the unit circle is any polynomial $P(x,y)$ in these same variables x,y, with the proviso that polynomials $P(x,y)$ and $Q(x,y)$ count as the same function on the circle if their difference $P(x,y)-Q(x,y)$ is a multiple of the defining polynomial $x^2+y^2-1=0$. When the polynomial coefficients are taken as real or complex numbers, then all the techniques of classical analysis apply. When they are taken in any field k, some analysis still applies since there is a familiar formal rule for the derivative of a polynomial. But classical techniques using limits or convergent power series do not apply when the field k has no topology (or no suitable topology) to support a notion of convergence. This happens in particular for fields of characteristic p, for a prime number p where multiplication by p counts as multiplication by 0. The algebraic geometry of these fields was ever more central to number theory following work by Bourbaki members Claude Chevalley and Weil, among others.

Dieudonné made up for a large part of the loss by abandoning topological convergence and working formally with arbitrary infinite power series. A *formal group* is roughly an algebraic space where the coordinate functions are not only polynomials but infinite series, and such that the space is also a group, like the classical groups. Through the 1950s Dieudonné made many classical analytic techniques apply in very useful ways without using the classical notion of convergence (later collected in Dieudonné, 1973).

Scheme Theory. In 1952 Dieudonné accepted a one-year professorship at the University of Michigan. That led to a professorship at Northwestern University from 1953 to 1959, where he gave the lectures on analysis that became *Foundations of Modern Analysis* (1960), the final result of Bourbaki's original plan for a textbook on analysis. This book has been a strong, immediate influence on far more mathematicians than have ever read anything else that Dieudonné wrote. It violates a stereotype of Bourbaki as it is thoroughly geometrical, but it is typical Dieudonné: It is axiomatic, quite general, and uses that generality entirely to simplify the theory. It defines derivatives as linear approximations to functions between (finite or infinite dimensional) Banach spaces and yet proves not one nontrivial theorem on Banach spaces. It uses the Banach space axioms because they assume all and only the structure needed for the basic theorems of differential calculus. They are to the point. Deep considerations on Banach spaces have no place here—simple, general facts about derivatives do.

Dieudonné left Northwestern to become the first professor of Mathematics at the Institut des Hautes Études Scientifiques (IHES) near Paris, modeled on the Institute for Advanced Study in Princeton, New Jersey. He brought his student Grothendieck, instantly making the IHES a power in mathematics. Grothendieck in fact had abandoned analysis, though, and begun the sweeping recreation of algebraic geometry around his new notion of *scheme*.

Roughly speaking, a scheme is an algebraic space, defined like most kinds of manifolds by coordinate functions on patches of the space, with the astonishing innovation that these "functions" need not be polynomials or even functions in any set theoretic sense. Rather, any ring in the sense of abstract algebra can be the ring of "coordinate functions" on a patch of a scheme, with the ring elements treated as coordinate functions. This appalling abstraction and generality struck many mathematicians as impervious to geometric intuition. But Grothendieck and Dieudonné knew better. They saw it not as general but as simple: The apparatus of analysis and classical topology is dropped in favor of the mere ring operations of addition and multiplication.

Much fundamental geometric intuition does survive. Notably, an algebraic triviality says that a subset S of a ring R generates the unit ideal if and only if some finite subset T of S already does. In scheme theory this has two immediate, fundamental consequences: the basic schemes are compact, and they admit analogues to Dieudonné's partitions of unity with the difference that the "functions" f_i are elements of arbitrary rings and are in no sense bounded between 0 and 1. At each point they do add up to 1.

Dieudonné took up another historic multi-volume collaboration, this time with Grothendieck as his single co-author. He did this "with the sole goal of bringing to the public the brilliant ideas of his young collaborator. One rarely sees such disinterested effort" (Cartan, 1993, p. 4). Dieudonné painstakingly organized a flood of Grothendieck's notes into *Les Éléments de géométrie algébrique* (1960–1967), still the standard reference on schemes in the twenty-first century.

Move to Nice. In 1964 Dieudonné became the first dean of the faculty of science at the newly created University of Nice, where the Mathematics Institute is named after him. He held the deanship until 1968 and faced student unrest with his life-long respect for other people's intentions yet rejection of all leftist politics. The professorship became honorary in 1969. He was elected to the Académie des Sciences of France in 1968, and quickly got a number of his comrades from Bourbaki into it.

He was a visiting professor at the University of Notre Dame (United States) in fall 1966 and again for two years, 1969–1971. At this time he took up his analysis textbook again and expanded to the nine-volume *Éléments d'analyse* (1968–1982). No doubt the first volume, and then the first few volumes, had more direct influence on more mathematicians than the later volumes, but the whole was a fantastic achievement and shaped the general conception of analysis for decades. The capstone of his academic career was organizing the World Congress of Mathematics in Nice in 1970. He turned to writing the history of mathematics.

In common with Weil, Dieudonné believed the history of mathematics should be impersonal, not about anecdotes, and not about priority disputes, but about the development of the leading ideas. His three key works are the historical part of his course on algebraic geometry (1974; translated to English, and expanded, 1985); his expert history of functional analysis (1981); and the massive, detailed history of twentieth-century algebraic and differential topology (1989). Any one can be recommended to graduate mathematics students learning those subjects—and any one can be faulted in detail by specialist historians. Nevertheless, they are invaluable documents. He wrote numerous entries for the *Dictionary of Scientific Biography* (Dugac, 1995, p. 119).

Tall and impressive, though not given to physical exercise, Dieudonné had an energetic enthusiasm that was punctuated by explosive bursts of temper. Friends found him optimistic, generous, honest, and with a strong sense of responsibility—although he said history precluded optimism. He distrusted political reform and was pleased to be received into the generally conservative Légion d'Honneur. He inherited strong discipline from his parents but in no ascetic way. He enjoyed good food and great wine and conversation. He was a skilled pianist and played for an hour or two each morning. Five or six hours of sleep per night was enough.

Dieudonné called himself happy. In old age he said Socrates and Michel de Montaigne were his models for taking difficulties in the best possible way, and expressed confidence that with death, "like all animals, I will entirely disappear." He died surrounded by his wife and children, keeping the attitude he expressed five years earlier: "Now I am ready to go. If one tells me 'it will be in one month' that is perfect. I ask no more. I have had everything that I wanted in life" (quoted in Dugac, 1995, p. 20).

Honors. Among the very many honors he received, the Académie des Sciences of Paris awarded Dieudonné their Grand Prize in 1944 and the Petit D'Ormoy Prize in 1966 and made him a member in 1968. In 1966 Dieudonné received the Gaston Julia Prize. He became a correspondent of the National Academy of Sciences (United States) in 1965 and a member in 1968, at the same time as he was elected to the Académie des Sciences of France. He became a foreign member of the Real Academia de Ciencias of Spain in 1970, and of the Académie Royale de Belgique in 1974. The American Mathematical Society awarded him the Steele Prize in 1971, and the London Mathematical Society made him an honorary member in 1972. In 1978 he was made an Officer of the Légion d'Honneur.

BIBLIOGRAPHY

WORKS BY DIEUDONNÉ

As Nicolas Bourbaki. *Éléments de Mathématique,* 27 vol. Paris: Hermann et Masson, 1939–1998. Translated into English as *Elements of Mathematics.* Paris: Hermann, 1974–. There are also translations into Japanese and Russian. Written under a pseudonym of a variable and purportedly secret group, Dieudonné wrote all the final drafts into the 1950s.

As Nicolas Bourbaki. "The Architecture of Mathematics." *The American Mathematical Monthly* 57 (1950): 221–232.

As Nicolas Bourbaki, with André Weil. *Elements d'histoire des mathématiques.* Paris: Hermann, 1960. Reprints of the historical notes from Bourbaki's *Elements.* Translated into English, German, Spanish, Russian.

"Recherches sur quelques problèmes relatifs aux polynômes et aux fonctions bornées d'une variable complexe." *Annales scientifiques de l'École Normale Supérieure* 48 (1931): 247–358.

"Les méthodes axiomatiques modernes et les fondements des mathématiques." *Revue Scientifique* 77 (1939): 224–232.

Théorie analytique des polynômes d'une variable. Paris: Gauthier-Villars, 1939.

Sur les groupes classiques. Paris: Hermann, 1958.

Foundations of Modern Analysis. New York: Academic Press, 1960.

Éléments d'analyse, 9 vols. Paris: Gauthier-Villars, 1968–1982. Volume I is a translation of Dieudonné 1960. Volumes 1–8

translated as *Treatise on Analysis,* 8 vols. New York: Academic Press, 1969–1993.

"The work of Nicholas Bourbaki." *American Mathematical Monthly* 77 (2, 1970): 134–145.

Introduction to the Theory of Formal Lie Groups. New York: Marcel Dekker, 1973.

Editor, and author with others. *Abrégé d'histoire des mathématiques: 1700–1900,* 2 vols. Paris: Hermann, 1978.

Choix d'OEuvres Mathématiques, 2 vol. Paris: Hermann, 1981.

History of Functional Analysis. Amsterdam: North Holland, 1981.

Panorama des mathématiques pures: le choix bourbachique. Paris: Gauthier-Villars, 1977. Translated into English by I. G. Macdonald as *A Panorama of Pure Mathematics, as seen by N. Bourbaki.* New York: Academic Press, 1982.

Cours de géométrie algébrique, 2 vol. Paris: Presses Universitaires de France 1974. The first volume is translated into English, with an additional chapter on recent work, by Judith Sally as *History of Algebraic Geometry.* Monterey, CA: Wadsworth, 1985.

A History of Algebraic and Differential Topology, 1900–1960. Boston: Birkhäuser, 1989.

Pour l'honneur de l'esprit humain—les mathématiques aujourd'hui. Paris: Hachette, 1987. This popularization, published in English as *Mathematic—the Music of Reason,* was translated by Harold G. and H. C. Dales. Berlin: Springer-Verlag, 1992.

With Henri Cartan. "Notes de tératopologie," I, II, III. *Revue Scientifique* 77 (1939): 39–40, 180–181, 413–414.

With Alexander Grothendieck. *Les Éléments de géométrie algébrique.* 4 vols. Bures-sur-Yvette, France: Publications Mathématiques de l'IHÉS, 1960–1967.

OTHER SOURCES

Borel, Armand. "Twenty-Five Years with Nicolas Bourbaki, (1949–1973)." *Notices of the American Mathematical Society* 45, no. 3 (1998): 373–380.

Bourbaki, Nicolas (pseud. of André Weil). "Foundations of Mathematics for the Working Mathematician." *Journal of Symbolic Logic* 14 (1949): 1–8.

Cartan, Henri. "Jean Dieudonné." *Gazette des Mathematiciens* 55 (1993): 3–4. This consists largely of quotes from Dieudonné (1981).

Cartier, Pierre. *Jean Dieudonné (1906–1992): Mathematician.* Bures-sur-Yvette, France: Institut des Hautes Études Scientifiques, 2005. A keenly observed biographical and mathematical account by a member of Bourbaki during the 1950s. It is available online from the IHES.

Dugac, Pierre. *Jean Dieudonné: Mathématicien complet.* Paris: Gabay, 1995. A colleague in history of mathematics assembles quotes from Dieudonné's less accessible publications and some unpublished writing, testimony by others, and photographs.

Eguether, Gérard. "Jean Delsarte." *1903–2003: Un siècle de mathématiques à Nancy,* edited by Daniel Barlet. Nancy: Institut Élie Cartan, 2003.

Goursat, Édouard. *Cours d'Analyse mathématique,* 2 vol. Paris: Gauthier-Villars, 1902–1905.

Hicks, Judith. "The Educational Theories of John Ruskin: A Reappraisal." *British Journal of Educational Studies* 22 (1, 1974): 56–77.

Mashaal, Maurice. *Bourbaki: Une Société Secrète de Mathématiciens.* Paris: Belin, Pour la Science, 2000.

Senechal, Marjorie. "The Continuing Silence of Bourbaki: An Interview with Pierre Cartier." *Mathematical Intelligencer* 20 (1998): 22–28.

Colin McLarty

DIJKSTRA, WYBE EDSGER (*b.* Rotterdam, Netherlands, 11 May 1930; *d.* Nuenen, Netherlands, 6 August 2002), *computer science, logic, mathematics.*

In 1972 Wybe Dijkstra became the first Dutch computer scientist to win the Turing Award, at the young age of forty-two. He counts as one of the founders of the discipline of computer science itself. He wrote the first Dutch textbook on programming, between 1952 and 1955. His work aimed at developing a theory of computing without computers. He was a member of the Royal Netherlands Academy of Arts and Sciences and a foreign honorary member of the American Academy of Arts and Sciences. He received a large number of prizes and distinctions.

Biographical and Career Details. Dijkstra grew up within an intellectual environment. Both his parents had taken university degrees: his mother was a mathematician, and his father was a chemist. In 1948 he finished *gymnasium,* the highest level of high school in the Netherlands (pupils receive education in Latin and Greek). He was groomed for a scientific career. His parents thought it would be a pity not to devote his life to science, and he followed their advice. He studied theoretical physics at one of the oldest Dutch universities, in Leiden.

In 1952 he started his career at the Mathematical Center in Amsterdam. He finished his university studies in 1956, and received his PhD in 1959 on "Communication with an Automatic Computer." In 1962 he became a professor at the Technical University in Eindhoven. In 1973 he became research fellow for the Burroughs Corporation. In 1984 he moved to Texas, to the University of Texas in Austin, retiring in 1999. He was married and had three children. He died of cancer in 2002 at age seventy-two.

Professionalization of Programming. Maurice Wilkes built one of the first electronic digital stored-program computers in the world, the EDSAC (Electronic Delay Storage Automatic Calculator) at the University of Cam-

bridge. He also developed one of the first programming courses in Europe, and in 1951 Dijkstra became one of his first students. This course was Dijkstra's first encounter with electronic digital computing machines. Dijkstra's entrance into the field of computing via knowledge of and experience with programming influenced Dijkstra's further career: although he participated in the logical design of some early digital electronic machines, he never involved himself with the material construction of a computer. People from all over the world joined Wilkes's courses, which means that Dijkstra belonged to the international community of computer experts from the start. It also means that Dijkstra entered the field in the context of scientific computing.

Dijkstra started working at the Center for Mathematics and Computer Science in Amsterdam (the former Mathematical Center), not yet having finished his studies. This center was subsidized by the national government, aiming at making mathematics useful for society. Numerical analysis and statistics were the core business, and this work involved a lot of computation. Therefore, the center had a computation department, which was headed by Adriaan van Wijngaarden. The first professor in computing science in the Netherlands, Van Wijngaarden was one of the key figures in the development of the computer language ALGOL 68. This computation department emerged as one of the leading institutions in the pioneering era of Dutch and European computer science in the context of scientific computing. Van Wijngaarden convinced Dijkstra to become a programmer, arguing that "computers are here to stay" (Dijkstra, EWD1308, p. 1).

In 1953 Dijkstra developed a programming manual for the first Dutch electronic digital computer, which was still being built at the time, the ARRA (Automatisch Relais Reken Apparaat, or Automatic Relay Calculator). Thus, he developed his first thoughts about programming without a machine at his disposal. Given the fact that early computers were rare, and that these were rather laboratory experiments than proper working machines, this was not so exceptional. For example, Arthur W. Burks and John von Neumann developed ideas about coding in 1946–1947, before the IAS (Institute for Advanced Study) machine had been built.

Dijkstra wrote, together with Van Wijngaarden, the first programming textbook, which was well entrenched in current knowledge and practice of the early 1950s. It included a discussion of the computer itself (the ARRA), a section on flowcharting, a library of subroutines, examples of programs, and a discussion of interpretative programming. In this textbook, one chapter is fully devoted on reliability of the results. This is a topic that Dijkstra continued working on throughout his career, especially with regard to software.

In his very first manual about "the programmer's task" in 1953, he initiated the professionalization of the programming activity (without coining it as such). He described the task of the programmer in terms of five steps, each in line with ideas about programming in the emergent scientific computing community. The first step was the mathematical formulation of the problem; the second was the mathematical solution. The third step was the construction of the numerical process that would produce the right result; the fourth step was the actual programming in terms of operations; and the final step was the coding. Flowcharting was used in the fourth step: information technology (IT) was a central concept to represent the structure of the problem, independent of the code that was specific to the machine.

Dijkstra called himself the first programmer in the Netherlands. Whether or not that was the case, he definitely was among the first people in the Netherlands who wrote about programming as a separate activity. In 1962 he described it as follows: "I should like to draw your attention in particular to those efforts and considerations which try to improve 'the state of the Art of Programming,' maybe to such extent that at some time in the future we may speak of 'the state of the Science of Programming'" (Dijkstra, EWD32, p. 1). Throughout his career he put his work in the perspective of professionalization of programming, in theory as well as in practice.

In 1967 he wrote in *Informatie,* the leading Dutch IT journal, "Het einde van een ambacht" (The end of a craft), in which he made a plea for properly (that is, academically) educated programmers. Dijkstra was a very good teacher himself, and used his teaching activities to spread his ideas. Those who knew him generally say that he was at his best in front of a class, explaining his latest insights. In his view, the key to a good computing science program was to consider it as a branch of mathematics. It is important to realize at this point that at the technical universities in the Netherlands there were programs in "technical mathematics," which taught numerical analysis, modeling, and early computing science. He himself had an appointment at such a program. So, mathematics was a natural context for him. He taught numerical analysis himself in the first years of his professorship.

Another aspect of academic professionalization is the definition of the object at the core of a discipline. For Dijkstra, the core object of computing science was the "abstract mechanism," a notion that he introduced in a number of EWD papers (EWD51, for example) and finalized in his 1976 *A Discipline of Programming.* In this book he writes: "I view a programming language primarily as a vehicle for the description of abstract mechanisms" (p. 9). An abstract mechanism is an algorithm that can be executed by an automaton and that produces an unique result when the input is given. Dijkstra was only interested in the formal aspects of the algorithm, and not in the physical machine that performed the execution. All his work was actually devoted to defining foundations for computing science as *science.* In contrast to many others of his time, he did not conceive computing science as a mixture of disciplines (electrical engineering, mathematics, and so on), but as proper mathematics. In 1961 he had already written that the mathematician "has theorems, we have subroutines" (Dijkstra, 1961, p. 4).

An academic discipline needs an object and a method. Together with a Dutch colleague Wim Feijen, he wrote *A Method of Programming* (1984, in Dutch), which was translated into English in 1988. In this book programming is presented as a "formal branch of mathematics."

Operating Systems. From the start, Dijkstra not only programmed but also reflected on the activity itself. He tried to find what he called "general" technologies and "general" statements, by which he meant technologies and statements that were independent of the specific computer and the specific program. Dijkstra used this word *general* throughout his career.

His first attempt to find such a general technology was the interrupt. One of the major problems at the time was that input and output devices were much slower than the clock of the computer. When the computer had to print a result, while the printer was still being occupied printing a previous result, the computer had to wait until the output device had finished typing (for example). That was considered to be inefficient. An interrupt told the computer to continue executing its orders, and to store the result that should be printed. The computer continued executing its program. When the printer was ready printing, the interrupt told the computer, and a connection was made between the stored result and the printer. Generally, this was coined as a synchronization problem, and the interrupt prevented waiting time. Already in 1955, he had written *Het communicatieprogramma van de ARRA* (Communication program of the ARRA), which shows his early interest in what would, in the early twenty-first century, be called the operating system of the computer.

Between 1956 and 1959 he worked on his PhD dissertation, "Communication with an Automatic Computer," published as a book in 1959, in which he developed an interrupt mechanism for the first Dutch commercial computer, the Electrologica X1. The book contained only the programming aspects of the mechanism (the hardware side of the interrupt was built by Bram Loopstra and Carel Scholten). The interrupt was at the vanguard of research at that time. For example,

Frederick Phillips Brooks Jr. and Dura Sweeney patented an interrupt system for the Stretch Computer, built at IBM during 1956–1959. However, Dijkstra did not cite their work in his dissertation. In 1968 Donald Knuth argued in *The Art of Computer Programming* that most fundamental techniques until then (and the interrupt system was one of them) had been independently developed by a number of different people. About Dijkstra, Knuth wrote in 1968: "An interrupt system which enabled buffering of input and output was independently developed by E. W. Dijkstra between 1957–1958. His thesis mentions buffering techniques, which in this case involved very long circles of buffers since the routines were primarily concerned with paper tape and type-writer I/O. Each buffer contained either a single character or a single number" (p. 227).

Dijkstra continued his work on parts of what would be called operating systems. The first paper on semaphores, "Multiprogrammering en de X8," was circulated in Dutch in 1962 (EWD51). Multiprogramming meant that the central processor was able to divide its time among a variety of jobs. (This is different from concurrent programming, in which several processors carry out the same job). In this paper he introduced his idea about *seinpalen* (semaphores), explaining that he used a metaphor derived from the railways because that was how he conceived of the regulation of concurrent sequential processes. How do several machines, either concrete or abstract, know that they can send or receive jobs or data? Generally, semaphores regulated the synchronization between loosely connected sequential processes, for example, the synchronization between an abstract mechanism (the program) and the input/output devices.

This work would finally result in a very influential paper, "Cooperating Sequential Processes" (EWD123, 1965). He proved the correctness of the logic of the semaphores. This paper was widely read, and many of the concepts that he introduced in that paper were quickly adopted by the pioneering computing science experts. In the early 1970s, the first books on operating systems came out, among them in the Netherlands by professor Arie J. W. Duijvestijn in 1973 (who had been the first programming expert at Royal Philips Electronics NV and was professor at the Twente University) and in the United States in 1973 by Per Brinch Hansen, who had developed a multiprogramming system for the RC 4000 computer at the Regnecentrale in Denmark. These works show that Dijkstra's concepts (semaphore, deadlock, critical regions, message buffers) were highly influential at the time. An example is the banker's algorithm, an algorithm that prevented deadlock during the execution of concurrent processes by one single processor. A deadlock situation is, for example, the case when two processes wait for each other during the execution of the program. Dijkstra introduced it internationally in EWD123, although a more primitive version of it had already been introduced in EWD108 in Dutch. This banker's algorithm was almost literally adopted in Brinch Hansen's book on operating systems (pp. 42–45). Dijkstra also introduced (internationally) the structure of hierarchical levels in his 1968 paper "The Structure of the 'THE'-multiprogramming system" ("THE" stood for Technical University Eindhoven).

Programming Languages and Compilers. The Mathematical Center was involved in the development of ALGOL 60, and was one of the central actors in the development of ALGOL 68. These were algorithmic languages, partly developed in competition with IBM's FORTRAN. The Mathematical Center provided a good environment for working on programming languages and compilers. Dijkstra was not directly involved in the development of ALGOL 60, as he was working on a compiler for the Electrologica X1 computer. However, his book *A Primer of ALGOL 60 Programming* was reprinted almost yearly and was the standard textbook on ALGOL in the 1960s.

A compiler translates the high-level language code into machine language code. Together with Jaap van Zonneveld, Dijkstra wrote the first ALGOL-compiler in the summer of 1961. The code of this compiler has recently been documented by Frans E. J. Kruseman Aretz (2003). This work proved to be very influential. He developed several concepts, the most famous of which is probably the "stack." The stack referred to a specific way of organizing memory during the executional process, following the principle of "first in, first out." It used recent developments by the German computer pioneers Friedrich Bauer and Klaus Samelson. This work became very well known, as is shown by textbooks in computing science *avant la lettre*. These early books within a discipline are mostly collections of important papers as long as a core body of knowledge is still lacking. In 1967 Saul Rosen, a professor in computer science at Purdue University, edited a collection of important articles on programming systems and languages, and Dijkstra's article on the stack was one of them:

> "Recursive Programming" by Professor Dijkstra is an early and important contribution to the art of writing compilers. The problems involved in permitting recursive calls on subroutines are attacked and handled in a simple elegant fashion. Almost everyone who has been involved in writing an Algol compiler has used some of the ideas developed in connection with the Algol compiler written by Professor Dijkstra and his colleagues at the Mathematical Centre at Amsterdam. (p. 181)

In 1968 Dijkstra published one of his most widely known articles, "GoTo Statement Considered Harmful."

It was about the statement "GoTo" in high-level programming languages (the original title of this paper was "A Case against the GoTo Statement" EWD215). In this article he addressed one of his central concerns: the gap between the static program text and the dynamic process of its execution. Dijkstra's striving for logic and proof of correctness originated from his conviction that the human mind was not very good at thinking through the process of execution of a program (executional abstraction). In many of his papers, he addressed this fundamental problem. In the course of his career, he increasingly considered programming to be a mental activity.

This problem, the confusion between a program and its execution, is also the key to his famous notion of "separation of concerns" (EWD447, 1974). According to Dijkstra, in the daily practice of programming, the separation between the preparation of the program and its execution was unclear. That caused a lot of problems. In his view, being well-defined rather than being implemented was a vital characteristic of a programming language. In this paper he asks which should take priority:

> On the one hand we have the physical equipment (the implementation), on the other hand we have the formal system (programming language). It is perhaps a question of taste—I don't believe so—to whom of the two we give the primacy, that is whether it is the task of the formal system to give an accurate description of (certain aspects of) the physical equipment, or whether it is the task of the physical equipment to provide an accurate model for the formal system—and I prefer the latter. (EWD447, 1974, p. 3)

This closed the circle in a way: after having freed programming from being dictated by the electronics of the machine, now the construction of the machine should enable the implementation of a well-defined and consistent programming language. That was what Dijkstra found at Burroughs when he started working there as an independent researcher. The computer there was one of the few expressly designed to implement ALGOL.

Algorithms. Already in 1957 Dijkstra conceived of his shortest path algorithm, published it in 1959 in *Numerische Mathematik*. A concise history of the shortest path algorithm is given by Helená Durnová (2004). Dijkstra has become known for several other algorithms, of which the banker's algorithm was already mentioned.

Context, Further Career, and Working Style. One of Dijkstra's most important Dutch colleagues, and competitor at the same time, was Willem van der Poel, who also joined the programming courses with Wilkes, and who constructed one of the first computing machines in the Netherlands. Van der Poel became a professor at Delft University of Technology, and was among other things chairman of Working Group 2.1 of the International Federation for Information Processing (IFIP WG 2.1) Dijkstra also participated in IFIP WG 2.1, and later in 2.3.

IFIP was established in 1960. Working group 2.1 was established to work on ALGOL—it still exists under the name of algorithmic languages and calculi. Van Wijngaarden led this working group when they started working on ALGOL 68. Charles Lindsey gave a very neat personal history about the reasons why this group of people, while they worked on ALGOL 68, finally split up: Dijkstra and Niklaus Wirth, who developed the high-level programming language PASCAL, founded (among others) a new working group 2.3, called programming methodology.

Dijkstra and Van der Poel developed quite different conceptions of programming. The key difference is that Dijkstra abstracted from the computer, while Van der Poel remained loyal to the machine. The boundary between hardware and software was Van der Poel's object of research.

Dijkstra was never good at citing others. "For the absence of a bibliography I offer neither explanation nor apology," he wrote in his preface to *A Discipline of Programming* (1976, p. xvii). On the one hand, Dijkstra has left thousands of pages of beautiful text, but on the other hand, it is sometimes difficult to trace his own intellectual inspiration.

From the 1970s, he was the principal motivator of the Tuesday Afternoon Club of the Technical University Eindhoven. This was a weekly seminar where recent work was discussed. This was continued in Eindhoven as well as at the University of Austin after he had moved there. These meetings were inspiring for people who belonged to Dijkstra's inner circle. Increasingly however, Dijkstra's behavior became off-putting now and then; some people experienced him as very offensive in social gatherings. Dijkstra established his reputation through his writings; his style is very elegant to read. Some people, however, tried to avoid meeting Dijkstra, while at the same time tried very hard to get his most recent EWD paper. Dijkstra had four PhD students: Netty van Gasteren, Nico Habermann, David Naumann, and Martin Rem. Habermann worked with him on the THE-multiprogramming system.

Paul Ceruzzi argues in his *History of Modern Computing* that Dijkstra was actually the exponent of a community that aimed at constructing a theoretical basis for computing science. This is a fair statement in the sense that Dijkstra was one of the software pioneers who addressed fundamental issues in such an elegant and rigorous way that he strongly influenced the early community. It is also true in the sense that many of his terms, such as "structured programming" or "separation of concerns," have almost become common sense language in computer science and software practice.

However, people from industry, and people from data processing were not that responsive to Dijkstra's ideas. Throughout his career he made a plea for proving correctness of small pieces (mechanisms) of a big program. People in industry felt that Dijkstra did not understand their problems: problems of large scale and problems of efficiency. In a world where time and money mattered, Dijkstra's programming methodology could not always work. Dijkstra, for his part, did not take the industrial and business context very seriously:

> One of the standard objections raised from the floor is along the following lines: "What you have shown is very nice for the little mathematical examples with which you illustrated the techniques, but we are afraid that they are not applicable in the world of data business processing, where the problems are much harder, because there one always has to work with imperfect and ambiguous specifications." From a logical point of view, this objection is nonsense: if your specifications are contradictory, life is easy, for then you know that no program will satisfy them, so make "no program"; if your specifications are ambiguous, the greater the ambiguity, the easier the specifications are to satisfy. (EWD447, 1974, p. 2)

BIBLIOGRAPHY

Dijkstra corresponded extensively with colleagues in academia and industry by means of numbered papers, reports, commentaries, and so forth, which are known as EWDs. Many of his publications started out as EWDs, but most EWDs were never published; however, they are readily available through archival sources. The Center for American History at the University of Texas, Austin, houses Dijkstra's original manuscripts. All the papers by Dijkstra, including all the references, are available from the "E. W. Dijkstra Archive" at http://www.cs.utexas.edu/users/EWD/welcome.html.

WORKS BY DIJKSTRA

Unpublished Manuscripts

"Some Meditations on Advanced Programming." EWD32, 1962.

"Multiprogrammering en de X8." EWD51.

"Cooperating Sequential Processes." EWD123, 1965.

"Een algorithme ter voorkoming van de dodelijke omarming." EWD108.

"A Case against the Go To Statement." EWD215.

"The Humble Programmer." EWD340.

"On the Role of Scientific Thought." EWD447, 1974.

"From My Life." EWD1166.

"What Led to 'Notes on Structured Programming.'" EWD1308.

Published Works

Het communicatieprogramma van de ARRA. MR21. Amsterdam: Stichting Mathematisch Centrum, 1955. Available from the "E. W. Dijkstra Archive."

With A. van Wijngaarden. *Programmeren voor Automatische Rekenmachines.* Amsterdam: Mathematisch Centrum, Rekenafdeling, 1955. Several further editions of this textbook were coauthored with Th. J. Dekker.

Communication with an Automatic Computer. Rijswijk, Netherlands: Excelsior, 1959. Dijkstra's PhD dissertation, in book format.

"On the Design of Machine Independent Programming Languages." MR34. Amsterdam: Mathematisch Centrum, 1961. Available from the "E. W. Dijkstra Archive" at http://www.cs.utexas.edu/users/EWD/welcome.html.

A Primer of ALGOL 60 Programming. London: Academic, 1962.

With Charles Antony Richard Hoare and Ole-Johan Dahl. *Structured Programming.* London: Academic, 1972.

A Discipline of Programming. Englewood Cliffs, NJ: Prentice-Hall, 1976.

With Wim H. J. Feijen. *Een methode van programmeren.* The Hague: Academic Service, 1984. Translated by Joke Sterringa as *A Method of Programming* (Reading, MA: Addison-Wesley, 1988).

OTHER SOURCES

Apt, Krzystof. "Edsger Wybe Dijkstra (1930–2002): A Portrait of a Genius." *Formal Aspects of Computing* 14 (2002): 92–98.

Bauer, Friedrich, and Klaus Samelson. "Sequentielle Formelübersetzung." *Elektronische Rechenanlagen.* 1, H. 4. (1959): 176–182.

Brinch Hansen, Per. *Operating System Principles.* Englewood Cliffs, NJ: Prentice-Hall, 1973.

Ceruzzi, Paul. *A History of Modern Computing.* Cambridge, MA: MIT Press, 2003. First published 1998.

Durnová, Helená. "A History of Discrete Optimization." In *Mathematics throughout the Ages II,* edited by Eduard Fuchs, 51–184. History of Mathematics 25. Prague: Research Centre for the History of Sciences and Humanities, 2004.

Goldstine, Herman H., and John von Neumann. "Planning and Coding for an Electronic Computing Instrument." Reprinted in *Charles Babbage Institute Reprint Series for the History of Computing,* vol. 12, pp. 145–308. Los Angeles: Tomash, 1982–1992.

Knuth, Donald E. *The Art of Computer Programming.* Vol. 1, *Fundamental Algorithms.* Reading, MA: Addison-Wesley, 1968.

Kruseman Aretz, Frans E. J. "The Dijkstra-Zonneveld ALGOL-60 Compiler for the Electrologica X1 (historical note SEN, 2)." CWI-report Note SEN-N0301. Amsterdam: Centrumvoor Wiskundeen Informatica, June 2003. Available from http://www.cwi.nl/ftp/CWIreports/SEN/SEN-N0301.pdf.

Lindsey, Charles H. "ALGOL 68 Session." In *History of Programming Languages II,* edited by Thomas J. Bergin and Richard G. Gibson, 27–96. New York: ACM Press, 1996.

MacKenzie, Donald. *Mechanizing Proof: Computing, Risk, and Trust.* Cambridge, MA: MIT Press, 2001.

———. "A View from Sonnenbichl: On the Historical Sociology of Software and System Dependability." In *History of Computing: Software Issues,* edited by Ulf Hashagen, Reinhard Keil-Slawik, and Arthur Norberg, 95–136. New York: Springer, 2002.

Rem, Martin, and Hans Schippers. "Edsger Dijkstra en zijn THE systeem" [Edsger Dijkstra and his THE-system]. In *TU/E Gedreven door nieuwsgierigheid* [TU/E driven by curiosity], edited by Harry W. Lintsen and Hans Schippers, 225–231. Zutphen, Netherlands: Walburg Pers, 2006.

Rosen, Saul. *Programming Systems and Languages.* New York: McGraw-Hill, 1967.

Adrienne van den Bogaard

DING WENJIANG (V. K. TING) (*b.* Huangqiao Village, Taixing, Jiangsu Province, China, 13 April 1887; *d.* Changsha, Hunan Province, 5 January 1936), *geologist, educator in geology.*

Ding Wenjiang was one of the founders of geological undertakings in China, especially of the renowned Geological Survey of China that began in 1916. Ding's geological studies were mainly carried out in Yunnan, Guizhou, and Guangxi provinces in the second and third decades of the twentieth century; they contributed greatly to the understanding of Palaeozoic stratigraphy and geological structures in southwestern China. He was later a research professor of geology at Peking University (1931–1934).

Early Life. Ding was born into a local gentry family. His father, Ding Zengqi, married Miss Shan and had four children. Ding Wenjiang was their second son. His exceptional intelligence was shown in one of his examination papers when was eleven years old. In his paper he wrote about the accomplishment of the Emperor Han Wu Ti (140–87 BCE) in developing the southwestern areas of China. His interest in this region seemed to predict his later geological career.

Ding was educated first in Japan (1902–1904) and then in the United Kingdom (1904–1911). He stayed in Tokyo learning Japanese only one and a half years and then went to England where he studied at Cambridge University (1904–1906) and Glasgow University (1907), majoring in zoology and geology. He received two bachelor's degrees from Glasgow in 1911 at the age of twenty-four.

Geological Survey of China. In 1913, Ding was appointed chief of the Section of Geology under the Ministry of Industry and Commerce of the Peking govern-

ment of China. From early on he recognized the urgent need to train young Chinese geologists to do research. Through negotiations with the authorities in the Geology Department of Peking University, which had not accepted students since 1903, Ding and his colleagues, Zhang Hongzhao and Weng Wenhao, were able to use the building and equipment of the department to establish in 1913 the Geological Institute of China, which was actually a training college in geology. Some thirty students were enrolled and received three years of serious training. In this temporary educational institute, Ding taught geology and paleontology and was especially rigorous in field training and mapping. In 1916, eighteen students graduated. They were the first generation of Chinese-trained geologists and became the backbone of the newly established Geological Survey of China.

Ding was director of the Geological Survey of China from 1916 to 1921. In that post he initiated systematic prospecting of mineral resources and regional geological mapping. He established the National Geological Library and the National Geological Museum, both in Beijing, and authored various geological publications, including the *Bulletin of the Geological Society of China*, which was initially published annually and became a quarterly in 1948. The journal was renamed as *Acta Geologica Sinica*, affiliated with The Geological Society of China since 1952.

Palaeontologia Sinica. Of special note was Ding's role in the development and publication of the multivolume *Palaeontologia Sinica,* one of the most important palaeontological publications. Ding organized it with the help of Johan Gunnar Anderson of Sweden. Ding was the chief editor from 1921 (its first year of publication) until his death in 1936. Another contribution of note was the first issue of the Special Report of the Survey, titled *A General Statement on the Mining Industry of China,* by Ding and Weng Wen Hao, published in 1921. In it the authors point out that unsuccessful prospecting for oil in northern Shensi (Shaanxi) Province was probably the result of insufficient drilling, not lack of oil. This supposition proved correct, and the area later became one of the biggest oil and gas basins in North China.

Geological Society and Peking University. In 1922, Ding helped establish the Geological Society of China in Beijing, one of the earliest natural science organizations in China. He was president of the society in 1923 and was reelected in 1929.

Ding was a renowned geological educator. The Geology Department of Peking University, founded in 1909, but closed in 1912, was restored in 1917. In 1920, Ding invited Amadeus William Grabau from the United States and Li Siguang (J. S. Lee) from England to assume professorships in Peking University, and they greatly improved the department. From 1931 to 1934, Ding was himself a research professor at the university. The joint efforts of Ding, Li, and Grabau brought about the first era of success for the department in the 1920s and 1930s.

Travel in Europe. In 1933, Ding attended the Sixteenth International Geological Congress in Washington, DC, with Grabau and presented papers on the subdivision of Carboniferous and Permian, then a much-discussed problem in stratigraphy. Afterward he visited the United Kingdom and returned to the University of Glasgow. Then he traveled in Europe and spent more than a month visiting geological institutes in the Soviet Union. He was deeply interested in that country and wrote an article for the *Independence Review* in Beijing, praising the great efforts made by the Soviets in geology.

Central Academy of Sciences. In the summer of 1934, Ding was appointed secretary general of the Central Academy of Sciences of China in Shanghai. During his tenure of eighteen months, he contributed significantly to reforming the administration of the academy. He helped change the senate and the funding and budget systems, establishing the Adademician Committee, which enabled the senate to qualify academicians. These changes greatly enhanced the efficiency of the academy and improved the working efficiency of its research institutes. He also did his best to support independent scientific research free of prejudices.

Work in Southwestern China. Ding emphasized the importance of firsthand geological field observations and originality in geological studies. En route back to China from abroad in 1912, he visited Haiphong, Vietnam, and then traveled to Kunming, China, to begin a geological reconnaissance through the Yunnan, Guizhou, and western Hunan provinces. His routine geological survey was Ding's first fieldwork in southwestern China and this and his subsequent work there was of monumental importance to both Ding and Chinese geology. He revisited southwestern China twice, in 1914 and again in 1930. In 1914, he studied the Carboniferous, Permian, and Triassic sequences in northwestern Guizhou and established the Late Palaeozoic stratigraphic successions. In 1929–1930, he organized several groups for a systematic, comprehensive survey of the southwest region. These groups investigated from the perspectives of paleontology, geology, mineral resources, geography, and anthropology. On the basis of the rich material obtained, Ding established the Fengninian system of the Lower Carboniferous Age, the system that had been in use for many years in China.

Ding remained interested in paleontology and in 1932 published a paper on the brachiopod species, *Spirifer tingi* and *Spirifer hsiehi*, using statistical research methods.

Social and Political Contributions. Ding possessed wide interests in geology and mining. As a geologist and natural scientist, he contributed to mining exploration and industrial administration. Ding contributed eminently to academic and social enterprises. He wrote social and political commentaries and criticisms for many journals and led the well-known countrywide debate regarding his article "Metaphysics and Science" (1923) and "Science and Outlook of Life," the latter a compilation of articles including three papers by Ding. This was an intense debate about life outlook and points of view on social problems. Ding attempted to make "Mr. Science" an integral part of China's everyday life.

Death and Legacy. In the winter of 1935, the Ministry of Railways invited Ding to survey the Xiangtan coal mine in Hunan province to find coal for use by the Canton-Hankow Railway. Simultaneously, the Ministry of Education asked him to propose a new site for Tsinghua University. He began his work from Hengshan in Hunan. Ding lived in the Tanjiashan coal mine and was poisoned by the old-fashioned coal stove in his bedroom. He was sent to the Xiangya Hospital in Changsha for first aid, and some of the best Beijing doctors were sent to treat him. They were too late. He died on 5 January 1936, and was buried at the foot of Yuelushan Hill, west of Changsha His grave was restored in 1986.

Long after his death, Dr. Huang Jiqing (T. K. Huang) edited his manuscripts and created a volume with many attached maps, titled *Geological Reports of Dr. V. K. Ting* (1947), published by the Geological Survey in Nanjing.

Ding Wenjiang was first of all a patriot and then a most renowned geologist, natural scientist, scholar, and the most eminent and competent organizer and administrator in China of his time. He was awarded the fourth A. W. Grabau Medal by the Geological Society of China in 1932.

BIBLIOGRAPHY

WORKS BY DING

With F. Solger and H. B. Wang. 调查正太铁路附近地质矿务报告书 (Report on the Geology and mining industry along the Zhengding-taiyuan Railway). *Journal of the Ministry of Agriculture and Commerce Republic of China* 1, no. 1 (1914): 14–17; no. 2 (1914): 15–19.

With J. C. Zhang. 直隶山西间蔚县、广灵、阳原煤田报告 (Report on the coal fields of Yu-hsien, Yang-yuan, and Kuang-ling of Shansi-Hebei Provinces). *Geological Society of*

China Bulletin 1 (1919): 1–14. Includes an English-language abstract.

With W. H. Wong. "General Statement on the Mining Industry of China." *Special Report of the Geological Society of China,* Series C, no. 1 (1921): 1–36.

"Metaphysics and Science." *Nuli Zhoubao* (Endeavor weekly) no. 48 (15 April 1923) and no. 49 (22 April 1923).

"The Orogenic Movements in China." *Geological Society of China Bulletin* 8 (1929): 151–170. Ding's presidential address at the sixth annual meeting of the Geological Society of China.

"On the Stratigraphy of the Fengninian System." *Geological Society of China Bulletin* 10 (1931): 1–48.

谢石燕与丁石燕宽高比例的不同的统计研究 (A statistical study of the difference between the width–height ratio of *Spirifer tingi* and that of S*pirifer hsieh). Geological Society of China Bulletin* 11, no. 4 (June 1932): 465–472.

With Y. L. Wang. "Cambrian and Silurian Formations of Malung and Chutsing Districts, Yunnan." *Geological Society of China Bulletin* 16 (1937): 1–28. This issue appeared in the bulletin's V. K. Ting memorial volume, compiled and completed by T. H. Yin.

Geological Reports of Dr. V. K. Ting. Edited by Huang Jiqing. Nanking, China: Geological Survey in Nanking (1947).

OTHER SOURCES

Furth, Charlotte. *Ting Wen-chiang: Science and China's New Culture.* East Asian series no. 42. Cambridge, MA: Harvard University Press, 1970.

Hu Shih. *Biography of Dr. V. K. Ting.* Haikou, China: Hainan Publishing House, 1993.

Huang Jiqing, Pan Yuntang, and Xie Guanglian, eds. 丁文江选集. (Selected works of Ding Wenjiang [V. K. Ting].) Beijing: Peking University Press, 1993. Includes an English-language introduction.

Pan Yuntang and Cheng Yuqi. "Ding Wenjiang." In *Chinese Encyclopedia: Geology.* Beijing: Chinese Encyclopedia Press, 1993. In Chinese.

Wang Hongzhen, Sun Ronggui, and Cui Guangzhen. 中国地质事业早期史. (The early history of geological undertaking in China, in commemoration of the 100th anniversary of Dr. V. K. Ting's birth and the 110th anniversary of Prof. H. T. Chang's birth.) Peking: Peking University Press, 1990. Includes an English-language abstract.

You Zhendong

DIOCLES OF CARYSTUS (b. Carystus [?];
Greece; fourth century BCE), *medicine, anatomy.* For the original article on Diocles see *DSB,* vol. 4.

Diocles of Carystus (a major town on the south end of the Greek island of Euboea, facing the East Coast of Attica) is enjoying renewed attention from historians of medicine, science, and philosophy. His significance as a major thinker, practitioner, and writer of the fourth cen-

tury BCE had always been recognised from antiquity onwards, but the details of his role in the history of medicine and related areas like botany—and possibly even meteorology—are now more accurately being grasped (see van der Eijk, 2000–2001; Hankinson,2002; Vivian Nutton, 2004).

This renewed interest comes after several decades of considerable neglect. Early and mid-twentieth century attempts to date and relate Diocles's medical ideas to other intellectual traditions (such as Max Wellmann's claim [1901] that Diocles belonged to the Sicilian school of medicine, or Werner Jaeger's thesis [1938; 1940; 1951; 1952] that Diocles was a pupil of Aristotle's) have proven too speculative and failed to find universal agreement (for surveys of earlier scholarship see von Staden, 1992, and Longrigg, 1993). A period of scepticism followed, and scholarship was aporetically stuck in "Probleme um Diokles von Karystos" (Kudlien, 1963). The chief difficulties were the fragmentary nature of the evidence (none of Diocles's works have survived in their entirety) and the bias of the sources reporting or quoting his views. The absence of a reliable collection, interpretation, and evaluation of the surviving evidence (Wellmann's 1901 collection widely being regarded as obsolete) presented a serious obstacle to a fresh and comprehensive investigation of his views.

New Historical Methods. Yet two related trends in classical scholarship addressed this situation and helped to restore Diocles's prominent position in the history of thought. First, there has been a renewed and systematic examination of medical and philosophical doxography and, more generally, of ancient authors' methods and strategies for quoting, reporting, and representing the views of earlier authorities. (Mansfeld and Runia, 1996; van der Eijk, 1999b). Scholars' knowledge of Diocles's ideas depends entirely on what later authors tell about him—authors such as Galen, Celsus, Pliny the Elder, Oribasius, Soranus, Caelius Aurelianus, the so-called 'Anonymous of Paris' (probably first century CE), Aëtius the doxographer, and Athenaeus of Naucratis's *Sophists at Dinner* (a voluminous work from the second century CE full of quotations from earlier authors). It is therefore important to determine how well informed they were (e.g. whether they had direct access to Diocles's writings or relied on intermediary sources), how they viewed his role in the history of medicine and his relationship to other medical authors, for what reasons they were interested in him, for what reasons they were citing or quoting him, what the peculiarities were of their methods of reporting, and how selective they may have been in directing their attention to specific areas of Diocles's output. Such determination is important not only in order to estimate the extent to which all these factors may have colored their representation of Diocles's views and scientific activity, but also to evaluate the information these source authors provide and to have some idea as to what one can expect them to say.

Secondly, and on the basis of this development, there has been a new approach to fragment collecting in classical scholarship that takes due account of the context in which a fragment is embedded and of the role of the reporting author in the representation of a thinker's views (Burkert,1998; van der Eijk, 1999a; Hanson, 1997). This then feeds into the reconstruction of the thinker's views in that, during the process of piecing together the surviving evidence, the material is differentially weighted in accordance with its relative evidential value.

In the case of Diocles, these scholarly developments led to a new collection, English translation, and comprehensive interpretation of the fragments (van der Eijk 2000–2001), which provides a basis for renewed study. The net result is a substantial collection of 234 fragments (more than fifty more than in Wellmann's collection), surviving in Greek, Latin, and Arabic; of these, nearly forty fragments lay claim to being direct *verbatim* quotations from his works (although in some cases their reliability is somewhat dubious), ranging in size from a few words to ten pages of text (fr. 182); the rest are reports in indirect speech, sometimes paraphrase, sometimes openly polemical in nature (for example, Caelius Aurelianus, our major source for Diocles's therapeutic views, heavily criticised him), or associating Diocles's views with those of other medical writers (such as many testimonies in Galen, who on the whole tends to downplay Diocles's originality in favor of his own achievements). The evidence adds up to an overall picture of a very self-conscious scientific thinker/practitioner with wide-ranging interests and a substantial output.

The titles surviving from his works are *Anatomy* (according to Galen the first handbook of its kind), *Affection, Cause, Treatment* (Diocles's major work on pathology), *On Treatments* (a detailed work in at least four books on the treatment of a wide range of different diseases), *On Prognosis, On Fevers, On Digestion, On Catarrhs, On Matters related to Women* (an extensive work in at least three books), *On Matters of Health to Pleistarchus* (Diocles's major work on regimen in health), *Archidamus* (on the medicinal usage of olive oil), *On Evacuations, On Bandages, On External Remedies, On Lethal Drugs, On Vegetables, On Rootcutting, In the Surgery, On Sexual Activity, Letter on the Preservation of Health to Antigonus,* and *On Cookery* (the evidence for the latter three works is, however, not entirely secure). It is reasonably certain that at least some of these works were widely available in the Hellenistic and early Imperial age, and some were subjected to close textual and medical analysis: Thus the first century BCE writer Apollonius of Citium quotes from Diocles's

work on surgery (fr. 163), Galen reports textual variants in different copies of Diocles's *Matters of Health* (fr. 188), and Oribasius in the fourth century preserved some extensive excerpts from Diocles's dietetic and therapeutic works. In the Byzantine era, however, direct access to Diocles's works seems to have become rare, and Arabic authors citing him seem to have been familiar with his views through Galen and other intermediaries only.

Research Approach. It is clear that, in antiquity, Diocles played a key role in the development of dissection and comparative anatomical research (fr. 24b refers to repeated animal dissection to prove a point in human anatomy), in systematic pathology (carefully distinguishing causes, symptoms, and therapies), in the further differentiation and refinement of therapeutics and surgery (where he earned fame for his *spoon* for the removal of arrow heads [fr. 167] and for his *bowl,* a particular type of bandage [fr. 166]), in gynaecology and especially dietetics and regimen in health—a field in which he acquired the greatest reputation (although again our view may be somewhat distorted by bias on the part of the sources and in the subsequent selective transmission of his ideas). He collected and systematised a large number of foods and drinks, herbs, and poisons. He went into great detail specifying their qualities and powers (*dunameis*) and differentiating according to mode of preparation, environmental factors such as season and climate, and according to age, living pattern, and constitution of the patient. Furthermore, his views on the role of *pneuma* in the psychophysiology of human cognition (in which both the heart and the brain are involved), emotion, movement, and action, as well as on blockage of the flow of *pneuma* as the major cause of a number of diseases, clearly paved the way for later developments in Hellenistic medicine and Stoic philosophy; and his account of *hypochondriac melancholy* (fr. 109) continued to be cited by later authors (Greek as well as Arabic) as the authoritative treatment of the subject.

Apart from this, Diocles is also being appreciated by historians of ancient philosophy for his methodological awareness and his theoretical views on causal explanation, inference from signs, for his careful balancing of reason and experience, and for the overall consistency and coherence of his views (Frede, 1987; Hankinson, 1998 and 2002). Diocles was not an armchair physician, and he clearly had a keen interest in the phenomena and in the practical aspects of medical care. Yet at the same time, he displayed a strong theoretical outlook, a desire to build his medical views on a general theory of nature, and a belief that the treatment of specific bodily parts has to be based on a consideration of the patient's body (and mind) as a whole—characteristics that prompted later Greek medical writers reflecting on the history of their own subject to speak of him as a member of the Rationalist (*logikos*) or

Dogmatist (*dogmatikos*) sect of medicine. It is true that Diocles sometimes showed himself eager to back up physiological reasoning by empirical evidence (e.g., in frs. 109 and 176), and he insisted that causal explanations must be empirically verifiable and relevant to the situation at hand (fr. 176). At the same time, he did not shy away from referring to hidden causes (fr. 178) and other invisible entities like *pneuma*; he seems to have adopted rather uncritically the principle that healing takes place by means of opposite qualities, and he shared several more speculative interests of some of the Hippocratic writers, such as the notion of critical days and the belief in the determining role of the number seven in areas like embryological development.

It is further clear that Diocles was a prolific writer and medical communicator using a variety of literary forms (including doxographical discourse and possibly letters and dialogues) and an elegance of style that would have contributed to the dissemination of medical ideas among wider audiences. He was part of a movement aiming for expansion of the area of expertise commanded by the medical profession of his time, comprising areas like wine-tasting, cookery, gymnastics, travel, and other life-style features, even the raising of children—all of which belonged to the matters of health (*hugieina*) covered by the health expert (*hugieinos*).

In all this, Diocles was most likely aware of a considerable number of other medical, scientific, and philosophical views of his time. He is seen on a number of occasions taking account of existing ideas, including some of the views found in the so-called Hippocratic writings, with which he sometimes took issue, but claims that he possessed, or even created, a Hippocratic Corpus go beyond the evidence (and there is no certainty that he took these writings to be by Hippocrates). On other occasions, he quoted or reported the works of Aristotle (fr. 40) and of a physician named Archidamus (fr. 185)—perhaps his father, although again this is not certain—and he displayed a more general concern with medical language and nomenclature. Considering his high reputation in Athens, it is plausible to assume that he was in touch with the main currents and centers of scientific thinking, such as Plato's Academy and Aristotle's Lyceum, and probably also the Athenian physician Mnesitheus and other dietetic writers, and although it is difficult to prove influence, similarities with Aristotelian and Peripatetic ideas and styles of reasoning and arguing are unmistakable. Yet there is no evidence that Diocles was a member or pupil at Aristotle's school, and there is good reason to believe that any intellectual exchange there may have been in both directions (the oldest reference to Diocles being found in Theophrastus's work *On Stones*).

On the negative side, associations of Diocles with Sicilian medicine (as represented by Empedocles, Philistion, and Plato) must be considered doubtful, and something similar applies to his putative connections with empiricism or scepticism: These are constructs of twentieth-century scholarship that fail to find corroboration by the evidence. Likewise, the hotly disputed question of Diocles's date must be regarded as insoluble for lack of secure independent evidence. All that can be said with some degree of certainty is that Diocles lived somewhat later than Hippocrates and somewhat earlier than Erasistratus and Herophilus. Considering the difficulties involved in dating these medical writers, the question must remain open, and any reasonable pair of dates within the broad time-frame of the fourth century must be deemed possible.

SUPPLEMENTARY BIBLIOGRAPHY

WORKS BY DIOCLES OF CARYSTUS

Eijk, Philip J. van der. *Diocles of Carystus. A Collection of the Fragments with Translation and Commentary.* Vol. 1: *Text and Translation.* Leiden, Germany: Brill (Studies in Ancient Medicine 22), 2000; Vol. 2: *Commentary.* Leiden, Germany: Brill (Studies in Ancient Medicine 23), 2001. This replaces the older editions by Max Wellmann *Die Fragmente der sikelischen Ärzte Akron, Philistion und des Diokles von Karystos* (Fragmentsammlung der griechischen Ärzte, Band 1), Berlin: Weidmann, 1901, and Moritz Fraenkel, *Dioclis Carystii fragmenta quae supersunt*, Berlin: Typus Haynianis, 1840. Collection of the fragments of Diocles.

OTHER SOURCES

Burkert, Walter, ed. *Fragmentsammlungen philosophischer Texte der Antike—Le raccolte dei frammenti di filosofi antichi.* Göttingen, Germany: Van den Hoeck & Rupprecht, 1998.

Eijk, Philip J. van der. "Some methodological issues in collecting the fragments of Diocles of Carystus." In *I testi medici greci III. Tradizione e ecdotica,* edited by Antonio Garzya and Jacques Jouanna. Naples: M. d'Auria, 1999a.

———, ed. *Ancient Histories of Medicine. Essays in Medical Historiography and Doxography in Classical Antiquity.* Leiden, Germany: Brill, 1999b.

———. "Diocles and the Hippocratic writings on the method of dietetics and the limits of causal explanation." In *Medicine and Philosophy in Classical Antiquity. Doctors and Philosophers on Nature, Soul, Health and Disease,* by Philip J. van der Eijk. Cambridge, U.K.: Cambridge University Press, 2005.

———. "The Heart, the Brain, the Blood and the Pneuma: Hippocrates, Diocles and Aristotle on the Location of Cognitive Processes." In *Medicine and Philosophy in Classical Antiquity. Doctors and Philosophers on Nature, Soul, Health and Disease,* by Philip J. van der Eijk. Cambridge, U.K.: Cambridge University Press, 2005.

———. "To Help, or to Do no Harm. Principles and Practices of Therapeutics in the Hippocratic Corpus and in the Work of Diocles of Carystus." In *Medicine and Philosophy in Classical Antiquity. Doctors and Philosophers on Nature, Soul,*

Health and Disease, by Philip J. van der Eijk. Cambridge, U.K.: Cambridge University Press, 2005.

Frede, Michael. "The Original Notion of Cause." In *Essays in Ancient Philosophy*, edited by Michael Frede. Oxford: Clarendon Press 1987.

Hankinson, R James. *Cause and Explanation in Ancient Greek Thought*. Oxford: Clarendon Press, 1998.

———. "Doctoring history: ancient medical historiography and Diocles of Carystus," *Apeiron* 35 (2002): 65–81.

Hanson, Ann Ellis. "Fragmentation and the Greek medical writers." In *Collecting Fragments—Fragmente sammeln*, edited by Glenn W. Most. Göttingen, Germany: Van den Hoeck & Rupprecht, 1997.

Harig, Gerhard, and Kollesch, Jutta. "Diokles von Karystos und die zoologische Systematik." *NTM Schriftenreihe zur Geschichte der Naturwissenschaften, Technik und Medizin* 11 (1974): 24–31.

Jaeger, Werner Wilhelm. *Diokles von Karystos. Die griechische Medizin und die Schule des Aristoteles*, Berlin: Weidmann, 1938a.

———. "Vergessene Fragmente des Peripatetikers Diokles von Karystos. Nebst zwei Abhandlungen zur Chronologie der dogmatischen Ärzteschule." *Abhandlungen der preussischen Akademie der Wissenschaften*, Philosophisch–historische Klasse, 1938b.

———. "Diocles. A New Pupil of Aristotle." *Philosophical Review* 49 (1940): 393–414.

———. "Diokles von Karystos. Ein neuer Schüler des Aristoteles." *Zeitschrift für philosophische Forschung* 5 (1951): 25–46.

———. "Diokles von Karystos und Aristoxenos über die Prinzipien." In *Hermeneia. Festschrift für Otto Regenbogen*. Heidelberg, 1952.

Kudlien, Fridolf. "Probleme um Diokles von Karystos." *Sudhoffs Archiv* 47 (1963): 456–464.

———. "Diokles von Karystos." *Der kleine Pauly* 2 (1967): 56–57.

Kullmann, Wolfgang. *Wissenschaft und Methode. Interpretationen zur aristotelischen Theorie der Naturwissenschaft*. Berlin: De Gruyter, 1974.

Longrigg, James. *Greek Rational Medicine*, London: Routledge, 1993.

———. *Greek Medicine from the Heroic to the Hellenistic Age*. New York: Routledge, 1998.

Mansfeld, Jaap, and Runia, David T., *Aetiana. The Method and Intellectual Context of an Ancient Doxographer*, Vol. 1: *The Sources*. Leiden, Germany: Brill, 1996.

Nutton, Vivian. "Diokles von Karystos." *Der neue Pauly* 3 (1997): 610–613.

———. *Ancient Medicine*. London: Routledge, 2004.

Sconocchia, Sergio. "La lettere di Diocle ad Antigono e le sue traduzioni latine." In *Prefazioni, prologhi, proemi di opere technico-scientifiche latine*, edited by Carlo Santini and Nino Scivoletto, Vol. 3. Rome: Herder,1998.

Staden, Heinrich von. "Jaeger's 'Skandalon der historischen Vernunft': Diocles, Aristotle, and Theophrastus." In *Werner Jaeger Reconsidered: Proceedings of the Second Oldfather Conference, University of Illinois, 26–28 April 1990*, edited by William M. Calder III. Atlanta: Scholar's Press, 1992.

Torraca, Luigi. "Diocle di Caristo, il Corpus Hippocraticum ed Aristotele." *Sophia* 33 (1965): 105–115.

Vallance, J. "Diocles (3)." In *Oxford Classical Dictionary*, edited by Simon Hornblower and Anthony Spawforth. Oxford: Oxford Unviersity Press, 1996, 470.

Wöhrle, Georg. *Studien zur Theorie der antiken Gesundheitslehre* (Hermes Einzelschriften 56). Stuttgart, Germany: Steiner Verlag, 1990.

Philip J. van der Eijk

DIODORUS OF ALEXANDRIA (*fl.* first century BCE), *gnomonics, astronomy.*

Diodorus of Alexandria was the author of the first treatise on sundials from which any significant amount of material has survived, and he is described in *The Palatine Anthology* as "famous among the gnomonists." (The gnomon is, in this context, the rod that casts a shadow in a sundial.) He is also known as one who attempted a proof of Euclid's famous parallel postulate "with a number of different figures."

Among the nonmathematical writings of Diodorus are treatises on physics and uranography. Although some have suggested that the authors in the three areas were different people, all three are referred to as "a mathematician" in ancient sources and, as Don R. Edwards has put it (1984, p. 153), "if little leads one to identify the three, nothing whatever prevents one." On the basis of the identification of these three writers named Diodorus as being one and the same person, then, Diodorus of Alexandria may be dated to the first century BCE. This is largely because of his having disagreed with Posidonius (c. 135–50 BCE) on the Milky Way and his having been quoted by the philosopher Eudorus (d. c. 25 BCE). More than this the sources do not reveal.

Work on the Heavens. His writing on uranography (that branch of Greek astronomy which describes the appearance of the stars and their constellations) appears, from the surviving references, to have been a commentary on Aratus's versified form of Eudoxus's *Phenomena*. For example, a scholium on Aratus cites Diodorus as commenting on a controversy between Attalus and Hipparchus about the position of stars in the constellation Draco. It is not clear if this is the same work as one referred to in both an ancient catalog of writers and a Byzantine scholium as one of those who "wrote about the pole [of the cosmos]." (Ernst Maass takes this, quite plausibly, to refer to a treatise on celestial phenomena.)

In physics, Macrobius cites Diodorus as arguing that the Milky Way is made of fiery particles. As regards the differences between mathematics and physics, Diodorus argues that although there is a conceptual difference between physical and mathematical argument one ought, when investigating a question where both are relevant, to ignore the conceptual distinction.

Work on Sundials. It was, however, his *Analemma,* a treatise on sundials, which brought Diodorus a lasting reputation. His writing in this area first appears in the first century CE incorporated in the writings of the Roman surveyor Hyginus Gromaticus, who describes a method for finding the local meridian (north-south) line. Hyginus does not name his source, but from Arabic works (below) we know that Diodorus invented the method. Then Pappus of Alexandria (c. 300 CE) composed a commentary on Diodorus's *Analemma* in which, as he says (in Book IV of his *Collection*), "we used the aforesaid line [the cochloid of Nicomedes] when we sought to trisect the angle." Indeed, because a circular arc representing the period of daylight on the face of a sundial would have to be divided into twelve segments (corresponding to the twelve hours into which the ancients divided the period of daylight), the problem of constructing sundials immediately leads one to the problem of trisecting an arc.

The word *analemma* is also used in a mathematical sense by Vitruvius Pollio, who lived at the time of Augustus, in his *Architecture* IX, 7 to describe a geometrical construction to determine the length of the noon shadow at a locality of given latitude when the sun has a given declination. Later, Heron of Alexandria applies the word to a similar method for determining the distance between Alexandria and Rome. Most famously the word is part of the title of Claudius Ptolemy's treatise on sundials, *On the Analemma.* In all these cases, the context is a solution to a problem by rotating geometrical objects—angles, circular arcs, or triangles—associated with the celestial sphere into a working plane where angles and arcs can be faithfully represented and measured. (The working plane represents a plane in the celestial sphere—often the local meridian—and the object is rotated about the line of the intersection of the working plane and the plane containing the object.) Thus, in Vitruvius's analemma, circle ABC represents the local meridian of the celestial sphere, which provides the working plane. The horizontal line represents the local horizon, and semicircle ADB represents the eastern half of the circle traced out by the sun (during the course of a given twenty-four-hour day) rotated 90° about AB into the working plane. The perpendicular DE represents the intersection of the semicircle with the horizon and hence arc AD measures half the length of daylight on the given day.

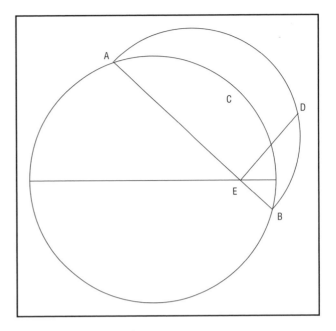

Figure 1. *A simple analemma.*

Diodorus's treatise used such methods to design sundials. But to orient the completed dial properly one would need to know the local meridian. And in the surviving extract from his book, Diodorus shows how to construct a geometrical diagram in the horizontal plane to determine this meridian. In his method, three triangles formed by a gnomon and its shadow in the planes of three altitude circles at different times during the day are represented by similar triangles in the plane of the horizon. And it is these triangles that allow the construction of the local north-south line.

Arabic References. Diodorus's *Analemma* was translated into Arabic and quoted by the gifted mathematician Ibrāhīm ibn Sinān of Baghdad (908–946). In his *Treatise on Shadow Instruments,* Ibn Sinān writes, "we take the tip of the gnomon as center of the [celestial] sphere as well as of all great circles which are on the sphere, such as the horizon and others. Diodorus and others took this as a principle in their works on the instrument."

Later in the tenth century, a little-known geometer, Abū Saʿīd al-Darīr ("the blind"), in his treatise *On the Determination of the Local Meridian,* cites a work titled *The Analemma* as the source of most of his treatise. That it was Diodorus's *Analemma* referred to is clear from Abū Rayḥān al-Bīrūnī's (d. 1048) *Exhaustive Treatise on Shadows,* where the method found in Abū Saʿīd is attributed to Diodorus's *Analemma.* (It is a curious turn of fate that, although Ptolemy did not mention Diodorus's *Analemma* in his work of the same name, it was via Diodorus's treatise, and not that of Ptolemy, which was unknown in medieval Islam, that the method of the analemma was introduced to medieval Islam.)

An important part of Abū Saʿīd's proof is a demonstration that two lines occurring in the procedure intersect on a certain side of a transversal. The proof of this demands, of course, a use of Euclid's parallel postulate, and it may be significant in this regard that the tenth-century writer al-Nairīzī, following Simplicius, mentions that Diodorus proved the parallel postulate by means of many different figures.

Finally, in addition to the above-cited discussion of the parallel postulate it appears that Diodorus also wrote on Euclid's *Data*. Because the *Data* shows that if certain features of a geometrical configuration are given, other features are given as well, it was useful in the analysis of geometrical problems. There was, however, some discussion of what, exactly, Euclid meant by "given," and Marinus of Neapolis cites Diodorus as taking "given" to mean "known…and whatsoever comes to a certain comprehension…even if it is not rational."

BIBLIOGRAPHY

WORK BY DIODORUS OF ALEXANDRIA

Bīrūnī, Muhammad ibn Ahmad. *The Exhaustive Treatise on Shadows by Abū Rayhān al-Bīrūnī* [Ifrād al-maqāl fi amr al-zilāl], translated by Edward S. Kennedy. 2 vols. Aleppo, Syria: University of Aleppo, 1976. Contains an English translation of the Arabic version of the surviving fragment from Diodorus's *Analemma*.

OTHER SOURCES

Besthorn, Rasmus O., and Johann L. Heiberg, eds. *Euclidis Elementa ex interpretatione al-Hadschdschadschī cum commentaries al-Nairīzī*. Part 1. Copenhagen, 1907.

Blume, Friedrich, Karl Lachmann, and Adolf Rudorff, eds. *Die Schriften der römischen Feldmesser*. Berlin: O. Reimer, 1848. Reprinted, Hildesheim, Germany: Olms, 1967.

Edwards, Don R. *Ptolemy's Περι αναλημματος: An Annotated Transcription of Moerbeke's Latin Translation and of the Surviving Greek Fragments with an English Version and Commentary*. Thesis, Brown University, 1984.

Kennedy, Edward S. "Bīrūnī's Graphical Determination of the Local Meridian." *Scripta Mathematica* 24 (1959): 251–255. Reprinted in *Studies in the Islamic Exact Sciences*, edited by Edward S. Kennedy, et al. Beirut: American University of Beirut Press, 1983.

Maass, Ernst. "Aratea." In *Philologische Untersuchungen*, vol. 12. Berlin: Weidmann, 1892.

Neugebauer, Otto N. *A History of Ancient Mathematical Astronomy*. 3 parts. New York: Springer-Verlag, 1975.

Schoy, Carl. "Abhandlung über die Ziehung der Mittagslinie, dem Buche über das Analemma entnommen, samt dem Beweis dazu von Abū Saʿīd ad-Darīr." *Annalen der*

Hydrographie und maritimen Meteorologie 10 (1922): 265–271.

　　　　　　　　　　　　　　　　J. Lennart Berggren

DOBSON, GORDON MILLER BOURNE

(*b.* Windermere, Cumbria, United Kingdom, 25 February 1889; *d.* Oxford, United Kingdom, 10 March 1976), *atmospheric ozone, atmospheric physics, atmospheric chemistry, meteorology.*

Dobson made the first systematic measurements of stratospheric ozone in the 1920s and 1930s. He elucidated how its behavior varied with latitude and season, using equipment that he developed.

Education and War Years. Gordon Dobson was born the youngest of four children (sisters Alice and Kate, brother Harry). His father, Thomas Dobson, was a medical practitioner in Windermere; his mother was Marianne Bourne. The family had a large house close to the lake. He was educated at Sedbergh School then at Gonville and Caius College, Cambridge University, from which he graduated in 1910 with a first-class BA in natural sciences. During his final year he studied geophysics and came across work by George Chrystal on seiches (oscillations in the water level) in Scottish lochs. This prompted him to build a simple chart recorder, which he used at his family boathouse on Lake Windermere. The lake is 18 kilometers long and displays various modes of oscillation that Dobson was able to isolate and successfully compare with elementary theory. The results were published in *Nature* in 1911.

Dobson had shown a clear bent for experimental physics from his time at school, having built a Tesla coil and a Wimshurst machine from rudimentary materials, and his later skill as an instrument designer and builder was already evident in a photograph of his seiche recorder.

His *Nature* paper led to a job offer from (William) Napier Shaw, director of the British Meteorological Office, to work at Kew Observatory, jointly funded by the Meteorological Office and Gonville and Caius College. While at Kew he worked with Charles Thomas Rees Wilson (on vertical wind velocity measurement) and William Henry Dines (assisting with balloon flights) amongst others, and he had a short spell running the Eskdalemuir magnetic observatory. In 1913, he was appointed meteorological advisor to the new military Central Flying School on Salisbury Plain (a 1917 paper gives his position as captain in the Royal Flying Corps) where he began pioneering work measuring the vertical wind profile. This led to a close association with the fluid dynamicist Geoffrey

Ingram Taylor, who had predicted the wind behavior in the boundary layer theoretically.

At the outbreak of war in 1914, his duties changed to instrument design, for example overseeing the development of the Aldis signaling lamp, leading to his appointment in 1916 as director of the Experimental Department of the Royal Aircraft Establishment (RAE), Farnborough. This carried a wide remit given his youth, including oversight of areas well outside his expertise. At a time when science was thought to have little relevance to the war effort, the RAE was a powerhouse for invention: Thus Dobson was fortunate to have found himself there working with a group of very able scientists and mathematicians. One of these was Frederick Alexander Lindemann, who was later to become Lord Cherwell, scientific advisor to and close confidant of Sir Winston Churchill during World War II. Together Dobson and Lindemann worked on projects such as one of the first automatic pilots and balloon cable cutters for aircraft. In 1919, Lindemann took the post of head of the Oxford University Physics Department (the Clarendon Laboratory) and quickly initiated a period of several decades of growth and success. Dobson was recruited as meteorology demonstrator in 1920.

Temperature and Ozone. Together Dobson and Lindemann undertook pioneering analysis (later described by Richard Goody as brilliant) of the height at which meteors burn up, leading to the conclusion that the atmospheric density above the 50-kilometer region was 100–1,000 times larger than previously assumed. This implied that temperature must increase substantially at lower levels, whereas currently it was assumed to be constant above the limit of balloon measurements (25 km). This was later corroborated by analysis of long-range sound propagation patterns, and with sounding rockets in the late 1940s. They proposed that the increase was caused by solar radiative heating of ozone that had been formed by ultraviolet dissociation of oxygen, which has proved to be correct.

This discovery led Dobson to develop methods to measure atmospheric ozone distribution. Work by Alfred Cornu, Walter Hartley, Alfred Fowler, and Robert Strutt had demonstrated ozone features in solar ultraviolet spectra. In 1921, Charles Fabry and Henri Buisson had determined the equivalent thickness of the atmospheric ozone layer by comparing the ultraviolet intensity in the Sun's direct beam at a single ozone absorbing wavelength with the Sun at two or more different zenith angles. They allowed for the effects of scattering by air molecules but were unable to correct for any aerosol absorption. Dobson and Douglas Neill Harrison improved this technique. By employing two nearby wavelengths with differing ozone absorptions and by assuming the same aerosol absorption in each, they were able to mainly eliminate aerosol contributions. Several pairs were normally used.

This work was performed with a spectrophotometer that Dobson designed and built, which employed a Féry prism, and a cell containing a mixture of chlorine and

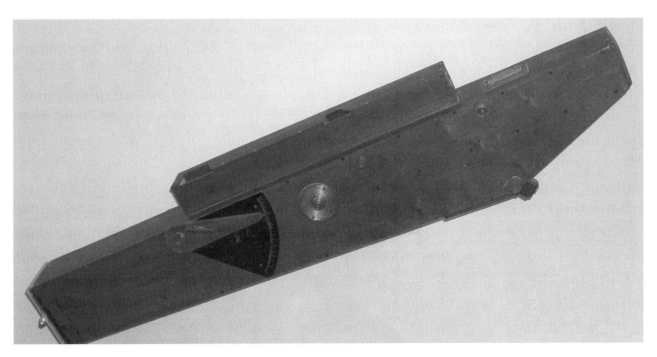

Spectrophotometer. *Fery prism photographic ozone spectrophotometer #3 built by Dobson in 1925.* **COURTESY OF JOHN BARNETT.**

bromine that transmits in the ultraviolet but blocks stronger and longer wavelengths. The cell enabled the instrument to be smaller than Fabry and Buisson's double monochromator, and portable. A photographic plate recorded the spectrum, and a neutral density wedge was arranged to give a known linear gradation perpendicular to the wavelength direction (so that features produced a signature whose size on the emulsion was proportional to their intensity). Development of the plate required a consistent procedure and a purpose-designed development tank. He built probably the first electronic densitometer to measure the degree of absorption on the plates, employing photocells developed elsewhere in the Clarendon. He wrote a book about the photographic aspects in 1926.

The first spectra were obtained in September 1924, and the results were so encouraging that a year later he began to build five more instruments partly funded by the Royal Society. These were placed at various European locations; the Smithsonian Institution funded another that was placed in Chile. Observations began in July 1926, with the photographic plates being returned to Oxford for processing. Dobson maintained the enthusiasm of the observers by mailing back results, annotated weather maps, etc. More than five thousand plates were measured during this campaign.

The instruments were then redeployed worldwide to California (Table Mountain Observatory), Egypt (Helwan), India (Kodaikanal), New Zealand (Christchurch), Switzerland (Arosa), plus Oxford. By the end of 1929, Dobson and his associates had established the main seasonal and latitudinal behavior of column ozone, apart from at high latitudes. A strong correlation with weather systems was found in both campaigns, and was later known to be due to the column mass of the stratosphere varying with tropopause height.

During this campaign, Dobson was working on a very much more advanced design that replaced photographic emulsion by photocells and could therefore benefit from current and future detector advances. It employed a rotary chopper and a double Féry monochromator (i.e., two in tandem) but in an unconventional configuration, to reduce stray light. Moveable neutral density wedges were used in a null arrangement that directly found the intensity ratio for two wavelengths.

The first observation considered publishable was made in July 1930. Measurements could then be made much more quickly (a few minutes) and the analysis performed on-site without sending the plates to Oxford. The technique was much more sensitive, and opened the way to making measurements with the Sun obscured by cloud.

It also enabled *Umkehr* measurements to be made: Paul Götz had recently shown that measurement of the intensity ratios for scattered light using a zenith view at several different wavelengths would allow a height-resolved profile to be obtained. This showed that the ozone concentration peaked at about 25 kilometers, half that of earlier results by others using views of the Sun at angles near the horizon. Balloon flights by Erich and Victor Regener confirmed this lower altitude, which was later known to be correct. *Umkehr* (a term Götz suggested to describe the way the graphs turned back at low sun angles) measurements opened up a new dimension which Dobson continued to explore throughout his life. The instrument was too complex for Dobson to manufacture in quantity himself, and a commercial instrument maker started limited production in about 1932.

Water Vapor. The outbreak of World War II forced a national change in scientific activity. While his Clarendon colleagues moved to radar and isotope separation work, Dobson was asked to help understand the formation of aircraft condensation trails, which were unpredictable and causing many losses because they made aircraft very prominent (a small dot of an aircraft can leave behind a huge trail that couldn't be missed). Existing humidity sensors were completely inadequate for the low dew points existing at high altitudes, and Dobson designed and built a new frost point hygrometer for aircraft use. The Meteorological Office provided Alan W. Brewer to lead the measurement program. By 1942, Dobson and Brewer had completed extensive measurements and achieved a good understanding of quite subtle behavior. Using a Flying Fortress they were able to reach above 11 kilometers altitude in 1943, and found that above the tropopause (then at 9 km) the frost point fell rapidly while the temperature rose.

Dobson presented the 1945 Royal Society Bakerian Lecture and showed clear evidence, based on thirteen ascents, of a much drier stratosphere than was expected. No firm explanations were proposed. He suggested that air might be entering the stratosphere via the tropics where the tropopause was very cold and thereby being freeze-dried, but he still assumed the classical picture of a stationary stratosphere in radiative balance, whereby the incoming and outgoing radiation were thought to balance each other, with no significant vertical motion to cause adiabatic heating or cooling. Brewer was recruited to Oxford in 1948 as meteorology lecturer, and in 1949, Brewer published a seminal paper proposing a circulation where air rises in the tropics, and falls over the poles in a circular fashion that would largely explain the water vapor observations, but departs a long way from radiative balance. Dobson seems to have been unconvinced by this theory (on the grounds that angular momentum would not be conserved) until further evidence mounted up by 1957. Not until the 1980s was the *Brewer-Dobson circulation,* as it came to be called, generally accepted.

Later Work. Dobson undertook work on the formation of ice particles in the 1950s, building cloud chambers which his research students used, but his main effort was concentrated on ozone measurement, both improving the spectrophotometer design (e.g., fitting photomultipliers, with greater sensitivity and enabling use of shorter wavelengths), and supporting the worldwide network that he had built up (forty-four Dobson spectrometers by 1956, and as of 2005 the primary standard for ozone column measurements with about one hundred active stations). He was assisted by Sir Charles Normand, who had retired from the Indian Meteorological Service, and by C. D. Walshaw. The International Geophysical Year (1957) brought new results, including the observation that the Antarctic seasonal cycle was very different from that of the Arctic.

Dobson was made a DSc of Oxford in 1924, based on a submission of fourteen scientific papers, and elected as a Fellow of the Royal Society in 1927, being awarded their Rumford Medal in 1942. In 1938, he was awarded the Royal Meteorological Society Symons Medal. He was appointed a professor in 1945, and was president of the Royal Meteorological Society from 1947 to 1949. He was award the CBE honor in 1951 and retired in 1956. He was president of the newly founded International Ozone Commission between 1948 and 1960, and the commission provided important funding to support the observing network. Between 1934 and 1950, he was chair of the U.K. government Atmospheric Pollution Committee and undertook some research in this area.

Dobson married Winifred Duncombe Rimer in 1914, and they had a daughter (Kathleen) and two sons (Desmond and Robert). A major outside interest was sheep farming, and their move in 1937 to a large new house on Shotover Hill on the outskirts of Oxford, with extensive grounds, enabled him to pursue this hobby as well as gardening, particularly of fruit and vegetables. He also inherited three farms in Cumbria from his father.

A necessary feature of his new house was an uninterrupted view to the south to permit ozone observation. He built a new observatory and workshop, both of which were featured in an article in the *Oxford Times* newspaper (1957). He was one of the last of a long series of scientists to undertake world-class research in their own facilities using partly their own funding (Winifred had a private income; Dobson had a significant inheritance); indeed, much of his own and his students' research was conducted from home rather than at the university. Before electricity was connected in the early 1920s students would cycle several kilometers to his house from central Oxford with lead-acid batteries to supply the equipment.

His other interests included music (he played the piano and violin), and he was a warden at St. Aldates Anglican Church, Oxford. Winifred died in 1952, and in 1954, he married Olive Mary Bacon who survived him. His last paper was written in 1973. A day after making an ozone observation he suffered a stroke, from which he died six weeks later on 10 March 1976.

After his death Dobson's name became well known even to the general public because of widespread concern about ozone depletion, and also the use of the Dobson Unit to describe the ozone column amount. In 2004, the International Ozone Commission established the quadrennial Dobson Award to a young scientist for the most significant contribution to ozone research in the previous four years.

The Dobson Unit is defined as the column amount of ozone given in units of 0.01 millimeter at 1 bar pressure and 0° Celsius. That is, if the total quantity of ozone (between the surface and space) is brought to a single layer of pure ozone at 1 bar pressure and 0° Celsius, the measurement in Dobson Units is the vertical thickness of that layer in units of 0.01 millimeter. A typical quantity is 300 Dobson Units, that is, a 3-millimeter thick equivalent layer and could correspond to an actual layer of ozone in the stratosphere 10 kilometers thick at a mean pressure of 0.01 bar and at −50° C with one atmospheric molecule in 300,000 being ozone.

BIBLIOGRAPHY

WORKS BY DOBSON

"Seiches in Windermere." *Nature* 86 (1911): 278–279. His first geophysical paper.

With Frederick A. Lindemann. "A Theory of Meteors and the Density and Temperature of the Outer Atmosphere to which It Leads." *Proceedings of the Royal Society of London,* Series A, 102 (1922): 411–437. See also next item.

With Frederick A. Lindemann. "A Note on the Temperature of the Air at Great Heights." *Proceedings of the Royal Society of London,* Series A, 103 (1923): 339–342.

Photographic Photometry. Oxford: Clarendon Press, 1926.

The Uppermost Regions of the Earth's Atmosphere: Being the Halley Lecture Delivered on 5 May, 1926. Oxford: Clarendon Press, 1926.

With Douglas N. Harrison and J. Lawrence. "Observations of the Amount of Ozone in the Earth's Atmosphere and Its Relation to Other Geophysical Conditions. Part III." *Proceedings of the Royal Society of London,* Series A, 122 (1929): 456–486.

With Alan W. Brewer and B. M. Cwilong. "Bakerian Lecture: Meteorology of the Lower Stratosphere." *Proceedings of the Royal Society of London, Series A Mathematical and Physical Sciences* 185 (1946): 144–175.

Exploring the Atmosphere. Oxford: Clarendon Press, 1963, 2nd ed. (much revised), 1968.

"Forty Years' Research on Atmospheric Ozone at Oxford: A History." *Applied Optics* 7 (1968): 387–405. Also available from http://ao.osa.org/abstract.cfm?id=15127&CFID= 34822189&CFTOKEN=38993172.

"The Laminated Structure of the Ozone in the Atmosphere."
Quarterly Journal of the Royal Meteorological Society 99
(1973): 599–607.

OTHER SOURCES

Brewer, Alan. "The Stratospheric Circulation: A Personal
History." *SPARC Newsletter,* 15 July 2000. Available from
http://www.aero.jussieu.fr/ɾsparc/News15/15_Norton.html.

Brönnimann, Stefan, Johannes Staehelin, S. F. G. Farmer, et al.
"Total Ozone Observations prior to the IGY. I: A History."
Quarterly Journal of the Royal Meteorological Society 129 (July
2003): 2797–2817. Also available from http://sinus.unibe.ch/
ɾbroenn/QJRMS_1.pdf.

Fort, Adrian. *Prof: The Life of Frederick Lindemann.* London:
Jonathan Cape, 2003.

Houghton, John T., and C. Desmond Walshaw. "Gordon Miller
Bourne Dobson." *Biographical Memoirs of Fellows of the Royal
Society* 23 (1977): 40–57. This contains a complete
bibliography.

"One of the Very Last Private Laboratories." *The Oxford Times,* 8
February 1957.

Walshaw, C. Desmond. "G. M. B. Dobson—The Man and His
Work." *Planetary and Space Science* 37 (1989): 1485–1507.

John Barnett

DODGSON, CHARLES LUTWIDGE

(*b.* Daresbury, Cheshire, England, 27 January 1832; *d.* Guildford, Surrey, England, 14 January 1898), *mathematics, logic, political science.* For the original article on Dodgson see *DSB,* vol. 3.

Thanks to the increasing publication and reprinting of original material and criticism since the 1950s, Dodgson's scientific work has become better known and more widely appreciated. In addition to his contributions as a teacher, popularizer, and puzzle-maker, these publications shed a new light on his social life and his original inventions in mathematics, political science, and logic.

Scientific Acquaintances. Since the 1950s, the progressive publication of new original material (diaries, letters, various manuscripts), the reprint of many of Dodgson's mathematical writings, and the creation of active Carrollian societies have cast a new light on both the personality of Dodgson and his scientific achievements. This new evidence refutes the legend that he was a reclusive man who lived cloistered at Christ Church. He liked meeting the celebrities of the time (actors, scientists, royalty, poets, and painters) and took numerous photographs of them. He had many adult friends (both male and female), and more surprisingly a good deal of his so-called "child-friends" were in fact adult women. Dodgson also participated in many public debates that took place in both university and society settings, and wrote letters to journals and published pamphlets on matters as various as vaccination, teaching science at the university, child actors, and vivisection.

A look at both his published work and private writings shows that Dodgson was acquainted with the scientific players of his time and their achievements. He visited Charles Babbage, met Arthur Cayley, and corresponded with Henry J. S. Smith, Isaac Todhunter, John Venn, Charles Darwin, William Spottiswoode, Francis H. Bradley, and many others. The catalog of his private library shows that he owned the major works of his time in a wide range of scientific interests. Contrary to what Norman T. Gridgeman wrote in the original *DSB* entry, two purely nineteenth-century subjects (non-Euclidean geometry and symbolic logic) may illustrate Dodgson's keeping abreast of the mathematical advances of the time in Britain, but like the majority of his contemporary British mathematicians, he ignored many advances made on the continent. For instance, Francine F. Abeles shows clearly that Dodgson knew the existence of the new non-Euclidean geometries, although he did not accept them (Abeles, 1994, p. 16). Dodgson owned copies of the main works on symbolic logic, which was a purely British subject at the time. In his *Symbolic Logic,* he referred to George Boole, Augustus de Morgan, William S. Jevons, John N. Keynes, Venn, and the members of Johns Hopkins University (the school of Charles Sanders Peirce). In his diaries, he mentioned Boole's work on logic as early as 25 May 1876. But like his contemporary British colleagues he ignored the work of the German logician Gottlob Frege.

Scientific Achievements. Dodgson's work is fully recognized in at least two areas of the mathematical sciences: the theory of determinants and the theory of voting. On the former, he invented a new rule for the evaluation of determinants by condensation in a paper that was first delivered to the Royal Society on 17 May 1866. On the latter, he published several pamphlets dealing with the issues of proportional representation, choice theory and elections, betting and rationality in tennis tournaments. Mathematicians and historians of mathematics evoke with respect Dodgson's work in logic and geometry, but in the early 2000s there was an ongoing dispute about its importance.

As a geometer, Dodgson is essentially remembered for his defense of Euclid against the new teaching methods, which flourished at the time. Euclid's rivals aimed to replace his *Elements* as a textbook for teaching geometry with other modern manuals. In *Euclid and His Modern Rivals* (first published in 1879 and then enlarged in 1885), Dodgson collected the main rival manuals, discussed them, and then claimed the superiority of Euclid's

Charles Lutwidge Dodgson. *Charles Lutwidge Dodgson, also known as Lewis Carroll.* © **BETTMANN/CORBIS.**

use of logical trees. More influential are Dodgson's two contributions to the philosophical journal *Mind*: "A Logical Paradox" (1894) and particularly "What the Tortoise Said to Achilles" (1895). These two problems, dealing with hypotheticals, have been widely reprinted; they were commented on and discussed by leading logicians of the nineteenth and twentieth centuries, including Venn, Hugh McColl, Bertrand Russell, Gilbert Ryle, and Willard V. Quine.

There are some other mathematical areas where Dodgson made contributions worth noting: his *Pillow Problems* (1893) included twelve interesting probability problems together with a thirteenth, controversial joke-problem in "transcendental probabilities." He also invented five cipher systems, and published numerous arithmetic methods and problems in the *Educational Times* and the journal *Nature*. Better known are Dodgson's contributions to recreational mathematics. His popular books and pamphlets; his numerous contributions to newspapers and journals; his private diaries, letters, and manuscripts; and even his literary works contain a rich collection of games, mathematical puzzles, and word plays. In the 1890s Dodgson planned to publish a book of original games and puzzles, but he never finished it. However, many posthumous compilations appeared and give a good idea of the richness of his work. Dodgson's fictional works have also been widely quoted, and their main characters (Alice, the Cheshire cat, the Red Queen, the Snark, Humpty Dumpty, Tweedledee and Tweedledum) became recurrent symbols in scientific literature.

textbook. On this matter he shared the view of some of Britain's leading mathematicians, including Cayley and de Morgan. Dodgson was, however, not completely against change: he introduced some minor modifications to Euclid in his numerous textbooks on geometry. More interesting is his *New Theory of Parallels* (1888), where he presented a new Euclidean parallels axiom.

Although he is generally considered a traditionalist logician merely concerned with recreational issues, Dodgson's writings on logic contain many original inventions that reveal a high understanding of the logical advances of his time. Dodgson signed with his pseudonym (Lewis Carroll) his two books on the subject: *The Game of Logic* (1886) and *Symbolic Logic, Part 1* (1896). These works present his new diagrammatic scheme for the representation of logical classes and propositions, which despite its numerous advantages in comparison to Venn diagrams, has been seldom used since. In 1977, William W. Bartley III published large fragments from the lost second part of Dodgson's *Symbolic Logic*, which notably included an original method for solving elimination problems with the

SUPPLEMENTARY BIBLIOGRAPHY

WORKS BY DODGSON

Abeles, Francine F., ed. *The Mathematical Pamphlets of Charles Lutwidge Dodgson and Related Pieces.* New York: Lewis Carroll Society of North America, 1994.

———. *The Political Pamphlets and Letters of Charles Lutwidge Dodgson and Related Pieces: A Mathematical Approach.* New York: Lewis Carroll Society of North America, 2001.

Bartley, William Warren, III, ed. *Lewis Carroll's Symbolic Logic.* New York: Potter, 1986. A commented edition of the first and (presumed lost) second parts of Dodgson's *Symbolic Logic.*

Cohen, Morton N., and Roger Lancelyn Green, eds. *The Letters of Lewis Carroll.* 2 vols. New York: Oxford University Press, 1979. A voluminous collection that however contains little in the way of letters of scientific content.

Dodgson, Charles L., ed. *Euclid. Books I, II.* London: Macmillan, 1882.

———. *Euclid and His Modern Rivals.* 2nd ed. London: Macmillan, 1885. Reprinted by Dover in 1973 and 2004.

———. *Curiosa Mathematica. Part I: A New Theory of Parallels.* 3rd ed. London: Macmillan, 1890.

Gardner, Martin, ed. *The Annotated Alice: The Definitive Edition.* New York: Norton, 2000. A good annotated edition of Dodgson's Alice tales, including "The Wasp in a Wig," a suppressed episode discovered in 1974.

Lovett, Charles C. *Lewis Carroll and the Press.* New Castle, DE: Oak Knoll Press, 1999. A descriptive bibliography of Dodgson's contributions to periodicals.

———. *Lewis Carroll among His Books: A Descriptive Catalogue of the Private Library of Charles L. Dodgson.* Jefferson, NC: McFarland, 2005.

Wakeling, Edward, ed. *Lewis Carroll's Diaries: The Private Journals of Charles Lutwidge Dodgson.* 9 vols. Luton, U.K.: The Lewis Carroll Society, 1993–2005. The complete version of Dodgson's surviving diaries. Richly annotated.

———, ed. *The Oxford Pamphlets, Leaflets, and Circulars of Charles Lutwidge Dodgson.* Charlottesville, VA: Lewis Carroll Society of North America, 1993.

Williams, Sidney Herbert, Falconer Madan, Roger Lancelyn Green, et al. *The Lewis Carroll Handbook.* Folkestone, Kent, U.K.: Dawson, 1979. The standard (but incomplete) bibliography of Dodgson's works. To be used with caution.

OTHER SOURCES

Abeles, Francine F. "Determinants and Linear Systems: Charles L. Dodgson's View." *The British Journal for the History of Science* 19 (November 1986): 331–335.

———. "Lewis Carroll's Formal Logic." *History and Philosophy of Logic* 26 (February 2005): 33–46.

———. "Lewis Carroll's Ciphers: The Literary Connections." *Advances in Applied Mathematics* 34 (May 2005): 697–708. See the *Erratum* in *Advances in Applied Mathematics* 37 (July 2006): 1. The best overview to date of Dodgson's work in cryptology.

———. "Lewis Carroll's Visual Logic." *History and Philosophy of Logic* 28 (February 2007): 1–17.

Bartley, William Warren, III. "Lewis Carroll's Lost Book on Logic." *Scientific American* 227 (July 1972): 39–46.

Cohen, Morton N. *Lewis Carroll: A Biography.* New York: Knopf, 1995. The best biography to date.

Englebresten, George. "Two Important Logical Insights by Lewis Carroll." In *Reflections on Lewis Carroll,* edited by Fernando J. Soto and Dayna McCausland. The Lewis Carroll Society of Canada, 2000.

Gardner, Martin. *The Universe in a Handkerchief: Lewis Carroll's Mathematical Recreations, Games, Puzzles, and Word Plays.* New York: Copernicus, 1996. A good overview of Dodgson's recreational work.

Jabberwocky. The journal of the Lewis Carroll Society since 1969. It became *The Carrollian* in 1998. Available from http://www.lewiscarrollsociety.org.uk.

Knight Letter. The magazine of the Lewis Carroll Society of North America since 1974. Available from http://www.lewiscarroll.org.

Leach, Karoline. *In the Shadow of the Dreamchild: A New Understanding of Lewis Carroll.* London: Peter Owen, 1999. A very controversial book with a brilliant discussion of the Carroll myth and a much disputed new assessment of his personal and social life.

McLean, Iain, Alistair McMillan, and Burt L Monroe, eds. *A Mathematical Approach to Proportional Representation: Duncan Black on Lewis Carroll.* Boston: Kluwer, 1996.

Moktefi, Amirouche. "How Did Lewis Carroll Become a Logician?" *Proceedings of the Canadian Society for the History and Philosophy of Mathematics* 18 (2005): 136–144.

Seneta, Eugene. "Lewis Carroll as a Probabilist and Mathematician." *The Mathematical Scientist* 9 (1984): 79–94.

Wilson, Robin. "Alice in Numberland: An Informal Dramatic Presentation in 8 Fits." *The College Mathematics Journal* 33 (November 2002): 354–377. A good overview for the general reader.

Amirouche Moktefi

DUBOIS, MARIE EUGÈNE FRANÇOIS THOMAS

(*b.* Eijsden, Limburg, The Netherlands, 28 January 1858; *d.* Haelen, Limburg, The Netherlands, 16 December 1940), *paleoanthropology, comparative anatomy, paleontology, geology, hydrology.*

Dubois earned worldwide fame through his discovery of *Pithecanthropus erectus* ("Java Man," now *Homo erectus*) in the years 1891–1893. The remains of this hominid, which according to Dubois represented the "missing link" between apes and humans, were the first fossils ever to be accepted as convincing paleontological evidence for human evolution.

Career. Eugène Dubois was the oldest son of Jean Joseph Balthasar Dubois (1832–1893), a country apothecary and burgomaster of Eijsden, and Maria Catharina Floriberta Agnes Roebroeck (1830–1911). His parents were devout Catholics, and it testifies to the high value they set on a good education that they allowed their son to attend the Rijks Hogere Burgerschool (State High School), which was looked upon as a dangerously liberal institution by the Catholic clergy. In 1877, Dubois was registered at the University of Amsterdam as a student of medicine. Among his teachers were the botanist Hugo de Vries, the physiologist Thomas Place, and the anatomist Max Fürbringer, a pupil of Carl Gegenbaur. Dubois became an assistant to Fürbringer in 1881. In the same year, he was appointed as teacher of anatomy at both the State Training School for Art Teachers and the State School of Applied Art, filling both posts until 1887. Dubois qualified as a medical doctor in 1884, and he became lecturer in anatomy at Amsterdam University in 1886. In that year he married Anna Geertruida Lojenga (1862–1943) from Elburg. They were to have three children.

In 1887, Dubois gave up his career in Amsterdam and enlisted for eight years as a medical officer second class in the Royal Dutch East Indies Army with the express purpose of mounting a search for the missing link between humans and apes in the Dutch Indies (later Indonesia). He was first stationed on Sumatra and then transferred to Java, where he discovered the remains of *Pithecanthropus erectus*. After his return from the Indies in 1895, Dubois was awarded a honorary doctorate in botany and zoology in 1897 and became a professor of crystallography, mineralogy, geology, and paleontology at the University of Amsterdam in 1899. In 1907, physical geography was added to his teaching duties. From 1897 onwards, Dubois was also curator of Teylers Museum in Haarlem, the city where he and his family settled in the same year. He retired in 1929.

Search for the Missing Link. Dubois's hunt for human ancestral remains in the Dutch East Indies was inspired by his conviction that only paleontological data could provide conclusive evidence for the descent of humans from a more apelike ancestor. The main protagonists of the German morphological approach to questions of descent, such as Dubois's mentor Fürbringer, Gegenbaur and, particularly, Ernst Haeckel, felt that the reconstruction of phylogenies should primarily be based on comparative anatomical and embryological studies. Dubois was trained as a morphologist and wrote several articles on the comparative anatomy of the larynx, yet he became dissatisfied with this approach and, having been an avid collector of fossils since his youth, turned his attention to paleontology.

Although he was seen as the most likely successor of Fürbringer after the latter's intended return to Germany, Dubois, reading the works on human descent by Charles Darwin, Thomas Henry Huxley, and Ernst Haeckel, became so fascinated with the problem of human evolution that he decided to give up his academic career and travel to the Dutch East Indies as a medical officer in order to find an opportunity to search for the paleontological "missing link" between humans and apes. In the 1880s, there were as yet no known fossils that were accepted as evidence for human evolution. The nineteenth-century anthropological framework allowed for a broad range of variation of the human races, and fossil hominids, such as the Neanderthal remains discovered in 1856, were easily accommodated within this range. Dubois's decision to try his luck in the Indies rather than in Africa (where Darwin had situated the cradle of humanity) was inspired by the discovery, in Pliocene deposits in the Indian Siwalik Hills in 1878, of a fossil ape that was believed to resemble humans more closely than any of the living anthropoid apes.

Furthermore, Dubois believed that not the African great apes, but the gibbons of Southeast Asia were the closest relatives of humans, since according to Darwin the

upright posture had come first in the evolution of humans and the gibbons were able to walk upright—albeit only to a limited extent. In 1887, Dubois wrote an article about the prospects for paleontological and paleoanthropological research in the Indies that attracted the attention of the colonial government, not least because Dubois appealed to feelings of national prestige by pointing to the growing interest taken by foreign scientists in the paleontological exploration of the Indies. As a result, he obtained a grant from the colonial government to begin his search. Two sergeants of the Engineering Corps were assigned to his party, along with fifty forced laborers.

On Sumatra, Dubois discovered a fossil fauna that according to his estimate was too young to contain intermediate forms between humans and apes. On his request, he was transferred to Java, where a promising find of a fossil hominid skull had been made near Wadjak in 1888. After having installed his family in the village of Tulungagung on Central Java, Dubois soon found a second skull in the Wadjak caves, yet he had to conclude now that both skulls, though fossilized, did not represent intermediate forms but were human. He then made the important decision to redirect his work from the exploration of caves, the customary site for the search for hominid fossils, to the exploration of open territory. This decision proved crucial for the success of his campaign.

In 1891, after an exploration of several promising sites in the Kendeng Hills, Dubois began excavations in the banks of the river Solo near the hamlet of Trinil. An enormous number of vertebrate fossils, dated by Dubois to the late Pliocene or early Pleistocene age, were unearthed. Among them were a molar and a skullcap of a primate. Dubois initially ascribed these fossils to a new species of chimpanzee, *Anthropopithecus*, noting however that the cranium was more humanlike than that of any known anthropoid. A year later a well-preserved fossil thigh bone was found at the same site. Its characteristics were almost completely human, indicating that its owner must have walked upright. Dubois considered the three skeletal elements to belong to the same species and accordingly christened his fossil chimpanzee *Anthropopithecus erectus*. Yet further study convinced him that the remains represented exactly what he had been looking for: the missing link between apes and humans. He therefore decided that it was more appropriate to designate his find an ape-man, *Pithecanthropus*, instead of a man-ape, *Anthropopithecus*, being well aware that the name *Pithecanthropus* had been coined by Ernst Haeckel in 1868 for the hypothetical link between humans and apes. In 1894, Dubois published the results of his studies, under the title Pithecanthropus erectus: *Eine menschenähnliche Uebergangsform aus Java* (Pithecanthropus erectus: A humanlike transitional form from Java). In later publications he would add a jaw fragment, found in

Kedung Brubus in the Kendeng Hills, and another molar, dug up in Trinil, to the remains of *Pithecanthropus*.

Dubois's anatomical analysis of the *Pithecanthropus* fossils in his 1894 monograph bears clear witness of his training in the German morphological tradition in phylogenetic research, which had its roots in pre-Darwinian idealistic or typological morphology. Dubois compared the distinguishing features of the fossils with those of various apes and humans and on this basis characterized them as either "primitive" or "modern," his unspoken assumption being that apes and humans represented distinct morphological types, each with its own typical features. In the early 2000s paleoanthropologists criticized this approach for failing to acknowledge the possibility of anatomical features having been shaped as adaptations to local circumstances. Such adaptations cannot unproblematically be taken to indicate phylogenetic affinities. It was mainly due to Dubois's typological perspective that he became convinced that *Pithecanthropus* was a veritable ape-man, exhibiting an equal mix of ape-like and human-like characteristics.

What Dubois envisaged *Pithecanthropus* to have looked like in the flesh can be gleaned from the life-size reconstruction that he sculpted with his own hands for the World Exhibition in Paris in 1900. As the reconstruction nicely illustrates, the fundamental idea underlying it was that *Pithecanthropus* stood halfway between apes and humans.

Reception of *Pithecanthropus*. After his return to Europe in 1895, Dubois spent several years endeavoring to convince the international scientific community of the importance of his discovery. He widely publicized his *Pithecanthropus* finds and displayed them at several international conferences and scientific meetings. Opinions on his discovery varied widely. Some critics did not accept Dubois's contention that the fossils belonged together, ascribing the skull to an ape and the thighbone to a human. Others contested the transitional status of *Pithecanthropus,* claiming that it must have been a gibbon-like ape, while still others felt that the remains derived from a primitive human. Dubois did not fail to exploit this difference of opinion, arguing that it underscored the intermediate status of his find, given that he had established beyond reasonable doubt that the remains belonged together.

Dubois's interpretation of *Pithecanthropus* as exactly intermediate between humans and apes was supported by authorities such as Haeckel, the German anatomist Gustav Schwalbe, and the American paleontologist Othniel C. Marsh, and a significant number of scientists accepted at least its evolutionary transitional status. Thus Dubois's find was the first to be widely accepted as paleontological

proof for human evolution, and in this sense his high hopes may be said to have been fulfilled. Furthermore, Dubois's work served to initiate a debate, led by Schwalbe, that opened up the possibility of an evolutionary interpretation of the Neanderthal remains as an intermediate form between *Pithecanthropus* and modern humans.

Dubois, however, took a more somber view of the appreciation that his discovery met with. He soon became irritated by the opposition to his interpretation of the fossils. Matters became worse after 1900. In accordance with the then prevailing progressive view of evolution, Dubois had envisaged the development of humans as a simple linear process, from an anthropoid ape (possibly the primate found in the Siwalik Hills) to *Pithecanthropus* to modern humans. In the early twentieth century, however, when more and more fossil remains came to light, this view was exchanged for a branching model of human evolution with many dead ends. Support for this view came from the discovery, in 1912, of the supposedly early Pleistocene Piltdown remains, which showed a surprising combination of an apelike mandible and a fully human skull. (Only in 1953 would it become clear that "Piltdown Man" was a hoax and that the bones were forgeries.) The humanity of the Piltdown skull seemed to indicate that not the upright gait but enlargement of the capacity of the brain had come first in human evolution, a view that was elaborated in detail by the English anatomist Grafton Elliot Smith. This "brain first" hypothesis was reinforced by nationalistic and racist sentiments which favored an early origin of the genus *Homo*, since this allowed for a long period of separate development of the human races.

Since the Piltdown remains were taken to be only slightly (if at all) younger than the fossils of the much more apelike *Pithecanthropus,* the latter was removed from the line of human ancestry and relegated to a side branch. Dubois clung to his own view of *Pithecanthropus* as a missing link, but he no longer took part in the debates. He locked his fossils away and even his supporters were denied access to them. This behavior added in no small measure to the image of Dubois as an idiosyncratic and paranoid recluse. No doubt Dubois was a difficult man—the countless incidents that marked his career amply illustrate this—but his secretiveness was also motivated by his plan to publish an extensive and hopefully definitive monograph on his finds. As it turned out, however, he lacked the patience for such work. Likewise, he would publish very little on the collection of thousands of vertebrate fossils that he had unearthed in the Dutch Indies. He could only bring himself to write on them in 1907, when his priority in describing the new species in the collection was threatened by a paleontological expedition to Java led by Margarethe Selenka, wife of the zoologist Emil Selenka. It took international pressure, placed upon him via the Dutch Academy of Science in the 1920s, to make

314

Dubois relieve the ban on investigation of the *Pithecanthropus* remains. Before doing so, he quickly churned out the most detailed description of the fossils he had ever written.

Pithecanthropus and Cephalization. After having withdrawn from the paleoanthropological scene, Dubois took up different interests and investigated a wide variety of geological problems. He explored the Teglian Clay, a geological formation that marks the boundary between the Pliocene and Pleistocene. He studied the climates of the geological past, having already in 1891 ventured the hypothesis that climatic changes were connected with the evolution of the Sun. Further he investigated the carbon cycle and produced an estimate of Earth's age on the basis of his findings. He delved into the genesis of the Dutch sand dunes and linked their formation with that of the Strait of Dover. Finally he published on the origin of the Dutch peat bogs and contributed to the discussion on the drinking-water supply in the coastal provinces with studies on ground- and dune-water.

Still, Dubois did not turn his back on *Pithecanthropus* altogether. One of the new areas of research that he ventured into, the evolutionary development of cephalization in vertebrates, had attracted his interest because of its relevance to human evolution. With his cephalization studies, Dubois—and, in his footsteps, the French physiologist Louis Lapicque—undertook a pioneering attempt in the field of quantitative morphology, particularly of allometry (study of growth of one body part relative to growth of the rest). Dubois's work aimed to show that there is a distinct mathematical relation between the development of an animal's body (represented by its body weight) and the development of its central nervous system (represented by its brain weight), a relation that Dubois called its cephalization. He further argued that degrees of cephalization can be distinguished, according to the degree of evolutionary development of animals. These different degrees could also be expressed mathematically, as coefficients of cephalization, and animals that represented the same level of evolutionary development of the brain had the same cephalization coefficient. According to Dubois, the coefficients tallied nicely with the zoological system, with humans having the highest coefficient, followed by the apes, the ungulates, carnivores, rodents, insectivores, etc.

These results provided Dubois with additional support for his interpretation of *Pithecanthropus erectus*. For on the basis of an estimate of its brain weight (derived from the endocranial capacity of the skullcap) and its body weight (gauged from the measures of the thighbone) Dubois was able to calculate a coefficient of cephalization for *Pithecanthropus* that was indeed roughly half that of

the human coefficient and double that of the great apes. Dubois was to continue his cephalization research in ever-greater detail in the 1910s and 1920s. He amassed a great amount of data, yet his interpretation of the results became more and more speculative. (Severe criticism of his work published in the 1930s and 1940s would throw the whole field into disrepute for several decades.)

Slowly but surely Dubois became convinced that cephalization in vertebrates had increased stepwise, brought about by a series of directed mutations that each entailed a doubling of the number of cells of the foremost part of the brain, dubbed the *psychencephalon*. Thus, Dubois argued in 1924, the psychencephalon of *Pithecanthropus* had had exactly twice the number of cells of that of apes and half that of humans, which again confirmed its intermediate position. This calculation required Dubois to assume a rather high body weight for *Pithecanthropus* of some 100 kilograms. Yet such a weight was plausible, he contended, provided it was assumed that *Pithecanthropus* had had rather apelike, particularly gibbonlike bodily proportions.

In 1935, Dubois published an article titled "On the Gibbon-Like Appearance of *Pithecanthropus erectus*." Contemporaneous authors and later historians have claimed that this article indicated a sudden about-face in Dubois's thinking, since he now seemed to reinterpret his fossils as deriving from an ape. Yet the article merely summarized the results of anatomical studies Dubois had undertaken to lend support to his assumption that *Pithecanthropus* had had a relatively high body weight, as required by his argument about its cephalization.

Viewed from this perspective, it is not difficult to understand why Dubois was unwilling to accept any relation between his *Pithecanthropus* and the new pithecanthropine finds made by the Canadian anatomist Davidson Black in China (described by him as *Sinanthropus pekinensis*) and by the German paleontologist Gustav Heinrich Ralph von Koenigswald on Java in the late 1920s and 1930s. From their study of these new fossils, Black, von Koenigswald, and the German anatomist Franz Weidenreich concluded that *Pithecanthropus* and *Sinanthropus* were much closer to *Homo sapiens*, a viewpoint that would later find expression in a new name for the species, *Homo erectus*. Dubois spent the last years of his life disputing this interpretation, arguing that the new finds derived from a primitive, yet fully human form, identical with the Wadjak remains he had found on Java. It was to no avail; Dubois lost all support for his by now highly labored and deviant interpretation.

In an obituary notice, Arthur Keith accurately characterized Dubois as an idealist who held to his ideas so firmly that his mind tended to bend facts rather than alter his ideas to fit them. To do justice to his life's work, however, it should be added that it was exactly his imaginative mind and unbending faith in his convictions that made Dubois into the unorthodox and colorful pioneer of paleoanthropology that he was.

BIBLIOGRAPHY

The principal collection of archival material relating to Dubois's life and work, containing diaries, correspondence, (field) notebooks, manuscripts, lecture notes, Dubois's paleoanthropological and paleontological library, his reprint collection, drawings, photographs, etc., is kept in Naturalis, National Museum of Natural History, Leiden, The Netherlands, which also houses the thousands of fossils that Dubois excavated in the Indies, the Pithecanthropus *remains included.*

WORKS BY DUBOIS

"Zur Morphologie des Larynx." *Anatomische Anzeiger* 1 (1886): 178–186, 225–231.

"Over de wenschelijkheid van een onderzoek naar de diluviale fauna van Ned. Indië, in het bijzonder van Sumatra." *Natuurkundig Tijdschrift voor Nederlandsch-Indië* 48 (1889): 148–165.

Pithecanthropus erectus: *Eine menschenähnliche Uebergangsform aus Java.* Batavia: Landesdruckerei, 1894. Reprint: New York: Stechert, 1915.

The Climates of the Geological Past and Their Relation to the Evolution of the Sun. London: S. Sonnenschein, 1895.

"On *Pithecanthropus erectus:* A Transitional Form between Man and the Apes." *Scientific Transactions of the Royal Dublin Society,* series 2, 6 (1896): 1–18.

"Ueber die Abhängigkeit des Hirngewichtes von der Körpergrösse bei den Säugethieren." *Archiv für Anthropologie* 25 (1898): 1–28.

"Eenige van Nederlandschen kant verkregen uitkomsten met betrekking tot de kennis der Kendeng-fauna (fauna van Trinil)." *Tijdschrift van het Koninklijk Nederlandsch Aardrijkskundig Genootschap,* series 2, 24 (1907): 449–458.

"Das geologische Alter der Kendeng- oder Trinil-Fauna." *Tijdschrift van het Koninklijk Nederlandsch Aardrijkskundig Genootschap,* series 2, 25 (1908): 1235–1270.

"On the Relation between the Quantity of Brain and the Size of the Body in Vertebrates." *Proceedings of the Royal Dutch Academy of Science* 16 (1914): 647–668.

"Phylogenetic and Ontogenetic Increase of the Volume of the Brain in Vertebrates." *Proceedings of the Royal Dutch Academy of Science* 25 (1923): 230–255.

"On the Principal Characters of the Cranium and the Brain, the Mandible and the Teeth of *Pithecanthropus erectus.*" *Proceedings of the Royal Dutch Academy of Science* 27 (1924): 265–278, 459–464.

"On the Principal Characters of the Femur of *Pithecanthropus erectus.*" *Proceedings of the Royal Dutch Academy of Science* 29 (1926): 730–743.

"The Law of the Necessary Phylogenetic Perfection of the Psychencephalon." *Proceedings of the Royal Dutch Academy of Science* 31 (1928): 304–314.

"Die phylogenetische Grosshirnzunahme autonome Vervollkommnung der animalen Funktionen." *Biologia Generalis* 6 (1930): 247–292.

"The Distinct Organization of *Pithecanthropus* of Which the Femur Bears Evidence, Now Confirmed from Other Individuals of the Described Species." *Proceedings of the Royal Dutch Academy of Science* 35 (1932): 716–722.

"On the Gibbon-Like Appearance of *Pithecanthropus erectus.*" *Proceedings of the Royal Dutch Academy of Science* 38 (1935): 578–585.

"Racial Identity of *Homo soloensis* Oppenoort (Including *Homo modjokertensis* von Koenigswald) and *Sinanthropus pekinensis* Davidson Black." *Proceedings of the Royal Dutch Academy of Science* 39 (1936): 1180–1185.

"The Fossil Human Remains Discovered in Java by Dr. G. H. R. von Koenigswald and Attributed by Him to *Pithecanthropus erectus,* in Reality Remains of *Homo wadjakensis* (syn. *Homo soloensis*)." *Proceedings of the Royal Dutch Academy of Science* 43 (1940): 494–496, 842–851, 1268–1275.

OTHER SOURCES

Bowler, Peter J. *Theories of Human Evolution: A Century of Debate, 1844–1944.* Baltimore. MD: Johns Hopkins University Press, 1986.

Brongersma, L. D. "De verzameling van Indische fossielen (Collectie Dubois)." *De Indische Gids* 63 (1941): 97–116.

Franzen, J. L. *Auf den Spuren des Pithecanthropus: Leben und Werk von Prof. Dr. Gustav Heinrich Ralph von Koenigswald (1902–1982).* Frankfurt am Main, Germany: Senckenberg Museum, 1984.

Hrdlička, Aleš. *Skeletal Remains of Early Man.* Smithsonian Miscellaneous Collections, vol. 83. Washington, DC: Smithsonian Institution, 1930. See pages 28–65.

Koenigswald, G. H. R. von. *Begegnungen mit dem Vormenschen.* Düsseldorf, Germany: Diederichs, 1955.

Reader, John. *Missing Links: The Hunt for Earliest Man.* London: Collins 1981.

Shipman, Pat. *The Man Who Found the Missing Link: The Extraordinary Life of Eugène Dubois.* London: Weidenfeld & Nicholson, 2001.

Spencer, Frank, ed. *History of Physical Anthropology: An Encyclopedia,* 2 vols. New York: Garland, 1997.

Theunissen, Bert. *Eugène Dubois and the Ape-Man from Java: The History of the First Missing Link and Its Discoverer.* London: Kluwer, 1988.

———, John de Vos, Paul Y. Sondaar, and Fachroel Aziz. "The Establishment of a Chronological Framework for the Hominid-Bearing Deposits of Java: A Historical Survey." In *Establishment of a Geologic Framework for Paleoanthropology,* edited by Léo F. Laporte. Special paper 242. Boulder, CO: Geological Society of America, 1990.

Bert Theunissen

DUBOS, RENÉ JULES (*b.* Saint-Brice-sous-Forêt, France, 20 February 1901; *d.* New York City, 20 February 1982), *microbiologist, disease ecologist, environmentalist.*

As a microbiologist and environmentalist, Dubos demonstrated a distinctively French fascination with *terroir* and *milieu,* prompted perhaps by his nostalgia for the imagined harmonies of rural existence. His life in biomedical research offers many paradoxes. French in sentiment and intellectual heritage, he lived and worked in the United States. A meticulous laboratory researcher, he abjured reductionism in modern biomedical science. Ecologically minded, he gave little heed to the science of ecology. A pioneer in discovering antibiotics, he discounted their value in medical practice. A frail man, afflicted with rheumatic heart disease, he asserted a sort of "despairing optimism." Shy and reserved, he became in the 1960s and 1970s a leading environmentalist and a dramatic, passionate public speaker. Temperamentally reclusive, he showed a knack for coining slogans such as "Think Globally, Act Locally" (c. 1978). His words provoked and galvanized millions of people.

Early Years. Dubos grew up in the village of Hénonville, in Île-de-France, one of three children of Georges Alexandre Dubos, a butcher, and Madeleine Adéline (née de Bloedt), a former seamstress who assisted her husband in his shop. Once a boisterous child, Dubos suffered a bout of rheumatic fever at eight years of age, which left him with permanent damage to his heart valves. He remained sickly, unable to participate in sport, but he found plenty of time to read widely and excelled at school. When he was thirteen, his family moved to Paris, where he attended high school at the Collège Chaptal on a scholarship. A reserved, myopic adolescent, Dubos spent most of the war years longing to return to the French countryside. In 1919 his father died suddenly, soon after coming home from war service. The family moved to the Paris suburbs, where his mother ran a small *épicerie,* or grocer's shop.

After obtaining his baccalaureate, Dubos enrolled in the Institut National Agronomique to train as an agricultural expert. Although microbiology and chemistry bored him, he displayed some interest in rural sociology and economics. On receiving his diploma, Dubos took courses at the Institut National d'Agronomie Coloniale in Nogent-sur-Marne, hoping to work as a colonial administrator in Indochina. His heart disease and poor eyesight, however, excluded him from such a career. In 1923 Dubos used his ability to review and abstract technical articles in several languages to secure a position in Rome as associate editor of the *Journal of International Agricultural Intelligence.* But these routine tasks left him listless and uninspired.

Travel to the United States. Visiting American scientists urged Dubos to travel to the United States. On the passage across the Atlantic he met Selman Waksman, who offered the charming young Frenchman a position in the PhD program at Rutgers University. A Russian émigré, Waksman was a soil microbiologist at the New Jersey Agricultural Experiment Station who later became interested in microorganisms that produced substances antagonistic to their competitors. He encouraged his graduate students to employ the experimental techniques of Sergei Winogradsky, a scientist at the Institut Pasteur who advocated "dynamic" soil microbiology. That is, rather than study microorganisms in isolation, Winogradsky wanted to examine their life cycles and interactions in soil under natural conditions. Years later, Dubos would come to recognize the "ecological" underpinnings of this approach. In 1927 Dubos completed his dissertation identifying the microbes responsible for the decomposition of cellulose in various circumstances. His conclusions emphasized the interaction of these organisms and their dependence on the particular character of the soil.

Unsure of what to do next, Dubos made contact with his compatriot Alexis Carrel, a scientist at the Rockefeller Institute in New York City, the leading medical research center in the United States. They lunched with Carrel's colleague Oswald T. Avery, who impressed on Dubos that he might possess the skills to decompose the polysaccharide capsule of the pneumococcus, the major cause of pneumonia. Appointed to Avery's laboratory of biochemical bacteriology, Dubos found soils in which organic materials decomposed then cleverly enriched them with the purified capsular polysaccharide of type III pneumococcus to see which microorganisms thrived on this nutrient. Having cultivated the responsive microbe from soil in a New Jersey cranberry bog, he extracted and purified the enzyme active against the capsular material. But tests in animals proved disappointing and the development of sulfa drugs in the 1930s seemed to make further investigation of this "antibacterial" enzyme unnecessary.

Through working with Avery, Dubos came to experience the thrill of scientific investigation. In his memoir of Avery (1976), he recalled, surprisingly, that the scientist observed biological phenomena as a naturalist, sensitive to the interplay between the life processes of parasite and host. His example confirmed Dubos's general biological orientation to the study of microbes.

Despite the satisfactions of laboratory studies, Dubos during the early 1930s remained unwell, poor, and homesick. He supplemented his wages teaching French to Franz Boas, professor of anthropology at Columbia University. In 1934 Dubos married Marie Louise Bonnet, another French immigrant with severe rheumatic heart disease, who was studying French symbolist poetry at Columbia.

She died in 1942 from tuberculosis. In 1946 he married (Letha) Jean Porter, his research assistant, who also developed tuberculosis but survived. They acquired a farm in the Hudson River valley and spent a large part of each year there, enjoying country life and planting trees.

Lab Work. The isolation of gramicidin in the late 1930s became Dubos's major laboratory achievement. In a series of experiments, he "fed" soil samples a nutrient broth containing intact bacteria associated with various common infections. Eventually he found a microbe, *Bacillus brevis,* which secreted a substance that killed some of the harmful bacteria. With Rollin Hotchkiss he refined the substance, tyrothricin, into two separate materials. One proved effective only in laboratory cultures and was toxic to animals. The other, gramicidin, was bacteriostatic, inhibiting growth of some bacteria, and safe to apply to skin infections. From 1941, it was used commonly as a topical antibiotic. Dubos's investigations inspired others to search systematically for antibacterial substances.

Dubos's reputation as an experimentalist reached its peak in the 1940s. In 1940 he received the John Phillips Memorial Award from the American College of Physicians; and the following year, the E. Mead Johnson Award of the American Academy of Pediatrics. He was elected to the National Academy of Sciences and made a full member of the Rockefeller Institute in 1941. With Waksman he shared the 1948 Albert Lasker Medical Research Award, for the discovery of soil antibiotics. Yet his success in the laboratory during this period was meager. Using common detergents, Dubos developed a more convenient growth medium for the tubercle bacillus, the cause of tuberculosis, but his efforts to find a flaw in its capsular armor failed.

Move to Harvard. In 1942 Dubos became George Fabyan Professor of Comparative Pathology and Tropical Medicine at the Harvard School of Public Health. Mourning his first wife, he never fully adjusted to his new environment. He did, however, become immersed in the study of infectious disease from evolutionary and ecological perspectives, especially through his reading of the work of Theobald Smith and Frank Macfarlane Burnet. It was Dubos who recommended Burnet as the 1944 Dunham lecturer at Harvard, thus beginning a lifelong association. That same year Dubos delivered the Lowell Lectures, which became the core of his first book, *The Bacterial Cell* (1945). Dubos sought to abandon the implicit anthropocentrism of contemporary microbiology, urging instead the investigation of the bacterium as a functioning cell, as an independent organism, in relation to its environment. That is, rather than focus solely on the implications for human disease, he wanted to view parasite and host in broader ecological perspective. Deploying "classical biology," he would, like Burnet, determine the "natural history" of infectious disease agents and so derive a more complex epidemiology. His musings on bacterial variability and natural selection also led him to restate carefully his warning, first improvised in 1942, of the likelihood of resistance emerging to new antibiotics.

Science Writing. Returning to the Rockefeller Institute in 1944, Dubos began gradually to move away from laboratory investigation and refashion himself as a popular writer and commentator. First he wrote *Louis Pasteur, Free Lance of Science* (1950), in which he distinguished the man of scientific sensibility and insight (such as himself and Pasteur) from the mere researcher. Dubos and his wife Jean then worked together on *The White Plague: Tuberculosis, Man, and Society* (1952), writing the biography of a disease they knew intimately. In this book they argued that microbes require a fertile soil for infection to grow into disease. They described the social and economic setting of tuberculosis, seeking to identify the forces that disturbed the equilibrium between parasite and host, giving rise to illness. Skeptical of antibiotics, they advocated avoidance of social environments promoting infection and return to a "physiological" way of living.

Inspired by the popular success of these books, Dubos wrote prolifically for the next thirty years. In *Mirage of Health* (1959), he recommended peaceful coexistence of humans and microbes, decrying technological fixes and medical utopias, including efforts to eradicate specific diseases. He deplored recourse to military metaphors such as the notion of a fight against disease agents, suggesting scientists might focus instead on mutualism and symbiosis. He condemned narrow physicochemical reductionism and favored an integrative, and sometimes even holistic, biological approach. But the emphasis on the harmony of the organism and its environment was now more Hippocratic than Darwinian in tone. He sought, above all, a balance between people and their environment in other to preserve the health and values of humanity.

In *Man Adapting* (1965), Dubos continued his exploration of microbial virulence and host resistance, the balance between parasitism and predation, but increasingly he also recognized direct environmental dangers to human health, following the attention given to toxins and pollutants in Rachel Carson's *Silent Spring* (1962). His appreciation of threats to "human values" became ever more acute. Dubos warned that adaptation to civilized life—for him epitomized in overcrowding, urban life, pollution, and stress—might prove hazardous to humanity. Humanistic value judgments thus often supplemented ecological analysis, perhaps making his observations more popularly appealing during this period. *So Human an Animal* (1968), a hyperbolic elaboration on *Man Adapting,* won a Pulitzer Prize in 1969.

By the time Dubos retired from Rockefeller University in 1971 he was giving some forty public lectures each year. With his French accent, his taste for drama, and his charm and enthusiasm, he was a strikingly effective speaker. In the last decade of his life, before his death from pancreatic cancer, Dubos asserted that the simple survival or sustainability of humanity is not enough. Humans must intervene to improve on nature, to humanize Earth. His land ethic, a term picked up from the environmentalist Aldo Leopold, implied stewardship of Earth, not detachment from it. Moreover, Dubos increasingly envisioned more creative adaptation of humans to their environments, which meant making conscious choices and new associations, the active transformation of selves. Other disease ecologists, such as Burnet, regarded this revival of the ideas of philosophers Henri-Louis Bergson (1859–1941) and Alfred North Whitehead (1861–1947) as a romantic's retreat from fundamental biological principles. All the same, Dubos, tirelessly writing and speaking, did perhaps more than anyone else to encourage the public to think in broad ecological terms about health and disease, and to recognize above all that the seed depends on the soil.

BIBLIOGRAPHY

Dubos's manuscripts are in the Rockefeller University Archives at the Rockefeller Archive Center, Sleepy Hollow, New York. The transcript of interviews Saul Benison conducted with Dubos in 1956 is in the Columbia University Oral History Research Office, Butler Library, Columbia University, New York City.

WORKS BY DUBOS

The Bacterial Cell in Relation to Problems of Virulence, Immunity, and Chemotherapy. Cambridge, MA: Harvard University Press, 1945.

Louis Pasteur, Free Lance of Science. Boston: Little, Brown, 1950.

With Jean Dubos. *The White Plague: Tuberculosis, Man, and Society.* Boston: Little, Brown, 1952.

Mirage of Health: Utopias, Progress, and Biological Change. Planned and edited by Ruth Nanda Anshen. New York: Harper & Brothers, 1959.

The Dreams of Reason: Science and Utopias. New York: Columbia University Press, 1961.

Man Adapting. New Haven, CT: Yale University Press, 1965.

So Human an Animal. New York: Scribner, 1968.

Reason Awake: Science for Man. New York: Columbia University Press, 1970.

With Barbara Ward. *Only One Earth: The Care and Maintenance of a Small Planet.* New York: Norton, 1972.

The Professor, the Institute, and DNA: Oswald T. Avery, His Life and Scientific Achievements. New York: Rockefeller University Press, 1976.

The Wooing of the Earth. New York: Scribner, 1980.

OTHER SOURCES

Davis, Bernard D. "Two Perspectives: On René Dubos, and on Antibiotic Actions." *Perspectives in Biology and Medicine* 35 (1991): 37–48.

Litsios, Socrates. "René Dubos and Fred L. Soper: Their Contrasting Views on Vector and Disease Eradication." *Perspectives in Biology and Medicine* 41 (1997): 138–149.

Moberg, Carol F. *René Dubos, Friend of the Good Earth: Microbiologist, Medical Scientist, Environmentalist.* Washington, DC: ASM, 2005.

Rosenkrantz, Barbara Gutmann. "Dubos and Tuberculosis, Master Teachers." In *The White Plague: Tuberculosis, Man, and Society,* by René Dubos and Jean Dubos. New Brunswick, NJ: Rutgers University Press, 1987.

———. "René Jules Dubos." *American National Biography Online.* Available from http://www.anb.org/articles/12/12-01795.html.

Warwick Anderson

DUHEM, PIERRE-MAURICE-MARIE
(*b.* Paris, France, 10 June 1861; *d.* Cabrespine, France, 14 September 1916), *physics, rational mechanics, physical chemistry, history of science, philosophy of science.* For the original article on Duhem see *DSB,* vol. 4.

Donald Miller's article gives an excellent overview of Duhem's scientific work and describes the main lines of Duhem's historical work. A manuscript in which Duhem summarizes the main lines of argument in his 10-volume *Le Système du Monde* was subsequently published as *L'aube du savoir: épitomé du système du monde,* with a comprehensive critical introduction by the editor. Extensive discussions of biographical material have been given in Jaki's *Uneasy Genius,* which also relates Duhem's work in philosophy to Thomist philosophy as well as discussing his work in history and physics, and Brouzeng's *Duhem: Science et Providence,* which also traces the first developments in irreversible thermodynamics to Duhem's *Traité d'énergétique.* Miller presents what was the standard interpretation of Duhem's philosophical position as aligned in important respects with contemporary positivism and as reserving truth for theology. This article will be mainly concerned with the interpretation of Duhem's philosophical position and its relation to his historical and scientific interests in chemistry.

Natural Classification. The classic source of the antirealist interpretation of Duhem is his discussion of Plato's dictum "to save the phenomena" in his book of the same name. As Duhem described there, ancient and medieval astronomers concluded that where one mathematical construction reproducing the observable features of planetary motions could be produced, others were possible. Yet there were also attempts to describe the real motions of the planets. The debate continued in the early twenty-first century.

Tycho Brahe devised a model of the Solar System that was observationally equivalent to Copernicus's system in the sense that the motions of the planets did not distinguish between these models. Antirealists argue that in the absence of crucial observation tests supporting the one and contradicting the other, there is no reason to believe the underlying explanation of the one rather than the other. But such cases hold only for a limited domain, and it is open for an advocate of one system to point to further observations that would justify preferring it. In fact, Tycho thought the way heavy bodies fall in a straight line and the absence of centrifugal forces counted against Copernicus's system, and Galileo tried to argue that observation of the tides favored Copernicus's system. The antirealist who wishes to make a general argument for not accepting the truth of theories must be assured that the observations supporting them are not limited to some restricted class, but cover all possible observations. Even with respect to some restricted class of observations, it is usually difficult enough to produce one adequate theory, and it is unusual to find alternative, equally well-developed mathematical theories of phenomena in the history of science.

Duhem, whose philosophical position was intimately connected with his reading of the history of science, would have been well aware of such historical facts, and he certainly made no attempt to develop the antirealist argument by arguing for the existence in principle of observational equivalents of theories with respect to all possible observations, as, for example, Quine has tried to do in "On Empirically Equivalent Systems." Further, his holistic view of theory, which shows, as Miller puts it, "that there can be no such thing as simply observing and reporting an experiment" (p. 227), throws into grave doubt the assumption that he would have allowed the notion of observation presupposed by the antirealist argument under consideration. Again, Quine's efforts in *Word and Object* and later writings well illustrate the need for a specific account of observation sentences within a general holistic framework. Nothing of the sort is to be found in Duhem's writings. None of this detracts from the good sense of refraining from taking a stand on what the evidence and theoretical discussion leaves indeterminate. But that is not antirealism.

On the contrary, Duhem thought the aim of physical theory was to develop into a natural classification. This is the limiting form of physical theory that finally becomes a "reflection of the true order according to which the realities escaping us are organized" (*La théorie physique*, p. 41), to which Duhem thought the history of science points by showing that those aspects which have proved their worth by "anticipating observation" (p. 39) and facilitating correct predications are retained and integrated into an ever more coherent and unified body of theory more adequately mirroring a coherent world.

Energetics. Miller discusses Duhem's conception of energetics as a unifying theory incorporating the well-established results of science under a range of conditions, which he developed in the 1911 book *Traité d'énergétique*, although he failed to cover electromagnetic radiation. The term *energetics* came to prominence as a term for theories developed by Georg Helm and by Wilhelm Ostwald. These were so heavily criticized by Ludwig Boltzmann and Max Planck after a famous meeting in Lübeck in 1895 that it may seem surprising that Duhem continued to use the term. Duhem made no allusion to these authors' understanding of energetics in his own developments of the subject, however, and was undaunted by the criticisms. The charges of making technical errors, such as confounding exact and inexact differentials, and of failing to understand and incorporate the notion of entropy into the theory of energy certainly could not be directed against him. And their philosophical motivations of energetics—the explicitly positivist eschewing of theoretical in favor of observational terms in the case of Helm, and the reification of energy to which matter and all other physical concepts were to be reduced in the case of Ostwald—were not his. Although, like them, he was critical of the nineteenth-century project of attempting to reduce all science to mechanics, he entertained no vision of replacing it with an alternative reductive project of reducing theoretical terms to observational terms or treating energy as the only ultimate physical reality. As he put it in an early study, having "constituted, under the name Thermodynamics, a science which covers in shared principles all the changes of state of bodies, including both changes of position and changes in physical qualities," he hoped it would be "easier to get away from what has hitherto been the most dangerous stumbling block of theoretical Physics, the search for a mechanical explanation of the Universe" ("Commentaire aux principes de la Thermodynamique. Troisième Partie," p. 285).

All energeticists, Duhem included, opposed atomism. Although such opposition is often construed as a form of antirealism, this can hardly be said of Duhem's antireductive stance, which has it that science should incorporate systematically whatever principles are needed to cover new discoveries rather than dogmatically adhere to previously conceived reductionist theses which cannot be shown to save the phenomena. There is nothing in his texts to suggest that he sought anything but a literal interpretation of such principles.

Anti-atomism. The antirealist interpretation of Duhem is naturally associated with his critical view of atomic theories. There is, however, certainly no suggestion of observationally equivalent theories in his arguments against the atomic view, which he is better understood as taking not to be a theory at all. As Miller emphasizes, Duhem regarded scientific theories as logically organized structures with a clear axiomatic base from which their import can be properly developed in terms of its logical consequences. Of course, first formulations may not achieve this ideal. But they are to be clearly distinguished from pictures and models, which have no comparably clear import. They were regarded by Duhem as a haven for ad hoc and conflicting speculations, and, the contrary claims of their proponents notwithstanding, as providing no real explanation of phenomena. Although he accepted that "as Dalton showed, it is easy to deduce the fundamental laws of chemistry" ("Notation atomique," p. 441), by which he meant the laws of constant and multiple proportions, this was only because they were directly read into the nature of the atoms. Later in the century, Adolf Wurtz described the role of atoms in chemistry in terms of their "atomicities." But once more, Duhem discounted this as simply reading the notion of valency as codified in the macroscopic behavior of the elements into the atoms, rather than as actually providing an explanation of valency in terms of characteristics of atoms ascribed to them by some systematic theory. This stood in sharp contrast to the genuine theory of chemical combination that Duhem was helping to develop in the last two decades of the nineteenth century on the basis of thermodynamic potentials.

None of this led Duhem to approve of the policy enforced by Marcelin Bertholet of banishing any mention of atoms from the science curriculum in France. But he thought that it was important to properly understand the import which science could justifiably ascribe to the chemical formulas usually described as based on the notion of an atom. His 1892 article "Notation atomique et hypothèses atomistiques" and much of *Le mixte et la combinaison chimique* are devoted to spelling this out. Building on a detailed statement of the doctrine of chemical proportions that is neutral with respect to the atomic or continuous view of matter, he established the notion of a compositional formula (*formule chimique brute*). Defining a notion of chemical type in the manner of Dumas on the basis of chemical substitution, elaborated to incorporate distinctions of valency, he then established the notion of a structural formula (*formule développée*), which can

Pierre Duhem. AIP EMILIO SEGRE VISUAL ARCHIVES, BRITTLE BOOKS COLLECTION.

distinguish isomers sharing the same compositional formula. These essentially topological (not two-dimensional) structures are finally elaborated with "a new element taken from geometry" (*Le mixte et la combinaison chimique*, p. 128) allowing the three-dimensional representation of optical isomers. Even here he would not allow that the van't Hoff structure should be viewed as literally picturing the spatial arrangement of atoms in a molecule because there was still no account of what the atoms were, and certainly no explanation of the rotation of plane polarized light in terms of atomic features.

Conception of Mixture. Duhem thought the foundation underlying chemical formulas had "yet to be discovered" (*Le mixte et la combinaison chimique*, p. 147), and clearly understood his account as abstracting from the concrete interpretation imposed by any specific theory of the nature of matter, whether atomic or continuous, so as to provide a statement of what could justifiably be held as true. He was interested in this foundational question, however, and clearly favored a view of compounds inspired by Aristotle's theory of mixing, according to which the original ingredients are no longer actually present in the resulting homogeneous mixture. This is usually understood to be a continuous theory of matter because Aristotle developed it in opposition to Democratian atomism. But the dichotomy in terms of which Duhem describes the historical development of the concept of a *mixt* in *Le mixte et la combinaison chimique* is based on the issue of whether the original ingredients are present in the *mixt* or not. He interprets ancient atomism to take the negative line. However, Descartes's theory, which is continuous and not atomic, is also classified as non-Aristotelian because, according to Duhem, it treats the original ingredients as present in a *mixt*. Perhaps, although he gives no example of this, an atomic theory might conceivably be Aristotelian in this sense. The Aristotelian view needs to be complemented, Duhem says, to accommodate later discoveries such as the law of constant proportions on which the distinction, not recognized by Aristotle and many after him, between compounds and solutions is based. (This is one reason why Duhem uses the term "mixt.") But nothing, he maintained, had been discovered which directly contradicted the Aristotelian notion. How, exactly, it is to be considered compatible with the general analysis of mixtures in Gibbs's phase rule raises some questions, but beyond the brief discussion of some simple, single-phase examples, Duhem does not really say.

An idiosyncrasy in Duhem's view of mixture is the principle of co-occupancy—according to which different bodies or quantities of matter can occupy the same place at the same time—which he very clearly states in some of his thermodynamics texts, such as the 1892 paper "Commentaire aux principes de la thermodynamique. Première partie" and the 1911 book *Traité d'énergétique*. This principle was emphatically denied by Aristotle, raising a question about Duhem's claim that nothing new in science contradicts the original Aristotelian conception of a mixt. The principle was adopted by the Stoics after Aristotle as a way of allowing that the original ingredients are actually present in a mixt without adopting the atomic view of matter, as Duhem discusses in a section of *Le Système du Monde* entitled "La physique Stoïcienne et la compénétration des corps" (Vol. I, Ch. V, §IX). The Stoic view of mixture is normally thought of as opposed to Aristotle's, and is anti-Aristotelian according to the dichotomy in *Le mixte et la combinaison chimique*, although nothing is said of it there. Nevertheless, Duhem seems not to have thought there was any tension.

BIBLIOGRAPHY

WORKS BY DUHEM

"Commentaire aux principes de la thermodynamique" *Journal de mathématiques pures et appliquées* 8: (1892): 269; 9: (1893):293; 10 (1893): 207.

"Notation atomique et hypothèses atomistiques." *Revue des questions scientifiques*, 31 (1892): 391–457. Translated by Paul Needham as "Atomic Notation and Atomistic Hypotheses." *Foundations of Chemistry* 2 (2000): 127–180.

Le mixte et la combinaison chimique: Essai sur l'évolution d'une idée. Paris: C. Naud, 1902; reprinted Paris: Fayard, 1985. Translated in *Mixture and Chemical Combination, and Related Essays,* translated and edited by Paul Needham. Dordrecht, Holland and Boston: Kluwer, 2002.

ΣΩΖΕΙΝ ΤΑ ΦΑΙΝΟΜΕΝΑ: *Essai sur la notion de théorie physique de Platon à Galilée.* Paris: A. Hermann et Fils, 1908. Translated by Edmund Doland and Chaninah Maschler as *To Save the Phenomena: An Essay on the Idea of Physical Theory from Plato to Galileo.* Chicago: University of Chicago Press, 1969.

Traité d'énergétique ou de thermodynamique générale. Paris: Gauthier-Villars, 1911.

La théorie physique: Son objet – sa structure, 2nd ed. Paris: Marcel Rivière & Cie, 1914; reprinted Paris: Vrin, 1981.

The Evolution of Mechanics. Translated by Michael Cole. Alphen aan den Rijn, The Netherlands: Sijthoff & Noordhoff, 1980.

Medieval Cosmology: Theories of Infinity, Place, Time, Void, and the Plurality of Worlds. Edited and translated by Roger Ariew. Chicago: University of Chicago Press, 1985. Abridged English translation of parts of *Le Système du Monde.*

Pinkava, Jindrich, ed. *The Correspondence of the Czech Chemist Frantisek Wald with W. Ostwald, E. Mach, P. Duhem, J. W. Gibbs and other Scientists of That Time.* Praha: Academia, 1987.

German Science. Translated by John Lyon. La Salle, IL: Open Court, 1991.

The Origins of Statics. Translated by Grant F. Leneaux, Victor N. Vagliente and Guy H. Wagener. Dordrecht, Netherlands, and Boston: Kluwer, 1991.

Essays in the History and Philosophy of Science. Translated and edited by Roger Ariew and Peter Barker. Indianapolis, IN: Hackett, 1996.

L'aube du savoir: épitomé du système du monde. Textes établis et présentés par Anastasios Brenner. (Collection histoire de la pensée.) Paris: Hermann, 1997.

OTHER SOURCES

Brenner, Anastasios. *Duhem: Science, Réalité et Apparence.* Paris: Vrin, 1990.

Brouzeng, Paul. *Duhem: Science et Providence.* Paris: Belin, 1987.

Jaki, Stanley L. *Uneasy Genius: The Life and Work of Pierre Duhem.* The Hague and Boston: Nijhoff, 1984. Includes a complete biography of Duhem's works.

Martin, Russell N. D. *Pierre Duhem: Philosophy and History in the Work of a Believing Physicist.* La Salle, IL: Open Court, 1991.

Needham, Paul. "Duhem's Theory of Mixture in the Light of the Stoic Challenge to the Aristotelian Conception." *Studies in History and Philosophy of Science* 33 (2002): 685–708.

Quine, Willard V. O. *Word and Object.* Cambridge, MA: MIT Press, 1960.

_____. "On Empirically Equivalent Systems of the World." *Erkenntnis* 9 (1975): 313–328.

Paul Needham

DUMAS, JEAN-BAPTISTE-ANDRE

(*b.* Alais [now Alès], Gard, France, 14 July 1800; *d.* Cannes, France, 11 April 1884), *chemistry.* For the original article on Dumas see *DSB,* vol. 4.

Dumas was one of the most eminent chemists in the world in the second quarter of the nineteenth century, overshadowed only by the fame of Justus von Liebig. Liebig's own reputation was built on what he had learned in the same Paris milieu. Dumas's greatest contribution was to organic chemistry but two significant areas of Dumas's influence hitherto unexamined are his research school and his advocacy of the importance of Antoine Lavoisier in the history of chemistry.

Although the work of the novelist Alexandre Dumas is better known to the general public, this was apparently not so evident in the mid-nineteenth century when the novelist wrote to the scientist: "You have made our name known throughout Europe" (Académie des Sciences Archives, Carton 28). By 1832 Dumas had established a name for himself and had even been elected to the prestigious Academy of Sciences. He was able that same year to establish his own private chemical laboratory and to invite students to work with him. He was soon to form a laboratory-based research school, comparable to the school established by Liebig.

The Research School. As a professor of chemistry and an outstanding lecturer, Dumas came into contact with thousands of science students. A small proportion of these were enthused by the prospect of chemical research and, if they were accepted by Dumas in his private laboratory in the rue Cuvier, they would often later identify themselves by publications in which they would express their indebtedness to their master as "chef d'école." The pharmacist Polydore Boullay was Dumas's first research student, since he started working in Dumas's laboratory at the École Polytechnique in 1826, when he was only twenty. Most of the later research students were under thirty, many working on their doctorates, supervised by Dumas. Of the twenty-two students who worked in Dumas's laboratory, seventeen were French citizens, of whom the most eminent included Auguste Cahours, Charles Gerhardt, Auguste Laurent, Louis Pasteur, Eugène Péligot, Henri-Étienne Sainte-Claire Deville, and Adolphe Wurtz.

Dumas encouraged collaboration in research, both with himself and with fellow students. For example, he

Jean-Baptiste-Andre Dumas. *Jean-Baptiste-Andre Dumas, circa 1845.* HULTON ARCHIVE/GETTY IMAGES

collaborated with Boullay on ethers. He asked Péligot to join him in his investigation of ordinary alcohol and they were able to show that "wood spirit" was also an alcohol. Analogy was a valuable guide in their research and they established that ethal was also an alcohol. A difficult revision of the precise atomic weight of carbon was carried out with the collaboration of the Belgian Jean-Servais Stas, whose later reputation was built on his determination of atomic weights. With the help of Cahours Dumas carried out many analyses of proteins. The most famous collaboration between his students was that over many years between Gerhardt and Laurent.

The basic characteristics of a research school are a talented leader, a pool of committed juniors, and one or more research programs. It is also usual for the research to end in publication. This was, of course, a period when organic chemistry was in its infancy. Whereas Liebig's basic research program was focused on the simple analysis of organic compounds, Dumas was determined to go further with a goal of their general classification. Inspired by Lavoisier's success in classifying mineral compounds Dumas was determined to penetrate the forest of the organic world. Casting aside the traditional separate classification of natural and artificial organic compounds, Dumas and Boullay published a new classification in

1828. Based largely on analogy with the binary constitution of ammonium salts, they were able to present the respective formulas of ether, alcohol, and alcohol derivatives in this way. Also there was also now work in inorganic chemistry arising from the rapidly expanding number of new elements and compounds.

It is possible to distinguish five research programs, of which three were in organic chemistry. In some ways they merged one into the other as research proceeded. The ether program together with his chlorination studies led to the theory of substitution (program 2). His later rejection of simple ideas of substitution led to program 3, the type theory. Dumas later returned to his early physiological studies in Geneva (program 4). The fifth program was the redetermination of atomic weights of all the elements, for which he was helped by his special interest in vapor density. All this was obviously much more than could ever be achieved by one man and indeed it involved his whole research school.

Dumas's study of ethers began with the simple study of acids on ordinary alcohol. With sulfuric acid this would produce common ether. He was assisted by Faustino Malaguti in the chlorination of ether. A full year's laboratory work with Péligot led to the discovery that "wood spirit" was analogous to ordinary alcohol, hence laying the foundation for a study of a group of similar compounds. The existence of a whole class of alcohols was confirmed by Cahours's discovery that potato oil was another alcohol.

Substitution reactions are important in organic chemistry but work in this area presented a challenge. Dumas was early convinced by Jöns Jakob Berzelius's theory of electrochemical dualism that made a firm distinction between electropositive and electronegative elements. A major problem arose when Dumas found in 1838 that, in the chlorination of acetic acid, the intensely electronegative chlorine could replace the electropositive hydrogen to produce a similar acid. It was only in 1840, after considerable hesitation, that Dumas finally abandoned Berzelius's theory for a unitary theory more helpful for classification.

The third program, therefore, was the theory of chemical types, which owed something to botany in so far as Dumas and his students now thought of compounds as belonging to a genus. Compounds might belong to a particular type if they had the same number of equivalents. Ordinary alcohol belonged to the acetic acid group, while ethylene was linked with marsh gas (methane). The theory stimulated the search for new compounds. For example, in 1842 Dumas was able to predict the existence of seventeen fatty acids, of which only nine were known. The series went from margaric acid down to the simplest, formic acid. Within three years nearly all the other acids had been isolated. This was an early example of a homologous series, the term being introduced by Gerhardt. Although Dumas received great credit for the type theory, he was criticized by Laurent, who claimed that it was similar to his earlier nuclear theory. It was, however, Dumas whom most chemists followed.

Dumas made great efforts to secure academic positions for his students, many at the École Centrale in Paris. He was also able to secure appointments for them in faculties of science in many provincial universities. Most appointees were grateful but Gerhardt and particularly Laurent complained that living in the provinces deprived them of contact with the key academic center, Paris, and even that Dumas was claiming credit for ideas that were originally their own. In 1837 Dumas in a joint paper with Liebig made interesting remarks about collaboration that echo some used by Lavoisier in the introduction to his *Traité elémentaire de chimie* about the pooling of ideas between colleagues.

> We have opened our laboratory to many young men. … We have worked under their eyes and we have made them work under ours in such a way that we have surrounded ourselves with young people eager to emulate us. They are the future hope of science, *whose work* will be added to ours, *may even be confounded with ours.* (Dumas and Liebig, 1837, pp. 567–572; italics added)

The Rediscovery of Lavoisier. Dumas also has a place in the historiography of science. After Lavoisier's show trial and execution at the height of the French Revolution, memory of his pioneering work in bringing about the "chemical revolution" had quickly faded. Not only was his execution an embarrassment for his surviving colleagues and for the French state, but the new oxygen theory quickly came to be taken for granted in France and new ideas gained prominence, particularly electrochemistry and John Dalton's atomic theory, both fields foreign to Lavoisier's inheritance. Lavoisier's widow was a solitary figure in trying to perpetuate his memory, calling for the condemnation of those who had condoned the crime. It was only after her death in February 1836 that others felt able to remind the scientific community of the work of their fellow countryman, whose chemistry had previously been taken for granted.

Dumas had obviously been waiting for the earliest opportunity to remind French scientists of their debt to Lavoisier, for in May 1836 he used the anniversary of the death of the chemist to deliver a series of lectures at the Collège de France (*Leçons sur la philosophie chimique*, 1837) to make an emotional appeal, deploring the neglect of his predecessor. Using religious language, he pledged to work to prepare a complete edition of the writings of Lavoisier, saying: "I will present chemists with their sacred text (*leur évangile*)." When in 1843 Dumas was elected to the honorary position of annual president of the Academy of Sciences, he took advantage of his position to write to the minister of education, asking for government funds to defray the cost of a complete edition of Lavoisier's works. Dumas himself was able to supervise the publication of the first four (1864–1869) of six volumes. He was also the author of a *Traité élémentaire de chimie* (1st ed., 4 vols., Paris, 1813–1815; 6th ed., 5 vols. 1834–1836).

A Powerful Figure. In 1828 he was one of the cofounders of the École Centrale des Arts et Manufactures, one of the first institutions that could be properly called an industrial school—very different from the elitist École Polytechnique. In Dumas's early years he was heavily committed to this institution and to joint editorship of a related periodical. In 1840 he was appointed as one of the editors of the key journal for chemistry, the *Annales de chimie et de physique*. His position gave him control over the publication of papers on chemical research. Gerhardt and Laurent, unhappy by his treatment of their work, founded their own journal.

Many of the positions Dumas held were largely due to the patronage of Louis Jacques Thenard, culminating in the important post of dean in the Paris Faculty of Science (1842). Even more prestigious was the post of secretary to the Academy of Sciences, to which he was elected in 1848. His earlier career had been considerably assisted by his marriage (1826), to the daughter of the wealthy director of the Sèvres porcelain factory and professor of mineralogy Alexandre Brongniart, without which he might not have been able to set up his own laboratory.

SUPPLEMENTARY BIBLIOGRAPHY

WORKS BY DUMAS

Traité élémentaire de chimie. Paris: Cuchet, 1789.

Leçons sur la philosophie chimique. Edited by M. Bineau. Paris: Ébrard, 1837.

With Justus Liebig. "Sur l'état de la chimie organique." *Comptes rendus de l'Académie des Sciences* 5 (1837): 567–572.

OTHER SOURCES

Crosland, Maurice. *In the Shadow of Lavoisier: The* Annales de chimie *and the Establishment of a New Science.* Oxford: British Society for the History of Science, 1994.

———. "Research Schools of Chemistry from Lavoisier to Wurtz." *British Journal for the History of Science* 36 (2003): 333–361.

Jacques, Jean. "Auguste Laurent et J. B. Dumas d'après leur correspondance inédite." *Revue d'Histoire des Sciences* 6 (1953): 329–349.

Klein, Ursula. *Experiments, Models, Paper Trails: Cultures of Organic Chemistry in the Nineteenth Century.* Stanford, CA: Stanford University Press, 2003.

Klosterman, Leo. "Studies in the Life and Work of Jean Baptiste André Dumas (1800–84): The Period up to 1850." Thesis, University of Kent, Canterbury, 1976.

———. "A Research School of Chemistry in the 19th Century: Jean Baptiste Dumas and His Students." Parts 1 and 2. *Annals of Science* 42 (1985): 1–40, 41–80.

Rocke, Alan J. *Nationalizing Science: Adolphe Wurtz and the Battle for French Chemistry.* Cambridge, MA: MIT Press, 2001.

　　　　　　　　　　　　　　　　　Maurice Crosland

DUMBLETON, JOHN (*b.* England; *d.* c. 1349), *natural philosophy.* For the original article on John Dumbleton (alphabetized under John) see *DSB*, vol. 7.

Dumbleton's *Summa logicae et philosophiae naturalis* (The whole of logic and natural philosophy, about 1340) is a large work found in more than twenty manuscripts, typically large, well-crafted folio volumes. Whereas many of the works of Dumbleton's Merton College contemporaries, known collectively under the labels the Merton School, or the Oxford Calculatores, received early printed editions, Dumbleton's *Summa* did not, probably because of its great length and the fact that it was not used as a textbook, as were Thomas Bradwardine's *Tractatus de Proportionibus* (1328; Treatise on proportions), William Heytesbury's *Regulae Solvendi Sophismatum* (1335; Rules for solving sophismata), and even Richard Swineshead's *Liber Calculationum* (before 1350; Book of calculations). Nevertheless, the *Summa* is perhaps the best single existing exemplar of fourteenth-century Oxford natural philosophy.

Influences. More is known about the life of John Dumbleton than was known when the original *Dictionary of Scientific Biography* article about him was written. He is listed at Merton College, Oxford, for 1338 and 1347–1348 and as one of the original fellows of Queen's College, Oxford, in 1341, but he likely left to study theology in Paris in the early 1340s. As Zenon Kaluza argues, Dumbleton was a fellow of the Sorbonne at about the same time as Étienne Gaudet; that is, perhaps between around 1344 and 1347. Gaudet was the owner or copyist, or both, of several manuscripts that were later owned by Thomas of Cracow around 1400 (and are now at the Bibliothèque Nationale de France in Paris). Manuscript Paris BNF lat. 16621, which was likely copied by Gaudet, contains parts of Dumbleton's *Summa*, Bradwardine's *De proportionibus* (On proportions), Roger Swineshead's *Descriptiones motuum* (Descriptions of motions), and Walter Burley's *De primo et ultimo instanti* (On the first and the last instant), as well as works by John Buridan and Nicole Oresme. Two other manuscripts, in the midst of theological questions, refer to "Master John Dumbleton, one time fellow of the Sorbonne, in his *Summa*. ..." The conclusion they refer to is, indeed, one of Dumbleton's significant ones, namely that there is no real or imaginary latitude to which all the degrees of perfection may be applied—the reason being that degrees of perfection are indivisible and so do not together compose a continuum.

One "Master Clay," also from England, was at the Sorbonne at the same time and disputed a question with Dumbleton there. The handsome fourteenth-century copy of Dumbleton's *Summa* that is at present-day Paris, Universitaire, MS 599, once belonged to the Oxford University Library and was later in the possession of Thomas Allen and Kenelm Digby, whose notes are found in the margins. In the copy of the *Summa* now found in Padua, Bibl. Antoniana MS. XVII, 375, f. 21v, Dumbleton is labeled B. Th. at the end of Part I, so it is likely that he completed his theological education at least to the level of bachelor. He seems to have returned to Oxford by 1347–1348, when he is again listed at Merton College, and he probably died in the plague, because nothing is heard of him after 1348.

John of Casali, who was in England as lector at the Franciscan convent in Cambridge in 1341–1342, copied the suppositions of his work, *De velocitate motus alterationis* (1346; On the velocity of motions of alteration), from Dumbleton's *Summa*, and also copied the definitions from Roger Swineshead's *Descriptiones motuum*. Casali's use of triangles to represent the intensity of illumination as it decreases with distance from the light source follows Dumbleton's approach rather than the later approach of Nicole Oresme. Thus, although Dumbleton did not become as well-known on the Continent as did his fellow Mertonians, Bradwardine and Swineshead (not to mention the earlier Walter Burley), his work was, nevertheless, not without influence. In commenting on Heytesbury's work on motion in the three categories of place, quality, and quantity, for instance, the Italian Angelus de Fossambruno compares the opinion of Dumbleton to those of Bradwardine and Heytesbury.

The *Summa logicae et philosophiae naturalis*. The contents of the *Summa* may be seen in the following short outline (each item contains a book within the work:

1. On the significance of terms and their imposition; the relation of definitions to what is defined; on the principles of doctrine and on the intension and remission of hesitation, belief, and knowledge.

2. First principles, matter and form; opinions about substantial forms; how qualities are intended and remitted.

3. On motion in the categories of place, quality, and quantity. On the causes of motion. How velocity is produced and caused. How alteration and augmentation are measured. The definitions of motion and time.

4. On the nature of the elements and their qualities. If each element has two qualities in the highest degree. The action and reaction of elements on each other. The relations of elemental and qualitative forms. Density and rarity and their variation. How the powers of natural bodies depend on their magnitudes. The relative weights of pure and mixed bodies.

5. On spiritual action and light. Whether light belongs particularly to some element or compound. On the nature of the medium receiving spiritual action, such as light. On the variation of spiritual action in a medium. Whether spiritual agents act instantaneously or in time.

6. On the limits of active and passive powers. On the difficulty of action. On the limits of the powers of natural bodies by their natural places. Do the powers of elemental forms seek rest as well as motion? On the motions of the heavens and their movers. On the limits of size of natural bodies. How some bodies are moved by an intrinsic mover (*ex se*) and some are not.

7. On the cause of individuals and species of generable and corruptible things with regard to their numbers and the potencies of matter and agent. Whether the Prime Mover is of infinite power and whether it has been proved by a physical argument that the world and motion had no beginning.

8. On the generation of substances by like substances and animals by complete animals and by putrefaction. On the numerical unity of the soul with respect to the sensitive and intelligible and on the operations of the nutritive soul.

9. On material related to *On the Soul*, Book II, concerning the five senses.

10. On universals that are called "Ideas" by the Platonists and on the passive intellect. On the simple and complex operations of the human intellect. (This part may never have been completed, since it is not found in any manuscript.)

Thus, after explaining the fundamental logical approach of medieval natural philosophy in Part I, Dumbleton ranges through metaphysics, physics, the elements and their interactions, optics, biology, and psychology. Parts VIII and IX, on biology and psychology, take up almost 40 percent of the entire work. The basic framework is Aristotelian, but there are some Platonic elements. The topics of most of the parts of the *Summa* correspond to books by Aristotle that were part of fourteenth-century university curricula, but in many cases Dumbleton alternates between sections discussing typical Aristotelian questions and sections using the analytical tools for which the Oxford Calculators are famous, such as the proportions of velocities in motions, the intension and remission of forms, first and last instants, maxima and minima, and so forth. Dumbleton devotes particular attention to the properties and relations of continua and indivisibles, emphasizing that there is no proportion between a point and a line or between an indivisible degree and a latitude of form. He pairs the latitude of proportion to the latitude of velocity as a way to express Bradwardine's view of the relation of velocities to the proportions of forces to resistances producing them. Whereas the works of William Heytesbury and Richard Swineshead seem designed to help undergraduate students prepare for disputations, especially disputations on *sophismata* (ambiguous or paradoxical sounding statements) in the case of Heytesbury, Dumbleton's *Summa* more consistently advocates a point of view in natural philosophy, one which includes, upon a foundation of Aristotle, both the nominalism of William of Ockham and the quantification or mathematization associated with Bradwardine's *De proportionibus*. It has yet to be established with certainty whether Dumbleton's *Summa* was composed before or after Richard Swineshead's *Liber Calculationum*. Because the *Summa* likely was never completed and the *Liber Calculationum* is found in varying states of completion, perhaps the times of composition of the two works are best seen as overlapping.

SUPPLEMENTARY BIBLIOGRAPHY

The original DSB *article cites Weisheipl's "Repertorium Mertonense," where he lists manuscripts of the* Summa. *It also mentions Weisheipl's edition of a "rather banal" work by Dumbleton in his dissertation. No single library has especially significant unpublished manuscripts of Dumbleton—libraries have at most a manuscript of the* Summa. *Other than the short work edited in Weisheipl's dissertation, there are no works of Dumbleton that have been published. The outline in Latin in my dissertation using sentences from the* Summa *is the closest thing to publication that exists for any of his works.*

Caroti, Stefano. "*Reactio* in English Authors." In *La nouvelle physique du XIVe Siècle*, edited by Stefano Caroti and Pierre Souffrin. Biblioteca di Nuncius. Studi e Testi 24. Florence, Italy: Leo S. Olschki, 1997. See pp. 247–248 and note 58 for the relation between Dumbleton and Richard Swineshead on the question of reaction.

Kaluza, Zenon. *Thomas de Cracovie: Contribution à l'histoire du collège de la Sorbonne.* Wroclaw, Poland: Ossolineum, 1978. This work contains evidence of Dumbleton's presence at the Sorbonne in the 1340s.

Sylla, Edith Dudley. "Medieval Concepts of the Latitude of Forms: The 'Oxford Calculators.'" *Archives d'histoire doctrinale et littéraire du moyen âge* 40 (1973): 223–283.

———. "The Oxford Calculators and Mathematical Physics: John Dumbleton's *Summa Logicae et Philosophiae Naturalis*, Parts II and III." In *Physics, Cosmology, and Astronomy, 1300–1700: Tension and Accommodation*, edited by Sabetai Unguru. Boston Studies in the Philosophy of Science, vol. 126. Dordrecht, The Netherlands: Kluwer Academic Publishers, 1991.

———. *The Oxford Calculators and the Mathematics of Motion, 1320–1350: Physics and Measurement by Latitudes.* New York; London: Garland Publishing, 1991. While Dumbleton's *Summa logicae et philosophiae naturalis* is still available only in manuscript, a detailed outline of the main sections of Parts II through VI of the *Summa* is contained in this work.

———. "Imaginary Space: John Dumbleton and Isaac Newton." In *Raum und Raumvorstellungen im Mittelalter*, edited by Jan Aertsen and Andreas Speer. Miscellanea Mediaevalia, 25. Berlin: Walter de Gruyter, 1998.

———. "Creation and Nature." In *The Cambridge Companion to Medieval Philosophy*, edited by Arthur S. Mcgrade. Cambridge, U.K. and New York: Cambridge University Press, 2003. This article uses an outline of Dumbleton's *Summa* as a way to characterize fourteenth-century natural philosophy.

Edith Dudley Sylla

E

ECCLES, JOHN CAREW (*b.* Melbourne, Australia, 27 January 1903; *d.* Contra, Switzerland, 2 May 1997), *spinal cord, cerebellum, neurophysiology, synapse.*

John ("Jack") Eccles was a pioneer of the physiology of the nerve cell, a leader in the rise of modern neuroscience in the middle of the twentieth century. He led the way in characterizing the mechanisms of the contacts (synapses) between nerve cells in the central nervous system. He was the first to identify a central neurotransmitter, the action of a central inhibitory neuron, and central circuits formed by synaptic contacts and synaptic actions.

Early Life and Career. Eccles was born and raised in Australia. His parents were both schoolteachers and Catholics, a family background that shaped his future career. He received his undergraduate and medical training at the University of Melbourne, graduating in 1925 with first-class honors. He won a Rhodes Scholarship for study at Oxford University, where he joined the group of outstanding young investigators, which included Derek Denny-Brown, John Farquhar Fulton, R. S. Creed, and E. G. T. Liddell, producing a series of studies under Charles Sherrington on spinal cord reflexes. This resulted in the landmark book *Reflex Activity of the Spinal Cord* (1932) by Creed and others. The book was believed to have played a significant role in the awarding of the Nobel Prize to Sherrington (together with E. G. Adrian of Cambridge) that year.

Eccles completed a BS at Oxford in 1927 and a DPhil in 1929, and then became a tutor at Magdalen College and a university demonstrator in 1934. Sherrington took him on as his research assistant for Sherrington's last experiments on excitation and inhibition of spinal cord reflexes. Eccles then developed his own studies of synaptic transmission in sympathetic ganglia, in which he interpreted his findings in terms of electrical transmission between the stimulated nerves and the postsynaptic cells. This brought him into conflict with the emerging pharmacological evidence by Henry H. Dale, Wilhelm Feldberg, Lindor Brown, and others for the release and action of chemical transmitters at the synaptic junctions between nerve cell fiber terminals and their target glands and muscles. Thus was engendered the "soup versus sparks" debates, which often involved pitched battles between the participants at one meeting after the other throughout the 1930s. Bernard Katz, who came to England in the mid-1930s as a refugee from Germany, described his amazement at how violently the younger Eccles and the older Dale would attack each other during these meetings, and his further amazement at how they would then retire to sherry and a convivial dinner together.

Return to the Antipodes. Sherrington retired in 1935 (at the age of seventy-five, having been granted a personal extension). Although Eccles was an obvious candidate to succeed him, his youth, brashness, and pugnacity were not a good fit with Oxford traditions and John Mellanby was appointed instead. In 1937 Eccles left to return to Australia (a common career trajectory after training in England) to head a small medical research unit in the Kanematsu Institute of Pathology in Sydney. It was near oblivion for him, with no university connection, no access to students, and an unsympathetic administration. Soon the onset of the war in Europe in September 1939 diverted most of his attention to the war effort. By good fortune, he was joined by both Katz and another refugee, Stephen Kuffler. There is an often reproduced photograph of the three young neuroscience greats strolling together down a street in Sydney (a painting of the photograph hangs in the physiological laboratory in Oxford). In 1939 Eccles reported electrophysiological recordings from the neuromuscular junction with evidence of chemical transmission, simultaneously with similar reports by T. P. Feng (Feng De-Pei) in China and H. Gopfert and H. Schaefer in Germany. Although this was a great breakthrough in the analysis of the physiology of the synapse, it also disproved his own electrical hypothesis, at least for peripheral synaptic transmission.

With prospects for building his research efforts dim at the institute, in 1944 Eccles accepted the professorship of physiology at the University of Otago, in Dunedin, New Zealand. Despite the remote location, it gave him the opportunity to return to an academic setting for his research, though with a heavy teaching load. He describes how in his first year he gave all the physiology lectures, totaling some 500 contact hours. On the positive side, it gave him discipline in using his time and a broad grasp of physiological principles.

Eccles was still depressed over the failure of his theoretical predictions in the 1930s, until meeting the philosopher Karl Popper in New Zealand just after the war. Popper was developing his philosophy of science, with the dictum that science can never prove a hypothesis correct, it can only falsify it, the goal of the scientist being to erect hypotheses that can be tested and disproven. According to this view, Eccles had been advancing science by proving himself wrong. The two became lifelong friends. The new concept of doing science rescued Eccles from his depression. "I was urged by Popper to formulate the hypotheses of electrical excitation and inhibition in models that invited experimental testing and falsification" (Eccles, 1977)—to which Eccles added a corollary: only Eccles would be allowed to disprove Eccles's hypotheses!

Despite the isolation of Dunedin, after the war he assembled a group of outstanding young students and colleagues from New Zealand and abroad, including the electrophysiologist Archibald ("Archie") McIntyre and the American biophysicist Wilfrid Rall. For several years he pursued his hypothesis of electrical transmission in the spinal cord. This required convoluted reasoning to account for current flows that could cause postsynaptic inhibition. In his remote location, one less motivated might have lost out in the postwar era of gearing up for modern cellular research and drifted out of the mainstream.

However, around 1950 McIntyre returned from the Rockefeller Institute with the circuit for the new state-of-the-art amplifier built by Jan Friedrich Toennies, an out-

standing German-trained engineer (who before the war had trained Alan Hodgkin in cathode followers for his squid axon studies). Dexter Easton came with the news that J. Walter Woodbury and Harry Patton in Seattle were beginning to make intracellular recordings in the spinal cord. This galvanized Eccles to a single-minded focus on this goal, with an intensity that could not be matched by the Seattle group.

It was a singular moment for Eccles, "a crisis in my life." Spurred by fear of the competition, he resolved to get there first. He needed hands to do it. Eccles asked John ("Jack") Coombs, a physicist, to find help with the electronics for doing the microelectrode work. Coombs decided it was interesting and would do it himself, constructing the needed cathode follower amplifier with high input impedance to reduce input capacitance and neutralize pipette capacitance by negative feedback.

Laurence Brock had just completed his medical course; he was good with his hands, and he pulled the micropipettes. This was done on a "microforge," requiring extreme concentration to pull the pipettes to a fine tip, and luck to get them fully filled with the electrode solution. Rall had started earlier work with Eccles, but decided he would do his own project for his PhD thesis. Archie MacIntyre was a mild-mannered person at an early stage in his career. Eccles at the time was using the classical mechano-electric Lucas pendulum breaks for stimulators, recording the data on glass negatives that were developed as they went along. When he realized he needed McIntyre's state-of-the-art equipment, he simply took it over. All efforts were bent on beating the Americans.

Eccles plunged into making intracellular recordings from the motor neurons in the spinal cord in response to an electrical shock to the motor neuron axons in the ventral roots. This approach enabled him to identify a motor neuron by the action potential in its axon invading backwardly (antidromically). He could then analyze the response of the cell to injected current and to synaptic activation over the normal (orthodromic) route by a shock delivered to sensory axons in the dorsal roots. The recordings immediately showed that stimulation of the sensory nerves from an agonist muscle set up depolarizing, excitatory postsynaptic potentials in a motoneuron, whereas from an antagonist muscle, hyperpolarizing inhibitory postsynaptic potentials were set up. These responses showed clearly the properties of chemical rather than electrical transmission. The electrical hypothesis was triumphantly demolished by its own Popperian architect.

These results were published in the *Journal of Physiology* beginning in 1951. In that year Eccles accepted the opportunity to move back to Australia, to be professor of physiology in the newly established Australian National University (ANU) in Canberra. It took fifteen months for the new laboratories to be ready, an interim that might have been fatal to most research workers at that critical juncture. However, Eccles typically used it to full advantage. He spent five months traveling in early 1952, first to a Cold Spring Harbor symposium on the neuron, where he learned about the Hodgkin-Huxley action potential model and the Katz neuromuscular junction work, then back to England to summarize the new results in the Waynflete Lectures, delivered at Magdalen College in Oxford in 1952 and published in his *The Neurophysiological Basis of Mind: The Principles of Neurophysiology* in 1953.

Neurophysiology. In many ways, this work and the book launched the modern cellular physiology of the central nervous system. It established the basic functions of chemical excitatory and inhibitory synapses, just before they were visualized morphologically for the first time in the electron microscope. They were furthermore developed firmly within the context of the emerging modern concepts of the properties of cell membranes, thanks to his rapid assimilation of the work of Alan L. Hodgkin and Andrew F. Huxley in developing their model of the action potential in the squid axon, and of Katz and Paul Fatt in their model of the neuromuscular junction. It immediately laid out the future of cellular and circuit neuroscience, at a time when neurophysiology ruled studies of the nervous system, before the advent of the biochemical and pharmacological approaches that we take for granted today.

Starting in the new laboratories in early 1953, Eccles, with Fatt and Kyozo Koketsu, identified the circuit mediating recurrent inhibition, from the collateral branches of the motor neuron axon to an inerneuron and back onto the same and neighboring motor neurons. The inhibition of a motoneuron by an interneuron had previously been predicted from recordings around 1940 by a young investigator at Harvard University, Birdsey Renshaw, who subsequently died at an early age of polio in 1947. Eccles termed these "Renshaw cells" in his honor, and they became the paradigmatic form of self and lateral feedback inhibition, with examples being found subsequently in many different regions of the nervous system. Paradoxically, in those regions specific functions for the inhibition could be proposed, whereas the functions in the spinal cord remained elusive. A new synthesis of these results with intracellular recordings in other nerve cells was summarized in his widely read book *The Physiology of the Nerve Cell* in 1957.

These findings on central synaptic transmission in the spinal cord were paralleled by the reports of Katz and his collaborators Fatt and José del Castillo revealing the mechanisms of chemical transmission at the neuromuscular junction. The air was suddenly cleared; chemical trans-

John Eccles. HULTON ARCHIVE/GETTY IMAGES.

mission appeared to be the way neurons communicate by means of synapses. This soon received strong support from the revelations of the electron microscope of the fine structure of the chemical synapse by Sanford Palay and George Palade in the United States and Eduardo de Robertis and H. S. Bennett in Argentina. However, within a few years electrical synapses were described by Ed Furshpan and David Potter, and their basis in gap junctions was shown, to give the present understanding of both chemical and electrical transmission in the central nervous system.

During the 1950s Eccles engaged in several unduly harsh efforts to apply the Popper doctrine to falsifying the findings of colleagues. One was David P. C. Lloyd, a former student at Oxford, over details of synaptic connectivity in the spinal cord. Another was his former student Rall, who brought forward evidence from Eccles's own recordings for dendritic dominance of synaptic integration. Eccles would brook no opposition, claiming another explanation based on a postulated persistent current. Rall refuted this explanation, and Eccles eventually abandoned it. But as late as 1960 he was still defending the idea that dendrites had mostly nutritive roles, being too distant to affect synaptic integration, which he believed was focused at the cell body where his recordings were made. His opposition greatly impeded recognition of the significance of Rall's work and the value of theory in neuroscience, in which Rall first adapted basic cable theory followed by his new methods of compartmental analysis to show that most synaptic integration takes place in the dendrites. However, as was typical of Eccles, harkening back to his interactions with Dale, when Rall and his colleagues came forward with evidence for novel interactions between dendrites, it was Eccles who organized and invited Rall to co-chair with him a meeting in 1968 where these new findings were presented. The reason for his harsh attacks may be traced back to his training in England, where such exchanges, as described above, could take place between colleagues within the clubby atmosphere of the Physiological Society. However, in the outside world, they were interpreted as doing unnecessary harm.

During the 1950s Eccles's laboratory in Canberra was a magnet for a new generation of cellular neurophysiologists from around the world. More than 100 of his approximately 200 students and collaborators came from that time. The several experimental rigs were in use around the clock, experiments often lasting through the night and sometimes through the next day (as in other electrophysiological laboratories of that era). For social variety there were the famous parties at Eccles's home, where he and his wife Irene Francis would entertain the group with square dancing, party games, and sports.

In the 1960s Eccles broadened his interests from the spinal cord to other brain regions, assisted by several outstanding students. A leading strategy was to test the generality of the Renshaw cell inhibitory feedback pathway. To this end he carried out a series of experiments, with Per Andersen from Norway, extending the model to inhibitory circuits in the thalamus and hippocampus. The productivity of that collaboration can be judged by the twenty-four papers produced in their two years together. With Masao Ito and others, Eccles carried out a series of intracellular experiments on neuronal interactions in the cerebellum. This produced evidence for the basket cell as an inhibitory interneuron, one of the first extensions of the Renshaw cell concept (along with the granule cell of the olfactory bulb) to the brain. This resulted in the book *The Cerebellum as a Neuronal Machine* (1966), written with Ito and the neuroanatomist John Szentagothai. These investigations increasingly used pharmacological tools to characterize the nature of chemical transmission in these different areas, which were summarized in another widely read book, *The Physiology of Synapses* (1964). From a current perspective it is noteworthy that all of this work was in anesthetized animals, predating the introduction of the brain slice preparation in 1971.

Late Career. As Eccles approached retirement age in the 1960s, his wish to remain active at the ANU went unheeded, so he left in 1966 to carry on his studies at a new private Institute of Biomedical Research set up by the American Medical Association in Chicago. Rodolfo Llinas, among other young investigators, joined him there. When this institute collapsed, he went to the State University of New York at Buffalo, together with his second wife Helena, also a neurophysiologist. There he continued to pursue his work on the cerebellum with a new generation of young neurophysiologists, including visiting former colleagues such as Don Faber, Henri Korn, Robert Schmidt, and Yamakazu Oshima. He also began to be interested in the interactions between the cerebellum and the neocortex, intrigued by the fact that 88 percent of the human cerebellum is oriented exclusively to the contralateral cerebrum. However, the grant to support this work ended in 1975, leading to his retirement in that year at the age of seventy-two.

He moved to a mountain village in Switzerland, which might seem remote, but not for Eccles. His retirement did not mean the end of his career in neuroscience, but rather a refocusing of his interests. An omnivorous reader and indefatigable traveler, he followed closely the current research, particularly on the cerebral cortex. The role of Ca2+ in synaptic integration in cortical neurons engaged his interest and prompted a series of articles well into the 1980s.

Retirement also meant the opportunity to pursue his lifelong absorption in the relation of brain circuits to cognition, philosophy, and religion. This had started with the last chapter in *The Neurophysiological Basis of Mind* in 1953, a rather startling—and some felt irrelevant—distraction from the solid science in the book, but this was his life view from the start. As a Catholic, he attacked the problem of the mind and the brain with the same vigor that he used in his scientific endeavors. He was inspired in this by his Oxford years with Sherrington, who set forth his own philosophical views on Cartesian dualism in *Man on His Nature* in 1940. Eccles published many articles and several books on resolving the mind-body problem (106 of his 588 publications according to Andersen and Lundberg, 1997), his most extensive attempt in a dialogue between himself, a dualist, with his old friend Popper, an agnostic, laid out in the book *The Self and Its Brain: An Argument for Interactionism* in 1977. It continued his attempt to probe the neural basis of consciousness, which has lately become a fashionable topic in cognitive neuroscience. So he can be called a pioneer in this field as well.

Many honors were bestowed on Eccles during his career. Among them, he was a member of the Royal Society, and Nobel laureate in 1963 with Hodgkin and

Huxley, recognized for his discoveries of the ionic basis of the function of nerve cells in the central nervous system.

In summing up his career, several themes are of interest to early twenty-first century scientists. One is his odyssey, as he described it himself, across the oceans, from Australia to Britain, back to Australia, to New Zealand, back to Australia, and to the United States and finally Switzerland; a scientist goes where the opportunities are greatest to realize one's career goals. Another is his life as an educator: he was willing in Dunedin to assume overwhelming teaching responsibilities that not only served his institution but grounded him in the fundamentals of his field. He was also an educator through his research: his 200 students and collaborators populated academia and industry with the new science. Scientists are supposed to write original research articles, not books, yet his books were instrumental in shaping modern neuroscience.

To those who knew him, his was a personality truly larger than life. He had a vigorous physique, with prodigious stamina at the experimental rig, at his desk, or traveling the world with his message. The voice was penetrating, with a broad Australian accent, overwhelming in debate and naturally dominating in conversation. He had a wide mouth, ready instantly to break out into a broad grin or hearty laugh to express a life-embracing sense of humor. There was total engagement in whatever issue was being discussed, with an encyclopedic grasp of the literature. He was courteous and generous to his friends and colleagues. Finally, he was a scientist who reserved a place in his life for his spiritual side. To those who knew him, he was the embodiment of a great era in the creation of modern neuroscience.

BIBLIOGRAPHY

A full account of all aspects of Eccles's life and works may be found in the numerous articles in a memorial issue: Stuart, D. G., ed. "The Contributions of John Carew Eccles to Contemporary Neuroscience." Progress in Neurobiology 78, no. 3–5 (2006): 135–326.

WORKS BY ECCLES

The Neurophysiological Basis of Mind: The Principles of Neurophysiology. Oxford: Clarendon Press, 1953.

The Physiology of the Nerve Cell. Baltimore, MD: Johns Hopkins Press, 1957.

The Physiology of Synapses. New York: Academic Press, 1964.

With Masao Ito and John Szentagothai. *The Cerebellum as a Neuronal Machine.* Berlin and New York: Springer-Verlag, 1966.

With Karl Popper. *The Self and Its Brain: An Argument for Interactionism.* New York: Springer International, 1977. The most complete account of his philosophy and spiritual beliefs.

"My Scientific Odyssey." *Annual Review of Physiology* 39 (1997): 1–18.

OTHER SOURCES

Andersen, Per, and Anders Lundberg. "John C. Eccles (1903–1997)." *Trends in Neuroscience* 20 (1997): 324–325.

Burke, R. E. "John Eccles' Pioneering Role in Understanding Central Synaptic Transmission." *Progress in Neurobiology* 78 (2006): 173–188.

Stuart, Douglas G., and Patricia A. Pierce. "The Academic Lineage of Sir John Carew Eccles (1903–1997)." *Progress in Neurobiology* 78 (2006): 136–155.

Gordon M. Shepherd

ECKERT, J. (JOHN ADAM) PRESPER, JR.

(*b.* Philadelphia, Pennsylvania, 9 April 1919; *d.* Bryn Mawr, Pennsylvania, 3 June 1995), *electrical engineering, computer engineering.*

J. Presper Eckert is best known for his role as chief engineer in the project that created the ENIAC (Electronic Numerical Integrator and Computer) at the University of Pennsylvania during World War II. Later he helped establish one of the first American computer companies and oversaw technical development of its first commercial computers.

Upbringing and Education. Eckert was the only child of a prominent Philadelphia real estate developer, John Eckert, and Ethel Hallowell Eckert. His parents valued education highly, and he attended the prestigious private William Penn Charter School. He also traveled extensively with his family both in the United States and abroad, visiting all forty-eight contiguous states, Alaska, and many major foreign cities. He showed a strong interest in electronics from an early age, tinkering with radios and phonographs. In addition to his formal schooling, he worked on electronics projects with staff at the Franklin Institute and at Philo Farnsworth's television laboratory.

Initially Eckert aspired to study electrical engineering at the Massachusetts Institute of Technology (MIT), but his father convinced him instead to enroll at the business-orientated Wharton School at the nearby University of Pennsylvania. Eckert was accepted at Wharton in 1937 but found it unsuited to his interests and transferred to the university's Moore School of Electrical Engineering. Its dean, Harold Pender, had recently been recruited from MIT, and was striving to increase the Moore School's standing as a national research center. While only a middling student, Eckert continued his self-directed tinkering on the side. He also assisted his electronics professor and mentor, Carl Chambers, with consulting projects. Eckert remembered that Chambers "really indoctrinated me with being as careful as I was in designs. I did some circuit design for him, and he always had me test it for all the variations possible" (Eckstein, 1996, p. 38).

In 1941 Eckert graduated and considered offers from Philco and RCA Laboratories, but elected instead to stay at the Moore School to begin graduate education and serve as a teaching assistant. One of his first assignments was as a laboratory supervisor in a summer course the Moore School was conducting for the military. There he met a colleague who became a lifelong partner, John Mauchly, a physics professor at nearby Ursinus College.

The Development of ENIAC. Mauchly, then thirty-four, and Eckert, twenty-two, spent hours talking about scientific and engineering topics. Both had a fascination with different ways to use the speed of electronic circuits to improve measurement and calculation. Mauchly was soon hired by the Moore School as an instructor, and Eckert became involved in a variety of projects. Most notable was time he spent on a Moore School contract with the MIT Radiation Laboratory for a switching amplifier. He experimented with timing equipment for a moving-target indicator (MTI) and developed a device called a mercury delay line, which used acoustic wave patterns in mercury to store and measure the intervals between signal pulses. He would return to the idea later in his career.

Eckert also worked with the Moore School's differential analyzer, a specialized piece of equipment used to compute solutions to differential equations. Developed by Vannevar Bush at MIT, the differential analyzer was a complex and intricate analogue device consisting of numerous gears, wheels, and shafts that were carefully selected and adjusted to solve each new problem. Pender had convinced the military to buy one for the Moore School, and even before Pearl Harbor, staff there were cooperating with the U.S. Army's Ballistics Research Laboratory (BRL) in computing firing tables. Eckert joined a group working with the analyzer and began trying to improve its performance with electronic components. With his assistance, the team added photocells, more than four hundred vacuum tubes, generators, and server motors that dramatically improved both the speed and the performance of the analyzer.

As requirements for more and faster computations grew, staff continued to consider other innovations. In August 1942, Mauchly dictated a memorandum describing an "electronic computor [*sic*]" that would be more accurate than the differential analyzer and far faster than either it or hand calculating with desktop calculators. The idea grew in part out of ongoing discussions with Eckert about electronic circuits and components. Mauchly sub-

mitted the memorandum to the Moore School deans, but they were unimpressed and failed to act on it. Mauchly remained enthusiastic about the idea, however, and brought it up again in discussions with Lieutenant Herman Goldstine, a PhD mathematician who served as the liaison between the BRL and the Moore School. By the spring of 1943, Goldstine was convinced that Mauchly's idea for an all-electronic computer should be considered seriously. Unfortunately, no one could locate the original memorandum proposing the computer that Mauchly had written six months earlier. It was re-created from notes.

On 9 April 1942, a formal meeting was convened with Mauchly, Eckert, the research director of the Moore School, Goldstine, and the director of the BRL. It was Eckert's twenty-third birthday. He later remembered that even as the meeting was going on, he and Mauchly were writing the technical appendices backing up the proposal. The plan was approved, and the Moore School soon began Project PX: to design and construct what became known as ENIAC, or Electronic Numerical Integrator and Computer. Originally the plan was for a machine containing around five thousand tubes and costing $150,000. Before the project was completed, however, the number of tubes had grown to eighteen thousand and the cost to $400,000. ENIAC would also require seventy thousand resistors, ten thousand capacitors, six thousand switches, and fifteen hundred relays, and would fill a room 9.1 meters (30 feet) wide by 15.2 meters (50 feet) long. The expansion was due to new requirements from the army, which insisted on having a machine that could solve a wide range of problems.

Although Goldstine had convinced the army to support the idea for ENIAC, others were skeptical. Doubts had begun with the Moore School's own dean. Leading scientists in the National Defense Research Committee, the organization designed to coordinate all university research and development during the war, did not support the idea. Most critics pointed to the growing complexity of the circuitry and the propensity of vacuum tubes to fail. By one naive calculation, if the mean life of a tube was around three thousand hours, then there would be a tube failure every ten minutes.

Making ENIAC work would require engineering genius. Eckert supplied it. While Mauchly had the overall vision for ENIAC and contributed innovations to programming it, Eckert oversaw the detailed hardware design. He specified circuits and wiring plans. He carefully tested each type of tube, and made sure that it would be powered at levels that would give it maximum life. Goldstine later wrote,

> Eckert fully understood at the start, as perhaps none of his colleagues did, that the overall success of the project was to depend entirely on a totally

new concept of component reliability and on utmost care in setting up criteria for everything from quality of insulation to types of tubes.... Eckert's standards were the highest, his energies almost limitless, his ingenuity remarkable, and his intelligence extraordinary.... It was Eckert's omnipresence that drove everything forward at whatever cost to humans including himself." (1972, pp. 153–154)

Although designed to meet a wartime emergency, ENIAC was not completed until after the war. It debuted with a formal dedication on 15 February 1946. The army proclaimed it a "new machine that is expected to revolutionize the mathematics of engineering and change many of our industrial design methods" (U.S. War Department). Well before the gala announcement, however, the ENIAC designers knew their machine, while a major step forward, had severe weaknesses. Their view was amplified and extended in the summer of 1944 during several visits from the famous mathematician John von Neumann, who became very interested in the development of computers. With his involvement and support, the ENIAC group won army approval for a new project, PY, to create EDVAC, or an Electronic Discrete Variable Automatic Computer. Two critical innovations underlay the new project. The first was mercury delay lines, which could be used to store numbers in the machine, vastly extending its storage capability. This grew from Eckert's previous work on mercury storage for the MIT project. The second—made possible by the first—was the simple but fundamental idea of stored programs: the computer's storage device would be used to hold both the instructions of a program and the numbers on which it operated. The specific originator of this idea is disputed. It is likely that once the possibility of extensive storage became realistic, several of those involved in the discussion conceived it independently. But unquestionably von Neumann's involvement catalyzed the idea, and he went on to articulate it most clearly in his famous "First Draft of a Report on the EDVAC (1945)." In retrospect, it has become recognized as a foundational document of computer science.

The ENIAC Patent Dispute. Besides considering technical improvements in ENIAC in 1944, Eckert and Mauchly also began thinking seriously about the commercial applications of the work they had been doing. In September 1944 Eckert wrote to his Moore School colleagues that he and Mauchly planned to apply for a patent on the ENIAC. Although some would later claim they had been left out of the application, at the time all agreed that the patent application should be in Eckert's and Mauchly's names. The school was also agreeable to the application, but insisted that patent rights be assigned to the university. Eckert and Mauchly balked, saying they should retain

the rights. After a bitter fight, the university finally accepted their position, and in March 1945, let the two men retain the rights. But the issue was not over. A year later, soon after ENIAC was dedicated to the public, the Moore School clarified its patent policy and now insisted that any future patent rights of researchers had to come to the university. By this time, with the war over, Eckert and Mauchly were already considering other career possibilities, and the new policy became a determining factor. They both refused to sign and resigned from the university. While both had several job possibilities, they decided they should take a bold step. In March 1946, they established the Electronic Control Company, the first commercial computer company in the United States.

Even after the departure of Eckert and Mauchly from the Moore School, the ENIAC patent dispute lived on. The application was finally filed on 26 June 1947, but the patent, U.S. Patent 3,120,606, was not finally granted until 4 February 1964. At that time, the rights were owned by Sperry Rand, where Eckert then worked. When the company began trying to collect royalties on the patent, some firms, such as International Business Machines (IBM), reached negotiated settlements. Honeywell Corporation, in contrast, decided to challenge the patent, and filed suit in 1967. A trial finally began in 1971, and ran until 13 March 1972. In a dramatic conclusion, Judge Earl R. Larson ruled the ENIAC patent invalid. While he noted many findings, he gave two primary reasons. First he concluded that Mauchly had not conceived his idea independently, but had derived it from knowledge of the work of John V. Atanasoff at Iowa State University. Atanasoff had developed an electronic computing device in the late 1930s, and Mauchly had visited him for four days in June 1941. Although Mauchly argued that this interaction was not the source of his idea, the judge ruled against him. The judge also concluded that there had been substantial public disclosure before the patent was filed. One example was the gala ENIAC announcement in February 1946.

While some believed the judge's decision rightly accorded Atanasoff credit for his pioneering work, Eckert and Mauchly both thought the ruling robbed them of due recognition for their role in creating ENIAC and launching the American computer industry. Eckert never accepted that Atanasoff should be known as some sort of "forgotten father" of the digital computer.

Creating a Computer Company. In the postwar period, there was little venture capital available to finance start-up companies, and no established market for digital computers. When creating their computer company, Eckert and Mauchly had to start small and continually struggle to finance company operations. Their first customer was the

J. Presper Eckert with James Wiener and John Mauchly. *J. Presper Eckert (center), James R. Wiener, and John W. Mauchly look over memory section of a computer.* **AP IMAGES.**

U.S. Census Bureau, which had received $300,000 from the U.S. Army Ordnance Department to develop a computer. Although some Census Bureau reviewers were lukewarm about the plans of Eckert and Mauchly, the bureau issued a $75,000 contract to the Electronic Control Company in September 1946 to conduct research on mercury delay storage units for computer use. Given that ENIAC had cost $400,000, this was a paltry sum. The expectation was that the project could develop into a larger contract for a full computer. Eckert and Mauchly were now envisioning a general purpose computer that could be used by many organizations, which they would soon call UNIVAC (Universal Automatic Computer).

In December 1947, the two incorporated their company and renamed it the Eckert-Mauchly Computer Company. Funding from the Census Bureau would not keep them afloat, especially as they added employees, so they continually sought new customers. Over the next several years, they succeeded in selling their proposed UNIVAC to the Prudential Life Insurance Company and the ACNielsen Company. They also negotiated a contract for a special purpose computer, the BINAC (Binary Auto-

matic Computer), with the Northrop Aircraft Company. BINAC first ran in February 1949, and was arguably the first successful stored computer in the United States. It was not fully a success, however, as it was delivered more than a year late. Northrop was never able to run the computer reliably once it had been transferred to them.

Building UNIVACs. The company was more successful with UNIVACs. Again, development took longer than expected. The first UNIVAC was released to the Census Bureau on 31 March 1951. Because of delays and cost escalation, Prudential and Nielsen ultimately canceled their contracts. However, other government agencies and private companies bought machines. In all, forty-six UNIVACs were produced. The most famous was serial number 5, which was sold to the Atomic Energy Commission and installed at the University of California Radiation Laboratory. In 1952 the CBS television network used it to predict the outcome of the presidential election between Adlai Stevenson and Dwight Eisenhower. On election night, with only 3.4 million votes counted, the computer predicted a landslide for Eisenhower: forty-three states to only five. The prediction was so lopsided that CBS decided not to air it, but the computer turned out to be close. Eisenhower won by thirty-nine states to nine, with a total of 61.5 million votes cast.

Throughout the development of the UNIVAC, Eckert had been the acknowledged technology leader of his company, inspiring his coworkers. One of them, Herman Lukoff, later remembered "Shift work didn't mean anything to Pres; he worked all shifts. He was there whenever anyone else was, working on the nagging problems of the moment. The only way his poor wife, Hester, got to see him was by coming in during the evening and idly standing by" (1979, p. 101).

Although Eckert and Mauchly had produced the first successful business computer in the United States, they were not themselves successful businessmen. They grossly underestimated both the cost of developing their products and the time required. Their company remained in financial difficulty. The problem was finally solved when the Remington Rand Company, a major producer of office equipment, bought the Eckert-Mauchly Computer Company on 1 February 1950. In 1952 Remington Rand also acquired Engineering Research Associates, another fledgling computer company, and thus became one of the leading computer companies in the United States. Other mergers would follow. It was Remington Rand who successfully negotiated cancellation of the Prudential and ACNielsen contracts, and substantially increased the price of subsequent UNIVACs. In 1955, Remington Rand merged with Sperry Gyroscope to form Sperry Rand, and in 1986, that company joined with Burroughs Corporation to form the Unisys Corporation.

In the mid-1950s, it seemed that Remington Rand was poised to take the lead in the new business of computer development, but the company was unable to turn a profit with computers. Not until the early 1960s did the computer division make money, and by that time, Remington Rand was being overshadowed in the market by rival IBM. Although Sperry Rand remained in IBM's shadow, it gradually became a successful computer company. In contrast, other firms that entered the business in the 1950s gave up after years of major losses.

Eckert's Legacy. Mauchly left Remington Rand in 1959 to form a consulting firm, Mauchly Associates. Eckert, however, stayed with the company. He served as director of engineering, 1950–1955; vice president and director of commercial engineering, 1955–1959; vice president and executive assistant to the general manager, 1959–1963; and vice president and technical advisor to the president, 1963–1982.

Eckert published few technical papers during his career. His most important contribution was "A Survey of

Digital Computer Memory Systems," which appeared in the *Proceedings of the Institute of Radio Engineers* in 1953. In the article he summarized the range of memory devices then being used or explored for use in computer systems. They ranged from vacuum tubes, such as were employed in ENIAC, to ferromagnetic cells, which would form the foundation of magnetic core memories. Eckert gave special attention to delay-line memories, which he had personally pioneered. The article makes clear, however, that he knew other techniques would soon surpass what could be done with delay-line systems.

A better measure of Eckert's technical expertise is his patents. He was issued ninety during his career: twenty-nine to him personally, ten jointly with Mauchly, and fifty-one jointly with other inventors. The topics ranged from electronic circuits, to memory systems, to printers. Patent 2,629,827, for example, was the first patent Eckert and Mauchly received on the ideas inherent in the mercury delay memory system. Clearly Eckert saw patents as more important to his legacy as an engineer than publications.

Eckert was elected to the National Academy of Engineering in 1967. In 1968 he was awarded the National Medal of Science "for pioneering and continuing contributions in creating, developing, and improving the high-speed electronic digital computer" (National Science Foundation Internet page). He fully retired in 1989, and died of leukemia in 1995. In 1986, after noting the remarkable progress in computer development over four decades, he penned his own wry epitaph. "The ENIAC was built as a system that has led directly to today's computers," he said. "I look back at the scenario and ask you to consider the following question: How would you like to see your life's work end up on a tenth of a square inch of silicon?" (1986).

BIBLIOGRAPHY

WORKS BY ECKERT

"A Survey of Digital Computer Memory Systems." *Proceedings of the Institute of Radio Engineers* 41 (October 1953): 1393–1406. Reprinted in *IEEE Annals of the History of Computing* 20, no. 4 (1998): 15–28.

"The ENIAC." In *A History of Computing in the Twentieth Century*, edited by N. Metropolis, J. Howlett, and Gian-Carlo Rota. New York: Academic Press, 1980.

"The Electronic Numerical Integrator and Computer." *Computer Museum Report* 16 (Summer 1986). Available from http://www.ed-thelen.org/comp-hist/TheCompMusRep/TCMR-V16.html#ENIAC.

Allison, David K. "Transcript of an Interview with J. Presper Eckert." Development of the ENIAC interviews, Smithsonian Videohistory Collection, Record Unit 9537. Smithsonian Institution Archives, Washington, DC. Available

from http://americanhistory.si.edu/collections/comphist/
eckert.htm.

OTHER SOURCES

Allison, David K. "The ENIAC." *Bulletin of the Scientific Instrument Society* 63 (1999): 15–17.

Brainerd, John G. "Genesis of the ENIAC." *Technology and Culture* 17 (1976): 482–488.

Burks, Alice R., and Arthur W. Burks. *The First Electronic Computer: The Atanasoff Story.* Ann Arbor: University of Michigan Press, 1988. A polemical account that argues the case for Atanasoff as inventor of the computer.

Campbell-Kelly, Martin, and William Aspray. *Computer: A History of the Information Machine.* New York: Basic, 1996. This overview puts ENIAC in context.

Eckstein, Peter. "J. Presper Eckert." *IEEE Annals of the History of Computing* 18 (1996): 25–44.

Goldstine, Herman. *The Computer from Pascal to von Neumann.* Princeton, NJ: Princeton University Press, 1972.

Gray, George. "Univac I: The First Mass-Produced Computer." *Unisys History Newsletter* 5 (2001).

Lee, J. A. N. "J. Presper Eckert, 1919–1995." *IEEE Annals of the History of Computing* 17, no. 3 (1995): 3–5.

Lukoff, Herman. *From Dits to Bits: A Personal History of the Electronic Computer.* Portland, OR: Robotics, 1979. A memoir that gives the flavor of working with Eckert.

McCartney, Scott. *ENIAC: The Triumphs and Tragedies of the World's First Computer.* New York: Walker, 1999. A lively journalistic account, but one that should be used with care.

Moore School of Electrical Engineering and United States, Army, Ordnance Dept. *A Report on the ENIAC (Electronic Numerical Integrator and Computer).* Philadelphia: Moore School of Engineering, University of Pennsylvania, 1946. This report, part of the documentation of the original ENIAC project, is the best available source on its technical structure, set-up, and operations.

National Science Foundation. "The President's National Medal of Science: Recipient Details: J. Presper Eckert, Jr." Available from http://www.nsf.gov/od/nms/recip_details. cfm?recip_id=115.

Norberg, Arthur. *Computers and Commerce: A Study of the Technology and Management at Eckert-Mauchly Computer Company, Engineering Research Associates, and Remington Rand, 1946–1957.* Cambridge, MA: MIT Press, 2005.

Stern, Nancy. *From ENIAC to UNIVAC: An Appraisal of the Eckert-Mauchly Computers.* Bedford, MA: Digital, 1981.

University Archives and Records Center, University of Pennsylvania. "Guide to the ENIAC Trial Exhibits Master Collection, 1864–1973 [1938–1971 bulk]." Available from http://www.archives.upenn.edu/faids/upd/eniactrial/ eniac.html. This collection at the University of Pennsylvania is the best single source for researching the massive documentation related to the ENIAC patent trial.

U.S. War Department. "Ordnance Department Develops All-Electronic Calculating Machine." Press release, 15 February 1946. Available from http://americanhistory.si.edu/ collections/comphist/pr1.pdf.

von Neumann, John. "First Draft of a Report on the EDVAC (1945)." Reprinted in *The Origins of Digital Computers: Selected Papers,* edited by Brian Randell. New York: Springer-Verlag, 1982.

David K. Allison

EDDINGTON, ARTHUR STANLEY

(*b.* Kendal, United Kingdom, 28 December 1882; *d.* Cambridge, United Kingdom, 22 November 1944), *astronomy, astrophysics, relativity, science and religion.* For the original article on Eddington see *DSB,* vol. 4.

Scholarship following the original *DSB* article provided new insights into Eddington's educational background, his work in relativity and the 1919 eclipse expedition, his role in teaching and training physicists, his contributions to stellar physics, and the significance of his popular and philosophical writings.

Education. An important feature of Eddington's education was his location in Manchester, which just before and during his time was the site of a movement known as the "Quaker Renaissance." This involved a body of Quakers who argued that their religious tradition needed to embrace modernity. In particular, they sought harmonious relationships between religion and "modern thought" (largely science). Eddington was mentored by the leaders of this movement such as John William Graham, and their emphasis on values of mysticism, internationalism, pacifism, and civic engagement can be seen in many parts of Eddington's career.

Relativity and the 1919 Eclipse Expedition. By the early 2000s, it was clear that Eddington's advocacy of Albert Einstein and relativity was also a defense of internationalism in science, which he felt was seriously threatened by Great War jingoism. Eddington's Quaker values of pacifism and internationalism made supporting Einstein's theory a religious task as well as a scientific one, which helps explain why Eddington was virtually alone among British scientists in embracing German science during the war. He thus promoted the 1919 eclipse expedition as a landmark of scientific internationalism triumphing over war, in addition to its technical significance.

A controversial topic has been whether Eddington's interest in relativity led him to manipulate the data of the expedition to provide a favorable outcome. This accusation of fraud usually rests on the rejection as unreliable of one of the three sets of data brought back in 1919. It is noted by critics that that discarded set was the only one of the three which did not support Einstein's prediction, and

Eddington is typically accused of a conspiracy to hide the unfavorable results. However, this claim ignores several important issues. First, the data were discarded because of optical problems during the eclipse observation in Brazil. These problems were noted in the field by the observers there (who did not include Eddington) long before the photographs were analyzed as being favorable or unfavorable to Einstein. Further, all three sets of data were made publicly available to the scientific community, and there were no objections from contemporary astronomers about the rejection of the corrupted data. Astronomers around the world were able to make their own measurements of the plates and agreed with Eddington's analysis. It seems that the conspiracy theory is based on a misunderstanding of the optical techniques and data analysis methods in use at the time. Eddington's contemporaries, well versed in the tacit knowledge involved in such difficult measurements, understood that the eclipse expedition results were well within the contemporary standards of scientific practice.

Teaching and Training. Historians interested in scientific training and pedagogy have examined Eddington's difficulty in learning the technical details of general relativity without direct contact with Einstein. He took nearly two years to become skilled enough to make original contributions in the theory, even though he had significant advantages over most of his British colleagues: he had been taught differential geometry as an undergraduate, and was introduced to general relativity through Willem de Sitter, who had important experience in presenting Einstein's theory in a comprehensible fashion. A tight relationship between Eddington's pedagogy and his scientific work can be seen in the fact that Eddington's first two books on relativity were almost certainly slight elaborations of his lecture notes for the first classes he taught on relativity. Virtually an entire generation of British scientists learned relativity from Eddington, and important aspects of his teaching can be traced through later developments in physics and astronomy.

Stellar Physics. Early twenty-first century historians of astronomy and physics have stressed that one of the difficulties Eddington encountered in his development of stellar models was that the physics of the day did not allow for a complete description of stellar interiors. This incompleteness led many physicists and astronomers holding to a deductive model of scientific truth to simply discard the problem as unworkable. For example, James Jeans argued that a physical model could not involve any unknown or partially understood agencies.

Eddington persevered and built a methodology on the idea that theories were pragmatic, approximate tools and did not need to be deductively certain. He con-

Arthur Stanley Eddington. © HULTON-DEUTSCH COLLECTION/CORBIS.

structed his theoretical models on a variety of physical assumptions (often based on novel, hypothetical physics such as quantum mechanics), all designed to bring model and observation together as quickly as possible. Eddington argued that his method produced useful results (such as the mass-luminosity relation and the correct radii of stars) and avoided the sterile rigidity of the deductive approaches favored by his opponents. The debates over the sources of stellar energy provide a useful case study in the difficulty Eddington had in establishing his new theoretical astrophysics and in how he skillfully deployed cutting-edge work from both astronomy and physics.

Eddington's later work in stellar physics led to his controversial exchanges with Subrahmanyan Chandrasekhar on the properties of dwarf stars and degenerate matter. The story has usually been told based on Chandrasekhar's personal recollections and typically accuses Eddington of intentional cruelty and racist motivations in rejecting the Indian scientist's theory. However, there is no evidence to suggest that this was the case. Eddington was famously vigorous in intellectual debate, and he treated Chandrasekhar just as he did his other rivals James Jeans and Edward Arthur Milne. Further, there is no reason to assume racism: for several years Eddington was the head of an organization which worked for Indian liberation.

Popular and Philosophical Writings. Eddington's popular and philosophical works were analyzed closely by the early 2000s with respect to their cultural, intellectual, and social context. They were shown to not be completely idiosyncratic, but rather coherent parts of ongoing debates in interwar Britain. In the wake of the Great War, the cultural position of science was seriously contested.

Eddington's popular books and lectures were designed to defend a liberal position in which science was perfectly compatible with traditional values, thus retaining both religion and science as critical elements of British identity and culture. He was particularly concerned with rejecting Marxist, materialist appropriations of science and their deterministic implications. However, he also rejected classical natural theology with its proofs of religion and rigid dogmatism. Eddington argued from a novel interpretation of positivism that religious experience and scientific experience were equally valid parts of human life, but that neither could prove any particular sectarian dogma. This ecumenical, reassuring position was quite popular in the interwar period with the last surge of liberal theology, but became less relevant with the death of that movement around World War II.

SUPPLEMENTARY BIBLIOGRAPHY

Bowler, Peter. *Reconciling Science and Religion: The Debate in Early-Twentieth-Century Britain.* Chicago: University of Chicago Press, 2001. Broad study of the relationship between science and religion in the interwar period.

Graham, Loren. *Between Science and Values.* New York: Columbia University Press, 1981. Chapters 2 and 3 discuss Eddington, particularly in contrast to Soviet expositors of relativity.

Hufbauer, Karl. "Astronomers Take up the Stellar-Energy Problem, 1917–1920." *Historical Studies in the Physical Sciences* 11 (1981): 277–303.

Kenat, Ralph. "Physical Interpretation: Eddington, Idealization and the Origin of Stellar Structure Theory (Realism)." PhD diss., University of Maryland College Park, 1987.

Paul, Erich Robert. *The Milky Way Galaxy and Statistical Cosmology.* Cambridge, U.K.: Cambridge University Press, 1993. Discusses Eddington's work in statistical cosmology.

Stanley, Matthew. "An Expedition to Heal the Wounds of War: The 1919 Eclipse Expedition and Eddington as Quaker Adventurer." *Isis* 94 (2003): 57–89.

———. *Practical Mystic: Religion and Science in the Life and Work of A. S. Eddington.* Chicago: University of Chicago Press, 2007.

———. "So Simple a Thing as a Star: The Eddington-Jeans Debate over Astrophysical Phenomenology." *British Journal for the History of Science* (2007).

Warwick, Andrew. *Masters of Theory: Cambridge and the Rise of Mathematical Physics.* Chicago: University of Chicago Press, 2003. Chapter 9 examines Eddington's work on relativity in a pedagogical context.

Wilson, David. "On Removing 'Science' and 'Religion' from the Discussion of Science and Religion: The Cases of Eddington and Jeans." In *Facets of Faith and Science,* edited by Jitse M. van der Meer. Lanham, MD: Pascal Centre for Advanced Studies in Faith and Science, University Press of America, 1996.

Matthew Stanley

EDINGER, LUDWIG (*b.* Worms, Rhineland-Palatinate, Germany, 13 April 1855, *d.* January 1918), *internal medicine, neurology, neuroanatomy, brain research.*

Edinger is one of the world pioneers of neuroscience, and one of the founders of comparative neuroanatomy. He dealt particularly with the relations between brain anatomy and brain functions in vertebrates. Because of his detailed knowledge of the macroscopic and microscopic anatomy of the brain of various vertebrate species and his studies of animal behavior of these same species, he was able to relate structures of the brain to its functions in various species, such as fishes, amphibians, reptiles, frogs and dogs. His revised nomenclature of the vertebrate brain is valid even in the early twenty-first century.

Edinger was born on 13 April 1885 in Worms, a small city along the Rhine River near Frankfurt am Main. His father, Marcus Edinger (1820–1879), was a well-known Jewish democratic member of the Worms parliament; his mother, Julie Hochstätter Edinger (1829–1893), was the daughter of a physician. Ludwig Edinger grew up in Worms, and studied medicine in Strasbourg and Heidelberg. Edinger earned his Medicine Doctor (M.D.) in 1878 at the University of Heidelberg. He was nominated university lecturer of internal medicine in (*Privatdozent*) in 1881 at the University of Giessen. Faced with marked anti-Semitism there, he decided not to continue his scientific career but settled in Frankfurt am Main in 1883 as a physician specializing in internal medicine and neurology. He soon became one of the first specialists of neurology in Germany. In 1886, Edinger married Anna Goldschmidt in Frankfurt. They had two children, Tilly and Fritz.

During the following years, Edinger began to study the anatomy of brains, beginning with the brains of animals, including fish, reptiles, birds, and mammals, as well as fetal human brains. He compared the macroscopic form and internal structure of these brains and thus became one of the founders of comparative neuroanatomy. At the request of his colleagues in Frankfurt, he presented these studies in lectures before the

340

association of local physicians. The lectures were highly successful, and they were published, for the first time in 1885 and thereafter in eleven reprints ("Vorlesungen über den Bau der nervösen Zentralorgane").

From the beginning, Edinger tried to relate the form and structure of brains to the functional capabilities of the relevant animals and of humans. Therefore, he made efforts to study the psychology and behavior of animals. He studied the form, structure, and function of the brain in many species. Edinger found that the lower parts of the brain (brain stem) in all vertebrates have a similar structure and are responsible for elementary, life-supporting functions such as respiration, blood pressure, hunger, and thirst, whereas the higher parts of the brain (diencephalon, telencephalon) are built very differently depending on the abilities of the relevant species, e.g. their olfactory, visual and acoustic perception, motor functions, recognition and memory. He was wise enough, however, not to extend these comparative studies of structure and function to the cerebral cortex of humans, rightly claiming that methods to investigate the finer structure of this part of the brain were not yet available.

In 1885, Edinger arranged for his friend, anatomist Carl Weigert (1845–1904) to become head of the renowned Senckenberg Institute of Anatomy in Frankfurt. In return, Weigert offered Edinger a room at the institute in 1902. This arrangement is considered to be the genesis of the Institute of Neurology in Frankfurt, later named the Edinger Institute. A fruitful cooperation between Edinger and Weigert followed, which lasted until Weigert's death in 1904. Guests and scientists from all parts of the world visited Edinger's laboratory to study the brain during that period. In 1907, Edinger moved to the newly built Institute of Pathology, where the entire second floor was offered to him for his institute, which was divided into a neuranatomy and neuropathology department. Financial support of the institute was provided exclusively by Edinger himself. In addition, Edinger founded, together with colleagues, a clinical department of neurology at the Frankfurter Poliklinik für Nervenkranke, where indigent patients suffering from neurological diseases were treated free of charge.

The main result of Edinger's comparative anatomical studies was the establishment of an inferior part of the brain consisting mainly of the diencephalon, mesencephalon, metencephalon, and medulla oblongata, which showed, in all species investigated, nearly the same form and internal structure and which is responsible for vital functions such as respiration, circulation, motivation, and awareness; he called this the brain's "own" or "proper" apparatus (Eigenapparat). In contrast, the telencephalon was found to display significant evolutionary variation. Edinger divided the telencephalon into older parts, desig-

nated the archipallium (with the archicortex), consisting mainly of the hippocampus, amygdala, and olfactory brain; and the neopallium (with the neocortex), consisting of all other cortical regions and their appropriate fiber bundles, bearing the end points of tactile, optic, and auditory pathways and the starting point of motor fibers. The neopallium increased markedly in size during evolution, depending on evolutionary requirements, according to Charles Darwin's theory. In his autobiography, *Mein Lebensgang* (published in 2005 on the occasion of his 150th birthday), Edinger describes the day when he detected the first traces of neocortex in the lizard brain as the happiest day of his scientific life. ("Das war der glücklichste Tag meines wissenschaftlichen Lebens.") The terms *archicortex* and *neocortex* were rapidly and widely integrated into the nomenclature of brain anatomy, but Edinger's authorship of these names has been nearly forgotten.

During the following years, Edinger, using the myelin staining techniques of Franz Nissl, Camillo Golgi, and especially Carl Weigert, detected many hitherto unknown brain structures, for example, the medial forebrain bundle joining the mesencephalon and the diencephalon. He found that, in the human brain, the termination of the spinal tractus spino-thalamicus (responsible for the perception of pain and temperature) was in the thalamus, instead of the cerebellum, as stated in contemporary textbooks. At the same time, Edinger recommended to the international conference Nomina Anatomica in Basel in 1899 that the fiber bundles of the human brain should not be named after the discoverer, as had been customary until that time, but by the anatomical starting and end points. The conference agreed, and this practice remained in place.

Edinger also described the exact location of the autonomous part of the mesencephalic oculomotor nucleus (which became known as the Edinger-Westphal-nucleus). He made high-quality histologic drawings of all his subjects of analysis, which are collected and stored at the Institute of Neurology in Frankfurt. In addition, a large macroscopic collection of animal brains, called the Edinger Collection, is carefully preserved there. Moreover, the archive of the institute possesses copies and originals of approximately four hundred letters Edinger received from friends and pupils from all over the world.

When the University of Frankfurt am Main was founded in 1914 by the king of Prussia, who was responsible at that time for the district of Frankfurt, Edinger's Institute of Neurology was integrated into the university as one of the twelve constituting institutes and clinics. At the same time Edinger was nominated professor of neurology. He extended his anatomical studies to the pathomorphology of human diseases, especially degenerative and infectious diseases, such as Friedreich's ataxia, Tabes dorsalis, and neuritis, as well as brain tumors. He also verified that increase and misuse of function, in connection with genetic factors, could contribute to the origin of neurological diseases, by exhausting energy for the relevant anatomical structure. These studies were published under the title "Edinger's energy exhausting theory" of neurological diseases ("Aufbrauchtheorie," 1904).

During World War I, Edinger, in his characteristic attitude of helping whenever possible, changed his focus of study to the trauma of the peripheral nerves found in soldiers returning from battles. He studied the methods for rejoining, reparation, and regeneration of nerves, and learned that precise adaptation of the proximal and distal stumps of transsected peripheral nerves is of paramount significance for the following regeneration. He published the results of these studies in several papers in 1916 and 1917 and presented a review of this topic in 1917, one year before his death, at the Annual Meeting of Neurologists in Bonn.

Ludwig Edinger died in his Frankfurt home on 26 January 1918 from heart failure following surgery for prostate cancer. His brain anatomy was examined and published by his pupils W. Riese and K. Goldstein, with emphasis on Edinger's mental ability and his left-handedness. Edinger is buried in the central cemetery in Frankfurt am Main.

Edinger's successor as director of his institute was his pupil Kurt Goldstein, who emigrated to the United States before the period of the Nazi regime and was later known as one of the pioneers of neuropsychology and neurolinguistics. Edinger's daughter, Tilly Edinger, emigrated to England and became known as the founder of paleoneurology. In the early 2000s Edinger's Institute of Neurology remained part of the University of Frankfurt, specializing in research in neuropathology, neurocytology, and neurobiology.

BIBLIOGRAPHY

WORKS BY EDINGER

Zehn Vorklesunger über den Bau der nervösen Zentralorgane. Leipzig: F. C. W. Vogel, 1885.

"Verlust des Sprechvemögens und doppelseitige Hypoglossusprarese, bedlingt durch einen kleinen Herd im Zentrum semiovale." *Deutsche Medizinische Wochenschrift* 12 (1886): 232–235.

"Einiges vom Verlaufe der Gefühlsbahnen im zentralen Nervensystem." *Deutsche Medizinische Wochenschrift* 16 (1890): 421–426.

"Eine neue Theorie über die Ursachen einiger Nervenkrankheiten, insbesondere der Neuritls und der Tabes." In *Vohmanns Sammlungen klinischer Vorträge*, no. 106, Neue Folge (Innere Medizin Nr. 32) (1894): 87–116.

The Anatomy of the Central Nervous System of Man and of Vertebrates in General, 5th ed. Translated by Winfield S. Hall. Philadelphia and New York: F. A. Davis, 1896.

"Die Entwicklung der Gehirnbahnen in der Tierreihe." *Deutsche Medizinische Wochenschrift* 22 (1896): 621–626.

Beiträge zur vergleichenden Anatomie des Gehims. Frankfurt am Main: Abhandlungen der Senckenbergischen Narurforschenden Gesellschaft, 1898.

"Himanatomie und Psychologie." *Berliner klinische Wochenscrift* 37.56 (1900): 561–564.

Wie lange kann ein intracerebraler großer Tumor sympromtos getragen warden? Leyden-Festschrift Bd. 1. Berlin: Hirschwald, 1901.

Bericht über die Tängkeit der Frankfurter Poliklinik für Nervenkranke. Frankfurt am Main: Knauer, 1903.

"Die Aufbrauchkrankheiten des Nervensystems." *Deutsche Medizinische Wochenschrift* 30 (1904): 1633–1636; 1800–1803; 1921–1924.

"Einiges vom 'Gehirn' des Amphioxus." *Anatomischer Anzeiger* 26 (1907): 417–428.

"Bericht über das Dr. Senckenbergische Neurologische Institut 1885–1906." *Frankfurter Zeitschrift für Pathologie* 1 (1907): 200–204.

Vorlesungen über den Bau der nervösen Zentralorgane des Menschen und der Tiere. Band 11: *Vergleichende Anatomie des Gehims.* 7. Auflage. Leipzig: F. C. W. Vogel, 1908a.

Der Antel der Funktion an der Entstehung von Nervenkrankheiten. Wiesbanden: J. F. Bergmann, 1908b.

"The Relations of Comparative Anatomy to Comparative Psychology." *Journal of Comparative Neurology and Psychology* 18 (1908c): 437–457.

Vorlesungen über den Bau der nervösen Zentralorgane des Menschen und der Tiere. Band 1: *Das Zentralnervensystem.* Leipzig: F. C. W. Vogel, 1911.

"Welche Bezeihungen bestehen zwischen dem Aufbau des Nervensystems und seiner Tätigkeit?" In his *Einführung in die Lehre vom Bau und den Verrichtungen des Nervensystems*, 2nd ed. Leipzig: F. C. W. Vogel, 1912.

With B. Fischer. "Ein Mensch ohne Großhim." *Archiv für die Gesamte Psychologie* 152 (1913): 535–562.

"Wege und Ziele der Himforschung. Die interakademischen Himforschungsinstitute." *Naturwissenschaften* 1 (1913): 441–444.

"Über die Regeneration durchschnittener Nerven." *Naturwissenschaften* 4 (1916): 226–230.

"Über die Vereinigung getrennter Nerven. Grundsätzliches und Mitteilung eines neuen Verfahrens." *Münchener Medizinische Wochenschrift* 63 (1916): 225–228.

"Bericht über die Symptomatologie und Therapie der peripheren Lähmungen auf Grund der Kriegsbeobachtungen. IX: Jahresversammlung der Gesellschaft deutscher Nervenerzte. 1917 in Bonn." *Deutsche Zeitschrift für Nervenheilkunde* 59 (1917): 12–32.

"Untersuchungen über die Neubildung des durchtrennten Nerven." *Deutsche Zeitschrift für Nervenheilkunde* 58 (1918): 1–32.

Gedenkschrift zu seinem 100. Geburtstag und zum 50-jährigen Bestehen des Neurologischen Instituts (Edinger Institut) der Universitst Frankfurt am Main und Wiesbaden: Franz Steiner, 1959.

OTHER SOURCES

Emisch, Heidemarie. *Ludwig Edinger—Hirnanatomie und Psychologie.* Leipzig: Gustav Fischer, 1991.

Goldstein, Kurt. "Ludwig Edinger (1855–1918)." *Zeitschrift für Die Gesamte Neurologie und Psychiatrie* 44 (1918): 114–149.

Kreft, Gerald. "The Work of Ludwig Edinger and His Neurology Institute." In *Neuroendocrinology: Retrospect and Perspectives,* edited by H.-W. Korf and K.-H. Usdael. Berlin-Heidelberg: Springer, 1997.

———, and Wolfgang Schlote. "Ludwig Edinger (1855–1918)—Hirnforscher und Neurologie in Franfurt am Main." In *Festschrift zur 500. Versammlung der Frandfurter Medizinischen Gesellschaft,* edited by H. W. Doer and H. W. Korf. Lamperdin: Alpha, 1995.

Riese, Walther, and Kurt Goldstein. "The Brain of Ludwig Edinger: An Inquiry into the Cerebral Morphology of Mental Ability and Lefthandedness." *Journal of Comparative Neurology* 92 (April 1950): 133–168.

Schlote, Wolfgang, and Gerald Kreft. "Der zweckentfremdete Küchentisch—Ludwig Edinger und die Anfänge der Hirnforschung in Frankfurt." *Forschung Frankfurt* 1, 46–59. Frankfurt am Main: Johann Wolfgang Goethe-Universität, 1997.

Scholte, Wolfgang. "Ludwig Edinger (1855–1918)—Neurologe, frankfurter Arzt und Weltbürger." In *Die Frankfurter Gelehrtenrepublik, Neue Folge.* Idstein: Schulz-Kirchner, 2002.

Wolfgang Schlote

EDLÉN, BENGT

EDLÉN, BENGT (*b.* Gusum, Sweden, 2 November 1906; *d.* Lund, Sweden, 10 February 1993), *physics, especially ultraviolet and astronomical spectroscopy.*

A physicist who devoted more than six decades to studying the spectra of high-temperature ions, Edlén achieved wide recognition in the early 1940s when he identified the ions that give rise to the long-mysterious coronal-line spectrum. The apex of his research life, this interdisciplinary breakthrough launched him into a long career as honoree, institution builder, and arbiter of scientific promise and achievement.

The eldest of five children of Gustaf Fridolf Edlén and Maria Amalia née Rundberg, Edlén spent his early years in Gusum, a small industrial town in central Sweden where his father worked as an accountant. When eleven, he enrolled in nearby Norrköping's upper school. During his nine years as a student there, he received particularly good marks in biology and physics. He later recalled that his instructor Harald Mohlin (whose doctoral advisor had

been Knut Ångström of Uppsala University) had those in the physics class conduct laboratory studies of the Sun's Fraunhofer spectrum. He also remembered participating in the school's astronomy club. The combined influence of his father's numeracy and these experiences surely helped prepare the way for his later contributions to spectroscopy.

In early 1927, after a stint of mandatory military training, Edlén matriculated at Uppsala University. He soon decided to study physics. This was a fortunate choice because Manne Siegbahn, an x-ray spectroscopist who had recently been recruited from Lund University and more recently been awarded the Nobel Prize in Physics, was busily updating the Physics Institute's spectroscopic armamentarium. Among other things, he was developing apparatus for measuring extreme ultraviolet (EUV) spectra so that he could calibrate his x-ray wavelength scale. In early 1929, Siegbahn asked Edlén, who already had one publication on x-ray measurements to his credit, and fellow student Algot Ericson to inaugurate the institute's first vacuum spectrograph for studying EUV spectra produced by spark discharges. Swiftly distinguishing himself, Edlén was picked to describe the instrument and some of its initial results in a paper at the Scandinavian Scientific Congress in Copenhagen that August.

Edlén and Ericson followed up on this report, which received encouraging praise from Niels Bohr, with a flurry of papers in *Nature,* the *Zeitschrift für Physik,* and the French Academy's *Comptes rendus.* Their last collaborative paper—submitted May 1930 with Ericson posthumously on the byline—dealt with the EUV spectra of the isoelectronic lithium-like ions C IV (i.e., trebly ionized carbon), N V und O VI. Continuing this line of research, Edlén went on to use the institute's EUV spectrograph to measure lines from nearly all the high-temperature ions of the elements between lithium and oxygen. Moreover, displaying the same industry and adeptness with the institute's calculating machines as its vacuum spectrograph, he identified the atomic transitions giving rise to these lines and investigated how the energy of specific atomic states varied along isoelectronic sequences. He brought all this work together in a doctoral thesis that he defended in April 1934. The following month Edlén, who was then twenty-seven, received a doctorate, a prestigious Bjurzons Prize for his dissertation, and an appointment as a Dozent (instructor) in physics.

The one consequential diversion from Edlén's arduous experimental inquiries during the preceding three years arose from his curiosity about the bearing of his results on astronomical spectroscopy. This curiosity may have been piqued by the example of Ira Bowen, an EUV spectroscopist at the California Institute of Technology who had caused quite a stir in the late 1920s with his

Bengt Edlén. *Formal portrait of Bengt Edlén.* COURTESY OF
THE DEPARTMENT OF PHYSICS, LUND UNIVERSITY, SWEDEN.

compelling attribution of the chief nebular emission lines
to familiar ions undergoing "forbidden" transitions—i.e.,
exceptional transitions that occur in sufficient numbers to
be observed in highly rarefied gases in which collisions are
so infrequent that excited atoms have fairly long lifetimes.
In any case, Edlén had familiarized himself with astronomical spectroscopy's current state by auditing the
course on the field that Dozent Carl Schalén offered at
Uppsala in the fall of 1931. Having learned from Schalén
that N IV was the source of two emission lines observed
in the hot Wolf-Rayet stars, Edlén had gone on to use his
own hard-won knowledge of the energy levels of multiply
ionized carbon, nitrogen, and oxygen to identify the transitions giving rise to many more unknown Wolf-Rayet
lines. Pleased with these findings, he had ventured into
the astronomical literature for the first time by announcing them in Britain's *Observatory* (1932) and discussing
them fully in Germany's *Zeitschrift für Astrophysik* (1933).

Edlén's pace during the half decade following his doctorate must have made his student days seem like a
leisurely stroll. His marriage with Ruth Grönwall in winter
1935 yielded Inga, Per, and Ruth by late 1937. Although
family life must have laid claim to some of his time, Edlén

seems to have been entirely preoccupied with research and
career through the winter 1939. In his research he first followed up on his doctoral work with a series of articles on
EUV spectra from numerous ions ranging from C II to Cu
XIX. Then around 1937, having reached the point of
diminishing returns from the institute's EUV spectrograph, he turned to developing better apparatus and to
seeking further applications of his results in astronomical
spectroscopy. In the meantime, with Siegbahn's departure
for Stockholm as head of the Swedish Academy of Science's
new Nobel Institute for Physics in 1936 and Axel Lindh's
appointment as his successor, Edlén was given the responsibility for teaching spring-term lecture courses on spectroscopy in 1936 and 1937, atomic physics in 1938, and
physical optics in 1938 and 1939.

All the while, aware that Sweden's academic gatekeep-
ers attached great importance to international recognition, Edlén was building relations with spectroscopists
abroad through collaborations and on research trips.
Seven of these relations ended up having particular significance for him—that with the Belgian astronomical spectroscopist Pol Swings, who journeyed from Liége to
Uppsala in 1934 particularly to work with him and
became a close friend and collaborator; those with the
German senior spectroscopist Friedrich Paschen and
astronomical spectroscopist Walter Grotrian, with whom
he became well acquainted during a sojourn in Berlin during 1935; those with the American EUV spectroscopists
Joseph Boyce, who passed through Uppsala en route to
the 1936 eclipse and invited him to come to the United
States the following year, and Ira Bowen, who followed up
Edlén's visit to Pasadena in 1937 by proposing a year later
that they collaborate in identifying emission lines on a
spectrogram from Nova RR Pictoris (1925); and those
with the American theoretical astrophysicists Donald
Menzel, whom he met at Harvard during his 1937 trip,
and Henry Norris Russell, who visited his laboratory in
Uppsala during the International Astronomical Union's
Congress in Stockholm in 1938. Two, indeed, wrote articles that stimulated Edlén to take up the coronal-line
problem in April 1939.

Seven decades earlier, during the total eclipse of
1869, Charles Young and William Harkness had been the
first to detect the solar corona's distinctive green emission
line. In the intervening period, eclipse observers, who
were joined by Bernard Lyot with his coronagraph during
the 1930s, had gradually identified and measured some
twenty emission lines that could be said with fair confidence to originate in the corona. However, none of the
numerous attempts to explain this unique spectrum had
been successful. The early failures to find matches
between laboratory and coronal lines had given rise to the
notion that an unknown element—dubbed "coronium"—produced the coronal spectrum. During the late

1920s, this speculation had fallen by the wayside for two reasons. On the one hand, the successes of chemists and physicists in filling most of the remaining gaps in the periodic table of elements had raised doubts about the very existence of coronium. On the other, Bowen's 1927 attribution of the chief nebular lines to rare transitions in oxygen and nitrogen ions—instead of to the equally hypothetical element "nebulium"—had pointed to an alternative path for seeking a solution. After Bowen's breakthrough, spectroscopists had presumed that the corona's spectrum would be traced back to ions of known elements. Their putative solutions had all been found wanting because, at best, only two line matches had been proposed, not nearly enough to strike those familiar with the problem as more than lucky coincidences. Through the 1930s, therefore, the coronal-line problem was widely regarded as the last great riddle of astronomical spectroscopy.

Edlén's own interest in the coronal-line problem was engendered by two publications he read in early spring 1939. One was an essay review on the problem by Swings. His Belgian friend not only stressed the problem's recalcitrance but also provided an up-to-date table of twenty-five coronal lines, including ten for which Lyot had determined the wavelengths and relative intensities. The more provocative one was a proposal by Grotrian in *Die Naturwissenschaften* suggesting that two coronal lines came from highly ionized iron. Edlén must have been struck by his German colleague's opening lines:

> Since I. S. Bowen and B. Edlén have recently shown that forbidden lines of Fe VII appeared in the spectrum of Nova RR Pictoris 1925, since W. S. Adams and A. H. Joy earlier showed that 5 coronal lines made an unambiguous appearance in the spectrum of RS Ophiuchi during a nova-like outbreak in 1933, since finally there are more and more indications that conditions for the excitation of spectral lines exist in the outer regions of the solar atmosphere that greatly exceed what would be expected in thermal equilibrium, it no longer seems completely amiss to discuss whether coronal lines are to be interpreted as forbidden lines from highly ionized atoms. (p. 214)

This was Edlén's first serious encounter with the counterintuitive—and quite original—idea that the temperature in the sun's atmosphere increased in rising from the photosphere through the chromosphere to the corona. Suddenly the prospect of scrutinizing his published and unpublished hot-ion spectral data for further matches with the coronal-line spectrum was quite alluring. Needing an accomplishment that would dramatize the larger significance of EUV spectroscopy, he could appreciate that following up Grotrian's line of attack on the coronal-

line problem might just give him a superb opportunity to demonstrate his own and his specialty's worth.

Edlén's first step was to search his unpublished hot-ion spectral data for forbidden transitions that matched further lines on Swings's list. He made four new tentative matches, including two that were analogous to those proposed by Grotrian. Much encouraged, he continued by examining hot ions of iron on account of this element's high cosmic abundance. Using isoelectronic extrapolation techniques, he soon found four more prospective matches. His success here in matching the bright green coronal line at 5,303 Å convinced him by later April 1939 that he was indeed on the right track. Through the spring, Edlén carried through more isoelectronic calculations, making seven further provisional matches. However, as his list of matches grew, he came up with several alternatives for lines that he had already tentatively matched. By early July, when he left Uppsala for a month of research with Swings in Liége and a conference on astronomical spectroscopy in Paris, he had gone well beyond Grotrian's two suggested identifications. He had provisionally matched one or more hot-ion transitions to fifteen additional coronal lines. Pleased, he showed Swings his results. But eager to tie up remaining loose ends, he asked his Belgian friend not to tell anyone.

Upon returning to Sweden, Edlén resumed his coronal calculations. His examination of a wider range of forbidden transitions yielded another nine tentative identifications, three for previously matched lines and six for unmatched lines. At this juncture, he drew up a fresh cumulative list of identifications, provisionally matching twenty-two of the twenty-five lines listed in Swings's review article. Surprisingly, rather than announce his progress, Edlén set aside his research on the coronal-line problem for more than a year. He later recalled feeling under great obligation to Swings to complete their collaboration on Fe III's spectrum. He also recalled being daunted by the abundance of lines on the EUV plates that he had made with the goal of refining his wavelength determinations. He may have been bothered as well by the way in which certain lines stubbornly defied all attempts at identification, thereby challenging his customary standards for completeness. Other matters probably claimed Edlén's attention as well. Germany had attacked Poland, and everyone, even in neutral Sweden, was worried about the future. His divorce from the mother of his three young children must also have been unsettling. In any case, after his marriage with Elfriede Mühlbach at the end of June 1940 and three months of military duty, Edlén began mulling over the coronal problem again.

Edlén finally decided in early 1941 to announce the matches that he regarded as most solid. He had not yet finished up the spectrum of Fe III. Nor had he extracted any useful information from his new EUV plates or come up with even provisional matches for some lines. But in order to continue getting support from Uppsala University, he needed to bring an end to the hiatus in his scientific production that stretched back to the Paris conference. The best way to do so, Edlén evidently concluded, was to get out a preliminary report on his coronal research. He arranged for the submission of a four-page account of this research in March to the Swedish Academy of Sciences for publication in the *Arkiv för Matematik, Astronomi och Fysik*. In the account, titled "An Attempt to Identify the Emission Lines in the Spectrum of the Solar Corona," he argued that fifteen coronal lines, including Grotrian's two, could be attributed to forbidden transitions of iron, nickel, and calcium ions. As warrant for these identifications, he pointed out that these lines accounted for more than 97 percent of the coronal emission spectrum's intensity, that the average intensity ratio of the iron and nickel lines was about ten to one in accord with the cosmic abundances of these two elements, that the ions involved had a relatively narrow range of ionization potentials, and that lines arising from ions with similar ionization potentials behaved, according to Lyot's observations, similarly to one another. Edlén estimated that the average ionization potential of the ions involved was 400 electron volts, which indicated—along with Lyot's estimates of the thermal broadening of certain lines—a coronal temperature well over 1,000,000 degrees. Such a high temperature would explain, he remarked, both the uniqueness of the coronal spectrum and "the failure of all previous attempts to connect it with any known atomic or molecular spectrum." Over a year later, he followed up this preliminary report with a comprehensive paper on the coronal-line problem in the *Zeitschrift für Astrophysik*. There, besides greatly amplifying his discussion of his investigative pathway and the implications of his putative findings, he proposed four further line identifications. It attests to Edlén's care in scrutinizing his tentative matches that nearly all nineteen identifications (including Grotrian's two) he listed—eight iron lines, six nickel lines, three calcium lines, and two argon lines—turned out to be quite robust.

Meanwhile, Edlén was eager to get his solution to the coronal-line problem into circulation. Its acceptance as a breakthrough on this long-standing conundrum would greatly enhance his career prospects. The trouble was that the times were not propitious. It was fairly easy to make his identifications known in neutral Sweden and neighboring Denmark by following up his paper in the Academy's *Arkiv* with a lecture, seminars, and a semipopular article. But it was quite a different matter to place his results before the international experts whose judgments would be crucial. Europe was sinking ever deeper into war, and many ordinary channels of communication were

constricted or closed. Moreover, scientists in the leading scientific nations were increasingly preoccupied with military matters. He overcame these obstacles by mailing advance copies of one or both of his papers to scientists who had earlier published on the coronal-line problem whom he knew personally—the Americans Bowen, Boyce, Menzel, and Russell; the Belgian Swings (who by this time was in America), and the Germans Grotrian and Paschen.

Once started on its way, Edlén's solution was not only rapidly disseminated but enthusiastically received. This warm welcome in the midst of World War II was a result both of its Swedish provenance and its robustness. Had Edlén been a citizen of one of the belligerent powers, his interpretation of the coronal emission spectrum might well have had great difficulty spreading beyond that power's alliance system. But as a Swedish physicist with good contacts in the United States and Germany alike, Edlén easily reached interested audiences on both sides of the battle lines. Once out, of course, his solution's reception depended upon its ability to satisfy the criteria that astronomical spectroscopists had set for the problem in the course of evaluating and rejecting earlier proposed solutions. His case that many of the known coronal lines could be attributed to forbidden transitions of highly excited iron, nickel, calcium, and argon ions swiftly came to be seen as not only compelling but also full of promise for future research into the corona's physical state. The quick international recognition accorded his breakthrough gave Edlén a decisive edge in the competition that resulted in his appointment at the age of thirty-eight to Lund University's chair of physics in 1944. His solution of what was then astronomical spectroscopy's last great riddle won him numerous honors in the ensuing decades, most notably the Royal Astronomical Society's Gold Medal (1945), the National Academy of Sciences' Henry Draper Medal (1968), and election to the Académie des sciences as a foreign member (1972).

Well positioned and much honored, Edlén continued his research in spectroscopy for the remainder of his long career. His passion for the field was so deep that, when asked once about his favorite pastimes, he replied "spectroscopy and gardening." Besides his research, Edlén presided effectively over a major postwar expansion of Lund University's Physics Institute until his retirement in 1973. Among his many national and international committee responsibilities over the decades, the most important was his long service on the Swedish Academy's Nobel Committee for Physics (1961–1976). While serious in demeanor, he was certainly not without a sense of humor. For instance, when a colleague told him near the end of his life of a foreign scientist's recent inquiry about the academy's failure to recognize his coronal breakthrough with a Nobel Prize, he commented that he would much rather that someone asked that than "Why did Edlén receive the Nobel?" Edlén died in 1993, less than half a year after several happy celebrations of the fiftieth anniversary of his comprehensive 1942 paper on the coronal spectrum.

BIBLIOGRAPHY

WORKS BY EDLÉN

"Zur Deutung der Spektren der heißen Sterne." *Zeitschrift für Astrophysik* 71 (1933): 378–390.

Wellenlängen und Termsysteme zu den Atomspektren der Elemente Lithium, Beryllium, Bor, Kohlenstoff, Stickstoff und Sauerstoff. Nova Acta Regiae Societatis Scientiarum Upsaliensis, ser. 4, vol. 9, no. 6. Uppsala, Sweden: Almqvist & Wiksell, 1934. Edlén's dissertation.

"Edlén, Bengt." In *Uppsala Universitets Matrikel, Höstterminen 1936*, edited by Thoralf Fries and Ernst von Döbeln. Uppsala: Almqvist & Wiksells, 1937. Edlen's curriculum vitae to 1936.

"An Attempt to Identify the Emission Lines in the Spectrum of the Solar Corona." *Arkiv för Matematik, Astronomi och Fysik* 28B, no. 1 (1941): 1–4.

"Die Deutung der Emissionslinien im Spektrum der Sonnenkorona." *Zeitschrift für Astrophysik* 22 (1942): 30–64.

"The Identification of the Coronal Lines." *Monthly Notices of the Royal Astronomical Society* 105 (1945): 323–333.

"Edlén, Bengt." In *Uppsala Universitets Matrikel 1937–1950*, edited by Åke Dintler and J. C. Sune Lindqvist. Uppsala: Almqvist & Wiksells, 1953.

"Edlén, Bengt." In *Lunds Universitets Matrikel 1967–68*, edited by Eva Gerle. Lund: Gleerup, 1968.

OTHER SOURCES

Friedman, Robert Marc. "Siegbahn, Karl Manne Georg." In *Dictionary of Scientific Biography*, edited by Frederic L. Holmes. New York: Charles Scribner's Sons, 1990.

Grotrian, Walter. "Zur Frage der Deutung der Linien im Spektrum der Sonnenkorona." *Naturwissenschaften* 27 (1939): 214.

Hufbauer, Karl. "Breakthrough on the Periphery: Bengt Edlén and the Identification of the Coronal Lines, 1939–1945." In *Center on the Periphery: Historical Aspects of 20th-Century Swedish Physics*, edited by Svante Lindqvist. Canton, MA.: Science History Publications, 1993.

———. "Artificial Eclipses: Bernard Lyot and the Coronagraph, 1929–1939." *Historical Studies in the Physical and Biological Sciences* 24 (1994): 337–394.

Litzén, Ulf. "Atomspektroskopi, klassisk mark i Lund: Bengt Edléns forskning under 1950-talet." In *Virvlande visioner: Fysiken i Lund under det senare 1900-talet*, edited by Hans Ryde. Lund, Sweden: Ugglan, 2002.

Martinson, Indrek. "Bengt Edlén's Scientific Work." In *Trends in Physics 1981: Papers presented at the Fifth General Conference of the European Physical Society, Istanbul, Turkey, 17–11 September 1981*, edited by I. A. Dorobantu. Bucharest, Romania: Central Institute of Physics, 1982.

Milne, Edward Arthur. "Address … on the Award of the Gold Medal to Professor Bengt Edlén, Professor of Physics in the University of Lund." *Monthly Notices of the Royal Astronomical Society* 105 (1945): 138–145.

Swings, Pol. "Une grande énigme de la spectroscopie astronomique actuelle: Le spectre de raies d'émission de la couronne solaire." *Scientia* 65 (1939): 69–78.

———. "Edlén's Identification of the Coronal Lines with Forbidden Lines of *Fe* X, XI, XIII, XIV, XV; *Ni* XII, XIII, XV, XVI; *Ca* XII, XIII, XV; *A* X, XIV." *Astrophysical Journal* 98 (1943): 116–128.

Karl Hufbauer

EDMAN, PEHR VICTOR

(*b.* Stockholm, Sweden, 14 April 1916; *d.* Munich, Germany, 19 March 1977), *chemistry, protein structure, amino acid sequence.*

In the history of protein chemistry Pehr Edman will be remembered for his work on amino acid sequences in proteins. He developed a technique by which amino acids in the protein molecule can be removed and identified one after the other in a stepwise fashion. The fast developments in molecular biology would not have been possible without this method, known as the Edman degradation, which is virtually the only tool for this purpose.

Edman set out already in the 1940s to solve the problem of rapid and accurate stepwise degradation of protein chains. Throughout his career he resisted all temptation to deviate from his set course until he considered the task completed and well done. Rewards for early application of his method to interesting biological and medical problems went to others. At the time of his death in 1977 he was still engaged in optimizing the method.

Origin and Early Education. Edman was born in Stockholm, Sweden, on 14 April 1916. His father, Victor Edman, a judge, was a serious man and a devoted Christian. His mother, Alba Edman, was joyous, lively, and neat. Edman attended public elementary school in Stockholm. He began high school with a focus on the humanities, but soon switched to a focus on mathematics and the natural sciences. In 1935 Edman passed his matriculation examination with excellent records.

Medical and Biochemical Studies. Edman began medical studies at Karolinska Institutet in Stockholm, Sweden. He received the bachelor of medicine degree in 1938 and graduated as a physician in 1946. Concurrently with his studies in medicine he trained in biochemistry under the guidance of Professor Erik Jorpes (famous for his studies on heparin; an inhibitor of blood coagulation). For a time he also studied in Professor Hugo Theorell's department (Theorell received the Nobel Prize in 1955 for his studies on oxidative enzymes). He became interested in protein chemistry and started on a project of his own—isolation and characterization of angiotensin (also called hypertensin or angiotonin). One of his tools during the work was column chromatography, and, seeing the need for collection of fractions at short regular intervals, he invented the first automatic fraction collector. This work resulted in a thesis that was presented at the Karolinska Institutet in 1945, receiving the mark of summa cum laude. The thesis work took place during World War II, and for a time Edman was drafted to serve as a physician in the armed forces. After his dissertation, Edman was admitted as docent, or lecturer, at the Karolinska Institutet. In order to widen his experience and perspectives in protein chemistry he spent one year (1946–1947) at the Rockefeller Institute in Princeton, New Jersey (a division of the Rockefeller Institute in New York). The institute was, at the time, one of the most prestigious places for protein chemists. Two of its members, John Northrop and Wendell M. Stanley, received the Nobel Prize in 1946 for preparation of enzymes and virus proteins in pure form. Edman studied in the laboratory of Northrop and Moses Kunitz, the latter a master in preparing proteins in crystalline form.

Studies on Protein Structure. By 1950 the realization had dawned that individual proteins contained molecules that were identical replicas, had exact molecular masses and amino acid compositions, and had identical packing of the polypeptide chains. This view gained final acceptance when crystalline preparations of proteins became available for analysis of their x-ray diffraction pattern; it was found that crystals gave rise to diffraction patterns that could be interpreted on the same basis as the crystals of simple inorganic salt compounds, although this required tremendous computer capabilities.

Although isolation of proteins and the analysis of amino acid composition had essentially become routine, the sequence of the amino acids in the polypeptide chain was still unknown. The first successful attack on the problem of sequence determination in proteins was mounted by Frederick Sanger at the University of Cambridge, England, and published during the period 1945 to 1951. Sanger received the Nobel Prize in 1958 for his work on the structure of proteins, especially that of insulin, his model protein. Sanger's idea for establishing the sequence was simple. First, all that is necessary for the determination of the sequence of a dipeptide is amino acid analysis and a method of determining which amino acid is N-terminal (that is, the amino acid having a free NH_2 group) or which is C-terminal (having a free COOH group) (see Figure 1). This reasoning could be applied to

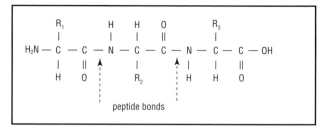

Figure 1. *Representation of a dipeptide with free NH_2- and COOH- groups. The amino acids are held together by peptide bond, CO-HN as indicated by arrows.*

a protein with known N-terminal amino acid provided it could be broken down to smaller peptides by random partial acid hydrolysis or by digestion with proteolytic enzymes. After labeling the N-terminal amino acid of the isolated peptides with 1-fluoro-2,4-dinitrobenzene, the peptides were exposed to acid hydrolysis and the components of the hydrolysate identified by chromatography. The labeled N-terminal amino acid had a bright yellow color, facilitating its identification. By fitting overlapping short sequences extending from the N-terminal to the C-terminal end of the protein, the complete amino acid sequence could eventually be deduced.

There is now strong evidence that the biological activity of a protein is somehow linked to its amino acid sequence, that is, to its primary structure. Attachment of prosthetic groups (such as sulfur, phosphorus, lipids, and so forth) to the peptide chains as well as their folding into a tertiary structure are also important for biological activity, but both attachment and folding are dependent on the primary structure. This view reflects Edman's thinking in the early 1960s. At that time it received experimental support from Chinese scientists, at the Academia Sinica in Shanghai, who synthesized insulin chains de novo from synthesized amino acids and showed that the compound formed had almost full biological insulin activity. During his earlier work on angiotensin it had become clear to Edman that molecular mass and amino acid compositions were insufficient to explain the biological activity of a protein. Most likely this must somehow reside in the amino acid sequence of the protein.

A New Idea Is Born. During his time at the Rockefeller Institute in 1946 and 1947, Edman made the first attempts toward solving the sequence problem using stepwise degradation of proteins by removing amino acids one after the other. The problem was how to break a terminal peptide bond while leaving the rest unaffected. He was convinced that the method used by Sanger would have severe limitations when it came to sequencing large protein molecules.

Whereas Sanger wanted a stable label on the N-terminal that could survive acid hydrolysis of all peptide bonds, Edman turned his attention to chemical reagents that would allow both labeling of the N-terminal amino acid residue in proteins and subsequent rearrangement and release of the N-terminal amino acid under conditions that would not lead to breakage of other peptide bonds. This approach was initially influenced by the work of previous investigators. Max Bergman and coworkers had in 1927 used phenylisocyanate to label the N-terminal amino acid in dipeptides and had shown that on subsequent acid hydrolysis the phenylhydantoin of the N-terminal was formed. In 1930, Emil Abderhalden and Hans Brockmann had been the first to use phenylisocyanate for stepwise degradation of polypeptides. However, it was inconvenient for sequence purpose because the labeled N-terminal amino acid could not be released without breaking other peptide bonds. Edman wanted to find another, more efficient, nucleophile, that is, a label on the N-terminal that would present the CO-group of the linkage to the next amino acid with an energetically more favorable reaction partner (than the NH-group) and thus cause fission of the bond without breaking other peptide bonds. Edman considered phenylisothiocyanate to be such a nucleophile, because the ketonic sulphur in this compound would be expected to be a good supplier of electrons (see Figure 2-1).

On his return to Sweden in 1947, Edman was appointed associate professor at the University of Lund and there he continued to work on the use of phenylisothiocyanate for sequence analysis. He continued work on other problems in protein chemistry, but sequence analysis was his major scientific interest. In 1949 the first version of Edman's method for determination of the amino acid sequence of peptides was ready for publication. It featured a concept of sequencing that was novel and which ultimately had far greater potential than Sanger's method, both for development and also for automation. In this first method Edman showed that coupling of phenylisothiocyanate to amino groups of peptides and proteins occurred easily in slightly alkaline buffers (see Figure 2-2). Furthermore, the labeled N-terminal amino acid was, in anhydrous acid media, swiftly rearranged and released as, he believed, a "phenylthiohydantoin" derivative of the N-terminal amino acid (see Figure 2-5). Following investigations on the reaction mechanisms and procedures for characterization of the "thiohydantoins" of different amino acids, a second version of Edman's method was published in 1950.

At the time of the above studies, Edman was unaware of an intermediate released from the labeled peptide in anhydrous acid media. He discovered this intermediate during a thorough study on the reaction mechanism of the thiohydantoin formation. The resulting publication in

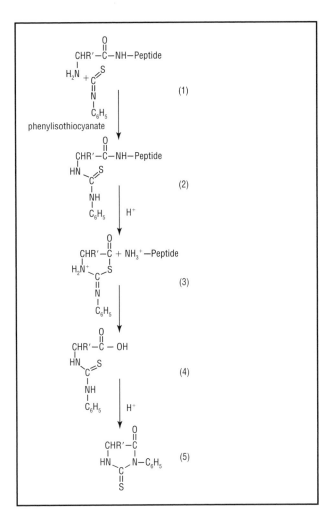

Figure 2. *Edman's final reaction scheme with intermediary thiazolinone formation. 1. Coupling with phenylisothiocyanate. 2. Carbamylated peptide. 3. Release of N-terminal as thiazolinone. 4. Hydrolysis of thiazolinone to carbamylated amino acid. 5. Ring closure in acid to thiohydantoin.*

1956 was of utmost importance for the practical execution of stepwise amino acid sequencing, as it now became evident that the product formed in anhydrous acid media was not a phenylthiohydantoin (PTH) derivative, as Edman had assumed before, but rather a novel compound, the isomeric anilinothiazolinone (2-anilino-5-thiazolinone) (see Figure 2-3). This derivative has different absorption spectrum in ultraviolet light and different migration during paper chromatography, which, presumably, is what initially led Edman to make a thorough chemical characterization of the compound. Its formation following the nucleophilic attack on the peptide bond by the thioketonic sulfur in phenylisothiocyanate was extremely fast. Its importance for the success of stepwise degradation lies in its speed of formation and in the fact that its formation is not due to a hydrolytic process but occurs under water-free acid conditions. The risk for cleavage of other peptide bonds than that involving the N-terminal amino acid is thus negligible. After its release it can be removed from the residual peptide by extraction and subsequently under hydrolytic acid conditions transformed to the thiohydantoin. The latter occurs in two steps. First the thiazolinone undergoes rearrangement in water to the corresponding thiocarbamyl derivative of the amino acid (see Figure 2-4) and then under hydrous acid conditions cyclization to the thiohydantoin takes place (see Figure 2-5). The latter reaction is slower than the thiazolinone formation. All PTH derivatives of amino acids show strong absorption in the ultraviolet (with a maximum around 268 nm), which is useful for their quantification.

It was now clear that three discrete reaction steps were involved in stepwise degradation as shown in Figure 2: first, labeling of N-terminal amino acid of peptide or protein with phenylisothiocyanate (1-2); second, cleavage to form anilinothiazolinone derivative under anhydrous acid conditions (3); followed by rearrangement to thiocarbamyl derivative of N-terminal amino acid (4); and, third, conversion to phenylthiohydantoin derivative under hydrous acid conditions (5).

The generality of thiazolinone formation in stepwise amino acid sequencing has been demonstrated in many other stepwise reactions using other reagents but where the key reaction is always the formation of a thiazolinone. Edman's mother reflected on the importance to Edman of the discovery of the three-stage reaction: "One day Pehr came home to me and asked me to sit down with him because he had something interesting to tell me. He then told me that he had discovered a way to analyze proteins which had not been possible before and that this discovery would certainly be of great importance for biochemistry in the future" (personal recollection of the author).

Edman characterized PTH derivatives of most of the naturally occurring amino acids by melting point and elementary analysis. With a few exceptions the chemical stability of PTH amino acids was excellent. Edman's coworker John Sjöquist developed paper chromatography systems for resolution of PTH amino acids. These systems permitted a direct identification and quantification of all amino acids as PTH derivatives instead of, as previously, indirectly by amino acid analysis after alkaline hydrolysis of the PTH derivatives. Later, a whole arsenal of procedures for rapid identification of the PTH amino acids was developed, for example, thin-layer and gas chromatography, mass spectroscopy, and high performance liquid chromatography.

Edman's approach of successively removing and identifying the N-terminal amino acid from a long polypeptide demanded that each step should be as precise and as free from side reactions as possible. This stepwise degradation must end as soon as the product of the side reactions reached concentrations comparable with those of the linear degradation. By eliminating side reactions and modifying the reaction mechanisms, Edman strived, up to the end of his life, to increase the repetitive yield of the N-terminal amino acid from one degradation cycle to the next. Edman illustrated the importance of high repetitive yields with a simple calculation: repetitive yields of 97, 98, and 99 percent make possible 30, 60, and 120 degradation cycles, respectively.

Some researchers modified Edman's method so that identification of the N-terminal amino acid was not performed directly, but instead by comparison of the amino acid composition of acid hydrolysates of the peptide before and after release of the N-terminal amino acid. Edman repudiated this approach on the grounds that it relates only to the hydrolysate of the peptide and, furthermore, that certain amino acids such as asparagines, glutamine, and tryptophan could not be indentified.

In 1957 Edman accepted a position as director of research at the newly established St. Vincent's School of Medical Research in Melbourne, Australia, where he remained for fifteen years and also became an Australian citizen. There, Edman perfected the manual three-stage degradation technique. Briefly, the manual three-stage method was performed as follows: protein or peptide is coupled with phenylisothiocyanate. After coupling, excess phenylisothiocyanate and by-products are removed by extraction with benzene and the water phase freeze-dried. The residue is extracted with ethyl acetate and dissolved in water-free trifluoroacetic acid, which leads to the release of the amino terminal amino acid as an anilinothiazolinone derivative. Trifluoroacetic acid has the advantage of being both a good catalyst for cyclization and a good solvent for proteins. From this solution the residual protein or peptide is precipitated with ethylene chloride and is now ready for the next degradation cycle. The ethylene chloride phase containing the thiazolinone is evaporated and the residue taken up in diluted hydrochloric acid for conversion of the thiazolinone to thiohydantoin at elevated temperature.

Except for his nearest coworkers, very few in the scientific community knew about the three-stage method. Edman refused to publish it as it stood at that time. He thought it could still be improved. Margareta Blombäck and this author worked in Edman's laboratory as visiting scientists in 1961 and tried the three-stage technique on a 16–amino acid residue peptide from fibrinogen, the clotting protein in blood. (Release of the peptide activates fibrinogen.) We were able to make a complete stepwise degradation with good yields up to the very last residues. These results impressed Edman and strengthened his conviction that longer peptides could be degraded in even better yield.

Automated Procedure. The need for automation was evident by 1962. Edman and his laboratory assistant Geoffrey Begg explored different possibilities to solve the automation problem. The problem was first to find a single physical process that could accommodate the various operations in the manual procedure. At the very start of this endeavor they conceived the idea of the spinning cylindrical cup, in which all reaction media were spread out as thin films on the vessel wall (see Figure 3). This established a large surface and accomplished the equivalent of rapid stirring. The rotating film containing the protein would be well suited for extraction with a solvent, because the extraction fluid is continuously fed at the bottom of the cup, glides over the surface of the protein film, and is subsequently removed in the upper part of the cup. The surface film is also well suited for carrying out drying and other procedures, and, furthermore, the whole degradation cycle could be programmed.

This instrument was designed to contain reservoirs to hold all the reagents required for the reaction cycles together with receivers for effluents and means for controlling reaction temperature. A system of feed tubes and automated valves was provided and programmed to supply the reagents and extraction solvents to the spinning cup in the correct order at preset time intervals. The process embraced the coupling step with formation of the phenylthiocarbamyl derivation of the protein and release of the N-terminal amino acid as anilinothiazolinone. The thiazolinones of each N-terminal amino acid were automatically transferred to tubes in a fraction collector and were then, in a separate operation, converted to the corresponding PTHs for identification by thin-layer chromatography or other suitable procedures. The steps in the sequenator were largely copies of the manual three-stage method, but for logistic or other reasons certain changes had to be made. For example, trifluoroacetic acid in the cleavage step was changed to heptafluorobutyric acid to avoid excessive evaporation.

The instrument enabled the degradation of even large polypeptides to an extent that had never before been possible. The degradation cycle proceeded at a rate of about fifteen cycles in twenty-four hours, as compared to one or two cycles per day with the manual technique. The three-stage sequence method had changed the strategy of sequence determination, and automation made it widely available. It was no longer necessary to begin by cleaving the protein backbone into many small peptides, since long direct sequences were possible. Later on Edman applied the process to apomyoglobin from the humpback whale and showed that it was possible to establish the sequence

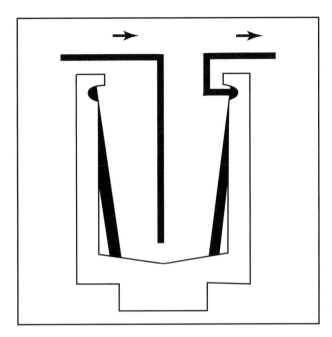

Figure 3. *Schematic presentation of the spinning cup. An aqueous solution containing protein and reaction components on the surface (white) is being extracted by an organic solvent (black).*

of the first sixty amino acids from the N-terminal end. The value of a sequencing technique depends to a large extent on the length of the amino acid sequence that may be determined. Therefore an important factor is high repetitive yield, that is, the yield of amino acid calculated from one degradation cycle to the next. With apomyoglobin this yield was 98 percent. In 1967 the work on the automated sequence analysis was finished and published. Edman's work became well known by the international science community at large and clarification of protein structures worldwide sped up tremendously. Up to that time most sequencing had been made using the earlier versions of Edman's method or with the Sanger technique.

In 1972 Edman accepted a position as director of the Department of Protein Chemistry I of the Max-Planck-Institut für Biochemie in Martinsried, near Munich, West Germany. His laboratory was endowed with a wealth of hard-won experience in sequencing and was engaged in a number of sequence projects. Nevertheless, during the last years of his life Edman continued to work on improving repetitive yield in the sequence procedure, which he thought was crucial for fast elucidation of protein sequences. With the advance of molecular genetics, high repetitive yields may have lost some of its former imperative. Relatively short amino acid sequences of a protein are required for identifying the cDNA sequence corresponding to the protein, and that sequence is subsequently translated into a (virtual) amino acid sequence.

Another concern that Edman had at this time was the necessity for the establishment of adequate arrangements for data storage, data retrieval, and data processing when a large number of protein sequences became clarified. For Edman, one of the most potentially powerful applications of sequence studies lay in the search for evolutionary relationships between different proteins, but this becomes valuable only when a large number of sequences are available for comparison. In his own words, "we may in time expect the unraveling of a new *systema naturalis* among biomolecules" (personal recollection by the author). He also foresaw early that mutational events in primary structure could change the function of a protein. Vernon Ingram had already in 1958 shown that a single point mutation in hemoglobin gave rise to sickle-cell anemia. Likewise in 1968 Birger Blombäck and others demonstrated that a point mutation in fibrinogen led to a severe bleeding diathesis.

Though Edman's most important work was concerned with stepwise degradation of proteins, he also worked in other areas of biochemistry. His work on hypertensin has already been mentioned. Early on he worked on constituents in nerve tissues. He later developed a technique for partition chromatography on starch and used it for separation of nucleic acid components. He experimented with the coupling of proteins to insoluble matrices. He studied the mechanism of cleavage of proteins by cyanogen bromide in order to obtain convenient fragments for stepwise degradation. He observed as early as the 1930s that some proteins such as fibrinogen had a lower solubility in the cold and consequently could be frozen out of solution. Much later, other workers were using this physical property for purification of fibrinogen, antihemophilic factor, and von Willebrand factor.

Edman preferred to work in a modest setting with only a few people around him. In his group in Lund, Sjöquist worked on a method for amino acid analysis using their PTH derivatives and Lars Josephsson studied reversible breakage of peptide bonds in anhydrous acid solution, the so-called N-O acyl shift. His group in Melbourne also consisted of a small number of people: Frank Morgan and Hugh Niall worked mainly on applications of the phenylisothiocyanate degradation technique. Derek Ilse studied the mechanism of the reaction. In Melbourne and during the time in Martinsried, Agnes Henschen and her group studied the structure of fibrinogen and were able to determine the larger part of the amino acid sequence of this protein with more than a thousand amino acid residues.

Edman received several honors for his achievements in science: the Britannica Australia Award, the Berzelius Gold Medal, the Gold Medal of the Swedish Academy of Engineering, and the Linderström-Lang Medal. He was a Fellow of the Australian Academy of Science, Fellow of the Royal Society of London, and a scientific member of the Max Planck Society.

Edman, the Person. People who met Edman for the first time may have gotten the impression of a courteous, kind, but reclusive man with a hint of shyness. People who came closer to him could appreciate other qualities: generosity, warmth, humor, sympathy. Edman had a vast knowledge in many areas. His mind was logical and he was stringent in expression. The integrity on which his opinions were based was admirable and respected. At the core of his personality was a sincere humanism.

Edman had an urge for purity and perfection in life and work. This quality was very likely in play when he joined the socialist group Clarté as a young man in the 1930s and when he chose self-imposed expatriation in the 1950s, and it was probably a strong driving force in his scientific accomplishments. This urge was most likely a prerequisite for his motivation to spend so much time and effort on perfection of the phenylisothiocyanate method. Edman was suspicious of fortuitous experiments for the simple reason that if successful they would be difficult to reproduce.

Pehr Edman had broad interests outside science. His love for nature derived from his childhood. He was especially interested in birds, and his knowledge of ornithology was impressive. Music, classical or contemporary, and literature were other favorite preoccupations.

Edman had many friends, many of them from circles outside the scientific field. Among them his shyness seemed to disappear and his humor blossomed—sometimes drastic but to the point. Edman's first marriage with Barbro Bergström produced two children, Martin and Gudrun. Edman met Agnes Henschen in Melbourne in 1966, and they were married in 1968. They had two children, Carl and Helena. Henschen later moved to the United States and worked in the Department of Molecular Biology and Biochemistry at the University of California, Irvine.

In February 1977, when leaving a scientific lecture in Martinsried, Edman suddenly fell down, unconscious. After a few weeks of illness he died on 19 March. A tumor of the brain was diagnosed; there had been no symptoms before he was struck unconscious.

BIBLIOGRAPHY

WORKS BY EDMAN

"A Method for the Determination of the Amino Acid Sequences in Peptides." *Archives of Biochemistry and Biophysics* 22 (1949): 475–490.

"Preparation of Phenylthiohydantoin from Some Natural Amino Acids." *Acta Chemica Scandinavica* 4 (1950): 277–282.

"Method for Determination of the Amino Acid Sequence in Peptides." *Acta Chemica Scandinavica* 4 (1950): 283–293.

"Selective Cleavage of Peptides." In *The Chemical Structure of Proteins,* edited by G. E. W. Wolstenholme and Margaret P. Cameron. London: Churchill, 1953.

"Mechanism of the Phenyl Isothiocyanate Degradation of Peptides." *Nature* 177 (1956): 667–668.

"On the Mechanism of the Phenyl Isothiocyanate Degradation of Peptides." *Acta Chemica Scandinavica* 10 (1956): 761–768.

With John Sjöquist. "Identification and Semiquantitative Determination of 3-Phenyl 2-Thiohydantoins." *Acta Chemica Scandinavica* 10 (1956): 1507–1509.

With K. Lauber. "Preparation of Phenylthiohydantoins from Glutamine, S-carboxymethylcysteine and Cysteic Acid." *Acta Chemica Scandinavica* 10 (1956): 466–467.

With K. Heirwegh. "Purification and N-terminal Determination of Crystalline Pepsin." *Biochimica et Biophysica Acta* 24 (1957): 219–220.

"Phenylthiohydantoins in Protein Analysis." *Annals of the New York Academy of Sciences* 88 (1960): 602–610.

"Determination of Amino Acid Sequences in Proteins." *Thrombosis et Diathesis Haemorrhagica, Supplementum* 13 (1963): 17–20.

With Geoffrey Begg. "A Protein Sequenator." *European Journal of Biochemistry* 1 (1967): 80–91.

With Agnes Henschen. "Sequence Determination. In *Protein Sequence Determination: A Sourcebook of Methods and Techniques,* edited by Saul B. Needleman. 2nd rev. and enl. ed., 232–279. Berlin: Springer-Verlag, 1975.

"Unwinding the Protein." *Carlsberg Research Communications* 42 (1977): 1–9.

OTHER SOURCES

Blombäck, Birger. "Pehr Victor Edman: The Solitary Genius." In *Comprehensive Biochemistry* 42, edited by Giorgio Semenza and Anthony John Turner, chapter 3, 103–135. Amsterdam: Elsevier Science BV, 2003.

Partridge, S. Miles, and Birger Blombäck. "Pehr Victor Edman." In *Biographical Memoirs of Fellows of the Royal Society* 25 (1979): 241–265.

Birger Blombäck

EDMONDSON, WALLIS THOMAS

(*b.* Milwaukee, Wisconsin, 24 April 1916; *d.* Seattle, Washington, 10 January 2000), *ecology, limnology, oceanography, environmental science.*

An American ecologist and limnologist, Edmondson was famous for his pioneering work on the effects of nutrient pollution upon freshwater environments. In collaboration with his wife, Yvette Hardman Edmondson, he developed a quantitative method connecting ratios between eggs and females in zooplankton to calculate population and birth rates. His research formed the foundation for the basic study of polluted aquatic environments, while informing political and technological solutions for their recovery. In tracing how nutrient loading, the excessive concentration of phosphorous and nitrogen, boosted the rapid growth of blue-green algae, which stripped water of oxygen and often killed all other life, Edmondson demonstrated how human alterations to aquatic ecosystems had negative but ultimately reversible effects.

Childhood and Education. Edmondson, known to friends and colleagues by his nickname, "Tommy," came to his calling early. As a young boy, he spent many hours collecting microscopic flora and fauna from the lakes, ponds, and vernal pools dotting the glaciated hills of Wisconsin. His parents gave him his first microscope at the age of twelve and a copy of Henry Baldwin Ward and George Chandler Whipple's classic text, *Freshwater Biology,* as a birthday present the following year. As an eighteen-year-old in New Haven, Connecticut, where he had moved with his widowed mother, Edmondson befriended Yale zoologist and ecologist, G. Evelyn Hutchinson, while still a student at Hillhouse High School. The precocious boy impressed the eminent scholar, who gave Edmondson access to his collection of rotifers from India, Hispaniola, and across North America at Yale's Osborn Memorial Laboratories. Edmondson enrolled at Yale in 1934, and by the time he graduated had already published eight articles, including one in *Science.* His first publications, based upon Hutchinson's collection, focused on systematics, fixation methods, and substrate effects derived from his work on one of his future specialties, the phylum *Rotifera,* one of the most abundant and prominent types of zooplankton. By focusing on *Rotifera,* Edmondson grounded his future career firmly in the tradition of population ecology established by his mentor, Hutchinson.

After graduation, Edmondson received a research assistantship in 1938 to attend the University of Wisconsin, where he worked with the noted limnologists Chauncey Juday and Edward A. Birge at their famed Trout Lake site. At Madison, Edmondson studied the chemical ecology of sessile rotifers, correlating the separate effects of pH, alkalinity, and ionic strength upon their reproduction and movement. Juday and Birge pushed the young scientist to hone his aptitude for observational fieldwork as carefully has he had perfected his experimental laboratory skills. While in Wisconsin, Edmondson also met his future wife, Yvette Hardman, then a doctoral candidate in microbial ecology, who later became his lifelong collaborator. Returning to Yale in 1939, he pursued his PhD under the direction of his old mentor, Hutchinson, and in 1941 defended his thesis on the population dynamics and ecology of sessile rotifers. In his doctoral research he had discovered that survival rates for rotifers increased if they lived in colonies instead of as individuals. Several hours after his thesis defense, he married Hardman, who had also completed her PhD at Wisconsin, in Yale's Dwight Chapel. Although Edmondson saw himself as part of the great Hutchinson lineage, his time at Wisconsin spent outdoors, on the water, would later prove to be as valuable as his training at Yale in hypothesis testing and mathematical modeling.

Edmondson's Egg Ratio Method. Before Edmondson embarked on his academic career, he joined the war effort against the Axis, working as a physical oceanographer for the U.S. Navy. His wartime duties took him first to the American Museum of Natural History, then the Woods Hole Oceanographic Institution, where he collaborated with Walter Munk, Henry Stommel, George Clarke, and Maurice Ewing on predicting wave heights to aid amphibious assaults and using sound refraction to detect downed aircraft and submersibles. (Yvette, at this time, was teaching biology at Bennington College, her alma mater.) After the war, Edmondson stayed briefly at Woods Hole before moving to Harvard University in 1946. There, reunited with Yvette, he began research on the effects of nutrient fertilization on primary production, the fundamental ecological process whereby organic compounds are created from inorganic compounds, usually by plants using photosynthesis. Secondary production, in contrast, is the process whereby other creatures take primary producers and consume them as food or nutrients, as a cow, might consume grass. This work eventually became the cornerstone of his professional reputation.

In 1949, the Edmondsons moved west, where he accepted a permanent faculty position at the University of Washington. He remained in Seattle for the rest of his career. The institution was a good match; under the leadership of Trevor Kincaid at the beginning of the twentieth century, Washington had already established a strong reputation in zoology and botany. During the Cold War decades, the university grew rapidly thanks to a vibrant local economy and aggressive efforts by its leaders to boost federal and private funding. Backed by numerous grants and fellowships, including several from the new National Science Foundation, created in 1950, Edmondson helped to make Washington's zoology and oceanography programs internationally famous. Together with Yvette and his growing group of graduate students, Edmondson pursued his work on the effect of nutrient enrichment on primary production. At the time, calculating biological productivity as a combined property of aquatic ecosystems was an innovative program, embraced by only a few oceanographers and limnoecologists like Edmondson. His research path blended his experiences at Yale and Wisconsin to produce one of the most important analytical concepts in freshwater ecology: the egg ratio method.

Publishing his findings initially in 1960 after a sabbatical at Istituto Italiano di Idrobiologia in Pallanza, Italy, Edmondson stated that the ratios between eggs and females in zooplankton, like rotifers, yielded quantitative estimates of birth rates. Suddenly, previously intractable problems became solvable, from complex relationships between primary production and secondary production to predator-prey interactions and their effects upon community structure. The egg-ratio method gave ecologists a powerful quantitative tool. Now, they could measure planktonic population dynamics historically, often in the field, without disturbing natural populations or resorting to inaccurate estimates. Before, scientists looked at aquatic ecosystems as something akin to a black box; now they began to raise further questions about species composition, community formation, and evolutionary dynamics as observed through ecological processes.

The Lake Washington Story. The Pacific Northwest was a near-perfect setting for Edmondson's research, with its mosaic of deep saltwater inlets and abundant lakes. Edmondson had learned that atypical lakes provided the best research opportunities, so he and his students scoured the region, looking for suitable locations. On the Columbia Plateau of eastern Washington, they found Soap Lake and Lake Lenore, high in salinity and home to unique biota. In the Puget Sound lowlands north of Seattle, Hall Lake, a glacial kettle, was a textbook example of biogenic meromixis, or the limited mixing of water due to heavy accumulations of sediment or decayed bacteria. Yet no place proved more fruitful for his studies than Lake Washington, located a short walk from his campus office. At first, Edmondson was uninterested in the lake. Two of his doctoral students, however, made it their laboratory, George C. Anderson focusing on phytoplankton, microscopic plants, and Gabriel W. Comita on copepods, microscopic crustaceans that fed on phytoplankton. On a June day in 1955, after a sailing trip on Lake Washington, Anderson returned to Edmondson's laboratory with a beer bottle full of water, telling his mentor that the lake had changed. Puzzled, the two graduate students, together with Edmondson, explained what swimmers and boaters had already noticed: the dramatic increase of a noxious growth, the blue-green alga *Oscillatoria rubescens*.

"This, of course," Edmondson recalled later in *The Uses of Ecology: Lake Washington and Beyond*, "was wildly exciting to us" (p. 13). He had found an unparalleled opportunity to test the association between primary productivity and lake organisms through time. Edmondson knew of earlier studies from Switzerland's Lake Zürich that identified the algae species as an indicator of human-induced eutrophication—a condition whereby excess nutrients such as phosphates, abundant in untreated sewage, hastened algal growth. The fast-growing algae stripped the waters of dissolved oxygen and killed all but the hardiest animals. Since sewage effluent was an extremely effective fertilizer, nutrients liberated by dying algae could continue the cycle unabated. In subsequent experiments, Edmondson and his students found that the visibility in the lake's previously clear waters, which once exceeded three meters in depth, had diminished to less than one meter. Even more alarming was how quickly the lake had changed; a 1939 study had found the waters clear and free of organic material. Now, during the hot summer months, the water looked like pea soup. Rafts of rotting, stinking algae clogged the lake, washing up on beaches and forcing health officials to close popular swimming spots. Alarmed, Edmondson and his students rushed to publish their findings.

As Edmondson's research became widely known throughout the metropolitan Seattle area, local newspapers turned to him for explanation and cited his research. Soon the scientist found himself recruited in a battle to save Lake Washington. A group of concerned citizens led by James R. Ellis, a crusading young attorney, had helped to form the Metropolitan Problems Advisory Council to address the mounting problems facing Seattle and its environs, from poor transportation to inadequate pollution control. Ellis and others had long worried that unchecked sewage dumping would imperil Lake Washington; now they seemed to have scientific proof. In 1956, Ellis asked Edmondson to explain his findings to the council. The ecologist's eight-page memo explained, in lay language, free of jargon, the grim state of Lake Washington and the possibilities for its revival. The combined effluent dumped into the lake by the ten suburban sewage treatment plants topped 20 million gallons daily. The rate of algal growth was directly proportional to the increase in sewage, and poisoning the algae or scooping it from the lake for removal would not solve the problem. Without definite and immediate action, he warned, the lake would continue to deteriorate.

Armed with Edmondson's findings, Ellis and the Metropolitan Problems Advisory Council proposed creating a new regional governmental agency, the Municipality of Metropolitan Seattle, or Metro, to eliminate the pollution threat. Metro would eliminate the pollution threat by building massive interceptor sewer and treatement system to remove sewage from Lake Washington permanently. Edmondson was now in the middle of a bitter political struggle pitting political reformers, like Ellis, against angry suburban homeowners resistant to higher taxes and bigger government. The first Metro referendum, which went to the voters in March 1958, was defeated in the suburbs

surrounding Lake Washington. As pollution increased later that summer, Metro proponents submitted a revised version that won approval in September 1958, with 58 percent of Seattle residents and 67 percent in the rest of King County voting in favor. Construction on the new sewer system began soon thereafter. During both elections, Edmondson gave numerous interviews and held debates with Metro opponents on the science behind Lake Washington's decline. The situation in the late 1950s, he later wrote, "was an example in which the results of basic research could be put to immediate application," and Edmondson soon earned a national reputation as a scientist who could link research to policy without simplifying the science (1991, p. 286).

After the elections, Edmondson confidently predicted that once sewage was treated and diverted away, Lake Washington would rebound and water quality would recover. By 1969, Secchi disk sampling indicated that water column transparency had increased from less than one meter six years before to more than three meters. The revival of Lake Washington became a textbook staple of how bioremediation could pull aquatic ecosystems back from the brink of collapse. Scientists and politicians in Ontario and Switzerland later turned to Edmondson's findings to resuscitate Lake Erie and Lake Zürich. The National Research Council would later conclude that Lake Washington's revival, guided by Edmondson's work, helped to set the course for effective restoration of other aquatic environments around the world. Ray T. Oglesby, a Cornell University limnologist, later wrote: "The 'Lake Washington Story' has become to the limnologist what the Lord's Prayer is to a preacher, a vital, uniquely clear, well-documented statement of what the profession is all about" (quoted in Lehman, 1988, p. 1237).

Accolades and Awards. Edmondson remained an active researcher with his wife, Yvette, continuing to track long-term changes in Lake Washington by studying nutrient addition, enhanced grazer abundance, and elevated alkalinity over time. Indeed, Yvette was an important figure in her own right, serving as editor of *Limnology and Oceanography* for nineteen years and helping to establish the journal as a leading publication in both fields. Even after their joint retirement in 1986, both continued to publish and attend conferences. Honors flowed to them, focused primarily on Edmondson's initial studies of fertilization and productivity in Lake Washington, work made possible, in large part, because of Yvette's laboratory assistance. Tommy Edmondson joined the National Academy of Sciences in 1973, the same year he received the academy's Frederick Garner Cottrell Award for Environmental Quality. Other tributes among many included Ecological Society of America's Eminent Ecologist Award, the Einar Naumann–August Thienemann Medal of the Societas

Internationalis Limnologiae, and a special resolution by the Washington State legislature commemorating his contributions to public welfare and environmental protection. Edmondson died in Seattle.

BIBLIOGRAPHY

The Special Collections of the University of Washington Libraries contains his complete personal papers.

WORKS BY EDMONDSON

With G. C. Anderson and D. R. Peterson. "Artificial Eutrophication of Lake Washington." *Limnology and Oceanography* 1 (January 1956): 47–53. The first publication on the changing conditions in Lake Washington, near Seattle.

"Reproductive Rate of Rotifers in Natural Populations." *Memorie dell'Istituto Italiano di Idrobiologia* 12 (1960): 21–77. The original explanation of Edmondson's egg ratio method.

"Reproductive Rate of Planktonic Rotifers as Related to Food and Temperature in Nature." *Ecological Monographs* 35 (1965): 61–111.

"The Present Condition of Lake Washington." *Verhandlungen der Internationalen Vereinigung für theoretische und angewandte Limnologie* 18 (1972): 284–291.

The Uses of Ecology: Lake Washington and Beyond. Seattle: University of Washington Press, 1991. A series of essays based upon the John and Jesse Danz Lectures at the University of Washington in 1990.

OTHER SOURCES

"Bibliography of W. T. Edmondson," In "W. T. Edmondson Celebratory Issue," edited by Nelson G. Hairston Jr., John T. Lehman, and John G. Stockner. Special Issue, *Limnology and Oceanography* 33 (1988): 1241–1243. Complete bibliography of Edmondson's publications and theses directed through 1988.

Hutchinson, G. E. "W. Thomas Edmondson." In "W. T. Edmondson Celebratory Issue," edited by Nelson G. Hairston Jr., John T. Lehman, and John G. Stockner. Special Issue, *Limnology and Oceanography* 33 (1988): 1231–1233.

Lehman, J. T. "Good Professor Edmondson," In "W. T. Edmondson Celebratory Issue," edited by Nelson G. Hairston Jr., John T. Lehman, and John G. Stockner. Special Issue, *Limnology and Oceanography* 33 (1988): 1234–1240.

Matthew Klingle

EHRENFEST-AFANAS'EVA, TATIANA A. (also Afanasyeva, Afanassjewa, Tatyana, Tatjana, b. T. Alekseevna Afanas'eva, m. Ehrenfest) (*b.* Kiev, in Ukraine, Russian Empire 19 November 1876; *d.* Leiden, The Netherlands 14 April 1964), *mathematics, statistical mechanics, mathematics education.*

Tatiana Ehrenfest-Afanas'eva was a Russian-Dutch mathematician. She was married to the Austrian physicist and mathematician Paul Ehrenfest (1880–1933). Tatiana and Paul Ehrenfest were a couple in science; they collaborated closely together, especially on their classical review of the statistical mechanics (1911) of Ludwig Boltzmann (1844–1906). She published articles on different topics, including randomness (1956), entropy (1958), and methodological problems concerning how to teach children in mathematics and geometry (1931). She also collaborated with the German-Dutch mathematician and historian of mathematics Hans Freudenthal (1905–1990) and the Dutch historian of science Eduard Jan Dijksterhuis (1892–1965).

Tatiana and Paul Ehrenfest had two daughters and two sons: The oldest daughter, Tatiana (Tanja) P. Ehrenfest, married Tanja van Aardenne-Ehrenfest (1905–1984), and became a mathematician too; Galja (also Anna), married A. van Bommel-Ehrenfest (1910–1979), and became an author and illustrator of children's books; Paul Jr. (1915–1939) studied physics. The youngest son Vassily (1918–1933) had been born with Down syndrome. In 1933 Paul Ehrenfest, suffering from depression, shot Vassily and then killed himself.

Early Years. Tatiana Alekseevna Afanas'eva was born in Kiev in the Ukraine, which at the time belonged to the Russian Empire. Little is known about her parents and her childhood. After the death of her father she lived with an uncle in St. Petersburg. She received a good education at a girl's school in St. Petersburg and attended a women's pedagogical school. Becoming a teacher was an acceptable profession for a young woman in that period. Furthermore, she could attend the Women's College in St. Petersburg where young women could obtain relatively good scientific training. As was the case with many women from Russia, Tatiana Afanas'eva went to Germany after graduating from school and became one of several Russian women students at the University of Goettingen. She studied mathematics and in 1902 met Paul Ehrenfest, who received his doctoral degree in 1904. They wed the same year.

The couple lived in Germany and Austria, but because of the then-normal anti-Semitism at German and Austrian universities, it was difficult for him, a Jew, to get an academic position. His marriage to a Russian woman, a foreigner, made the situation even more complicated. In 1907 the couple moved to St. Petersburg, but he had no chance at a permanent position in academia because he was an Austrian and a Jew. After arriving in St. Petersburg, Tatiana and Paul Ehrenfest made contacts with the younger generation of Russian physicists and mathematicians, including Jakov Davidovich Tamarkin (1888–

1945), Aleksandr Aleksandrovich Fridman (Friedmann; 1888–1925); the elder Orest Daniilovich Chwolson (Khvol'son; 1852–1934), Vladimir Andreevich Steklov (1864–1925), and Abram Fedorovich Joffe (Ioffe; 1880–1960). Joffe and Paul Ehrenfest (Pavel Sigismundovich, as friends called him in Russia) became close friends. Tatiana and Paul invited these physicists and mathematicians to an informal, unofficial colloquium that was held every other week at Ehrenfest's home, where they discussed recently published works and other scientific subjects. The colloquium also was called the physics discussion club. Little is known about the work of the Ehrenfests in St. Petersburg; they spent five years there and although they made good friends, they were isolated as well. In that time both worked on their famous article, the review about statistical mechanics, which was published in 1911 in the famous *Encyklopädie der mathematischen Wissenschaften.* Felix Klein (1849–1925) edited the volume, and the Ehrenfests were familiar with him from Goettingen University.

Move to Leiden. Because of the political situation in Russia after 1911, the Ehrenfests, now with two little daughters, looked for better living and working conditions outside of Russia. In 1912 Paul Ehrenfest embarked on a two-month-long lecture and visiting tour through several German-speaking universities, including in Zurich and Prague, where he first met Albert Einstein (1879–1955). Finally, on the advice of Hendrik Anton Lorentz (1853–1928), Paul Ehrenfest luckily received an academic position: He was appointed as professor at the University of Leiden as Lorentz's successor. In autumn 1912 the couple arrived in Leiden and remained there for the rest of their lives. Because of World War I, Paul obtained Dutch citizenship only in 1922; his wife probably did, too. Whereas each detail of the academic career of Paul Ehrenfest in Leiden is known—his research and his teaching activities, how he organized seminars and his famous colloquium Ehrenfestii (the Wednesday Physics Colloquium), how he managed the visits of all the important physicists of that time, including Niels Bohr (1885–1962) and his friend Albert Einstein—little is known about the scientific work of Tatiana in this period. From several letters it is obvious that she participated in the Wednesday discussions, and she was remembered as the intelligent partner of her husband. In 1931 she published her study on teaching mathematics problems, the *Exercises in Experimental Geometry.*

After Paul's death in 1933, Tatiana had to independently care for the education and life of her three children, and she also began worrying about the developments in neighboring Nazi Germany. During the occupation of the Netherlands by German troops the Ehrenfest daughters survived all dangers (they were half Jews by Nazi defini-

tion). It seems from her list of publications that Tatiana could work in science again only after the liberation of the Netherlands in 1945. In 1956 and in 1958 her important articles on thermodynamics were published, in Leiden and in the *American Journal of Physics,* respectively.

Tatiana Ehrenfest-Afanas'eva belonged to the rare and small group of talented women mathematicians who luckily received professional training at universities in the beginning of the twentieth century and who worked in the fields of mathematics and science. Her marriage had a double and paradoxical effect on her career. Thanks to her husband she came in contact with many important physicists of her time, but she was mostly considered simply his wife, and his secretary or private assistant. It is difficult to reconstruct her ideas and her own scientific work. Thanks to such colleagues as Albert Einstein and Niels Bohr, the scientific work of Tatiana Ehrenfest was acknowledged in the 1920s, and thanks to colleagues such as Hans Freudenthal and E. J. Dijksterhuis, she was accepted as an intellectual in the 1950s.

Ehrenfest published several articles on different topics, first together with her husband, especially their famous article in 1911, but also alone, such on randomness (1956) and entropy (1958). She also wrote about methodological problems on the didactics of mathematics, and how to teach children mathematics and geometry (1931, 1960). The work of Tatiana and Paul Ehrenfest on the foundations of statistical mechanics and statistical thermodynamics was important to the development of those fields.

BIBLIOGRAPHY

WORKS BY EHRENFEST-AFANAS'EVA

With Paul Ehrenfest. "Bemerkung zur Theorie der Entropiezunahme in der 'Statistischen Mechanik' von W. Gibbs." *Wien Berichte* 115 (1906): 89.

With Paul Ehrenfest. "Über eine Aufgabe aus der Wahrscheinlichkeitsrechnung, die mit der kinetischen Deutung der Entropievermehrung zusammenhängt." *Mathematisch-Naturwissenschaftliche Blätter* 3 (1906).

With Paul Ehrenfest. "Über zwei bekannte Einwände gegen das Boltzmannsche H-Theorem." *Physikalische Zeitschrift* 8 (1907): 311.

With Paul Ehrenfest. "Begriffliche Grundlagen der statistischen Auffassung in der Mechanik." In *Enzyklopädie der mathematischen Wissenschaften,* Vol. 4, Teil 32, Leipzig, Germany: Teubner, 1911.

"Die Anwendung der Wahrscheinlichkeitsrechnung auf gesetzmässige Erscheinungen." *Journal der Russ. Physikalischen Gesellschaft* 43 (1911): 256.

Exercises in Experimental Geometry. 1931. Available from http://www.pims.math.ca/~hoek/teageo/TEA.pdf

Die Grundlagen der Thermodynamik. Leiden, the Netherlands: E. J. Brill, 1956.

"On the Use of the Notion 'Probability' in Physics." *American Journal of Physics* 26 (1958): 388.

With Paul Ehrenfest. *The Conceptual Foundations of the Statistical Approach in Mechanics.* Ithaca, New York: Cornell University Press, 1959.

Wiskunde: Didactische opstellen. Zutphen, the Netherlands, 1961. A treatise on the teaching of mathematics, in Dutch.

OTHER SOURCES

Klein, Martin J., and Paul Ehrenfest. *The Making of a Theoretical Physicist*, Vol. 1. Amsterdam: North-Holland Publishing Company, 1970.

Kochina, P. Ja. *Nauka, ljudi, gody. Vospominanija i vystuplenija.* Moscow: Nauka, 1988. Memories of the female mathematician P. La. Kochina (1899–1999), who attended the women courses in St. Petersburg.

"References on T. Ehrenfest." In *Twentieth Century Physics*, Vol. I–III, edited by Laurie M. Brown, Abraham Pais, and Sir Brian Pippard. New York: Institute of Physics Publishing and American Institute of Physics Press, 1995.

Annette B. Vogt

EICHENGRÜN, ARTHUR (*b.* Aachen, Germany, 13 August 1867; *d.* Bad Wiessee, Germany, 23 December 1949), *macromolecular chemistry, plastics industry, pharmaceutical chemistry, photochemistry.*

In the late 1890s, Eichengrün discovered protargol, a very successful drug against gonorrhea, and co-discovered aspirin. He went on to develop processes for the manufacture of cellulose acetate materials and devoted the rest of his life to the technical and economic development of plastics, lacquers, enamels, and artificial fibers based on cellulose acetate. During World War I his relatively non-inflammable synthetic cellulose acetate lacquers were important in the aircraft industry. He also pioneered the influential technique of injection molding.

Arthur Eichengrün was born in Aachen, Germany, on 13 August 1867 into a Jewish family of cloth manufacturers and was educated at the Kaiser Karl Gymnasium before entering the Aachen Technische Hochschule. He completed his undergraduate studies at Berlin under A. Wilhelm Hofmann and Carl Liebermann, then returned to Aachen in 1888 to prepare a PhD thesis titled *Über das Methoxy-oxy-dihydrocarbostyril*, supervised by Alfred Einhorn (for formal reasons Eichengrün obtained his PhD from the University of Erlangen in 1890, because at that time the Technische Hochschule did not yet have the right to grant the doctorate). He remained with Einhorn in Aachen to study the degradation of cocaine, then became a private assistant to Carl Graebe at the University of Geneva. In 1892 he was invited to introduce cocaine pro-

duction at the firm of C. H. Boehringer Sohn of Ingelheim am Rhein. A year later, he moved to Balzer & Co. in Grünau near Berlin, but soon transferred to L. C. Marquardt of Bonn-Beuel. In 1894 he married the American Elizabeth Fechheimer, with whom he had four children. After a divorce, in 1905 he married a Dutch woman, Madeleine Mijnssen, who gave him two children. This marriage broke up in 1921, and he married Lucie Henriette Gartsche in 1927.

Work at Bayer. While working at L. C. Marquardt Eichengrün developed a complex of iodoform with hexamine as an odorless antiseptic and investigated a silver-protein complex as an alternative to silver nitrate for the topical treatment of gonorrhea. Lacking the facilities to evaluate this, he approached Theobald Floret, company physician to the Farbenfabriken vormals Friedrich Bayer & Co. of Elberfeld. This resulted in his preparation being shown to be effective, and the rights to it were then purchased by F. Bayer & Co. On 1 October 1896, Eichengrün became employed by the company with responsibility for developing new drugs. His silver-protein complex was marketed the following year as Protargol and was the drug of choice for treating gonorrhea until the 1940s. As single inventor of this successful drug, Eichengrün received 5 percent of the net profit as a royalty. This made him a relatively wealthy man, who could start his own company when he left Bayer in 1908.

Eichengrün also produced iron somatose, another protein complex, as an oral iron preparation that would not irritate the stomach wall. These early drugs were followed by several others, including the antiseptics Helmitol (hexamethylenetetramine) and Citarin (the sodium salt of methylene citric acid), the famous drug aspirin (acetylsalicylic acid), and the odorless methyl salicylate substitute Mesotan (methoxymethyl salicylate).

The work on aspirin was carried out by Felix Hoffmann, acting under Eichengrün's direction. For many years Hoffmann was credited with the discovery of aspirin on his own on the basis of an anecdotal footnote in an encyclopedia published in Nazi Germany in 1934. As a Jew, Eichengrün was unable to challenge this in public at that time, but he did refute it in 1944 in a long letter sent from the Theriesenstadt concentration camp to the management of I. G. Farben, into which F. Bayer & Co. had been incorporated. This was a plea for help from his former employer, in which his contributions to the success of the company were laid out. The text relating to aspirin was slightly modified for publication in *Die Pharmazie* shortly before Eichengrün's death during the fiftieth anniversary year of its marketing by Bayer.

Although this detailed his claim to have co-discovered aspirin, and despite the fact that Hoffmann had never claimed credit for it in print, most authorities continued to believe that Hoffmann alone discovered it because of his synthesis of it on 10 August 1897. Yet careful examination of the text of the laboratory report reveals that this was not the first aspirin synthesis in the Bayer laboratories. It was also thought that Hoffmann discovered aspirin because his name was on the U.S. patent, but this overlooks the fact that the name of another colleague, Otto Bonhoeffer, appeared on the prior German patent application. It is not without significance that shortly after the introduction of aspirin Eichengrün, in 1901, became director of pharmaceutical and photographic research, whereas Hoffmann became director of sales. Eichengrün was the first director of pharmaceutical research at Bayer.

In his new role, Eichengrün introduced a variety of products, including the rapidly acting photographic developer Edinol (the hydrochloride salt of 3-amino salicyl alcohol), the automatic room disinfectant Autan (a complex of barium hydroxide and polymerized formaldehyde), and Cellit. The latter was the outcome of work with Theodor Becker to find a substitute for the highly flammable cellulose nitrate film being used in the rapidly expanding cinematographic industry. A process they devised in 1901 for the direct acetylation of cellulose at a low temperature to prevent its degradation also permitted the degree of acetylation to be controlled, thereby avoiding total conversion to its triacetate. This enabled Eichengrün and Becker, in 1904, to introduce a reliable synthesis of Cellit, a stable, non-brittle cellulose acetate polymer that could be dissolved in acetone for further processing. Cellit was then used to manufacture non-flammable cinematographic film, which Eastman Kodak and the Pathé Fréres began to use in 1909.

Eichengrün also devised a dry spinning process in which Cellit was sprayed into a heated chamber during production of acetate rayon fiber. This was licensed to the textile manufacturer Kunstseidenfabrik Jülich, which used it to begin production of artificial silk in 1907. Difficulties with the application of dyes to the new fabric led to its abandonment until the 1920s.

Research Laboratory and Factory. Eichengrün left Bayer in 1908 and established his own research laboratory in Berlin to manufacture materials based on cellulose acetate. Within a year or two he had devised two novel products. The first was Cellon, a flame resistant plastic that served as a replacement for celluloid. During World War I it was in considerable demand for manufacture of pilots' goggles, windshields, and gas masks. The second product was a cellulose acetate fire-resistant substitute for the rubber-based dope applied to the fabric of aircraft wings to render them water-resistant. This was also used in Zeppelin airships to additionally prevent gas leakage. These novel

products were produced under license by other companies, but in 1915 Eichengrün established his own factory in Berlin, which in 1919 was renamed the Cellon-Werke Dr. Arthur Eichengrün, with almost seventy workers. This was the year in which he pioneered injection molding, utilizing cellulose acetate to form a plastic that was initially named Lonarit. Injection molding has since been used worldwide in the manufacture of modern plastics.

The Cellon-Werke prospered, but in 1933 Eichengrün had to sell part of his share in the company to Germans of Aryan descent. In 1938 the Nazis forced him to withdraw completely from his company, and as a result he sold his firm to the Chemische Fabrik Dr. Joachim Wiernik & Co. in Berlin-Waidmannslust. Due to his reputation and influential contacts, Eichengrün remained free and continued his research at home until he was imprisoned for four months in 1943 for failing to include the statutory "Israel" as part of his name in a letter to a Reich official. In May 1944, he was deported to Theriesenstadt concentration camp until its liberation by the Red Army. He returned to Berlin after the war to continue his scientific work in private.

Eichengrün received honorary doctorates from the Technical Universities of Hannover (1929) and Berlin (1947). In 1948 he moved to Bad Wiessee in Bavaria, where he died on 23 December 1949.

BIBLIOGRAPHY

WORKS BY EICHENGRÜN

"Pharmazeutisch wissenschaftliche Abteilung." In *Geschichte und Entwicklung der Farbenfabriken vormals Friedrich Bayer & Co.*, Vol. 2. "Böttinger Schrift", 409–416. Elberfeld, Germany: Farbenfabriken, 1918.

"Photographische und technische Abteilung." In *Geschichte und Entwicklung der Farbenfabriken vormals Friedrich Bayer & Co.*, Vol. 2. "Böttinger Schrift", 457–462. Elberfeld, Germany: Farbenfabriken, 1918.

"Acetylcellulosen (Celluloseacetate)." In *Enzyklopädie der technischen Chemie*, edited by Fritz Ullmann., 2nd ed., Vol. 1. Berlin: Urban & Schwarzenberg, 1928.

"Cellit (I.G.)." In *Enzyklopädie der technischen Chemie*, edited by Fritz Ullmann., 2nd ed., Vol. 3. Berlin: Urban & Schwarzenberg, 1929.

"Cellon-Lacke." In *Enzyklopädie der technischen Chemie*, edited by Fritz Ullmann., 2nd ed., Vol. 3. Berlin: Urban & Schwarzenberg, 1929

"50 Jahre Aspirin." *Die Pharmazie* 4 (1949): 582–584.

OTHER SOURCES

Bodenbender, H. G. "A. Eichengrün zum 80. Geburtstag." *Angewandte Chemie* 60 (1948): A111–A112. On Eichengrün's contributions to the plastics industry, written on the occasion of his eightieth birthday.

Sneader, Walter. "The Discovery of Aspirin: A Reappraisal." *British Medical Journal* 321 (2000): 1591–1594.

Vaupel, Elisabeth. "Arthur Eichengrün—Tribute to a Forgotten Chemist, Entrepreneur, and German Jew." *Angewandte Chemie International Edition* 44 (2005): 3344–3355.

———. "Cellit-Lacke und Cellon-Fenster: Die Kunstoffe des Chemikers Arthur Eichengrün und ihre Bedeutung für den Zeppelinbau." In *Wissenschaftliches Jahrbuch 2006*, edited by Zeppelin Museum Friedrichshafen. Friedrichshafen, Germany: Verlag Robert Gessler, 2006. On Eichengrün's contributions to the plastics and aircraft industry.

Wimmer, Wolfgang. *Wir haben fast immer was Neues: Gesundheitswesen und Innovationen der Pharma-Industrie in Deutschland, 1880–1935*. Berlin: Duncker & Humblot, 1994. An overview of the German pharmaceutical industry.

Walter Sneader

EILENBERG, SAMUEL

EILENBERG, SAMUEL (*b.* Warsaw, Russian Empire [later Poland], 13 September 1913; *d.* New York, New York, 30 January 1998), *mathematics, specifically algebraic topology, category theory, and automata theory.*

Eilenberg, one of the architects of twentieth-century mathematics, transformed mathematicians' ways of thinking about topology and, in the process, helped found two major branches of mathematics—homological algebra and category theory—that he later applied to the theory of automata. Topology is an elastic version of geometry that retains the idea of continuity but relaxes rigid metric notions of distance. Its ideas were first introduced by Henri Poincaré in the early twentieth century, but topology became a central frontier of mathematical research only in the latter half of that century, with the introduction of powerful algebraic methods, largely pioneered by Eilenberg.

Early Life and Career. Little is known of Eilenberg's family life in Poland. Eilenberg recounted in a conversation with Peter Freyd, "My mother's father had the town brewery and he had one child, a daughter. He went to the head of the town Yeshiva and asked for the best student. ... So my future father became a brewer instead of a rabbi" (Bass et al, p. 1350). As a personal presence Eilenberg was, throughout his life, short, energetic (for example, an enthusiastic swimmer in his youth), expressive, charismatic, quick witted, often confrontational, and a brilliant thinker and good-humored conversationalist. He was single, except for his marriage to Natasha Chterenzon from 1960 to 1969. His development as a mathematician began at the University of Warsaw, in the vibrant Polish school of general topology. After receiving his master of arts degree in 1934, Eilenberg began his thesis, concerned with the topology of the plane and written under the direction of Karol Borsuk. It was well received abroad as

Samuel Eilenberg. WITH PERMISSION OF THE UNIVERSITY ARCHIVES, COLUMBIA UNIVERSITY IN THE CITY OF NEW YORK.

well as in Poland, and Eilenberg received his PhD in 1936. He published prodigiously, largely in French, during his early years in Poland, and so he already had an international reputation when he left that nation.

Early in 1939, on the advice of his father, Eilenberg left Poland for New York. Soon after his arrival he went to Princeton, New Jersey, where Oswald Veblen and Solomon Lefschetz of Princeton University were welcoming refugee mathematicians and finding them suitable positions at American universities. By this time, Eilenberg had already come to be called "Sammy" by all mathematicians who knew him. He joined the Topology Group then being developed by Ray Wilder at the University of Michigan, which came to include such major figures as Norman Steenrod, Deane Montgomery, Hans Samelson, Raoul Bott, and Steven Smale.

At Michigan: Eilenberg and Steenrod. At the University of Michigan began Eilenberg's collaboration with Steenrod, which led to their axiomatization of homology theory and to their landmark book, *Foundations of Algebraic Topology* (1952), which synthesized and crystallized the then-chaotic state of the field. Eilenberg's contributions to this work earned him the Leroy P. Steele Prize of the American Mathematical Society in 1987. Axiomatization afforded important advantages. Verification of the axioms became an elegantly efficient way to establish the equivalence of different definitions of homology. Moreover, the axioms and variations on them provided a general and uniform framework for mathematical development, the results of which apply to all models of the axioms, often well beyond those that first motivated their introduction.

Such a program of development was vigorously pursued in what, after this Eilenberg-Steenrod publication, came to be called Algebraic Topology. In building up the vast algebraic machinery for the development of algebraic topology, Eilenberg began long-term collaborations with Henri Cartan of the Université de Paris and with Saunders Mac Lane of the University of Chicago. Though his mathematical ideas may have seemed to have a kind of crystalline austerity, Eilenberg was a warm, robust, and very animated human being, for whom mathematics was a social activity—whence his many collaborations. He liked to do mathematics on his feet, often prancing while he explained his thoughts. When something connected, one could read it in his impish smile and the sparkle in his eyes.

At Columbia: Eilenberg and Cartan, and Bourbaki. Eilenberg first met Cartan in 1947 in New York City, when he began his thirty-five-year career at Columbia University. Eilenberg also later lectured in Paris in the "Séminaire Cartan" (Cartan Seminar) at the École normale supérieure (Superior normal school), then attended by the students Jean-Pierre Serre and Armand Borel. His collaboration with Cartan evolved into the epochal work, *Homological Algebra* (1956). This book identified and systematized the fundamental algebraic structures that supported the new Algebraic Topology but put them on an autonomous algebraic footing—a grand work of distillation and synthesis. The tools and language of homological algebra later infiltrated, often in deep ways, every branch of mathematics.

Eilenberg's French connection went deeper. In 1949, André Weil invited Eilenberg to participate in what was called Bourbaki, an illustrious but anonymous group of French mathematicians who were writing, under the pseudonym of Nicolas Bourbaki, a multivolume tome aimed at providing a coherent and rigorous treatment of the fundamental structures of all of contemporary mathematics. Eilenberg, as one of the rare non-French members, collaborated actively with Bourbaki for the next fifteen years.

Eilenberg and Mac Lane. Eilenberg's other great collaboration, with Saunders Mac Lane, began when, in 1940, the latter came to lecture in Michigan on "group extensions," a fundamental construction in the theory of groups, which is the mathematical theory of symmetry. Eilenberg immediately saw connections that answered a problem that had been raised by Steenrod. Eilenberg and Mac Lane stayed up the night working out details of what later evolved into a major series of papers that founded the cohomology theory of groups, among other things. (This research was done partly in the spare hours of wartime work on the mathematics of ballistics.) Much of the early work of Eilenberg and Mac Lane, beyond its important contributions to algebraic topology, served as a precursor to *Homological Algebra*.

Most significantly, Mac Lane understood and came to embrace Eilenberg's mathematical spirit and method, which was to look always for fundamental explanatory structures, unencumbered by anything extraneous, that made the mathematics flow naturally, almost inevitably, in a way that demystified the complex. Eilenberg believed philosophically that all mathematics, once properly understood, would submit to such treatment. Mac Lane captured part of Eilenberg's spirit with the maxim, "Dig deep and deeper, till you get to the bottom of each issue." Eilenberg's student, Alex Heller, expressed it as "his radical insistence on lucidity, order, and understanding as opposed to trophy hunting." Peter Freyd, another of Eilenberg's students, expressed it more lyrically as a "triumph of style over substance" (all quotations from Bass et al.) Eilenberg's honorary degree from the University of Pennsylvania in 1985 cited him as "our greatest mathematical stylist."

Eilenberg's Mathematical Legacy. In the words of Eilenberg's Columbia colleague, John Morgan, "The theme that runs through Sammy's mathematics is always to find the absolutely essential ingredients in any problem and work only with those ingredients and nothing else—in other words, get rid of all the superfluous information." For example, when someone once asked Eilenberg if he could eat Chinese food with three chopsticks, he answered, "Of course." The questioner then asked, "How are you going to do it?" and Eilenberg replied, "I'll take the three chopsticks, I'll put one of them aside on the table, and I'll use the other two" (Pace, p. B9).

The greatest monument of Eilenberg and Mac Lane's work is the field of category theory, substantially created by them and their students and disciples. While some of the seeds of category theory were already visible in *Homological Algebra*, it emerges as a kind of reification of the formalisms of all of mathematics, in terms of "matter" (objects) and "motion" (transformations, or arrows).

What is remarkable, at this extreme level of abstraction and voiding of internal meaning, is how much interesting and useful mathematics remains to be done, and discovered. Indeed, the innocuous-seeming 1945 paper of Eilenberg and Mac Lane, "General Theory of Natural Equivalences," in which categories were first defined, was first rejected by the editor of an inauspicious journal as "more devoid of content than any I have read." To which Mac Lane is said to have replied, "That's the point." Besides becoming, in the hands of Eilenberg's students—notably William Lawvere—a vigorous field in its own right, category theory also helped shape Alexandre Grothendieck's refounding of modern algebraic geometry, and it has had significant applications in logic, theoretical computer science, linguistics, and philosophy. Eilenberg and Mac Lane continued throughout their careers to nurture the lively international community of category theorists, for which they became venerated and generous patriarchs. The fifteen joint papers of Eilenberg and Mac Lane are assembled in *Eilenberg-Mac Lane, Collected Works* (1986).

Eilenberg also adopted a categorical approach to the last phase of his mathematical work, which was in automata theory, a branch of theoretical computer science. This resulted in the two-volume work, *Automata, Languages, and Machines* (1974–1976).

Eilenberg and Columbia University. Eilenberg spent most of his mathematical career in the Mathematics Department of Columbia University, which he twice chaired. He helped develop it into a major center of pure mathematical research. Beyond his many doctoral students, including David Buchsbaum, Peter Freyd, Alex Heller, Daniel Kan, William Lawvere, Fred Linton, and Steven Schanuel, he was an important mentor to many of the postdoctoral fellows at Columbia, this author included. In 1982, Columbia named Eilenberg a university professor, the highest faculty distinction that the university confers.

Eilenberg was a member of the National Academy of Sciences (U.S.A.) and the American Academy of Arts and Sciences. In 1986, Eilenberg shared the Wolf Prize in mathematics, "for his fundamental work in algebraic topology and homological algebra." His co-awardee was the number theorist, Atle Selberg.

Art Collector and Dealer. Though a celebrated and well-liked mathematician on the world stage, Eilenberg also lived in another world, separate and almost parallel to that of mathematics, but intersecting it, by design, only near the end of his career. In one world lived "Sammy," the mathematician; in the other world lived the "Professor," famous as a dealer in and collector of art, a world where few who knew the "Professor" knew that he was also a celebrated mathematician. The "Professor's" interest was specifically Southeast Asian sculpture, of which Eilenberg gradually accumulated a rare and valuable collection. His collecting began on excursions during mathematical visits to India in the mid-1950s. He found in ancient Hindu sculpture a formal elegance and imagination that resonated well with the same aesthetic sensibility—"classical rather than romantic," in the words of Alex Heller—that animated his mathematical work.

Not being particularly wealthy, he chose a niche that leveraged his modest material resources, refined aesthetic judgment, and acute skills as a dealer to best advantage. He generally gathered small pieces from regions and periods that were not yet saturated by the current art market. He often found his way to primary sources and became a world expert—widely consulted by dealers and curators—in the genre, on both authentic and counterfeit pieces. His collection of Javanese bronzes was said to be the most important group outside Indonesia and the Netherlands. After thirty years of collecting, his collection was estimated in 1989 to be worth more than $5 million. Parts of his collection have been exhibited in major museums—the Metropolitan Museum of Art in New York City, the Arthur M. Sackler Gallery in Washington, D.C., the Dallas Museum of Art, the Cleveland Museum of Art, the Brooklyn Museum, and the British Museum in London, as well as the Victoria and Albert Museum in London. Mathematician friends of Eilenberg could glimpse some of the gems of his collections in his apartments, one on Riverside Drive in New York City, the other in London, near Buckingham Palace. They seemed among the principal occupants of these templelike living spaces.

Eilenberg's art and mathematical worlds intersected when, in 1989, he donated more than four hundred valuable sculptures to the Metropolitan Museum of Art. In turn, the Metropolitan raised, through general funds and with contributions by others, most of the $1.5 million needed to endow the Samuel Eilenberg Visiting Professorship of Mathematics at Columbia University. This elegant maneuver, optimizing outcomes for all concerned, was a vintage Eilenberg design. The Eilenberg Visiting Professorship has brought many of the world's leading mathematicians to Columbia.

Eilenberg's aesthetic sensibility also valued the artisanship and imagination of more mundane objects, as shown in another collection he assembled, this time of Indian betel nut cutters. These are often ornate hinged devices, typically made of brass, for cutting the hard betel nut that is commonly chewed in South Asia. The forms and ornamentation of them can be extravagantly imaginative and expressive. Previously little recognized in the art world, Eilenberg's collection, described in Henry

Brownrigg's *Betel Cutters from the Samuel Eilenberg Collection* (1992), helped create a niche for these objects in the art collectors' world.

Eilenberg led a full and active life till, in 1995, in New York City, he suffered a stroke. He remained mentally alert but was bedridden; sadly, he lost his ability to speak. His health remained frail. In June 1997, he fell into a coma, a state in which he lingered until his death of cardiac arrest at a geriatric center in New York City in January 1998, at the age of eighty-four.

BIBLIOGRAPHY

WORKS BY EILENBERG

With Saunders Mac Lane. "General Theory of Natural Equivalences." *Transactions of the American Mathematical Society* 58 (1945): 231–294. This modest paper is generally considered the birthplace of category theory.

With Norman Steenrod. *Foundations of Algebraic Topology.* Princeton, NJ: Princeton University Press, 1952.

With Henri Cartan. *Homological Algebra.* Princeton, NJ: Princeton University Press, 1956. Translated into Spanish and Russian.

With Calvin C. Elgot. *Recursiveness.* New York: Academic Press, 1970.

Automata, Languages, and Machines. 2 vols. New York, Academic Press, 1974–1976.

With Saunders Mac Lane. *Eilenberg-Mac Lane, Collected Works.* Orlando, FL: Academic Press, 1986.

OTHER SOURCES

Bass, Hyman, et al. "Samuel Eilenberg (1913–1998)." *Notices of the American Mathematical Society* 45, no. 10 (1998): 1344–1352. An extended memorial article.

Brownrigg, Henry. *Betel Cutters: From the Samuel Eilenberg Collection.* London; New York: Thames and Hudson, 1992.

Lerner, Martin, and Steven Kossak. *The Lotus Transcendent: Indian and Southeast Asian Art from the Samuel Eilenberg Collection.* New York: Metropolitan Museum of Art, 1991.

Pace, Eric. "Samuel Eilenberg, 84, Dies; Mathematician at Columbia." *New York Times,* 3 February 1998, p. B9.

Hyman Bass

EINSTEIN, ALBERT (*b.* Ulm, Germany, 14 March 1879; *d.* Princeton, New Jersey, 18 April 1955) *physics.* For the original article on Einstein see *DSB,* vol. 4.

This essay extends and corrects the original entries by Martin J. Klein and Nandor L. Balazs, drawing on recent work in a variety of areas: experimental tests of general relativity and the role of the cosmological constant; new topics based on recently available information, such as the Einstein family business and its influence on young Einstein; his love affairs, first and second marriages, and other women in his life; black hole physics; and inadequate discussions of the nature of Einstein's light quantum hypothesis; the reasons for his discontent with quantum mechanics; the origins of special relativity and the role of local time; the development of general relativity and the role of metric, affine connection, and Riemann tensor in the theory; his views on the significance of general relativity and the relation between physics and geometry; and his hopes for a unified field theory.

Einstein Family Business. The Einstein brothers' Munich electrical engineering firm built and installed dynamos, power plants, and electric lighting systems, largely invented and patented by Albert's uncle Jakob (1850–1912), an engineer. The new, enlarged factory, started in 1885 with financial help from his mother Pauline's (1858–1920) wealthy father, was managed by his father Hermann (1847–1902), a businessman. The dynamo division alone employed some fifty people. The firm was initially rather successful, and total employment at its height has been estimated at 150–200 (for the family business in Munich, see Hettler, 1996). But after an acrimonious dispute with its larger German rivals, the firm lost the lighting contract for the city of Munich in 1893.

The brothers decided to move to Northern Italy, where they had already installed several power plants, and in 1895 they built a large factory in Pavia. Their efforts to secure a contract to supply the city with electrical power failed due to various local intrigues, and they again had to liquidate their firm in 1896, losing almost everything in the process (for the Italian firm, see Winteler-Einstein, 1924). Uncle Jakob went to work for another firm but, despite Albert's warnings, his father opened a small electrical firm in Milan. Albert helped out from time to time during school vacations, but was able to finish his education only with financial help from his mother's wealthy family.

Prematurely aged by his financial troubles, Hermann died in 1902 deeply in debt to Rudolf Einstein (1843–1928), his cousin and brother-in-law. Young Albert had just started work at the Swiss Patent Office and was unable to support his mother or sister Maja (1881–1951). He had originally been destined to take over the family business and, as an adolescent, demonstrated considerable technical aptitude in electrotechnology, which later stood him in good stead at the Patent Office (1902–1909). But his father's business failures and the attendant stress on the family contributed to an aversion to commercial activities for profit that ultimately led to his critique of capitalism and espousal of socialism (for Albert's early development, see *The Collected Papers,* vol. 1, passim; and John Stachel,

"New Introduction" to Einstein, 2005). "I was also originally supposed to be a technical worker. But the thought of having to expend my inventive power on things, which would only make workaday life more complicated with the goal of dreary oppression by capital, was unbearable to me" (translation from Stachel, 2005, "New Introduction," p. xxxiii; see Einstein, 1949, for his later condemnation of the profit system).

Einstein's Love Affairs. The plaster saint image of Einstein, carefully cultivated by his executors, has been shaken by the disclosure of his many love affairs before, during, and after his two marriages. There is now a danger that the myth of the white-haired saint will be replaced by that of a devil incarnate ("father of the atom bomb," "plagiarist," "thief of his wife's ideas"), but what is starting to emerge is something much more interesting than saint or devil: the rounded portrait of a human being (for a discussion of some common myths, see Brian, 2005).

While a student at the Aargau Kantonsschule (a Realschule, not a Gymnasium) in Aarau (1895–1896), Einstein boarded with the family of Jost ("Papa," 1846–1929) Winteler, a teacher at the school and his wife Pauline ("Momma," 1845–1906), with whom he developed close and lasting relationships. His sister later married Paul (1882–1952), one of the Winteler sons, and he had a brief love affair with their daughter Marie (1877–1957), which she later described as "innig [deep]" but "durchaus ideal [completely ideal]." It ended when he moved to Zurich in 1896 to attend the Zurich Poly (1896–1900), where he met Mileva Marić (1875–1948), the only other physics student to enter the program for teachers of mathematics and physics. The two began to study physics together and became intensely involved emotionally during their last years at the Poly. His letters to her from this period (see Einstein, 1992) are the major contemporary source of information on his scientific interests before his first published paper (1901). There is no evidence in his letters or in hers to support claims that she played more than a supporting role in his early research activities (for discussions of their relationship, see Stachel, 2002c; Stachel, 1996; and Martinez, 2005); she was the first of a series of "sounding boards" that he needed in order to help put the fruits of his research, carried out alone and with the aid of non-verbal symbolic systems, into a form that could be communicated to others (for further discussion, including an account of his mode of thought, see the "Introduction to the Centenary Edition" of Einstein, 2005).

After he graduated (she failed the final examinations twice due to poor grades in mathematics), they had a daughter out of wedlock, Lieserl (b. 1902), whose fate is unknown. But they lived apart until his job at the Swiss Patent Office (1902–1909) enabled their marriage in 1903. During these years Einstein did much of his research during working hours, and later stated, "The work on the final formulation of technical patents was a true blessing … and also provided important inspiration for physical ideas" (Einstein, 1956, p. 12). His first biographer reports: "He recognizes a definite connection between the knowledge acquired at the patent office and the theoretical results which, at that same time, emerged as examples of the acuteness of his thinking" (Moszkowski, 1921, p. 22).

In 1909 Einstein obtained his first academic post in theoretical physics at the University of Zurich, and his career slowly began to prosper, with successive posts in Prague and the Zurich Poly. He drifted away from Marić, later attributing his alienation to her taciturnity, jealousy, and depressive personality. By 1912 he was having an affair with Elsa Löwenthal (1876–1936), his cousin and childhood friend. She was a divorcee living in Berlin with her parents—her father Rudolf had been his father's chief creditor. Albert's move to Berlin in 1914 as a newly-elected member of Prussian Academy of Sciences precipitated a crisis in the marriage and Mileva returned to Zurich with their two sons, where she remained for the rest of her life.

After Albert's divorce from Mileva and marriage to Elsa in 1919, he continued to have numerous affairs. In Berlin, the women included Betty Neumann, his secretary; Tony Mendel; and Margarete Lebach; after his move to Princeton in 1933 they included Margarita Konenkova, a Russian citizen living in the United States who has been accused of being a spy (see Pogrebin, 1998, for excerpts from his letters to Konenkova after her return to Russia in 1945; and Schneir, 1998, for contradictions in the spy story). His last close companion was Princeton librarian Johanna Fantova, an old friend from Europe (see Calaprice, 2005 for Fantova's diary of her conversations with Einstein).

Einstein's Light Quantum Hypothesis. In 1905 Einstein characterized only one of his papers as "very revolutionary," the one that "deals with radiation and the energetic properties of light." Klein comments: "Einstein leaped to the conclusion that the radiation … must consist of independent particle of energy" (p. 315), but a reading of the 1905 light quantum paper shows that he did not. He characterizes his demonstration that, in a certain limit, black body radiation behaves as if it were composed of energy quanta, as "a heuristic viewpoint"; and in 1909 warned against just this misunderstanding: "In fact, I am not at all of the opinion that light can be thought of as composed of quanta that are independent of each other and localized in relatively small spaces. This would indeed be the most convenient explanation of the Wien region of the radiation spectrum. But just the division of a light ray at the surface of a refracting medium completely forbids this outlook. A light ray divides itself, but a light quantum cannot divide without a change of frequency" (Einstein to H. A. Lorentz, 23 May 1909, Collected Papers, vol. 5, p. 193). It was only in 1915 that other considerations led him to attribute momentum to a light quantum (see p. 317), and only a decade later, after Bose's work (see pp. 317–318) had shown that elementary particles need not be statistically independent, did he describe them as particles (see Stachel, 2000).

Speaking of Einstein's first paper on mass-energy equivalence, Balazs writes: "[Einstein] observed that the exchange of radiation between bodies should involve an exchange of mass; light quanta have mass exactly as do ordinary molecules" (p. 323). But in his derivation of this result, Einstein speaks about a "light complex," an entirely classical concept, rather than about a light quantum. In his early works, Einstein never mixed concepts from his quantum papers with those from his relativity papers. And when, after Bose's work, he did attribute corpuscular properties to light quanta, he distinguished clearly between photons (a word he did not use), zero rest mass bosons (another word introduced later) whose number need not be conserved; and massive bosons, whose number must be conserved. His prediction of a condensed state for massive bosons (see Einstein, 1925), now called a Bose-Einstein condensate, offered the first theoretical explanation of a transition between two phases of a system. The prediction was spectacularly confirmed some seventy years later, winning its discoverers the 2001 Nobel prize in physics.

Discontent [*Unbehagen*] with Quantum Mechanics. Speaking of Einstein's "Discontent with Quantum Mechanics," Klein cites (p. 318) its basically statistical nature and presumed incompleteness as the reasons. Actually, Einstein believed that, if one adopted the statistical ensemble interpretation of quantum mechanics (which he referred to as the Born interpretation, but had actually adumbrated; see Stachel, 1986, Sections 5 and 7), there was no problem with the theory. For him, the problem came when the theory was applied to an individual system: it was here that the issue arose of completeness of the quantum mechanical description. A careful reading of his comments on this topic (see Stachel, 1986) shows that the issue of non-separability was the most fundamental cause of his "*Unbehagen.*" As Wolfgang Pauli explained: "Einstein does not consider the concept of 'determinism' to be as fundamental as it is frequently held to be. … he *disputes* that he uses as a criterion for the admissibility of a theory the question 'Is it rigorously deterministic?'" (Pauli to Max Born, 31 March 1954, quoted from Stachel, 1991, p. 411). Once they interact, two quantum systems remain entangled, no

matter how far apart in time and space they may have traveled. To Einstein, this seemed to contradict his expectation, based on the role of space-time in his relativity theories, that two systems, sufficiently separated in space-time, should not exert any physical influence on each other.

> Does it make sense to say that two parts *A* and *B* of a system do exist independently of each other if they are (in ordinary language) located in different parts of space at a certain time, if there are no considerable interactions between those parts … at the considered time? … I mean by "independent of each other" that an action on *A* has no immediate influence on the part *B*. In this sense I express a principle a) independent existence of the spatially separated. This has to be considered with the other thesis b) the ψ-function is the complete description of the individual physical situation. My thesis is that a) and b) cannot be true together …. The majority of quantum theorists discard a) tacitly to be able to conserve b). I, however, have strong confidence in a), so I feel compelled to relinquish b). (Einstein to Leon Cooper, 31 October 1949, quoted from Stachel, 1986, p. 375)

Since then the formulation of Bell's inequality and its experimental testing by Clauser, Horne, and Shimony, and by Aspect, have convinced most physicists that quantum entanglement is not the result of an incompleteness due to neglected statistical correlations, as Einstein suggested. Whatever the ultimate fate of contemporary quantum mechanics, entanglement seems destined to remain a fundamental feature of any future physical theory (for a review of this topic, with references to the original literature, see Shimony, 2006).

Origin of Special Relativity. Balazs points out: "By [Einstein's] own testimony the failure of the ether-drift experiments did not play a determinative role in his thinking but merely provided additional evidence in favor of his belief that inasmuch as the phenomena of electrodynamics were 'relativistic,' the theory would have to be reconstructed accordingly" (p. 320). In fact, the phenomena of the optics of moving bodies also played a major role in the development of his ideas. In 1952 he wrote: "My direct path to the special theory of relativity was mainly determined by the conviction that the electromotive force induced in a conductor moving in a magnetic field is nothing other than an electric field. But the result of Fizeau's experiment and the phenomenon of aberration also guided me" (quoted from Stachel, 1989, p. 262).

As Balazs explains (p. 320), the conductor-magnet example suggested to Einstein that the relativity principle must be extended from mechanics to electromagnetic theory. He then attempted to reconcile the relativity principle with well-known optical phenomena, in particular the

Albert Einstein. *Physicist Albert Einstein writing an equation on a blackboard.* © BETTMANN/CORBIS.

constancy of the velocity of light. Two main alternatives presented themselves: (1) The velocity of light is independent of that of its source, constant relative to the ether; or (2) The velocity of light is constant relative to its source (ballistic theory of light—light behaves like a bullet).

Lorentz's version of Maxwell's theory, based on the first alternative, was able to explain the result of Fizeau's experiment and the phenomenon of aberration, but did not seem to be compatible with the relativity principle—the ether frame of reference is special. So Einstein explored the second alternative, where the situation was just the reverse: The relativity principle presented no problem if one assumed that a moving medium dragged the ether along within it. But Fizeau's experiment on the velocity of light in moving water, interpreted within the framework of an ether theory, seemed to preclude the idea that ether was totally dragged along by matter. Rather, it confirmed Fresnel's formula, which had been developed to account for aberration and predicted a partial dragging of the ether (see Stachel, 2005a).

Attempts to explain Fizeau's experiment using the second alternative led to more and more complications, so Einstein returned to the first, but with a crucial difference: he dropped the ether. He realized that the relativity principle then requires the velocity of light to be a universal constant, the same in all inertial frames of reference. But how is this possible? He pondered this question for several years. Finally in 1905 came the insight that removed the puzzle. It is possible if one gives up the Galileian law of addition of relative velocities! A reanalysis of the concept of time showed that the proof of this law depended on the existence of an absolute time, which implies that one can always say whether two events are simultaneous, however far apart. But careful analysis of the concept of simultaneity showed that one must *define* when two events occurring at some distance from each other are simultaneous. He showed that one could adopt definition that made the velocity of light the same in all inertial frames—but this definition gives a different answer in each inertial frame and results in a new law for addition of relative velocities.

Einstein's new definition of frame-dependent time is closely related to Lorentz's concept of local time, as Balazs points out "Although Lorentz appears to have viewed local time as a mathematical artifice, it represented in embryo a concept of time that Einstein would later justify adopting for the whole of physics" (p. 321). In 1900 Poincaré had given a physical interpretation of the local time within the ether-theoretical framework: It is the time that clocks in a moving frame of reference would read (compared with clocks at rest in the ether, which read the true, absolute time) if they were synchronized using light signals, but without correcting for the effects of motion through the ether on the propagation of light. Einstein may well have been familiar with Poincaré's work, but his crucial idea was to drop all reference to the ether and accept the local time of each inertial frame as just as good as that of any other.

Development of General Relativity. Einstein divided his work on general relativity into three key steps (for the first two steps, see Stachel, 2002b; for the third step, see Janssen et al., 2007, vol. 2.).

The first step, in 1907, was his "basic idea for the general theory of relativity" (Stachel, 2002b, p. 261). He was referring to his formulation of the equivalence principle—the inability to uniquely separate gravitation and inertia. Balazs states: "Einstein published two remarkable memoirs in 1912 which were efforts to construct a complete theory of gravitation incorporating the equivalence principle" (p. 326). Actually, they were an attempt to construct equations only for a static field, as well as the equations of motion of a test particle in such a field. His recognition that the latter equations describe the geodesics of a non-flat space-time was a major clue that led to the second step, in 1912: his "recognition of the non-Euclidean nature of the metric and of its physical determination by gravitation" (Stachel, 2002b, p. 261). He was referring to the adoption of the metric tensor as the representation of the gravitational potentials.

The third step came with his "1915 field equations of gravitation. Explanation of the perihelion motion of Mercury" (Stachel 2002b, p. 261). Einstein was referring to the final form of the field equations, which he announced on 25 November 1915. This corrects the erroneous date of 25 March given in the table on p. 324 and on p. 327. The correct date, when combined with Balazs' statement: "[O]n 20 November, David Hilbert, in Göttingen, independently found the same field equations" (p. 327). might suggest that Hilbert actually had priority, a claim that is still maintained by some scholars in the face of new evidence to the contrary (for a review of Hilbert's role in the development of general relativity, see Renn and Stachel, 2007).

Role of the Affine Connection. A fourth key step may be added: Recognition of the affine connection and parallel displacement as the correct mathematical representation of the inerto-gravitational field (for a discussion of the role of the affine connection in the development of gravitation theory, see Stachel, 2007). This step was first taken by Tullio Levi-Civita in 1917, but Einstein came to recognize its crucial importance:

It is the essential achievement of the general theory of relativity that it freed physics from the necessity of introducing the "inertial system" (or inertial systems). (*The Meaning of Relativity*, p. 139)

The development ... of the mathematical theories essential for the setting up of general relativity had the result that at first the Riemannian metric was considered the fundamental concept on which the general theory of relativity and thus the avoidance of the inertial system were based. Later, however, Levi-Civita rightly pointed out that the element of the theory that makes it possible to avoid the inertial system is rather the infinitesimal [parallel] displacement field Γ^l_{ik}. The metric or the symmetric tensor field g_{ik} which defines it is only indirectly connected with the avoidance of the inertial system in so far as it determines a displacement field. (*The Meaning of Relativity*, p. 141)

The mathematical formulation of the equivalence principle is that "the displacement field," also called the affine connection, represents a single inertio-gravitational field.

In all previous physical theories, including the special theory, the space-time structures, metric and connection, had been fixed, background fields, determining the kinematics of space-time: the stage, on which the drama of matter and dynamical fields takes place. With the dynamization of these space-time structures, the stage now became part of the play; moreover a new kind of physics was born, now called background-independent to contrast it with all theories based on fixed background space-time.

Balazs writes: "Gravitation is a universal manifestation because it is a property of space-time, and hence everything that is in space-time (which is, literally, everything) must experience it" (p. 331). But Einstein opposed such a "container" or absolute concept of space-time and forcefully advocated a relational approach to space-time (see, for example, Einstein, 1954), preferring to say that space-time is a property of the gravitational field:

[A]ccording to the special theory of relativity, space (space-time) has an existence independent of matter or field. In order to be able to describe at all that which fills up space ..., space-time or the inertial system with its metrical properties must be thought of at once as existing, for otherwise the description of "that which fills up space" would have no meaning. On the basis of the general theory of relativity, on the other hand, space as opposed to "what fills space" ... has no separate existence. ... If we imagine the gravitational field, i.e., the functions g_{ik} to be removed, there does not remain a space of the type (1) [Minkowski space-time], but absolutely *nothing*, and also no "topological space". ... There is no such thing as an empty space, i.e., a space without field. Space-time does not claim existence on its own, but only as a structural quality of the field. (Einstein, 1952, p. 155).

Balazs writes: "In this way Einstein showed that gravitational fields influence the motion of clocks" (p. 325). Presumably, Balazs meant the rate of clocks, but even that statement would be inaccurate. General relativity is built precisely on the assumption that (ideal) clocks and measuring rods are *not* affected by the presence of an inertio-gravitational field. However, the rates of two clocks at different places in a gravitational field cannot be directly compared. (If the two clocks are brought to the same place for direct comparison, according to general relativity they will always agree!) Some signal must pass between them. It is the difference between the frequency with which a signal is emitted by one clock and the frequency with which the signal is detected at the position of the other clock that is responsible for gravitational effects on time measurements, such as the gravitational red shift.

Balazs writes "In particular [Einstein] assumed that ... the history of a body will be a geodesic ... the curve in space-time for which $\int ds$ is a minimum, $\delta \int ds = 0$" (p. 227). While this integral is always an *extremal* of the space-time interval for geodesic curves, for time-like paths it is a *maximum*. This is the basis of the twin paradox: The stay-at-home, non-accelerating twin will be much older than his adventurous, accelerating sibling when the two meet again.

Balazs writes "$\Theta_{\mu\nu}$ contains the material sources of the field ... In any given physical situation, the $\Theta_{\mu\nu}$ may be assumed known" (p. 227). In fact, the expression for $\Theta_{\mu\nu}$, the stress-energy-momentum tensor (later in the article symbolized by $T_{\mu\nu}$), almost always contains the metric tensor, so the gravitational field equations cannot be solved separately. Rather, one must solve the coupled sets of equations for the source fields and for the metric field.

Curvature Tensors and Field Equations. Balazs writes "[T]he gravitational field can be characterized by Riemann's curvature tensor $G_{\mu\nu}$ .... [Einstein] wrote the gravitational field equations as $G_{\mu\nu} = K(T_{\mu\nu} - 1/2\, g_{\mu\nu}T)$, where T is the scalar of the material energy tensor $T_{\mu\nu}$ and K is a gravitational constant. ... The curvature of space-time at a point is determined by the amount of matter and electromagnetic field and their motion at that point" (p. 328). There are several errors here. First, Balazs' $G_{\mu\nu}$ is the Ricci tensor, not the Riemann curvature tensor. The Riemann tensor is a four-index tensor $R^\kappa_{\mu\lambda\nu}$, the trace of which is equal to the Ricci tensor: $R^\kappa_{\mu\kappa\nu} = G_{\mu\nu}$, in Balazs' notation. The Ricci tensor is more commonly denoted by $R_{\mu\nu}$, whereas $G_{\mu\nu}$ is used to denote the Einstein tensor $R_{\mu\nu} - 1/2\, g_{\mu\nu}R$, where R is the trace of the Ricci tensor. The gravitational field equations are now more commonly written in the form: $R_{\mu\nu} - 1/2\, g_{\mu\nu}R = KT_{\mu\nu}$, which is equivalent to Einstein's original form.

Second, according to Einstein, it is the affine connection that defines the inertio-gravitational field, not the Riemann tensor:

What characterizes the existence of a gravitational field from the empirical standpoint is the non-vanishing of the Γ^l_{ik} [components of the affine connection], not the non-vanishing of the R_{iklm} [the components of the Riemann tensor]. If one does not think in such intuitive ways, one cannot comprehend why something like curvature should have anything at all to do with gravitation. (Einstein to Max von Laue 1950; English translation from Stachel, 1989, p. 326)

The affine connection is not a tensor between systems of such particles. The Riemann tensor is built from its components and their first derivatives. The affine connection enters the geodesic equation—it would actually be better to say the equation for autoparallel or straightest lines—describing the motion of freely falling sructureless particles, while the Riemann tensor enters the equation of geodesic deviation, which characterizes the tidal gravitational forces between such particles.

A metric affine connection, as in general relativity, is built from the components of the metric and their first derivatives. In this case, the autoparallel lines are also metric geodesics. It follows that a metric Riemann tensor depends on the metric tensor and its first and second derivatives. In spite of Einstein's comments cited above, general relativity is still often presented entirely in terms of the metric tensor and its derivatives, without proper emphasis on the role of the connection.

The third error is that the curvature at a point of space-time is *not* "determined by the amount of matter and electromagnetic field and their motion *at that point.*" The Riemann tensor determined by a metric has twenty independent components at each point, and only the ten components of the Ricci tensor are so determined. It is the additional ten components that enable the propagation of gravitational waves, even in "empty" regions of space-time, that is, regions in which the Ricci tensor vanishes.

Tests of the General Theory. The theory has survived much more precise observations of the three classic predictions: the anomalous precession of Mercury's orbit, the gravitational red shift, and the apparent bending of light beams in strong gravitational fields. Indeed, the relativistic effects are now so well confirmed that they are routinely used in many new applications (for surveys, see Damour, 2006 and Will, 2005).

The gravitational bending effect is the basis of the phenomenon known as gravitational lensing, originally predicted by Einstein around 1912, but not published by him until 1936 (for Einstein's role, see Renn, Sauer, and Stachel, 1997). It is now a major tool in observational cosmology, particularly the study of the effects of "dark matter" in galaxies and clusters on light propagation (for gravitational lensing, see Schneider, Ehlers, and Falco, 1992). On a more everyday level, the ubiquitous Global Positioning System (GPS) could not operate without taking into account both special and general relativistic effects (see Ashby, 2005).

The major outstanding project is the direct detection of gravitational waves. Indirect confirmation of the emission of quadrupole gravitational radiation by the binary pulsar PSR 1913+16 through measurement of the resulting modification of the presumed back reaction on their orbits has been extremely successful, winning its observers the Nobel Prize for Physics in 1993 (see Will, 2005). But instruments designed to detect the radiation itself, notably the Laser Interferometer Gravitational-Wave Observatory (LIGO), did not attain sufficient sensitivity to "see" the extremely weak radiation predicted from astrophysical sources (see Saulson, 2005), or the even weaker background cosmological gravitational radiation predicted by some models of the early universe.

The Cosmological Constant. As Balazs points out, Einstein originally introduced the cosmological constant Λ in 1916 order to implement what he called Mach's principle: On a cosmological scale, the metric tensor field should be completely determined by matter. Einstein took it for granted that, on the average, the universe was static, so he developed such a static cosmological model, for which he needed Λ. When Alexander Friedmann first showed that there are non-static cosmological models with and without the cosmological constant, Einstein thought he had found an error in Friedmann's work. He quickly withdrew that claim, but regarded the expanding universe solutions as mere mathematical curiosities until the observations of Hubble around 1930 showed their importance for cosmology. By this time Einstein had abandoned Mach's principle in favor of the reverse, unified field viewpoint: The properties of matter should be completely determined by solutions to some set of unified field equations. Thus, the cosmological constant was no longer needed for its original purpose and there were expanding cosmological models without it, so Einstein abandoned the concept. Others, such as Eddington, kept Λ for other reasons, and it maintained a precarious foothold in cosmological speculations.

In the latter third of the twentieth century, the situation in cosmology began to change dramatically. Theoretical cosmology became more and more closely associated with elementary particle theory, and observational cosmology began to accumulate more and more data limiting the possibilities for and influencing the construction of cosmological models. The cosmological constant has had a dramatic rebirth with the accumulating observation evidence that, rather than slowing down as current theories had predicted, the expansion of the universe is actually accelerating with cosmic time. By an appropriate choice of sign and value for Λ, cosmological models with this property are easily constructed. The problem is to give a physical explanation for such a choice of Λ. One favored explanation as of 2007 is that the Λ-term in the field equations is actually the stress-energy-momentum tensor for "dark energy," a hitherto unobserved component pervading the entire universe. If this explanation stands the test of time, it may also turn out that the "cosmological constant" is not constant, but varies with cosmological time! (For a review of developments in cosmology, see Padmanabhan, 2005.)

Black Hole Physics. Since the original edition of the *DSB*, an entire industry has grown up within theoretical physics and observational astronomy known as "black hole physics" (for reviews, see Carter, 2006, and Price, 2005). It is based theoretically on the existence of two solutions to the homogeneous Einstein field equations: the static, spherically symmetric Schwarzschild solution, dating from 1916, and the stationary, axially symmetric Kerr solution, dating from 1963. (For reviews of these and other exact solutions to the Einstein equations, see Bičak, 2000.) Astrophysics predicts that sufficiently massive astrophysical objects ultimately undergo gravitational collapse as gravitation overwhelms the pressures and stresses that keep them from collapsing. If they are massive enough, this process will not be halted by the formation of a neutron star, but will continue until the system passes through an event horizon and forms a black hole, which ultimately ends in a singularity, signaling the breakdown of classical general relativity. This is the upshot of the famous Penrose-Hawking singularity theorems. The external gravitational field outside the horizon must ultimately take the form of either the Schwarzschild field if the system has no net angular momentum, or the Kerr solution if it does. This result was picturesquely stated as "black holes have no hair" by John Wheeler, who coined the term "black hole." Classically, except for their gravitational fields, such black holes have no influence on their exterior, but Stephen Hawking showed that a semi-classical treatment of quantum-mechanical effects predicts the formation of a radiation field outside the black hole that behaves like black-body radiation at a temperature dependent on the mass of the black hole. Much theoretical work is being done in the early 2000s in the attempt to find an exact quantum-gravitational treatment of black holes, and much observational work on the search for black holes in the cosmos.

Relation Between Geometry and Physics. Balazs asserts: "Minkowski recast the special theory of relativity in a form which had a decisive influence in the geometrization of physics. … This very strong geometrical point of view … led to Einstein's belief that all laws of nature should be geometrical propositions concerning space-time" (p. 323). Einstein's supposed "views on the geometrization of physics" are repeated: "He felt that not only the gravitational but also electromagnetic effects should be manifes-

tations of the geometry of space-time" (p. 325). Although many people continue to hold this view of Einstein's accomplishment and attribute it to him, Einstein explicitly rejected it. In 1928 he wrote: "I cannot agree that the assertion relativity reduces physics to geometry has a clear meaning. One can more correctly say that it follows from the theory of relativity that (metric) geometry has lost its independent existence with respect to the laws usually classified as physical. … That this metric tensor is designated as 'geometrical' is simply connected with the fact that the formal structures concerned first appeared in the science called 'geometry.' But this is not at all sufficient to justify applying the name 'geometry' to every science in which this formal structure plays a role, even when for purposes of visualization [*Veranschaulichung*] representations are used, to which geometry has habituated us. …" He explicitly rejected the idea that the search for a unified field theory was an attempt to geometrize the electromagnetic field: "The essential thing in Weyl's and Eddington's theoretical representations of the electromagnetic field does not lie in their having embedded the field in geometry, but that they have shown a possible way to represent gravitation and electromagnetism from a unified point of view" (Einstein, 1928; translated from the German manuscript, *The Einstein Archives Online*, Call Nr. [1-68.00]). Peter Bergmann has suggested that "physicalization of geometry" would be a more appropriate phrase (see Bergmann, 1979; the phrase had been used in Zubirini, 1934).

Balazs asserts: "[T]he geometrization of gravitation led eventually to the general theory of relativity; the additional geometrization of the electromagnetic fields of force led to the invention of the unified field theories." Apart from the use of geometrization language, criticized above, the statement may be misleading. The most successful "geometrization of the electromagnetic fields of force" has been achieved as part of the modern gauge theory of Yang-Mills fields. This has served to unify the electromagnetic and weak nuclear forces, and to a lesser extent, in the theory of quantum chromodynamics, the strong nuclear forces, in the so-called Standard Model. The formulation and quantization of these theories is based on the mathematics of gauge natural fiber bundles, while the standard formulation of general relativity only requires natural bundles. While classical gravitation theory also can be formulated as a gauge natural bundle theory, as of 2007 no successful quantization based on this approach has been accomplished—let alone a unified quantum theory including gravitation (for natural and/or gauge natural theories see Fatibene and Francaviglia, 2003).

Einstein and Unified Field Theory. Balazs states: "Between 1907 and 1911 … [Einstein] came to understand that the solution to the dualism [of fields and particles] problem was to write physics in terms of continuous field quantities and nonlinear partial differential equations that would yield singularity-free particle solutions" (pp. 325–326). Similarly, Klein states "[Einstein] never lost his hope that a field theory of the right kind might eventually reach this goal" (pp. 318–319). Actually, as early as 1916, Einstein was presenting arguments suggesting that the continuum was too rich a structure for the treatment of quantum phenomena (for the evolution of his ideas between 1902 and 1954, see Stachel, 1993). While he continued to work on the topic, his hopes for a satisfactory unified field theory grew weaker in his later years, as Balazs himself suggests: "In 1953 Einstein said to the author that … it is doubtful that a unified field theory of the type he was seeking could exist" (p. 330).

Here is Einstein's last published comment on the subject, written shortly before he died:

> One can give good reasons why reality cannot at all be represented by a continuous field. From the quantum phenomena it appears to follow with certainty that a finite system of finite energy can be completely described by a finite set of numbers (quantum numbers). This does not seem to be in accordance with a continuum theory, and must lead to an attempt to find a purely algebraic theory for the description of reality. But nobody knows how to obtain the basis of such a theory. ("Appendix II" to *The Meaning of Relativity*, 5th ed. Princeton, 1955, p. 166)

Much recent work on quantum gravity has been based on attempts to set up just such a "purely algebraic theory." For reviews of some attempts, see Gambini and Pullin, 2005; Dowker, 2005; and Ambjorn, Jurkiewicz, and Loll, 2006.

SUPPLEMENTARY BIBLIOGRAPHY

For the Einstein Archives in the Hebrew University of Jerusalem, consult http://www.albert-einstein.org. For the Einstein Papers Project, consult http://www.einstein.caltech.edu. For updated reviews of most topics in general relativity, consult http://relativity.livingreviews.org.

WORKS BY EINSTEIN

"Quantentheorie des einatomigen idealen Gases. Zweite Abhandlung." *Preussische Akademie der Wissenschaften* (Berlin) *Physikalisch-mathematische Klasse. Sitzunsberichte* (1925): 3–14.

"A propos de la déduction relativiste de M. Emile Meyerson." *Revue Philosophique* 105 (1928): 161–166.

"Lens-Like Action of a Star by the Deviation of Light in a Gravitational Field." *Science* 84 (1936): 506–507.

"Why Socialism." *Monthly Review* (May 1949). Reprinted in *Ideas and Opinions*. New York: Crown Publishers, 1954, 151–158.

"Relativity and the Problem of Space." In *Relativity: The Special and the General Theory.* 15th ed. New York: Crown, 1952. Reprinted in *Ideas and Opinions.* New York: Crown Publishers, 1954.

"Foreword." In *Concepts of Space*, by Max Jammer. Cambridge, MA: Harvard University Press, 1954.

"Autobiographische Skizze." In *Helle Zeit- Dunkle Zeit In Memoriam Albert Einstein,* edited by Carl Seelig. Zürich: Europa, 1956.

The Collected Papers of Albert Einstein. Translated by Anna Beck. Princeton, NJ: Princeton University Press, 1987–2004. Vol. 1: *The Early Years, 1879–1902.* Vol. 2: *The Swiss Years: Writings, 1900–1909.* Vol. 3: *The Swiss Years: Writings, 1909–1911.* Vol. 4: *The Swiss Years: Writings, 1912–1914.* Vol. 5: *The Swiss Years: Correspondence, 1902–1914.* Vol. 6: *The Berlin Years: Writings, 1914–1917.* Vol. 7: *The Berlin Years: Writings, 1918–1921.* Vol. 8: *The Berlin Years: Correspondence, 1914–1918.* Vol. 9: *The Berlin Years: Correspondence, January 1919–April 1920.* Vol. 10: *The Berlin Years: Correspondence, May-December 1920, and Supplementary Correspondence, 1909–1920.* Cited as *Collected Papers.* These volumes are making available a wealth of new material about his personal life, his scientific work, and his political-social activities. Each volume has an English translation supplement.

Albert Einstein, Mileva Maric: The Love Letters, edited by Jürgen Renn and Robert Schulmann, translated by Shawn Smith. Princeton, NJ: Princeton University Press, 1992.

Einstein's Miraculous Year: Five Papers that Changed the Face of Physics. New introduction by John Stachel; foreword by Roger Penrose. 2nd ed. Princeton, NJ: Princeton University Press, 2005. Translations of all the 1905 papers, with commentary and notes.

The New Quotable Einstein. Edited by Alice Calaprice; foreword by Freeman Dyson. Princeton, NJ: Princeton University Press, 2005.

The Political Einstein. Edited and translated by David Rowe and Robert Schulmann. Princeton, NJ: Princeton University Press, 2007.

OTHER SOURCES

Ambjorn, Jan, J. Jurkiewicz, and Renate Loll. "Quantum Gravity, or the Art of Building Spacetime." In *Approaches to Quantum Gravity,* edited by Danielle Oriti Cambridge, U.K.: Cambridge University Press, 2007.

Ashby, Niel. "Relativity in the Global Positioning System." In *100 Years of Relativity Space-Time Structure,* edited by Abhay Ashtekar. Hackensack, NJ: World Scientific, 2005.

Ashtekar, Abhay, ed. *100 Years of Relativity Space-Time Structure: Einstein and Beyond.* Hackensack, NJ: World Scientific, 2005.

Bergmann, Peter G. "Unitary Field Theory, Geometrization of Physics or Physicalization of Geometry?" In *Einstein Symposion, Berlin: aus Anlaß der 100. Wiederkehr seines Geburtstages 25. bis 30. März 1979,* edited by Horst Nelkowski, A. Hermann, and H. Poser. Lecture Notes in Physics, vol. 100. Berlin and New York: Springer, 1979.

Bičak, Jiri. "Selected Solutions of Einstein's Field Equations: Their Role in General Relativity and Astrophysics." *Lecture Notes in Physics* 540 (2000): 1–126.

Brian, Denis. *The Unexpected Einstein: The Real Man behind the Icon.* Hoboken, NJ: Wiley, 2005.

Carter, Brandon. "Half Century of Black-Hole Theory: From Physicists' Purgatory to Mathematicians' Paradise." In *A Century of Relativity Physics*, edited by Lysiane Mornas and Joaquin Diaz Alonso. Melville, NY: American Institute of Physics, 2006.

Damour, Thibault. "100 Years of Relativity: Was Einstein 100% Right?" In *A Century of Relativity Physics*, edited by Lysiane Mornas and Joaquin Diaz Alonso. Melville, NY: American Institute of Physics, 2006.

Dowker, Fay. "Causal Sets and the Deep Structure of Spacetime." In *100 Years of Relativity Space-Time Structure*, edited by Abhay Ashtekar. Hackensack, NJ: World Scientific, 2005.

Fatibene, Lorenzo, and Mauro Francaviglia, *Natural and Gauge Natural Formalism for Classical Field Theories: A Geometric Perspective including Spinors and Gauge Theories.* Dordrecht, Netherlands, and Boston: Kluwer, 2003.

Fölsing, Albrecht. *Albert Einstein: A Biography.* New York and London: Viking, 1997. Good on biographical information, weak on science.

Gambini, Rodolfo, and Jorge Pullin. "Consistent Discrete Space-Time." In *100 Years of Relativity Space-Time Structure*, edited by Abhay Ashtekar. Hackensack, NJ: World Scientific, 2005.

Goenner, Hubert F. M. "On the History of Unified Field Theories." *Living Reviews in Relativity* 7 (2004). Available from http://relativity.livingreviews.org/lrr-2004-2.

Hettler, Nicolaus. "Die Elektrotechnische Firma J. Einstein u. Cie in München—1876–1894." PhD diss. Stuttgart University, 1996.

Highfield, Roger, and Paul Carter. *The Private Lives of Albert Einstein.* London: Faber, 1993; Boston: St, Martin's, 1994.

Janssen, Michel, John D. Norton, Jürgen Renn, et al. *The Genesis of General Relativity*, vol. 1: *Einstein's Zurich Notebook: Introduction and Source*, vol. 2: *Einstein's Zurich Notebook: Commentary and Essays.* Dordrecht, Netherlands: Springer, 2007.

Martinez, Alberto. "Handling Evidence in History: The Case of Einstein's Wife." *Science School Review* 86 (2005): 51–52.

Moszkowski, Alexander. *Einstein, Einblicke in seine Gedankenwelt: Gemeinverständliche Betrachtungen über die Relativitätstheorie und ein neues Weltsystem, Entwickelt aus Gesprächen mit Einstein.* Hamburg, Germany: Hoffmann und Campe, 1921.

Oriti, Daniele, ed. *Approaches to Quantum Gravity.* Cambridge, U.K.: Cambridge University Press, 2007.

Overbye, Dennis. *Einstein in Love: A Scientific Romance.* New York: Viking, 2000.

Padmanabhan, Thanu. "Understanding Our Universe: Current Status and Open Issues." In *100 Years of Relativity Space-Time Structure*, edited by Abhay Ashtekar. Hackensack, NJ: World Scientific, 2005.

Pais, Abraham. *'Subtle is the Lord …' The Science and the Life of Albert Einstein.* New York: Oxford University Press, 1982. The best overall analysis of Einstein's scientific work.

Pogrebin, Robin. "Love Letters by Einstein at Auction." *New York Times*, 1 June 1998.

Price, Richard H. "The Physical Basis of Black Hole Astrophysics." In *100 Years of Relativity Space-Time Structure*, edited by Abhay Ashtekar.

Renn, Jürgen, and John Stachel. "Hilbert's Foundation of Physics: From a Theory of Everything to a Constituent of General Relativity." In *The Genesis of General Relativity*, vol. 3, *Gravitation in the Twilight of Classical Physics: Between Mechanics, Field Theory and Astronomy*, edited by Jürgen Renn and Matthias Schimmel. Dordrecht, Netherlands: Springer, 2007.

Renn, Jürgen, Tilman Sauer, and John Stachel. "The Origin of Gravitational Lensing: A Postscript to Einstein's 1936 *Science* Paper." *Science* 275 (1997): 184–186. Reprinted in Stachel, *Einstein from "B" to "Z."*

Saulson, Peter R. "Receiving Gravitational Radiation." In *100 Years of Relativity Space-Time Structure*, edited by Abhay Ashtekar.

Sayen, Jamie. *Einstein in America: The Scientist's Conscience in the Age of Hitler and Hiroshima.* New York, Crown, 1985.

Schneider, Peter, Jürgen Ehlers, and Emilio E. Falco. *Gravitational Lenses.* Berlin and London: Springer, 1992.

Schneir, Walter. "Letter to the Editor." *New York Times*, 5 June 1998.

Shimony, Abner. "Bell's Theorem." *Stanford Encyclopedia of Philosophy* (Fall 2006), edited by Edward N. Zalta. Available from http://plato.stanford.edu/archives/fall2006/entries/bell-theorem.

Stachel, John. "Einstein and the Quantum: Fifty Years of Struggle." In *From Quarks to Quasars: Philosophical Problems of Modern Physics*, edited by Robert Colodny. Pittsburgh, PA: University of Pittsburgh Press, 1986. Reprinted in Stachel, *Einstein from "B" to "Z."* Boston, Berlin, and Basel: Birkhauser, 2002a.

———. "Einstein on the Theory of Relativity," 1987. In *Collected Papers*, vol. 1, pp. 253–274. Reprinted in Stachel, *Einstein from "B" to "Z."* Boston, Berlin, and Basel: Birkhauser, 2002a.

———. "Einstein's Search for General Covariance." In *Einstein and the History of General Relativity*, edited by Don Howard and John Stachel. Einstein Studies, vol. 1. Boston/Berlin/Basel: Birkhauser, 1989. Reprinted in Stachel, *Einstein from "B" to "Z."* Boston, Berlin, and Basel: Birkhauser, 2002a.

———. "Einstein and Quantum Mechanics." In *Conceptual Problems of Quantum Gravity*, edited by Abhay Ashtekar and John Stachel. Einstein Studies, vol. 2. Boston, Berlin, Basel: Birkhauser, 1991. Reprinted in Stachel, *Einstein from "B" to "Z."* Boston, Berlin, and Basel: Birkhauser, 2002a.

———. "The Other Einstein: Einstein Contra Field Theory." *Science in Context* 6 (1993): 275–290. Reprinted in Stachel, *Einstein from "B" to "Z."* Boston, Berlin, and Basel: Birkhauser, 2002a.

———. "Einstein and Marić: A Collaboration that Failed to Develop." In *Creative Couples in the Sciences*, edited by Helena M. Pycior, Nancy G. Slack, and Pnina Abir-Am. New Brunswick, NJ: Rutgers University Press, 1996. Reprinted in Satchel, *Einstein from "B" to "Z."* Boston, Berlin, and Basel: Birkhäuser, 2002a.

———. "Einstein's Light Quantum Hypothesis, or Why Didn't Einstein Propose a Quantum Gas a Decade-and-a-Half Earlier?" In *Einstein: The Formative Years, 1879–1909*, edited by Don Howard and John Stachel. Boston: Birkhäuser, 2000. Reprinted in *Einstein from "B" to "Z."* Boston, Berlin, and Basel: Birkhäuser, 2002a.

———. *Einstein from "B" to "Z."* Boston, Berlin, and Basel: Birkhäuser, 2002a.

———. "The First Two Acts," 2002b. In *Einstein from "B" to "Z."* Boston, Berlin, and Basel: Birkhäuser, 2002a.

———. "The Young Einstein: Poetry and Truth," 2002c. In *Einstein from "B" to "Z."* Boston, Berlin, and Basel: Birkhäuser, 2002a.

———. "Fresnel's (Dragging) Coefficient as a Challenge to 19th Century Optics of Moving Bodies." In *The Universe of General Relativity*, edited by A. J. Cox and Jean Einsenstaedt. Einstein Studies, vol. 11. Boston, Basel, Berlin: Birkhäuser, 2005a.

———. "Introduction to the Centenary Edition," 2005b. In *Einstein's Miraculous Year: Five Papers that Changed the Face of Physics*. New introduction by John Stachel; foreword by Roger Penrose. 2nd ed., 2005b. Princeton, NJ: Princeton University Press, 2005.

———. "The Story of Newstein: Or Is Gravity Just Another Pretty Force?" In *The Genesis of General Relativity*, vol. 4, *Gravitation in the Twilight of Classical Physics: The Promise of Mathematics*, edited by Jürgen Renn and Matthias Schimmel. Berlin: Springer, 2007.

Will, Clifford. "Was Einstein Right? Testing Relativity at the Centenary." In *100 Years of Relativity Space-Time Structure*, edited by Abhay Ashtekar. Hackensack, NJ: World Scientific, 2005.

Winteler-Einstein, Maja. "Albert Einstein—Beitrag für Sein Lebensbild," 1924. In *Collected Papers*, vol. 1.

Zubirini, Xavier. "La idea de naturaleza: la nueva fisica." Translation in *Nature, History, God*. Washington, DC: University Press of America, 1981.

John Stachel

ELION, GERTRUDE BELLE (*b.* New York, New York, 23 January 1918; *d.* Chapel Hill, North Carolina, 21 February 1999), *pharmacology, antimetabolites, immunosuppressors, anticancer drugs, antiviral drugs.*

Elion shared the 1988 Nobel Prize in Physiology or Medicine with James Black, who discovered beta-blockers and H_2–receptor antagonists, and George H. Hitchings, with whom she had collaborated for more than forty years, the two being responsible for the discovery of many major therapeutic agents—anticancer, antiviral, antibacterial, immunosuppressive, anti-gout—whose common characteristic was that they were specifically targeted at nucleic acids. Elion may thus be considered a founder of molecular pharmacology. Although she was the fifth woman to receive the Nobel Prize in Physiology or Medicine, she was the first who was neither a physician nor the holder of a doctoral degree.

Elion was born in New York on 23 January 1918. Her father, Robert Elion, had immigrated from Lithuania at the age of twelve and studied dental surgery in New York. Her mother, Bertha Cohen, had arrived in the United States from the Russian-Polish borderlands at age fourteen. Their daughter graduated from Hunter College in 1937. Academia was scarcely welcoming to women in those days, and she was unable to pursue her studies immediately. She taught for a semester at the New York Hospital School of Nursing and volunteered at a chemistry laboratory. Only in 1939 did she embark on postgraduate studies at New York University, where, two years later, the sole female candidate, she was awarded a master of science degree in chemistry.

When her grandfather died of cancer, Elion began to dream of a career in medical research, but she was obliged to start out as a food analyst for the Quaker Maid Company. The American mobilization for World War II, by opening up many positions to women, gave her a chance to enter the pharmaceutical industry. In 1944, after a few months with Johnson & Johnson, she was offered employment with Burroughs Wellcome as an assistant chemist in the laboratory of Hitchings in Tuckahoe, New York. There she began, ten years before the discovery of the double helix, to investigate modifiers of nucleic-acid metabolism.

Contemporary advances in antineoplastic chemotherapy prompted the reorientation of this research toward cancer. The first concrete results began to appear in 1947, with the formulation of the antileukemics 6-mercaptopurine and 6-thioguanine. Elion and her colleagues subsequently developed azathioprine, a powerful immunosuppressive drug. Another line of inquiry led to allopurinol, a treatment for gout and hyperuricemia.

Elion's work culminated in a great discovery, that of the strong antiherpetic action of acyclovir. From 1967 on, she headed Burroughs Wellcome's Experimental Therapy Department. Her name appeared on forty-five patents. She received twenty-five honorary doctorates and was elected president of the American Association for Cancer Research. She entered semiretirement in 1983, but was invited to teach at Duke University (Durham, North Carolina) and at the University of North Carolina at Chapel Hill. She also worked for the World Health Organization and strove to increase support for young researchers, notably through the Wellcome Foundation. The Nobel Prize was a fitting coda to her remarkable career.

Gertrude Belle Elion, known to her friends as "Trudy," died at the age of eighty-one on 21 February 1999 in Chapel Hill.

Research Program. In the mid-1940s, the idea of producing drugs designed to treat viral conditions seemed incongruous, for hitherto almost all efforts had been bent toward the development of vaccines capable of preventing such conditions. The aim now was to intervene early, at the beginning of the reproductive cycle of viruses. One of the difficulties facing Elion and her coworkers was the relative crudeness of the techniques available: Their physical and chemical apparatus was of the most basic kind, and they had little by way of spectroscopic or radiological equipment.

Antimetabolites. The theory of antimetabolites, conceived in 1940, was the brainchild of the Oxford biochemist Donald Woods, who argued that exogenous substances could compete with the natural substrates necessary to the anabolism of microorganisms and thus inhibit their replication. Woods observed that brewer's yeast impeded the action of sulfonamides, and concluded that this yeast contained a substance closely resembling sulfanilamide and capable of competing with it. Based on this competition between sulfonamides and *p*-aminobenzoic acid (PABA), a natural substrate of bacterial metabolism, the term *antimetabolite* was applied to any substance capable of exercising such an inhibitory function.

Following a similar line of inquiry, Hitchings showed that different antimetabolites could prevent the growth of microorganisms. Thus pyrimethamine, a dihydrofolate-reductase inhibitor in protozoa, was proposed as an antimalarial agent.

In 1966 other chemical modifications brought about in the benzene cycle of 5-benzyl-2,4-diaminopyrimidine made it possible to obtain a derivative that was active against *Proteus vulgaris*. This was trimethoprim, an inhibitor fifty thousand times stronger than the human enzyme with respect to bacterial dihydrofolate reductase. A combination of trimethoprim with the sulfonamide sulfamethoxazole (co-trimoxazole) was offered by Burroughs Wellcome.

Hitchings was convinced that it should be possible to arrest the growth of rapidly dividing cells (bacteria or cancerous cells) by means of antagonists of the nucleic-acid bases their division depended on. The object was to exploit the high speed of their proliferation as compared with normal mammalian cells and ultimately to classify the bio-

chemical differences between cell types according to the ways in which they responded to these antimetabolites.

The importance of dihydrofolate reductase inhibitors was recognized because this enzyme is an important rate-limiting step in the *de novo* folate synthesis pathway, which is an universal step in cell life cycle in eucaryote and procaryote cells as well. That is why the pharmacological targets of those inhibitors are so various: For instance, methotrexate is a cancer chemotherapeutic agent, whereas trimethoprim is an antibiotic. This is explained through the fact that despite both being dihydrofolate reductase inhibitors, methotrexate has a selective affinity for mammalian dihydrofolate reductase, while trimethoprim has a selective affinity for the bacterial enzyme.

Possible targets of research were provided by the various enzymes of nucleic acids then known: nucleases, nucleotidases, nucleosidases, deaminases, xanthine oxydase, and uricase. Hitchings and Elion began by studying guanase and xanthine oxydase in order to learn whether purines acted as substrates or as inhibitors of these enzymes. In 1948 they discovered that 2,6-diaminopurine was a powerful growth inhibitor for *Lactobacillus casei*, except when adenine was present. A strain of *Lactobacillus casei* resistant to diaminopurine made it possible to demonstrate that adenine and 2,6-diaminopurine were both modified by the same enzyme, namely adenylate pyrophosphorylase, described in 1955 by Arthur Kornberg (Nobel laureate, 1959).

Antileukemic Drugs. At the beginning of the 1950s, methotrexate was the only anticancer drug available. A leukemic child had a life expectancy of only three to four months once diagnosed, and only 30 percent of children survived for more than a year. In the late 1940s, the administration of 2,6-diaminopurine to leukemic mice (mice that are highly susceptible to development of spontaneous leukemias) and the exposure of tumor cells to it in vitro resulted in strong inhibitory activity. When it was tried out on patients, in 1951, impressive remissions of chronic myeloid leukemia were observed, as well as an in vitro inhibition of vaccinia virus. Unfortunately an excessive toxicity put an end to the clinical application of 2,6-diaminopurine.

In 1951 Elion and Hitchings synthesized and evaluated more than one hundred purine derivatives, finding that the replacement of the oxygen atom by a sulfur atom at the 6-position of guanine and hypoxanthine produced inhibitors of purine utilization, namely 6-thioguanine (6-TG) and 6-mercaptopurine (6-MP). Following toxicological testing of these agents on animals, Joseph Burchenal of the Sloan-Kettering Institute in New York carried out clinical trials with children suffering from acute lymphoblastic leukemia. Some complete remissions were recorded, though most patients relapsed in the medium term. Consequently, in 1953, the U.S. Food and Drug Administration approved the use of 6-MP for acute leukemia in patients of this type, and the median survival rate for children thus treated rose from three to twelve months. A combination of thioguanine and cytosine arabinoside was later used to treat acute leukemias in adults.

Immunosuppression and Transplantation. In 1958 a team of Boston researchers led by William Dameshek and Robert Schwartz achieved an immuno-pharmacological breakthrough when they showed that prolonged and simultaneous administration of 6-MP and an antigen prevented the development of antibodies against the antigen in question. An immunological screening test allowed Schwartz and Elion to identify a new agent, 1-methyl-4-nitro 5-imidazolyl, or azathioprine (Imuran®), a prodrug for the 6-MP produced by the red blood cells under the influence of glutathion. At the suggestion of Schwartz and Elion, the British surgeon Roy Calne achieved a very good outcome when he replaced 6-MP by azathioprine in his already successful canine kidney homograft studies: With 6-MP, Calne had achieved a forty-four-day survival in a dog that had received a kidney from an unrelated donor—far longer than the nine- or ten-day graft survival expectation for control animals—furthermore, azathioprine proved to be even more effective in preventing rejection.

In humans, kidney transplantation from unrelated donors became possible in 1962, thanks to the use of immunosuppressive treatments combining azathioprine and cortisone derivatives. In the early twenty-first century, azathioprine was still a mainstay of transplantation. Its immunosuppressive properties are also called on in the treatment of a variety of autoimmune disorders.

Gout and Hyperuricemia. It was while searching for additional antileukemia agents that Elion and Hitchings came upon a treatment for gout. The biosynthesis of 6-thiouric acid, a product of the catabolism of 6-MP, is inhibited by xanthine oxidase. To evaluate the inhibition of xanthine oxidase in vivo, Elion and Hitchings used an analog of hypoxanthine, namely 4-hydroxypyrazolo-(3,4-d)-pyrimidine (allopurinol). They found that when allopurinol and 6-MP were administered simultaneously to mice, oxidation of the 6-MP was indeed inhibited. The antineoplastic and immunosuppressive properties of 6-MP were multiplied by a factor of three or four, whereas its toxicity was "only" doubled. Wayne Rundles studied leukemic patients on this basis, but found that in humans, unfortunately, toxicity increased in proportion to antitumoral action.

Another line of research with xanthine oxidase concerned the formation of uric acid from hypoxanthine and xanthine. It was found that treatment with allopurinol (a xanthine oxidase inhibitor) brought about a significant reduction in uric acid in blood and urine. This finding raised several questions. Would the pharmacokinetics of allopurinol ensure a durable impact on the metabolism of purines and uric-acid production? Would other metabolic products accumulate, such as hypoxanthine or xanthine? Did excess hypoxanthine and xanthine induce increased enzyme synthesis, thus indicating the administration of higher dosages of allopurinol? What would be the long-term effects of this drug?

All these questions were carefully explored, first with animals and then with human subjects. Allopurinol was determined to be a competitive inhibitor as well as a substrate of xanthine oxydase. Its oxidation produces the corresponding analog of xanthine, oxypurinol (or alloxantine), which is also a potent xanthine-oxydase inhibitor. Whereas allopurinol was found to have a plasma elimination half-life of just 90–120 minutes, that of oxypurinol was 18–30 hours: with a single daily dose of allopurinol, it was possible after a few days to maintain a roughly constant oxypurinol concentration. By adjusting the dosage, uric-acid concentration could be kept at the desired level. Completely absorbed after administration by mouth, allopurinol could become an ideal "prodrug." It was the first radical treatment for gout.

Antiviral Drugs. In 1968, Hitchings and Elion and their team turned their attention once more to a working hypothesis—framed twenty years earlier but prematurely set aside—concerning the antiviral action of 2,6-diaminopurine. The idea of using this agent had been abandoned in view of its high toxicity, but the discovery of the antiviral properties of adenine arabinoside (ara-A) justified revisiting it and also considering 2,4-diaminopurine-arabinoside, synthesized by Janet Rideout and subjected to virological study by John Bauer at the Wellcome Research Laboratories in the United Kingdom. This new derivative was effective not only against the vaccinia virus but also against herpes simplex, implicated in a variety of pathologies of the skin and mucous membranes. Furthermore, it was less cytotoxic than ara-A for eukaryotic cells. Hitchings and Elion had been right on target, and this was the beginning of what Elion called their "antiviral odyssey." For several years they worked with purine arabinosides, investigating the relations between their structure and their action, searching for the best syntheses, and studying not only their metabolism but also their antiviral effectiveness. Among the most intriguing derivates of diaminopurine arabinoside (ara-DAP) were guanine arabinoside (ara-G), a more potent antiviral than the deamination product of ara-A, hypoxanthine arabinoside. Did this superiority warrant a full-scale development of ara-DAP? The answer was soon to come.

Gertrude Belle Elion. AP IMAGES.

When Hitchings and Elion's research laboratory moved to North Carolina in 1970, Howard Schaeffer, a specialist in analogs of adenosine, joined them as head of the organic chemistry department. Schaeffer had studied the effect of various changes on acyclic side-chains at the 9-position of adenine, and found that 9-(2-hydrox-yethoxymethyl)-adenine was a constant substrate of adenosine deaminase. It followed logically that other enzymes too might likewise be able to mimic such side-chains and that nucleoside analogs of this kind might have antimetabolic properties. Research was therefore focused on acyclic nucleoside analogs. Schaeffer's syntheses were followed by antiviral testing by Bauer and Peter Collins, while Elion's group explored the mechanisms of action and conducted in vivo enzymological and metabolic studies. This was the context in which the potency of acy-cloguanosine (acyclovir) came to light.

Acyclovir. Elion's most celebrated article was published in *Proceedings of the National Academy of Sciences* (*PNAS*) in December 1977, barely two months after she submitted it. The advent of acycloguanosine amounted to a thera-

peutic revolution. Acyclovir proved effective with respect to herpes simplex, just as, in the case of the purines, the analog of 2,6-diaminopurine had done. The big surprise was that acycloguanosine was more than one hundred times as active as the "diamino" compound. Four days after the Elion team's pioneering article was sent to *PNAS*, they submitted to *Nature* a contribution that was largely concerned with clinical issues and already included, as well as recommendations on inhibitory dosages, some discussion of experimental pathology (experimental herpetic encephalitis and herpetic keratitis) and of pharmacokinetics. This was the start of the pharmacological career of acyclovir, an analog of guanine whose performance far surpassed that of 2,6-diaminopurine.

Acyclovir's spectrum of action was found to cover herpes simplex virus types 1 and 2 and varicella zoster virus. It also had interesting properties in connection with Epstein-Barr virus (EBv). Unfortunately, it turned out to be less active with cytomegalovirus (CMV). Its great virtue was its very low toxicity. Acyclovir was manifestly more effective than all previously proposed antiviral agents. The utility of this new inhibitor resided not only in its potency but also in its very high selectivity, for it was not cytotoxic to mammalian cells in which herpes viruses grow.

The reasons for this selectivity were explored by the virologist Philip Furman. Although acyclic substitution at the 9-position did not, properly speaking, confer the structure of a nucleoside on it, acyclovir nevertheless behaved like an arabinoside-type derivative. Its chief chemical property lay in its ability to be triphosphory-lated, an indispensable trait for any antimetabolite.

Ordinary derivatives can be phosphorylated by cellular kinases; in contrast, a viral kinase was solely responsible for the activity of acyclovir. Vero cell cultures, uninfected or infected in advance with strains of herpes simplex virus type 1 were incubated with radioactive acyclovir labeled with carbon 14 (^{14}C) at the 8-position of the guanine and with tritium (^{3}H) in the side-chain. Extracts of the cells were examined, after separation, by chromatography. The uninfected cells were found to contain only nonphosphorylated acyclovir. By contrast, three new radioactive compounds appeared on the chromatograms of the HSV-infected cells: these were identified as the monophosphate (ACV-MP), diphosphate (ACV-DP), and triphosphate (ACV-TP) of acyclovir.

Once the first phosphate had been added, the second was formed by a cellular guanylate kinase, while the third could be formed by several other thymidine kinases. Since the cellular thymidine kinase could not use acyclovir as a substrate, very little ACV-TP formed in noninfected cells. Once formed, the ACV-TP became a potent inhibitor of the viral DNA polymerase, which was also inactivated by the formation of an enzyme-template-acyclovirmonophosphate complex (an inactivation that did not occur with cellular DNA polymerase).

Pharmacokinetic and metabolic studies of acyclovir in several animal species and in humans revealed that it had a remarkable metabolic stability. Because its plasma half-life was about three hours, intravenous infusion of acyclovir (Zovirax®) was generally ordered on an eight-hourly basis. It was also possible to administer it via the genital, ophthalmic, or labial mucous membranes, or by mouth. Since the mid-1990s, the drug has been widely used to treat varied conditions in which herpes virus is implicated: first episodes of genital herpes infection, herpes zoster, prevention of herpes infection in immunode-pressed patients, herpetic encephalitis, and so on.

The discovery of acyclovir was a major therapeutic breakthrough per se, but the lessons learned from its history have also turned out to be extremely fruitful for subsequent research on antivirals, most notably in connection with AIDS. In-depth study of its mechanism of action has led to a better grasp of the enzymatic differences between healthy and virus-infected cells and helped assess the impact of the specific properties of enzymes on their therapeutic applications.

The introduction of acyclovir was undoubtedly the high point of Elion's career. It is a remarkable fact that, more than fifty years after she began her work, the discoveries of this extraordinary pharmacologist were still indispensable and unsurpassed therapeutic tools.

BIBLIOGRAPHY

WORKS BY ELION

With George H. Hitchings, Gertrude B. Elion, Elvira A. Falco, et al. "Antagonists of nucleic acid derivatives. I. The lactobacillus casei model." *Journal of Biological Chemistry* 183 (March 1950): 1–9.

With Sandra Callahan, R. Wayne Rundles, and George H. Hitchings. "Relationship between Metabolic Fates and Antitumor Activities of Thiopurines." *Cancer Research* 23 (1963): 1207–1217.

With R. Wayne Rundles, James B. Wyngaarden, George H. Hitchings, et al. "Effects of a Xanthine Oxidase Inhibitor on Thiopurine Metabolism, Hyperuricemia, and Gout." *Transactions of the Association of American Physicians* 76 (1963): 126–140.

"Enzymatic and Metabolic Studies with Allopurinol." *Annals of the Rheumatic Diseases* 25 (1966): 608–614.

With S. Singer and George H. Hitchings. "Resistance to Inhibitors of Dihydrofolate Reductase in Strains of *Lactobacillus casei* and *Proteus vulgaris*." *Journal of General Microbiology* 42, no. 2 (1966): 185–196.

With Vincent Massey, Hirochika Komai, and Graham Palmer. "On the Mechanism of Inactivation of Xanthine Oxidase by Allopurinol and Other Pyrazolo [3,4-*d*]-pyrimidines." *Journal of Biological Chemistry* 245 (1970): 2837–2844.

With Paulo de Miranda, Lowrie M. Beacham III, and Teresa H. Creagh. "The Metabolic Fate of the Methylnitroimidazole Moiety of Azathioprine in the Rat." *Journal of Pharmacology and Experimental Therapeutics* 187, no. 3 (1973): 588–601.

With Janet L. Rideout, Paulo de Miranda, Peter Collins, et al. "Biological Activities of Some Purine Arabinosides." *Annals of the New York Academy of Science* 255 (1975): 468–480.

With Phillip A. Furman, James A. Fyfe, Paulo de Miranda, et al. "Selectivity of Action of an Antiherpetic Agent, 9-(2-hydroxyethoxymethyl)guanine." *Proceedings of the National Academy of Sciences of the United States of America* 74, no. 12 (1977): 5716–5720.

With Howard J. Schaeffer, Lilia Beauchamp, Paulo de Miranda, et al. "9-(2-hydroxyethoxymethyl)guanine Activity against Viruses of the Herpes Group." *Nature* 272 (1978): 583–585.

With Karen K. Biron." *In Vitro* Susceptibility of Varicella-Zoster Virus to Acyclovir." *Antimicrobial Agents and Chemotherapy* 18 (1980): 443–447.

With Brenda M. Colby, James E. Shaw, and Joseph S. Pagano. "Effect of Acyclovir [9-(2-hydroxyethoxymethyl)guanine] on Epstein-Barr Virus DNA Replication." *Journal of Virology* 34 (1980): 560–568.

With Marty H. St Clair, Phillip A. Furman, and Carol M. Lubbers. "Inhibition of Cellular Alpha and Virally Induced Deoxyribonucleic Acid Polymerases by the Triphosphate of Acyclovir." *Antimicrobial Agents and Chemotherapy* 18 (1980): 741–745.

With Phillip A. Furman, Paulo de Miranda, and Marty H. St Clair. "Metabolism of Acyclovir in Virus-Infected and Uninfected Cells." *Antimicrobial Agents and Chemotherapy* 20 (1981): 518–524.

With Paul M. Keller, James A. Fyfe, Lilia Beauchamp, et al. "Enzymatic Phosphorylation of Acyclic Nucleoside Analogs and Correlations with Antiherpetic Activities." *Biochemical Pharmacology* 30 (1981): 3071–3077.

With Goerge H. Hitchings. "Layer on Layer: The Bruce F. Cain Memorial Award Lecture." *Cancer Research* 45 (1985): 2415–2420.

"Nobel Lecture: The Purine Path to Chemotherapy." In *The Nobel Prizes 1988*, edited by Tore Frängsmyr. Stockholm: Nobel Foundation, 1989.

With F. Chast, C. Chastel, N. Postel-Vinay, et al. *Virus Herpès et pensée médicale, de l'empirisme au Prix Nobel* [Herpes Virus and Medical Thought: From Empiricism to the Nobel Prize]. Paris: Imothep-Maloine, 1997.

OTHER SOURCES

Chast, François. *Histoire contemporaine des médicaments* [Contemporary History of Drugs]. Paris: La Découverte, 2002.

"Gertrude Belle Elion: A Lifeline." Chemical Heritage Foundation. Available from http://www.chemheritage.org/EducationalServices/pharm/chemo/readings/lifeline.htm.

François Chast

ELSASSER, WALTER MAURICE (*b.* Mannheim, Germany, 20 March 1904; *d.* Baltimore, Maryland, 14 October 1991), *physics, geophysics, biophysics.*

Elsasser trained originally in physics (especially quantum mechanics), but worked for most of his career in atmospheric dynamics, geomagnetism, seismology, and theoretical biology. His development of early dynamo theories of Earth's main magnetic field ultimately gained him wide recognition and several important awards. More than once in his career, however, Elsasser produced theoretical aperçus that were received with skepticism; subsequent theoretical elaboration and experimental work demonstrated the value of his insights, but the development was made by others. In the words of Victor Weisskopf, Elsasser generated "great flashes of ideas; and it was not Elsasser's style to elaborate details" (1979, p. 759). The wide-ranging character of his fields of activity was paralleled, not coincidentally, by a rather peripatetic career. Elsasser's memoirs frankly portray these aspects of his scientific work and reflect on the psychological underpinnings of scientific creativity.

Early Years. Both sides of Elsasser's family ran prosperous businesses: burlap manufacturing for the family of his mother, Johanna Masius, and fruit brandy distilling for that of his father, Moritz. Moritz Elsasser obtained a law degree, entered the civil service, and was eventually appointed a judge in Mannheim—where Walter and his sister Maria were born—then later Pforzheim and Heidelberg, along with a period of military duty in Konstanz during World War I. Walter attended a humanistic-classical *Gymnasium*, but his mathematics teacher encouraged him to pursue science professionally. A brief stint in his grandfather's firm convinced him that science—specifically, physics—was a better career choice than business, and he entered the University of Heidelberg in 1922.

Elsasser's parents were both Protestant converts, though not very religious; heretofore he had been conscious of his Jewish family background only in an abstract, philosophical sense. At the university, however, Elsasser witnessed students' enthusiasm for the anti-Semitic, ultranationalist sentiments of the physicist Philipp Lenard, and he was warned that he would face extreme antagonism in Lenard's laboratory. Elsasser therefore transferred to Munich, where he studied with Wilhelm Wien and Arnold Sommerfeld. But once again he sensed strong undercurrents of anti-Semitism and took advice to go to Göttingen, which had a more congenial reputation.

Interests in Physics. Elsasser arrived in 1925, just as Göttingen was becoming a center of the new quantum mechanics, and he became a student of the experimentalist James Franck. In Max Born's seminar on atomic structure, Elsasser learned of an experiment by Clinton Davisson and Charles Henry Kunsman at Bell Laboratories in which the angular distribution of electrons scattered from a platinum plate showed maxima and minima. Contemporaneously, Franck, Born, and their students were discussing Albert Einstein's notion of gas degeneracy as a wave phenomenon, which referred in turn to Louis de Broglie's thesis on electron orbital wavelengths. Juxtaposing these results, Elsasser suggested that the electron scattering patterns, as well as the Ramsauer effect, might be interference phenomena. Franck and Born encouraged Elsasser to publish a note in *Naturwissenschaften*. Most readers—including Einstein, who refereed the brief article—were apparently intrigued but not entirely convinced; Davisson himself regarded this explanation of his experiment skeptically. Elsasser's own experiments to confirm the result were unsuccessful and convinced his mentors that his talents lay primarily in theory. The theorist Born therefore took over as the *Doktorvater* of a 1927 thesis on the quantum mechanics of electron-hydrogen atom collisions. Meanwhile, Davisson returned to the scattering problem with methodological innovations that produced definitive results, and with the benefit of Erwin Schrödinger's widely noted adoption of de Broglie's thesis. For this work, Davisson received the Nobel Prize in 1937.

After receiving his doctorate Elsasser became an assistant to Paul Ehrenfest in Leiden, apparently through the recommendation of Robert Oppenheimer, who had become acquainted with Elsasser in Göttingen and who had previously been Ehrenfest's assistant. Ehrenfest and Elsasser, both sensitive personalities, found it impossible to get along with each other, and after several weeks of escalating tension, Elsasser departed in a state of depression for Berlin, where his parents now lived. After another postdoctoral semester, this time with Wolfgang Pauli in Zürich, Elsasser took up an adjunct research assistantship with Fritz Houtermans at the Technische Hochschule Berlin. In summer 1930, Elsasser became a technical specialist at the new Physico-Technical Institute in Kharkiv, Ukraine; ill health compelled his return to Berlin after only six months, but Elsasser was profoundly affected by his experience in the Soviet Union. The following summer, he was appointed to an assistantship with Erwin Madelung in Frankfurt. There Elsasser also began an extended psychoanalysis with Karl Landauer. His interest in psychology also led, subsequently, to extensive reading in the works of Carl Jung.

With an apparently stable job and a fresh psychological perspective, Elsasser started his time in Frankfurt promisingly. However, the National Socialists' rise to power in 1933 presaged even more virulent anti-Semitism. At Landauer's urging, Elsasser departed in April for

Zürich. Soon after his arrival, Pauli matched him with an opening for a theorist in Frédéric Joliot-Curie's laboratory.

In Paris, Elsasser's attention turned to nuclear structure. Rejecting a then widespread idea that alpha particles constituted a kind of primary building block for heavier nuclei, Elsasser instead picked up a suggestion by James Holley Bartlett and theorized, based on Pauli's exclusion principle, that nucleons resided in shells analogous to the electron shells. Elsasser found evidence for this in patterns in the number of stable isotopes for a given atomic number, in the relative abundance of isotopes, and in nuclear binding energies. However, the theory remained suggestive rather than comprehensive. A much greater accumulation of data on nuclear reactions enabled Maria Goeppert-Mayer and Hans Jensen to develop a more thorough theory of nuclear shell structure in the 1940s—once again, Nobel Prize–winning work.

Elsasser felt welcome in Joliot's laboratory but was daunted by the prospect of a permanent accommodation to French culture and nationality; moreover, he remained concerned by the European political situation, particularly for the sake of his parents. On a 1935 trip exploring options for emigration to the United States he met several useful contacts—as well as a young American woman, Margaret Trahey, whom he married in 1937—but he did not land a job. On a return trip in 1936, Elsasser took up California Institute of Technology (Caltech) president Robert Millikan's suggestion that he move into meteorology, a field that Millikan was seeking to bolster at Caltech. Elsasser surmised that the next fruitful arena for physics after the breakthroughs of quantum theory would be an attempt to apply physical principles to complex systems, and he saw in meteorology a chance to try out this conjecture. Specifically, he decided to study the process of heat transfer in the atmosphere via infrared radiation, a topic still relatively unfamiliar to meteorologists.

Meteorology. Meteorology at Caltech was officially under the purview of the fluid dynamicist Theodore von Kármán. In 1941 the head of research of the U.S. Weather Bureau attempted to persuade Caltech to make Elsasser head of the department, and Kármán took this perceived outside interference as a reason to dismiss Elsasser. After a brief period at Harvard's Blue Hill Meteorological Observatory, where he published a widely noted monograph on his infrared radiation studies, Elsasser joined the Army Signal Corps as a civilian expert, working first on electronics (at Fort Monmouth) and then on meteorological effects in the use of radar (in New York). After the war there followed short stints at RCA's Princeton laboratories and at the University of Pennsylvania. With some relief, in 1950 he accepted an invitation to develop a physics graduate program at the University of Utah.

When Elsasser arrived in Utah, his main attention became focused on a research field he had been cultivating almost as a diversion alongside his official duties since the late 1930s: geomagnetism. Discounting a hypothesis popularized by Einstein and Patrick Maynard Stuart Blackett that Earth's magnetic field is a property of its rotation per se, he thought instead of a self-sustaining dynamo in the molten metallic core. A key clue for Elsasser in his approach to the problem was a similarity between maps of the long-term variations in Earth's magnetic field and the maps of atmospheric flows familiar from his work in meteorology. Elsasser theorized that Coriolis forces and convection currents in the conductive liquid combined to produce poloidal magnetic and toroidal electric fields (the former extending beyond Earth's surface, the latter interior to it) that had a feedback effect on each other. Though some details were unclear, he argued that the dynamo theory gave the right order of magnitude for the magnetic field's strength and potentially accounted for its secular variations. By the mid-1950s, Elsasser's junior colleague at Utah, Eugene Newman Parker, and the British physicists Edward Crisp Bullard and the Australian-born George Keith Batchelor had explored alternative dynamo models and elaborated the mathematics showing that the field was self-sustaining. The dynamo theory ultimately received wide acceptance. It subsequently also became a key element of Hannes Alfvén's Nobel Prize–winning work on plasma electrodynamics. In the 1960s, Elsasser's geophysical interests moved into modeling seismic deformation in the context of the burgeoning theory of plate tectonics.

Largely in recognition of this breakthrough in the theory of terrestrial magnetism, but also in acknowledgment of his earlier work in quantum physics and meteorology, Elsasser was elected to the National Academy of Sciences (1957), later receiving the Bowie and Fleming medals of the American Geophysical Union (in 1959 and 1971, respectively), the Gauss Medal in Germany (1977), the Penrose Medal of the Geological Society of America (1979), and the U.S. National Medal of Science (1987).

Theoretical Biology. While at Utah, Elsasser also began publishing in yet another field, theoretical biology. His earlier experiences and reading in psychology were great influences on his work in this direction, giving him an intuition that the workings of the mind, and therefore by implication biological systems in general, were in some way "irrational." Another major influence was his former colleague in Paris, the physiologist Theophile Kahn, who emphasized the uniqueness of individual organisms and the difficulty in treating them as homogeneous classes, something that Elsasser felt was consonant with his own first-hand experiences of the attempt to forge a collectivist society in the Soviet Union.

Walter Maurice Elsasser. SCIENCE PHOTO LIBRARY/PHOTO
RESEARCHERS, INC.

Elsasser's central concern as a theoretical biologist
thus became the complexity and individuality of living
systems, which he contrasted with the simplicity and
reproducibility of those systems studied in the physico-
chemical laboratory. He became convinced that it was not
possible simply to extrapolate the methods of physics and
chemistry to the study of biology, except in certain limited
circumstances. The laws of quantum physics arose precisely out of the identity of its objects—all electrons, for
example, were mutually indistinguishable. Living organisms, by contrast, represented unique individuals within a
range of hypothetically possible molecular arrangements
that was immensely large. Elsasser expressed this formally
in "the principle of finite classes"—the fact that biological
entities such as proteins or pathways have an astronomical
number of potential states, far more than can possibly be
instantiated in the real world—and he used the term "generalized complementarity," adopted from the Copenhagen
Interpretation founder Niels Bohr, to describe the impossibility of a full, quantum-level, description of a living system. In short, for Elsasser reductionist approaches to, and
mechanistic or deterministic explanations of, biology were
inadequate for a complete understanding of organisms.
For example, he suggested the likelihood of indeterminate
behavior in protein molecules, on the basis of the fact that
John von Neumann's quantum mechanical proof of determinism at the macroscopic level was invalid when applied
to finite classes. Later experimental evidence suggests that

this is untrue (possibly as a result of quantum decoherence
within individual proteins), but a formal demonstration
of exactly *why* Elsasser was wrong about this had not yet
been obtained by the early twenty-first century.

In the light of the principle of finite classes, therefore,
it was the task of biology to account for the extant organisms functionally and holistically. Toward this end,
Elsasser advocated attention to several key concepts: "var-
iostability," the tendency for regularity to appear in
macroscopic structure despite irregularity in the finite
class of the underlying molecular structure; "creativity,"
the process whereby an organism navigates the states of a
finite class; and "operative symbolism," the use of control
structures, for example, genetic switches, to release creativity. Memory, for example, when analyzed from an
information-theoretic viewpoint was more than a problem of chemical storage, but had to be understood as a
manifestation of these concepts. Likewise, after some early
skepticism that DNA could be the carrier of hereditary
information in the organism, he produced the subtler
modified argument that, while DNA was the molecule of
heredity, it did not completely specify the organism but
rather acted as a trigger for its holistic morphological
development. Elsasser thus proposed that biology should
be treated as an essentially inductive science where the
"irrational" organism is the central focus of experimentation rather than the suborganismic components such as
molecules.

Whereas Elsasser's contributions to atomic physics
and geophysics are of acknowledged importance, his theoretical biology remains controversial. Many of his critics
were dismissive, seeing his efforts as an attempt to reintro-
duce vitalism into biological discourse, something that
Elsasser always denied. By the late 1960s Elsasser had
decided that his early theoretical biology was impaired by
his reluctance to offend the biological "establishment,"
many of whom were indeed evidently offended, and this
is reflected in the more speculative character of his subsequent writings. As a result, he was rather marginalized
from the scientific mainstream during the last fifteen years
of his life.

Nevertheless, with the expansion of systems biology
since the late 1990s, Elsasser has once again begun to be
discussed by biologists, for whom the problems of
extremely complex systems have continuing relevance.
Many of the specifics of Elsasser's biological work have
come to be considered obsolete—for instance, his early
skepticism concerning the role of DNA in information
storage and his prediction of indeterminate behavior by
proteins on the basis of the principle of finite classes.
Rather it is the questions that Elsasser asked, questions
neglected in the first fifty years of molecular biology, that
are his legacy in that field.

Alongside successes and challenges in his professional life, Elsasser experienced a hard personal loss with the death of his wife Margaret in 1954. He married his second wife Susanne Rosenfeld, a childhood friend (and relative), a decade later. The peripatetic pattern of his career continued, with moves to physics, later oceanography, at the University of California, San Diego (1956), to geology at Princeton (1962), to a research professorship at the Institute for Fluid Dynamics and Applied Mathematics at Maryland (1967) and, finally, to an adjunct professorship of earth and planetary science at Johns Hopkins (1974). This last post—after his formal retirement—proved to be the longest lasting of his multifarious career.

BIBLIOGRAPHY

Correspondence and manuscripts, primarily from the 1950s onward, are available from the Walter M. Elsasser Papers, Special Collections, Milton S. Eisenhower Library, Johns Hopkins University, Baltimore, Maryland. Elsasser's narrative response to a survey on the history of geophysics and the responses by several of Elsasser's colleagues to it are available from the Niels Bohr Library, American Center for Physics (NBL-ACP), College Park, Maryland. Oral history interviews with Elsasser and several of his teachers and colleagues are available from the Archives for the History of Quantum Physics (AHQP), at NBL-ACP and several other deposit libraries.

WORKS BY ELSASSER

"Bemerkungen zur Quantenmechanik freier Elektronen." *Naturwissenschaften* 13 (1925): 711.

"Interferenzerscheinigungen bei Korpuskularstrahlen." *Naturwissenschaften* 16 (1928): 720–725.

"Sur le principe de Pauli dans les noyaux." Pts. 1 and 2. *Journal de physique et le radium*, 7th ser., 4 (1933): 549–556; 5 (1934): 389–397, 635–639.

"On the Origin of the Earth's Magnetic Field." *Physical Review* 55 (1939): 489–498.

Heat Transfer by Infrared Radiation in the Atmosphere. Milton, MA: Harvard University, Blue Hill Meteorological Observatory, 1942. Rev. ed., with Margaret F. Culbertson, as *Atmospheric Radiation Tables*, Meteorological Monographs 4, no. 23. Boston: American Meteorological Society, 1960.

"Induction Effects in Terrestrial Magnetism." Parts 1, 2, and 3. *Physical Review* 69 (1946): 106–116, 202–212; 72 (1947): 832–833.

"The Earth's Interior and Geomagnetism." *Reviews of Modern Physics* 22 (1950): 1–35.

"The Hydromagnetic Equations." *Physical Review* 79 (1950): 183.

"Hydromagnetic Dynamo Theory." *Reviews of Modern Physics* 28 (1956): 135–163.

The Physical Foundation of Biology: An Analytical Study. New York: Pergamon, 1958.

Atom and Organism: A New Approach to Theoretical Biology. Princeton, NJ: Princeton University Press, 1966.

"Thermal Structure of the Upper Mantle and Convection." In *Advances in Earth Science: Contributions*, edited by Patrick M. Hurley. Cambridge, MA: MIT Press, 1966.

"Convection and Stress Propagation in the Upper Mantle." In *The Application of Modern Physics to the Earth and Planetary Interiors*, edited by Stanley K. Runcorn. London: Wiley-Interscience, 1969.

"Sea-Floor Spreading as Thermal Convection." *Journal of Geophysical Research* 76 (1971): 1101–1112.

The Chief Abstractions of Biology. Amsterdam: North-Holland; New York: American Elsevier, 1975.

Memoirs of a Physicist in the Atomic Age. New York: Science History Publications, 1978.

Reflections on a Theory of Organisms: Holism in Biology. Frelighsburg, Que.: Editions Orbis, 1987. Rev. ed., Baltimore: Johns Hopkins University Press, 1998.

OTHER SOURCES

Alfvén, Hannes, and Carl-Gunne Fälthammar. *Cosmical Electrodynamics: Fundamental Principles.* 2nd ed. Oxford: Clarendon Press, 1963.

Goeppert-Mayer, Maria. "The Shell Model" [Nobel Prize Lecture, 1963]. In *Physics, 1963–1970*, edited by Bengt Samuelsson and Michael Sohlman. *Nobel Lectures, Including Presentation Speeches and Laureates' Biographies.* Singapore and River Edge, NJ: World Scientific, 1998.

Jammer, Max. *The Conceptual Development of Quantum Mechanics.* New York: McGraw-Hill, 1966.

Kragh, Helge. *Quantum Generations: A History of Physics in the Twentieth Century.* Princeton, NJ: Princeton University Press, 1999.

Laudan, Rachel. "Terrestrial Magnetism." In *The Oxford Companion to the History of Modern Science*, edited by John L. Heilbron. Oxford: Oxford University Press, 2003.

Medicus, Heinrich. "Fifty Years of Matter Waves." *Physics Today* 27, no. 2 (1974): 38–45.

Parker, Eugene N. "Adventures with the Geomagnetic Field." In *Discovery of the Magnetosphere*, edited by C. Stewart Gillmor and John R. Spreiter. History of Geophysics, no. 7. Washington, DC: American Geophysical Union, 1997.

Rubin, Harry. "Walter M. Elsasser." *Biographical Memoirs* 68 (1995): 103–165.

———. "Complexity, the Core of Elsasser's Theory of Organisms." *Complexity* 7 (2002): 17–20.

Russo, Arturo. "Fundamental Research at Bell Laboratories: The Discovery of Electron Diffraction." *Historical Studies in the Physical and Biological Sciences* 12 (1981): 117–160.

Schaffner, Kenneth F. "Antireductionism and Molecular Biology. *Science* 157 (1967), 644–647.

Weisskopf, Victor F. "Physics as Natural Philosophy." *Nature* 278 (1979): 759–760.

Richard H. Beyler
Derek Gatherer

ELTON, CHARLES SUTHERLAND

(b. Manchester, England, 29 March 1900; d. Oxford, England, 1 May 1991) *animal ecology, conservation.*

Often considered the father of animal ecology, Elton published the field's first general synthesis, formulating principles that would shape subsequent concepts and methods. He founded a small research center, the Bureau of Animal Population, at Oxford University in 1932, and directed it until its dissolution upon his retirement in 1967. The bureau became an internationally significant center for research and scholarly exchange, influencing two generations of ecologists. Elton was the founding editor of the *Journal of Animal Ecology,* a position he held for two decades. He also contributed to Great Britain's nature conservation policies and agencies, and to defining the relevance of ecological science to economic and environmental concerns.

Early Life and Education. Charles Elton was the youngest of three sons of middle class, scholarly, and socially well-connected parents. Their father Oliver was an Oxford-educated professor of English at Liverpool University: a literary scholar, translator, and critic. Their mother Letitia Maynard (née MacColl) was a writer.

Geoffrey, the eldest son, attended Cambridge, served in the army during World War I, worked in fisheries research and finally as an English teacher. As children, Geoffrey and Charles rambled the countryside, studying nature near Liverpool and during holidays in the Malvern Hills. Years later Charles recalled that without Geoffrey's inspiration, he might never have become an ecologist. When Geoffrey died unexpectedly in 1927, Elton dedicated his first book to him, and also vowed to create a research institution in his memory.

Elton attended Liverpool College, and trained with the Army Cadet School (Royal Engineers), but escaped battlefield service. He entered New College, Oxford in 1919, graduating in 1922 with first-class honors in zoology. These Oxford years proved to be formative: He was mentored by the anatomist Edwin S. Goodrich and tutored by the zoologist Julian Huxley. Alexander Carr-Saunders was also influential, with Elton eventually applying his sociological ideas to animal populations. Studies near Liverpool, in the Lake District, and at Oxford—of ponds, an estuarine stream, and sand dunes—confirmed his interest in ecology. In Victor Shelford's *Animal Communities in Temperate America* (1913), he found models for the study of ecological communities.

Elton's relationship with Huxley was fruitful: Through him he gained his first experience with Arctic ecology, and he wrote his first book, *Animal Ecology* (1927), at Huxley's behest. Huxley's efforts to expand Oxford zoology beyond anatomy and embryology also created opportunities for Elton (and others) to pursue their interests in ecology. But the relationship was sometimes tense: Peter Crowcroft recorded Elton's terse comment, "I don't really mind when Julian steals my ideas. But I strongly object when he takes out a notebook and writes them down in front of me" (1991, p. 2).

After graduating in 1922, Elton remained at Oxford; he was at first employed part-time as a departmental demonstrator, then was promoted in 1929 to permanent status as university demonstrator. He retained this position until 1936, when he became university reader in animal ecology—a title he retained until retirement in September 1967.

In the early 1920s polar exploration had captured the British imagination, inspiring Oxford scientific expeditions to Spitsbergen (now Svalbard). These expeditions, part of an Oxford tradition of scientific study in remote locations, were seen as providing not just training in field sciences, but opportunities to build character and a spirit of teamwork. They would also prove essential to Elton's formation as an ecologist. He accompanied expeditions in 1921, 1923, and 1924, undertaking ecological surveys of arctic islands. In the latter two expeditions Elton served as ecologist and chief scientist. The relatively small number of species in northern ecological communities—a simplicity that presented the possibility of their full description—was of special interest to him. This complemented another environmental perspective that Elton gained through his northern experience. George Binney, the expedition leader, introduced aircraft and aerial photography as research tools, and used these to develop overviews of the northern landscape. This "view from above" would long influence Elton's perspective on nature: When describing ecological communities his perspective would be that of an elevated observer, able to perceive all the relations between species and their environment, and, in principle at least, to construct a comprehensive account of an ecological community. Although his Arctic research ended with a 1930 expedition to Lapland, these experiences would shape his perspective on ecology throughout his career.

Elton went on to play a large role in organizing expeditions, serving from 1927 to 1932 as the first chairman of the Oxford Exploration Club, and two more years as treasurer. The club organized thirteen expeditions before World War II, providing formative experiences for many later prominent ecologists and conservationists, including Max Nicholson, Nicholas Polunin, and Colin Trapnell.

Populations and Communities. While still in his early twenties, Elton drew on these experiences to construct a series of novel ecological perspectives. In 1923 he and botanist Victor Summerhayes published a paper, based on the 1921 expedition, in which they described the habitats and plant and animal communities found on Spitsbergen and Bear Island. Concluding that animal communities could be best described in terms of the food relations between species, they seized the opportunity presented by the relatively small number of species on Bear Island to present in diagram form a complete overview of their ecological interactions. In effect, they synthesized their knowledge of the natural history of the island by representing it in terms of the feeding relationships linking all animal species.

The following year Elton examined another phenomenon commonly associated with northern animal species. On the voyage home from the 1923 expedition, he had bought a book by the Norwegian biologist Robert Collett, *Norges Pattedyr*. He translated it, and studied Collett's discussion of northern animal populations, including his credulous accounts of the population explosions, migrations, and mass drownings of lemmings (stories, as eventually became evident, that were more folklore than fact). These convinced Elton that dramatic fluctuations were a characteristic feature of northern animal populations. Their existence, he thought, must overturn the widespread but erroneous assumption that populations maintain a state of balance. Understanding why these fluctuations occur could also illuminate the mechanisms by which populations are regulated. In a 1924 paper, "Periodic Fluctuations in the Numbers of Animals: Their Causes and Effects," Elton surveyed an extensive literature, including Collett, as well as C. Gordon Hewitt's *The Conservation of the Wildlife of Canada* (1921), which discussed fluctuations in Canadian populations of fur-bearing animals. Believing that the cause of these fluctuations lay in external factors, and specifically variations in climate, he explored the possibility of correlating them with an eleven-year cycle of sunspot activity. These fluctuations, he also argued, both had economic implications and were relevant to understanding the action of natural section.

In subsequent years Elton pursued a series of research projects, applying diverse methods but with a common focus on the regulation of animal populations. The first project began in 1925, when the Hudson's Bay Company hired him as a consultant. The position owed itself to George Binney's intervention; more generally, it reflected the company's interest in predicting variations in fur-bearing animal populations. For five years Elton immersed himself in the company's London archives. Its fur trade records extending back to 1736 would, he hoped, throw light on fluctuations in fur-bearing animals in Canada. Supplementary data were provided by the fur records of the Moravian Missions in Canada, extending from 1834 to 1925. In a second project, also beginning in 1925, he conducted field studies of mice and vole populations in Bagley Wood near Oxford, tracking their reproduction and mor-

tality. In this project Elton collaborated with other biologists, including John R. Baker and ecological geneticist Edmund B. Ford; they styled themselves the "Mouse Gesellschaft." This project ended in 1928, the same year Elton began a study of vole populations that drew not just on his own fieldwork, but on reports from a wide range of observers, collected through a self-styled "intelligence system." This project would continue until 1939.

Animal Ecology. While pursuing these studies on animal populations, Elton also wrote his first book, *Animal Ecology*, published in 1927. He had already demonstrated by his papers on animal communities and populations his interest in synthetic perspectives, but the immediate impetus for this book came from Huxley, who invited him to contribute to his series on biology. Their shared ambition, shaped in the context of a research community still focused on laboratory study of animals, was to demonstrate that ecology could also be studied scientifically. Animal ecologists, though, needed their own distinctive concepts, so as to be able to cease borrowing them from plant ecology (as they had with the concept of succession, for example).

Elton drew together decades of accumulated observations, and explained how these could be understood in terms of a small number of principles governing the structure and function of animal populations and communities. These included: the arrangement of species in food chains and cycles (or webs); the niche, as a description of an animal's place in its community, especially its relation to food and predators; and the principles of food size and pyramid of numbers, meaning that large numbers of small prey tend to be at one end of a food chain, and small numbers of large predators at the other. Such ideas were not entirely new—food chains of course were familiar, and Charles Darwin and other naturalists had discussed the niche concept. Elton, however, placed these ideas in new contexts; he explained, for example, the relation of an animal's size to its position on the food chain, or the value of viewing its niche in terms of functional (feeding) relationships.

Animal Ecology was noteworthy for its clear style and simplicity of language. Its significance also lay in its demonstration that ecological communities, in all their diversity and complexity, could be understood in terms of basic principles, that were based, in turn, on a classification of species as producers or consumers—an economic view of the natural order that was widely persuasive. This view of nature as an economy epitomized the ties of analogy and inspiration linking Elton's views of animal communities and human society. Humans, indeed, were at the heart of Elton's ecology: as he explained, his book was "chiefly concerned with ... the sociology and economics of animals" (p. vii). He often drew the parallels implied by this comment, perhaps most notably when he explained the niche concept in terms of an analogy between the "occupation" of a badger and that of a vicar (p. 64). In drawing these ties Elton exhibited the influence of Carr-Saunders, whose work Elton had studied closely. In *The Population Problem*, published in 1922, Carr-Saunders had applied a neo-Malthusian perspective to human populations, examining how societies differentiated in terms of traditions or level of development proved able or unable to restrict their increase in population, and so to live within the limits of their resources. To some extent, Elton read Carr-Saunders's sociology into nature; the sociologist's explanations of social and economic cycles, classes and conflicts influenced Elton's discussion of animal populations and relations between species.

Elton was somewhat unusual among ecologists in considering evolution—most ecologists at this time did not, and even he decided that the relevant chapter in *Animal Ecology* required some explanation. His interest undoubtedly reflected Huxley's influence, as well as his youthful reading of Darwin and Alfred Russell Wallace. Yet, like many British and American naturalists, he found unpersuasive strict Darwinian accounts that relied solely on natural selection. Some features, such as color, or differences between closely related species, could not, he believed, be explained in terms of selective advantage. Natural selection, he concluded, varies in its intensity, is only one of a number of agents of evolution, and sometimes fades into irrelevance. Population ecology, in fact, could illuminate this varying role of selection: the abundance of a species—whether it was crowded or scarce—would shape the selective pressures imposed by its environment, or, indeed, determine whether an animal might migrate elsewhere, thereby effectively upending Darwinian assumptions by selecting its environment, rather than the reverse.

Animal Ecology epitomized the approach Elton would follow in his research over the next few decades. The book opened with the disarming claim that "Ecology is a new name for a very old subject. It simply means scientific natural history" (p. 1). This captured Elton's intent: Throughout the book he discussed not just the concepts, but the practice of ecology, emphasizing that it was preeminently a field science, requiring careful observation of animals in their habitats. *Animal Ecology* also established a research agenda, outlining the topics requiring attention, including the significance of physical and biological factors to ecological interactions, and the implications of space and time. It also demonstrated the links between topics usually considered separately. For example, the pyramid of numbers and niche concepts showed how to relate research on feeding by individual organisms to the study of population size and animal community structure.

More generally, his view of how ecological communities are organized provided a basis for organizing work in the discipline—the order of ecological knowledge and practice paralleling the order of nature.

The view presented in *Animal Ecology* was eventually superseded by other approaches to theory, methods, and modeling. Nevertheless, two generations of ecologists testified to the influence of the framework presented by Elton, and his principles became staples of ecological training. The book was reprinted nine times and translated into several languages.

In two subsequent books, *Animal Ecology and Evolution*, published in 1930 (based on three 1929 lectures at the University of London), and *The Ecology of Animals*, appearing in 1933 as part of a series of popular accounts of biology, Elton presented his ideas to wider audiences. During these years his own views regarding theory were evolving, as well. Reflecting his wariness of efforts to represent the complexity of nature in mathematical terms, *Animal Ecology* had contained little discussion of work by theorists such as Alfred Lotka and Vito Volterra. Nevertheless, he would eventually find their work helpful, particularly the argument that not just environmental factors, but also interactions between or within species (including competition, the significance of which he had once viewed skeptically), could cause populations to fluctuate. He added a brief discussion of recent theoretical work to the second edition of *Animal Ecology* in 1935.

In 1928 Elton married Rose Montague (1906–1997). The match was dissolved amicably in 1937. Late that year, he married poet Edith Joy Scovell. They had two children, Catherine (1940) and Robert Andrew (1943). The marriage of Charles and Joy was happy—it was once described as a "true conversation." Elton's decision to make family life a priority may explain his reluctance to travel over much of the rest of his career. (He also disliked crowds, and his refusal to attend large meetings was perhaps also a factor.)

The Bureau of Animal Population. By the early 1930s Elton had developed a sophisticated perspective on animal populations and communities. The perspective would prove highly productive, yet it also embodied a tension. In *Animal Ecology* he had presented ecological communities as integrated, self-regulating entities tending towards equilibrium. At the same time, these communities could be highly unstable: the "balance of nature," he insisted, was a myth, and populations constantly varied as a result of disease, migration, or environmental change. It was a tension not unlike that facing Elton himself: living in a society that valued stability, yet that gave many only uncertainty and insecurity—a reality that a young and ambitious scientist of uncertain status in his own university could not but be aware.

British ecologists had to struggle for decades to obtain support for their research. Elton was no exception. Temporary positions at Oxford and elsewhere had supported him during the 1920s, but in 1930 the most significant one, his consultancy with the Hudson's Bay Company, fell victim to the economic crisis. Yet in the same year a new opportunity emerged. At Binney's instigation, American industrialist Copley Amory enlisted Elton to help organize his 1931 Conference on Biological Cycles, held at Matamek, Quebec. The conference was well attended, testifying to the interest in fluctuating populations, particularly of species with economic significance—several of which were in a state of ruinous scarcity in that region. As conference secretary Elton met many of the most active scientists in the field, including Canadian wildlife officials and biologists, and American game biologist Aldo Leopold, with whom he would develop a lengthy and friendly professional relationship. But he had another interest in participating, as well: the opportunity to discuss his research plans with potential funders. This effort was successful, and Elton returned home with a grant of 564 pounds per year for two and three-quarter years from the New York Zoological Society. These funds enabled Elton to persuade Oxford to give provisional approval for his most ambitious enterprise: the Bureau of Animal Population.

The bureau's purpose was to study fluctuations in animal populations, with special reference to the role of disease. More specifically, Elton envisaged several functions. One was to enable research on the causes of these fluctuations, through projects such as his study of vole populations. A second was to collect and store population data, including the output from two new studies: the Canadian Arctic Wild Life Enquiry, and the Snowshoe Rabbit Enquiry. Each involved the coordination of hundreds of observers—game managers, police officers, and trappers—who, using questionnaires distributed with the assistance of the Canadian National Parks Bureau, reported on animal population changes in their area. Elton considered this approach superior to his archival studies: It could provide a picture of fluctuations over a large area, and the data were not inferred from fur returns, but based on direct surveillance by knowledgeable observers.

These questionnaire studies—dubbed "mail-order zoology"—were pursued until the late 1940s, generating a series of papers, most written by other bureau ecologists and staff, including Dennis Chitty, Helen Chitty, and Mary Nicholson. The projects accumulated evidence of cycles of abundance of lynx, rabbits, and other species; these data were then tabulated on maps, illustrating Elton's view that population phenomena, including,

among other factors, the consequences of migration and environmental change, may be best understood in spatial terms. Yet explanations for these cycles remained elusive, and Elton eventually came to doubt that this method could find them.

Beyond field research and analysis of population data, the small group that Elton assembled at the bureau pursued a variety of tasks, all focused on population phenomena. These included breeding of laboratory animals for experimental work, research on reproduction, mortality, and the pathology of diseases, development of census methods, and application of statistical and mathematical methods to ecological problems. Whereas Elton himself never made extensive use of mathematics, he recognized its importance, drawing on the work of Lotka and other mathematically inclined scientists, even as he occasionally complained that they gave too little assistance to ecologists hoping to apply their techniques to nature. The value he attached to mathematics was evident in the role he gave Patrick Leslie, who joined the bureau in 1935 as assistant in biomathematics. Leslie worked closely with ecologists, introducing them to statistical and modeling techniques.

In its early years, financial security for the bureau proved elusive. Besides the crucial support of the New York Zoological Society, the bureau received funds from other sources, including the Royal Society of London, the Agricultural Research Council (ARC), and the chemical firm ICI. Elton saw fundraising as a waste of time and a distraction from research, but he pursued the task energetically. During one year alone (1937–1938) the bureau listed support from thirteen external agencies—the product of more than 100 letters of request. These supporters, particularly the ARC, also pressed Oxford itself to provide stable funding, and in 1935 it began to do so, albeit with the proviso that the Bureau continue to pursue outside support. Elton was also named a senior research fellow of Corpus Christi College in 1936.

While at times unsteady financially, and with only a small staff, the bureau nevertheless gained an international reputation for population research, attracting visiting scientists and students from many countries. It was said that almost everyone of note in ecology made a "pilgrimage" to the bureau, such that it served, as Crowcroft described it, as "the venue of a thirty-five-year international conference" (1991, p. 12). Many students, British and foreign, also came to study, several as Rhodes Scholars. They found not just research opportunities, but an outstanding library, and opportunities for discussion and collaboration. They also enjoyed the close-knit, collegial atmosphere of the bureau, even if most were conscious of their status as colleagues or students, but not friends, of "the boss." Elton himself did not travel extensively. In 1938, however, he and Joy toured Canada and the United States visiting colleagues, including Canadian biologists and conservationists, as well as Aldo Leopold in Wisconsin.

In 1932 the British Ecological Society, acknowledging the distinctive identity of Elton's field, permitted him to establish the *Journal of Animal Ecology*. He would edit it until 1951. In addition to conventional research articles, the journal presented abstracts of reports published elsewhere, including the publications of local natural history societies. This exemplified Elton's view that information collected by amateur but knowledgeable observers could also be an essential resource for ecologists—a view evident in his population research during the 1920s and 1930s, and that would be presented most expansively in his 1942 monograph, *Voles, Mice, and Lemmings*. He echoed this point in his communication with wider audiences. When in 1932, for example, the British Broadcasting Corporation invited him to present a series of radio lectures (these eventually appeared in book form as *Exploring the Animal World*, 1933), Elton encouraged his listeners to record systematically their observations of birds and other fauna.

Information provided by careful observers was, of course, only useful if it was organized. This was, as has been seen, one of the functions of the bureau, and this illustrates how Elton saw this task of organizing—of information, research collaborations, expeditions, publications—as a priority, and one which placed him at the center of diverse social networks combining amateurs and professionals. In addition, the bureau itself, as a storehouse of ecological information, and a crossroads in the professional terrain of ecology, reinforced his role in coordinating ecological research and knowledge. Together, these ambitious efforts constituted, in effect, partial fulfillment of plans for the organization of knowledge of the natural world along ecological lines that Elton had himself sketched on the last page of *Animal Ecology*.

Wytham Woods. Just as in the 1920s Elton formulated the perspectives that would guide his research over the following decade, the 1940s would be similarly formative. This time, however, he reconsidered, revised, even rejected, some of his earlier ideas. First, however, urgent events intervened. Shortly before war began in September 1939, Elton had proposed to the Ministry of Agriculture a study of the control of rodent pests endangering food stocks. This proposal—reflecting both Elton's interest in the practical implications of ecology, and his now well-honed ability to pursue funding opportunities—received quick approval, and until 1947 the survey and elimination of rodents (mostly rats, but also the house mouse) preoccupied Elton and other bureau ecologists. This work, apparently such a sharp departure from his previous studies, in fact drew on the research he and his colleagues had

done on rodent population dynamics, while branching into new directions, including animal behavior and the chemistry of poisons.

But in 1942 Elton also published a work distant in both conception and results from his work on rodent control. *Voles, Mice, and Lemmings* summarized years of research and collation of data relating to animal populations. Ranging widely, from Britain to Lapland to northern Canada, he demonstrated the existence of cycles in various species. Causes proved more elusive, with various possibilities considered—climate, interactions between populations, migration, environmental change—but with each able to account for only some observations. G. Evelyn Hutchinson of Yale University, who practiced an ecology more focused on theory and the testing of hypotheses, was both impressed by the book's avalanche of empirical observations, and frustrated by its lack of a conclusion. He titled his review, "Nati Sunt Mures, et Facta est Confusio" (Mice are born, and the result is confusion).

Elton was himself moving toward at least partial agreement with Hutchinson. He eventually concluded that the approach followed in *Voles, Mice, and Lemmings*, of induction from data collected by observers scattered over a large area, was unlikely to generate satisfying explanations. Helen Chitty had maintained the Canadian wildlife questionnaire surveys while the rest of the bureau was preoccupied with rodent control, but in the late 1940s they were suspended.

Long before then—indeed, the same year that he published *Voles, Mice, and Lemmings*—Elton had begun exploring an alternative approach to ecological survey, involving studies of population dynamics, interactions between species, and habitats, with the ultimate goal of building a detailed understanding of the ecology of a specific site. This approach reflected his growing interest, shared with other British ecologists, including Arthur Tansley (who had coined in 1935 the term *ecosystem*), in breaking down the division between plant and animal ecology, with the aim instead of formulating a synthetic perspective on ecological communities and their habitats.

An opportunity soon arose to put these plans into effect. Elton had originally envisaged an ambitious ecological survey of Oxfordshire, Berkshire, and Buckinghamshire, but in 1943 a more limited and therefore more practical terrain became available when the thousand-acre Wytham Woods estate near Oxford was donated to the university. It possessed abundant possibilities for ecological studies: As Elton described the scene in 1966, "a rich series of habitats from open ground and limestone to woodland with many springs and marshes interspersed occupies a hill set in riverine surroundings" (p. 17). It also had the security of tenure necessary for long-term studies—a valuable feature, given British ecologists' experience of losing research sites to development. A further advantage was the support now available from the Nature Conservancy, provided in recognition of the project's status as a pilot program for the ecological survey of nature reserves. As it did for British ecology generally, the Conservancy provided Elton with the novelty of reliable research funding. (Incorporation within the university's Department of Zoological Field Studies in 1947 had also given the bureau firmer institutional status.)

For two decades after the war, Wytham Woods was the site of intensive research, with Elton hosting field ecology courses, entertaining visiting scientists, supervising projects and graduate theses—providing, in short, the terrain on which he could apply his aptitude for organizing ecological research and information. These studies also contributed to the Wytham Biological Survey, an approach to data collection based on a system of habitat classification devised by Elton and Richard Miller, an American postgraduate.

In 1966 Elton summarized the findings of the first two decades of the survey in *The Pattern of Animal Communities*. As he did so, he distinguished his approach from that of ecologists who, overly "dazzled by the technical and mathematical triumphs of physics and chemistry," in his view embraced quantitative approaches at the expense of understanding nature's complexities (p. 374). Whereas, as has been observed, Elton valued mathematics, he never risked retreating into formulae. Always stressing the need for careful observation, often illustrating points through anecdotes drawn from the field, at heart he remained a field naturalist, with a strong aesthetic sense and a naturalist's joy at observing life. And as he once noted, fieldwork was essential if one was to have time to think!

Nature Conservation. Elton's affinity for nature was expressed not only through his research, but through his long-standing concern for the practical implications of ecology. These implications—fluctuations in the Canadian fur trade, or the impacts of rodents on food stocks, for example—commonly reflected, but went beyond, the priorities of his patrons. Elton was also a determined communicator, incorporating conservation concerns into his popular writings and radio talks.

During and after World War II Elton contributed to ecologists' advocacy for nature conservation. He served on the British Ecological Society's committee on nature conservation, and then worked with Tansley and other ecologists on the Wild Life Conservation Special Committee. Its 1947 report presented a plan for the Nature Conservancy, duly established two years later as the national agency responsible for ecological research, protection and management of nature reserves, and provision of advice on conservation. Like Tansley, John Baker (his Oxford colleague and Bagley Wood collaborator), and other British ecologists who were members of the Society for Freedom in Science, Elton combined these practical concerns with a belief in the need for science to remain independent of utilitarian compulsion. He continued until 1956 to serve on the Conservancy's Scientific Policy Committee; in more subtle ways his impact was expressed through his influence on individuals such as Max Nicholson, the Conservancy's dynamic Director-General.

The most prominent of Elton's practical concerns related to the ecological consequences of the movement of species. To his geographical perspective and interest in migration, already evident in his research on wildlife population cycles, Elton added a fascination with (as an ecologist) and an alarm regarding (as a conservationist) what he called "the breakdown in Wallace's realms": the establishment of populations of plants and animals in new areas as a result (intentionally or otherwise) of human actions. In 1958 he published *The Ecology of Invasions by Animals and Plants*, where he explained why he considered this phenomenon deeply problematic: "we are living in a period of the world's history when the mingling of thousands of kinds of organisms from different parts of the world is setting up terrific dislocations in nature" (p. 18). Presenting evidence that more diverse ecological communities are more stable and so better able to resist these dislocations, he concluded that conservation must encompass the preservation of diversity.

Elton retired in September 1967. To his chagrin, and in spite of his advocacy, the university took this occasion to close the bureau. This was partly the consequence of changing views regarding the organization of research at Oxford. It also reflected, however, how research in animal ecology had shifted away from Elton's "scientific natural history." The style of patient observation and data collection represented by the Wytham Biological Survey was less suited to newer trends in theoretical ecology, or to an increasingly competitive scientific world that demanded immediate results. Young ecologists such as Robert MacArthur were pursuing new approaches to theory, modeling and experimentation with populations; ecosystem ecology, with its focus on flows of energy and nutrients, was attracting much attention. To some, Elton's continued focus on accumulation of data and induction of general principles had begun to appear as the relic of an earlier generation. Elton himself conducted relatively little research after retirement, although visits to South and Central America in 1965, 1968, and 1970 provided the basis for a study of the invertebrate ecology of the neotropical rain forest.

Yet Elton had an enormous influence on the field—a legacy testified to by countless students and colleagues. The concepts he elucidated: of food chains and cycles, the pyramid of numbers, and the niche, became staples of ecological training—so intrinsic to the grammar of the field that many no longer associated them with an actual individual. The broader approach they represented: of understanding ecological communities in terms of feeding relationships—generalized as flows of nutrients and energy—gained a similar status, and eventually underpinned the study of ecoenergetics and ecosystem ecology.

Elton's influence was also expressed through his organizational vision, most immediately by the formation and nurturing of the Bureau of Animal Population into an institution that influenced the careers of dozens of ecologists. This vision was also evident in his contributions to constructing animal ecology as a distinct field of study, the formation of the Nature Conservancy as the chief postwar institution for British ecology, and the emergence of environmentalism through his writings and lectures. The more recent revival of his *Ecology of Invasions*, celebrated by some as a prescient commentary on the new field of "invasion biology," testifies to his continuing significance.

Elton received many honors. In 1931 he was named a fellow of the New York Zoological Society, in 1953 a fellow of the Royal Society, and in 1983 an honorary fellow of the Institute of Biology in London. He also became in 1961 the first foreigner to be named an eminent ecologist by the Ecological Society of America, and in 1968 was named a foreign honorary member by the American Academy of Arts and Sciences. Additional awards included the Linnean Society Gold Medal (1967), the Darwin Medal of the Royal Society (1970), and the Tyler Award (1976). A succession of organizations named him an honorary life member: the Chicago Academy of Science (1946), The Wildlife Society (1949), the British Ecological Society (1960), the American Society of Mammalogists (1973), and the American Society of Zoologists (1985). He resided in Oxford with his wife Joy until his death in 1991. Elton's unpublished materials are held by the Bodleian Library, Oxford University.

BIBLIOGRAPHY

WORKS BY ELTON

With Victor S. Summerhayes. "Contributions to the Ecology of Spitsbergen and Bear Island." *Journal of Ecology* 11 (1923): 214–268.

"Periodic Fluctuations in the Numbers of Animals: Their Causes and Effects." *British Journal of Experimental Biology* 2 (1924): 119–163.

Animal Ecology. London: Sidgwick & Jackson, 1927.

Animal Ecology and Evolution. Oxford, U.K.: Clarendon Press, 1930.

The Ecology of Animals. London: Methuen, 1933.

Voles, Mice, and Lemmings: Problems in Population Dynamics. Oxford, U.K.: Clarendon Press, 1942.

"Population Interspersion: An Essay on Animal Community Patterns." *Journal of Ecology* 37 (1949): 1–23.

"Research on Rodent Control by the Bureau of Animal Population September 1939 to July 1947." In *Control of Rats and Mice*, 3 vols., edited by Dennis Chitty. Oxford, U.K.: Clarendon Press, 1954.

With Richard S. Miller. "The Ecological Survey of Animal Communities: With a Practical System of Classifying Habitats by Structural Characters." *Journal of Ecology* 42 (2, 1954): 460–496.

The Ecology of Invasions by Animals and Plants. London: Methuen, 1958.

The Pattern of Animal Communities. London: Methuen, 1966.

OTHER SOURCES

Anker, Peder. *Imperial Ecology: Environmental Order in the British Empire, 1895–1945*. Cambridge, MA: Harvard University Press, 2001.

Chitty, Dennis. *Do Lemmings Commit Suicide? Beautiful Hypotheses and Ugly Facts*. New York: Oxford University Press, 1996.

Cox, David L. "Charles Elton and the Emergence of Modern Ecology." PhD diss. St. Louis, MO: Washington University, Department of Biology, 1979.

Crowcroft, Peter. *Elton's Ecologists: A History of the Bureau of Animal Population*. Chicago: University of Chicago Press, 1991.

Hagen, Joel. *An Entangled Bank: The Origins of Ecosystem Ecology*. New Brunswick, NJ: Rutgers University Press, 1992.

Hardy, Alister. "Charles Elton's Influence in Ecology." *Journal of Animal Ecology* 37 (1968): 3–8.

Hutchinson, G. Evelyn. "Nati sunt mures, et facta est confusion." *Quarterly Review of Biology* 17, no. 4 (1942): 354–357. Review of Charles Elton's *Voles, Mice and Lemmings*.

Kingsland, Sharon E. *Modeling Nature: Episodes in the History of Population Ecology*. Chicago: University of Chicago Press, 1985.

Lindström, Jan, Esa Ranta, Hanna Kokko, et al. "From Arctic Lemmings to Adaptive Dynamics: Charles Elton's Legacy in Population Ecology." *Biological Reviews* 76 (2001): 129–158.

Macfadyen, Amyan. "Obituary: Charles Sutherland Elton." *Journal of Animal Ecology* 61 (1992): 499–502.

Morrell, Jack. *Science at Oxford 1914–1939: Transforming an Arts University*. Oxford, U.K.: Clarendon Press, 1997.

Paviour-Smith, Kitty. "Elton, Charles Sutherland (1901–1991)." *Oxford Dictionary of National Biography*. Oxford: Oxford University Press, 2004. Available from http://www.oxforddnb.com.

Southwood, Richard, and J.R. Clarke. "Charles Sutherland Elton." *Biographical Memoirs of Fellows of the Royal Society* 45 (1999): 129–146. Includes a complete Elton bibliography.

Stephen Bocking

EMERSON, ALFRED EDWARDS (*b.* Ithaca, New York, 31 December 1896; *d.* Huletts Landing, New York, 3 October 1976), *biogeography, ecology, entomology, evolutionary biology, systematic biology.*

Emerson was a leading authority on the classification, anatomy, and biogeography of termites, noted for his writing on the concept of the "superorganism." He used termite nest structure and termite colony behavior as important traits in his classifications. He also made significant contributions to the "Chicago school" of ecology and debates over evolutionary speciation, drawing generalizations from data and observations on adaptations, behavior, geographical distribution, and physiology.

Early Life and Education. Emerson was born in Ithaca, New York, on 31 December 1896, the youngest of four children of Alfred Emerson, a classical archaeologist then teaching at Cornell University, and Alice Louisa (Edwards) Emerson, a concert pianist and instructor in the history of music. He grew up in Chicago after his father joined the staff of the University of Chicago's Art Institute as curator of antiquities. Family life revolved around the arts, and Emerson developed an early interest in music. Thoughts of a career in music, however, gave way to a fascination with biology, after he was placed in charge of building and maintaining a poultry farm at the Interlaken School, Rolling Prairie, Indiana, which he attended from 1910 to 1914. Emerson later described himself as the Emerson family's "scientific mutant." In 1914 he returned to Ithaca and enrolled at Cornell University for its agricultural program, but he soon found that the program lacked the intellectual challenge he desired.

After taking courses in all of Cornell's scientific departments, he decided to major in entomology, studying at the premier entomology department in the United States under Professors John Henry Comstock and James G. Needham. The Comstock school of entomology focused on an evolutionary approach to insect systematics that included analysis of embryological, ecological, and behavioral characters. In the Cornell "Insectary," students observed living organisms in their natural environments. Needham was also a pioneer in the emerging fields of ecology and limnology, introducing students to insect life in its dynamic aquatic environments. Emerson built on this strong base in his own career. He also formed a close friendship with the Comstocks and Needhams. Professor Comstock's wife, Anna Botsford Comstock, was a leading figure in the Nature Study movement in the United States. Emerson attended Cornell with Karl Patterson Schmidt, a lifelong friend and collaborator, who was later curator of herpetology at the Chicago Natural History Museum, now the Field Museum.

Career in Termite Systematics. After receiving his BS from Cornell in 1918, Emerson served in the U.S. Army during World War I, but he did not see combat. Following his discharge in December 1918, he made the first of several field trips to the tropics, visiting the New York Zoological Society's Station at Kartabo in British Guiana. The trip proved to be a pivotal moment in his life, when the New York Zoological Society naturalist and pioneering marine biologist William Bebee suggested that Emerson focus his research on termites, setting the course of his scientific career. Emerson completed the MA at Cornell in 1920 and returned to Kartabo for additional fieldwork that year and again in 1924, serving as assistant director of the station and amassing a large taxonomic collection and behavioral observations that would be the basis for years of research. In 1925 he was awarded the PhD from Cornell, with a dissertation on "The Termites of Kartabo, Bartica District, British Guiana," which was subsequently published in *Zoologica*. In 1921 he had been appointed an instructor at the University of Pittsburgh; after receiving his doctorate, he advanced to associate professor there from 1925 to 1929. He was also a Guggenheim Fellow in 1925 and 1926, conducting research at laboratories in Italy and Sweden on the ontogenetic and phylogenetic origin of the castes of termites.

In 1929 Emerson was appointed associate professor of zoology at the University of Chicago, where he remained until his retirement in 1962. In 1934 he advanced to full professor. This highly regarded department had been founded in 1892 as a research center by the noted embryologist Charles Otis Whitman, who also directed the Marine Biological Laboratory at Woods Hole, Massachusetts. At the time of Emerson's appointment, the Department of Zoology was chaired by embryologist Frank R. Lillie. Colleagues in the department included Sewall Wright, a pioneer in the application of statistical analysis to genetics and evolutionary biology, and Warder Clyde Allee, an ecologist interested in the evolutionary significance of animal societies. Emerson was an active participant in the development of a revitalized undergraduate curriculum in biology at Chicago, known as the "New Plan." In earlier years, undergraduate biology education had languished at the university. Under Lillie's leadership, a series of four basic courses in biological sciences were developed and taught by all department faculty. While research remained the highest priority of the department, undergraduate and graduate teaching were now required of all professors. Faculty and student interaction was also fostered by meetings of the "Zoology Club," a weekly social gathering followed by a lecture and discussion. During his career, Emerson also held visiting appointments as an instructor in the biology laboratory at Cold Spring Harbor in 1922, at the University of California at Berkeley in the summer of 1949, and as

Distinguished Professor of Natural Science at Michigan State University in the spring of 1960.

Emerson published more than one hundred articles on the natural history, classification, evolution, and biogeography of termites. He was probably the most prolific of the termite systematists, publishing species descriptions as well as revisions of higher taxa. He was a research associate of the Chicago Museum of Natural History from 1942 and the American Museum of Natural History from 1940 until his death. In 1935 he conducted field work at the Canal Zone Biological Area on Barro Colorado Island in Panama, now the Smithsonian Tropical Research Institute. During his career, he conducted fieldwork in North, Central, and South America; the Caribbean; Asia; the Indian subcontinent; Pacific islands; Australia; Africa; and Europe. His collection contained specimens of 1,745 species, some 91 percent of the known taxa; it was acquired by the American Museum of Natural History. Emerson was deeply interested in termite physiology, morphology, and behavior. His observations focused on the social behavior and complex division of labor into separate castes in the termite colony, a stable environment that termites create, monitor, regulate, and defend. He was especially interested in using such behavioral traits as geographically specific nest-building techniques to differentiate taxonomic groups. Emerson called the structure of termite nests "frozen behavior"—a character that could be observed, illustrated, and weighed as accurately as any anatomical character. He demonstrated that species of *Apicotermes* termites that looked similar could be differentiated by their nest-building habits. He also studied the other organisms that had evolved within the environment created by the termite colony. Emerson also distinguished between stable, nonfunctional characters and rapidly evolving functional characters in his classifications. Emerson's work was highly influential in integrating behavioral characters into systematic and evolutionary biology.

Emerson was also an expert on the geographical distribution of termite taxa, publishing such works as "The Biogeography of Termites" in 1952. His significant publications on the geographical range and evolution of termites ensured that termite—and insect—distribution was an important component of the emerging field of biogeography. Emerson was among the group of thinkers who developed the "evolutionary synthesis" in the 1940s, integrating modern genetic theory with Charles Darwin's theory of evolution of species. He was a founding member of the Society for the Study of Evolution, and he participated in symposia surrounding the centennial of the publication of Darwin's *On the Origin of Species* in 1859.

The Chicago School. At the University of Chicago, Emerson, Warder Clyde Allee, and Thomas Park became the leading figures in the "Chicago school" of ecology, which shared a conceptual framework that emphasized the importance of cooperation in the natural world and focused on the population, not the individual, as the unit of ecological study and evolutionary selection. The Chicago school became primarily known through their 1949 seminal work, *Principles of Animal Ecology*, which synthesized contemporary ecological thought and highlighted the emerging field of population biology. The volume was known popularly as "The Great AEPPS" for its authors: Warder Clyde Allee, Alfred Edwards Emerson, Orlando Park, Thomas Park, and Emerson's old friend, Karl Patterson Schmidt. Allee, Emerson, and Thomas Park were on the University of Chicago faculty. The Park brothers were both students of Allee; Orlando Park then joined the faculty at nearby Northwestern University. Schmidt, who attended Cornell with Emerson, was then curator of herpetology at the Chicago Natural History or Field Museum. The five biologists formed the core of the "Ecology Group," an informal seminar that met on alternate Monday evenings to discuss contemporary ideas. Thomas Park focused his research on the experimental analysis of population phenomenon, and his 1939 paper to the group, "Concerning Ecological Principles," stimulated work on the volume. For the next decade, the five met on Sunday evenings to carefully review and discuss each chapter.

The AEPPS text is credited with stimulating much population biology and community ecology in the 1950s and 1960s. It also created the model for later ecology textbooks, such as Eugene P. Odum's 1953 *Fundamentals of Ecology*. Emerson's most distinctive contribution was to highlight the importance of studying behavior in the social insects. The Chicago school members believed that only group selection could account for many of the ecological and evolutionary processes they observed in populations. They were influenced by their colleague Sewall Wright's interdemic model of selection in which evolution is the result of natural selection operating on a set of demes or small semi-isolated groups. They also focused on the concept of cooperation, arguing that competition, at the group level, could be either beneficial and therefore a form of cooperation, or it could be dysfunctional. Their work on cooperation had been stimulated by the 1939 book *Bio-Ecology*, by Frederick Clements and Victor Shelford, which coined the term *disoperation* to describe interactions between organisms that had immediate harmful effects. In his work on termites, Emerson argued that evolution could only be understood by studying the action of selection on populations, rather than individuals, and used the concept of cooperation to explain the origins of sociality and social organizations in insect communities. Emerson believed that cooperation was superior because it created a division of labor, allowed selection to act at a group level, and tended to create homeostasis. The cooperative and productive work of the Chicago school of ecology was itself a demonstration of Emerson's belief than organisms functioned best in groups.

The Concept of the Superorganism. Emerson is perhaps best known for his use of the concept of the "superorganism" in evolutionary biology, a concept first developed by the noted ant specialist William Morton Wheeler in the early twentieth century. Wheeler had taught at the University of Chicago prior to Emerson's arrival. Both men were influenced by their observations and studies of complex insect societies that differentiated members through a division of labor. Emerson integrated thinking on homeostasis and equilibrium theory with Darwin's principle of natural selection to develop his theory of biological and social evolution. In publications such as his 1952 essay, "The Superorganismic Aspects of the Society," Emerson used the behavioral and structural characters of the colony, as well as the anatomical and physiological characters of individual organisms. For Emerson, the social group—in his research, the entire termite colony—was the unit of selection in evolution, not the individual organism. Competition within and between species, he argued, occurred at multiple levels within an ecological system and created either cooperation or conflict. He concluded that reproductive behavior and the division of labor were the fundamental group adaptations that controlled the social evolution of the group. In 1950s essays such as "Dynamic Homeostasis: A Unifying Principle in Organic, Social, and Ethical Evolution" and "Homeostasis and Comparison of Systems," he argued that the social insects were the exemplification of "dynamic homeostasis," that is, their group level adaptations led to a greater overall functional efficiency and ecological equilibrium, a concept that he believed would prove to be a unifying principle of evolutionary biology. Emerson's concept of the "superorganism" had little long-term impact on a field that was to move away from holistic approaches to research, focusing on more specialized studies. However, Emerson's work was an important influence in the "units of selection" debate that stimulated much work in evolutionary biology throughout the second half of the twentieth century.

Emerson also extended his analysis of the evolution of social dynamics to human populations in essays such as "Biological Sociology" in 1941, "Biological Principles of Human Social Integration" in 1948, "Human Cultural Evolution and Its Relation to Organic Evolution of Termites" in 1962, and in 1973 "Some Biological Antecedents of Human Purpose." Emerson acknowledged a difference between animal and human social evolution, based on human ability to communicate through learned symbols, but argued that such communication was sub-

ject to the same forces as genes. Emerson and Allee were regarded as highly principled men, and their scientific views were integrally related to their social views. Indeed, during World War II, they publicly argued against the misuse of Darwin's principle of the survival of the fittest to justify nationalist aggression and genocide. They maintained that cooperation was more often the key to survival and well-being among social organisms, especially humans. Allee's views, influenced by his Quaker religion, held that cooperation was an absolute good. Emerson's concept of cooperation was based on a relativistic natural ethics that held that the good and right were those things and actions that functioned to ensure efficient homeostasis for all members of the society. Human ethics served as an integrating mechanism at many levels in human societies that led toward greater homeostasis. Both Allee and Emerson advocated social democracy, based on peaceful intergroup competition, similar to Wright's interdemic selection. Emerson rejected the communism and socialism of his day, arguing that competitive capitalism, under strong social control, produced better results.

Emerson also engaged in the discussions of science and religion in his 1960 article "The Impact of the Theory of Evolution on Religion." Throughout his career, Emerson addressed popular, as well as scholarly, audiences, likely reflecting the influence of Anna Botsford Comstock and the Nature Study approach he had learned at Cornell. Indeed, Emerson's first publication, "A Willy-Nilly Stepmother and Other Disasters," appeared in 1917 in the *Nature Study Review*. He also wrote for such popular journals as *Classroom Teacher, Natural History,* and *New Republic.* In 1937 he coauthored a children's book on termite biology and society, *Termite City,* with Eleanor Fish.

Emerson's professional activities reflected his broad interests in contemporary biology. Emerson was an influential member of the Ecological Society of America, serving as editor of *Ecology* from 1932 to 1939, as well as secretary-treasurer in 1931 and president in 1941. He was an active member of the Society for Systematic Zoology, serving as its president in 1958, and of the Entomological Society of America, serving as vice president. He was a co-organizer of the Society for the Study of Evolution, and he served as its president in 1960. He was a fellow of the New York Zoological Society and the Animal Behavior Society. He was active in the American Association for the Advancement of Science, serving as Section F, Zoological Sciences, vice president in 1946, and in the Illinois State Academy of Science, serving as president from 1945 to 1946. Emerson also served on the Cornell University Committee on Systematics, Evolution, and Environmental Biology; the Atlantica Foundation, an organization that supported research, especially the Atlantica Ecological Research Station in Southern Rhodesia; and the Belgian American Educational Foundation, a group that supported technical schools, libraries, and scientific research. In recognition of his contributions to zoology, Emerson received an honorary DSc from Michigan State University in 1961. He was elected a Fellow of the National Academy of Sciences in 1962 and served as chair of the board of its Bache Fund. He received the Eminent Ecologist Award of the Ecological Society of America in 1967.

Family Life and Interests. In 1920 Emerson married Winifred Jelliffe, whom he had met at Cornell. She was the daughter of the prominent psychiatrist Smith Ely Jelliffe. They had two children, Helena Emerson (Wilkening) and William Jelliffe Emerson. After Winifred's sudden death in 1949, while Emerson was a visiting instructor in biology at the University of California at Berkeley, Emerson married Eleanor Fish in 1950. An old friend, she had coauthored the children's book *Termite City* with him; she died in 1971. Emerson's younger sister, Gertrude (Mrs. Boshi Sen), lived in India and became editor of *Asia Magazine*. Because of her extensive connections there, Emerson visited the subcontinent several times and formed a friendship with Indian Prime Minister Indira Gandhi in his later years.

After retirement from the University of Chicago in 1962, Emerson was named professor emeritus and moved to Huletts Landing, New York. He made his second "around the world" tour, continuing his taxonomic collecting and ecological observations. He and his wife, Eleanor, returned to Chicago for several months each year to conduct research at the university's libraries and laboratories, as well as to enjoy the music and arts offerings of the city. He continued to write and publish in his later years, especially on fossil termites. In 1976, the year of his death, he revised two papers for inclusion in *External Constructions of Animals*. He died in Huletts Landing, New York, on 3 October 1976, following a heart attack.

BIBLIOGRAPHY

The Alfred E. Emerson Papers, 1917–1976, are held by the University of Chicago Library, Special Collections Research Center.

WORKS BY EMERSON

"A Willy-Nilly Stepmother and Other Disasters." *Nature Study Review* 13 (1917): 198–199.

"The Termites of Kartabo, Bartica District, British Guiana." *Zoologica* 6 (1925): 291–459; 7 (1926): 69–100.

Second Year College Sequence in Botany, Zoology, and Physiology. Syllabus for Zoology. Chicago: University of Chicago Press, 1931.

With Eleanor Fish. *Termite City.* Chicago: Rand McNally, 1937.

"Biological Sociology." *Journal of the Scientific Laboratories, Denison University* 36 (1941): 146–155.

"Biological Principles of Human Social Integration." *Intercultural Education News* 9 (1948): 8–9.

With Warder Clyde Allee, Orlando Park, Thomas Park, and Karl P. Schmidt. *Principles of Animal Ecology.* Philadelphia: W.B. Saunders Co., 1949.

"The Biogeography of Termites." *Bulletin of the American Museum of Natural History* 99 (1952): 217–225.

"Phylogeny of Social Behavior as Illustrated by the Termite Genus *Apicotermes*." *Bulletin of the Ecological Society of America* 33 (1952): 66.

"The Supraorganismic Aspects of the Society." In *Structure et Physiologie des Societes animals.* Colloquium International de Centre National de la Recherche Scientifique, no. 34, 1952.

"The Biological Foundations of Ethics and Social Progress." In *Goals of Economic Life,* edited by A. D. Ward. New York: Harper and Brothers, 1953.

"Dynamic Homeostasis: A Unifying Principle in Organic, Social, and Ethical Evolution." *Scientific Monthly* 78 (1954): 67–85.

"Homeostasis and Comparison of Systems." In *Toward a Unified Theory of Human Behavior,* edited by Roy R. Grinker Sr. New York: Basic Books, 1956.

"Ethospecies, Ethotypes, Taxonomy, and Evolution of *Apicotermes* and *Allognathotermes* (Isoptera: Termitidae)." *American Museum Novitates* 1771 (1956): 1–31.

"The Impact of the Theory of Evolution on Religion." In *Science Ponders Religion,* edited by Harlow Shapley. New York: Appleton-Century-Crofts, 1960.

"The Impact of Darwin on Biology." *Acta Biotheoretica* 15 (1962): 175–216.

"Human Cultural Evolution and Its Relation to Organic Evolution of Termites." In *Termites of the Humid Tropics,* Proceedings of the New Delhi Symposium, 4–12 October 1960. Paris: UNESCO, 1962.

"A Revision of the Tertiary Fossil Species of the Kalotermitidae (Isoptera)." *American Museum Novitates* 2359 (1969): 1–57.

"Some Biological Antecedents of Human Purpose." *Zygon* 8, no. 3–4 (1973): 294–309.

"Termite Nests: A Study of the Phylogeny of Behavior" and "Changes in the Biological Basis of Termite Ethology with More Recent Bibliography." In *External Constructions by Animals,* Benchmark Papers in Behavior, edited by Nicholas Collias and E. Collias. Stroudsburg, PA: Dowden, Hutchinson and Ross, 1976.

OTHER SOURCES

Guide to the Alfred E. Emerson Papers, 1917–1976. Chicago: University of Chicago Library, Special Collections Research Center, 1999.

Mitman, Gregg. "From Population to Society: The Cooperative Metaphors of W. C. Allee and A. E. Emerson." *Journal of the History of Biology* 21, no. 2 (1988): 173–194.

Newman, Horatio H. "History of the Department of Zoology in the University of Chicago." *Bios* 19 (1948): 215–239.

Park, Thomas. "Alfred Edwards Emerson, Eminent Ecologist—1967." *Bulletin of the Ecological Society of America* 48 (1967): 104–107.

"Prof. Alfred Emerson, Pioneer in Ecology, Dies." *Chicago Tribune*, 5 October 1976, B7.

Wilson, Edward O., and Charles D. Michener. "Alfred Edwards Emerson, December 31, 1896–October 3, 1976." *National Academy of Sciences Biographical Memoirs* 53: 159–177. Washington, DC: National Academy Press, 1982.

Pamela M. Henson

EMMETT, PAUL HUGH (*b.* Portland, Oregon, 22 September 1900; *d.* Portland, 22 April 1985), *chemistry, catalysis.*

Emmett devoted sixty years of research to unraveling the myriad complexities and subtleties of chemical catalysis. After the turn of the twentieth century, industrial chemists were increasingly employing metal catalysts to make chemical reactions fast and efficient. However, the scientific understanding of catalysis lagged far behind its technical importance throughout the first half of the century. Emmett was one of a small group of chemists, beginning in the 1920s, who were undaunted by the complexity of the phenomena they were investigating. His most important contribution was his research in the mid-1930s on determining the surface area of catalyst particles. Before this work, researchers could not distinguish between catalysts that very efficiently expedited chemical reactions and those that reacted molecules more slowly over a very large surface area. In order to investigate the actual mechanism of catalysis, it was critical to normalize experiments by accounting for differences in surface area. Working with a colleague, Stephen Brunauer, and physicist Edward Teller, Emmett developed a straightforward experimental method for determining the surface area of a catalyst particle. Their classic paper, "Adsorption of Gases in Multimolecular Layers," was published in 1938; their surface area formula soon became known as the BET (Brunauer-Emmett-Teller) equation.

Over his long, productive career, Emmett published 164 papers and edited 8 books. Perhaps reflecting the scientific ethos of his formative years—the 1920s—his approach to research was to investigate what were deemed at the time the "fundamentals" of catalysis—that is, to explain the various physical and chemical properties that determined how a particular catalyst worked. The goal of this work, of course, was to develop a more general understanding of the phenomena involved. His methodology can be characterized as scientific puzzle solving. Emmett became highly skilled at designing experiments and interpreting the data they yielded. His extensive study of catalysts used to make ammonia was cited by catalysis pioneer Hugh S. Taylor as a model for others to emulate. In recog-

nition of his stature in catalysis, Emmett was elected to the National Academy of Sciences in 1955.

Childhood and Education. Emmett was born in Portland, Oregon, on 22 September 1900, to John Hugh and Vina (Hutchens). His father worked for a railroad and had become an expert on explosives. In high school, Emmett took no science classes until his senior year, when a guidance counselor suggested that he take chemistry and physics. His chemistry teacher, William Green, inspired him to continue studying chemistry in college. Green apparently had a similar effect on another young man, Linus Pauling. Emmett, who was a friend of Pauling, followed him to the Oregon Agricultural College (now Oregon State University) at Corvallis and then for graduate school to the new California Institute of Technology (Caltech) in 1922. (They would publish a paper together in 1925, "The Crystal Structure of Barite," on the crystal structure of barium sulfate.) Emmett was attracted to Caltech because of its eminent faculty members, including Arthur A. Noyes in chemistry and Robert Millikan in physics, and the fact that its graduate stipends were double those of other schools. At Caltech, Emmett worked with Arthur F. Benton, who had been a student of Hugh S. Taylor at Princeton University in New Jersey. Benton was an accomplished experimentalist working on the role of adsorption in catalysis. For his thesis, Emmett studied a number of metal oxide systems to determine whether during reduction with hydrogen, the reduced metal atoms became catalytic sites that accelerated the reaction rate. This was his initiation into the emerging science of catalysis.

The BET Equation. After earning his doctorate at Caltech in 1925, Emmett taught for one year at his undergraduate alma mater before joining the Fixed Nitrogen Research Laboratory (FNRL) in Washington, D.C., during 1926. The FNRL had been founded in 1919 as a continuation of wartime efforts to develop an American "fixed" nitrogen industry for the production of synthetic ammonia. At the outbreak of World War I, most of the world's supply of nitrates, an essential ingredient in explosives and fertilizer, came from mines in Chile. Germany, which had stockpiled only enough nitrates for a short war, came to rely on the new Haber-Bosch process that produced ammonia from the high-pressure catalytic reaction of nitrogen and hydrogen. In the early 1920s the FNRL developed its own ammonia process, a key component of which was an effective catalyst.

When Emmett joined the FNRL, located at American University, he was assigned to work on the iron catalyst used in the process. As part of his extensive studies on ammonia catalysts, he realized that it would be important to know the surface area of catalyst particles; his research on this matter led to the famous BET equation. The scientific challenge was to correlate what could be measured, which in this case was curves of the mass of gas adsorbed on a catalyst surface as a function of pressure at a constant temperature. Emmett's mentor, Benton, had conducted experiments with nitrogen that showed several kinks in this curve. Benton had hypothesized that these kinks might signal the completion of the first and then additional layers of gas molecules surrounding the catalyst surface. However, Emmett determined that the kinks could be accounted for by deviations from the ideal gas law. Upon further study of these curves, Emmett surmised that the beginning of the linear section might indicate the completion of a monolayer and the beginning of a second layer of adsorbed molecules. Using a number of different gases and catalysts, Emmett became convinced that his hypothesis was correct. At this point, in 1937, Brunauer, who was doing the experimental work and also had helped analyze the curves, told a former teacher and fellow Hungarian, Teller, about this research. Teller had left Hungary in 1935 and taken a position in the Physics Department at George Washington University in Washington, D.C. Starting with the earlier work of Irving Langmuir on adsorbed monolayers, Teller developed a theory of multilayer adsorption, which included the equation for calculating surface area from adsorption data.

In his eleven years at the FNRL and—after 1927—its successor, the U.S. Department of Agriculture's Bureau of Chemistry and Soils, Emmett also developed methods for determining the surface composition of multicomponent catalysts. (The ammonia catalyst was a three-component one.) One of Emmett's favorite projects was one which showed that an anomaly in the predicted and measured equilibrium constant in the important water gas reaction ($H_2O + CO = H_2 + CO_2$) was the result of thermal diffusion effects in standard apparatus.

Mellon Institute and Johns Hopkins. In 1937 Emmett moved to Johns Hopkins University, where he became the first head of its Department of Chemical Engineering. He later noted that during the late 1930s and early 1940s, it was very difficult to find money to finance basic research. In 1943 Emmett left Hopkins and joined the Manhattan Project, where he did mostly administrative work before moving on the following year to the Mellon Institute in Pittsburgh to work on research sponsored by Gulf Oil, which had its headquarters there. His research at the Mellon Institute focused on sorting out the complex set of reactions occurring in the Fischer-Tropsch process that produced gasoline from carbon monoxide and hydrogen. This process had been commercialized in Germany, and American oil companies saw it as a potential alternative to processes based on petroleum should supplies of it

become scarce and expensive. To follow the complex path of reactions, Emmett used molecules that were tagged with radioactive carbon-14 atoms. As concerns about the future supply of oil faded in the 1950s, Emmett shifted to studying catalytic cracking of petroleum fractions to make gasoline. Catalytic cracking, which had been developed by Eugene Houdry in the 1930s, produced high-octane gasoline, but chemists did not understand how the mixture of molecules in petroleum were broken up and reformed. To comprehend this, he developed a microcatalytic pulse reactor that could be put in the gas stream of a gas chromatograph. This allowed him to analyze the compounds that are produced by reactions on the surface of the catalyst. His research on catalytic cracking demonstrated that the larger molecules in gasoline were built up by reactions of smaller molecules generated by cracking.

In 1955 Emmett left the Mellon Institute and returned to Johns Hopkins, this time as the W. R. Grace Professor in the Chemistry Department. He continued his research on catalytic cracking and did more general studies to investigate the nature of catalysis. After retiring from Johns Hopkins in 1971, he returned to his native Oregon where he served as visiting research professor at Portland State University until his death on 22 April 1985.

Encyclopedist of Catalysis. In addition to his research, Emmett was widely recognized for his encyclopedic knowledge of the catalysis literature and his willingness to share his information with others. His expertise, in part, resulted from his editing of seven volumes on catalysis between 1954 and 1960. In 1965 he coauthored a text titled *Catalysis Then and Now.* Emmett wrote Part 1, which was a general survey of catalysis, with emphasis on his areas of expertise. Part 2 was a reprint of a translation of catalyst pioneer Paul Sabatier's 1913 treatise, *La catalyse en chimie organique* (translated as *Catalysis in Organic Chemistry*). It is rather unusual in science that a general survey of a field, like Emmett's contribution to *Catalysis Then and Now,* would still be relevant over forty years after its publication. But catalysis had always been a highly empirical art, so the careful experimental results of early investigators were never completely replaced by later investigations or more general theoretical treatments. It was perhaps the hallmark of Emmett's career that his work has held up to the test of time in spite of advances in the field, especially in instrumentation, which has allowed much more intimate examination of chemical reactions on catalyst surfaces.

BIBLIOGRAPHY

Emmett's papers are at Oregon State University in Corvallis, Oregon. (See http://osulibrary.oregonstate.edu/specialcollections/coll/emmett/index.html.) "Publications by Professor Paul H.

Emmett," in Journal of Physical Chemistry *90 (1986): 4706–4710, provides a complete bibliography of Emmett's published works.*

WORKS BY EMMETT

With Linus Pauling. "The Crystal Structure of Barite." *Journal of the American Chemical Society* 46 (1925): 1026–1030.

With Stephen Brunauer and Edward Teller. "Adsorption of Gases in Multimolecular Layers." *Journal of the American Chemical Society* 60 (1938): 309–319.

Editor. *Catalysis.* 7 vols. New York: Reinhold, 1954–1960.

With Paul Sabatier. *Catalysis Then and Now.* Englewood Cliffs, NJ: Franklin Publishing, 1965. Emmett wrote Part 1, *A Survey of the Advances in Catalysis.*

"The Fixed Nitrogen Research Laboratory." In *Heterogeneous Catalysis: Selected American Histories,* edited by Burtron H. Davis and William P. Hettinger Jr. Washington, DC: American Chemical Society, 1983.

OTHER SOURCES

Brasted, Robert C., and Peter Farago, eds. "Interview with Paul H. Emmett." *Journal of Chemical Education* 55, no. 4 (April 1978): 248–252.

Davis, Burtron H. "Paul H. Emmett (1900–1985): Six Decades of Catalysis." *Journal of Physical Chemistry* 90, no. 20 (1986): 4701–4706. This article is in the Emmett Memorial Issue of the journal.

Garten, Robert L. "Paul H. Emmett: Six Decades of Contributions to Catalysis." In *Heterogeneous Catalysis: Selected American Histories,* edited by Burtron H. Davis and William P. Hettinger Jr. Washington, DC: American Chemical Society, 1983.

Koski, Walter S. "Paul Hugh Emmett, September 22, 1900–April 22, 1985." *Biographical Memoirs of the National Academy of Sciences* 67 (1995): 118–129. Also available from http://www.nap.edu/readingroom/books/biomems/pemmett.pdf.

John K. Smith

EMPEDOCLES OF ACRAGAS (*b.* Acragas [now Agrigento, Sicily], c. 492 BCE; *d.* c. 432 BCE), *natural philosophy.* For the original article on Empedocles of Acragas see *DSB,* vol. 4.

The early Greek poet, natural scientist, and philosopher Empedocles is the author of two (or perhaps one) lost didactic epics, the *On Nature* and *The Purifications.* Empedocles is best known as the oldest exponent of the four-element theory of matter—earth, air (or *aether*), fire, and water—which endured until the advent of modern chemistry, although with some serious modifications by later thinkers and despite strong criticisms from the ancient atomists. Writing in the wake of Parmenides' critique of earlier philosophers, Empedocles posited four

eternally stable and indestructible elements, which he sometimes also referred to by using the names of the Olympian gods. In addition to the four elements, he also advanced two motive forces, the quasi-psychological powers Love and Strife. Intuitively enough, Love is a force of attraction, combining the elements into mixtures, while Strife separates them. These six "first principles" underlie all phenomena. Further, while Love and Strife are equals, their sway over the elements rises and falls in alternation, each giving way before the other. The result of this alternation is that the world as a whole, including its inhabitants, is periodically dissolved and recombined. This alternation is known as his doctrine of the cosmic cycle. Along with his physical teachings, Empedocles was also a firm believer in reincarnation, along Pythagorean lines, and even makes personal claims to divine status as a fallen god. In accordance with these beliefs, he abhorred meat-eating and proposed to do away with the sacrificial slaughter of animals, a main source of meat in his day and the central ritual practice of Greek religion. How this side of his thought relates to his physical teachings, if at all, is one of the central problems in the interpretation of his thought.

Biography and Biographical Tradition. The biographical tradition on Empedocles is rich and rather fanciful, as one might expect for someone who claimed to be god, but also includes some reliable information. Our only source is Diogenes Laertius' "Life of Empedocles," chapters 51–77 of book eight in his *Lives of the Philosophers.* Writing probably in the early third century CE, Diogenes is a mere compiler of earlier material. The most famous story of all, which took on a life of its own as the great example of philosophical megalomania, told how Empedocles cast himself into the volcanic flames of Mount Aetna in order to prove himself a god (book eight, chapter 69). But Diogenes also records other variants on his death and further tales of wonder-working. Since it is unlikely that much biographical detail can have survived beyond the work itself, it is probably safest to see in these stories a biographical extrapolation from the work (see Lefkowitz in bibliography). Further, some of these tales are known to have circulated in nonhistorical works, so that they need not have been originally written with a biographical intent and were only employed as such much later. For instance, the oldest known mention of the leap into Aetna occurs in a philosophical dialogue by Heraclides Ponticus, an older contemporary of Aristotle. It seems that Heraclides, known for his fabulous afterlife myths, only related it so as to refute it with an equally fanciful apotheosis of his own invention (see Diogenes 8.69). From less spectacular material we are told that Empedocles's family was prominent at Acragas, and wealthy enough to equip and win the chariot race at the Olympic games. Aristotle (fragment 66,

Empedocles of Acragas. HULTON ARCHIVE/GETTY IMAGES.

Rose ed.) and the historian Timaeus (*Fragmente der Griechischen Historiker* [ed. F. Jacoby] no. 566, fragment 2) relate his efforts to sustain the fledgling democracy after the fall of the previous tyranny, and Timaeus remarks that his democratic leanings seem to clash with the conceited and pretentious tone he strikes in his poetry. The latter, precisely because of this contrast, seems to indicate some independent authority.

Works: *On Nature* and/or *The Purifications.* Empedocles presented his doctrines in the traditional poetic medium of hexameter verse, the format used by Homer and Hesiod two centuries earlier. This choice had precedents in Xenophanes (c. 570–c. 468 BCE) and Parmenides (fl. c. 490), who also used poetry to convey their ideas. As a philosophical didactic poet, he was the champion of the genre and was the model for the first-century BCE Latin poet Lucretius, who emulated him in his own poem *On The Nature of Things*, devoted to Epicurean, atomistic physics.

Empedocles' poetry has not survived entire but is known to readers mostly through fragments, that is, ancient citations, especially from Aristotle and Simplicius, the sixth-century CE Aristotelian commentator. In 1999 a papyrus was published, *PStrasb. Gr. 1665–1666*, from the first or second century CE, containing about seventy-four full or partial original lines, twenty of which overlap with previously known passages. This new text, from an ancient copy of Empedocles' poetry, was assembled from numerous smaller scraps by its editors and contains four longer continuous sections named *a, b, c,* and *d* (discounting a few remainders). It raised the total number of surviving verses to a little over five hundred, plus or minus

some half-lines. In addition to these fragments we have a substantial number of testimonies in the form of ancient reports and discussions of Empedoclean doctrine, which also add to our understanding.

The reconstruction of Empedocles' literary output is controversial because the evidence is conflicting. The fundamental question is whether he wrote one or two main philosophical poems. Diogenes Laertius, at 8.77 of his "Life of Empedocles," gives a *single* verse total of five thousand lines along with *two* apparent titles, the *On Nature* and *The Purifications*. This is the only ancient passage that mentions both titles together. Otherwise, the majority of the fragments are given without a title, which might incline people to think that Empedocles was known for only one work. But then again, a small number of citations do mention one or the other title, which counterbalances that inference. After some hesitations in the first half of the nineteenth century, scholarly opinion thereafter opted strongly for the assumption of two works and sought to classify the unidentified fragments according to their thematic link with each title. Thus, the *On Nature* was given all the physical, cosmological, and biological fragments, while to *The Purifications* were attributed the teachings on reincarnation and religious reform. The most influential edition of this type remains that found in Diels-Kranz, *Die Fragmente der Vorsokratiker*, volume 1 (Berlin, 1903; 5th ed., 1934, with numerous reprints). Over the last twenty years, however, a number of challenges have been made to this older consensus, in favor of the assumption of a single original work. No new consensus has yet emerged. More recently, since 1999, the papyrus, while it does not contain a title, has contributed some new evidence to the debate. Although sections *a, b,* and *c* show overlap with fragments that Simplicius gives from the *On Nature*, section *d* overlaps in part with a passage linked by its source to "purifications." Even more significantly, section *d* contains a transition from a discussion of reincarnation to cosmological material. At a minimum, then, it seems that the *On Nature* must also have discussed reincarnation; or perhaps there was only one work, which went under alternative titles.

Doctrines. If the number of Empedoclean works remains an open question, this is no longer the case for the reconstruction of his thought. Section *d* implies very clearly that however problematic people may find the unity of his thought, Empedocles nevertheless presented it as a unity. Accordingly, perhaps the best way to approach Empedocles is as an early philosophical system builder. The components from which he constructed his system include the Ionian tradition of natural philosophy, Pythagorean beliefs about the soul, and Parmenides' critique of earlier philosophy. His debt to the Ionian tradition of natural science is reflected in his continued commitment to its scientific project of explaining the world, especially in the form of a cosmology, which had been put into question by Parmenides' critique of change. As for his response to Parmenides, there is general agreement that it is to be found in his doctrine of the cosmic cycle, but less agreement as to the precise form of the doctrine or how well it succeeds in responding to Parmenides' critique. However exactly it be understood, it seems that the main motivation of the theory is a commitment to nonemergence, that is, the goal is to show how changes in the world, properly understood, do not involve anything coming "from nothing."

Scholarly opinion on the cosmic cycle is divided between two main types of reconstruction. Different labels have been applied to them, but there is no consistent usage. Here they will be called the *symmetrical view* and the *hierarchical interpretation.*

The symmetrical view is characterized in the main by an emphasis on the equality of Love and Strife. This equality entails that both powers achieve, in alternation, complete domination over the elements. Under Love, the elements become harmoniously fused into a cosmic superorganism, which Empedocles calls the *Sphairos* god; under Strife, the four are completely separated, so that no mixture can endure. (It is unclear whether the elements under Strife simply descend into chaos or whether they form some kind of structured pattern.) Worlds like ours occur in the middle periods, when both powers temper each other's rule. According to Aristotle in *On Coming-To-Be and Passing-Away* (*De generatione et corruptione* or *GC*) 334a5–7, Empedocles held that the current world was a "world of Strife"; this appears confirmed by extant passages describing how Strife shattered the *Sphairos* and thereby brought the world into being.

Provided such a reconstruction is correct, there are at least two ways in which it might provide a response to Parmenides. One is through the notion of elemental stability, the degree to which the individual elements, while retaining their separate properties, seem separately to inherit the permanency of Parmenides' unique eternal "being." This approach can invoke in its support Parmenides' own cosmology in the Way of Appearance. Another possibility is to stress the permanent status of the whole cosmic cycle, especially the two-directional process of becoming. This way, neither the elements nor the *Sphairos* is recognized as more fundamental or ontologically prior to the other, while the cycle itself is shown to be invariant within limits. Some support for this interpretation is given by Aristotle, when he wonders at *GC* 315a19–20, if the *Sphairos* does not deserve also to be considered a principle, alongside the four elements. Against the symmetrical interpretation of the cycle, there is no dominant alternative reconstruction. By and large, however, the alternatives tend to negate the full equality of the powers and place

Love above Strife in a more hierarchical relation. It is in fact easier to characterize this approach negatively, in terms of the objections made to the alternative. One objection is that the symmetrical view commits Empedocles to an unheard-of double cosmogony: one world of Love and one of Strife. A second objection is that both powers would, on the symmetrical view, prove profoundly ambivalent factors in human life, since both would be creative as well as destructive. Yet extant fragments show Empedocles as a consistent devotee of Love. Potent objections though these are, one strong consideration against them is that, while the asymmetrical reading seems more intuitive, it is much more difficult to see how it can be framed as a response to Parmenides.

Another notable feature of his work is that, within the framework of his four-element and two-power theory, it appears that Empedocles sought to be as encyclopedic as possible. The extant fragments cover numerous topics, including cosmology, geology, botany, physiology, reproduction, and embryology as well as sense perception (Empedocles is the oldest known theorist of the senses as captors of "emissions" from bodies). Particularly noteworthy in this respect is his use of elaborate poetic analogies from crafts and technology to explain natural structures and processes, for example fragment 84 Diels-Kranz on the eye, which is compared to a storm lantern.

Finally, there remains the problem of relating Empedocles' views on reincarnation to his physics. Since the nineteenth century, scholars have often denied, sometimes vehemently, any possible reconciliation between an immortal reincarnated soul and elemental physics. Strictly, however, an important distinction should be made, which is often simply ignored, namely that Empedocles' reincarnated soul need not be understood as an immaterial, immortal Platonic soul. That doctrine was Plato's achievement in the *Phaedo*, two full philosophical generations later. As for Empedocles' own view, despite the obvious difficulties, a number of fragments attest to his belief in some kind of postmortem survival. This is bizarre, but based on the physiological knowledge of the day, hardly to be excluded as a strict impossibility, and had strong local Pythagorean precedent. Moreover, this survival need not be equated with a claim of complete immortality, which the cyclical destruction of the world in any case denies. From other fragments we also know that Empedocles postulated the existence of what he calls "long-lived gods." He mentions these more than once, in the context of a list of all the varied products of the combined elements, alongside fishes, birds, land animals, and men and women. If the epithet "long-lived" seems to imply their status as mortals or animals of some kind, the word "gods" nevertheless implies that they rank above humans in the natural world. Perhaps, but this remains highly conjectural, this is what he meant when he claimed to be a fallen god: he had once been of their number, and entertained hopes of imminent return.

SUPPLEMENTARY BIBLIOGRAPHY

WORKS BY EMPEDOCLES OF ACRAGAS

Bollack, Jean, ed. *Empédocle*. 3 vols. Paris: Éditions de Minuit, 1969. Reprinted, Paris: Gallimard, 1992. In French. Very full commentary, but idiosyncratic and now out of date.

Wright, M. R, ed. *Empedocles: The Extant Fragments*. New Haven, CT: Yale University Press, 1981; 2nd ed., London: Duckworth, 1995. Reliable text, translation and commentary.

Inwood, Brad, ed. *The Poem of Empedocles*. Toronto: University of Toronto Press, 1992; 2nd ed., 2001. Edition with translation based on single-work approach.

Martin, Alain, and Oliver Primavesi, eds. *L'Empédocle de Strasbourg (P. Strasb. gr. 1665–1666): Introduction, édition et commentaire*. Berlin, New York, and Strasbourg: Walter de Gruyter, 1999. High-quality first edition of the papyrus.

Vítek, Tomás, ed. *Empedoklés*. 3 vols. Prague: Herrmann & Synové, 2006. In Czech. Fullest, completely up-to-date edition, commentary, and bibliography. For specialists.

OTHER SOURCES

Curd, Patricia. *The Legacy of Parmenides: Eleatic Monism and Later Presocratic Thought*. Princeton, NJ: Princeton University Press, 1998.

Furley, David J. *The Greek Cosmologists*. Cambridge, U.K.: Cambridge University Press, 1987.

Goulet, Richard. "Empédocle." In *Dictionnaire des philosophes antiques*. Vol. 3, pp. 66–88. Paris: Presses du CNRS, 2000.

Graham, Daniel W. "Symmetry in the Empedoclean Cycle." *Classical Quarterly* 38 (1988): 297–312.

Kingsley, Peter. *Ancient Philosophy, Mystery, and Magic: Empedocles and the Pythagorean Tradition*. Oxford: Oxford University Press, 1995.

Kirk, G. S., J. E. Raven, and M. Scholfield. *The Presocratic Philosophers*. 2nd ed. Cambridge, U.K.: Cambridge University Press, 1983.

Lefkowitz, Mary R. *Lives of the Greek Poets*. London: Duckworth, 1981.

Long, Anthony, ed. *The Cambridge Companion to Early Greek Philosophy*. Cambridge, U.K.: Cambridge University Press, 1999.

Mourelatos, Alexander P. D. "Quality, Structure, and Emergence in Later Pre-Socratic Philosophy." *Proceedings of the Boston Area Colloquium in Ancient Philosophy* 2 (1986): 127–194.

O'Brien, Denis. *Empedocles' Cosmic Cycle: A Reconstruction from the Fragments and Secondary Sources*. Cambridge, U.K.: Cambridge University Press, 1969.

Osborne, Catherine. "Empedocles Recycled." *Classical Quarterly* 37 (1987): 24–50.

Pierris, Apostolos, ed. *The Empedoclean Kosmos: Structure, Process, and the Question of Cyclicity*. Patras, Greece: Institute for Philosophical Research, 2005. Multiple articles on new papyrological material and other questions. For specialists.

Sedley, David. *Lucretius and the Transformation of Greek Wisdom*. Cambridge, U.K.: Cambridge University Press, 1998. See chapter 1, "The Empedoclean Opening."

Trépanier, Simon. *Empedocles: An Interpretation*. London and New York: Routledge, 2004.

Simon Trépanier

EPHRUSSI, BORIS (*b.* Moscow, Russia, 9 May 1901; *d.* Paris, France, 2 May 1979), *embryology, development, physiology, genetics.*

Ephrussi was a Russian-born French geneticist who emigrated to France through Romania, after the Bolshevik revolution. Awarded the Louisa Gross Horwitz Prize from Columbia University in 1975, he was a pioneer in developmental and physiological genetics, and made fundamental contributions to understanding the biochemical processes depending on gene action, to understanding the role of genes in biochemical processes, and in articulating the significance of cytoplasmic factors in inheritance and development. Ephrussi was perhaps the most important of several French biologists who together were crucial to the emergence and development of French genetics in the twentieth century; he held the first chair in genetics at the Sorbonne.

Ephrussi was married to Harriet Taylor Ephrussi (1918–1968), who was a biologist that worked on the structure of DNA. They had a daughter, Anne.

Early Education. Ephrussi was trained as an embryologist in the 1920s at the Marine Biological Station at Roscoff, in France. His earliest work, under the biochemist Louis Rapkine, focused on environmental factors influencing embryological development; in particular, he studied the effects of temperature on the development of sea urchin embryos. Ephrussi, in a second thesis (which was typical at the time), also did research on tissue cultures, under Emmanuel Fauré-Fremiet, with less than satisfactory results. In the end, he concluded in this project that some "intrinsic factors" played a role in development. The more fundamental interest reflected in these theses concerned the role of intracellular and extracellular processes in the regulation of development (Ephrussi, 1932). Throughout, Ephrussi later said, his interest was in understanding "the chain of reactions connecting the gene with the character" (1938, p. 6). This interest continued throughout his life, as did his commitment to the idea that both intracellular and extracellular factors were crucial to understanding development, and that, among the intracellular factors, both nuclear and extranuclear factors affected development and function.

Ephrussi's training in morphogenesis and development, at the time, would have been thought of as embryology; that is, he was engaged in understanding the various contributions that led from a fertilized egg to an organism, where those contributions were both internal and external to the organism. In the context of French biology during the 1930s, physiological geneticists and embryologists recognized substantial cytological control of development, emphasizing pathways, and chemical determinants beyond the gene (cf. Sapp, 1987). Mendelians, by contrast, tended to assume that the nucleus contained "factors" sufficient to determine ontogeny; that is, they assumed genes were what determined development. Developmentalists, in France and elsewhere, generally felt they needed to recognize both internal and external causes: given the acknowledged fact that cells have *the same* genetic material whatever their morphological fates, it seemed inevitable that epigenetic factors had to govern cell fate. In France, the role of the cytoplasm was broadly assumed to be crucial to understanding development. There was, in any case, no established Mendelian tradition in France in the years immediately following World War II, and, if anything, an antagonism to Mendelian thinking before the war. Ephrussi was unusual in being sympathetic with Mendelian inheritance, and simultaneously embedded in a robust developmental tradition. Throughout his career, Ephrussi also had considerable sympathy for cytoplasmic inheritance. His Mendelian sympathies fit somewhat uncomfortably with the more conservative French sympathies with Larmarckian inheritance; his developmental sympathies fit equally uncomfortably with the prevailing influence of Mendelian genetics led by Thomas Hunt Morgan (1866–1945) and his followers.

Work in Physiological Genetics. Ephrussi began working in genetics in the 1930s after finishing his embryological training. During that decade, the best understood organism from a genetic viewpoint was clearly *Drosophila*. Ephrussi wanted to approach the problems of cellular differentiation from a genetic *and* a physiological standpoint; this dual perspective required integrating information concerning cytoplasmic and environmental effects on development with the well-known and elaborate emphasis on chromosomal genetics characteristic of Mendelian work. Because there was no established tradition of Mendelian genetics in France at this point, from 1934 to 1935, supported by the Rockefeller Foundation, Ephrussi moved to the California Institute of Technology (Caltech), to work under Morgan. (Morgan had moved from Columbia to Caltech in 1928, with Alfred Henry Sturtevant and others following him.) It was during this period that Ephrussi began his seminal work with George Wells Beadle. Beadle at that point was a Cornell-trained corn geneticist who was a postdoctoral fellow in Morgan's lab, engaged in studying crossing over in *Drosophila*. When

Ephrussi moved back to Paris in 1935, Beadle followed him there.

The ultimate goal of Beadle and Ephrussi's collaborative work was to gain an increased understanding of gene expression and development. In terms that would have been natural to Ephrussi, they were interested in the physiology of gene action. There were a number of significant influences on this work, some embryological and some genetic. Within experimental embryology, the transplantation of tissues had become an accepted technique, following the work by Ernst Wolfgang Caspari in Alfred Kühn's zoological institute at Göttingen. Essentially, the transplantation of tissue enabled experimentalists to explore the influence of surrounding tissues on developing embryos, and so to see the several factors affecting development. So if at early embryological stages, some tissue (or cell) is displaced to a different context, one can see how the development of the displaced tissue is changed. Ephrussi and Beadle extended that technique to *Drosophila*. *Drosophila* is an organism that was well understood from a genetic point of view at the time, but developmentally it was a difficult organism to work with. Ephrussi and Beadle were able to turn the micromanipulator into a device to implant imaginal disks (which develop into eyes) onto *Drosophila* larvae. The implantation eventually allowed them to see how development (specifically of eye color) was affected by the larger context of the developing organism. Within *Drosophila* genetics, the nonautonomous control of development offered a useful target. Crossbreeding had already shown that the normal, or wild-type, eye color in *Drosophila* was the result of two pigments, one brown and one red. Either could be inhibited by mutations, with observably different outcomes. The resulting mutant colors are vermilion and cinnabar. Sturtevant, one of the most respected of Morgan's protégés, had shown in 1919 that eye color in *Drosophila* could be altered under the influence of other tissues. Its development is in this sense nonautonomous, because it is not determined entirely by the intrinsic genetic constitution. So, for example, working with a gynandromorph—a mosaic fly with both male and female constitution—whose head showed characteristics that would require it to have vermilion eyes, Sturtevant found it in fact developed a wild-type eye color. The intrinsic genetic constitution failed to determine the eye color. Sturtevant concluded that development was somehow or other modified by "diffusible substances." The result was intriguing, but unexplained, until Beadle and Ephrussi revealed their results.

Beadle and Ephrussi implanted imaginal disks onto embryos of flies with a different genetic constitution from the donor eyes (Ephrussi and Beadle, 1936; Ephrussi and Beadle, 1937). The goal was one of illustrating various influences on eye color. They already knew from genetic studies that there are two mutant forms, each thwarting the development of the wild-type (brown) eye color in *Drosophila*. The actual color of the eye would then be influenced both by the intrinsic constitution of the imaginal disk, and by the surrounding tissue. It was not surprising, in light of Sturtevant's work, that the eye color would have these dual influences. What was surprising was the pattern of outcomes.

There were, then, three genotypes in play: vermilion (v), cinnabar (cn), and wild type (v+). These were available both in the imaginal disks and the hosts. As a result, there were six possible reciprocal implantations, as exhibited in Table 1. (It was not necessary to implant disks into hosts of the same genotype.)

TABLE 1

Implanted Imaginal Disk Host	Body Type	Color of Resulting Eye
Vermilion (v)	Wild Type (v+)	Wild Type (v+)
Vermilion (v)	Cinnabar (cn)	Wild Type (v+)
Cinnabar (cn)	Vermilion (v)	Cinnabar (cn)
Cinnabar (cn)	Wild Type (v+)	Wild Type (v+)
Wild Type (v+)	Cinnabar (cn)	Wild Type (v+)
Wild Type (v+)	Vermilion (v)	Wild Type (v+)

The wild-type imaginal implants develop, as predicted, into wild-type eyes. Vermilion and cinnabar imaginal disks transplanted into a wild-type larvae likewise both develop into eyes with the wild-type color. These results are compatible with Sturtevant's earlier observations. They are also compatible with the view that cinnabar and vermilion are simple Mendelian recessives. The wild-type dominates in development as well. The crucial cases are the reciprocal implants between cinnabar and vermilion, given in the second and third rows in the table above. When a vermilion disk is implanted onto a cinnabar larvae it develops a wild-type color, whereas when a cinnabar disk is implanted onto a vermilion larvae it retains its cinnabar color. These outcomes could be accommodated only by assuming the two genes occupy sequential positions in the metabolic pathway responsible for the production of the pigments, rather than providing independent contributions. Ephrussi wrote, somewhat later,

> There are two different substances, one responsible for the change from vermilion to wild type and the other for the change from cinnabar to wild type. The wild type lymph contains both these substances. The lymph of the mutant

cinnabar contains only one of them, namely the substance responsible for the change from vermilion to wild type. The mutant vermilion contains none of these substances.... [The] two substances are formed in the course of a single chain of reactions, of which the v+ substance represents the first and the cn+ the second link: ⇒ v+ ⇒ cn+. (1942, pp. 329–330)

Beadle and Ephrussi thus concluded that there are at least two diffusible substances, and, developmentally, they are organized sequentially. The vermilion mutant fails to carry out the first reaction, and therefore also cannot synthesize the second of the diffusible substances. So the vermilion host cannot supplement the cinnabar implant. The cinnabar mutant can perform the first reaction, but not the second. As a host, therefore, it would supplement the needed material for the vermilion implant, resulting in a normal eye color.

The next logical step would have been to identify the specific substances involved. Because at this time the genetic code was unknown, they could not predict the substances directly from the genetic structure. The only alternative was to begin with the phenotypic effects, and infer from them what physiological pathways produce the observed effects on development. It was clear these factors shaping development were not genes, but they were relatively simple substances. By 1939 Beadle and Ephrussi concluded that the blockage of reactions was due to a lack of specific enzymes. They also concluded that it was necessary to work with some organism that was developmentally and physiologically less complex than *Drosophila*. Beadle returned to the United States, where he eventually took up work on *Neurospora*. Ephrussi continued with the *Drosophila* project until the Germans invaded France. In the end, they were able to identify one of the "hormones" involved in the *Drosophila* cases (tryptophan, an amino acid), but the other eluded them.

Interruption during World War II. Ephrussi's work was interrupted by World War II. During that period, Ephrussi's work was centered at Johns Hopkins University in Baltimore, Maryland, as a refugee. By 1944 he had assumed an active role in the forces of French liberation, and was ready to return to France after the war. Following the war's conclusion, the French undertook, under the auspices of Centre national de la recherché scientifique (CNRS), to establish an institutional profile in genetics— one that had been lacking prior to 1945. Ephrussi was named the first chair of genetics at the Sorbonne. Ephrussi applied to the Rockefeller Foundation to obtain support for an Institute of Genetics at Gif under CNRS. After some controversy, this was approved in April 1950. In the end, these funds were never expended, and Ephrussi remained in Paris at the Institut de Biologie Physicochimique (the Rothschild Institute), and later at CNRS.

Yeast and Adaptive Mutations after the War. Ephrussi's work continued to focus on the interaction of nuclear and cytoplasmic factors on development. He was convinced that both factors were crucial to development. At this point, he abandoned the use of *Drosophila,* thinking that yeast (*Saccharomyces*) was a more promising organism, while Beadle switched to *Neurospora.* Yeast was a commonly used organism for biochemical studies. With Louis Pasteur's legacy, and the lucrative benefits connected with the beer industry in France, a great deal was known about the biochemistry associated with yeast. Considerably less was known about yeast genetics, with the first systematic studies only in the late 1930s. Yeast also exhibited what were called "adaptive mutations," but the processes of mutations in yeast were not known. Initially, Ephrussi was interested in understanding whether these mutations were induced by environmental causes or were already present in the cultures at low frequencies; that is, the question was whether environmental stress led to mutant forms that were adaptive, or whether they were already present and the environment promoted them by selection. The former view, which Ephrussi eventually embraced, would have required cytoplasmic elements playing a significant role in development.

In the end, Ephrussi's work went in a direction rather different than did that pursued by Beadle and Edward L. Tatum in the United States, although it started out allied with that work. Ephrussi and his collaborators raised yeast on a medium containing acriflavine (an antibacterial agent), and found the resulting colonies consisted almost exclusively of a slow-growing, and respiratory-deficient, form. The strain could not use oxygen. They called these mutants petites. The changes induced were irreversible: subsequent generations did not shift back to a respiring form, even in a more benign environment. The change was inherited, but it was not inherited in a Mendelian fashion. The implication was that it was nonchromosomal inheritance. By crossing wild types with these so-called petite strains that were respiration deficient, Ephrussi was able to observe the expression of various nuclear genes in different cytoplasmic contexts. Eventually, it became clear that the slow growth of these forms was the result of a deficiency in respiratory enzymes. (Yeast is a facultative anaerobe.) The real focus of Ephrussi's interest was in the contribution of cytoplasmic factors to development. He and his collaborators managed to show that there was crucial information contained in the cytoplasm—later identified as residing in mitochondria—that is necessary for respiration. These cytoplasmic properties were not nuclear genes, though they did appear to depend on them.

Boris Ephrussi. COURTESY OF THE ARCHIVES, CALIFORNIA INSTITUTE OF TECHNOLOGY.

For the next decade, the mechanism responsible for this adaptive modification in yeast was the subject of considerable controversy. Ephrussi subjected the yeast to a series of anaerobic conditions. He and his collaborators were eventually able to produce adaptive responses that were reversible. In the end, Ephrussi concluded that nuclear genes, the cytoplasm, and the environment codetermine the constitution of the cell. This led Ephrussi to reject the view that cellular enzymes were exclusively under the control of nuclear genes, a view most forcibly defended by his former collaborator, Beadle. Ephrussi denied there was any evidence for the nuclear origin of the cytoplasmic factors in yeast.

It turns out that the activity of mitochondria is necessary for respiration. Without the enzymes provided by the mitochondria, respiration ceases, and the loss is irreversible. It also turns out that there are a number of distinct mitochondrial genes involved, which can be lost separately. Sometimes this shows up because cells capable of respiration occasionally yield some progeny that are competent and others that are not; this is due to the inheritance of different portions of the mitochondrial particles.

Somatic Cell Hybrids. In the 1950s Ephrussi continued his exploration of somatic cell differentiation (e.g., Ephrussi, Davidson, and Yamamoto, 1966). The general theme remained the same. As an embryologist, he was interested in the factors that contribute to cell differentiation, and how those factors limit developmental potentials. More conventional geneticists were convinced that all cells had the same potentialities for development because they are genetically identical, which meant that their nuclear genes were equally endowed (cf. Ephrussi, 1970). That, of course, again left the differences among cells unexplained.

In 1962 Ephrussi moved to Western Reserve University in Cleveland, Ohio, where he stayed until 1967, focusing on intraspecific and interspecific somatic cell hybrids. Interspecific hybrids are formed by encouraging the fusion of cells from different species, including both the cytoplasm and the nuclear materials. This often leads to chromosome loss, and allows the association of specific genes with selected chromosomes. (In this way it is fundamentally different from the more recent work using nuclear implantation.) He developed a number of techniques using hybrids formed from mouse and human cells in culture. Ephrussi's *Hybridization of Somatic Cells* (1972) provides a detailed review of the work conducted in his laboratory.

Intraspecific hybrids offered the opportunity to address the same problems that had occupied Ephrussi throughout his career, though without depending on the vicissitudes of sexual reproduction (see Zallen and Burian, 1992). As the technique had originally been developed by Georges Barski, Serge Sorieul, and Francine Cornefert at the Institut Gustave Roussy in France, hybrid cells were identifiable only by chromosomal features. Ephrussi's laboratory developed a number of other markers, including biochemical ones. Once again, he was able to return to the question of cell differentiation. He distinguished between "household" and "luxury" functions—the former being required for fundamental metabolic functions in all cells, and the latter being what distinguishes particular cells from one another. One intriguing observation will illustrate the kind of results they achieved. When they created fusions between differentiated cells from different lines, it turned out that the "luxury" functions were lost. Ephrussi took this as evidence that the hybridization repressed the "luxury" functions. Similar results were found in a number of laboratories working with hybrid cell lines.

Throughout his career, Ephrussi maintained a focus on issues of cell differentiation and development. His var-

ious shifts in the kinds of organisms he used, and his development of novel techniques, reflect his willingness to modify the tools used in his research to address the fundamental problems concerning the regulation of development and the interaction between nuclear and cytoplasmic factors.

BIBLIOGRAPHY

Ephrussi resources can be found at the Rockefeller Archive Center and the Archive of the Institut Pasteur.

WORKS BY EPHRUSSI

"D'une temperature elevée sur la mitose de segmentation des oeufs d'oursin." *Comptes rendus de l'Académie des Sciences, Paris* 177 (1932): 152–154.

"Contribution a l'analyse de premiers stades du développement de l'oerouf." *Action de lat termperérature.* Impremature de l'Academie, Paris.

"The Absence of Autonomy in the Development of the Effects of Certain Deficiencies in *Drosophila melanogaster*." *Proceedings of the National Academy of Sciences of the United States of America* 20 (1934): 420–422.

With George W. Beadle. "La transplantation des disques imaginaux chez la *Drosophile*." *Comptes rendus de l'Académie des Sciences, Paris* 201 (1935): 98–100.

———. "The Differentiation of Eye Pigments in *Drosophila* as Studied by Transplantation." *Genetics* 21 (1936): 225–247.

———. "Development of Eye Colors in *Drosophila*: Diffusible Substances and Their Interactions." *Genetics* 22 (1937): 76–86.

"Aspects of the Physiology of Gene Action." *American Naturalist* 72, no. 738 (1938): 5–23.

"Chemistry of 'Eye Color Hormones' of *Drosophila*." *Quarterly Review of Biology* 17 (1942): 327–338.

"The Interplay of Heredity and Environment in the Synthesis of Respiratory Enzymes in Yeast." *Harvey Lectures* 46 (1950): 45–67.

Nucleo-Cytoplasmic Relations in Microorganisms: Their Bearing on Cell Heredity and Differentiation. Oxford: Clarendon Press, 1953.

With Richard L. Davidson and Kohtaro Yamamoto. "Regulation of Pigment Synthesis in Mammalian Cells, as Studied by Somatic Hybridization." *Proceedings of the National Academy of Sciences of the United States of America* 56 (1966): 1437–1440.

"Somatic Hybridization as a Tool for the Study of Normal and Abnormal Growth and Differentiation." In *Genetic Concepts and Neoplasia.* Baltimore, MD: Williams and Wilkins, 1970.

Hybridization of Somatic Cells. Princeton, NJ: Princeton University Press, 1972.

OTHER SOURCES

Burian, Richard M., Jean Gayon, and Doris Zallen. "The Singular Fate of Genetics in the History of French Biology, 1900–1940." *Journal of the History of Biology* 21 (1988): 357–402.

————. "Boris Ephrussi and the Synthesis of Genetics and Embryology." In *A Conceptual History of Embryology*, edited by Scott F. Gilbert, 207–227, New York: Plenum Press, 1991.

Lwoff, André. "Recollections of Boris Ephrussi." *Somatic Cell and Molecular Genetics* 5 (1979): 677–679.

Roman, Herschel. "Boris Ephrussi." *Annual Review of Genetics* 14 (1980): 447–450.

Sapp, Jan. *Beyond the Gene: Cytoplasmic Inheritance and the Struggle for Authority in Genetics*. New York: Oxford University Press, 1987.

Weiss, Mary C. "Contributions of Boris Ephrussi to the Development of Somatic Cell Genetics." *BioEssays* 14 (1992): 349–353.

Zallen, Doris T., and Richard M. Burian. "On the Beginnings of Somatic Cell Hybridization: Boris Ephrussi and Chromosome Transplantation." *Genetics* 132 (1992): 1–8.

Robert C. Richardson

ERDÖS, PAUL (PÁL) (*b.* Budapest, Hungary, 26 March 1923; *d.* Warsaw, Poland, 20 September 1996), *mathematics, number theory.*

Erdös was a Hungarian mathematician who spent much of his life traveling and working with colleagues around the world on mathematical problems of many kinds. He published some 1500 papers, making him the most prolific major mathematician of the twentieth century, and had more than 450 collaborators and coauthors. His work falls into a number of fields, some of which he created, but which can mostly be embraced under the general heading of discrete mathematics, one of the major developments of twentieth-century mathematics. It also exerted a major influence on computer science, a field in which Erdös himself never worked.

Early Life. Erdös's parents, Anna and Lajos Erdös, were both mathematics teachers, and he was brought up by his very protective mother, who was ever mindful of the fact that she had lost two daughters to scarlet fever just before Paul was born. His father was taken prisoner by the Russians during the World War I and sent to Siberia for six years. His parents kept Paul out of school after a few years to foster his evident talent, and at age twenty he became well known for finding an elegant new proof of a famous theorem in mathematics. This was Tchebychev's theorem, which states that for every natural number n there is always a prime number between n and $2n$. Erdös retained a lifelong interest in prime numbers; one of his best-known achievements is the so-called elementary proof of the prime number theorem that he and Atle Selberg published in 1949. The theorem says that the number of prime numbers less than x is approximately $x / \log x$, as x gets larger and larger. Their proof is far from simple; it is elementary because it avoids the use of complex function theory, which is not needed for the statement of the theorem but is a central feature of most of its proofs. He and Selberg had planned to publish their proof in two papers in the same issue of a journal, but at the last minute Erdös changed his mind and published first. The next year, however, Selberg was awarded a Fields Medal for this and other achievements.

Erdös obtained his PhD from the University of Budapest in 1934 and came to the University of Manchester in England on a post-doctoral fellowship. It was by now clear that the Nazi takeover in Germany threatened the lives of Jews in Europe, and Erdös was able to leave for the United States. In the 1950s his political naivety caused him problems with the immigration authorities of the United States, and he emigrated to Israel, where he remained until the 1960s. Then, joined by his mother who was now in her eighties, Erdös began the extremely peripatetic life for which he became famous. He would arrive at a friend's home, stay with him for a few days working exclusively on mathematics and talking about nothing else, and then move on by mutual agreement. Close friends, such as Ronald L. Graham, the director of the information sciences research center at AT&T Laboratories, who set aside a room in his house for Erdös, took care of the financial side of Erdös's life; Graham was one of a number of people who provided Erdös with food and clothes and sorted out his tax returns. Erdös earned money from invitations to give lectures and work with mathematicians around the world, and usually donated it to struggling young mathematicians or gave it away in the form of prizes for the solution of problems he found particularly noteworthy. For example, when he won the Wolf Prize in 1983, which was then the most lucrative award available to mathematicians, he kept only $720 of the $50,000 prize.

Relations with Contemporaries. Erdös spoke of the world in a private language that reflected his cosseted upbringing. Thus SF (for Supreme Fascist) was his name for God, whom he regarded as a malign deity he believed had created the universe and tormented people; "epsilon" (traditionally a very small quantity in mathematics) was his name for a child—Erdös was very fond of children; and "bosses" his name for women, with whom he was less comfortable and who occasionally protested at the way people attracted to the cult around Erdös glossed over the sexism inherent in the term. Men were called "slaves" and people who had given up mathematics were said to have "died." Erdös often spoke of what he called "The Book," supposedly in the possession of the SF, in which were collected all the best proofs of all the important results in

Paul Erdos. WOLF FOUNDATION. REPRODUCED BY
PERMISSION.

mathematics, and which it was the job of mathematicians to discover. After his death mathematicians began to publish a book called *Proofs from the Book*, a compilation of exceptionally elegant proofs of various results.

It is fair to say that Erdös divided the mathematical community more than any other mathematician of his stature. To his friends and admirers, especially those who worked with him and who regarded their collaboration as a rare opportunity to experience a first-rate mathematical mind close up, he was one of the great mathematicians of the century if not of all time, to be compared with Leonhard Euler for his originality. Others, while impressed, were less convinced. The disagreement goes back to a familiar tension in twentieth-century mathematics between the theory builders and the problem solvers. Much of the mathematics of the twentieth century, and indeed the nineteenth century, was conceptual and highly structured. Elaborate and profound general theories were constructed that are admired as much for their breadth of insight as for the problems they solve. The mathematicians most associated with this kind of mathematics, David Hilbert and his followers, especially Emmy Noether, and then the successive members of the Bourbaki

group after World War II, not only promoted this style of mathematics through their own work but maintained it as the core activity of the mathematician. Erdös's obsessive interest in problems that seemed to lack a general theory was completely the opposite of this and led some to see his contributions as remarkable and yet somehow marginal.

To make matters worse, his problems were mostly combinatorial and can be difficult without seeming deep. The large and difficult topic of differential equations, especially partial differential equations, is similarly full of difficult problems that yield only to delicate and often ad hoc analysis. It, too, is a branch of mathematics that has not been overwhelmed by the structural style of mathematics, but here no one disputes its depth or importance: Almost all of mathematical physics is written and studied in the language of partial differential equations. Lacking, apparently, depth and applications, Erdös's problems could seem shallow and artificial, and his success in attracting interest in them even counterproductive. It was even suggested that by attracting so many Hungarian mathematicians to the pursuit of his problems he had unbalanced the whole study of mathematics in Hungary, which, before World War II, had been remarkable for its breadth and vigor. Erdös compounded the issue by his prizes and the fame that attached to anyone who solved one of his more challenging problems. The underlying significance of Erdös's work seems likely to lie in concepts that he articulated only imperfectly and that his flurry of problem solving partly obscured.

Analytic Number Theory. The easiest way to see the depth of Erdös's problems is to approach them via one of the most difficult and delicate branches of classical mathematics, analytic number theory, in which Erdös was profoundly immersed. The prime number theorem is just one of a large collection of results that make claims about the number of numbers less than some bound n with a specific property as the bound n increases indefinitely. It says, as was noted above, that the number of prime numbers less than x is well approximated by $x / \log x$. It is well known that the sum of the reciprocals of the integers is infinite, but the sum of the reciprocals of the squares $(1/1 + 1/4 + 1/9 + \dots)$ is finite (a result first established by Euler). This gives a way of saying that although there are infinitely many square numbers they form a rather sparse subset of the set of all integers. What about the prime numbers? In fact, as Euler also showed, the sum of the reciprocals of the primes is also infinite, which says not only that there are infinitely many primes but that they are rather numerous, and more numerous than the squares, according to the ways in which number theorists distinguish between the "sizes" of infinite sets.

Now consider an arithmetic progression, which is a set of numbers of the form $a + bk$, $k = 0, 1, 2, \ldots$ where a and b are positive integers with no common factor (so for example one might have $a = 6$ and $b = 35$). In 1927 Bartel van der Waerden proved that if the natural numbers are divided into k subsets then at least one of these sets contains arbitrarily long arithmetic progressions. Erdös and Paul Turan then conjectured in 1936 that any subset of the natural numbers that has positive density contains arbitrarily long arithmetic progressions. (To say that a subset A of the natural numbers has positive density is to say that as n increases indefinitely, the ratio of the number of numbers less than n that are in A to the number of numbers less than n tends to a limit greater than zero.) This result was proved in 1974 by the Hungarian mathematician Emre Szemeredi, for which he was awarded $1,000 by Erdös. But the prime numbers thin out; they do not form a set of positive density, and in 1936 Erdös and Turan had also asked if any subset of the natural numbers with the property that the sum of its reciprocals is infinite also contains arbitrarily long arithmetic progressions. This is a profound generalization of the earlier conjecture, one that would locate a deep property of prime numbers in a more general setting.

In 2006 the young mathematician Terence Tao was awarded a Fields Medal for solving many remarkable problems in diverse areas of mathematics; one of these was his work with Ben Green that shows that the set of prime numbers does indeed contain arbitrarily long arithmetic progressions. Erdös and Turan's question remains unsolved in general.

So Erdös reminded mathematicians of how little they know about prime numbers despite all their grand theorems. The prime numbers are the building blocks of arithmetic, and Erdös's remarkable insights into their properties led not only to good theorems but directed mathematicians back to the task of exploring this core part of their subject.

Erdös's understanding of analytic number theory also helped create what has come to be called probabilistic number theory. In September 1939 he was at Princeton University listening to a lecture by Mark Kac on the behavior of the function that counts the number of prime divisors of a number. Heuristically, Kac regarded divisibility by 2, 3, 5 and so on as independent events and treated this function using ideas from probability theory. He suggested that the distribution of the number of prime divisors was a normal distribution, which would considerably sharpen some classical results in number theory, but was unable to prove it. Before the lecture was over Erdös had used his knowledge of what are called sieve methods to establish Kac's conjecture. Ever since, probabilistic methods have spread in analytic number theory to the mutual advantage of both subjects. Ironically, Erdös's knowledge of probability theory matched Kac's grasp of number theory: Erdös did not even know the central limit theorem at that time.

Combinatorics. Another of Erdös's major achievements is that he established combinatorial questions in mathematics as a central, new field of enquiry. The subject was reinvented in the decades after World War II, having become unfashionable. Whereas others may have done as much to reinvigorate the connections between combinatorics and other branches of mathematics that have their roots in the work of the previous two centuries, Erdös directed attention to novel but equally significant questions in the subject. Here two topics stand out: Ramsey theory and Random graphs.

Ramsey theory was initiated by the English mathematician Frank Plumpton Ramsey, and concerns problems that ask for the smallest set of objects in which a certain pattern must appear. For example, how many people must there be in a room together before one can be certain that at least two have the same sex? Here the answer is obviously three. How many people must there be in a room together before one can be certain that either three know each other or three do not (assuming that if Jack knows Jill then Jill knows Jack)? Here the answer is six, but the way to prove this is not to list all the sets of three there can be, because there are a lot. The same problem can be asked for foursomes, and here Erdös, Graham, and others proved that the answer is 18, but all that is known for fivesomes is that the answer lies between 43 and 49. Erdös discovered profound implications of Ramsey theory in the study of graphs, both finite graphs and, perhaps more remarkably, infinite graphs.

Whenever it is asked if an infinite graph has a certain property, it is likely that the question turns into one about the independence, or otherwise, of this or a related property from the fundamental axioms of set theory (usually ZFC or Zermelo-Frankel set theory with the axiom of choice). In 1943 Erdös and Alfred Tarski wrote a joint paper that showed that some of these questions led to the construction of what are called inaccessible cardinals (sets of a vastly greater size than are usually encountered in mathematics). The theory of these and other huge sets is today an active branch of modern set theory.

Random graph theory is the application of probabilistic methods to combinatorial questions, and combines numerical estimates with probability theory to establish the existence of graphs with properties that ought to occur quite often. It was created in a series of papers by Erdös and Alfréd Rényi in the 1960s. The basic idea is that a graph with a certain number, n, of vertices is specified by assigning the edges at random. When a suitable number of edges have been specified, the graph ought to have certain properties. For example, after a time one expects all the vertices to be connected, and Erdös and Rényi gave sharp estimates of when this will occur (roughly $n \log (n/2)$ edges have to be assigned). More remarkably, they showed that after about $n/2$ edges have been chosen one can expect a giant component to appear, which then steadily absorbs the remaining components as the number of edges further increases. This is a good model for a phase transition, such as occurs in percolation theory, and in many branches of physics.

BIBLIOGRAPHY

It is possible to list only a small selection of his papers here.

WORKS BY PAUL ERDÖS

With Mark Kac. The Gaussian Law of Errors in the Theory of Additive Number Theoretic Functions. *American Journal of Mathematics* 62 (1940): 738–742.

With Alfred Tarski. On Families of Mutually Exclusive Sets. *Annals of Mathematics* 44 (1943): 315–329.

"On a New Method in Elementary Number Theory which Leads to an Elementary Proof of the Prime Number Theorem." *Proceedings of the National Academy of Sciences* 35 (1949): 374–384.

With Alfréd Rényi. "On the Evolution of Random Graphs." *Magyar Tudomanyos Akademia Matematikai Kutato Intezetenek Kozlemenyei* 5 (1960): 17–61.

Paul Erdös: The Art of Counting. Selected Writings. Edited by Joel Spencer and with a dedication by Richard Rado. *Mathematicians of Our Time,* Vol. 5. Cambridge, MA and London. MIT Press, 1973.

With Joel Spencer. *Probabilistic Methods in Combinatorics. Probability and Mathematical Statistics,* Vol. 17. New York and London: Academic Press, 1974.

With Ronald L. Graham. "Old and New Problems and Results in Combinatorial Number Theory: Van der Waerden's Theorem and Related Topics." *L'Enseignement Mathématique* 25 (1979): 325–344. Also in *Monograph No. 28 de L'Enseignement Mathématique* (1980).

OTHER SOURCES

Babai, László. *Paul Erdös (1913–1996): His Influence on the Theory of Computing. Proceedings of the Twenty-ninth Annual ACM Symposium on the Theory of Computing,* 1997. New York: Association for Computing Machinery, 1999, pp. 383–401. (Electronic.)

———. "Finite and Transfinite Combinatorics." *Notices of the American Mathematical Society* 45 (1998): 23–28.

Babai, László, Carl Pomerance, and Peter Vértesi. "The Mathematics of Paul Erdös." *Notices of the American Mathematical Society* 45 (1998): 19–23.

Babai, László, and Joel Spencer. "Paul Erdös (1913–1996)." *Notices of the American Mathematical Society* 45 (1998): 64–66.

Hajnal, András. *Paul Erdös' Set Theory. The Mathematics of Paul Erdös*, Vol. 2, *Algorithms Combin.* 14 (1997): 352–393. Reprinted in *The Mathematics of Paul Erdös,* edited by Ronald L. Graham and Jaroslav Nešetřil. Berlin and New York: Springer, 1997.

Hoffman, Paul. *The Man Who Loved Only Numbers.* London: Fourth Estate, 1998.

Jeremy Gray

ERIKSON, ERIK HOMBURGER (*b.* Frankfurt, Germany, 15 June 1902; *d.* Harwich, Massachusetts, 12 May 1994), *psychoanalytic theory, psychohistory and psychobiography, child and adolescent psychotherapy, developmental psychology.*

Erikson is best known for identifying eight stages of psychosocial development in the human life cycle and for his concept of the identity crisis. He expanded psychoanalytic theory to include the influence of cultural variations on individual ego development, and showed how personality development in certain key individuals can induce widespread cultural changes. For his book *Gandhi's Truth,* he won a Pulitzer Prize and a National Book Award. By improving Sigmund Freud's case-history research methods and extending their application beyond childhood to the entire life span, Erikson became the father of contemporary psychobiographical research.

Early Development. Erik Erikson entered the world in the midst of an identity crisis. Conceived in Denmark, he was born in Germany. His mother, Karla Abrahamsen, was a Danish Jew; his father was probably a Danish Gentile, perhaps an artist or photographer. She had been very briefly married to another man several years earlier, but never revealed the identity of Erik's father. To avoid scandalizing her family, she moved from Copenhagen to Frankfurt before the birth. Baby Erik was blond and blue-eyed, resembling no one in the family. He became well aware of his differences from those around him as he grew older. On his third birthday his mother married a German Jewish pediatrician; she told Erik that the doctor was his birth father. Little Erik had his suspicions, entertaining the sort of fantasy that Freud called the "family romance": that both his true parents must be much finer than these obvious imposters. Erik was not officially told about his adoptive status until late childhood; he remained bitter about how his mother and stepfather had lied to him, as a brief autobiography written nearly sixty years later indicates:

> I grew up in Karlsruhe in Baden as the son of a pediatrician, Dr. Theodor Homburger, and his wife Karla, née Abrahamsen, a native of

Copenhagen, Denmark. All through my earlier childhood they kept secret from me the fact that my mother had been married previously and that I was the son of a Dane who had abandoned her before my birth. (1970, p. 742)

Except for such questions about his true identity, Erik Homburger had a comfortable childhood, with a solid classical education at the local Gymnasium. He displayed artistic talent and was encouraged in that direction by his mother's artist friends. His stepfather wanted Erik to follow in his footsteps as a pediatrician; Erik chose instead to pursue the wandering life of an art student from his late teens until age twenty-five. It was not unusual at that time for the sons of well-to-do German families to pursue a *Wanderjahr* (literally, wandering year) or a longer *Wanderschaft* (period of journeying). (He later wrote about such socially approved postponements of full adulthood, referring to them as "psychosocial moratoria.") Erik's mother provided occasional financial support, and he was able to sell or barter sketches to people he met on his travels. Eventually he realized that he was not sufficiently talented to become a full-time artist, so he returned to Karlsruhe to become an art teacher. At that point a friend of his from the Gymnasium, Peter Blos, told him of a more interesting possibility. In Vienna, Sigmund Freud's daughter Anna had become close to a wealthy American heiress, Dorothy Tiffany Burlingham, who needed a tutor for her four children. Erik was first hired to sketch the children, then took over their tutoring from Blos. Erik impressed the children and both women with his competence and empathy. Other members of the Freud circle, including analysts and patients, also had children who needed to be educated. Blos was invited to set up a small psychoanalytically oriented school, with himself and Erik as the faculty.

Psychoanalytic Training. In 1927, when Erik Homburger joined Blos in Vienna, he knew little or nothing about psychoanalysis. But it was an exciting time to get to know the Freuds and the ideas they were advancing. Sigmund Freud had recently proposed a new theory of anxiety, emphasizing its use by the ego to keep other parts of the personality in line. Anna Freud was beginning to develop her own ideas, building on her father's concepts about unconscious defenses to understand how adolescents cope with inner and outer threats to their continuing psychological development. She was also analyzing children directly, rather than waiting for them to enter analysis as adults with problems left over from childhood. Other members of the Freudian circle were similarly reshaping Sigmund Freud's earlier concepts into a more reality-oriented "ego psychology," in contrast to the earlier "id psychology" that emphasized unconscious urges for immediate satisfaction. Sigmund Freud, who gave Anna a

training analysis though she had no advanced degrees in medicine or otherwise, had begun to encourage the practice of "lay analysis" by other nonmedical psychoanalysts in Europe and America.

Anna Freud was eager to expand the practice of child analysis, whether by psychoanalytically trained psychiatrists or by analysts with talents in other directions. Recognizing Erik Homburger's promise in the way he taught young children, she offered him a nearly free training analysis. He hesitantly accepted her offer, at first having no intention to practice as a psychoanalyst. During his four years of almost daily analysis with Anna, he often encountered Sigmund in the waiting room between their offices, but all his substantive conversations were with Anna alone. Erik was shy, and he knew that Sigmund was already suffering badly from the oral cancer that would eventually kill him, so they rarely said anything more to each other than hello. Erik learned his psychoanalytic theory and practice directly from Anna Freud, from reading Sigmund Freud's works, and from seminars with prominent analysts at the Vienna Psychoanalytic Institute. As Erik's ideas about psychoanalytic theory and practice began to emerge, he offered them in a soft-spoken and thoughtful manner, avoiding the loud rebelliousness of some of Freud's former disciples. In Lawrence Friedman's accurate characterization, Erik engaged in a "process of embracing while amplifying and subtly criticizing" Freudian theory (1999, p. 88), not only as a student in Vienna but throughout his psychoanalytic career.

Professional Beginnings. At a Viennese masked ball in 1929, Erik Homburger met a Canadian-American teacher and student of modern dance named Joan Serson. They fell in love, moved in together, and married shortly after they found she was pregnant. Joan was Episcopalian, doubted the value of psychoanalysis, and disliked Anna Freud. But she was a believer in Erik's capabilities, brought increased order to his life, and gradually helped him to develop an eloquence in his English-language writings that he might not have otherwise achieved. After he finished his clinical training and became a full member both of the Vienna Psychoanalytic Society and the International Psychoanalytical Association, they decided together that it was time to leave Vienna. Erik wanted to establish his own psychoanalytic practice, somewhere beyond the tight circle around Sigmund and Anna Freud. The Nazis were gaining strength in Austria as well as in Germany, and Joan was dismayed by the thought of raising children in such an ugly political atmosphere. They left Vienna in spring 1933, going first to Copenhagen, where Erik still had a number of maternal relatives and where he hoped to find traces of his birth father. But psychoanalysis was in official disfavor there, and the Danish government refused to give Erik a work permit. Rather

Erik Erikson. © TED STRESHINSKY/CORBIS.

than returning to Vienna, the Homburgers headed for America.

Erik had been encouraged by Hanns Sachs, an early Freud disciple who had moved to Boston, to set up a child analysis practice there. Joan's mother also lived there and promised to help them. They arrived in fall 1933 with two small sons in tow. In spite of his limited facility in English, Erik quickly gained a strong reputation as a child analyst, achieving impressive success in treating several adults as well. Despite his lack of higher-educational degrees (or indeed any degrees beyond his graduation from the Gymnasium in Karlsruhe and a diploma in Montessori education), he was offered part-time professional positions in several Boston-area clinical settings. Most significantly in terms of his subsequent career, he was hired by Henry A. Murray to join the staff of the Harvard Psychological Clinic.

The clinic did not operate primarily as a treatment facility but as a research center, empirically testing psychoanalytic concepts and other approaches to personality. Murray quickly made Erik a member of the center's Diagnostic Council, an elite group of experts in one or another approach to personality assessment. Murray asked him to apply a modified version of a technique that Erik had already used successfully with children, in which the child patient creates a doll family out of clay and then acts out various family interactions among the dolls, to the center's Harvard undergraduate volunteer subjects. When the results of the center's first major study were published in 1938 as the now-classic volume *Explorations in Personality,* Erik was listed on the title page as one of Murray's coauthors, still under the name of Erik Homburger.

By that time, however, Erik and his family (now including a daughter) had moved on. His reputation as a child analyst was spreading rapidly, attracting particular attention at a campus that was active both in research on children and in the incorporation of psychoanalytic theory into academic psychology: Yale University. Erikson was offered a position there—again, not as a full-time faculty member in one department, but as a part-timer with his time split among several programs. Henry Murray was unhappy to see him go, but Erik was beginning to express ambitions that the largely experiment-oriented Harvard psychology department was unlikely to let him fulfill. The move to Yale also enabled Erik to start over again personally, by changing his last name from his stepfather's "Homburger" to the self-created "Erikson." He kept Homburger as his middle name, to honor his stepfather's contributions to his upbringing; he thought of Erikson as recognizing his birth father—who, according to some Copenhagen rumors, shared the given name of Erik. Both Erik and Joan adopted the Erikson name when they became naturalized U.S. citizens in 1938, and also gave the name to their three children, who were happy that other children would not be calling them "Hamburger" any more. That was one of the reasons Erik Erikson later gave for the change in the family name.

Though Erikson was welcomed by some child psychologists at Yale, others disdained his empathic approach to understanding children. He lasted no longer there than at Harvard. By now, however, his reputation had spread as far as the West Coast, where in 1939 he was offered another package of part-time positions at the University of California's (UC) Berkeley campus. Those part-time positions included the chance to work with samples of psychologically healthy children, rather than the disturbed ones he had mostly been observing and treating. Complementing an earlier research trip to an Oglala Sioux reservation, he also visited a Yurok tribe in Northern California, where he questioned and observed adults and children concerning tribal child-raising practices. Such cross-cultural excursions added to his own contrasting observations of childhood in Germany, Austria, and America. During World War II, he employed his cross-cultural expertise to provide U.S. government agencies with analyses of German national character, including the development of Adolf Hitler's charismatic appeal to German youth.

Erikson's initial appointments at UC Berkeley were not renewed, partly as a result of personal and theoretical clashes with sponsoring faculty members. During most of the 1940s he supported himself largely through private clinical practice in the San Francisco Bay Area. He also wrote a series of important papers, which he began to see as the foundation for his first book. His growing professional reputation and the impending publication of this book, as well as a competing offer from Yale, led UC Berkeley to offer him a tenured full professorship in 1949. That was a remarkable achievement for a man who had never earned a formal degree and who had begun to learn English only at age thirty-one. Erikson was delighted to receive such recognition from the academic establishment, and soon accepted the offer. But after a year in this prestigious new position, he joined a faculty protest against a loyalty oath imposed by the UC's Board of Regents, resigning his professorship along with several other members of the psychology department. For several months he maintained a temporary research appointment at Berkeley, but the Northeast was calling again.

Midlife Achievement and Influence. In October 1950, three months after submitting his statement of resignation to UC, Erikson published his first and most influential book, *Childhood and Society*. The book was not a systematic explication of his ideas but included examples from each of the several related lines of his psychoanalytic research and writing. Four underlying themes were evident throughout: the constant work of the individual ego in mediating between the demands of biology and society; the influence of an individual's distinctive social world on his or her psychological development; the developmental challenges faced by the individual from early childhood throughout adulthood and into old age; and the promotion of healthy psychological development rather than a focus on the neurotic struggles of the usual clinical case history. Each of these themes represented modifications and expansions in the perspectives of Sigmund Freud and his immediate followers, and were therefore controversial among orthodox psychoanalysts. But Erikson's discussion of psychological development across the whole human life span attracted the enthusiastic attention of many readers outside Freudian circles.

Like Freud, Erikson conceptualized personality development as proceeding through a series of distinct stages, with the possibility of becoming fixated at a given stage when the individual is unable to cope effectively with that stage's distinctive developmental crisis. But whereas Freud focused on what he called "psychosexual" stages and crises, Erikson concluded that those early developmental stages were much broader in scope, involving "psychosocial" crises as well. In Freud's oral stage, the developmental crisis is weaning; Erikson saw the broader crisis the child faces there as whether to develop a basic sense of trust in the parents or to retain a sense of mistrust. In

Stages in the Development of the Personality

Stage	Age (Years)							
	1	2	3	4	5	6	7	8
VIII								INTEGRITY vs. DESPAIR
VII							GENERATIVITY vs. STAGNATION	
VI						INTIMACY vs. ISOLATION		
V	Temporal Perspective vs. Time Confusion	Self-Certainty vs. Self-Consciousness	Role Experimentation vs. Role Fixation	Apprenticeship vs. Work Paralysis	IDENTITY vs. IDENTITY CONFUSION	Sexual Polarization vs. Bisexual Confusion	Leader- and Followership vs. Authority Confusion	Ideological Commitment vs. Confusion of Values
IV				INDUSTRY vs. INFERIORITY	Task Identification vs. Sense of Futility			
III			INITIATIVE vs. GUILT		Anticipation of Roles vs. Role Inhibition			
II		AUTONOMY vs. SHAME, DOUBT			Will to be Oneself vs. Self-Doubt			
I	TRUST vs. MISTRUST				Mutual Recognition vs. Autistic Isolation			

SOURCE: Table from Erikson, Erik H. "The Life Cycle: Epigenesis of Identity," *Identity: Youth and Crisis*, W. W. Norton: New York, 1968, 94.

"Stages in the Development of the Personality" Table of Erik Erikson's stages in personality development.

Freud's anal stage, the crisis is toilet training; Erikson identified the broader crisis as developing a sense of autonomy or becoming overwhelmed by shame and self-doubt. In Freud's phallic stage, the crisis involves the child's assertion of sexual or sensual attraction to the opposite-sexed parent and a perception of threat from the same-sexed parent; Erikson saw the issue more broadly (and not just sexually) as a matter of displaying initiative or of developing "a sense of guilt over the goals contemplated and the acts initiated in one's exuberant enjoyment of new locomotor and mental power" (1963, p. 255). In Freud's latency stage, the child represses Oedipal concerns while undergoing asexual cognitive development; Erikson likewise sees the stage as one where the child "develops a sense of industry. … In all cultures, at this stage, children receive some *systematic instruction*" (1963, p. 259), which may instead yield a sense of inferiority. In Freud's genital stage, the crisis is one of attaining full adult sexual capabilities; Erikson sees it as just as significantly concerned with attaining a sense of one's individual identity, in terms not only of gender but of occupational interests and other personal enthusiasms and social roles. Erikson also identified several additional developmental stages beyond the achievement of genital maturity and ego identity. In these further stages, Freud's psychosexual emphasis recedes as the psychosocial issues of full adulthood come to the fore.

The stages of psychosocial development that Erikson diagramed and discussed in *Childhood and Society*'s central chapter, "Eight Ages of Man," have become a standard feature of introductory psychology textbooks and self-help best sellers (with the latter often disguising their Eriksonian sources behind new terminology). His book was not an immediate best seller, but within less than a decade after its publication the Eriksonian psychosocial stages were recognized by many developmental psychologists and other mental health professionals as a good way to organize thinking about major turning points across the individual's life cycle. Though Erikson's resignation from his tenured full professorship at Berkeley was a courageous form of protest against an abridgment of academic freedom, the publication of *Childhood and Society* meant that he had little need to worry about getting another job fairly quickly.

Indeed, his next job offered advantages that Berkeley did not. He joined the clinical staff of the Austen Riggs Center, a private psychiatric hospital in Stockbridge, Massachusetts. The center's staff included several other distinguished psychoanalysts, who were happy to have Erikson as a colleague. He was given a light patient load, mostly troubled adolescents who provided case material for his study of identity issues, and he was allowed substantial time to write. He became a prolific writer during his Austen Riggs years, most significantly producing his first full-length psychobiography, *Young Man Luther* (1958). In his earlier and much briefer study of Hitler's childhood, he traced the role of certain Germanic cultural influences as they interacted with Adolf's particular family circumstances to produce a massively destructive personality pattern. In *Young Man Luther,* Erikson examined other Germanic cultural patterns in interaction with Luther's childhood circumstances as they led to a similarly society-changing but more constructive outcome. He used Luther's example to discuss in much greater detail than before the fifth stage of his eight-stage psychosocial schema, Ego Identity versus Role Confusion, as it culminates in an identity crisis. Martin Luther resolved his identity crisis, according to Erikson, by advancing a new concept of man's relationship to God, thus initiating the Protestant Reformation.

Erikson also used his discussion of Luther to offer advice to other biographers on how to do psychobiography responsibly: look for the sources of the subject's psychological strengths, not only for serious flaws; avoid "originology," which Erikson defined as focusing only on childhood sources of adult personality without recognizing the contributions of later developmental stages; pay attention to obvious gaps in the biographical record (such as, in this case, any significant mention of Luther's mother) and look for evidence that might productively bridge those gaps. Although some Luther scholars have criticized Erikson's analysis of Luther, others have praised his book as insightful and as stimulating further scholarship. (See the volume edited by Capps, Capps, and Bradford, 1977, for several perspectives.) His methodological suggestions have also been seen as advancing psychobiog-

raphy significantly beyond Freud's initial contributions to the field.

After spending most of the 1950s at the Austen Riggs Center, Erikson was offered a position at Harvard University that was tailor-made for him: a full-time appointment as professor of human development—a title that he chose, with no obligations to any specific academic department, but with freedom to teach on the topics of his expertise and to associate with friendly and influential colleagues in several areas. He was also named as a lecturer in the Harvard Medical School's department of psychiatry, though he had no medical degree. By this time, as Erikson remarked in his "Autobiographic Notes on the Identity Crisis," he had come as close as possible to being a pediatrician (his stepfather's original aim for him) without going to medical school.

At Harvard, Erikson taught a course on the human life cycle to undergraduates for the first time. The course was quite popular; over the years he was assigned a variety of graduate teaching assistants to help him with the large enrollments. Several of these assistants later went on to prominence in the social and behavioral sciences themselves, including Robert Coles, Kenneth Keniston, Carol Gilligan, and Mary Catherine Bateson. Perhaps in part because he gained so much satisfaction by nurturing both undergraduate students and graduate assistants in this course, Erikson focused in his next book on the seventh stage of his life cycle schema, generativity versus stagnation. (It should be noted that Stage Seven issues had earlier become painfully salient to Erikson himself after Joan gave birth to a Down syndrome child in 1944. At Erikson's direction, the child was quickly placed in a private institution and died there in 1965 without parental contact or acknowledgment.)

Like his earlier work on Luther, *Gandhi's Truth* (1969) is a psychobiography of a revolutionary figure who resolves a developmental crisis in his own life while initiating a major religious and political movement that changes the culture around him. Though Mohandas Gandhi had identity issues as a young man, Erikson saw his crucial psychosocial crisis as that of middle age: accepting or rejecting one's responsibilities to other people. Erikson's carefully chosen word for the positive pole of Stage Seven's crisis, "generativity," most often refers to taking care of one's own children, but it can also encompass taking care of others' children (as in a classroom), taking care of one's community (as expressed in political responsibilities), and in Gandhi's case, taking care of a whole nation—initiating and guiding the cultural and political changes that ultimately freed India from British rule. Erikson gave special attention to Gandhi's development of *satyagraha,* usually translated as "truth force" or (more passively) "nonviolent resistance," which involves caring

410

for one's opponents as well as for one's fellow citizens. Erikson did not judge Gandhi's motives as altogether virtuous, however; a major point of his book was the need not only for "Gandhi's Truth" in the form of *satyagraha,* but for "Freud's Truth" in the form of self-exploration and self-criticism of one's less conscious motives. (In Gandhi's case, according to Erikson, these included unstated urges toward violence in addition to his endorsement of peaceful goal-seeking). Erikson also continued to elaborate his methodological advice to other psychobiographers, especially in terms of what to make of a subject's autobiographical accounts. As he pointed out, Gandhi wrote several versions of his autobiography at different times in his life; the astute psychobiographer needs to pay attention to Gandhi's intended audience and underlying aims when interpreting and assessing each autobiographical version.

Moving into Old Age. Erikson retired from the Harvard teaching faculty in 1970, but he hardly retired from writing. Although he did not complete any more long psychobiographies along the lines of the Luther and Gandhi books, he wrote thoughtful shorter works on Thomas Jefferson and on Jesus. With the full participation of his wife Joan, he continued to write about the later stages of the life cycle. Perhaps his most interesting treatment of the final stage, dealing with the crisis he called "ego integrity versus despair," was a paper he had originally developed for his Harvard undergraduate course as a commentary on the Ingmar Bergman film *Wild Strawberries.* The film depicts an elderly Scandinavian professor's review of his entire life cycle on the day he is to receive an honorary degree for his life's work—no doubt a personally resonant film for Erikson, but also an excellent medium for him to communicate to young people what it means to look back on one's life at its end and to assess whether it has been emotionally and morally rewarding or deeply disappointing.

In his late seventies Erikson thought about writing a full-scale autobiography, perhaps as a further illustration of that final stage of psychosocial development. But he did not do it; as he moved into his eighties, his memories and his eloquence began to fade. Continuing the pattern he had followed throughout his life, he moved every few years from one part of the country to another, though by now the places he moved to were mostly returns: back for a while to Stockbridge, Massachusetts, then to Tiburon in the San Francisco Bay Area, then across the continent again to Cape Cod and to Cambridge, near Harvard. During his final years he was unable to write anything or to remember much of what had gone before. He died on Cape Cod at age ninety-one. His wife Joan continued to write about the life cycle until her own death three years later.

BIBLIOGRAPHY

The primary archival collection of Erikson's papers is in the Houghton Library, Harvard College Library, Harvard University.

WORKS BY ERIKSON

"Dramatic Productions Test." In *Explorations in Personality,* by Henry A. Murray et al., pp. 552–582. New York: Oxford University Press, 1938.

Childhood and Society. New York: Norton, 1950. 2nd, enlarged ed., 1963.

"The Dream Specimen of Psychoanalysis." *Journal of the American Psychoanalytic Association* 2 (1954): 5–56.

Young Man Luther: A Study in Psychoanalysis and History. New York: Norton, 1958.

Identity: Youth and Crisis. New York: Norton, 1968.

Gandhi's Truth: The Origins of Militant Nonviolence. New York: Norton, 1969.

"Autobiographic Notes on the Identity Crisis." *Daedalus* 99, no. 4 (1970): 730–759.

Dimensions of a New Identity. New York: Norton, 1974.

Life History and the Historical Moment. New York: Norton, 1975.

"Reflections on Dr. Borg's Life Cycle." *Daedalus* 105, no. 2 (1976): 1–31.

"The Galilean Sayings and the Sense of 'I'." *Yale Review* 70, no. 3 (1981): 321–362.

The Life Cycle Completed. New York: Norton, 1982.

A Way of Looking at Things: Selected Papers from 1930 to 1980. Edited by Stephen Schlein. New York: Norton, 1987. Includes a complete bibliography of Erikson's published work.

The Erik Erikson Reader. Edited by Robert Coles. New York: Norton, 2000.

OTHER SOURCES

Alexander, Irving L. "Erikson and Psychobiography, Psychobiography and Erikson." In *Handbook of Psychobiography,* edited by William Todd Schultz. New York: Oxford University Press, 2005.

Bloland, Sue Erikson. *In the Shadow of Fame.* New York: Viking, 2005. A memoir of family life by Erikson's daughter, who is a psychotherapist.

Capps, Donald, Walter H. Capps, and M. Gerald Bradford, eds. *Encounter with Erikson: Historical Interpretation and Religious Biography.* Missoula, MT: Scholars Press, 1977.

Coles, Robert. *Erik H. Erikson: The Growth of His Work.* Boston: Little, Brown, 1970. A sympathetic biography by one of Erikson's most distinguished students.

Evans, Richard I. *Dialogue with Erik Erikson.* New York: Harper & Row, 1967. Transcripts of several filmed interviews with Erikson.

Friedman, Lawrence J. *Identity's Architect: A Biography of Erik H. Erikson.* New York: Scribner, 1999. The most extensive and detailed biography.

Roazen, Paul. *Erik H. Erikson: The Power and Limits of a Vision.* New York: Free Press, 1976. A critical biography; Erikson privately disputed some details.

Stevens, Richard. *Erik Erikson: An Introduction.* New York: St. Martin's Press, 1983. A brief and clear presentation of Erikson's life and work.

Alan C. Elms

ERIUGENA, JOHANNES SCOTTUS

(*b.* Ireland, early ninth century; *d.* England [?], c. 875), *natural philosophy, theology.* For the original article on Eriugena see *DSB,* vol. 4.

New editions (including the *Periphyseon*) and a considerable amount of new scholarly literature since the publication of the original *DSB* article have contributed to a better understanding of Eriugena's work.

John the Scot ("Irishman") or Eriugena ("of Irish birth") was a scholar at the court of Charles the Bald in Laon, France, around 845–875. John got his reputation as a master in the liberal arts, which was the main subject in the curriculum of the palace school. He was the first to write a commentary on Martianus Capella's handbook *De nuptiis.* Asked to intervene in a debate on predestination, he composed a controversial treatise, *De praedestinatione,* in which he attributed the misunderstanding of the Christian doctrine of predestination to insufficient training in the liberal arts. He also acquired a knowledge of Greek that was exceptional in the West at that time. At the request of the emperor, he made a Latin translation of the works of Dionysius the Areopagite, which was followed later by translations of Maximus Confessor and Gregory of Nyssa. Through those translations he came deeply influenced by the Neoplatonic interpretation of the Christian doctrine, toward which he was already inclined because of his previous acquaintance with Platonism through the Latin theological tradition, in particular Augustine. After the completion of the Dionysius translation he started working on his own theo-philosophical synthesis, the *Periphyseon,* which was finished by 866. The commentary and homily on Saint John date probably from the last period of his life.

Metaphysical Views. The *Periphyseon* is an attempt to explain the "division" of the universe (Nature) into a manifold of species from the most general to the most particular, and to reduce its manifold divisions to unity. In the Neoplatonic tradition *diairesis* (which divides a genus into specific forms) and *synopsis* (which brings a dispersed plurality under a single form) are not just two logical procedures of dialectics. They correspond to the very

movements of reality: the procession of multiplicity from the One and its return into the One; in Christian terms, creation and redemption. Following the dialectical method of dividing a genus into species by differences, John presents a division that can be applied to the whole universe. The most fundamental difference in Nature is that between "creating" and "being created." Through applying this distinction he defines the four fundamental species of Nature: (1) that which creates and is not created; (2) that which creates and is created; (3) that which is created and does not create; (4) that which neither is created nor creates. The *first* species of nature is God, the uncaused cause of everything. The *third* species, diametrically opposite to the first, stands for the sensible world, comprehending the numerous species of animals and plants that come to be in times and places. The *second* species has attributes of both extremes: it is both created and creative. This is the level of the "primordial ideas" wherein God has from all eternity created all species. The *fourth* nature must be understood again as God: not, however, as the creative cause from which all things proceed, but as the ultimate Good toward which all things return. In this division, the divine nature is that which comes first and last. God, however, is not simply a species among many, because He "transcends everything that is or can be" and thus seems to fall outside all system. But one could as well say that God is the whole system in its unfolding and that all four divisions of nature are moments within the circular process whereby the divine nature proceeds from and returns to itself. If the being of the creature is nothing but a participation in the being of its creator, one may also understand the creation of the world in its manifold species as God's creation of himself. In this sense creation is God's revelation and the whole world must be understood as a *theophany,* that is, an "appearing of God."

In the last part of the work Eriugena explains how all creatures return to the One by the same stages through which the division had previously started into multiplicity. At the "end," all things will return to their primordial causes and the human beings, blessed and damned alike, will return to the perfection of one and the same asexual human nature. Yet they will be individually distinguished by the different access each shall be granted to God's self-revelation. Those who led a virtuous life will be beatified and allowed to see God in differing gradations of his theophanies. The damned, on the contrary, will be refused access to that vision and will be eternally tormented with the "vain dreams" of those things which incited their desires.

Eriugena stands apart from any of his contemporaries in his daring speculations on creation and redemption, showing a great confidence in the harmony of reason and revelation. Yet he exercised only a limited indirect influence in the Middle Ages, where he was mostly appreciated as a translator and glossator of Dionysius. The *Periphyseon* was condemned as heresy in 1225 and copies of it were burned. From a philosophical viewpoint, Eriugena's greatest accomplishment is his understanding of creation as the self-creation of God. This doctrine attracted the admiration of idealist philosophers such as Friedrich von Schelling and G. W. F. Hegel, which led to his rediscovery in the twentieth century.

Duhem's Interpretation. In the history of science, Eriugena is often quoted because he is considered to defend a mixed geo-heliocentric system, wherein Earth remains in the center of the cosmos, but the Sun functions as center around which the planets Mercury, Venus, Mars, and Jupiter orbit. Eriugena owes this fame in the history of astronomy to the historian Pierre Duhem, who recognized in the cosmological section of *Periphyseon* III (3257–3277 ed. Jeauneau) a prefiguration of the system that was later developed by the Danish astronomer Tycho Brahe as an alternative to Nicholas Copernicus's heliocentricism. Some passages in the annotations on Martianus, too, seem to support this innovative astronomical view. A careful analysis of all texts (Eastwood, 2001) makes the claim of Duhem implausible. Eriugena is original in his cosmological speculations, but not as an astronomer. He attempts to integrate the often disparate information on the planetary movements he found in his late antique sources (Pliny and Martianus) and likes to use the metaphors of circles and orbits in his speculation.

SUPPLEMENTARY BIBLIOGRAPHY

WORKS BY ERIUGENA

Jean Scot: Commentaire sur l'Évangile de Jean. Sources Chrétiennes 180. Edited by Édouard Jeauneau. Paris: Éditions du Cerf, 1972.

Iohannis Scoti Eriugenae Expositiones in Ierarchiam coelestem. Corpus Christianorum: Continuatio Mediaevalis, vol. 21. Edited by Jeanne Barbet. Turnhout, Belgium: Brepols, 1975.

Iohannis Scotti De divina praedestinatione liber. Edited by Goulven Madec. Corpus Christianorum: Series Latina, vol. 50. Turnhout, Belgium: Brepols, 1978.

Maximi Confessoris Quaestiones ad Thalassium una cum latina interpretatione Iohannis Scotti Eriugenae. Edited by Carl Laga and Carlos Steel. Corpus Christianorum: Series Graeca, vol. 7 and 22. Turnhout, Belgium: Brepols/Leuven University Press, 1980–1990.

Periphyseon. The Division of Nature. Translated by Inglis Sheldon-Williams and John J. O'Meara. Montreal: Bellarmin, 1987.

Maximi Confessoris Ambigua ad Iohannem iuxta Iohannis Scotti Eriugenae latinam interpretationem. Corpus Christianorum: Series Graeca, vol. 18. Edited by Édouard Jeauneau. Turnhout, Belgium: Brepols/Leuven University Press, 1988.

Iohannis Scotti seu Eriugenae Periphyseon. Corpus Christianorum: Continuatio Mediaevalis, vol. 164–165. Edited by Édouard Jeauneau. Turnhout, Belgium: Brepols, 1996–2003.

Treatise on Divine Predestination. Translated by Mary Brennan. Notre Dame, IN: University of Notre Dame Press, 1998.

OTHER SOURCES

Beierwaltes, Werner. *Eriugena. Grundzüge seines Denkens.* Frankfurt am Main, Germany: Vittorio Klostermann, 1994.

Brennan, Mary. *A Guide to Eriugenian Studies. A Survey of Publications 1930–1987.* Fribourg, Switzerland: Editions Universitaires, 1989.

Carabine, Deirdre. *John Scottus Eriugena.* Oxford and New York: Oxford University Press, 2000.

Eastwood, Bruce Stansfield. "Johannes Scottus Eriugena, Sun-Centred Planets and Carolingian Astronomy." *Journal of the History of Astronomy* 32 (2001): 281–324.

Jeauneau, Édouard. *Études érigéniennes*, Paris: Études Augustiniennes, 1987.

McEvoy, James, and Michael Dunne, eds. *History and Eschatology in John Scottus Eriugena and His Time.* Proceedings of the Society for the Promotion of Eriugenian Studies, 2002. Leuven, Belgium: Leuven University Press, 2002. Contains an exhaustive bibliography for 1996–2000.

Moran, Dermot. *The Philosophy of John Scottus Eriugena. A Study of Idealism in the Middle Ages,* Cambridge, U.K., and New York: Cambridge University Press, 1989.

———. "John Scottus Eriugena." *Stanford Encyclopedia of Philosophy.* October 17, 2004. Available from http://plato.stanford.edu/entries/scottus-eriugena/.

Van Riel, Gerd, Carlos Steel, and James McEvoy, eds. *Iohannes Scottus Eriugena. The Bible and Hermeneutics.* Proceedings of the Society for the Promotion of Eriugenian Studies, 1995. Leuven, Belgium: Leuven University Press, 1996. Contains an exhaustive bibliography for 1987–1995.

Carlos Steel

ESAU, KATHERINE (*b.* Yekaterinoslav [also spelled Ekaterinoslav], Russia [later Dnepropetrovsk, Ukraine], 3 April, 1898; *d.* Santa Barbara, California, 4 June 1997), *plant anatomy, phloem structure and function, transmission electron microscopy, plant ultrastructure, plant viruses.*

Esau was the quintessential botanist of the twentieth century, a century that echoed her own long lifespan of ninety-nine years. Best known for her textbooks on plant structure and development, Esau literally wrote the book on plant anatomy for U.S. botanists. Her textbooks *Plant Anatomy* ("Big Esau," 1953, 2nd ed., 1965; 3rd ed. by Ray F. Evert, 2006) and especially *Anatomy of Seed Plants* ("Little Esau," 1960, 2nd ed., 1977) directly or indirectly served to educate several generations of American plant biologists in plant anatomy with a clarity of presentation and illustration that has remained unparalleled. Botanists who never knew her personally nevertheless happily count themselves among her students.

As essential to botany as her textbooks have been, Esau's research contributions reach far beyond that of textbook author. For more than six decades she undertook pure and applied research, studying pathological and normal tissue development. Her work, initially based on field studies in plant breeding and genetics of crop plants, led to a definitive structure-function understanding of phloem (food conducting) tissue, first at the level of light microscopy and later, in pioneering studies with transmission electron microscopy, at the ultrastructural level. Her research questions included understanding the pathways of several economically important plant viruses (long before the basic structure of viruses was clearly understood), their relationship to the infected phloem tissues, and the elusive structure of the phloem itself. Her treatise *The Phloem*, published in 1969 as Volume 5 of the *Handbuch der Pflanzenanatomie*, reviewed studies of phloem from their inception and relied much on information from her own research efforts. This volume has been hailed as the most important of this series and essentially the bible of phloem.

By the early 1960s already the preeminent American plant anatomist, Esau moved beyond the level of light microscopy and embarked on the use of transmission electron microscopy (TEM) for the study of plant subcellular (ultrastructural) features, pioneering the use of this tool for plant cellular biology. In 1963, at an age when many would be considering retirement, she left her position at the University of California at Davis to follow her colleague and collaborator Vernon Cheadle to UC–Santa Barbara, where he became chancellor, and where she established a TEM laboratory that was later given her name. During the next twenty-two years, which she counted as the most productive of her career, she maintained a highly active research program on plant and plant-viral ultrastructure and function, securing National Science Foundation funds for TEM facilities and refining techniques for ultrastructural study of plant tissues. The TEM provided a magnificent tool for further elucidating the fine details of both normal and pathological tissues, for documenting the mode of infection and propagation of plant viruses, and for better understanding the development of phloem structure. These studies lay the groundwork for the current understanding of plant viruses and phloem structure and function.

Esau received considerable recognition throughout her career. Among her honors were a Guggenheim fellowship in 1940 for work at Harvard, a Faculty Research Lectureship at the University of California, Davis (the highest

honor the faculty can give to a peer) in 1946; election to the National Academy of Sciences (the sixth woman to receive this honor) in 1957 and to the American Philosophical Society in 1964. She served as president of the Botanical Society of America in 1951 and received from this group one of the first of its Merit Awards in its Fiftieth (Golden) Anniversary year in 1956. In 1989 Esau was the first trained botanist to receive the President's National Medal of Science from George H. W. Bush, at age ninety-one.

Family Background and Career Path. Esau was born in Russia (now Ukraine) to Johan (John) Esau and Margrethe Toews Esau, both of whom came from highly educated German Mennonite families. Her great-great grandfather Aron Esau had emigrated to the Ukraine from Prussia in 1804 along with many German Mennonites in response to Catherine the Great's invitation to foreigners who could help to improve Russian agriculture. Mennonites as a religious group had been alternately tolerated and exiled throughout Europe, in part because of their pacifist beliefs. Many had a reputation as excellent farmers, and rural communities in various parts of Europe benefited from the establishment of Mennonite colonies. Strong community, a serious work ethic, a simple life, and an appreciation of education were values deeply ingrained in Esau's character. She honored this background with a highly disciplined, ascetic life that ultimately contributed to her remarkable academic success.

In 1869 Esau's father, Johan, and his brother Jacob became the first Mennonite boys in their community to go to a Russian school. Her father became a mechanical engineer and later went on to establish much of the infrastructure of the city of Yekaterinoslav, of which he later became mayor, and her uncle became a physician. In an ironic turn of fate these children of immigrant ancestry had to flee their own homes in 1917, during the Bolshevik Revolution, as Johan Esau was now considered loyal to the tsarist regime. Esau's family went to Germany, where they had relatives. For the next two years she studied agriculture, first at the Berlin Landwirtschaftliche Hochschule and then at the Hohenheim College of Agriculture near Stuttgart, returning to Berlin to obtain the title *Landwirtschaftlehrerin* and later to pass the *Zusatzprufung* in plant breeding. Her father's skill in managing money enabled the family to emigrate to the United States in 1922.

The Esau family relocated in Reedley, California, near Fresno, because there was a strong Mennonite community there. Within a few years Esau began working as a plant breeder in fields first near Oxnard and later Salinas, studying the curly top viral disease in sugar beets. Her interests in selecting for disease-resistant strains of the plants culminated in her first research paper in 1930 in *Hilgardia*, the University of California's journal of agriculture. At that time basic viral structure, let alone the mode of viral transmission, was poorly known. Esau began to study the tissues of pathological and normal plants comparatively, and as she did this, began to realize the need for understanding normal development.

A shift from plant geneticist to plant anatomist came about as Esau entered graduate school in 1928. Her work was centered at the relatively young agricultural school at UC–Davis; however, because Davis did not have a graduate degree program, her graduate work was administrated through Berkeley, where she also took several courses. At the time of her studies, other researchers at Davis began a program on standardizing beet varieties. Because they did not want their study sites to be infected with curly top and because the leafhoppers who were vectors for its transmission did not grow well in Davis, Esau's work became less field-oriented and more anatomical. In her dissertation research she did a comprehensive comparison of the cells and tissues of infected and normal plants, in particular the phloem tissues. Upon completion of her dissertation in 1932, she was hired as a lecturer and researcher at the University of California at Davis, where she worked until 1963. Her work continued at Santa Barbara thereafter well into her nineties, and she lived in Santa Barbara until her death in 1997.

Legacy. Esau's most important contributions depended on her exceptionally careful and clear comparative study of the cells and tissues of healthy and infected plants. Whereas other plant anatomists took a static view of structures, her studies were dynamic, following the development and differentiation of tissues. Her descriptions are a clear, concise, cell-by-cell account of the changes that occur with development or with infection. As a writer her considerable facility with language (including fluency in German, Russian, English, French, Spanish, and Portuguese) was essential to the work; she was well acquainted with the German and Russian literature and was able to incorporate this information into her English-language texts. She consulted regularly with her colleague, the writer Celeste Turner Wright, to improve her writing.

Esau's talents in writing, illustrating, and communicating also made her an excellent teacher and public speaker. She had a droll sense of humor that delighted her students and audiences. She was known to start her lectures with the words "Once upon a time," which led students to refer to the lectures as "Esau's fables." She invented a continuing story, "The Saga of Vladimir the Virus, or the Account of the Tragic Fate of Norman the Nucleus," to illustrate the progress of viral infection of a cell's nucleus with a series of electron micrographs.

Esau was a very successful collaborator, working with Robert Gill on phloem ultrastructure, James Cronshaw on the characterization of P-protein (formerly called "slime" in phloem), and Lynn Hoefert on plant virus research. She also collaborated with Vernon Cheadle on the comparative anatomy of phloem and its evolutionary significance. Esau directed fifteen PhD students, mostly at Davis, and numerous postdoctoral associates. Her students included Hugh Wilcox (mycorrhizae) and Peter Kaufman (gravitropic response; gibberellins). Perhaps her best-known student is Ray F. Evert, who continued her studies of phloem ultrastructure, wrote plant biology textbooks, and in 2006 revised Esau's *Plant Anatomy.* Jennifer Thorsch became Esau's last graduate student when Esau was eighty-one years old and remained close to her in her final years.

Esau's legacy is rooted in the fundamental descriptive science of plant anatomy precisely because it is a highly practical and necessary field of endeavor. She trained not only pure but applied scientists who needed to understand the economically important plants that she studied with such rigor. With exceptional skill, dedication, and good humor she became a fundamental figure in understanding and teaching plant anatomy, and she remains foremost in the minds of those who care about plant structure and function.

In 1993 she established the Katherine Esau Fellowship Program at the University of California at Davis for junior faculty members, visiting scholars, and postdoctoral researchers. In recognition of her legacy, the Katherine Esau Award of Botanical Society of America is given annually at the society's meeting.

BIBLIOGRAPHY

Katherine Esau's papers are deposited in the Department of Special Collections, Donald C. Davidson Library, University of California, Santa Barbara. Details are available at http://www.library.ucsb.edu/speccoll/ua.html. Prepared slides, photographs, and other materials from the research of Esau and her colleague and collaborator Vernon Cheadle are housed in the Vernon I. Cheadle and Katherine Esau Structural Botanical Collections, University of California, Santa Barbara; information is available from http://www.lifesci.ucsb.edu/~mseweb/cheadle_esau/index.html.

WORKS BY ESAU

"Studies of the Breeding of Sugar Beets for Resistance to Curly Top." *Hilgardia* 4 (1930): 417–441. Esau's first paper, based on her early work in plant breeding for resistant crops, drawn on her work at the Spreckle Seed Company near Salinas, California.

"Origin and Development of Primary Vascular Tissues in Seed Plants." *Botanical Review* 9 (1943): 125–206.

Plant Anatomy. New York: Wiley, 1953; 2nd ed., 1965. A complete and detailed text on the development and structure of the vegetative structures (leaves, stems, roots, wood, and bark) of vascular plants. The long-anticipated revision of this text has been published as Evert, Ray F., *Esau's Plant Anatomy: Meristems, Cells, and Tissues of the Plant Body: Their Structure, Function, and Development*, 3rd ed., Hoboken, NJ: Wiley, 2006. This edition includes many of the original figures from Esau's original texts and research and is an updated discussion of developments in the field.

"Primary Vascular Differentiation in Plants." *Biological Review* 29 (1954): 46–86.

With Vernon I. Cheadle. "Secondary Phloem of Calycanthaceae." *University of California Press, Publications in Botany, Berkeley* 29 (1958): 397–510. A paper surveying variations in secondary phloem tissue and its value for comparative taxonomic purposes.

Anatomy of Seed Plants. New York: Wiley, 1960; 2nd ed., 1977. A more streamlined version of the principles of plant anatomy that also includes chapters on plant reproductive structures (flowers, fruits, seeds), this text has been used extensively in plant anatomy courses and in the early 2000s forms the basis for how many botanists teach the discipline.

Plants, Viruses, and Insects. Cambridge, MA: Harvard University Press, 1961.

Vascular Differentiation in Plants. New York: Holt, Rinehart and Winston, 1965.

"Anatomy of Plant Virus Infections." *Annual Review of Phytopathology* 5 (1967): 45–76.

With James Cronshaw. "Relation of Tobacco Mosaic Virus to the Host Cells." *Journal of Cell Biology* 33 (June 1967): 665–678.

Viruses in Plant Hosts: Form, Distribution, and Pathologic Effects. Madison: University of Wisconsin Press, 1968.

The Phloem: Handbuch der Pflanzenanatomie. Band V, Teil 2, Histologie. Berlin-Stuttgart: Gebrüder Borntraeger, 1969. Part of a series of books that treat detailed topics in plant anatomy, this volume details the structure, function, and variation known in the phloem tissue in the late 1960s, including some of Esau's first electron micrographs.

With Robert H. Gill. "Aggregation of Endoplasmic Reticulum and Its Relation to the Nucleus in a Differentiating Sieve Element." *Journal of Ultrastructure Research* 34 (1971): 144–158.

With Lynn L. Hoefert. "Ultrastructure of Sugar Beet Leaves Infected with Beet Western Yellows Virus." *Journal of Ultrastructure Research* 40 (1972): 556–571.

With Jennifer Thorsch. "Sieve Plate Pores and Plasmodesmata, the Communication Channels of the Symplast: Ultrastructural Aspects and Developmental Relations." *American Journal of Botany* 72 (October 1985): 1641–1653. (Special paper.)

With Robert H. Gill. "Distribution of Vacuoles and Some Other Organelles in Dividing Cells." *Botanical Gazette* 152 (1991): 397–407. Esau's last paper, at age ninety-one.

OTHER SOURCES

Evert, Ray F. "Commentary: The Contributions of Katherine Esau." *International Journal of Plant Sciences* 153 (September 1992): v-ix. This commentary is part of a special Festscrift dedicated to Katherine Esau which includes contributed

papers from the Katherine Esau International Symposium, held at UC Davis March 28–31, 1992.

———. "Katherine Esau: Address Given by President-Elect Ray F. Evert." *Plant Science Bulletin* 3 (October 1985). Available from http://www.botany.org/bsa/misc/esau.html. One of Esau's most prominent graduate students, Evert focused his address as president-elect of the Botanical Society of America on Esau's life and scientific accomplishments.

O'Hearn, Elizabeth Moot. "Profiles of Pioneer Women Scientists: Katherine Esau." *Botanical Review* (July 1996): 209–271. New York Botanical Garden. This source includes detailed information on Esau's research studies, honors, and graduate students; reminiscences from her academic peer and friend Celeste Turner Wright, and an addendum containing a biography of her father, Johan Esau.

Ruddat, Manfred, and Edward D. Garber. "Editorial." *International Journal of Plant Sciences* 153 (September 1992): iii-iv. This editorial introduces a special Festscrift dedicated to Katherine Esau which includes contributed papers from the Katherine Esau International Symposium, held at UC Davis March 28–31, 1992.

Stebbins, George Ledyard. "Katherine Esau (3 April 1898–4 June 1997)." *Proceedings of the American Philosophical Society* 143 (December 1999): 665–672. Available from http://www.aps-pub.com/proceedings/1434/Esau.pdf. This summary provides insight from one of Esau's most prominent botanical contemporaries and colleagues on the broad significance of her work.

Thorsch, Jennifer, and Ray F. Evert. "Katherine Esau." *American Journal of Botany* 84 (November 1997): 1621–1623.

———. "Katherine Esau, 1898–1997." *Annual Review of Phytopathology* 36 (September 1998): 27–40. These two final references are coauthored by Jennifer Thorsch, Esau's last graduate student, who cared for her in her later years, and Evert, who carried on much of Esau's work on phloem. They provide an outline to Esau's professional activities as well as some personal reminiscences.

Kathleen E. Pigg

EUCLID (*fl.* Alexandria [?], third century BCE), *mathematics.* For the original article on Euclid see *DSB*, vol. 4 (part [i]: Life and Works, by Ivor Bulmer Thomas, pp. 414-437; [ii]: Transmission of the Elements, by John Murdoch, pp. 437–459).

This postscript addresses only two points: the discussions concerning the authenticity of certain of Euclid's writings (*Phænomena, Optics, Catoptrica, Sectio Canonis*) considered minor works, at least in size, when compared to the *Elements;* and the transmission of the *Elements* during the ancient and medieval periods.

Discussion of Certain Minor Works. Any even mildly ambitious interpretation of Euclidian writings immediately

Euclid. HULTON ARCHIVE/GETTY IMAGES.

could not have engaged in this type of study. Pushed to its limits, this reasoning would also lead to the exclusion of the *Optics* and the *Phænomena.* However, nobody knows Euclid's philosophic orientation, or even if he had one; in any case, to adopt the point of view of Proclus of Lycia (fifth century) who identifies Euclid as a Platonist does not prevent attributing to him an *Optics,* a *Catoptrica,* and a musical treatise.

Hence another criterion: taking the exposition of the *Elements* as a standard, one presumed to be able to differentiate between the works that could, from the formal point of view of the characteristics of the demonstration (the position of the postulates, the rigor of the proofs) stand in favorable comparison versus those that were unworthy of the great geometer's reputation.

Basing his thought on these very uncertain presumptions, Heiberg concluded that the *Optics* was authentic (at least in the recension that he had just recently discovered), but he rejected the *Catoptrica,* which he attributed to Theon. Paul Tannery condemned the *Sectio Canonis* in a like manner. Some less clear-cut positions were also adopted that sought to identify a Euclidian nucleus or, what amounted to almost the same thing, simply to reject certain portions of the treatises.

Recent studies devoted to the *scripta minora* (minor works) of Euclid have properly called into question conclusions that were once believed definitive. Of the two recensions of the *Phænomena,* the one that Heiberg considered closest to the Euclidian original is identified by J. L. Berggren and Robert S. D. Thomas as the work of Theon; the other, which Heiberg designated as Theonian and which appears in the oldest Greek manuscript of the collection known as *The Little Astronomy* (MS Vat. graec. 204), is even later. Both were modified according to information provided by Pappus (beginning of the fourth century) in Book VI of his *Collection.*

Alexander Jones and Wilbur Knorr arrive at similar conclusions for the *Optics,* especially concerning Pappus's influence on the two preserved recensions and their mutual contaminations. Furthermore, their order of precedence must be reversed: the one that Heiberg attributed to Theon is closest to the original! There is an interesting consequence: the terminological connection that exists between this version of the *Optics* and the *Catoptrica,* a connection that for Heiberg constituted an argument in favor of his position, now becomes a sign of authenticity for the treatise on reflected vision. In addition, the same studies show that the shortcomings of the *Catoptrica* when it is compared to the *Optics* do not really exist. Except for some local alterations that are inevitable in ancient texts, the two pieces are rather comparable with regard to their success and their deficiencies in the partial mathematicization of direct and reflected vision.

encounters philological problems concerning the reliability of the text that has survived, questions of total or partial authenticity, and choices to be made between different versions when those exist. From the 1890s until recently, historians had regarded these questions as wholly settled and sanctioned by the monumental edition of Euclid's *Opera omnia,* the work of Johan L. Heiberg and Heinrich Menge. The manuscript traditions had transmitted two recensions (at least) of the *Elements,* the *Data,* the *Optics,* and the *Phænomena,* but, for each treatise, Heiberg believed he could determine precisely which was the most faithful version. He attributed to Theon of Alexandria (second half of the fourth century) the others, which he considered reworkings. If this attribution was in a certain way justifiable for the two treatises on geometry (cf. Euclid, *DSB* 4, part [ii], p. 437), it was certainly not the case for either the *Optics* or the *Phænomena.*

For the *Catoptrica* and the *Sectio Canonis,* the problem was different: at issue was their attribution to Euclid. There were two points to consider: first, the fact that it is a question of the mathematicization of certain sensible phenomena, in this case the reflection of visual rays on the one hand and the consonance or dissonance of certain musical intervals on the other. In the opinion of some, Euclid, the champion of abstract geometry and under the influence of the Platonic conception of mathematics,

In a similar way, the works of Andrew Barker and Alan and William Bowen have highlighted the coherence of the plan that underlies the Propositions of the *Sectio Canonis*. However, these three specialists do not agree on the authenticity of the introduction that precedes the theorems that follow. This example shows clearly that the debate has not ended. It must be recognized that the philological certainties that seemed obvious in the wake of Heiberg's works on the *Scripta minora* of Euclid are no longer appropriate today.

Transmission of the *Elements*. The situation is much the same for the *Elements*. In this case, the problem does not really reside in the evaluation of the two complete versions transmitted by the Greek manuscripts. Heiberg had identified them respectively as: (1) pre-Theonian (in the sole MS Vat. graec. 190 = *P*); and (2) the product of the re-edition by Theon of Alexandria. Essentially the debate rests on the comparison of the Greek text with the indirect tradition of the medieval translations. Martin Klamroth and Heiberg had already raised the issue in the 1880s. They disagreed with each other concerning the reliability and the purity of the Arabic translations, which were themselves the source of a large part of the so-called indirect medieval tradition (Latin, Hebrew, Syrian, Persian, and so forth) (cf. Euclid, *DSB* 4, part [ii], p. 442; pp. 444–448). Heiberg thought he could resolve the question in favor of the direct tradition of the Greek manuscripts by linking the Arabic translations to a hypothetical abridged Byzantine version for which he thought he had found partial evidence (MS Bononiensis, bibl. comun. 18–19 = *b*) for Propositions XI. 36-XII. 17. Most specialists, notably Thomas L. Heath and Murdoch (cf. Euclid, *DSB* IV, part [ii], p. 439), subscribed to the textual history that Heiberg had proposed. It was based on a very incomplete knowledge of the medieval versions, which had not been thoroughly studied at the time and whose heterogeneity was greatly underestimated, including by Klamroth.

The Indirect Medieval Tradition. The richness and the variety of the above-mentioned versions are infinitely better recognized in the early twenty-first century. One of the most striking features of the Arabic-Latin tradition, after the phase of reappropriation and its three twelfth-century translations (Adelard of Bath, Hermann of Carinthia, Gerard of Cremona), is the malleability of the transmission of the text of the *Elements* in the multiple recensions that derive from them. The most celebrated are the one known as "Adelard II," attributed to Robert of Chester by its recent publishers, and the one by Campanus of Novara. The former is contaminated by other texts (such as the so-called Boethian tradition of Euclid, the arithmetic of Jordanus de Nemore, and certain commentaries translated from the Arabic). The liberties that were taken

particularly with the proofs, which others replaced or omitted in favor of metamathematic information, suggested that it was believed that one could treat the demonstrations as though they were commentaries. The idea that the authentically Euclidian nucleus resides essentially in the enunciations is perhaps the cause or the consequence of this.

As for the Arabic and Hebrew versions, the situation is a little less favorable, for complete critical editions of the different versions are not available. Nevertheless, the inventory and the description of what has been preserved (translations, recensions, commentaries), although not complete, have improved greatly since the redaction of Murdoch's note, particularly for the Ishāq-Thābit version (translation by Ishāq ibn Hunayn, revision by Thābit ibn Qurra). Two provisional editions (because they were not based on the collation of all the known manuscripts) have been compiled respectively for Books V (William Engroff) and VII–IX (Gregg De Young). In these books, there are important differences in structure (additions and omissions of material; changes in order; substitution of proofs), style, and terminology among certain groups of manuscripts. A number of marginal glosses, the addition of alternative proofs explicitly attributed to the translation by al-Hajjāj (a translator who preceded Ishāq), and indications by the authors of several recensions affirming their consultation of the two versions (al-Hajjāj, Ishāq-Thābit) are all evidence of much contamination among the different branches of the tradition. The same observation holds for the Hebrew tradition.

This increased knowledge of the primary Arabic transmission permitted Engroff to refute the thesis that the Leiden manuscript contained the (revised) translation by al-Hajjāj of Books I to VI, glossed by the Persian mathematician an-Nayrizī (cf. Euclid, *DSB* 4, part [ii], p. 439). Rather, an-Nayrizī in preparing this recension contaminated different traditions, in particular those of al-Hajjāj and that of Ishāq-Thābit, and he had recourse to (at least) two Greek commentaries translated into Arabic, those of Hero of Alexandria and of Simplicius. This example in itself summarizes the state of current understanding of the medieval tradition: thanks to recent studies, there has become available a much greater wealth of information, but the time for synthesis and certainty has not yet arrived. No longer possessing a version of al-Hajjāj as was believed in 1970 and not yet having available a critical edition of Ishāq-Thābit's translation, specialists of the Arabic Euclid are now compelled to take into consideration the transmission of secondary works (commentaries, epitomes, recensions, and various adaptations) in order to gather information on the different translations that circulated in the Islamic countries. This broadening of the documentary base complicates their task, all the more so because these pieces of information are not always consonant.

Ancient History of the Greek Text. The medieval phase of the reappropriation of Euclid has an intrinsic interest for the history of mathematics and more generally for the culture of the time. It is also not without consequences for knowledge of the ancient phase of the imperial period and Late Antiquity. In fact, scholars know almost nothing certain about the history of the text during the last three centuries before the Common era. Proclus gives some information on the subject of alternative definitions or proofs, in particular by Apollonius of Perga and Poseidonius of Apamea, as well as on the polemic that pitted the latter against Zeno of Sidon and that seems to have had as a backdrop the first Book of the *Elements*. The debate between Epicureans and Stoics regarding geometry had raged since the third century (Polyaenus), but the connection with Euclid and his treatise was perhaps accentuated, indeed even created, by the exegetic orientation of Proclus or one of his predecessors.

The first person who seems to have played an important role in the transmission of the text is Hero of Alexandria (first century). The Arab bibliographers mention a book *On the Difficulties of Euclid* (*Kitāb Hall Shukūk Uqlīdis*). This is certainly the source of Proclus's citations. Unfortunately, it has been lost, but fragments have been transmitted by several medieval commentators. Its exact nature remains uncertain. Focused on the logico-mathematic difficulties of the treatise, it would probably have also suggested a large number of textual changes, which, in other terms, correspond to a (re)edition in the Alexandrian sense of the word, not necessarily implying the production of a new copy of the text but establishing a sort of "instruction manual with commentary." Others might later have referred to it to produce their versions, and indeed it seems that this was what occurred with Thābit ibn Qurra when he was working on his revision.

As in the case of Apollonius's *Conics,* somewhat better known thanks to Eutocius, a constant exegetic work on the proofs, additional cases, interpolated lemmas, marginal annotations continued and interfered with the text of the *Elements*. The medieval versions, however, permit formulation of some reasonable conjectures, in particular concerning the occurrence of double proofs, which are rather frequent in the *Elements*. This phenomenon was probably accentuated by the compilation activities of the Byzantine scribes responsible for the composition of the oldest extant copies, contemporary with or subsequent to the operation of transliteration (the passage from the majuscule writing known as uncial to the minuscule), in Constantinople, from the end of the eighth century on.

They clearly tried to preserve as much as possible of the richness of the ancient tradition.

Wilbur Knorr took up again the detailed comparison of the different Greek and Arabic-Latin versions for the portion XI. 36-XII. 17. It is hardly favorable to the hypotheses that Heiberg had formulated concerning the history of the text, especially regarding the partial alternative version of the Bolognese manuscript (*b*). Knorr reverses Heiberg's conclusions and allies himself with the position previously maintained by Klamroth concerning the primacy of the indirect tradition. In the early twenty-first century, however, the more complete knowledge that scholars have of this tradition precludes such a facile conclusion. In seeking to determine the version that is least distant from the original, one notices that the result seems to depend either on the books concerned (what one finds in Books I to IX, or in Book X, is rather different from what appears in the stereometric books), or on the nature of the textual element concerned (principles or enunciations *versus* proofs), or on the criterion that one chooses (addition or suppression of material, changes in order, modification or replacement of proofs).

As the medieval history of the text clearly demonstrates, the transmission of the text from antiquity onward has been much more malleable than what philologists are generally willing to admit. Heiberg as well as Klamroth and Knorr accepted certain linear patterns in order to account for the textual development of the *Elements*. For Heiberg the text became progressively corrupt; for the partisans of the indirect tradition it was greatly enriched and made more sophisticated, albeit in a trivial manner, because of the pedagogic and exegetic methods. These simple approaches were supposed to permit identification of a globally "purer" version; for Heiberg it was the so-called pre-Theonian version, while for Klamroth and Knorr it was the alleged archetype of the Arabic translations, notably slimmer and thus purer. These patterns do not work, partly because of the generalized contamination and perhaps also because certain epitomes have played a role. Furthermore, one must not forget the interventions of the revisers of the two Arabic translations (al-Hajjāj for his own work, Thābit ibn Qurra for the translation of Ishāq). Such modalities of transmission are perhaps valid for all the mathematic texts of Greek antiquity, but they are easier to perceive in the case of the *Elements*. This investigation has not ended. Future scholars may receive some fine surprises.

SUPPLEMENTARY BIBLIOGRAPHY

There has been no new critical edition of the Greek text of Euclid's principal works since that of Heiberg and Menge (references in DSB *4, part [i], 435), but it has served as the basis for new translations.*

NEW TRANSLATIONS OF EUCLID'S WORKS

Elements

Euclide d'Alexandrie. *Les Eléments* [The Elements]. General introduction by Maurice Caveing. French translation and commentaries by Bernard Vitrac. Paris: Presses universitaires de France, Bibliothèque d'histoire des sciences. Vol. 1. Books I–IV, 1990. Vol. 2. Books V–IX, 1994. Vol. 3. Book X, 1998. Vol. 4. Books XI–XIII, 2001.

Euclides. *Elementos* [The Elements]. Introduction by Luis Vega. Translation and notes by Maria-Luisa Puertas Castaños. Madrid: Biblioteca Clasica Gredos (155, 191, 228). Vol. 1. Books I–IV, 1991. Vol. 2. Books V–IX, 1994. Vol. 3. Books X–XIII, 1996.

Scripta minora *(Minor Works)*

Dedomena [ΔΕΔΟΜΕΝΑ]: *Euclid's Data or, The Importance of Being Given,* by Christian Marinus Taisbak. Copenhagen: Museum Tusculanum Press, University of Copenhagen, 2003.

Euclid's Phænomena. *A Translation and Study of a Hellenistic Treatise in Spherical Astronomy,* by J. L. Berggren & Robert S. D. Thomas. New York and London: Garland Publishing Inc., 1996.

Euclides. *Optica, Catoptrica, Fenomenos* [Optics, Catoptrica, Phænomena]. In *Sobre las líneas indivisibles,* by Aristotle. Introduction, translation, and notes by Paloma Ortiz Garcia. Madrid: Biblioteca Clasica Gredos (277), 2000.

GENERAL SOURCES

Vitrac, Bernard. "Euclide." In *Dictionnaire des Philosophes antiques* [Dictionary of ancient philosophers], edited by Richard Goulet. Vol. 3. Paris: Éditions du Centre national de la recherche scientifique (CNRS), 2000, pp. 252–272.

AUTHENTICITY OF CERTAIN MINOR WORKS

The Phænomena

Berggren, J. L., and Robert S. D. Thomas. "Introduction." In *Euclid's Phænomena. A Translation and Study of a Hellenistic Treatise in Spherical Astronomy.* New York and London: Garland Publishing Inc., 1996, pp. 10–18.

The Optics

Jones, Alexander. "Peripatetic and Euclidean Theories of the Visual Ray." *Physis* 31 (1994): 47–76. Also see the bibliography.

Knorr, Wilbur R. "Pseudo-Euclidean Reflections in Ancient Optics: A Re-examination of Textual Issues Pertaining to the Euclidean *Optica* and *Catoptrica.*" *Physis* 31 (1994): 1–45. Also see the bibliography.

The Catoptrica

Knorr, Wilbur R. "Archimedes and the Pseudo-Euclidean *Catoptrics:* Early Stages in the Ancient Geometric Theory of Mirrors." *Archives Internationales d'Histoire des Sciences* 35 (1985): 28–105.

The Sectio Canonis

Barker, Andrew D. "Method and Aims in the Euclidean *Sectio Canonis.*" *Journal of Hellenic Studies* 101 (1981): 1–16.

Bowen, Alan C., and William R. Bowen. "The Translator as Interpreter: Euclid's *Sectio Canonis* and Ptolemy's *Harmonica* in the Latin Tradition." In *Music Discourse from Classical to Early Modern Times,* edited by Maria R. Maniates. Toronto; Buffalo, NY; and London: University of Toronto Press, 1997. 97–148.

TRANSMISSION OF THE *ELEMENTS* IN ANTIQUITY AND IN THE MIDDLE AGES

General

Folkerts, Menso. *Euclid in Medieval Europe.* Winnipeg, MB: Benjamin, 1989.

The Elements *in Greek Antiquity*

Knorr, Wilbur R. "The Wrong Text of Euclid: On Heiberg's Text and Its Alternatives." *Centaurus* 36 (1996): 208–276.

Rommevaux, Sabine, Ahmed Djebbar, and Bernard Vitrac. "Remarques sur l'Histoire du Texte des *Éléments* d'Euclide" [Remarks on the history of the text of Euclid's *Elements*]. *Archive for History of Exact Sciences* 55 (2001): 221–295.

Vitrac, Bernard. "Notices Pertaining to the History of the Text." In *Les Eléments,* by Euclide d'Alexandrie. Paris: Presses universitaires de France. Vol. 3, 1998, 381–411; and Vol. 4, 2001, 32–71.

———. "Les scholies grecques aux *Éléments* d'Euclide" [The Greek scholia to Euclid's *Elements*]. *Revue d'Histoire des Sciences* 56 (2003): 275–292.

———. "A propos des démonstrations alternatives et autres substitutions de preuve dans les *Éléments* d'Euclide" [On alternative demonstrations and other substitutions of proofs in Euclid's *Elements*]. *Archive for History of Exact Sciences* 59 (2004): 1–44.

The Medieval Arabic Euclid

Brentjes, Sonia. "Observations on Hermann of Carinthia's Version of the *Elements* and Its Relation to the Arabic Transmission." *Science in Context* 14 (2001): 39–47.

De Young, Gregg. "The Arabic Version of Euclid's *Elements* by al-Hajjāj ibn Yūsuf ibn Matar: New Light on a Submerged Tradition." *Zeitschrift für Geschichte der arabisch-islamischen Wissenchaften* 15 (2002/2003): 125–129.

———. "The Latin Translation of Euclid's *Elements* Attributed to Gerard of Cremona in Relation to the Arabic Transmission." *Suhayl* 4 (2004): 311–318.

Djebbar, Ahmed. "Quelques Commentaires sur les Versions arabes des *Eléments* d'Euclide et sur leur Transmission à l'Occident Musulman" [Some commentaries on the Arabic versions of Euclid's *Elements* and on their transmission to the Islamic west]. In *Mathematische Probleme im Mittelalter. Der lateinische und arabische Sprachbereich* [Mathematic problems in the Middle Ages. The Latin and Arabic language regions], edited by Menso Folkerts, 91–114. Wiesbaden, Germany: Harrassowitz Verlag, 1996.

The Medieval Latin Euclid: The Arabic-Latin Phase

Busard, Hubert L. L. *Campanus of Novara and Euclid's* Elements. Boethius, Band 51. 1–2. Stuttgart, Germany: Franz Steiner Verlag, 2005.

The First Latin Translation of Euclid's Elements *Commonly Ascribed to Adelard of Bath.* Edited by Hubert L. L. Busard. Toronto: Pontifical Institute of Mediaeval Studies, 1983.

Johannes de Tinemue's Redaction of Euclid's Elements, *The So-Called Adelard III Version.* Edited by Hubert L. L. Busard. Boethius, Band 45. 1–2. Stuttgart, Germany: Franz Steiner Verlag, 2001.

The Latin Translation of the Arabic Version of Euclid's Elements *Commonly Ascribed to Gerard of Cremona.* Edited by Hubert L. L. Busard. Leiden, Netherlands: Brill, 1984.

Robert of Chester's (?) Redaction of Euclid's Elements, *the So-Called Adelard II Version.* Edited by Hubert L. L. Busard and Menso Folkerts. Basel, Switzerland; Boston; and Berlin: Birkhäuser Verlag, 1992.

A Thirteenth-Century Adaptation of Robert of Chester's Version of Euclid's Elements. Edited by Hubert L. L. Busard. Munich, Germany: Institut für Geschichte der Naturwissenschaften, 1996.

The Medieval Hebrew Euclid

Lévy, Tony. "Les *Eléments* d'Euclide en hébreu (XIIIe–XVIe siècles)" [Euclid's *Elements* in Hebrew, Thirteenth–Sixteenth Centuries]. In *Perspectives arabes et médiévales sur la tradition scientifique et philosophique grecque,* edited by Ahmed Hasnawi, Abdelali Elamrani-Jamal, and Maroun Aouad, 79–94. Leuven, Belgium: Peters; and Paris: Institut du monde arabe, 1997.

———. "Une version hébraïque inédite des *Eléments* d'Euclide" [An unpublished Hebrew version of Euclid's *Elements*]. In *Les voies de la science grecque. Études sur la transmission des textes de l'Antiquité au dix-neuvième siècle,* edited by Danielle Jacquart, 181–239. Geneva: Droz, 1997.

Bernard Vitrac

EULER, LEONHARD

EULER, LEONHARD (*b.* Basel, Switzerland, 15 April 1707; *d.* St. Petersburg, Russia, 18 September 1783), *mathematics, mechanics, astronomy, physics.* For the original article on Euler see *DSB,* vol. 4.

Euler's mathematics had its own characteristics and was based upon principles that distinguished it both from Leibnizian and Newtonian mathematics and nineteenth-century mathematics. In the period from 1975 to 2005 the most interesting historical studies on Euler have tried to highlight these characteristics and to reconstruct the conceptual background to Euler's mathematics and the reasons underlying his work.

Analysis and Geometry. Euler's scientific work was crucial in the process of transformation of analysis into an autonomous field of mathematics. He thought that analysis and geometry were characterized by different methods. In geometry a part of the reasoning was unloaded onto figures in the sense that some steps of the deductive process were based on the intuitive inspection of a figure, without a verbal formulation. Instead analysis was understood as a conceptual system where deduction was merely linguistic and mediated: It proceeded from one proposition to another discursively, without inference derived from the immediate evidence of a diagram.

Even though this concept of analysis was the necessary premise for nineteenth- and twentieth-century concepts, Euler's idea of mathematical theory was radically different from the modern one. In his opinion mathematics was not a free creation of the mind and was not constituted from a set of propositions syntactically derived from explicit axioms. Mathematics was viewed as a mirror of reality; its objects were idealizations derived from the physical world and had an intrinsic existence before and independent from their definition. Theorems were not merely hypothetical but concerned reality, and were true or false according to whether or not they corresponded to the facts. This led to a lack of distinction between syntactical and semantic aspects of mathematical theories (see Ferraro, 2001).

Quantity, Function, and Formal Methodology. The transformation of analysis into an exclusively linguistic deductive system was based on the notions of general quantity and function. A general quantity was what all geometrical quantities had in common, namely, it was an abstract entity characterized by the capacity of being increased or decreased in a continuous way (see Panza, 1996). A general quantity was measured by numbers and could have any numerical value; however, it was a mathematical object different from the set of real numbers.

In Euler's opinion the proposition "y is a function of x" meant that there was a particular relationship between general quantities x and y and that this relationship could be expressed by an appropriate analytical expression. A function therefore was not a mere analytical expression: It was a pair that consisted of a relationship between general quantities and the analytical expression of this relationship. This twofold aspect of the notion of a function gave rise to a tension that also appears in the apparently different definitions found in *Introductio in analysin infinitorum* (1748) and in *Institutiones calculi differentialis* (1755)(see Ferraro, 2000a, pp. 113–114).

The importance of the analytical expression in the concept of a function was due to the fact that only the relationships that were analytically expressed by means of certain determined analytical expressions were accepted as functions. More precisely, an explicit function was given by one analytical expression constructed from variables in a finite number of steps using exponential, logarithmic, and trigonometric functions, algebraic operations, and composition of functions (see Fraser, 1989, p. 325). A function could also be given in an implicit form $f(x,y) = 0$, where f is an analytical expression in the above sense.

Euler realized that elementary functions were not sufficient to the development of analysis. He also investigated certain relations between quantities that could not be expressed using elementary functions and sometimes termed them "functions." However, the knowledge of these transcendental nonelementary functions was considered incomplete and unsatisfactory, and Euler did not put these functions and elementary ones on the same plane. In his opinion a function was an entirely known object, to such a degree that it could be accepted as the final solution to a problem. During the eighteenth century only elementary functions were thought to be known objects to the point that they could be accepted as the final solution to a problem: For this reason, only elementary functions were considered as functions in the proper sense of the term. Nonelementary transcendental functions were objects to be investigated and made known, rather than effectively given functions. Euler believed that they could be accepted as functions (in the proper sense) when their knowledge was improved (on Euler's concept of a function see Fraser, 1989; Panza, 1996; and Ferraro, 2000a).

Euler's notion of function was characterized in an essential way by the use of a formal methodology that made it possible to operate upon analytical expressions independently of their meaning. This formal methodology was based upon two closely connected analogical principles:

1. (Principle of the generality of algebra.) If formulas or equations were derived by using the rules of analysis and were valid over an interval I_x of values of variables, then it was thought to be valid in general.

2. (Principle of extension of rules and procedures from the finite to the infinite.) If a rule R was valid for finite expressions or if a procedure P depended on a finite number n of steps S_1, S_2, S_3, ... , S_n, then it was legitimate to apply the rule R and the procedure P to infinite expressions and in an unending number of steps S_1, S_2, S_3, ...

Infinite Series. Infinite series were not themselves regarded as functions. They were conceived as the development of functions or other quantities and served to represent them (see Fraser, 1989, p. 322). The procedures for developing a function into a series were based upon principle 2. Following the pioneer of series theory, Euler initially thought that a series represented a quantity only if it converged to it. Principle 2, however, posed the problem of the relationship between formal manipulation and convergence. The eighteenth-century accepted solution con-

Leonhard Euler. HULTON ARCHIVE/GETTY IMAGES.

sisted in assuming that the usual procedures of development transformed a given function $f(x)$ into a series $\sum_{n=0}^{\infty} a_n x^n$ converging to $f(x)$ at least over an interval of values of the variable x. The actual determination of the interval of convergence was an a posteriori question, which occurred only when, in dealing with numerical, geometric, and mechanical problems, it was necessary to compute the values of $f(x)$ by means of its series expansion (on Euler's theory of series see Ferraro, 2000b, and Ferraro and Panza, 2003).

This way of treating series worked well enough as concerns the ordinary power series deriving from elementary functions and did not involve the consideration of the sum of divergent series. However, formal manipulation led Euler to consider asymptotic series and series with the radius of convergence equal to zero. He also came to regard certain power series only from a combinatorial viewpoint. This yielded an aware shift to a more formal concept and led to Euler's notion of the sum of a series as the function that *generated* the series. The latter notion solved some complications in series theory and had significant developments during the second part of the eighteenth century (for instance, Laplace's theory of generating functions) but prevented Euler from achieving a real understanding of trigonometric functions and from using series to investigate special functions appropriately.

Differential and Integration. In *Institutiones calculi differentialis* Euler stated that the true object of the calculus was not the differential dy of a function $y = y(x)$ but the differential ratio $\frac{dy}{dx}$. However, this idea was not sufficiently developed, and Euler's calculus continued to be based on the use of differentials. These were thought of as fictitious quantities, namely as symbols that represented quantities tending to zero and that were manipulated in the same way as numbers (on Euler's notion of number and infinitesimal, see Ferraro, 2003).

The fact that a function was a relationship between general quantities involved some implicit assumptions. General quantities (and consequently functions) were thought to possess properties such as continuity, differentiability, and Taylor expansion (in the modern sense of the terms), which corresponded to the usual properties of a "nice" curve, lack of jumps, presence of the tangent, curvature radius, and so on. This was due to the fact that general quantities were abstractions from geometrical objects. Thus, even if Euler's analysis dispensed with figures, it retained a remarkably geometric characterization.

Euler's approach to the calculus was global; namely, he did not considered a certain property of a function $f(x)$, such as differentiability, as a local property valid in a neighborhood of given values x_o of the variable. He rather considered them as global properties valid for every value of the variable quantity x (see Fraser, 1989, pp. 328–329). If a certain property failed at a value x_o of x, this was not considered significant. The generality of algebra was the basis of this approach.

Euler did not appreciate the difference between complex and real variables and, therefore, between complex and real analysis. Even if he obtained some results, which can be interpreted a posteriori as being related to the functions of complex variables, complex functions were not an autonomous object of study (see Fraser, 1989, pp. 327–328).

Euler defined integration as the inverse operation of differentiation or derivation, namely the integral $\int f(x)dx$ of the function $f(x)$ was defined as a function $F(x)$ such that $dF = f(x)dx$. He was aware that many simple functions could not be integrated by means of elementary functions and that this concept of integration posed the problem of nonelementarily integrable functions. However, the problem of establishing a priori the existence of the integral or of the solution of a differential equation

was not tackled. Euler limited himself to comparing integration with inverse arithmetical operations. In his opinion integration led to new transcendental "quantities" in the same manner as the operations of subtraction, division, and extracting a root led to negative, rational, and irrational numbers. Even if Euler devoted many pages to the investigation of new transcendental quantities, such as

$$\int_0^\infty t^{z-1}e^{-t}dt$$

his concept of a function prevented him from giving them adequate treatment.

Calculus of Variations and Applied Mathematics. Although Euler was a student of Johann Bernoulli, Euler's calculus of variations was much influenced by Jacob Bernoulli and Brook Taylor, in particular, "the essential analytical innovations that distinguished Euler's approach from the Bernoullis were provided by Taylor" (Fraser, 1994, pp. 138–139). Taylor was not the only English mathematician to influence Euler. For instance, Euler's theory of series was rooted in Isaac Newton's method of series and in Abraham de Moivre's work on recurrent series.

Euler did not employ limiting processes or finite approximations in order to minimize and maximize an integral

$$\int_a^b Z(x, y, \frac{dy}{dx})\,dx$$

where F is a function of x, y, and $\frac{dy}{dx}$ He rather considered the integral

$$\int_a^b Z\,dx$$

as an infinite sum of the form $\ldots + Z_{\prime}dx + Zdx + Z'dx + \ldots$, where dx is an infinitesimal and $Z_{\prime}, Z, Z'$ are the values of Z at $\ldots$, $x-dx$, x, $x+dx$, $\ldots$ (Fraser, 1999, p. 359). In his *Methodus inveniendi lineas curvas maximi minimive proprietate gaudentes* (1744) Euler treated the calculus of variations geometrically; however, his reasonings were very general and did not depend on the particular geometrical representation. He also called for the development of a simple method or an algorithm to obtain variational equation. This algorithm was developed by Lagrange, who recognized the dual usage of the symbol dy in Euler's paper, where it denoted both the differential dy of y with respect to x and the variation of the curve $y(x)$ (on Euler's calculus of variation see Fraser, 1992, 1994, and 1997).

Euler strongly developed analytical methods in applied mathematics. He thought that while analysis considered general quantities, applied mathematics concerned the specific types of quantities, such as areas, lengths, and force. His concept of mechanics had wide success and paved the way for analytical mechanics (Euler's mechanics as discussed here refer to Fraser, 1991; Maltese, 2000; Panza, 1995; and Cordoso and Penha, 1999, in particular for the relationship between mathematical technique and physical conception, for the notion of a motion, and for his conception of the principle of least action). Euler also investigated the theory of music. In his *Tentamen novae theoriae musicae* (1739), he tried to make music part of mathematics and calculated the degrees of order associated with chords and sequences of chords.

BIBLIOGRAPHY

WORKS BY EULER

Leonhardi Euleri Opera omnia. Berlin, Leipzig, Heidelberg, Zurich, and Basel: 1911– .The plan of Euler's *Opera omnia* originally involved three series, containing the works that Euler personally prepared for publication. Between 1911 and 2006 seventy volumes of series 1, 2, and 3 were published. Volumes 26 and 27 of series 2 were expected to be published in 2010. The publication of series 4 began in 1985. It is devoted to Euler's correspondence (series 4A) and manuscripts (series 4B). Series 4A was planned to consist of ten volumes (four volumes were published by 2006). Series 4B was anticpated to contain Euler's hitherto unpublished manuscripts, notebooks, and diaries.

The Euler Archive. Available from http://math.dartmouth.edu/~euler. An online resource for Leonhard Euler's original works and modern Euler scholarship.

OTHER SOURCES

Bailhache, Patrice. "Deux mathématiciens musiciens: Euler et d'Alembert." *Physis Rivista Internazionale Storia Scienza (N.S.)* 32 (1995): 1–35.

Calinger Ronald. "Leonhard Euler: The First St. Petersburg Years (1727–1741)." *Historia Mathematica* 23 (1996): 121–166.

Cardoso Dias, Maria Penha. "Euler's 'Harmony' between the Principles of 'Rest' and 'Least Action': The Conceptual Making of Analytical Mechanics." *Archive for History of Exact Sciences* 54 (1999): 67–86.

Engelsman, Steven B. *Families of Curves and the Origins of Partial Differentiation.* Amsterdam: North-Holland, 1984.

Ferraro, Giovanni. "Some Aspects of Euler's Theory of Series: Inexplicable Functions and the Euler-Maclaurin Summation Formula." *Historia Mathematica* 25 (1998): 290–317.

———. "Functions, Functional Relations, and the Laws of Continuity in Euler." *Historia Mathematica* 27 (2000a): 107–132.

———. "The Value of an Infinite Sum: Some Observations on the Eulerian Theory of Series." *Sciences et Techniques en Perspective* 4 (2000b): 73–113.

———. "Analytical Symbols and Geometrical Figures: Eighteenth-Century Analysis as Nonfigural Geometry." *Studies in History and Philosophy of Science* 32 (2001): 535–555.

———. "Differentials and Differential Coefficients in the Eulerian Foundations of the Calculus." *Historia Mathematica* 31 (2004): 34–61.

Ferraro, Giovanni, and Marco Panza. "Developing into Series and Returning from Series: A Note on the Foundations of Eighteenth-Century Analysis." *Historia Mathematica* 30 (2003): 17–46.

Fraser, Craig G. "The Calculus as Algebraic Analysis: Some Observations on Mathematical Analysis in the 18th Century." *Archive for History of Exact Sciences* 39 (1989): 317–335. A crucial essay that clarifies the conceptual foundation of analysis in the eighteenth century.

———. "Mathematical Technique and Physical Conception in Euler's Investigation of the Elastica." *Centaurus* 34, no. 3 (1991): 211–246.

———. "Isoperimetric Problems in the Variational Calculus of Euler and Lagrange. *Historia Mathematica* 19 (1992): 4–23.

———. "The Origins of Euler's Variational Calculus." *Archive for History of Exact Sciences* 47 (1994): 103–141.

———. "The Concept of Elastic Stress in Eighteenth-Century Mechanics: Some Examples from Euler." In *Hamiltonian Dynamical Systems: History, Theory, and Applications*, edited by H. Scott Dumas, Kenneth R. Meyer, and Dieter S. Schmidt. Heidelberg: Springer-Verlag, 1995.

———. "The Background to and Early Emergence of Euler's Analysis." In *Analysis and Synthesis in Mathematics: History and Philosophy*, edited by Michael Otte and Marco Panza. Dordrecht, Boston, and London: Kluwer, 1997.

———. "The Calculus of Variations: A Historical Survey." In *A History of Analysis*, edited by Hans Niels Jahnke. Providence, RI: American Mathematical Society, 2003.

Golland, Louise Ahrndt, and Ronald William Golland. "Euler's Troublesome Series: An Early Example of the Use of Trigonometric Series." *Historia Mathematica* 20 (1993): 54–67.

Maltese, Giulio. "On the Relativity of Motion in Leonhard Euler's Science." *Archive for History of Exact Sciences* 54 (2000): 319–348.

Panza, Marco. *La forma della quantità. Analisi algebrica e analisi superiore: Il problema dell'unità della matematica nel secolo dell'illuminismo.* Vols. 38–39 of the *Cahiers d'historie et de philosophie des sciences.* Nantes, France: 1992. A wide investigation (almost eight hundred pages) of eighteenth-century mathematics. Several aspects of Euler's work are dealt with (Italian).

———. "Concept of Function, between Quantity and Form, in the Eighteenth Century." In *History of Mathematics and Education: Ideas and Experiences*, edited by Hans Niels Jahnke, Norbert Knoche, and Michael Otte. Göttingen, Germany: Vandenhoeck & Ruprecht, 1996.

———. "De la nature épargnante aux forces généreuses: Le principe de moindre action entre mathématiques et métaphysique Maupertuis et Euler, 1740–1751." *Revue d'Histoire des Sciences* 4 (1995): 435–520.

Steele, Brett D. "Muskets and Pendulums: Benjamin Robins, Leonhard Euler, and the Ballistics Revolution." *Technology and Culture* 35 (1994): 348–382.

Wilson, Curtis. "D'Alembert versus Euler on the Precession of the Equinoxes and the Mechanics of Rigid Bodies." *Archive for History of Exact Sciences* 37 (1987): 233–273.

Giovanni Ferraro

EXNER-EWARTEN, FELIX MARIA VON

(*b.* Vienna, Austria, 23 August 1876; *d.* Vienna, 7 February 1930), *atmospheric physics, meteorology, weather forecasting.*

Exner is counted among the pioneers who introduced theoretical mechanics into meteorology with the aim of calculating future atmospheric states from initial conditions known from measurements. During the first decade of the twentieth century, using an approximated and therefore tractable set of equations, he successfully calculated the four-hourly change of surface pressure over the contiguous United States. His textbook *Dynamische Meteorologie* (Dynamical Meteorology, 1917) was internationally influential for at least two decades. As professor of physics of the Earth and director of the Austrian weather service, he furthermore pioneered laboratory experiments to study the general circulation of the atmosphere and initiated the publication of *World Weather Records*, a series that has continued under the auspices of the *World Meteorological Organization (WMO)*. In the early 2000s, the pressure-dependent factor to convert temperature into potential temperature, the *Exner function*, carries his name.

Felix Maria Exner originated from a Viennese family of renowned scientists and university professors. His grandfather Franz was professor of philosophy in Prague and member of the imperial Academy of Sciences in Vienna, his uncle Adolf taught jurisprudence at the universities of Zurich and Vienna before becoming a state politician, his uncle Karl was professor of mathematics in Innsbruck, his uncle Franz Serafin held a chair of physics in Vienna. His father Sigmund Exner, a celebrated professor of physiology, was raised to hereditary nobility (Ritter von Ewarten) in 1917. His mother, Emilie, née von Winiwarter, also had roots in the liberal bourgeoisie of Vienna.

Felix Exner was educated in a liberal thinking family and the *Gymnasium* (classical secondary school). Then he studied mathematics, physics, and chemistry at the University of Vienna, where he graduated after two semesters abroad (Berlin, Göttingen) in 1900 (PhD) and obtained *Habilitation* in 1904.

In 1901, Exner started his professional career as a scientific assistant at the Zentralanstalt für Meteorologie und Erdmagnetismus (since 1904, Zentralanstalt für Meteorologie und Geodynamik; abbreviated ZAMG) in Vienna where he used his broad background as a mathematically oriented physicist to teach himself about atmospheric problems. Eventually he adopted an intermediate position between the vast descriptive climatologies of Julius von Hann (retired director of ZAMG) and the abstract theoretical deductions of Max Margules (an older fellow scientist). Until 1910, Exner laid some foundations for numerical weather prediction by using analytically tractable approximations of the governing equations to calculate the surface pressure change on a regular latitude-longitude grid. During a one-year world tour (1904–1905) he used a visit to Washington, DC, to obtain observational data from the entire North American continent. He used it to achieve a significant, yet little known, milestone for a successful calculation of surface pressure change on a purely physical basis (the single case result given in Figure 1) Notably, it was much more successful and was published fourteen years earlier than the well-known attempt by Lewis Fry Richardson. Technically Exner's final refined approach amounted to computing manually the advective rate of change of a layer of uniform potential temperature; it was based upon incorporating the hydrostatic and geostrophic approximations into the thermodynamic equation. Exner also tried this method for European cases but came to recognize that the

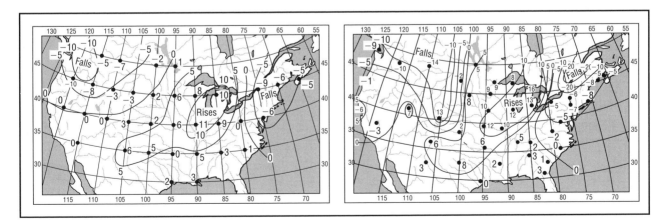

Figure 1. *4 hourly change in surface pressure over the contiguous United States for 3 January 1895 in units of 0.01 inch Hg (approximately 0.33 hPa); left: calculated for a regular 5° x 5° geographical grid; right: observed at a network of 35 stations. Both charts contain manually analyzed isolines and exhibit a sequence of regions where pressure falls and rises.*

disregard of tropopause-level effects often tended to induce substantial errors.

During this period Exner assisted the ZAMG director Josef Pernter with the compilation of a handbook for meteorological optics, which he completed after Pertner's death in 1908. In 1910, Exner embarked on an academic career by moving to the chair for cosmic physics (an old-fashioned term for the combination of meteorology and high altitude physics) at the University of Innsbruck. During the last years of the Habsburg Empire of Austria-Hungary, he condensed his vast knowledge of physical concepts and meteorological observations into the first modern textbook for dynamical meteorology (which appeared in 1917 after a delay of two years due to World War I). Ninety-six short sections were grouped in thirteen chapters dealing inter alia with the general dynamical equations: statics, kinematics, and dynamics of the atmosphere and its general circulation. Rigorous mathematical treatment was mixed with sufficient explanatory text and numerous sketches as well as with observational diagrams.

From 1915, Exner headed the newly established military weather service, and from 1917 until his untimely death, he held the traditionally combined positions of professor for physics of the Earth at the Viennese university and of director of ZAMG, first the imperial and then the republican Austrian weather service. In his academic capacity, he enlarged the fluid dynamics laboratory's novel rotating-tank experiments, forerunners of the famous dishpan experiments of the 1950s (best known in Chicago). He first observed axisymmetric flow at small rotation rates and turbulence in the form of growing and decaying cyclonic and anticyclonic eddies at higher rates (Figure 2). Secondly, Exner inferred that the east-west pressure gradients associated with the large-scale eddies would be an effective brake on the development of strong zonal flow. As director of the weather service, he extended the Viennese analyses of large-scale variations in planetary flow patterns. He constructed one-point correlation (teleconnection) maps based upon Northern Hemisphere station data for the 1897–1906 period, and later for the entire globe for the 1887–1916 period. Thus he documented in a pioneering sense the essence of what was later termed North Atlantic Oscillation (NAO), alongside with the independent, later renowned investigations by Gilbert Walker in India (whom Exner had met on his world tour). At a conference of the International Meteorological Organization, Exner suggested in 1923 the establishment of *World Weather Records* (first realized in 1927 by the Smithsonian Institution in Washington). They contain quality-controlled decadal statistics of daily measurements for climate studies. The corresponding data collection and reduction continued into the twenty-first century.

Figure 2. *Image of rotating tank experiment to simulate atmospheric turbulence. The water-filled annulus was heated at the circumference and cooled at the center by a round block of ice. Ink released at the cool center made it possible to mark the temperature contrasts which developed in both zonal and meridional directions.*

Exner's insights and personal opinion regarding the Norwegian cyclone model were documented in the written version of a presentation at a conference convened by Vilhelm Bjerknes in Bergen in summer 1920. It reveals that important ingredients of the textbook standard for the coming decades had also been found by the Viennese school of meteorology. Their conceptualization, however, was less focused and their widespread publication much less energetic. After Hann's death in 1921, Exner took on the onerous task of coediting *Meteorologische Zeitschrift*, one of the leading journals for meteorology of the era from 1870 to 1940, and he continued this work until his own death. Official recognition of Exner's achievements is evident through his full membership in the Austrian Academy of Science (since 1922) and corresponding memberships with the Prussian Academy of Science (Berlin) and the Royal Society (London).

Undoubtedly Felix Maria Exner of Austria belongs to the trio of great pioneers who, in the first third of the twentieth century, turned meteorology into atmospheric physics. Napier Shaw of Great Britain and Vilhelm Bjerknes of Norway stand at his side. Exner was scientifically very productive and took pioneering steps into a number of research avenues that are of continuing relevance. As a geophysical all-rounder beyond meteorology, he observed the time dependence of sandbanks in rivers as well as the movement of sand dunes and proposed simplified equations to describe the observations. Early in his career, he obviously profited from being well connected in scientific circles in one of the political centers of Europe. He was married for twenty-five years to Christiane, née baroness

Popp von Böhmstetten, and was the father of two daughters and two sons, one of whom, Christoph Exner, became a professor of geology. Exner's personality and position provided ideal links between innovative academic research and routine data collection and analysis. The summit of his career coincided with an era of rapid economic decline and political turmoil in his home country during and after World War I. In combination with his early death, this may explain why Exner's name, quite undeservedly, does not loom very large in early twenty-first century histories of meteorological thought. The barrier between the German text of all of Exner's publications and a potential reception in the English-speaking world of the early 2000s may add to this fact as well as the usage of the renowned, though not widely circulated, transactions of the Viennese academy as his main medium for publications. However, a change in perception emerged in the early 2000s with a special focus on an Austrian school of probabilistic reasoning in science at the beginning of the twentieth century. In this context Felix Maria Exner and other members of the "Exner dynasty of scientists" are being considered as prototypical characters.

BIBLIOGRAPHY

Exner's archival material is stored at the Austrian Academy of Science; contact http://www.oeaw.ac.at/biblio/en/Archiv/ Archiv.html for details.

WORKS BY EXNER

"Über eine erste Annäherung zur Vorausberechnung synoptischer Wetterkarten." *Meteorologische Zeitschrift* 25 (1908): 57–67. English translation and accompanying material in Shields, Lisa. *A First Approach towards Calculating Synoptic Forecast Charts.* Historical Note, no. 1. Dublin: Meteorological Service, 1995. Contains the first convincing juxtaposition of calculated and observed change in surface pressure for a case study (3 January 1895).

With J. M. Pernter. *Meteorologische Optik* [Meteorological optics]. Vienna: W. Braum‚ller, 1910. Second ed. 1922. Still classical handbook for this branch of meteorology. Exner contributed section 4 to the first edition and took over completion of the book from his teacher Pernter after the latter's death.

Dynamische Meteorologie [Dynamical meteorology]. Leipzig: Teubner, 1917. Second ed. Vienna: J. Springer, 1925. First textbook to combine mathematical techniques of theoretical physics with empirical findings of synoptic meteorology.

"Anschauungen über kalte und warme Luftströmungen nahe der Erdoberfläche und ihre Rolle in den niedrigen Zyklonen" [Perceptions about Cold and Warm Airflows near the Earth's Surface and their Role in Shallow Cyclones]. *Geografiske Annaler* 3 (1920): 225–236. Written version of an oral presentation given at a conference in Bergen, Norway, August 1920, which summarizes the insights of the Viennese school of meteorology concerning cyclogenesis and atmospheric fronts.

"Zur Physik der Dünen" [On the Physics of Dunes]. *Sitzungsberichte Wiener Akademie der Wissenschaften* 129 (1920): 929–954.

"Über die Bildung von Windhosen und Zyklonen" [On the Formation of Tornados and Cyclones]. *Sitzungsberichte Wiener Akademie der Wissenschaften* 132 (1923): 1-14. Contains photographs of one of the earliest rotating-tank experiments.

"Monatliche Luftdruck- und Temperaturanomalien auf der Erde (Korrelationen des Luftdrucks auf Island mit anderen Orten)" [Monthly Pressure and Temperature Anomalies on the Globe (Pressure Correlations on Iceland with Other Locations)]. *Sitzungsberichte Wiener Akademie der Wissenschaften* 133 (1924): 307-408. Contains one-point correlation (teleconnection) maps.

"Über die Wechselwirkung zwischen Wasser und Geschiebe in Flüssen" [On the Interaction between Water and Gravel Deposits in Rivers]. *Sitzungsberichte Wiener Akademie der Wissenschaften* 134 (1925): 165–203. Contains observations of banks in the river Mur at different times during the previous year and theoretical calculations.

OTHER SOURCES

Coen, Deborah. "Felix Exner and the Probabilistic Turn in Austrian Meteorology." In *From Beaufort to Bjerknes and Beyond: Critical Perspectives on Observing, Analyzing, and Predicting Weather and Climate,* edited by S. Emeis and C. Lüdecke. Series Algorismus 52, Munich, Germany: Rauner, 2005.

Davies, H. C. "Vienna and the Founding of Dynamical Meteorology." In *Die Zentralanstalt für Meteorologie und Geodynamik 1851–2001* [Central Institute for Meteorology and Geodynamics 1851–2001], edited by C. Hammerl, W. Lenhardt, R. Steinacker, and P. Steinhauser. Graz, Austria: Leykam Buchverlagsgesellschaft, 2001. Exner's achievements are reviewed and embedded in the overall findings of a group of Austrian researchers working between 1890 and 1930.

Ficker, Heinrich. "Von Hann bis Exner" [From Hann to Exner]. *Meteorologische Zeitschrift* 48 (1931): 454–461. Very personal speech given at an international meteorological conference one year after Exner's sudden death.

Fortak, Heinz C. "Felix Maria Exner und die österreichische Schule der Meteorologie" [F. M. Exner and the Austrian School of Meteorology]. In *Die Zentralanstalt für Meteorologie und Geodynamik 1851–2001.* [Central Institute for Meteorology and Geodynamics 1851–2001], edited by C. Hammerl, W. Lenhardt, R. Steinacker, and P. Steinhauser. Graz, Austria: Leykam Buchverlagsgesellschaft, 2001. Exner's achievements and personality are outlined and juxtaposed to those of his predecessors and successors; the extensive bibliography contains fifty-four titles authored or coauthored by Exner (mostly as a single author).

Leliavsky, S. *An Introduction to Fluvial Hydraulics.* London: Constable, 1955. Makes several detailed references of Exner's pioneering observational and theoretical studies concerning the time dependence of river sediments and sand dunes.

Toperczer, Max. "Felix Maria Ritter Exner von Ewarten." *Neue Deutsche Biographie,* vol. 4. Berlin: Duncker & Humblot, 1959.

"World Weather Records." Deutscher Wetterdienst [German Weather Service]. Available from http://www.dwd.de/en/FundE/Klima/KLIS/daten/online/wwr/index.htm. Continuation of quality-controlled decadal statistics of daily measurements for climate studies.

Hans Volkert

EYSENCK, HANS JÜRGEN (*b*. Berlin, Germany, 4 March 1916; *d*. London, United Kingdom, 4 September 1997), *psychology, personality and intellectual differences, popular science.*

Eysenck was a prominent and polarizing figure in postwar British psychology, noted for the expansive scope of his research and the forthright, often controversial, views he expressed. He developed a distinctive dimensional model of personality based on factor-analytic summaries and biogenetic processes. Eysenck married descriptive statistics with physiological experimentation, collapsing the distinction between pure and applied science. He was an outspoken advocate of the biogenetic basis of individual differences in intelligence and personality, as well as a trenchant critic of psychoanalytic psychotherapy. The author of eighty-five books and more than one thousand scientific papers, Eysenck was a renowned popularizer of psychological science.

Life and Career. Eysenck was born an only child in Berlin in 1916. His mother, Ruth Werner, was a notable silent film actress (with the stage name Helga Molander) in the early years of the German film industry, and his Catholic father, Eduard Eysenck, was a stage performer. Soon after he was born his parents separated, and he was raised by his Jewish maternal grandmother. Eysenck completed his secondary schooling at Prinz-Heinrichs-Gymnasium in Berlin in 1934. However, his ambiguous ethnic background left him with a difficult choice: He could either toe the National Socialist line or leave. His mother and her de facto partner, Jewish film producer Max Glass, had already fled to France. Eysenck chose to join them, spending a few months in Dijon in the summer of 1934 before moving on to London in August. His father Eduard stayed on, joining the Nazi Party in May 1937, much to Hans's disgust.

Eysenck did bridging courses at Pitman's College in London in the winter of 1934–1935 and then applied to study physics at University College London, in October 1935. He found he lacked the necessary prerequisites, however, and instead enrolled in psychology. After taking his degree in 1938, Eysenck remained at University College, rapidly completing a PhD on the experimental

analysis of aesthetic preferences, supervised by Cyril Burt. The war escalated just as Eysenck completed his doctorate in June 1940. Still a German national, he narrowly avoided being interned. Unable to enlist or get a job, he had a spell as a firewatcher. As restrictions eased, Eysenck landed a job at the Mill Hill Hospital in Northern London in June 1942. Headed by the imposing psychiatrist Aubrey Lewis, Mill Hill functioned as the relocated Maudsley psychiatric hospital. After the war, the Maudsley hospital was reestablished in South London and merged with Bethlem Hospital. A new Institute of Psychiatry (IoP) in London was added as a postgraduate training and research facility. Eysenck turned down offers at several other universities to head the IoP psychology department. It was his first and only job, providing a stable institutional environment until his retirement in 1983. He was given an unusual degree of bureaucratic freedom to organize the department around his research priorities. In 1938 Eysenck married Canadian graduate student Margaret Davies and they had one child, Michael Eysenck, born in 1944 and a notable psychologist in the early twenty-first century. The marriage, however, foundered soon after the war. In 1955 Hans Eysenck became a full professor at the IoP and a British citizen.

The Dimensional Approach to Personality. Eysenck began at Mill Hill with little in the way of equipment or money, but he was drawn to psychometric descriptions of personality. He factor-analyzed the data sheets Lewis kept on new hospital arrivals, correlating the results with questionnaire and experimental data. The various results were summarized in 1947 in *Dimensions of Personality*, Eysenck's first and most important book. *Dimensions of Personality* outlined two personality factors of neuroticism (N) and introversion-extraversion (I-E), creating an inverted "T" grid with an I-E base and an N vertex. Eysenck was guided by the idea that two common psychiatric diagnoses, dysthymia and hysteria, were the introverted and extraverted manifestations of a highly neurotic personality. Eysenck deliberately contrasted these continuums with the discrete typologies of psychiatry and attempted to clear up the confusing and speculative trait lists of personality psychology. It was a work unprecedented in Britain, but Eysenck drew inspiration from the trait approach of Gordon Allport and James Cattell in the United States and the typological theories of Carl Jung and Ernst Kretschmer on the Continent. In 1952 *The Scientific Study of Personality* introduced a third factor, psychoticism (P), again constructed around the idea that psychotic disorders differed in terms of introversion-extraversion.

Eysenck looked to go beyond descriptive level theory, however, well aware that factor-analytic models were inherently arbitrary. Mind and body were a continuum,

Eysenck wrote in his memoirs, *Rebel with a Cause* (1997), an assumption he always thought "too obvious to require supporting argument" (p. 64). Thus, he investigated the relationship of his dimensions to both specific behavior and brain processes. In his landmark 1957 book, *The Dynamics of Anxiety and Hysteria,* Eysenck argued that I-E was related to a simplified version of Ivan Pavlov's notion of excitation and inhibition, while N was vaguely linked with anxiety drive strength. This allowed Eysenck to connect personality differences with conditioned learning; in particular, he suggested that introverts were far more responsive than extroverts, learning quicker, better, and for longer periods. As a consequence, introverts also tended to have a more developed sense of morality and a greater capacity for academic achievement. While critics such as Lowell Storms and John Sigal demurred, it remained the most sustained and ambitious attempt to combine trait description with neurological subsystems defined in terms of their behavior control function.

By the mid-1960s, classical behaviorism had fallen out of favor, especially the formalism of Clark Hull that framed Eysenck's first biological model of personality. Ambiguous results from a range of researchers suggested that modifications were necessary. Armed with a more sophisticated appreciation of Russian work courtesy of young student Jeffrey Gray, Eysenck outlined a revised model in his 1967 book, *The Biological Basis of Personality.* I-E was linked to cortical arousal levels in the brain stem's activation systems. Learning was now seen as an interaction between external stimulation and internal activation levels, with introverts and extroverts having characteristically different optimal bandwidths. Conversely, N was more straightforwardly related to limbic system activation. It was a feed-forward model, wherein basic differences in neurobiology influenced more complex cerebral capacities that determined the rate and pattern of learning in any particular situation. Eysenck was an interactionist rather than a reductionist, arguing that behavior was the sum effect of genetic endowment and environment. From the early 1950s he collaborated on pioneering kinship studies concerning the inheritance of personality dimensions. Early work suggested extremely high heritability estimates, for N especially. More extensive sampling and sophisticated models produced lower estimates but still indicated substantial heritabilities for all three dimensions, as well as mostly unique, nonfamily environmental influences.

Many additional implications could be drawn from Eysenck's personality theories, including the prediction of various forms of social distress from extreme positions on at least one of these dimensions. In the mid-1960s Eysenck raised eyebrows by likening conscience to a conditioned reflex. He suggested that personalities with a lower capacity for conditioned learning (i.e., extroverts)

were slower to develop socially acceptable behavior. Moreover, emotionally labile persons (i.e., high N) with antisocial tendencies were more likely to act out than emotionally stable people with similar tendencies. These suggestions did not fare particularly well, however, and provided additional impetus for an overhaul of his three-dimensional factor structure. High N was finally made up of traits such as anxiety, guilt, and tension and suggested a propensity for neurotic breakdown. Less theoretically driven, P was reworked to be more indicative of the sociopathy of current psychiatric nomenclature. P never received a clearly articulated biological basis either, with high P associated with impulsivity and creativity, as well as the persistence and severity of criminality. Neither extreme on the I-E dimension per se carried quite the same implications. High E was characterized by sociability, assertiveness, and sensation seeking, the introverted end by low levels of these traits.

In a bid to provide standardized measures for his dimensions, Eysenck developed a series of relatively short, accessible questionnaires. The first appeared in 1959 as the Maudsley Personality Inventory (measuring I-E and N) and was soon revised as the Eysenck Personality Inventory. With considerable input from his second wife, Sybil (née Rostal), the 1975 version was renamed the Eysenck Personality Questionnaire and included a measure of P as well. These inventories became some of the most widely used of their type in the world and served as valuable research tools for those researching Eysenck-related topics.

Clinical Psychology and Behavior Therapy. Eysenck also played a founding role in clinical psychology in Britain and was a key promoter of behavior therapy. When Eysenck was placed in charge of psychology at the IoP after the war, there were no formally recognized training courses, although other programs would soon commence at the Tavistock Clinic in London and the Crichton Royal Hospital in Dumfries, Scotland. Eysenck hired Monte Shapiro to head the clinical section, overseeing the new graduate training course for clinical psychologists to the hospital. However, Eysenck dominated as the professional spokesperson, even though he had little to do with clinical teaching and never treated patients.

In the early 1950s, Eysenck argued for a research-based clinical discipline that put science ahead of social need. He saw the rapid development of clinical psychology in America as a mistake, a craven subservience to medical imperatives accompanied by a misplaced enthusiasm for psychotherapy. These pronouncements were accompanied by a research program highlighting the inadequacies of psychiatry. Eysenck and his clinical colleagues attacked the reliability of psychiatric diagnosis and the validity of projective tests like the Rorschach. His widely cited 1952 article, "The Effects of Psychotherapy: An Evaluation," also famously questioned the efficacy of talk psychotherapy. Over the years, Eysenck's antipathy to psychoanalysis became legendary. Psychoanalysis was, he wrote, insular and imprecise and seldom supported by the limited empirical testing it allowed. While hardly a lone anti-Freudian in Britain, Eysenck was probably the most vociferous, clearing the way for his preferred therapeutic alternative.

In the mid-1950s, Maudsley psychologists had begun treating patients with a new form of behavioral treatment, disguising it as case-based research. They borrowed from work done in the United States and South Africa, especially the work of Joseph Wolpe, mindful to put it in a Pavlovian learning framework. Reputedly demanding no empathy from the therapist, "behavior therapy" was perfectly in tune with Eysenck's perspective of the detached clinical scientist. Behavior therapy was less talk and more a targeted course of remedial training summed up by Eysenck's pithy 1959 slogan: "Get rid of the symptom and you have eliminated the neurosis."

By late 1958 Eysenck began to advocate openly that psychologists practice behavioral treatment. This provoked a furious medical backlash, not least from Eysenck's superior, Aubrey Lewis, who was scandalized by the idea of nonmedical practitioners treating patients rather than behavior therapy per se. Despite the bad interdisciplinary blood, the 1960s became the era of behavior therapy in British clinical psychology. Eysenck edited several books on the subject, linking up diverse practices into a seemingly coherent international movement. He also started the journal *Behaviour Research and Therapy* (*BRAT*) in 1963. The Maudsley program dominated in this period, supplying the rationale and most of the trained personnel for a small but growing profession. Maudsley graduates came to head many of the clinical courses started in the late 1950s and 1960s across the United Kingdom.

Nonetheless, Eysenck's vision of the clinical psychologist as a research-oriented scientist did not map easily onto the structure and demands of the public-sector National Health Service, which employed the majority of clincial psychologists in Britain. As the most visible and dominant psychological treatment, behavior therapy also proved vulnerable to the radical social critiques of the period. Advocates of behavioral interventions were obliged to soften their style, so diagnosis and directed therapy gave way to helping the patients help themselves.

While psychoanalysts learned to ignore his attacks, Eysenck helped ensure that clinical psychology became a more accountable, empirically based practice. However, his vision of clinical psychology as the research-based application of learning principles has been swamped by a more diverse, service-oriented profession wielding a hybrid variety of humanistic and cognitive-behavioral techniques. Eysenck would concede that cognitive factors were important, but he redescribed them in a manner which suggested that behavior therapy always allowed for them.

Personality and Politics. Eysenck extended his early success in getting a grip on personality via factor-analysis into the political realm. Although he published several more papers afterward, his 1954 book, *The Psychology of Politics,* remained his major statement in the area. Eysenck summarized social and political attitudes with two bipolar dimensions. One dimension made the usual distinction between radicalism and conservativism, the other contrasted tough- and tender-mindedness, following the thinking of William James. This produced a four-quadrant space, the most provocative implication being that the extremes of Fascism and Communism were separated by ideology but were similar in terms of personal style. For Eysenck, this balanced out the political picture, explaining the "same but different" paradox he had witnessed in pre-war Germany. His work clashed directly with postwar research on the authoritarian personality, with Eysenck controversially arguing that Theodor Adorno and his coauthors' measure of Fascist potential in *The Authoritarian Personality* (1950) was practically synonymous with tough-mindedness. It led to an acrimonious, highly technical debate with Milton Rokeach and Richard Christie over the reality of left-wing authoritarianism in Western democratic societies. Although Eysenck largely left political attitudes research alone after this mid-1950s skirmish, the political fallout would carry over into the nature-nurture wars a decade and a half later.

Intellectual Differences. Eysenck's latter-day public reputation came to be overshadowed by his popular writings on intelligence—even though he came to it late as a research topic—because these musings touched on some sensitive areas of public concern. In the late 1960s, just as his four children from his second marriage were beginning their secondary education, the British government foreshadowed sweeping reforms aimed at leveling the tripartite structure of the secondary school system. Eysenck quickly identified himself as an enemy of these reforms, and further argued that compensatory measures such as more money for facilities and teacher salaries in the poorer regions of the country would be ineffective or even counterproductive for those they targeted. He raised his profile still further with his breezy 1971 book supporting Arthur Jensen's contention that black-white differences in IQ scores were in part hereditary. While *Race, Intelligence, and Education* was poorly received by many of his peers, violent protests from leftist groups saw Eysenck transformed into an icon for freedom of scientific expression.

Hans J. Eysenck. *Eysenck using a Swedish machine for measuring eye blinks, 1968.* **HULTON ARCHIVE/GETTY IMAGES.**

concept of general intelligence, or *g*, originated by his intellectual forefather Charles Spearman. True to his London School perspective, Eysenck focused on individual differences rather than component mechanisms of intelligence. He attempted to avoid the circularities of psychometric definitions of intelligence by looking beyond IQ tests to investigate the relationship between intellectual differences and central nervous system functioning.

In the early 1980s, Eysenck urged psychologists to have another look at the contention of Francis Galton (1822–1911) that processing speed was an important factor in intellectual differences. Eysenck touted reaction time and electroencephalogram (EEG) measures of brain activity as holding great promise. However, Eysenck's own postretirement EEG research of the early 1990s proved frustratingly inconsistent, and the biological basis of intelligence remained a work in progress. Speed was an important but not overriding factor, with Eysenck speculating that it was a by-product of more efficient, errorless neural transmission.

Personality, Smoking, and Physical Disease. Eysenck's other major postretirement initiative examined the link between temperament with physical health. An early 1960s collaboration with oncologist David Kissen suggested an association between cancer and personality. Eysenck soon attracted more attention by claiming the causal role of cigarettes in cancer had not been convincingly proven. Certain types of people smoked, he argued, some of whom were also susceptible to cancer. Eysenck took a welter of criticism from public health advocates as the antismoking message became more visible and forceful in the late 1960s.

Eysenck revisited the issue in the early 1980s and presented new genetic evidence linking personality, smoking, and disease. Although mostly declared, the financial support he received from the tobacco industry left him open to charge of a conflict of interest. In a series of papers in the late 1980s and early 1990s, Eysenck and the little-known Yugoslav researcher Ronald Grossarth-Maticek reported on a series of longitudinal studies apparently demonstrating a striking association between personality types and cancer and coronary heart disease. While Eysenck did not set up these studies, his input helped fine-tune the presentation and analyses. A number of interventions were carried out suggesting that psychotherapy could have remarkably beneficial effects for cancer sufferers and those with unhealthy lifestyles. While the scope and ambition of these investigations were applauded, critics complained of a lack methodological controls and descriptive detail. Some, such as Anthony Pelosi and Louis Appleby, even suggested that the results were "too good to be true."

Nevertheless, the public hounding he endured was enough to ensure he largely avoided debating the race issue.

The Cyril Burt scandal in the mid-1970s, in which Burt was accused of manufacturing data to show that intelligence is inherited, brought Eysenck back into the nature-nurture debate. He eventually and reluctantly distanced himself from his old mentor's questionable practices but not his general ideas. Eysenck would repeat to the grave his contention that intellectual differences were 80 percent heritable—a high-end estimate in this field—most notably defending this position in a 1981 confrontation with Leon Kamin, the coauthored book *The Intelligence Controversy.* In the latter part of his postretirement career, Eysenck also played a key role in attempts to increase intelligence with vitamins. In an about-face of sorts, he even suggested that nutritional factors may account for race differences.

Eysenck's research on intelligence did not take off until the late 1970s, with Eysenck also playing a senior role in defining concepts and arbitrating debates. Throughout his career, he remained committed to the

Popular Writings. Over the years Eysenck authored a number of extremely popular paperbacks and made numerous media appearances. He was the people's psychologist in Britain; his best-selling Pelican paperbacks of the 1950s and 1960s helped introduce the discipline to many would-be students. Eysenck's rigorous empiricism was matched by a skeptical attitude that entertained nearly all except those he targeted. Eysenck's race and IQ book was an extension of this popular role, a calculated provocation of his liberal critics. Yet it polarized his reputation to such an extent that it stalled his career as a mainstream spokesman. Afterward, Eysenck tended to turn to more offbeat topics both for serious research and popular presentations—including gender, sex and marriage, parapsychology, and astrology. One last set of writings looked at genius, creativity, and madness, exploring links with the P dimension in particular.

Legacy and Wider Influence. Eysenck's three-dimensional view of personality was always countered by more complex descriptive systems in the United States, particularly the sixteen personality factors of Raymond Cattell. However, Eysenck never compromised on his view that three dimensions were sufficient to describe the underlying, culturally universal structure of personality. In the early twenty-first century, five factors are seen as the most defensible, two of which are similar to Eysenck's I-E and N. Eysenck dominated the study of the biological basis for personality and introduced testable theoretical accounts into an area that had appeared to avoid them. In hindsight, though, Eysenck was only partially successful in bridging Lee Cronbach's two disciplines of psychology. The physiological aspects of his work alienated social psychologists, whereas experimentalists did not appreciate his insistence on accounting for individual variation in their search for basic mechanisms. Only a handful of researchers have shared his integrative approach. Within this tradition have come several major challenges, notably from his successor at the IoP, Jeffrey Gray.

Without qualification, Eysenck was the most influential psychologist in postwar Britain. Yet he received only belated acknowledgment in the United States and was never truly honored in his adopted homeland. He was, his supporters recalled, a foreigner in many senses—too ambitious, too much the nonconformist. A pronounced introvert, Eysenck was uninterested in the more usual forms of social networking. He gave up on dominating or remodeling existing disciplinary bodies and instead created his own. People joined him rather than the other way around. However, to call him an outsider would be partly to buy into the rebel image he constructed for himself in wake of latter-day controversies.

Eysenck trained hundreds of research students. They were a key to his immense output, co-opted into an all-embracing, programmatic setup. Many subsequently took up key positions in universities in the United Kingdom and abroad. Although he was reluctant to push the idea of a dogmatic "Eysenckian school," his ideas and approach continue to evolve in the hands of an international network centered on journals such as *Personality and Individual Differences* and *BRAT* and the International Society for the Study of Individual Differences—all of which Eysenck was pivotal in founding.

Eysenck's detached, hands-off approach to his work was both a strength and a weakness. Always with an eye on the big picture, Eysenck was able to see connections and consistencies others did not. But he came across as insensitive to the nuances and complexity at the heart of the many disputations he engaged in. Eysenck's reputation as a controversial figure derived in part from his involvement in issues that were already controversial. However, his propensity to step over intellectual boundaries divided his peers. His brilliant and intimidating debating skills rallied the troops but left a pack of defeated opponents nursing a grudge. To his coterie he was stimulating and supportive, inclusive and trusting. To outsiders his style was confrontational, resembling that of a prosecuting lawyer selectively marshaling data and arguments. Eysenck claimed he never deliberately provoked debate, and certainly he could not have enjoyed the more vituperative attacks he and his family endured. However, he clearly wished to have his ideas actively discussed and saw something sinister in any kind of enforced consensus.

BIBLIOGRAPHY

See Personality and Individual Differences *31 (2001): 45–99 for a full bibliography of Eysenck's work. All personal papers have been destroyed. Limited Eysenck correspondence and other material is scattered in other archival collections, most notably at the Archives of the History of American Psychology, and the Tobacco Documents Online, available from http://tobaccodocuments.org.*

WORKS BY EYSENCK

Dimensions of Personality: A Record of Research Carried out in Collaboration with H. T. Himmelweit. London: Kegan Paul, 1947.

"The Effects of Psychotherapy: An Evaluation." *Journal of Consulting Psychology* 16 (1952): 319–324.

The Scientific Study of Personality. London: Routledge and Kegan Paul, 1952.

Uses and Abuses of Psychology. London and Baltimore, MD: Penguin Books, 1953.

The Psychology of Politics. London: Routledge and Kegan Paul, 1954.

The Dynamics of Anxiety and Hysteria: An Experimental Application of Modern Learning Theory to Psychiatry. New York: Praeger, 1957.

"Learning Theory and Behavior Therapy." *Journal of Mental Science* 105 (1959): 61–75.

The Biological Basis of Personality. Springfield, IL: Charles C. Thomas, 1967.

The IQ Argument: Race, Intelligence, and Education. New York: Library Press, 1971. Published in the United Kingdom as *Race, Intelligence, and Education* (1971).

With Leon J. Kamin. *The Intelligence Controversy.* New York: John Wiley, 1981. This volume was published in the United Kingdom as *The Battle for the Mind* (1981).

With Lindon J. Eaves and Nick G. Martin. *Genes, Culture, and Personality: An Empirical Approach.* London and San Diego, CA: Academic Press, 1989.

"Personality, Stress, and Disease: An Interactionist Perspective." *Psychological Inquiry* 2 (1991): 221–232.

Rebel with a Cause: The Autobiography of Hans Eysenck. Rev. and exp. ed. New Brunswick, NJ: Transaction, 1997. The first edition of his autobiography appeared in 1990.

OTHER SOURCES

Buchanan, Rod. *Playing with Fire: The Controversial Career of Hans J. Eysenck.* Oxford: Oxford University Press, forthcoming.

Christie, Richard. "Eysenck's Treatment of the Personality of Communists." *Psychological Bulletin* 53 (1956): 411–430.

Gibson, Hamilton Bertie. *Hans Eysenck: The Man and His Work.* London: Peter Owen, 1981. The first, somewhat incomplete, biography of Eysenck. Gibson was a student and colleague of Eysenck's, and this relatively friendly work reflects that perspective.

Lynn, Richard, ed. *Dimensions of Personality: Papers in Honour of H.J. Eysenck.* Oxford: Pergamon Press, 1981.

Modgil, Sohan, and Celia Modgil, eds. *Hans Eysenck: Consensus and Controversy.* London and Philadelphia: Falmer Press, 1986.

Nyborg, Helmuth, ed. *The Scientific Study of Human Nature: Tribute to Hans J. Eysenck at Eighty.* Oxford and New York: Elsevier, 1997.

Pelosi, Anthony J., and Louis Appleby. "Psychological Influences on Cancer and Ischaemic Heart Disease." *British Medical Journal* 304 (1992): 1295–1298.

Storms, Lowell H., and John J. Sigal. "Eysenck's Personality Theory with Special Reference to *The Dynamics of Anxiety and Hysteria.*" *British Journal of Medical Psychology* 31 (1958): 228–246.

Rod Buchanan